# CASES AND MATERIALS ON

# TORTS

## Second Edition

By

## John L. Diamond

*Professor of Law*
*University of California, Hastings College of the Law*

**Edited by**
**Lucia M. Diamond**
*The Robbins Collection, School of Law,*
*University of California, Berkeley*

## AMERICAN CASEBOOK SERIES®

THOMSON
WEST

Mat #40264561

© West, a Thomson business, 2001
© 2008 Thomson/West
    610 Opperman Drive
    P.O. Box 64526
    St. Paul, MN 55123
    1–800–313–9378

Printed in the United States of America

**ISBN:** 978–0–314–15410–1

 TEXT IS PRINTED ON 10% POST CONSUMER RECYCLED PAPER

*With love to my wife, Lucia,
my son, Danny,
and my mother, Rhoda,
and in loving memory of my father,
Monroe Thomas Diamond.*

\*

# Acknowledgments to the Second Edition

I would first like to thank my wife, Lucia M. Diamond, for her insightful and creative editing of this new edition.

I would also like to thank the following University of California, Hastings College of the Law students who, as research assistants, did outstanding work discovering new cases and drafting notes to enrich this edition: Edward H. Ahn, Ronak Daylami, Mark P. Diperna, Anton L. Hasenkampf, Ondrej Likar and John J. Roach.

I am also very indebted to Divina Morgan of the University of California, Hastings College of the Law Faculty Support Department, for expert and professional preparation of this manuscript.

As always, I remain very grateful to my students for the wonderful privilege to share the exploration of torts with them and for all they continue to teach me.

\*

# Acknowledgments to the First Edition

The creation of this casebook has very much been a collaborative effort. A team of nine University of California, Hastings College of the Law students helped produce over the course of several years a variety of the notes appearing in this book. I would like to recognize the areas where each made most of their contributions. Mark J. Seifert did a truly extraordinary job of coordinating and organizing the work of others along with outstanding research, drafting, and editing contributions throughout the book. I am very much indebted for his dedication. I am also very indebted to Lela T. Juarez who over a two-year period discovered wonderful cases. Her excellent research and drafting contributions are reflected throughout the intentional and negligence sections. I would also like to thank Sanjeeu Rajan for his excellent research, drafting, and editing contributions to the strict liability, nuisance, and workers' compensation sections. I am also very indebted for the excellent research and drafting contributions provided by James N. McDermott, Julie M. Pietrantoni, and Nicholas J. Wenbourne for many of the negligence sections; Tiffany S. Madsen for failure to act sections; and Paul J. Myslin for products liability and a variety of other sections. Finally, Justin N. Bezis made invaluable contributions of research, editing, and proofreading to help see the book through completion. I am grateful for all their work.

I would also very much like to express my thanks to my two co-authors of our concise treatise, *Understanding Torts* (2d ed. 2000), Professor Lawrence C. Levine and Professor M. Stuart Madden. I have learned from them and their insights are reflected throughout the book. I have defied citation protocol to include all the authors in every citation of *Understanding Torts* to emphasize that references to the text are in the majority of cases references to the work of my co-authors. In addition I would like to express my sincere appreciation to my colleagues at the University of California, Hastings College of the Law including Professors Ashutosh Bhagwat, Marsha N. Cohen, David J. Jung, David I. Levine, Naomi Roht-Arriaza, and Francis R. Walsh for their many insights and generous guidance.

I am also very indebted for enormous and unsparing assistance of the University of California, Hastings College of the Law Faculty Support group, directed by Stephen R. Lothrop. The text was word processed with great intelligence and care by Suzanne P. Menne and Barbara A. Topchov. I would also like to express my sincere appreciation for the very generous reference assistance of University of California, Hastings College of the Law librarians including Charles H. Marcus, Vincent C. Moyer, Jenni Parrish, and Linda M. Weir. I would also like to express my sincere gratitude for the very helpful assistance of Kathy A. Walters of West Group.

I would like to express my appreciation to the American Law Institute for permission to reprint sections from its restatements.

I am also very truly indebted for the invaluable help and encouragement of my wife, Lucia M. Diamond.

Finally, I would like to thank all my torts students for sharing the adventures of torts with me and teaching so much along the way.

# Preface

Since there are already a large number of excellent tort casebooks available to law professors and students, I thought I should briefly outline the contributions I hope this book can make.

The casebook strives to invigorate the study of intentional torts by going beyond the traditional personal injury approach. Battery is considered not simply in its traditional personal injury context, but also in its increasing application in environmental litigation. Students are presented with a second-hand smoke case and another case of university students suing for battery after being exposed to radiation on a field trip.

False imprisonment is studied as it interacts with malicious prosecution and abuse of process. Students consider this interaction in a provocative case in which a university arranges a sham mental commitment to keep a first year student from dropping out of school. The important role of these torts in defining society's relative permissiveness toward litigation is explored along with possible trends toward expanding the torts.

The torts of intentional interference with contractual and economic relations, which almost all students will encounter in whatever field of practice (e.g. corporate, entertainment, public interest) they ultimately choose, are introduced in the basic intentional tort section. The torts are considered in contexts ranging from a lawyer losing his client, the case that nearly bankrupt Texaco, and the potential liability of an environmental public interest group for encouraging a boycott. The notes articulate the issues posed by the increasing pervasiveness of these economic torts.

After a brief introduction to the highly limited tort of assault, and its historical recognition of psychological harm as damage, the tort of intentional infliction of mental distress is considered as it applies in different contexts including sexual harassment. The civil case prompting President Clinton's impeachment is included as a principal case.

Wrongful termination is briefly considered in one principal case that raises issues of when tort law should overrule a contractual relationship and provide potential punitive damages. Similarly, another principal case introduces tortious breach of the covenant of good faith and fair dealing and, in the context of a plaintiff dependant on his insurance company, explores when, if ever, tort remedies may need to supplement a contract remedy. Intentional misrepresentation is explored in a case brought by consumer advocate Ralph Nader, and in a lawsuit against the tobacco industry. The necessity defense is considered in the context of the Katrina hurricane.

The negligence section provides focus on current issues confronting tort law and includes cases concerning parental liability for failure to prevent a child from committing homicide and mental distress for exposure to toxic pollutants. The O.J. Simpson case is utilized to help illustrate wrongful death issues. Contemporary issues in causation including medical uncertainty, informed consent, and environmental issues are explored. Negligence is critiqued from feminist, economic, and other perspectives. The products liability section includes cases addressing tobacco liability and changes to the law proposed in the new Restatement (Third).

Statutory replacements to torts including workers' compensation and no-fault are available for exploration. No-fault is compared with the traditional torts regime under perspectives ranging from corrective justice to economic efficiency. Defamation and privacy sections emphasize new approaches utilized by litigants to attempt to impose media liability. Reprints from pages of the *National Enquirer* and *New York Times* are included to help illustrate defamation controversies. Special issues related to internet defamation are also considered. Trespass and nuisance are treated together in the context of environmental litigation.

Most importantly, cases (both new and classics) have been selected for their teachability and stimulation for students. Notes are straightforward and designed to allow professors freedom to explore policy concerns rather than struggle with clarifying black letter law. Newspaper articles and editorials have been reprinted to emphasize the public controversies surrounding tort law decisions.

Torts is an incredibly exciting subject to study. Many fundamental social issues are confronted and addressed in tort decisions. Despite increasing statutory modifications, torts remain a common law subject empowering the courts (its judges, law clerks, and litigants) to formulate new rules and solutions for a society seeking to be more just. I hope these materials convey this excitement.

# Summary of Contents

# Table of Contents

*

# Table of Cases

The principal cases are in bold type. Cases cited or discussed in the text are roman type. References are to pages. Cases cited in principal cases and within other quoted materials are not included.

*

# CASES AND MATERIALS ON
# TORTS
## Second Edition

*

# Chapter I

## SELECTED INTENTIONAL TORTS

---

### SECTION A.  THE CONCEPT OF INTENT

#### GARRATT v. DAILEY

Supreme Court of Washington, Department 2.
46 Wash.2d 197, 279 P.2d 1091 (1955).

HILL, Justice.—The liability of an infant for an alleged battery is presented to this court for the first time. Brian Dailey (age five years, nine months) was visiting with Naomi Garratt, an adult and a sister of the plaintiff, Ruth Garratt, likewise an adult, in the back yard of the plaintiff's home, on July 16, 1951. It is plaintiff's contention that she came out into the back yard to talk with Naomi and that, as she started to sit down in a wood and canvas lawn chair, Brian deliberately pulled it out from under her. The only one of the three persons present so testifying was Naomi Garratt. (Ruth Garratt, the plaintiff, did not testify as to how or why she fell.) The trial court, unwilling to accept this testimony, adopted instead Brian Dailey's version of what happened, and made the following findings:

"III. * * * that while Naomi Garratt and Brian Dailey were in the back yard the plaintiff, Ruth Garratt, came out of her house into the back yard. Some time subsequent thereto defendant, Brian Dailey, picked up a lightly built wood and canvas lawn chair which was then and there located in the back yard of the above described premises, moved it sideways a few feet and seated himself therein, at which time he discovered the plaintiff, Ruth Garratt, about to sit down at the place where the lawn chair had formerly been, at which time he hurriedly got up from the chair and attempted to move it toward Ruth Garratt to aid her in sitting down in the chair; that due to the defendant's small size and lack of dexterity he was unable to get the lawn chair under the plaintiff in time to prevent her from falling to the ground. That plaintiff fell to the ground and sustained a fracture of her hip, and other injuries and damages as hereinafter set forth.

1

"IV. That the preponderance of the evidence in this case establishes that when the defendant, Brian Dailey, moved the chair in question *he did not have any wilful or unlawful purpose* in doing so; that *he did not have any intent to injure the plaintiff, or any intent to bring about any unauthorized or offensive contact with her person* or any objects appurtenant thereto; that the circumstances which immediately preceded the fall of the plaintiff established that the defendant, *Brian Dailey, did not have purpose, intent or design to perform a prank or to effect an assault and battery upon the person of the plaintiff.*" (Italics ours, for a purpose hereinafter indicated.)

It is conceded that Ruth Garratt's fall resulted in a fractured hip and other painful and serious injuries. To obviate the necessity of a retrial in the event this court determines that she was entitled to a judgment against Brian Dailey, the amount of her damage was found to be $11,000. Plaintiff appeals from a judgment dismissing the action and asks for the entry of a judgment in that amount or a new trial.

The authorities generally, but with certain notable exceptions, see Bohlen, 'Liability in Tort of Infants and Insane Persons,' 23 Mich.L.Rev. 9, state that when a minor has committed a tort with force he is liable to be proceeded against as any other person would be. *Paul v. Hummel*, 1868, 43 Mo. 119, 97 Am.Dec. 381; *Huchting v. Engel*, 1863, 17 Wis. 230, 84 Am.Dec. 741; *Briese v. Maechtle*, 1911, 146 Wis. 89, 130 N.W. 893, 35 L.R.A.,N.S., 574; 1 Cooley on Torts (4th ed.) 194, § 66; Prosser on Torts 1085, § 108; 2 Kent's Commentaries 241; 27 Am.Jur. 812, Infants, § 90.

In our analysis of the applicable law, we start with the basic premise that Brian, whether five or fifty-five, must have committed some wrongful act before he could be liable for appellant's injuries.

The trial court's finding that Brian was a visitor in the Garratt back yard is supported by the evidence and negatives appellant's assertion that Brian was a trespasser and had no right to touch, move, or sit in any chair in that yard, and that contention will not receive further consideration.

It is urged that Brian's action in moving the chair constituted a battery. A definition (not all-inclusive but sufficient for our purpose) of a battery is the intentional infliction of a harmful bodily contact upon another. The rule that determines liability for battery is given in 1 Restatement, Torts, 29, § 13, as:

"An act which, directly or indirectly, is the legal cause of a harmful contact with another's person makes the actor liable to the other, if

"(a) the act is done with the intention of bringing about a harmful or offensive contact or an apprehension thereof to the other or a third person, and

"(b) the contact is not consented to by the other or the other's consent thereto is procured by fraud or duress, and

"(c) the contact is not otherwise privileged."

We have in this case no question of consent or privilege. We therefore proceed to an immediate consideration of intent and its place in the law of battery. In the comment on clause (a), the Restatement says:

> "*Character of actor's intention.* In order that an act may be done with the intention of bringing about a harmful or offensive contact or an apprehension thereof to a particular person, either the other or a third person, the act must be done for the purpose of causing the contact or apprehension or with knowledge on the part of the actor that such contact or apprehension is substantially certain to be produced." See, also, Prosser on Torts 41, § 8.

We have here the conceded volitional act of Brian, *i.e.*, the moving of a chair. Had the plaintiff proved to the satisfaction of the trial court that Brian moved the chair while she was in the act of sitting down, Brian's action would patently have been for the purpose or with the intent of causing the plaintiff's bodily contact with the ground, and she would be entitled to a judgment against him for the resulting damages. *Vosburg v. Putney*, 1891, 80 Wis. 523, 50 N.W. 403, 14 L.R.A. 226; *Briese v. Maechtle, supra.*

The plaintiff based her case on that theory, and the trial court held that she failed in her proof and accepted Brian's version of the facts rather than that given by the eyewitness who testified for the plaintiff. After the trial court determined that the plaintiff had not established her theory of a battery (*i. e.*, that Brian had pulled the chair out from under the plaintiff while she was in the act of sitting down), it then became concerned with whether a battery was established under the facts as it found them to be.

\* \* \*

A battery would be established if, in addition to plaintiff's fall, it was proved that, when Brian moved the chair, he knew with substantial certainty that the plaintiff would attempt to sit down where the chair had been. If Brian had any of the intents which the trial court found, in the italicized portions of the findings of fact quoted above, that he did not have, he would of course have had the knowledge to which we have referred. The mere absence of any intent to injure the plaintiff or to play a prank on her or to embarrass her, or to commit an assault and battery on her would not absolve him from liability if in fact he had such knowledge. *Mercer v. Corbin*, 1889, 117 Ind. 450, 20 N.E. 132, 3 L.R.A. 221. Without such knowledge, there would be nothing wrongful about Brian's act in moving the chair and, there being no wrongful act, there would be no liability.

While a finding that Brian had no such knowledge can be inferred from the findings made, we believe that before the plaintiff's action in such a case should be dismissed there should be no question but that the trial court had passed upon that issue; hence, the case should be remanded for clarification of the findings to specifically cover the question of Brian's knowledge, because intent could be inferred therefrom. If the court finds that he had such knowledge the necessary intent will be established and the plaintiff will be entitled to recover, even though there was no purpose to injure or embarrass the plaintiff. *Vosburg v. Putney, supra.* If Brian did not have such knowledge, there was no wrongful act by him and the basic premise of liability on the theory of a battery was not established.

It will be noted that the law of battery as we have discussed it is the law applicable to adults, and no significance has been attached to the fact that Brian was a child less than six years of age when the alleged battery occurred. The only circumstance where Brian's age is of any consequence is in determining what he knew, and there his experience, capacity, and understanding are of course material.

From what has been said, it is clear that we find no merit in plaintiff's contention that we can direct the entry of a judgment for $11,000 in her favor on the record now before us.

Nor do we find any error in the record that warrants a new trial.

* * *

Remanded for clarification.

<h2 style="text-align:center">NOTES</h2>

**1. Subsequent Case History.** On remand the trial judge concluded, contrary to his earlier finding of fact, that Brian had removed the chair after the plaintiff had started to sit, and concluded the defendant "knew, with substantial certainty, at that time she would attempt to sit in the place where the chair had been." See *Garratt v. Dailey*, 49 Wash.2d 499, 304 P.2d 681 (1956). Do you think it is more likely Brian "desired" or was "substantially certain" the plaintiff would fall?

**2. Intent.** Intentional torts require that the defendant intentionally commit the elements that define the tort. Merely engaging in voluntary acts does not suffice unless the actor intended all the elements of the tort to occur. In the case of battery this would include, as the principal case indicates, harmful or offensive contact. The Restatement (Second) of Torts articulates the generally accepted view as follows:

> The word "intent" is used throughout the Restatement of this subject to denote that the actor desires to cause consequences of his act or that he believes that the consequences are substantially certain to result from it.

Restatement (Second) of Torts § 8A (1965). See Keeton, *Prosser and Keeton on the Law of Torts*, § 8 (5th ed. 1984), Dobbs, *The Law of Torts* § 24, (2000) and Diamond, Levine & Madden, *Understanding Torts* § 1.01 (2nd ed. 2000). Do you agree with both alternative ways the Restatement defines intent? Is it counter-intuitive to include substantial certainty as one definition for intent?

Consider the proposed Restatement (Third) definition of intent:

> A person acts with the intent to produce a consequence if:
>
>> (a) the person acts with the purpose of producing that consequence; or

(b) the person acts knowing that the consequence is substantially certain to result.

Proposed Final Draft Restatement (Third) of Torts § 1. Whereas the Restatement Second tended to blend desire and substantial certainty into one definition of intent, The Restatement (Third) of Torts separates "purpose" and "knowledge" into subsections (a) and (b). For most intentional torts both definitions will still apply. The Restatement (Third) recognizes that there is a division among courts whether to limit liability to "purpose" in areas such as workplace litigation where finding intent can allow tort liability to supersede workers' compensation. The Restatement (Third) also advises limiting the "substantial certainty" definition to situations involving a small identifiable group of victims within a localized area, thus limiting liability for large manufacturers and others who know over an extended period of time some vague group of people will eventually be injured.

**3. Desire or Substantial Certainty Intent.** As the Restatement indicates, intent can be satisfied either when the defendant desires or is substantially certain the elements of the tort will occur. An inadvertent result of an action is not intentional. Consider *Ricca v. U.S.*, 488 F.Supp. 1317 (E.D.N.Y. 1980), where a police officer accidentally shot the plaintiff near the ear. The court rejected the plaintiff's claim that the officer "intended" a battery since he neither desired nor knew the bullet would hit the plaintiff. By contrast consider *Mauri v. Smith*, 324 Or. 476, 929 P.2d 307 (Or. 1996), where the Supreme Court of Oregon reasoned that the defendant police officers' alleged desire to cause an unauthorized intrusion or their alleged belief that the unauthorized entry was substantially certain to result would constitute an intentional intrusion.

**4. Substantial Certainty as Intent in Environmental and Workplace Litigation.** Defining intent to include substantial certainty significantly expands the use of intentional torts in environmental and workplace litigation. When plaintiffs argue intent based on the defendant's alleged "substantial certainty" that the consequences of the tort will occur, courts, however, are usually very strict in requiring proof of the defendant's "certainty."

Consider *Vogel v. Grant–Lafayette Electric Cooperative*, 201 Wis.2d 416, 548 N.W.2d 829 (Wis. 1996), where dairy farmers alleged an electric company intentionally interfered with the use and enjoyment of their property (constituting intentional nuisance). The Supreme Court of Wisconsin held that while the electric company knew some stray electrical current would invade the dairy, there was no evidence the electric company knew with substantial certainty and thereby intended to expose the dairy to sufficient electric current to interfere with the dairy's use and enjoyment of its property. Similarly, in *Pariseau v. Wedge Products, Inc.*, 36 Ohio St.3d 124, 522 N.E.2d 511 (Ohio 1988), an employee brought an action against his employer alleging intentional tortious conduct due to injuries the plaintiff sustained because of the malfunctioning of the employer's punch press. The Supreme Court of Ohio held that the employer's actions did not rise to the level of an intentional tort because the injury did not result from circumstances where the employer was "substantially certain" that the malfunctioning would occur.

But consider *Turner v. PCR, Inc.*, 754 So.2d 683 (Fla.2000), where employee technicians were killed as a result of an explosion in the defendant's chemical plant. The court held it was an issue of fact whether the plant was so unsuited for the large quantities of highly flammable substances used by the plant that the defendant owner of the plant was substantially certain injury or death would result. Consider also *Connelly v. Arrow Air, Inc.*, 568 So.2d 448 (Fla.Ct.App., 3d Dist.1990), where the court held it was an issue of fact whether "a passenger aircraft which is routinely overloaded and poorly maintained with known mechanical deficiencies ... will to a substantial certainty eventually succumb to the incessant forces of gravity causing serious injury to, or the death of, those aboard."

Some courts decline to accept the Restatement's expanded definition of intent to include substantial certainty as well as desire. For example, in *Ferris v. V.I. Industrial Gases, Inc.*, 1987 WL 10225 (D.Virgin Islands 1987), the court held plaintiff's claims that his employer's maintenance of a dangerous workplace could not constitute an intentional injury without proof that his injuries were "the result of the employer's conscious design." The decision precluded a tort action since the relevant workers compensation statute (see Chapter 7, Sec. A, *infra*) only allowed law suits for intentional torts. Consider also *Fenner v. Municipality of Anchorage*, 53 P.3d 573, 577 (Ala. 2002), where the Supreme Court of Alaska declined to accept substantial certainty as intent in workplace litigation, and instead required that the employer have a "specific intent" to injure. Should intent include "substantial certainty?" For successful environmental battery cases based on substantial certainty, see Notes 4, 6, and 7 in Section B, *infra*.

**5. Infancy as a Defense.** As the principal case demonstrates, children are not usually excused from liability for intentional torts. In *Cornell v. Cornell*, 42 B.R. 860 (Bankr.Ct., E.D. Wash.1984), for example the court held a seven-year-old boy could be liable for an intentional tort for intentionally setting chicken coops on fire. Should it make any difference that Brian Dailey in the principal case was only five years old? Under the common law, parents are not automatically liable for their children's torts, although many states have statutes imposing vicarious liability against parents up to a specific amount (e.g., $3,000 in the *Cornell* case cited above). Parents can, however, potentially be liable for unlimited amounts if they negligently fail to control their children. Parental liability is discussed infra at pages 298–305 (negligent control) and pages 653–656 (vicarious liability).

Although infancy does not excuse children from intentional torts, the requisite intent for a tort may be sufficiently complex that it is possible to argue a young child lacked the capacity to form the alleged intent. For example, a very young child may not intend harmful contact when she pulls what adults would know to be a loaded gun's trigger. Consider *Allstate Insurance Company v. Patterson*, 904 F.Supp. 1270 (1995), where the court held that older boys may not have had the requisite intent to cause "bodily harm" when engaging in sexual contact with younger boys because of the older boys' immaturity. Consider, however, *Bailey v. C.S.*, 12 S.W.3d 159 (Tex.App.2000), in which the Court of Appeals of Texas held that even though the defendant was only four years of age when he angrily hit his babysitter in the throat, crushed her larynx and caused loss/impairment of her voice, his status as a minor was insufficient to establish that he lacked intent as a matter of law.

**6.   Further Study.** For further study, see Simons, *Rethinking Mental States*, 72 B.U. L. Rev. 463 (1992), which discusses intent in respect to each category of tort law, and Jung & Levine, *Whence Knowledge Intent? Whither Knowledge Intent*, 20 U.C. Davis L. Rev. 551 (1987).

## WILLIAMS v. KEARBEY

Court of Appeals of Kansas.
13 Kan.App.2d 564, 775 P.2d 670 (1989).

DAVIS, Judge.

Defendant Alan Kearbey, a minor, shot and wounded plaintiff Don Harris and plaintiff Daniel Williams, also a minor. Plaintiffs brought this action against Kearbey for battery. The jury found for plaintiffs. It also found, in answer to a special question, that Kearbey was insane at the time. The trial court entered judgment for plaintiffs and Kearbey appeals, arguing: (1) that an insane person should not be held civilly liable for his torts; and (2) that an insane person cannot commit a battery because he is incapable of forming the necessary intent.

Highly summarized, the material facts are as follows: On January 21, 1985, Alan Kearbey, who was then 14 years old, shot several people at Goddard Junior High School. The principal was killed and three other people were wounded. Among the wounded were plaintiff Don Harris, a teacher at the school, and plaintiff Daniel Williams, a student at the school. Both were shot in the leg.

* * *

In 1927, the Kansas Supreme Court held that "[a]n insane person who shoots and kills another is civilly liable in damages to those injured by his tort." *Seals v. Snow,* 123 Kan. 88, Syl. ¶ 1, 254 P. 348 (1927). In 1940, the Supreme Court reaffirmed this holding in dicta, saying: "It is definitely settled in this state that the defendant, Toepffer, if in fact insane, would have been civilly liable in damages for his torts." *Toepffer v. Toepffer,* 151 Kan. 924, 929, 101 P.2d 904 (1940). The appellate courts of this state have not spoken on this subject since 1940.

The tort liability of insane persons presents a policy question. In resolving this question, American courts have unanimously chosen to impose liability on an insane person rather than leaving the loss on the innocent victim. *Seals v. Snow* is a leading case in support of this view.

In *Seals v. Snow,* Martin Snow shot and killed Arthur Seals. Seals' widow brought an action for wrongful death. Snow answered that he had acted in self-defense. The jury returned a general verdict for the plaintiff, and found in answer to special questions that Snow had not acted in self-defense, that he was insane when he shot Seals, and that he was not able "to distinguish right from wrong" at the time he shot Seals. 123 Kan. at 88–89, 254 P. 348.

On appeal, Snow argued that he should not be held liable for his torts since he was insane. The court responded:

"It is conceded that the great weight of authority is that an insane person is civilly liable for his torts. This liability has been based on a number of grounds, one that where one of two innocent persons must suffer a loss, it should be borne by the one who occasioned it. Another, that public policy requires the enforcement of such liability in order that relatives of the insane person shall be led to restrain him and that tort-feasors shall not simulate or pretend insanity to defend their wrongful acts causing damage to others, and that if he was not liable there would be no redress for injuries, and we might have the anomaly of an insane person having abundant wealth depriving another of his rights without compensation." 123 Kan. at 90, 254 P. 348.

Kearbey argues (1) the loss should fall upon plaintiffs rather than himself since he was not capable of avoiding his conduct and, hence, was not at fault; (2) it no longer makes sense to impose liability on an insane person in order to encourage his relatives to confine him since public policy no longer favors confinement of the mentally ill unless the insane person presents a danger to other people, in which case liability should be imposed directly on the insane person's relatives for failing to confine him, rather than on the insane person himself; and (3) concern over feigned insanity is no longer warranted since psychiatrists and psychologists now have improved methods of proving or disproving insanity.

Taking up Kearbey's arguments in reverse order, it is obvious that Kearbey's confidence in modern psychiatry is not widely shared. Comments to the Restatement (Second) of Torts list several valid reasons why liability is still imposed on insane persons. These reasons include:

"the unsatisfactory character of the evidence of mental deficiency in many cases, together with the ease with which it can be feigned, the difficulty of estimating its existence, nature and extent; and some fear of introducing into the law of torts the confusion that has surrounded the defense of insanity in the criminal law." Restatement (Second) of Torts § 895J comment a (1977).

Next, Kearbey argues that liability should not be imposed on an insane person in order to encourage his relatives to confine him since public policy no longer favors confinement of the mentally ill. We agree that this is not a particularly strong reason for imposing liability. It is also clear, however, that removing this rationale would not have changed the court's decision in *Seals v. Snow.*

The main rationale of *Seals v. Snow* and the one which keys our affirmance of the trial court in this case is that, as between an insane person who injures another and an innocent person, it is more just for the insane person to bear the loss he caused than to visit the loss on the injured person. As stated in *Seals v. Snow:*

"Undoubtedly, there is some appearance of hardship, even of injustice, in compelling one to respond for that which, for want of the control of reason, he was unable to avoid; that it is imposing upon a person already visited with the inexpressible calamity of mental obscurity an obligation to observe the same care and precaution respecting the rights of others that the law demands of one in the full possession of his faculties. But the question of liability in these cases, as well as in others, is a question of policy; and it is to be disposed of as would be the question whether the incompetent person should be supported at the expense of the public, or of his neighbors, or at the expense of his own estate. If his mental disorder makes him dependent, and at the same time prompts him to commit injuries, there seems to be no greater reason for imposing upon the neighbors or the public one set of these consequences, rather than the other; no more propriety or justice in making others bear the losses resulting from his unreasoning fury, when it is spent upon them or their property, than there would be in calling upon them to pay the expense of his confinement in an asylum, when his own estate is ample for the purpose." 123 Kan. at 90–91, 254 P. 348 (quoting 1 Cooley on Torts 172 [3d ed.1906]).

Although the above language is somewhat dated, the reasoning is still well grounded in sound public policy. Someone must bear the loss and, as between the tortfeasor, the injured party, and the general public, sound public policy favors placing the loss on the person who caused it, whether sane or not.

\* \* \*

Kearbey argues that he did not commit the tort of battery because his insanity prevented him from forming the intent necessary for that tort. The prevailing American view as set forth above is that a finding of insanity does not preclude a finding that a defendant acted intentionally. A jury may find that an insane person acted intentionally if he intended to do what he did, even though his reasons and motives were entirely irrational. Restatement (Second of Torts § 895J comment c (1977)); Prosser & Keeton on Torts § 135, p. 1074 (5th ed.1984).

The requirements of the prevailing American view for imposing liability for an intentional tort are satisfied in this case. In finding for the plaintiffs, the jury necessarily found that Alan Kearbey touched or struck the plaintiffs "with the intent of bringing about either a contact or an apprehension of contact, that is harmful or offensive." The fact that Kearbey did not "understand the nature of his acts" or did not "understand that what he was doing was prohibited by law" does not preclude the jury from finding that Kearbey acted intentionally in discharging a weapon in Goddard Junior High School.

Affirmed.

### NOTE

**1. Insanity is not a Defense to Intentional Torts.** In contrast to criminal law, insanity is not a defense to intentional torts. See Diamond, Levine & Madden, *Understanding Torts* § 1.01[F] (2nd ed. 2000); Keeton, *Prosser and Keeton on the Law of Torts* §§ 134, 135 (5th ed. 1984); Dobbs, *The Law of Torts* § 25 (2000).

Consider *Delahanty v. Hinckley*, 799 F.Supp. 184 (D.D.C.1992), where the court held that the defendant who claimed "he was in a 'deluded and psychotic state of mind' [when] he fired at the President of the United States" could be held liable for compensatory tort damages even though a criminal court found the would-be assassin of President Reagan legally insane at the time of his action. The court did hold, however, that an insane person could not be liable for punitive damages designed only to punish the defendant when he acted with malice. (For discussion of punitive damages see Chapter 5, Sec. C, infra). Consider also *Miele v. United States*, 800 F.2d 50 (2d Cir.1986), holding that a soldier, adjudicated insane in a criminal proceeding, nevertheless could be held liable for intentionally throwing sulphuric acid into the face of a child. Similarly, in *Colman v. Notre Dame Convalescent Home*, 968 F.Supp. 809 (D.Conn. 1997), the court held that a patient in a convalescent home suffering from senile dementia, who had been declared legally incompetent to manage her affairs, could nevertheless be liable for attacking a performer entertaining patients at the convalescent home with the performer's own guitar.

Are you persuaded by the policy arguments advanced in the principal case to justify its decision? Can the different approaches toward insanity taken by criminal law and torts consistently be reconciled by the different purposes served by torts and criminal law?

# SECTION B.   BATTERY

## LEICHTMAN v. WLW JACOR COMMUNICATIONS, INC.
Court of Appeals of Ohio, First District, Hamilton County.
92 Ohio App.3d 232, 634 N.E.2d 697 (1994).

PER CURIAM.

\* \* \*

In his complaint, Leichtman claims to be "a nationally known" antismoking advocate. Leichtman alleges that, on the date of the Great American Smokeout, he was invited to appear on the WLW Bill Cunningham radio talk show to discuss the harmful effects of smoking and breathing secondary smoke. He also alleges that, while he was in the studio, Furman, another WLW talk-show host, lit a cigar and repeatedly blew smoke in Leichtman's face "for the purpose of causing physical discomfort, humiliation and distress."

Leichtman contends that Furman's intentional act constituted a battery. The Restatement of the Law 2d, Torts (1965), states:

"An actor is subject to liability to another for battery if

"(a) he acts intending to cause a harmful or offensive contact with the person of the other * * *, and

"(b) a harmful contact with the person of the other directly or indirectly results[; or]

"(c) an offensive contact with the person of the other directly or indirectly results."

In determining if a person is liable for a battery, the Supreme Court has adopted the rule that "[c]ontact which is offensive to a reasonable sense of personal dignity is offensive contact." *Love v. Port Clinton* (1988), 37 Ohio St.3d 98, 99, 524 N.E.2d 166, 167. It has defined "offensive" to mean "disagreeable or nauseating or painful because of outrage to taste and sensibilities or affronting insultingness." *State v. Phipps* (1979), 58 Ohio St.2d 271, 274, 12 O.O.3d 273, 275, 389 N.E.2d 1128, 1131. Furthermore, tobacco smoke, as "particulate matter," has the physical properties capable of making contact. R.C. 3704.01(B) and 5709.20(A); Ohio Adm.Code 3745–17.

As alleged in Leichtman's complaint, when Furman intentionally blew cigar smoke in Leichtman's face, under Ohio common law, he committed a battery. No matter how trivial the incident, a battery is actionable, even if damages are only one dollar. *Lacey v. Laird* (1956), 166 Ohio St. 12, 1 O.O.2d 158, 139 N.E.2d 25, paragraph two of the syllabus. The rationale is explained by Roscoe Pound in his essay "Liability": "[I]n civilized society men must be able to assume that others will do them no intentional injury—that others will commit no intentioned aggressions upon them." Pound, An Introduction to the Philosophy of Law (1922) 169.

Other jurisdictions also have concluded that a person can commit a battery by intentionally directing tobacco smoke at another. *Richardson v. Hennly* (1993), 209 Ga.App. 868, 871, 434 S.E.2d 772, 774–775. We do not, however, adopt or lend credence to the theory of a "smoker's battery," which imposes liability if there is substantial certainty that exhaled smoke will predictably contact a nonsmoker. Ezra, Smoker Battery: An Antidote to Second–Hand Smoke (1990), 63 S.Cal.L.Rev. 1061, 1090.... [As] Leichtman alleges that Furman deliberately blew smoke into his face, we find it unnecessary to address offensive contact from passive or secondary smoke....

\* \* \*

Arguably, trivial cases are responsible for an avalanche of lawsuits in the courts. They delay cases that are important to individuals and corporations and that involve important social issues. The result is justice denied to litigants and their counsel who must wait for their day in court. However, absent circumstances that warrant sanctions for frivolous appeals under App.R. 23, we refuse to limit one's right to sue. Section 16, Article I, Ohio Constitution states, "All courts shall be open, and every person, for an injury done him in his land, goods, person, or reputation, shall have remedy by due course of law, and shall have justice administered without denial or delay."

This case emphasizes the need for some form of alternative dispute resolution operating totally outside the court system as a means to provide an attentive ear to the parties and a resolution of disputes in a nominal case. Some need a forum in which they can express corrosive contempt for another without dragging their antagonist through the expense inherent in a lawsuit. Until such an alternative forum is created, Leichtman's battery claim, previously knocked out by the trial judge in the first round, now survives round two to advance again through the courts into round three.

\* \* \*

Judgment accordingly.

## BOHRMANN v. MAINE YANKEE ATOMIC POWER CO.

United States District Court, D. Maine.
926 F.Supp. 211 (1996).

CARTER, Chief Judge.

Plaintiffs, several University of Southern Maine students, have filed the present action against Maine Yankee Atomic Power Company ("Maine Yankee") for injuries they allegedly sustained after being exposed to radiation when touring Defendant's nuclear power plant in Wiscasset, Maine. . . .

The facts alleged in the Complaint are as follows. Plaintiffs are five University of Southern Maine students who were among a group of chemistry students invited to tour Defendant's facility. Plaintiffs allege that approximately two weeks before their tour, there was a radioactive gas leak in Defendant's primary auxiliary building (PAB) as a result of design flaws and faulty engineering when Defendant "sluiced the demineralizers in its Chemical and Volume Control System." The students toured Maine Yankee on the morning of October 11, 1994, at which time, Defendant allegedly was in the process of repairing the leakage problem. Plaintiffs claim that "Maine Yankee officials had decided to flush out resin 'hot spots' in the demineralizer" and scheduled the procedure to occur during Plaintiffs' tour. Plaintiffs further allege that the officials were aware that the flushing procedure would release radioactive gases. Plaintiffs claim that they were never apprised of the problems at Defendant's facility.

Plaintiffs allege that each student was given a pocket-sized Self–Reading Dosimeter, which measures only gamma radiation. The students were not provided with Thermo–Luminescent Dosimeters, which also measure beta radiation and which are worn by the employees of Defendant.

Plaintiffs claim that despite his being warned that radioactive gases would be released in the PAB, the lead tour guide led the students into the "hot" side of the plant. Plaintiffs allege that the tour guides knowingly took the students through a plume of unfiltered radioactive gases. While the students were walking through the radioactive gases, the continuous air monitor in the PAB was sounding an alarm. After spending thirty to forty minutes on the "hot" side of the plant, the students returned to the "hot" side's entry point and stepped into portal monitors. Plaintiffs and the tour guides allegedly "alarmed out," indicating that they had all been exposed to excessive radioactive contamination from the tour. In fact, Plaintiffs Bohrmann and Ortman continued to "alarm out" up to twenty minutes after they left the PAB.

Plaintiffs allege that Maine Yankee employees never suggested that the students remove their contaminated clothing or that the students take a shower and wash themselves. Two hours after the exposure to radioactive gases, Defendant told a few students that they needed to go for a "whole body count" to assess their radiation exposure. Plaintiff Gagnon allegedly was told that he had nothing to worry about and was not told to undergo a whole body count. Plaintiffs claim that Maine Yankee employees falsely told them that they had not been subjected to gamma radiation and that only gamma radiation was "bad." Defendant's employees allegedly told Plaintiffs that they had not been exposed to anything that would pose a health risk.

\* \* \*

Plaintiff Bohrmann claims to have suffered a significant decrease in his white blood cell count. In addition, Plaintiffs allege that they live with "the significant distress and uncertainty caused by exposure to unreasonably high levels of nuclear radiation." Plaintiffs now seek compensatory and punitive damages.

\* \* \*

As concerns Plaintiffs' claims for damages pursuant to theories of . . . battery, the Court concludes that such intentional tort claims are not inconsistent with the federal safety standards. To recover . . . Plaintiffs must demonstrate that Defendant intentionally exposed Plaintiffs to radiation without their consent, and that such intentional conduct on the part of Defendant caused them damages. See, e.g. . . . . *Pattershall v. Jenness,* 485 A.2d 980, 984 (Me.1984) (an element of battery is an intentional act).[10]

There is no reason apparent to this Court to believe that Congress intended that a defendant be insulated from liability for its intentional acts solely by complying with the federal safety standards. Instead, compliance with the federal regulations merely demonstrates the absence of negligence. See *Coley,* 768 F.Supp. at 629. The federal safety standards have no bearing on a defendant's liability for its intentional acts. While a plaintiff may recover on an intentional tort theory without proving exposure to radiation exceeding the federal safety standards, a plaintiff may not recover without first proving that he sustained damages, and such proof may be difficult to establish in the absence of proving a violation of the federal safety standards. See, e.g., *Laswell v. Brown,* 683 F.2d 261, 269 (8th Cir.1982) (concluding that "lawsuit for personal injuries cannot be based only upon the mere possibility of some future harm"), *cert. denied,* 459 U.S. 1210, 103 S.Ct. 1205, 75 L.Ed.2d 446 (1983); *Johnston v. United States,* 597 F.Supp. 374, 425–26 (D.Kan. 1984); *Bubash v. Philadelphia Elec. Co.,* 717 F.Supp. 297, 300 (M.D.Pa. 1989) (concluding that mere exposure to radiation is not an actionable physical injury). Nevertheless, the absence of a violation of the federal standards does not necessarily establish the absence of an actual injury.

\* \* \*

**10.** The Court intimates no opinion as to whether the facts as alleged by Plaintiffs amount to physical contact so as to constitute a battery.

*NOTES*

**1. Restatement Definition.** Battery has historically compensated both harmful and offensive contact. The Restatement (Second) of Torts articulates the generally accepted view as follows:

> An actor is subject to liability to another for battery if (a) he acts intending to cause a harmful or offensive contact with the person of the other or a third person, or an imminent apprehension of such contact and (b) a *harmful* contact with the person of the other directly or indirectly results.

> An actor is subject to liability to another for battery if (a) he acts intending to cause a harmful or offensive contact with the person of the other or a third person, or an imminent apprehension of such contact and (b) an *offensive* contact with the person of the other directly or indirectly results.

Restatement (Second) of Torts §§ 13, 18 (1965). See Keeton, *Prosser and Keeton on the Law of Torts*, § 9 (5th ed. 1984); Dobbs, *The Law of Torts* §§ 28–31 (2000), and Diamond, Levine & Madden, *Understanding Torts* § 1.02 (2nd ed. 2000).

**2. Intent to Harm is Not Required.** Since battery requires either the intent to make a harmful or offensive contact, the intent does not necessarily have to be to do harm. For example, in *White v. University of Idaho*, 115 Idaho 564, 768 P.2d 827 (Idaho Ct.App.1989), a music professor suddenly walked up behind the plaintiff and "touched her back with both of his hands in a movement later described as one a pianist would make in striking and lifting the fingers from a keyboard" causing the victim to suffer unexpected harmful injuries requiring the surgical removal of a rib. The professor argued that although he "intentionally touched the victim's back" ... his purpose was to demonstrate the sensation of the particular movement by a pianist, not to cause any harm. The court deciding for the plaintiff held that the intent element of battery "is satisfied if the actor's affirmative act causes an intended contact which is unpermittable and which is harmful or offensive." See also *Caudle v. Betts*, 512 So.2d 389 (La.1987), where the Supreme Court of Louisiana held a CEO liable for battery for inadvertently injuring his employee while administering an electrical shock as a practical joke.

Also consider *Lambertson v. United States*, 528 F.2d 441 (2d Cir.1976), where a government meat inspector playfully and without warning jumped on the back of an employee at a meat company, screaming "boo" and pulling the victim's stocking hat over his eyes, riding him piggyback. As a result, the victim's face fell forward into a meathook severely injuring his mouth and teeth. The court held the defendant's action was not negligence but an intentional battery since the defendant had intended contact defined as offensive. The distinction was significant since the then current governmental immunity statute allowed liability for negligence but not battery.

**3. Offensive Contact as Battery.** As the ancient English case of *Cole v. Turner*, 90 Eng. Rep. 958 (nisi prius 1704), established, "the least touching of another in anger is battery." The contact need only be offensive and no minimal physical harm is required. This early case helps illustrate tort law's historic willingness to recognize liability where meaningful physical injury is absent. Do you agree that mere offensive contact should be compensated? Indeed, contact to the plaintiff's clothes or item she is holding can constitute a battery. Consider *Fisher v. Carrousel Motor Hotel, Inc.*, 424 S.W.2d 627 (Tex.1967), where the intentional snatching of a plate from the plaintiff because he was black was held to be battery.

In order for a contact to be an offensive battery, it must be such that it would offend the personal dignity of an ordinary person. See Restatement (Second) of Torts § 19. The Restatement takes no position on whether an actor should be liable for contact, normally not offensive, if he knows the recipient would be offended. Id., caveat.

Do you agree that mere offensive contact should be compensated?

**4. Environmental Battery Cases.** In addition to the principal cases, consider *Cunningham v. Anchor Hocking Corporation*, 558 So.2d 93 (Fla. App. 1990). Employees alleged that the owners of a glass manufacturing plant committed battery by exposing employees to hazardous levels of sulphur and graphite, acidic vapors and other toxic fumes. The court upheld the complaint based on claims the plaintiffs could prove the employer knew with substantial certainty contact to the employees would occur.

See also *Werlein v. United States*, 746 F.Supp. 887 (D.Minn.1990), holding that defendant's disposal of a "highly toxic substance into sandy ground directly above a regional aquifer" at an army ammunition site was sufficient evidence to hold that the defendant was substantially certain harmful or offensive contact would occur to nearby residents and preclude summary judgment against a claim of battery.

Consider also *Gulden v. Crown Zellerbach Corporation*, 890 F.2d 195 (9th Cir.1989). The Ninth Circuit upheld battery claims against an employer who had ordered employees to finish cleaning up toxic levels of PCB even after hazardous waste specialists had reported to the employer that contamination remained at unsafe levels. As a result of the exposure, plaintiff employees absorbed unsafe body levels of PCBs. The court held a jury could conclude that "the intention to injure [by exposing plaintiffs to toxic levels] was deliberate where the employer had an opportunity to weigh the consequences and make a conscious choice." Since workers' compensation law usually precludes all but intentional tort liability against employers, characterizing the employee's injury as intentional can be critical. (See Chapter 7, Sec. A, infra.)

**5. HIV Cases.** Courts have held that engaging in sexual contact without disclosing HIV-positive status can constitute a battery. Consider *Robinson v. Louie*, 213 B.R. 754 (U.S. Bankr. Ct., N.D. Cal. 1997), where the court held a life partner's assurances that it was safe to have unprotected sex, despite being diagnosed HIV-positive, constituted at least an offensive if not harmful contact sufficient to establish battery even in the absence of evidence that the plaintiff had contracted the virus. Consider also *Doe v. Johnson*, 817 F.Supp. 1382 (W.D.Mich.1993), where the court held that plaintiff had adequately alleged a claim of battery by asserting her sex partner had failed to disclose HIV-positive status prior to sexual relations.

By contrast in *Brzoska v. Olson*, 668 A.2d 1355 (Del.1995), the Supreme Court of Delaware held that the "incidental touch of a patient by an HIV-infected dentist [whose HIV status was unknown to patient], while performing ordinary, consented-to dental procedures is insufficient to sustain a battery claim ... in the absence of actual exposure to the HIV virus." The court rejected the plaintiff patient's "speculative" arguments and concluded there was no evidence that any bleeding, wound, or lesions from the dentist came into contact with the plaintiff's skin or mucous membranes.

**6. Tobacco Smoke as Battery.** Consider in addition to the *Leichtman* case, *Richardson v. Hennly*, 209 Ga.App. 868, 434 S.E.2d 772 (1993), where the Georgia Court of Appeals held that pipe smoke is capable of touching or making contact with one's person. Consequently, plaintiff's allegation that she had been harmed by a co-worker's pipe smoke supported a claim for battery.

But consider also *Shaw v. Brown & Williamson Tobacco Corp.*, 973 F.Supp. 539 (D.Md. 1997), where the District Court of Maryland held that a cigarette manufacturer lacked the requisite intent to be liable for battery to a non-smoker who developed cancer as a result of exposure to second-hand smoke from a co-worker. The court reasoned that the defendant manufacturer had not manufactured its cigarettes with a desire to "touch" non-smokers with second-hand smoke; nor did the defendant "know with a substantial certainty that second-hand smoke would touch any particular non-smoker." Any generalized knowledge that the defendant may have had that second-hand smoke would reach some non-smokers was insufficient to satisfy the intent requirement because such generalized knowledge is more characteristic of "accidental contact." Consider also, *Bell v. Elmhurst Chicago Stone Company*, 919 F.Supp. 308 (N.D.Ill. 1996), where an employee brought a claim alleging that his employer had "committed the intentional tort of battery by authorizing his coworkers to inflict their cigarette smoke on him." The court rejected the claim despite the plaintiff's allegations that his co-workers know of his severe reaction to smoke, noting that those employees who smoked did not do so out of any desire to harm the plaintiff. The knowledge that the plaintiff might be harmed "simply does not transform his co-workers' desire to smoke into an intentional tort."

Do you agree with the *Shaw* court that the tobacco company should not be responsible for an intentional battery? Should substantial certainty require that the defendant know who the particular victim will be to constitute "intent"? How would this affect liability for the environmental batteries discussed in Note 4?

**7. Radiation Exposure as Battery.** In *Corcoran v. New York Power Authority*, 935 F.Supp. 376 (S.D.N.Y.1996), the deceased plaintiff had been employed to do maintenance work at the New York Power Authority's Indian Point Nuclear Power Plant. Plaintiff alleged that the Power Authority and Westinghouse knowingly sent the plaintiff to work in an area "dangerously contaminated by radiation" and that they "failed to timely alert and warn" him. *Id.* at 382. The plaintiff wore no protective clothing and no equipment to warn him of the presence of radiation. He was consequently exposed to radiation levels "in excess of applicable regulatory standards." The court held that, "If, as plaintiff alleges, the defendants know of the dangerous condition and nonetheless intentionally assigned the deceased to work there with the intent that he become exposed to the radiation without his consent, then plaintiff may have stated a claim of battery." *Id.* at 387–388. Unlike in the *Maine Yankee Atomic Power Co.* case, the court required the plaintiff to also plead in the battery action that he was exposed to levels of radiation in excess of federal regulations governing allowable occupational dose limits. The plaintiff's battery claim was later dismissed because it had not been filed within the time limit imposed by the statute of limitations applicable for intentional battery. See *Corcoran v. New York Power Authority*, 202 F.3d 530 (2d Cir.1999).

Should radiation and other toxic exposures be a basis for alleging battery where the defendant has the requisite intent? Should both purposeful and substantial certainty satisfy intent in this context? Should liability be limited to harmful contact or should offensive contact also suffice to establish liability?

**8. Proposed Final Draft to the Restatement (Third) of Torts, Intentional Torts.** The Restatement (Second) finds intent when the defendant either desires or is substantially certain the tortuous consequences would occur. The proposed Restatement (Third), unlike the Restatement (Second) would limit intent liability based on substantial certainty to "a small class of [persons] within a localized area." Restatement (Third) of Torts § 1, Comment e. In addition, the proposed Restatement recognizes courts may choose in some cases only to find intent where the consequences were purposeful. Restatement (Third) of Torts § 1, Comment a. *See* Sec. A, Note 2, *supra* at pages 4–5. Are these proposed changes limiting intentional liability appropriate? How would they impact on the environmental cases discussed in the previous notes?

**9. Further Study.** For further study see McAuliffe, *Resurrecting An Old Cause of Action for a New Wrong: Battery as a Toxic Tort*, 20 Environmental Affairs 265 (1993); Rimer, *Secondhand Smoke Damages: Extending a Cause of Action for Battery Against a Tobacco Manufacturer*, 24 S.W.U.L. Rev. 1237 (1995).

# SECTION C.  ASSAULT

### I DE S ET UX v. W DE S
At the Assizes, 1348.
Y.B.Lib.Ass. folio 99, placitum 60.

I de S and M, his wife, complain of W de S concerning this, that the said W, in the year, etc., with force and arms did make an assault upon the said M at S and beat her. And W pleaded not guilty. And it was found by the verdict of the inquest that the said W came at night to the house of the said I and sought to buy his wine, but the door of the tavern was shut and he beat upon the door with a hatchet which he had in his hand, and the wife of the plaintiff put her head out of the window and commanded him to stop, and he saw and he struck with the hatchet but did not hit the woman. Whereupon the inquest said that it seemed to them that there was no trespass since no harm was done.

THORPE, C.J. There is harm done and a trespass for which he shall recover damages since he made an assault upon the woman, as has been found, although he did no other harm. Wherefore tax the damages, etc. And they taxed the damages at half a mark. Thorpe awarded that they should recover their damages, etc., and that other should be taken. And so note that for an assault a man shall recover damages, etc.

## CASTRO v. LOCAL 1199, NATIONAL HEALTH & HUMAN SERVICES EMPLOYEES UNION

United States District Court, S.D. New York.
964 F.Supp. 719 (1997).

PRESKA, District Judge:

\* \* \*

The facts, drawing all justifiable inferences in favor of the non-movant, are as follows: Plaintiff is an Hispanic woman, now in her mid-forties, who has asthma. She obtained a position with the defendant union in 1986 to work as an organizer. Plaintiff's position required that she work both indoors and outdoors. Plaintiff spent a majority of her time indoors working at her desk or attending meetings. As necessary, plaintiff also occasionally led picket lines outdoors. Plaintiff's doctor advised her to avoid extreme temperatures because it aggravated her asthma symptoms. This was the only restriction that plaintiff was required to observe that limited her employment. In her deposition, plaintiff stated, "I was willing and capable of performing my duties. The only accommodation that I got—I wanted was that in extreme cold or heat, that I was not to be standing outside in the cold."

\* \* \*

Plaintiff's assault claim against Frankel arises out of events that allegedly took place at a routine meeting on Friday, April 8, 1994. Those attending the meeting were defendant Frankel, plaintiff's supervisor, Patricia Harris, and four other union employees. Plaintiff had returned from an extended disability leave that Monday and had not received her usual assignment. When plaintiff questioned Harris about this matter at the meeting, Harris was unresponsive. Harris then assigned plaintiff to assist another organizer in preparing for an arbitration, an assignment which plaintiff found to be unsatisfactory. Plaintiff became upset at this point and pleaded with her supervisor to "level" with her and tell her "what the hell was going on."

At this point, plaintiff claims that Steve Frankel, screamed, "You know something, if I was you, I would take whatever assignment they give me and that's it." When plaintiff asked Frankel what he meant, Frankel slammed his hand on the table again and responded, "If I was you, I would take whatever they give me, because you could lose more than your job." Plaintiff claims that Frankel was visibly angry during the course of the exchange as he was "red in the face," slamming the table, and "coming at" her by wheeling his chair closer and closer to her. Plaintiff implored Frankel to clarify his statement by asking, "What do you mean I could lose more than my job? Are you threatening my life?" Frankel then stated, "Take it any way you want." Plaintiff gathered her things and stated, "Well, it seems, Pat, you're not going to give me an assignment. It seems I am amongst enemies here," and left the meeting.

Under New York law, assault is the intentional placing of another person in apprehension of imminent harmful or offensive contact. *United*

*National Ins., Co. v. Waterfront New York Realty Corp.,* 994 F.2d 105, 108 (2d Cir.1993); *Cohen v. Davis,* 926 F.Supp. 399, 402 (S.D.N.Y.1996); *Hayes v. Schultz,* 150 A.D.2d 522, 541 N.Y.S.2d 115, 116 (2d Dep't 1989). With respect to verbal threats, "words not accompanied by circumstances inducing a reasonable apprehension of bodily harm, such as movements of drawing back a fist, aiming a blow, or the show of a weapon, do not constitute an assault." *Williams v. Port Authority of New York and New Jersey,* 880 F.Supp. 980, 994 (E.D.N.Y.1995). The facts of *Williams* are similar to the present case. In *Williams,* the plaintiff, an employee of defendant Port Authority, was called into his supervisor's office where his supervisor reprimanded him. Once inside the office, the plaintiff claimed that the supervisor used a racial slur, backed him against the wall, and threatened to "get him." The *Williams* court dismissed the complaint finding that no assault occurred because the supervisor's threat was "forward-looking," and not of such nature as to lead the plaintiff to believe that his supervisor was going to strike him at or near that point in time.

Similarly, in the present case, the actions that plaintiff asserts constitute an assault—plaintiff's interpretation of Frankel's remarks as a threat, Frankel "slamming" the table with his hand and moving his chair closer to plaintiff during the course of the exchange—were "forward-looking" and were not accompanied by gestures that would cause plaintiff to reasonably believe that she was in danger of imminent bodily harm. Furthermore, plaintiff's own admission indicates that her apprehension of bodily harm was not imminent. Accordingly, defendant Frankel's motion for summary judgment is granted as to plaintiff's assault claim.

\* \* \*

## NOTES

**1. Restatement Definition.** Assault occurs where the defendant's acts intentionally cause the plaintiff reasonable apprehension of an immediate harmful or offensive contact. The Restatement (Second) of Torts articulates the tort as follows:

> An actor is subject to liability to another for assault if (a) he acts intending to cause a harmful or offensive contact with the person of the other or a third person, or an imminent apprehension of such a contact, and (b) the other is thereby put in such imminent apprehension.

Restatement (Second) of Torts § 21 (1965). See also Keeton, *Prosser and Keeton on the Law of Torts* § 10; Diamond, Levine & Madden, *Understanding Torts* § 1.03 (2nd ed. 2000) and Dobbs, *The Law of Torts* §§ 33–35 (2000). The Restatement, unlike most courts, does not require that the apprehension be reasonable.

**2. Compensation for Mental Distress.** Do you agree with the court in *I de S et Ux v. W de S* that the victim suffered harm and that, at least in this context, mental distress should be compensated? Despite its early origin, compensation for mental distress, particularly in the context of negligence (see Chapter 2, Sec. H, infra) remains controversial.

**3. The Requirement of Imminent Apprehension.** To state a claim for assault, the plaintiff must apprehend an imminent harmful or offensive contact. For example, in *Yale v. Town of Allenstown*, 969 F.Supp. 798, (D.N.H. 1997), a police officer brought an action against another officer. The plaintiff was working on an exam for a promotion when the other officer walked approximately five feet behind her and drew his firearm, leading her to believe she was about to be shot. The District Court of New Hampshire held that the officer was put in imminent apprehension of a harmful contact. Consider also, *Sides v. Cleland*, 436 Pa.Super. 618, 648 A.2d 793 (1994), where the defendant, along with his two friends, approached the plaintiff, wielding chainsaws and screamed, "Bring on the chainsaws!" The men responded by cutting the tree in which the plaintiff sat. The Supreme Court of Pennsylvania held that a factfinder could not only reasonably conclude that an assault had occurred, but that the court was at "a loss to understand how a factfinder could arrive at any other conclusion."

But consider cases where the court determined that the plaintiff failed to state a claim for assault because the requisite imminent apprehension had not been satisfied. In *Stump v. Wal–Mart Stores, Inc.*, 942 F.Supp. 347 (E.D.Ky.1996), the court held that the alleged act of "striking the table" and demanding that an employee admit that she had failed to charge a customer for $19 worth of merchandise did not constitute assault. The court concluded that a "forced and harassing interrogation" by itself does not create imminent apprehension of harmful or offensive contact. Consider also *Newman v. Gehl Corporation*, 731 F.Supp. 1048 (M.D.Fla.1990) where the court held a threat against a former employee contemplating a sexual harassment action that "anyone who might do anything against the company should think twice" because he could make a phone call and the person would be "taken care of" did not establish the necessary "fear of imminent peril" to establish assault.

By contrast, consider *Campbell v. Kansas State University*, 780 F.Supp. 755 (D.Kan.1991), where a university department head's verbal remark that he felt like hitting his assistant on the buttocks, after he had already slapped her on the buttocks, constituted assault. The court reasoned that it was an intentional threat, made with apparent ability to inflict offensive contact on the assistant, resulting in the assistant's immediate apprehension of the offensive contact.

Do you agree that assault should limit recovery to victims who suffer apprehension of imminent contact? Why shouldn't a serious threat of future harm constitute assault?

**4. Reasonable Apprehension.** Most courts, unlike the Restatement (see Note 1, *supra*), require that apprehension of a harmful or offensive contact be reasonable. For example in *Cohen v. Davis*, 926 F.Supp. 399 (S.D.N.Y.1996), the plaintiff alleged a security guard pursued her in order to retrieve her office keys after she had been dismissed from her job. The court held that whether the security guard's actions constituted assault was dependent on the jury concluding "whether the ordinary person would ... be in apprehension of harmful or offensive contact."

**5. Contemporaneous Perception.** In *Tom v. Lenox Hill Hospital*, 165 Misc.2d 313, 627 N.Y.S.2d 874 (N.Y. 1995), the court rejected a patient's assault claim against a surgeon for an alleged unconsented surgical procedure, since the patient was unconscious and was therefore unable to be apprehensive of imminent harmful or offensive contact. Consider also *Haines v. Fisher*, 82 F.3d 1503 (10th Cir.1996), where three police officers and a police dispatcher played a practical joke on a Seven–Eleven clerk by orchestrating a fake armed robbery. Police officers in disguise fired blanks at the store clerk. The victim was not amused and sued for assault. The court upheld the jury's finding that the victim had recognized the police officer in time to be aware he was not actually endangered and therefore did not suffer apprehension of imminent harmful or offensive contact.

The requirement of contemporaneous perception in assault should be contrasted with battery which does not require that the victim be conscious at the time that contact occurred. Is there a justification for this distinction between battery and assault liability?

**6. Tort versus Criminal Law Definition of Assault.** The tort definition of assault differs significantly from the traditional common law criminal definition of assault. Criminal assault occurs when the defendant attempts to inflict harmful or offensive contact. See Lafave & Scott, *Criminal Law* § 7.16(A) (3rd ed. 2000). Under the criminal law definition, perception by the victim is not required to constitute assault. Under the tort but not criminal law definition, an actual attempt to inflict contact is not required, only the intent to create apprehension. Consequently, pulling the trigger of an unloaded gun can constitute tort but not criminal assault. Can a policy rationally justify the difference between the tort and criminal law approach?

# SECTION D.   THE CONCEPT OF TRANSFERRED INTENT

## ALTEIRI v. COLASSO

Supreme Court of Connecticut.
168 Conn. 329, 362 A.2d 798 (1975).

LOISELLE, Associate Justice.

This action is one for battery brought by a minor, the plaintiff Richard Alteiri, to recover for injuries he suffered, and by his mother, the named plaintiff, to recover for expenses incurred. The complaint alleges that while the minor plaintiff was playing in the back yard of a home at which he was visiting, the defendant threw a rock, stone or other missile into the yard and struck the minor plaintiff in the eye and "[a]s a result of said battery by the defendant, the plaintiff Richard Alteiri suffered severe, painful and permanent injuries."

\* \* \*

Six interrogatories were submitted to the jury. Two interrogatories were answered in the affirmative as follows: "On April 2, 1966, did the defendant, John Colasso, throw a stone which struck the plaintiff, Richard Alteiri, in the right eye?" Answer: "Yes." "[W]as that stone thrown by John Colasso with the intent to scare any person other than Richard Alteiri?" Answer: "Yes." The jury answered "No" to four other questions concerning whether the defendant had intended to strike either the minor plaintiff or any other person and whether he had thrown the stone either negligently or wantonly and recklessly. A plaintiffs' verdict was returned. The defendant has appealed from the judgment rendered.

\* \* \*

Error is assigned in the court's denial of the defendant's motions to set aside the verdict and for judgment notwithstanding the verdict. The defendant claims that the jury could not have reasonably and logically rendered a verdict under our law when in their answers to the interrogatories they expressly found that the defendant did not throw the stone with intent to strike either the minor plaintiff or any other person. . . .

\* \* \*

By their answers to the interrogatories it is clear that the jury found that the battery to the minor plaintiff was one committed willfully. The issue to be determined on this appeal is whether a jury upon finding that the defendant threw the stone with the intent to scare someone other than the one who was struck by the stone can legally and logically return a verdict for the plaintiffs for a willful battery.

\* \* \*

It is not essential that the precise injury which was done be the one intended. 1 Cooley, Torts (4th Ed.). § 98. An act designed to cause bodily injury to a particular person is actionable as a battery not only by the person intended by the actor to be injured but also by another who is in fact so injured. Restatement (Second), 1 Torts § 13; *Singer v. Marx*, 144 Cal.App.2d 637, 301 P.2d 440; *Smith v. Moran*, 43 Ill.App.2d 373, 193 N.E.2d 466; *McGee v. Vanover*, 148 Ky. 737, 147 S.W. 742; *Talmage v. Smith*, 101 Mich. 370, 59 N.W. 656; *Carnes v. Thompson*, 48 S.W.2d 903 (Mo.); *Morrow v. Flores*, 255 S.W.2d 621 (Tex.Civ.App.); *Bannister v. Mitchell*, 127 Va. 578, 104 S.E. 800; Prosser, Torts (4th Ed.) § 8; 1 Harper & James, Torts § 3.3, p. 218. This principle of 'transferred intent' applies as well to the action of assault. See *Davis v. McKey*, 167 So.2d 416 (La.App.); *Jeppsen v. Jensen*, 47 Utah 536, 155 P. 429; Prosser, *supra*; 6 Am.Jur.2d, Assault and Battery, § 115. And where one intends merely an assault, if bodily injury results to one other than the person whom the actor intended to put in apprehension of bodily harm, it is battery actionable by the injured person. Restatement (Second), 1 Torts § 16; *Brown v. Martinez*, 68 N.M. 271, 361 P.2d 152; *Daingerfield v. Thompson*, 74 Va. (33 Gratt.) 136; Prosser, *supra*.

The defendant claims that comment b to subsection 2 of § 16 of the Restatement (Second) indicates that subsection 2 applies only to negligent acts where a person not intended to be injured is injured. The comment states in pertinent part that "[i]t is not necessary that the actor know or have reason even to suspect that the other is in the vicinity of the third person whom the actor intends to affect and, therefore, that he should recognize that his act, though directed against a third person, involves a risk of causing bodily harm to the other so that the act would be negligent toward him." It is clear that the gist of this comment is that the actor need not know or suspect the presence of the third party, that is, need not be negligent.

It follows that the jury could logically and legally return a plaintiffs' verdict for willful battery, and that the court in accepting that verdict and denying the defendant's motions was not in error.

There is no error.

In this opinion the other judges concurred.

### NOTES

**1. The Doctrine of Transferred Intent.** The doctrine of transferred intent has traditionally been applied to five intentional torts: battery; assault; false imprisonment (see Chapter 1, Sec. E, infra); trespass to land (see Chapter 4, infra); and trespass to chattel (personal property). Under the doctrine a defendant's intent to commit any of these five torts can constitute the necessary intent to commit any of the other of these five torts. As *Alteiri v. Colasso* also illustrates, under the doctrine of transferred intent, an intent to commit any of these five torts against a particular victim constitutes intent against any other person, no matter how unforeseeable, who is instead or also a victim of one of these five torts.

Consequently, if A intends to commit battery against B but instead only assaults B and/or C, the intent to commit battery constitutes the necessary intent to assault B and/or C.

Historically the five torts were merged in a single action of trespass which encompassed injuries representing all five of the torts. Consequently, it has been argued that the transferred intent doctrine reflects the historical unification of the five torts. See Keeton, *Prosser and Keeton on the Law of Torts*, § 8 (5th ed. 1984); Diamond, Levine & Madden, *Understanding Torts* § 1.01[D] (2nd ed. 2000) and Dobbs, *The Law of Torts* § 40 (2000). While many courts and treatises continue to accept the doctrine, the Restatement (Second) of Torts does not endorse it generally but incorporates it in its definition of the intent required for the torts of assault and battery. See Restatement (Second) of Tort §§ 13, 21 (1965).

**2. Examples of Transferred Intent.** Consider *Hall v. McBryde*, 919 P.2d 910 (Colo.App.1996), where a youth, in an attempt to scare away a motorist, exchanged gunfire with the passing motorist who had begun shooting toward the youth's home. One bullet inadvertently struck the plaintiff, who lived next door to the youth, causing serious injury. The Colorado Court of Appeals held that, if the bullet that struck the plaintiff was fired by the youth, the doctrine of transferred intent would apply. Where one intends an assault against one person and bodily injury results to another, then it is a battery, actionable by the injured person. Similarly, in *Davis v. White*, 18 B.R. 246 (Bankr.E.D.Va.1982), the plaintiff was inadvertently struck in the stomach with a bullet fired by the defendant, but intended for another person. The Bankruptcy Court of Virginia held that "Under the doctrine of transferred intent, one who intends a battery is liable for that battery when he unexpectedly hits a stranger instead of the intended victim." Consider also, *Smith v. Moran*, 43 Ill.App.2d 373, 193 N.E.2d 466 (1963), where the Appellate Court of Illinois held that the doctrine of transferred intent applied where the defendant entered a restaurant with the intent to shoot one waitress and not only shot the intended victim, but the plaintiff as well. Consider also, *Holloway v. Wachovia Bank and Trust Company*, 109 N.C.App. 403, 428 S.E.2d 453 (1993), where the defendant pointed a gun at the driver of an automobile in an effort to repossess the automobile. Although the gun was not pointed directly at the passenger-plaintiff, because the plaintiff suffered imminent apprehension of a harmful contact, the Court of Appeals of North Carolina held that the doctrine of transferred intent was applicable.

But consider *Allstate Insurance Company v. Lewis*, 732 F.Supp. 1112 (D.Colo.1990), where a juvenile intended to pull the trigger on a gun, whose chamber the youngster believed to be empty. The juvenile's intention was neither to fire bullets nor to shoot the victim. Thus, the District Court of Colorado held that the doctrine of transferred intent was not applicable. The court reasoned that if the youngster had intended to fire the gun in order to frighten the plaintiff, he could have been held liable for battery if the bullet had unexpectedly hit the plaintiff because the juvenile's intent to assault the plaintiff then could have been transferred to the shooting. But, as was the case here, "the shooting was accidental and not the ordinary consequence of the assault."

**3. Doctrine is Not Applied to Other Intentional Torts.** Also consider *In the Matter of EDC, Incorporated*, 930 F.2d 1275 (7th Cir.1991), which illustrates the courts' unwillingness to extend the doctrine of transferred intent beyond the traditional five torts. The Seventh Circuit held that the plaintiffs had standing to sue for fraud even though they were not its primary victims. The court was careful, however, to assert, "That is not because this is a case of transferred intent. . . . transferred intent is not the general rule in fraud cases." Rather, the court reasoned that because fooling the plaintiffs was an intended intermediate step in the defendant's scheme to defraud another and although the defendant "would have been happy if the [plaintiffs] had not been hurt, it [did] not defeat the plaintiff's rights." Ultimately, the court decided that it was not because of the "fiction of transferred intent" that the plaintiffs were defrauded, but because the defendant knew that the plaintiffs would be hurt, which the court equated to deliberateness.

**4. The Policy of Transferred Intent.** Is it fair to transform the intent from a property tort to a personal injury tort? Is the defendant's moral culpability the same for all torts? Is transferred intent appropriate in torts but not criminal law? Note that most states under felony murder impose murder convictions on defendants who only intended a felony like robbery when a victim is accidentally killed. Does transferred intent help deter wrongful conduct?

**5. Mistake Doctrine.** Under the mistake doctrine in intentional torts it is no defense that the defendant mistakes, even reasonably, the identity of the property or person he acts against. For example, under *Ranson v. Kitner*, 31 Ill.App. 241 (1889), the defendant was held liable for shooting a dog even when it was reasonable to mistake the dog for a wolf which the defendant would have been privileged to kill. Similarly, in *Perry v. Jefferies*, 61 S.C. 292, 39 S.E. 515 (S.C. 1901), the defendant was held liable for intentional trespass when he removed trees from plaintiff's land even though he thought it was his own land. The mistake doctrine, while often acknowledged, is not endorsed generally by the Restatement. Restatement 2nd § 164 does specifically adopt the mistake doctrine for trespass. Does the mistake doctrine expand the concept of intent beyond appropriate limits? Can it be justified to prevent unjust enrichment, particularly in the context of property? See Diamond, Levine & Madden, *supra*, § 10.1[E]; Keeton, *supra*, § 17; Dobbs, *supra*, § 69.

# SECTION E.  FALSE IMPRISONMENT; MALICIOUS PROSECUTION; ABUSE OF PROCESS

## DUPLER v. SEUBERT

Supreme Court of Wisconsin.

69 Wis.2d 373, 230 N.W.2d 626 (1975).

WILKIE, Chief Justice.

This is a false imprisonment action. On April 23, 1971, plaintiff-appellant Ethel M. Dupler was fired from her job with the defendant-respondent Wisconsin Telephone Company. She was informed of her discharge during an hour-and-a-half session with her two superiors, defendants-respondents Keith Peterson and Helen Seubert, who Dupler claims, falsely imprisoned her during a portion of this time period. A jury found that Peterson and Seubert did falsely imprison Dupler and fixed damages at $7,500. The trial court gave Dupler the option of accepting a lower amount—$500—or a new trial on the issue of damages. The option was not exercised, judgment for $500 was entered, and Mrs. Dupler appeals. We reverse and remand for a new trial on the issue of damages, but give plaintiff-appellant an option to accept $1,000 damages in lieu of a new trial.

Dupler had worked for the Telephone Company as a customer service representative since 1960. At approximately 4:30 on April 23rd, Seubert asked Dupler to come to Peterson's office. When all three were inside, sitting down, with the door closed, Seubert told Dupler the Telephone Company would no longer employ her and that she could choose either to resign or be fired. Dupler testified that she refused to resign and that in the conversation that followed, Peterson discussed several alternatives short of dismissal, all of which had been considered but rejected.

At approximately 5 o'clock, Dupler testified, she began to feel sick to her stomach and said "You have already fired me. Why don't you just let me go." She made a motion to get up but Peterson told her to sit down in "a very loud harsh voice." Then, Dupler testified, she began to feel violently ill and stated "I got to go. I can't take this any more. I'm sick to my stomach. I know I'm going to throw up." She got up and started for the door but Seubert also arose and stood in front of the door. After Dupler repeated that she was sick, Seubert allowed her to exit, but followed her to the men's washroom, where Dupler did throw up. Following this, at approximately 5:25, Seubert asked Dupler to return to Peterson's office where she had left her purse to discuss the situation further. Dupler testified that she went back to the office and reached for her purse; Seubert again closed the door and Peterson said "[i]n a loud voice 'Sit down. I'm still your boss. I'm not through with you.'" At approximately 5:40 Dupler told Peterson her husband was waiting for her outside in a car and Peterson told her to go outside and ask her husband to come inside. Dupler then went outside and explained the situation to her husband who said "You get back in there and get your coat and if you aren't right out I'll call the police." Dupler returned to Peterson's office and was again told in a loud tone of voice to sit down. She said Seubert and Peterson were trying to convince her to resign rather than be fired and again reviewed the alternatives that had been considered. Dupler then said: "What's the sense of all this. Why keep torturing me. Let me go. Let me go." She stated that Peterson replied "No, we still aren't finished. We have a lot of things to discuss, your retirement pay, your vacation, other things." Finally, at approximately 6:00 Peterson told Dupler they could talk further on the phone or at her house, and Dupler left. When asked why she had stayed in Peterson's office for such a long time, Dupler replied:

> "Well, for one thing, Helen, Mrs. Seubert, had blocked the door, and tempers had been raised with all the shouting and screaming, I was just plain scared to make an effort. There were two against one."

Peterson and Seubert did not dispute that Dupler had been fired on April 23rd, or that the conference lasted from 4:30 to 6 p.m., or that Dupler became very upset and sick to her stomach and had to leave to throw up. Peterson admitted that Dupler had asked to leave and that he requested that she stay and continue talking so she could indicate whether she wished to resign or be fired. Seubert said Dupler did not so indicate until 'within three minutes of her leaving.' Both denied that any loud or threatening language had been used, or that Dupler was detained against her will. Peterson said neither he nor Seubert even raised their voices. He said the session was so lengthy because Dupler continued to plead for another chance, and to request reasons for the dismissal.

The jury found that both Peterson and Seubert falsely imprisoned Dupler and fixed her damages at $7,500.

\* \* \*

Is the jury's verdict, finding that Dupler was falsely imprisoned, supported by the evidence?

The essence of false imprisonment is the intentional, unlawful, and unconsented restraint by one person of the physical liberty of another. In *Maniaci v. Marquette University*, the court adopted the definition of false imprisonment contained in sec. 35 of the Restatement of Torts 2d, which provides in part:

> "False Imprisonment
>
> "(1) An actor is subject to liability to another for false imprisonment if
>
> > "(a) he acts intending to confine the other or a third person within boundaries fixed by the actor, and

"(b) his act directly or indirectly results in such a confinement of the other, and

"(c) the other is conscious of the confinement or is harmed by it."[8]

Secs. 39[9] and 40[10] provide that the confinement may be caused by physical force or the threat of physical force, and the comment to sec. 40 indicates the threat may either be express, or inferred from the person's conduct. As Prosser comments:

*"Character of Defendant's Act*

"The restraint may be by means of physical barriers, or by threats of force which intimidate the plaintiff into compliance with orders. It is sufficient that he submits to an apprehension of force reasonably to be understood from the conduct of the defendant, although no force is used or even expressly threatened.... This gives rise, in borderline cases, to questions of fact, turning upon the details of the testimony, as to what was reasonably to be understood and implied from the defendant's conduct, tone of voice and the like, which seldom can be reflected accurately in an appellate record, and normally are for the jury."[11]

This is precisely such a case and we conclude that the record contains sufficient evidence from which the jury could have concluded that Mrs. Dupler was intentionally confined, against her will, by an implied threat of actual physical restraint. She testified that defendant Peterson ordered her in a loud voice to remain seated several times, after she expressed the desire to leave. She reported being "berrated, screamed and hollered at," and said the reason she did not just walk out of the room was that "Mrs. Seubert had blocked the door, and tempers had been raised with all the shouting and screaming, I was just plain scared to make an effort. There were two against one." The jury obviously believed Mrs. Dupler's rather than the defendants' account of what transpired, as it had the right to do, and we conclude her testimony was sufficient to support the jury's verdict.

Defendants rely upon the 1926 case of *Weiler v. Herzfeld–Phillipson Co.*,[12] where this court held that an employer, who had detained an employee in his office for several hours upon suspicion of theft and then discharged her, was not liable for false imprisonment. This case is distinguishable, however, principally upon the ground that in Weiler the court emphasized several times that during the entire session the plaintiff was still employed by defendant and "was compensated for

---

**8.**  Restatement, 1 Torts 2d, p. 52, sec. 35.

**9.**  *Id.* at page 59: "39. Confinement by Physical Force"

"The confinement may be by overpowering physical force, or by submission to physical force."

**10.**  *Id.*: "40. Confinement by Threats of Physical Force"

"The confinement may be by submission to a threat to apply physical force to the other's person immediately upon the other's going or attempting to go beyond the area in which the actor intends to confine him."

**11.**  Prosser, Torts (4th ed. 1971), sec. 11, p. 44.

**12.**  (1926), 189 Wis. 554, 208 N.W. 599.

every minute of the time spent by her in the office.'' In the instant case, Dupler was compensated only through 5 p.m., and according to her testimony, she was not ordered to remain in the office, after she requested to leave, until after 5 p.m.

We conclude that Weiler is not controlling here and that the jury could properly find that defendants falsely imprisoned Dupler by compelling her to remain in Peterson's office against her will after 5 p.m. We conclude the imprisonment ceased when Dupler left the building to visit her husband, but resumed when she reentered Peterson's office to get her coat in order to leave, but was commanded to stay.

Order affirmed; judgment modified with new trial ordered on the issue of damages unless, within twenty days of remittitur, plaintiff-appellant Ethel Dupler elects to accept judgment for $1,000, and, as modified affirmed.

### NOTES

**1. Restatement Definition.** False imprisonment is defined as the unlawful and intentional confinement or restraint of the victim by the defendant, within a bounded area. The Restatement (Second) of Torts § 35 (1965), quoted in the principal case, articulates the generally accepted view. See also Keeton, *Prosser and Keeton on the Law of Torts* § 11 (5th ed. 1984); Diamond, Levine & Madden, *Understanding Torts* § 1.04 (2nd ed. 2000) and Dobbs, *The Law of Torts* §§ 36–39 (2000).

**2. Means of Confinement.** The confinement or restraint in false imprisonment can be accomplished by: (1) physical barriers; (2) force or threat of immediate force; (3) omissions where there is a duty to act; (4) improper assertions of legal authority (false arrest). See Restatement (Second) of Torts §§ 37, 38, 39.

Consider *Bureerong v. Uvawas*, 959 F.Supp. 1231 (C.D.Cal. 1997), where immigrant garment workers who were involuntarily held and employed in a complex brought an action for false imprisonment against both the operators of the complex and the manufacturer who contracted with the operators. Defendants accomplished restraint through express and implied threats of physical force including threatening harm to the plaintiffs and their families if they attempted to escape. The California District Court held that the facts alleged were sufficient to state a cause of action for false imprisonment. Consider also *Fischer v. Famous–Barr Co.*, 646 S.W.2d 819 (Mo.App.1982), where a store employee seized plaintiff's bag and the plaintiff refused to abandon her property and followed the employee into the store. The court held that the employee's action against the victim's bag constituted false imprisonment in light of her unwillingness to abandon the bag.

As observed above, an omission can lead to liability. In *Whittaker v. Sandford*, 110 Me. 77, 85 A. 399 (Maine 1912), for example, defendant's failure to bring plaintiff back to shore, pursuant to an earlier promise, resulting in the victim's confinement on a boat, was held to constitute false imprisonment since the defendant breached his obligation to return the victim to land.

**3. Victim Must be Confined in Bounded Area.** Consider that it is not false imprisonment if the victim can proceed in any direction, even though she may be prevented from going in the direction she prefers. For example, in *Smith v. Comair Incorporated*, 134 F.3d 254 (4th Cir.1998), a passenger sued Delta Airlines for false imprisonment based on the airline's refusal to permit him to board his flight after a layover. The airline had previously failed to ask for the passenger's photo at the point of original departure. The Fourth Circuit Court held that because the passenger was "free at all times to leave the airport or leave Cincinnati altogether by any means he could arrange other than on a Comair flight," the allegations were not sufficient to state a claim for false imprisonment. However, the area of the confinement can be large. In *Albright v. Oliver*, 975 F.2d 343 (7th Cir.1992), the court suggested wrongful confinement in an entire state could constitute false imprisonment, claiming: "if Denmark was a dungeon to Hamlet ... we suppose Illinois could be a prison to Kevin Albright." However, consider also *Shen v. Leo A. Daly Company*, 222 F.3d 472 (8th Cir.2000), where the Eighth Circuit Court of Appeals held that an employee who was not allowed to leave the country of Taiwan due to his employer's refusal to pay taxes was not falsely imprisoned. The court stated, "although it is difficult to define exactly how close the level of restraint must be, in this case, the country of Taiwan is clearly too great an area within which to be falsely imprisoned."

**4. Consciousness of Confinement.** The tort of false imprisonment traditionally required that the victim be conscious of his or her confinement. The Restatement (Second) of Torts § 35 allows liability without consciousness if the victim is harmed. Some courts have gone even further. For example, in *Kajtazi v. Kajtazi*, 488 F.Supp. 15 (E.D.N.Y. 1978), a mother brought an action for false imprisonment against her child's father when the father abducted the child and removed the child to Yugoslavia. The District Court of New York held regarding the element of awareness of confinement that "where a person by infancy or incompetency has no such will as enables him to exercise intelligent and legal volition as to his custody, the action may be predicated upon his restraint or removal against the will of the party having his legal custody." Should consciousness of confinement or harm be a predicate to recovery?

**5. Coercion Must Be Immediate and Physical.** Consider that the tort of false imprisonment generally fails to recognize highly coercive, non-immediate physical threats. For example, in *Snyder v. Evangelical Orthodox Church*, 216 Cal.App.3d 297, 264 Cal.Rptr. 640 (1989), the California Court of Appeal held that a church bishop was not falsely imprisoned when members of a church ordered him to meditate in isolation for one week on a threat of revealing his adulterous relationship with the church's parishioner and of not absolving him of his sins. The bishop was free to leave at any time since he was subject to no physical restraints. Consider also, *Molko v. Holy Spirit Association for the Unification of World Christianity*, 46 Cal.3d 1092, 252 Cal.Rptr. 122, 762 P.2d 46 (1988), where the California Supreme Court held that threats of divine Retribution by the church against former members were insufficient to state a claim for false imprisonment because the members had not been subject to physical restraints.

Similarly, the tort of false imprisonment fails to recognize the use of threats of economic retaliation or termination of employment to coerce a victim to remain. For example, in *Trahan v. Bellsouth Telecommunications, Inc.*, 881 F.Supp. 1080 (W.D.La.1995), the Louisiana District Court held that an employee who was threatened with the loss of his job if he did not remain on company premises could not state a claim for false imprisonment where there was no evidence of physical restraint.

Consider also *Lopez v. Winchell's Donut House*, 126 Ill.App.3d 46, 81 Ill.Dec. 507, 466 N.E.2d 1309 (Ill.Ct.App.1984), where the court held that an employee suspected of theft had agreed to go into a back room to be interrogated in response only to moral pressure and, therefore, had not been falsely imprisoned.

**6.   Should Tort Be Expanded?** Should the tort of false imprisonment be expanded to include non-immediate physical threats or even intense economic coercion? Would such an expansion dangerously blur the distinction between legitimate persuasion and illegal coercion? Are most workers economically coerced to be in places against their will? Was the defendant in the principal case economically, morally or physically coerced?

## MANIACI v. MARQUETTE UNIVERSITY

Supreme Court of Wisconsin.
50 Wis.2d 287, 184 N.W.2d 168 (1971).

Appeal from a judgment of the circuit court for Milwaukee County: Robert J. Parins, Circuit Judge for the Fourteenth Circuit, Presiding. Reversed and remanded.

In September of 1966, Saralee Maniaci left her home in Windsor, Ontario, Canada, to attend school at Marquette University in Milwaukee. She was sixteen years old at the time. She arrived at the airport in Milwaukee carrying a check for $2,000, which was to be used to pay the year's expenses. She was met at the airport by Father Thomas A. Stemper, a Jesuit priest employed by the university and an old Maniaci family friend. He took her to Heraty Hall, which was to be her dormitory.

In the following months Saralee Maniaci became very dissatisfied with life at Marquette. She found the quality of education unimpressive, and she was bored with her courses. She was also unhappy with the social life. She complained to her father about the "fast" social life at the university. She spent three of the first seven weekends at her parents' home in Windsor. She travelled from Milwaukee to Windsor with Leonard McGravey, a thirty-two-year-old former priest, whom she had known since she was in high school. Each time she went home, she told her parents of her desire to leave Marquette. Her father each time convinced her that things would get better and that she should give the school another chance. She returned to Marquette on October 30, 1966, with the idea that she would give Marquette one more chance, but that if things did not work out, she would have her parents' permission to quit.

On Wednesday, November 2, 1966, she decided to quit school. She told her closest friend, Jean Huby, that she was leaving, and Jean said she wanted to leave too. Jean asked to go home with Saralee to Windsor, because Jean thought her father would send her back to Marquette if she tried to go to her own home. Saralee agreed to this request. Jean got Saralee to promise, however, that she would not tell anyone where they were going.

On Thursday, November 3, 1966, Saralee went to the Student Credit Bank and withdrew the $1300 she had remaining on deposit there. She then went to the railroad station and purchased two tickets to Detroit, which was across the river from Windsor, and as close as she could get to Windsor by train. She then returned to Heraty Hall and began packing.

A representative of the student bank notified the dean of women's office that Saralee had said that she was leaving school. Assistant Dean of Women Patricia Watson notified Esther Morgan, the head resident at Heraty Hall. Esther Morgan notified Joseph Maniaci that his daughter Saralee was intending to run away from school to marry an older man. When Maniaci learned that the man was Leonard McGravey, he said there must be some mistake and gave his approval of whatever plans Leonard McGravey had.

Esther Morgan told Saralee that on Friday morning, November 4, 1966, she was to report to the office of the dean of women. When Saralee failed to report, Dean of Women Mary Alice Cannon went with Assistant Dean Watson to Heraty Hall to persuade Saralee to remain at the school. Saralee admitted that she intended to leave Milwaukee that evening and refused to state her destination. She stated a number of reasons for leaving, including hostility toward her parents, dissatisfaction with education at the university, a desire to act, sing, and write, and a belief that she was more mature than the other students she knew. She insisted that she was going to leave by train at 8 o'clock that evening and that she would notify her father later. She did not state that she had, in fact, received her father's permission to leave. The discussion continued through the morning.

Father Stemper was called about 11:30 a.m. to help persuade Saralee to remain at the school until her parents could be notified. Dean Cannon concluded that Student Health Physician Dean D. Miller should be called. Doctor Miller arrived at Heraty Hall at about 1:30 p.m. accompanied by Nurse June B. Steiner. Doctor Miller conferred with Saralee for about two hours. During that time, Dean Cannon and Assistant Dean Watson persuaded Jean not to leave with Saralee. Throughout the afternoon, unsuccessful attempts were made by Saralee and the dean of women to contact Saralee's father. At 3:30 p.m., Doctor Miller suggested to Dean Cannon that Saralee be hospitalized. Father Stemper saw nothing abnormal about Saralee's conduct and disagreed with Doctor Miller, although he did not know Doctor Miller proposed commitment to a mental hospital.

Milwaukee police officers were called and asked to bring the proper papers for temporary detention of Saralee Maniaci under the emergency provisions of sec. 51.04(1), Stats.[1] The officers arrived at about 4:30 p.m.

---

**1.** "51.04 Temporary detention of persons. (1) Emergency provisions. The sheriff or any other police officer may take into temporary custody any person who is violent or who threatens violence and who appears irresponsible and dangerous. The sheriff or other police officer shall take temporary custody of any person when it appears by application delivered to such officer and executed by 3 persons, one of whom shall be a physician licensed to practice medicine and surgery in this state, that such person has a mental illness, is in need of hospitalization, and is irresponsible and dangerous to himself or others. The application shall set forth the name and address of

The "Application for Temporary Custody" was filled out by Doctor Miller and signed by him, by Dean Cannon, and by Nurse Steiner. The "Application for Temporary Custody" stated:

"That each of the applicants is an adult resident of the State of Wisconsin, and that one of the applicants, Dean D. Miller M.D., is a physician licensed to practice medicine and surgery in this state.

"That Sara Lee Maniaci of the City of Milwaukee, in said county, hereinafter called the patient, is believed to be mentally ill for the reason (state facts observed or information known tending to show existence of mental illness, mental infirmity, or mental deficiency): Sara Lee is a 16 yr. old freshman at Marquette University, wishes to leave the University without the consent of the University officials or her parents, to an unknown destination. Her plans for the future are indefinite and it is obvious that she cannot give rational reasons for leaving.

"That the patient is in need of hospitalization and is irresponsible and dangerous to self or others, so as to require immediate temporary detention by reason of she has persuaded other girls to leave the University with her for reasons which are illogical to us. As a minor we cannot permit her to leave, and feel that she should be confined until her parents have been informed of the situation, and appear on her behalf, and until she has been thoroughly evaluated by a psychiatrist.

"WHEREFORE, your applicants pray for immediate temporary detention of the patient in the custody of the sheriff or other police officer, not exceeding five days, and for a judicial inquiry to determine the mental condition of the patient and for such orders of temporary or permanent nature as may be necessary.

Dean D. Miller M.D., 1945 Wauwatosa Ave. Wauwatosa, Wisc.
Mary Alice Cannon 731 Glenview Ave. Wauwatosa
June B. Steiner RN. 3731 W. Linden Pl. Milwaukee"

The police officers took Saralee to the Milwaukee County General Hospital, where she was taken to a locked ward on the fifth floor for mental observation. The officers said they had an intelligent conversation with Saralee and that she was cooperative and displayed no tendencies toward violence.

\* \* \*

She persuaded a social worker at the hospital to notify Leonard McGravey what had happened to her. At about 11 p.m., McGravey

the patient together with a statement by the physician which describes the illness and reasons why the patient is considered irresponsible and dangerous. This is an emergency provision intended for the protection of persons and property. Such person may be kept in custody until regular proceedings are instituted to cope with the case, but not exceeding 5 days. The application provided for herein shall be presented by such sheriff or other officer to the county * * * court of the county in which the patient is found, and shall be considered an application for mental examination within the meaning of s. 51.01(1)(a)."

arrived at the hospital and was permitted to talk to Saralee after she told the nurse he was her fiancé. She told him what had happened, and he relayed the message to her father. Her father contacted Doctor Miller and insisted that his daughter be released. Doctor Miller was unable to have Saralee released at that time of night, but he arranged to have Saralee transferred from a larger ward on the fifth floor to a locked private room. Doctor Miller did not tell Joseph Maniaci that Saralee would continue to be confined in a mental hospital. She was, however, released from the hospital at about 9 o'clock the next morning. She returned to her dormitory, gathered up her belongings, and went to Windsor. She never returned to Marquette.

On November 29, 1967, an action was commenced by Saralee Maniaci through her guardian ad litem, Andrew C. Shane, and by her father, Joseph Maniaci, against Marquette University, Doctor Dean D. Miller, Dean Mary Alice Cannon, and Nurse June B. Steiner. During the course of the trial, all causes of action were dismissed except Saralee's action against the defendants for false imprisonment. That matter was submitted to the jury, and it returned a general verdict for the plaintiff and assessed her damages as follows: (1) compensatory damages—$5,000; (2) punitive damages: Marquette University—$35,000; Doctor Miller—$2,000; Dean Cannon—$5,000; and Nurse Steiner—$1.

On motions after verdict, the trial court upheld the compensatory damages award, but reduced the punitive damages assessment against Marquette University to $12,000 and the assessment against Dean Cannon to $1,000. Judgment was entered on the verdict as so modified. The defendants appeal from this judgment. The plaintiff also cross-appealed from the judgment.

HEFFERNAN, Justice.

The defendants' appeal is premised upon the contention that the trial court erroneously permitted the trial to proceed, and the jury verdict to be rendered, on the question of false imprisonment. Defendants contend that plaintiff's only possible cause of action was for malicious prosecution, and, as a corollary to that contention, take the position that the evidence was insufficient to sustain a verdict for malicious prosecution, and that the damages were excessive.

Plaintiffs, respondents herein, take the position that the facts spelled out a cause of action for false imprisonment, that the verdict is supported by sufficient evidence, and that the damages found by the jury were reasonable.

We agree with the defendants in their contention that no cause of action has been proved under the theory of false imprisonment.

This court has defined the tort of false imprisonment as, "The unlawful restraint by one person of the physical liberty of another." *Lane v. Collins* (1965), 29 Wis.2d 66, 69, 138 N.W.2d 264, 266. It is apparent, therefore, that a "lawful" restraint does not constitute false imprisonment, though it may well constitute some other tort. Restatement, Torts 2d, page 52, sec. 35, points out:

"(1) An actor is subject to liability to another for false imprisonment if (a) he acts intending to confine the other or a third person within boundaries fixed by the actor, and (b) his act directly or indirectly results in such a confinement of the other * * *."

The commentary on this section states, however, that an act which makes an actor liable for confinement otherwise than by a lawful arrest is not false imprisonment, but may be malicious prosecution or abuse of process.

Restatement, Torts 2d, p. 69, sec. 45A, points out that, "One who instigates or participates in the unlawful confinement of another is subject to liability to the other for false imprisonment." Comment (b) to the chapter states in part:

"In order for this Section to be applicable to an arrest, it must be a false arrest, made without legal authority. One who instigates or partici-pates in a lawful arrest, as for example an arrest made under a properly issued warrant by an officer charged with the duty of enforcing it, may become liable for malicious prosecution, as stated in Chapter 29, or for abuse of process, as stated in Chapter 31, but he is not liable for false imprisonment, since no false imprisonment has occurred."

Prosser points out that no cause of action for false imprisonment will lie:

"If the defendant complies with the formal requirements of the law, as by swearing out a valid warrant, so that the arrest of the plaintiff is legally authorized * * *. He is therefore liable, if at all, only for a misuse of legal process to effect a valid arrest for an improper purpose." Prosser, Law of Torts (Hornbook series, 3d ed.), p. 62, sec. 12.

Harper and James, 1 The Law of Torts, p. 232, sec. 3.9, states: "If it (confinement) has been extra judicial, without legal process, it is false imprisonment."

In the instant case it is clear that the type of tort that the concept of "false imprisonment" encompasses did not take place. There was not an "unlawful" restraint of freedom.

Since the plaintiff Saralee was confined pursuant to the mandate of sec. 51.04(1), Stats., and by a petition that conformed, prima facie at least, to the jurisdictional requirements of the statute, the confinement was pursuant to law. She was arrested by legal process in the sense that the document executed by the defendants under the statute conferred authority or jurisdiction upon the police officers to take physical custody of the plaintiff's person and to deliver her to the mental hospital.

Although the tort committed was not that of false imprisonment as contended by the plaintiff, neither can we agree with defendants' conten-tion that the insult to plaintiff's liberty can properly be denominated as "malicious prosecution." The reason why defendants assert plaintiff's only cause of action is malicious prosecution is clear, for defendants point out, after setting up the "strawman" of malicious prosecution, that plaintiff cannot prove significant facts to maintain her action. In this contention they are correct, but their argument proves too much in that, by so doing, they demonstrate that plaintiff's cause is not one of malicious prosecution, irrespective of the factual lacunae upon which defendants would rely.

Harper and James, *supra*, page 300, sec. 4.1, states:

"The tort of malicious prosecution of criminal proceedings occurs when one citizen initiates or procures the initiation of criminal proceedings against an innocent person, for an improper purpose and without probable cause therefore, if the proceedings terminate favorably for the person thus prosecuted."

Prosser, *supra*, page 852, sec. 113, explains that the cause of action for malicious prosecution is designed to afford redress for invasions of the right to be free from unjustifiable litigation. Four elements originally were requisite to a cause of action for malicious prosecution:

"1. A criminal proceeding instituted or continued by the defendant against the plaintiff.

"2. Termination of the proceeding in favor of the accused.

"3. Absence of probable cause for the proceeding.

"4. 'Malice,' or a primary purpose other than that of bringing an offender to justice." Prosser, *supra*, p. 853, sec. 113.

Prosser demonstrates that malicious prosecution lies only when a plaintiff's interests are invaded by an ostensibly legal process. The essence of the tort is the "perversion of proper legal procedure." (P. 853) He distinguishes it from false imprisonment in that the latter tort occurs only when a plaintiff is arrested or confined without a warrant or legal authority. As stated above, the tort alleged here is clearly not that of false arrest. It is equally clear that the facts do not spell out an action for malicious prosecution.

In *Elmer v. Chicago & N. W. Ry. Co.* (1950), 257 Wis. 228, 231, 43 N.W.2d 244, 246, this court stated the six essential elements of malicious prosecution:

"1. There must have been a prior institution or continuation of some regular judicial proceedings against the plaintiff in this action for malicious prosecution.

"2. Such former proceedings must have been by, or at the instance of the defendant in this action for malicious prosecution.

"3. The former proceedings must have terminated in favor of the defendant therein, the plaintiff in the action for malicious prosecution.

"4. There must have been malice in instituting the former proceedings.

"5. There must have been want of probable cause for the institution of the former proceedings.

"6. There must have been injury or damage resulting to the plaintiff from the former proceedings."

It should be noted that Wisconsin takes the position that the unjustifiable litigation need not be criminal in nature—that any prior regular but unjustifiable judicial proceedings, civil or criminal, will suffice.

In *Yelk v. Seefeldt* (1967), 35 Wis.2d 271, 277, 278, 151 N.W.2d 4, 7, we specifically pointed out that "the institution of a *proceeding* to inquire into the mental health of a person is grounds for a suit for malicious prosecution." (Emphasis supplied.)

In the instant case, however, elements that must be present to characterize the action as one of malicious prosecution are absent.

Here, unlike the situation in *Yelk v. Seefeldt, supra*, the petition was never presented to a court, and no order of a court ever provided for the institution of a mental inquiry. Whatever proceedings antedated this action did not terminate in favor of the plaintiff. In the instant case the defendants simply chose not to proceed and released Saralee from the mental hospital.

There was no "malice" in the conduct of the defendants that led to Saralee's confinement in a mental ward. *Yelk v. Seefeldt, supra*, page 280, 151 N.W.2d page 8, referred to the element of "malice" as one that would be demonstrated by evidence as "wanton or willful disregard for the facts or law in (a) manner * * * that would evince any ill will or vindictiveness."

However the conduct of the defendants may be described, it was not malicious in the sense referred to in *Yelk*. The evidence showed defendants had a genuine concern for the plaintiff's welfare, and they prevented her from leaving the university to protect what they conceived to be Saralee's own best interests.

Other elements of malicious prosecution are arguably present. Although the plaintiff would contend that no probable cause existed for the confinement, and defendants would argue that no injury or damage resulted as the result of the occurrence, these are determinations that need not be made in view of the disposition we make of this appeal. Suffice it to say that the plaintiff failed to properly prove up a cause of action in either false imprisonment or malicious prosecution. We, however, do not for that reason dismiss her complaint, for we are satisfied that the proof submitted would, skeletally at least, support an alternate cause of action—that of abuse of process.

Abuse of process is defined by the Restatement, Torts, page 464, sec. 682, in the following terms:

> "One who uses a legal process, whether criminal or civil, against another to accomplish a purpose for which it is not designed is liable to the other for the pecuniary loss caused thereby."

Prosser, *supra*, page 876, sec. 115, points out that abuse of process supplies a remedy that is denied under the theory of malicious prosecution. Abuse of process lies even in those instances where:

"... legal procedure has been set in motion in proper form, with probable cause, and even with ultimate success, but nevertheless has been perverted to accomplish an ulterior purpose for which it was not designed."

The gist of the tort is:

"... misusing or misapplying process justified in itself for an end other than that which it was designed to accomplish. The purpose for which the process is used * * * is the only thing of importance." Prosser, *supra*, p. 876, sec. 115.

Malice is not required. Probable cause does not defeat the plaintiff's action, and there need not have been a termination in the plaintiff's favor.

Our appraisal of the evidence leads to the conclusion that the plaintiff's proof spells out a cause of action for abuse of process. It is clear that the purpose of all the individual defendants was not essentially to have inquiry into Saralee's mental condition, though Dean Cannon, at least, was concerned about her "illogical" state of mind. Rather, the purpose of the three defendants was to detain her until such time as her parent had been notified and he had either given his permission for Saralee to leave or had directed Saralee to stay at school. The purpose was to have her physically detained until the problem of her withdrawal from school was resolved to the satisfaction of the school authorities. Doctor Miller acknowledged that he told Saralee he could not release her without her parent's permission. To assure her non-release until that time, he struck upon the idea of using the statute that permits the temporary detention of persons who demonstrate symptoms of dangerous mental illness.

On the facts before us, this was a perversion of the purpose of the law and constituted an abuse of process. After Saralee's father was contacted, Saralee was released—all interest in her mental condition vanished, and the pretense of proceeding with a mental inquiry was abandoned.

The trial judge made the specific finding that the purpose of the petition was to detain the plaintiff and not to examine the condition of her mental health. These facts, which appear in the record on the instant appeal, are facts which would support a cause of action for abuse of process. However, the lawsuit was not tried upon that theory, and the jury was not instructed in respect to factual issues that must be resolved in the trial of an abuse-of-process tort.

... [I]t is apparent that the real controversy has not been tried and that the liability of the defendants, as applied to these facts, was founded upon an erroneous view of the law, an error in which both plaintiff and defendants participated, since neither conceived of the case as involving a tort other than false imprisonment or malicious prosecution.

... [I]t is apparent that the defendants had no opportunity to defend on the basis of legal theories that are available to defendants in abuse-of-process actions. Moreover, the nature of both plaintiff's and defendants' proof in an action brought solely for abuse of process might well be different and of an emphasis at variance from that presented at this trial. It is, therefore, the conclusion of the court the interests of justice require that the judgment be reversed and the cause remanded for a new trial, and that, prior to such new trial, the plaintiff be required to amend her complaint, to allege, if she can, a cause of action for abuse of process. Inasmuch as we do not dismiss the complaint, it remains viable and may be amended on remand.

The portion of plaintiff's cause of action, insofar as it relates to false imprisonment, is dismissed.

\* \* \*

*By the Court.*—Judgment is reversed under the provisions of sec. 251.09, Stats., and cause is remanded for such other and further action and proceedings as may be consistent with this opinion and for a new trial. No costs are to be taxed on this appeal.

## NOTES

**1.  False Arrest.** False arrest is a form of false imprisonment whereby the improper assertion of legal authority can unlawfully restrain a victim. In *Asgari v. City of Los Angeles*, 15 Cal.4th 744, 63 Cal.Rptr.2d 842, 937 P.2d 273 (Cal. 1997), a plaintiff was arrested by a police officer, without probable cause. The California Supreme Court held that false imprisonment lasted for seven days at which time the plaintiff was arraigned in municipal court on a felony complaint; from that point on, "his confinement was pursuant to a lawful process and no longer constituted false imprisonment." Consider also, *Taylor v. Gregg*, 36 F.3d 453 (5th Cir.1994), where the 5th Circuit held that where the plaintiffs were arrested due to having been unruly on an airline flight, any basis for a claim of false imprisonment ended once plaintiffs were placed before a magistrate and grand jury, as they were henceforth confined pursuant to a lawful process. Consider also, *Du Lac v. Perma Trans Products, Inc.*, 103 Cal.App.3d 937, 163 Cal.Rptr. 335 (1980), where the California Court of Appeal held that to result in false imprisonment, false statements knowingly made to the police must have been made with the intent to induce arrest. The court reasoned that a defendant should not be liable for an unlawful arrest which follows solely upon false accusations that create no recognizable risk of arrest. Rather, the false accusations must have been of a character as to foreseeably induce an arrest, such as "false accusations that others have 'stolen' particular property."

**2.  Malicious Prosecution—Restatement Definition.** Malicious prosecution is characterized as the institution of wrongful criminal proceedings against another, resulting in damage to the plaintiff. The Restatement (Second) of Torts articulates the tort as follows:

> A private person who initiates or procures the institution of criminal proceedings against another who is not guilty of the offense charged is subject to liability for malicious prosecution if
>
> > (a) he initiates or procures the proceedings without probable cause and primarily for a purpose other than that of bringing an offender to justice, and
> >
> > (b) the proceedings have terminated in favor of the accused.

Restatement (Second) of Torts § 653 (1965). See also Keeton, *Prosser and Keeton on the Law of Torts* § 119 (5th ed. 1984); Diamond, Levine & Madden, *Understanding Torts* § 20.02 (2nd ed. 2000); Dobbs, *The Law of Torts* §§ 430–435 (2000). Some jurisdictions, as in the principal case, include the initiation of wrongful civil as well as criminal actions. Other jurisdictions, consistent with the Restatement, have a parallel tort of "wrongful institution of civil proceedings" with similar elements as in malicious prosecution. Consequently, whether wrongful civil actions are included in the malicious prosecution tort or a separate tort is ordinarily not significant.

**3. Parties Subject to Liability.** It should be noted that prosecutors and judges are immune from liability for malicious prosecution for their official actions. Nevertheless, police and private parties can be held liable for wrongfully instituting criminal as well as civil proceedings.

Consider *Cook v. Sheldon*, 41 F.3d 73 (2d Cir. 1994), where the plaintiff sued state troopers for malicious prosecution. The Second Circuit Court of Appeals held that the plaintiff stated a claim for malicious prosecution because the state troopers instituted a criminal proceeding against the plaintiff by charging the plaintiff with violation of a statute and having him arraigned. The court concluded the necessary elements of the tort were satisfied. The proceeding ended in the plaintiff's favor, since the charges were dismissed. The troopers lacked probable cause because the criminal proceedings were instituted when it was highly unlikely the plaintiff had actually violated the statute. Moreover, the state troopers were "driven by vengeance" since the criminal proceedings were instituted only after the plaintiff suggested that his companion "assert his rights," in respect to the companion's dealings with the state troopers. Consider also the case of *DiNicola v. DiPaolo*, 945 F.Supp. 848 (W.D.Pa.1996), where the plaintiff brought an action against a hypnotist, arising from the plaintiff's arrest and conviction for arson and second-degree murder for which the plaintiff was retried and acquitted. The District Court held that the plaintiff stated a claim for malicious prosecution against the hypnotist because the testimony of the principal prosecution witness was the false product of intentional hypnotic suggestion.

**4. Requirement That Legal Proceedings be Instituted.** Consider cases where the plaintiff did not state a claim for malicious prosecution because the defendant did not initiate a legal proceeding against the plaintiff. In *Boschette v. Buck*, 916 F.Supp. 91 (D.Puerto Rico 1996), plaintiffs brought an action against the defendant, whom plaintiffs believed had stolen a sexually explicit videotape. The defendant counterclaimed for malicious prosecution. The District Court of Puerto Rico held that the defendant was not subjected to malicious prosecution because the district attorney merely reviewed the plaintiff's claim and never actually prosecuted the claim. The court reasoned that "criminal proceedings are not commenced until process is issued to bring the accused before a judicial officer." Because there had been no criminal proceedings against the defendant, there was no cause of action for malicious prosecution.

Similarly, in *Adams v. Superior Court*, 2 Cal.App.4th 521, 3 Cal.Rptr.2d 49 (1992), the Court of Appeal of California held that a motion for reconsideration filed by the alleged victims of the defendant's fraud, in a legal proceeding to have defendant's convictions overturned, was not an independent action necessary to support a claim for malicious prosecution. The court determined that a malicious prosecution action "[could] not be grounded upon subsidiary activity within a pending lawsuit." Instead, malicious prosecution requires the initiation of a "full-blown action."

**5.  Termination in Favor of Plaintiff.** Suits based on malicious prosecution require the termination of the proceedings in favor of the individual bringing the claim for malicious prosecution. The requirement can be onerous. Plaintiff is precluded from bringing the action until the litigation she is complaining of is terminated. Furthermore, criminal charges or litigation that are simply dropped by the prosecutor or suing party are not ordinarily considered termination in favor of the accused. Some modern courts are becoming a bit more flexible. For example, in *Davis v. City of San Antonio*, 752 S.W.2d 518, 519 (Tex.1988), the plaintiff's criminal charge was dropped by the prosecutor after eighteen months. The court in a malicious prosecution action held that if "there was *some evidence* . . . that the criminal proceedings were terminated in favor" of the plaintiff, a verdict of malicious prosecution could be sustained. In any event, the vindication must be unconditional. Vindication, for example, based on a statute of limitations claim is not adequate. See *Lackner v. LaCroix*, 25 Cal.3d 747, 159 Cal.Rptr. 693, 602 P.2d 393 (Cal. 1979). Consider also *Pawlicki v. City of Ithaca*, 993 F.Supp. 140 (N.D.N.Y. 1998), where under New York law dismissal of the criminal charges against the plaintiff was conditional on the plaintiff's payment of restitution. The District Court held that this did not constitute termination of the matter in a manner favorable to the plaintiff, so that the plaintiff could recover for malicious prosecution.

**6.  Absence of Probable Cause.** Suits based on malicious prosecution require an absence of probable cause. In *Dzinanka v. County of Suffolk*, 932 F.Supp. 59 (E.D.N.Y.1996), the plaintiff brought an action against the president and a co-worker of the plaintiff's former employer for malicious prosecution arising from the plaintiff's arrest as a result of affidavits submitted by the president and the co-worker. The affidavits stated that the plaintiff had stolen money or property from the employer. The District Court of New York held that the affidavits established probable cause because the defendants were credible witnesses, and therefore, an action for malicious prosecution was precluded. Similarly, in *Collom v. Incorporated Village of Freeport, New York*, 691 F.Supp. 637 (E.D.N.Y.1988), the New York District Court held that where probable cause legitimately supported the plaintiff's arrest, there were no grounds for malicious prosecution unless a jury found "that between the arrests and the prosecution the authorities [had become] aware of evidence exonerating the accused," and nevertheless continued the legal proceeding against the plaintiff. See also, *Wolford v. Lasater*, 78 F.3d 484 (10th Cir.1996), where the Tenth Circuit held that there was a lack of evidence that the county sheriff's department had filed criminal charges against a former employee in order to retaliate against her for politically supporting the former sheriff and that, therefore, the former employee failed to establish absence of probable cause for her arrest.

**7.  Malice or Improper Purpose.** The Restatement replaces the traditional element of "malice" with the requirement that the defendant acted with a purpose "other than of bringing the defender to justice." Whether the defendant felt malice or "ill-will" toward the victim is considered irrelevant to the Restatement. How does this change affect the analysis in the principal case?

Requiring an improper purpose means that even a criminal charge or civil proceeding without any probable cause is not actionable without bad faith on the part of the accuser. Is this too high a standard before allowing recovery?

**8. Expanding Malicious Prosecution?** In England the losing party pays the other party's legal costs in civil litigation. This is not ordinarily the case in the United States. The malicious prosecution tort, if successful, awards more than legal fees, including consequential economic losses and mental distress caused by the litigation. The cumulative requirements of the tort make recovery quite difficult. Should innocent victims of litigation be able to recover more often or would this overly deter individuals from bringing lawsuits?

**9. Restatement Definition of Abuse of Process.** Abuse of process is generally characterized as misuse of either a criminal or civil legal process for an ulterior purpose, which results in damage to the plaintiff. The Restatement (Second) of Torts articulates the generally accepted view as follows:

> One who uses a legal process, whether criminal or civil, against another primarily to accomplish a purpose for which it is not designed, is subject to liability to the other for harm caused by the abuse of process.

Restatement (Second) of Torts § 682 (1965). See also Keeton, *supra*, § 121; Diamond, Levine & Madden, *supra*, § 20.05 and Dobbs, *supra*, § 438.

**10. Distinguishing Malicious Prosecution from Abuse of Process.** Abuse of process, as the principal case indicates, does not, unlike malicious prosecution, require the favorable termination of the litigation complained of by the plaintiff. Consequently, the abuse of process tort can be filed immediately. The tort focuses on the misuse of subpoenas, attachments and other legal processes within the litigation. For example, in *Board of Education of Farmingdale Union Free School District v. Farmingdale Classroom Teachers Association*, 38 N.Y.2d 397, 380 N.Y.S.2d 635, 343 N.E.2d 278 (N.Y. 1975), the court held it was a prima facie case of abuse of process to subpoena 87 teachers from a school to appear at the same time rather than stagger the required appearances, thereby forcing the school to hire 71 substitute teachers.

Consider *Rosen v. Tesoro Petroleum Corporation*, 399 Pa.Super. 226, 582 A.2d 27 (1990), where the plaintiffs brought an action against a corporation and its officers and directors for abuse of process alleging that the institution of an earlier cause of action had been out of retaliation for the plaintiffs' participation in a class action against the corporation and its officers and directors. The Superior Court of Pennsylvania held that the pleadings charged that the institution of litigation was for a wrongful purpose, but failed to state a claim for abuse of process since there were no assertions the defendants had "perverted any legal process" within the litigation.

Consider also *Doctor's Associates, Inc. v. Weible*, 92 F.3d 108 (2d Cir. 1996), where a fast food franchisor (the national chain) brought an action against a franchisee (the local restaurant) for the alleged violation of privacy and wiretapping laws. The local restaurant counterclaimed, alleging abuse of process based on the restaurant's belief that the purpose of the national chain's cause of action was to force the restaurant to abandon an earlier lawsuit against the national chain. The Second Circuit Court of Appeals held that abuse of process could not be based upon motive for commencement of a cause of action. Rather, "liability for abuse of process exists only when the defendant overtly misuses a process once a proceeding has begun" and sets forth evidence demonstrating the misapplication of the legal process.

**11. Further Study.** For further study see O'Brien, *Misuse of Administrative Process Provides Grounds For Malicious Prosecution and Abuse of Process*—Hillside Associates v. Stravato, 29 Suffolk U. L. Rev. 541 (1995), which makes an effort to clarify the overlapping elements of malicious prosecution and abuse of process.

# SECTION F. INTENTIONAL INFLICTION OF EMOTIONAL DISTRESS

## SLOCUM v. FOOD FAIR STORES OF FLORIDA, INC.
Supreme Court of Florida.
100 So.2d 396 (1958).

DREW, Justice.

This appeal is from an order dismissing a complaint for failure to state a cause of action. Simply stated, the plaintiff sought money damages for mental suffering or emotional distress, and an ensuing heart attack and aggravation of pre-existing heart disease, allegedly caused by insulting language of the defendant's employee directed toward her while she was a customer in its store. Specifically, in reply to her inquiry as to the price of an item he was marking, he replied: "If you want to know the price, you'll have to find out the best way you can * * * you stink to me." She asserts, in the alternative, that the language was used in a malicious or grossly reckless manner, "or with intent to inflict great mental and emotional disturbance to said plaintiff."

No great difficulty is involved in the preliminary point raised as to the sufficiency of damages alleged, the only direct injury being mental or emotional with physical symptoms merely derivative therefrom. *Kirksey v. Jernigan, Fla.*, 45 So.2d 188, 17 A.L.R.2d 766. While that decision would apparently allow recovery for mental suffering, even absent physical consequences, inflicted in the course of other intentional or malicious torts, it does not resolve the central problem in this case, i.e. whether the conduct here claimed to have caused the injury, the use of insulting language under the circumstances described, constituted an actionable invasion of a legally protected right. Query: does such an assertion of a deliberate disturbance of emotional equanimity state an independent cause of action in tort?

Appellant's fundamental argument is addressed to that proposition. The case is one of first impression in this jurisdiction, and she contends that this Court should recognize the existence of a new tort, an independent cause of action for intentional infliction of emotional distress.

A study of the numerous references on the subject indicates a strong current of opinion in support of such recognition, in lieu of the strained reasoning so often apparent when liability for such injury is predicated upon one or another of several traditional tort theories. See annotation 15 A.L.R.2d 108; Wade, Tort Liability for Abusive Language, 4 Vanderbilt L.Rev., p. 63; Prosser, intentional Infliction of Mental Suffering; a New Tort, 37 Mich.L.Rev. 874; Magruder, Mental and Emotional Disturbance and the Law of Torts, 49 Harv.L.Rev. 1033. Cf. *Cason v. Baskin*, 155 Fla. 198, 20 So.2d 243, 168 A.L.R. 430, quoting Sec. 4, Declaration of Rights, Fla.Const. F.S.A.

\* \* \*

A most cogent statement of the doctrine covering tort liability for insult has been incorporated in the Restatement of the Law of Torts, 1948 supplement, sec. 46, entitled "Conduct intended to cause emotional distress only." It makes a blanket provision for liability on the part of "one, who, without a privilege to do so, intentionally causes severe emotional distress to another," indicating that the requisite intention exists "when the act is done for the purpose of causing the distress or with knowledge \* \* \* that severe emotional distress is substantially certain to be produced by (such) conduct." Comment (a), Sec. 46, *supra*. Abusive language is, of course, only one of the many means by which the tort could be committed.

However, even if we assume, without deciding, the legal propriety of that doctrine, a study of its factual applications shows that line of demarcation should be drawn between conduct likely to cause mere "emotional distress" and that causing "severe emotional distress," so as to exclude the situation at bar. Illus. 5, sec. 46, *supra*. "So far as it is possible to generalize from the cases, the rule which seems to be emerging is that there is liability only for conduct exceeding all bounds which could be tolerated by society, of a nature especially calculated to cause mental damage of a very serious kind." Prosser, Mental Suffering, 37 Mich.L.R. 889. And the most practicable view is that the functions of court and jury are no different than in other tort actions where there is at the outset a question as to whether the conduct alleged is so legally innocuous as to present no issue for a jury. Wade, p. 91, *supra*. See also 7 Miss.L.J. 390.

This tendency to hinge the cause of action upon the degree of the insult has led some courts to reject the doctrine in toto. *Wallace v. Shoreham Hotel Corp., D.C. Mun.App.*, 49 A.2d 81. Whether or not this is desirable, it is uniformly agreed that the determination of whether words or conduct are actionable in character is to be made on an objective rather than subjective standard, from common acceptation. The unwarranted intrusion must be calculated to cause "severe emotional distress" to a person of ordinary sensibilities, in the absence of special knowledge or notice. There is no inclination to include all instances of mere vulgarities, obviously intended as meaningless abusive expressions. While the manner in which language is used may no doubt determine its actionable character, appellant's assertion that the statement involved in this case was made to her with gross recklessness, etc., cannot take the place of allegations showing that the words were intended to have real meaning or serious effect.

A broader rule has been developed in a particular class of cases, usually treated as a distinct and separate area of liability originally applied to common carriers. Rest.Torts, per.ed., sec. 48. The courts have from an early date granted relief for offense reasonably suffered by a patron from insult by a servant or employee of a carrier, hotel, theater, and most recently, a telegraph office. The existence of a special relationship, arising either from contract or from the inherent nature of a non-competitive public utility, supports a right and correlative duty of courtesy beyond that legally required in general mercantile or personal relationships. Cases collected, section 14, annotation 15 A.L.R.2d 108, 136. *Republic Iron & Steel Co. v. Self*, 192 Ala. 403, 68 So. 328, L.R.A.1915F, 516; *Wallace v. Shoreham Hotel*, *supra*.

In view of the concurrent development of the cause of action first above described, there is no impelling reason to extend the rule of the latter cases. Their rationale does not of necessity cover the area of business invitees generally, where the theory of respondeat superior underlying most liabilities of the employer would dictate some degree of conformity to standards of individual liability. This factor, together with the stringent standards of care imposed in a number of the carrier cases (*Haile v. New Orleans R. Co.*, 135 La. 229, 65 So. 225, 51 L.R.A.N.S. 1171), may have influenced the treatment of the subject by editors of the Restatement, where the statement of the carrier doctrine is quite limited in scope and classified separately from the section covering the more general area of liability under consideration. But whether or not these rules are ultimately adopted in this jurisdiction, the facts of the present case cannot be brought with their reasonable intendment.

Affirmed.

### NOTES

**1. Restatement Definition.** The tort of intentional infliction of mental or emotional distress is not a historic tort, as the principal case suggests, but a product of the 20th Century. Intentional infliction of emotional distress occurs when the defendant, through extreme and outrageous conduct, intentionally or recklessly causes the victim severe emotional distress. See Keeton, *Prosser and Keeton on the Law of Torts*, § 12 (5th ed. 1984), Dobbs, *The Law of Torts* §§ 303–307 (2000) and Diamond, Levine & Madden, *Understanding Torts* § 51.06 (2nd ed. 2000). The Restatement (Second) of Torts articulates the tort as follows:

(1) One who by extreme and outrageous conduct intentionally or recklessly causes severe emotional distress to another is subject to liability for such emotional distress, and if bodily harm to the other results from it, for such bodily harm.

(2) Where such conduct is directed at a third person, the actor is subject to liability if he intentionally or recklessly causes severe emotional distress

(a) to a member of such person's immediate family who is present at the time, whether or not such distress results in bodily harm, or

(b) to any person who is present at the time, if such distress results in bodily harm.

Restatement (Second) of Torts § 46.

In addition the Restatement provides:

A common carrier or other public utility is subject to liability to patrons utilizing its facilities for gross insults which reasonably offend them, inflicted by the utility's servants while otherwise acting within the scope of their employment.

Restatement (Second) of Torts § 48 (1965).

Is the tort's definition too vague and uncertain or do its flexible elements make the tort more useful?

**2. Recklessness.** Recklessness is not a component of intent which, as noted at Note 2, (p. 4, *supra*), is generally defined as acting with desire or substantial certainty the elements of the tort will occur. Recklessness is a variant of negligence, and in this context encompasses when the defendant acted with a "deliberate disregard of a high degree of probability" that severe mental distress will result. See Restatement (Second) of Torts § 46 comment i. Nevertheless, liability for intentional infliction of mental distress has included, consistent with the Restatement definition, liability for reckless as well as intentional conduct. For example, where B attempted to commit suicide in A's kitchen by cutting his throat, knowing with a high degree of probability A would return to see the gore, the requisite culpability for the tort is satisfied. See Restatement (Second) of Torts § 46, ill. 15. The need to include recklessness with intent for the tort of intentional infliction of emotional distress is mostly superfluous today with the more recent acceptance of liability for the separate tort for negligent infliction of mental distress, discussed infra Chapter 2, Sec. H(2).

**3. Extreme and Outrageous Conduct.** The tort requires that the defendant act with extreme and outrageous conduct. The Restatement elaborates by commenting:

"Liability has been found only where the conduct has been so outrageous in character, and so extreme in degree, as to go beyond all possible bounds of decency, and to be regarded as atrocious, and utterly intolerable in a civilized community."

Restatement (Second) of Torts § 46 comment d.

Consider *Field v. Philadelphia Electric Company*, 388 Pa.Super. 400, 565 A.2d 1170 (Pa. Sup.Ct. 1988), where the plaintiff, a safety expert, was intentionally exposed to high levels of radioactive steam after previously warning operators of the danger of such exposure. In addition, the power company attempted to conceal from the plaintiff the high radioactive readings indicated on his survey meter. The court concluded that

"We can visualize no conduct more outrageous in character, so extreme in degree, that went beyond all bounds of decency and to be regarded as atrocious and utterly intolerable in a civilized community, than to vent highly radioactive steam upon another ... and then [attempt] to conceal the resulting situation."

Consider also *Miller v. National Broadcasting Company*, 187 Cal.App.3d 1463, 232 Cal.Rptr. 668 (Ct. App., 2d Dist., Div. 1, Cal. 1986), holding that a widow had stated a claim for intentional infliction of mental distress against a television network after she viewed television film made without the family's consent by the network. The film showed her husband being treated by paramedics for a fatal coronary in their home. The plaintiff did not know about the filming until she observed it while "flipping channels looking for a soap opera." Consider also *Larijani v. Georgetown University*, 791 A.2d 41 (2002), where the court held that it was an issue of fact whether exposure to the sound from a noise making machine over the course of nine months constituted extreme and outrageous behavior. The plaintiff in this case repeatedly complained of the "piercing" noise made by the machine constantly throughout the workday and also complained that it had serious effects both on the plaintiff's physical health and mental wellbeing.

    **4. Common Carriers.** As the Restatement (Second) of Torts § 48, quoted in note one, *supra*, indicates, common carriers (e.g., trains and buses) and utilities (e.g., telephone and telegraph companies) are liable for mere gross insults to customers. There is no requirement that intentional infliction of extreme mental distress be intended or suffered. Although the Restatement does not include innkeepers, many courts would expand the rule to these classes of defendants as well. See Diamond, Levine & Madden, *supra*, § 1.06 [E]; Keeton, *supra*, § 12 Dobbs, *supra*, *The Law Of Torts* § 303 (2000). Some courts have justified this special treatment since utilities, common carriers and often inns historically were monopolies. Others have suggested class attitude toward the employees of these industries prompted the rule. Are there any justifications for treating these industries differently today?

## RULON–MILLER v. INTERNATIONAL BUSINESS MACHINES CORPORATION

California Court of Appeal, First District, California.
162 Cal.App.3d 241, 208 Cal.Rptr. 524 (1984).

RUSHING, Judge:

International Business Machines (IBM) appeals from the judgment entered against it after a jury awarded $100,000 compensatory and $200,000 punitive damages to respondent (Virginia Rulon–Miller) on claims of wrongful discharge and intentional infliction of emotional distress. Rulon–Miller was a low-level marketing manager at IBM in its office products division in San Francisco. Her termination as a marketing manager at IBM came about as a result of an accusation made by her immediate supervisor, defendant Callahan, of a romantic relationship with the manager of a rival office products firm, QYX.

### Factual Background

IBM is an international manufacturer of computers, office equipment and telecommunications systems. As well, it offers broad general services in the data processing field. It is reputed to be the single most successful high technology firm in the world. It is also a major force in the low technology field of typewriters and office equipment.

IBM is an employer traditionally thought to provide great security to its employees as well as an environment of openness and dignity. The company is organized into divisions, and each division is, to an extent, independent of others. The company prides itself on providing career opportunities to its employees, and respondent represents a good example of this. She started in 1967 as a receptionist in the Philadelphia Data Center. She was told that "career opportunities are available to [employees] as long as they are performing satisfactorily and are willing to accept new challenges." While she worked at the data center in Philadelphia, she attended night school and earned a baccalaureate degree. She was promoted to equipment scheduler and not long after received her first merit award. The company moved her to Atlanta, Georgia where she spent 15 months as a data processor. She was transferred to the office products division and was assigned the position of "marketing support representative" in San Francisco where she trained users (i.e., customers) of newly-purchased IBM equipment. Respondent was promoted to "product planner" in 1973 where her duties included overseeing the performance of new office products in the marketplace. As a product planner, she moved to Austin, Texas and later to Lexington, Kentucky. Thereafter, at the urging of her managers that she go into sales in the office products division, she enrolled at the IBM sales school in Dallas. After graduation, she was assigned to San Francisco.

Her territory was the financial district. She was given a performance plan by her management which set forth the company's expectations of her. She was from time to time thereafter graded against that plan on a scale of one through five with a grade of one being the highest. After her first year on the job, she was given a rating of one and was felt by her manager to be a person who rated at the top of IBM's scale.

A little over a year after she began in San Francisco, IBM reorganized its office products division into two separate functions, one called office systems and another called office products. Respondent was assigned to office systems; again she was given ratings of one and while there received a series of congratulatory letters from her superiors and was promoted to marketing representative. She was one of the most successful sales persons in the office and received a number of prizes and awards for her sales efforts. IBM's system of rewarding salespersons has a formalistic aspect about it that allows for subtle distinctions to be made while putting great emphasis on performance; respondent exercised that reward system to its fullest. She was a very successful seller of typewriters and other office equipment.

She was then put into a program called "Accelerated Career Development Program" which was a way of rewarding certain persons who were seen by their superiors as having management potential. IBM's prediction of her future came true and in 1978 she was named a marketing manager in the office products branch.

IBM knew about respondent's relationship with Matt Blum well before her appointment as a manager. Respondent met Blum in 1976 when he was an account manager for IBM. That they were dating was widely known within the organization. In 1977 Blum left IBM to join

QYX, an IBM competitor, and was transferred to Philadelphia. When Blum returned to San Francisco in the summer of 1978, IBM personnel were aware that he and respondent began dating again. This seemed to present no problems to respondent's superiors, as Callahan confirmed when she was promoted to manager. Respondent testified: "Somewhat in passing, Phil said: I heard the other day you were dating Matt Blum, and I said: Oh. And he said, I don't have any problem with that. You're my number one pick. I just want to assure you that you are my selection." The relationship with Blum was also known to Regional Manager Gary Nelson who agreed with Callahan. Neither Callahan nor Nelson raised any issue of conflict of interest because of the Blum relationship.

Respondent flourished in her management position, and the company, apparently grateful for her efforts, gave her a $4,000 merit raise in 1979 and told her that she was doing a good job. A week later, her manager, Phillip Callahan, left a message that he wanted to see her.

When she walked into Callahan's office he confronted her with the question of whether she was dating Matt Blum. She wondered at the relevance of the inquiry and he said the dating constituted a "conflict of interest," and told her to stop dating Blum or lose her job and said she had a "couple of days to a week" to think about it.

The next day Callahan called her in again, told her "he had made up her mind for her," and when she protested, dismissed her. IBM and Callahan claim that he merely "transferred" respondent to another division.

\* \* \*

### Intentional Infliction of Emotional Distress

... [T]he question is whether ... IBM ... should ... be liable for ... intentional infliction of emotional distress. The issue is whether the conduct of the marketing manager of IBM was "extreme and outrageous," a question involving the objective facts of what happened in the confrontation between the employee and employer as well as the special susceptibility of suffering of the employee.

The general rule is that this tort, in essence, requires the defendant's conduct to be so extreme and outrageous as to go beyond all possible bounds of decency, and to be regarded as atrocious and utterly intolerable in a civilized community....

The question is reduced to the inquiry of whether Callahan's statements and conduct could be found by the jury to fall within doctrinal requirements. "It is for the court to determine whether on the evidence severe emotional distress can be found; it is for the jury to determine whether, on the evidence, it has in fact existed." (*Fletcher v. Western National Life Ins. Co.* (1970) 10 Cal.App.3d 376, 397.) "Where reasonable men may differ" the court must instruct the jury on the law and entrust the factual determination to it. (*Fuentes v. Perez* (1977) 66 Cal.App.3d 163, 172.) The finding on this cause of action as reflected herein is sufficient to support the award of punitive damages. (*Fletcher, supra*, at p. 404.)

To determine if Callahan's conduct could reach the level of extreme, outrageous, and atrocious conduct, requires detailed examination. First, there was a decided element of deception in Callahan acting as if the relationship with Blum was something new. The evidence was clear he knew of the involvement of respondent and Blum well before her promotion. Second, he acted in flagrant disregard of IBM policies prohibiting him from inquiring into respondent's "off job behavior." By giving respondent "a few days" to think about the choice between job and lover, he implied that if she gave up Blum she could have her job. He then acted without giving her "a few days to think about it" or giving her the right to choose.

So far the conduct is certainly unfair but not atrocious. What brings Callahan's conduct to an actionable level is the way he brought these several elements together in the second meeting with respondent. He said, after calling her in, "I'm making the decision for you." The implications of his statement were richly ambiguous, meaning she could not act or think for herself, or that he was acting in her best interest, or that she persisted in a romantic involvement inconsistent with her job. When she protested, he fired her.

The combination of statements and conduct would under any reasoned view tend to humiliate and degrade respondent. To be denied a right granted to all other employees for conduct unrelated to her work was to degrade her as a person. His unilateral action in purporting to remove any free choice on her part contrary to his earlier assurances also would support a conclusion that his conduct was intended to emphasize that she was powerless to do anything to assert her rights as an IBM employee. And such powerlessness is one of the most debilitating kinds of human oppression. The sum of such evidence clearly supports the jury finding of extreme and outrageous conduct.

Accordingly we conclude that the emotional distress cause of action was amply proved and supports the award of punitive damages. (*Neal v. Farmers Ins. Exchange, supra*, 21 Cal.3d 910, 927–928.)

The judgment is affirmed.

### NOTES

**1. Relationship Between Defendant and Plaintiff.** The relationship between the defendant and plaintiff can impact the courts' characterization of the defendant's conduct as extreme and outrageous. For example, in *Scamardo v. Dunaway*, 650 So.2d 417 (La.App.1995), a husband brought an action against a doctor for intentional infliction of emotional distress, alleging that while the husband and wife were consulting with the doctor for treatment for infertility, the doctor and wife had an affair which ultimately led to the dissolution of the marriage. The Court of Appeal of Louisiana held that "because this case involves the doctor-patient relationship, in which both husband and wife sought the services of the physician, we recognize that appellant may have an individual cause of action for intentional infliction of emotional distress." See Diamond, Levine & Madden, *Understanding Torts* § 1.06 (2nd ed. 2000); Dobbs, *The Law of Torts* § 304 (2000). Similarly, in *Figueiredo-Torres v. Nickel*, 321 Md. 642, 584 A.2d 69 (Md.

1991), the court held that a husband's allegation against a psychologist that he had commenced a romantic relationship with the plaintiff's wife, while treating the couple for marital problems, stated a claim for intentional infliction of emotional distress.

Consider also *Hester v. Barnett*, 723 S.W.2d 544 (Mo. Ct. App., W.D. 1987), where the court held a claim of intentional infliction of mental distress could be alleged against a minister who, while counseling a married couple, attempted to have the couple's children removed from their custody by fabricating that the parents physically abused the children. But consider *Strauss v. Cilek*, 418 N.W.2d 378 (Iowa Ct.App.1987), where the court held that it was not intentional infliction of mental distress for defendant to participate in a sexual relationship with his friend's (the plaintiff) wife. The court observed "A recitation of the facts of this case to an average member of the community would not lend him to exclaim, 'Outrageous!' "

**2. Termination of Employees.** Do you agree with the principal case that the supervisor in addition to potential liability for wrongful termination for wrongfully dismissing the employee (see Chapter 1, Sec. I(1), infra) should also be liable for intentional infliction of mental distress for the way he terminated her? Consider *Jaffe v. National League for Nursing*, 222 A.D.2d 233, 635 N.Y.S.2d 9 (N.Y.App.Div.1995), where the court rejected a claim for intentional infliction of mental distress for allegations of "harassment and intimidation, leading to forced resignation" and noted "courts will closely scrutinize complaints which seek to circumvent 'the right of employer to terminate an at will employee.' "

But consider *Wilson v. Monarch Paper Company*, 939 F.2d 1138 (5th Cir.1991), where the court upheld a jury verdict for intentional infliction of emotional distress against a company that reassigned a vice president with a college education and 30 years experience to do janitorial duties. The demotion was part of a year-long campaign to force the vice president out of his job and effectuate a corporate "goal of getting rid of old employees." Consider also *Dean v. Ford Motor Credit Company*, 885 F.2d 300 (5th Cir.1989). The plaintiff offered evidence that her supervisor had intentionally planted checks in the plaintiff's purse for purpose of framing her for theft. The court ruled this was sufficient evidence to submit a claim of intentional infliction of emotional distress to the jury.

Some courts have precluded intentional infliction of mental distress torts against employers because of the existence of workers' compensation systems (see Chapter 7, Sec. A, infra) designed to limit tort litigation between employers and employees. While allowing most other intentional torts, these courts are concerned employees could allege intentional infliction of mental distress too often and thereby undermine a goal of workers' compensation to limit litigation between employers and employees. See *Fermino v. Fedco, Inc.*, 7 Cal.4th 701, 30 Cal.Rptr.2d 18, 872 P.2d 559 (1994) (reprinted in Chapter 7 at p. 669, infra). Do you agree?

**3. Divorce Context.** Consider cases where claims of intentional infliction of emotional distress arise from the divorce context. What constitutes "extreme and outrageous" may not be consistent from court to court. In *Raftery v. Scott*, 756 F.2d 335 (4th Cir.1985), for example, a former husband brought an action against his former wife for intentional infliction of emotional distress resulting from the former wife's effort to destroy his father-son relationship with their child. The Fourth Circuit Court held that the former wife's continuing and successful effort to destroy the relationship between her former husband and their son supported a claim for intentional infliction of emotional distress. The court reasoned that "where there is no remedy available to a parent who as a result was psychologically damaged, strikes us as more potentially a danger to society" than the "implicit threat of an avalanche of cases arising whenever one parent makes an uncomplimentary remark about the other." Consider also, *Twyman v. Twyman*, 855 S.W.2d 619 (Tex. 1993), where the Texas Supreme Court held that a claim for intentional infliction of emotional distress could be brought in a divorce proceeding where the wife claimed that her husband "intentionally and cruelly" attempted to force her to engage in "deviate sexual acts."

But consider cases where the court declined to find extreme and outrageous conduct. For example, in *Hetfeld v. Bostwick*, 136 Or.App. 305, 901 P.2d 986 (Or.Ct.App.1995), the plaintiff alleged his former wife and her present husband "embarked on a course of conduct aimed at estranging him from his children" including withholding visitation, disparaging his character, planning activities in conflict with proposed visitation and encouraging children to call him by his first name. The court dismissed the intentional infliction of mental distress claim and reasoned that "many of the alleged behaviors are all too common in the context of a hostile dissolution involving children [and] [c]ertainly, no single act alleged to have been committed here was 'outrageous in the extreme.'"

Consider also *Cochran v. Cochran*, 65 Cal.App.4th 488, 76 Cal.Rptr.2d 540 (1998), where the court rejected the prominent attorney's wife's claim of intentional infliction of emotional distress against her estranged husband. The defendant had left on an answering machine a suggestion that his wife travel on "Value–Jet," an airline shut down after a fatal crash. The court concludes, "there must still be freedom to express an unflattering opinion and some safety valve must be left through which irascible tempers may blow off relatively harmless steam...."

**4. Vulnerability of Victim.** If the defendant is prewarned that the victim of his or her conduct is vulnerable or hypersensitive, this knowledge in conjunction with the defendant's conduct may be sufficient to characterize it as extreme and outrageous. For example, the standard of acceptable conduct may be higher when the victim is a child. Consider *KOVR–TV v. Superior Court*, 31 Cal.App.4th 1023, 37 Cal.Rptr.2d 431 (1995), where TV news reporters told three young children that a next door neighbor had murdered her two children before killing herself. The reporter with "camera rolling" interrogated the children while aware that the children were home without any adult supervision. The court ruled the trial court had properly denied defendant's summary judgment and allowed the children's intentional infliction of mental distress action to proceed.

Consider also the classic case of the defendants who played a practical joke on a woman who believed long-dead relatives had planted a pot of gold in a yard and spent each day digging for the pot. The defendants planted their own pot, but with dirt instead of gold. The neighbors rushed over when the woman found the pot and watched when she later opened it in front of several people at the bank. The practical joke caused her extreme distress. Ultimately the court compensated the woman's heirs for her extreme distress. (*Nickerson v. Hodges*, 146 La. 735, 84 So. 37 (La.1920)).

## JONES v. CLINTON

United States District Court for the Eastern District of Arkansas.
990 F.Supp. 657 (1998).

WRIGHT, District Judge.

The plaintiff in this lawsuit, Paula Corbin Jones, seeks civil damages from William Jefferson Clinton, President of the United States, and Danny Ferguson, a former Arkansas State Police Officer, for alleged actions beginning with an incident in a hotel suite in Little Rock, Arkansas. . . .

This lawsuit is based on an incident that is said to have taken place on the afternoon of May 8, 1991, in a suite at the Excelsior Hotel in Little Rock, Arkansas. President Clinton was Governor of the State of Arkansas at the time, and plaintiff was a State employee with the Arkansas Industrial Development Commission ("AIDC"), having begun her State employment on March 11, 1991. . . .

\* \* \*

. . . [T]he Court addresses plaintiff's state law claim of intentional infliction of emotional distress. . . . Arkansas recognizes a claim of intentional infliction of emotional distress based on sexual harassment. *Davis v. Tri–State Mack Distribs., Inc.,* 981 F.2d 340, 342 (8th Cir.1992) (citing *Hale v. Ladd,* 308 Ark. 567, 826 S.W.2d 244 (1992)). To establish a claim of intentional infliction of emotional distress, a plaintiff must prove that: (1) the defendant intended to inflict emotional distress or knew or should have known that emotional distress was the likely result of his conduct; (2) the conduct was extreme and outrageous and utterly intolerable in a civilized community; (3) the defendant's conduct was the cause of the plaintiff's distress; and (4) the plaintiff's emotional distress was so severe in nature that no reasonable person could be expected to endure it. *Milam v. Bank of Cabot,* 327 Ark. 256, 264–66, 937 S.W.2d 653, 658 (1997); *Hollomon v. Keadle,* 326 Ark. 168, 170–71, 931 S.W.2d 413, 415 (1996); *Cherepski v. Walker,* 323 Ark. 43, 913 S.W.2d 761, 767 (1996); *Croom v. Younts,* 323 Ark. 95, 913 S.W.2d 283, 286 (1996).

The President argues that the alleged conduct of which plaintiff complains was brief and isolated; did not result in any physical harm or objective symptoms of the requisite severe distress; did not result in distress so severe that no reasonable person could be expected to endure it; and he had no knowledge of any special condition of plaintiff that would render her particularly susceptible to distress. He argues that plaintiff has failed to identify the kind of clear cut proof that Arkansas courts require for a claim of outrage and that he is therefore entitled to summary judgment. The Court agrees.

One is subject to liability for the tort of outrage or intentional infliction of emotional distress if he or she wilfully or wantonly causes severe emotional distress to another by extreme and outrageous conduct. *Sterling Drug Inc. v. Oxford,* 294 Ark. 239, 243–44, 743 S.W.2d 380, 382 (1988). See also *Ingram v. Pirelli Cable Corp.,* 295 Ark. 154, 157–59, 747

S.W.2d 103, 105 (1988). In *M.B.M. Co. v. Counce*, 268 Ark. 269, 280, 596 S.W.2d 681, 687 (1980), the Arkansas Supreme Court stated that "[b]y extreme and outrageous conduct, we mean conduct that is so outrageous in character, and so extreme in degree, as to go beyond all possible bounds of decency, and to be regarded as atrocious, and utterly intolerable in civilized society." Whether conduct is "extreme and outrageous" is determined by looking at "the conduct at issue; the period of time over which the conduct took place; the relation between plaintiff and defendant; and defendant's knowledge that plaintiff is particularly susceptible to emotional distress by reason of some physical or mental peculiarity." *Doe v. Wright*, 82 F.3d 265, 269 (8th Cir.1996) (citing *Hamaker*, 51 F.3d at 111). The tort is clearly not intended to provide legal redress for every slight insult or indignity that one must endure. *Manning*, 127 F.3d at 690 (citing *Hamaker*, 51 F.3d at 110). The Arkansas courts take a strict approach and give a narrow view to claims of outrage, see *id.*, and merely describing conduct as outrageous does not make it so. *Ross*, 817 S.W.2d at 420.

Plaintiff seems to base her claim of outrage on her erroneous belief that the allegations she has presented are sufficient to constitute criminal sexual assault. She states that "Mr. Clinton's outrageous conduct includes offensive language, an offensive proposition, offensive touching (constituting sexual assault under both federal and state definitions), and *actual exposure of an intimate private body part*," and that "[t]here are few more outrageous acts than a criminal sexual assault followed by unwanted exposure, coupled with a demand for oral sex by the most powerful man in the state against a very young, low-level employee." Pl.'s Opp'n to Def. Clinton's Mot. for Summ. J. at 66 (emphasis in original).

While the Court will certainly agree that plaintiff's allegations describe offensive conduct, the Court, as previously noted, has found that the Governor's alleged conduct does not constitute sexual assault. Rather, the conduct as alleged by plaintiff describes a mere sexual proposition or encounter, albeit an odious one, that was relatively brief in duration, did not involve any coercion or threats of reprisal, and was abandoned as soon as plaintiff made clear that the advance was not welcome. The Court is not aware of any authority holding that such a sexual encounter or proposition of the type alleged in this case, without more, gives rise to a claim of outrage. *Cf. Croom*, 913 S.W.2d at 287 (use of wine and medication by a vastly older relative to foist sex on a minor cousin went "beyond a mere sexual encounter" and offended all sense of decency).

Moreover, notwithstanding the offensive nature of the Governor's alleged conduct, plaintiff admits that she never missed a day of work following the alleged incident, she continued to work at AIDC another nineteen months (leaving only because of her husband's job transfer), she continued to go on a daily basis to the Governor's Office to deliver items and never asked to be relieved of that duty, she never filed a formal complaint or told her supervisors of the incident while at AIDC, she never consulted a psychiatrist, psychologist, or incurred medical bills as a result of the alleged incident, and she acknowledges that her two subsequent contacts with the Governor involved comments made "in a light vein" and nonsexual contact that was done in a "friendly fashion." Further, despite earlier claiming that she suffered marital discord and humiliation, plaintiff stated in her deposition that she was not claiming damages to her marriage as a result of the Governor's alleged conduct, *see* Pl.'s Depo. at 122, and she acknowledged the request to drop her claim of injury to reputation by stating, "I didn't really care if it was dropped or not personally." *Id.* at 261–62. Plaintiff's actions and statements in this case do not portray someone who experienced emotional distress so severe in nature that no reasonable person could be expected to endure it. *Cf. Hamaker,* 51 F.3d 108 (no claim of outrage where plaintiff, who had a speech impediment and an I.Q. of between 75 and 100, was "red-faced and angry," had an "increased heart rate and blood pressure," and had trouble sleeping four days after incident involving "rather nasty" practical joke).

Nevertheless, plaintiff submits a declaration from a purported expert with a Ph.D. in education and counseling, Patrick J. Carnes, who, after a 3.5 hour meeting with plaintiff and her husband a mere four days prior to the filing of President Clinton's motion for summary judgment, opines that her alleged encounter with Governor Clinton in 1991, "and the ensuing events," have caused plaintiff to suffer severe emotional distress and "consequent sexual aversion." The Court does not credit this declaration.

In *Angle v. Alexander,* 328 Ark. 714, 945 S.W.2d 933 (1997), the Arkansas Supreme Court noted that absent physical harm, courts look for more in the way of extreme outrage as an assurance that the mental disturbance claimed is not fictitious. *Id.* at 936–37. In that case, the plaintiffs offered their own testimony that they had experienced emotional distress, thoughts of death, fear, anger, and worry, but little else. *Id.* In concluding that there was no evidence of extreme emotional distress required to prevail on an outrage claim, the Court found it significant that none had seen a physician or mental health professional for these concerns. *Id.* The Court did not allow the fact that one plaintiff "on the advice of her attorney, spoke to a psychologist," to overcome her failure of proof on this point. *Id.* at 937 n. 3.

Aside from other deficiencies with the Carnes' declaration (including the fact that the substance of this declaration apparently was not disclosed in accordance with rules governing pre-trial discovery), the opinions stated therein are vague and conclusory and, as in *Angle,* do not suffice to overcome plaintiff's failure of proof on her claim of outrage. *Cf. Crenshaw v. Georgia–Pacific Corp.,* 915 F.Supp. 93, 99 (W.D.Ark.1995) (affidavit prepared after opposing motion for summary judgment filed detailing symptoms of weight loss, lack of sleep, headache, worry, and nausea, failed to present sufficient evidence of emotional distress).

In sum, plaintiff's allegations fall far short of the rigorous standards for establishing a claim of outrage under Arkansas law and the Court therefore grants the President's motion for summary judgment on this claim.

* * *

## *NOTES*

**1. Sexual and Racial Harassment.** Traditionally, many courts have been reluctant to characterize instances of sexual and racial harassment as "extreme and outrageous conduct." For example, in *Ward v. Goldman Sachs & Co.*, 1996 WL 3930 (S.D.N.Y.), the plaintiff brought an action for intentional infliction of emotional distress against his former employer resulting from his subjection to office gossip and derogatory comments concerning his sexual orientation. The District Court of New York held that this conduct suggested homophobia on the part of his co-workers but did "not, however, demonstrate that plaintiff's co-workers engaged in conduct so extreme in degree as to go beyond all possible bounds of decency." Consider also *Wilson v. Bellamy*, 105 N.C.App. 446, 414 S.E.2d 347 (N.C.Ct.App.1992), where the court found defendant's fondling and kissing of a female student while intoxicated and not fully conscious did constitute a sexual battery but not intentional infliction of emotional distress. But consider *Demby v. Preston Trucking Company, Inc.*, 961 F.Supp. 873 (D.Md.1997), where a former employee brought an action against his former employer for intentional infliction of emotional distress resulting from the employer's sanctioning of racial bigotry in the workplace. The court did not disagree that the conduct may have been extreme and outrageous. Rather, the employee's allegations were insufficient to state a claim for intentional infliction of emotional distress only because the employee failed to demonstrate that he suffered severe emotional distress.

What constitutes extreme and outrageous reflects current societal attitudes and evolves as social values change. See Diamond, Levine & Madden, *Understanding Torts* § 1.06[A] (2nd ed. 2000); Dobbs, *The Law of Torts* § 305 (2000); Love, *Discriminatory Speech and the Tort of Intentional Infliction of Emotional Distress*, 47 Wash. & Lee L. Rev. 123 (1990).

**2. Extreme Mental Distress.** The tort of intentional infliction of mental distress requires as an independent element that the plaintiff actually suffer extreme mental distress. Originally courts required that the extreme distress be manifested physically by a heart attack, ulcer, or even merely serious stomach trouble. Most courts today, consistent with the Restatement (Second) of Torts § 46, do not require physical manifestation. A majority of courts still, however, require physical manifestation for negligent infliction of mental distress. See Chapter 2, Sec. H(2), *infra*. Is there a serious policy rationale for retaining the physical manifestation requirement?

As the principal case and *Demby v. Preston Trucking Co.*, discussed in Note 1, *supra*, indicate by their results for the defendants, courts still can be quite rigorous in requiring that the plaintiff, even though not required to prove physical manifestation, must still prove his or her mental distress was severe.

**3. Third Party Recovery.** The Restatement (Second) of Torts provides the following special rule for third party recovery for intentional infliction of severe emotional distress:

> (2) Where such conduct is directed at a third person, the actor is subject to liability if he intentionally or recklessly causes severe emotional distress

(a) to a member of such person's immediate family who is present at the time, whether or not such distress results in bodily harm, or

(b) to any other person who is present at the time, if such distress results in bodily harm.

Restatement (Second) of Torts § 46.

The Restatement position is more expansive than most courts, which have thus far allowed third party recovery only to close relatives who witness outrageous conduct against other family members when the defendant knows the third party is present and a close relative. See, for example, *Taylor v. Vallelunga*, 171 Cal.App.2d 107, 339 P.2d 910 (1959), where a daughter who did not allege she was present to witness beating of her father nor pled that defendant knew she was present could not recover. See Keeton, *supra*, § 12 (5th ed. 1984); Diamond, Levine & Madden, *supra*, § 1.06[D] (1996); and Dobbs, *supra*, § 307. While concerns over excessive liability may influence these limits, the issue of third party recovery is far more extensively debated in the context of negligent infliction of mental distress as, for example, when one family member witnesses another family member injured by a negligently driven car. See Chapter 2, Sec. H(2), infra.

**4. The Clinton Case.** Alleged perjury and obstruction of justice in the principal case was the basis for President Clinton's impeachment proceedings in the House of Representatives. The case also included federal sexual harassment allegations which were also dismissed.

## HUSTLER MAGAZINE v. FALWELL

Supreme Court of the United States.
485 U.S. 46, 108 S.Ct. 876, 99 L.Ed.2d 41 (1988).

Chief Justice REHNQUIST delivered the opinion of the Court.

Petitioner Hustler Magazine, Inc., is a magazine of nationwide circulation. Respondent Jerry Falwell, a nationally known minister who has been active as a commentator on politics and public affairs, sued petitioner and its publisher, petitioner Larry Flynt, to recover damages for invasion of privacy, libel, and intentional infliction of emotional distress. The District Court directed a verdict against respondent on the privacy claim, and submitted the other two claims to a jury. The jury found for petitioners on the defamation claim, but found for respondent on the claim for intentional infliction of emotional distress and awarded damages. We now consider whether this award is consistent with the First and Fourteenth Amendments of the United States Constitution.

The inside front cover of the November 1983 issue of Hustler Magazine featured a "parody" of an advertisement for Campari Liqueur that contained the name and picture of respondent and was entitled "Jerry Falwell talks about his first time." This parody was modeled after actual Campari ads that included interviews with various celebrities about their "first times." Although it was apparent by the end of each interview that this meant the first time they sampled Campari, the ads clearly played on the sexual double entendre of the general subject of "first times." Copying the form and layout of these Campari ads, Hustler's editors chose respondent as the featured celebrity and drafted an alleged "interview" with him in which he states that his "first time" was during a drunken incestuous rendezvous with his mother in an outhouse. The Hustler parody portrays respondent and his mother as drunk and immoral, and suggests that respondent is a hypocrite who preaches only when he is drunk. In small print at the bottom of the page, the ad contains the disclaimer, "ad parody—not to be taken seriously." The magazine's table of contents also lists the ad as "Fiction; Ad and Personality Parody."

\* \* \*

This case presents us with a novel question involving First Amendment limitations upon a State's authority to protect its citizens from the intentional infliction of emotional distress. We must decide whether a public figure may recover damages for emotional harm caused by the publication of an ad parody offensive to him, and doubtless gross and repugnant in the eyes of most. Respondent would have us find that a State's interest in protecting public figures from emotional distress is sufficient to deny First Amendment protection to speech that is patently offensive and is intended to inflict emotional injury, even when that speech could not reasonably have been interpreted as stating actual facts about the public figure involved. This we decline to do.

At the heart of the First Amendment is the recognition of the fundamental importance of the free flow of ideas and opinions on matters of public interest and concern. "[T]he freedom to speak one's mind is not only an aspect of individual liberty—and thus a good unto itself—but also is essential to the common quest for truth and the vitality of society as a whole." *Bose Corp. v. Consumers Union of United States, Inc.,* 466 U.S. 485, 503–504, 104 S.Ct. 1949, 1961, 80 L.Ed.2d 502 (1984).

\* \* \*

The sort of robust political debate encouraged by the First Amendment is bound to produce speech that is critical of those who hold public office or those public figures who are "intimately involved in the resolution of important public questions or, by reason of their fame, shape events in areas of concern to society at large." *Associated Press v. Walker,* decided with *Curtis Publishing Co. v. Butts,* 388 U.S. 130, 164, 87 S.Ct. 1975, 1996, 18 L.Ed.2d 1094 (1967) (Warren, C.J., concurring in result). Justice Frankfurter put it succinctly in *Baumgartner v. United States,* 322 U.S. 665, 673–674, 64 S.Ct. 1240, 1245, 88 L.Ed. 1525 (1944), when he said that "[o]ne of the prerogatives of American citizenship is the right to criticize public men and measures." Such criticism, inevitably, will not always be reasoned or moderate; public figures as well as public officials will be subject to "vehement, caustic, and sometimes unpleasantly sharp attacks," *New York Times, supra,* 376 U.S., at 270, 84 S.Ct., at 721. "[T]he candidate who vaunts his spotless record and sterling integrity cannot convincingly cry 'Foul!' when an opponent or an industrious reporter attempts to demonstrate the contrary." *Monitor Patriot Co. v. Roy,* 401 U.S. 265, 274, 91 S.Ct. 621, 626, 28 L.Ed.2d 35 (1971).

Of course, this does not mean that *any* speech about a public figure is immune from sanction in the form of damages. Since *New York Times Co. v. Sullivan,* 376 U.S. 254, 84 S.Ct. 710, 11 L.Ed.2d 686 (1964), we have consistently ruled that a public figure may hold a speaker liable for the damage to reputation caused by publication of a defamatory falsehood, but only if the statement was made "with knowledge that it was false or with reckless disregard of whether it was false or not." *Id.,* 376 U.S., at 279–280, 84 S.Ct., at 726.

\* \* \*

Respondent argues, however, that a different standard should apply in this case because here the State seeks to prevent not reputational damage, but the severe emotional distress suffered by the person who is the subject of an offensive publication. Cf. *Zacchini v. Scripps–Howard Broadcasting Co.,* 433 U.S. 562, 97 S.Ct. 2849, 53 L.Ed.2d 965 (1977) (ruling that the "actual malice" standard does not apply to the tort of appropriation of a right of publicity). In respondent's view, and in the view of the Court of Appeals, so long as the utterance was intended to inflict emotional distress, was outrageous, and did in fact inflict serious emotional distress, it is of no constitutional import whether the statement was a fact or an opinion, or whether it was true or false. It is the intent to cause injury that is the gravamen of the tort, and the State's interest in preventing emotional harm simply outweighs whatever interest a speaker may have in speech of this type.

Generally speaking the law does not regard the intent to inflict emotional distress as one which should receive much solicitude, and it is quite understandable that most if not all jurisdictions have chosen to make it civilly culpable where the conduct in question is sufficiently "outrageous." But in the world of debate about public affairs, many things done with motives that are less than admirable are protected by the First Amendment. In *Garrison v. Louisiana,* 379 U.S. 64, 85 S.Ct. 209, 13 L.Ed.2d 125 (1964), we held that even when a speaker or writer is motivated by hatred or ill will his expression was protected by the First Amendment:

> "Debate on public issues will not be uninhibited if the speaker must run the risk that it will be proved in court that he spoke out of hatred; even if he did speak out of hatred, utterances honestly believed contribute to the free interchange of ideas and the ascertainment of truth." *Id.,* at 73, 85 S.Ct., at 215.

Thus while such a bad motive may be deemed controlling for purposes of tort liability in other areas of the law, we think the First Amendment prohibits such a result in the area of public debate about public figures.

Were we to hold otherwise, there can be little doubt that political cartoonists and satirists would be subjected to damages awards without any showing that their work falsely defamed its subject. Webster's defines a caricature as "the deliberately distorted picturing or imitating of a person, literary style, etc. by exaggerating features or mannerisms for satirical effect." Webster's New Unabridged Twentieth Century

Dictionary of the English Language 275 (2d ed. 1979). The appeal of the political cartoon or caricature is often based on exploitation of unfortunate physical traits or politically embarrassing events—an exploitation often calculated to injure the feelings of the subject of the portrayal. The art of the cartoonist is often not reasoned or evenhanded, but slashing and one-sided. One cartoonist expressed the nature of the art in these words:

> "The political cartoon is a weapon of attack, of scorn and ridicule and satire; it is least effective when it tries to pat some politician on the back. It is usually as welcome as a bee sting and is always controversial in some quarters." Long, The Political Cartoon: Journalism's Strongest Weapon, The Quill 56, 57 (Nov. 1962).

Several famous examples of this type of intentionally injurious speech were drawn by Thomas Nast, probably the greatest American cartoonist to date, who was associated for many years during the post-Civil War era with Harper's Weekly. In the pages of that publication Nast conducted a graphic vendetta against William M. "Boss" Tweed and his corrupt associates in New York City's "Tweed Ring." It has been described by one historian of the subject as "a sustained attack which in its passion and effectiveness stands alone in the history of American graphic art." M. Keller, The Art and Politics of Thomas Nast 177 (1968). Another writer explains that the success of the Nast cartoon was achieved "because of the emotional impact of its presentation. It continuously goes beyond the bounds of good taste and conventional manners." C. Press, The Political Cartoon 251 (1981).

Despite their sometimes caustic nature, from the early cartoon portraying George Washington as an ass down to the present day, graphic depictions and satirical cartoons have played a prominent role in public and political debate. Nast's castigation of the Tweed Ring, Walt McDougall's characterization of Presidential candidate James G. Blaine's banquet with the millionaires at Delmonico's as "The Royal Feast of Belshazzar," and numerous other efforts have undoubtedly had an effect on the course and outcome of contemporaneous debate. Lincoln's tall, gangling posture, Teddy Roosevelt's glasses and teeth, and Franklin D. Roosevelt's jutting jaw and cigarette holder have been memorialized by political cartoons with an effect that could not have been obtained by the photographer or the portrait artist. From the viewpoint of history it is clear that our political discourse would have been considerably poorer without them.

Respondent contends, however, that the caricature in question here was so "outrageous" as to distinguish it from more traditional political cartoons. There is no doubt that the caricature of respondent and his mother published in Hustler is at best a distant cousin of the political cartoons described above, and a rather poor relation at that. If it were possible by laying down a principled standard to separate the one from the other, public discourse would probably suffer little or no harm. But we doubt that there is any such standard, and we are quite sure that the pejorative description "outrageous" does not supply one. "Outrageous-

ness" in the area of political and social discourse has an ~~\~~.
subjectiveness about it which would allow a jury to impose liabil.
the basis of the jurors' tastes or views, or perhaps on the basis of t~~\~~.
dislike of a particular expression. An "outrageousness" standard thu~~\~~.
runs afoul of our longstanding refusal to allow damages to be awarded
because the speech in question may have an adverse emotional impact on
the audience. See *NAACP v. Claiborne Hardware Co.*, 458 U.S. 886, 910,
102 S.Ct. 3409, 3424, 73 L.Ed.2d 1215 (1982) ("Speech does not lose its
protected character ... simply because it may embarrass others or
coerce them into action"). And, as we stated in *FCC v. Pacifica Foundation*, 438 U.S. 726, 98 S.Ct. 3026, 57 L.Ed.2d 1073 (1978):

> "[T]he fact that society may find speech offensive is not a
> sufficient reason for suppressing it. Indeed, if it is the speaker's
> opinion that gives offense, that consequence is a reason for
> according it constitutional protection. For it is a central tenet of
> the First Amendment that the government must remain neutral
> in the marketplace of ideas." *Id.*, at 745–746, 98 S.Ct., at 3038.

See also *Street v. New York*, 394 U.S. 576, 592, 89 S.Ct. 1354, 1366,
22 L.Ed.2d 572 (1969) ("It is firmly settled that ... the public expression of ideas may not be prohibited merely because the ideas are
themselves offensive to some of their hearers").

Admittedly, these oft-repeated First Amendment principles, like
other principles, are subject to limitations. We recognized in *Pacifica
Foundation*, that speech that is " 'vulgar,' 'offensive,' and 'shocking' " is
"not entitled to absolute constitutional protection under all circumstances." 438 U.S., at 747, 98 S.Ct., at 3039. In *Chaplinsky v. New
Hampshire*, 315 U.S. 568, 62 S.Ct. 766, 86 L.Ed. 1031 (1942), we held
that a State could lawfully punish an individual for the use of insulting
" 'fighting' words—those which by their very utterance inflict injury or
tend to incite an immediate breach of the peace." *Id.*, at 571–572, 62
S.Ct., at 769. These limitations are but recognition of the observation in
*Dun & Bradstreet, Inc. v. Greenmoss Builders, Inc.*, 472 U.S. 749, 758,
105 S.Ct. 2939, 2945, 86 L.Ed.2d 593 (1985), that this Court has "long
recognized that not all speech is of equal First Amendment importance."
But the sort of expression involved in this case does not seem to us to be
governed by any exception to the general First Amendment principles
stated above.

We conclude that public figures and public officials may not recover
for the tort of intentional infliction of emotional distress by reason of
publications such as the one here at issue without showing in addition
that the publication contains a false statement of fact which was made
with "actual malice," *i.e.*, with knowledge that the statement was false
or with reckless disregard as to whether or not it was true. This is not
merely a "blind application" of the *New York Times* standard, see *Time,
Inc. v. Hill*, 385 U.S. 374, 390, 87 S.Ct. 534, 543, 17 L.Ed.2d 456 (1967),
it reflects our considered judgment that such a standard is necessary to
give adequate "breathing space" to the freedoms protected by the First
Amendment.

Here it is clear that respondent Falwell is a "public figure" for purposes of First Amendment law. The jury found against respondent on his libel claim when it decided that the Hustler ad parody could not "reasonably be understood as describing actual facts about [respondent] or actual events in which [he] participated." App. to Pet. for Cert. C1. The Court of Appeals interpreted the jury's finding to be that the ad parody "as not reasonably believable," 97 F.2d, at 1278, and in accordance with our custom we accept this finding. Respondent is thus relegated to his claim for damages awarded by the jury for the intentional infliction of emotional distress by "outrageous" conduct. But for reasons heretofore stated this claim cannot, consistently with the First Amendment, form a basis for the award of damages when the conduct in question is the publication of a caricature such as the ad parody involved here. The judgment of the Court of Appeals is accordingly reversed.

## *NOTES*

**1. Public Figure.** Public figures must prove *New York Times* malice in addition to the usual elements to recover for intentional infliction of emotional distress caused by publications. *New York Times* malice, devised by United States Supreme Court in *New York Times Co. v. Sullivan*, 376 U.S. 254, 84 S.Ct. 710, 11 L.Ed.2d 686 (1964), see Chapter 8, Sec. D, infra, requires that the plaintiff prove the defendant communicated with "knowledge that the statement was false or with reckless disregard as to whether or not it is true." The burden to prove this culpability requirement is imposed now on public officials and public figures suing for defamation. The defamation tort compensates for falsehoods that injure the plaintiff's reputation. Why is the standard relevant to intentional infliction of emotional distress? Does truth or falsehood have anything to do with the tort? Does the requirement effectively eliminate the tort as a remedy for public plaintiffs for published derision except where defamation exists?

**2. Common Law Malice Distinguished.** *New York Times* (sometimes labeled constitutional) malice should be distinguished from ordinary common law malice. Common law malice is generally defined as ill will, hatred, or reckless disregard toward the rights of the victim. Where common law malice exists in the context of a tort, most jurisdictions allow the jury to award the plaintiff punitive damages as discussed infra in Chapter 5, Sec. C.

**3. Private Plaintiffs.** Courts have not required private plaintiffs to prove *New York Times* malice to recover for intentional infliction of emotional distress. Consider *Esposito–Hilder v. SFX Broadcasting Inc.*, 236 A.D.2d 186, 665 N.Y.S.2d 697 (N.Y. Sup. Ct., App. Div. 1997). Defendant radio station and its disc jockeys regularly broadcast an "Ugliest Bride" contest. In a departure from routine practice, the disc jockeys broadcast the full name, place, and position of employment and names of her business superiors. The court held the plaintiff bride, as a private plaintiff, was not precluded from alleging intentional infliction of emotional distress and did not impose *New York Times* malice as a prerequisite to recovery. Does the tort pose a First Amendment threat when private plaintiffs sue for statements made by others? Should opinions or truthful statements lead to liability? Is the tort too vague to provide potential defendants guidance as to what will be characterized as outrageous? See Franklin, Anderson & Cate, *Mass Media Law* (6th ed. 2000).

# SECTION G.  DEFENSES TO INTENTIONAL TORTS

## DRABEK v. SABLEY
Supreme Court of Wisconsin.
31 Wis.2d 184, 142 N.W.2d 798 (1966).

Action for false imprisonment and assault and battery.

The jury found no false imprisonment and no assault and battery. On September 14, 1965, the court entered judgment dismissing the complaint. Plaintiff has appealed.

Plaintiff Thomas Drabek, 10 years old, lived with his parents on highway 67, just north of the village of Williams Bay. On February 23, 1964, shortly before 6:00 p.m., Tom and four other boys were across the highway from the Drabek home, throwing snowballs at passing cars. Defendant, Dr. Nanito Sabley, drove by, and his car was hit by a snowball, apparently thrown by one of the other boys. Dr. Sabley stopped his car and the boys ran. Dr. Sabley pursued Tom for about 100 yards, caught him, and, holding him by the arm, took him to the car and directed him to enter it. Dr. Sabley asked and was told Tom's name, but did not ask where he lived. Dr. Sabley, who had been driving north, turned his car around and drove into the village. He located a police officer, and turned Tom over to him. Tom told the officer the names of the other boys involved, and the officer took Tom to his home. Tom was with the defendant some 15 to 20 minutes.

Additional facts will be referred to in the opinion.

FAIRCHILD, Justice.

Interpreting the evidence, where in conflict, most favorably to the verdict, defendant effectively restrained Tom's physical liberty, and took him into the village for the purpose of having him tell the police officer the names of the other boys. Defendant held Tom by the arm both on the way to the car before driving into the village, and, at times, while they were in the village.

Thus there was false imprisonment unless the restraint was legally justified. Except for possible justification, the offensive holding of the arm was also a battery, albeit nominal.

Defendant claims justification in that he witnessed acts that were dangerous to defendant and others and took reasonable steps to prevent further dangerous activities.

It is recognized that one may be privileged to interfere with the liberty of another, within limits, for the purpose of defending one's self, defending a third person, or preventing the commission of a crime. Dr. Sabley did not act in self defense, since he was no longer in danger. It is true that the boys momentarily terminated their offensive activity when he stopped his car, but it was reasonable to expect them to renew it. We perceive that throwing snowballs at moving cars creates danger, as much because of the likelihood of startling the driver as of damage to the cars. Although it is a close question whether the threat to the safety of others was sufficiently immediate, after the boys had run away, it seems to us that Dr. Sabley, though not an officer, was privileged to take reasonable steps to prevent the resumption of the activity.

We conclude that Dr. Sabley's actions presented a jury question of reasonableness up to the time he put the boy in his car and drove away. Up to that time he had obtained the boy's name, and admonished him, according to the defendant's testimony, against carrying on the activity. The jury was entitled to believe that in holding the boy he used only such force as was reasonable for the purpose. Dr. Sabley may well have been justified in marching Tom across the road to his home and notifying his parents. We conclude, however, that it was unreasonable, as a matter of law, for Dr. Sabley to put 10–year-old Tom in his car a few yards from his home and drive him into the village for the purposes he did and under the circumstances of this case.

We note that where a child is taken into immediate custody under the children's code, his parents "shall be notified as soon as possible" and that "The person taking the child into custody shall, unless it is impracticable, undesirable, or has been otherwise ordered by the court, return the child to his parent, guardian or legal custodian on the promise of such person to bring the child to the court...."

Accordingly we conclude that the jury finding, in effect, that Dr. Sabley's conduct was reasonable exonerates him up to the time he put Tom in the car, but not afterward. The restraint of Tom's liberty continued, and after that point there was false imprisonment. Dr. Sabley admitted holding Tom while they looked for the officer, and this was a battery, though nominal.

It follows that there must be a determination of compensatory damages, though the record will not support a very substantial award, for the period of false imprisonment after the point just mentioned, and for the battery, consisting of the holding of the arm for a time after reaching the village. We think the first jury's findings that there was no false imprisonment and no assault and battery, imply a finding that there was no malice, and hence no punitive damages are recoverable. The only issue on the new trial will be compensatory damages.

Judgment reversed, cause remanded for further proceedings.

### *NOTES*

**1. Restatement Formulation of Self–Defense Privilege.** Self-defense constitutes a defense which can justify and therefore negate liability for intentional torts. Under self-defense the actor may use reasonable force that is reasonably perceived by the actor as necessary to protect from the threat of immediate force. The Restatement of Torts articulates self-defense as follows:

(1) An actor is privileged to use reasonable force, not intended or likely to cause death or serious bodily harm, to defend himself against unprivileged harmful or offensive contact or other bodily harm which he reasonably believes that another is about to inflict intentionally upon him.

(2) Self-defense is privileged under the conditions stated in Subsection (1), although the actor correctly or reasonably believes that he can avoid the necessity of so defending himself,

(a) by retreating or otherwise giving up a right or privilege, or

(b) by complying with a command with which the actor is under no duty to comply or which the other is not privileged to enforce by the means threatened.

(1) ... an actor is privileged to defend himself against another by force intended or likely to cause death or serious bodily harm, when he reasonably believes that

(a) the other is about to inflict upon him an intentional contact or other bodily harm, and that

(b) he is thereby put in peril of death or serious bodily harm or ravishment, which can safely be prevented only by the immediate use of such force.

As the Restatement indicates, force intended to inflict death or serious bodily injury is only reasonable in response to the immediate threat of serious bodily injury or death. Furthermore, the Restatement requires retreat, if safely possible (except from the victim's own dwelling), before the victim can respond with force intended to inflict serious bodily injury or death. See Restatement (Second) of Torts § 65 cmt. g. The majority of courts disagree with the Restatement on this point and would never require the victim to retreat from a lawful location. Which position do you find most persuasive?

Restatement (Second) of Torts §§ 63 and 65. See also Keeton, *Prosser and Keeton on the Law of Torts*, § 19 (5th ed. 1984); Diamond, Levine & Madden, *Understanding Torts* § 2.02 (2nd ed. 2000) and Dobbs, *The Law of Torts* §§ 70–73 (2000).

**2.   Immediate Threat.** Self-defense must be in response to an immediate threat of harm. In *Juarez-Martinez v. Deans*, 108 N.C.App. 486, 424 S.E.2d 154 (1993), for example, the Court of Appeals of North Carolina held that an employee was acting in self-defense where the employee attacked his employer after he awoke to his employer standing over him pouring beer on the employee's face with one hand and a metal pin in the other. The court reasoned, "a person in the [employee's] situation would feel a reasonable apprehension of apparent danger." But consider, *Holbrook v. Swabley*, 1996 WL 277679 (Ohio App. 6 Dist.), where the Court of Appeals of Ohio held that the defendant's theory that he had acted in self-defense, based on an altercation a year prior between himself and the plaintiff, did not show that the defendant held a belief that he was "in such imminent danger of harm so as to justify hitting the plaintiff in the face."

**3.   Spousal Abuse.** The generally accepted requirement that the threat be immediate to establish self-defense has prompted controversy in spousal abuse cases. Some commentators have argued that to require a smaller spouse to wait until a physical threat is immediate, thereby putting the victim at great physical disadvantage, is unrealistic and also ignores that the spouse may effectively find herself in an entrapped situation. Other commentators have emphasized the danger toward spiraling violence by authorizing preemptive violence. See generally Faigman, *Note, The Battered Woman Syndrome and Self–Defense: A Legal and Empirical Dissent*, 72 Va. L. Rev. 619 (1986). See also Maguigan, 140 U. Pa. L. Rev. 379 (1991).

**4.  Reasonable Belief.** A sincere but unreasonable belief that force is necessary will not constitute a defense. Consider cases that assess whether the victim's response was reasonable. In *Coleman v. Strohman*, 821 P.2d 88 (1991), for example, the Supreme Court of Wyoming held that refusal of the plaintiff's instruction that the defendant had negligently used force to repel a perceived attack was not error. The court reasoned that such an instruction is unnecessary because in order to establish the defense of self-defense, the defendant was required to show that the defendant honestly and reasonably believed that it was necessary for him to use force and that he used no more force than a reasonably prudent person would have used. Thus, the self-defense instruction given to the jury was sufficient for the jury to find that the defendant's use of self-defense was reasonable and without excessive force. Consider also, *Goldfuss v. Davidson*, 79 Ohio St.3d 116, 679 N.E.2d 1099 (Ohio 1997), where the Supreme Court of Ohio held that the defendant's use of deadly force against a trespasser attempting to break into the defendant's barn was unreasonable. The court reasoned that there was insufficient evidence for a jury to find that the defendant believed that he and his family were in imminent danger of death or great bodily harm. The defendant and his family were safely in their house with all the doors locked, and the trespasser was approximately one hundred feet away at the barn.

**5.  Self–Defense Against Excessive Police Force.** Consider also cases involving a right to self-defense against excessive police force. In *State v. Panella*, 43 Conn.App. 76, 682 A.2d 532 (1996), the Appellate Court of Connecticut held that a self-defense instruction was appropriate. The defendant testified that an officer attacked him with a flashlight without provocation and without informing the defendant that he was under arrest, that the defendant resisted arrest because he feared for his life, and that this fear was based on his belief that the police officers had a reputation for beating and assaults. Similarly, consider *Robinson v. United States*, 649 A.2d 584 (D.C.App.1994), where the District of Columbia Court of Appeals asserted that, while one cannot normally invoke a right of self-defense to justify assaultive behavior toward a police officer, a limited right of self-defense arises if the defendant shows evidence that the officer used excessive force in carrying out his duties. For further study, see Ytreberg, *Right to Resist Excessive Force Used in Accomplishing Lawful Arrest*, 77 A.L.R.3d 281 (1977).

**6.  Defense of Others: Should Good Samaritans be Encouraged to Intervene?** The Restatement, as articulated below, provides a privilege that allows reasonable force to protect a third party:

The actor is privileged to defend a third person from a harmful or offensive contact or other invasion of his interests of personality under the same conditions and by the same means as those under and by which he is privileged to defend himself if the actor correctly or reasonably believes that

(a) the circumstances are such as to give the third person a privilege of self-defense, and

(b) his intervention is necessary for the protection of the third person.

The Restatement view rejects the traditional rule still adhered to by many courts. Under the traditional rule, the actor is only privileged to intervene to defend another when the person he is defending is, in fact, privileged. The Restatement would protect the Good Samaritan who makes a reasonable mistake and intervenes on behalf of someone who in fact does not have the right of self-defense. Consider, for example, A sees B being attacked by C and A therefore assists B in resisting C. In fact, B is a serial killer and C is an undercover police officer using reasonable force to arrest B. Under the traditional rule, A's intervention, no matter how reasonable and in good faith, is not privileged since B enjoyed no privilege of self-defense. The Restatement and modern trend would excuse the Good Samaritan provided his mistaken intervention was reasonable from his perspective. Should the law encourage Good Samaritan intervention or would it be better to encourage Good Samaritans to seek professional assistance and avoid the risk even professionals face of intervening on the wrong side?

Restatement (Second) of Torts § 76. See Keeton, *supra*, § 20 (5th ed. 1984); Diamond, Levine & Madden, *supra*, § 2.03 and Dobbs, *supra*, § 74.

**7. Imminent Danger to Third Party Required.** Consider *Morgan v. State*, 545 S.W.2d 811 (Tex.Crim.App. 1977), where the Court of Appeals of Texas held that the evidence was insufficient to raise the issue of defense of third person because, even though the defendant allegedly saw the victim grab the defendant's sister around her neck with a beer bottle in his hand, the sister was out of danger at the time the defendant inflicted serious stab wounds on the victim. See also, *State v. Pounders*, 913 S.W.2d 904 (Mo.App. 1996), where the Missouri Court of Appeals held that the defendant was not entitled to an instruction on use of deadly force in defense of a third person. The victim's punching with his fists was merely a threat of assault and battery that could not justify use of deadly force. Neither was the third person in imminent danger of death or serious injury by the victim, because the third person had left the scene before the defendant applied the deadly force to the victim.

But consider *State v. Wright*, 163 Ariz. 184, 786 P.2d 1035 (Ariz.App. 1989), where the Court of Appeals of Arizona held that the court committed error by denying the defendant's defense-of-a-third-person instruction where the defendant entered a fight between his friend and the victim allegedly in order to save his friend. Consider also, *Deakyne v. Selective Insurance Company of America*, 728 A.2d 569 (Del.Super.1997), where the Superior Court of Delaware held that an insurance company was required to provide defense and indemnification to the plaintiff, as the plaintiff had acted in defense of his mother and sister against two trespassers on his property. In fact, only after receiving injuries himself, did the plaintiff resort to physical force against the two trespassers. Consider *Devincenzi v. Faulkner*, 174 Cal.App.2d 250, 344 P.2d 322 (1959), where the District Court of Appeal held that the defendant was justified in hitting a large dog with his vehicle in an effort to prevent the dog from attacking a fifteen-year-old boy.

**8. Defense of Unborn Fetuses.** Consider *Boushey v. State*, 804 S.W.2d 148 (Tex.App. 1990), where the Court of Appeals of Texas held that defense of a third person did not include defense of the unborn and therefore was not available to a pro-life demonstrator who had obstructed a passageway to an abortion clinic. See also, *Brumley v. State*, 804 S.W.2d 659 (Tex.App. 1991), where the Court of Appeals of Texas held that because fetuses were not "persons" under Texas law, protection of a third person was unavailable as a defense in a trespass action arising from the defendant's blocking of an entrance to a physician's office because the defendant believed the physician was about to perform an abortion.

**9. Further Study.** For further study, see Bendinelli and Edsall, *Defense of Others: Origins, Requirements, Limitations and Ramifications*, 5 Regent U.L.Rev. 153 (1995).

**10. Defense of Property.** Reasonable force can be used to protect personal and real property. Force intended to inflict death or serious bodily injury is never reasonable to merely protect property. The Restatement articulates the prevailing rule:

> An actor is privileged to use reasonable force, not intended or likely to cause death or serious bodily harm, to prevent or terminate another's intrusion upon the actor's land or chattels, if
>
> > (a) the intrusion is not privileged or the other intentionally or negligently causes the actor to believe that it is not privileged, and
> >
> > (b) the actor reasonably believes that the intrusion can be prevented or terminated only by the force used, and
> >
> > (c) the actor has first requested the other to desist and the other has disregarded the request, or the actor reasonably believes that a request will be useless or that substantial harm will be done before it can be made.

Restatement (Second) of Torts § 77.

As the Restatement indicates, the privilege doesn't apply if the actor utilizes force against an innocent person in fact privileged to use the property who has not intentionally or negligently induced the mistake. Although a reasonable mistake excuses the actor in the case of self-defense, courts are less tolerant of mistakes in defense of property and the actor largely acts at his own peril. An exception exists for merchants who are generally provided a privilege to use reasonable force against possible shoplifters and other thieves even if the alleged perpetrator is innocent. See, e.g., Cal. Penal Code § 490.5(f)(1); see also Diamond, Levine & Madden, *supra*, § 2.04; Keeton, *supra*, §§ 21–22 and Dobbs, *supra*, §§ 76–81.

Consider also the classic case of *Katko v. Briney*, 183 N.W.2d 657 (Iowa 1971), where a trespasser was shot by a mechanical spring gun set up to automatically fire at an intruder in an uninhabited farm structure. The court held the landowners who set the mechanical device were liable since human life had not been endangered. The Restatement (Second) would make privileged the infliction by mechanical device of serious bodily injury or death only when in fact the actor would be privileged to use such force if present. See Restatement § 85.

**11. Privilege to Arrest.** Arrests pursuant to an apparently valid warrant are privileged. Furthermore, under the common law, a private citizen has the right to use reasonable force to arrest an individual for a felony (a crime subject to punishment of over a year's imprisonment), when either the individual is in fact guilty of the felony or the felony actually occurred and the citizen reasonably believes the person he arrests is guilty.

In addition, a private citizen has the right to use reasonable force to arrest someone she witnesses committing a misdemeanor (a crime which has a maximum penalty of under a year) when the misdemeanor constitutes a breach of the peace. A police officer under the common law has in addition to these privileges the privilege to arrest an individual when she has a reasonable basis to believe the person is guilty of a felony even if no felony actually in fact occurred. As the principal case indicates, these common law rules are subject to specific statutory provisions. Consequently the defendant in the principal case could not rely on a privilege based on the "citizen's arrest" of the child without conforming to the statutory requirement that the parents be notified as soon as possible and normally returned to the parent's and not the police's custody. See Dobbs, *The Law of Torts* §§ 82–83 (2000); Restatement (Second) of Torts §§ 119; 122.

**12. What is Reasonable Force?** Do you agree with the judge in the principal case that the force and confinement against the ten-year-old was excessive and the jury verdict required reversal?

## VINCENT v. LAKE ERIE TRANSP. CO.

Supreme Court of Minnesota.
109 Minn. 456, 124 N.W. 221 (1910).

O'BRIEN, J.

The steamship Reynolds, owned by the defendant, was for the purpose of discharging her cargo on November 27, 1905, moored to plaintiff's dock in Duluth. While the unloading of the boat was taking place a storm from the northeast developed, which at about 10 o'clock p. m., when the unloading was completed, had so grown in violence that the wind was then moving at 50 miles per hour and continued to increase during the night. There is some evidence that one, and perhaps two, boats were able to enter the harbor that night, but it is plain that navigation was practically suspended from the hour mentioned until the morning of the 29th, when the storm abated, and during that time no master would have been justified in attempting to navigate his vessel, if he could avoid doing so. After the discharge of the cargo the Reynolds signaled for a tug to tow her from the dock, but none could be obtained because of the severity of the storm. If the lines holding the ship to the dock had been cast off, she would doubtless have drifted away; but, instead, the lines were kept fast, and as soon as one parted or chafed it was replaced, sometimes with a larger one. The vessel lay upon the outside of the dock, her bow to the east, the wind and waves striking her starboard quarter with such force that she was constantly being lifted and thrown against the dock, resulting in its damage, as found by the jury, to the amount of $500.

\* \* \*

The situation was one in which the ordinary rules regulating property rights were suspended by forces beyond human control, and if, without the direct intervention of some act by the one sought to be held liable, the property of another was injured, such injury must be attributed to the act of God, and not to the wrongful act of the person sought to be charged. If during the storm the Reynolds had entered the harbor, and while there had become disabled and been thrown against the plaintiffs' dock, the plaintiffs could not have recovered. Again, if while attempting to hold fast to the dock the lines had parted, without any negligence, and the vessel carried against some other boat or dock in the harbor, there would be no liability upon her owner. But here those in charge of the vessel deliberately and by their direct efforts held her in such a position that the damage to the dock resulted, and, having thus preserved the ship at the expense of the dock, it seems to us that her owners are responsible to the dock owners to the extent of the injury inflicted.

* * *

In *Ploof v. Putnam*, 71 Atl. 188, 20 L. R. A. (N. S.) 152, the Supreme Court of Vermont held that where, under stress of weather, a vessel was without permission moored to a private dock at an island in Lake Champlain owned by the defendant, the plaintiff was not guilty of trespass, and that the defendant was responsible in damages because his representative upon the island unmoored the vessel, permitting it to drift upon the shore, with resultant injuries to it. If, in that case, the vessel had been permitted to remain, and the dock had suffered an injury, we believe the shipowner would have been held liable for the injury done.

Theologians hold that a starving man may, without moral guilt, take what is necessary to sustain life; but it could hardly be said that the obligation would not be upon such person to pay the value of the property so taken when he became able to do so. . . .

Let us imagine in this case that for the better mooring of the vessel those in charge of her had appropriated a valuable cable lying upon the dock. No matter how justifiable such appropriation might have been, it would not be claimed that, because of the overwhelming necessity of the situation, the owner of the cable could not recover its value.

This is not a case where life or property was menaced by any object or thing belonging to the plaintiff, the destruction of which became necessary to prevent the threatened disaster. Nor is it a case where, because of the act of God, or unavoidable accident, the infliction of the injury was beyond the control of the defendant, but is one where the defendant prudently and advisedly availed itself of the plaintiffs' property for the purpose of preserving its own more valuable property, and the plaintiffs are entitled to compensation for the injury done.

Order affirmed.

## NOTES

**1. Private Necessity.** Private necessity is a privilege which allows the defendant to interfere with the property interests of an innocent party in an effort to avoid a greater injury. The privilege is incomplete since the actor must still compensate the victim for the property. The privilege can benefit the actor since she is not a trespasser or wrongfully using the property. Any force directed against the actor's presence on the property or appropriation of the personal property when used out of necessity can therefore be a tort against the actor. Furthermore, trespassers, as discussed in Chapter 2, Sec. H(6), infra, enjoy fewer rights to sue landowners for injuries they suffer from unsafe conditions on the land. See Restatement (Second) of Torts §§ 197, 263; Keeton, *Prosser and Keeton on the Law of Torts*, § 24 (5th ed. 1984); Diamond, Levine & Madden, *Understanding Torts* § 2.05 (2nd ed. 2000) and Dobbs, *The Law of Torts* § 107 (2000). For further study, see Finan and Ritson, *Tortious Necessity; The Privileged Defense*, 26 Akron Law Review 1 (1992).

Clearly protecting one's safety or health justifies the emergency use of property under necessity. As the principle case indicates, protecting the greater value of the boat justified intentional damage to the dock. Would this principle justify removing a less expensive car from higher ground to safeguard a more expensive car from flooding if no other safe area was immediately available? Would necessity justify destroying a less expensive house to save a more expensive one? How far should the principle extend?

**2.  Reasonable Perception of Need Required.** To constitute the defense of necessity, the defendant must have reasonably perceived an immediate need to appropriate the victim's property to avoid a greater damage to property or life. Consider *Benamon v. Soo Line Railroad Company*, 294 Ill.App.3d 85, 228 Ill.Dec. 494, 689 N.E.2d 366 (1997), where the Appellate Court of Illinois held that a juvenile's presence on a railroad track was not a private necessity entitling the youngster to a higher standard of care than would ordinarily apply to trespassers. The court explained that the private necessity privilege permits one to enter the premises of another without permission in an emergency situation when such entry is reasonably necessary to avoid serious harm. The court went further to assert that the plaintiff's action, hiding from his assailants near the girders on the railroad tracks, was unreasonable where the plaintiff had "other, more safe, options available to him." Thus, the plaintiff was not a permissive user such that the railroad company owed plaintiff a duty of reasonable care and was therefore, not liable for the injuries the plaintiff sustained. Consider also, *Pacific Alaska Fuel Services v. M/V Miyoshima Maru*, 1994 WL 739434 (D.Alaska), where the United States District Court of Alaska held that the doctrine of private necessity was inapplicable where the master of a group of vessels caused damage to a dock due to the master's failure to get the vessels away from the dock prior to a storm. Because it was determined that the master could have safely departed at an earlier time, the master's failure to depart was perceived as unreasonable.

But consider *Trisuzzi v. Tabatchnik*, 285 N.J.Super. 15, 666 A.2d 543 (1995), where the Superior Court of New Jersey held that a dog bite victim had a right to be on the property of the dog owner if the victim was there to protect himself or his wife and child. The court reasoned that simply asking the jury whether the plaintiff was bitten while lawfully on the defendant's property was an inadequate instruction. Rather, the jury should have been permitted to consider whether the plaintiff "was acting pursuant to the privilege of private necessity if he entered upon the defendant's land." In

*Kavanaugh v. Midwest Club, Inc.*, 164 Ill.App.3d 213, 115 Ill.Dec. 245, 517 N.E.2d 656 (1987), however, the Appellate Court of Illinois held that an owner of land adjacent to a roadway did not owe a duty to a motorist, who suffered an epileptic seizure and left the roadway, to protect the motorist from the retention pond located on the owner's land. The court reasoned that the motorist was not a rightful entrant under the doctrine of private necessity. The motorist did not actually "leave the roadway out of private necessity to protect his own interest, but, instead, deviated due to an apparent involuntary epileptic seizure."

**3. Public Necessity.** The defense of public necessity allows the appropriation of property to avoid a greater harm to the public. Unlike private necessity, the defendant under the common law privilege is not required to compensate the innocent victim. See Diamond, Levine & Madden, *supra*, § 2.05[C]; Keeton, *supra*, § 24 and Dobbs, *supra*, §§ 108–109. Consider the classic case of *Surocco v. Geary*, 3 Cal. 69 (1853), where a San Francisco public official ordered the destruction of a building to create a gap that would help put out a massive fire engulfing much of the city. The owners of the building were denied compensation for property they would have had time to save if the building and contents had not been destroyed prior to the fire reaching the building.

More recently in *Customer Co. v. City of Sacramento*, 10 Cal.4th 368, 41 Cal.Rptr.2d 658, 895 P.2d 900 (1995), the Supreme Court of California held that a store owner could not recover for damage to his store caused by the police, "who were under pressure of public necessity," due to a dangerous suspect's presence in the store. Thus, the city was not liable for the damage caused by the tear gas fired into the store by police in an effort to subdue and arrest the barricaded suspect. Some courts decline to apply the defense of public necessity in all cases. Consider, *Wegner v. Milwaukee Mutual Insurance Company*, 479 N.W.2d 38 (Minn.1991), where the Supreme Court of Minnesota held that the doctrine of public necessity did not insulate a municipality from its liability to pay just compensation to a homeowner for damages caused by the police who fired tear gas into the home in their attempt to apprehend the armed suspect barricaded in the home. The Court reasoned that in situations where an innocent third party's property is taken, damaged or destroyed by the police in the course of apprehending a suspect, the municipality should compensate the innocent party because this comports with our "basic notions of fairness and justice." Similarly, in *Steele v. City of Houston*, 603 S.W.2d 786 (Tex.1980), the Supreme Court of Texas held that the doctrine of public necessity did not prevent the plaintiff from recovering for damages to the plaintiff's house caused by police officers, who set fire to the plaintiff's house in an effort to recapture escaped convicts hiding in the house.

### 4.  Katrina Hurricane.

*Tue Aug 30,11:31 AM ET*

 Associated Press

A young man walks through chest deep flood water after looting a grocery store in New Orleans on Tuesday, Aug. 30, 2005. Flood waters continue to rise in New Orleans after Hurricane Katrina did extensive damage when it made landfall on Monday. (AP Photo/Dave Martin) (Reprinted by permission.)

*Tue Aug 30, 3:47 AM ET*

Two residents wade through chest-deep water after finding bread and
soda from a local grocery store after Hurricane Katrina came through
the area in New Orleans, Louisiana.(AFP/Getty Images/Chris
Graythen)(Reprinted by permission.)

Consider the two photographs of individuals attempting to survive the
Katrina Hurricane in New Orleans. Is it correct to characterize the man as
looting? Did private or public necessity justify taking food in an emergency
where aid was not yet available? Would a store be liable for actively
preventing access to food and other supplies even if the survivors could not
pay at the time?

**5. Intentional Infliction of Personal Injury or Death.** Although
there is some old favorable dictum, courts have not exonerated the intentional infliction of personal injury or death against a small number to avoid the
personal injury or death to a greater number of people. The Restatement
(Second) of Torts limits its adoption of the necessity privilege to interference
with property. See Restatement (Second) of Torts §§ 199 and 262. In *United
States v. Holmes*, 26 F. Cas. 360 (C.C.E.D.Pa.1842) (No. 15,383), the crew
threw male passengers out of a lifeboat to save the remainder from sinking.
The criminal court convicted the crew but in dictum said if a fair lottery had
selected the victim, the action would have been justified. In *Regina v. Dudley
& Stephens*, 14 Q.B.D 273 (1884), three adult seamen killed and ate a 17-

year-old boy in an effort to survive a period during which they were stranded on a lifeboat. Two of the seamen, who had actually carried out the killing, were sentenced to death, but the punishment was later commuted to six months' imprisonment.

Should necessity justify intentional killing to avoid more deaths? Unlike the Restatement (Second) of Torts, the Model Penal Code in criminal law considers necessity should be a defense to intentional killing since more lives will be saved. See Model Penal Code § 3.03. Is there a moral difference between intentional killing of the innocent and imposing a substantial but justified risk such as in a rescue operation or military campaign?

**6. Civil Disobedience.** The necessity defense is often used to defend torts or crimes arising out of civil disobedience. In most instances, courts have ruled a lawful alternative existed and do not accept the defense. Consider *United States v. Schoon*, 955 F.2d 1238 (9th Cir.1991), where the defendants, gaining admittance to an IRS office in Tucson, splashed simulated blood on the counters, walls, and carpeting, and generally obstructed the office's operation. The defendants asserted the necessity defense, claiming that their acts in protest of American involvement in El Salvador were necessary to avoid further bloodshed in that country. The Ninth Circuit held that the necessity defense was inapplicable to cases involving indirect civil disobedience, reasoning that the actions taken by the defendants were unlikely to abate the killings in El Salvador and that there were alternative lawful political means to mitigate the "harm." For further study, see Finan & Ritson, *Tortious Necessity: The Privileged Defense*, 26 Akron L. Rev. 1 (1992).

**7. Consent.** A potential plaintiff's consent to acts that would otherwise constitute a tort ordinarily is a defense to the tort. Controversy concerning the validity of the consent often focuses on whether the actions of the defendant went beyond what was consented or whether the consent was induced by duress or material fraud. In addition, children and the incapacitated are often deemed not to have the capacity to consent. See Diamond, Levine & Madden, *supra*, § 2.01; Keeton, *supra*, § 18, and Dobbs, *supra*, (2000); § 95.

The issue of consent in the context of medical treatment is considered in *Cobbs v. Grant*, at page 180, infra.

# SECTION H. INTENTIONAL INTERFERENCE WITH CONTRACTUAL AND ECONOMIC RELATIONS

## CALBOM v. KNUDTZON
Supreme Court of Washington.
65 Wash.2d 157, 396 P.2d 148 (1964).

HAMILTON, Judge.

Plaintiff (respondent) instituted this action seeking recovery of damages upon the grounds that defendants (appellants) had interfered with and induced a breach of an attorney-client relationship. Defendants appeal from an adverse judgment.

On May 1, 1958, K. T. Henderson, sole proprietor of a successful general contracting business, unexpectedly died of a heart attack. His death created pressing problems pertaining to the continuing operations of his business. Mrs. Jessie Bridges, Mr. Henderson's office manager, immediately contacted plaintiff, who was personally acquainted with the Hendersons and who, as a practicing attorney, had served them occasionally. Plaintiff, in substance, advised Mrs. Bridges that before he could intelligently give counsel he would have to know whether Mr. Henderson left a will and, if so, who was named as executor or executrix therein, and the provisions thereof. Mrs. Bridges then contacted Mrs. Henderson and a meeting was arranged between plaintiff, Mrs. Henderson, and Mrs. Bridges. At this meeting, it was disclosed that Mr. Henderson had left a will naming Mrs. Henderson his executrix, and that she desired to continue the business. She requested that plaintiff make arrangements to carry out her wishes.

Plaintiff prepared the necessary papers and at 4 p.m. on May 1, 1958, appeared with Mrs. Henderson and Mrs. Bridges before the Superior Court of Cowlitz County, at which time the will was offered for probate, Mrs. Henderson designated as executrix, and an order authorizing continuance of the business was entered. The following day, Mrs. Henderson was fully qualified as executrix and, with plaintiff's assistance, accounts at the bank were adjusted whereby business obligations, including the payroll of the business then due, were met, and a letter relating to and confirming an outstanding bid to a local school district for school construction dispatched. Plaintiff prepared to perfect and continue probate of the estate.

On May 6th, it was necessary for plaintiff to go to California. Before leaving, he checked with Mrs. Bridges to ascertain any immediate needs, and was informed there was none. Between May 6th and May 8th, Halvor Knudtzon, Sr., the senior member of the firm of Knudtzon and Associates, certified public accountants, returned from a trip. On May 8th, he was consulted by Mrs. Henderson relative to performing the tax work in connection with the estate. At this meeting, Mr. Knudtzon inquired of Mrs. Henderson if she had selected an attorney, to which she replied "Yes, I suppose Harry Calbom." Whereupon, Mr. Knudtzon shook his head and indicated, by inference at least, that plaintiff was unsatisfactory. Mr. Knudtzon thereupon recommended a list of attorneys from which one was selected.

On May 9th, plaintiff returned and was advised by Mrs. Bridges that another attorney was handling the probate matter. Thereupon, he contacted Mr. Knudtzon, Sr., and requested a meeting, which was arranged for that morning. Mr. Knudtzon, who was at home when contacted by plaintiff, telephoned his son at the office and advised him that plaintiff was coming in to confer with them, and that they would give him "a line of hot air." When confronted by plaintiff at their office, plaintiff was advised by Mr. Knudtzon, Sr., that they, as accountants, hired and fired attorneys for their clients and made reference to a former probate matter in which they had been instrumental in discharging the attorney.

Subsequently, an effort was made to pay plaintiff for services he had performed and secure his signature upon a notice of substitution of attorneys. Plaintiff refused to submit a bill for his services up to the time of his termination, refused to agree to a substitution of attorneys, and instituted the present action against the defendants alleging intentional interference with plaintiff's employment contract.

\* \* \*

Intentional and unjustified third-party interference with valid contractual relations or business expectancies constitutes a tort, with its taproot embedded in early decisions of the courts of England, e.g.: *Keeble v. Hickeringill*, 11 East 574, 11 Mod. 74, 130, 3 Salk 9, 103 Eng.Rep. 1127 (1809); *Lumley v. Gye*, 2 El. & Bl. 216, 118 Eng.Rep. 749 (1853); *Bowen v. Hall*, 6 Q.B.D. 333, 50 L.J.Q.B. 305 (1881); *Temperton v. Russell*, 1 Q.B. 715, 62 L.J.Q.B. 412 (1893); *South Wales Miners' Federation v. Glamorgan Coal Co.*, A.C. 239, 74 L.J.K.B. 525 (1905).

From and with the English decisions, the tort has become engraved upon American law, generally unsullied in principle, although with some case by case distinctions. See, Carpenter, Interference with Contract Relations, 41 Harv.L.Rev. 728; Prosser on Torts (3rd ed.) § 123, p. 950; 30 Am.Jur., Interference § 61, p. 95; 84 A.L.R. 43; 9 A.L.R.2d 228; 26 A.L.R.2d 1227.

We have recognized the tort in its various forms. [citations omitted]

The fundamental premise of the tort—that a person has a right to pursue his valid contractual and business expectancies unmolested by the wrongful and officious intermeddling of a third party—has been crystallized and defined in Restatement, Torts § 766, as follows:

> "Except as stated in Section 698 (betrothal promises), one who, without a privilege to do so, induces or otherwise purposely causes a third person not to

> "(a) perform a contract with another, or

> "(b) enter into or continue a business relation with another

> is liable to the other for the harm caused thereby."

Clause (a) relates to those cases in which the purposeful interference of a third party induces or causes a breach of an existing and valid contract relationship. Clause (b) embraces two types of situations. One is that in which the interferor purposely induces or causes a party not to enter into a business relationship with another. The second is where a business relationship, terminable at the will of the parties thereto, exists, and the intermeddler purposely induces or causes a termination of such relationship. The distinction between the situations propounded by clauses (a) and (b) lies not so much in the nature of the wrong, as in the existence or nonexistence, and availability as a defense, of privilege or justification for the interference. Restatement, Torts § 766, Comment c.

The basic elements going into a prima facie establishment of the tort are (1) the existence of a valid contractual relationship or business expectancy; (2) knowledge of the relationship or expectancy on the part of the interferor; (3) intentional interference inducing or causing a breach or termination of the relationship or expectancy; and (4) resultant damage to the party whose relationship or expectancy has been disrupted. Ill will, spite, defamation, fraud, force, or coercion, on the part of the interferor, are not essential ingredients, although such may be shown for such bearing as they may have upon the defense of privilege.

The burden of showing privilege for interference with the expectancy involved rests upon the interferor. Prosser on Torts (3rd ed.) § 123, p. 967; 30 Am.Jur., Interference § 57, p. 93. The basic issue raised by the assertion of the defense is whether, under the circumstances of the particular case, the interferor's conduct is justifiable, bearing in mind such factors as the nature of the interferor's conduct, the character of the expectancy with which the conduct interferes, the relationship between the various parties, the interest sought to be advanced by the interferor, and the social desirability of protecting the expectancy or the interferor's freedom of action. Restatement, Torts § 767. Some of the privileges and their limitations, which have been recognized, depending upon the circumstances and the factors involved, are legitimate business competition (Restatement, Torts § 768), financial interest (Restatement, Torts § 769), responsibility for the welfare of another (Restatement, Torts § 770), directing business policy (Restatement, Torts § 771), and the giving of requested advice (Restatement, Torts § 772).

Against the backdrop of the foregoing, we turn to defendants' contentions.

Defendants first assert that the evidence does not support the trial court's finding concerning the existence of an attorney-client relationship between plaintiff and Mrs. Henderson whereby plaintiff would undertake the "long term" probate of the estate. This assertion is predicated upon the argument that the testimony of Mrs. Henderson and Mrs. Bridges, coupled with the surrounding circumstances, indicate that Mrs. Henderson only intended to engage plaintiff's services for the limited purpose of admitting the will to probate and securing an order authorizing continuation of the business.

We agree that the evidence presented by defendants upon this point is susceptible of the interpretation defendants would place upon it. However, such is not the only interpretation finding support in the evidence as a whole. The evidence reveals that at the meeting on May 1, 1958, after plaintiff had explained the necessity for probate proceedings, Mrs. Henderson stated to plaintiff she wanted him to "handle this thing for me." Plaintiff thereupon prepared all papers incidental to the admission of the will to probate; arranged for the testimony of the witnesses to the will; appeared in court and presented the testimony of Mrs. Henderson, Mrs. Bridges, and the witnesses to the will; provided for, counseled, and participated in arrangements to meet pending business obligations; and, to all intents and purposes, became the attorney in fact and of record for the estate. Although the relationship thus established was terminable at the will of the parties, we are convinced the evidence and the reasonable inferences therefrom amply support the trial court's finding of an existing attorney-client relationship which plaintiff had every right to anticipate would continue, and which would have continued but for the intervention of defendants. Under such circumstances, we will not disturb the trial court's finding. *Thorndike v. Hesperian Orchards, Inc.*, 54 Wash.2d 570, 343 P.2d 183 (1959).

Defendants next assert that the evidence does not support the trial court's finding that they had knowledge of the existence of the attorney-client relationship in issue. Here again, the evidence and the inferences therefrom produce a conflict. On the one hand, defendants claim they were advised by Mrs. Bridges that plaintiff's employment was limited. On the other hand, plaintiff's evidence indicates that defendants were not only aware of plaintiff's position as attorney in fact and of record for the estate, but in fact boasted of their ability to terminate that relationship. Additional evidence supportive of plaintiff's version is the admission of defendants that they determined to give plaintiff a "line of hot air" when he called upon them, rather than rely upon what they now assert was their knowledge of his status in the estate.

Although knowledge of the existence of the business relationship in issue is an essential element in establishing liability for interference therewith, it is sufficient if the evidence reveals that the alleged interferor had knowledge of facts giving rise to the existence of the relationship. It is not necessary that the interferor understand the legal significance of such facts. Restatement, Torts § 766, Comment e.

We are satisfied that the evidence presented supports the trial court's finding of the requisite knowledge of the circumstances on the part of defendants. The finding falls within the ambit of the rule of *Thorndike v. Hesperian Orchards, Inc., supra*, and will not be disturbed.

Defendants next contention is that plaintiff's employment as attorney for the estate created a conflict of interest with his duties as a member of the local school board, and was, therefore, contrary to public policy and invalid. This is predicated upon the fact that the Henderson Construction Company had pending before the school board a bid for school construction at the time plaintiff initiated the probate proceedings.

We find no merit in this contention because (a) plaintiff stepped down from the school board at the time it considered the bid; (b) the board did not consider the bid until May 12, 1958, at which time plaintiff's services with the estate had been terminated; (c) the board, upon advice of the prosecuting attorney, rejected the bid; and (d) neither plaintiff nor his successor represented the estate before the school board. It is possible that had plaintiff continued as counsel for the estate he would have been confronted with a choice between his position upon the school board and as attorney for the estate. The fact is, however, that he was not afforded this opportunity, and speculation that he might have made a wrong choice cannot now form the basis of a declaration that his continued employment as attorney for the estate would have been invalid. Particularly is this so in the face of the unchallenged finding by the trial court that plaintiff acted "at all times herein material * * * with the highest degree of integrity consistent with the professional ethics of an attorney at law."

Defendants next contend that their interference with plaintiff's relationship to the estate was privileged. Defendants predicate this assertion upon the claim that they occupied a confidential relationship with Mrs. Henderson by virtue of their long time service to the Hendersons as tax consultants. In essence, defendants rely upon the privileges capsulized in Restatement, Torts §§ 770[1] and 772,[2] or a combination thereof.

The basic reason supporting both of the mentioned privileges is the protection of public and private interests in freedom of communication, decent conduct, and professional as well as lay counsel. Such privileges, however, do not justify officious, self-serving, or presumptuous assumption of responsibility and interference with the rights of others. The burden of establishing the existence of such a privilege or privileges rests, as heretofore indicated, upon the one asserting justification thereby.

We are satisfied, from our examination of the record, that defendants have not sustained their burden of proof. Suffice it to say the evidence supports the trial court's finding that defendants' interference was malicious, intentional and without justification.

The judgment is affirmed.

# Restatement (Second) of Torts*

## § 766. INTENTIONAL INTERFERENCE WITH PERFORMANCE OF CONTRACT BY THIRD PERSON

One who intentionally and improperly interferes with the performance of a contract (except a contract to marry) between another and a third person by inducing or otherwise causing the third person not to perform the contract, is subject to liability to the other for the pecuniary loss resulting to the other from the failure of the third person to perform the contract.

## § 766A. INTENTIONAL INTERFERENCE WITH ANOTHER'S PERFORMANCE OF HIS OWN CONTRACT

One who intentionally and improperly interferes with the performance of a contract (except a contract to marry) between another and a third person, by preventing the other from performing the contract or causing

---

**1.** "One who is charged with responsibility for the welfare of another is privileged purposely to cause him not to perform a contract, or enter into or continue a business relation, with a third person if the actor

   (a) does not employ improper means and

   (b) acts to protect the welfare of the other."

Restatement, Torts § 770.

**2.** "One is privileged purposely to cause another not to perform a contract, or enter into or continue a business relation, with a third person by giving honest advice to the other within the scope of a request for advice made by him, except that, if the actor is under a special duty to the third person with reference to the accuracy of the advice, he is subject to liability for breach of that duty." Restatement, Torts § 772.

\* © 1979 by the American Law Institute. Reprinted with permission.

his performance to be more expensive or burdensome, is subject to liability to the other for the pecuniary loss resulting to him.

## § 766B. INTENTIONAL INTERFERENCE WITH PROSPECTIVE CONTRACTUAL RELATION

One who intentionally and improperly interferes with another's prospective contractual relation (except a contract to marry) is subject to liability to the other for the pecuniary harm resulting from loss of the benefits of the relation, whether the interference consists of

(a) inducing or otherwise causing a third person not to enter into or continue the prospective relation or

(b) preventing the other from acquiring or continuing the prospective relation.

## § 767.  FACTORS IN DETERMINING WHETHER INTERFERENCE IS IMPROPER

In determining whether an actor's conduct in intentionally interfering with a contract or a prospective contractual relation of another is improper or not, consideration is given to the following factors:

(a) the nature of the actor's conduct,

(b) the actor's motive,

(c) the interests of the other with which the actor's conduct interferes,

(d) the interests sought to be advanced by the actor,

(e) the social interests in protecting the freedom of action of the actor and the contractual interests of the other,

(f) the proximity or remoteness of the actor's conduct to the interference and

(g) the relations between the parties.

## § 768.  COMPETITION AS PROPER OR IMPROPER INTERFERENCE

(1) One who intentionally causes a third person not to enter into a prospective contractual relation with another who is his competitor or not to continue an existing contract terminable at will does not interfere improperly with the other's relation if

(a) the relation concerns a matter involved in the competition between the actor and the other and

(b) the actor does not employ wrongful means and

(c) his action does not create or continue an unlawful restraint of trade and

(d) his purpose is at least in part to advance his interest in competing with the other.

(2) The fact that one is a competitor of another for the business of a third person does not prevent his causing a breach of an existing

contract with the other from being an improper interference if the contract is not terminable at will.

## § 769. ACTOR HAVING FINANCIAL INTEREST IN BUSINESS OF PERSON INDUCED

One who, having a financial interest in the business of a third person intentionally causes that person not to enter into a prospective contractual relation with another, does not interfere improperly with the other's relation if he

(a) does not employ wrongful means and

(b) acts to protect his interest from being prejudiced by the relation.

## § 770. ACTOR RESPONSIBLE FOR WELFARE OF ANOTHER

One who, charged with responsibility for the welfare of a third person, intentionally causes that person not to perform a contract or enter into a prospective contractual relation with another, does not interfere improperly with the other's relation if the actor

(a) does not employ wrongful means and

(b) acts to protect the welfare of the third person.

## § 771. INDUCEMENT TO INFLUENCE ANOTHER'S BUSINESS POLICY

One who intentionally causes a third person not to enter into a prospective contractual relation with another in order to influence the other's policy in the conduct of his business does not interfere improperly with the other's relation if

(a) the actor has an economic interest in the matter with reference to which he wishes to influence the policy of the other and

(b) the desired policy does not unlawfully restrain trade or otherwise violate an established public policy and

(c) the means employed are not wrongful.

## § 772. ADVICE AS PROPER OR IMPROPER INTERFERENCE

One who intentionally causes a third person not to perform a contract or not to enter into a prospective contractual relation with another does not interfere improperly with the other's contractual relation, by giving the third person

(a) truthful information, or

(b) honest advice within the scope of a request for the advice.

## § 773. ASSERTING BONA FIDE CLAIM

One who, by asserting in good faith a legally protected interest of his own or threatening in good faith to protect the interest by appropriate means, intentionally causes a third person not to perform an existing contract or enter into a prospective contractual relation with another does not interfere improperly with the other's relation if the actor believes that his interest may otherwise be impaired or destroyed by the performance of the contract or transaction.

## § 774.  AGREEMENT ILLEGAL OR CONTRARY TO PUBLIC POLICY

One who by appropriate means causes the nonperformance of an illegal agreement or an agreement having a purpose or effect in violation of an established public policy is not liable for pecuniary harm resulting from the nonperformance.

## § 774A.  DAMAGES

(1) One who is liable to another for interference with a contract or prospective contractual relation is liable for damages for

(a) the pecuniary loss of the benefits of the contract or the prospective relation;

(b) consequential losses for which the interference is a legal cause; and

(c) emotional distress or actual harm to reputation, if they are reasonably to be expected to result from the interference.

(2) In an action for interference with a contract by inducing or causing a third person to break the contract with the other, the fact that the third person is liable for the breach does not affect the amount of damages awardable against the actor; but any damages in fact paid by the third person will reduce the damages actually recoverable on the judgment.

### *NOTES*

**1.  Elements of the Tort.** The tort of intentional interference with contract and the parallel tort of intentional interference of prospective contractual relations (also known as prospective economic relationship, economic expectations or opportunities, or business advantage) both provide tort remedies when the defendant without justification interferes with the plaintiff's contractual or prospective business relationship with another. The Restatement of Torts (Second) reprinted above articulates the generally accepted elements and justifications. In essence the elements of the two torts are:

(1) A valid contract (for the tort of interference of contract) or a valid economic expectancy (for the tort of interference of economic expectancy).

(2) Knowledge of the valid contract or economic expectancy by the defendant.

(3) Intent by the defendant to interfere with the contract or economic expectancy.

(4) Interference caused by the defendant.

(5) Damage to plaintiff.

See Diamond, Levine & Madden, *Understanding Torts* § 19.02 (2nd ed. 2000); Keeton, *Prosser and Keeton on the Law of Torts*, §§ 129–130 (5th ed. 1984) and Dobbs, *The Law of Torts* §§ 445–450 (2000).

It should be emphasized that the tort does not impose liability against either of the parties of a contract or prospective economic relationship, but punishes the third party intermeddler who unjustifiably induces one of the parties to breach the contract or sever the prospective business relationship or otherwise makes it impossible for one of the parties to perform the contract or continue the relationship. The parties who wrongfully breach a contract may, themselves, be liable under contract law for breach of contract. The tort liability for the intermeddler can be more severe, however, since liability for either of the torts includes emotional distress and potentially punitive damages (see Chapter 5, Sec. C, infra), in addition to economic consequences caused by the interference.

2.  **Justifications.** Once the plaintiff has established the prima facie elements noted above for either tort, a variety of justifications, as noted in the Restatement excerpt above, can negate liability. While traditionally the defendant has the burden of proving the justifications, an increasing number of courts are requiring the plaintiff to prove, in addition to the prima facie case, the lack of any arguable justifications. See, e.g., *Della Penna v. Toyota Motor Sales, U.S.A., Inc.*, 11 Cal.4th 376, 45 Cal.Rptr.2d 436, 902 P.2d 740 (Cal. 1995). Note that the Restatement avoids taking a position on whether the plaintiff or defendant has the burden of disproving or proving the justifications. The argument for requiring the plaintiff to prove the lack of a justification is particularly compelling in the case of intentional interference of economic expectation since interfering with another's economic expectations (where no contract exists) is at the core of competitive capitalism. Consider that Pepsi Cola's attempts to win over consumers predisposed to purchase Coca Cola is an example of classic American capitalism.

The first two specific justifications articulated by the Restatement—(1) fair competition (§ 768), and (2) proper protection of one's financial interest (§ 769)—only provide a justification for interfering with prospective contractual relations or a contract that is freely terminable at will. Consequently, it is justifiable for Coca Cola to freely compete for Pepsi's customers provided the company does not persuade a contracted customer (not terminable at will) to breach a purchase agreement. Similarly, a stockholder with a financial interest in a company can, through proper means as specified in Restatement § 769, argue against hiring an employee to protect the financial profitability of his stock interest but cannot urge wrongful breach of a contract with a current employee.

Section 771 of the Restatement, as reprinted above, provides a justification sufficient only for interfering with a prospective contractual relation to advance a legitimate business policy for which the actor has an economic interest. For example, a business could encourage other businesses in their industry not to purchase products from foreign manufacturers which do not meet certain factory standards or pay a living wage, even if such conditions are not illegal.

The additional specific justifications noted by the Restatement—(1) protecting the welfare of another one is responsible for (§ 770); (2) providing truthful information or honest (even if not accurate) advice within the scope of a request (§ 772); (3) assertion of a bona fide property right (e.g., preventing a thief from selling the victim's own car) (§ 773); and (4) interfering with an agreement either illegal or against public policy—are sufficiently strong justifications to preclude liability for interfering with any contract or prospective contractual relationship.

In addition to the specific justifications, Section 767 of the Restatement, as reprinted above, authorizes the jury to consider other justifications and articulates a broad range of factors to help the jury evaluate the propriety of the interference in specific cases. Do the factors specified in Section 767 provide any real guidance to the jury or any predictive value to the litigants?

**3. Evaluating the Justifications in the Principal Case.** Did the widow breach a contract by dismissing the plaintiff's attorney from providing additional legal services? What impact does this have on the available justifications for the accountants? Why did the court reject the defendant's justifications based on Restatement sections 770 and 772? What did the defendants do wrong? Suppose a patient tells her family doctor that she has contracted with a surgeon to operate on her. The family doctor honestly believes the surgeon, while licensed, is incompetent and would place the patient needlessly at risk. In light of the principal case and the Restatement justifications, what advice could you give the family doctor about the risk of encouraging the patient to retain a different surgeon than the one the patient had contracted to do surgery on her?

**4. Interference With Economic Relationships.** Consider *Small v. Juniata College*, 452 Pa.Super. 410, 682 A.2d 350 (1996), where a football coach sued three football players for intentional interference with contract after the football coach was terminated due to the player's complaints to the college administrators regarding the plaintiff's coaching tactics. The Superior Court of Pennsylvania held that the college player's complaints did not constitute intentional interference with contract because student criticism of an employee with whom the players routinely interacted was justified, in that the "rules of the game in the academic world encourage students to voice their opinions." Consider also, *Farrington v. Buttrey Food and Drug Stores Company*, 272 Mont. 140, 900 P.2d 277 (1995), where an employee brought an action against a grocery store chain, alleging that the chain's banning of him from their stores had caused him to lose his job as a grocery store supplier. The defendant argued that its banning of the employee was due to the employee's misconduct while employed at another store and temporarily working on assignment at the defendant's grocery store. The Supreme Court of Montana held that it was a question for the jury whether the banning of the employee from the store was justified, considering that the misconduct had occurred over one year prior to the banning of the plaintiff from the defendant's stores and the plaintiff's duties at the time of the banning were substantially different from those at the time of the plaintiff's earlier misconduct, so as to make further misconduct nearly impossible. Compare with *Fankhanel v. M & H Construction Company, Inc.*, 559 N.W.2d 229 (N.D.1997), where a truck driver brought an action against a contractor for intentional interference with the driver's employment contract after the contractor requested that the driver no longer make deliveries to the contractor's job sites. The Supreme Court of North Dakota held that the contractor's interference was justified because the driver's earlier failure to pay a debt to the contractor provided the contractor with a legitimate business reason to exclude the driver from the contractor's job sites.

Consider *Brown Mackie College v. Graham*, 768 F.Supp. 1457 (D.Kan. 1991), where a lawyer representing a college student contacted several other students who were unhappy with a program offered by the college. The students later withdrew and asked the lawyer for legal advice. The college sued the lawyer for interference with contractual relations. However, the court held that the defendant's interference with the contracts between the students and the school was privileged and not tortious. The court pointed out that the defendant, as the students' attorney, was responsible for their welfare and so was privileged to advise or induce the students to breach their contracts with the college. Consider also *Nathanson v. Medical College of Pennsylvania*, 926 F.2d 1368 (3d Cir.1991), where a medical student who took a leave of absence following an accident sued her college for tortious interference with existing contractual relationship. In her complaint, plaintiff alleged that defendant had notified another medical school of plaintiff's matriculation with defendant college, which had caused the other school to withdraw its offer of acceptance. The district court granted summary judgement to the defendant. The circuit court affirmed, holding that the defendant's communication with the other school was proper insofar as it protected defendant's contractual interests. Plaintiff failed also to prove that this information adversely affected her applications to other schools.

# LOWELL v. MOTHER'S CAKE & COOKIE CO.

Court of Appeal, First District, Division 2, California.
79 Cal.App.3d 13, 144 Cal.Rptr. 664 (1978).

KANE, J., Associate Justice.

Plaintiff, Fred Lowell, Jr., the sole owner of Lowell Freight Lines, Inc., a common carrier, appeals from a judgment of dismissal entered after respondent's demurrer to the second amended complaint was sustained without leave to amend.

\* \* \*

The principal issues on appeal are whether the complaints to which the demurrers were sustained without leave to amend alleged actionable wrongs ... for tortious interference with prospective business advantage; ...

*Intentional Interference With Prospective Business Advantage:* In addressing the first issue, we initially note that the basic principles underlying the tort of inducing breach of contract have been extended to impose liability for intentional interference with business relations or advantages which are merely prospective and not subject to an existing, legally binding agreement (*Buckaloo v. Johnson* (1975) 14 Cal.3d 815, 823 [122 Cal.Rptr. 745, 537 P.2d 865]; *Dryden v. Tri–Valley Growers* (1977) 65 Cal.App.3d 990, 994 [135 Cal.Rptr. 720]; 4 Witkin, Summary of Cal. Law (8th ed. 1974) § 392, p. 2643). While the criteria of this new tort are developing and admittedly vague, it is widely recognized that in order to be actionable the interference with prospective economic advantage or advantageous business relationship must be *unjustified and/or without privilege.* As has been pointed out, "one who *unjustifiably* interferes with an advantageous business relationship to another's damage may be held liable therefor." (*Diodes, Inc. v. Franzen* (1968) 260

Cal.App.2d 244, 255 [67 Cal.Rptr. 19], italics added. See also *Speegle v. Board of Fire Underwriters* (1946) 29 Cal.2d 34, 39 [172 P.2d 867]; *Shida v. Japan Food Corp.* (1967) 251 Cal.App.2d 864, 866 [60 Cal.Rptr. 43]; *Masoni v. Board of Trade of S.F.* (1953) 119 Cal.App.2d 738, 741 [260 P.2d 205].) Restatement of Torts section 766, likewise provides in part that "one who, *without a privilege* to do so, induces or otherwise purposely causes a third person not to . . . (b) enter into or continue a business relation with another is liable to the other for the harm caused thereby." (Italics added.)

The unjustifiability or wrongfulness of the act may consist of the *methods* used *and/or* the *purpose* or motive of the actor. On one hand it is emphasized that the wrong consists of intentional and *improper methods* of diverting or taking business from another which are not within the privilege of fair competition (*A. F. Arnold & Co. v. Pacific Professional Ins., Inc.* (1972) 27 Cal.App.3d 710, 715 [104 Cal.Rptr. 96]; 4 Witkin, Summary of Cal. Law, *supra.*). On the other, it is underscored that the cases involving interference with prospective business advantage " 'have turned almost entirely upon the *defendant's motive or purpose, and the means* by which he has sought to accomplish it. As in the case of interference with contract, *any manner of intentional invasion of the plaintiff's interests may be sufficient if the purpose is not a privileged one . . .* ' " (*A. F. Arnold & Co. v. Pacific Professional Ins., Inc.*, *supra.*, at p. 716, italics added; Prosser on Torts (4th ed. 1971) p. 952). In accordance therewith it has been held that an action for interference with prospective business advantage will lie where the right to pursue a lawful business is intentionally interfered with either by unlawful means or by means otherwise lawful when there is a lack of sufficient justification (*Chicago Title Ins. Co. v. Great Western Financial Corp.* (1968) 69 Cal.2d 305, 319 [70 Cal.Rptr. 849, 444 P.2d 481]; *Willis v. Santa Ana etc. Hospital Assn.* (1962) 58 Cal.2d 806, 810 [26 Cal.Rptr. 640, 376 P.2d 568]; *Guillory v. Godfrey* (1955) 134 Cal.App.2d 628, 632 [286 P.2d 474]; *Masoni v. Board of Trade of S.F.*, *supra.*, 119 Cal.App.2d at p. 741). (2) Finally, it bears special emphasis that while the defendant's culpable intent and the damages resulting from the interference are elements of the cause of action which must be pleaded and proved by the plaintiff, the defendant's justification is not an ingredient of the cause of action, but rather constitutes an affirmative defense (*A. F. Arnold & Co. v. Pacific Professional Ins., Inc.*, *supra.*, at p. 714; Prosser on Torts, *supra.*, at p. 953). As has been said in *Herron v. State Farm Mutual Ins. Co.* (1961) 56 Cal.2d 202, 207 [14 Cal.Rptr. 294, 363 P.2d 310], "Justification is an affirmative defense and may not be considered as supporting the trial court's action in sustaining a demurrer unless it appears on the face of the complaint." (Accord: *Gold v. Los Angeles Democratic League* (1975) 49 Cal.App.3d 365, 376 [122 Cal.Rptr. 732]; *A. F. Arnold & Co. v. Pacific Professional Ins., Inc.*, *supra.*)

When examined in light of the foregoing principles we believe the Second Complaint alleges facts sufficient to state a cause of action for tortious interference with prospective business advantage and at the same time the requisite justification fails to appear upon the face of the complaint. As a consequence, we hold that the trial court erred in sustaining respondent's demurrer to the Second Complaint and in dismissing appellant's action.

The Second Complaint in essence avers that appellant was the sole owner of Lowell Freight Lines, Inc., a trucking firm (Company). For over five years the Company performed delivery services for respondent pursuant to an oral contract. The revenue derived from that contract amounted to approximately 40 percent of the gross income of appellant's business. Appellant intended to sell the Company, and he received several offers from potential purchasers. One of these offers, which was conditioned on the Company's continued business with respondent, was for approximately $200,000. Respondent, however, intentionally interfered with the consummation of this agreement by informing the prospective purchasers that the delivery contract would be terminated if the Company was sold to a third person. The purpose of the interference was to discourage potential buyers from purchasing the Company from appellant and thereby depress its purchase price substantially below its market value. Respondent succeeded in its scheme. The Company was sold to respondent for about $17,400 instead of its true market value of $200,000, and as a result appellant suffered damages in the sum of $183,000.

The facts alleged in the Second Complaint, which for the purpose of a demurrer must be regarded as true (*Mercer v. Elliott* (1962) 208 Cal.App.2d 275, 279 [25 Cal.Rptr. 217]), thus clearly establish that respondent intentionally interfered with a prospective advantageous business relationship, and that the interference resulted in substantial damages to appellant. These allegations, of course, are sufficient to state a valid cause of action for interference with prospective economic advantage *unless it can be said that the facts averred in the complaint show justification or privilege as a matter of law* (*A. F. Arnold & Co. v. Pacific Professional Ins., Inc., supra.*; Prosser on Torts, *supra.*, at p. 953).

This leads us to the very heart of the dispute, i.e., whether the facts alleged in the Second Complaint divulge upon their face that the acts complained of were justified or privileged. Respondent, in effect, argues that in the absence of a binding contract it was free to terminate its business relationship with appellant or any potential successor, and was also at liberty to inform the future buyers that respondent did not intend to utilize the services of the Company if the latter changed hands. Since the means adopted and utilized by respondent were entirely proper and lawful, continues the argument, no actionable wrong was alleged or committed, even if the Second Complaint charged that the steps complained of were taken for an improper purpose or motive. Respondent's position is unacceptable for a number of considerations.

One, as spelled out above, even if the means used by the defendant are entirely lawful, intentional interference with prospective economic advantage constitutes actionable wrong *if* it results in damages to the plaintiff, and the defendant's conduct is not excused by a legally recognized privilege or justification (*Chicago Title Ins. Co. v. Great Western*

*Financial Corp., supra.*, 69 Cal.2d 305, 319; *A. F. Arnold & Co. v. Pacific Professional Ins., Inc., supra.*, at p. 716; Rest., Torts, § 766).[1]

Two, as a general rule, the determination of whether the defendant's conduct of interfering with existing contracts with third persons or prospective economic advantage is privileged comprises a factual issue to be decided upon all the circumstances of the case. "*Whether an intentional interference by a third party is justifiable depends upon* a balancing of the importance, social and private, of the objective advanced by the interference against the importance of the interest interfered with, *considering all circumstances* including the nature of the actor's conduct and the relationship between the parties." (*Herron v. State Farm Mutual Ins. Co., supra.*, 56 Cal.2d at p. 206, italics added; *Greenberg v. Hollywood Turf Club* (1970) 7 Cal.App.3d 968, 977 [86 Cal.Rptr. 885]; see also *Freed v. Manchester Service, Inc.* (1958) 165 Cal.App.2d 186 [331 P.2d 689]; *Masoni v. Board of Trade of S.F., supra.*, 119 Cal.App.2d 738.) In harmony therewith, Restatement of Torts section 767, provides that "In determining whether there is a privilege to act in the manner stated in § 766, the following are important factors: (a) the nature of the actor's conduct, (b) the nature of the expectancy with which his conduct interferes, (c) the relations between the parties, (d) the interest sought to be advanced by the actor and (e) the social interests in protecting the expectancy on the one hand and the actor's freedom of action on the other hand." Significantly enough, comment d to section 767 spells out that "*the question on the issue of privilege is whether the actor's conduct was fair and reasonable under the circumstances . . .*" (Emphasis added).

Three, but aside from the general rule, respondent's interference here may not *eo ipso* be justified by virtue of certain special privileges carved out for competitors and persons having a financial interest in the business of the person induced either (Rest., Torts, §§ 768, 769). Section 768 of the Restatement of Torts explicitly provides that the privilege accorded therein applies only to a competitor of the defendant.[2] Appellant and respondent here were involved in entirely different kinds of businesses, and by no stretch of the imagination may they be said to have been competitors to each other. At the same time respondent fails to qualify for an *ipso jure* privilege under Restatement of Torts, section 769, as well. The latter states that "One who has a financial interest in the business of another is privileged purposely to cause him not to enter into or continue a relation with a third person in that business if the actor (a) does not employ improper means, and (b) acts to protect his

---

**1.** Respondent at oral argument advanced for the first time the theory of justification based upon the giving of advice as described in the Restatement of Torts section 772, and discussed in *Walsh v. Glendale Fed. Sav. & Loan Assn.* (1969) 1 Cal. App.3d 578, 588–589 [81 Cal.Rptr. 804]. Reliance on this theory is misplaced since, as pointed out in comment a to the Restatement of Torts section 772, one of the conditions of such justification is "(1) that the advice be requested, . . ." In the case at bench nothing in the allegations of the Sec-

ond Complaint remotely suggests that respondent was requested by the prospective purchasers to give them any advice concerning the purchase of appellant's business.

**2.** Restatement of Torts section 768, sets out in part that "(1) One is privileged purposely to cause a third person not to enter into or continue a business relation *with a competitor of the actor.*" (Emphasis added.)

interest from being prejudiced by the relation." Clarifying the meaning of this section, comment a emphasizes that the financial interest privileged under section 769 is an interest in the nature of an investment (i.e., interest of a part owner, partner, stockholder and the like). However, it is made clear that the interest of a person who looks to the other for business and will lose business opportunities if the other enters into the business relations involved is not a financial interest within the meaning of section 769. (7)Even more to the point, the case law underlines that the privilege that arises by reason of section 769 is at most a qualified privilege which depends for its existence upon the circumstances of the case. It is essentially a state-of-mind privilege, and therefore its existence cannot be satisfactorily determined on the basis of the pleadings alone. The resolution of the issue turns on the defendant's predominant purpose in inducing the breach and consequently the matter is to be determined on the basis of proof rather than of pleading (*Culcal Stylco, Inc. v. Vornado, Inc.* (1972) 26 Cal.App.3d 879, 883 [103 Cal.Rptr. 419]; see also *Tye v. Finkelstein* (D.Mass. 1958) 160 F.Supp. 666, 668; Rest., Torts, § 769, com. b).

The foregoing discussion clearly indicates that the privilege or justification which would exempt respondent from liability as a matter of law does not appear on the face of the Second Complaint. It follows that it constitutes an affirmative defense which may be raised only by answer (Code Civ. Proc., § 430.30).

\* \* \*

### NOTES

**1. Wrongful Conduct.** Unlike many other intentional torts, the uniqueness of what constitutes sufficient justification for intentional interference with prospective contractual relations can make it difficult for attorneys to predict exactly when courts will impose liability. How persuasive are the arguments that Mother's Cookies' actions were wrongful intermeddling? Would it be proper for Mother's Cookies to allow the sale to go through without interference and then start its own trucking department and abandon its relationship with the sold company? Would this have been fair to the new buyer? How much consideration should be given to the fact that Mother's Cookies was not bound by contract to continue its relationship with the trucking company? Did the original price or the actual sale price more accurately reflect the trucking company's value or its terminable relationship with Mother's Cookies?

**2. Modifying the Tort.** The tort of intentional interference with prospective contract, prior to considering justifications such as fair and ethical competition (see Note 2, *supra*, after *Calbom* principal case), makes legitimate economic competitive behavior tortious. Consequently, some more recent court decisions require the plaintiff to prove as part of its affirmative case that the defendant does not have a justification. See, e.g., *Della Penna v. Toyota Motor Sales, U.S.A., Inc.*, 11 Cal.4th 376, 45 Cal.Rptr.2d 436, 902 P.2d 740 (Cal. 1995). The *Della Penna* decision also held that the intentional interference with prospective contract tort must include interference which is "wrongful by some legal measures other than the fact of interference itself." The phrase is unfortunately ambiguous and the court declined to simply define wrongful to be behavior that is criminal or independently tortious. Should bad motives suffice to constitute improper interference or should the court allow otherwise legal tactics against an economic rival? How do you think the requirement of "wrongful" interference would have impacted on the principal case?

Consider also *Korea Supply Co. v. Lockheed Martin*, 29 Cal.4th 1134, 131 Cal.Rptr.2d 29, 63 P.3d 937 (2003), where the broker for an unsuccessful bidder on a military contract with the Republic of Korea sued the successful bidder for intentional interference with prospective economic advantage. The court there noted that "the tort of intentional interference with prospective economic advantage does not require a plaintiff to plead that the defendant acted with specific intent, or purpose, of disrupting the plaintiff's prospective economic advantage. Instead, to satisfy the intent requirement for this tort, it is sufficient to plead that the defendant knew that the interference was certain or substantially certain to occur as a result of its action." The court also reaffirmed the *Della Penna* requirement that intentional interference with a prospective contract must be wrongful by some other means, noting that "such a requirement sensibly redresses the balance between providing a remedy for predatory economic behavior and keeping legitimate business competition outside litigative bounds (internal quotations omitted)."

**3. Examples of Interferences.** In *Fishman v. Wirtz*, 807 F.2d 520 (7th Cir.1986), the court held it was wrongful interference for a competing purchaser for the Chicago Bulls, a professional basketball team, to refuse in violation of antitrust law to permit a competitor purchaser to use its basketball stadium thereby disrupting the sale. Consider also *Monette v. AM–7–7 Baking Co., Ltd.*, 929 F.2d 276 (1991), where the owner of a bread distribution route sued his supplier for intentional interference with prospective economic advantage after the supplier stopped selling him bread, and, stealing one of his customer lists, sold to customers off the list. The district court found for the plaintiff, and the circuit court affirmed, noting that plaintiff's business relations with his customers need not be reduced to formal binding contracts, and in consideration of defendant's deception and the resulting illicit profits, the plaintiff was entitled to recovery.

Consider *American Airlines, Inc. v. Platinum Worlds Travel*, 769 F.Supp. 1203 (D.Utah 1990), where an airline sued a broker of frequent flyer awards for interference with contractual relations by arranging for the sale of free airline travel awards in violation of the rules imposed by the frequent travel programs. The court held the broker liable for purposely inducing travelers to breach their contracts with the airlines. The court rejected the broker's argument that improper interference required deception directed toward the consumer.

### TEXACO, INC. v. PENNZOIL, CO.
Court of Appeals of Texas, Houston.
729 S.W.2d 768 (1987).

WARREN, Justice.

This is an appeal from a judgment awarding Pennzoil damages for Texaco's tortious interference with a contract between Pennzoil and the

"Getty entities" (Getty Oil Company, the Sarah C. Getty Trust, and the J. Paul Getty Museum).

The jury found, among other things, that:

(1) At the end of a board meeting on January 3, 1984, the Getty entities intended to bind themselves to an agreement providing for the purchase of Getty Oil stock, whereby the Sarah C. Getty Trust would own 4/7 th of the stock and Pennzoil the remaining 3/7 th; and providing for a division of Getty Oil's assets, according to their respective ownership if the Trust and Pennzoil were unable to agree on a restructuring of Getty Oil by December 31, 1984;

(2) Texaco knowingly interfered with the agreement between Pennzoil and the Getty entities;

(3) As a result of Texaco's interference, Pennzoil suffered damages of $7.53 billion;

(4) Texaco's actions were intentional, willful, and in wanton disregard of Pennzoil's rights; and,

(5) Pennzoil was entitled to punitive damages of $3 billion.

The main questions for our determination are: (1) whether the evidence supports the jury's finding that there was a binding contract between the Getty entities and Pennzoil, and that Texaco knowingly induced a breach of such contract;

\* \* \*

Texaco argues first that there was no evidence or there was insufficient evidence to support the jury's answers to Special Issue No. 1. The jury found that the Trust, the Museum, and Getty Oil Company intended to bind themselves to an agreement with Pennzoil containing certain enumerated terms at the end of the Getty Oil Company board meeting on January 3, 1984. Texaco claims that not only is there insufficient evidence of any intent to be bound but also that the "agreement" referred to in Special Issue No. 1 is too indefinite to be a legally enforceable contract.

Second, Texaco asserts that the evidence is legally and factually insufficient to support the jury's answer to Special Issue No. 2, which inquired whether Texaco knowingly interfered with any agreement that the jury had found between Pennzoil and the Getty entities. Texaco contends that there is insufficient evidence that it had actual knowledge of a legally enforceable contract, or that Texaco actively induced a breach of the alleged contract. Texaco further asserts that the alleged contract was not valid and enforceable, because it was based on a mutual mistake, because it would violate SEC Rule 10b–13 and the statute of frauds, and because it would be a breach by Gordon Getty and by the Getty Oil directors of their fiduciary duties; thus, Texaco argues, the alleged contract will not support a tort action for inducement of breach.

SPECIAL ISSUE NO. 1

Texaco contends that under controlling principles of New York law, there was insufficient evidence to support the jury's finding that at the end of the Getty Oil board meeting on January 3, the Getty entities intended to bind themselves to an agreement with Pennzoil.

\* \* \*

Under New York law, if parties do not intend to be bound to an agreement until it is reduced to writing and signed by both parties, then there is no contract until that event occurs. *Scheck v. Francis,* 26 N.Y.2d 466, 311 N.Y.S.2d 841, 260 N.E.2d 493 (1970). If there is no understanding that a signed writing is necessary before the parties will be bound, and the parties have agreed upon all substantial terms, then an informal agreement can be binding, even though the parties contemplate evidencing their agreement in a formal document later. *Municipal Consultants & Publishers, Inc. v. Town of Ramapo,* 47 N.Y.2d 144, 417 N.Y.S.2d 218, 220, 390 N.E.2d 1143, 1145 (1979); *R.G. Group, Inc. v. Horn & Hardart Co.,* 751 F.2d 69, 74 (2d Cir.1984).

If the parties do intend to contract orally, the mere intention to commit the agreement to writing does not prevent contract formation before execution of that writing, *Winston v. Mediafare Entertainment Corp.,* 777 F.2d 78, 80 (2d Cir.1985), and even a failure to reduce their promises to writing is immaterial to whether they are bound. *Schwartz v. Greenberg,* 304 N.Y. 250, 107 N.E.2d 65 (1952).

However, if either party communicates the intent not to be bound before a final formal document is executed, then no oral expression of agreement to specific terms will constitute a binding contract. *Winston,* 777 F.2d at 80; *R.G. Group,* 751 F.2d at 74.

Thus, under New York law, the parties are given the power to obligate themselves informally or only by a formal signed writing, as they wish. *R.G. Group,* 751 F.2d at 74. The emphasis in deciding when a binding contract exists is on intent rather than on form. *Reprosystem, B.V. v. SCM Corp.,* 727 F.2d 257, 261 (2d Cir.), *cert. denied,* 469 U.S. 828, 105 S.Ct. 110, 83 L.Ed.2d 54 (1984).

It is the parties' expressed intent that controls which rule of contract formation applies. To determine intent, a court must examine the words and deeds of the parties, because these constitute the objective signs of such intent. *Winston,* 777 F.2d at 80; *R.G. Group,* 751 F.2d at 74. Only the outward expressions of intent are considered—secret or subjective intent is immaterial to the question of whether the parties were bound. *Porter v. Commercial Casualty Insurance Co.,* 292 N.Y. 176, 54 N.E.2d 353 (1944).

\* \* \*

There was sufficient evidence for the jury to conclude that the parties had reached agreement on all essential terms of the transaction with only the mechanics and details left to be supplied by the parties' attorneys. Although there may have been many specific items relating to the transaction agreement draft that had yet to be put in final form, there is sufficient evidence to support a conclusion by the jury that the parties did not consider any of Texaco's asserted "open items" significant obstacles precluding an intent to be bound.

\* \* \*

Although the magnitude of the transaction here was such that normally a signed writing would be expected, there was sufficient evidence to support an inference by the jury that that expectation was satisfied here initially by the Memorandum of Agreement, signed by a majority of shareholders of Getty Oil and approved by the board with a higher price, and by the transaction agreement in progress that had been intended to memorialize the agreement previously reached.

The record as a whole demonstrates that there was legally and factually sufficient evidence to support the jury's finding in Special Issue No. 1 that the Trust, the Museum, and the Company intended to bind themselves to an agreement with Pennzoil at the end of the Getty Oil board meeting on January 3, 1984. Point of Error 46 is overruled.

Texaco next claims that even if the parties intended to bind themselves before a definitive document was signed, no binding contract could result because the terms that they intended to include in their agreement were too vague and incomplete to be enforceable as a matter of law. Texaco attacks the terms, found by the jury, of the alleged agreement as being so uncertain as to render the alleged contract fatally indefinite.

\* \* \*

For a contract to be enforceable, the terms of the agreement must be ascertainable to a reasonable degree of certainty. *Candid Productions, Inc. v. International Skating Union,* 530 F.Supp. 1330, 1333 (S.D.N.Y. 1982). The question of whether the agreement is sufficiently definite to be enforceable is a difficult one. The facts of the individual case are decisively important. *Mason v. Rose,* 85 F.Supp. 300, 311 (S.D.N.Y.1948), *aff'd,* 176 F.2d 486 (2d Cir.1949). "The agreement need not be so definite that all the possibilities that might occur to a party in bad faith are explicitly provided for, but it must be sufficiently complete so that parties in good faith can find in the agreement words that will fairly define their respective duties and liabilities." *Id.* On review, the agreement must be sufficiently definite for the court to be able to recognize a breach and to fashion a remedy for that breach. *Candid Productions, Inc.,* 530 F.Supp. at 1333–34.

Texaco does not assert that a specific essential term was completely omitted from the agreement, but rather alleges very briefly why the terms of the agreement found by the jury are fatally incomplete. Texaco cites to the lack of description of the mechanics of various aspects of the transaction, e.g., how and when the determined price would be paid to shareholders, how the agreed stock ownership ratio was to be achieved, how a potential tax penalty on Getty's purchasing the Museum shares would be resolved, and what limitations, if any, existed on the option granted to Pennzoil to buy 8 million shares of Getty Oil stock.

Texaco's attempts to create additional "essential" terms from the mechanics of implementing the agreement's existing provisions are unpersuasive. The terms of the agreement found by the jury are supported by the evidence, and the promises of the parties are clear enough for a court to recognize a breach and to determine the damages resulting from that breach. Point of Error 47 is overruled.

Special Issue No. 2

Texaco's next points of error concern the jury's finding in Special Issue No. 2 that Texaco knowingly interfered with the agreement, if so found, between Pennzoil and the Getty entities. Texaco contends that the evidence is legally and factually insufficient to show that Texaco had actual knowledge of any agreement, that it actively induced breach of the alleged contract, and that the alleged contract was valid and capable of being interfered with.

First, Texaco asserts that Pennzoil failed to prove that Texaco had actual knowledge that a contract existed.

New York law requires knowledge by a defendant of the existence of contractual rights as an element of the tort of inducing a breach of that contract. *Hornstein v. Podwitz,* 254 N.Y. 443, 173 N.E. 674 (1930). However, the defendant need not have full knowledge of all the detailed terms of the contract. *Guard-Life Corp. v. S. Parker Hardware Manufacturing Corp.,* 50 N.Y.2d 183, 428 N.Y.S.2d 628, 406 N.E.2d 445 (1980); *Gold Medal Farms, Inc. v. Rutland County Co-operative Creamery, Inc.,* 10 A.D.2d 584, 9 A.D.2d 473, 195 N.Y.S.2d 179, 185 (App.Div.1959).

There is even some indication that a defendant need not have an accurate understanding of the exact legal significance of the facts giving rise to a contractual duty, but rather may be liable if he knows those facts, but is mistaken about whether they constitute a contract. Restatement (Second) of Torts § 766, comment i (1977); see *Entertainment Events, Inc. v. Metro-Goldwyn–Mayer Inc.,* No. 74 Civ. 2959, slip op. at 15 (S.D.N.Y., May 31, 1978).

For example, the commentary to the Restatement (Second) of Torts describes the knowledge requirement as follows:

> *Actor's knowledge of other's contract.* To be subject to liability ... the actor must have knowledge of the contract with which he is interfering.... [I]t is not necessary that the actor appreciate the legal significance of the facts giving rise to the contractual duty ... If he knows those facts, he is subject to liability even though he is mistaken as to their legal significance and believes that the agreement is not legally binding....

Sec. 766, comment i. New York's highest court has followed the principles and precepts embodied in the Restatement in this developing area of tort law. See, e.g., *Guard-Life Corp.,* 50 N.Y.2d 183, 428 N.Y.S.2d 628, 406 N.E.2d 445.

The element of knowledge by the defendant is a question of fact, and proof may be predicated on circumstantial evidence. See *American Cyanamid Co. v. Elizabeth Arden Sales Corp.,* 331 F.Supp. 597 (S.D.N.Y.

1971). Since there was no direct evidence of Texaco's knowledge of a contract in this case, the question is whether there was legally and factually sufficient circumstantial evidence from which the trier of fact reasonably could have inferred knowledge.

... Texaco presented evidence that it was told repeatedly that Pennzoil had no binding agreement with the Getty interests. But there was other circumstantial evidence, as discussed above, from which the jury could conclude that Texaco did indeed have knowledge of the parties' obligations to Pennzoil.

The jury was not required to accept Texaco's version of events in this case, and this Court may not substitute its own interpretation of the evidence for the decision of the trier of fact. There was legally and factually sufficient evidence to support an inference by the jury that Texaco had the required knowledge of an agreement. Point of Error 49 is overruled.

The second major issue Texaco raises under Special Issue No. 2 is that the evidence was legally and factually insufficient to show that Texaco actively induced breach of the alleged Pennzoil/Getty contract.

A necessary element of the plaintiff's cause of action is a showing that the defendant took an active part in persuading a party to a contract to breach it. *State Enterprises, Inc. v. Southridge Cooperative Section 1, Inc.*, 18 A.D.2d 226, 238 N.Y.S.2d 724 (App.Div.1963). Merely entering into a contract with a party with the knowledge of that party's contractual obligations to someone else is not the same as inducing a breach. *P.P.X. Enterprises, Inc. v. Catala*, 17 A.D.2d 808, 232 N.Y.S.2d 959 (App.Div.1962). It is necessary that there be some act of interference or of persuading a party to breach, for example by offering better terms or other incentives, for tort liability to arise. *State Enterprises, Inc.*, 238 N.Y.S.2d at 726; *Cosmopolitan Film Distributors, Inc. v. Feuchtwanger Corp.*, 226 N.Y.S.2d 584, 591 (Sup.Ct.1962). The issue of whether a defendant affirmatively took steps to induce the breach of an existing contract is a question of fact for the jury. See *State Enterprises, Inc.*, 238 N.Y.S.2d at 726.

Texaco contends that it did not actively procure the alleged breach and that the required inducement did not occur. Texaco argues that it merely responded to a campaign of active solicitation by Getty Oil and the Museum, who were dissatisfied by the terms of Pennzoil's offer.

\* \* \*

Texaco argues that its testimony shows that Getty Oil and the Museum were the real moving forces that eventually led to the Texaco contract. However, we find that there is legally and factually sufficient evidence in the record to support the jury's finding that Texaco actively induced the breach of the Getty entities' agreement with Pennzoil.

\* \* \*

... It was no defense that Getty was not happy with the Pennzoil price, or might have been dissatisfied with the agreement. See *Gold Medal Farms, Inc.*, 195 N.Y.S.2d at 185. We overrule Points of Error 48 and 50, contending that there was no evidence or factually insufficient evidence to support the jury's finding that Texaco knowingly induced the breach of Pennzoil's agreement.

### VALIDITY OF THE CONTRACT

Texaco's last contention regarding the sufficiency of the evidence is that Pennzoil failed to prove that the alleged contract was valid and enforceable, so there could be no interference. Texaco argues that the alleged contract would have violated SEC Rule 10b–13;

\* \* \*

Rule 10b–13 was promulgated to protect the interests of shareholders who have already tendered their shares pursuant to a publicly announced tender offer, by prohibiting the offeror from making purchases outside the tender offer on different terms. *Wellman v. Dickinson,* 475 F.Supp. 783, 833 (S.D.N.Y.1979), *aff'd,* 682 F.2d 355 (2d Cir.1982), *cert. denied,* 460 U.S. 1069, 103 S.Ct. 1522, 75 L.Ed.2d 946 (1983); *Heine v. Signal Companies, Inc.* [1976–77 Transfer Binder] Fed.Sec.L.Rep. (CCH) par. 95,898 (S.D.N.Y. March 4, 1977). In particular, the rule seeks to prevent outside purchases by the offeror at a different price than that stated in the tender offer. *Wellman,* 475 F.Supp. at 833.

The rule itself provides a mechanism by which an exemption from its coverage can be obtained. In subsection (d), it provides that the rule will not prohibit a transaction if the Commission, upon written request or on its own motion, exempts the transaction as not constituting a manipulative, fraudulent, or deceptive device, act, or practice as comprehended by the purpose of the section. 17 C.F.R. § 10b–13(d). The emphasis is thus on applying the rule to further its stated purposes.

Although Texaco is not a party whom the rule is intended to protect in any way, it complains that Pennzoil's transaction violated the rule, was automatically void for that reason, and therefore could not give rise to an action for tortious interference. The express exemption provision of the rule negates the suggestion that *any* infraction of the rule automatically makes the transaction void. If the transaction is only voidable, Texaco has no standing to assert the rule, and we may not speculate on whether a proper party would have successfully asserted it.

We disagree with Texaco's contention that it was irrelevant that Pennzoil might have obtained an exemption from the prohibitions of the rule, because it did not. Pennzoil had no control over the timing of Texaco's interference with its agreement with Getty entities. If an exemption had been obtained, the rule would not have prevented the purchase of Getty shares outside the tender offer, and Texaco's argument about the invalidity of the agreement for this reason fails.

\* \* \*

Considering the type of action, the conduct involved, and the need for deterrence, we are of the opinion that the punitive damages are excessive and that the trial court abused its discretion in not suggesting a remittitur. Though our Texas guidelines are similar to those of New York, New York courts have adopted a more conservative stance on punitive damages. There is a point where punitive damages may overstate their purpose and serve to confiscate rather than to deter or punish. In this case, punitive damages of one billion dollars are sufficient to satisfy any reason for their being awarded, whether it be punishment, deterrence, or encouragement of the victim to bring legal action. We conclude that the award of punitive damages is excessive by two billion dollars. Point of Error 67 is sustained.

If within 30 days from the date of this opinion, Pennzoil files in this Court a remittitur of two billion dollars, the judgment of the trial court will be reformed, and the award of one billion dollars punitive damages will be affirmed; otherwise, the cause will be reversed and remanded.

Finally, we respectfully refuse to certify to the Texas Supreme Court the question of the judgment's propriety under New York law. We are of the opinion that this question is not an appropriate one for certification.

Texaco's Points of Error 1 through 66, and 68 through 90 are overruled. Point of Error 67 is sustained.

If within thirty days from the date of this judgment, Pennzoil files in this Court a remittitur of two billion dollars, as suggested above, the judgment will be reformed and affirmed as to the award of $7.53 billion in compensatory damages and $1 billion in exemplary damages; otherwise the judgment will be reversed and remanded.

* * *

### NOTES

**1. Distinguishing Interference With Contract From Prospective Contract.** As the notes indicate after the first principal case addressing these torts, fair and ethical competition is a justification for interference with prospective contract but not a nonterminable contract. The *Texaco* case illustrates the hazards of misinterpreting whether an oral agreement in fact constituted a contract. The tort allows no defense for a good faith error. Should it?

**2. Bringing Harm to Texaco and Prominence to a Tort.** The decision threatened to bankrupt Texaco and led to a three billion dollar settlement. The damages were deemed so high in part because Texaco, confident of victory, had failed to contest the plaintiff's measure of damages. The decision brought the relatively obscure tort to great prominence as a factor to be reckoned with for corporate and other high stake disputes. Unlike mere contract breach between parties, tort remedies against third parties who "wrongfully disrupt" a relationship can lead to punitive damages (in part determined by the wealth of the defendant; see Damages Chapter 5, Sec. C, infra) and also mental distress damages where appropriate. See generally Shannon, *Texaco and the $10 Billion Jury* (1988).

**3. The Plaintiff's Attorney.** Joseph D. Jamail, a very prominent Texas tort attorney, led the plaintiff's legal litigation against Texaco. Anxious first year law students may be interested to learn that Mr. Jamail's first exposure to tort law was inauspicious. He reports he received an "F" in Torts at the University of Texas School of Law. The law school's library is now named after him. (Interview with Joseph Jamail, conducted for casebook 1/17/01.)

## ENVIRONMENTAL PLANNING AND INFORMATION COUNCIL OF WESTERN EL DORADO COUNTY, INC., SUPERIOR COURT

Supreme Court of California.
36 Cal.3d 188, 203 Cal.Rptr. 127, 680 P.2d 1086 (1984).

GRODIN, J., Justice.

This writ proceeding stems from an action by Detmold Publishing Company (Detmold), publisher of a newspaper, the Foothill Times, against Environmental Planning and Information Council of Western El Dorado County, Inc. (EPIC), a nonprofit corporation, and several of its officers. The gist of the complaint, insofar as it concerns this proceeding, is that EPIC published a newsletter criticizing the newspaper's editorial policies on environmental matters, and calling upon readers of the newsletter not to patronize businesses that advertise in the Foothill Times. The complaint seeks injunctive relief, and both punitive and compensatory damages. Defendants moved for summary judgment with supporting affidavits and, when their motion was denied, filed this petition in mandate to compel reversal of the trial court's order of denial.

* * *

EPIC is a nonprofit corporation with a membership of approximately 100 persons in El Dorado County. Its purpose is to promote citizen participation in public affairs and, according to its articles of incorporation, "conservation and preservation of, and general public appreciation for, the unique historical and natural resources" of western El Dorado County.

EPIC's April 1982 newsletters criticized the editorial policies of the Foothill Times. In the context of a discussion of the alleged prodevelopment bias of the El Dorado Irrigation District (EID) directors, the newsletter stated in part: "[T]he western county areas are flooded by the *Foothill Times*, a newspaper that doesn't deserve to be called one. This is the rag that played a major role in last November's election of George Gribkoff and John Smith. Since then it has continued to *ignore established facts, print inaccuracies, and blatantly editorialize* in its 'news' articles." The newsletter complained that the four directors of the EID, backed by the newspaper, had taken over the irrigation district on behalf of a "very limited development group."

The newsletter went on to ask, "What can be done about this outrageous situation?" It then suggested three courses of action. First, "The most important step is for *you to be informed*. An adequately informed citizenry is the only hope for curing bad government. ...If you read newspaper articles thoughtfully, talk to people, and attend some EID meetings, you'll develop a fair grasp of what's going on."

Second, the newsletter suggested; "Whenever something puzzles you or infuriates you, *write a letter to the editor*. Small letters are big tools. Encourage other concerned people to do the same."

The third possible course of action was phrased as a question: "What about *contacting businesses advertising in the Foothill Times* and requesting that they discontinue that advertising? Freedom of speech is one thing; vicious, irresponsible journalism is another, and perhaps you would prefer not to patronize businesses that advertise in such a publication." The newsletter went on to propose a recall of the four EID directors.

Nothing more was said in the newsletter about the Foothill Times, except that attached to the two-page newsletter was a list of eighty nonclassified advertisers in two issues of the weekly newspaper. At the top of the list, the newsletter cautioned, "This is not a black list! No condemnation of these businesses is implied! This list is merely for your convenience should you wish to contact *Foothill Times* advertisers."

\* \* \*

We begin with the common law. The courts of this state have recognized that an unjustified, or unprivileged, intentional interference with the prospective economic advantage of another may subject the actor to liability in tort, even when that interference does not take the form of inducing a breach of contract. (*Buckaloo v. Johnson* (1975) 14 Cal.3d 815, 822–823 [122 Cal.Rptr. 745, 537 P.2d 865]).

The contours of justification, or privilege, are not precisely defined. In relation to the tort of interference with contract, we have said: "Whether an intentional interference by a third party is justifiable depends upon a balancing of the importance, social and private, of the objective advanced by the interference against the importance of the interest interfered with, considering all circumstances including the nature of the actor's conduct and the relationship between the parties." (*Herron* v. *State Farm Mutual Ins. Co.* (1961) 56 Cal.2d 202, 206 [14 Cal.Rptr. 294, 363 P.2d 310].) When the defendant's action does not interfere with the performance of existing contracts, the range of acceptable justification is broader; for example, a competitor's stake in advancing his own economic interest will not justify the intentional inducement of a contract breach (*Imperial Ice Co. v. Rossier* (1941) 18 Cal.2d 33, 36 [112 P.2d 631]), whereas such interests will suffice where contractual relations are merely contemplated or potential. (*Buckaloo v. Johnson, supra*, 14 Cal.3d 815, 828.)

Most of the cases in which claims of tortious interference have been considered have involved either pure commercial relationships or union-management relationships. There is a paucity of authority in the application of common law principles to a situation such as this, in which a group organized for political purposes allegedly undertakes a consumer boycott to achieve its ends. What authority does exist in this arena strongly suggests, even apart from constitutional doctrine, that such action will not give rise to liability. Certainly the defendants' objective— to change the editorial policies of the Foothill Times in relation to public issues affecting the environment—is a lawful one, and the means used— a peaceful secondary boycott—have likewise been held to be lawful under the common law of this state. (*Fortenbury v. Superior Court* (1940) 16 Cal.2d 405, 409 [106 P.2d 411].) And, in somewhat analogous context, the Supreme Court of Pennsylvania has held that no cause of action exists against church leaders who threatened to lead a boycott of church members against a department store in order to influence the broadcasting policies of a radio station which was under the same ownership (*Watch Tower Bible & Tract Soc. v. Dougherty* (1940) 337 Pa. 286 [11 A.2d 147, 148]; see also, *Kuryer Pub. Co. v. Messmer* (1916) 162 Wis. 565 [156 N.W. 948] [Catholic boycott of newspaper gave rise to no cause of action]).

This case cannot realistically be viewed from an exclusively common law perspective, however, since the very nature of the activities complained of invites constitutional analysis as well. In a case of this sort, constitutional principles impose outer limits upon the category of conduct that may be subject to liability on the basis of common law doctrine, and thus serve to shape the doctrine itself. Moreover, it is precisely the constitutional aspect of this case that warrants appellate intervention through extraordinary writ.

The United States Supreme Court recently had occasion to consider First Amendment limitations upon the power of a state to regulate secondary consumer boycotts directed at political objectives. *NAACP v. Claiborne Hardware Co., supra,* 458 U.S. 886, involved a boycott by black citizens in Port Gibson, Mississippi, against white merchants in that city, aimed at putting pressure on white elected officials to accede to the citizens' demands for racial equality and integration. The Mississippi Supreme Court upheld, on common law tort grounds, a judgment for injunctive relief and damages against certain civil rights organizations, their leaders, and their members responsible for the boycott. The basis for the state court holding was that the boycott was accompanied by some acts and threats of violence. In reversing that holding, the high court declared: "The right of the States to regulate economic activity could not justify a complete prohibition against a nonviolent, politically motivated boycott designed to force governmental and economic change and to effectuate rights guaranteed by the Constitution itself." (*Id.*, at p. 914 [73 L.Ed.2d at p. 1237], fn. omitted.) Accordingly, the court held that the nonviolent elements of the petitioners' activities were entitled to First Amendment protection. (*Id.*, at p. 915 [73 L.Ed.2d at p. 1237].)

*Claiborne Hardware* draws a crucial distinction between solely economic boycott activity which can be and has been regulated, i.e., by antitrust laws, and political boycotts. The same distinction is present in this case. Justice Stevens pointed out for a unanimous court in *Claiborne Hardware*: "While States have broad power to regulate economic activity, we do not find a comparable right to prohibit peaceful political activity such as that found in the boycott in this case. This Court has recognized that expression on public issues 'has always rested on the highest rung of the hierarchy of First Amendment values.' " (*Id.*, at p. 913 [73 L.Ed.2d at p. 1236], quoting from *Carey v. Brown* (1980) 447 U.S. 455, 467 [65 L.Ed.2d 263, 273, 100 S.Ct. 2286].)

Detmold would have us distinguish *Claiborne Hardware* on the basis of the objective sought by the boycott in that case. The activities of those defendants, Detmold suggests, were "clearly entitled to full First Amendment protections as the objective of their boycott was to vindicate rights of equality and freedom that lie at the heart of the Fourteenth Amendment," whereas these defendants—an "irresponsible few," according to Detmold—are seeking to further merely their private views on environmental matters, and at the expense of Detmold's own rights of free expression.

Detmold's argument might have merit if this were an ordinary case of interference with advantageous economic relationships in the commercial context; for there, as we have observed, courts may be called upon to balance the social and private importance of the defendant's objective against the substantiality of the interest which plaintiff asserts. As in *Claiborne Hardware*, however, defendants' activities constitute a "politically motivated boycott designed to force governmental and economic change" (458 U.S. at p. 914 [73 L.Ed.2d at p. 1237]), and the fact that the change which they seek bears upon environmental quality rather than racial equality, can hardly support a different result. On the contrary, we are precluded by the First Amendment itself from gauging the degree of constitutional protection by the content or subject matter of the speech: "[T]here is an 'equality of status' in the field of ideas" (*Police Department of Chicago v. Mosley* (1972) 408 U.S. 92, 95–96 [33 L.Ed.2d, 212, 216–217, 92 S.Ct. 2286]).

Nor is a different result dictated by the fact that the boycott in this case is aimed at changing the editorial policies of a newspaper. The freedom of a newspaper to formulate editorial policies is obviously of great value in our society, and the spectacle of different groups seeking to influence those policies through the use of economic boycott is troublesome to contemplate. Yet, the newspaper is not in a position to claim infringement of its own constitutional rights by such conduct, since no governmental action is implicated, and the degree of economic coercion which exists may be no greater than that which might lawfully be exerted by an advertiser who, on his own, seeks to influence editorial policy by withdrawing or threatening to withdraw its patronage. The market place of ideas contemplated by the First Amendment (*Lamont v. Postmaster General* (1965) 381 U.S. 301, 308 [14 L.Ed.2d 398, 403, 85 S.Ct. 1493] [Brennan, J., conc.]) cannot be so insulated. Moreover, this case is not distinguishable from *Claiborne Hardware* on that basis, since in that case, as well, the boycott sought to influence political expression and behavior by private citizens. (*NAACP v. Claiborne Hardware Co., supra*, 458 U.S. 886, 911–912 [73 L.Ed.2d 1215, 1234–1235].)

Applying common law principles, and construing them in light of the First Amendment and article I, section 2 of the state Constitution (see *Robins* v. *Pruneyard Shopping Center, supra*, 23 Cal.3d 899, 908), we conclude that petitioners are entitled to summary judgment as a matter of law.

Let a writ of mandate issue commanding respondent court to vacate its order denying petitioners' motion for summary judgment and directing it to enter a new and different order granting said motion and dismissing this action. Costs to petitioners.

### NOTES

**1. Liability for Political Expression and Protests.** As the principal case suggests, intentional interference with contracts or prospective contracts can bring potential liability to public interest organizations and activists. Would the defendants in the principal case have escaped liability if they had used physical means such as a sit-in to enforce their boycott? Consider *Northeast Women's Center, Inc. v. McMonagle*, 670 F.Supp. 1300, (E.D.Pa.1987), where a group of anti-abortion protesters prevented two staff members of a women's health center from going inside. The center sued the protesters for tortious interference with contractual relations. The court held that in regard to the employment contracts between the health center and two of its staff members, the center had made a prima facie case for interference with contractual relations. Compare with *Worldwide Primates, Inc. v. McGreal*, 26 F.3d 1089 (11th Cir. 1994), where a commercial wildlife company sued an animal rights activist for tortious interference with a business relationship, after the activist sent two letters critical of the company to one of its clients. The court held that the company could establish no cause of action for interference with its business relationship because the activist only gave truthful information to the client.

Consider also *Tarleton State University v. Rosiere*, 867 S.W.2d 948 (Tex.App.1993), where a professor who failed to make tenure sued the university president and the vice-president of student services for tortious interference with his business relationship with the university. Plaintiff based his claim on the defendant vice-president's telling the president that plaintiff had "objected loudly" at a school activity to the president's decision to sell a university ranch. The court held that the university's vice-president's report to the president was not improper interference with the professor's employment relationship. Compare with *Estate of Braude v. U.S.*, 35 Fed.Cl. 99 (1996), where a United States Information Agency officer who was terminated in 1953 for loyalty and security reasons and blacklisted by USIA officials brought suit to recover back pay. Plaintiff argued that he was unable to obtain a federal position until 1988. The court held for the plaintiff, since the blacklisting activities constituted intentional interference with prospective contractual relations. The court pointed out that if the USIA had only disclosed its reasons for firing the plaintiff, instead of blacklisting him and including a recommendation that he not be employed, no tort would have been committed.

**2. Sexual Harassment as Interference.** Consider *Boyle v. Boston Foundation, Inc.*, 788 F.Supp. 627 (D.Mass.1992), where a woman sued her supervisor for intentional interference with contractual relationship with her employer, claiming she was forced to quit as a result of defendant's harassment. The court upheld the cause of action, stating that liability did not require that interference be so great as to cause the employer to breach the employment contract, but that liability could exist if defendant's interference kept plaintiff from performing the contract or increased the burden of her performance sufficiently to prompt her resignation.

**3. Interference With Election Results.** Consider *Gold v. Los Angeles Democratic League*, 49 Cal.App.3d 365, 122 Cal.Rptr. 732 (1975), described by the California Supreme Court in the following excerpt from its opinion in *Youst v. Longo*, 43 Cal.3d 64, 233 Cal.Rptr. 294, 729 P.2d 728 (1987):

> In *Gold*, the plaintiff, a candidate for Los Angeles City Controller, claimed that defendants had interfered with his opportunity to win an election to political office. The defendants, including several

political supporters of plaintiff's opponent, had sent a false and misleading mailing to voters stating their candidate, and not plaintiff, was the candidate officially endorsed by the Democratic Party. The opponent was in fact not so endorsed; he was a Republican. Plaintiff alleged that his defeat by the voters was a result of defendants' misrepresentations. The trial court in *Gold* sustained defendants' demurrer, but the Court of Appeal majority held defendants' actions stated a cause of action for interference with prospective economic advantage; plaintiff's expectancy was the salary he would have earned had he won the election. Defendants failed to petition for hearing with this court.

The *Gold* court seemed to place little emphasis on the general tort requirement that the plaintiff show a probability of the prospective advantage, that is, that plaintiff would have benefitted economically but for the interference. The Court of Appeal here noted that the *Gold* majority "was not concerned about what some might call the 'speculative nature' of plaintiff's injury. Actually plaintiff had lost the election by a four-to-one margin.... It seems most unlikely plaintiff would have won election and the economic advantage of serving in that office even if defendants had refrained from sending out this one misleading brochure. But this factor did not bother the California court. It upheld the cause of action for interfering with a contestant's opportunity to win a contest."

The California Supreme Court endorsed the plaintiff's recovery in *Gold*, despite the plaintiff's obvious failure to demonstrate that he would have won the election without the defendant's wrongful conduct. Ordinarily recovery for intentional interference with perspective economic advantage requires proof that the plaintiff had a valid economic expectancy, and not merely the aspiration or hope of economic success, which was wrongly interfered with by the defendant's conduct. The California Supreme Court in *Youst* affirmed the general rule but indicated that "compelling public policy" justified substantially relaxing the expectation element of the tort in an election context. Conversely, the California Supreme Court held public policy would normally preclude the tort's use by a participant in a sporting event who asserted another participant unfairly interfered with her victory, even if the aggrieved participant had a valid economic expectation of winning the sporting event. In *Youst*, the court held that the tort of intentional interference with economic advantage was not available to the owners of a horse who alleged wrongful interference by a competing jockey who had caused the plaintiff's horse to lose its first place position. Do you agree with the California Supreme Court that the tort should be applied in political contexts even when economic expectation has not been established and not applied more readily than ordinarily and in sporting contexts even when economic expectation has been established? Most courts have not adopted this approach.

**4. Intimidating Journalists.** The prominent CBS news show "60 Minutes" was required by its corporate attorneys not to televise an interview by Mike Wallace with Dr. Jeffrey Wigand, an ex-executive of a tobacco company, since Dr. Wigand had signed a severance contract requiring that he not reveal information about the tobacco company's practices. CBS attorneys were concerned the telecast would constitute intentional interference with the tobacco's company contract with Dr. Wigand. The cancellation created much controversy and is dramatized by a major movie, "The Insider." CBS subsequently broadcast the interview much later, after the *Wall Street Journal* published the interview. In describing CBS's initial decision to cancel the interview, the *Wall Street Journal* reported that "the nearly universal opinion of commentators in the past week has been that wimpy network lawyers, fearful of a huge lawsuit, used an arcane legal theory [tortious interference with contract] as a pretext for caving in to the tobacco industry." See Freedman, Jensen & Stevens, "Tort TV: CBS Legal Guarantees to '60 Minutes' Source Muddy Tobacco Story," *Wall Street Journal* (11/16/95) at Al. Were CBS's lawyers "wimpy" or were there valid legal concerns?

# SECTION I. WRONGFUL TERMINATION OF EMPLOYMENT CONTRACTS AND TORTIOUS BREACH OF THE COVENANT OF GOOD FAITH AND FAIR DEALING

## 1. Wrongful Termination of Employment

### FOLEY v. INTERACTIVE DATA CORP.

Supreme Court of California.

47 Cal.3d 654, 254 Cal.Rptr. 211, 765 P.2d 373 (1988).

LUCAS, C. J., Chief Justice.

After Interactive Data Corporation (defendant) fired plaintiff Daniel D. Foley, an executive employee, he filed this action seeking compensatory and punitive damages for wrongful discharge. . . .

\* \* \*

According to the complaint, plaintiff is a former employee of defendant, a wholly owned subsidiary of Chase Manhattan Bank that markets computer-based decision-support services. Defendant hired plaintiff in June 1976 as an assistant product manager at a starting salary of $18,500.

\* \* \*

Over the next six years and nine months, plaintiff received a steady series of salary increases, promotions, bonuses, awards and superior performance evaluations. In 1979 defendant named him consultant manager of the year and in 1981 promoted him to branch manager of its Los Angeles office. His annual salary rose to $56,164 and he received an additional $6,762 merit bonus two days before his discharge in March 1983. He alleges defendant's officers made repeated oral assurances of job security so long as his performance remained adequate.

Plaintiff also alleged that during his employment, defendant maintained written "Termination Guidelines" that set forth express grounds for discharge and a mandatory seven-step pretermination procedure. Plaintiff understood that these guidelines applied not only to employees under plaintiff's supervision, but to him as well. On the basis of these representations, plaintiff alleged that he reasonably believed defendant would not discharge him except for good cause, and therefore he refrained from accepting or pursuing other job opportunities.

The event that led to plaintiff's discharge was a private conversation in January 1983 with his former supervisor, Vice President Richard Earnest. During the previous year defendant had hired Robert Kuhne and subsequently named Kuhne to replace Earnest as plaintiff's immediate supervisor. Plaintiff learned that Kuhne was currently under investigation by the Federal Bureau of Investigation for embezzlement from his former employer, Bank of America.[1] Plaintiff reported what he knew about Kuhne to Earnest, because he was "worried about working for Kuhne and having him in a supervisory position ... , in view of Kuhne's suspected criminal conduct." Plaintiff asserted he "made this disclosure in the interest and for the benefit of his employer," allegedly because he believed that because defendant and its parent do business with the financial community on a confidential basis, the company would have a legitimate interest in knowing about a high executive's alleged prior criminal conduct.

In response, Earnest allegedly told plaintiff not to discuss "rumors" and to "forget what he heard" about Kuhne's past. In early March, Kuhne informed plaintiff that defendant had decided to replace him for "performance reasons" and that he could transfer to a position in another division in Waltham, Massachusetts. Plaintiff was told that if he did not accept a transfer, he might be demoted but not fired. One week later, in Waltham, Earnest informed plaintiff he was not doing a good job, and six days later, he notified plaintiff he could continue as branch manager if he "agreed to go on a 'performance plan.' Plaintiff asserts he agreed to consider such an arrangement." The next day, when Kuhne met with plaintiff, purportedly to present him with a written "performance plan" proposal, Kuhne instead informed plaintiff he had the choice of resigning or being fired. Kuhne offered neither a performance plan nor an option to transfer to another position.

## I. Tortious Discharge in Contravention of Public Policy

We turn first to plaintiff's cause of action alleging he was discharged in violation of public policy. Labor Code section 2922 provides in relevant part, "An employment, having no specified term, may be terminated at the will of either party on notice to the other. ..." (2) This presumption may be superseded by a contract, express or implied, limiting the employer's right to discharge the employee. (*Strauss v. A. L. Randall Co.* (1983) 144 Cal.App.3d 514, 517 [194 Cal.Rptr. 520]; *Drzewiecki v. H & R Block, Inc.* (1972) 24 Cal.App.3d 695, 703 [101 Cal.Rptr. 169]; see also cases cited in part II(B) of this opinion, *post*, p. 680 et seq.) Absent any contract, however, the employment is "at will," and the employee can be fired with or without good cause. But the employer's right to discharge an "at will" employee is still subject to limits imposed by public policy,

---

**1.** In September 1983, after plaintiff's discharge, Kuhne pleaded guilty in federal court to a felony count of embezzlement.

since otherwise the threat of discharge could be used to coerce employees into committing crimes, concealing wrongdoing, or taking other action harmful to the public weal.

. . . *Tameny v. Atlantic Richfield Co., supra,* [1980] 27 Cal.3d 167, 178, declared that a tort action for wrongful discharge may lie if the employer "condition[s] employment upon required participation in unlawful conduct by the employee." In *Tameny,* the plaintiff alleged he was fired for refusing to engage in price fixing in violation of the Cartwright Act and the Sherman Antitrust Act. (*Id.,* at p. 170.) We held the trial court erred in sustaining Atlantic Richfield's demurrer to plaintiff's tort action for wrongful discharge. Writing for the majority, Justice Tobriner concluded that "an employer's authority over its employee does not include the right to demand that the employee commit a criminal act to further its interests. . . . An employer engaging in such conduct violates a basic duty imposed by law upon all employers, and thus an employee who has suffered damages as a result of such discharge may maintain a tort action for wrongful discharge against the employer." (*Id.,* at p. 178.)

\* \* \*

We do not decide in this case whether a tort action alleging a breach of public policy under *Tameny* may be based only on policies derived from a statute or constitutional provision or whether nonlegislative sources may provide the basis for such a claim. Even where, as here, a statutory touchstone has been asserted, we must still inquire whether the discharge is against public policy and affects a duty which inures to the benefit of the public at large rather than to a particular employer or employee. For example, many statutes simply regulate conduct between private individuals, or impose requirements whose fulfillment does not implicate fundamental public policy concerns. Regardless of whether the existence of a statutory or constitutional link is required under *Tameny,* disparagement of a basic *public* policy must be alleged, and we turn now to determining whether plaintiff has done so here.

In the present case, plaintiff alleges that defendant discharged him in "sharp derogation" of a substantial public policy that imposes a legal duty on employees to report relevant business information to management. An employee is an agent, and as such "is required to disclose to [his] principal all information he has relevant to the subject matter of the agency." (2 Witkin, Summary of Cal. Law (9th ed. 1987) Agency & Employment, § 41, p. 53; see *Loughlin v. Idora Realty Co.* (1968) 259 Cal.App.2d 619, 629 [66 Cal.Rptr. 747]; *Jolton v. Minster Graf & Co.* (1942) 53 Cal.App.2d 516, 522 [128 P.2d 101].) Thus, plaintiff asserts, if he discovered information that might lead his employer to conclude that an employee was an embezzler, and should not be retained, plaintiff had a duty to communicate that information to his principal.

It is unclear whether the alleged duty is one founded in statute. No enactment expressly requires an employee to report relevant information concerning other employees to his employer, and none prohibits discharge of the employee for so doing.

Whether or not there is a statutory duty requiring an employee to report information relevant to his employer's interest, we do not find a substantial public policy prohibiting an employer from discharging an employee for performing that duty. Past decisions recognizing a tort action for discharge in violation of public policy seek to protect the public, by protecting the employee who refuses to commit a crime (*Tameny, supra,* 27 Cal.3d 167; *Petermann, supra,* 174 Cal.App.2d 184), who reports criminal activity to proper authorities (*Garibaldi v. Lucky Food Stores, Inc.* (9th Cir. 1984) 726 F.2d 1367, 1374; *Palmateer v. International Harvester Co., supra,* 421 N.E.2d 876, 879–880), or who discloses other illegal, unethical, or unsafe practices (*Hentzel v. Singer Co.* (1982) 138 Cal.App.3d 290 [188 Cal.Rptr. 159, 35 A.L.R.4th 1015] [working conditions hazardous to employees]). No equivalent public interest bars the discharge of the present plaintiff. When the duty of an employee to disclose information to his employer serves only the private interest of the employer, the rationale underlying the *Tameny* cause of action is not implicated.

We conclude that the Court of Appeal properly upheld the trial court's ruling sustaining the demurrer without leave to amend to plaintiff's first cause of action.

\* \* \*

## NOTES

**1. Wrongful Discharge or Termination Against Public Policy.** An employer may be liable for the tort of wrongful discharge (also called wrongful termination) where its termination of an employee contravenes public policy. The tort exists irrespective of whether the employee's termination violated the employment contract. The termination must, however, be for a reason that contradicts a significant public policy.

The California Supreme Court further clarified its requirements for the tort in *Stevenson v. Superior Court,* 16 Cal.4th 880, 66 Cal.Rptr.2d 888, 941 P.2d 1157 (1997). A former employee brought suit against Huntington Memorial Hospital for wrongful discharge in violation of the public policy against age discrimination. The court held that a wrongful discharge claim requires that the employee be discharged in violation of a public policy that is: (1) delineated in either constitutional or statutory provisions; (2) "public" in the sense that it inures to the benefit of the public rather than serving merely the interests of the individual; (3) well established at the time of discharge; (4) substantial and fundamental. The court concluded in *Stevenson* the public policy prohibiting employment discrimination against older workers, set forth in the Fair Employment and Housing Act, satisfied each criterion necessary to state a claim for wrongful discharge in violation of public policy: (1) the policy had been articulated in a statute; (2) the policy benefitted society at large, as age discrimination has the potential to affect all citizens; (3) the policy was well established; and (4) the policy was both substantial and fundamental. Do you agree with the California Supreme Court's decision in the principal case or should the tort have been ruled applicable?

In *Smith v. Bates Technical College,* 139 Wash.2d 793, 991 P.2d 1135 (2000), the court clarified that the tort of wrongful discharge was available

to employees with a collective bargaining agreement, who could only be terminated for cause, as well as for at will employees. The court acknowledged that such employees had other avenues available to seek redress not available to at will employees, but focused on the fact that the tort of wrongful discharge offers remedies unavailable in a contract action, and as such, serves a different function, mainly to deter wrongful conduct. Consider also *Harvey v. Care Initiatives, Inc.*, 634 N.W.2d 681 (Iowa 2001), where the Supreme Court of Iowa held that no cause of action existed for wrongful discharge of an independent contractor. The court noted that the independent contractor relationship lacks the inequity normally present in an employer-employee relationship, and also the concern that "judicial extension of tort remedies into contracts without clear legislative authority can essentially nullify terms agreed to by the parties to the contract."

**2. Terminations Found to Violate Public Policy.** Consider *Phillips v. Gemini Moving Specialists*, 63 Cal.App.4th 563, 74 Cal.Rptr.2d 29 (1998), where the plaintiff alleged that he was discharged from his employment because he questioned his employer about its right to make a deduction from his payroll check and because the plaintiff objected to the manner in which the deduction was made. The California Court of Appeal held that statutes mandating prompt payment of wages and prohibiting unauthorized deductions from pay, set forth a clear public policy and could reasonably form the basis of a wrongful discharge action. Similarly, in *Bleich v. Florence Crittenton Services of Baltimore, Inc.*, 98 Md.App. 123, 632 A.2d 463 (Md. 1993), a former teacher at a licensed child care facility brought suit against the facility and its executive director for wrongful discharge. The teacher alleged that she was terminated because she sent a letter to state licensing authorities complaining of child abuse at the child care facility. The Court of Special Appeals of Maryland held that the allegations of termination in retaliation for the letter were sufficient to state a claim for wrongful discharge in violation of the public policy found in statutes and regulations dealing with the protection of children from abuse and requiring that suspected abuse or neglect be reported to the authorities.

Consider also, *Mason v. Oklahoma Turnpike Authority*, 115 F.3d 1442 (10th Cir.1997), where a former employee of the Oklahoma Turnpike Authority alleged that his termination was due to his opposition to engage in the illegal activity of using surplus funds for the construction of a toll plaza. The 10th Circuit Court of Appeals held that the jury's conclusion that the plaintiff was wrongfully discharged for his refusal to violate the law was reasonable.

**3. Terminations Found Not in Violation of Public Policy.** Consider cases where the allegations were insufficient to state a claim for wrongful discharge. For example, in *Milton v. IIT Research Institute*, 138 F.3d 519 (4th Cir.1998), the Fourth Circuit Court of Appeals held that the employee's termination, allegedly for expressing concerns that the employer was abusing its tax-exempt status, did not constitute wrongful discharge in violation of public policy. The plaintiff merely claimed that he was terminated for fulfilling his fiduciary duty as a corporate officer to inform the Board of activities that might be injurious to the corporation's long-term interests. The court reasoned that even if the plaintiff had been fulfilling a recognized fiduciary duty, "his claim [fell] one critical step short of the goal—he [did] not [link] his duty to any explicit policy or 'clear mandate' that was violated by his discharge." Similarly, in *Wright v. Shriners Hospital For Crippled*

*Children*, 412 Mass. 469, 589 N.E.2d 1241 (Mass. 1992), a nurse brought a claim for wrongful discharge against a hospital, alleging that her termination was in retaliation for the critical remarks the nurse made to an internal survey team. The Supreme Judicial Court of Massachusetts held that public policy was not violated simply because the plaintiff claimed to have reported on issues that she felt were detrimental to health care. The court reasoned that the plaintiff's argument would require the court to convert an employment-at-will-contract that could be terminated at any time for any reason or for no reason, into a rule that requires just-cause to terminate an at-will employee.

Consider also, *Shea v. Emmanuel College*, 425 Mass. 761, 682 N.E.2d 1348 (Mass. 1997), where a former college employee alleged that she was wrongfully discharged by the college and her former supervisor for having reported criminal activity to the employer. Although the Supreme Judicial Court of Massachusetts held that an at-will employee who is discharged for reporting criminal activity to an employer is entitled to recover for wrongful discharge, the court ruled the plaintiff failed to provide evidence that she had been discharged for that reason. The court noted the plaintiff's employment record was full of incidents of troubles the plaintiff had been having on the job, which the employer asserted was the actual reason for the employee's termination. Similarly, in *Hinchey v. NYNEX Corporation*, 144 F.3d 134 (1st Cir.1998), the First Circuit Court of Appeals held that the plaintiff's claim that he had been wrongfully discharged in retaliation for having reported his employer's antitrust abuses, failed to provide support for this claim. Rather, the plaintiff made mere assertions and speculations that termination was prompted by his reporting of the antitrust abuses.

**4. Evaluating the Tort.** Do you agree that wrongful termination should provide an employee remedies even if, as is often the case, the employment contract allows the employer to discharge the employee at will? Should the tort be expanded to cover any unreasonable or unjustified discharge of an employee? What do you think are the positive and negative impacts of the tort on business and the hiring process? Does the wrongful termination tort inappropriately interfere with the contractual right to fire an employee?

## 2. Tortious Breach of the Covenant of Good Faith and Fair Dealing

# EGAN v. MUTUAL OF OMAHA INSURANCE CO.

Supreme Court of California, In Bank.
24 Cal.3d 809, 169 Cal.Rptr. 691, 620 P.2d 141 (1979).

MOSK, Justice.

\* \* \*

In 1962, plaintiff purchased a health and disability insurance policy from defendant Mutual through its Los Angeles representative, the Hall–Worthing Agency (agency). The policy provided for lifetime benefits of $200 per month in event the insured became totally disabled as a result of either an accidental injury "independent of sickness and other causes" or sickness sufficiently severe to cause confinement of the insured to his residence. Benefits for a nonconfining illness were payable for a period not to exceed three months.

\* \* \*

In addition to the duties imposed on contracting parties by the express terms of their agreement, the law implies in every contract a covenant of good faith and fair dealing. (*Comunale v. Traders & General Ins. Co.* (1958) 50 Cal.2d 654, 658 [328 P.2d 198, 68 A.L.R.2d 883]; see also Comment, *Extending the Insurer's Duty of Good Faith and Fair Dealing to Third Parties Under Liability Insurance Policies* (1978) 25 UCLA L.Rev. 1413, 1418–1424.) The implied promise requires each contracting party to refrain from doing anything to injure the right of the other to receive the benefits of the agreement. (*Murphy v. Allstate Ins. Co.* (1976) 17 Cal.3d 937, 940 [132 Cal.Rptr. 424, 553 P.2d 584]; *Crisci v. Security Ins. Co.* (1967) 66 Cal.2d 425, 429 [58 Cal.Rptr. 13, 426 P.2d 173]; *Comunale* v. *Traders & General Ins. Co., supra,* 50 Cal.2d at p. 658.) The precise nature and extent of the duty imposed by such an implied promise will depend on the contractual purposes.

\* \* \*

... "[W]hen the insurer unreasonably and in bad faith withholds payment of the claim of its insured, it is subject to liability in tort." (*Gruenberg,* at p. 575 of 9 Cal.3d; accord, *Silberg,* at p. 461 of 11 Cal.3d; *Fletcher,* at pp. 401–402 of 10 Cal.App.3d.) For the insurer to fulfill its obligation not to impair the right of the insured to receive the benefits of the agreement, it again must give at least as much consideration to the latter's interests as it does to its own. (*Silberg,* at p. 460 of 11 Cal.3d.)

The insured in a contract like the one before us does not seek to obtain a commercial advantage by purchasing the policy—rather, he seeks protection against calamity. As insurers are well aware, the major motivation for obtaining disability insurance is to provide funds during periods when the ordinary source of the insured's income—his earnings—has stopped. The purchase of such insurance provides peace of mind and security in the event the insured is unable to work. (See *Crisci v. Security Ins. Co., supra,* 66 Cal.2d at p. 434.) To protect these interests it is essential that an insurer fully inquire into possible bases that might support the insured's claim. Although we recognize that distinguishing fraudulent from legitimate claims may occasionally be difficult for insurers, especially in the context of disability policies, an insurer cannot reasonably and in good faith deny payments to its insured without thoroughly investigating the foundation for its denial.

Here the evidence is undisputed that Mutual failed to properly investigate plaintiff's claim; hence the trial court correctly instructed the jury that a breach of the implied covenant of good faith and fair dealing was established.

## II

Civil Code section 3294 provides: "In an action for the breach of an obligation not arising from contract, where the defendant has been guilty of oppression, fraud, or malice, express or implied, the plaintiff, in addition to the actual damages, may recover damages for the sake of example and by way of punishing the defendant." Section 3294 was originally enacted in 1872, a minor amendment was adopted in 1905, and the statute has remained intact ever since. It is true that the concept of punitive damages has been criticized; but unless at this late date we were to hold the section unconstitutional—a proposition that has been frequently rejected (see, e.g., *Fletcher v. Western National Life Ins. Co., supra*, 10 Cal.App.3d at pp. 404–405; *Toole* v. *Richardson-Merrell Inc.* (1967) 251 Cal.App.2d 689, 719 [60 Cal.Rptr. 398, 29 A.L.R.3d 988]; *United States v. Regan* (1914) 232 U.S. 37, 46–49 [58 L.Ed. 494, 497–499, 34 S.Ct. 213])—we cannot usurp the Legislature's determination that such damages should be recoverable in cases in which the statutory prerequisites are fulfilled. (*Merlo v. Standard Life & Acc. Ins. Co.* (1976) 59 Cal.App.3d 5, 19–20 [130 Cal.Rptr. 416]; *Ferraro v. Pacific Fin. Corp.* (1970) 8 Cal.App.3d 339, 355 [87 Cal.Rptr. 226].)

In the present context, the principal purpose of section 3294 is to deter acts deemed socially unacceptable and, consequently, to discourage the perpetuation of objectionable corporate policies. (See *Ferraro v. Pacific Fin. Corp., supra*, 8 Cal.App.3d at p. 353 [punitive award to deter corporate policy of repossessing automobiles despite bona fide claims of ownership by third parties].) Traditional arguments challenging the validity of exemplary damages lose force when a punitive award is based on this justification. (5) The special relationship between the insurer and the insured illustrates the public policy considerations that may support exemplary damages in cases such as this.

As one commentary has noted, "The insurers' obligations are ... rooted in their status as purveyors of a vital service labeled quasi-public in nature. Suppliers of services affected with a public interest must take the public's interest seriously, where necessary placing it before their interest in maximizing gains and limiting disbursements ... [A]s a supplier of a public service rather than a manufactured product, the obligations of insurers go beyond meeting reasonable expectations of coverage. The obligations of good faith and fair dealing encompass qualities of decency and humanity inherent in the responsibilities of a fiduciary. Insurers hold themselves out as fiduciaries, and with the public's trust must go private responsibility consonant with that trust." (Goodman & Seaton, *Foreword: Ripe for Decision, Internal Workings and Current Concerns of the California Supreme Court* (1974) 62 Cal.L.Rev. 309, 346–347.) Furthermore, the relationship of insurer and insured is inherently unbalanced; the adhesive nature of insurance contracts places the insurer in a superior bargaining position. The availability of punitive damages is thus compatible with recognition of insurers' underlying public obligations and reflects an attempt to restore balance in the contractual relationship. (Hirsch et al., *Strict Liability: A Response to the Gruenberg–Silberg Conflict Regarding Insurance Litigation Awards* (1975) 7 Sw.U.L.Rev. 310, 326; Comment, *Egan v. Mutual of Omaha Insurance Co.: The Expanding Use of Punitive Damages in Breach of Insurance Contract Actions* (1978) 15 San Diego L.Rev. 287, 298–301;

Note, *Contracting for Punitive Damages: Fletcher* v. *Western National Life Insurance Company* (1971) 4 Loyola L.A. L.Rev. 208, 219–224.)

\* \* \*

Plaintiff received his first payment from Mutual on the claim in issue herein only after a long delay and a personal visit to the claims office. When he requested additional payments as a result of his continuing inability to work, McEachen* visited him at his home. Testimony was introduced that McEachen, although aware of plaintiff's good faith efforts to work, called plaintiff a fraud and told him that he sought benefits only because he did not want to return to work. McEachen advised plaintiff he was not entitled to any further payments and that past benefits received were also unwarranted, despite plaintiff's bona fide claim of accidental injury. When plaintiff expressed his concern regarding the need for money during the approaching Christmas season and offered to submit to examination by a physician of Mutual's choice, McEachen only laughed, reducing plaintiff to tears in the presence of his wife and child.

After plaintiff received what Mutual designated his "final" payment, he was compelled to undergo back surgery. Segal visited plaintiff after he made further requests for total disability payments because he was confined to his home for medical reasons. Segal told him that he was not incapacitated from an accidental injury but had a "sickness" that could not qualify under the policy's total disability provision. Despite the lack of support for denying plaintiff's disability claim, Segal offered a "final" check under the policy's sickness provision, or a larger check if plaintiff would surrender the policy.[4] Other evidence reflected both Segal's and McEachen's knowledge that plaintiff had a 12-year-old child and a totally disabled wife. In short, the record as a whole contains substantial evidence from which the jury might reasonably find that defendant "acted maliciously, with an intent to oppress, and in conscious disregard of the rights of its insured." (*Neal v. Farmers Ins. Exchange* (1978) 21 Cal.3d 910, 923 [148 Cal.Rptr. 389, 582 P.2d 980].)

\* \* \*

We turn to the question whether the amount of the punitive damage award herein—$5 million—is excessive as a matter of law. We have recently reviewed the considerations governing appellate determination of such questions, and need not reiterate them at this time. (*Neal v. Farmers Ins. Exchange* (1978) *supra*, 21 Cal.3d 910, 927–928, and cases cited.) Applying those considerations to the case at bar, we observe first that the award of punitive damages is more than 40 times larger than the not-insubstantial assessment of $123,600 in compensatory damages against Mutual. In addition, the punitive damage figure herein represents two and one-half months of Mutual's entire net income in 1973,

---

* McEachen was an agency claims manager and Segal was an agency claims adjuster for Mutual of Omaha.

**4.** Of course, if there had been a reasonable and carefully investigated foundation for believing that plaintiff's injury did not fall within the scope of the policy coverage, the proposed settlement could not have been considered inappropriate and, accordingly, could not have entered into the jury's decision to award punitive damages.

and more than seven months of such income in 1974. Viewing the record as a whole and in the light most favorable to the judgments, we conclude that in these circumstances the punitive damage award against Mutual must be deemed the result of passion and prejudice on the part of the jurors and excessive as a matter of law.

\* \* \*

## *NOTES*

**1. Tortious Breach of the Implied Covenant of Good Faith and Fair Dealing.** The implied covenant of good faith and fair dealing is essentially a contract term:

> Every contract imposes upon each party a duty of good faith and fair dealing in its performance and enforcement.

Restatement (Second) of Contracts § 205. The implied covenant is imposed by law as an additional term in every contract. In this way each party to the contract is obligated to act fairly and in good faith toward the other party. The breach of the implied covenant by one of the parties constitutes a breach of contract and can lead to liability under contract law. In some types of contracts, courts have also held that a breach of the implied covenant of good faith and fair dealing can constitute a tort. This permits tort damages, including compensation for mental distress and punitive damages, in addition to contract remedies, which do not ordinarily provide for these kind of damages.

As the principal case indicates, in the context of insurance contracts, the tort with its threat of punitive and other large damages provides a deterrence against wrongfully denying or delaying compensation for legitimate insurance claims. See Diamond, Levine & Madden, *Understanding Torts* § 19.03 (2nd ed. 2000); Dobbs, *The Law of Torts* § 457 (2000). It should be emphasized that merely incorrectly failing to pay an insurance claim to a beneficiary as required by the contract does not automatically constitute a breach of the implied covenant of good faith and fair dealing. The insurance company must act in bad faith, intentionally obstructing or inappropriately delaying the payment of a valid claim.

Most states recognize the tort of breach of the implied covenant of good faith and fair dealing at least in the context of insurance contracts. Consider *Best Place Inc. v. Penn America Insurance Company*, 82 Hawai'i 120, 920 P.2d 334 (1996), where an insured brought suit against a fire insurer for tortious breach of the implied covenant of good faith and fair dealing, after the insurer wrongfully denied the insured's fire claim. The Supreme Court of Hawaii held that Hawaii recognizes the tort of breach of the implied covenant of good faith and fair dealing where an unequal bargaining position exists between the parties of a contract and particularly where an insurance company denies a claim in bad faith.

**2. Non–Insurance Breaches.** Consider *The Garshman Company Ltd. v. General Electric Company, Inc.*, 993 F.Supp. 25 (D.Mass.1998), where an auction company brought suit against a corporation for tortious breach of the implied covenant of good faith and fair dealing due to the corporation's breach of the auction agreement. The District Court of Massachusetts held that tort liability for breach of the implied covenant of good faith and fair dealing is only appropriate where there's evidence of unequal bargaining positions. Here, both the auction company and the corporation were commercial entities and there was no evidence of inherently unequal bargaining positions. Consider also, *Cenex, Inc. v. Arrow Gas Service*, 896 F.Supp. 1574 (D.Wyo.1995), where a seller of a propane business brought suit against a propane distributor for tortious breach of the implied covenant of good faith and fair dealing, alleging that the distributor operated the propane business in a manner that deliberately suppressed sales to lower the payments due to the seller of the business. The District Court of Wyoming held that the distributor was not liable for the tort. Rather, the court reasoned that a tortious breach of good faith claim requires proof that a special relationship of trust and reliance existed between the parties.

By contrast consider *Nicholson v. United Pacific Insurance*, 219 Mont. 32, 710 P.2d 1342 (1985). The parties agreed to a lease with the landlord agreeing to remodel the office to the future tenant's satisfaction. The would-be tenant repeatedly denied satisfaction with the landlord's successive efforts to remodel the office as a ruse to escape the lease agreement. The court held the tenant had tortiously breached the covenant of good faith and fair dealing. Consider also *State University and Community College System v. Sutton*, 120 Nev. 972, 103 P.3d 8 (Nev. 2004), where the Nevada Supreme Court recognized that liability for tortious breach of the implied covenant of good faith was not restricted only to the context of insurance, but also other situations where there is a special relationship between the contracting parties. Specifically the court held that "tort liability for breach of the implied covenant of good faith and fair dealing is appropriate where the party in the superior or entrusted position has engaged in grievous or perfidious misconduct (internal quotations omitted)." In the instant case, the court held that the employer/employee relationship between a university and a professor satisfied this relationship.

**3. Expanding the Tort to Non–Insurance Contexts.** Despite the examples above, most, but not all, courts have hesitated to extend the tort beyond the insurance context, where the beneficiary with an insured loss remains dependent on the insurance company to fairly evaluate the victim's claim. California in a very prominent case, *Seaman's Direct Buying Service, Inc. v. Standard Oil Co.*, 36 Cal.3d 752, 206 Cal.Rptr. 354, 686 P.2d 1158 (Cal. 1984), extended a portion of the tort to all commercial contracts where the bad faith breach consisted of in bad faith denying the very existence of the contract. In *Seaman*, Standard Oil was accused of wrongfully denying it had a contract with a marina to supply fuel, leading to the marina's bankruptcy. The extension proved unpopular and prompted much criticism including the following from Judge Kozinski in a concurring opinion in *Oki America, Inc. v. Microtech Int'l Inc.*, 872 F.2d 312, 314–315 (9th Cir.1989):

> "Nowhere but in the Cloud Cuckooland of modern tort theory could a case like this have been concocted. One large corporation is complaining that another obstinately refused to acknowledge they had a contract. For this shocking misconduct it is demanding millions of dollars in punitive damages. I suppose we will next be seeing lawsuits seeking punitive damages for maliciously refusing to return telephone calls or adopting a condescending tone in interoffice memos.... The intrusion of the courts into every aspect of life ... trivializes the law, and denies individuals and businesses the autonomy of adjusting mutual rights and responsibilities through voluntary contractual agreement."

In *Freeman & Mills, Inc. v. Belcher Oil Co.*, 11 Cal.4th 85, 44 Cal. Rptr.2d 420, 900 P.2d 669 (Cal. 1995), the California Supreme Court overruled *Seaman's* and restricted the tort to the insurance context. But see *Story v. Bozeman*, 242 Mont. 436, 791 P.2d 767, 776 (Mont. 1990), which applies the bad faith tort to all types of contracts where the parties primarily because of an unequal bargaining relationship have a special relationship. See also Slawson, *Binding Premises* (1996) p. 112, suggesting as many as 16 states out of 36 states that recognize the tort have applied the tort to some noninsurance contracts.

**4. Policy Alternatives.** The threat of punitive damages provided by the bad faith tort acts as a counterweight to the potential economic incentive for insurance companies to stonewall the payment of a valid claim. Contract remedies alone would only enforce the claim and do not provide punitive damages, so the insurance company (with lawyers on staff) could calculate it economically advantageous to deny claims intentionally. The worst result after contract litigation (if the beneficiary could afford to pursue the claim) would be payment with interest of the amount owed to the insured. Does the marketplace provide a sufficient alternative incentive for insurance companies to pay claims quickly in order to attract new customers? Since insurance companies are licensed and heavily regulated, do administrative remedies provide a sufficient safeguard against insurance company abuses? Should the bad faith tort be extended to other contexts, such as to employers or the examples where it was rejected in Note 2, *supra*? Should the bad faith tort be abolished?

# SECTION J.   INTENTIONAL MISREPRESENTATION

### NADER v. ALLEGHENY AIRLINES, INC.
United States District Court, District of Columbia.
445 F.Supp. 168 (1978).

CHARLES R. RICHEY, District Judge.

This action arose from the denied boarding of the plaintiff Ralph Nader from Allegheny Airlines Flight 864 on April 28, 1972. A trial was held before the Court, sitting without a jury, on September 4 and 10, 1973, and a decision awarding nominal and punitive damages to plaintiff Connecticut Citizens Action Group (CCAG) and compensatory and punitive damages to plaintiff Nader was filed on October 18, 1973. 365 F.Supp. 128. On appeal by the defendant, the Court of Appeals reversed in part and set aside the Court's 1973 judgment. *Nader v. Allegheny Airlines, Inc.*, 167 U.S.App.D.C. 350, 512 F.2d 527 (1975). That decision, insofar as it applied the doctrine of primary jurisdiction to stay plaintiffs' common law misrepresentation claims, was reversed by the Supreme Court in June 1976, 426 U.S. 290, 96 S.Ct. 1978, 48 L.Ed.2d 643. In short, the Supreme Court upheld this Court's determination that a bumped passenger, such as plaintiff Nader, need not await a determination by the Civil Aeronautics Board (CAB) before proceeding with his claim of common-law misrepresentation in the federal courts. Subsequently, the Court of Appeals entered an amended judgment on November 10, 1976.

The case is now on remand to this Court for final disposition in accordance with the decisions of the reviewing courts. Additional discovery has been undertaken and additional exhibits pertaining to the issues remaining for decision have been submitted. Upon review of the entire record herein, and in light of the opinions of the Court of Appeals and the Supreme Court, the Court now makes the following Findings of Fact and Conclusions of Law on remand. The Findings of Fact and Conclusions of Law filed by this Court on October 18, 1973, are hereby reaffirmed except to the extent they are inconsistent herewith or with the amended judgment of the Court of Appeals.

\* \* \*

## II.   *Plaintiff Nader's Fraudulent Misrepresentation Claim*

9.   This Court's judgment in favor of plaintiff Nader on his claim of fraudulent misrepresentation has been vacated, and this Court has been directed by the United States Court of Appeals for the District of Columbia Circuit to "reconsider the issue of fraudulent misrepresentation in light of the opinion(s) of the Supreme Court" and of the Court of Appeals. (United States Court of Appeals, Amended Judgment of November 10, 1976).

10.   Pursuant to the Court of Appeals' opinion, this Court must, and does, find that Allegheny made no affirmative misrepresentations to plaintiff Nader (*Nader v. Allegheny Airlines, Inc.*, 167 U.S.App.D.C. 350, 365, 512 F.2d 527, 542 (1975)). Further, this Court must, and does, find that Allegheny owed Nader no duty of full disclosure as a fiduciary (*Nader v. Allegheny Airlines, Inc.*, 167 U.S.App.D.C. 350, 375, 512 F.2d 527, 552 (1975)). What this Court must decide is whether Allegheny's failure to disclose its overbooking policies to plaintiff Nader was a fraudulent misrepresentation.

11.   The elements of the common-law tort of fraudulent misrepresentation that a plaintiff must prove in order to recover are:

(1) A false representation (2) in reference to a material fact (3) made with knowledge of its falsity (4) and with the intent to deceive (5) with action taken in reliance upon the representation.

*Nader v. Allegheny Airlines, Inc.*, 167 U.S.App.D.C. 350, 364, 512 F.2d 527, 541 n.32 (1976). In addition, since the Court of Appeals has held that defendant Allegheny did not affirmatively represent to plaintiff that he had a guaranteed seat on Flight 864, 167 U.S.App.D.C. at 365, 512 F.2d at 542, plaintiff Nader must prove that "Allegheny had a duty to disclose the possibility that its policy of deliberate overbooking could alter (public expectations of the meaning of 'confirmed reservation')." *Id*. The Court finds that plaintiff Nader has proved all of these elements by a preponderance of the evidence.

12.   *Falsity.* It is undisputed that defendant Allegheny communicated to plaintiff that he had a "confirmed reservation" on Flight 864 on April 28, 1972. It is also undisputed that defendant at no time (not in its tariffs, advertising, or other communications to the public) communicat-

ed to the plaintiff the existence of its overbooking practice. Defendant contends that a reasonable person would recognize that a "confirmed reservation" is not an absolute guarantee, but rather is a "reasonable assurance," of being flown, because any given flight may be cancelled as a result of meteorological conditions, mechanical problems, or the like. Defendant further contends that plaintiff had such a "reasonable assurance" of being flown on Flight 864 on April 28, 1972, notwithstanding defendant's overbooking policy, because only a very small percentage of reservation-holders were ever bumped.

The Court agrees with defendant's first contention, but disagrees entirely with its second contention. The "reasonable assurance" of flight that the term "confirmed reservation" connotes is a guarantee of flight subject only to contingencies beyond the control of the airline. The expectation of a reasonable person receiving a "confirmed reservation" is that the airline will do everything within reason to assure that the reservation-holder is flown on the flight for which he has a "confirmed reservation." Merely because any reservation is necessarily subject to unforeseen and uncontrollable contingencies is not license for the airline deliberately to impose its own additional contingencies on the "confirmed reservation," and no reasonable person would interpret the term "confirmed reservation" to incorporate such a license. Cf. *British Airways Board v. Taylor*, 1 All E.R. 65 (House of Lords 1976). The Court thus finds that defendant's nondisclosure of its overbooking practice was misleading and created a false understanding as to the chance of being flown on Flight 864.

13. *Materiality.* A material fact is one to which a reasonable person might attach importance in choosing his course of action, see W. Prosser, Law of Torts, § 108, at 719 (4th ed. 1971); in other words, it is a fact that could reasonably be expected to influence the conduct of a person with respect to the transaction in question. See ALI, Restatement of Restitution § 8(2) (1937).

The Court finds that the fact of the existence of defendant Allegheny's overbooking practice was such a material fact. There can be no doubt that the very essence of a "confirmed reservation" is the assurance of flight capacity. Thus, even though defendant contends that the statistical probability of any given passenger being bumped is not substantial, the knowledge that bumping is a possibility might well, for example, influence a reasonable person to arrive earlier for the flight than he otherwise would have. Moreover, defendant's contention that the fact of the existence of its overbooking practice is not material and would not likely influence passengers' behavior is irreconcilable with its admission in oral argument before the Supreme Court that Allegheny might well lose substantial business if it unilaterally (i.e., without like action by other airlines) notified passengers of its overbooking practice.

14. *Knowledge of Falsity.* Defendant Allegheny clearly knew that its representation to plaintiff Nader that he had a "confirmed reservation" was false and misleading because it knew that its practice of overbooking subjected Mr. Nader's reservation to the risk of being dishonored.

15. *Intent to Deceive*. There can be no doubt that the nondisclosure of the existence of defendant's overbooking practice was the result of a conscious and deliberate policy implemented by Allegheny in order to deprive passengers of information about its overbooking practice so as not to distinguish Allegheny's reservation practices from those of its competitors.

16. *Reliance*. Plaintiff Nader relied on his confirmed reservation as an assurance that he would be accommodated on Allegheny's flight, and the Court finds that such reliance was reasonable. Prior to April 28, 1972, plaintiff Nader was unaware of Allegheny's intentional overbooking policy. Although he knew from prior experience that other airlines had occasionally bumped passengers with confirmed reservations, he was unaware of Allegheny's overbooking practice, especially since the other airlines had always explained their oversales as purely accidental rather than the result of a deliberate overbooking practice. If Allegheny had revealed the existence of its overbooking practice to Mr. Nader, the Court finds that because of the importance that he attached to the fulfillment of his speaking engagement in Hartford, he would have taken appropriate steps to protect against the risk of bumping, such as arriving earlier at the gate, arranging for an earlier flight, or arranging an alternative way to travel to Hartford. Allegheny's purpose in making confirmed reservations is to induce just such reliance by persons making travel arrangements, and there is no basis to assume that Mr. Nader should have realized that his reservation was subject to the risk of overbooking. For these reasons, the Court finds that plaintiff Nader justifiably relied on defendant's representation that he had a "confirmed reservation" as a reasonable person would construe that term. See Finding #12 *supra*.

17. *Duty*. It is well-established in this jurisdiction that:

> [A] statement in a business transaction, which, while stating the truth as far as it goes, the maker knows or believes to be materially misleading because of his failure to state qualifying matter is a fraudulent misrepresentation; also that a statement containing a half-truth may be as misleading as a statement wholly false and thus that a statement which contains only those matters which are favorable and omits all reference to those which are unfavorable is as much a false representation as if all the facts stated were untrue. . . .

*Borzillo v. Thompson*, 57 A.2d 195, 197–98 (D.C.Mun.App.1948). Thus, "concealment or suppression of a material fact is as fraudulent as a positive direct misrepresentation." *Andolsun v. Berlitz School of Languages, Inc.*, 196 A.2d 926 (D.C.App.1964); *Baker v. Baker*, 54 App.D.C. 214, 217, 296 F. 961, 964 (1924). See Restatement (Second) of Torts § 529 (1977). It is also well-established that there is a duty upon one who undertakes to speak "not only to state truly what he tells" but also not to "suppress or conceal any facts within his own knowledge which materially qualify those stated. If he speaks at all he must make full and fair disclosure." *Kapiloff v. Abington Plaza Corp.*, 59 A.2d 516, 518

(D.C.Mun.App.1948). Accord, *Tucker v. Beazley*, 57 A.2d 191, 193 (D.C.Mun.App.1948).

In the instant case, defendant Allegheny intentionally failed to disclose to plaintiff Nader information within defendant's possession the existence of its overbooking practice see Finding #15 *supra*, which materially qualified the meaning of its statement to plaintiff Nader that he had a "confirmed reservation," see Finding #13 *supra* ; and this omission was misleading, see Finding #12 *supra*, and defendant knew it to be so, see Finding #14 *supra*. Thus, defendant Allegheny had a duty to disclose the existence of its overbooking practice and its failure to do so subjects it to liability for the common-law tort of misrepresentation.

18. Plaintiff Nader's injury as a result of his reliance on defendant's misrepresentation was $10.00; $7.00 for long-distance phone calls and $3.00 for the extra cost of a ticket to Boston. Since plaintiff is entitled to recover these damages from defendant on the basis of both the common-law tort of fraudulent misrepresentation and the nondiscrimination provision of 49 U.S.C. § 1374(b), see Finding #8 *supra*, defendant's total liability to plaintiff Nader for compensatory damages will be $10.00.

### III. *Plaintiff CCAG's Fraudulent Misrepresentation Claim*

19. This Court, in its initial opinion, held that plaintiff Connecticut Citizens Action Group (CCAG), the sponsor of the rally in Hartford to which plaintiff Nader was traveling on April 28, 1972, was entitled to recover its damages for reliance on defendant Allegheny's fraudulent misrepresentation that plaintiff Nader had a "confirmed reservation" despite the fact that plaintiff CCAG was not a direct party to the transaction in issue. 365 F.Supp. at 132–33. On appeal, the Court of Appeals reversed this holding on the ground that plaintiff CCAG was too remote from the transaction to be owed a duty by defendant Allegheny; and, it held, in the absence of such a duty, a plaintiff may not recover even if all the elements of the common-law tort of fraudulent misrepresentation have been proved. 167 U.S.App.D.C. at 372, 512 F.2d at 549.

20. On this remand, plaintiff CCAG has asserted that the evidence at trial proved (1) that its director, Toby Moffett, directly communicated on the phone with defendant Allegheny prior to April 28, 1974, "to confirm that Mr. Nader had a reservation" on Flight 864, and (2) that defendant's representative replied affirmatively without any disclosure of Allegheny's overbooking practice. Plaintiff CCAG contends that defendant's direct assurance to it that plaintiff Nader had a reservation on Flight 864 brings CCAG within the scope of defendant's duty.

21. The Court finds credible Mr. Moffett's testimony that he called Allegheny and that it directly represented to him that plaintiff had a reservation on Flight 864 on April 28, 1972. Mr. Moffett testified, however, that he "just" called and asked whether plaintiff Nader had such a reservation. There is absolutely no indication that Mr. Moffett identified himself, his organization, or his reason for calling, and the Court therefore finds that Mr. Moffett did not make such an identification to the Allegheny representative with whom he spoke.

22. In view of Mr. Moffett's failure to identify himself, his organization, or the reason for his call in any way, the Court must, under the standards articulated by the Court of Appeals herein, see 167 U.S.App. D.C. at 370–72, 512 F.2d at 547–49, conclude that plaintiff CCAG was not a member of the class of persons to whom defendant Allegheny's duty extended. Mr. Moffett's unidentified phone call does not change the fact that "(CCAG) was not identified to Allegheny until this law suit was instituted," and that "Allegheny had no special reason to know of CCAG's reliance or even of its existence." 167 U.S.App.D.C. at 372, 512 F.2d at 549. Since " 'the line (of duty) is definitely drawn' where the plaintiff is unidentified and the defendant has no special reason to expect that he may act in reliance," 167 U.S.App.D.C. at 371, 512 F.2d at 548, quoting Prosser, Misrepresentations and Third Persons, 19 Vand.L.Rev. 231, 251 (1966), Mr. Moffett's phone call was not sufficient to bring CCAG within the scope of defendant's duty.

### IV.  *Plaintiffs' Entitlement to Punitive Damages on Their Fraudulent Misrepresentation Claims*

23. Both plaintiff Nader and plaintiff CCAG pray this Court to assess punitive damages against the defendant for its fraudulent misrepresentation. Since only plaintiff Nader is entitled to recover from Allegheny for its fraudulent misrepresentation, the Court can only consider the appropriateness of a punitive damages award to plaintiff Nader.

27. Upon reconsideration of the entire record herein, the Court reaffirms its conclusion that punitive damages are appropriately assessed against defendant Allegheny for its fraudulent misrepresentation to plaintiff Nader that he had a "confirmed reservation" on Flight 864. First, it is well-established in this jurisdiction that "proof of fraudulent misrepresentation is itself sufficient to support an award of punitive damages, because of the state of mind rendering it fraudulent." *Day v. Avery*, 548 F.2d 1018, 1029 n.58 (D.C.Cir.1976), citing *Harris v. Wagshal*, 343 A.2d 283, 288 (D.C.App.1975), and *District Motor Co. v. Rodill*, 88 A.2d 489, 492–93 (D.C.Mun.App.1952).

*Second*, even if this principle were not applicable to the instant case, this case is plainly an appropriate case for the imposition of punitive damages against the defendant. The Court of Appeals expressly recognized in this case that it is appropriate to award punitive damages "to punish a defendant for the outrageous nature of his conduct and to deter the defendant and others from engaging in the same or similar acts." 167 U.S.App.D.C. at 374, 512 F.2d at 549.

\* \* \*

29. Having concluded that punitive damages are appropriately awarded herein, the Court must determine the appropriate amount of punitive damages to be awarded. In its initial decision, this Court assessed punitive damages in the amount of $50,000 against defendant Allegheny; $25,000 in favor of plaintiff Nader, and $25,000 in favor of plaintiff CCAG. Upon reconsideration of the entire record herein, including defendant's submissions and arguments with respect to its asserted "good faith" defense, the Court concludes that an award of $15,000

punitive damages is appropriate in the circumstances of this case. In making this determination, the Court is guided by the considerations set forth in *Afro-American Publishing Co. v. Jaffe*, 125 U.S.App.D.C. 70, 83, 366 F.2d 649, 662 (1966); *Town Center Management Corp. v. Chavez*, 373 A.2d 238, 245–46 (D.C.App.1977); and *Harris v. Wagshal*, 343 A.2d 283, 288 (D.C.App.1975). The Court finds that an award of $15,000 in punitive damages will adequately serve to punish defendant Allegheny for its willful and wanton policy of nondisclosure and misrepresentation and will adequately serve to deter defendant from engaging in such practices in the future. The Court is aware that in this jurisdiction it is appropriate in assessing punitive damages to consider the amount of attorneys' fees incurred by the prevailing plaintiff in the course of this litigation, *Afro-American Publishing Co. v. Jaffe, supra*; *Town Center Management Corp. v. Chavez, supra*, and the Court recognizes that the award of $15,000 will not fully compensate plaintiff Nader for the value of the many, many hours expended by his able counsel in pursuing this litigation to a successful conclusion. Nevertheless, in the circumstances of the present case, the Court concludes that the award of punitive damages should be limited to an amount adequate for the purposes of punishment and deterrence, and the Court concludes that the award of $15,000 in punitive damages is fair and reasonable and appropriate to satisfy the objectives of the law in applying punitive damages.

30. An Order in accordance with the foregoing will be issued of even date herewith.

## NOTES

**1. Subsequent Case History.** The court of appeal reversed Mr. Nader's recovery concluding that there was no "justifiable reliance" since the consumer advocate had been bumped several times before and was presumably aware of the airline's practice of overbooking. 626 F.2d 1031 (D.C.Cir.1980). The Nader litigation preceded and indeed began the process which prompted regulations requiring airlines to disclose their overbooking policies and compensate passengers bumped as a result. For a discussion of justifiable reliance, see Note 6, infra.

**2. Restatement Definition.** Intentional misrepresentation or fraud is the (1) material misrepresentation; (2) made with knowledge the statement is false or with reckless disregard as to its truth or falsity; (3) with the intention to induce reliance by the victim; (4) the victim justifiably relies on the misrepresentation; (5) and pecuniary damages result to the victim. The Restatement (Second) of Torts articulates the tort as follows:

> One who fraudulently makes a misrepresentation of fact, opinion, intention or law for the purpose of inducing another to act or to refrain from action in reliance upon it, is subject to liability to the other in deceit for pecuniary loss caused to him by his justifiable reliance upon the misrepresentation.

Restatement (Second) of Torts § 525 (1965). See also Keeton, *Prosser and Keeton on the Law of Torts*, § 107 (5th ed. 1984); Diamond, Levine & Madden, *Understanding Torts* § 19.01 (2nd ed. 2000) and Dobbs, *The Law of Torts* §§ 469–483 (2000).

**3.   Misrepresentations to Induce Sale of Products.** Consider *Radford v. J.J.B. Enterprises, Ltd.*, 163 Wis.2d 534, 472 N.W.2d 790 (1991), where the purchasers of a cabin cruiser brought an intentional misrepresentation claim against a boat retail business which had restored the boat, as well as the former owner of the boat, for their statements that the boat's hull was sound and that all the dry rot had been removed. The Wisconsin Court of Appeals concluded that the evidence satisfied the elements required to prove intentional misrepresentation. The defendants' misrepresentations were affirmative representations of facts falsely describing the condition of the boat at the time of the purchase negotiations. The defendants intended to induce and defraud the plaintiffs, as evidenced by body putty that was put directly on top of dry rot and then painted over. Moreover, the hull's defects were hidden and could not reasonably be detected until the boat was put into the water, where it promptly sank.

Similarly, in *Stev-Mar, Inc. v. Matvejs*, 678 So.2d 834 (Fla.App.1996), the District Court of Florida held that a buyer's course of conduct in buying property was justified, as the buyer had relied on the misrepresentations of the seller that the property had been zoned for a single family home, when it had in fact, not been. Since the buyer suffered economic damages, he sufficiently stated a claim for intentional misrepresentation.

Consider *Clark v. McDaniel*, 546 N.W.2d 590 (Iowa 1996), where the plaintiff brought suit against the private sellers of a used car and a used car salesman, who had originally sold the car to the private sellers. The suit was brought after the plaintiff discovered that the car had been "clipped", so that the front half of the car had been welded to the back half of another car of the same make but with an older model year. The Supreme Court of Iowa held that substantial evidence established that the used car salesman had misrepresented the condition of the car by not only failing to tell the original buyers that the car had been "clipped", but by leading the buyers to believe that the car had low mileage only because it had seldom been driven. Therefore, the court reasoned, the used car salesman intended to induce reliance and with the salesman's experience, he could reasonably have expected that his misrepresentation would be passed on to third parties.

Consider also *Tietsworth v. Harley–Davidson, Inc.*, 270 Wis.2d 146, 677 N.W.2d 233 (2004), where the court held that mere "puffery" was not actionable as misrepresentation. In this case, Harley–Davidson advertised that its line of motorcycles was "a masterpiece" of "premium quality" along with other advertising boasting the engine's quality despite a manufacturing defect causing a particular part to need more frequent replacement. The court noted that "one reason for excluding commercial puffs from the scope of actionable misrepresentation is that they are not capable of being substantiated or refuted (internal quotations omitted)." In this case, because the defendants did not make any affirmative statements regarding the engine beyond those classified as advertising puffery, they were not liable.

**4.   Misrepresentations to Join a College Team, Remain a TV Anchor, or Engage in Sex.** Consider *Hanks v. Hubbard Broadcasting, Inc.*, 493 N.W.2d 302 (Minn.App.1992), where a news anchor filed suit for intentional misrepresentation against a television station after the television station failed to promote her and reduced her role as a coequal anchor with her male counterpart. The Minnesota Court of Appeals held that the television station's representations to the plaintiff that her reduction of role would only be on a temporary basis in an effort to introduce the new male anchor to the market, was actionable as intentional misrepresentation. Ultimately, evidence showed that the plaintiff sufficiently stated a cause for intentional misrepresentation, as the plaintiff rejected her agent's advice to look for a position in a top ten market, in justifiable reliance upon television station's representations. This resulted in the plaintiff's pecuniary loss, since the plaintiff received a lower salaried job than she would have received if she had gained experience as a coequal anchor.

Similarly, in *Lesser v. Neosho County Community College*, 741 F.Supp. 854 (D.Kan.1990), the District Court of Kansas held that a reasonable jury could find that the defendant, a community college baseball coach, had fraudulently misrepresented to a student that he would not be cut from the team, preventing the student from receiving exposure to college and professional scouts while at the community college. In reliance upon the alleged misrepresentations, the student had foregone the opportunity to join other college teams. See also, *DiLeo v. Nugent*, 88 Md.App. 59, 592 A.2d 1126 (Md. 1991), where the Court of Special Appeals of Maryland held that the evidence sustained a finding of intentional misrepresentation where a physician intentionally misrepresented the purpose of his psychotherapy to induce sex from his patient. The patient suffered post traumatic stress disorder which needed to be medically treated, and therefore resulted in pecuniary loss.

**5. Misrepresentation in Adoption Cases.** Consider cases where intentional misrepresentation claims were asserted within the adoption context. In *Gibbs v. Northampton County Children and Youth*, 538 Pa. 193, 647 A.2d 882 (Pa. 1994), adoptive parents discovered that their child had a significant history of physical and sexual abuse that had not been disclosed to the parents, although they had requested the information on numerous occasions. The Supreme Court of Pennsylvania held that the plaintiffs sufficiently stated a claim for intentional misrepresentation. Compare with *M.H. & J.L.H. v. Caritas Family Services*, 488 N.W.2d 282 (Minn.1992), where adoptive parents sued an adoption agency for misrepresentations made regarding their child's prior sexual abuse. The Supreme Court of Minnesota held that there were insufficient allegations to support a claim of intentional misrepresentation since any misrepresentations were not designed to mislead the parents.

**6. Justifiable Reliance.** For the plaintiff to recover for intentional misrepresentation, the victim must have authentically relied on the misrepresentation. If the victim is not deceived and totally discounts the misrepresentation, there is no reliance. In addition, the reliance must be "justifiable." The Restatement considers "the qualities and characteristics of the particular plaintiff, and the circumstances of the particular case" (Restatement § 545A, cmt. b) in evaluating whether the plaintiff's reliance is justified. Does this explain the appellate court's reversal of Mr. Nader's verdict in the principal case as described in Note 1? The Restatement position gives more protection to fools than a victim who should know better. Should a fool who wrongfully thinks he has purchased the Empire State Building be able to recover? Consider *Chamberlin v. Fuller*, 59 Vt. 247, 9 A. 832, 836 (Vt. 1887): "No rogue should enjoy his ill-gotten plunder for the simple reason that his victim is by chance a fool." This is in contrast to negligent misrepresentation (see Chapter 2, Sec. H, infra) where, unlike the intentional tort, contributory or comparative negligence is a defense.

Consider *Burroughs v. Jackson National Life Insurance Company*, 618 So.2d 1329 (Ala.1993), where an investor brought suit against an insurer and its insurance agent for intentional misrepresentation regarding the terms of the insurance policy purchased for investment purposes. The Supreme Court of Alabama held that the evidence did not support a finding that the plaintiff had justifiably relied on the insurance agent's alleged statement that the plaintiff could get a portion of his investment returned to him at any time after the policy was issued. The plaintiff's own investigation, made prior to his investment, had indicated that the plaintiff could in fact not get his investment back until the policy had accumulated a sufficient cash surrender value.

**7. Material Misrepresentations.** The misrepresentation must be "material" to be actionable. The Restatement defines this to be an assertion that a reasonable person would attach importance to or the defendant should know the victim will personally consider important. See Restatement (Second) of Torts § 538. In addition to facts, opinions are actionable when they are articulated by an expert to a nonexpert, fiduciaries, and actors who mislead a victim about their objectivity. See Restatement (Second) of Torts § 542.

While misrepresentations of present or past facts are actionable, traditionally misrepresentation of future facts are not. Consider *Morgan v. Celender*, 780 F.Supp. 307 (W.D.Pa.1992), where a reporter promised a mother that statements regarding the sexual abuse of her children by their father, a former police officer, were "off the record" and that no names would be used with the photograph and article published by the reporter. The District Court of Pennsylvania held that this did not constitute intentional misrepresentation since the assurance to keep the information confidential was a mere promise to do something in the future, instead of an affirmative representation of fact.

Courts have justified excluding promises from liability for intentional misrepresentation since it places in jeopardy people who fail to keep a promise, such as finishing a job or paying a bill on time. While, in some instances, breach of a promise may also constitute a breach of a contract, contract remedies are generally not as harsh as tort remedies and do not include potential punitive damages.

The Restatement and an increasing majority of modern courts would include, as a present fact qualifying for liability under the tort, misrepresentation of a current intention as a present fact. See Restatement (Second) of Torts § 530, cmt. a. The Restatement view represents confidence courts will distinguish between a promise which is a lie, and consequently a misrepresentation of current intention, and the subsequent failure to keep a sincerely uttered promise. Does the Restatement view represent an appropriate expansion upon the traditional view?

**8. Failure to Disclose.** A failure to disclose was traditionally not a basis for liability under misrepresentation. There are exceptions, however, where there is a duty to disclose. Exceptions include those owed a fiduciary obligation (such as an attorney to a client), and where the actor realized he has concealed material information or misled another even if such earlier actions were unintentional. See Restatement (Second) of Torts § 551 and § 529. In addition, the Restatement more generally would impose a duty to disclose "facts basic to the transaction, if he knows that the other is about to enter under a mistake as to them, and that the other, because of the relationship between them, the customs of the trade or other objective circumstances, would reasonably expect a disclosure of those facts." See Restatement (Second) of Torts § 551(2)(e).

Consider *Ensminger v. Terminix International*, 102 F.3d 1571 (10th Cir.1996), where a termite inspection company performed an inspection of a home at the request of the seller. The termite company owed a fiduciary duty to the buyer to disclose information regarding the condition of the home with respect to termites. Thus, the failure of the company to make disclosure of the termite infestation was held to constitute the tort of misrepresentation since the condition of the home was material information leading the buyer to accept the bargain or to abandon the deal. The court reasoned the company had undertaken an obligation for the seller for the benefit and use of the prospective buyer, who would have no ability to detect the termite problem even with the exercise of reasonable diligence. But see *America's Favorite Chicken Company v. Copeland*, 130 F.3d 180 (5th Cir. 1997), where the Fifth Circuit Court of Appeals held that a franchisor did not have a duty to inform a prospective franchisee about certain equipment problems with one restaurant location and a competitor's plan to relocate next to another location. The court reasoned that the franchisee was a relatively sophisticated consumer with the ability to independently investigate the condition of the locations.

When, if ever, should a seller be legally obligated to warn a prospective buyer about defects or other reasons not to consummate the purchase? Does the Restatement (Second) of Tort § 551(2)e, quoted above, provide adequate guidance as to when there is an obligation to disclose? Should the prospective purchaser of a rare baseball card be obligated to warn the seller that the card he is selling is vastly underpriced? Brian Wrzesinski, a twelve-year-old boy, paid $12 for a Nolan Ryan rookie baseball card that the store had incorrectly marked down from its intended price of $1200. A civil suit against the boy was settled by an agreement to auction the card for charity where it fetched $5,000. See Woodward, *Disputed Ryan Card Gets $5,000*, USA Today (6/24/91) at C2.

Should a real estate developer be obligated to tell prospective out of state purchasers that the homes she is selling are more expensive than comparable homes in adjacent neighborhoods? Several real estate developers were criminally charged and convicted based on their failure to disclose a lower price. An appellate court adapted a more traditional approach and reversed the convictions. See *United States v. Brown*, 79 F.3d 1550 (11th Cir. 1996); Coffee, Jr., "If Silence Equals Fraud, The Rules Shift," *National Law Journal* (10/5/92) at 18. Should the home buyers be able to recover in tort for misrepresentation against the developers?

## NEW JERSEY CARPENTERS HEALTH
## FUND v. PHILIP MORRIS, INC.

United States District Court, D. New Jersey.

17 F.Supp.2d 324 (1998).

BARRY, District Judge.

Plaintiffs, six multi-employer health and welfare trust funds operating in New Jersey (the "Funds") and providing comprehensive health care benefits to union workers, to their families, and to covered retirees (collectively "participants"), have filed this action against the leading tobacco companies and their lobbying and public relations agents (collectively as "defendants").

In their behemoth 124–page, 350–paragraph complaint, the Funds set forth virtually the entire history of the marketing of cigarettes and allege that for decades the defendants have collectively engaged in systematic and calculated misconduct, including, among other things: fraudulently failing to disclose accurate information as to the health risks of smoking, intentionally misrepresenting the addictiveness of nicotine, secretly manipulating and controlling nicotine levels to assure addiction, and purposefully inhibiting the development and marketing of safer, less-addictive cigarettes. Defendants' falsehoods and misrepresentations, it is alleged, resulted in an increase in tobacco-related injuries suffered by participants and heightened health care costs for which the Funds were responsible.

The Funds are pursuing claims of fraud (Count VI), federal RICO (Counts I and II), federal and state antitrust (Count III and IV), as well as claims of undertaking and failing to perform a special duty (Count VII), and unjust enrichment (Count XI). They seek to recover damages presumably in the multi-millions of dollars, including but not limited to the health care costs they paid allegedly because of defendants' activities—the big ticket item, to be sure. They also seek, among other things, injunctive relief requiring the defendants to disclose research and information, fund corrective public education, fund cessation programs for dependent smokers, disclose nicotine yields in their cigarettes, and cease advertising and promoting smoking to minors. Prayer for Relief, Compl. at 121–122. Aside from common law and statutory claims specific to a particular state, the virtually identical complaint has been filed by the relevant Funds in about forty states. The success of these actions thus far has been less than ringing.

Defendants now move to dismiss the complaint, pursuant to Fed. R.Civ.P. 12(b)(6), for failure to state a claim. . . .

The recent explosion of litigation and proposed legislation centering around the tobacco industry has brought many issues to the forefront of public debate. The most fundamental issue, at least in this court's view, is whether smokers should be responsible for their own behavior or whether that behavior should be excused—or at least explained—by supposedly wicked forces beyond the control of these malleable and helpless victims, such as advertising. Somewhat related thereto is the issue of whether, as long as tobacco is legal, the tobacco industry should be liable for successfully marketing its legal products. Other issues surface more regularly in the burgeoning litigation. When did the tobacco industry become aware of the health risks of tobacco and the addictiveness of nicotine? Did the tobacco industry knowingly conspire to mislead the public into wrongfully believing that a link between cancer and tobacco use was still an "open question"? Are the risks associated with tobacco products so well-known as to foreclose any claim of justifiable reliance? Would public health organizations and consumers have acted any differently had they been given full disclosure by the tobacco industry? These issues, and more, raise questions which are both complex and important. At this juncture, however, this court must look only to the complaint and decide whether, as alleged, each count of the Funds' complaint states a claim upon which relief can be granted.

\* \* \*

## A.  *Fraud Claim*

Count VI of the complaint alleges that defendants intentionally engaged in fraudulent misrepresentations and concealment of the health hazards of smoking and its addictiveness which induced participants to smoke and continue to smoke, causing the Funds to incur increased health care costs. Defendants make two arguments in support of their motion to dismiss Count VI. First, defendants argue that the fraud claim fails because the Funds' injuries, if any, are too remote from defendants' alleged misconduct. Specifically, defendants assert that any fraudulent misrepresentations or concealment by defendants and any injuries or damages incurred because of that misconduct were directed at and suffered by smokers and potential smokers, *not* the health and welfare funds bringing suit here. Second, defendants argue that, aside from what has come to be referred to as "remoteness," the Funds' fraud claim has not been pled with particularity, as required by Fed.R.Civ.P. 9(b).

### 1.  *Remoteness*

To effectively analyze the issue of remoteness, it is imperative to recognize that the Funds allege misconduct essentially directed at two different groups: participants who smoked and the Funds themselves. Although seeking relief for fraud perpetrated by the defendants against both groups, it is the fraud allegedly directed at the Funds themselves which is the supposed "focus" of the Funds' fraud claim. Thus, the argument goes, the tobacco defendants aimed misconduct directly at the Funds as providers of health care services to "shield themselves from having to pay the health care costs of tobacco-related diseases and to shift those costs to others, including [p]laintiffs...." By virtue of this misconduct, the Funds were prevented from restructuring their health care programs to discourage or reduce tobacco use by their participants. See Compl. at ¶ 304 (as a result of defendants' misconduct, the Funds "relied on false or incomplete information in taking or not taking actions to discourage and reduce tobacco use by [p]laintiffs' participants"); Compl. at ¶ 309 (by relying on defendants' misrepresentations and nondisclosures, the Funds' "failed to take or would have taken sooner actions to more appropriately treat tobacco-related injuries and diseases as well as to discourage and reduce cigarette and smokeless tobacco use, and the costs associated therewith").

\* \* \*

### a.  *Allegations of Misconduct Directed at Participants*

Taking the Funds' "secondary" claim first, the Funds may not recover for any damages incurred due to fraud directed at the Funds' participants because the Funds' injuries are too remote.... While the Funds' increased health care costs may have been a foreseeable consequence of an alleged fraud levied against participant smokers, not every foreseeable harm is recoverable. Indeed, courts have established parameters by which to determine, as a matter of law, whether injuries are too remote to warrant recovery.

It has long been recognized that

[a]s a practical matter, legal responsibility must be limited to those causes which are so closely connected with the result and of such significance that the law is justified in imposing liability. Some boundary must be set to liability for the consequences of any act, upon the basis of some social idea of justice or policy.

*Caputzal v. Lindsay Co.,* 48 N.J. 69, 78, 222 A.2d 513 (1966)....

One such fixed point is this: one who pays the medical expenses of another may not bring a direct action to recover those expenses from the tortfeasor who caused the increased medical expenses. See *Anthony v. Slaid*, 52 Mass. (11 Met.) 290, 291 (1846) (plaintiff, who agreed to support all of the town paupers, could not recover against defendant for the assault and battery by defendant's wife of one of the paupers, thereby increasing plaintiff's expenses, because the injury was too remote). This rule is traditionally invoked in the context of insurers who attempt to recover their increased costs directly from the tortfeasor. Courts have consistently disallowed such direct recovery, holding that because the tortfeasor directly harmed the insured individual, the insurer's damages were too remote to be recovered in a direct action.

\* \* \*

### b. *Allegations of Misconduct Directed at the Funds*

Although nearly all of the Funds' massive complaint addresses misconduct levied against participants and smokers, parsing through Count VI this court has managed to tease out from the complaint the claimed "focus" of the Funds' fraud claim: a claim of fraud directed at the Funds themselves. As noted above, the Funds assert that for the purpose of shifting health care costs from themselves, defendants aimed misrepresentations and nondisclosures directly at the Funds intending that the Funds would rely upon those representations (or lack thereof) in structuring their health care programs. Because the Funds relied on those misrepresentations and nondisclosures, the Funds failed to treat tobacco-related injuries and diseases and failed to discourage and reduce tobacco use, and the costs associated therewith. The imposition of these health care costs damaged the institutional interests of the Funds by "diminish[ing] the assets of the Funds and depriv[ing] the participants as a whole of resources to pay for health care benefits." Pl. Opp. Br. at 9.

Injuries premised upon misconduct directed at the Funds cannot be dismissed as remote because the Funds are not suing on behalf of their participants to recover for smoking-related injuries that the participants sustained, but are suing to recover for the economic injuries that they, as health care organizations, suffered due [to] fraudulent conduct directed at them. Proximate cause is no longer a hurdle and subrogation would be inappropriate because the Funds' claims are independent of any misrepresentation toward, or reliance by, smokers.

Defendants argue, however, that the Funds' "purported 'direct' claim" must be rejected because it is simply a recharacterization of the fraud claim vis-a-vis the Funds' participants as to which the Funds cannot recover as remote payors. Def. Br. at 17; Tr. 24–25; Def. Reply Br. at 4. Moreover, defendants argue, "in the absence of participants who purchased and smoked cigarettes . . . , the Funds have no legally cognizable injuries regardless of their now asserted failure to take action to 'protect' themselves." Def. Reply Br. at 4; Tr. 34–35 (the Funds' claims "fall on the remoteness doctrine because all of the[ir] injury is still derivative and derives through the individual smokers who were injured"). This court will take each of these concerns in turn.

First, fraud against the Funds in order to shift health care costs onto the Funds is a separate claim—involving different considerations as to each element of the offense—than that of fraud against participants in order to encourage them to begin or continue smoking. Fraud against participants would require, for example, proof of justifiable reliance by the participants. Reliance by participants, however, is irrelevant to a claim of fraud against the Funds themselves and whether the Funds justifiably relied by failing to institute smoking cessation programs or impose other cost-saving mechanisms. Defendants are simply incorrect in saying that "[t]he fraud or deception that [the Funds] allege [was] directed at them [requires that] the smoker . . . be deceived by the fraud." Tr. 24.

Secondly, the fact that the bulk of the Funds' injuries stem directly from injuries suffered by participants does not make the Funds' claim of injuries from fraud as to them any less direct. An example is helpful. Supposing the inventor of Procedure X approached the Funds and informed them, in order to persuade them to offer health insurance coverage for Procedure X, that it is perfectly safe. Relying on the representation made by the inventor, the Funds offer coverage to their participants for Procedure X. As it turns out, however, Procedure X is extremely dangerous and causes numerous health problems which its inventor knew it would when he or she fraudulently represented its safety to the Funds. The damage to the Funds' business as a result of this fraud would be the money the Funds lost as a result of relying upon the misrepresentation. The fact that those costs would stem from the injuries suffered by the Funds' participants would not make the Funds' fraud claim any less direct or actionable.

Here, the allegations of fraud directed at the Funds are significantly less impressive than the allegation in the above example and, indeed, are not very impressive at all. However, because—and only because—this motion is brought pursuant to Fed.R.Civ.P.12(b)(6), those allegations state a claim.

Accordingly, the Funds' claim that fraud was directed against them will not be dismissed on the ground that the Funds' injuries are too remote.

## 2. *Particularity*

The Funds' claim that defendants perpetrated a fraud directly upon the Funds, although not remote, must still be pled with particularity pursuant to Fed.R.Civ.P. 9(b). The elements of fraud are

> (1) a material misrepresentation of a presently existing or past fact; (2) knowledge or belief by the defendant of its falsity; (3) an intention that the other person rely on it; (4) reasonable reliance thereon by the other person; and (5) resulting damages.

*Gennari v. Weichert Co. Realtors,* 148 N.J. 582, 610, 691 A.2d 350 (1997).

The Funds allege that for decades defendants knowingly made material misrepresentations and omissions (Compl. ¶ 300) as to, among other things, the addictiveness of nicotine (Compl. ¶ 53), the link between cancer and tobacco (Compl. ¶ 140), whether defendants manipulated the nicotine levels in their products (Compl. ¶¶ 192–94), whether defendants added ammonia to enhance nicotine absorption (Compl. ¶ 173), and whether defendants bred special tobacco plants which yielded higher levels of nicotine (Compl. ¶¶ 166–71). Again, as teased out above, defendants sought to induce the Funds to rely upon these misrepresentations in order to "shield themselves from having to pay the health care costs of tobacco-related diseases and to shift those costs to others, including [p]laintiffs. . . ." Compl. ¶ 307. By reasonably relying on defendants' misrepresentations and nondisclosures, the Funds allegedly "failed to take or would have taken sooner actions to more appropriately treat tobacco-related injuries and diseases as well as to discourage and reduce cigarette and smokeless tobacco use, and the costs associated therewith[.]" Compl. ¶ 309.

While the Funds will assuredly have a hard time demonstrating that defendants' intent in misrepresenting or concealing information was to dupe the Funds into paying for health care (as opposed to duping consumers into smoking or into continuing to smoke), *and* that the Funds' reliance was justifiable in light of widely-available information about the dangers of tobacco, *and* that their costs would in fact have been reduced but for the defendants' misrepresentations and omissions, for purposes of this motion to dismiss, this court must accept the allegations of the complaint as true. *Cruz,* 405 U.S. at 322, 92 S.Ct. 1079. At this early stage, as the Funds have reminded this court, see pp. 328–329, *supra,* "[t]he issue is not whether a plaintiff will ultimately prevail but whether the claimant is entitled to offer evidence to support the claims." *Scheuer v. Rhodes,* 416 U.S. 232, 236, 94 S.Ct. 1683, 40 L.Ed.2d 90 (1974). "Indeed it may appear on the face of the pleadings that a recovery is very remote and unlikely but that is not the test." *Id.* While recovery here is certainly "very remote", the fraud claim is set forth—again, just barely—with sufficient particularity.

\* \* \*

## NOTES

**1. Tobacco Litigation.** The resurgence in litigation against the tobacco companies has most recently been based on release of industry documents which revealed alleged deception about the industry's perception of the addictiveness of nicotine and the health hazards of cigarettes. Consequently, misrepresentation has been a popular tort to apply on behalf of large entities, such as insurance plans and state and local governments. These entities, such as the plaintiff in the principal case, allege the misrepresentations were intentionally directed at them and, consequently, the massive economic expenses related to the health impact of tobacco to health and government care should be the responsibility of the tobacco industry. As the principal case indicates, however, proving insurance companies and governments were the target of these representations can be difficult. Nevertheless, the enormity of the potential liability and the legal expenses these plaintiffs, such as state governments, can incur forces the industry to take any marginal risk of liability very seriously. The unpopularity of the tobacco industry only adds to their concern. Do you agree with the principal case? Are the plaintiffs' arguments credible? See Barry Meier, "Cigarette Makers in $368 Billion Accord to Curb Lawsuits and Control Marketing," *New York Times*, 6/21/97, p.1.

In *Steamfitters Local Union 420 v. Philip Morris, Inc.*, 171 F.3d 912 (3d Cir. 1999), the appellate court, criticizing the principal case and finding causation too indirect, dismissed a similar union insurance fund against the tobacco company but did note that 9 out of 20 similar cases have allowed some actions against the tobacco industry to survive dismissal. Tobacco companies' potential liability for manufacturing "defective products" is considered in the product liability section (Chapter 3, Sec. B(2) at page 532 and in a much older case at Sec. (B)(1) page 516). Plaintiff's claims against the industry based on misrepresentation avoid the need to prove a defect and avoid an assumption of risk defense.

In addition to common law fraud claims, plaintiffs have also pursued claims against tobacco companies under federal antitrust law, and the federal conspiracy law RICO (Racketeer Influenced and Corrupt Organizations Act). In *Schwab v. Philip Morris USA*, 449 F.Supp.2d 992 (E.D.N.Y. 2006), plaintiffs alleged that Philip Morris and other tobacco companies deceptively marketed "light cigarettes" as being safer than other cigarettes, and that this misinformation lead to their paying higher prices for light cigarettes than they were worth. In a massive 300 page opinion, the court sustained the plaintiffs' cause of action, declining to grant the defendant's motion for summary judgment.

**2. Intent to Induce Plaintiff.** As observed in Note 1 above, the plaintiff must prove in intentional misrepresentation that he or she was an intended victim or at the very least, if the Restatement (quoted below) is followed, that the defendant had reason to expect the plaintiff will hear and justifiably rely on the misrepresentation. This proved difficult in the tobacco case above and impossible for the organization expecting Mr. Nader to speak in the previous principal case. The Restatement articulates the requirement as follows:

> The maker of a fraudulent misrepresentation is subject to liability for pecuniary loss to another who acts in justifiable reliance upon it if the misrepresentation, although not made directly to the other, is made to a third person and the maker intends or has reason to expect that its terms will be repeated or its substance communicat-

ed to the other, and that it will influence his conduct in the transaction or type of transaction involved.

Restatement (Second) § 533.

A caveat, however, expresses no opinion whether liability can be extended beyond the ambit of the provision. How far would you extend liability to third parties for intentional misrepresentation? Negligent, as opposed to intentional, misrepresentation liability to third parties is usually extremely limited. See Chapter 2, Sec. H, infra.

**3. Remote Causation.** The principal case required the health fund plaintiffs to prove that they were direct victims of the tobacco companies' misrepresentations. Note that the court rejected arguments that the health funds could recover because misrepresentations directed at tobacco smokers caused the smokers to become ill from continued smoking and ultimately caused the funds to spend money on their medical care.

Usually in intentional torts the injuries are so direct that courts rarely have to discuss how far to extend the chain of cause and effect. In negligence actions, however, governing liability for accidental injuries, courts regularly consider whether the plaintiff's injuries are sufficiently connected to the defendant's tortious conduct to find "proximate" or "legal" cause and impose liability. The subject of proximate cause is discussed extensively in Chapter 2, Section F, infra.

Insurance companies often do have contract provisions, known as subrogation clauses, with the insured. This allows the insurance companies to claim any recovery the victim receives in a tort action, if the insurance company had compensated the victim for that injury. See Chapter 5, page 614, infra.

# Chapter II

# NEGLIGENCE

## SECTION A.   OVERVIEW

### PITRE v. EMPLOYERS LIABILITY ASSURANCE CORPORATION

Court of Appeal of Louisiana, First Circuit.
234 So.2d 847 (1970).

LANDRY, Judge.

This appeal by defendants, Employers Liability Assurance Corporation, Ltd. and Maryland Casualty Company, insurers of the Thibodaux Fireman's Fair, is from the judgment of the trial court awarding Mr. and Mrs. Merville N. Pitre damages for the death of their nine and one-half year old son, Anthony Pitre, who died [of] injuries received when he was struck in the head by the hand of a fair patron winding up to pitch a baseball at a concession stand. The trial court rendered no reasons for judgment. We reverse the judgment and dismiss plaintiffs' actions with prejudice upon finding defendants' insured free of negligence.

\* \* \*

The determinative facts of this case are not in dispute. The unfortunate accident occurred at approximately 8:00 P.M., April 29, 1967, at the baseball concession stand operated at the annual Fireman's Fair conducted upon public school grounds in the City of Thibodaux by the Fire Department. The funds raised are used exclusively to purchase equipment for the companies concerned. It appears that the fairs, which have been held for several successive years, are considerable in scope and grow larger each year. The fair is designed to attract people of all ages. It offers a variety of mechanical rides and amusement devices such as a ferris wheel, merry-go-round, and similar contraptions. Additionally, it offers food in the form of hot dogs, hamburgers and similar fare. Drinks include soft drinks, lemonade and beer. From the record, it is safe to infer the enterprise nets the Fire Department approximately $40,000–$45,000 yearly.

The baseball concession stand consisted of two 'alleys' at the rear of which was a canopy type cover of canvas or similar material. At the other end, about 20–25 feet distant, was a counter approximately two feet in height. Beneath the canopy was some sort of rack on which were mounted canvas flaps or dolls which could be knocked down if struck with a baseball. Between the counter and canopy ropes were strung to keep spectators from walking between the counter and the dolls. For the sum of 25 cents a participant was furnished three baseballs from a supply kept on the counter. The object of the game was to knock over the 'dolls' and win a prize. Participants were required to stand outside the enclosure and throw from beyond the counter. Beyond the counter there were no barriers, ropes or other devices to restrain the thrower or isolate or separate him from spectators or other patrons attending the fair. Two members of the Fire Department operated the concession from posts which they assumed inside the counter near the restraining side ropes. At no time did the attendants leave the alleys to supervise the activity of a patron standing on the opposite side of the counter to pitch balls.

It is conceded that LeBouef, who was seventeen years of age at the time, in the act of "winding up" to pitch a baseball at the concession, struck young Anthony Pitre in the left temple region.

\* \* \*

George Everett Henderson, an expert on conducting fairs, testified he has had twenty years experience in the business, the last sixteen as Concessions Manager for Playland Amusements, Incorporated, Pontchartrain Beach, New Orleans. As manager, he is in charge of all concessions at Pontchartrain Beach including design, construction and safety aspects. He has operated approximately 48 similar baseball concessions or stands and at present is operating three such concessions. He noted that safety is not considered as large a problem with concessions of this type as in the case of mechanical rides and amusement devices. He provided such stands with baffles at the end where the targets are situated. The battles prevented baseballs from ricocheting since experience proved ricocheting balls were the greatest hazard in operating a concession of this nature. His visits to hundreds of similar concessions at other fairs showed the only significant hazard was that incident to richocheting baseballs. He has never seen or used restraining ropes or barriers to isolate participants from spectators. He conceded that professional fairs draw a line on the ground six feet from the counter and require participants to stand within this line when throwing. He explained that since the thrower must cast down at the targets, the closer the participant is to the target, the less accurate he is because of the trajectory involved at a short distance. The farther away the thrower stands, the more level his trajectory and the greater the accuracy. He noted that the six foot restraining line used by professionals has no relation to safety. He further noted that insurance company safety engineers have always approved the operation of his baseball stands without barriers and even though his employees remain inside the concession area as did defendant's operators in the instant case. He also stated that, as a matter of policy, he did not permit very young persons to patronize such a game because they lacked physical strength to knock over the dolls.

\* \* \*

Fault is determined by asking the question: How would a reasonably prudent individual have acted or what precautions would he have taken under the same or similar circumstances? *Tucker v. Travelers Insurance Company*, La.App., 160 So.2d 440. Negligent conduct is determined in the light of the facts and environmental circumstances of each case. *Zorick v. Maryland Casualty Company*, La.App., 172 So.2d 706.

Failure to take every precaution against all foreseeable injury to another does not necessarily constitute negligence. On the contrary, negligence requires that the risk be both foreseeable and unreasonable. *Turner v. Caddo Parish School Board*, 252 La. 810, 214 So.2d 153. Failure to take a particular precaution to guard against injury to another in connection with a risk constitutes negligence only where it appears such a precaution would have been undertaken under the circumstances by a reasonably prudent individual. *Turner v. School Board*, above. One is bound to protect against what usually happens or what is likely to happen under the circumstances. *Wilson v. Scurlock Oil Co.*, La.App., 126 So.2d 429. Ordinary care requires only that precautions be taken against occurrences that can and should be foreseen; it does not require that one anticipate unusual and improbable, though entirely possible happenings. *Rouseo v. Gauche Connor Co.*, 8 Orleans App. 216.

Plaintiffs, relying principally upon *Gilliam v. Serrano*, 162 So.2d 32, maintain that the Fire Department owned the affirmative duty to either warn or guard participants and spectators against the inherent danger of being struck by a person winding up to throw at the targets. It is contended that the attendants should have stayed on the outside of the counter to keep spectators at a safe distance from participants. It is also argued that restraining ropes or other barriers could have effectively isolated pitchers from spectators and other participants.

We find Gilliam, above, clearly distinguishable from the case at hand. In Gilliam, the fair operators were operating a mechanical amusement device at a 'fair' designed expressly to attract children of pre-school age. In essence, Gilliam holds that where pre-school children are concerned, the operator of amusement devices owes a high degree of care. With this general rule, we are in accord. To hold as plaintiffs urge herein would make operators of amusement devices insurers of the safety of their patrons. Such is not the law. The operator is required only to exercise that degree of care commensurate with foreseeable dangers inherent under the circumstances, including the age bracket of his anticipated patrons. Plaintiff has not shown that children of decedent's age were permitted to participate in the baseball concession involved herein. Mr. Henderson's testimony justifies the assumption that persons of decedent's age were not allowed to indulge in this particular sport.

It is well settled that custom and usage are properly considered in determining whether sufficient care has been taken in a particular instance, but custom and usage are not controlling or decisive since the customary way of doing a thing may be negligent and may create a false standard of care. *Harris Drilling Co. v. Delafield*, 222 La. 416, 62 So.2d 627. Here the record shows it is customary only to protect against ricocheting balls. It is not normal or customary to station attendants outside the enclosed concession area nor is it standard procedure to rope off or barricade the pitching area. Although the custom shown does not conclusively establish that the Fire Department discharged its duty to decedent, it is one factor to be considered in determining whether a reasonably prudent person would or should have foreseen the danger of injury from the source encountered here. It does not appear that the same or a similar accident had previously occurred. We find that there were no latent or hidden dangers to spectators in the throwing of baseballs under the circumstances shown. The pitching was conducted openly, in full view of all who watched. It involved forcibly throwing an object which could produce injury if misdirected, but the injury here did not result in their manner. Such danger as attended a participant stepping back, winding up to throw and actually throwing a ball was clearly visible to all.

\* \* \*

The national popularity of baseball as a sport warrants the conclusion that even a nine and one-half year old lad is aware of such danger as attends his remaining in proximity to persons throwing baseballs. Although the type of accident in question is one that was perhaps foreseeable, and certainly of a type possible, its probability of occurrence was not so great as to render the operators negligent for failing to take measures to prevent its happening. As stated above, failure to take precautions does not constitute negligence unless the danger is both foreseeable and unreasonable. Here, such danger as existed was not unreasonable. Here, a nonprofit organization, performing a vital public service, took such precaution as was deemed advisable by persons engaged in a similar enterprise as a business. In this instance, we find that the risk of foreseeable harm to others, and the probability of an accident of this nature occurring is outweighed by the utility of purpose for which the enterprise was conducted.

We find therefore that the trial court erred in finding that, as a matter of law, the Fire Department was negligent in this instance.

\* \* \*

It is ordered, adjudged and decreed that the judgment of the trial court be and the same is hereby reversed and set aside and judgment rendered herein in favor of defendants, Employers Liability Assurance Corporation and Maryland Casualty Company, rejecting and dismissing the demands of plaintiffs Merville N. Pitre and Florence Theresa Barrilleaux Pitre, with prejudice, at plaintiffs' cost.

Reversed and rendered.

### NOTES

**1. The Tort of Negligence.** The tort of negligence is the dominant method by which the courts determine whether an actor is liable for accidentally injuring another's person or property. Negligence developed as a formal tort in the nineteenth century from the breakdown of writ systems which divided liability based on direct and indirect injuries. To impose liability, negligence requires proof that the defendant acted unreasonably. This contrasts with strict liability (see Chapter 3, infra) where liability is imposed even when defendant acts reasonably and is without fault. Some scholars argue that the emergence of negligence with its numerous prerequisites for imposing liability contributed to America's economic development. Dangerous new industries could injure and kill and often escape responsibility. The victims, by often absorbing the cost of their own injuries, effectively subsidized the growth of new industries. Others extol negligence as a method for encouraging efficient conduct. Still others praise negligence as a fault based system which imposes liability for only wrongful conduct. Negligence has its critics as well. Some argue fairness compels that the injurer should always compensate the injured. Others critique the notion that reasonableness should be the central standard for determining liability. These issues are explored throughout the book.

The contemporary tort of negligence consists of the following elements that must be proven to establish liability: (1) a duty by the defendant to conform to (2) a standard of conduct; (3) breach by the defendant of the standard of conduct; (4) cause-in-fact; (5) proximate or legal cause; and (6) damages.

In essence, duty addresses whether the defendant has an obligation to the plaintiff to conform to a minimum standard of reasonable conduct. The standard of conduct elements address precisely what constitutes the minimum required conduct, usually a reasonable person standard. The breach element requires that the plaintiff prove that the defendant failed to conform to the requisite standard. Cause-in-fact generally addresses whether the defendant's wrongful conduct was a but-for cause of the plaintiff's injury. Proximate or legal cause focuses on whether the damage is sufficiently foreseeable or whether other policy considerations should preclude defendant's liability. Finally the damage element focuses on what losses are compensable.

The following cases explore these elements in detail. Each provides an additional hurdle that the plaintiff must overcome in order to win a negligence action. See Diamond, Levine & Madden, *Understanding Torts* § 3.01 (2nd. ed. 2000). See also Keeton, *Prosser and Keeton on* The Law of Torts § 30 (5th ed. 1984), and Dobbs, *The Law of Torts* § 115 (2000).

**2. Defining the Reasonable Person.** Virtually all courts utilize a variant of the "reasonable person" standard to establish the appropriate standard of conduct required in most circumstances to avoid negligence liability. The Restatement (Second) of Torts articulates the generally accepted view as follows:

> "Unless the actor is a child, the standard of conduct to which he must conform to avoid being negligent is that of a reasonable man under like circumstances."

Restatement (Second) of Torts § 283. See also Keeton, supra, § 32, and Diamond, Levine & Madden, supra, § 3.04.

The reasonable person doctrine originated with *Vaughan v. Menlove*, 132 Eng. Rep. 490 (1837). The defendant had stacked hay next to wood and thatch buildings on his own property; these buildings in turn stood close to buildings on the plaintiff's property. The haystack spontaneously caught fire, and the fire spread to and destroyed the plaintiff's buildings. The Court of Common Pleas rejected the defendant's argument that the court should take mental disability into account in the negligence analysis:

> It is contended . . . that the learned Judge was wrong in leaving this to the jury as a case of gross negligence, and that the question of negligence was so mixed up with reference to what would be the conduct of a man of ordinary prudence that the jury might have thought the latter the rule by which they were to decide; that such a rule would be too uncertain to act upon; and that the question ought to have been whether the Defendant had acted honestly and bona fide to the best of his own judgment. That, however, would leave so vague a line as to afford no rule at all, the degree of judgment belonging to each individual being infinitely various: and though it has been urged that the care which a prudent man would take, is not an intelligible proposition as a rule of law, yet such has always been the rule adopted in cases of bailment, as laid down in *Coggs v. Bernard* (2 Ld. Raym. 909).

> \* \* \*

> Instead . . . of saying that the liability for negligence should be co-extensive with the judgment of each individual, which would be as variable as the length of the foot of each individual, we ought rather to adhere to the rule which requires in all cases a regard to caution such as a man of ordinary prudence would observe.

132 Eng. Rep. at 490.

Do you agree with the court that a defendant should be compared to a hypothetical reasonable person even if the defendant did her best? Is the defendant who does her best really at "fault"? See generally Kirkland, *Of Horses, Helpers, and Hayricks: A Brief Re-examination of Some Basic Principles of the Law of Negligence*, 39 S. Tex. L. Rev. 87 (1997).

**3. Critiquing the Reasonable Person Standard.** Note that the Restatement (Second) of Torts, supra Note 3, speaks of "a reasonable *man*" standard (emphasis added). This traditional phraseology, which is supposed to be a generic term encompassing both men and women, has been criticized as anachronistic and sexist. Many courts have responded to this criticism by employing a "reasonable *person*" standard. However, some scholars argue that this still does not go far enough to remedy the problem. In addition to gender bias, some scholars have also questioned whether a reasonable person standard can adequately reflect cultural diversity. Consider Professor Leslie Bender's critique:

> That implicit male norms have been used to skew legal analysis can be seen in tort negligence law. To assess whether a defendant's conduct is negligent, and hence subject to liability, we ask whether the defendant has a duty to the plaintiff and whether she has met the legally required standard of conduct or care. "Standard of care" is a term of art in the law. It is alternatively described as the care required of a reasonably prudent person under the same or similar circumstances, or of a reasonable person of ordinary prudence, an ordinary prudent man, or a man of average prudence. Prosser and

Keeton explain the standard as some "blend of reason and caution." A "reasonable person" standard is an attempt to establish a universally applicable measure for conduct. This reasonable person is a hypothetical construct, not a real person, and is allegedly objective rather than subjective.

Not surprisingly, the standard was first articulated as a reasonable *man* or *man* of ordinary prudence. Recognizing the original standard's overt sexism, many courts and legal scholars now use a "reasonable person" standard. My concern with the "reasonable person" standard is twofold. Does converting a "reasonable man" to a "reasonable person" in an attempt to eradicate the term's sexism actually exorcise the sexism or instead embed it? My second concern is related. Should our standard of care focus on "reason and caution" or something else?

It was originally believed that the "reasonable man" standard was gender neutral. "Man" was used in the generic sense to mean person or human being. But man is not generic except to other men. Would men regard a "prudent woman" standard as an appropriate measure of their due care? As our social sensitivity to sexism developed, our legal institutions did the "gentlemanly" thing and substituted the neutral word "person" for "man." Because "reasonable man" was intended to be a universal term, the change to "reasonable person" was thought to continue the same universal standard without utilizing the gendered term "man." The language of tort law protected itself from allegations of sexism, it did not change its content and character.

This "resolution" of the standard's sexism ignores several important feminist insights. The original phrase "reasonable man" failed in its claim to represent an abstract, universal person. Even if such a creature could be imagined, the "reasonable man" standard was postulated by men, who, because they were the only people who wrote and argued the law, philosophy, and politics at that time, only theorized about themselves. When the standard was written into judicial opinions, treatises, and casebooks, it was written about and by men. The case law and treatises explaining the standard are full of examples explaining how the "reasonable man" is the "man on the Clapham Omnibus" or "the man who takes the magazines at home and in the evening pushes the lawn mower in his shirt sleeves." When the authors of such works said "reasonable man," they meant "male," "man" in a gendered sense. The legal world that generated the "reasonable man" was predominantly, if not wholly, male. What other connotations or meanings could the phrase have had? When it was converted to "reasonable person," it still meant "person who is reasonable by my standards" almost exclusively from the perspective of a male judge, lawyer, or law professor, or even a female lawyer trained to be "the same as" a male lawyer.

Changing the word without changing the underlying model does not work. Specifically addressing the "reasonable person" tort standard, Guido Calabresi challenges whether the "reasonable person" is in any way meant to include women or, for that matter, people of non-WASP beliefs or attitudes. Calabresi explains that use of a universal standard is intended to cause those who are "different" from that standard to adopt the dominant ideological stance. Like the notion of America as a melting pot, the reasonable person standard encourages conformism and the suppression of different voices.

Not only does "reasonable person" still mean "reasonable man"—"reason" and "reasonableness" are gendered concepts as well. Gender distinctions have often been reinforced by dualistic attributions of reason and rationality to men, emotion and intuition (or instinct) to women. Much of Western philosophy is built on that distinction.

\* \* \*

If we have been culturally and socially informed by a concept of "woman" that does not correlate with notions of reason or reasonableness, then how is the phrase "reasonable person" or the notion of "reasonableness" as a tort standard of conduct going to connote women's thinking, values, attitudes, or approaches to problem solving?

We would be hard pressed today to find many people who would openly assert that women cannot be reasonable. Today we are taught to consider women reasonable when they act as men would under the same circumstances, and unreasonable when they act more as they themselves or as other women act. If it is true that somewhere, at some subconscious level, we believe men's behavior is more reasonable and objective than women's, then changing the phrase "reasonable man" to "reasonable person" does not really change the hypothetical character against whom we measure the actors in torts problems. By appending the very term "reasonable," we attach connotations and characteristics of maleness to the standard of conduct. If we are wedded to the idea of an objective measure, would it not be better to measure the conduct of a tortfeasor by the care that would be taken by a "neighbor" or "social acquaintance" or "reasonable person with conscious care and concern for another's safety"?

Perhaps we have gone astray in tort-law analysis because we use "reason" and caution as our standard of care, rather than focusing on care and concern.

\* \* \*

Leslie Bender, *A Lawyer's Primer on Feminist Theory and Tort*, 38 J.Legal Educ. 3, 20–25 (1988).\* See also Cahn, *The Looseness of Legal Language: The Reasonable Woman Standard in Theory and in Practice*, 77 Cornell L. Rev. 1398 (1992). See generally Diamond, Levine & Madden, supra, § 3.04.

Do you agree or disagree that the reasonable person standard is flawed? How should the law respond?

\* Reprinted with permission of Journal of Legal Education.

The popularity of the reasonable person standard has even prompted at least some courts to extend the concept to animals. See *Kirkham v. Will*, 311 Ill.App.3d 787, 244 Ill.Dec. 174, 724 N.E.2d 1062 (Ill. App. 2000), upholding a "reasonable dog" standard in evaluating whether the dog's bite was adequately provoked.

**4. Precautions at Water Park.** In 1997, a high school in Napa, California, took a group of students on a trip to a recreational water park. At one point several students rode down a waterslide together in an effort to set a record for "clogging" the slide. The slide collapsed under the weight of the students, which was four times the maximum load that the slide could withstand. One student died and several were injured. Allegedly "clogging" was a popular activity familiar to the water park industry. It was also alleged that the students had rushed past a lifeguard in order to all ride the slide at once. The families of the dead and injured students sued the water park and the school district (school officials had allegedly encouraged the students to set a new record for "clogging"). See Goodyear, *Mom Sues in Death at Waterworld*, San Francisco Chronicle, Feb. 3, 1998, at A11.

Given these facts, what will the parties argue in this case? Will the water park have more difficulty defending this case than the defendants in *Pitre*? If "clogging" really is a common phenomenon, should the water park have prepared against it by building stronger slides? How common does an activity have to be in order for it to be "foreseeable"? Should it have been enough that a lifeguard was on duty to try preventing the students from rushing onto the slide? Should the park have warned customers of the dangers of clogging? Should the students have been aware of the dangers of "clogging," just as Anthony Pitre should have, according to the court, been aware of the danger of standing too close to someone throwing baseballs? Do you think that courts give weight to peripheral facts such as the fact that the *Pitre* defendants' insurees were firefighters operating a fair to raise funds for their department? Which way does each fact push your analysis?

**5. Proposed Final Draft to the Restatement (Third) of Torts, Negligence.** The Restatement (Third) § 3 elaborates negligence as follows:

> A person acts negligently if the person does not exercise reasonable care under all circumstances. Primary factors to consider in ascertaining whether the person's conduct lacks reasonable care are the foreseeable likelihood that the person's conduct will result in harm, the foreseeable severity of any harm that may ensue, and the burden of precautions to eliminate the risk of harm.

The Restatement (Third) keeps the same reasonable person standard of conduct by emphasizing that one who "exercises reasonable care" is the same as a "reasonably careful person." The primary factors to consider indicate an endorsement of the Hand Formula (Note 1 in Section A, infra), where negligence can be established by showing that the disadvantages (likelihood of harm, severity of harm) of an act outweigh the advantages (foregoing the burden of precaution). This cost-benefit analysis works best when it can be shown that an actor appreciated the risk but continued the action because the burden of taking precaution was too great. In cases where the actor was simply not paying attention and did not notice the risk, his conduct can best be evaluated by determining whether a reasonably careful person would have noticed. Restatement (Third) of Torts, § 3, comments a, b, k.

# UNITED STATES FIDELITY & GUARANTY COMPANY v. PLOVIDBA

United States Court of Appeals, Seventh Circuit.
683 F.2d 1022 (1982).

POSNER, Circuit Judge.

This is an appeal from a judgment exonerating the defendant, a Yugoslavian enterprise that owns the M/V *Makarska*, from negligence in connection with the death of a longshoreman, Patrick Huck, who fell into a hold.

The *Makarska* has five holds, numbered 1 through 5 from bow to stern, as shown in the following diagram:

Schematic Cross-Section of M/V Makarska

Each has three decks. From top to bottom they are the weather deck, the upper 'tween deck, and the lower 'tween deck. Below the lower 'tween deck is the main cargo area of the hold. Each deck contains a hatch roughly 30 feet across. When all three hatches in a hold are open, cargo can be loaded into (or unloaded from) the main cargo area. Hatchways of the typical maritime type (smaller than regular doorways, and with high thresholds) connect the holds laterally at each deck.

\* \* \*

On the morning of the day he was killed, Huck was working with a party of longshoremen on the upper 'tween deck of hold number 1. The hatch above them (in the weather deck) was open to give them light, and the hatch beneath their feet (in the upper 'tween deck) was closed. The longshoremen completed their work in hold number 1 at noon and took their lunch break. When work resumed it was in hold number 4, but by the end of the afternoon the longshoremen were working on the weather deck of hold number 2, which is to say on the same level as, and adjacent to, the upper 'tween deck of hold number 1.

After the longshoremen had completed their work in hold number 1 and broken for lunch, the ship's crew had come in and closed the hatch in the weather deck but opened the two hatches below it (the hatches in the upper 'tween and lower 'tween decks). This is a customary practice to facilitate a prompt start on loading and unloading cargo at the next port of call, for it can take as long as 30 minutes to open each hatch.

The closing of the hatch in the weather deck of hold number 1 plunged the entire hold into pitch darkness. Sometime during the late afternoon Huck, unobserved, entered hold number 1. He did so by stepping through the hatchway between the weather deck of hold number 2, where the longshoremen were then working, and the upper 'tween deck of hold number 1, now in darkness. It is unclear whether he opened the door in the hatchway or whether it was open already. It would not have been locked, but only latched, so if it was not already open he could easily have opened it. The hatch in the upper 'tween deck of hold number 1—now open, but in darkness—begins about 6 to 10 feet in from the hatchway where Huck entered. But Huck's body was found at the bottom of the forward part of hold number 1, some 40 feet in from the hatchway. This suggests that he had not walked directly into the open hatch, but rather had fallen in from the forward part of the upper 'tween deck after having successfully skirted the open hatch when he first entered.

The other longshoremen left the ship without noticing that Huck was not among them. His body was not found till the next morning. No one knows why Huck was in hold number 1. But it was stipulated that crates of liquor were stored in the forward part of the hold on the upper 'tween deck, the part from which Huck apparently fell, and it is conjectured that he was planning to steal some of the liquor on his way off the ship.

* * *

Under the regime of *Sieracki* the shipowner was liable even if the defect or unreasonably dangerous condition had been created by the stevedore, that is, by the longshoreman's employer. But in such a case the shipowner could get indemnity from the stevedore, so that liability ultimately came to rest on the party that could have avoided the accident at least cost. See *Ryan Stevedoring Co. v. Pan–Atlantic S.S. Corp.*, 350 U.S. 124, 76 S.Ct. 232, 100 L.Ed. 133 (1956); *Italia Societa per Azioni di Navigazione v. Oregon Stevedoring Co.*, 376 U.S. 315, 324, 84 S.Ct. 748, 754, 11 L.Ed.2d 732 (1964).

... [I]n 1972, when Congress amended the Longshoremen's and Harbor Workers' Compensation Act ... they ... substituted negligence for unseaworthiness as the standard of liability in actions by longshoremen against shipowners ... [under] 33 U.S.C. § 905(b). Congress did not attempt to define negligence; after 200 years of judicial experience with the negligence standard it would have been redundant and confusing to do so. Any necessary fine tuning was left to the courts....

... But we find nothing ... inconsistent with the negligence formula proposed in *Johnson v. A/S Ivarans Rederi*, supra, 613 F.2d at 348, which requires "balancing the usefulness to the ship of the dangerous condition and the burden involved in curing it against the probability and severity of the harm it poses." This formula echoes that of Judge Learned Hand in *United States v. Carroll Towing Co.*, 159 F.2d 169, 173 (2d Cir. 1947), also a maritime negligence case, though Johnson does not cite *Carroll Towing*. Judge Hand, designating by "B" the burden of the precautions necessary to avert an accident, by "L" the magnitude of the loss if the accident occurred, and by "P" the probability that if the precautions were not taken the accident would occur, reasoned that a shipowner or other alleged tortfeasor was negligent if B<PL, that is, if the burden of precautions was less than the harm if the accident occurred discounted (i.e., multiplied) by the probability that it would occur. The higher P and L are, and the lower B is, the likelier is a finding of negligence.

Though mathematical in form, the Hand formula does not yield mathematically precise results in practice; that would require that B, P, and L all be quantified, which so far as we know has never been done in an actual lawsuit. Nevertheless, the formula is a valuable aid to clear thinking about the factors that are relevant to a judgment of negligence and about the relationship among those factors. It gives federal district courts in maritime cases, where the liability standard is a matter of federal rather than state law, a useful framework for evaluating proposed jury instructions, for deciding motions for directed verdict and for judgment notwithstanding the verdict. . . . We do not want to force the district courts into a straitjacket, so we do not hold that they must use the Hand formula in all maritime negligence cases. We merely commend it to them as a useful tool—one we have found helpful in this case in evaluating the plaintiff's challenge to the jury instructions and its contention that negligence was shown as a matter of law.

. . . [J]ury instructions are challenged. The first reads: "A shipowner's duty to provide longshoremen with a reasonably safe place to work is confined to those areas of the vessel where longshoremen may reasonably be expected to go." This instruction is consistent with the Hand formula. Of course it is possible that a longshoreman will stray into a part of the ship where he has no business, but the probability (P in the Hand formula) seems too low to warrant the shipowner's taking precautions against an accident to him. If Huck had wandered into the captain's stateroom and slipped on a throw rug there, it would be unreasonable to impose liability on the shipowner even if the cost of doing without the throw rug would have been slight. Hold number 1 was not so remote from Huck's work area as the captain's stateroom would be, but all the challenged instruction did was ask the jury to decide whether it was a place where the shipowner should have expected Huck to be when the accident occurred, and this was proper.

* * *

The plaintiff also contends that even if the instructions were satisfactory, the undisputed facts showed negligence by the shipowner as a matter of law. We again use the Hand formula to frame this issue. L, the loss if the accident occurred, was large. There was a 25 foot drop from the upper 'tween deck of hold number 1 to the bottom of the hold, and a fall from that height was very likely to cause serious injury or, as in this case, death. As to B, the burden of precautions, there were various ways the shipowner could have prevented the accident. He could have lit the hold, locked the hatchway leading to it from the weather deck of hold number 2, roped off the open hatch, or placed a sign at the hatchway (though the effectiveness of this last precaution may be doubted). Probably the cheapest way of avoiding the accident, however, would have been for the ship's crew not to open the hatches until all the longshoremen had left the ship. This would have meant either the crew's working after normal working hours, or, if the opening of the hatches was postponed till the following morning, delay in beginning stevedoring operations at the next port of call. We doubt that either alternative would be very costly so we judge B in this case to have been, at most, moderate, and possibly small.

If P, the probability of an accident if the precautions that would avert it were not taken, was high, then it would appear, in light of our discussion of L and B, that the shipowner was negligent in failing to take one of the precautions that we have mentioned. But probably P was low. There was no reason for a longshoreman to reenter a hold after he had completed his work there and moved on to another part of the ship. The plaintiff speculates that Huck may have left a piece of clothing in hold number 1 and gone back to retrieve it. It does not seem very likely that anyone would enter a pitch-black hold to retrieve a glove or a sock or a jacket, when he could easily ask for light. It is far more likely that Huck entered for an illicit purpose. This would not defeat a recovery if the shipowner were negligent; neither assumption of risk nor contributory negligence is a defense to liability in a negligence action under section 905(b). See S.Rep.No.1125, supra, at 12; 1A Benedict on Admiralty §§ 116–17 (7th ed. 1981). But Huck's motive in entering hold number 1 bears on the probability of the accident and hence on the cost-justified level of precautions by the shipowner. Cf. *Clemons v. Mitsui O.S.K. Lines, Ltd.*, 596 F.2d 746, 750 n.17 (7th Cir. 1979). Unless it is common for longshoremen to try to pilfer from darkened holds—and it was the plaintiff's burden to show that it is—the shipowner would have no reason to think it so likely that a longshoreman would be in a darkened hold as to require precautions against his falling through an open hatch.

Moreover, the relevant probability, so far as the Hand formula is concerned, is not the probability that a longshoreman would enter a darkened hold but the probability that he would fall into an open hatch in such a hold. The probability was small. The darkness was as effective a warning of danger as a sign would have been. Any longshoreman would know that there was a hatch on the floor and he could not rationally assume that it was closed. Only a reckless person would walk about in the hold in these circumstances, especially if he had no flashlight; Huck had none. There are reckless people as there are dishonest people; but the plaintiff did not try to prove that there are so many reckless dishonest longshoremen as to require the precautions that the defendant in this case would have had to take to avert injury to them.

We do not know whether Huck was aware of the custom of opening the hatches after the longshoremen left the hold, and for the reasons just suggested it is not critical whether he was or not. But probably he was. His body was found well forward of where he would have fallen had he walked straight into the hold. No doubt he was trying to skirt what he knew to be an open hatch. The shipowner was not required to anticipate that a longshoreman knowing of the open shaft would not be able to avoid it; this was possible—it happened—but the probability was too remote to warrant precautions beyond the implicit warning of darkness itself.

Another factor bearing on the probability of an accident is that Huck was under the general supervision of the stevedore company that employed him. Even if the defendant should have regarded Huck as no better than a sheep wandering about the ship with no rational concern for his own safety, it was entitled to regard the stevedore as his principal shepherd. The stevedore had a work rule forbidding longshoremen to be anywhere on the ship except where stevedoring operations were actually in progress. The shipowner was entitled to rely on the stevedore to enforce this rule, if not 100 percent at least enough to make it highly improbable, in light of the other circumstances that we have discussed, that one of the longshoremen would stray away from the rest and fall into a darkened hold.

The fact that the practice of leaving the hatches open in darkened holds was customary (or so the jury could find) and not just an idiosyncrasy of this Yugoslavian ship or shipowner has additional relevance to this case. Although custom is not a defense to a charge of negligence, The T. J. Hooper, 60 F.2d 737, 740 (2d Cir. 1932), it is a material consideration in evaluating the charge, especially where the victim and the alleged tortfeasor are linked, even if indirectly, in a voluntary relationship, as they were here. If a shipowner were to follow a practice that flunked the Hand formula—that in other words was not cost-justified, because the expected accident costs associated with the practice exceeded the costs of abandoning the practice and so preventing any accident from happening—then he would have to pay his stevedores higher rates, to compensate them for the additional risk to their employees, the longshoremen, whom the stevedores must compensate under 33 U.S.C. § 904, regardless of fault, for any injury the longshoremen sustain in the course of their employment. And since by hypothesis the cost to the stevedores of the additional compensation—the expected accident cost, in other words—would exceed the cost of abandoning the practice (for otherwise the practice would be cost-justified), it would pay the shipowner to abandon it. Cf. Coase, *The Problem of Social Cost*, 3 J.L. & Econ. 1 (1961). Hence if the shipowner persists in a dangerous practice—if the whole trade persists in the practice-that is some evidence, though not conclusive, that the practice is cost-justified, and not negligent.

But all this is not to say that the defendant's conduct in this case was, in fact, nonnegligent. We are not the triers of fact. The jury found the defendant nonnegligent and our job is just to decide whether a reasonable jury could have so found. Obviously we think the jury's finding was reasonable, just like the district court's finding of nonnegligence in *Grayson v. Cordial Shipping Co.*, 496 F.2d 710, 715 (7th Cir. 1974), a previous darkened-hold case in this circuit. The plaintiff has cited to us a number of darkened-hold cases where jury verdicts for plaintiffs were upheld, but none where a jury verdict for the defendant was set aside on the ground that the facts showed negligence as a matter of law. *Badalamenti v. United States*, 160 F.2d 422 (2d Cir. 1947), heavily relied on by the plaintiff, is an example of a case where a finding of negligence was upheld. Like the other cases cited by the plaintiff it is factually distinguishable from the present case. There was no partition between the lighted and unlighted parts of the cargo area; and the longshoreman was injured while searching for rope that the shipowner had undertaken to provide for stevedoring operations and had left in an unlighted part of the deck. P was therefore higher than in this case. Also, there was no mention of any evidence of a custom of leaving the hatch open in darkened holds. But the more fundamental distinction is that the court in *Badalamenti* was upholding a judgment for the longshoreman, not, as we are being asked to do here, reversing a judgment against him.

\* \* \*

The judgment appealed from is

AFFIRMED.

### NOTES

**1. The Hand Formula.** In *United States v. Carroll Towing Co.*, 159 F.2d 169 (2d Cir.1947), the defendant's tug caused the plaintiff's barge to become unmoored. The barge collided against a tanker and began taking in water. Since the plaintiff's bargee was not on the barge at the time of the accident, the leak was not discovered and the barge sank. Had the bargee been on board, he would have promptly discovered the leak and would have been able to enlist the help of other ships to tow it to shore, thus saving the barge and the cargo. In evaluating the issue of the plaintiff's contributory negligence, the court had to consider the reasonableness of the bargee's absence from the ship during normal working hours. To aid his analysis of reasonableness, Judge Learned Hand articulated and applied what is now known as the "Hand formula," which has now been used to analyze negligence of both plaintiffs and defendants:

> [T]here is no general rule to determine when the absence of a bargee or other attendant will make the owner of the barge liable for injuries to other vessels if she breaks away from her moorings. However, in any cases where he would be so liable for injuries to others obviously he must reduce his damages proportionately, if the injury is to his own barge. It becomes apparent why there can be no such general rule, when we consider the grounds for such a liability. Since there are occasions when every vessel will break from her moorings, and since, if she does, she becomes a menace to those about her; the owner's duty, as in other similar situations, to provide against resulting injuries is a function of three variables: (1) The probability that she will break away; (2) the gravity of the resulting injury, if she does; (3) the burden of adequate precautions. Possibly it serves to bring this notion into relief to state it in algebraic terms: if the probability be called P; the injury, L; and the burden, B; liability depends upon whether B is less than L multiplied by P: i.e., whether $B < PL$. Applied to the situation at bar, the likelihood that a barge will break from her fasts and the damage she will do, vary with the place and time; for example, if a storm threatens, the danger is greater; so it is, if she is in a crowded harbor where moored barges are constantly being shifted about. On the other hand, the barge must not be the bargee's prison, even

though he lives aboard; he must go ashore at times. We need not say whether, even in such crowded waters as New York Harbor a bargee must be aboard at night at all; it may be that the custom is otherwise ... and that, if so, the situation is one where custom should control. We leave that question open; but we hold that it is not in all cases a sufficient answer to a bargee's absence without excuse, during working hours, that he has properly made fast his barge to a pier, when he leaves her. In the case at bar the bargee left at five o'clock in the afternoon of January 3rd, and the flotilla broke away at about two o'clock in the afternoon of the following day, twenty-one hours afterwards. The bargee had been away all the time, and we hold that ... he had no excuse for his absence. At the locus in quo—especially during the short January days and in the full tide of war activity—barges were being constantly "drilled" in and out. Certainly it was not beyond reasonable expectation that, with the inevitable haste and bustle, the work might not be done with adequate care. In such circumstances we hold—and it is all that we do hold—that it was a fair requirement that the [plaintiff] Conners Company should have a bargee aboard (unless he had some excuse for his absence), during the working hours of daylight.

**2. The Value of the Hand Formula.** Do you agree with Judge Posner that the Hand formula (Burden (B) < Probability (P) X Loss (L)) is a useful way to determine whether or not the defendant has acted reasonably or breached the requisite standard of conduct? Should it be possible in some cases to translate the risks versus the benefits of a defendant's behavior into quantitative terms? Under negligence the factfinder must also evaluate what the reasonable person of ordinary intelligence would have found reasonable. Consequently proof that conduct was unreasonably dangerous does not necessarily demonstrate that the reasonable person would have been intelligent and knowledgeable enough to realize his conduct violated the risk versus benefit formula inherent in the Hand formula. See Diamond, Levine & Madden, Understanding Torts (2nd Ed. 2000), § 4.02; Dobbs, The Law of Torts (2000) §§ 143–146.

**3. The Restatement.** The Restatement (Second) of Torts also uses a risk/utility analysis to determine the reasonableness of an actor's conduct. See Restatement (Second) of Torts § 291. To guide the analysis, section 293 lists the following criteria for evaluating risk:

(a) the social value which the law attaches to the interests which are imperiled;

(b) the extent of the chance that the actor's conduct will cause an invasion of any interest of the other or of one of a class of which the other is a member;

(c) the extent of the harm likely to be caused to the interests imperiled;

(d) the number of persons whose interests are likely to be invaded if the risk takes effect in harm.

As for the utility of the actor's conduct, section 292 lists the following factors:

(a) the social value which the law attaches to the interest which is to be advanced or protected by the conduct;

(b) the extent of the chance that this interest will be advanced or protected by the particular course of conduct;

(c) the extent of the chance that such interest can be adequately advanced or protected by another and less dangerous course of conduct.

In *Moning v. Alfono*, 400 Mich. 425, 254 N.W.2d 759 (Mich. 1977), a case involving a child who was blinded in one eye when a pellet fired from his friend's slingshot ricocheted off a tree, the Supreme Court of Michigan applied the Restatement rubric and reversed a directed verdict for the defendants, who had marketed the slingshots directly to children. Regarding risk, the court noted the high social value in preventing blindness, the danger of slingshots, the seriousness of potential injuries, and the large number of children at risk of injury. The court attached little utility to marketing slingshots directly to children, noting that social opinion tends to oppose it, that children are more likely to acquire slingshots that are marketed directly to children, and that marketing slingshots to adults instead of children would help reduce risk since adults who know a particular child are in a better position to judge the child's responsibility and since the adults would be liable for any damage caused.

**4. An Economic Approach to Negligence.** As a University of Chicago law professor prior to his appointment to the United States Court of Appeals, Judge Posner, author of the principal case, became one of the most prominent leaders of the law and economics school of legal thought. Consider his characterization of the Hand formula in economic terms:

> Hand was adumbrating, perhaps unwittingly, an economic meaning of negligence. Discounting (multiplying) the cost of an accident if it occurs by the probability of occurrence yields a measure of the economic benefit to be anticipated from incurring the costs necessary to prevent the accident. The cost of prevention is what Hand meant by the burden of taking precautions against the accident. It may be the cost of installing safety equipment or otherwise making the activity safer, or the benefit forgone by curtailing or eliminating the activity. If the cost of safety measures or of curtailment— whichever cost is lower—exceeds the benefit in accident avoidance to be gained by incurring that cost, society would be better off, in economic terms, to forgo accident prevention. A rule making the enterprise liable for the accidents that occur in such cases cannot be justified on the ground that it will induce the enterprise to increase the safety of its operations. When the cost of accidents is less than the cost of prevention, a rational profit-maximizing enterprise will pay tort judgments to the accident victims rather than incur the larger cost of avoiding liability. Furthermore, overall economic value or welfare would be diminished rather than increased by incurring a higher accident-prevention cost in order to avoid a lower accident cost. If, on the other hand, the benefits in accident avoidance exceed the cost of prevention, society is better off if those costs are incurred and the accident averted, and so in this case the enterprise is made liable, in the expectation that self-interest will lead it to adopt the precautions in order to avoid a greater cost in tort judgments.

Posner, *A Theory of Negligence*, 1 J. Legal Stud. 29 (1972). This theory is of course consistent with an approach to law that has as its goal the minimization of costs to society. But if other functions of tort law are held to be more important than social efficiency, such as compensation for damages, accident prevention, or some scheme of fairness, might a different approach to tort liability be more viable than the above cost/benefit approach? As you read the strict liability materials, Chapter 5, Sec. A, infra, see if your perspective on these issues changes.

**5. Custom.** As the principal case indicates, custom is generally accepted as evidence of what constitutes reasonable conduct. Nevertheless, in most negligence cases (the professional standard is an exception, see infra Chapter 2, Sec. B), the finder of fact, ordinarily the jury, is free to determine that an industry's or community's custom is unreasonable and hence negligent. Do you agree with Judge Posner's conclusion in the principal case that an industry's custom ordinarily reflects efficient behavior? Consider how important you think the jury considered the local food industry's customary temperature to heat coffee in the McDonald's case below. See generally Diamond, Levine & Madden, supra, § 4.03, and Keeton, supra, § 33.

**6. The McDonald's Coffee Case.** In 1994 a McDonald's customer purchased coffee at a drive-through window. As the customer drove off, she held the coffee in her lap and removed the lid to add cream and sugar. The coffee spilled and caused third degree burns which required skin grafts and a week-long hospital stay. She sued.

McDonald's serves its coffee at 180 to 190 degrees in order to meet the demand of its customers, who, according to the results of McDonald's focus groups, desire coffee that is hot enough to steam. Coffee industry spokespersons say that McDonald's conforms to industry standards regarding the temperature of its coffee. Additionally, one coffee connoisseur has said that 175 degrees is the optimal temperature for brewing coffee. But when McDonald's began defending the suit, it hired a law student to check the temperature of coffee at other local restaurants. The student found that none served coffee hotter than about 160 degrees.

At the trial, a burn expert testified that 190 degree coffee takes about three seconds to cause a third degree burn, 180 degree coffee about twelve to fifteen seconds, and 160 degree coffee about twenty seconds. In the decade prior to the case, McDonald's had received over 700 reports of coffee burns and paid out over $500,000 in burn related settlements. But another expert testified that since McDonald's sells about one billion cups of coffee annually, this was a negligible number of complaints.

The jury disagreed. It returned a verdict for $2.9 million consisting of nearly $200,000 in compensatory damages, and punitive damages equal to two days of McDonald's coffee sales, or about $2.7 million. The judge, however, reduced the award to approximately half of a million dollars. The parties eventually settled.

See Gerlin, *A Matter of Degree: How a Jury Decided That a Coffee Spill is Worth 2.9 Million*, Wall Street Journal, Sept. 1, 1994, at A1. See also Rhode, *Too Much Law, Too Little Justice: Too Much Rhetoric, Too Little Reform*, 11 Geo. J. Legal Ethics 989 (1998).

How would you analyze these facts in terms of the Hand formula? Do you agree with the jury's evaluation? Bear the Hand formula in mind as you read the following article.

Peter Fimrite, *Cables to Plug Fatal Bridge GAP\**
San Francisco Chronicle, Dec. 24, 1997, at A1.

Golden Gate Bridge workers will begin stringing cables today across a gap on the north bridge approach where a 2–year-old girl fell to her death during a family outing.

The system of two parallel cables was designed hurriedly amid accusations that bridge officials allowed a dangerous condition to exist in violation of state regulations.

Bridge district engineer Mervin Giacomini said yesterday that two horizontal cables four inches apart will be installed by the end of the month on the east-side pedestrian walkway, where the accident occurred.

"We think this is the very best way we can close the gap," Giacomini said at a news conference yesterday. "It provides a barrier, and it also allows for simple installation quickly."

The girl, Gauri Govil of Fremont, tripped over a curb Sunday and fell through a 9 1/2–inch gap between the sidewalk and the roadway. She plunged 170 feet to her death as family members screamed in horror. Her father captured the scene on videotape.

The resulting uproar forced bridge officials to develop a system quickly to block access to the opening, which extends 1,200 feet on both sides of the north viaduct of the bridge, near Vista Point.

The gap is between five and six inches wide along the rest of the 1.7–mile suspension bridge because a steel reinforcing beam blocks a portion of the opening. Giacomini said cables will not be strung immediately on the suspension portion of the bridge, pending further evaluation.

\* \* \*

"Even though the probability of this happening again would be very low, this is the prudent thing to do," Giacomini said.

The walkway where the accident occurred was replaced in 1985 as part of a project to widen the highway from 60 to 62 feet. At the same time, the sidewalk was widened from 4 ½ feet to about 10 feet, and the design allowed for a 9 1/2–inch gap between the roadway and walkway.

*Design Reasons for the Gap*

The space was included so water and debris can drain off the bridge and to minimize rocking during high winds. It also was designed as a buffer in the event that a car slams into the divider separating the sidewalk and roadway.

Giacomini said the gap complied with the state Uniform Building Code when the designs were completed in the late 1970s. The code, however, was changed to allow only a six-inch gap between the time the designs were drawn and the project was completed.

\* \* \*

\* © The San Francisco Chronicle reprinted with permission.

*Changing State Codes*

Giacomini said the district would need to change the design of the bridge every few years if it attempted to comply with every code change. He said that until the fatal accident, nobody had ever complained about the gap, let alone fallen into it.

"We have a very good record of recognizing hazards, but it was not evident that this was a hazard," Giacomini said. "The issue is whether you replace a large component of the bridge to comply with changing codes."

Giacomini said a damage claim filed by a New York man who was thrown onto the roadway after his tire allegedly got caught in the same gap is a different issue. A bicycle railing, now being designed, would solve that problem, he said.

# SECTION B.   STANDARD OF CONDUCT

## CORDAS v. PEERLESS TRANSP. CO.

City Court of New York, New York County.
27 N.Y.S.2d 198 (1941).

CARLIN, Justice.

This case presents the ordinary man—that problem child of the law—in a most bizarre setting. As a lowly chauffeur in defendant's employ he became in a trice the protagonist in a breach-bating drama with a denouement almost tragic. It appears that a man, whose identity it would be indelicate to divulge, was feloniously relieved of his portable goods by two nondescript highwaymen in an alley near 26th Street and Third Avenue, Manhattan; they induced him to relinquish his possessions by a strong argument ad hominem couched in the convincing cant of the criminal and pressed at the point of a most persuasive pistol. Laden with their loot, but not thereby impeded, they took an abrupt departure and he, shuffling off the coil of that discretion which enmeshed him in the alley, quickly gave chase through 26th Street toward 2nd Avenue, whither they were resorting 'with expedition swift as thought' for most obvious reasons. Somewhere on that thoroughfare of escape they indulged the stratagem of separation ostensibly to disconcert their pursuer and allay the ardor of his pursuit. He then centered on for capture the man with the pistol whom he saw board defendant's taxicab, which quickly veered south toward 25th Street on 2nd Avenue where he saw the chauffeur jump out while the cab, still in motion, continued toward 24th Street; after the chauffeur relieved himself of the cumbersome burden of his fare the latter also is said to have similarly departed from the cab before it reached 24th Street. The chauffeur's story is substantially the same except that he states that his uninvited guest boarded the cab at 25th Street while it was at a standstill waiting for a less colorful fare; that his 'passenger' immediately advised him 'to stand not upon the order of his going but to go at once' and added finality to his command by an appropriate gesture with a pistol addressed to his sacroiliac. The chauffeur in reluctant acquiescence proceeded about fifteen feet, when his hair, like unto the quills of the fretful porcupine, was made to stand on end by the hue and cry of the man despoiled accompanied by a clamourous concourse of the law-abiding which paced him as he ran; the concatenation of 'stop thief', to which the patter of persistent feet did maddingly beat time, rang in his ears as the pursuing posse all the while gained on the receding cab with its quarry therein contained. The hold-up man sensing his insecurity suggested to the chauffeur that in the event there was the slightest lapse in obedience to his curt command that he, the chauffeur, would suffer the loss of his brains, a prospect as horrible to an humble chauffeur as it undoubtedly would be to one of the intelligentsia. The chauffeur apprehensive of certain dissolution from either Scylla, the pursuers, or Charybdis, the pursued, quickly threw his car out of first speed in which he was proceeding, pulled on the emergency, jammed on his brakes and, although he thinks the motor was still running, swung open the door to his left and jumped out of his car. He confesses that the only act that smacked of intelligence was that by which he jammed the brakes in order to throw off balance the hold-up man who was half-standing and half-sitting with his pistol menacingly poised. Thus abandoning his car and passenger the chauffeur sped toward 26th Street and then turned to look; he saw the cab proceeding south toward 24th Street where it mounted the sidewalk. The plaintiff-mother and her two infant children were there injured by the cab which, at the time, appeared to be also minus its passenger who, it appears, was apprehended in the cellar of a local hospital where he was pointed out to a police officer by a remnant of the posse, hereinbefore mentioned. He did not appear at the trial. The three aforesaid plaintiffs and the husband-father sue the defendant for damages predicating their respective causes of action upon the contention that the chauffeur was negligent in abandoning the cab under the aforesaid circumstances. Fortunately the injuries sustained were comparatively slight. Negligence has been variously defined but the common legal acceptation is the failure to exercise that care and caution which a reasonable and prudent person ordinarily would exercise under like conditions or circumstances. It has been most authoritatively held that "negligence in the abstract, apart from things related, is surely not a tort, if indeed it is understandable at all." Cardozo, C. J., in *Palsgraf v. Long Island Railroad Co.*, 248 N.Y. 339, 345, 162 N.E. 99, 101, 59 A.L.R. 1253. In *Steinbrenner v. M. W. Forney Co.*, 143 App.Div. 73, 127 N.Y.S. 620, 622 it is said, 'The test of actionable negligence is what reasonably prudent men would have done under the same circumstances'; *Connell v. New York Central & Hudson River Railroad Co.*, 144 App.Div. 664, 129 N.Y.S. 666, 669, holds that actionable negligence must be predicated upon "a breach of duty to the plaintiff. Negligence is 'not absolute or intrinsic,' but 'is always relevant to some circumstances of time, place or person.'" In slight paraphrase of the world's first bard it may be truly observed that the expedition of the chauffeur's violent love of his own security outran the pauser, reason, when he was suddenly confronted with unusual emergency which 'took his reason prisoner'. The learned attorney for the plaintiffs concedes that the chauffeur acted in an emergency but claims a right to recovery upon the following proposition taken verbatim from his brief: 'It is respectfully submitted that the value of the interests of the public at large to be immune from being injured by a dangerous instrumentality such as a car unattended while in motion is very superior to the right of a driver of a motor vehicle to abandon same while it is in motion even when acting under the belief that his life is in danger and by abandoning same he will save his life'. To hold thus under the facts adduced herein would be tantamount to a repeal by implication of the primal law of nature written in indelible characters upon the fleshy tablets of sentient creation by the Almighty Law-giver, 'the supernal Judge who sits on high'. There are those who stem the turbulent current for bubble fame, or who bridge the yawning chasm with a leap for the leap's sake or who 'outstare the sternest eyes that look outbrave the heart most daring on the earth, pluck the young sucking cubs from the she-bear, yea, mock the lion when he roars for prey' to win a fair lady and these are the admiration of the generality of men; but they are made of sterner stuff than the ordinary man upon whom the law places no duty of emulation. The law would indeed be fond if it imposed upon the ordinary man the obligation to so demean himself when suddenly confronted with a danger, not of his creation, disregarding the likelihood that such a contingency may darken the intellect and palsy the will of the common legion of the earth, the fraternity of ordinary men,—whose acts or omissions under certain conditions or circumstances make the yardstick by which the law measures culpability or innocence, negligence or care. If a person is placed in a sudden peril from which death might ensue, the law does not impel another to the rescue of the person endangered nor does it condemn him for his unmoral failure to rescue when he can; this is in recognition of the immutable law written in frail flesh. Returning to our chauffeur. If the philosophic Horatio and the martial companions of his watch were 'distilled almost to jelly with the act of fear' when they beheld "in the dead vast and middle of the night" the disembodied spirit of Hamlet's father stalk majestically by "with a countenance more in sorrow than in anger" was not the chauffeur, though unacquainted with the example of these eminent men-at-arms, more amply justified in his fearsome reactions when he was more palpably confronted by a thing of flesh and blood bearing in its hand an engine of destruction which depended for its lethal purpose upon the quiver of a hair? When Macbeth was cross-examined by Macduff as to any reason he could advance for his sudden despatch of Duncan's grooms he said in plausible answer 'Who can be wise, amazed, temperate and furious, loyal and neutral, in a moment? No ma''. Macbeth did not by a 'tricksy word' thereby stand justified as he criminally created the emergency from which he sought escape by indulgence in added felonies to divert suspicion to the innocent. However, his words may be wrested to the advantage of the defendant's chauffeur whose acts cannot be legally construed as the proximate cause of plaintiff's injuries, however regrettable, unless nature's first law is arbitrarily disregarded. Plaintiff's attorney in his brief cites the cases of *Grunfelder v. Brooklyn Heights Railroad Co.*, 143 App.Div. 89, 127 N.Y.S. 1085, and *Savage v. Joseph H. Bauland Co.*, 42 App.Div. 285, 58 N.Y.S. 1014, as authorities for a contrary holding. Neither case is apposite in fact nor principle. In the classic case of *Laidlaw v. Sage*, 158 N.Y. 73, 89, 90, 52 N.E. 679, 685, 44 L.R.A. 216, is found a statement of the law peculiarly apropos: "That the duties and responsibilities of a person confronted with such a danger are different and unlike those which follow his actions in performing the ordinary duties of life under other conditions is a well-established principle of law. * * * 'The law presumes that *an act or omission done or neglected under the influence of pressing danger was done or neglected involuntarily.*' It is there said that this rule seems to be founded upon the maxim that self-preservation is the first law of nature, and that, where it is a question whether one of two men shall suffer, each is justified in doing the best he can for himself". (Italics ours.) *Kolanka v. Erie Railroad Co.*, 215 App.Div. 82, 86, 212 N.Y.S. 714, 717, says: "The law in this state does not hold one in an emergency to the exercise of that mature judgment required of him under circumstances where he has an opportunity for deliberate action. He is not required to exercise unerring judgment, which would be expected of him, were he not confronted with an emergency requiring prompt action". The circumstances provide the foil by which the act is brought into relief to determine whether it is or is not negligent. If under normal circumstances an act is done which might be considered negligent it does not follow as a corollary that a similar act is negligent if performed by a person acting under an emergency, not of his own making, in which he suddenly is faced with a patent danger with a moment left to adopt a means of extrication. The chauffeur—the ordinary man in this case—acted in a split second in a most harrowing experience. To call him negligent would be to brand him coward; the court does not do so in spite of what those swaggering heroes, 'whose valor plucks dead lions by the beard', may bluster to the contrary. The court is loathe to see the plaintiffs go without recovery even though their damages were slight, but cannot hold the defendant liable upon the facts adduced at the trial. Motions, upon which decision was reserved, to dismiss the complaint are granted with exceptions to plaintiffs. Judgment for defendant against plaintiffs dismissing their complaint upon the merits. Ten days' stay and thirty days to make a case.

### NOTES

**1. Reasonableness in the Context of Circumstance.** Courts evaluate the "reasonableness" of the defendant's conduct in the context of the circumstances confronting the defendant. Consequently, courts allow the jury to consider, in its determination of the defendant's reasonableness, evidence that the defendant was acting under emergency circumstances. The Restatement (Second) of Torts articulates the generally accepted view as follows:

> (1) In determining whether the conduct is negligent toward another, the fact that the actor is confronted with a sudden emergency which requires a rapid decision is a factor in determining the reasonable character of his choice of action.

(2) The fact that the actor is not negligent after the emergency has arisen does not preclude his liability for his tortious conduct which has produced the emergency.

Restatement (Second) of Torts § 296. See also Keeton, *Prosser and Keeton on* The Law of Torts § 33 (5th ed. 1984); Diamond, Levine & Madden, *Understanding Torts* § 3.04 (2nd ed. 2000); and Dobbs, *The Law of Torts* § 129 (2000).

**2. Anticipated Emergencies.** Even courts that accept the emergency charge find it inappropriate where the emergency should have been anticipated. Consider *Roberts v. The Estate of Randall*, 51 P.3d 204 (2002) where two parties snowmobiling in opposite directions collided at the crest of a hill when both swerved in the same direction to avoid a collision. The Montana court found the sudden emergency doctrine inapplicable to the case of a snowmobiling accident. It noted that "some emergencies must be anticipated, and the actor must be prepared to meet with them when he engages in an activity in which they are likely to arise." In this case, the court noted that "this very emergency was one that Roberts should have anticipated . . . when he engaged in snowmobiling activity. Consider also *Malinowski v. United Parcel Service*, 727 A.2d 194 (1999), where the driver of a UPS truck claimed that it was a sudden emergency when a fourteen year old boy was pushed by his friend in front of the truck, even though he had seen the boys playing from 300 feet away. The Supreme Court of Rhode Island held that the sudden emergency charge was inapplicable. The court found "that the maxim that one is not bound to anticipate another's negligence is at odds with the duties placed upon drivers to exercise due care to avoid colliding with any pedestrians."

**3. Emergency Charge.** Traditionally trial courts have been required to give the jury a special instruction or "charge" underscoring that a reasonable person in a sudden emergency should not be expected to respond as wisely as a reasonable person allowed the luxury to contemplate his actions under more leisurely and less pressured circumstances. For example, in *Rivera v. New York City Transit Authority*, 77 N.Y.2d 322, 567 N.Y.S.2d 629, 569 N.E.2d 432 (N.Y. 1991), the court overturned a judgment against the Transit Authority based on the failure of a subway motorman to stop a train after the victim had fallen onto the track. The court reversed the verdict for the plaintiff since a special emergency charge was not given to the jury. The court reasoned "[a] person in such an emergency situation cannot reasonably be held to the same accuracy of judgment or conduct as one who has had full opportunity to reflect even though it later appears that the actor made the wrong decision."

**4. Recent Rejection of Emergency Charge.** Some recent decisions have rejected the practice of an "emergency" instruction as redundant and misleading since negligence liability is only imposed when the defendant acted unreasonably under the circumstances. For example, in *Lyons v. Midnight Sun Trans. Servs. Inc.*, 928 P.2d 1202 (Alaska 1996), the Supreme Court of Alaska concluded:

We believe that the sudden emergency instruction is a generally useless appendage to the law of negligence. With or without an emergency, the standard of care a person must exercise is still that of a reasonable person under the circumstances. With or without the instruction, parties are still entitled to present evidence at trial which will establish what the circumstances were, and are also entitled to argue to the jury that they acted as a reasonable person would have in light of those circumstances. Thus, barring circumstances that we cannot at the moment hypothesize, a sudden emergency instruction serves no positive function.

But also consider *Lockhart v. List*, 542 Pa. 141, 665 A.2d 1176 (Pa. 1995), where the Supreme Court of Pennsylvania rejected arguments to abolish the emergency charge:

> The trial court ... found that the doctrine is nothing more than a redefinition of standard negligence principles, i.e., a person is always held to a standard of reasonable care under the circumstances, and that to give such a charge produces confusion. We disagree.
>
> Admittedly, a handful of other states have abolished or severely limited the use of the sudden emergency doctrine based principally upon the belief that the doctrine implies that ordinary rules of negligence are inapplicable to circumstances constituting a so-called emergency. We think, however, that a properly drawn instruction explaining the sudden emergency doctrine, in the proper circumstances, only serves to further clarify for the jury the applicable law. The doctrine itself is far from complex. It does not obliterate the "reasonable man" standard or serve to excuse one from fault, but rather explains to the jury the standard by which to judge the person's behavior in consideration of the emergency.

The Proposed Final Draft to the Restatement (Third) of Torts acknowledges the advantages and disadvantages of giving an emergency charge to the jury, but does not endorse one side over the other. Restatement (Third) of Torts, § 7 comments a, c, d.

## BREUNIG v. AMERICAN FAMILY INSURANCE COMPANY

Supreme Court of Wisconsin.
45 Wis.2d 536, 173 N.W.2d 619 (1970).

Appeal from a judgment of the Circuit Court for Dane County: Norris E. Maloney, Circuit Judge. *Affirmed.*

This is an action by Phillip A. Breunig to recover damages for personal injuries which he received when his truck was struck by an automobile driven by Erma Veith and insured by the defendant American Family Insurance Company (Insurance Company). The accident happened about 7:00 o'clock in the morning of January 28, 1966, on highway 19 a mile west of Sun Prairie, while Mrs. Veith was returning home from taking her husband to work. Mrs. Veith's car was proceeding west in the eastbound lane and struck the left side of the plaintiff's car near its rear end while Breunig was attempting to get off the road to his right and avoid a head-on collision.

The Insurance Company alleged Erma Veith was not negligent because just prior to the collision she suddenly and without warning was seized with a mental aberration or delusion which rendered her unable to operate the automobile with her conscious mind.

The jury returned a verdict finding her causally negligent on the theory she had knowledge or forewarning of her mental delusions or disability. The jury also found Breunig's damages to be $10,000. The court, on motions after verdict, reduced the amount of damages to $7,000, approved the verdict's finding of negligence, and gave Breunig the option of a new trial or the lower amount of damages. Breunig elected to accept the lower amount and judgment was accordingly entered. The defendant insurance company appeals.

HALLOWS, Chief Justice.

There is no question that Erma Veith was subject at the time of the accident to an insane delusion which directly affected her ability to operate her car in an ordinarily prudent manner and caused the accident. The specific question considered by the jury under the negligence inquiry was whether she had such foreknowledge of her susceptibility to such a mental aberration, delusion or hallucination as to make her negligent in driving a car at all under such conditions.

At the trial Erma Veith testified she could not remember all the circumstances of the accident and this was confirmed by her psychiatrist who testified this loss of memory was due to his treatment of Erma Veith for her mental illness. This expert also testified to what Erma Veith had told him but could no longer recall. The evidence established that Mrs. Veith, while returning home after taking her husband to work, saw a white light on the back of a car ahead of her. She followed this light for three or four blocks. Mrs. Veith did not remember anything else except landing in a field, lying on the side of the road and people talking. She recalled awaking in the hospital.

The psychiatrist testified Mrs. Veith told him she was driving on a road when she believed that God was taking ahold of the steering wheel and was directing her car. She saw the truck coming and stepped on the gas in order to become air-borne because she knew she could fly because Batman does it. To her surprise she was not air-borne before striking the truck but after the impact she was flying.

Actually, Mrs. Veith's car continued west on highway 19 for about a mile. The road was straight for this distance and then made a gradual turn to the right. At this turn her car left the road in a straight line, negotiated a deep ditch and came to rest in a cornfield. When a traffic officer came to the car to investigate the accident, he found Mrs. Veith sitting behind the wheel looking off into space. He could not get a statement of any kind from her. She was taken to the Methodist Hospital and later transferred to the psychiatric ward of the Madison General Hospital.

The psychiatrist testified Erma Veith was suffering from "schizophrenic reaction, paranoid type, acute."[1] He stated that from the time

---

1. In layman's language, the doctor explained: "The schizophrenic reaction is a thinking disorder of a severe type usually implying disorientation with the world. Usually implying a break with reality. The paranoid type is a subdivision of the think-ing disorder in which one perceives oneself either as a very powerful or being persecuted or being attacked by other people. And acute implies that the rapidity of the onset of the illness, the speed of onset is meant by acute."

Mrs. Veith commenced following the car with the white light and ending with the stopping of her vehicle in the cornfield, she was not able to operate the vehicle with her conscious mind and that she had no knowledge or forewarning that such illness or disability would likely occur.

The Insurance Company argues Erma Veith was not negligent as a matter of law because there is no evidence upon which the jury could find that she had knowledge or warning or should have reasonably foreseen that she might be subject to a mental delusion which would suddenly cause her to lose control of the car. Plaintiff argues there was such evidence of forewarning and also suggests Erma Veith should be liable because insanity should not be a defense in negligence cases.

The case was tried on the theory that some forms of insanity are a defense to and preclude liability for negligence under the doctrine of *Theisen v. Milwaukee Automobile Mut. Ins. Co.* (1962), 18 Wis.2d 91, 118 N.W.2d 140, 119 N.W.2d 393. We agree. Not all types of insanity vitiate responsibility for a negligent tort. The question of liability in every case must depend upon the kind and nature of the insanity. The effect of the mental illness or mental hallucinations or disorder must be such as to affect the person's ability to understand and appreciate the duty which rests upon him to drive his car with ordinary care, or if the insanity does not affect such understanding and appreciation, it must affect his ability to control his car in an ordinarily prudent manner. And in addition, there must be an absence of notice of forewarning to the person that he may be suddenly subject to such a type of insanity or mental illness.

In *Theisen* we recognized one was not negligent if he was unable to conform his conduct through no fault of his own but held a sleeping driver negligent as a matter of law because one is always given conscious warnings of drowsiness and if a person does not heed such warnings and continues to drive his car, he is negligent for continuing to drive under such conditions. But we distinguished those exceptional cases of loss of consciousness resulting from injury inflicted by an outside force, or fainting, or heart attack, or epileptic seizure, or other illness which suddenly incapacitates the driver of an automobile when the occurrence of such disability is not attended with sufficient warning or should not have been reasonably foreseen.

*Theisen* followed *Eleason v. Western Casualty & Surety Co.* (1948), 254 Wis. 134, 135 N.W.2d 301, and *Wisconsin Natural Gas Co. v. Employers Mutual Liability Ins. Co.* (1953), 263 Wis. 633, 58 N.W.2d 424. In *Eleason* we held the driver, an epileptic, possessed knowledge that he was likely to have a seizure and therefore was negligent in driving a car and responsible for the accident occurring while he had an epileptic seizure. In *Wisconsin Natural Gas Co. v. Employers Mutual Liability Ins. Co., supra*, the sleeping driver possessed knowledge that he was likely to fall asleep and his attempts to stay awake were not sufficient to relieve him of negligence because it was within his control to take effective means to stay awake or cease driving.

There are authorities which generally hold insanity is not a defense in tort cases ... Restatement of Torts, 2d Ed., p. 16, sec. 283B, and appendix (1966) and cases cited therein. These cases rest on the historical view of strict liability without regard to the fault of the individual. Prosser, in his *Law of Torts*, 3d Ed. p. 1028, states this view is a historical survival which originated in the dictum in *Weaver v. Ward* (1616), Hob. 134, 80 English Reports 284, when the action of trespass still rested upon strict liability. He points out that when the modern law developed to the point of holding the defendant liable for negligence, the dictum was repeated in some cases.

The policy basis of holding a permanently insane person liable for his tort is: (1) Where one of two innocent persons must suffer a loss it should be borne by the one who occasioned it; (2) to induce those interested in the estate of the insane person (if he has one) to restrain and control him; and (3) the fear an insanity defense would lead to false claims of insanity to avoid liability. These three grounds were mentioned in the *Guardianship of Meyer* (1935), 218 Wis. 381, 261 N.W. 211, where a farm hand who was insane set fire to his employer's barn. The insurance company paid the loss and filed a claim against the estate of the insane person and was allowed to recover.

In an earlier Wisconsin case involving arson, the same view was taken. *Karow v. Continental Ins. Co.* (1883), 57 Wis. 56, 64, 15 N.W. 27, 30. But it was said in *Karow* that an insane person cannot be said to be negligent. The cases holding an insane person liable for his torts have generally dealt with pre-existing insanity of a permanent nature and the question here presented was neither discussed nor decided. The plaintiff cites *Sforza v. Green Bus Lines* (1934), 150 Misc. 180, 268 N.Y.S. 446; *Shapiro v. Tchernowitz* (1956), 3 Misc.2d 617, 115 N.Y.S.2d 1011; *Johnson v. Lombotte* (1961), 147 Colo. 203, 363 P.2d 165, for holding insanity is not a defense in negligence cases. *Sforza* and *Shapiro* are New York trial court decisions which do not discuss the question here presented and are unconvincing. In *Johnson*, the defendant was under observation by order of the county court and was being treated in a hospital for "chronic schizophrenic state of paranoid type." On the day in question, she wanted to leave the hospital and escaped therefrom and found an automobile standing on a street with its motor running a few blocks from the hospital. She got into the car and drove off, having little or no control of the car. She soon collided with the plaintiff. Later she was adjudged mentally incompetent and committed to a state hospital. *Johnson* is not a case of sudden mental seizure with no forewarning. The defendant knew she was being treated for a mental disorder and hence would not have come under the nonliability rule herein stated.

We think the statement that insanity is no defense is too broad when it is applied to a negligence case where the driver is suddenly overcome without forewarning by a mental disability or disorder which incapacitates him from conforming his conduct to the standards of a reasonable man under like circumstances. These are rare cases indeed, but their rarity is no reason for overlooking their existence and the justification which is the basis of the whole doctrine of liability for negligence, i.e., that it is unjust to hold a man responsible for his conduct which he is incapable of avoiding and which incapability was unknown to him prior to the accident.

We need not reach the question of contributory negligence of an insane person or the question of comparative negligence as those problems are not now presented. All we hold is that a sudden mental incapacity equivalent in its effect to such physical causes as a sudden heart attack, epileptic seizure, stroke, or fainting should be treated alike and not under the general rule of insanity.

An interesting case holding this view in Canada is *Buckley & Toronto Transp. Comm'n v. Smith Transport, Ltd.*, 1946 Ont.Rep. 798, 4 Dom.L.Rep. 721, which is almost identical on the facts with the case at bar. There, the court found no negligence when a truck driver was overcome by a sudden insane delusion that his truck was being operated by remote control of his employer and as a result he was in fact helpless to avert a collision.

The insurance company argues that since the psychiatrist was the only expert witness who testified concerning the mental disability of Mrs. Veith and the lack of forewarning that as a matter of law there was no forewarning and she could not be held negligent; and the trial court should have so held. While there was testimony of friends indicating she was normal for some months prior to the accident, the psychiatrist testifies the origin of her mental illness appeared in August, 1965, prior to the accident. In that month Mrs. Veith visited the Necedah Shrine where she was told the Blessed Virgin had sent her to the shrine. She was told to pray for survival. Since that time she felt it had been revealed to her the end of the world was coming and that she was picked by God to survive. Later she had visions of God judging people and sentencing them to Heaven or Hell; she thought Batman was good and was trying to help save the world and her husband was possessed of the devil. Mrs. Veith told her daughter about her visions.

The question is whether she had warning or knowledge which would reasonably lead her to believe that hallucinations would occur and be such as to affect her driving an automobile. Even though the doctor's testimony is uncontradicted, it need not be accepted by the jury. It is an expert's opinion but it is not conclusive. It is for the jury to decide whether the facts underpinning an expert opinion are true. *Dreher v. United Commercial Travelers* (1921), 173 Wis. 173, 179, 180 N.W. 815; *Bucher v. Wisconsin Centr. R.R.* (1909), 139 Wis. 597, 611, 120 N.W. 518; *Massachusetts Bonding & Ins. Co. v. Industrial Comm.* (1959), 8 Wis.2d 606, 610, 99 N.W.2d 809. The jury could find that a woman, who believed she had a special relationship to God and was the chosen one to survive the end of the world, could believe that God would take over the direction of her life to the extent of driving her car. Since these mental aberrations were not constant, the jury could infer she had knowledge of her condition and the likelihood of a hallucination just as one who has knowledge of a heart condition knows the possibility of an attack. While the evidence may not be strong upon which to base an inference, especially in view of the fact that two jurors dissented on this verdict and expressly stated they could find no evidence of forewarning, nevertheless, the evidence to sustain the verdict of the jury need not constitute the great weight and clear preponderance.

The insurance company claims the jury was perverse because the verdict is contrary both to the evidence and to the law. We think this argument is without merit.

## NOTES

1. **Mental Disability Irrelevant.** The traditional majority rule holds an insane adult person and/or mentally deficient adult person to a reasonable person standard of care. Unlike in criminal law, no dispensation is made under the majority rule for even extreme mental disability. The Restatement (Second) of Torts articulates the generally accepted view as follows:

> Unless the actor is a child, his insanity or other mental deficiency does not relieve the actor from liability for conduct which does not conform to the standard of a reasonable man under like circumstances.

Restatement (Second) of Torts § 283B. See also Keeton, *Prosser and Keeton on* The Law of Torts, § 32 (5th ed. 1984); Diamond, Levine & Madden, *Understanding Torts* § 3.04 (2nd ed. 2000) and Dobbs, *The Law of Torts* § 120 (2000). Is there a reason to distinguish the criminal law's general willingness to allow an insanity defense from the tort law's general rejection of the insanity defense?

2. **Physical Disability Considered.** Note that so-called "physical" as opposed to "mental" disabilities, such as blindness, hearing impairment, heart attack, or seizure, have always been considered "circumstances" which are taken into account in determining whether the individual behaved reasonably. See Restatement (Second) of Torts § 283C. See also *Hammontree v. Jenner*, 20 Cal.App.3d 528, 97 Cal.Rptr. 739 (Cal.Ct.App.1971) (finding no liability for an accident caused by an epileptic seizure). Is the distinction between mental and physical disability valid?

3. **Sudden Insanity.** The majority does not follow the *Breunig* exception, instead holding a mentally ill individual to the reasonable person standard without exception. Consider also, *Burch v. American Family Mutual Insurance Company*, 198 Wis.2d 465, 543 N.W.2d 277 (Wis. 1996), another Wisconsin case, where the court held that the lower court's reliance on the *Breunig* exception was erroneous because the mental deficiency of the plaintiff was not sudden. Rather, the mentally retarded driver was held to the same standard as that applied to a reasonable person for her negligence in operating a vehicle.

4. **Mentally Disabled Can be Contributorily Negligent.** The majority rule refuses to make allowances for mental deficiencies regardless of whether the mentally disabled person is the defendant or the plaintiff. When the mentally disabled is a plaintiff, the issue of his or her conduct becomes central in determining when the recovery is limited by contributory or comparative negligence. (See Defenses Chapter 2, Sec. I, infra.) For example, in *Galindo v. TMT Transport, Inc.*, 152 Ariz. 434, 733 P.2d 631 (App.1986), a man suffering from a paranoid schizophrenic episode ran erratically onto the freeway and was killed. The Court of Appeals of Arizona held that the standard of care in determining whether such a mentally deficient person was contributorily negligent was the same standard of care as was required of an ordinarily careful person under like circumstances. But consider *Jankee v. Clark County*, 235 Wis.2d 700, 612 N.W.2d 297 (2000), in which

the Wisconsin Supreme Court held that the requirement of sudden unanticipated insanity also applied to an analysis of the plaintiff's comparative negligence. In *Jankee* the plaintiff had forewarning of his medical disability because his doctors warned him of this risk if he suspended his medication.

**5. Some New Decisions Consider Plaintiff's Mental Disability.** In what the Supreme Court of New Jersey in *Cowan v. Doering*, 111 N.J. 451, 545 A.2d 159 (1988) characterizes as "the modern trend," several recent decisions have evaluated contributory or comparative negligence in light of the plaintiff's mental capacity. In *Cowan*, the patient brought action for injuries she sustained when she jumped from a second-story window while being treated at the hospital for overdose of sleeping pills. The court held that the behavior of mentally disturbed plaintiffs should not be measured in light of the objective reasonable person standard, but rather "a mentally disturbed plaintiff's conduct should be measured in light of his or her mental capacity." Similarly in *Maunz v. Perales*, 276 Kan. 313, 76 P.3d 1027 (2003), the Supreme Court of Kansas held that the standard of evaluation of fault should be under a capacity-based standard. Maunz, 16 years of age, was released from a mental hospital after a few days of medication and suicide watch on the condition that his parents remove all guns from the house. Maunz shot himself with a shotgun on the second night of his release. The court held that because Maunz had not been completely incapable of caring for himself the jury could rightfully allocate a degree of fault to him. Consider also *Brandvain v. Ridgeview Institute, Inc.*, 188 Ga.App. 106, 372 S.E.2d 265 (App.1988), where a mentally deficient patient's act of suicide did not bar his administratrix, due to contributory negligence, from seeking to recover against the hospital at which he had been a patient. See also *Mochen v. State of New York*, 43 A.D.2d 484, 352 N.Y.S.2d 290 (N.Y.App.Div.1974), where a seventeen-year-old mental patient was able to recover damages resulting from a state hospital's negligence occasioned by the patient's inability to comprehend possible consequences of an attempt to exit from a second story window. Should courts be more inclined to consider mental disability when the mentally disabled person is a plaintiff? Many of the newer decisions considering the plaintiff's mental disability in determining contributory or comparative negligence occur where the defendant is the mentally disabled person's caregiver. Consider, however, *Stacy v. Jedco Construction Inc.*, 119 N.C.App. 115, 457 S.E.2d 875 (1995), where the guardian of a senile man brought action against a construction company for injuries the man sustained while walking without authorization in a construction area of his home. The court held that the man would be held to the standard of care of a person of like mental capacity under similar circumstances.

**6. Caretakers Suing Mentally Disabled Patients.** Some courts have considered the mental deficiency of a defendant when the plaintiff was his or her caretaker. See *Gould v. American Family Mutual Insurance Co.*, 198 Wis.2d 450, 543 N.W.2d 282 (1996), where the Supreme Court of Wisconsin held that a person institutionalized with a mental disability and who did not have the capacity to control or appreciate his behavior could not be held liable in negligence for personal injuries caused to his employed caretaker. Similarly, consider *Colman v. Notre Dame Convalescent Home*, 968 F.Supp. 809 (D.Conn.1997), where the court held that an institutionalized patient was not liable for injuries to a paid caregiver resulting from the patient's negligence. Consider also *Berberian v. Lynn, As Guardian of the*

Incompetent Edmund Gernannt, *179 N.J. 290, 845 A.2d 122 (2004), in which the Supreme Court of New Jersey held that the reasonable person standard did not apply in this case where Gernannt, suffering from senile dementia, pushed the head nurse while attempting to leave the institution, causing the nurse to fall and break her leg. The court held that there is no duty of care owed to caregivers by mentally disabled patients when that patient is incapable of controlling his or her conduct. The defense of assumption of risk is also relevant to these cases. See Chapter 2, Sec. I, infra.*

**7. Further Study.** For further study, see Goldstein, *Asking the Impossible: The Negligence Liability of the Mentally Ill*, 12 J. Contemp. Health L. & Pol'y 67 (1995), which advocates the adoption of a limited objective standard for the mentally ill.

## NEUMANN v. SHLANSKY

Westchester County Court.
58 Misc.2d 128, 294 N.Y.S.2d 628 (1968).

JOHN C. MARBACH, Justice.

Defendant moves to set aside the verdict and for a new trial on the ground that the verdict was contrary to the law of the case since the charge given by me, as trial judge, was erroneous as a matter of law.

The question presented here is, as far as can be determined, a case of first impression not only in this state but also in the nation. The issue is the standard of care which must be exercised by an 11–year-old infant defendant when he is playing golf.

The facts are relatively simple and may be summarized as follows: Defendant, an 11–year-old boy, was playing in a foursome at the Harrison Country Club with his mother and two other adults. The infant defendant was on the tee of a par three hole of about 170 yards. Plaintiff had just left the green on the par three hole and was crossing a foot bridge, which his caddy was about to cross, about 150 to 160 yards from the tee, in plain view of the tee, when he was hit in the knee by the ball driven from the tee by the infant defendant. The infant testified that he saw the plaintiff before he hit. There was testimony that indicated that infant had yelled "fore", the traditional warning given on the golf course when a golfer sees that someone may be hit by a golf ball. Plaintiff testified he did not hear the warning. There was further testimony which indicated that the infant was a boy who had been playing golf two to three times a week during the season for the past two years. It was apparent on the trial, from the shot hit by the infant, that he had at least some proficiency in hitting the golf ball.

The court charged the jury that the infant in this case was to be held to the standard of care of an adult and not to the usual standard of care of a child. The jury returned with a verdict for the plaintiff.

At the outset it should be established that a golfer owes a duty to use reasonable care to avoid injuring other players on the golf course. (*Trauman v. City of New York*, 208 Misc. 252; *Johnston v. Blanchard*, 276 App. Div. 839 [1st Dept., 1949]; *Toohey v. Webster*, 97 N. J. L. 545; *Walsh v. Machlin*, 128 Conn. 412.) Furthermore, a golf ball is a dangerous missile which can cause serious injury if it hits someone while in flight. (*Povanda v. Powers*, 152 Misc. 75 [Sup. Ct., N. Y. County, 1934].) See, also, *Ratcliffe v. Whitehead* (3 West. Week. Rep. 447 [Manitoba, 1933]) where the court stated that, in some ways, hitting a golf ball can be more dangerous than firing a gun or throwing a stone since one is likely to have more control over the direction of a gunshot or a thrown stone than a golf ball. The ordinary rules of negligence apply to games and in the playing of games as in other transactions in life a person must exercise reasonable care. (*Cleghorn v. Oldham*, 43 Times L.R. 465 [Eng. 1927].) It is for this court to determine based upon all the factors involved whether this infant defendant while he was on the golf course is to be held to the standard of care of the reasonably prudent infant or the reasonably prudent man.

This court holds that this infant should be held to the standard of care of the reasonable man. This raises several questions and the court will proceed to discuss the relevant considerations.

\* \* \*

## II.

The ancient and honorable game of golf has been with us since around 1100. It is only within the last few decades that it has evolved into a game which is either played or played at by some eight million people throughout the world. The pastime that was at one time "indulged in by only kings and the nobility" *Gleason v. Hillcrest Golf Course*, 148 Misc. 246, 248 and was described by Andrew Carnegie as an "indispensable adjunct of high civilization" (The Complete Golfer, edited by Herbert Warren Wind, Simon and Schuster, New York, 1954, at xvi of preface), has now become a game which is played by people of all classes from all walks of life. Hand in hand with the increasing popularity of the sport has been a rise in the number and type of accidents occurring on the golf course. One of the most common accidents results when one of the participants, or a person in the gallery, is struck by an errant golf ball projected from the club of a competitor who never dreamed he or she would ever hit anyone with that shot.

\* \* \*

## III.

An infant may be held civilly liable for damages occasioned by his tortious acts. (See, e.g., *Taksen v. Kramer*, 239 App. Div. 756; *Rozell v. Rozell*, 281 N. Y. 106.) The general rule is that, if the actor is a child, the standard of conduct to which he must conform to avoid being negligent is that of a reasonable person of like age, intelligence and experience under the like circumstances. Restatement, Torts 2d, § 283A.

\* \* \*

## IV.

There is an exception to the general rules for infants who engage in adult activities. Restatement of Torts, Second Section 283A, Subsection C provides:

"Child engaging in adult activity. An exception to the rule . . . may arise where the child engages in an activity which is normally undertaken only by adults, and for which adult qualifications are required. As in the case of one entering upon a professional activity which requires special skill . . ., he may be held to the standard of adult skill, knowledge and competence, and no allowance may be made for his immaturity."

It has been held that an infant must exercise the same standard of care as an adult when he is driving a motorboat or airplane (*Dellwo v. Pearson*, 259 Minn. 452, *supra*); a go-cart (*Ewing v. Biddle*, 216 N.E. 2d 863 [Ind.]); a motor vehicle or motorcycle (*Daniels v. Evans*, 107 N. H. 407). There are several other cases in various jurisdictions concerning infants driving power-operated machines such as the above. The rationale for these decisions is that when a minor engages in such activities as the operation of an automobile or similar power-driven device, he forfeits his rights to have the reasonableness of his conduct measured by a standard commensurate with his age and is thenceforth held to the same standard as all other persons. (Ann. 97 A.L.R. 2d 872 at 875). The underlying theory for this view would seem to be that the very nature of a power-driven vehicle makes it a dangerous instrument whether driven by an adult or a child since it obviously makes little difference to the maimed pedestrian or occupant of a vehicle that his mechanized nemesis was a minor.

This Court cannot adopt the theory advocated by some in support of this standard, that licensing statutes automatically impose the adult standard on the driver. If this were so, the unlicensed minor driver who would, presumably, be an even greater menace on the highways, would be held only to the mitigated standard, (Ann. 97 A.L.R. 2d, *supra* at 876), the absence of a license being then only a portion of the proof of the infant's lack of experience. Likewise, compliance with the administrative and quasi-criminal requirements of licensing laws is not controlling on the issue of negligence as between adult drivers and it is equally unimportant in the case of a minor and therefore should not be the criterion determining the standard by which the minor is to be judged. (7 Am.Jur. 2d Automobiles and Highway Traffic #367 and the cases cited therein).

## V.

As applied to the instant case, one of the critical elements in the opinion of the Court is the risk involved when a dangerous missile is hit by a golfer. Just as a motor vehicle or other power-driven vehicle is dangerous, so is a golf ball hit with a club. Driving a car, an airplane or powerboat has been referred to as adult activity even though actively engaged in by infants. (*Dellwo v. Pearson, supra*). Likewise, golf can easily be determined to be an adult activity engaged in by infants. Both involve dangerous instruments. (*Povanda v. Powers, supra*). No matter what the age of a driver of a car or a driver of a golf ball, if he fails to exercise due care serious injury may result. Driving a car, it is true, is not a game as golf may be. However, golf is not a game in the same way that football, baseball, basketball or tennis is a game. It is a game played by an individual which in order to be played well demands an abundance of skill and personal discipline, not to mention constant practice and dedication. Custom, rules and etiquette play an important role in this game. Foremost among these is the fact, as is indicated on many scorecards, that one does not hit a ball when it is likely that the ball could or will hit someone else, for the obvious reason that someone could get hurt. In the definitive work on the subject the rule of etiquette is stated as follows: "No player should play until the party in front is out of range". "Golf, Its Rules and Decisions", Richard S. Francis, Norwood Press, Norwood, Massachusetts, p. 369.

The risks attendant in the game of golf have long been recognized. As early as 1905 the Scottish court in *Andrew v. Stevenson* (13 Scot. L.T. 581, 582 [1905]) stated that the risks of accident in golf are such, that no one is entitled to take part in the game without paying attention to what is going on around and near him. No mention was made of this not applying to people under 21, or under 18 or 15 or 10. The nature of the game is the same, even if the age of the participant varies. In the case at bar we have an 11–year-old boy playing in the company of three adults. He has taken lessons and plays regularly at his club. On a par three hole of about 170 yards he sees the plaintiff within the realm of foreseeable danger and he hits a golf ball, a dangerous missile, 150 to 160 yards where it hits the plaintiff. Had it hit the plaintiff in the head it may have seriously injured or even killed him. The boy knew or should have known that a golf ball can inflict serious injury. He could have waited for a few seconds until plaintiff was clear, yet he chose to hit in breach of his duty and injury resulted. This particular infant defendant was for all purposes on the golf course as an adult golfer. He was playing in a foursome with adults; he had played this course in the company of adults before and he hit the ball, as well as, if not better than many adults. If this court were to say that the standard of care which this defendant must bring to a golf course is only that of an infant it would be ignoring the realities of the game as well as the situation applicable to this case.

It might be argued that the applicable standard should be that of an 11–year-old boy who possesses the experience or intelligence of one who has played a great deal of golf. This subjective standard does not adequately consider the objective nature of the game, the inherent risks involved and the undisputed fact that a golf ball is a dangerous missile capable of inflicting grievous harm no matter who hits it. *Povanda v. Powers, supra.*

It is not uncommon today that teenagers are outstanding amateur golfers. Indeed, the 1968 United States amateur championship was won by Bruce Fleisher, a 19–year-old, and youths of varying ages were at the top of the leader boards all during this tournament. Craig Harmon was the amateur champion of this county at a young age. Members of high school teams in this area regularly shoot scores of championship caliber, as do competitors in "junior" golf. These facts are well known, and are not only particular to this county but are also applicable to other areas throughout the state and nation.

Should this Court say that all of these competitors are to be held to a different standard than adults playing golf? Even if we adopted a subjective standard based on the experience and intelligence of a 16–year-old infant tournament golfer, is his experience and intelligence on the golf course less than that of an adult? Is the cutoff point a matter of age? I think not. When you have, as we have here, a situation where there is potentially an inherently dangerous object hit by someone who despite his age is for all practical purposes just like an adult on the golf course then it is this Court's opinion that he should be treated like an adult and held to an adult standard of care. It may be true that, hypothetically, a six-year-old could appear on the course for the first time and hit a ball which would hurt someone and the objective standard might not be applicable, but that would be the exception rather than the rule. People who play golf on a golf course know or should know that a golf ball can cause serious injury just as a car may cause serious injury and they should exercise the same degree of care.

In conclusion, this Court holds that golf involves special factors which when considered together in the abstract and in conjunction with the fact situation in this particular case require that this infant be held to the standard of the reasonable man on the golf course. Motion denied.

## *NOTES*

**1. Special Child Standard.** Courts do not ordinarily impose an adult reasonable person standard when evaluating the conduct of children under negligence. The Restatement (Second) of Torts articulates the generally accepted view as follows:

> If the actor is a child, the standard of conduct to which he must conform to avoid being negligent is that of a reasonable person of like age, intelligence, and experience under like circumstances. An exception to this rule may arise where the child engages in an activity which is normally undertaken only by adults, and for which adult qualifications are required.

Restatement (Second) of Torts § 283A. See also, Keeton, *Prosser and Keeton on* The Law of Torts § 32 (5th ed. 1984); Diamond, Levine & Madden, *Understanding Torts* § 3.05 (2nd ed. 2000); and Dobbs, *The Law of Torts,* §§ 124–127 (2000). Note that it is generally easier to find liability for a child's intentional tortious acts than for a child's negligent acts. See Note 5, infra.

**2. Accounting for Child's Individual Characteristics.** Unlike the adult reasonable person standard, the child standard adjusts to take into account the individual intelligence and experience of the particular child. The lower the intelligence of the child the more difficult it can be to establish negligence. Consequently, a mentally disabled 15–year-old is treated very differently than a mentally disabled 25–year-old under the Restatement standards. Is it rational policy to take into account variations in intelligence and experience for children (including teenagers under 18) but not adults?

**3. Very Young Children.** Historically some courts automatically precluded a finding of negligence for children under seven and utilized a rebuttable presumption that children between seven and fourteen were not negligent. Modern courts generally do not utilize these age categories, although the younger the child the more difficult it is to establish negligence.

Consider *Standard v. Shine*, 278 S.C. 337, 295 S.E.2d 786 (1982), where an action was brought against a six-year-old child for the child's negligence in setting fire to leased premises. The Supreme Court of South Carolina held that the minor's conduct should be judged by the standard of behavior expected of a child of like age, intelligence, and experience under like circumstances. Consider also *Vandine v. Marley*, 1996 WL 92224 (Conn.Super.), where the court held that a "two-year-old plaintiff, compared to the standard of an ordinary child of comparable age, knowledge, and experience would inevitably result in the common sense conclusion that she could, under no circumstances, be capable of negligence."

**4. Teenagers.** Courts have applied the child standard to teenagers as old as seventeen. For example, in *Goss v. Allen*, 70 N.J. 442, 360 A.2d 388 (1976), the Supreme Court of New Jersey utilized the child standard for a 17–year-old defendant sued for negligent skiing. On the other hand, the Supreme Court of New Hampshire in *Dorais v. Paquin*, 113 N.H. 187, 304 A.2d 369 (1973), applied the adult standard to a 17-year-old pedestrian walking on the right-hand side of a highway in dark clothing and without a flashlight. The court noted that "[o]nce a youth's intelligence, experience and judgment mature to a point where his capacity to perceive, appreciate and avoid situations involving an unreasonable risk of harm to himself or others approximates the capacity of an adult, the youth will be held to the adult standard of care."

**5. Negligence Versus Intentional Torts.** Contrast the special standard for children in negligence with the lack of a special standard for intentional torts. Recall *Garratt v. Dailey*, 46 Wash.2d 197, 279 P.2d 1091 (1955) discussed in the Intent chapter, supra. Is there a good reason for the distinction in approach?

**6. Exception for Adult Activities.** As the Restatement indicates (see Note 1, supra), children are subject to the adult standard when engaging in adult activities requiring adult qualifications. Typically, most cases where a child is held to the adult standard involve children driving motorized vehicles. For example, in *Burch v. American Family Mutual Insurance Company*, 198 Wis.2d 465, 543 N.W.2d 277 (1996), a fifteen-year-old, mentally retarded child was held to an adult standard of conduct for injury she caused while operating an automobile. Consider also *Dellwo v. Pearson*, 259 Minn. 452, 107 N.W.2d 859 (1961), where a plaintiff brought an action for injuries sustained due to the negligence of a twelve-year-old defendant in driving a powerboat. While behind the boat in which the plaintiff was fishing, the powerboat's propeller caught a fishing line, causing the rod to jerk, the reel to come apart and part of the reel to fly through the plaintiff's glasses, injuring her eye. The Supreme Court of Minnesota held that the twelve-year-old defendant should be held to an adult standard of conduct where a child engages in an adult activity requiring adult qualifications because, while one can anticipate conduct that does not reach an adult standard of care when a child engages in childhood activities, one cannot know whether an operator of a powerboat is an adult or child, and "usually cannot protect herself against youthful imprudence even if warned." But consider *Hudson–Conner v. Putney*, 192 Ore.App. 488, 86 P.3d 106 (App.

2004), in which a court denied the application of the adult standard to an 11-year-old who drove a golf cart and accidentally hit the accelerator when attempting to stop, causing him to run into the plaintiff. The court distinguished a motorized golf cart driven on private premises from a motor vehicle because golf carts do not require a license to be driven on private property, are designed to operate at 15 mph or less, are subject to statutory restrictions on where they can be operated, and are not in need of the more demanding adult skills such as understanding of traffic laws, signs and signals, road surface conditions, traffic conditions, and safe stopping distances which are associated with cars driven on public highways.

**7. Courts Hesitant to Apply Adult Standard.** Unlike the principal case, most courts are very hesitant to apply the adult standard when children are not driving a motorized vehicle. Consider *Strait v. Crary*, 173 Wis.2d 377, 496 N.W.2d 634 (App.1992), where a sixteen-year-old passenger, while intoxicated, attempted to climb out of the passenger window and into the box of the moving truck. In the attempt he fell and sustained injury. In bringing suit against the twenty-one-year-old driver for negligence, the Court of Appeals of Wisconsin held that the sixteen-year-old plaintiff "should be held to the 'special' standard of care applicable to children because while drinking to the point of intoxication is—generally, but certainly not exclusively—an adult-type activity, climbing around the outside of a moving vehicle may well not be." Also consider *Goss v. Allen*, 70 N.J. 442, 360 A.2d 388 (1976), noted above, where a seventeen-year-old defendant, while skiing, was held to a child standard due to the determination that skiing as a recreational sport is engaged in by persons of all ages and is therefore not an adult activity.

**8. Use of Firearms.** In applying the adult standard to children, the activity must not only require "adult qualifications," but also be "normally undertaken only by adults." Consequently, using the Restatement principle, courts have applied the child standard to youths in firearm accidents. Consider *Purtle v. Shelton*, 251 Ark. 519, 474 S.W.2d 123 (1971), where a seventeen-year-old defendant injured a sixteen-year-old plaintiff while both parties were deer hunting. The court held that the seventeen-year-old defendant should be held to a child standard of care because a child could lawfully hunt without a license at any age under sixteen and that it would therefore be unreasonable to suggest that hunting is an activity normally engaged in by adults only. Do you agree that children using firearms should benefit from the special child standard?

**9. Alternative "Inherently Dangerous" Standard.** Not all courts utilize the majority Restatement test for determining when to apply the adult standard to children. In *Robinson v. Lindsay*, 92 Wash.2d 410, 598 P.2d 392 (1979), the Supreme Court of Washington instead held that the adult standard would apply when the activity engaged in was "inherently dangerous." In *Robinson* an action was brought for injuries sustained by a girl in an accident involving a snowmobile driven by a thirteen-year-old defendant. The court held that because the boy was operating a powerful motorized vehicle, a 30–horsepower snowmobile, he should be held to the standard of conduct expected of an adult. The court reasoned that such a rule "discourages immature individuals from engaging in inherently dangerous activities." In *Huebner v. Koelfgren*, 519 N.W.2d 488 (Minn.App.1994), the Minnesota Court of Appeals also rejected the Restatement standard in a case where the plaintiff was struck by a BB gun fired by a fourteen-year-old defendant. The court held that an adult standard of care applied to a minor handling a gun because "the public has a right to expect a single, adult standard of care from individuals who handle guns."

**10. Further Study.** For further study, see Gray, *The Standard of Care for Children Revisited*, 45 Mo. L. Rev. 597 (1980).

## MELVILLE v. SOUTHWARD

Supreme Court of Colorado.
791 P.2d 383 (1990).

Chief Justice QUINN delivered the Opinion of the Court.

The question in this case is whether a plaintiff in a medical malpractice action against a podiatrist, who performed foot surgery and rendered post-operative care and treatment to the plaintiff, may elicit expert opinion testimony from a practitioner of another school of medicine, namely orthopedic surgery, on the standard of care applicable to podiatric surgery and post-operative care and treatment. The trial court permitted the plaintiff, over the defendant's objection, to elicit an expert opinion from an orthopedic surgeon that the podiatric surgery performed on the plaintiff's foot and the post-operative treatment rendered to the plaintiff fell below the standard of care applicable to the surgery in question and also fell below the standard of care applicable to the post-operative care and treatment of the patient.... We agree with the court of appeals that the lack of any foundation for the orthopedic surgeon's familiarity with the podiatric standard of care for the surgery in question and the post-operative care and treatment of the patient rendered the orthopedic surgeon's opinion testimony inadmissible. However, contrary to the court of appeals' decision, we believe that the proper disposition of this matter is to return the case to the trial court for a new trial.

### I.

The plaintiff-petitioner, Lulu Melville (plaintiff), filed a negligence action in the district court of Fremont County against the defendant-respondent, Dr. Stanton C. Southward (defendant), a licensed podiatrist. The complaint, as pertinent here, alleged that on or about August 14, 1980, the defendant performed a surgical procedure in his office on the plaintiff's right foot, that the surgical procedure fell below the standard of reasonably careful podiatric surgery, that defendant failed to provide adequate post-operative care and treatment, and that the plaintiff sustained a serious infection and developed osteomyelitis as a result of defendant's negligence. The defendant denied the allegations of negligence and asserted that any injury suffered by the plaintiff was a result of her own negligence.

The case proceeded to a jury trial on May 27, 1986, at which the defendant represented himself. The evidence at trial established the following sequence of events. The plaintiff first consulted the defendant in July 1980 for an ingrown toenail. The defendant removed the ingrown toenail and subsequently, on August 14, 1980, recommended that plaintiff undergo a surgical procedure known as a metatarsal osteotomy in order to relieve the discomfort that the plaintiff had been experiencing.

The recommended surgery consisted of the cutting and shortening of the metatarsal shaft of the second toe in the right foot.

The plaintiff agreed to the surgery, and it was performed on August 14 in the defendant's office. The defendant applied a local anesthesia to the plaintiff's foot and made a minimal incision, about a quarter-inch wide, through the top of the foot and then used a drill to fracture the metatarsal shaft and a dental burr to remove any bone fragments. After completing the surgery, he instructed the plaintiff to soak her foot in vinegar and water. The defendant wrapped the foot in a Unna boot, which basically is an ace bandage soaked in an antibiotic, placed plaintiff's foot in a half shoe, and provided the plaintiff with a pamphlet containing post-operative instructions.

The plaintiff returned home after the surgery and resumed her usual activities, which consisted primarily of gardening. She wore the half shoe, soaked her foot daily as directed, and returned to the defendant's office approximately one week later for a check-up. Upon examining the foot the defendant commented, "I don't like the looks of this," and then medicated and rewrapped the foot and provided the plaintiff with an antibiotic medication.

On August 26, 1980, the plaintiff telephoned the defendant and complained that her foot was swollen, red, and quite painful. The defendant advised her to increase the amount of vinegar in the prescribed solution and to soak the foot more frequently, and stated that he would check the foot again in two days at the plaintiff's scheduled office appointment. The defendant, at the scheduled office visit, told the plaintiff that her foot was healing, and he rewrapped the foot with clean bandages. The next day, August 29, the plaintiff noticed a sore spot near the surgical site and a fluid exuding from that area when it was touched. The plaintiff telephoned her family physician, Joseph R. McGarry, for an appointment.

Doctor McGarry, a medical doctor, saw the plaintiff on September 3, 1980. The plaintiff told Doctor McGarry that she had undergone surgery on the foot two weeks previously and that the foot had become swollen and red and had been draining at the surgical site. Upon examination of the foot, McGarry saw that the surgical site was badly infected. McGarry instructed the plaintiff to keep her foot elevated, prescribed an antibiotic, and told her that her infection was quite serious and to return to his office for a check-up. When the plaintiff experienced more drainage from the surgical site, McGarry admitted her to a hospital for X-rays and for the administration of antibiotics intravenously. McGarry diagnosed the plaintiff's condition as a compound fracture of the second metatarsal on the right foot, with concomitant infection resulting from the surgery, and recommended that plaintiff see Doctor Michael Barnard, an orthopedic surgeon practicing in the area.

Doctor Barnard first saw the plaintiff on October 17, 1980, and noted that the plaintiff's foot was swollen and slightly red. X-rays revealed an erosion of the bone in the area of the second metatarsal. Such bone erosion, according to Barnard, was consistent with osteomyelitis which, in his view, had been caused by the osteotomy performed by the defendant.

Plaintiff's counsel asked Doctor Barnard whether he had an opinion to a reasonable medical probability on whether the osteotomy was performed below the standard of care for such a surgical procedure. The defendant objected to this line of questioning on the basis that no foundation had been laid regarding Barnard's knowledge of the standard of care applicable to podiatry. The trial court overruled the objection and permitted Barnard to testify. Barnard testified that the osteotomy performed by the defendant was below the standard of care for two reasons: first, the surgery was unnecessary because none of the pre-surgical X-rays indicated a deformity in the metatarsal; and second, even assuming the surgery was necessary, the osteotomy was performed in an unsterile office environment and thereby subjected the bone to a high risk of infection. Barnard acknowledged in his testimony that he was unfamiliar with the standards applicable to podiatric foot surgery, was not familiar with podiatric literature, had never received any instruction on podiatry, and had never performed the surgical procedure involved in this case.

Doctor Barnard also testified, again over the defendant's objection, that the defendant's post-operative treatment of the plaintiff fell below the proper standard of care for treating an osteotomy. . . .

Doctor Barnard also testified that he performed a surgical procedure on the plaintiff's right foot on July 30, 1981, for the purpose of removing some degenerative osteophytes that had formed around the second metatarsal. It was Barnard's opinion that the plaintiff had sustained a permanent disability as a result of the defendant's surgery and would have difficulty walking and balancing herself.

\* \* \*

The defendant testified on his own behalf. He stated that the plaintiff had failed to follow some of his post-operative instructions and, in that respect, was responsible for some of the post-operative complications in her right foot. He also testified that the plaintiff made use of her foot more often than he had recommended and that, contrary to his instructions, she had tried to wear a full shoe. In addition, he claimed that during the post-operative period the plaintiff had bumped her foot against some object and had irritated the surgical site.

The jury found that the plaintiff had sustained damage in the amount of $56,000 as a result of the defendant's negligence. The defendant appealed to the court of appeals, contending that, because the plaintiff's only expert on the standard of care was a practicing orthopedic surgeon, the plaintiff had failed to establish a *prima facie* case of negligence. . . .

## II.

In a medical malpractice case, the burden is on the plaintiff to establish a *prima facie* case of negligence. E.g., *Maercklein v. Smith*, 129 Colo. 72, 266 P.2d 1095 (1954); *Hanley v. Spencer*, 108 Colo. 184, 115 P.2d 399 (1941). To establish a *prima facie* case, the plaintiff must establish that the defendant failed to conform to the standard of care ordinarily possessed and exercised by members of the same school of medicine practiced by the defendant. See, e.g., *Bloskas v. Murray,* 646 P.2d 907 (Colo.1982); *Dixon v. Norberg,* 113 Colo. 352, 157 P.2d 131 (1945); *Norkett v. Martin,* 63 Colo. 220, 165 P. 256 (1917); *McGraw v. Kerr,* 23 Colo.App. 163, 128 P. 870 (1912). The standard of care in a medical malpractice action is measured by whether a reasonably careful physician of the same school of medicine as the defendant would have acted in the same manner as did the defendant in treating and caring for the plaintiff. E.g., *Norkett,* 63 Colo. 220, 165 P. 256; *Jackson v. Burnham,* 20 Colo. 532, 39 P. 577 (1895).

Unless the subject matter of a medical malpractice action lies within the ambit of common knowledge or experience of ordinary persons, the plaintiff must establish the controlling standard of care, as well as the defendant's failure to adhere to that standard, by expert opinion testimony. See, e.g., *Bloskas,* 646 P.2d at 914; *Daly v. Lininger,* 87 Colo. 401, 406, 288 P. 633, 636 (1930); *Farrah v. Patton,* 99 Colo. 41, 44, 59 P.2d 76, 78 (1936); *Norkett,* 63 Colo. at 221, 165 P. at 257; *Jackson,* 20 Colo. at 536, 39 P. at 580; *Mudd v. Dorr,* 40 Colo.App. 74, 574 P.2d 97 (1977). The reason for the requirement of expert opinion testimony in most medical malpractice cases is obvious: matters relating to medical diagnosis and treatment ordinarily involve a level of technical knowledge and skill beyond the realm of lay knowledge and experience. Without expert opinion testimony in such cases, the trier of fact would be left with no standard at all against which to evaluate the defendant's conduct. *McGraw,* 23 Colo.App. at 172, 128 P. at 873.

\* \* \*

The evidentiary standard for determining whether a member of one school of medicine may offer an opinion concerning the standard of care applicable to another school has been articulated by several appellate courts in various ways. One line of cases places emphasis on whether the expert witness is sufficiently knowledgeable of and familiar with the standard of care governing the defendant's specialty to offer an informed opinion on that issue.... Another line of cases focuses primarily on whether the standard of diagnosis or treatment applicable to the expert witness' specialty is substantially identical to the standard for the defendant's practice....

There is merit in both of the above approaches.... In our view, therefore, the dispositive consideration in ruling on the admissibility of expert opinion testimony by a medical witness regarding whether the defendant, who practices in another school of medicine, has adhered to or deviated from the requisite standard of care in diagnosing or treating the plaintiff should be the following: (1) whether the testifying expert, although practicing a specialty different from that of the defendant, nonetheless is, by reason of knowledge, skill, experience, training, or education, so substantially familiar with the standard of care applicable to the defendant's specialty as to render the witness' opinion testimony as well-informed as would be the opinion of an expert witness practicing the same specialty as the defendant; or (2) whether the standard of care for the condition in question is substantially identical for both specialties. If a proper foundation establishes either of these evidentiary predicates for admissibility, the witness should be permitted to offer an expert opinion on the standard of care applicable to the defendant's specialty and on whether the defendant breached that standard of care. On the other hand, absent the proper foundation evidence, the expert witness practicing a specialty different from that of the defendant should not be permitted to offer an expert opinion on those matters.

## III.

The practice of podiatry is defined by statute as "the diagnosis and the medical, surgical, mechanical, manipulative, and electrical treatment of disorders of the human toe and foot, including the ankle and tendons that insert into the foot." § 12–32–101(3), 5 C.R.S. (1985). The practice of medicine, in contrast, includes the diagnosis, treatment, or prevention of "any human disease, ailment, pain, injury, deformity, or physical or mental condition, whether by the use of drugs, surgery, manipulation, electricity, or any physical, mechanical, or other means whatsoever." Section 12–36–106(1)(a), 5 C.R.S. (1985). Orthopedic surgery is a medical subspecialty that involves the utilization of medical, surgical, and physical methods in treating the extremities, spine, and associated structures, and, as such, includes not only foot surgery encompassed by the practice of podiatry but also other treatments and medical practices not within podiatric practices. 6 *Lawyers' Medical Cyclopedia* § 41.1, at 188 (1977).

The fact that practicing podiatrists and orthopedic surgeons are authorized to perform surgical procedures on a patient's foot is not to say that the standard of care applicable to each discipline is necessarily the same. . . .

The trial court ruled that, because an orthopedic surgeon receives more training and education than a podiatrist, Doctor Barnard was qualified to render an opinion on the standard of care exercised by the defendant in performing the metatarsal osteotomy on the plaintiff's foot. The court of appeals disagreed with the trial court's ruling and held that Barnard's opinion testimony was nothing more than an expression of opinion that the general practice of podiatry did not meet the standard of care observed by an orthopedic surgeon in performing foot surgery. We agree with the court of appeals that the trial court erred in its evidentiary ruling.

The plaintiff failed to establish an evidentiary foundation that Doctor Barnard, by reason of his knowledge, skill, experience, training, or education, was so substantially familiar with the standard of care for podiatric surgery as to render his opinion testimony as well-informed as that of a podiatrist. . . . Nor did the plaintiff establish by way of an evidentiary predicate that the standard of care for a metatarsal osteotomy was substantially identical for both the practice of orthopedic surgery and podiatry. . . .

* * *

IV.

Although the trial court erred in permitting Doctor Barnard to offer opinion testimony on the defendant's failure to use reasonable care in the performance of the metatarsal osteotomy and in his post-operative care and treatment of the plaintiff, we believe the proper disposition of this case is not a dismissal of the plaintiff's complaint with prejudice, as ordered by the court of appeals, but a remand of the case for a new trial. In ordering the dismissal of the plaintiff's complaint, the court of appeals reasoned that when Doctor Barnard's opinion testimony was excluded from consideration, the other evidence offered by the plaintiff failed to establish a prima facie case of negligence. The plaintiff, however, never had reason to establish an adequate foundation for Barnard's opinion testimony because the trial court simply overruled the defendant's objection and thus admitted the opinion testimony without requiring any further foundation.

If the trial court had sustained the defendant's objections to Doctor Barnard's opinion testimony, as it should have done, the plaintiff might have been able to lay an adequate foundation for at least some of the doctor's opinion testimony. Although Barnard acknowledged that he was not familiar with the standard of care applicable to a podiatric metatarsal osteotomy, he might have been sufficiently familiar with the podiatric standard of care applicable to post-operative care and treatment or might have been of the view that the post-operative standard of care for a metatarsal osteotomy was identical for both orthopedic surgery and podiatry. Moreover, in the event the defendant's objection had been sustained, the plaintiff might have been able to present an adequate foundation through Doctor McGarry or some other expert witness for eliciting opinion testimony on the issue of the defendant's alleged post-operative negligence. In light of the particular circumstances of this case, we believe the appropriate disposition is to remand the case to the court of appeals with directions to return the case to the district court for a new trial. . . .

* * *

## NOTES

**1.  Standard of Conduct for Professionals.** Generally, professionals have been held to a special standard of conduct while engaging in their professional activities. The Restatement (Second) of Torts articulates this approach as follows:

> Unless he represents that he has greater or less skill or knowledge, one who undertakes to render services in the practice of a profession or trade is required to exercise the skill and knowledge normally possessed by members of that profession or trade in good standing in similar communities.

Restatement (Second) of Torts § 299A. See also Keeton, *Prosser and Keeton on* The Law of Torts § 32 (5th ed. 1984); Diamond, Levine & Madden, *Understanding Torts* § 7.01 (2nd ed. 2000); and Dobbs, *The Law of Torts* §§ 242–247 (2000).

**2. Expert Testimony Required.** As the principal case indicates, to establish professional negligence, often referred to as malpractice, a qualified expert witness must provide evidence that the defendant did not meet the minimum applicable professional standard. For example in *Roberson v. Jeffrey M. Waltner, M.D., Inc.*, 108 P.3d 567 (Okla.Civ.App.Div.3 2005), the Court of Appeals of Oklahoma found that the testimony of the defendant physician could also serve as evidence of the medical standard of the community. But consider also *Kranis v. Scott*, 178 F.Supp.2d 330 (E.D.N.Y. 2002), in which the plaintiff, a disbarred attorney, attempted to act as an expert on the professional standard of care for attorneys, specifically on the issue of legal malpractice. The District Court in New York found that the plaintiff presented no evidence that he ever specialized in malpractice law or that he had adequate familiarity with basic rules of practice and procedure and in fact appeared in his pretrial motions to the court to be at a substandard level of legal skill. As such, the court held that the plaintiff was not qualified to serve as a legal expert.

Unlike the hypothetical reasonable person standard where the jury is free to determine what is "reasonable," the professional standard limits the jury's discretion. The jury must factually determine what the profession's customary standard of competence is as reported by witnesses knowledgeable about that standard. In this sense, the courts have delegated to the profession's establishment the appropriate standard below which a professional can be held negligent.

In a highly unusual and extensively discussed decision, *Helling v. Carey*, 83 Wash.2d 514, 519 P.2d 981 (1974), the Washington Supreme Court rebelled against the generally accepted judicial deference to the medical profession's right to determine the appropriate standard for the diagnosis and treatment of patients. Accepted medical practice prescribed that only patients over 40 years old should be routinely tested for glaucoma, an eye disease which can lead to blindness if not timely treated. The court articulated a rule of law (see Chapter 2, Sec. 2, infra) requiring opthamologists to routinely test patients under 40. The court, in response to state legislation, ultimately replaced this rule with a "reasonable prudence" standard for medical malpractice to be decided by a jury. Under this approach, the jury is free to decide a medical practice accepted as appropriate by most physicians is nonetheless negligent. Do you agree with this distinctly minority approach? See *Harris v. Groth*, 99 Wash.2d 438, 663 P.2d 113 (1983); Dobbs, supra § 247.

**3. Professional Elitism?** The Restatement, quoted in Note one above, applies the professional standard to professions and trades. Nevertheless, many courts have only applied the professional standard to elite professions such as medicine, law and architecture. Should juries be required to defer to a profession's or trade's determination as to what is or is not acceptable practice? Should it depend on the particular profession or trade of the defendant?

**4. Geographical Considerations.** Geography has in the past been a critical factor in determining which medical expert can testify in a medical malpractice action. Originally physicians were held to the professional standard in their own community. Courts reasoned that rural physicians could not be expected to utilize the latest advances available in urban medical centers. As a result of this rule, only experts in the same community were held competent to testify on the standard in that community. In communities where very few, if any, other doctors practiced, plaintiffs found it extremely difficult if not impossible to find expert witnesses prepared to testify against their local colleagues. Some commentators characterized this as a "conspiracy of silence." The Restatement, Note one supra, reflects the current majority view that experts in "similar" communities can testify as to what constitutes negligent medicine. Consider *Gambill v. Stroud*, 258 Ark. 766, 531 S.W.2d 945 (1976), where the Supreme Court of Arkansas held that the standard of care to which a physician would be held for his alleged negligent performance of a medical procedure was the standard of care of physicians in the same or similar communities. Similarly, in *Erickson v. United States*, 504 F.Supp. 646 (D.S.D.1980), the court held that a physician performing a medical procedure, or making a diagnosis, had a duty to use the degree of care and skill ordinarily exercised in similar cases by other members of the profession in good standing, in the "same or similar locality."

Courts generally apply a national standard for medical specialists and an increasing number of courts are applying a national standard for general practitioners. For example, in *Vergara v. Doan*, 593 N.E.2d 185 (Ind.1992), the Supreme Court of Indiana adopted a national standard of care, rationalizing that "with advances in communication, travel, and medical education, the disparity between rural and urban health care diminished and justification for the locality rule waned." Do current communications technology and transportation make obsolete different local standards for professionals? For a discussion of the relationship among technology, information and the law of medical malpractice, see Kacmar, *The Impact of Computerized Medical Literature Databases on Medical Malpractice Litigation: Time for Another* Helling v. Carey *Wake-Up Call?*, 58 Ohio St. L.J. 617 (1997).

**5. Common Knowledge and Experience.** As the principal case briefly indicates, courts will not require medical experts when the negligence is so obvious a lay jury can make the determination without expert assistance. The common knowledge exception helps to mitigate, in extreme cases, the difficulty a plaintiff can have in obtaining expert medical testimony against a defendant physician.

**6. Higher Standard for Specialists.** Specialists are held to a higher standard of skill than non-specialists. See *Baker v. Story*, 621 S.W.2d 639 (Tex.Civ.App.1981), where the Court of Civil Appeals of Texas determined that the supervising surgeon, a specialist in the field of neurosurgery who had supervised a non-specialist surgeon, would be held to a higher standard of care than that which would be applied to the surgeon who had performed the neurosurgery because more was expected from one holding himself out as a specialist.

**7. HMO and Insurance Liability.** Congress and some state legislatures have recently focused on whether health maintenance organizations (HMOs) and other insurance companies should be liable for negligently failing to authorize or approve medical services. Historically, federal law has effectively immunized insurance companies from liability, particularly when the medical insurance is part of an employment benefit package. Versions of legislation authorizing suits have been passed separately by both the Senate and the House of Representatives. A few states, e.g., California and Texas, have adopted legislation facilitating suits against insurance companies. See

Robert Pear, "House Passes Bill to Expand Rights on Medical Care," New York Times, p.1 (October, 1999). However, proposed federal legislation on this matter has never been adopted. Consider *Aetna Health Inc. v. Davila*, 542 U.S. 200, 124 S.Ct. 2488, 159 L.Ed.2d 312 (2004) where the Supreme Court held that state law claims alleging injury caused by defendants' decisions not to provide coverage for physician-recommended treatment were preempted by Employee Retirement Income Security Act (ERISA). "Congress' intent to make the ERISA civil enforcement mechanism exclusive would be undermined if state causes of action that supplement the ERISA § 502(a) remedies were permitted, even if the elements of the state cause of action did not precisely duplicate the elements of an ERISA claim." This ruling has the effect of preempting state law claims for denial of benefits under any "ERISA regulated benefit plan." What are the arguments for an against authorizing lawsuits against health insurance companies that negligently refuse to authorize health care payments? Should the bad faith tort be applied here? (See Chapter 1, Sec. I, supra.)

**8.  Malpractice Liability Reforms.** Some states limit the damages and attorneys' fees recoverable for malpractice actions to limit the cost of malpractice insurance to doctors, hospitals, and other health care providers. Other reforms have focused on providing arbitration and allowing courts to consider whether the patient's losses due to malpractice will be compensated by the patient's own insurance protection. The issue is explored in Chapter 5, Sec. D, infra.

**9.  Attorney Malpractice.** Consider cases addressing attorney malpractice. In *Wright v. Williams*, 121 Cal.Rptr. 194, 47 Cal.App.3d 802 (1975) an admiralty lawyer failed to advise his clients of the implications of an endorsement in a purchase document precluding the vessel's use in commercial trade. The court held that the "attorney-client relationship imposes upon the lawyer to represent his client with such skill, prudence,and diligence commonly possess[ed]" by other attorneys "in the same or similar locality under similar circumstances." In *Lucas v. Hamm*, 56 Cal.2d 583, 15 Cal.Rptr. 821, 364 P.2d 685 (1961), the Supreme Court of California, held that an attorney who had drafted a will that violated the rule against perpetuities was *not* liable for malpractice. The court, noting that Professor Leach had described the rule as a "technicality-ridden legal nightmare," declined "to hold that defendant failed to use such skill, prudence, and diligence as lawyers of ordinary skill and capacity commonly exercise." See also *Russo v. Griffin*, 147 Vt. 20, 510 A.2d 436 (1986), where, as with medical malpractice suits, the Supreme Court of Vermont rejected the "locality" standard previously in place. Instead, the court adopted a statewide standard as the relevant geographic area because the state where an attorney practices "is the jurisdiction in which the attorney is licensed to practice."

**10.  Police Officer Training.** Police officers have also been held liable for negligence in the performance of their jobs. In *District of Columbia v. Peters*, 527 A.2d 1269 (D.C.App.1987), the court held that whether the District of Columbia was negligent for failing to train its police officers adequately to interact with the mentally disturbed or persons under the influence of drugs could be evaluated only if the jury was informed of recognized standards concerning such training. Testimony by a professor, an expert in the field of criminology, was held sufficient to document the training standards used by other police departments to prepare their officers to respond to the mentally disabled.

**11. Clergy Malpractice.** Some courts have argued that there should be a clergy malpractice tort, but declined to find it on the facts of the case, while others have claimed that no clergy malpractice tort exists to begin with. See, for example, *Hester v. Barnett*, 723 S.W.2d 544 (Mo.Ct.App. 1987), in which the court recognized the tort of clergy malpractice but declined to find the defendant liable for it on the facts. See also *Strock v. Pressnell*, 38 Ohio St.3d 207, 527 N.E.2d 1235 (1988), where the defendant minister allegedly had a sexual relationship with the plaintiff's wife during a period when the plaintiff and his wife were seeing the minister for marriage counseling. The Supreme Court of Ohio dismissed the clergy malpractice claim on the grounds that it was a separate cause of action from any alleged intentional torts, one that must concern the counseling relationship itself and not merely be associated with it. Consider also *Langford v. Roman Catholic Diocese of Brooklyn*, 271 A.D.2d 494, 705 N.Y.S.2d 661 (N.Y.A.D. 2 Dept. 2000), in which Monsignor Sivillo had counseled the plaintiff on her personal and health problems, depression, marriage and her future, even claiming that his prayers made her multiple sclerosis go into remission. For the next three years, the parties engaged in a sexual relationship, at one point Sivillo advising plaintiff's husband that their marriage was not salvageable. The Supreme Court of New York upheld the dismissal of the plaintiff's case because "any attempt to define the duty of care owed by a member of the clergy to a parishioner fosters excessive entanglement with religion." Recall cases discussing clergy liability for intentional infliction of mental distress. See Chapter 1, Sec. F at page 50, supra. For further study, see Fain, *Clergy Malpractice: Liability for Negligent Counseling and Sexual Misconduct*, 12 Miss. C. L. Rev. 97 (1991), which traces clergy malpractice cases and discusses possible standards of conduct for members of the clergy (secular, professional psychotherapist, and denominationally specific).

## COBBS v. GRANT

Supreme Court of California, In Bank.
8 Cal.3d 229, 104 Cal.Rptr. 505, 502 P.2d 1 (1972).

MOSK, Justice.

This medical malpractice case involves two issues: first, whether there was sufficient evidence of negligence in the performing of surgery to sustain a jury verdict for plaintiff; second, whether, under plaintiff's alternative theory, the instructions to the jury adequately set forth the nature of a medical doctor's duty to obtain the informed consent of a patient before undertaking treatment. We conclude there was insufficient evidence to support the jury's verdict under the theory that defendant was negligent during the operation. Since there was a general verdict and we are unable to ascertain upon which of the two concepts the jury relied, we must reverse the judgment and remand for a new trial. To assist the trial court upon remand we analyze the doctor's duty to obtain the patient's informed consent and suggest principles for guidance in drafting new instructions on this question.

Plaintiff was admitted to the hospital in August 1964 for treatment of a duodenal ulcer. He was given a series of tests to ascertain the severity of his condition and, though administered medication to ease his discomfort, he continued to complain of lower abdominal pain and nausea. His family physician, Dr. Jerome Sands, concluding that surgery was indicated, discussed prospective surgery with plaintiff and advised him in general terms of the risks of undergoing a general anesthetic. Dr. Sands called in defendant, Dr. Dudley F. P. Grant, a surgeon, who after examining plaintiff, agreed with Dr. Sands that plaintiff had an intractable peptic duodenal ulcer and that surgery was indicated. Although Dr. Grant explained the nature of the operation to plaintiff, he did not discuss any of the inherent risks of the surgery.

A two-hour operation was performed the next day, in the course of which the presence of a small ulcer was confirmed. Following the surgery the ulcer disappeared. Plaintiff's recovery appeared to be uneventful, and he was permitted to go home eight days later. However, the day after he returned home, plaintiff began to experience intense pain in his abdomen. He immediately called Dr. Sands who advised him to return to the hospital. Two hours after his readmission plaintiff went into shock and emergency surgery was performed. It was discovered plaintiff was bleeding internally as a result of a severed artery at the hilum of his spleen. Because of the seriousness of the hemorrhaging and since the spleen of an adult may be removed without adverse effects, defendant decided to remove the spleen. Injuries to the spleen that compel a subsequent operation are a risk inherent in the type of surgery performed on plaintiff and occur in approximately 5 percent of such operations.

After removal of his spleen, plaintiff recuperated for two weeks in the hospital. A month after discharge he was readmitted because of sharp pains in his stomach. X-rays disclosed plaintiff was developing a gastric ulcer. The evolution of a new ulcer is another risk inherent in surgery performed to relieve a duodenal ulcer. Dr. Sands initially decided to attempt to treat this nascent gastric ulcer with antacids and a strict diet. However, some four months later plaintiff was again hospitalized when the gastric ulcer continued to deteriorate and he experienced severe pain. When plaintiff began to vomit blood the defendant and Dr. Sands concluded that a third operation was indicated: a gastrectomy with removal of 50 percent of plaintiff's stomach to reduce its acid-producing capacity. Some time after the surgery, plaintiff was discharged, but subsequently had to be hospitalized yet again when he began to bleed internally due to the premature absorption of a suture, another inherent risk of surgery. After plaintiff was hospitalized, the bleeding began to abate and a week later he was finally discharged.

Plaintiff brought this malpractice suit against his surgeon, Dr. Grant. The action was consolidated for trial with a similar action against the hospital. The jury returned a general verdict against the hospital in the amount of $45,000. This judgment has been satisfied. The jury also returned a general verdict against defendant Grant in the amount of $23,800. He appeals.

The jury could have found for plaintiff either by determining that defendant negligently performed the operation, or on the theory that defendant's failure to disclose the inherent risks of the initial surgery vitiated plaintiff's consent to operate. Defendant attacks both possible grounds of the verdict. He contends, first, there was insufficient evidence to sustain a verdict of negligence, and, second, the court committed prejudicial error in its instruction to the jury on the issue of informed consent.

## I

\* \* \*

[In Section I of the opinion, the court concluded that the lack of expert testimony precluded finding negligence either in the decision to operate or in the performance of the surgery.]

## II

Since the question of informed consent is likely to arise on retrial, we address ourselves to that issue. (Code Civ. Proc., § 43.) In giving its instruction the trial court relied upon *Berkey v. Anderson* (1969) 1 Cal.App.3d 790, 803 [82 Cal.Rptr. 67], a case in which it was held that if the defendant failed to make a sufficient disclosure of the risks inherent in the operation, he was guilty of a "technical battery" (also see *Pedesky v. Bleiberg,* (1967) 251 Cal.App.2d 119, 123 [59 Cal.Rptr. 294]; *Hundley v. St. Francis Hospital* (1958) 161 Cal.App.2d 800, 802 [327 P.2d 131]). While a battery instruction may have been warranted under the facts alleged in *Berkey*, in the case before us the instruction should have been framed in terms of negligence.

Where a doctor obtains consent of the patient to perform one type of treatment and subsequently performs a substantially different treatment for which consent was not obtained, there is a clear case of battery. (*Berkey v. Anderson* (1969) *supra*, 1 Cal.App.3d 790 (allegation of consent to permit doctor to perform a procedure no more complicated than the electromyograms plaintiff had previously undergone, when the actual procedure was a myelogram involving a spinal puncture); *Bang v. Charles T. Miller Hosp.* (1958) 251 Minn. 427 [88 N.W.2d 186] (plaintiff consented to a prostate resection when uninformed that this procedure involved tying off his sperm ducts); *Corn v. French* (1955) 71 Nev. 280 [289 P.2d 173] (patient consented to exploratory surgery; doctor performed a mastectomy); *Zoterell v. Repp* (1915) 187 Mich. 319 [153 N.W. 692] (consent given for a hernia operation during which doctor also removed both ovaries).)

However, when an undisclosed potential complication results, the occurrence of which was not an integral part of the treatment procedure but merely a known risk, the courts are divided on the issue of whether this should be deemed to be a battery or negligence. (*Gray* v. *Grunnagle* (1966) 423 Pa. 144 [223 A.2d 663] (failure to warn a patient a spinal operation involved an inherent risk of permanent paralysis; battery); *Belcher v. Carter* (1967) 13 Ohio App.2d 113 [234 N.E.2d 311] (failure to warn of danger of radiation burns; battery); *Nolan v. Kechijian* (1949) 75 R.I. 165 [64 A.2d 866] (operation to strengthen ligaments of spleen when spleen was removed; trespass to the body and negligence); *Natanson* v.

*Kline* (1960) 186 Kan. 393 [350 P.2d 1093] (radiation treatment produced a severe burn; *semble* battery or negligence); *Natanson* v. *Kline* (1960) 187 Kan., 186 [354 P.2d 670] (rehearing of previous case; negligence); *Mitchell v. Robinson* (Mo. 1960) 334 S.W.2d 11 (vertebrae broken during insulin shock treatment; negligence).) California authorities have favored a negligence theory. (*Carmichael* v. *Reitz* (1971) 17 Cal.App.3d 958 [95 Cal.Rptr. 381] (pulmonary embolism caused by adverse reaction to drug; negligence); *Dunlap v. Marine* (1966) 242 Cal.App.2d 162 [51 Cal.Rptr. 158] (cardiac arrest allegedly caused by administration of anesthetic; negligence); *Tangora v. Matanky* (1964) 231 Cal.App.2d 468 [42 Cal.Rptr. 348] (anaphylactic shock as a result of intramuscular penicillin shot; negligence); *Salgo v. Leland Stanford etc. Bd. Trustees* (1957) 154 Cal.App.2d 560 [317 P.2d 170] (paralysis of lower extremities after aortographic examination; negligence).)

Dean Prosser surveyed the decisions in this area and concluded, "The earliest cases treated this as a matter of vitiating the consent, so that there was liability for battery. Beginning with a decision in Kansas in 1960 [*Natanson v. Kline* (1960) *supra*, 187. Kan. 186], it began to be recognized that this was really a matter of the standard of professional conduct.... [T]he prevailing view now is that the action ... is in reality one for negligence in failing to conform to the proper standard...." (Fns. omitted; Prosser on Torts (4th ed. 1971) pp. 165–166.)

Although this is a close question, either prong of which is supportable by authority, the trend appears to be towards categorizing failure to obtain informed consent as negligence. That this result now appears with growing frequency is of more than academic interest; it reflects an appreciation of the several significant consequences of favoring negligence over a battery theory. As will be discussed *infra*, most jurisdictions have permitted a doctor in an informed consent action to interpose a defense that the disclosure he omitted to make was not required within his medical community. However, expert opinion as to community standard is not required in a battery count, in which the patient must merely prove failure to give informed consent and a mere touching absent consent. Moreover a doctor could be held liable for punitive damages under a battery count, and if held liable for the intentional tort of battery he might not be covered by his malpractice insurance. (Comment, *Informed Consent in Medical Malpractice* (1967) 55 Cal.L.Rev. 1396.) Additionally, in some jurisdictions the patient has a longer statute of limitations if he sues in negligence.

We agree with the majority trend. The battery theory should be reserved for those circumstances when a doctor performs an operation to which the patient has not consented. When the patient gives permission to perform one type of treatment and the doctor performs another, the requisite element of deliberate intent to deviate from the consent given is present. However, when the patient consents to certain treatment and the doctor performs that treatment but an undisclosed inherent complication with a low probability occurs, no intentional deviation from the consent given appears; rather, the doctor in obtaining consent may have failed to meet his due care duty to disclose pertinent information. In that situation the action should be pleaded in negligence.

The facts of this case constitute a classic illustration of an action that sounds in negligence. Defendant performed the identical operation to which plaintiff had consented. The spleen injury, development of the gastric ulcer, gastrectomy and internal bleeding as a result of the premature absorption of a suture, were all links in a chain of low probability events inherent in the initial operation.

### III

Since this is an appropriate case for the application of a negligence theory, it remains for us to determine if the standard of care described in the jury instruction on this subject properly delineates defendant's duty to inform plaintiff of the inherent risks of the surgery. In pertinent part, the court gave the following instruction: "A physician's duty to disclose is not governed by the standard practice in the community; rather it is a duty imposed by law. A physician violates his duty to his patient and subjects himself to liability if he withholds any facts which are necessary to form the basis of an intelligent consent by the patient to the proposed treatment."

Defendant raises two objections to the foregoing instruction. First, he points out that the majority of the California cases have measured the duty to disclose not in terms of an absolute, but as a duty to reveal such information as would be disclosed by a doctor in good standing within the medical community. (*Carmichael v. Reitz* (1971) *supra*, 17 Cal. App.3d 958, 976; *Dunlap v. Marine* (1966) *supra*, 242 Cal.App.2d 162; *Tangora v. Matanky* (1964) *supra*, 231 Cal.App.2d 468; contra, *Berkey v. Anderson* (1969) *supra*, 1 Cal.App.3d 790.) One commentator has imperiously declared that "good medical practice is good law." (Hagman, *The Medical Patient's Right to Know* (1970) 17 U.C.L.A. L.Rev. 758, 764.) Moreover, with one state and one federal exception every jurisdiction that has considered this question has adopted the community standard as the applicable test. Defendant's second contention is that this near unanimity reflects strong policy reasons for vesting in the medical community the unquestioned discretion to determine if the withholding of information by a doctor from his patient is justified at the time the patient weighs the risks of the treatment against the risks of refusing treatment.

The thesis that medical doctors are invested with discretion to withhold information from their patients has been frequently ventilated in both legal and medical literature. (See, e.g., *Salgo v. Leland Stanford etc. Bd. Trustees* (1957) *supra*, 154 Cal.App.2d 560, 578; *Mitchell v. Robinson* (Mo. 1960) *supra*, 334 S.W.2d 11 (even though patient was upset, agitated, depressed, crying, had marital problems and had been drinking, the court found that since no emergency existed and he was legally competent he should have been advised of the risks of shock therapy); Mosely, Textbook of Surgery (3d ed. 1959) pp. 93–95; Laufman, Surgical Judgment, in Christopher's Textbook of Surgery (Davis ed. 1968) pp. 1459, 1461; Louisell & Williams, Medical Malpractice (1970) § 22.02; McCoid, *A Reappraisal of Liability for Unauthorized Medical Treatment* (1957) 41 Minn.L.Rev. 381; Plante, *An Analysis of "Informed Consent"* (1968) 36 Fordham L.Rev. 639.) Despite what defendant characterizes as the prevailing rule, it has never been unequivocally adopted by an authoritative source. Therefore we probe anew into the rationale which purportedly justifies, in accordance with medical rather than legal standards, the withholding of information from a patient.

Preliminarily we employ several postulates. The first is that patients are generally persons unlearned in the medical sciences and therefore, except in rare cases, courts may safely assume the knowledge of patient and physician are not in parity. The second is that a person of adult years and in sound mind has the right, in the exercise of control over his own body, to determine whether or not to submit to lawful medical treatment. The third is that the patient's consent to treatment, to be effective, must be an informed consent. And the fourth is that the patient, being unlearned in medical sciences, has an abject dependence upon and trust in his physician for the information upon which he relies during the decisional process, thus raising an obligation in the physician that transcends arms-length transactions.

From the foregoing axiomatic ingredients emerges a necessity, and a resultant requirement, for divulgence by the physician to his patient of all information relevant to a meaningful decisional process. In many instances, to the physician, whose training and experience enable a self-satisfying evaluation, the particular treatment which should be undertaken may seem evident, but it is the prerogative of the patient, not the physician, to determine for himself the direction in which he believes his interests lie. To enable the patient to chart his course knowledgeably, reasonable familiarity with the therapeutic alternatives and their hazards becomes essential.

Therefore, we hold, as an integral part of the physician's overall obligation to the patient there is a duty of reasonable disclosure of the available choices with respect to proposed therapy and of the dangers inherently and potentially involved in each.

A concomitant issue is the yardstick to be applied in determining reasonableness of disclosure. This defendant and the majority of courts have related the duty to the custom of physicians practicing in the community. (*Aiken v. Clary* (Mo. 1965) 396 S.W.2d 668, 675; *Roberts v. Young* (1963) 369 Mich. 133 [119 N.W.2d 627, 630]; *Haggerty* v. *McCarthy* (1962) 344 Mass. 136 [181 N.E.2d 562, 565]; *DiFilippo v. Preston* (1961) 53 Del. 539 [173 A.2d 333, 339].) The majority rule is needlessly overbroad. Even if there can be said to be a medical community standard as to the disclosure requirement for any prescribed treatment, it appears so nebulous that doctors become, in effect, vested with virtual absolute discretion. (See Note, *Physicians and Surgeons* (1962) 75 Harv.L.Rev. 1445; Waltz and Scheuneman, *Informed Consent to Therapy* (1970) 64 Nw.U.L.Rev. 628.) The court in *Canterbury v. Spence, supra,* 464 F.2d 772, 784, bluntly observed: "Nor can we ignore the fact that to bind the disclosure obligation to medical usage is to arrogate the decision on revelation to the physician alone. Respect for the patient's right of self-determination on particular therapy demands a standard set by law for physicians rather than one which physicians may or may not impose upon themselves." Unlimited discretion in the physician is irreconcilable with the basic right of the patient to make the ultimate informed decision regarding the course of treatment to which he knowledgeably consents to be subjected.

A medical doctor, being the expert, appreciates the risks inherent in the procedure he is prescribing, the risks of a decision not to undergo the treatment, and the probability of a successful outcome of the treatment. But once this information has been disclosed, that aspect of the doctor's expert function has been performed. The weighing of these risks against the individual subjective fears and hopes of the patient is not an expert skill. Such evaluation and decision is a nonmedical judgment reserved to the patient alone. A patient should be denied the opportunity to weigh the risks only where it is evident he cannot evaluate the data, as for example, where there is an emergency or the patient is a child or incompetent. For this reason the law provides that in an emergency consent is implied (*Wheeler v. Barker* (1949) 92 Cal.App.2d 776, 785 [208 P.2d 68]; *Preston v. Hubbell* (1948) 87 Cal.App.2d 53, 57–58, [196 P.2d 113]), and if the patient is a minor or incompetent, the authority to consent is transferred to the patient's legal guardian or closest available relative (*Ballard v. Anderson* (1971) 4 Cal.3d 873, 883 [95 Cal.Rptr. 1, 484 P.2d 1345]; *Doyle* v. *Giuliucci* (1965) 62 Cal.2d 606 [43 Cal.Rptr. 697]; *Bonner v. Moran* (1941) 126 F.2d 121 [75 App.D.C. 156]. In all cases other than the foregoing, the decision whether or not to undertake treatment is vested in the party most directly affected: the patient.

The scope of the disclosure required of physicians defies simple definition. Some courts have spoken of "full disclosure" (e.g., *Berkey v. Anderson, supra*, 1 Cal.App.3d 790, 804; *Salgo v. Leland Stanford etc. Bd. Trustees, supra*, 154 Cal.App.2d 560, 578) and others refer to "full and complete" disclosure (*Stafford v. Shultz* (1954) 42 Cal.2d 767, 777 [270 P.2d 1]; *Pashley v. Pacific Elec. Ry. Co.* (1944) 25 Cal.2d 226, 235 [153 P.2d 325]), but such facile expressions obscure common practicalities. Two qualifications to a requirement of "full disclosure" need little explication. First, the patient's interest in information does not extend to a lengthy polysyllabic discourse on all possible complications. A mini-course in medical science is not required; the patient is concerned with the risk of death or bodily harm, and problems of recuperation. Second, there is no physician's duty to discuss the relatively minor risks inherent in common procedures, when it is common knowledge that such risks inherent in the procedure are of very low incidence. When there is a common procedure a doctor must, of course, make such inquiries as are required to determine if for the particular patient the treatment under consideration is contraindicated—for example, to determine if the patient has had adverse reactions to medication; but no warning beyond such inquiries is required as to the remote possibility of death or serious bodily harm.

However, when there is a more complicated procedure, as the surgery in the case before us, the jury should be instructed that when a given procedure inherently involves a known risk of death or serious bodily harm, a medical doctor has a duty to disclose to his patient the potential of death or serious harm, and to explain in lay terms the complications that might possibly occur. Beyond the foregoing minimal disclosure, a doctor must also reveal to his patient such additional information as a skilled practitioner of good standing would provide under similar circumstances.

In sum, the patient's right of self-decision is the measure of the physician's duty to reveal. That right can be effectively exercised only if the patient possesses adequate information to enable an intelligent choice. The scope of the physician's communications to the patient, then, must be measured by the patient's need, and that need is whatever information is material to the decision. Thus the test for determining whether a potential peril must be divulged is its materiality to the patient's decision. (*Canterbury v. Spence, supra*, 464 F.2d 772, 786.)

We point out, for guidance on retrial, an additional problem which suggests itself. There must be a causal relationship between the physician's failure to inform and the injury to the plaintiff. Such causal connection arises only if it is established that had revelation been made consent to treatment would not have been given. Here the record discloses no testimony that had plaintiff been informed of the risks of surgery he would not have consented to the operation. (*Shetter* v. *Rochelle* (1965) 2 Ariz.App. 358 [409 P.2d 74]; *Sharpe v. Pugh* (1967) 270 N.C. 598 [155 S.E.2d 108]; cf. *Aiken* v. *Clary* (Mo. 1965) *supra*, 396 S.W.2d 668.)

The patient-plaintiff may testify on this subject but the issue extends beyond his credibility. Since at the time of trial the uncommunicated hazard has materialized, it would be surprising if the patient-plaintiff did not claim that had he been informed of the dangers he would have declined treatment. Subjectively he may believe so, with the 20/20 vision of hindsight, but we doubt that justice will be served by placing the physician in jeopardy of the patient's bitterness and disillusionment. Thus an objective test is preferable: i.e., what would a prudent person in the patient's position have decided if adequately informed of all significant perils. (*Canterbury v. Spence, supra*, 464 F.2d 772, 791.)

The burden of going forward with evidence of nondisclosure rests on the plaintiff. Once such evidence has been produced, then the burden of going forward with evidence pertaining to justification for failure to disclose shifts to the physician.

Whenever appropriate, the court should instruct the jury on the defenses available to a doctor who has failed to make the disclosure required by law. Thus, a medical doctor need not make disclosure of risks when the patient requests that he not be so informed. (See discussion of waiver: Hagman, *The Medical Patient's Right to Know, supra*, 17 U.C.L.A. L.Rev. 758, 785.) Such a disclosure need not be made if the procedure is simple and the danger remote and commonly appreciated to be remote. A disclosure need not be made beyond that required within the medical community when a doctor can prove by a preponderance of the evidence he relied upon facts which would demonstrate to a reasonable man the disclosure would have so seriously upset the patient that the patient would not have been able to dispassionately weigh the risks of refusing to undergo the recommended treatment. (E.g., see discussion of informing the dying patient: Hagman, *The Medical Pa-*

*tient's Right to Know, supra*, 17 U.C.L.A. L.Rev. 758, 778.) Any defense, of course, must be consistent with what has been termed the "fiducial qualities" of the physician-patient relationship. (*Emmett v. Eastern Dispensary and Casualty Hospital* (1967) 396 F.2d 931, 935 [130 App. D.C. 50].)

The judgment is reversed.

## NOTES

**1. Informed Consent.** As the principal case indicates, a physician's failure to inform a patient of material risks entailed in treatment can subject a physician to negligence liability. Today, only in extreme cases where the medical practitioner misrepresents the entire procedure, will most courts characterize such behavior as an intentional battery. See Keeton, *Prosser and Keeton on* The Law of Torts § 32 (5th ed. 1984); Diamond, Levine & Madden, *Understanding Torts*, § 7.03 (2nd ed. 2000) and Dobbs, *The Law of Torts* § 250 (2000).

**2. The "Physician Rule" and the "Patient Rule."** Courts are divided over whether the standard to inform should be determined by the professional standard or a reasonable person standard. Some courts under the so-called "physician rule" treat the duty to inform like any other medical malpractice claim. The medical profession in the community determines when a competent physician should inform the patient. Consider *Roberts v. Young*, 369 Mich. 133, 119 N.W.2d 627 (1963). The court held that the extent of the duty of a physician to warn of the risks associated with a caesarian section procedure was "determined with reference to the general practice customarily followed by the medical profession in the locality."

Other courts, as in the principal case, use the so-called "patient rule" which allows jurors to determine when the "reasonable" physician should inform regardless of current medical practice. Such courts distinguish between medical treatment, where jurors must defer to what the medical profession accepts as competent, and the informing of risks, where expert medical testimony is not required. In such jurisdictions the jurors are considered competent to evaluate when the doctor should inform and, when appropriate, find current dominant medical practices on informing to be inadequate. Which approach seems better?

**3. Causation.** Even when the plaintiff proves the defendant doctor breached the standard of conduct and failed to adequately inform the patient of risks, the plaintiff must also prove that the failure to inform caused the patient harm. (See Cause–In–Fact Chapter 2, Sec. E, infra.) If the patient would have accepted the treatment even if the risk had been disclosed, the doctor's failure to properly inform made no difference. The principal case analyzes this issue as what a hypothetical reasonable patient would do, while other courts ask what the particular patient would have done. Which approach do you think is fairer?

**4. Materiality of Risks.** Informed consent concerns only those risks that are "material" (Note 1, supra). What should constitute a "material" risk? Should the likelihood of a particular risk be factored against its gravity? *Canterbury v. Spence*, 464 F.2d 772 (D.C.Cir.1972), which was mentioned repeatedly in the principal case, concerned a 1% risk of paralysis. Consider also *Curtis v. MRI Imaging Services II*, 327 Or. 9, 956 P.2d 960

(1998), which allowed a malpractice claim where a patient was not informed that an MRI could cause him emotional distress by triggering his claustrophobia. At least one court held that it is not material to inform a patient of other doctors in the area that are more qualified ... do you agree? See *Goldberg v. Boone*, 167 Md.App. 410, 893 A.2d 625 (App. 2006), in which the Court of Special Appeals of Maryland rejected the argument by the plaintiff that the defendant, a specialist who had performed the specific type of surgery only once during the previous three years should have informed the plaintiff of his lack of experience and should have provided a referral to another doctor who performed that type of surgery regularly. The court held that the duty to obtain the patient's informed consent does not require the physician to advise the plaintiff that he might make a mistake during the surgery, or that there are more experienced surgeons in the area who are less likely to make a mistake.

Would it be wise to consider the context of the particular procedure in evaluating the materiality of risks involved? That is, should doctors have less of a duty to disclose when the procedure is necessary to prevent grave harm, as opposed to elective surgery? Or would this go too far in undercutting patient autonomy?

**5.  Danger of Not Having Treatment.** In *Truman v. Thomas*, 27 Cal.3d 285, 165 Cal.Rptr. 308, 611 P.2d 902 (1980), the patient declined a pap smear and subsequently died of cancer of the cervix. The California Supreme Court expanded the disclosure requirements adopted in *Cobbs* and held that "[i]f a patient indicates that he or she is going to *decline* the risk-free test or treatment, then the doctor has the additional duty of advising of all material risks of which a reasonable person would want to be informed before deciding not to undergo the procedure." Do you agree physicians should have the duty to warn their patients of the risks of declining medical treatment?

# SECTION C.  RULES OF LAW

## AKINS v. GLENS FALLS CITY SCHOOL DISTRICT

Court of Appeals of New York.
53 N.Y.2d 325, 441 N.Y.S.2d 644, 424 N.E.2d 531 (1981).

JASEN, Judge.

On this appeal, we are called upon to define the scope of the duty owed by a proprietor of a baseball field to the spectators attending its games. The specific question presented is whether such an owner, having provided protective screening for the area behind home plate, is liable in negligence for the injuries sustained by a spectator as a result of being struck by a foul ball while standing in an unscreened section of the field. . . .

\* \* \*

Plaintiff arrived while the game was in progress and elected to view the contest from a position behind the three-foot fence along the third base line, approximately 10 to 15 feet from the end of the backstop and 60 feet from home plate. As there were no seating facilities for spectators along the base lines, plaintiff had to stand in order to watch the game. At the time, other spectators were also standing along the base lines behind the three-foot fence. . . . Approximately 10 minutes after arriving at the baseball field, plaintiff was struck in the eye by a sharply hit foul ball, causing her serious and permanent injury.

The present action was then commenced by the plaintiff against the defendant school district. Alleging that the school district was negligent in failing to provide safe and proper screening devices along the base lines of its field, plaintiff sought judgment against the school district in the sum of $250,000. After trial, the jury returned a verdict in plaintiff's favor, assessing damages in the amount of $100,000. . . .

\* \* \*

We hold that, in the exercise of reasonable care, the proprietor of a ball park need only provide screening for the area of the field behind home plate where the danger of being struck by a ball is the greatest. . . .

\* \* \*

As the dissent correctly notes, what constitutes reasonable care under the circumstances ordinarily is a question for the jury. This is not to say, however, that in every case involving a landowner's liability in negligence the question whether reasonable care was exercised must be determined by the jury. . . .

\* \* \*

COOKE, Chief Judge (dissenting).

The majority today engages in an unfortunate exercise in judicial rule making in an area that should be left to the jury. . . . I therefore dissent and vote to affirm.

\* \* \*

The majority errs . . . in deciding as a matter of law exactly what steps by a baseball field proprietor will constitute reasonable care under the circumstances. Such a determination, by its very dependence upon the "circumstances", hinges upon the facts of the individual situation and should be left for the jury. Indeed, those exceptions to this rule that have been made by courts occur only in those narrow classes of cases where an identical set of facts is likely to recur with regularity, and "[s]uch holdings today are rare" (2 Harper and James, Torts, p 977).

\* \* \*

The majority has in effect undertaken the task of prescribing the size, shape and location of backstops and other protective devices that will satisfy a baseball field owner's duty of reasonable care under the circumstances. This attempt to impose a straightjacket upon the relationship between a baseball field proprietor and spectators, regardless of the particular circumstances, is arbitrary and unrealistic. It is reminiscent of the Supreme Court's attempt, in the early years of the automobile, to impose upon the operator the duty of leaving the vehicle and examining each railroad grade crossing on foot, if necessary for a better view of the tracks (*Baltimore & Ohio R. R. v. Goodman*, 275 U.S. 66 [per Holmes, J.]). This standard enjoyed little favor among State courts, engendered confusion among lower Federal courts attempting to apply it and was quickly repudiated by the Supreme Court (*Pokora v. Wabash Ry. Co.*, 292 U.S. 98).

In *Pokora*, Justice Cardozo noted that the problems springing from the grade-crossing rule emphasized "the need for caution in framing standards of behavior that amount to rules of law" (*id.* at p 105). Indeed, railroad crossing cases provide a good example of this court's reluctance to impose blanket rules of conduct divorced from actual events. More than a century ago, this court stated that "[i]t is a general rule that care commensurate with the danger must be exercised, and it is also a general rule that it is the province of the jury, and not of the court, to determine whether such care has been exercised" (*Dolan v. Delaware & Hudson Canal Co.*, 71 N.Y. 285, 288; see, also, *Beisiegel v. New York Cent. R. R. Co.*, 34 N.Y. 622, 625–626). . . .

The wisdom of eschewing such blanket rules where negligence is concerned is obvious. In the present context, the majority has held as a matter of law that the proprietor of the baseball field fulfilled his duty of reasonable care by erecting a backstop that was 24 feet high and 50 feet wide. The court issues this rule with no more expertise available to it than Justice Holmes had in 1927 when he recommended that motorists venture on foot onto railroad grade crossings for a better view. It has selected one of a variety of forms of protection currently in use at professional ballparks and school playgrounds—what in reality is nothing more than a straight, high fence behind home plate—and has designated it as sufficient protection as a matter of law.

Such a ruling robs the jury of its ability to pass on whether the circumstances here might have made this type of backstop inadequate. In the present case, the majority has taken from the jury its ability to consider the following evidence: that the cost of placing "wings" on the backstop extending to first and third base would have been only $209 when the backstop was built; that other baseball diamonds do have such wings; that the type of game being played at the field was not a softball game between young tykes but rather a varsity high school hardball game involving players such as the batter in this incident, who was six-foot two-inches tall, weighed 190 pounds and was advanced enough in ability to later play professional ball; that school authorities were aware that line drives "frequently" went over the low fence that ran along the base lines, and that there were no signs or other warnings of the dangers of standing behind this fence. Because of public familiarity with the "national pastime", no expert testimony would generally be required to make out a showing of failure to exercise due care in such a case (see *Meiselman v. Crown Hgts. Hosp.*, 285 N.Y. 389, 396). In this case, however, the jury even had before it the testimony of a civil engineer as to the feasibility and minimal cost of ensuring greater safety for spectators. This makes an even stronger argument for sending this case to the jury.

The court's ruling will also foreclose juries in the future from considering the wide range of circumstances of individual cases, as well as new developments in safety devices or procedures. Unless the court plans to periodically take up such cases in the future to adjust its rule, it has frozen a position that is certain to become outdated, if it is not already. It would make as much sense for the court to decree, as a matter of law, what sort of batting helmet or catcher's mask a school district should supply to its baseball team. Baseball may be a sport steeped in tradition, but it is hardly immune from technological change and shifts in public perception of what constitute reasonable safety measures. It has traditionally been the jury that reflects these shifts and changes.

\* \* \*

## NOTES

**1. Rules of Law.** In most cases juries must determine what is reasonable under the circumstances to determine negligence. Consequently, a jury in a negligence case must not only decide what the disputed facts surrounding the accident were, but also must agree on what behavior constitutes negligent conduct. On occasion judges have enunciated rules that under certain circumstances a particular conduct is negligent or not negligent, which may establish a precedent for other cases where the facts are substantially the same. To that extent, the standard of reasonable conduct may be defined by this precedent. The Restatement (Second) of Torts articulates this approach as follows:

The standard of conduct of a reasonable man may be

. . .

(C) established by judicial decision;

. . .

. . . Certain situations, or combinations of situations, recur with such frequency that it is possible to find a fairly definite expression of judicial opinion as to the manner in which persons who find themselves therein should conduct themselves. . . .

Restatement (Second) of Torts § 285(c), cmt. e. See also Keeton, *Prosser and Keeton on* The Law of Torts § 35 (5th ed. 1984); Diamond, Levine & Madden, *Understanding Torts* § 4.04 (2nd ed. 2000) and Dobbs, *The Law of Torts* § 132 (2000).

The principal case describes the ultimately rejected efforts of Justice Holmes to establish rules of behavior when a driver crosses railroad tracks. Consider a more recent decision, *Trevino v. Union Pacific Railroad Co.*, 916 F.2d 1230 (7th Cir.1990), which rejected a rule of law requiring a driver to notice a railroad car standing at a crossing:

Under Holmes' ["Stop, Look, and Listen"] approach the railroad has no liability to a traveler who fails to stop, and under the standing-car-rule it has no liability to a traveler who collides with a railroad car that is at rest in the crossing. In both cases the burden of prevention rests wholly on the traveler; if the accident occurs, he is solely at fault for having failed to prevent it. Both rules buck the twentieth century trends toward leaving questions of care to the jury to decide under the broad unelaborated standard of negligence.

Thus, the standing-car-rule was held inapplicable by the court in defining the standard of conduct in this case.

**2. A "Legal Dinosaur"?** As the principal case demonstrates, courts still may on occasion adopt a rule of law establishing the required standard of conduct. In *Hurst v. Union Pacific Railroad Co.*, 958 F.2d 1002 (10th Cir.1992) the majority upheld Oklahoma's "occupied crossing rule" requiring that the driver must notice a railroad car, whether moving or not on the crossing, despite evidence it was a dark, foggy night and that seconds later another collision between a car and the same train occurred. Consider the dissent's vigorous commentary:

> This appeal unlooses a legal dinosaur, which, once out, tramples twentieth century negligence law and then lumbers back to its dark cave only to await another victim. The jurisprudential fossils it leaves behind are truly daunting as this case illustrates. However, absent any contra-indication from the Oklahoma Supreme Court, the dinosaur prevails.

* * *

> Plaintiff's complaint alleged, at approximately 3:05 a.m., their 17–year-old son Roy was driving north on South Rock Creek Road in Pottawatomie County, Oklahoma, in an extremely heavy fog when he collided with a train owned by Union Pacific and driven by Marlyn Coleman. The complaint stated because of the heavy fog, "the train was not visible three cars away." As further evidence of the density of the fog, the complaint stated that within seconds after Roy Hurst's fatal collision another automobile traveling south on South Rock Creek Road ran into the other side of the same train. The complaint alleged that neither the moving train not the crossing was equipped with any warning devices except for the standard wooden crossbuck railroad marker positioned on either side of the railroad crossing. The complaint alleged two similar collisions occurred at this crossing; the area around it was heavily populated; a school was located only 1,250 feet away; and on a particular day, 640 vehicles used the crossing. Plaintiffs alleged Union Pacific's knowledge of other fatal accidents "coupled with the dangerous nature of the crossing, the foggy conditions, heavy traffic count, dense population, and proximity to school, combined to create unusual circumstances under Oklahoma law" requiring Union Pacific to construct additional safety devices and its employee to drop flares to warn oncoming vehicles of the presence of trains. Having failed to perform that duty, plaintiffs alleged Union Pacific and its employee were negligent.

* * *

> That both accidents occurred in the dense fog with the second driver traveling well under the legal speed limit must raise the inference that "the presence" of the train on this crossing was not discernible until the traveling public was so close that stopping was impossible. Nevertheless, under Oklahoma law, it is not relevant

that a driver can "see" the presence of the train as long as the train occupies the crossing.

How persuasive is the argument that rules of law avoid excessive litigation and provide society with an appropriate degree of certainty on what constitutes negligent and non-negligent conduct? Did the majority in the principal case rule incorrectly?

# SECTION D.   NEGLIGENCE PER SE

## WAWANESA MUTUAL INSURANCE CO. v. MATLOCK

Court of Appeal, Fourth District, Division 3, California.
60 Cal.App.4th 583, 70 Cal.Rptr.2d 512 (1997).

SILLS, P. J.

\* \* \*

Timothy Matlock, age seventeen, bought two packs of cigarettes from a gas station one day in April 1993. Tim gave one of the packs to his friend, Eric Erdley, age fifteen. Smoking as they walked, the two trespassed onto a private storage facility in Huntington Beach, where a couple of hundred telephone poles were stacked up high upon the ground, held in place by two vertical poles sticking out of the ground. The two had climbed on the logs many times before.

Timothy and Eric were joined by 2 younger boys, about 10 or 11 years old, who walked with them on the logs. Eric was smoking a cigarette held in his left hand. Timothy began to tease the younger boys, telling them the logs were going to fall. The boys started to run, though perhaps more out of laughter than of fear. One of the younger boys ran right into Eric's left arm. Eric dropped his cigarette down between the logs, where it landed on a bed of sand. For about 20 seconds Eric tried to retrieve the cigarette, but he couldn't reach it. He stood up and tried to extinguish it by spitting on it, and again was unsuccessful.

Then Eric caught up with Timothy, who was about 10 feet ahead. They went into some bunkers about 50 feet away; when they came out again after about 20 minutes, they saw flames at the base of the logs. They were seen running from the location.

The Woodman Pole Company suffered considerable property damage because of the fire. . . .

After a bench trial, the court awarded the insurer $44,500 against Timothy and [his father] Paul, which included $25,000 against Paul based on a statute which fixes liability on a custodial parent for the willful misconduct of a minor. (See Civ. Code, § 1714.1, subd. (a.).) . . . . The judge stated that the statute that makes it unlawful to give cigarettes to minors, Penal Code section 308, had to have been enacted in 1891 with "more than health concerns" in mind, "since the health issues on tobacco are of considerably more recent concern."

Timothy and his father Paul now appeal, arguing that there is no basis on which to hold Timothy liable for the damage caused when Eric dropped the cigarette.

We agree. There is no valid basis on which to hold Timothy liable.

## II.

### Negligence Per Se[2]

(1) Just because a statute has been violated does not mean that the violator is necessarily liable for any damage that might be ultimately traced back to the violation. As the court stated in *Olsen v. McGillicuddy* (1971) 15 Cal.App.3d 897, 902–903 [93 Cal.Rptr. 530]: "The doctrine of negligence per se does not apply even though a statute has been violated if the plaintiff was not in the class of persons designed to be protected or the type of harm which occurred was not one which the statute was designed to prevent." Mere "but for" causation, as is urged in Wawanesa's brief, is simply not enough. The statute must be designed to protect against the *kind of harm* which occurred.

(2a) The statute that makes it illegal to furnish tobacco to minors, Penal Code section 308, has nothing to do with fire suppression. As it *now* stands, it is intended to prevent early *addiction* to tobacco. It may be true, as the trial court opined, that when the first version of the statute was enacted in 1891 (see Stats. 1891, ch. 70, § 1, p. 64) it was not directed primarily at protecting minors' health.[3] But it is most certainly a health statute as it exists *today*. As our Supreme Court recently noted in *Mangini v. R. J. Reynolds Tobacco Co.* (1994) 7 Cal.4th 1057, 1060 [31 Cal.Rptr.2d 358, 875 P.2d 73] (quoting from an affirmed decision of the Court of Appeal), section 308 " 'reflects a statutory policy of protecting minors from addiction to cigarettes.' " The connection of section 308 with health is emphasized by the court's specifically analogizing section 308 to former Health and Safety Code section 25967, which states that preventing children from "beginning to use tobacco products"is "among the highest priorities in *disease* prevention for the State of California." (*Mangini, supra,* 7 Cal.4th at pp. 1061–1062, italics added [quoting from appellate opinion quoting statute].)

---

**2.** .... (See Evid. Code, § 669, subd. (a)(1) ["The failure of a person to exercise due care is presumed if: [¶] ... He violated a statute ..."].)

**3.** Which raises the question—why *was* it originally enacted? The trial judge may have been a little hasty in concluding that health was not the reason behind the 1891 statute. The noxiousness of tobacco was known long before 1891. Back in 1604 James I called it a custom "dangerous to the lungs" in his Counterblaste to Tobacco. By 1630 (give or take a few years), Sultan Murad IV tried to ban the use of tobacco. He failed. For their part, the Puritans of the Massachusetts Bay Colony tried to prohibit smoking about the same time as Murad. They failed as well.

Assuming, for sake of argument, that the Legislature did not have minors' health at heart when it prohibited giving tobacco to them in 1891, the placement of section 308 in chapter 7 of title 9 of the Penal Code, dealing with crimes against religion, conscience and "good morals," furnishes another answer. While we do not have the legislative history from 1891, it appears the statute was most probably enacted to protect minors from the general licentiousness associated with the consumption of cigarettes in the 1890's. (These days-though we recognize that there is altogether too much teenage tobacco smoking-cigarettes tend to be associated more with the World War II generation than with cheesy dens of iniquity.) However, we have found nothing, and certainly Wawanesa has cited us to nothing, which would show that section 308 was ever enacted out of some concern that minors with cigarettes would pose a fire hazard.

Nothing suggests that section 308 is part of any scheme to prevent fires. Its placement in the general morals section of the Penal Code belies such an intent.

\* \* \*

# STACHNIEWICZ v. MAR–CAM CORPORATION
Supreme Court of Oregon.
259 Or. 583, 488 P.2d 436 (1971).

HOLMAN, Justice.

The patron of a drinking establishment seeks to recover against the operator for personal injuries allegedly inflicted by other customers during a barroom brawl. The jury returned a verdict for defendant. Plaintiff appealed.

\* \* \*

The principal issue is whether, as plaintiff contends, violations of ORS 471.410(3) and of Oregon Liquor Control Regulation No. 10–065(2) constitute negligence as a matter of law. The portion of the statute relied on by plaintiff reads as follows:

"(3) No person shall give or otherwise make available any alcoholic liquor to a person visibly intoxicated \* \* \*."

The portion of the regulation to which plaintiff points provides:

"(2) No licensee shall permit or suffer any loud, noisy, disorderly or boisterous conduct, or any profane or abusive language, in or upon his licensed premises, or permit any visibly intoxicated person to enter or remain upon his licensed premises."

The trial court held that a violation of either the statute or the regulation did not constitute negligence per se. It refused requested instructions and withdrew allegations of negligence which were based on their violation.

A violation of a statute or regulation constitutes negligence as a matter of law when the violation results in injury to a member of the class of persons intended to be protected by the legislation and when the harm is of the kind which the statute or regulation was enacted to prevent. *Dimick v. Linnell*, 240 Or. 509, 511, 402 P.2d 734 (1965); *Smith v. Portland Traction Co.*, 226 Or. 221, 359 P.2d 899 (1961). The reason behind the rule is that when a legislative body has generalized a standard from the experience of the community and prohibits conduct that is likely to cause harm, the court accepts the formulation. Justice Traynor in *Clinkscales v. Carver*, 22 Cal.2d 72, 136 P.2d 777 (1943).

However, in addition, it is proper for the court to examine preliminarily the appropriateness of the standard as a measure of care for civil litigation under the circumstances presented. F. James, Jr., "Statutory Standards and Negligence in Accident Cases," 11 La.L.Rev. 95, 111–12 (1950–51); Restatement (Second) of Torts § 286, comment d (1965). The statute in question prevents making available alcohol to a person who is *already visibly intoxicated*. This makes the standard particularly inappropriate for the awarding of civil damages because of the extreme difficulty, if not impossibility, of determining whether a third party's injuries would have been caused, in any event, by the already inebriated person. Unless we are prepared to say that an alcoholic drink given after visible intoxication is the cause of a third party's injuries as a matter of law, a concept not advanced by anyone, the standard would be one almost impossible of application by a factfinder in most circumstances.

. . . . Hence, we agree with the trial court that a violation of the statute should not constitute negligence as a matter of law in a civil action for damages against its violator.

The regulation promulgated by the commission is an altogether different matter. The regulation requires certain conduct of licensees in the operation of bars. The regulation was issued under ORS 471.730(5) which provides:

"The function, duties and powers of the commission include the following:

"* * *.

"(5) To adopt such regulations as are necessary and feasible for carrying out the provisions of this chapter and to amend or repeal such regulations. When such regulations are adopted they shall have the full force and effect of law."

ORS 471.030, entitled "Purpose of Liquor Control Act," provides, in part, as follows:

"(1) The Liquor Control Act shall be liberally construed so as:

"(a) To prevent the recurrence of abuses associated with saloons or resorts for the consumption of alcoholic beverages.

"* * *."

An examination of the regulation discloses that it concerns matters having a direct relation to the creation of physical disturbances in bars which would, in turn, create a likelihood of injury to customers. A common feature of our western past, now preserved in story and reproduced on the screen hundreds of times, was the carnage of the barroom brawl. No citation of authority is needed to establish that the "abuses associated with saloons," which the Liquor Control Act seeks to prevent, included permitting on the premises profane, abusive conduct and drunken clientele (now prohibited by the regulation) which results in serious personal injuries to customers in breach of the bar owner's duty to protect his patrons from harm. We find it reasonable to assume that the commission, in promulgating the regulation, intended to prevent these abuses, and that they had in mind the safety of patrons of bars as well as the general peace and quietude of the community. In view of the quoted purpose of the Act and of the history of injury to innocent patrons of saloons, we cannot assume otherwise.

In addition, we see no reason why the standard is not an appropriate one for use in the awarding of civil damages. Because plaintiff was within the class of persons intended to be protected by the regulation and the harm caused to him was the kind the statute was intended to prevent, we hold that the trial court erred in not treating the alleged violations of the regulation as negligence as a matter of law.

Besides contending that the regulation should not be used as a standard of care for the protection of plaintiff, defendant also contends that, in any event, there was insufficient evidence to submit to the jury the questions of whether permitting visibly intoxicated persons to remain upon the premises, and failing to remove them therefrom after they had threatened violence, were causes of the injuries to plaintiff. Defendant argues that there is no proof of causation because it was not shown the one of the persons in the booth inflicted the injuries upon plaintiff, nor, if it is inferred that one of them did, could it be shown that it was as the result of defendant's failure to remove such person from the premises. We believe it would be fair for the jury to infer, in the circumstances set forth in the statement of the facts, that plaintiff was injured by one of the persons in the booth who had created the disturbance and that the injuries would not have occurred except for defendant's violation of the commission's regulation, as alleged.

The judgment of the trial court is reversed and the case is remanded for a new trial.

## NOTES

**1. Negligence Per Se.** On occasion courts in a negligence action will adopt the standard of conduct from a criminal statute, administrative regulation, or other legislative enactment. In such instances the jury no longer determines the standard of conduct by deciding what a "reasonable person" would do. Instead the conduct required by the criminal law or regulation is used by the judge to determine the proper conduct that the defendant should have followed. The adoption of the legislative standard is called "negligence per se." The jury still must determine, if contested, whether factually the defendant transgressed the standard and whether the breach was the cause of the plaintiff's injury. The Restatement (Second) of Torts articulates this approach as follows:

> The court may adopt as the standard of conduct of a reasonable man the requirements of a legislative enactment or an administrative regulation whose purpose is found exclusively or in part
>
> (a) to protect a class of persons which includes the one whose interest is invaded, and
>
> (b) to protect the particular interest which is invaded, and
>
> (c) to protect that interest against the kind of harm which has resulted, and
>
> (d) to protect that interest against the particular hazard from which the harm results.

Restatement (Second) of Torts § 286 (1965). See also Keeton, *Prosser and Keeton on* The Law of Torts § 32 (5th ed. 1984); Diamond, Levine & Madden, *Understanding Torts* § 6.02 (2nd ed. 2000); and Dobbs, *The Law of Torts* §§ 133–142 (2000).

2. **Type of Harm and Class of Persons.** As indicated by the Restatement section quoted above, the judge may, but is not required to, adopt the statutory standard in the negligence suit when the type of harm to be prevented and the class of persons to be protected are the same in the statute and the tort action. Consider, for example, *Martin v. Herzog*, 228 N.Y. 164, 126 N.E. 814 (1920), where the plaintiff's wagon collided with the defendant's automobile coming from the opposite direction, killing plaintiff's husband. The plaintiff's failure to use headlights on the wagon constituted negligence per se as this was a violation of a highway law intended to protect motorists from injury. Consider also *Sinclair v. Okata*, 874 F.Supp. 1051 (D.Alaska 1994), where the defendant's failure to comply with a section of a code requiring a person who owns a dog or cat to keep the animal under restraint at all times constituted negligence per se when the dog bit and injured the two-year-old plaintiff.

Compare *Randi W. v. Muroc Joint Unified School District*, 14 Cal.4th 1066, 60 Cal.Rptr.2d 263, 929 P.2d 582 (1997), where the defendant's alleged failure to report to the authorities various incidents of sexual misconduct of one of its former employees did not constitute negligence per se because the plaintiff, a student of another school district, was "not a member of the class for whose protection the Reporting Act was enacted."

3. **Unattended Vehicles Statutes.** Courts are divided over whether "unattended vehicle" statutes can be a basis for establishing negligence per se when the plaintiff is injured by a car thief driving a stolen vehicle. Consider *Vining v. Avis Rent–A–Car Systems*, 354 So.2d 54 (Fla.1977). The court held that Florida's unattended vehicle statute requiring that "no person permit a vehicle to stand unattended without stopping the engine, locking the car, and removing the key" was designed to protect the general public from a car thief's dangerous driving. But consider *DeCastro v. Boylan*, 367 So.2d 83 (La. App. 1979) where the defendant in violation of a similar statute left the car keys in his unlocked car in front of a construction site where it was stolen. The court held the statute was designed to protect auto owners and the police but not members of the public injured by a car thief.

4. **Licensing Statutes.** Consider also licensing statutes, which the majority of courts have refused to use as a standard of care. For example, in *Hertz Driv–Ur–Self System v. Hendrickson*, 109 Colo. 1, 121 P.2d 483 (1942), a nineteen-year-old unlicensed driver was involved in an automobile accident while driving friends back from the top of a mountain lookout site. The court refused to allow a negligence per se standard to serve as a pretext for establishing negligence when, in fact, the driver was not necessarily negligent—only unlicensed. Consider also *Rentschler v. Lewis*, 33 S.W.3d 518 (2000) where a driver whose license had been suspended for failing to attend alcohol classes following an alcohol related motorcycle accident, collided with another car in a parking lot. The court refused to allow a negligence per se standard to serve as a pretext for establishing negligence when the fact that the driver had a suspended license "could not be considered as evidence of negligence because that fact had no causal relationship to the accident."

5. **Consistency Between Civil and Criminal Law.** The use of negligence per se enables courts to apply a consistent standard in torts and criminal cases. Generally, it would appear awkward for a jury to conclude that it was not negligent for the defendant to have violated a criminal law adopted to protect the same class of potential victims and prevent the same

type of harm. Nevertheless, courts are free to determine that a statutory standard should not be adopted in the negligence action. The court may determine the statute is antiquated or does not provide a sufficiently clear standard. See, for example, *Weston v. Washington Metropolitan Area Transit Authority*, 78 F.3d 682 (D.C.Cir.1996), where an alleged violation of a particular statute did not constitute negligence per se because at the time of the alleged violation, the statute had been repealed. See also *Dougherty v. Santa Fe Marine, Inc.*, 698 F.2d 232 (5th Cir.1983), where the 5th Circuit held that because it is "[i]mplicit in virtually all discussions of negligence per se . . . that the regulation in question establishes a clear minimum standard of care," where two regulations offer conflicting directions, there is no clear minimum standard of care and, therefore, no negligence per se.

**6. Negligence Per Se and the Child Standard.** Negligence per se is generally not applied in lieu of the child standard (see Chapter 2, Sec. B, supra). Consider *Bauman v. Crawford*, 104 Wash.2d 241, 704 P.2d 1181 (Wash. 1985), where the Supreme Court of Washington held that a "minor's violation of a statute does not constitute proof of negligence per se, but may, in proper cases, be introduced as evidence of a minor's negligence."

**7. Excuses for Violations.** Even when a statutory standard is adopted, most jurisdictions will allow the defendant to offer an excuse for violations when compliance would be more dangerous than non-compliance or when compliance would be impossible. Alternatively, other jurisdictions utilize the statutory standard as a presumptive standard which the defendant can rebut. For instance, suppose driver A goes over a double yellow line to the wrong side of the road in violation of the traffic code and collides into an oncoming car. If A did so in order to avoid hitting a jaywalker, the court could accept A's excuse and not find negligence per se. In very unusual instances, the court will not allow any excuse, effectively establishing strict liability (see Chapter 3, Sec. A, infra).

**8. Criminal Statutes Only?** Some courts differ from the Restatement approach and will apply negligence per se only to criminal statutes, and not to administrative rules or municipal ordinances. These courts often will, however, allow the ordinance or regulations to serve as evidence of the proper standard of conduct.

**9. Civil Liability Statutes Compared.** Negligence per se should be distinguished from civil statutes which impose civil liability for certain conduct. In negligence per se, the standard for negligence is being adopted from a statute that was not enacted to impose civil liability.

**10. Reasonableness Per Se.** Courts do not automatically conclude that compliance with a criminal statute or regulation means the defendant has acted reasonably. Most such statutory standards are viewed as minimum requirements, and do not necessarily suggest that compliance will protect the defendant from negligence liability. See Keeton, *supra*, § 36.

# SECTION E.    CAUSE–IN–FACT

## EAST TEXAS THEATRES, INC. v. RUTLEDGE

Supreme Court of Texas.
453 S.W.2d 466 (1970).

SMITH, Justice.

This is a damage suit alleging personal injuries were sustained by Sheila Rutledge, on or about September 25, 1966, while attending a midnight movie in a theatre owned and operated by East Texas Theatres, Inc. . . . The jury found the defendant guilty of negligence in failing to remove certain unidentified "rowdy persons" from the theatre and that such negligence was a proximate cause of Sheila's injuries. Damages were assessed by the jury at $31,250.00. Based upon the jury findings, the trial court entered judgment for the plaintiffs. The Court of Civil Appeals has affirmed. 445 S.W.2d 538. We reverse the judgments of both courts and here render judgment that the plaintiffs take nothing.

* * *

On September 24 and the early morning of September 25, 1966, Sheila, a paying guest, was attending a special "midnight show" at the Paramount Theatre, one of the several theatres owned by the defendant. The interior of the theatre was arranged with a lower floor and a balcony for the seating of patrons. Sheila and her friends took seats on the lower floor in the left section close to an aisle which ran parallel with the left wall and out beyond the overhang of the balcony. When the picture came to an end, Sheila started making her exit, after the lights were turned on, using the aisle between the left section and the wall. As she proceeded up the aisle toward the front of the building for the purpose of leaving the theatre and just before she walked under the balcony overhang, some unidentified person in the balcony threw a bottle which struck her on the side of her head just above her left ear.

### Conduct of the Theatre Patrons

Since the jury found that the patrons in the balcony were acting in a "rowdy" manner and that the defendant, its agents, servants and employees, negligently failed to remove such rowdy persons from the premises and that such negligence proximately caused the injuries sustained by Sheila, we deem it important to particularly point out the evidence bearing on the conduct of the patrons during the evening. The evidence favorable to the verdict is that during the progress of the show, the patrons in the theatre, both on the lower floor and in the balcony, were engaged in "hollering." Sheila, in describing the "hollering," said that "a few slang words" were used. This "hollering" was intermittent; it occurred "off and on" during "parts of" the movie. One witness testified that " * * * they would holler and maybe slack off a few minutes and then holler again." Buddy Henderson testified that he saw paper or cold drink cups either "drifting down" or being thrown down toward the front of the theatre. Sheila did not see throwing of any type. Henderson testified that he did not recall anything drifting down or being thrown down other than the paper cold drink cups. In regard to the duration of the commotion in the theatre, the evidence shows that there was more commotion on the lower floor than in the balcony. Henderson testified that he thought that the 'hollering' seemed to get worse toward the end of the show. Sheila was certain that " * * * (a)bout 30 minutes before the show was over it seemed to be quieter; they didn't seem to be as rowdy then." Sheila, Henderson and an officer by the name of Burt, all agreed in their testimony that before the show was over, and, thus, before the accident, all commotion in the theatre had ceased. The last disturbance of any kind before the show was over was not throwing but "hollering." Henderson further testified that nothing happened, whether "hollering" or the throwing of paper cups, to make him think that something bad was going to happen; he was not worried about the safety of himself or the safety of his friends or anybody that was there.

### THE BALCONY PATRONS AND THEIR CONDUCT

The balcony, which would seat 263 people, was "just about full." The witness, Burt, estimated that about 175 of the balcony seats were occupied. The disturbance in the balcony seemed to come from the balcony generally, "just all over it." The evidence does not identify any particular person as being a "rowdy person." No witness could state which persons in the balcony were rowdy and which were not. No witness could identify the person who threw the bottle. Incidentally, there is no evidence that a hard substance of any character was thrown, other than the bottle which struck Sheila. The witness, Henderson, testified that he could not identify the person who threw the bottle, but that out of the corner of his eye, he saw a "movement, a jerking motion" by someone in the balcony and then saw the bottle hit Sheila. No witness testified that the bottle thrower had been engaged in "hollering" or throwing paper cups. The jury found that Sheila's injuries were not solely caused by the action of "some unknown person who threw a bottle * * *."

Assuming without deciding that the finding of negligence is supported by evidence of probative force, we go direct to the question of whether there is in the record evidence or probative force to support the finding of proximate cause. We hold that there is no evidence to support the finding of the jury that the failure of the defendant to remove "rowdy persons" from its premises was a proximate cause of Sheila's injuries.

"Proximate cause" was defined by the trial court exactly as the definition of the term was given by the trial court in the case of *Baumler v. Hazelwood*, 162 Tex. 361, 347 S.W.2d 560 (1961). Just as we said in *Baumler v. Hazelwood* and later in *Texas & Pacific Railway Co. v. McCleery*, 418 S.W.2d 494 (Tex. Sup.1967), it is well settled that proximate cause includes two essential elements: (1) there must be cause in fact—a cause which produces an event and without which the event would not have occurred; and (2) foreseeability. See also, *Hopson v. Gulf Oil Corp.*, 150 Tex. 1, 237 S.W.2d 352 (1951). "An essential element of the plaintiff's cause of action for negligence is that there be some reasonable connection between the act or omission of the defendant and the damage which the plaintiff has suffered." Prosser, Law of Torts (3rd Ed.) 240–41, "Causation", 41 (1964). We base our decision here on the ground that the plaintiffs have failed to offer evidence of probative force to establish the cause-in-fact element of proximate cause. In particular, the plaintiffs contend that the act of omission in failing to remove "rowdy persons" from the theatre was a proximate cause of the injuries resulting from the throwing of the bottle by an unknown patron of the theatre. We recognize that cause-in-fact covers the defendant's omissions as well as its acts. However, it cannot be said from this record that had the defendant removed the "rowdy persons" from the premises, the bottle thrower would not have thrown the bottle. The record in this case clearly shows a complete lack of proof that the bottle would not have been thrown "but for" the failure of the defendant to remove "rowdy persons" from the premises. There is no evidence that the bottle thrower was one of the "rowdy persons" engaged in "hollering" and throwing paper cups from the balcony. We cannot say from this evidence what persons would have been removed. We agree with the defendant's contention as made in its Motion for Instructed Verdict; Motion for Judgment non obstante veredicto; Amended Motion for New Trial; points in the Court of Civil Appeals and in this Court that the judgment of the trial court cannot be sustained in that there is no evidence that the alleged injuries were proximately caused by any act of commission or omission of the defendant. As said by this Court in *Enloe v. Barfield*, 422 S.W.2d 905 (Tex.Sup.1967), "a finding of 'proximate cause' cannot be sustained unless there is proof of cause in fact and foreseeability." See *Whitfield v. Cox*, 189 Va. 219, 52 S.E.2d 72 (1949).

The plaintiffs further contend that cause-in-fact was proved on the theory that "it would be considerably more probable that had even minimum supervision, such as a request by theatre employees to cease such rowdy behavior, or for the policeman to even go to the balcony and stand so that he might be seen by the patrons in the balcony, would have prevented the person who did throw the bottle from doing so because of his fear of being apprehended. That the theatre, by and through its employees, in failing to give this minimum supervision or yet, the more burdensome elements submitted upon the part of the plaintiff, failure to oust persons engaging in rowdy behavior, encouraged the wrongdoer by guaranteeing his anonymity in a crowd to the point that he felt he could and did in fact, get away with throwing the bottle." This theory is related in no way to the single act of throwing the bottle. It is purely speculative as to what would have happened had the defendant attempted to remove the "rowdy persons" from the theatre. The bottle thrower may not have been present at a time when the "rowdy persons" were being ejected. If present at the time of removal of the persons who were "hollering" and throwing paper cups, it would be just a guess as to what subjective effect such action may have had upon the bottle thrower. To adopt the "guaranteed anonymity" theory would be allowing a presumption of fact to rest upon a fact presumed. This cannot be permitted . . . . . " 'One presumption cannot be based upon another presumption.' *Mo. Pac. Ry. Co. v. Porter*, 73 Tex. 304, 11 S.W. 324, * * *."

We recognize that the theatre was under a duty to exercise reasonable care for the safety of its patrons. *Marek v. Southern Enterprises, Inc.*, 128 Tex. 377, 99 S.W.2d 594 (1936). However, operators of theatres are not insurers of their patrons' safety. *Vance v. Obadal*, 256 S.W.2d 139, 140 (Tex.Civ.App.1953, writ ref.).

The judgments of the Court of Civil Appeals and the trial court are reversed and judgment is here rendered that plaintiffs take nothing.

### NOTES

1. **"But For" Test.** The main approach to determining whether a defendant's conduct in fact caused a plaintiff's harm is the "but for" test. Under this approach, the plaintiff must prove by a preponderance of the evidence that *but for* the defendant's conduct, the plaintiff would not have been harmed. To illustrate, suppose A negligently constructs a building in a city known for earthquakes so that the building is not strong enough to withstand a mild "routine" earthquake. If the routine earthquake strikes, A's negligence is a "but for" cause of the building's collapse. However, if a catastrophic earthquake strikes that would have destroyed even a well-built building just as quickly as A's building, A is not a "but for" cause of the building's destruction. See generally Diamond, Levine & Madden, *Understanding Torts* § 11.02 (2nd ed. 2000); Keeton, *Prosser and Keeton on* The Law of Torts § 41 (5th ed. 1984) and Dobbs, *The Law of Torts* §§ 166–179 (2000). Consider also the following illustration from the Restatement (Second) of Torts:

> A dams a stream running through his own land. The dam is negligently constructed in that it is not sufficiently strong to confine the water from the freshets which occur from time to time in the spring. A sudden cloudburst of unprecedented severity sweeps the dam away, causing the water collected by it to overflow the land of B. The flood caused by the cloudburst is so great that it would have burst the dam even had it been properly constructed. A's negligent construction of the dam is not a cause of the inundation of B's land.

Restatement (Second) of Torts § 432(1) cmt. b, illus. 2.

In *Sullivan v. Boone*, 205 Minn. 437, 286 N.W. 350 (1939), passengers in a truck sued a railroad after the truck collided with the sixty-eighth car of a passing train. In reviewing a judgment notwithstanding the verdict for the defendants, the Supreme Court of Minnesota considered the effect of a statute requiring a railroad to continue sounding a bell or whistle on the locomotive as the entire train passes a crossing. The court held that, even assuming the railroad had failed to maintain the signal, that failure could not have caused the accident since at the time of the impact the locomotive would have been a half mile away from the crossing, making the signal inaudible to the truck's driver.

Might a defendant always try to evade liability by arguing that a plaintiff's harm would have happened regardless of the defendant's negligence? Consider *Reynolds v. Texas and Pacific Railway Co.*, 37 La. Ann. 694 (1885), where the evidence showed that passengers on a train that was running late were told to hurry off of the train. The plaintiff's wife, a heavyset woman, emerged from a bright room on the train and rushed down unlighted steps. She tripped, fell to the platform, and sustained serious injuries. The defendant argued that, even if it were to concede that the steps were unlighted, the plaintiff still had not established that darkness was a cause in fact of the plaintiff's injury since she might have tripped even in daylight. The court rejected this argument, stating that "where the negligence of the defendant greatly multiplies the chances of accident to the plaintiff, and is of a character naturally leading to its occurrence, the mere possibility that it might have happened without the negligence is not sufficient to break the chain of cause and effect between the negligence and the injury."

**2. Multiple Causes.** Note that in the context of multiple causes that combine to produce a plaintiff's harm, each cause may be considered a "but for" cause as long as the harm would not have happened without it.

For example, in *Washington & G. R. Co. v. Hickey*, 166 U.S. 521, 17 S.Ct. 661, 41 L.Ed. 1101 (1897), the plaintiff, a passenger in a horse-drawn street car, was injured during the commotion that ensued when the car became trapped on a railroad crossing. The driver was negligent in trying to cross the tracks as a train approached. Additionally, the guard at the crossing was negligent in lowering the gates while the car was still on the tracks, thus penning it in place. The Court held that the jury could find that the cause of the injurious commotion was the combined, simultaneous negligence of the driver and the guard. "But for" the negligence of both defendants, the accident wouldn't have happened.

Consider also *Lloyd v. Lloyd*, 479 S.W.2d 623 (Ky.1972), where a father brought his infant son with him as he rode on the defendant's power lawnmower. The lawnmower jerked and threw the father and son to the ground, where they were both severely injured by the lawnmower's blades. The father and son sued the owner since the owner had been on notice that the lawnmower was defective yet failed to warn the father. Regarding the son's action against the owner, the court held that despite the father's negligence in taking a two-year-old on a power lawnmower, the owner's negligence could nevertheless be a "but for" cause of the infant's injuries.

A similar causation analysis appears in *Nisbet v. Bucher*, 949 S.W.2d 111 (Mo.Ct.App.1997), where the parents of a college freshman who died during alleged hazing activities brought a wrongful death action against two fraternities, a campus organization, and several members of the organization. The student had sought to join a planning board for an upcoming "St. Pat's" celebration. Membership on the board allegedly required participating in an initiation that involved consuming a heated concoction of grain alcohol and green peas. After the student became unconscious, several of the defendants left him unattended face down on the floor, even though green fluid oozed from his nose and mouth. The defendants did not aid the student themselves, nor did they call for help. The student suffocated from the fluid. The court held that the case could not be dismissed as a matter of law since the facts as pleaded established a prima facie negligence claim, including cause in fact. The court distinguished cases in which defendants had merely furnished a plaintiff with alcohol, noting that this was "a situation where defendants pressured [the decedent] to drink alcoholic concoctions for the specific purpose of inducing intoxication." The court remanded the case for findings "as to what degree [the decedent] was coerced by defendants to consume excessive quantities of alcohol and as to what extent his will to make a conscious decision about his alcohol consumption was overcome." In short, the complaint sufficiently alleged facts showing that *but for* the social pressure, the decedent would not have drunk to the point of death.

**3. The Restatement.** Although the Restatement (Second) of Torts does not utilize the precise term "but for", it does generally require proof that the harm would not have been sustained if the actor had not been negligent. Section 431(a) describes a cause as "a substantial factor in bringing about the harm." Section 432 states: "... the actor's negligent conduct is not a substantial factor in bringing about harm to another if the harm would have been sustained even if the actor had not been negligent."

**4. Proximate Causation Compared.** Strictly speaking, a fortuitous chain of events that starts with a defendant's negligent conduct and eventually results in a remote plaintiff's harm may satisfy the "but for" test. Recall *Wawanesa Mutual Insurance Co. v. Matlock*, 60 Cal.App.4th 583, 70 Cal. Rptr.2d 512 (Cal.Ct.App.1997), which was presented with the negligence per se materials in Chapter 2, Sec. D at p. 194, supra. That case involved a minor (insured by the plaintiff), whom the defendant had negligently given cigarettes. The property damage at issue was caused by a fire when the minor dropped a burning cigarette into a pile of telephone poles. Consider the chain of causal events, about which the court quotes from the plaintiff's brief: "But-for" Timothy Matlock's illegal act ... of procuring tobacco for minor Eric Erdley (who was unable to purchase the cigarettes himself), and "but-for" Timothy Matlock's participation as a co-conspirator ... in an agreement to trespass to smoke these cigarettes with Eric Erdley on Wood–Man Pole Company land, and "but-for" Timothy Matlock's act of causing the younger children to rush off of the wood pile (because of Timothy Matlock's acts of jumping on the logs), Eric Erdley would not have been on top of the Wood–Man Pole Company telephone poles smoking a cigarette at the time that he was bumped by the younger children and dropped the lit cigarette which started the fire.... "Cause in fact is indeed satisfied here." But note that the doctrine of proximate causation cuts off liability when the connection between the defendant's conduct and plaintiff's harm is unforeseeable or so attenuated, that public policy precludes liability. See Chapter 2, Sec. F, infra.

**5. Further Study.** For further study, see Robertson, *The Common Sense of Cause in Fact*, 75 Tex. L. Rev. 1765 (1997). See also Wright, *Causation in Tort Law*, 73 Cal. L. Rev. 1735 (1985).

# ANDERSON v. MINNEAPOLIS, ST. P. & S. S. M. RY. CO.

Supreme Court of Minnesota.
146 Minn. 430, 179 N.W. 45 (1920).

LEES, C.

This is a fire case, brought against the defendant railway company and the Director General of Railroads. For convenience, we shall refer to the railway company, throughout this opinion, as the defendant. Plaintiff had a verdict. The appeal is from an order denying a motion in the alternative for judgment notwithstanding the verdict or for a new trial.

The complaint alleged that early in August, 1918, sparks from one of defendant's locomotive engines set a fire on or near the right of way, and that this fire spread until it finally reached plaintiff's land, where it destroyed some of his property. The answer was a general denial, followed by an allegation that, if plaintiff was damaged by fire, the fire was not due to any act of defendant, was of unknown origin, and, by reason of extraordinary weather conditions, became a huge conflagration. The reply put these allegations in issue.

Plaintiff's case in chief was directed to proving that in August, 1918, one of defendant's engines started a fire in a bog near the west side of plaintiff's land; that it smoldered there until October 12, 1918, when it flared up and burned his property, shortly before it was reached by one of the great fires which swept through Northeastern Minnesota at the close of that day. Defendant introduced evidence to show that on and prior to October 12th fires were burning west and northwest of, and were swept by the wind towards, plaintiff's premises. It did not show how such fires originated, neither did it clearly and certainly trace the destruction of plaintiff's property to them.

\* \* \*

The following proposition is stated in defendant's brief and relied on for a reversal:

"If plaintiff's property was damaged by a number of fires combining, one being the fire pleaded, and the others being of no responsible origin, but of such sufficient or superior force that they would have produced the damage to plaintiff's property, regardless of the fire pleaded, then defendant was not liable."

This proposition is based upon *Cook v. M., St. P. & S. S. M. Ry. Co.*, 98 Wis. 624, 74 N.W. 561, 40 L. R. A. 457, 67 Am. St. Rep. 830. In *Farrell v. M. & R. R. Ry. Co.*, 121 Minn. 357, 141 N.W. 491, 45 L. R. A. (N. S.) 215, this court considered the *Cook* Case, but refrained from expressing approval or disapproval of its doctrine. The Supreme Court of Michigan has referred to it as good law. *Pluchak v. Crawford*, 137 Mich. 509, 100 N. W. 765. The Supreme Court of Idaho says the opinion is logical and well reasoned, but the discussion is in a large measure theoretical and academic. *Miller v. N. P. Ry. Co.*, 24 Idaho, 567, 135 Pac. 845, 48 L. R. A. (N. S.) 700, Ann. Cas. 1915C, 1214. Judge Thompson, in his work on Negligence (volume 1, § 739), says that the conclusion reached is so clearly wrong as not to deserve discussion. If the *Cook* Case merely decides that one who negligently sets a fire is not liable if another's property is damaged, unless it is made to appear that the fire was a material element in the destruction of the property, there can be no question about the soundness of the decision. But if it decides that if such fire combines with another of no responsible origin, and after the union of the two fires they destroy the property and either fire independently of the other would have destroyed it, then, irrespective of whether the first fire was or was not a material factor in the destruction of the property, there is no liability, we are not prepared to adopt the doctrine as the law of this state. If a fire set by the engine of one railroad company unites with a fire set by the engine of another company, there is joint and several liability, even though either fire would have destroyed plaintiff's property.

\* \* \*

We therefore hold that the trial court did not err in refusing to instruct the jury in accordance with the rule laid down in the *Cook* Case. In the foregoing discussion we have assumed, although it is doubtful, that the evidence was such that a foundation was laid for the application of the rule, if it was otherwise applicable.

\* \* \*

We find no error requiring a reversal, and hence the order appealed from is affirmed.

## NORTHINGTON v. MARIN

United States Court of Appeals, Tenth Circuit.
102 F.3d 1564 (1996).

BRISCOE, Circuit Judge.

Deputy Sheriff Jesse Marin appeals the judgment entered against him in this 42 U.S.C. § 1983 action brought by Craig Northington, a Denver County jail inmate, claiming Marin caused other inmates to assault Northington by labeling him a snitch. . . .

\* \* \*

In February 1990, Northington was serving a sentence at the Denver County Jail in a community corrections program. . . . Northington alleged Deputy Marin caused other inmates to assault him by labeling him a snitch or an informer.

. . . . The magistrate believed the testimony of several inmates that Deputy Marin had spread a rumor among inmates that Northington was a snitch, and found Northington was assaulted several times by inmates who accused him of being a snitch. Although Marin denied spreading the rumor, he testified that an inmate labeled a snitch would most likely be beaten. There was evidence that other deputies spread the snitch rumor about Northington, and the magistrate found there was no evidence that Marin rather than another deputy originated the rumor heard by the inmates who assaulted Northington.

\* \* \*

Marin himself testified that if he spread a rumor in the jail that an inmate was a snitch, the inmate would probably be beaten by other inmates. The magistrate found from this evidence that Marin knew the probable result of spreading the rumor would be to place Northington in serious jeopardy of assault by other inmates and concluded this amounted to obdurate and wanton disregard for Northington's safety. The district court adopted the magistrate's findings and agreed with his conclusions of law on this issue. . . .

Under the "but for" test of causation, Marin could not be the cause of Northington's beating. Had Marin not spread the rumor, the statements of other deputies to inmates would have spread rapidly with the probable result that Northington would have been beaten. However, Restatement (Second) of Torts § 432(2) states: "If two forces are actively operating, one because of the actor's negligence, the other not because of any misconduct on his part, and each of itself is sufficient to bring about harm to another, the actor's negligence may be found to be a substantial factor in bringing it about." See generally, e.g., *In re Bendectin Litigation,* 857 F.2d 290, 310–11 (6th Cir.1988), *cert. denied* 488 U.S. 1006, 109 S.Ct. 788, 102 L.Ed.2d 779 (1989); *Basko v. Sterling Drug,* 416 F.2d 417, 430–31 (2d Cir.1969); *Fleming v. Kellett,* 167 F.2d 265, 267 (10th Cir.1948) (Federal Employers' Liability Act case); W. Page Keeton, ed., *Prosser and Keeton on Torts* § 41, pp. 266–67 (5th ed. 1984).

Here, two forces were actively operating to spread the rumor—Marin and the other deputies. Because, as the magistrate found, rumors about snitches spread rapidly and inmates rumored to be snitches will probably be beaten, the conduct of each (Marin's circulation of the rumor, or the other deputies' circulation of the rumor) by itself was sufficient to cause Northington to be beaten.

The magistrate's findings also established that Marin's spreading of the rumor was a substantial factor in bringing about harm to Northington. Marin's actions were not insignificant in relation to those of the other deputies. The magistrate found Marin repeated the rumor to inmates on four occasions. There was no evidence of more than four other instances in which other deputies spread the rumor. See Restatement (Second) of Torts § 41, pp. 266–69. The magistrate's findings therefore established that Marin and the other deputies were substantial factors in bringing about harm to Northington, and thus were concurrent causes of the harm.

Multiple tortfeasors who concurrently cause an indivisible injury are jointly and severally liable; each can be held liable for the entire injury. It is not essential that all persons who concurrently caused the harm be joined as defendants. Restatement (Second) of Torts § 433A, comment i, § 433B, comments c and d, and §§ 879–82. See *Edmonds v. Compagnie Generale Transatlantique,* 443 U.S. 256, 260 n. 7 and 8, 99 S.Ct. 2753, 2756 n. 7 and 8, 61 L.Ed.2d 521 (1979); *Menne,* 861 F.2d at 1466; *Bell v. Mickelsen,* 710 F.2d 611, 619 (10th Cir.1983) (applying Wyoming law); Prosser and Keeton on Torts, § 47, p. 328 and § 52, pp. 347–48. Consequently, a tortfeasor who cannot prove the extent to which the harm resulted from other concurrent causes is liable for the entire harm. Subsection (2) of § 433B states the burden of proof also shifts to the defendant in the case of concurrent causes:

> "Where the tortious conduct of two or more actors has combined to bring about harm to the plaintiff, and one or more of the actors seeks to limit his liability on the ground that the harm is capable of apportionment among them, the burden of proof as to the apportionment is upon each such actor."

\* \* \*

AFFIRMED.

## *NOTES*

**1. The Substantial Factor Test.** The substantial factor test imposes liability on culpable defendants whose conduct is one of two or more *redundant* causes of a plaintiff's injury. As the *Anderson* case suggests, if defendant A is careless with fire on one side of a plaintiff's house, and defendant B is careless with fire on the other side of the house, and both fires merge to destroy it, then each defendant may be considered a substantial factor in causing the damage and thus be held liable. While the conduct of neither A nor B may be considered a "but for" cause of the damage, since with respect to each fire individually the damage would have occurred without it, it would seem unfair to exonerate both defendants in such a case.

The substantial factor test is therefore used by many courts instead of the "but for" test in cases of simultaneous *redundant* causes. See Diamond, Levine & Madden, *Understanding Torts* § 11.03 (2nd ed. 2000). See also Keeton, *Prosser and Keeton on* The Law of Torts § 41 (5th ed. 1984); Dobbs, *The Law of Torts* § 171 (2000). How is the substantial factor test applied in *Northington?*

**2. The Restatement.** The Restatement (Second) of Torts concurs with the general rule stated in *Anderson.* However, rather than using the "but for" terminology for most cases and the substantial factor terminology for cases with redundant causes, the Restatement uses the substantial factor test for both: "The actor's negligent conduct is a legal cause of harm to another if (a) his conduct is a substantial factor in bringing about the harm...." Restatement (Second) of Torts § 431(a). Restatement § 432 consequently reads:

> (1) Except as stated in Subsection (2), the actor's negligent conduct is not a substantial factor in bringing about harm to another if the harm would have been sustained even if the actor had not been negligent.

> (2) If two forces are actively operating, one because of the actor's negligence, the other not because of any misconduct on his part, and each of itself is sufficient to bring about harm to another, the actor's negligence may be found to be a substantial factor in bringing it about.

**3. Dispensing with "But For".** Some states follow the Restatement approach, dispensing with the term "but for" but effectively requiring "but for" causation outside the context of redundant causes. See, for example, *Mitchell v. Gonzales*, 54 Cal.3d 1041, 1 Cal.Rptr.2d 913, 819 P.2d 872 (1991), where the Supreme Court of California replaced a "but for" causation requirement with a "substantial factor" jury instruction. Note that this is in lieu of the traditional approach of utilizing the term "but for" except in redundant cause cases, where the term "substantial factor" would be used.

**4. Redundant Causes.** In *Corey v. Havener*, 182 Mass. 250, 65 N.E. 69 (1902), two defendants independently operating motor tricycles simultaneously rode by a horse. The smoke and noise from the vehicles startled the horse, resulting in injuries to the plaintiff. Since the causes were redundant, neither would be a "but for" cause of the injury, thus potentially barring any recovery by the plaintiff. However, the court found that each vehicle would have been sufficient to frighten the horse. Thus, each defendant was a substantial factor in producing plaintiff's harm and therefore liable.

**5. Incremental Loss.** In *Dillon v. Twin State Gas & Electric Co.*, 85 N.H. 449, 163 A. 111 (1932), a child was playing on the girders of a bridge when he lost his balance and grasped onto power lines which the defendant had strung along the girders. The wires were insufficiently insulated and the child was electrocuted. In considering what damages would be recoverable, the Supreme Court of New Hampshire held that, if the child would have fallen from the bridge and died moments later after he hit the ground regardless of the presence of the defendant's wires, then the only recoverable damage against the electric company would be for the extra increment of pain caused by the electrocution since the child's life expectancy while in the process of falling would be negligible.

**6. Slippery Slope?** Consider the following modification to the *Anderson* facts in light of *Dillon*. Suppose that the plaintiff's house were built on the edge of a cliff that was doomed to collapse in two years due to erosion. Defendant A negligently starts a fire that destroys the house. Under the "but for" approach used in *Dillon*, A would be liable for only two years' worth of the value of the house. Now suppose that the plaintiff's house is doomed to fall off the cliff at virtually the same moment A's fire reaches the house. Should not A be liable for only the brief "life" expectancy of the house? Yet under *Anderson* A's negligence would be a substantial factor in the destruction of the house and A would be fully liable for the whole value of the house. In essence, the substantial factor test produces a different result from the "but for" test in cases of simultaneous causes, but not in cases of *nearly* simultaneous causes. Is utilizing the "but for" test or the substantial factor test more equitable in cases of simultaneous causes? What about cases with nearly simultaneous causes? Note that some commentators have proposed that courts not utilize the substantial factor test when one or more of the causes is non-negligent. See, for example, Peaslee, *Multiple Causation and Damages*, 47 Harv. L. Rev. 1127 (1934). The Restatement rejects this approach and applies the substantial factor test for simultaneous causes even if one or more of the causes is natural. See Restatement (Second) of Torts § 432(2) cmt. d.

## HERSKOVITS v. GROUP HEALTH COOPERATIVE OF PUGET SOUND

Supreme Court of Washington.
99 Wash.2d 609, 664 P.2d 474 (1983).

DORE, Justice.

This appeal raises the issue of whether an estate can maintain an action for professional negligence as a result of failure to timely diagnose lung cancer, where the estate can show probable reduction in statistical chance for survival but cannot show and/or prove that with timely diagnosis and treatment, decedent probably would have lived to normal life expectancy.

Both counsel advised that for the purpose of this appeal we are to *assume* that the respondent Group Health Cooperative of Puget Sound and Dr. William Spencer negligently failed to diagnose Herskovits' cancer on his first visit to the hospital and *proximately* caused at 14 percent reduction in his chances of survival. It is undisputed that Herskovits had less than a 50 percent chance of survival at all times herein.

The main issue we will address in this opinion is whether a patient, with less than a 50 percent chance of survival, has a cause of action against the hospital and its employees if they are negligent in diagnosing a lung cancer which reduces his chances of survival by 14 percent.

The personal representative of Leslie Herskovits' estate initiated this survivorship action against Group Health Cooperative of Puget Sound (Group Health), alleging failure to make an early diagnosis of her husband's lung cancer. Group Health moved for summary judgment for dismissal on the basis that Herskovits *probably* would have died from lung cancer even if the diagnosis had been made earlier, which the trial court granted.

* * *

Dr. William Spencer, the physician from Group Health Hospital who cared for the deceased Herskovits, testified that in his opinion, based upon a reasonable medical probability, earlier diagnosis of the lung cancer that afflicted Herskovits would not have prevented his death, nor would it have lengthened his life. He testified that nothing the doctors at Group Health could have done would have prevented Herskovits' death, as death within several years is a virtual certainty with this type of lung cancer regardless of how early the diagnosis is made.

Plaintiff contends that medical testimony of a reduction of chance of survival from 39 percent to 25 percent is sufficient evidence to allow the proximate cause issue to go to the jury. Defendant Group Health argues conversely that Washington law does not permit such testimony on the issue of medical causation and requires that medical testimony must be at least sufficiently definite to establish that the act complained of "probably" or "more likely than not" caused the subsequent disability. It is Group Health's contention that plaintiff must prove that Herskovits "probably" would have survived had the defendant not been allegedly negligent; that is, the plaintiff must prove there was at least a 51 percent chance of survival.

Pursuant to CR 56(c), summary judgment is appropriate only where there is no genuine issue as to any material fact and the moving party is entitled to judgment as a matter of law. All reasonable inferences from the evidence must be resolved against the moving party, and in favor of the nonmoving party. *Lamon v. McDonnell Douglas Corp.,* 91 Wash.2d 345, 588 P.2d 1346 (1979).

## II

This court has held that a person who negligently renders aid and consequently increases the risk of harm to those he is trying to assist is liable for any physical damages he causes. *Brown v. MacPherson's, Inc.,* 86 Wash.2d 293, 299, 545 P.2d 13 (1975). In *Brown,* the court cited Restatement (Second) of Torts § 323 (1965), which reads:

> One who undertakes ... to render services to another which he should recognize as necessary for the protection of the other's person or things, is subject to liability to the other for physical harm resulting from his failure to exercise reasonable care to perform his undertaking, if
>
> (a) his failure to exercise such care increases the risk of such harm, ...

This court heretofore has not faced the issue of whether, under § 323(a), proof that the defendant's conduct increased the risk of death by decreasing the chances of survival is sufficient to take the issue of proximate cause to the jury. Some courts in other jurisdictions have allowed the proximate cause issue to go to the jury on this type of proof. See *McBride v. United States,* 462 F.2d 72 (9th Cir.1972); *Hamil v.*

*Bashline,* 481 Pa. 256, 392 A.2d 1280 (1978); *Kallenberg v. Beth Israel Hosp.,* 45 A.D.2d 177, 357 N.Y.S.2d 508 (1974); *Jeanes v. Milner,* 428 F.2d 598 (8th Cir.1970); *Hicks v. United States,* 368 F.2d 626 (4th Cir.1966). These courts emphasized the fact that defendants' conduct deprived the decedents of a "significant" chance to survive or recover, rather than requiring proof that with absolute certainty the defendants' conduct caused the physical injury. The underlying reason is that it is not for the wrongdoer, who put the possibility of recovery beyond realization, to say afterward that the result was inevitable. *See also* Wolfstone & Wolfstone, *Recovery of Damages for the Loss of a Chance,* Personal Injury Annual 744 (1978).

Other jurisdictions have rejected this approach, generally holding that unless the plaintiff is able to show that it was *more likely than not* that the harm was caused by the defendant's negligence, proof of a decreased chance of survival is not enough to take the proximate cause question to the jury. *Cooper v. Sisters of Charity of Cincinnati, Inc.,* 27 Ohio St.2d 242, 272 N.E.2d 97 (1971); *Hiser v. Randolph,* 126 Ariz. 608, 617 P.2d 774 (Ct.App.1980); *Hanselmann v. McCardle,* 275 S.C. 46, 267 S.E.2d 531 (1980); *Cornfeldt v. Tongen,* 295 N.W.2d 638 (Minn.1980). These courts have concluded that the defendant should not be liable where the decedent more than likely would have died anyway.

The ultimate question raised here is whether the relationship between the increased risk of harm and Herskovits' death is sufficient to hold Group Health responsible. Is a 36 percent (from 39 percent to 25 percent) reduction in the decedent's chance for survival sufficient evidence of causation to allow the jury to consider the possibility that the physician's failure to timely diagnose the illness was the proximate cause of his death? We answer in the affirmative. To decide otherwise would be a blanket release from liability for doctors and hospitals any time there was less than a 50 percent chance of survival, regardless of how flagrant the negligence.

### III

We are persuaded by the reasoning of the Pennsylvania Supreme Court in *Hamil v. Bashline, supra.* While *Hamil* involved an original survival chance of greater than 50 percent, we find the rationale used by the *Hamil* court to apply equally to cases such as the present one, where the original survival chance is less than 50 percent. The plaintiff's decedent was suffering from severe chest pains. His wife transported him to the hospital where he was negligently treated in the emergency unit. The wife, because of the lack of help, took her husband to a private physician's office, where he died. In an action brought under the wrongful death and survivorship statutes, the main medical witness testified that if the hospital had employed proper treatment, the decedent would have had a substantial chance of surviving the attack. The medical expert expressed his opinion in terms of a 75 percent chance of survival. It was also the doctor's opinion that the substantial loss of a chance of recovery was the result of the defendant hospital's failure to provide prompt treatment. The defendant's expert witness testified that the patient would have died regardless of any treatment provided by the defendant hospital.

The *Hamil* court reiterated the oft-repeated principle of tort law that the mere occurrence of an injury does not prove negligence, but the defendant's conduct must be a proximate cause of the plaintiff's injury. The court also referred to the traditional "but for" test, with the qualification that multiple causes may culminate in injury. *Hamil,* 481 Pa. at 266, 392 A.2d 1280.

The court then cited Restatement (Second) of Torts § 323 (1965) as authority to relax the degree of certitude normally required of plaintiff's evidence in order to make a case for the jury. The court held that once a plaintiff has introduced evidence that a defendant's negligent act or omission increased the risk of harm to a person in plaintiff's position, and that the harm was in fact sustained, "it becomes a question for the jury as to whether or not that increased risk was a substantial factor in producing the harm". *Hamil,* 481 Pa. at 269, 392 A.2d 1280. *See also* C. McCormick, *Damages* § 31 (1935); Wolfstone & Wolfstone, *supra* at 744.

The *Hamil* court distinguished the facts of that case from the general tort case in which a plaintiff alleges that a defendant's act or omission set in motion a force which resulted in harm. In the typical tort case, the "but for" test, requiring proof that damages or death probably would not have occurred "but for" the negligent conduct of the defendant, is appropriate. In *Hamil* and the instant case, however, the defendant's act or omission failed in a *duty* to protect against harm from *another source.* Thus, as the *Hamil* court noted, the fact finder is put in the position of having to consider not only what *did* occur, but also what *might have* occurred. *Hamil* states at 271, 392 A.2d 1280:

> Such cases by their very nature elude the degree of certainty one would prefer and upon which the law normally insists before a person may be held liable. Nevertheless, in order that an actor is not completely insulated because of uncertainties as to the consequences of his negligent conduct, Section 323(a) tacitly acknowledges this difficulty and permits the issue to go to the jury upon a less than normal threshold of proof.

The *Hamil* court held that once a plaintiff has demonstrated that the defendant's acts or omissions have increased the risk of harm to another, such evidence furnishes a basis for the jury to make a determination as to whether such increased risk was in turn a substantial factor in bringing about the resultant harm.

In *Hicks v. United States, supra,* the Court of Appeals set forth the rationale for deviation from the normal requirements of proof in a case such as the one presently before us. The following quotation from *Hicks,* at 632, is frequently cited in cases adopting loss of a chance because it succinctly defines the doctrine:

> Rarely is it possible to demonstrate to an absolute certainty what would have happened in circumstances that the wrongdoer did not allow to come to pass. The law does not in the existing circumstances require the plaintiff to show to a *certainty* that

the patient would have lived had she been hospitalized and operated on promptly.

Under the *Hamil* decision, once a plaintiff has demonstrated that defendant's acts or omissions in a situation to which § 323(a) applies have increased the risk of harm to another, such evidence furnishes a basis for the fact finder to go further and find that such increased risk was in turn a substantial factor in bringing about the resultant harm. The necessary proximate cause will be established if the jury finds such cause. It is not necessary for a plaintiff to introduce evidence to establish that the negligence resulted in the injury or death, but simply that the negligence increased the *risk* of injury or death. The step from the increased risk to causation is one for the jury to make. *Hamil*, 481 Pa. at 272, 392 A.2d 1280.

\* \* \*

## Conclusion

Both counsel have agreed for the purpose of arguing this summary judgment, that the defendants were negligent in failing to make a diagnosis of cancer on Herskovits' initial visit in December 1974, and that such negligence was the proximate cause of reducing his chances of survival by 14 percent. It is undisputed that Herskovits had less than a 50 percent chance of survival at that time. Based on this agreement and Dr. Ostrow's deposition and affidavit, a prima facie case is shown. We reject Group Health's argument that plaintiffs *must show* that Herskovits "probably" would have had a 51 percent chance of survival if the hospital had not been negligent. We hold that medical testimony of a reduction of chance of survival from 39 percent to 25 percent is sufficient evidence to allow the proximate cause issue to go to the jury.

Causing reduction of the opportunity to recover (loss of chance) by one's negligence, however, does not necessitate a total recovery against the negligent party for all damages caused by the victim's death. Damages should be awarded to the injured party or his family based only on damages caused directly by premature death, such as lost earnings and additional medical expenses, etc.

We reverse the trial court and reinstate the cause of action.

## *NOTES*

1. **Causation in Medical Malpractice Cases.** There are three generally accepted views regarding "but for" causation in medical malpractice cases. The traditional and majority approach requires that the negligence of the medical professional be a "but for" cause of the plaintiff's injury. Under this view, the plaintiff bears the burden of proving that more likely than not the defendant's negligence caused the plaintiff's harm. Under this approach, the *Herskovits* plaintiff would recover nothing.

The second view uses a relaxed "but for" test that dispenses with the stringency of the traditional "but for" standard. Under this approach, the court asks the jury whether or not causation is established under a more elastic concept of causation. Some courts borrow the terminology "substantial factor" utilized in redundant causation cases (see Note 1 following *Northington* supra) as a sufficiently flexible term to accomplish this purpose. A court using this standard would allow the jury to decide without the precise restraint of a "but for" test whether malpractice "caused" the death, and hence the doctor should be liable. Note that even where the plaintiff is allowed to recover for wrongful death under this approach, recovery is limited, as *Herskovits* mentions, to the types of damages typically recoverable in all wrongful death suits.

Under the third view, the defendant compensates the plaintiff for the plaintiff's so-called "lost opportunity" occasioned by the defendant's negligence. The court does not relax the requirements of "but for" causation. Rather, it assesses the value of the reduction in the plaintiff's chance of recovery and compensates for the value of the lost chance of recovery; in *Herskovits* that would have been 14% of wrongful death damages. See Diamond, Levine & Madden, *Understanding Torts* § 11.04 (2nd ed. 2000). See also Keeton, *Prosser and Keeton on the Law of Torts* § 41. (5th ed. 1984); Dobbs, *The Law of Torts* § 178 (2000). Which approach is fairest? Which approach most appropriately deters medical malpractice?

**2. States are Divided.** Courts are divided on the issue of which approach to use. Maryland, for instance, rejected the "lost opportunity" approach in *Fennell v. Southern Maryland Hospital Center, Inc.*, 320 Md. 776, 580 A.2d 206 (1990):

> Re-defining loss of chance of survival as a new form of damages so that the compensable injury is not the death, but is the loss of chance of survival itself, may really be an exercise in semantics. Loss of chance of survival in itself is not compensable unless and until death ensues. Thus, it would seem that the true injury is the death.
>
> While we should not award damages if there is no injury, the logical extension of the loss of chance damages theory arguably should allow loss of chance damages for negligence, even when the patient miraculously recovers....

The *Fennell* court also based its decision on practical matters, such as the unreliability of statistical evidence and concern about an increase in medical malpractice litigation and insurance premiums.

The modern trend, however, is toward greater acceptance of the "lost opportunity" approach. See, for example, in *Scafidi v. Seiler*, 119 N.J. 93, 574 A.2d 398 (1990), where the plaintiff sued her obstetrician for the wrongful death of her baby. The baby was born prematurely as a result of the obstetrician's negligence, which consisted of failing to properly administer drug therapy designed to arrest the plaintiff's premature labor. The plaintiff's expert witness testified that the drug therapy was 75% to 80% effective in patients. The defendant's expert witness, however, testified that proper treatment was effective in only 25% of patients. The court held that "[i]n the event of a jury verdict against defendant on liability and damages, the trial court will mold the verdict to limit defendant's liability to the value of the lost chance for recovery attributable to defendant's negligence."

Consider *Jorgenson v. Vener*, 616 N.W.2d 366, 371 (2000), where the Supreme Court of South Dakota held that the key to a successful application of the lost chance doctrine is recognizing and valuing the lost chance as a compensable injury, and not the underlying injury itself.

> "Adoption of the loss of chance doctrine properly balances the competing concerns of a patient who receives negligent treatment, against those of the doctor who practices in the inherently inexact science of medicine. Properly applied, the loss of chance doctrine does not alter or eliminate the requirement of proximate cause. Rather, a plaintiff must still prove ... more likely than not, that the defendant's actions reduced her chance of a better outcome.... Furthermore, although the doctrine relies on statistical evidence in order to assign a value to the lost chance, such use of mathematical calculations is already necessary under traditional standards of causation and valuation ... how else do we even know whether we are talking about a better than even chance when applying the all-or-nothing rule."

> "Nor should we reject the doctrine simple because it ostensibly places medical malpractice on a different plane of liability compared to other types of malpractice. The fact that the doctrine has thus far been applied only in a medical malpractice context in all likelihood derives from the availability of statistical probabilities in the field of medical science; such information is not widely available in other malpractice contexts."

Consider also *Williams v. Wraxall*, 33 Cal.App.4th 120, 39 Cal.Rptr.2d 658 (1995), where a former client of a forensic serologist sued for malpractice, claiming that the serologist's failure to disclose certain test results lead to his, the client's, conviction in a murder case. The court first noted that California has uniformly rejected the lost chance theory of causation, but also concluded that it was particularly inapplicable outside of the medical context because there was no "preexisting condition which rendered proof of a reasonable probability of causation difficult." Do you agree?

**3. Drawing the Line.** In *Delaney v. Cade*, 255 Kan. 199, 873 P.2d 175 (1994), a medical malpractice case, the court endorsed the "lost opportunity" approach but limited it to loss of a "substantial" opportunity. However, it declined to "draw a bright line rule on the percentage of lost chance that would be sufficient for the case to be submitted to the jury." Should courts give a "lost opportunity" jury instruction in cases involving small numbers? *Herskovits* concerned a 14% loss in opportunity to recover. Should a 5% loss be actionable? Does it depend how far below 50% the victim's chances of survival were? Do you see any problems with a jury trying to evaluate these percentages?

**4. Using Statistics to Limit Recovery.** Should courts that favor allowing plaintiffs to recover a "lost opportunity" apply this rule when the plaintiff would be able to recover full wrongful death damages under traditional causation rules because the chance of recovery fell, for example, from 55% to 45%? Should the plaintiff receive only a 10% lost opportunity or full 100% wrongful death recovery? Thus far, courts appear to have utilized "lost opportunity" only when plaintiff would not recover at all.

More generally, should tort law develop to allow juries to give percentage recoveries based on the likelihood the defendant's negligence caused the victim harm in other contexts rather than requiring purely yes or no verdicts on liability? Arguably cases that are settled before a verdict reflect in the size of the settlement each side's assessment of the likelihood the tort action would be successful.

**5. Causation in Non–Medical Cases.** There are undoubtedly difficult causation cases in a range of torts. For example, if A negligently fails to initiate a search and rescue operation in a timely manner, did the delay cause the victim's death? Ordinarily, the question is uncertain enough to allow the issue of causation to reach the jury. In the medical malpractice case, however, the professional statistics can be so precise, the court may be forced in many cases to find no causation as a matter of law without adopting a special rule. Does this argue for creating special rules for medical cases or creating a consistent set of causation rules for all tort cases? Should physicians specializing in treating patients with a poor prognosis be subject to special rules to ensure accountability?

**6. Further Study.** For further study, see King, *Causation, Valuation, and Chance in Personal Injury Torts Involving Pre-existing Conditions and Future Consequences*, 90 Yale L.J. 1353 (1981).

## SUMMERS v. TICE

Supreme Court of California.
33 Cal.2d 80, 199 P.2d 1 (1948).

CARTER, Justice.

Each of the two defendants appeals from a judgment against them in an action for personal injuries. Pursuant to stipulation the appeals have been consolidated.

Plaintiff's action was against both defendants for an injury to his right eye and face as the result of being struck by bird shot discharged from a shotgun. The case was tried by the court without a jury and the court found that on November 20, 1945, plaintiff and the two defendants were hunting quail on the open range. Each of the defendants was armed with a 12 gauge shotgun loaded with shells containing 7 ½ size shot. Prior to going hunting plaintiff discussed the hunting procedure with defendants, indicating that they were to exercise care when shooting and to "keep in line." In the course of hunting plaintiff proceeded up a hill, thus placing the hunters at the points of a triangle. The view of defendants with reference to plaintiff was unobstructed and they knew his location. Defendant Tice flushed a quail which rose in flight to a 10–foot elevation and flew between plaintiff and defendants. Both defendants shot at the quail, shooting in plaintiff's direction. At that time defendants were 75 yards from plaintiff. One shot struck plaintiff in his eye and another in his upper lip. Finally it was found by the court that as the direct result of the shooting by defendants the shots struck plaintiff as above mentioned and that defendants were negligent in so shooting and plaintiff was not contributorily negligent.

First, on the subject of negligence, defendant Simonson contends that the evidence is insufficient to sustain the finding on that score, but he does not point out wherein it is lacking. There is evidence that both defendants, at about the same time or one immediately after the other, shot at a quail and in so doing shot toward plaintiff who was uphill from them, and that they knew his location. That is sufficient from which the trial court could conclude that they acted with respect to plaintiff other than as persons of ordinary prudence. The issue was one of fact for the trial court. See, *Rudd v. Byrnes,* 156 Cal. 636 [105 P. 957, 20 Ann.Cas. 124, 26 L.R.A.N.S. 134].

Defendant Tice states in his opening brief, "we have decided not to argue the insufficiency of negligence on the part of defendant Tice." It is true he states in his answer to plaintiff's petition for a hearing in this court that he did not concede this point but he does not argue it. Nothing more need be said on the subject.

\* \* \*

The problem presented in this case is whether the judgment against both defendants may stand. It is argued by defendants that they are not joint tort feasors, and thus jointly and severally liable, as they were not acting in concert, and that there is not sufficient evidence to show which defendant was guilty of the negligence which caused the injuries—the shooting by Tice or that by Simonson.

\* \* \*

When we consider the relative position of the parties and the results that would flow if plaintiff was required to pin the injury on one of the defendants only, a requirement that the burden of proof on that subject be shifted to defendants becomes manifest. They are both wrongdoers— both negligent toward plaintiff. They brought about a situation where the negligence of one of them injured the plaintiff, hence it should rest with them each to absolve himself if he can. The injured party has been placed by defendants in the unfair position of pointing to which defendant caused the harm. If one can escape the other may also and plaintiff is remediless. Ordinarily defendants are in a far better position to offer evidence to determine which one caused the injury.

\* \* \*

It is urged that plaintiff now has changed the theory of his case in claiming a concert of action; that he did not plead or prove such concert. From what has been said it is clear that there has been no change in theory. The joint liability, as well as the lack of knowledge as to which defendant was liable, was pleaded and the proof developed the case under either theory. We have seen that for the reasons of policy discussed herein, the case is based upon the legal proposition that, under the circumstances here presented, each defendant is liable for the whole damage whether they are deemed to be acting in concert or independently.

The judgment is affirmed.

### NOTES

**1. Burden Shifting.** If the *Summers* court had decided to use a standard "but for" causation analysis, what result? To avoid the unfairness of no recovery where *both* of the defendants breached a duty towards the innocent plaintiff, the court shifted the burden of proof of causation onto the defendants to prove which one was responsible. If one or more defendants has not acted negligently toward a plaintiff, would *Summers* be controlling?

*Summers* has been widely accepted where a small number of defendants have acted tortiously toward an innocent plaintiff. A typical application of the *Summers* rule involves automobile collisions where both drivers were negligent. See, e.g., *Petersen v. Parry*, 92 Idaho 647, 448 P.2d 653 (1968). Typically, the defendants must have performed similar tortious acts toward the plaintiff, and at nearly the same time. Also, before shifting the burden of proving causation, many courts require that all of the tortfeasors be joined as defendants. See Diamond, Levine & Madden, *Understanding Torts* § 11.04 (2nd ed. 2000); Keeton, *Prosser and Keeton on The Law of Torts* § 42 (5th ed. 1984) and Dobbs, *The Law of Torts* § 175 (2000). The Restatement (Second) of Torts endorses the rule in *Summers*:

> Where the conduct of two or more actors is tortious, and it is proved that harm has been caused to the plaintiff by only one of them, but there is uncertainty as to which one has caused it, the burden is upon each such actor to prove that he has not caused the harm. Restatement (Second) of Torts § 433B(3).

**2.  Classroom Justice?** Consider the example of the fifth grade teacher who leaves a classroom of children alone only to find the class fish bowl shattered. Does the *Summers* rule support punishing all the students? What factors are different? Were all the students negligent?

**3.  Other Contexts.** Are there other rationales that might drive a court to shift the burden of proof of causation? For instance, what kind of a deterrent effect does this burden-shifting have? In what types of cases are these issues likely to occur? Consider, for example, *Haft v. Lone Palm Hotel*, 3 Cal.3d 756, 91 Cal.Rptr. 745, 478 P.2d 465 (1970), a wrongful death action to recover for the deaths of a father and son who had drowned in the defendant's pool. The defendant was negligent by having neither a lifeguard nor a warning sign at the pool as required by statute. But the plaintiff was unable to prove causation since there were no witnesses. The court used the defendant's negligence to justify shifting the burden of proof, similar to *Summers*. Do you see any differences from *Summers* on these facts? Do those differences matter?

## SINDELL v. ABBOTT LABORATORIES

Supreme Court of California.
26 Cal.3d 588, 163 Cal.Rptr. 132, 607 P.2d 924 (1980).

MOSK, Justice.

This case involves a complex problem both timely and significant: may a plaintiff, injured as the result of a drug administered to her mother during pregnancy, who knows the type of drug involved but cannot identify the manufacturer of the precise product, hold liable for her injuries a maker of a drug produced from an identical formula?

Plaintiff Judith Sindell brought an action against eleven drug companies and Does 1 through 100, on behalf of herself and other women similarly situated. The complaint alleges as follows:

Between 1941 and 1971, defendants were engaged in the business of manufacturing, promoting, and marketing diethylstilbestrol (DES), a drug which is a synthetic compound of the female hormone estrogen. The drug was administered to plaintiff's mother and the mothers of the class she represents, for the purpose of preventing miscarriage. In 1947, the Food and Drug Administration authorized the marketing of DES as a miscarriage preventative, but only on an experimental basis, with a requirement that the drug contain a warning label to that effect. DES may cause cancerous vaginal and cervical growths in the daughters exposed to it before birth, because their mothers took the drug during pregnancy. The form of cancer from which these daughters suffer is known as adenocarcinoma, and it manifests itself after a minimum latent period of 10 or 12 years. It is a fast-spreading and deadly disease, and radical surgery is required to prevent it from spreading. DES also causes adenosis, precancerous vaginal and cervical growths which may spread to other areas of the body. The treatment for adenosis is cauterization, surgery, or cryosurgery. Women who suffer from this condition must be monitored by biopsy or colposcopic examination twice a year, a painful and expensive procedure. Thousands of women whose mothers received DES during pregnancy are unaware of the effects of the drug.

In 1971, the Food and Drug Administration ordered defendants to cease marketing and promoting DES for the purpose of preventing miscarriages, and to warn physicians and the public that the drug should not be used by pregnant women because of the danger to their unborn children.

During the period defendants marketed DES, they knew or should have known that it was a carcinogenic substance, that there was a grave danger after varying periods of latency it would cause cancerous and precancerous growths in the daughters of the mothers who took it, and that it was ineffective to prevent miscarriage. Nevertheless, defendants continued to advertise and market the drug as a miscarriage preventative. They failed to test DES for efficacy and safety; the tests performed by others, upon which they relied, indicated that it was not safe or effective. In violation of the authorization of the Food and Drug Administration, defendants marketed DES on an unlimited basis rather than as an experimental drug, and they failed to warn of its potential danger.

Because of defendants' advertised assurances that DES was safe and effective to prevent miscarriage, plaintiff was exposed to the drug prior to her birth. She became aware of the danger from such exposure within one year of the time she filed her complaint. As a result of the DES ingested by her mother, plaintiff developed a malignant bladder tumor which was removed by surgery. She suffers from adenosis and must constantly be monitored by biopsy or colposcopy to insure early warning of further malignancy.

* * *

Plaintiff seeks compensatory damages of $1 million and punitive damages of $10 million for herself. For the members of her class, she prays for equitable relief in the form of an order that defendants warn physicians and others of the danger of DES and the necessity of performing certain tests to determine the presence of disease caused by the drug, and that they establish free clinics in California to perform such tests.

Defendants demurred to the complaint. While the complaint did not expressly allege that plaintiff could not identify the manufacturer of the precise drug ingested by her mother, she stated in her points and authorities in opposition to the demurrers filed by some of the defendants that she was unable to make the identification, and the trial court sustained the demurrers of these defendants without leave to amend on the ground that plaintiff did not and stated she could not identify which defendant had manufactured the drug responsible for her injuries. Thereupon, the court dismissed the action.

\* \* \*

This case is but one of a number filed throughout the country seeking to hold drug manufacturers liable for injuries allegedly resulting from DES prescribed to the plaintiffs' mothers since 1947. According to a note in the Fordham Law Review, estimates of the number of women who took the drug during pregnancy range from 1 ½ million to 3 million. Hundreds, perhaps thousands, of the daughters of these women suffer from adenocarcinoma, and the incidence of vaginal adenosis among them is 30 to 90 percent. (Comment, *DES and a Proposed Theory of Enterprise Liability* (1978) 46 Fordham L.Rev. 963, 964–967 [hereafter Fordham Comment].) Most of the cases are still pending. With two exceptions, those that have been decided resulted in judgments in favor of the drug company defendants because of the failure of the plaintiffs to identify the manufacturer of the DES prescribed to their mothers. The same result was reached in a recent California case. (*McCreery v. Eli Lilly & Co.* (1978) 87 Cal.App.3d 77, 82–84 [150 Cal.Rptr. 730].) The present action is another attempt to overcome this obstacle to recovery.

We begin with the proposition that, as a general rule, the imposition of liability depends upon a showing by the plaintiff that his or her injuries were caused by the act of the defendant or by an instrumentality under the defendant's control. The rule applies whether the injury resulted from an accidental event (e.g., *Shunk* v. *Bosworth* (6th Cir. 1964) 334 F.2d 309) or from the use of a defective product. (E.g., *Wetzel v. Eaton Corporation* (D.Minn. 1973) 62 F.R.D. 22, 29–30; *Garcia v. Joseph Vince Co.* (1978) 84 Cal.App.3d 868, 873–875 [148 Cal.Rptr. 843]; and see Annot. collection of cases in 51 A.L.R.3d 1344, 1351; 1 Hursh & Bailey, American Law of Products Liability (2d ed. 1974) p. 125.)

There are, however, exceptions to this rule. Plaintiff's complaint suggests several bases upon which defendants may be held liable for her injuries even though she cannot demonstrate the name of the manufacturer which produced the DES actually taken by her mother. The first of these theories, classically illustrated by *Summers v. Tice* (1948) 33 Cal.2d 80 [199 P.2d 1, 5 A.L.R.2d 91], places the burden of proof of causation upon tortious defendants in certain circumstances. The second basis of liability emerging from the complaint is that defendants acted in concert to cause injury to plaintiff. There is a third and novel approach to the problem, sometimes called the theory of "enterprise liability," but which we prefer to designate by the more accurate term of "industry-wide" liability, which might obviate the necessity for identifying the manufacturer of the injury-causing drug. We shall conclude that these doctrines, as previously interpreted, may not be applied to hold defendants liable under the allegations of this complaint. However, we shall propose and adopt a fourth basis for permitting the action to be tried, grounded upon an extension of the *Summers* doctrine.

I

Plaintiff places primary reliance upon cases which hold that if a party cannot identify which of two or more defendants caused an injury, the burden of proof may shift to the defendants to show that they were not responsible for the harm. This principle is sometimes referred to as the "alternative liability" theory.

The celebrated case of *Summers v. Tice, supra,* 33 Cal.2d 80, a unanimous opinion of this court, best exemplifies the rule. In *Summers,* the plaintiff was injured when two hunters negligently shot in his direction. It could not be determined which of them had fired the shot that actually caused the injury to the plaintiff's eye, but both defendants were nevertheless held jointly and severally liable for the whole of the damages. We reasoned that both were wrongdoers, both were negligent toward the plaintiff, and that it would be unfair to require plaintiff to isolate the defendant responsible, because if the one pointed out were to escape liability, the other might also, and the plaintiff-victim would be shorn of any remedy. In these circumstances, we held, the burden of proof shifted to the defendants, "each to absolve himself if he can." (*Id.,* p. 86.) We stated that under these or similar circumstances a defendant is ordinarily in a "far better position" to offer evidence to determine whether he or another defendant caused the injury.

* * *

Here, as in *Summers,* the circumstances of the injury appear to render identification of the manufacturer of the drug ingested by plaintiff's mother impossible by either plaintiff or defendants, and it cannot reasonably be said that one is in a better position than the other to make the identification. Because many years elapsed between the time the drug was taken and the manifestation of plaintiff's injuries she, and many other daughters of mothers who took DES, are unable to make such identification. Certainly there can be no implication that plaintiff is at fault in failing to do so—the event occurred while plaintiff was *in utero,* a generation ago.

* * *

Nevertheless, plaintiff may not prevail in her claim that the *Summers* rationale should be employed to fix the whole liability for her injuries upon defendants, at least as those principles have previously been applied. There is an important difference between the situation involved in *Summers* and the present case. There, all the parties who were or could have been responsible for the harm to the plaintiff were joined as defendants. Here, by contrast, there are approximately 200 drug companies which made DES, any of which might have manufactured the injury-producing drug.

Defendants maintain that, while in *Summers* there was a 50 percent chance that one of the two defendants was responsible for the plaintiff's injuries, here since any one of 200 companies which manufactured DES might have made the product that harmed plaintiff, there is no rational basis upon which to infer that any defendant in this action caused plaintiff's injuries, nor even a reasonable possibility that they were responsible.

These arguments are persuasive if we measure the chance that any one of the defendants supplied the injury-causing drug by the number of possible tortfeasors. In such a context, the possibility that any of the five defendants supplied the DES to plaintiff's mother is so remote that it would be unfair to require each defendant to exonerate itself. There may be a substantial likelihood that none of the five defendants joined in the action made the DES which caused the injury, and that the offending producer not named would escape liability altogether. While we propose, *infra*, an adaptation of the rule in *Summers* which will substantially overcome these difficulties, defendants appear to be correct that the rule, as previously applied, cannot relieve plaintiff of the burden of proving the identity of the manufacturer which made the drug causing her injuries.

## II

The second principle upon which plaintiff relies is the so-called "concert of action" theory....

.... The elements of this doctrine are prescribed in section 876 of the Restatement Second of Torts. The section provides, "For harm resulting to a third person from the tortious conduct of another, one is subject to liability if he (a) does a tortious act in concert with the other or pursuant to a common design with him, or (b) knows that the other's conduct constitutes a breach of duty and gives substantial assistance or encouragement to the other so to conduct himself, or (c) gives substantial assistance to the other in accomplishing a tortious result and his own conduct, separately considered, constitutes a breach of duty to the third person." With respect to this doctrine, Prosser states that "those who, in pursuance of a common plan or design to commit a tortious act, actively take part in it, or further it by cooperation or request, or who lend aid or encouragement to the wrongdoer, or ratify and adopt his acts done for their benefit, are equally liable with him. Express agreement is not necessary, and all that is required is that there be a tacit understanding...." (Prosser, Law of Torts (4th ed. 1971) § 46, p. 292.)

Plaintiff contends that her complaint states a cause of action under these principles. She alleges that defendants' wrongful conduct "is the result of planned and concerted action, express and implied agreements, collaboration in, reliance upon, acquiescence in and ratification, exploitation and adoption of each other's testing, marketing methods, lack of warnings ... and other acts or omissions ..." and that "acting individually and in concert, (defendants) promoted, approved, authorized, acquiesced in, and reaped profits from sales" of DES. These allegations, plaintiff claims, state a "tacit understanding" among defendants to commit a tortious act against her.

In our view, this litany of charges is insufficient to allege a cause of action under the rules stated above. The gravamen of the charge of concert is that defendants failed to adequately test the drug or to give sufficient warning of its dangers and that they relied upon the tests performed by one another and took advantage of each others' promotional and marketing techniques. These allegations do not amount to a charge that there was a tacit understanding or a common plan among defendants to fail to conduct adequate tests or give sufficient warnings, and that they substantially aided and encouraged one another in these omissions.

\* \* \*

None of the cases cited by plaintiff supports a conclusion that defendants may be held liable for concerted tortious acts. They involve conduct by a small number of individuals whose actions resulted in a tort against a single plaintiff, usually over a short span of time, and the defendant held liable was either a direct participant in the acts which caused damage, or encouraged and assisted the person who directly caused the injuries by participating in a joint activity.

*Orser v. George* (1967) 252 Cal.App.2d 660 [60 Cal.Rptr. 708], upon which plaintiff primarily relies, is also distinguishable. There, three hunters negligently shot at a mudhen in decedent's direction. Two of them shot alternately with the gun which released the bullet resulting in the fatal wound, and the third, using a different gun, fired alternately at the same target, shooting in the same line of fire, perhaps acting tortiously. It was held that there was a possibility the third hunter knew the conduct of the others was tortious toward the decedent and gave them substantial assistance and encouragement, and that it was also possible his conduct, separately considered, was a breach of duty toward decedent. Thus, the granting of summary judgment was reversed as to the third hunter.

. . . . There is no allegation here that each defendant knew the other defendants' conduct was tortious toward plaintiff, and that they assisted and encouraged one another to inadequately test DES and to provide inadequate warnings. Indeed, it seems dubious whether liability on the concert of action theory can be predicated upon substantial assistance and encouragement given by one alleged tortfeasor to another pursuant to a tacit understanding to fail to perform an act. Thus, there was no concert of action among defendants within the meaning of that doctrine.

### III

A third theory upon which plaintiff relies is the concept of industry-wide liability, or according to the terminology of the parties, "enterprise liability." This theory was suggested in *Hall v. E. I. Du Pont de Nemours & Co., Inc.* (E.D.N.Y. 1972) 345 F.Supp. 353. In that case, plaintiffs were 13 children injured by the explosion of blasting caps in 12 separate incidents which occurred in 10 different states between 1955 and 1959. The defendants were six blasting cap manufacturers, comprising virtually the entire blasting cap industry in the United States, and their trade association. There were, however, a number of Canadian blasting cap manufacturers which could have supplied the caps. The gravamen of the complaint was that the practice of the industry of omitting a warning on individual blasting caps and of failing to take other safety measures created an unreasonable risk of harm, resulting in the plaintiffs' injuries. The complaint did not identify a particular manufacturer of a cap which caused a particular injury.

The court reasoned as follows: there was evidence that defendants, acting independently, had adhered to an industry-wide standard with regard to the safety features of blasting caps, that they had in effect delegated some functions of safety investigation and design, such as labelling, to their trade association, and that there was industry-wide cooperation in the manufacture and design of blasting caps. In these circumstances, the evidence supported a conclusion that all the defendants jointly controlled the risk. Thus, if plaintiffs could establish by a preponderance of the evidence that the caps were manufactured by one of the defendants, the burden of proof as to causation would shift to all the defendants. The court noted that this theory of liability applied to industries composed of a small number of units, and that what would be fair and reasonable with regard to an industry of five or ten producers might be manifestly unreasonable if applied to a decentralized industry composed of countless small producers.

Plaintiff attempts to state a cause of action under the rationale of *Hall*. She alleges joint enterprise and collaboration among defendants in the production, marketing, promotion and testing of DES, and "concerted promulgation and adherence to industry-wide testing, safety, warning and efficacy standards" for the drug. We have concluded above that allegations that defendants relied upon one another's testing and promotion methods do not state a cause of action for concerted conduct to commit a tortious act. Under the theory of industry-wide liability, however, each manufacturer could be liable for all injuries caused by DES by virtue of adherence to an industry-wide standard of safety.

In the Fordham Comment, the industry-wide theory of liability is discussed and refined in the context of its applicability to actions alleging injuries resulting from DES. The author explains causation under that theory as follows, "... [T]he industrywide standard becomes itself the cause of plaintiff's injury, just as defendants' joint plan is the cause of injury in the traditional concert of action plea. Each defendant's adherence perpetuates this standard, which results in the manufacture of the particular, unidentifiable injury-producing product. Therefore, each industry member has contributed to plaintiff's injury." (Fordham Comment, *supra*, at p. 997.)

\* \* \*

We decline to apply this theory in the present case. At least 200 manufacturers produced DES; *Hall*, which involved 6 manufacturers representing the entire blasting cap industry in the United States, cautioned against application of the doctrine espoused therein to a large number of producers. (345 F.Supp. at p. 378.) Moreover, in *Hall*, the conclusion that the defendants jointly controlled the risk was based upon allegations that they had delegated some functions relating to safety to a trade association. There are no such allegations here, and we have concluded above that plaintiff has failed to allege liability on a concert of action theory.

Equally important, the drug industry is closely regulated by the Food and Drug Administration, which actively controls the testing and manufacture of drugs and the method by which they are marketed, including the contents of warning labels. To a considerable degree, therefore, the standards followed by drug manufacturers are suggested or compelled by the government. Adherence to those standards cannot, of course, absolve a manufacturer of liability to which it would otherwise be subject. (*Stevens v. Parke, Davis & Co.* (1973) 9 Cal.3d 51, 65, 107 Cal.Rptr. 45, 507 P.2d 653 [94 A.L.R.3d 1059].) But since the government plays such a pervasive role in formulating the criteria for the testing and marketing of drugs, it would be unfair to impose upon a manufacturer liability for injuries resulting from the use of a drug which it did not supply simply because it followed the standards of the industry.

### IV

If we were confined to the theories of *Summers* and *Hall*, we would be constrained to hold that the judgment must be sustained. Should we require that plaintiff identify the manufacturer which supplied the DES used by her mother or that all DES manufacturers be joined in the action, she would effectively be precluded from any recovery. As defendants candidly admit, there is little likelihood that all the manufacturers who made DES at the time in question are still in business or that they are subject to the jurisdiction of the California courts. There are, however, forceful arguments in favor of holding that plaintiff has a cause of action.

\* \* \*

The most persuasive reason for finding plaintiff states a cause of action is that advanced in *Summers*: as between an innocent plaintiff and negligent defendants, the latter should bear the cost of the injury. Here, as in *Summers*, plaintiff is not at fault in failing to provide evidence of causation, and although the absence of such evidence is not attributable to the defendants either, their conduct in marketing a drug the effects of which are delayed for many years played a significant role in creating the unavailability of proof.

\* \* \*

Where, as here, all defendants produced a drug from an identical formula and the manufacturer of the DES which caused plaintiff's injuries cannot be identified through no fault of plaintiff, a modification of the rule of *Summers* is warranted. As we have seen, an undiluted *Summers* rationale is inappropriate to shift the burden of proof of causation to defendants because if we measure the chance that any particular manufacturer supplied the injury-causing product by the number of producers of DES, there is a possibility that none of the five defendants in this case produced the offending substance and that the responsible manufacturer, not named in the action, will escape liability.

But we approach the issue of causation from a different perspective: we hold it to be reasonable in the present context to measure the likelihood that any of the defendants supplied the product which allegedly injured plaintiff by the percentage which the DES sold by each of them for the purpose of preventing miscarriage bears to the entire production of the drug sold by all for that purpose. Plaintiff asserts in her briefs that Eli Lilly and Company and five or six other companies produced 90 percent of the DES marketed. If at trial this is established to be the fact, then there is a corresponding likelihood that this comparative handful of producers manufactured the DES which caused plaintiff's injuries, and only a 10 percent likelihood that the offending producer would escape liability.[28]

If plaintiff joins in the action the manufacturers of a substantial share of the DES which her mother might have taken, the injustice of shifting the burden of proof to defendants to demonstrate that they could not have made the substance which injured plaintiff is significantly diminished. While 75 to 80 percent of the market is suggested as the requirement by the Fordham Comment (at p. 996), we hold only that a substantial percentage is required.

The presence in the action of a substantial share of the appropriate market also provides a ready means to apportion damages among the defendants. Each defendant will be held liable for the proportion of the judgment represented by its share of that market unless it demonstrates that it could not have made the product which caused plaintiff's injuries. In the present case, as we have seen, one DES manufacturer was dismissed from the action upon filing a declaration that it had not manufactured DES until after plaintiff was born. Once plaintiff has met her burden of joining the required defendants, they in turn may cross-complain against other DES manufacturers, not joined in the action, which they can allege might have supplied the injury-causing product.

Under this approach, each manufacturer's liability would approximate its responsibility for the injuries caused by its own products. Some minor discrepancy in the correlation between market share and liability is inevitable; therefore, a defendant may be held liable for a somewhat different percentage of the damage than its share of the appropriate market would justify. It is probably impossible, with the passage of time, to determine market share with mathematical exactitude. But just as a

**28.** The Fordham Comment explains the connection between percentage of market share and liability as follows: "[I]f X Manufacturer sold one-fifth of all the DES prescribed for pregnancy and identification could be made in all cases, X would be the sole defendant in approximately one-fifth of all cases and liable for all the damages in those cases. Under alternative liability, X would be joined in all cases in which identification could not be made, but liable for only one-fifth of the total damages in these cases. X would pay the same amount either way. Although the correlation is not, in practice, perfect (footnote omitted), it is close enough so that defendants' objections on the ground of fairness lose their value." (Fordham Comment, *supra*, at p. 994.)

jury cannot be expected to determine the precise relationship between fault and liability in applying the doctrine of comparative fault (*Li v. Yellow Cab Co.* (1975) 13 Cal.3d 804 [119 Cal.Rptr. 858, 532 P.2d 1226, 78 A.L.R.3d 393]) or partial indemnity (*American Motorcycle Assn.* v. *Superior Court* (1978) 20 Cal.3d 578 [146 Cal.Rptr. 182, 578 P.2d 899]), the difficulty of apportioning damages among the defendant producers in exact relation to their market share does not seriously militate against the rule we adopt. As we said in *Summers* with regard to the liability of independent tortfeasors, where a correct division of liability cannot be made "the trier of fact may make it the best it can." (33 Cal.2d at p. 88.)

We are not unmindful of the practical problems involved in defining the market and determining market share, but these are largely matters of proof which properly cannot be determined at the pleading stage of these proceedings. Defendants urge that it would be both unfair and contrary to public policy to hold them liable for plaintiff's injuries in the absence of proof that one of them supplied the drug responsible for the damage. Most of their arguments, however, are based upon the assumption that one manufacturer would be held responsible for the products of another or for those of all other manufacturers if plaintiff ultimately prevails. But under the rule we adopt, each manufacturer's liability for an injury would be approximately equivalent to the damage caused by the DES it manufactured.

The judgments are reversed.

### NOTES

**1. The Market Share Answer to Causation.** The theory of market share liability holds members of an industry liable for a plaintiff's harm in proportion to the share of the market they represent. California, Florida, New York and Washington have utilized market share liability in DES litigation. Michigan adopted an approach similar to *Summers v. Tice* where each defendant is jointly liable rather than merely liable for its market share. See *Abel v. Eli Lilly & Co.*, 418 Mich. 311, 343 N.W.2d 164 (Mich. 1984). However, in 1995, Michigan passed legislation which overruled *Abel*, by eliminating joint and several liability except in limited circumstances. See *Napier v. Osmose, Inc.*, 399 F.Supp.2d 811 (D. Mich. 2005). Wisconsin has adopted an apportioned liability system which varies based on an evaluation of the risk each manufacturer imposed on consumers for which market share is only a factor. See *Collins v. Eli Lilly & Co.*, 116 Wis.2d 166, 342 N.W.2d 37 (1984).

Most states have not adopted market share liability with the result that a plaintiff who could not identify the manufacturer would be unable to recover. See, for example, *Mulcahy v. Eli Lilly & Co.*, 386 N.W.2d 67 (Iowa 1986). See Diamond, Levine & Madden, *Understanding Torts* § 11.04 (2nd ed. 2000); Keeton, *Prosser and Keeton on* The Law of Torts § 42 (5th ed. 1984) and Dobbs, *The Law of Torts* § 176 (2000). How does market share liability vary from the principle of *Summers v. Tice*?

**2. Representative Samples.** Substantial debate centers around how to measure market share in an industry. Should the industry be evaluated nationally? Statewide? Locally? Consider *Conley v. Boyle Drug Co.*, 570 So.2d

275 (Fla.1990), where the Supreme Court of Florida used a local standard in applying market share liability. The court reasoned that a local standard would spare from liability those defendants who did not market the product in the plaintiff's area and thus could not have caused the plaintiff's harm. The court also noted that the market share liability should only be used where a plaintiff has shown due diligence in trying to ascertain which specific manufacturer caused the plaintiff's harm. In contrast, California and New York base liability on national market share liability where percentages are more easily ascertainable. See *Hymowitz v. Eli Lilly & Co.*, 73 N.Y.2d 487, 541 N.Y.S.2d 941, 539 N.E.2d 1069 (1989). Does varying the geographic basis for determining the market impact on the fairness of market share liability?

**3. Beyond Burden Shifting.** In the principal case, the California Supreme Court shifted the burden so that the defendant manufacturer is liable for its market share unless the defendant can prove it could not have provided the substance that injured a particular plaintiff. Do you agree that a manufacturer should not be liable if it can definitively prove its drug was not consumed by the plaintiff's mother? Consider *Hymowitz v. Eli Lilly & Co.*, 73 N.Y.2d 487, 541 N.Y.S.2d 941, 539 N.E.2d 1069 (1989), where the Court of Appeals of New York refused to allow individual defendants to prove that they could not have supplied DES to a particular plaintiff.

> [B]ecause liability here is based on the over-all risk produced, and not causation in a single case, there should be no exculpation of a defendant who, although a member of the market producing DES for pregnancy use, appears not to have caused a particular plaintiff's injury. It is merely a windfall for a producer to escape liability solely because it manufactured a more identifiable pill, or sold only to certain drugstores. These fortuities in no way diminish the culpability of a defendant for marketing the product, which is the basis of liability here.

*Id.* at 73 N.Y.2d 512, 541 N.Y.S.2d 950, 539 N.E.2d 1078. Is the New York court's approach fairer than the California approach?

**4. Joining Defendants.** *Sindell* requires that enough defendant manufacturers be joined as defendants so that a substantial share of the market is represented. In a decision subsequent to *Sindell*, the California Supreme Court in *Brown v. Superior Court*, 44 Cal.3d 1049, 245 Cal.Rptr. 412, 751 P.2d 470 (1988) held that the missing market share caused by defendants not represented in the lawsuit proportionally reduces the plaintiff's compensation. In other words, the defendants in the litigation will not share responsibility for the missing market share percentages. In light of *Brown*, is the requirement that a substantial share of the market be represented still necessary? Suppose, for example, a plaintiff can only gain jurisdiction over companies which represent only 50 percent of the market. Is imposing liability on these companies unfair?

**5. The Future of Market Share Liability.** Market share liability has been rarely used outside of DES litigation. For example, in *Sheffield v. Eli Lilly & Co.*, 144 Cal.App.3d 583, 192 Cal. Rptr. 870 (Cal.Ct.App.1983), the court declined to apply market share liability to manufacturers of Salk polio vaccine. The court noted that "the injuries did not result from the use of a drug generally defective ... but because some manufacturers made and distributed a defective product." *Id.* at 877. Consequently, unlike in the DES cases, the hazards posed by the "product" were not uniform. Furthermore, the court noted the latency period from drug use to injury was much shorter than in DES cases. Finally, the court noted the public policy of encouraging the manufacture of vaccines.

One exception where market share was applied to a non-DES case was in *Smith v. Cutter Biological, Inc.*, 72 Haw. 416, 823 P.2d 717 (Hawaii 1991), where the court imposed market share liability for a blood clotting protein.

**6. "Acting in Concert."** Although rejected as inapplicable in *Sindell*, liability for acting in concert is an important tort doctrine. In criminal law, accessories and co-conspirators are guilty of crimes they aid or encourage, even if another person physically did the crime. In tort law, the term "acting in concert" is used in lieu of the term accessory and co-conspirator, but the same principle applies. Consequently, if A encourages B to speed to the store before it closed, B as well as A is liable for the accident that results. See, e.g., *Loeb v. Kimmerle*, 215 Cal. 143, 9 P.2d 199 (1932), where a defendant was held liable for encouraging another person to commit an assault; and *Agovino v. Kunze*, 181 Cal.App.2d 591, 5 Cal.Rptr. 534 (1960), where one participant in a drag race was held liable for another participant's negligent collision with a third car, since by participating in the drag race he encouraged the opposing driver to speed negligently.

# AYERS v. TOWNSHIP OF JACKSON

Supreme Court of New Jersey.

106 N.J. 557, 525 A.2d 287 (1987).

STEIN, Justice.

In this case we consider the application of the New Jersey Tort Claims Act (the Act), *N.J.S.A.* 59:1–1 to 12–3, to the claims asserted by 339 residents of Jackson Township against that municipality.

The litigation involves claims for damages sustained because plaintiffs' well water was contaminated by toxic pollutants leaching into the Cohansey Aquifer from a landfill established and operated by Jackson Township. After an extensive trial, the jury found that the township had created a "nuisance" and a "dangerous condition" by virtue of its operation of the landfill, that its conduct was "palpably unreasonable,"—a prerequisite to recovery under *N.J.S.A.* 59:4–2—and that it was the proximate cause of the contamination of plaintiffs' water supply. . . .

\* \* \*

CLAIMS FOR ENHANCED RISK AND MEDICAL SURVEILLANCE

No claims were asserted by plaintiffs seeking recovery for specific illnesses caused by their exposure to chemicals. Rather, they claim damages for the enhanced risk of future illness attributable to such exposure. They also seek to recover the expenses of annual medical examinations to monitor their physical health and detect symptoms of disease at the earliest possible opportunity.

\* \* \*

1.

Our evaluation of the enhanced risk and medical surveillance claims requires that we focus on a critical issue in the management of toxic tort litigation: at what stage in the evolution of a toxic injury should tort law intercede by requiring the responsible party to pay damages?

\* \* \*

By far the most difficult problem for plaintiffs to overcome in toxic tort litigation is the burden of proving causation.... In the typical tort case, the plaintiff must prove tortious conduct, injury and proximate cause. W. Keeton, D. Dobbs, R. Keeton & D. Owen, *Prosser & Keeton on the Law of Torts* § 30, at 164–65 (1984). Ordinarily, proof of causation requires the establishment of a sufficient nexus between the defendant's conduct and the plaintiff's injury. In toxic tort cases, the task of proving causation is invariably made more complex because of the long latency period of illnesses caused by carcinogens or other toxic chemicals. The fact that ten or twenty years or more may intervene between the exposure and the manifestation of disease highlights the practical difficulties encountered in the effort to prove causation. Moreover, the fact that segments of the entire population are afflicted by cancer and other toxically-induced diseases requires plaintiffs, years after their exposure, to counter the argument that other intervening exposures or forces were the "cause" of their injury. The thoughtful analysis by District Judge Jenkins in *Allen v. United States,* 588 F.Supp. 247 (D. Utah 1984), rev'd on other grounds, 816 F.2d 1417 (10th Cir.1987), a case involving the causal relationship between nuclear fallout and cancer, graphically explains the causation problem in mass exposure litigation:

> In most cases, the factual connection between defendant's conduct and plaintiff's injury is not genuinely in dispute. Often, the cause-and-effect is obvious: A's vehicle strikes B, injuring him; a bottle of A's product explodes, injuring B; water impounded on A's property flows onto B's land, causing immediate damage.

> In this case, the factual connection singling out the defendant as the source of the plaintiffs' injuries and deaths is very much in genuine dispute. Determination of the cause-in-fact, or factual connection, issue is complicated by the nature of the injuries suffered (various forms of cancer and leukemia), the nature of the causation mechanism alleged (ionizing radiation from nuclear fallout \* \* \*), the extraordinary time factors and other variables involved in tracing any causal relationship between the two.

> At this point, there appears to be no question whether or not ionizing radiation causes cancer and leukemia. It does. Once more, however, it seems important to clarify what is meant by "cause" in relation to radiation and cancer.

>> When we refer to radiation as a cause, we do not mean that it causes every case of cancer or leukemia. Indeed, the evidence we have indicating radiation in the causation of

> cancer and leukemia shows that not all cases of cancer are caused by radiation. Second, when we refer to radiation as a cause of cancer, we do not mean that every individual exposed to a certain amount of radiation will develop cancer. We simply mean that a population exposed to a certain dose of radiation will show a greater incidence of cancer than that same population would have shown in the absence of the added radiation.

J. Gofman, M.D., *Radiation and Human Health* 54–55 (1981), PX–1046.

The question of cause-in-fact is additionally complicated by the long delay, known often as the *latency period,* between the exposure to radiation and the observed cancer or leukemia. Assuming that cancer originates in a single cell, or a few cells, in a particular organ or tissue, it may take years before those cells multiply into the millions or billions that comprise a detectable tumor.

\* \* \*

> The problem of the latency period is one factor distinguishing \* \* \* cancer causation questions from the cause-in-fact relationships found in most tort cases; normally "cause" is far more direct, immediate and observable, *e.g.,* A fires a gun at B, seriously wounding him. The great length of time involved \* \* \* allows the possible involvement of "intervening causes," sources of injury wholly apart from the defendant's activities, which obscure the factual connection between the plaintiff's injury and the defendant's purportedly wrongful conduct. The mere passage of time is sufficient to raise doubts about "cause" in the minds of a legal system accustomed to far more immediate chains of events. [*Id.* at 405–06 (citations omitted).]

... The same difficulties encountered in *Allen* have also troubled commentators assessing the application of common-law doctrines to toxic tort litigation. Hence, recommendations have been made for a legislative response to the problem of causation when the injury has been manifested....

Although we acknowledge, as we must, the array of complex practical and doctrinal problems that confound litigants and courts in toxic-tort mass-exposure litigation, we are confronted in this case with fairly narrow and manageable issues. A legally and financially responsible defendant has been identified and a jury has determined "fault...." No statute of limitations questions are raised in this litigation. Nor are we confronted with insurmountable issues of causation: the testimony of plaintiffs' experts has persuasively established the relationship between defendant's wrongful conduct and the contamination of plaintiffs' wells; and plaintiffs do not seek damages for presently-existing illness or disease attributable to defendant's wrongful conduct. The legal issue we must resolve, in the context of the jury's determination of defendant's liability under the Act, is whether the proof of an unquantified enhanced risk of illness or a need for medical surveillance is sufficient to justify compensation under the Tort Claims Act. In view of the acknowledged difficulties of proving causation once evidence of disease is manifest, a determination of the compensability of post-exposure, pre-symptom injuries is particularly important in assessing the ability of tort law to redress the claims of plaintiffs in toxic-tort litigation.

* * *

Our disposition of this difficult and important issue requires that we choose between two alternatives, each having a potential for imposing unfair and undesirable consequences on the affected interests. A holding that recognizes a cause of action for unquantified enhanced risk claims exposes the tort system, and the public it serves, to the task of litigating vast numbers of claims for compensation based on threats of injuries that may never occur. It imposes on judges and juries the burden of assessing damages for the risk of potential disease, without clear guidelines to determine what level of compensation may be appropriate. It would undoubtedly increase already escalating insurance rates. It is clear that the recognition of an "enhanced risk" cause of action, particularly when the risk is unquantified, would generate substantial litigation that would be difficult to manage and resolve.

Our dissenting colleague, arguing in favor of recognizing a cause of action based on an unquantified claim of enhanced risk, points out that "courts have not allowed the difficulty of quantifying injury to prevent them from offering compensation for assault, trespass, emotional distress, invasion of privacy or damage to reputation." *Post* at 318. Although lawsuits grounded in one or more of these causes of action may involve claims for damages that are difficult to quantify, such damages are awarded on the basis of events that have occurred and can be proved at the time of trial. In contrast, the compensability of the enhanced risk claim depends upon the likelihood of an event that has not yet occurred and may never occur—the contracting of one or more diseases the risk of which has been enhanced by defendant's conduct. It is the highly contingent and speculative quality of an unquantified claim based on enhanced risk that renders it novel and difficult to manage and resolve. If such claims were to be litigated, juries would be asked to award damages for the enhanced risk of a disease that may never be contracted, without the benefit of expert testimony sufficient to establish the likelihood that the contingent event will ever occur.

On the other hand, denial of the enhanced-risk cause of action may mean that some of these plaintiffs will be unable to obtain compensation for their injury. Despite the collateral estoppel effect of the jury's finding that defendant's wrongful conduct caused the contamination of plaintiffs' wells, those who contract diseases in the future because of their exposure to chemicals in their well water may be unable to prove a causal relationship between such exposure and their disease. We have already adverted to the substantial difficulties encountered by plaintiffs in attempting to prove causation in toxic tort litigation. Dismissal of the enhanced risk claims may effectively preclude any recovery for injuries caused by exposure to chemicals in plaintiffs' wells because of the difficulty of proving that injuries manifested in the future were not the product of intervening events or causes.

It may be that this dilemma could be mitigated by a legislative remedy that eases the burden of proving causation in toxic-tort cases where there has been a statistically significant incidence of disease among the exposed population. Other proposals for legislative intervention contemplate a funded source of compensation for persons significantly endangered by exposure to toxic chemicals. We invite the legislature's attention to this perplexing and serious problem.

In deciding between recognition or nonrecognition of plaintiffs' enhanced-risk claim, we feel constrained to choose the alternative that most closely reflects the legislative purpose in enacting the Tort Claims Act. We are conscious of the admonition that in construing the Act courts should "exercise restraint in the acceptance of novel causes of action against public entities." Comment, *N.J.S.A.* 59:2–1. In our view, the speculative nature of an unquantified enhanced risk claim, the difficulties inherent in adjudicating such claims, and the policies underlying the Tort Claims Act argue persuasively against the recognition of this cause of action. Accordingly, we decline to recognize plaintiffs' cause of action for the *unquantified* enhanced risk of disease, and affirm the judgment of the Appellate Division dismissing such claims. We need not and do not decide whether a claim based on enhanced risk of disease that is supported by testimony demonstrating that the onset of the disease is reasonably probable ... could be maintained under the Tort Claims Act.

\* \* \*

The claim for medical surveillance expenses stands on a different footing from the claim based on enhanced risk. It seeks to recover the cost of periodic medical examinations intended to monitor plaintiffs' health and facilitate early diagnosis and treatment of disease caused by plaintiffs' exposure to toxic chemicals. At trial, competent medical testimony was offered to prove that a program of regular medical testing and evaluation was reasonably necessary and consistent with contemporary scientific principles applied by physicians experienced in the diagnosis and treatment of chemically-induced injuries.

\* \* \*

This point is well-illustrated by the hypothetical case discussed in the opinion of the Court of Appeals in *Friends For All Children v. Lockheed Aircraft Corp.*, 746 F.2d 816 (D.C.Cir.1984):

> Jones is knocked down by a motorbike when Smith is riding through a red light. Jones lands on his head with some force. Understandably shaken, Jones enters a hospital where doctors recommend that he undergo a battery of tests to determine whether he has suffered any internal head injuries. The tests prove negative, but Jones sues Smith solely for what turns out to be the substantial cost of the diagnostic examinations.
>
> From our example, it is clear that even in the absence of physical injury Jones ought to be able to recover the cost for the various diagnostic examinations proximately caused by Smith's negligent action. A cause of action allowing

recovery for the expense of diagnostic examinations recommended by competent physicians will, in theory, deter misconduct, whether it be negligent motorbike riding or negligent aircraft manufacture. The cause of action also accords with commonly shared intuitions of normative justice which underlie the common law of tort. The motorbike rider, through his negligence, caused the plaintiff, in the opinion of medical experts, to need specific medical services—a cost that is neither inconsequential nor of a kind the community generally accepts as part of the wear and tear of daily life. Under these principles of tort law, the motorbiker should pay. [*Id.* at 825.]

\* \* \*

Accordingly, we hold that the cost of medical surveillance is a compensable item of damages where the proofs demonstrate, through reliable expert testimony predicated upon the significance and extent of exposure to chemicals, the toxicity of the chemicals, the seriousness of the diseases for which individuals are at risk, the relative increase in the chance of onset of disease in those exposed, and the value of early diagnosis, that such surveillance to monitor the effect of exposure to toxic chemicals is reasonable and necessary. In our view, this holding is thoroughly consistent with our rejection of plaintiffs' claim for damages based on their enhanced risk of injury. That claim seeks damages for the impairment of plaintiffs' health, without proof of its likelihood, extent, or monetary value. In contrast, the medical surveillance claim seeks reimbursement for the specific dollar costs of periodic examinations that are medically necessary notwithstanding the fact that the extent of plaintiffs' impaired health is unquantified.

\* \* \*

### NOTES

1. **Toxic Torts.** Toxic tort cases, such as those involving exposure to carcinogens in the workplace or to toxins in a nearby waste facility, present overwhelming causation problems to potential plaintiffs. These problems include proving that they were actually exposed to a particular toxic substance, that the defendant is responsible for the plaintiff's contact with that substance, and that the toxic substance has in fact caused their injury.

2. **Expert Testimony.** Parties almost always must rely on scientific testimony from experts. In the flagship case concerning the admissibility of scientific testimony, *Daubert v. Merrell Dow Pharmaceuticals, Inc.*, 509 U.S. 579, 113 S.Ct. 2786, 125 L.Ed.2d 469 (1993), the plaintiffs sued to recover for birth defects allegedly caused by the defendant's drug Bendectin, which the plaintiffs' mothers had taken. The defendants introduced evidence showing that no study to date had shown that Bendectin caused birth defects. The plaintiffs sought to challenge this evidence with evidence consisting of animal studies, pharmacological studies showing Bendectin was chemically similar to other drugs known to cause birth defects, and reevaluation of the results of existing studies on Bendectin. The district court granted summary judgment in favor of the defendants, noting that the plaintiffs' testimony

was not generally accepted in the scientific community, and the court of appeals affirmed. The Supreme Court reversed, however, and held that the "general acceptance" approach had been superseded by the Federal Rules of Evidence, which require that expert scientific testimony be admitted if it (1) consists of scientific knowledge and (2) assists the trier of fact in understanding or determining the relevant issue. The Court also noted that such scientific evidence typically, though not necessarily, will have been tested, subject to peer review, including publication, and be widely accepted. Does this strike the right balance between admitting evidence that will shed light on the truth and screening bogus testimony?

The *Daubert* standard was applied in *Allen v. Pennsylvania Engineering Corp.*, 102 F.3d 194 (5th Cir.1996), a suit against the manufacturer of ethylene oxide, which allegedly caused brain cancer in the plaintiffs' decedent. The court ruled that the plaintiff's expert's testimony did not satisfy *Daubert* since it was not based on reliable science. The evidence included animal testing that showed a carcinogenic effect in rats. However, the same effect was not seen in mice. Also, certain studies "suggested" a connection between the chemical and cancer; the court held that "suggestiveness" is not sufficient to satisfy *Daubert*. The plaintiffs also relied on a "weight of the evidence" methodology employed by health organizations. However, the court noted the preventive purpose of such organizations and found that they use a low threshold when classifying a substance as a carcinogen.

**3. Medical Monitoring.** Despite the plaintiffs' inability to recover for the "increased risk" that they will later develop diseases caused by the negligence of the defendant, the court in *Ayers* did open the door to recovery for the costs of medical monitoring. Does this allow sufficient recovery? Does it provide sufficient deterrence for wrongful conduct? Is it likely plaintiffs who later develop diseases will not be able to prove the defendant caused it? Should mental distress caused by knowledge of the increased risk of disease be compensable? This issue is considered in Chapter 2, Sec. H(2), infra at pages 337–344.

**4. Straining the Tort System.** Professor Rabin has noted that the tort system is under great strain to adequately address the problems posed by environmental torts. He notes that environmental torts do not fit neatly into the standard paradigm of a two-party tort suit. Problems include identifying injury, the dispersion of parties geographically and chronologically, and difficulties of determining who is responsible for the harm. See Rabin, *Environmental Liability and the Tort System*, 24 Hous. L. Rev. 27 (1986).

What might be the best solution? Should the cause-in-fact requirement in tort law be adjusted to reflect the plaintiff's proof difficulties? Should the burden of proof be shifted as in *Summers v. Tice* or should percentage recoveries be allowed as in some medical uncertainty cases? Is a legislative solution the best answer? Note that in mid–1999 Congress began hearings on a possible national system for compensating asbestosis sufferers. The plan would require industry to contribute to a fund which would pay claims to those who have suffered asbestos-related injury. See Labaton, *Asbestos Cases in for Overhaul by Lawmakers*, New York Times, June 28, 1999, at A1. What are the advantages of such a system? Lower transaction costs? What about the drawbacks? Will plaintiffs be adequately compensated? What about deterring harm?

# SECTION F.  DUTY AND PROXIMATE CAUSE

## ATLANTIC COAST LINE R. CO. v. DANIELS

Court of Appeals of Georgia.
8 Ga.App. 775, 70 S.E. 203 (1911).

POWELL, J.

\* \* \*

... We have read and re-read a multitude of cases on the subject of what relation must exist between a negligent act and an injury that follows, in order that the author of the one may be held liable in damages to the sufferer of the other. We have read of "proximate cause" and of "natural consequence," and of other phrases expressing the same general idea, until eyes have grown weak with reading ... trying to understand what learned judge after learned judge, and learned law-writer after learned law-writer have said on the subject....

Cause and effect find their beginning and end in the limitless and unknowable. Therefore courts, in their finitude, do not attempt to deal with cause and effect in any absolute degree, but only in such a limited way as is practical and as is within the scope of ordinary human understanding. Hence arbitrary limits have been set, and such qualifying words as "proximate" and "natural" have come into use as setting the limits beyond which the courts will not look in the attempt to trace the connection between a given cause and a given effect. A plaintiff comes into court alleging, as an effect, some injury that has been done to his person or to his property. He shows that antecedent to the injury a wrongful act of another person occurred, and that, if this wrongful act had not occurred, the injury complained of would not (as human probabilities go) have occurred. We then say, in common speech, that the wrong was a cause of the injury. But to make such a standard (that, if the cause had not existed, the effect would not have occurred) the basis of legal responsibility would soon prove very unsatisfactory; for a reduction ad absurdum may be promptly established by calling to mind, that, if the injured person had never been born, the injury would not have happened. So the courts ask another question: Was the wrongful act the proximate cause?

\* \* \*

## NOTES

1. **Proximate or Legal Cause.** The "proximate" or "legal" cause element of negligence presents an additional barrier to recovery for plaintiffs. Even when the defendant's negligence is the actual "but for" cause of the plaintiff's injury, courts may find that the injury is too remotely connected to the defendant's wrongdoing to fairly impose responsibility on the defendant. As the principal case suggests, without some additional limit, a defendant whose negligence led to a child's birth could potentially be held

responsible for that child's future child's own negligence. Since cause-in-fact proves too much, proximate or legal cause provides a limit.

As subsequent cases will indicate, proximate or legal cause is ultimately a method by which courts can protect the defendant from liability even when her unreasonable conduct has caused harm to the plaintiff. A variety of policy factors undoubtedly influence the rules and the actual application of proximate cause including but not limited to the foreseeability of the harm suffered by the plaintiff.

Do you agree that there should be some limits on what a negligent defendant should be responsible for even when he was a but for cause of the plaintiff's injury? Is it more fair to impose unexpected consequence on the victim or the actor who negligently caused the injury? Is it practical to impose unlimited liability on a defendant? Is it more efficient to ask the victim or negligent actor to insure for unforeseeable loss? Does excessive liability overdeter productive activity? Should the temporal or spatial immediacy of the defendant's acts and the plaintiff's injury affect liability? Consider these factors as you evaluate the approaches to proximate cause in the following cases.

**2. The Restatement.** Historically the term "proximate cause" was used by courts, but the Restatement of Torts has attempted to popularize the term "legal cause" as more accurately reflecting that policy concerns and not mere physical factors determine whether the plaintiff establishes liability under proximate or legal cause. See Restatement (Second) of Torts § 431.

**3. Intentional Torts.** Although proximate cause is required for intentional tort cases as well as negligence and strict liability, most intentional tort cases do not discuss the requirement since it is rarely an issue.

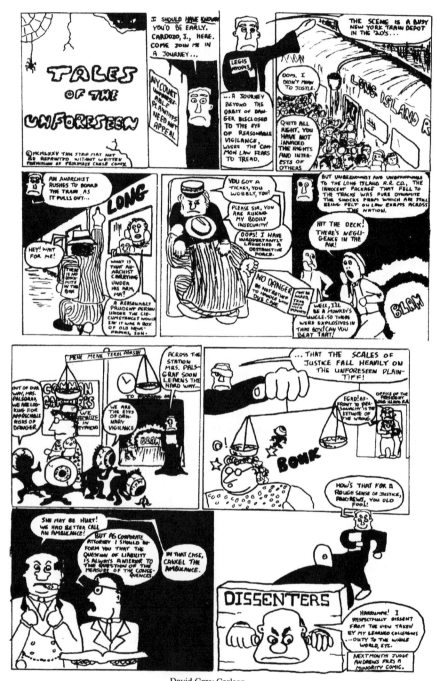

David Gray Carlson
Reprinted from 27 Hastings Law Journal 776-777 (1976) by permission.

# PALSGRAF v. THE LONG ISLAND RAILROAD COMPANY

Court of Appeals of New York.
248 N.Y. 339, 162 N.E. 99 (1928).

CARDOZO, C. J.

Plaintiff was standing on a platform of defendant's railroad after buying a ticket to go to Rockaway Beach. A train stopped at the station, bound for another place. Two men ran forward to catch it. One of the men reached the platform of the car without mishap, though the train was already moving. The other man, carrying a package, jumped aboard the car, but seemed unsteady as if about to fall. A guard on the car, who had held the door open, reached forward to help him in, and another guard on the platform pushed him from behind. In this act, the package was dislodged, and fell upon the rails. It was a package of small size, about fifteen inches long, and was covered by a newspaper. In fact it contained fireworks, but there was nothing in its appearance to give notice of its contents. The fireworks when they fell exploded. The shock of the explosion threw down some scales at the other end of the platform, many feet away. The scales struck the plaintiff, causing injuries for which she sues.

The conduct of the defendant's guard, if a wrong in its relation to the holder of the package, was not a wrong in its relation to the plaintiff, standing far away. Relatively to her it was not negligence at all. Nothing in the situation gave notice that the falling package had in it the potency of peril to persons thus removed. Negligence is not actionable unless it involves the invasion of a legally protected interest, the violation of a right. "Proof of negligence in the air, so to speak, will not do" (Pollock, Torts [11th ed.], p. 455; *Martin v. Herzog*, 228 N.Y. 164, 170; cf. Salmond, Torts [6th ed.], p. 24). "Negligence is the absence of care, according to the circumstances" (Willes, J., in *Vaughan v. Taff Vale Ry. Co.*, 5 H. & N. 679, 688; 1 Beven, Negligence [4th ed.], p. 7; *Paul v. Consol. Fireworks Co.*, 212 N.Y. 117; *Adams v. Bullock*, 227 N.Y. 208, 211; *Parrott v. Wells–Fargo Co.*, 15 Wall. [U.S.] 524). The plaintiff as she stood upon the platform of the station might claim to be protected against intentional invasion of her bodily security. Such invasion is not charged. She might claim to be protected against unintentional invasion by conduct involving in the thought of reasonable men an unreasonable hazard that such invasion would ensue. These, from the point of view of the law, were the bounds of her immunity, with perhaps some rare exceptions, survivals for the most part of ancient forms of liability, where conduct is held to be at the peril of the actor (*Sullivan v. Dunham*, 161 N.Y. 290). If no hazard was apparent to the eye of ordinary vigilance, an act innocent and harmless, at least to outward seeming, with reference to her, did not take to itself the quality of a tort because it happened to be a wrong, though apparently not one involving the risk of bodily insecurity, with reference to some one else. "In every instance, before negligence can be predicated of a given act, back of the act must be sought and found a duty to the individual complaining, the observance of which would have averted or avoided the injury" McSherry, C. J., in *W. Va. Central R. Co. v. State*, 96 Md. 652, 666; cf. *Norfolk & Western Ry. Co. v. Wood*, 99 Va. 156, 158, 159; *Hughes v. Boston & Maine R. R. Co.*, 71 N. H. 279, 284; *U. S. Express Co. v. Everest*, 72 Kan. 517; *Emry v. Roanoke Nav. Co.*, 111 N.C. 94, 95; *Vaughan v. Transit Dev. Co.*, 222 N.Y. 79; *Losee v. Clute*, 51 N.Y. 494; *DiCaprio v. N. Y. C. R. R. Co.*, 231 N.Y. 94; 1 Shearman & Redfield on Negligence, § 8, and cases cited; Cooley on Torts [3d ed.], p. 1411; Jaggard on Torts, vol. 2, p. 826; Wharton, Negligence, § 24; Bohlen, *Studies in the Law of Torts*, p. 601). "The ideas of negligence and duty are strictly correlative." Bowen, L. J., in *Thomas v. Quartermaine*, 18 Q. B. D. 685, 694. The plaintiff sues in her own right for a wrong personal to her, and not as the vicarious beneficiary of a breach of duty to another.

A different conclusion will involve us, and swiftly too, in a maze of contradictions. A guard stumbles over a package which has been left upon a platform. It seems to be a bundle of newspapers. It turns out to be a can of dynamite. To the eye of ordinary vigilance, the bundle is abandoned waste, which may be kicked or trod on with impunity. Is a passenger at the other end of the platform protected by the law against the unsuspected hazard concealed beneath the waste? If not, is the result to be any different, so far as the distant passenger is concerned, when the guard stumbles over a valise which a truckman or a porter has left upon the walk? The passenger far away, if the victim of a wrong at all, has a cause of action, not derivative, but original and primary. His claim to be protected against invasion of his bodily security is neither greater nor less because the act resulting in the invasion is a wrong to another far removed. In this case, the rights that are said to have been violated, the interests said to have been invaded, are not even of the same order. The man was not injured in his person nor even put in danger. The purpose of the act, as well as its effect, was to make his person safe. If there was a wrong to him at all, which may very well be doubted, it was a wrong to a property interest only, the safety of his package. Out of this wrong to property, which threatened injury to nothing else, there has passed, we are told, to the plaintiff by derivation or succession a right of action for the invasion of an interest of another order, the right to bodily security. The diversity of interests emphasizes the futility of the effort to build the plaintiff's right upon the basis of a wrong to some one else. The gain is one of emphasis, for a like result would follow if the interests were the same. Even then, the orbit of the danger as disclosed to the eye of reasonable vigilance would be the orbit of the duty. One who jostles one's neighbor in a crowd does not invade the rights of others standing at the outer fringe when the unintended contact casts a bomb upon the ground. The wrongdoer as to them is the man who carries the bomb, not the one who explodes it without suspicion of the danger. Life will have to be made over, and human nature transformed, before prevision so extravagant can be accepted as the norm of conduct, the customary standard to which behavior must conform.

The argument for the plaintiff is built upon the shifting meanings of such words as "wrong" and "wrongful," and shares their instability. What the plaintiff must show is "a wrong" to herself, i.e., a violation of her own right, and not merely a wrong to some one else, nor conduct "wrongful" because unsocial, but not "a wrong" to any one. We are told that one who drives at reckless speed through a crowded city street is guilty of a negligent act and, therefore, of a wrongful one irrespective of the consequences. Negligent the act is, and wrongful in the sense that it is unsocial, but wrongful and unsocial in relation to other travelers, only because the eye of vigilance perceives the risk of damage. If the same act were to be committed on a speedway or a race course, it would lose its wrongful quality. The risk reasonably to be perceived defines the duty to be obeyed, and risk imports relation; it is risk to another or to others within the range of apprehension Seavey, Negligence, Subjective or Objective, 41 H.L.Rv. 6; *Boronkay v. Robinson & Carpenter*, 247 N.Y. 365. This does not mean, of course, that one who launches a destructive force is always relieved of liability if the force, though known to be destructive, pursues an unexpected path. "It was not necessary that the defendant should have had notice of the particular method in which an accident would occur, if the possibility of an accident was clear to the ordinarily prudent eye." *Munsey v. Webb*, 231 U.S. 150, 156; *Condran v. Park & Tilford*, 213 N.Y. 341, 345; *Robert v. U. S. E. F. Corp.*, 240 N.Y. 474, 477. Some acts, such as shooting, are so imminently dangerous to any one who may come within reach of the missile, however unexpectedly, as to impose a duty of prevision not far from that of an insurer. Even today, and much oftener in earlier stages of the law, one acts sometimes at one's peril Jeremiah Smith, Tort and Absolute Liability, 30 H.L.Rv. 328; Street, Foundations of Legal Liability, vol. 1, pp. 77, 78. Under this head, it may be, fall certain cases of what is known as transferred intent, an act willfully dangerous to A resulting by misadventure in injury to B. *Talmage v. Smith*, 101 Mich. 370, 374. These cases aside, wrong is defined in terms of the natural or probable, at least when unintentional *Parrot v. Wells–Fargo Co.* (The Nitro–Glycerine Case), 15 Wall. [U.S.] 524. The range of reasonable apprehension is at times a question for the court, and at times, if varying inferences are possible, a question for the jury. Here, by concession, there was nothing in the situation to suggest to the most cautious mind that the parcel wrapped in newspaper would spread wreckage through the station. If the guard had thrown it down knowingly and willfully, he would not have threatened the plaintiff's safety, so far as appearances could warn him. His conduct would not have involved, even then, an unreasonable probability of invasion of her bodily security. Liability can be no greater where the act is inadvertent.

Negligence, like risk, is thus a term of relation. Negligence in the abstract, apart from things related, is surely not a tort, if indeed it is understandable at all. Bowen, L. J., in *Thomas v. Quartermaine*, 18 Q. B. D. 685, 694. Negligence is not a tort unless it results in the commission of a wrong, and the commission of a wrong imports the violation of a right, in this case, we are told, the right to be protected against interference with one's bodily security. But bodily security is protected, not against all forms of interference or aggression, but only against some. One who seeks redress at law does not make out a cause of action by showing without more that there has been damage to his person. If the harm was not willful, he must show that the act as to him had possibilities of danger so many and apparent as to entitle him to be protected against the doing of it though the harm was unintended. Affront to personality is still the keynote of the wrong. Confirmation of this view will be found in the history and development of the action on the case. Negligence as a basis of civil liability was unknown to mediae-val law. 8 Holdsworth, History of English Law, p. 449; Street, Founda-tions of Legal Liability, vol. 1, pp. 189, 190. For damage to the person, the sole remedy was trespass, and trespass did not lie in the absence of aggression, and that direct and personal. Holdsworth, op. cit. p. 453; Street, op. cit. vol. 3, pp. 258, 260, vol. 1, pp. 71, 74. Liability for other damage, as where a servant without orders from the master does or omits something to the damage of another, is a plant of later growth. Holdsworth, op. cit. 450, 457; Wigmore, Responsibility for Tortious Acts, vol. 3, Essays in Anglo–American Legal History, 520, 523, 526, 533. When it emerged out of the legal soil, it was thought of as a variant of trespass, an offshoot of the parent stock. This appears in the form of action, which was known as trespass on the case. Holdsworth, op. cit. p. 449; cf. *Scott v. Shepard*, 2 Wm. Black. 892; Green, Rationale of Proxi-mate Cause, p. 19. The victim does not sue derivatively, or by right of subrogation, to vindicate an interest invaded in the person of another. Thus to view his cause of action is to ignore the fundamental difference between tort and crime. Holland, Jurisprudence (12th ed.), p. 328. He sues for breach of a duty owing to himself.

The law of causation, remote or proximate, is thus foreign to the case before us. The question of liability is always anterior to the question of the measure of the consequences that go with liability. If there is no tort to be redressed, there is no occasion to consider what damage might be recovered if there were a finding of a tort. We may assume, without deciding, that negligence, not at large or in the abstract, but in relation to the plaintiff, would entail liability for any and all consequences, however novel or extraordinary. *Bird v. St. Paul F. & M. Ins. Co.*, 224 N.Y. 47, 54; *Ehrgott v. Mayor, etc., of N.Y.*, 96 N.Y. 264; *Smith v. London & S. W. Ry. Co.*, L.R. 6 C. P. 14; 1 Beven, Negligence, 106; Street, op. cit. vol. 1, p. 90; Green, Rationale of Proximate Cause, pp. 88, 118; cf. *Matter of Polemis*, L.R. 1921, 3 K.B. 560; 44 Law Quarterly Review, 142. There is room for argument that a distinction is to be drawn according to the diversity of interests invaded by the act, as where conduct negligent in that it threatens an insignificant invasion of an interest in property results in an unforeseeable invasion of an interest of another order, as, e.g., one of bodily security. Perhaps other distinctions may be necessary. We do not go into the question now. The consequences to be followed must first be rooted in a wrong.

The judgment of the Appellate Division and that of the Trial Term should be reversed, and the complaint dismissed, with costs in all courts.

ANDREWS, J. (dissenting).

Assisting a passenger to board a train, the defendant's servant negligently knocked a package from his arms. It fell between the plat-form and the cars. Of its contents the servant knew and could know nothing. A violent explosion followed. The concussion broke some scales standing a considerable distance away. In falling they injured the plaintiff, an intending passenger.

Upon these facts may she recover the damages she has suffered in an action brought against the master? The result we shall reach depends upon our theory as to the nature of negligence. Is it a relative concept— the breach of some duty owing to a particular person or to particular persons? Or where there is an act which unreasonably threatens the safety of others, is the doer liable for all its proximate consequences, even where they result in injury to one who would generally be thought to be outside the radius of danger? This is not a mere dispute as to words. We might not believe that to the average mind the dropping of the bundle would seem to involve the probability of harm to the plaintiff standing many feet away whatever might be the case as to the owner or to one so near as to be likely to be struck by its fall. If, however, we adopt the second hypothesis we have to inquire only as to the relation between cause and effect. We deal in terms of proximate cause, not of negligence.

Negligence may be defined roughly as an act or omission which unreasonably does or may affect the rights of others, or which unreasonably fails to protect oneself from the dangers resulting from such acts. Here I confine myself to the first branch of the definition. Nor do I comment on the word "unreasonable." For present purposes it sufficiently describes that average of conduct that society requires of its members.

There must be both the act or the omission, and the right. It is the act itself, not the intent of the actor, that is important. *Hover v. Barkhoof*, 44 N.Y. 113; *Mertz v. Connecticut Co.*, 217 N.Y. 475. In criminal law both the intent and the result are to be considered. Intent again is material in tort actions, where punitive damages are sought, dependent on actual malice—not on merely reckless conduct. But here neither insanity nor infancy lessens responsibility. *Williams v. Hays*, 143 N.Y. 442.

\* \* \*

But we are told that "there is no negligence unless there is in the particular case a legal duty to take care, and this duty must be one which is owed to the plaintiff himself and not merely to others." Salmond Torts (6th Ed.), 24. This, I think too narrow a conception. Where there is the unreasonable act, and some right that may be affected there is negligence whether damage does or does not result. That is immaterial. Should we drive down Broadway at a reckless speed, we are negligent whether we strike an approaching car or miss it by an inch. The act itself is wrongful. It is a wrong not only to those who happen to be within the radius of danger but to all who might have been there—a wrong to the public at large. Such is the language of the street. Such the language of the courts when speaking of contributory negligence. Such again and again their language in speaking of the duty of some defendant and discussing proximate cause in cases where such a discussion is wholly irrelevant on any other theory. *Perry v. Rochester*

*Line Co.*, 219 N. Y. 60. As was said by Mr. Justice Holmes many years ago:

> "The measure of the defendant's duty in determining whether a wrong has been committed is one thing, the measure of liability when a wrong has been committed is another." *Spade v. Lynn & Boston R. R. Co.*, 172 Mass. 488. Due care is a duty imposed on each one of us to protect society from unnecessary danger, not to protect A, B or C alone.

It may well be that there is no such thing as negligence in the abstract. "Proof of negligence in the air, so to speak, will not do." In an empty world negligence would not exist. It does involve a relationship between man and his fellows. But not merely a relationship between man and those whom he might reasonably expect his act would injure. Rather, a relationship between him and those whom he does in fact injure. If his act has a tendency to harm some one, it harms him a mile away as surely as it does those on the scene. We now permit children to recover for the negligent killing of the father. It was never prevented on the theory that no duty was owing to them. A husband may be compensated for the loss of his wife's services. To say that the wrongdoer was negligent as to the husband as well as to the wife is merely an attempt to fit facts to theory.

\* \* \*

The proposition is this. Every one owes to the world at large the duty of refraining from those acts that may unreasonably threaten the safety of others. Such an act occurs. Not only is he wronged to whom harm might reasonably be expected to result, but he also who is in fact injured, even if he be outside what would generally be thought the danger zone. There needs be duty due the one complaining but this is not a duty to a particular individual because as to him harm might be expected. Harm to some one being the natural result of the act, not only that one alone, but all those in fact injured may complain.

\* \* \*

The right to recover damages rests on additional considerations. The plaintiff's rights must be injured, and this injury must be caused by the negligence. We build a dam, but are negligent as to its foundations. Breaking, it injures property down stream. We are not liable if all this happened because of some reason other than the insecure foundation. But when injuries do result from our unlawful act we are liable for the consequences. It does not matter that they are unusual, unexpected, unforeseen and unforeseeable. But there is one limitation. The damages must be so connected with the negligence that the latter may be said to be the proximate cause of the former.

These two words have never been given an inclusive definition. What is a cause in a legal sense, still more what is a proximate cause, depend in each case upon many considerations, as does the existence of negligence itself. Any philosophical doctrine of causation does not help us. A boy throws a stone into a pond. The ripples spread. The water level rises. The history of that pond is altered to all eternity. It will be altered by other causes also. Yet it will be forever the resultant of all causes combined. Each one will have an influence. How great only omniscience can say. You may speak of a chain, or if you please, a net. An analogy is of little aid. Each cause brings about future events. Without each the future would not be the same. Each is proximate in the sense it is essential. But that is not what we mean by the word. Nor on the other hand do we mean sole cause. There is no such thing.

Should analogy be thought helpful, however, I prefer that of a stream. The spring, starting on its journey, is joined by tributary after tributary. The river, reaching the ocean, comes from a hundred sources. No man may say whence any drop of water is derived. Yet for a time distinction may be possible. Into the clear creek, brown swamp water flows from the left. Later, from the right comes water stained by its clay bed. The three may remain for a space, sharply divided. But at last, inevitably no trace of separation remains. They are so commingled that all distinction is lost.

As we have said, we cannot trace the effect of an act to the end, if end there is. Again, however, we may trace it part of the way. A murder at Serajevo may be the necessary antecedent to an assassination in London twenty years hence. An overturned lantern may burn all Chicago. We may follow the fire from the shed to the last building. We rightly say the fire started by the lantern caused its destruction.

A cause, but not the proximate cause. What we do mean by the word "proximate" is, that because of convenience, of public policy, of a rough sense of justice, the law arbitrarily declines to trace a series of events beyond a certain point. This is not logic. It is practical politics. Take our rule as to fires. Sparks from my burning haystack set on fire my house and my neighbor's. I may recover from a negligent railroad. He may not. Yet the wrongful act as directly harmed the one as the other. We may regret that the line was drawn just where it was, but drawn somewhere it had to be. We said the act of the railroad was not the proximate cause of our neighbor's fire. Cause it surely was. The words we used were simply indicative of our notions of public policy. Other courts think differently. But somewhere they reach the point where they cannot say the stream comes from any one source.

Take the illustration given in an unpublished manuscript by a distinguished and helpful writer on *The Law of Torts*. A chauffeur negligently collides with another car which is filled with dynamite, although he could not know it. An explosion follows. A, walking on the sidewalk nearby, is killed. B, sitting in a window of a building opposite, is cut by flying glass. C, likewise sitting in a window a block away, is similarly injured. And a further illustration. A nursemaid, ten blocks away, startled by the noise, involuntarily drops a baby from her arms to the walk. We are told that C may not recover while A may. As to B it is a question for court or jury. We will all agree that the baby might not. Because, we are again told, the chauffeur had no reason to believe his conduct involved any risk of injuring either C or the baby. As to them he was not negligent.

But the chauffeur, being negligent in risking the collision, his belief that the scope of the harm he might do would be limited is immaterial. His act unreasonably jeopardized the safety of any one who might be affected by it. C's injury and that of the baby were directly traceable to the collision. Without that, the injury would not have happened. C had the right to sit in his office, secure from such dangers. The baby was entitled to use the sidewalk with reasonable safety.

The true theory is, it seems to me, that the injury to C, if in truth he is to be denied recovery, and the injury to the baby is that their several injuries were not the proximate result of the negligence. And here not what the chauffeur had reason to believe would be the result of his conduct, but what the prudent would foresee, may have a bearing. May have some bearing, for the problem of proximate cause is not to be solved by any one consideration. It is all a question of expediency. There are no fixed rules to govern our judgment. There are simply matters of which we may take account. We have in a somewhat different connection spoken of "the stream of events." We have asked whether that stream was deflected—whether it was forced into new and unexpected channels. *Donnelly v. Piercy Contracting Co.*, 222 N.Y. 210. This is rather rhetoric than law. There is in truth little to guide us other than common sense.

There are some hints that may help us. The proximate cause, involved as it may be with many other causes, must be, at the least, something without which the event would not happen. The court must ask itself whether there was a natural and continuous sequence between cause and effect. Was the one a substantial factor in producing the other? Was there a direct connection between them, without too many intervening causes? Is the effect of cause on result not too attenuated? Is the cause likely, in the usual judgment of mankind, to produce the result? Or by the exercise of prudent foresight could the result be foreseen? Is the result too remote from the cause, and here we consider remoteness in time and space. *Bird v. St. Paul F. & M. Ins. Co.*, 224 N.Y. 47, where we passed upon the construction of a contract—but something was also said on this subject. Clearly we must so consider, for the greater the distance either in time or space, the more surely do other causes intervene to affect the result. When a lantern is overturned the firing of a shed is a fairly direct consequence. Many things contribute to the spread of the conflagration—the force of the wind, the direction and width of streets, the character of intervening structures, other factors. We draw an uncertain and wavering line, but draw it we must as best we can.

Once again, it is all a question of fair judgment, always keeping in mind the fact that we endeavor to make a rule in each case that will be practical and in keeping with the general understanding of mankind.

Here another question must be answered. In the case supposed it is said, and said correctly, that the chauffeur is liable for the direct effect of the explosion although he had no reason to suppose it would follow a collision. "The fact that the injury occurred in a different manner than that which might have been expected does not prevent the chauffeur's negligence from being in law the cause of the injury." But the natural results of a negligent act—the results which a prudent man would or should foresee—do have a bearing upon the decision as to proximate cause. We have said so repeatedly. What should be foreseen? No human foresight would suggest that a collision itself might injure one a block away. On the contrary, given an explosion, such a possibility might be reasonably expected. I think the direct connection, the foresight of which the courts speak, assumes prevision of the explosion, for the immediate results of which, at least, the chauffeur is responsible.

It may be said this is unjust. Why? In fairness he should make good every injury flowing from his negligence. Not because of tenderness toward him we say he need not answer for all that follows his wrong. We look back to the catastrophe, the fire kindled by the spark, or the explosion. We trace the consequences—not indefinitely, but to a certain point. And to aid us in fixing that point we ask what might ordinarily be expected to follow the fire or the explosion.

This last suggestion is the factor which must determine the case before us. The act upon which defendant's liability rests is knocking an apparently harmless package onto the platform. The act was negligent. For its proximate consequences the defendant is liable. If its contents were broken, to the owner; if it fell upon and crushed a passenger's foot, then to him. If it exploded and injured one in the immediate vicinity, to him also as to A in the illustration. Mrs. Palsgraf was standing some distance away. How far cannot be told from the record—apparently twenty-five or thirty feet. Perhaps less. Except for the explosion, she would not have been injured. We are told by the appellant in his brief "it cannot be denied that the explosion was the direct cause of the plaintiff's injuries." So it was a substantial factor in producing the result—there was here a natural and continuous sequence—direct connection. The only intervening cause was that instead of blowing her to the ground the concussion smashed the weighing machine which in turn fell upon her. There was no remoteness in time, little in space. And surely, given such an explosion as here it needed no great foresight to predict that the natural result would be to injure one on the platform at no greater distance from its scene than was the plaintiff. Just how no one might be able to predict. Whether by flying fragments, by broken glass, by wreckage of machines or structures no one could say. But injury in some form was most probable.

Under these circumstances I cannot say as a matter of law that the plaintiff's injuries were not the proximate result of the negligence. That is all we have before us. The court refused to so charge. No request was made to submit the matter to the jury as a question of fact, even would that have been proper upon the record before us.

The judgment appealed from should be affirmed, with costs.

### *NOTES*

**1. Duty Versus Proximate Cause Elements of Negligence.** Be careful to distinguish the element of duty from proximate cause (which is discussed in the subsequent principal cases). Both elements in negligence limit the defendant's responsibility for unreasonable conduct that caused the potential plaintiff injury. Arguably the "duty" and "proximate cause" elements could have been merged, but history developed the architecture of the tort differently.

Duty focuses on *"to whom"* the defendant owes an obligation to conform to a prescribed standard of reasonable conduct. The majority and dissenting opinions in the principal case disagree over whether that duty or obligation is limited to foreseeable victims as is discussed further in Note 3.

The proximate or legal cause element of negligence also potentially limits the defendant's liability. As will be seen in subsequent cases, proximate cause limits the *"type"* or *"kind"* of harm the defendant can be liable for. The majority in the principal case resolved the case using only the duty element in favor of the defense and never reached the proximate cause element. By contrast, the dissenting opinion discussed both elements in deciding the case for the plaintiff.

**2.  Palsgraf.** The *Palsgraf* case is probably the most famous case in all of torts and possibly all of American jurisprudence. Generations of law students and lawyers relished its weird sequence of facts (although contemporaneous news coverage does not support the court's findings of fact), and revered it as a foundation of American tort principles. See Keeton, *Prosser and Keeton on the Law of Torts*, § 43, note 35 (5th ed. 1984); Prosser, *Palsgraf Revisited*, 52 Mich. L. Rev. 1 (1953). Consider the accompanying cartoon written as a law student by Professor David Carlson. To some, if not many, current law students, the case is instead burdened with flowery language and speaks the obvious.

Consider the following haiku penned by Professor Neil M. Levy in tribute to *Palsgraf*:

> A man, a package,
> push, bang, the scales are falling.
> Poor Helen Palsgraf.

**3.  Duty and Foreseeability.** The fact that *Palsgraf* may speak the obvious indeed may emphasize its success in indoctrinating current culture with its approach to liability. *Palsgraf* introduced as law in the important jurisdiction of New York the concept of foreseeability as a limiting factor on the scope of liability for negligence. This limitation has since become well entrenched in American tort law. The majority opinion framed the foreseeability requirement in light of the presence or absence of duty. Justice Cardozo interpreted the element of duty as a relational concept whereby a defendant owes a duty to refrain from negligent conduct only to foreseeable victims. Thus, in order to establish this duty, the plaintiff must show that the plaintiff was in the foreseeable zone of danger. This represents the current majority view and is endorsed by the Restatement:

> "In order for the actor to be negligent with respect to the other, his conduct must create a recognizable risk of harm to the other individually, or to a class of persons—as, for example, all persons within a given area of danger—of which the other is a member. If the actor's conduct creates such a recognizable risk of harm only to a particular class of persons, the fact that it in fact causes harm to a person of a different class, to whom the actor could not reasonably

have anticipated injury, does not make the actor liable to the persons so injured."

Restatement (Second) of Torts § 43. See Diamond, Levine & Madden, *Understanding Torts* 133 (2nd ed. 2000); Dobbs, *The Law of Torts* § 182 (2000). Do you agree that liability should be limited to foreseeable victims? Should wrongdoers be spared the complete consequences of their negligence?

**4. Zone of Risk.** As the principal case illustrates, a plaintiff must be within the "zone of risk" in order to recover for injuries sustained. Because Mrs. Palsgraf was nowhere near the exploding package and there was no reason for the guards to believe the package contained explosives, she was outside of the area where she could have foreseeably been harmed. Therefore, the railroad did not owe a duty to Mrs. Palsgraf to keep her free from this specific harm. Consequently, even though the railroad may have breached the requisite standard of conduct and caused Mrs. Palsgraf's injuries, it was able to avoid liability because of the lines drawn around the zone of foreseeability. Could the facts have been rephrased to make Mrs. Palsgraf seem foreseeable? After all, she was a railroad customer and near the railroad scale.

Consider *Mellon Mortgage Co. v. Holder*, 5 S.W.3d 654, 42 Tex. Sup. J. 1159 (1999), where the Supreme Court of Texas only recently adopted *Palsgraf*'s requirement that the plaintiff be foreseeable. In *Mellon Mortgage* the plaintiff was sexually assaulted by an on-duty police officer who told her to follow him into the defendant's garage. The garage was located in a high crime area in Houston. The majority concluded that Mellon, the company managing the garage, did not owe a duty to the victim because she was not an employee or other person who used the garage and was therefore "not a member of this class or any other that Mellon would have reasonably foreseen would be a victim of a criminal act in its garage."

**5. Duty Owed to Rescuers.** Generally rescuers who voluntarily expose themselves to a risk are considered foreseeable plaintiffs, even if they were not initially within the zone of danger. Consider *Dillard v. Pittway Corp.*, 719 So.2d 188 (Ala.1998), where the court held that the manufacturer of a defective smoke detector owed a duty to a rescuer who was injured while attempting to rescue a fire victim.

**6. The *Palsgraf* Dissent.** Justice Andrews' dissent represents a viable minority view followed by courts today. Andrews rejected the majority's proposition that a duty is owed only to foreseeable victims; instead, the dissent proposed that "[e]very one owes to the world at large the duty of refraining from those acts that may unreasonably threaten the safety of others." However, the dissent recognized that a limitation was necessary. Instead, proximate cause serves as the element operating as the ultimate brake on the scope of liability. While the majority in *Palsgraf* never reached the question of proximate cause, Andrews, having found there was a duty owed the plaintiff, must analyze whether the railroad's negligence was the proximate cause of Mrs. Palsgraf's injury. Justice Andrews ultimately concluded that proximate cause is a question of public policy, fairness and justice, which could not be reduced to any mechanical formula. Justice Andrews' analysis of proximate cause is informed by a number of factors that help determine what is fair and just. Which of those factors, described in his dissent, do you think is most important? While Justice Andrews does not exclude foreseeability as a factor, consider how his use of the concept differs from the majority's application of foreseeability in its analysis of the duty element in negligence. Does Justice Andrews' approach of analyzing foreseeability from the perspective of what would appear to be the "the natural results of a negligent act [looking] back to the catastrophe" represent a fair or useful definition of "foreseeability"?

**7. Policy of Proximate Cause.** Modern courts will sometimes utilize Andrews' candid policy approach to proximate cause, especially when the majority's approach would produce an unfavorable result. See Note 5, infra, which follows the next principal case.

**8. Proposed Final Draft to the Restatement (Third) of Torts, Duty.** The Restatement (Third) defines duty as follows:

(a) An actor ordinarily has a duty to exercise reasonable care when the actor's conduct creates a risk of physical harm.

(b) In exceptional cases, when an articulated countervailing principle or policy warrants limiting or denying liability in a particular class of cases, a court may decide that the defendant has no duty or that the ordinary duty of care requires modification.

While not explicitly saying so, The Restatement (Third) effectively overrules Cardozo's holding in *Palsgraf* that a person only owes a duty to foreseeable victims. Like the Andrews dissent, The Restatement (Third) endorses the notion that there is a general duty of reasonable care to all. In certain circumstances, a court may decide to limit duty in the interest of public policy, such as when social hosts serve alcohol to guests. According to The Restatement (Third), foreseeability as a limiting factor is best left to proximate cause and should not be discussed in regard to duty. Further, the defendant has the obligation to raise the issue whether a no-duty rule should be applied. Restatement (Third) of Torts § 7, comments a, b, j.

## OVERSEAS TANKSHIP (U.K.) LTD. v. MORTS DOCK & ENGINEERING CO. (THE WAGON MOUND)
### PRIVY COUNCIL
On Appeal from the Supreme Court of New South Wales.
1961 A.C. 388 (P.C.).

Appeal (No. 23 of 1960) from an order of the Full Court of the Supreme Court of New South Wales (Owen, Maguire and Manning JJ.) (December 3, 1959) dismissing an appeal by the appellants, Overseas Tankship (U.K.) Ltd., from a judgment of Kinsella J. exercising the Admiralty Jurisdiction of that court (April 23, 1959) in an action in which the appellants were defendants and the respondents, Morts Dock & Engineering Co. Ltd., were plaintiffs.

The following facts are taken from the judgment of the Judicial Committee: In the action the respondents sought to recover from the appellants compensation for the damage which its property known as the Sheerlegs Wharf, in Sydney Harbour, and the equipment thereon had suffered by reason of fire which broke out on November 1, 1951. For that damage they claimed that the appellants were in law responsible.

The relevant facts can be comparatively shortly stated inasmuch as not one of the findings of fact in the exhaustive judgment of the trial judge had been challenged.

The respondents at the relevant time carried on the business of ship-building, ship-repairing and general engineering at Morts Bay, Balmain, in the Port of Sydney. They owned and used for their business the Sheerlegs Wharf, a timber wharf about 400 feet in length and 40 feet wide, where there was a quantity of tools and equipment. In October and November, 1951, a vessel known as the *Corrimel* was moored alongside the wharf and was being refitted by the respondents. Her mast was lying on the wharf and a number of the respondents' employees were working both upon it and upon the vessel itself, using for that purpose electric and oxy-acetylene welding equipment.

At the same time the appellants were charterers by demise of the s.s. *Wagon Mound,* an oil-burning vessel, which was moored at the Caltex Wharf on the northern shore of the harbour at a distance of about 600 feet from the Sheerlegs Wharf. She was there from about 9 a.m. on October 29 until 11 a.m. on October 30, 1951, for the purpose of discharging gasolene products and taking in bunkering oil.

During the early hours of October 30, 1951, a large quantity of bunkering oil was, through the carelessness of the appellants' servants, allowed to spill into the bay, and by 10.30 on the morning of that day it had spread over a considerable part of the bay, being thickly concentrated in some places and particularly along the foreshore near the respondents' property. The appellants made no attempt to disperse the oil. The *Wagon Mound* unberthed and set sail very shortly after.

When the respondents' works manager became aware of the condition of things in the vicinity of the wharf he instructed their workmen that no welding or burning was to be carried on until further orders. He inquired of the manager of the Caltex Oil Company, at whose wharf the *Wagon Mound* was then still berthed, whether they could safely continue their operations on the wharf or upon the *Corrimal.* The results of the inquiry coupled with his own belief as to the inflammability of furnace oil in the open led him to think that the respondents could safely carry on their operations. He gave instructions accordingly, but directed that all safety precautions should be taken to prevent inflammable material falling off the wharf into the oil.

For the remainder of October 30 and until about 2 p.m. on November 1 work was carried on as usual, the condition and congestion of the oil remaining substantially unaltered. But at about that time the oil under or near the wharf was ignited and a fire, fed initially by the oil, spread rapidly and burned with great intensity. The wharf and the *Corrimal* caught fire and considerable damage was done to the wharf and the equipment upon it.

The outbreak of fire was due, as the judge found, to the fact that there was floating in the oil underneath the wharf a piece of débris on which lay some smouldering cotton waste or rag which had been set on fire by molten metal falling from the wharf: that the cotton waste or rag burst into flames: that the flames from the cotton waste set the floating oil afire either directly or by first setting fire to a wooden pile coated with oil, and that after the floating oil became ignited the flames spread rapidly over the surface of the oil and quickly developed into a conflagration which severely damaged the wharf.

\* \* \*

It is inevitable that first consideration should be given to the case of *In re Polemis and Furness Withy & Co. Ltd.* which will henceforward be referred to as *Polemis*. For it was avowedly in deference to that decision and to decisions of the Court of Appeal that followed it that the Full Court was constrained to decide the present case in favour of the respondents.

\* \* \*

What, then, did *Polemis* decide? Their Lordships do not propose to spend time in examining whether the issue there lay in breach of contract or in tort. That might be relevant for a tribunal for which the decision was a binding authority: for their Lordships it is not. It may, however, be observed that in the proceedings there was some confusion. The case arose out of a charterparty and went to arbitration under a term of it, and the first contention of the charterers was that they were protected from liability by the exception of fire in the charterparty. But it is clear from the pleadings and other documents, copies of which were supplied from the Record Office, that alternative claims for breach of contract and negligence were advanced, and it is clear, too, that before Sankey J. and the Court of Appeal the case proceeded as one in which, independently of contractual obligations, the claim was for damages for negligence. It was upon this footing that the Court of Appeal held that the charterers were responsible for all the consequences of their negligent act even though those consequences could not reasonably have been anticipated. The negligent act was nothing more than the carelessness of stevedores (for whom the charterers were assumed to be responsible) in allowing a sling or rope by which it was hoisted to come into contact with certain boards, causing one of them to fall into the hold. The falling board hit some substances in the hold and caused a spark: the spark ignited petrol vapour in the hold: there was a rush of flames, and the ship was destroyed. The special case submitted by the arbitrators found that the causing of the spark could not reasonably have been anticipated from the falling of the board, though some damage to the ship might reasonably have been anticipated. They did not indicate what damage might have been so anticipated.

There can be no doubt that the decision of the Court of Appeal in *Polemis* plainly asserts that, if the defendant is guilty of negligence, he is responsible for all the consequences whether reasonably foreseeable or not. The generality of the proposition is perhaps qualified by the fact that each of the Lords Justices refers to the outbreak of fire as the direct result of the negligent act. There is thus introduced the conception that the negligent actor is not responsible for consequences which are not "direct," whatever that may mean. It has to be asked, then, why this conclusion should have been reached. The answer appears to be that it was reached upon a consideration of certain authorities, comparatively few in number, that were cited to the court. Of these, three are generally regarded as having influenced the decision. The earliest in point of date was *Smith v. London & South Western Railway Co.* In that case it was said that "when it has been once determined that there is evidence of negligence, the person guilty of it is equally liable for its consequences, whether he could have foreseen them or not": see *per* Channell B. Similar observations were made by other members of the court. Three things may be noted about this case: the first, that for the sweeping proposition laid down no authority was cited; the second, that the point to which the court directed its mind was not unforeseeable damage of a different kind from that which was foreseen, but more extensive damage of the same kind; and the third, that so little was the mind of the court directed to the problem which has now to be solved that no one of the seven judges who took part in the decision thought it necessary to qualify in any way the consequences for which the defendant was to be held responsible. It would perhaps not be improper to say that the law of negligence as an independent tort was then of recent growth and that its implications had not been fully examined.

* * *

Enough has been said to show that the authority of *Polemis* has been severely shaken though lip-service has from time to time been paid to it. In their Lordships' opinion it should no longer be regarded as good law. It is not probable that many cases will for that reason have a different result, though it is hoped that the law will be thereby simplified, and that in some cases, at least, palpable injustice will be avoided. For it does not seem consonant with current ideas of justice or morality that for an act of negligence, however slight or venial, which results in some trivial foreseeable damage the actor should be liable for all consequences however unforeseeable and however grave, so long as they can be said to be "direct." It is a principle of civil liability, subject only to qualifications which have no present relevance, that a man must be considered to be responsible for the probable consequences of his act. To demand more of him is too harsh a rule, to demand less is to ignore that civilised order requires the observance of a minimum standard of behaviour.

This concept applied to the slowly developing law of negligence has led to a great variety of expressions which can, as it appears to their Lordships, be harmonised with little difficulty with the single exception of the so-called rule in *Polemis*. For, if it is asked why a man should be responsible for the natural or necessary or probable consequences of his act (or any other similar description of them) the answer is that it is not because they are natural or necessary or probable, but because, since they have this quality, it is judged by the standard of the reasonable man that he ought to have foreseen them. Thus it is that over and over again it has happened that in different judgments in the same case, and sometimes in a single judgment, liability for a consequence has been imposed on the ground that it was reasonably foreseeable or, alternatively, on the ground that it was natural or necessary or probable. The two grounds have been treated as coterminous, and so they largely are. But, where they are not, the question arises to which the wrong answer was given in *Polemis*. For, if some limitation must be imposed upon the consequences for which the negligent actor is to be held responsible— and all are agreed that some limitation there must be—why should that test (reasonable foreseeability) be rejected which, since he is judged by what the reasonable man ought to foresee, corresponds with the common conscience of mankind, and a test (the "direct" consequence) be substituted which leads to no-where but the never-ending and insoluble problems of causation. "The lawyer," said Sir Frederick Pollock, "cannot afford to adventure himself with philosophers in the logical and metaphysical controversies that beset the idea of cause." Yet this is just what he has most unfortunately done and must continue to do if the rule in *Polemis* is to prevail A conspicuous example occurs when the actor seeks to escape liability on the ground that the "chain of causation" is broken by a "nova causa" or "novus actus interveniens."

\* \* \*

Their Lordships conclude this part of the case with some general observations. They have been concerned primarily to displace the proposition that unforeseeability is irrelevant if damage is "direct." In doing so they have inevitably insisted that the essential factor in determining liability is whether the damage is of such a kind as the reasonable man should have foreseen. This accords with the general view thus stated by Lord Atkin in *Donoghue v. Stevenson*: "The liability for negligence, whether you style it such or treat it as in other systems as a species of 'culpa,' is no doubt based upon a general public sentiment of moral wrongdoing for which the offender must pay." It is a departure from this sovereign principle if liability is made to depend solely on the damage being the "direct" or "natural" consequence of the precedent act. Who knows or can be assumed to know all the processes of nature? But if it would be wrong that a man should be held liable for damage unpredictable by a reasonable man because it was "direct" or "natural," equally it would be wrong that he should escape liability, however "indirect" the damage, if he foresaw or could reasonably foresee the intervening events which led to its being done: cf. *Woods v. Duncan*. Thus foreseeability becomes the effective test. In reasserting this principle their Lordships conceive that they do not depart from, but follow and develop, the law of negligence as laid down by Baron Alderson in *Blyth v. Birmingham Waterworks Co.*

\* \* \*

Their Lordships will humbly advise Her Majesty that this appeal should be allowed, and the respondents' action so far as it related to damage caused by the negligence of the appellants be dismissed with costs. . . .

### NOTES

**1. *In re Polemis* and the Direct Causation Test.** *Polemis*, discussed and overruled in the principal case, represented the state of proximate cause law in England prior to the decision handed down in *Wagon Mound*. In *Polemis*, the servants of the defendant dropped a plank into the hold of a leased yacht, causing a spark to ignite petrol fumes and the ship to explode. Although the explosion was found not to be a foreseeable consequence of the negligence, it was clear that the action of the defendant's servants was the direct cause of the catastrophe. The court held for plaintiffs, as the defendants were unsuccessful in convincing the court to replace the dominant direct test with the foreseeability test. See *In re Polemis, Furness, Withy and Co.*, 3 K.B. 560 (1921). Under the more expansive direct test the existence of new, intervening forces could possibly preclude a finding of proximate cause if the defendant's negligence was found to be only an "indirect cause" of the plaintiff's injury, but it was not necessary to prove the type of harm suffered by the plaintiff was foreseeable. As one court explained the *Polemis* approach, proper proximate cause (as evidenced by the direct test) is "a rule of physics and not a criterion of negligence." See *Collier v. Citizens Coach Co.*, 231 Ark. 489, 330 S.W.2d 74 (1959). Although perhaps a more mechanical and straightforward standard for proximate cause, the "direct test" is no longer accepted by modern courts. See Diamond, Levine & Madden, *Understanding Torts* 212 (1996).

2. ***Wagon Mound I.*** The *Wagon Mound* case espoused the principle that proximate cause should limit the defendant's liability to the kinds or types of consequences that were reasonably foreseeable. Liability could not ensue because the defendant could not reasonably be expected to know that the spilled oil was capable of being set on fire on the water. This decision was a logical consequence of Justice Cardozo's majority decision in *Palsgraf* (see page 241, supra), which required that the *plaintiff* be foreseeable under the *duty* element of negligence. *Wagon Mound* now required that the *type of harm* suffered be foreseeable as well under the *proximate cause* element of negligence.

3. ***Wagon Mound II.*** In a subsequent case, *Overseas Tankship (U.K.) Ltd. v. Miller Steamship Co.*, [1967] A.C. 617 (P.C. 1966) (*Wagon Mound II*), the owners of another ship burned in the same fire sued the same defendant for discharging the oil and thereby causing the fire which destroyed their ship. The court reversed its position somewhat and accepted the plaintiff's contentions that the resulting fire was a foreseeable risk from the oil spill. While acknowledging the ambiguity of the words "foreseeable" and "reasonably foreseeable," the court emphasized that the foreseeability required need not be great when the manifested risk would be significant, and there was no justification to incur the risk. The court concluded that where "it is clear that the reasonable man would have realized or foreseen or prevented the risk, then it must follow the appellant is liable." The differing opinions may to a certain extent be explained by adversarial tactics. Since the plaintiff's employees in *Wagon Mound I* had continued soldering the dock after noticing the spilled oil, the plaintiff may have been contributorily negligent, which at the time would have barred his recovery. Presumably the plaintiff in *Wagon Mound I* therefore had never argued that the fire was foreseeable in order to avoid this potential defense. The plaintiff ship owner in *Wagon Mound II*, however, would not have been concerned with a possible contributory negligence defense. Thus in *Wagon Mound II* the plaintiff could advance the claim that the fire was in fact foreseeable, and the court accepted his position. Whatever unique procedural factors were at play, the two cases emphasize the leeway enjoyed by courts determining proximate cause by manipulating what is determined to be foreseeable.

**4. *Kinsman I.*** Although most courts today require a finding of reasonable foreseeability, occasionally, despite the malleability of the language, this test does not comport with the court's preferred finding. In some such instances courts will fall back on the reasoning expressed by Justice Andrews' dissenting opinion in *Palsgraf*, approaching proximate cause as a policy analysis (see Note 6, page 251, supra). For example, in *Petition of Kinsman Transit Co.*, 338 F.2d 708 (2d Cir. 1964), a ship negligently moored in the Buffalo River was set adrift by floating ice and collided with a second (properly moored) ship which also was set adrift. The two ships then traveled down river towards a lift bridge, which the City negligently failed to raise, thus precipitating a second collision. Ultimately, this blockage acted as a dam, allowing the ice and water to rise, and caused severe flooding of surrounding property. The court, in an opinion by Judge Friendly, appeared to extend the parameters of what could be foreseeable:

> Foreseeability of danger is necessary to render conduct negligent; where as here the damage was caused by just those forces whose existence required the exercise of greater care than was taken ... the incurring of consequences other and greater than foreseen does not make the conduct less culpable or provide a reasoned basis for insulation.

> The weight of authority in this country rejects the limitation of damages to consequences foreseeable at the time of the negligent conduct when the consequences are "direct," and the damage, although other and greater than expectable, is of the same general sort that was risked.

As illustrated above, the *Kinsman* court tried to adhere to some variant of the foreseeability requirement, yet approached the problem in a very aggressive way. Once again this demonstrates the malleability of the proximate cause element and a court's ability to fashion language to the desired result.

**5. *Kinsman II.*** In a subsequent action for economic damages resulting from the need to transport ship cargoes around the blockage the court refused to extend liability to the defendants. *Petition of Kinsman Transit Co.*, 388 F.2d 821 (2d Cir. 1968). Oddly enough, the facts of *Kinsman II* would appear to be much more foreseeable than the first action, since a jam in a waterway would often lead to delays and increased costs in transporting goods around the blockage. However, the court did not utilize the same aggressive approach in determining that the damages were foreseeable. Rather, the court, citing Justice Andrews' dissent in *Palsgraf* that proximate cause is ultimately the court's evaluation of "public policy, of a rough sense of justice," held that the economic damages were too "tenuous and remote" to permit recovery. Clearly the policy ramifications of imposing liability for economic injury to all those delayed by an accident on a public waterway compelled the court to restrict liability. When courts are unable, as in *Kinsman II*, to manipulate foreseeability to the required result, courts, often citing Andrews' candid acknowledgment, concede that determining proximate cause is ultimately an issue of policy. Interestingly, the court could have avoided the proximate cause problem by relying on a limited duty for pure economic loss, see Chapter 2, Sec. H(9), infra.

**6. Foreseeable Consequences.** Regardless of the difficulties it presents, the leading test for proximate cause continues to focus on whether the consequences or type of harm suffered by the plaintiff were reasonably foreseeable. This test requires only that the type of harm suffered be foreseeable, but the precise manner and extent of the harm need not be foreseeable. In *Weirum v. RKO General, Inc.*, 15 Cal.3d 40, 123 Cal.Rptr. 468, 539 P.2d 36 (1975), for example, the court held a radio station was liable for the death that resulted when the station promoted a contest encouraging its teenage audience to be the first to reach the radio station's van since the teenager driver's auto accident was a foreseeable consequence. In *Braun v. Soldier of Fortune Magazine, Inc.*, 968 F.2d 1110 (11th Cir. 1992), Soldier of Fortune Magazine published for 10 months an advertisement titled, "GUN FOR HIRE," indicating, "All jobs considered." One response to the classified add resulted in a solicitation to murder a business partner. The murder took place and relatives of the deceased sued the magazine for negligence in running the advertisement. The court found the advertisement was a proximate cause of death since the "criminal act was reasonably foreseeable and, accordingly, that the chain of causation was not broken." Consider also, *Crankshaw v. Piedmont Driving Club*, 115 Ga.App. 820, 156 S.E.2d 208 (1967), holding that it was not foreseeable spoiled shrimp consumed by a customer would cause someone else to trip on his vomit.

**7.  Other Factors.** Occasionally, other factors such as the defendant's spatial proximity to the accident influence a court. Consider the result in *Depew v. Crocodile Enterprises, Inc.*, 63 Cal.App.4th 480, 73 Cal.Rptr.2d 673 (1998), where the defendant's employee fell asleep while returning home from a long shift at work. The employee subsequently rear-ended another car, killing the driver. The estate of the deceased driver brought suit alleging that the employer had acted negligently by subjecting the employee to excessive work hours and allowing him to drive home in a state of exhaustion. The court refused to sustain the action, reasoning that "[w]hat is required to bring the claimant within the ambit of liability is 'continuity of cause' ... combined with continuity in time and space." Contrast this approach with *Snowbarger v. Tri–County Electric Cooperative*, 793 S.W.2d 348 (Mo.1990), where the court did extend liability to an employer whose employee was killed after falling asleep at the wheel on his return from work. The court relied solely on the traditional foreseeability approach and found "the employer could have reasonably foreseen that its exhausted employee, who had been required to work over 27 hours without rest would pose a risk of harm to other motorists." Which result seems fairer? Does foreseeability comport more with contemporary sensibilities or is it too vague a term to be meaningful?

**8.** The foreseeability test is limited by the additional requirement that there be no superseding intervening force that caused the plaintiff's harm. This principle is further explained in the cases that follow.

## THOMAS v. UNITED STATES SOCCER FEDN.
Supreme Court of New York, Appellate Division.
236 A.D.2d 600, 653 N.Y.S.2d 958 (N.Y.A.D. 1997).

On the evening of June 18, 1992, the plaintiff, Octavio Thomas, was injured while participating in a game sponsored by the Cosmopolitan Soccer League (hereinafter Cosmopolitan). According to the plaintiff, the events leading to his injury were precipitated when the opposing team kicked the ball out of bounds. As the plaintiff picked up the ball and prepared to throw it back onto the playing field, he was suddenly attacked by an unidentified member of the opposing team, who punched him twice in the face. When the plaintiff hit his assailant back, 20 to 30 spectators allegedly ran onto the playing field, and some of these individuals jumped on top of the plaintiff. While the spectators and opposing team members held the plaintiff down, the player who had originally attacked him bit off the plaintiff's ear.

The plaintiff subsequently commenced this action against Cosmopolitan, the Eastern New York State Senior Soccer Association, Inc., and the United States Soccer Federation, Inc., alleging that the defendants had negligently failed to provide a properly trained referee to officiate at the game, and failed to maintain a safe playing environment for participants in the league-sponsored game. Following discovery, the defendants moved for summary judgment dismissing the complaint, contending that their alleged negligence was not the proximate cause of the plaintiff's injuries. The Supreme Court thereafter denied the defendants' motion, and the defendants now appeal.

Contrary to the conclusion reached by the Supreme Court, we find that the defendants' motion for summary judgment should be granted.

\* \* \*

The concept of proximate cause is an elusive one which cannot be precisely defined because it "stems from policy considerations that serve to place manageable limits upon the liability that flows from negligent conduct" (*Derdiarian v. Felix Const. Corp., supra*, at 314). Moreover, where, as here, an intentional or criminal act of a third person intervenes between the defendant's conduct and the plaintiff's injury, liability will turn upon whether the intervening act is a normal or foreseeable consequence of the situation created by the defendant's negligence (see *Derdiarian v. Felix Constr. Corp., supra*, at 315).

Applying these principals to the essentially undisputed facts set forth by the parties, we find that the defendants' alleged negligence was not the proximate cause of the plaintiff's injuries. Significantly, the plaintiff's deposition testimony reveals that there was no prior history of acrimony between the plaintiff's team and the opposing team, and that the attack on the plaintiff occurred suddenly and without warning (see, *Elba v. Billie's 1890 Saloon*, 227 A.D.2d 438; *Scotti v. W.M. Amusements*, 226 A.D.2d 522). In addition, the plaintiff admitted at his deposition that neither team had any problems with the acting referee's rulings prior to the time the plaintiff was attacked, and there is no indication that the presence of a trained referee could have prevented the assault upon the plaintiff. Under these circumstances, the plaintiff's injuries were not the foreseeable consequence of the defendants' alleged failure to provide adequate security or a properly trained referee (see, *Derdiarian v. Felix Constr. Corp., supra*).

Bracken, J.P., Santucci, Krausman and McGinity, J.J., concur.

### NOTES

1.  **Manner and Extent of Harm.** Under the foreseeability test established in *Wagon Mound* for proximate or legal cause, the consequences or

type of harm must be foreseeable, but the manner or scenario, by which the type of harm resulted, need *not* be foreseeable. In addition, the foreseeability test does not require that the extent or size of the harm be foreseeable, only the type. For example, if a fire is foreseeable, the size and extent of the fire need not be under the foreseeability test for proximate cause. Consider *United Novelty Co. v. Daniels*, 42 So.2d 395 (Miss.1949), where defendant negligently kept a lighted flame next to a gas outlet. A rat happened by the flame and his fur became ignited. The flaming rat scurried back towards the gas outlet and caused an explosion, which in turn caused injury to a nearby worker. Since the explosion was a foreseeable risk of keeping the flame near a gas outlet, the court held that proximate cause was satisfied because the exact manner in which the explosion occurred did not have to be foreseeable. See Diamond, Levine & Madden, *Understanding Torts* § 12.03 (2nd ed. 2000); Dobbs, *The Law of Torts* § 186 (2000).

**2. Superseding Intervening Force.** Even if the type of harm is foreseeable, courts will generally not find proximate cause if there is a *superseding* intervening force. To this extent, this is an exception to the general approach that the manner by which the accident occurs is not critical to a finding of proximate cause. An intervening force is one that joins with the defendant's conduct to cause the injury. Such a force, whether it be human, animal, mechanical, or natural is considered intervening because it occurs after the defendant's conduct. An intervening force will only act to cut off proximate cause if it is characterized as superseding. Superseding intervening forces are those new forces which are extraordinarily unexpected.

**3. Criminal Acts of Third Parties.** As a general matter, while courts are quick to find negligence of a third party foreseeable and hence not superseding, criminal acts are often characterized as extraordinarily unforeseeable and hence superseding. In *Shepard v. South Carolina Department of Corrections*, 299 S.C. 370, 385 S.E.2d 35 (S.C.Ct.App.1989), the court articulated the test as whether the "intervening act and the injury resulting therefrom are of such a character that the author of the primary negligence should have reasonably anticipated them in light of the attendant circumstances." In *Shepard* the Highway Department negligently allowed a minimum security prisoner to escape from roadside cleanup. The prisoner then went on to rape, rob and murder the plaintiff's decedent. The court held that the Highway Department personnel's negligent supervision did not lead to liability because the prisoner's violent behavior was unforeseeable and therefore a superseding intervening cause. Consider *State ex rel. Missouri Highway & Transportation Commission v. Dierker*, 961 S.W.2d 58 (Mo. 1998), where the estate of a woman who was killed by a broken piece of concrete obtained and thrown from a highway overpass was barred from recovering from the state. The court reasoned that the intervening superseding criminal act of the person who threw the concrete acted to break the chain of proximate cause and therefore held the poor condition of the overpass was not the legal cause of the injury.

Consider also the events leading up to *Graves v. Warner Bros.*, 253 Mich.App. 486, 656 N.W.2d 195 (Mich.Ct.App.2002). Jonathan Schmitz appeared on the Jenny Jones Show, and his friend, Scott Amedure, made a surprising revelation that he had a homosexual crush on him. Three days later, Schmitz found a suggestive note from Amedure, went to Amedure's trailer, and fired two shots into his chest, leaving him no chance for survival.

The personal representative of Amedure alleged that Schmitz shot and killed Amedure as a direct and proximate result of the actions of the Jenny Jones Show and that the show breached its duty to refrain from placing Amedure in a position that would unreasonably expose him to risk of harm because the defendants should have foreseen that their action would incite violence.

The Court of Appeals of Michigan disagreed, holding that the defendants in this case had no duty to anticipate and prevent the act of murder committed by Schmitz hundreds of miles away from the studio and three days after he left peacefully. Because there were no exceptional circumstances warranting departure from the general rule that a party is not liable for the criminal conduct of a third party, the court held that the Jenny Jones Show breached no duty to Amedure.

Consider also the foreseeability determination made in *Flaherty v. Walgreen Eastern Co.*, 18 Mass. L. Rptr. 661 (2005), where the court denied summary judgment to Walgreen, holding that a jury could find it responsible for injuries caused by the flight of a panicked shoplifter. Walgreen's employees pursued a woman suspected of shoplifting in violation of company policy, which stated that employees were not to chase shoplifters inside or outside the store. The woman ran to her car and then hit an employee who stood behind the car in an attempt to block her escape. The plaintiff attempted to come to the aid of the injured employee and was also run over by the shoplifter. The court held that "the assistant manager and the manager should have known that Ms. Crump was a desperate and panicked woman" and that "a jury could find that the intentional or negligent driving of Ms. Crump together with the negligence of the Walgreen's employee(s) jointly created a dangerous situation," which caused the plaintiff's injuries. Consider also *Cowart v. Kmart*, 20 S.W.3d 779 (Tex.App. 2000), where Kmart negligently sold ammunition to two teenagers. The boys spent the afternoon drinking beer and shooting cans. When they got bored, they picked up a third friend and went "cruising" looking for a fight. Believing the gun to be unloaded, the third friend aimed it at Richard Cowart, whom he had in a headlock, and fired it, killing him. The Cowarts sued all the boys, as well as Kmart, alleging that their negligence in selling bullets to a minor proximately caused their son's death. In finding that Kmart was not responsible, the court noted that criminal conduct of a third party is generally a superseding cause that extinguished liability except when such criminal conduct is a foreseeable result of the prior negligence. It found that a seventeen-year-old should be old enough to appreciate the danger of negligent or intentional misuse of ammunition and that "Kmart could not foresee that this sale to a seventeen year old minor would result in negligent or intentional misuse of the ammunition by Bell, who was not a party to the sale."

**4. Forces of Nature.** Consider *Johnson v. Kosmos Portland Cement Co.*, 64 F.2d 193 (6th Cir.1933), where the court held the defendant liable for carelessly allowing gas to collect in a barge, where it was struck by lightning causing an explosion. The court concluded that "[l]ightning is, at least at the time and place here involved, no extraordinary manifestation of natural force." While truly extraordinary and unexpected storms and other forces of nature may be characterized as superseding, courts are probably more hesitant to characterize forces of nature as superseding since it leaves the plaintiff without a potential human defendant.

**5. Dependent and Independent Forces.** Sometimes "intervening" forces are characterized as "dependent" or "independent." Independent intervening forces are forces which are not stimulated by the defendant's negligence, while dependent forces are so stimulated by the defendant. An ambulance driver's collision while rushing to the response to the defendant's accident is a dependent force. On the other hand, another car that was proceeding already on the highway and crashed into the accident site is an independent intervening force. The terms, while used by courts, are in some ways superfluous. While dependent intervening forces are more often foreseeable, ultimately the determinative issue is whether or not the intervening force is extraordinarily unexpected. See Diamond, Levine & Madden, *Understanding Torts* § 12.03[3] (2nd ed. 2000); Dobbs, *The Law of Torts* §§ 190–196 (2000).

## BIGBEE v. PACIFIC TELEPHONE AND TELEGRAPH CO.

Supreme Court of California, In Bank.
34 Cal.3d 49, 192 Cal.Rptr. 857, 665 P.2d 947 (1983).

BIRD, C. J.

On November 2, 1974, plaintiff, Charles Bigbee, was severely injured when an automobile driven by Leona North Roberts struck the telephone booth in which he was standing. Plaintiff thereafter brought an action for damages against Roberts and the companies allegedly responsible for serving her alcoholic beverages. A settlement was reached as to these defendants. In addition, plaintiff sued the companies allegedly responsible for the design, location, installation, and maintenance of the telephone booth, including Pacific Telephone and Telegraph Company (Pacific Telephone), the owner of the booth, Western Electric Company, Inc. (Western Electric), Western Industrial Services, Inc. (Western Industrial), and D.C. Decker Company (Decker).

* * *

Plaintiff saw Roberts' car coming toward him and realized that it would hit the telephone booth. He attempted to flee but was unable to do so. According to the allegations of the complaint, the telephone booth was so defective in design and/or manufacture, or so negligently installed or maintained that the door to the booth "jammed and stuck, trapping" plaintiff inside. Had the door operated freely, he averred, he would have been able to escape and would not have suffered injury.

Additionally, plaintiff alleged that the telephone booth was negligently located in that it was placed too close to Century Boulevard, where "traffic ... travelling easterly, generally and habitually speeded in excess of the posted speed limit," thereby creating an unreasonable risk of harm to anyone who used the telephone booth.

* * *

Defendants contend that their duty to use due care in the location, installation, and maintenance of telephone booths does not extend to the risk encountered by plaintiff and that neither their alleged negligence in carrying out these activities nor any defect in the booth was a proximate cause of plaintiff's injuries. These contentions present the same issue in different guises. Each involves this question—was the risk that a car might crash into the phone booth and injure plaintiff reasonably foreseeable in this case? (See, e.g., *Weirum v. RKO General, Inc., supra,* 15 Cal.3d 40, 45–46; *Akins v. County of Sonoma* (1967) 67 Cal.2d 185, 198–199 [60 Cal.Rptr. 499, 430 P.2d 57]; see generally, 2 Harper & James, Law of Torts (1956) §§ 18.2, 20.5, at pp. 1022, 1141–1143; Rest.2d Torts, § 281, coms. e, f and h; see also *Cronin v. J.B.E. Olson Corp.* (1972) 8 Cal.3d 121, 127 [104 Cal.Rptr. 433, 501 P.2d 1153].)

Ordinarily, foreseeability is a question of fact for the jury. (*Weirum v. RKO General, Inc., supra,* 15 Cal.3d 40, 46.) It may be decided as a question of law only if, "under the undisputed facts there is no room for a reasonable difference of opinion." (*Schrimscher v. Bryson* (1976) 58 Cal.App.3d 660, 664 [130 Cal.Rptr. 125]; accord *Richards v. Stanley* (1954) 43 Cal.2d 60, 66 [271 P.2d 23]; see generally, Rest.2d Torts, § 453, com. b.) Accordingly, this court must decide whether foreseeability remains a triable issue in this case. If any triable issue of fact exists, it is error for a trial court to grant a party's motion for summary judgment. (Code Civ. Proc., § 437c; see generally, *Stationers Corp. v. Dun & Bradstreet, Inc.* (1965) 62 Cal.2d 412, 417 [42 Cal.Rptr. 449, 398 P.2d 785].)

\* \* \*

Turning to the merits of this case, the question presented is a relatively simple one. Is there room for a reasonable difference of opinion as to whether the risk that a car might crash into the phone booth and injure an individual inside was reasonably foreseeable under the circumstances set forth above?

In pursuing this inquiry, it is well to remember that "foreseeability is not to be measured by what is more probable than not, but includes whatever is likely enough in the setting of modern life that a reasonably thoughtful [person] would take account of it in guiding practical conduct." (2 Harper & James, Law of Torts, *supra,* § 18.2, at p. 1020.) One may be held accountable for creating even " 'the risk of a slight possibility of injury if a reasonably prudent [person] would not do so.' " (*Ewart v. Southern Cal. Gas Co.* (1965) 237 Cal.App.2d 163, 172 [46 Cal.Rptr. 631], quoting from *Vasquez v. Alameda* (1958) 49 Cal.2d 674, 684 [321 P.2d 1] (dis. opn. of Traynor, J.); see also *Crane v. Smith* (1943) 23 Cal.2d 288, 299 [144 P.2d 356]; see generally, Rest.2d Torts, § 291.) Moreover, it is settled that what is required to be foreseeable is the general character of the event or harm—e.g., being struck by a car while standing in a phone booth—not its precise nature or manner of occurrence. (*Taylor v. Oakland Scavenger Co.* (1941) 17 Cal.2d 594, 600 [110 P.2d 1044]; *Gibson v. Garcia* (1950) 96 Cal.App.2d 681, 684 [216 P.2d 119]; see generally, Rest.2d Torts, § 435, subd. 1, com. a.)

Here, defendants placed a telephone booth, which was difficult to exit, in a parking lot 15 feet from the side of a major thoroughfare and near a driveway. Under these circumstances, this court cannot conclude as a matter of law that it was unforeseeable that the booth might be struck by a car and cause serious injury to a person trapped within. A jury could reasonably conclude that this risk was foreseeable. (Cf. *Barker v. Wah Low* (1971) 19 Cal.App.3d 710, 723 [97 Cal.Rptr. 85] [reasonable jurors could find that the chance that a car in the parking lot of a drive-in restaurant might strike a patron at the adjacent service counter was foreseeable].) This is particularly true where, as here, there is evidence that a booth at this same location had previously been struck. (See, *ante*, pp. 54–55 and fn. 6.)

Indeed, in light of the circumstances of modern life, it seems evident that a jury could reasonably find that defendants should have foreseen the possibility of the very accident which actually occurred here. Swift traffic on a major thoroughfare late at night is to be expected. Regrettably, so too are intoxicated drivers. (See *Coulter v. Superior Court, supra*, 21 Cal.3d 144, 154.) Moreover, it is not uncommon for speeding and/or intoxicated drivers to lose control of their cars and crash into poles, buildings or whatever else may be standing alongside the road they travel—no matter how straight and level that road may be.

Where a telephone booth, which is difficult to exit, is placed 15 feet from such a thoroughfare, the risk that it might be struck by a car veering off the street, thereby causing injury to a person trapped within, cannot be said to be unforeseeable as a matter of law.

It is of no consequence that the harm to plaintiff came about through the negligent or reckless acts of Roberts. "If the likelihood that a third person may act in a particular manner is the hazard or one of the hazards which makes the actor negligent, such an act whether innocent, negligent, intentionally tortious, or criminal does not prevent the actor from being liable for harm caused thereby." (Rest.2d Torts, § 449; accord *Weirum v. RKO General, Inc., supra*, 15 Cal.3d 40, 46; *Vesely* v. *Sager* (1971) 5 Cal.3d 153, 164 [95 Cal.Rptr. 623, 486 P.2d 151]; *Richardson* v. *Ham* (1955) 44 Cal.2d 772, 777 [285 P.2d 269]; see also *Cronin v. J.B.E. Olson Corp., supra*, 8 Cal.3d 121, 126–127.) Here, the risk that a car might hit the telephone booth could be found to constitute one of the hazards to which plaintiff was exposed.

Other courts considering cases presenting factual situations similar to this one have reached precisely the same conclusions. (See, e.g., *Noon v. Knavel* (1975) 234 Pa.Super. 198 [339 A.2d 545]; *Brinkley v. Southern Bell Telephone & Telegraph Company* (Fla.App. 1977) 353 So.2d 593; see generally, Annot., Liability of Telephone Company for Injury Resulting From Condition or Location of Telephone Booth, *supra*, 17 A.L.R.4th 1308.) In *Brinkley* a car, driven by a person who was allegedly drunk, struck a telephone booth in a shopping center parking lot. The court thought the question of foreseeability was so obviously a triable issue that it reversed a summary judgment for the telephone company in a two-paragraph opinion.

*Noon v. Knavel, supra*, 339 A.2d 545, involved an accident in which the plaintiff was struck by a car while standing in a telephone booth located on the premises of a gas station. The booth was situated at the bottom of a long downgrade about 10 feet from the edge of the street and about 5 feet from a railroad crossing. The accident occurred when the car's brakes failed and the car ricocheted off a train at the crossing and crashed through the telephone booth. (*Id.*, at pp. 547–548.)

The court affirmed a jury verdict against the telephone company after concluding that the company was under a duty to use due care to protect users of the booth from the accidental, negligent or reckless acts of drivers. The risk of a railroad crossing accident was found to be among the foreseeable hazards which made the location of the booth unreasonably dangerous. Accordingly, the court concluded that the telephone company's negligence, in failing to use due care in positioning the booth, was a proximate cause of plaintiff's injuries. (*Id.*, at pp. 549–552.)

Considering the case law and the circumstances of this case, this court cannot conclude as a matter of law that injury to plaintiff, inflicted by negligent or reckless third party drivers, was unforeseeable. "[J]ust as we may not rely upon our private judgment on this issue, so the trial court may not impose its private judgment upon a situation, such as this, in which reasonable minds may differ." (*Schwartz v. Helms Bakery Limited, supra*, 67 Cal.2d 232, 244.)

Since the foreseeability of harm to plaintiff remains a triable issue of fact, the judgment is reversed and the case is remanded to the trial court for further proceedings consistent with the views expressed in this opinion.

### *NOTES*

**1.  Foreseeable Intervening Forces.** Unlikely, but nevertheless foreseeable possible contingencies are often not found to be superseding intervening forces. Thus, automobile accidents and cases of medical malpractice, which occur after a defendant's negligence and are occasioned by it, have often been held not to be superseding causes. Although the odds of such events occurring may be slight and perhaps not highly foreseeable, courts have chosen to extend liability in many such incidents. For example, in *Lucas v. City of Juneau*, 127 F.Supp. 730 (D.Alaska 1955), the defendant who originally caused injury to the plaintiff was held responsible when the plaintiff was re-injured while being moved by hospital employees eighteen days after the initial injury.

On the other hand, some contingencies are too remote for the court to find proximate cause. In *Levitt v. Lenox Hill Hospital*, 184 A.D.2d 427, 585 N.Y.S.2d 401 (N.Y.App.Div.1992), the plaintiff attempted to hold the defendant responsible for an unfortunate chain of events: while being treated for a broken knee in defendant's hospital the plaintiff was given an addictive pain killer, despite the defendant's knowledge that he had previously been addicted to narcotics. Subsequently, the plaintiff became re-addicted, had to pass bad checks to satisfy his habit, was convicted and imprisoned for grand larceny, and became infected with the AIDS virus after using a shared needle to inject intravenous drugs while in jail. The court refused to expand the concept of proximate cause to include liability for the ultimate infection with the disease "irrespective of whether the disease may be contracted as a consequence of actions that are themselves foreseeable."

**2.  Foreseeability of Car Thefts.** Once the defendant's negligence is established, because some form of harm was to be expected, an intervening cause that could not reasonably be foreseen and that is not a normal part of the risk originally created, may bring about unexpected results. See Keeton, *Prosser and Keeton on* The Law of Torts § 44 (5th ed. 1984). One class of cases where this issue often arises involves those where defendant parks a car, leaving the key in the ignition and the car unlocked. Ultimately, the plaintiff is run down and injured by a thief who is making his getaway in the stolen vehicle. The great majority of decisions in this area have refused to hold the car owner liable. Yet special circumstances can persuade a court to depart from the majority approach. Consider *Kozicki v. Dragon*, 255 Neb. 248, 583 N.W.2d 336 (1998), where defendant was held liable after he left his car running and unlocked while he went into his house in a high-crime area where the danger of car thefts should be anticipated. The court concluded the defendant should have reasonably foreseen that thieves are more negligent drivers than law-abiding citizens.

**3. Policy Concerns.** Ultimately what courts determine to be "superseding" intervening forces, thereby precluding liability against the defendant may be influenced by the court's notion of fairness and other policy concerns. Is this appropriate or should the courts strive for as mechanical a rule as possible?

**4. Foreseeable Type of Harm.** As the cases thus far have illustrated, foreseeability of consequences is generally required to find liability. Courts, however, make an exception and do not require that the type of personal injury suffered by a victim be foreseeable. Rather, the defendant takes his plaintiff as he finds him. This concept, known as the "egg-shell plaintiff" rule, is further explored in the following case.

## STEINHAUSER v. HERTZ CORPORATION
United States Court of Appeals, Second Circuit.
421 F.2d 1169 (1970).

FRIENDLY, Circuit Judge:

On September 4, 1964, plaintiff Cynthia Steinhauser, a New Jersey citizen then 14 years old, her mother and father were driving south through Essex County, N.Y. A northbound car, owned by defendant Hertz Corporation, a Delaware corporation authorized to do business in New York, and operated by defendant Ponzini, a citizen of New York, crossed over a double yellow line in the highway into the southbound lane and struck the Steinhauser car heavily on the left side. The occupants did not suffer any bodily injuries.

The plaintiffs' evidence was that within a few minutes after the accident Cynthia began to behave in an unusual way. Her parents observed her to be "glassy-eyed," "upset," "highly agitated," "nervous" and "disturbed." When Ponzini came toward the Steinhauser car, she jumped up and down and made menacing gestures until restrained by her father. On the way home she complained of a headache and became uncommunicative. In the following days things went steadily worse. Cynthia thought that she was being attacked and that knives, guns and bullets were coming through the windows. She was hostile toward her parents and assaulted them; becoming depressed, she attempted suicide.

The family physician recommended hospitalization. After observation and treatment in three hospitals, with a final diagnosis of "schizophrenic reaction—acute—undifferentiated," she was released in December 1964 under the care of a psychiatrist, Dr. Royce, which continued until September 1966. His diagnosis, both at the beginning and at the end, was of a chronic schizophrenic reaction; he explained that by "chronic" he meant that Cynthia was not brought to him because of a sudden onset of symptoms. She then entered the Hospital of the University of Pennsylvania and, one month later, transferred to the Institute of Pennsylvania Hospital for long-term therapy. Discharged in January 1968, she has required the care of a psychiatrist. The evidence was that the need for this will continue, that reinstitutionalization is likely, and that her prognosis is bad.

As the recital makes evident, the important issue was the existence of a causal relationship between the rather slight accident and Cynthia's undoubtedly serious ailment. The testimony was uncontradicted that prior to the accident she had never displayed such exaggerated symptoms as thereafter. However, she had fallen from a horse about two years earlier and suffered what was diagnosed as a minor concussion; she was not hospitalized but missed a month of school. . . .

Dr. Royce testified that a person may have a predisposition to schizophrenia which, however, requires a "precipitating factor" to produce an outbreak. As a result of long observation he believed this to have been Cynthia's case—that "she was a rather sensitive child and frequently exaggerated things and distorted things that happened within in the family" but that the accident was "the precipitating cause" of her serious mental illness. Under cross-examination he stated that prior to the accident Cynthia had a "prepsychotic" personality but might have been able to lead a normal life. Dr. Stevens, attending psychiatrist at the Institute of Pennsylvania Hospital, who had treated Cynthia, in answer to a hypothetical question which included the incidents relied on by the defendants to show prior abnormality, was of the opinion that the accident "was the precipitating cause of the overt psychotic reaction," "the last straw that breaks the camel's back." . . . .

It is unnecessary to engage in exhaustive citation of authority sustaining the legal validity of plaintiffs' theory of the case. Since New York law governs, the oft-cited decision in *McCahill v. New York Transportation Co.*, 201 N.Y. 221, 94 N.E. 616, 48 L.R.A.,N.S. 131 (1911), which plaintiffs' appellate counsel has discovered, would alone suffice. There the defendant's taxicab negligently hit McCahill, broke his thigh and injured his knee. After being hospitalized, he died two days later of delirium tremens. A physician testified that "the injury precipitated his attack of delirium tremens, and understand I mean precipitated not induced"; he explained that by "precipitated," he meant "hurried up,"—just what plaintiffs' experts testified to be the role of the accident here. The Court of Appeals allowed recovery for wrongful death. In *Champlin Refining Co. v. Thomas*, 93 F.2d 133, 136 (10 Cir. 1937), the court held that "where one who has tubercular germs in his system suffers injuries due to the negligence of another, and the injuries so weaken the resistance of the tissues that as a direct consequence tubercular infection sets up therein, the negligence is the proximate cause of the tubercular infection and renders the negligent person liable in damages therefor." In *Pigney v. Pointer's Transport Services, Ltd.*, (1957) 1 W.L.R. 1121, recovery for wrongful death was allowed where head injuries induced an anxiety neurosis leading to suicide. Our own decision in *Evans v. S. J. Groves & Sons Co.*, 315 F.2d 335, 346–349 (1963) (thrombosis of sinus possibly due in part to ear disease but 'triggered' by blow to head) is also quite relevant.... For further discussion of this familiar tort doctrine,[4] see A.L.I. Restatement of Torts 2d § 461; Prosser, Torts 300–301 (3d ed. 1964); 2 Harper & James, *The Law of Torts* 1127–28 (1956); Hart and Honore Causation in the Law 160–62 (1959); Keeton, Legal Cause in *The Law of Torts* 67–69 (1963).

* * *

We add a further word that may be of importance on a new trial. Although the fact that Cynthia had latent psychotic tendencies would not defeat recovery if the accident was a precipitating cause of schizophrenia, this may have a significant bearing on the amount of damages. The defendants are entitled to explore the probability that the child might have developed schizophrenia in any event. While the evidence does not demonstrate that Cynthia already had the disease, it does suggest that she was a good prospect. Judge Hiscock said in *McCahill*, "it is easily seen that the probability of later death from existing causes for which a defendant was not responsible would probably be an important element in fixing damages, but it is not a defense." 201 N.Y. at 224, 94 N.E. at 617. In *Evans v. S. J. Groves & Sons Company, supra*, we noted that if a defendant "succeeds in establishing that the plaintiff's pre-existing condition was bound to worsen * * * an appropriate discount should be made for the damages that would have been suffered even in the absence of the defendant's negligence." 315 F.2d at 347–348.... It is no answer that exact prediction of Cynthia's future apart from the accident is difficult or even impossible. However taxing such a problem may be for men who have devoted their lives to psychiatry, it is one for which a jury is ideally suited.

Reversed for a new trial.

### NOTES

**1. The Egg–Shell Plaintiff Rule.** If the defendant is responsible for injuring a victim, courts will generally hold the defendant responsible for even highly unusual medical complications that result because the victim is extremely frail or otherwise vulnerable. If the plaintiff's egg-shell skull splatters instead of merely suffering a scratch like a normal skull as a result of a minor impact, the defendant is nevertheless still held as the "proximate cause" of the catastrophic injury. This is a generally accepted exception to the rule that the injury must be foreseeable.

While it is possible to group all personal injuries (e.g., a scratch and a splattered head) as one type of injury and therefore be consistent with the

---

**4.** The seeming severity of this doctrine is mitigated by the prevalence of liability insurance which spreads the risks.

general rule that the type of harm must be foreseeable, courts are usually candid in recognizing that unforeseen personal injuries are not subject to the general proximate cause rule that harm be foreseeable.

Do you agree that a defendant who negligently bumps into a victim with a weak heart should be responsible for the victim's heart attack?

2. **Emotional Injuries.** Controversy often arises when courts must determine whether to extend the egg-shell plaintiff rule to psychological sensitivity. Consider *Aflague v. Luger*, 8 Neb.App. 150, 589 N.W.2d 177 (Neb.Ct.App.1999). The court held that jury instructions as to the egg-shell plaintiff rule were appropriate where a minor auto accident caused the plaintiff to become agitated, unable to focus and ultimately unable to be employed. Eleven years earlier, the plaintiff had suffered a fall from horse-back that left her in a coma for 3 months with severe brain injury. Although the plaintiff had completely recovered from the earlier accident by the time of the collision, the defendant driver had to take the plaintiff "as he found her, including her preexisting susceptibility to brain injury." Consider also *Reese v. Home Budget Center*, 619 A.2d 907, (Del.1992), where the court allowed compensation to a worker who suffered an on-the-job back injury that ultimately led to post-traumatic stress disorders. The court ruled that the injuries of the worker, who had previously been addicted to drugs and alcohol and had a pre-existing disposition to emotional injury, were compensable as long as the accident provided the "setting" or "trigger" for the ailment. Thus, where an egg-shell plaintiff is concerned, the accident itself need not be the sole cause or even a substantial cause of the injury, but must satisfy "but for" causation.

3. **Damages.** Although a defendant is liable for the full extent of the harm suffered by an egg-shell plaintiff, the damages award, discussed in Chapter 5, Sec. A, infra, may be adjusted to reflect a plaintiff's preexisting condition. The jury may consider the life expectancy and prospective health of the plaintiff when determining the appropriate level of damages. See Diamond, Levine & Madden, *Understanding Torts* 211 (2nd ed. 2000); Dobbs, *The Law of the Torts* § 188 (2000). Consider the instructions given in *David v. DeLeon*, 250 Neb. 109, 547 N.W.2d 726 (1996), to assist the jury in determining damages for the plaintiff, who had a preexisting and ongoing back condition, "[i]f you cannot separate damages caused by the pre-existing conditions from those caused by the accident, then the defendant is liable for all of those damages."

4. **Alternative Approaches to Proximate Cause.** Do you agree that the defendants should be responsible for plaintiff's unusual medical vulnerability? Should damages be restricted to foreseeable injuries? Have the courts expanded the concept of foreseeability to an extent that the term has lost any real meaning? Should courts follow a consistent approach in evaluating proximate cause or should courts depend on an individual policy analysis of the facts of each case as Justice Andrews advocated in *Palsgraf*? Note that the jury generally determines proximate cause unless the court rules no reasonable jury could conclude other than what the court dictates.

# SECTION G.   PROOF OF NEGLIGENCE: RES IPSA LOQUITUR

## KREBS v. CORRIGAN

District of Columbia Court of Appeals.
321 A.2d 558 (1974).

YEAGLEY, Associate Judge:

This is an appeal from a directed verdict entered in favor of appellees (defendants) at the conclusion of appellant's (plaintiff's) case in chief. The complaint alleged that defendant Bronson negligently caused damage to personal property belonging to plaintiff and that defendant Donald Corrigan was liable for such damage as Bronson's principal.

The evidence reflected the following. Plaintiff is an artist who creates plexiglass sculptures. On the morning of the accident he entered his studio to find a station wagon parked within, just inside of a 10 roll-back garage door. The bumper was very close to a large sculpture. The car had been placed there by defendant Bronson so that he could avoid the chill of the morning while endeavoring to fix some dents in the automobile. Although plaintiff had not given Bronson permission to put the car in the studio, he did not order him to remove the car at once. However, after giving Bronson a dent-removing tool, so as to expedite his work, and instructing him on the use of the tool, he asked him to remove the car as soon as possible. At that moment the telephone (which was on a nearby wall) rang and plaintiff proceeded to answer it. From that position he could see the studio area, but his attention was away from Bronson as he talked on the telephone. While still on the phone, plaintiff glanced back toward where Bronson was working and saw him "flying through the air ... at least three feet off the ground-and he landed in the middle of (a plexiglass sculpture)." Four sculptures in all were destroyed.

Upon the conclusion of plaintiff's case, defendants moved for a directed verdict on the ground that plaintiff had not presented a prima facie case of negligence. After extended argument, mainly involving the doctrine of res ipsa loquitur, the court granted defendants' motion and directed a verdict in their favor. The judge, in explaining his decision to the jury, indicated that a verdict was directed because plaintiff could not show what caused defendant Bronson's body to fall or be thrown onto the sculptures.

This information was not only unknown to plaintiff but was peculiarly within the knowledge of the defendant Bronson. He, of course, never testified as to any explanation he might have had for the accident, since his motion for a directed verdict was granted. We do not believe a plaintiff ought to be held to that burden on these facts which, left unexplained, support, an inference of negligence. Accordingly, we reverse and remand for a new trial.

It is well established, to the extent that a citation of authority is unnecessary, that the mere happening of an accident does not give rise to any inference of negligence. On the other hand, it is established that the circumstances of certain accidents may be such as to justify an inference that negligence was involved. In the District of Columbia an inference that defendant may have been negligent is permitted when the following three conditions exist: first, the cause of the accident is known; second, the accident-producing instrumentality is under the exclusive control of the defendant; and third, the instrumentality is unlikely to do harm without negligence on the part of the person in control. *Powers v. Coates*, D.C.App., 203 A.2d 425 (1964), citing *Washington Loan & Trust Co. v. Hickey*, 78 U.S.App.D.C. 59, 61, 137 F.2d 677, 679 (1943). The presence of these factors distinguishes such cases from the vast majority that lack those features, concerning which it is said that negligence is not to be inferred from the mere happening of an accident.

In the case before us there is no doubt that the cause of the accident was known, i.e., the sculpture was damaged by Bronson's falling on it. To say that the cause of the accident was not known, because there was no evidence as to what caused Bronson to come into contact with the sculptures, "confuses the cause of the accident with the manner in which it was caused, lack of knowledge of which, in plaintiff, is a reason for the doctrine of res ipsa loquitur...." *Kerlin v. Washington Gas Light Co.*, 110 F.Supp. 487, 488 (D.D.C.1953) aff'd, 94 U.S.App.D.C. 39, 211 F.2d 649 (1954). The doctrine was applied in that case where the evidence reflected that plaintiff, while standing on the sidewalk was struck by an object propelled from an area where defendant's employees were digging with picks.

Nor is there any doubt that the accident-producing instrumentality, Bronson's body, was within his exclusive control. While falling cans in a supermarket may not be within the owner's exclusive control, we think it to be a fair presumption that a person's body usually is within his exclusive control; such is the sub silentio presumption in most medical malpractice cases. See also *Kohner v. Capital Traction Co.*, 22 App.D.C. 181 (1903). Defendants' contention that the dent-removing tool was the accident-producing instrumentality, and that Bronson did not have exclusive control over that tool, misses the mark. Moreover, the factual assumption, being without proof of this record, is no more than speculation. As stated, supra, the accident-producing instrumentality was Bronson's body, the dent-removing tool, if at all involved in this case, was in the control of defendant and would only be related to the "manner in which (the accident) was caused." *Kerlin, supra*.

Lastly, as in other situations permitting the application of res ipsa loquitur, we consider it of no small significance that the accident-producing instrumentality, Bronson's body, is one which is unlikely to do harm in the absence of negligence on the part of the person in control. Such a conclusion does not ignore the possibility of other explanations for the incident, explanations which might not involve negligence; but human bodies do not generally go crashing into breakable personal property. When they do, as here, we think the facts require the court of permit an inference of negligence. The person in control of the body or instrumentality may come forth with an explanation. To have to explain the actions of one's body is certainly not unreasonable and is less burdensome than to have to explain why a barrel of flour fell out of one's warehouse onto a pedestrian, a situation to which res ipsa loquitur was held applicable in *Byrne v. Boadle*, 159 Eng.Rep. 299 (Ex. 1863).

The instant situation, plaintiff's are objects being damaged by an inexplicably falling human body, is not unlike that of a parked automobile inexplicably being hit by a moving automobile. In the latter situation a prima facie case of negligence was found to have been presented, though there was no evidence as to why defendant's car struck plaintiff's car. *Bonbrest v. Lewis*, D.C.Mun.App., 54 A.2d 751, 752 (1947); *Schwartzbach v. Thompson*, D.C.Mun.App., 33 A.2d 624 (1943).

In a case which did involve a bodily collision, Kohner v. Capital Traction Co., supra, plaintiff established only that as he was riding on an open summer streetcar he was injured by "the violent contact of the right hand of the conductor of the car with the face of the appellant...." *Id.* at 182 of 22 App.D.C. Plaintiff was unable to testify as to any negligent act on the conductor's part or as to the manner in which the accident was caused. The court reversed a directed verdict for defendant finding that res ipsa loquitur was applicable.

In *Machanic v. Storey*, 115 U.S.App.D.C. 87, 317 F.2d 151 (1963), res ipsa loquitur was applied where a car driven by defendant, in which plaintiff was a sleeping passenger, went off the road causing injuries to plaintiff, although plaintiff was unable to produce any evidence as to why the car left the road.

Appellees contend that res ipsa loquitur does not apply when the accident-producing instrumentality is a human body. We find nothing in the law of this jurisdiction to indicate that res ipsa loquitur does not apply when the accident-producing instrumentality is a body rather than an inanimate object. In *Kohner, supra*, the instrumentality was a streetcar conductor's hand. Medical malpractice cases also involve bodily instrumentalities and it has been held that in a proper case res ipsa loquitur may be applied. *Raza v. Sullivan*, 139 U.S.App.D.C. 184, 432 F.2d 617 (1970). cert. denied, 400 U.S. 992, 91 S.Ct. 458, 27 L.Ed.2d 440 (1971); *Smith v. Reitman*, 128 U.S.App.D.C. 352, 389 F.2d 303 (1967).

Appellees also contend that appellant could not rely on the doctrine of res ipsa loquitur because there was an eyewitness to the accident, i.e., defendant Bronson, and that appellant should have called Bronson as a witness before being allowed to invoke res ipsa loquitur.

To our knowledge this court has never held that a plaintiff may not invoke the doctrine of res ipsa loquitur when the defendant is an eyewitness. In fact on many occasions we have noted that one of the main reasons for the doctrine is the superior, if not exclusive, knowledge which defendants sometimes have as to the cause of accidents. If requiring a plaintiff to call the defendant as an adverse witness was deemed a sufficient method of determining the cause of an accident, there would be no need for the doctrine of res ipsa loquitur. The doctrine exists because of the realization that examination of a defendant as an adverse witness is not a viable way to discover the cause of an accident.

Although there are no cases in this jurisdiction commenting on whether a plaintiff must call an eyewitness-defendant to testify before being allowed to rely on res ipsa loquitur, there have been several where res ipsa loquitur has been applied although an available eyewitness-defendant was not called by plaintiff.

In *Machanic v. Storey, supra,* res ipsa loquitur was applied although the eyewitness-defendant (the driver of the automobile which crashed) was not called by the plaintiff, who himself was unable to testify as to the manner in which the accident was caused.

In *Bonbrest v. Lewis, supra,* the court found plaintiff's evidence, that defendant's car hit plaintiff's parked car, sufficient to establish a prima facie case of negligence, although plaintiff did not call the eyewitness-defendant to testify. While the court phrased its opinion in terms of the establishment of a "prima facie case", rather than specifically using the term res ipsa loquitur, the effect is the same; plaintiff was allowed an inference of negligence although the eyewitness-defendant was not called as a witness.

Finally in *Raza v. Sullivan, supra,* res ipsa loquitur was found applicable though the facts indicated that the defendant-dentist was an eyewitness (he was the person who treated plaintiff) and that he was not called by plaintiff as a witness.

In deciding whether or not res ipsa loquitur is applicable, courts necessarily are mindful of the different effects which that decision will have on the parties and the trial. If res ipsa loquitur is not employed, plaintiff's case is terminated even though he suffered an injury that was caused by the defendant. If res ipsa loquitur is found applicable, defendant is put to no greater burden than to produce information peculiarly within his knowledge as to how the incident occurred. Even if that explanation is unsatisfactory or indeed even if no explanation is made, the jury is free to decline to draw an inference of negligence, and it is so instructed.

We find that the plaintiff's evidence, considered in the light most favorable to him, as must be done in ruling on the motion for a directed verdict by a defendant, was sufficient to raise an inference of negligence so as to survive the defendants' motion and to put them to their proof.

Reversed for a new trial.

### *NOTES*

**1. Res Ipsa Loquitur.** Res ipsa loquitur, literally meaning in Latin "the thing speaks for itself," allows the jury to infer from circumstantial evidence that the defendant was negligent. It is ordinarily used where the plaintiff is unable to make specific allegations as to how the defendant was negligent. The doctrine of res ipsa loquitur has the effect of creating a prima facie case of negligence sufficient for submission to the jury. Ordinarily, the jury is instructed, it may, but is not required to, draw an inference of negligence from the accident itself. Typically, in order to have the jury instructed on res ipsa loquitur, the plaintiff must demonstrate (1) that the accident is of such a nature that it does not usually occur in the absence of negligence, and (2) that the instrumentality causing the injury was within the defendant's exclusive control. Modern courts often broaden this second prong to simply require that the negligence can be attributed to the defendant and (3) the plaintiff was not at fault. As in the principal case, different courts may vary in how they exactly articulate when res ipsa loquitur may be used. See Diamond, Levine & Madden, *Understanding Torts* § 5.04 (2nd ed. 2000); Keeton, *Prosser and Keeton on* The Law of Torts § 39 (5th ed. 1984), and Dobbs, *The Law of Torts* §§ 154–161 (2000).

**2. The Restatement.** The Restatement (Second) of Torts articulates the prerequisites to a res ipsa loquitur charge with the following language:

> It may be inferred that harm suffered by the plaintiff is caused by negligence of the defendant when (a) the event is of a kind which ordinarily does not occur in the absence of negligence; (b) other responsible causes, including the conduct of the plaintiff and third persons, are sufficiently eliminated by the evidence; and (c) the indicated negligence is within the scope of the defendant's duty to the plaintiff.

Restatement (Second) of Torts § 328D.

**3. Evidentiary Inference of Negligence.** Res ipsa loquitur is simply an evidentiary doctrine, which reminds the court and the jury that the accident, itself, can be sufficient circumstantial evidence to infer the defendant negligently caused the accident. Its historical origin is derived from an old English case when the plaintiff's barrister, trained as most barristers were in Latin, uttered the phrase to argue negligence when a barrel of flour was dropped from a building onto the plaintiff. See Keeton, supra, § 39 at 243 discussing *Bryne v. Boadle*, 159 Eng. Rep. 299 (1863).

In essence, the doctrine just reiterates the common sense any parent uses when he or she returns to a room to find a child alone with a broken cookie jar. The culprit and his wrongdoing are apparent. When the accident more likely than not would not have occurred absent negligence and can be attributed to the defendant, the judge should not dismiss the case and should advise the jury that they may infer negligence. For example, in *Mintzer v. Wilson*, 21 Cal.App.2d 85, 68 P.2d 370 (1937), plaster from the ceiling fell on the plaintiff as he slept in a hotel bed. This was sufficient to support a finding of negligence without additional evidence.

**4. Exclusive Control.** Traditionally, res ipsa loquitur required proof that the instrument causing plaintiff's harm was in the exclusive control of defendant. For example, in *Kilgore v. Shepard Co.*, 52 R.I. 151, 158 A. 720 (1932), the plaintiff was sitting on a chair in defendant's store when the chair collapsed. The court refused to allow res ipsa loquitur since the defendant was not in complete control of the chair by virtue of plaintiff's use of it.

The purpose of the exclusive control requirement is logically to be able to attribute the negligence to the defendant. Consequently, many modern courts now have relaxed the requirement that the defendant must have been in exclusive control of the accident causing instrument provided that the negligence, more likely than not, can be attributed to the defendant. Consider *Robert v. Aircraft Investment Co.*, 575 N.W.2d 672 (N.D.1998), in which an airplane owner sought damages from the installer of a replacement engine alleging defendant was negligent in failing to install a rear cone which caused the crankshaft to crack. The plaintiff had hired the defendant to install an engine a few years prior to discovery of the missing part, which the defendant should have installed with the new engine. The court upheld the res ipsa loquitur charge, relying on the trial court's finding that in the intervening years, other mechanics had done only minor repairs and had not tampered with the section of the plane containing the missing part.

By contrast consider *Samson v. Riesing*, 62 Wis.2d 698, 215 N.W.2d 662 (1974). A number of parents of high school band members individually cooked turkeys at their homes which were collected and made into a turkey salad. The plaintiff suffered food poisoning from eating the salad. The court held res ipsa loquitur was not applicable since it was impossible to attribute negligence to any one parent.

**5. Pleading in the Alternative.** Res ipsa loquitur is often pleaded in the alternative to claims of specific acts of negligence. Consider *Weaks v. Rupp*, 966 S.W.2d 387 (Mo.Ct.App.1998), in which the plaintiffs alleged that they suffered carbon monoxide poisoning due to their landlord's failure to properly maintain a furnace. The court held that the plaintiffs could use res ipsa loquitur regardless of whether their evidence gave some indication of the cause of the negligent act.

Some jurisdictions, however, do not allow this. In *Bargmann v. Soll Oil Co.*, 253 Neb. 1018, 574 N.W.2d 478 (1998), the plaintiffs suffered loss as a result of petroleum contamination in and around their homes. The plaintiffs alleged that the owner of a gasoline service station and a bulk plant were negligent for not investigating the possibility of contamination after discovering oil tanks were leaking and for not investigating possible contamination in the soil underneath underground tanks that had been excavated. The court held that if specific acts of negligence are alleged, or if there is direct evidence of the precise cause of the accident, the doctrine of res ipsa loquitur is not applicable.

**6. Expert opinions in medical cases.** A minority of states do not allow the use of expert testimony in res ipsa loquitur cases, even ones involving complex medical issues, because the proof of alleged negligence should be based on common knowledge. See *Spears v. Capital Region Med. Ctr., Inc.*, 86 S.W.3d 58 (Mo.Ct.App. 2002). However, most courts do not accept this approach. In *Seavers v. Methodist Med. Ctr.*, 9 S.W.3d 86 (Tenn. 1999), the Supreme Court of Tennessee noted that the use of expert testimony served to bridge the gap between the jury's common knowledge and complex subject matter that is "common" only to experts in a designated field.

## YBARRA v. SPANGARD
Supreme Court of California.
25 Cal.2d 486, 154 P.2d 687 (1944).

In Bank.

GIBSON, Chief Justice.

This is an action for damages for personal injuries alleged to have been inflicted on plaintiff by defendants during the course of a surgical operation. The trial court entered judgments of nonsuit as to all defendants and plaintiff appealed.

On October 28, 1939, plaintiff consulted defendant Dr. Tilley, who diagnosed his ailment as appendicitis, and made arrangements for an appendectomy to be performed by defendant Dr. Spangard at a hospital owned and managed by defendant Dr. Swift. Plaintiff entered the hospital, was given a hypodermic injection, slept, and later was awakened by Doctors Tilley and Spangard and wheeled into the operating room by a nurse whom he believed to be defendant Gisler, an employee of Dr. Swift. Defendant Dr. Reser, the anesthetist, also an employee of Dr. Swift, adjusted plaintiff for the operation, pulling his body to the head of the operating table and, according to plaintiff's testimony, laying him back against two hard objects at the top of his shoulders, about an inch below his neck. Dr. Reser then administered the anesthetic and plaintiff lost consciousness. When he awoke early the following morning he was in his hospital room attended by defendant Thompson, the special nurse, and another nurse who was not made a defendant.

Plaintiff testified that prior to the operation he had never had any pain in, or injury to, his right arm or shoulder, but that when he awakened he felt a sharp pain about half way between the neck and the point of the right shoulder. He complained to the nurse, and then to Dr. Tilley, who gave him diathermy treatments while he remained in the hospital. The pain did not cease, but spread down to the lower part of his arm, and after his release from the hospital the condition grew worse. He was unable to rotate or lift his arm, and developed paralysis and atrophy of the muscles around the shoulder. He received further treatments from Dr. Tilley until March, 1940, and then returned to work, wearing his arm in a splint on the advice of Dr. Spangard.

Plaintiff also consulted Dr. Wilfred Sterling Clark, who had X-ray pictures taken which showed an area of diminished sensation below the shoulder and atrophy and wasting away of the muscles around the shoulder. In the opinion of Dr. Clark, plaintiff's condition was due to trauma or injury by pressure or strain, applied between his right shoulder and neck.

\* \* \*

Plaintiff's theory is that the foregoing evidence presents a proper case for the application of the doctrine of res ipsa loquitur, and that the inference of negligence arising therefrom makes the granting of a nonsuit improper. Defendants takes the position that, assuming that plaintiff's condition was in fact the result of an injury, there is no showing that the act of any particular defendant, nor any particular instrumentality, was the cause thereof. They attack plaintiff's action as an attempt to fix liability "en masse" on various defendants, some of whom were not responsible for the acts of others; and they further point to the failure to show which defendants had control of the instrumentalities that may have been involved. Their main defense may be briefly stated in two propositions: (1) that where there are several defendants, and there is a division of responsibility in the use of an instrumentality causing the injury, and the injury might have resulted from the separate act of either one of two or more persons, the rule of res ipsa loquitur cannot be invoked against any one of them; and (2) that where there are several instrumentalities, and no showing is made as to which caused the injury or as to the particular defendant in control of it, the doctrine cannot apply. We are satisfied, however, that these objections are not well taken in the circumstances of this case.

The doctrine of res ipsa loquitur has three conditions: "(1) the accident must be of a kind which ordinarily does not occur in the absence of someone's negligence; (2) it must be caused by an agency or instrumentality within the exclusive control of the defendant; (3) it must not have been due to any voluntary action or contribution on the part of the plaintiff." Prosser, Torts, p. 295. It is applied in a wide variety of situations, including cases of medical or dental treatment and hospital care. *Ales v. Ryan,* 8 Cal.2d 82 [64 P.2d 409]; *Brown v. Shortlidge,* 98 Cal.App. 352 [277 P. 134]; *Moore v. Steen,* 102 Cal.App. 723 [83 P. 833]; *Armstrong v. Wallace,* 8 Cal.App.2d 429 [47 P.2d 740]; *Meyer v. McNutt Hospital,* 173 Cal. 156 [159 P. 436]; *Vergeldt v. Hartzell,* 1 F.2d 633; *Maki v. Murray Hospital,* 91 Mont. 251 [7 P.2d 228]; *Whetstine v. Moravec,* 228 Iowa 352 [291 N.W. 425]; see Shain, *Res Ipsa Loquitur,* 17 So.Cal.L. Rev. 187, 196.

There is, however, some uncertainty as to the extent to which res ipsa loquitur may be invoked in cases of injury from medical treatment. This is in part due to the tendency, in some decisions, to lay undue emphasis on the limitations of the doctrine, and to give too little attention to its basic underlying purpose. The result has been that a simple, understandable rule of circumstantial evidence, with a sound background of common sense and human experience, has occasionally been transformed into a rigid legal formula, which arbitrarily precludes its application in many cases where it is most important that it should be applied. If the doctrine is to continue to serve a useful purpose, we should not forget that "the particular force and justice of the rule, regarded as a presumption throwing upon the party charged the duty of producing evidence, consists in the circumstance that the chief evidence of the true cause, whether culpable or innocent, is practically accessible to him but inaccessible to the injured person." 9 Wigmore, Evidence [3d ed.], § 2509, p. 382; see, also, *Whetstine v. Moravec,* 228 Iowa 352 [291 N.W. 425, 432]; *Ross v. Double Shoals Cotton Mills,* 140 N.C. 115 [52 S.E. 121; 1 L.R.A.N.S. 298]; *Maki v. Murray Hospital,* 91 Mont. 251 [7 P.2d 228, 231].) In the last-named case, where an unconscious patient in a hospital received injuries from a fall, the court declared that without the doctrine the maxim that for every wrong there is a remedy would be rendered nugatory, "by denying one, patently entitled to damages, satisfaction merely because he is ignorant of facts peculiarly within the knowledge of the party who should, in all justice, pay them."

The present case is of a type which comes within the reason and spirit of the doctrine more fully perhaps than any other. The passenger sitting awake in a railroad car at the time of a collision, the pedestrian walking along the street and struck by a falling object or the debris of an explosion, are surely not more entitled to an explanation than the unconscious patient on the operating table. Viewed from this aspect, it is difficult to see how the doctrine can, with any justification, be so restricted in its statement as to become inapplicable to a patient who submits himself to the care and custody of doctors and nurses, is rendered unconscious, and receives some injury from instrumentalities used in his treatment. Without the aid of the doctrine a patient who received permanent injuries of a serious character, obviously the result of someone's negligence, would be entirely unable to recover unless the doctors and nurses in attendance voluntarily chose to disclose the identity of the negligent person and the facts establishing liability. See *Maki v. Murray Hospital,* 91 Mont. 251 [7 P.2d 228].) If this were the state of the law of negligence, the courts, to avoid gross injustice, would be forced to invoke the principles of absolute liability, irrespective of negligence, in actions by persons suffering injuries during the course of treatment under anesthesia. But we think this juncture has not yet been reached, and that the doctrine of res ipsa loquitur is properly applicable to the case before us.

The condition that the injury must not have been due to the plaintiff's voluntary action is of course fully satisfied under the evidence produced herein; and the same is true of the condition that the accident must be one which ordinarily does not occur unless someone was negligent. We have here no problem of negligence in treatment, but of distinct injury to a healthy part of the body not the subject of treatment, nor within the area covered by the operation. The decisions in this state make it clear that such circumstances raise the inference of negligence, and call upon the defendant to explain the unusual result. See *Ales v. Ryan,* 8 Cal.2d 82 [64 P.2d 409]; *Brown v. Shortlidge,* 98 Cal.App. 352 [277 P. 134].)

The argument of defendants is simply that plaintiff has not shown an injury caused by an instrumentality under a defendant's control, because he has not shown which of the several instrumentalities that he came in contact with while in the hospital caused the injury; and he has not shown that any one defendant or his servants had exclusive control over any particular instrumentality. Defendants assert that some of them were not the employees of other defendants, that some did not stand in any permanent relationship from which liability in tort would follow, and that in view of the nature of the injury, the number of defendants and the different functions performed by each, they could not all be liable for the wrong, if any.

We have no doubt that in a modern hospital a patient is quite likely to come under the care of a number of persons in different types of contractual and other relationships with each other. For example, in the present case it appears that Doctors Smith, Spangard and Tilley were physicians or surgeons commonly placed in the legal category of independent contractors; and Dr. Reser, the anesthetist, and defendant Thompson, the special nurse, were employees of Dr. Swift and not of the other doctors. But we do not believe that either the number or relationship of the defendants alone determines whether the doctrine of res ipsa loquitur applies. Every defendant in whose custody the plaintiff was placed for any period was bound to exercise ordinary care to see that no unnecessary harm came to him and each would be liable for failure in this regard. Any defendant who negligently injured him, and any defendant charged with his care who so neglected him as to allow injury to occur, would be liable. The defendant employers would be liable for the neglect of their employees; and the doctor in charge of the operation would be liable for the negligence of those who became his temporary servants for the purpose of assisting in the operation.

In this connection, it should be noted that while the assisting physicians and nurses may be employed by the hospital, or engaged by the patient, they normally become the temporary servants or agents of the surgeon in charge while the operation is in progress, and liability may be imposed upon him for their negligent acts under the doctrine of respondeat superior. Thus a surgeon has been held liable for the negligence of an assisting nurse who leaves a sponge or other object inside a patient, and the fact that the duty of seeing that such mistakes do not occur is delegated to others does not absolve the doctor from responsibility for their negligence. See *Ales v. Ryan,* 8 Cal.2d 82 [64 P.2d 409]; *Armstrong v. Wallace,* 8 Cal.App.2d 429 [47 P.2d 740]; *Ault v. Hall,* 119 Ohio St. 422 [164 N.E. 518, 60 A.L.R. 128]; and see, also, *Maki v. Murray Hospital,* 91 Mont. 251 [7 P.2d 228, 233].

It may appear at the trial that, consistent with the principles outlined above, one or more defendants will be found liable and others absolved, but this should not preclude the application of the rule of res ipsa loquitur. The control, at one time or another, of one or more of the various agencies or instrumentalities which might have harmed the plaintiff was in the hands of every defendant or of his employees or temporary servants. This, we think, places upon them the burden of initial explanation. Plaintiff was rendered unconscious for the purpose of undergoing surgical treatment by the defendants; it is manifestly unreasonable for them to insist that he identify any one of them as the person who did the alleged negligent act.

The other aspect of the case which defendants so strongly emphasize is that plaintiff has not identified the instrumentality any more than he has the particular guilty defendant. Here, again, there is a misconception which, if carried to the extreme for which defendants contend, would unreasonably limit the application of the res ipsa loquitur rule. It should be enough that the plaintiff can show an injury resulting from an external force applied while he lay unconscious in the hospital; this is as clear a case of identification of the instrumentality as the plaintiff may ever be able to make.

An examination of the recent cases, particularly in this state, discloses that the test of actual exclusive control of an instrumentality has not been strictly followed, but exceptions have been recognized where the purpose of the doctrine of res ipsa loquitur would otherwise be defeated. Thus, the test has become one of right of control rather than actual control. See *Metx v. Southern Pac. Co.,* 51 Cal.App.2d 260, 268 [127 P.2d 670]. In the bursting bottle cases where the bottler has delivered the instrumentality to a retailer and thus has given up actual control, he will nevertheless be subject to the doctrine where it is shown that no change in the condition of the bottle occurred after it left the bottler's possession, and it can accordingly be said that he was in constructive control. *Escola v. Coca Cola Bottling Co.,* 24 Cal.2d 453.

[150 P.2d 436]. Moreover, this court departed from the single instrumentality theory in the colliding vehicle cases, where two defendants were involved, each in control of a separate vehicle. See *Smith v. O'Donnell,* 215 Cal. 714 [12 P.2d 933]; *Godfrey v. Brown,* 220 Cal. 57 [29 P.2d 165, 93 A.L.R. 1072]; Carpenter, 10 So.Cal.L.Rev. 170. Finally, it has been suggested that the hospital cases may properly be considered exceptional, and that the doctrine of res ipsa loquitur "should apply with equal force in cases wherein medical and nursing staffs take the place of machinery and may, through carelessness or lack of skill, inflict, or permit the infliction of, injury upon a patient who is thereafter in no position to say how he received his injuries." *Maki v. Murray Hospital,* 91 Mont. 251 [7 P.2d 228, 231]; see, also, *Whetstine v. Moravec,* 228 Iowa 352 [291 N.W. 425, 435], where the court refers to the "instrumentalities" as including "the unconscious body of the plaintiff."

In the face of these examples of liberalization of the tests for res ipsa loquitur, there can be no justification for the rejection of the doctrine in the instant case. As pointed out above, if we accept the contention of defendants herein, there will rarely be any compensation for patients injured while unconscious. A hospital today conducts a highly integrated system of activities, with many persons contributing their efforts. There may be, e.g., preparation for surgery by nurses and interns who are employees of the hospital; administering of an anesthetic by a doctor who may be an employee of the hospital, an employee of the operating surgeon, or an independent contractor; performance of an operation by a surgeon and assistants who may be his employees, employees of the hospital, or independent contractors; and post surgical care by the surgeon, a hospital physician, and nurses. The number of those in whose care the patient is placed is not a good reason for denying him all reasonable opportunity to recover for negligent harm. It is rather a good reason for re-examination of the statement of legal theories which supposedly compel such a shocking result.

We do not at this time undertake to state the extent to which the reasoning of this case may be applied to other situations in which the doctrine of res ipsa loquitur is invoked. We merely hold that where a plaintiff receives unusual injuries while unconscious and in the course of medical treatment, all those defendants who had any control over his body or the instrumentalities which might have caused the injuries may properly be called upon to meet the inference of negligence by giving an explanation of their conduct.

The judgment is reversed.

### NOTES

**1. Multiple Defendants.** The *Ybarra* court extended the rule of res ipsa loquitur and applied it in a medical case where multiple defendants did not have exclusive control of the instrumentality causing harm and were not all necessarily negligent. Should res ipsa loquitur be used in this manner? See Diamond, Levine & Madden, *Understanding Torts* § 5.04 (2nd ed. 2000); Keeton, *Prosser and Keeton on* The Law of Torts § 39 (5th ed. 1984) and Dobbs, *The Law of Torts* § 158 (2000). The *Ybarra* position is a minority one that has been adopted in about ten jurisdictions but has often been limited to its facts. See Teshima, *Applicability of Res Ipsa Loquitur in Case of Multiple Medical Defendants—Modern Status*, 67 A.L.R.4th 544 (1989 & Supp. 1998). In those states that follow *Ybarra*, some have limited it to cases involving medical malpractice. For a discussion of the standard of care used in medical malpractice cases, see Chapter 2, Sec. B at pages 173–192, supra.

Consider *Estate of Chin v. St. Barnabas Medical Center*, 312 N.J.Super. 81, 711 A.2d 352 (N.J.Super.Ct.App.Div.1998), in which an anesthetized patient underwent a hysteroscopy, a diagnostic procedure that typically does not involve an anticipated risk of death. The procedure was performed using a flow pump scope energized by a gas which then flows out of the pump through an exhaust line. The evidence established that the exhaust line was properly clipped when it left the manufacturer, but that the last clip was not on the apparatus when it was used during the plaintiff's procedure. This caused twenty-seven inches of the exhaust line to hang loose. The theory was that in such a state the exhaust line could have been mistaken for a suction line. Chin was killed when gas from the exhaust line entered her circulatory system via her body cavity and formed bubbles. The court found that a jury could conclude from the evidence that one or more of the nurses assisting in the procedure unclipped the exhaust line, facilitating its incorrect connection back to the scope. The jury could also infer that the doctor performing the procedure attached the loose exhaust line back onto the scope, or that one of the nurses connected the loose exhaust line to a suction canister. The court concluded that Chin was a blameless, anesthetized victim of an event not reasonably foreseeable or anticipated that would not have occurred in the absence of wrongdoing by one or more of the defendants. Each defendant, therefore, had the burden of persuading the jury that, as compared with the other defendants, he or she was blameless.

Compare *Esco Oil & Gas, Inc. v. Sooner Pipe & Supply Corp.*, 962 S.W.2d 193 (Tex. Ct. App. 1998), in which the plaintiff sued multiple defendants involved in the ordering, manufacturing, and shipping of the pipes it had purchased. The pipes leaked as a result of excessive nickel content in the joints. The plaintiff claimed that the negligence of one of the defendants had caused plaintiff's injury. The court held that res ipsa loquitur is not available to fix responsibility when any one of a number of defendants might have been responsible for plaintiff's injury, although the doctrine can be used to fix responsibility against multiple defendants when they had joint control of the instrumentality causing injury. The court concluded that the doctrine of res ipsa was not available to the plaintiff as none of the defendants had joint custody of the pipe.

Similarly, in *King v. Searle Pharmaceuticals, Inc.*, 832 P.2d 858 (Utah 1992), the plaintiff sued her physician and an IUD manufacturer when she suffered a spontaneous abortion after her IUD perforated her uterus. The court held that an unexplained and unexpected injury can be the basis for requiring multiple defendants collectively in control of the circumstances to explain how the injury occurred. The plaintiff here, however, could not use res ipsa loquitur to raise a presumption of negligence because her injury did not occur while she was within the observation and control of both defendants.

**2. Non–Medical Case.** On a few occasions, courts have been willing to infer negligence on the part of multiple defendants outside the medical malpractice context even when it would have been impossible for both defendants to be negligent. Consider *Martinides v. Mayer*, 208 Cal.App.3d 1185, 256 Cal.Rptr. 679 (1989), where the plaintiff was injured in a hit-and-run automobile accident, but could not establish which of two defendants was driving at the time of the injury. The court held that since the defendants had exclusive access to the vehicle, res ipsa loquitur could be used. The court allowed the inference that both defendants were in control of the vehicle during the accident, even though this would have been physically impossible. Does this strike you as an absurd result?

**3. Rejection of *Ybarra*.** Most states do not extend res ipsa loquitur as far as *Ybarra*. In *Darrah v. Bryan Memorial Hospital*, 253 Neb. 710, 571 N.W.2d 783 (1998), the plaintiff brought a medical malpractice action based on res ipsa loquitur against a hospital, claiming that he sustained ulnar nerve damage at some point during his hospitalization. The plaintiff underwent surgery for a ruptured disc but experienced pain and loss of strength in his left hand and arm after he left the hospital. The plaintiff alleged that a nurse had problems inserting an IV into his arm. The court noted that the exclusive control requirement of res ipsa loquitur is satisfied if the injury results from external force applied while the plaintiff was in the control of the defendants. Moreover, the control is exclusive for the purposes of res ipsa loquitur if it is shown that there was no possibility that a third party, not a defendant, could have caused the injury. The court determined that the plaintiff here did not satisfy the exclusive control element of res ipsa loquitur since the record was unclear as to when and where plaintiff's injuries occurred. A party other than the hospital could have caused the patient's injuries. Summary judgment for defendant was affirmed. Are factual differences from *Ybarra* driving the court's decision?

Consider also *Golden v. Kishwaukee Community Health Services Center, Inc.*, 269 Ill.App.3d 37, 206 Ill.Dec. 314, 645 N.E.2d 319 (1994), where the plaintiff, a motorcyclist injured in a collision, was first treated by physicians at one hospital, then taken for long term treatment to a second hospital. On arriving at the second hospital, the plaintiff could voluntarily move his limbs to some degree. The next day however, he was unable to move his extremities and remained paralyzed from the neck down. Plaintiff sued both hospitals and all treating physicians alleging that the treatment he received either caused or contributed to his paralysis. The court found that the plaintiff received treatment by different entities at different times and that the plaintiff failed to demonstrate joint or exclusive control on the part of the defendants. Thus, neither hospital to which plaintiff was taken, nor the physicians who treated him, could be liable to plaintiff under res ipsa loquitur. Again, can you distinguish this case from the facts of *Ybarra*?

**4. Rationales.** The *Ybarra* rule of imposing an inference of negligence against multiple defendants via res ipsa loquitur is often justified by virtue of defendants' superior knowledge of the cause of the accident. Each defendant has the duty to come forward with explanatory evidence.

Another rationale for the *Ybarra* extension appears in medical malpractice cases where the plaintiff is unconscious:

> In the ordinary case, the law will not assist an innocent plaintiff at the expense of an innocent defendant. However, in the type of case we have here, where an unconscious or helpless patient suffers an admitted mishap not reasonably foreseeable and unrelat-

ed to the scope of the surgery (such as cases where foreign objects are left in the body of the patient), those who had custody of the patient, and who owed him a duty of care as to medical treatment, or not to furnish a defective instrument for use in such treatment can be called to account for their default. They must prove their nonculpability, or else risk liability for the injuries suffered.

*Estate of Chin*, supra, Note one. Are you convinced? Is the *Ybarra* rule comparable to the fifth grade teacher who punished the entire class for breaking the fishbowl unless the guilty student was identified? Would the ruling in *Ybarra* be necessary if vicarious liability was extended beyond its normal limits of making an employer responsible for her employees' torts? (See Chapter 6, Sec. A, infra.) Should the head surgeon or hospital be responsible for all medical personnel working on a patient even if some of those personnel are not employees?

# SECTION H.   LIMITATIONS ON DUTY

## 1.   Failure to Act

### L. S. AYRES & CO. v. HICKS

Supreme Court of Indiana.
220 Ind. 86, 40 N.E.2d 334 (1942).

SHAKE, Chief Justice.

The appellee recovered a judgment against the appellant for personal injuries. The assigned errors relate to the overruling of the appellant's motion for a judgment on the interrogatories and the answers thereto and the motion for a new trial. Under the motion for a new trial it is charged that the verdict is not sustained by sufficient evidence; that it is contrary to law; that there was error in the giving and refusal of certain instructions; that appellee's counsel was guilty of misconduct; and that the damages are excessive.

John Hicks, the appellee, a six year old boy, visited the appellant's department store in company with his mother, who was engaged in shopping. While descending from the third floor on an escalator, the appellee fell at the second floor landing and some fingers of both his hands were caught in the moving parts of the escalator at the place where it disappears into the floor.

The appellee's complaint contained five distinct charges of negligence, as follows:

"1. In operating an escalator so constructed as to leave sufficient space between said ribs, said comb-plate and the teeth thereof to permit the fingers of small children, including plaintiff, to become caught and wedged therein when said escalator could then and prior thereto have been so constructed as defendant knew or should have known with ribs so close together and passing between the teeth and under the comb-plate with so little space between that fingers of children could not have been entangled or wedged therein.

"2. In failing to have a proper guard placed over the teeth of said comb-plate and the openings between said teeth to prevent objects and particularly fingers and other parts of the body of passengers on said escalators which might be drawn therein from being caught therein.

"3. In failing to take proper steps to stop the movement of said escalator with reasonable promptness when it knew, or by exercise of reasonable care should have known, of plaintiff's position of peril. That the means taken by defendant, if any, with reference to safeguarding passengers upon said escalators by having employees in a position to observe the same and stop said operation in the event of an accident, and the facts with reference to the stopping of the escalator after plaintiff's said fall are unknown to plaintiff, but are fully known to the defendant.

"4. In failing to take proper steps for the immediate release of plaintiff from said escalator following said accident. That the means taken by defendant with reference to reversing such mechanism upon the happening of an accident and the means adopted by defendant with reference thereto after plaintiff's said fall are unknown to plaintiff, except as hereinbefore stated, but are fully known to defendant.

"5. In failing to equip said mechanism so that it could be instantly reversed at or near the point of the accident in order to extricate therefrom persons who might become caught or entangled therein."

On review only the pleadings, the general verdict, and the interrogatories and answers will be considered in determining whether a judgment should have been entered on the answers to interrogatories. The evidence actually introduced at the trial will not be considered, but the court will suppose any evidence that might properly have been introduced under the issues. 2 Watson's Works Practice, § 1903.

The jury found that the escalators with which the appellant's store was equipped were purchased and installed in 1934; that no escalator was made prior to the accident that was safer than the one in use; that it was not the practice of stores installing escalators to have an attendant after a year; that the escalator on which appellee was injured was equipped with switch buttons at each floor landing by which it could be stopped in about 2 ½ steps; that appellant had clerks working within 50 feet of the place where appellee was injured, all of whom had not been instructed how to stop the escalator; that the escalator was moving at the rate of 90 feet per minute; that appellee's fingers were caught in the mechanism practically as soon as he fell; that the escalator ran "approximately 70 steps (of 15 inches) or more" before it was stopped; that it was from 3 to 5 minutes after appellee was first injured before his fingers were released; and that the appellee's injuries were increased by the grinding effect on his fingers which continued until the escalator was stopped.

The appellant asserts that it affirmatively appears from the answers to the interrogatories that it was not guilty of any act or omission of negligence charged in the complaint. The facts found by the jury conclusively establish that the appellant was not negligent with respect to the choice, construction, or manner of operating the escalator. This being true, there could have been no incidental duty on the appellant to anticipate an accident, to instruct its employees, or to keep someone in attendance when the machine was in operation. One is not bound to guard against a happening which there is no reason to anticipate or expect. *Parry Mfg. Co. v. Eaton*, 1908, 41 Ind.App. 81, 83 N.E. 510. Having concluded that the appellant was not responsible for the appellee's initial injury, the question arises whether it may, nevertheless, be held liable for an aggravation of such injury, and, if so, under what circumstances.

It may be observed, on the outset, that there is no general duty to go to the rescue of a person who is in peril. So, in *Hurley, Adm'r, v. Eddingfield*, 1901, 156 Ind. 416, 59 N.E. 1058, 53 L.R.A. 135, 83 Am.St.Rep. 198, it was held that a physician was not liable for failing without any reason to go to the aid of one who was violently ill and who died from want of medical attention which was otherwise unavailable. The effect of this rule was aptly illustrated by Carpenter, C.J., in *Buch v. Amory Mfg. Co.*, 1897, 69 N.H. 257, 260, 44 A. 809, 810, 76 Am.St.Rep. 163, 165, as follows: "With purely moral obligations the law does not deal. For example, the priest and Levite who passed by on the other side were not, it is supposed, liable at law for the continued suffering of the man who fell among thieves, which they might, and morally ought to have, prevented or relieved."

There may be principles of social conduct so universally recognized as to be demanded that they be observed as a legal duty, and the relationship of the parties may impose obligations that would not otherwise exist. Thus, it has been said that, under some circumstances, moral and humanitarian considerations may require one to render assistance to another who has been injured, even though the injury was not due to negligence on his part and may have been caused by the negligence of the injured person. Failure to render assistance in such a situation may constitute actionable negligence if the injury is aggravated through lack of due care. Am.Jur. Negligence, § 16; 69 L.R.A. 533. The case of *Depue v. Flatau*, 1907, 100 Minn. 299, 111 N.W. 1, 8 L.R.A.,N.S., 485, lends support to this rule. It was there held that one who invited into his house a cattle buyer who called to inspect cattle which were for sale owed him the duty, upon discovering that he had been taken severely ill, not to expose him to danger on a cold winter night by sending him away unattended while he was in a fainting and helpless condition.

After holding that a railroad company was liable for failing to provide medical and surgical assistance to an employee who was injured without its fault but who was rendered helpless, by reason of which the employee's injuries were aggravated, it was said with the subsequent approval of this court, in *Tippecanoe Loan, etc., Co. v. Cleveland, etc., R. Co.*, 1915, 57 Ind.App. 644, 649, 650, 104 N.E. 866, 868, 106 N.E. 739: "In some jurisdictions the doctrine has been extended much further than we are required to go in deciding this case. It has been held to apply to cases where one party has been so injured as to render him helpless by an instrumentality under the control of another, even though no relation of master and servant, or carrier and passenger, existed at the time. It has been said that the mere happening of an accident of this kind creates a relation which gives rise to a legal duty to render such aid to the injured party as may be reasonably necessary to save his life, or to prevent a serious aggravation of his injuries, and that this subsequent duty does not depend upon the negligence of the one party, or the freedom of the other party from contributory negligence, but that it exists irrespective of any legal responsibility for the original injury".

From the above cases it may be deduced that there may be a legal obligation to take positive or affirmative steps to effect the rescue of a person who is helpless and in a situation of peril, when the one proceeded against is a master or an invitor or when the injury resulted from use of an instrumentality under the control of the defendant. Such an obligation may exist although the accident or original injury was caused by the negligence of the plaintiff or through that of a third person and without any fault on the part of the defendant. Other relationships may impose a like obligation, but it is not necessary to pursue that inquiry further at this time.

In the case at bar the appellee was an invitee and he received his initial injury in using an instrumentality provided by the appellant and under its control. Under the rule stated above and on the authority of the cases cited this was a sufficient relationship to impose a duty upon the appellant. Since the duty with which we are presently concerned arose after the appellee's initial injury occurred, the appellant cannot be charged with its anticipation or prevention but only with failure to exercise reasonable care to avoid aggravation.

\* \* \*

Since the appellee was only entitled to recover for an aggravation of his injuries, the jury should have been limited and restricted in assessing the damages to the injuries that were the proximate result of the appellant's actionable negligence.

This opinion might be extended, but in view of the fact that a new trial will be ordered it is not deemed necessary or proper to say more. Both parties are represented by able counsel and the case was unusually well tried. It is unlikely that the alleged errors not discussed will recur.

The judgment is reversed with directions to sustain the appellant's motion for a new trial.

### NOTES

**1. Limitations on Duty.** While potential defendants usually have a "duty" to act like a reasonable person, for public policy reasons courts impose "limits" on the duty to act reasonably. These "limited" duties in effect allow defendants to act unreasonably and still remain immune from negligent tort liability. As the California Supreme Court has observed, "Whether a duty is owed is simply a shorthand way of phrasing what is the essential question—whether the plaintiff's interests are entitled to legal protection [under tort law] against the defendant's conduct." See *J'Aire Corp. v. Gregory* infra at p. 407. As a result of judicially formulated "limitations" on duty, some wrongful conduct resulting in injury to another is not accountable under tort law.

The principal case illustrates that there is generally "no duty to act." Consequently, an omission or nonfeasance will not ordinarily lead to tort liability. Common law judicial policy "limits the duty" in this way to act reasonably.

Do you agree with the no-duty rule? Do you think the law should manifest a stronger moral position on these issues? Commentators have argued vigorously for the expansion of duty in rescue situations. See, for example, Weinrib, *The Case for a Duty to Rescue*, 90 Yale L.J. 247 (1980). For the law and economics perspective on these issues, see Landes & Posner, *Salvors, Finders, Good Samaritans, and Other Rescuers: An Economic Study of Law and Altruism*, 7 J. Leg. Stud. 83 (1978). See Diamond, Levine & Madden, *Understanding Torts* § 8.02 (2d ed. 2000). See generally Keeton, *Prosser and Keeton on The Law of Torts* § 56 (5th ed. 1984) and Dobbs, *The Law of Torts* §§ 314–321 (2000).

In subsequent sections, consider other tort-free zones of conduct where there is no or less obligation to act as a reasonably prudent person. The duty of a landowner is a classic example. For an interesting discussion of the duty partners owe one another during intimacy, see *Doe v. Moe*, 63 Mass.App.Ct. 516, 827 N.E.2d 240 (2005), where the ensuing injuries and details are described more vividly than here.

**2. Exceptions to the General Rule.** Increasingly, courts have crafted exceptions to the general no-duty rule. These exceptions include the following: (a) when a special relationship exists between the parties; (b) when the defendant, or an instrument under her control, has created the peril; (c) when the defendant voluntarily undertakes to act and puts the plaintiff in a worse position.

*a. Special Relationships.* Courts have justified imposing a duty to give aid in situations where there is a special relationship between the parties. The Restatement (Second) of Torts endorses the special relationships exception:

(1) A common carrier is under a duty to its passengers to take reasonable action

(a) to protect them against unreasonable risk of physical harm, and

(b) to give them first aid after it knows or has reason to know that they are ill or injured, and to care for them until they can be cared for by others.

(2) An innkeeper is under a similar duty to his guests.

(3) A possessor of land who holds it open to the public is under a similar duty to members of the public who enter in response to his invitation.

(4) One who is required by law to take or who voluntarily takes the custody of another under circumstances such as to deprive the

other of his normal opportunities for protection is under a similar duty to the other.

Restatement (Second) of Torts § 314A. Comments a and b following section 314A indicate that the above list is not exhaustive and that other relationships, such as a business relationship, might suffice. Additionally, section 314B indicates that an employer has a duty to aid an employee who is threatened or injured on the job.

Courts have found that common carriers must take reasonable affirmative steps to help passengers in peril. See, for example, *Lopez v. Southern California Rapid Transit District,* 40 Cal.3d 780, 221 Cal.Rptr. 840, 710 P.2d 907 (1985), where a transit district was held liable for injuries sustained by a passenger during a violent argument between other passengers on a bus. The court noted that a common carrier has a duty of "utmost care and diligence" to protect passengers from assaults by fellow passengers. Consider also *Hinckley v. Palm Beach County Board of County Commissioners,* 801 So.2d 193 (Fla.App.4 Dist. 2001), where the parents of a mentally disabled woman who was molested by a bus driver sued the county. The court concluded that "the relationship between a care provider and a mentally or physically disabled individual has been said to create a special relationship giving rise to a duty to control the conduct of a third person." See Diamond, Levine & Madden, *Understanding Torts* § 8.02 (2d ed. 2000). See generally Keeton, *Prosser and Keeton on The Law of Torts* § 56 (5th ed. 1984) and Dobbs, *The Law of Torts* §§ 314–321 (2000).

b. *Defendant's Conduct, or Instrument Under Her Control, Creates the Peril.* When the defendant's own conduct, whether negligent or innocent, is responsible for the harm to the plaintiff, courts determine that this creates a relationship that justifies imposition of a duty to take reasonable efforts to assist the injured plaintiff and avoid any further harm. The Restatement expresses this position thus:

> If the actor knows or has reason to know that by his conduct, whether tortious or innocent, he has caused such bodily harm to another as to make him helpless and in danger of further harm, the actor is under a duty to exercise reasonable care to prevent such further harm.

Restatement (Second) of Torts § 322. Consider *South v. National Railroad Passenger Corp.,* 290 N.W.2d 819 (N.D.1980), in which the defendant's train collided with the plaintiff's truck. The court found that even though the plaintiff was contributorily negligent, the defendant still had a duty to give aid to the injured plaintiff because it was the railroad's conduct that helped create the danger. In adopting this standard, the court commented that section 322 of the Restatement "reflects the type of basic decency and human thoughtfulness which is generally characteristic of our people."

See also *Lewis v. United States,* 702 F.Supp. 231 (E.D.Mo.1988). In *Lewis,* the plaintiff went to a federal penitentiary to visit her husband. While she was inside, an inmate hosed off the driveway outside even though the temperature had dropped below freezing. The cold weather caused the water to freeze into an ice patch on the driveway. When the plaintiff was leaving, she slipped on the icy driveway and sustained injuries. The court held the government liable since it had created the hazard by hosing down the driveway in cold weather.

A defendant may be held liable for not correcting or warning of danger created by her conduct even if her initial conduct itself was non-negligent. This diverges from the traditional common law, which found no duty in such cases. Consider *Hardy v. Brooks*, 103 Ga.App. 124, 118 S.E.2d 492 (Ga.Ct. App.1961), where the defendant motorist, driving at night, non-negligently collided with a 900-pound black cow, killing it. The defendant left the dead cow on the road and failed to provide any warning to other motorists. The plaintiff subsequently drove down the road and hit the cow and another car. The court held that the defendant was under a duty to remedy the hazard he had created. See Keeton, supra, § 56.

*c. Duty Created by Voluntary Undertaking.* This exception to the general rule of no duty is discussed in the next principal case, *Miller v. Arnal Corp.*, and the notes accompanying it.

Consider *Nelson v. Driscoll*, 295 Mont. 363, 983 P.2d 972 (1999), where the Supreme Court of Montana held that a duty of care existed for a police officer who pulled over a woman on suspicion of drunk driving. Officer Driscoll told the plaintiff and his deceased wife that they could either walk home or that he would give them a ride, because he believed they had been drinking and that it would be unsafe for them to drive home in the dark and icy conditions. The plaintiff's wife was then struck and killed by a drunk driver while walking home. The Court rejected the plaintiff's arguments that because probable cause existed to arrest the deceased that the officer had assumed a duty of care, and that by ordering the deceased not to drive that the officer was in custody of her, creating a duty of care. However, the Court did find that this case fell under the maxim that "one who assumes to act, even though gratuitously, may thereby become subject to the duty of acting carefully if he acts at all (internal quotations omitted)." By preventing the deceased from driving home, and remaining in the area to make sure that she got home safely, the officer assumed a duty to act with reasonable care, and whether or not he had done so was a question for the jury.

**3. Criminal Liability.** A few states and many foreign countries have enacted statutes imposing criminal liability upon those who fail to help someone in peril. Such statutes typically involve only a small fine and do not require a potential rescuer to put herself in danger. France is one country that has a such a statute. It was used to prosecute several photographers who allegedly failed to aid Princess Diana after she was involved in a fatal accident in Paris in 1997. The French statute authorizes a fairly stiff penalty of up to $83,000 and five years in prison. See Whitney, *Death of the Princess: The Inquiry*, New York Times, Sept. 3, 1997, at A1. Should such statutes be enacted in more states? If there can be criminal liability for such omissions, do you think that victims should be able to recover damages as well? Consider these issues as you read the following article.

> For 19-year-old sophomore David Cash, life at Berkeley consists of going to his classes, lying low, and occasionally being yelled at or spat on.
>
> A year and a half ago, Cash chose not to intervene when his high school friend Jeremy Strohmeyer molested and killed a little girl in the bathroom of a Nevada casino. . . .
>
> The murder happened on May 25, 1997 at the Primadonna Casino near Las Vegas. Cash saw Strohmeyer struggling with 7-year old Sherrice Iverson in a restroom stall, but left before Stroh-

meyer started molesting her. Afterward, Strohmeyer confessed to him that he had strangled the second-grader, but Cash kept quiet until Strohmeyer turned himself in three days later. Cash was questioned about the crime but released, because Nevada doesn't have a "Good Samaritan" law, which would have made his silence a crime.

\* \* \*

The legal process has now run its course. Strohmeyer pleaded guilty and has been sentenced to life in prison, and Cash faces no . . . charges. . . .

\* \* \*

When he appeared on CBS–TV's . . . *Sixty Minutes* broadcast called "The Bad Samaritan," Cash seemed strangely disconnected from the crime. Soon after he saw Strohmeyer struggling with the girl, he told interviewer Ed Bradley, he left the bathroom. "Based on what I saw," he said, "this wasn't a situation where I wanted to be around." Why didn't he do anything after Strohmeyer confessed to him? "I knew his day of reckoning would come," said Cash. "I didn't want to be the one to turn him in." Finally, when Bradley asked him what he would do differently, if he could go back and do it all over again, Cash paused, then said, "I don't feel there's much I could have done differently."—William Rodarmor, *California Monthly* (vol. 109, no. 2, Nov. 1998) at 1–2.[1]

Note that in response to the Cash controversy, Nevada has Passed Assembly Bill 267 which requires bystanders to report to an enforcement agency such sexual and violent acts against children under the age of 18 "as soon as reasonably practicable but not later than 24 hours after the person knows or has reasonable cause to believe that the other person has committed the violent or sexual offense against the child" (subsection 2, subsection 1(b)). Anyone who violates this law is guilty of a misdemeanor (section 2, subsection 7).

What are the arguments for and against imposing tortious, if not criminal liability, for failing to report a crime or seek aid for a child in danger?

### MILLER v. ARNAL CORP.

Court of Appeals of Arizona.
129 Ariz. 484, 632 P.2d 987 (1981).

O'CONNOR, Presiding Judge.

This is an appeal from a denial of a motion for new trial following a jury verdict against the appellant and in favor of appellee in an action alleging that the appellee willfully, negligently, and unreasonably terminated a rescue effort to assist the appellant. The appeal raises the issue of whether certain jury instructions were properly refused by the trial court. We find no error and affirm the orders of the trial court.

The appellant, Clint Miller, and five companions hiked on Humphrey's Peak in the mountains near Flagstaff, Arizona, in December,

---

**1.** Copyright, 1998, California Monthly, Reprinted by permission.

1972. The group assembled for the hike in the parking lot of the Snow Bowl ski area and camped out overnight nearby on December 30, 1972. The next morning, they began their hike and set up camp for the night of December 31 in a ravine at an elevation of approximately 11,200 to 11,500 feet. During the night a severe storm developed, with high winds, blowing snow and extremely low temperatures. Much of the group's shelter and equipment was lost or destroyed in the storm. The following morning, four members of the group, including Douglas Rickard, decided to descend the mountain and to return to the Snow Bowl and try to obtain assistance for Mr. Miller and another companion, Allison Clay. Mr. Miller had suffered from exposure and frostbite during the preceding night and he did not want to attempt to walk down the mountain. Ms. Clay decided to remain with Mr. Miller.

The four who left the campsite arrived at the Snow Bowl Lodge at approximately 1:45 P.M. on January 1, 1973. They contacted Danny Rich, the assistant Director of the ski patrol, and told him of the predicament of Mr. Miller and Ms. Clay. Rich was a member of the ski patrol and an employee of the Snow Bowl, which was owned and operated by appellee, Arnal Corporation. Rich asked several other ski patrolmen whether they wanted to volunteer for the rescue attempt and told them to begin gathering their equipment and warm clothing. He also telephoned the Coconino County Sheriff's office to obtain assistance from their search and rescue unit. Rickard told Rich that the appellant and Ms. Clay were camped somewhere near the top of the chair life, indicating what he believed to be the general area on a map Rich showed him. In fact, the appellant's location was a substantial distance farther around the mountain. Rich planned to use the ski chair lift to ascend the mountain, and then traverse on skis over to the stranded hikers. However, another storm was developing and the wind was blowing so hard that the chair lift had been shut off. Rich asked his supervisor, Dave Kuntzleman, the appellee corporation's mountain manager, to start the ski lift for the rescue party to ascend. Kuntzleman refused on the ground that it was too dangerous in the existing high winds and he thought the chair lift cable might derail, and also because he wanted the ski patrol to remain on duty to protect skiers on Snow Bowl property. In making his decision, Kuntzleman testified that he was aware the hikers could suffer serious harm or death if they were forced to spend another night on the mountain. An argument ensued between Rich and Kuntzleman, but Kuntzleman refused to start the lift.

The Coconino County Sheriff's search and rescue party did not arrive at the Snow Bowl until approximately 5:30 P.M. Efforts were made to reach the two stranded hikers but the rescuers did not reach them until early morning on January 2. The storm during the night of January 1 was more severe than on the previous night. On arrival, the rescuers found appellant, Miller, in serious condition with hypothermia and frostbite; Ms. Clay had frozen to death. As a result of his exposure, Mr. Miller lost all ten toes, other portions of both feet, and all the fingers of his right hand.

Appellant's first contention is that the trial court erred in failing to submit his requested instruction 14 to the jury. It reads as follows:

One who undertakes, gratuitously or for consideration, to render services to another which he should recognize as necessary for the protection of the other's person or things, is subject to liability to the other for physical harm resulting from his failure to exercise reasonable care to perform his undertaking, if the harm is suffered because of the other's reliance upon the undertaking.

The requested instruction is taken directly from Restatement (Second) of Torts § 323 dealing with negligent performance of an undertaking to render services.[1] Appellant contends that he was put in a worse position by appellee's termination of a rescue attempt by its own ski patrol and the jury should have been allowed to compensate him for his loss of the chance of being rescued by the ski patrol.

Appellant concedes that the law presently imposes no liability upon those who stand idly by and fail to rescue a stranger who is in danger. See, e. g., *Union Pacific Ry. Co. v. Cappier*, 66 Kan. 649, 72 P. 281 (1903); *Buch v. Amory Mfg. Co.*, 69 N.H. 257, 44 A. 809 (1897); *Yania v. Bigan*, 397 Pa. 316, 155 A.2d 343 (1959). See also Annot., 33 A.L.R.3d 301 (1970); M. Shapo, *The Duty to Act* (1977); G. Gordon, *Moral Challenge to the Legal Doctrine of Rescue*, 14 Cleveland–Marshall L.Rev. 334 (1965); Note, *The Failure to Rescue: A Comparative Study*, 52 Columbia L.Rev. 631 (1952); Note, *The Duty to Rescue*, 47 Ind.L.J. 321 (1972); Comment, *The Duty to Rescue*, 28 U. of Pitts.L.Rev. 61 (1966).

W. Prosser, Handbook of The Law of Torts § 56 at 341–42 (4th ed. 1971) explains the general rule as follows:

Thus far the difficulties of setting any standards of unselfish service to fellow men, and of making any workable rule to cover possible situations where fifty people might fail to rescue one, has limited any tendency to depart from the rule to cases where some special relation between the parties has afforded a justification for the creation of a duty, without any question of setting up a rule of universal application. Thus a carrier has been required to take reasonable affirmative steps to aid a passenger in peril, and an innkeeper to aid his guest. Maritime law has long recognized the duty of a ship to save its seaman who has fallen overboard; and there is now quite a general tendency to extend the same duty to any employer when his employee is injured or endangered in the course of his employment. There is now respectable authority imposing the same duty upon a shopkeeper to his business visitor, upon a host to his social guest, upon a jailer to his prisoner, and upon a school to its pupil. There are undoubtedly other relations calling for the same conclusion. (footnotes omitted)

---

**1.** Restatement (Second) of Torts § 323, at 135, reads as follows:

One who undertakes, gratuitously or for consideration, to render services to another which he should recognize as necessary for the protection of the other's person or things, is subject to liability to the other for physical harm resulting from his failure to exercise reasonable care to perform his undertaking, if

(1) his failure to exercise such care increases the risk of such harm, or

(2) the harm is suffered because of the other's reliance upon the undertaking.

As noted by appellant, some states have created statutory duties to
render assistance in certain circumstances. See, e. g., A.R.S. § 28–663
(duty of a motorist involved in an accident to render aid to persons
injured in the accident). The Arizona Legislature has also limited the
liability of persons who render "emergency care" gratuitously and in
good faith to circumstances of gross rather than ordinary negligence,
whether liability is alleged to exist as a result of an act or a failure to act.
A.R.S. § 32–1471. The purpose of A.R.S. § 32–1471 has been described
as follows:

> The apparent purpose of this statute is to relieve the burden of
> liability on individuals who choose to or not to render aid to
> others in emergency situations. . . . An individual may in good
> faith help another in a crisis with untoward results for which he
> should not be penalized or the same person may not help,
> perhaps knowing that he lacks the necessary expertise to be of
> aid.

*Guerrero v. Copper Queen Hospital*, 112 Ariz. 104, 106, 537 P.2d
1329, 1331 (1975).

The applicability of this statute to a case such as this has not been
decided by the Arizona courts, although the language has been described
in one case as "notably broad." See *Barnum v. Rural Fire Protection Co.*,
24 Ariz.App. 233, 237 n.1, 537 P.2d 618, 622 n.1 (1975). However, the
Barnum opinion cites with approval Restatement (Second) of Torts
§ 323. It holds that reliance is a necessary element for recovery against a
volunteer, and that the element of reliance "bespeaks a voluntary choice
of conduct by the person harmed. It infers that the person exercising it
can decide between available alternatives." *Id.* at 237, 537 P.2d at 622.

Comment (a) to § 323 reads in part as follows:

> This Section applies to any undertaking to render services to
> another which the defendant should recognize as necessary for
> the protection of the other's person or things. It applies whether
> the harm to the other or his things results from the defendant's
> negligent conduct in the manner of his performance of the
> undertaking, or from his failure to exercise reasonable care to
> complete it or to protect the other when he discontinues it. It
> applies both to undertakings for a consideration, and to those
> which are gratuitous.

Comment (c) to § 323 deals with termination of services once begun,
and it reads:

> The fact that the actor gratuitously starts in to aid another does
> not necessarily require him to continue his services. He is not
> required to continue them indefinitely, or even until he has
> done everything in his power to aid and protect the other. *The
> actor may normally abandon his efforts at any time unless, by
> giving the aid, he has put the other in a worse position than he
> was in before the actor attempted to aid him.* His motives in
> discontinuing the services are immaterial. It is not necessary for
> him to justify his failure to continue the services by proving a

privilege to do so, based upon his private concerns which would suffer from the continuance of the service. He may without liability discontinue the services through mere caprice, or because of personal dislike or enmity toward the other.

Where, however, the actor's assistance has put the other in a worse position than he was in before, either because the actual danger of harm to the other has been increased by the partial performance, or because the other, in reliance upon the undertaking, has been induced to forego other opportunities of obtaining assistance, the actor is not free to discontinue his services where a reasonable man would not do so. He will then be required to exercise reasonable care to terminate his services in such a manner that there is no unreasonable risk of harm to the other, or to continue them until they can be so terminated. (emphasis added)

The trial court instructed the jury concerning the abandonment or termination of rescue services in its instruction number 1, which incorporates much of the language of comment (c) quoted above.[4]

We believe the trial court properly refused to give appellant's requested instruction 14 for several reasons. Appellant did not claim that his injuries were caused by the negligent performance by appellee of any duty owed to appellant, but rather claimed that his injuries were exacerbated by a termination of the initial plans and arrangements being made by the ski patrol to attempt his rescue. The Restatement (Second) of Torts § 323 explanation in comment (c) concerning termination or abandonment of rescue efforts was in fact incorporated into the court's instruction 1, which correctly and adequately covered the alleged wrong, namely, an unreasonable termination of rescue services. Moreover, we believe that any instruction concerning negligent performance of an undertaking to render services under these circumstances would have to be limited to acts or omissions amounting to gross negligence as required by A.R.S. § 32–1471. Appellant's requested instruction was based on a standard of ordinary negligence alone.

In determining whether an instruction is justified, we must consider the evidence in the strongest possible manner in support of the theory of

---

**4.** Court's instruction number 1 reads:

If the defendant gratuitously started to aid the plaintiff, this does not necessarily require it to continue its services.

Defendant is not required to continue the services indefinitely, or even until it has done everything in its power to aid and protect the plaintiff.

The defendant could abandon its efforts at any time, unless, by giving the aid, it put the plaintiff in a worse position than he was in before the defendant attempted to aid him.

Its motives in discontinuing the services are immaterial. It is not necessary for the defendant to justify its failure to continue the services. If, however, the defendant's assistance put the plaintiff in a worse position than he was in before, either because the actual danger of harm to the plaintiff has been increased by the partial performance, or because the plaintiff or those acting on his behalf, in reliance upon the undertaking, has been induced to forego other opportunities of obtaining assistance, the defendant is not free to discontinue its services where a reasonable man would not do so.

The defendant would then be required to exercise reasonable care to terminate its services in such a manner that there is no unreasonable risk of harm to the plaintiff, or to continue them until they can be so terminated.

the party asking for the instruction. *Evans v. Pickett*, 102 Ariz. 393, 430 P.2d 413 (1967). Even viewed in this light, there is no evidence that appellant relied on any rescue undertaking by appellee in the sense that he chose rescue by the ski patrol over any other available alternative. Appellant's companions did not rely on appellee by choosing not to pursue other possible avenues of rescue on his behalf. Appellee's employee Rich telephoned the county search and rescue unit almost immediately after appellant's companions arrived at the lodge. The county unit then began organizing equipment and personnel for its rescue attempt. The evidence shows that the county's rescue efforts were not delayed, discouraged, or prevented by any act of appellee's. It is error to instruct in relation to a matter not supported by the evidence. *De Elena v. Southern Pacific Co.*, 121 Ariz. 563, 592 P.2d 759 (1979). Thus, the trial court properly refused to give appellant's requested instruction 14.

Appellant next contends that the trial court erred in refusing to give his requested instructions 2 and 9. They read as follows:

> 2. Defendant is liable if you find that it unreasonably terminated a rescue attempt once it had begun.

> 9. The defendant is liable if it began to assist plaintiff, knowing its services were necessary to prevent serious harm to him, and then unreasonably abandoned the effort.

It is not error for the trial court to refuse to give a requested instruction where the subject of the requested instruction was adequately covered by other instructions which were given. *Tucson Utility Supplies, Inc. v. Gallagher*, 102 Ariz. 499, 433 P.2d 629 (1967). Appellant's requested instructions 2 and 9 were clearly covered by court's instruction 1, which defined the circumstances in which a rescue effort may be abandoned in accordance with the comment (c) to § 323. In a caveat to § 323, the Restatement notes at 135–36:

> The Institute expresses no opinion as to whether:

> there may not be other situations in which one may be liable where he has entered upon performance, and cannot withdraw from his undertaking without leaving an unreasonable risk of serious harm to the other.

In comment (e) to § 323 at 139, the caveat is clarified as follows:

> The Caveat also leaves open the question whether there may not be cases in which one who has entered on performance of his undertaking, and cannot withdraw from it without leaving an unreasonable risk of serious harm to another, may be subject to liability even though his conduct has induced no reliance and he has in no way increased the risk. Clear authority is lacking, but it is possible that a court may hold that one who has thrown rope to a drowning man, pulled him half way to shore, and then unreasonably abandoned the effort and left him to drown, is liable even though there were no other possible sources of aid, and the situation is made no worse than it was.

Appellant urges us to implement comment (e) to § 323 of the Restatement by holding it to be the law in this jurisdiction that a rescue effort, once begun in any manner and in any degree whatsoever, may not thereafter be abandoned or terminated if it would leave the other person with an unreasonable risk of serious harm, even though there has been no reliance on the rescue effort and the extent of the risk has not been increased. We decline to so hold. The trial court properly refused to give appellant's requested instructions 2 and 9.

\* \* \*

### NOTES

**1. Voluntary Undertakings.** Although there is generally no duty to act, barring a special relationship or the defendant's creation of the risk, where a person does choose to give aid, a duty arises to avoid putting the victim in a worse position. A defendant may put a victim in a worse position by harming the victim directly, preventing aid from another source, or inducing the victim to rely detrimentally on the defendant's aid. See Diamond, Levine & Madden, *Understanding Torts* § 8.02 (2nd ed. 2000); Keeton, *Prosser and Keeton on* The Law of Torts § 56 (5th ed. 1984) and Dobbs, *The Law of Torts*, § 319 (2000). The Restatement (Second) of Torts expresses this duty as follows:

> One who undertakes, gratuitously or for consideration, to render services to another which he should recognize as necessary for the protection of the other's person or things, is subject to liability to the other for physical harm resulting from his failure to exercise reasonable care to perform his undertaking, if
>
> (a) his failure to exercise such care increases the risk of such harm, or
>
> (b) the harm is suffered because of the other's reliance upon the undertaking.

Restatement (Second) of Torts § 323.

Although an actor may initially be under no duty to provide assistance, once she does, she must use reasonable care not to not harm the victim further. Consider, for example, *United States v. Lawter,* 219 F.2d 559 (5th Cir.1955), where the U.S. Coast Guard voluntarily undertook to search by helicopter for any vessels that might have been caught in rough waters. The plaintiff, his wife, the decedent, and two other people had been on the water in a small boat, but, when high waves swamped their boat, they jumped overboard. The Coast Guard found the group and lowered a rescue cable from the helicopter. The cable operator was inexperienced and began hoisting up the decedent before she had a chance to properly attach the harness, requiring the decedent to hold onto the cable with just her hands. The cable operator then stopped the hoist before the decedent was high enough to board the helicopter, causing her to lose her grip and fall. In holding the government liable, the court stated that it was "hornbook law" that one who undertakes a rescue, even voluntarily, is under a duty to perform it with due care.

Courts are split as to whether a gratuitous promise by itself, without any performance on the part of the defendant, may give rise to a duty to act under tort law if the plaintiff relies on the promise. In the leading case of *Thorne v. Deas,* 4 Johns. 84 (N.Y.1809), the defendant had promised to purchase insurance for a ship he co-owned with the plaintiff; the plaintiff thus did not seek insurance himself. The defendant failed to buy the insurance, so when the ship was subsequently lost at sea the plaintiff suffered heavy pecuniary loss. Nevertheless, the court refused to impose a duty and permitted no tort recovery.

Many courts have followed *Thorne*. But others have departed from its rule, holding that a promise itself can give rise to a duty to act. Consider *Mixon v. Dobbs Houses, Inc.*, 149 Ga.App. 481, 254 S.E.2d 864 (1979), in which an employee informed his employer that his wife was due to go into labor and that if she called he would need the message immediately. The employer agreed. But on the day that the wife called, the employer failed to relay the message to her husband. She called again and said she was at home and in labor, but the message was still not given to her husband. She called a third time, asking with increasing urgency why her husband had not yet returned home. She was told that he was on his way, even though he had still not been informed of the phone calls. She eventually gave birth at home by herself and without any medication. She sued the employer for failing to give the message and the court held that the employer had, by its promise, induced the husband's reliance and thus could be held liable for the harm caused by its subsequent failure to act.

**2. Good Samaritan Statutes.** Might the risk of liability deter potential rescuers from aiding an injured person? To avoid this effect, most states have enacted Good Samaritan statutes, which exempt rescuers from liability for ordinary negligence. These statutes only apply to rescuers acting outside the course of their employment, and in some states, to professional rescuers only, such as doctors, nurses and paramedics.

## WELLS v. HICKMAN

Court of Appeals of Indiana.
657 N.E.2d 172 (1995).

NAJAM, Judge.

Cheryl Wells ("Wells") filed a complaint for the wrongful death of her son, D.E., at the hands of L.H., the son of Gloria Hickman ("Hickman") and the grandson of Albert and Geneva Hickman (the "Grandparents"). L.H. beat D.E. to death while the two boys were in the woods behind the Grandparents' home. Wells alleged that Hickman and the Grandparents failed to control L.H. when they were aware or should have been aware that injury to D.E. was possible and that their negligence resulted in D.E.'s death....

\* \* \*

D.E. and his mother, Cheryl Wells, were neighbors to L.H. and his mother, Gloria Hickman. L.H. and Hickman lived in a trailer located on land owned by L.H.'s grandparents, Albert and Geneva Hickman. The trailer was parked within 100 feet of the Grandparents' house and L.H. was often at their home. Hickman worked the night shift and usually left for work at 10:00 p.m. The Grandparents cared for L.H. while Hickman was at work, and L.H. often ate his meals and snacks at the Grandparents' home. Either Hickman or the Grandparents always knew L.H.'s whereabouts.

Between the Fall of 1990 and October 15, 1991, L.H. killed a pet dog by beating it to death, and he killed a pet hamster. L.H. had also expressed his desire to commit suicide. L.H. often exhibited anger and, on one occasion, he came home from school with a black eye, cuts and bruises. Upon the recommendation of his school principal, L.H. attended counseling sessions at Southern Hills Counseling Center.

On October 15, 1991, D.E. was celebrating his twelfth birthday. After school, fifteen year old L.H. invited D.E. over to play video games. Wells, D.E.'s mother, agreed. The boys did not play video games and neither Hickman nor the Grandparents were aware that D.E. and L.H. were together. Around 6:30 p.m., L.H. returned home and appeared to be very nervous. Later, L.H. told his mother that he thought he had killed D.E. After a search, D.E.'s body was found lying beside a fallen tree on the Grandparents' property.

\* \* \*

A negligence action is rarely an appropriate case for summary judgment. *Miller,* 626 N.E.2d at 541. Even if a trial court does not believe the party will be successful at trial, summary judgment should not be entered where material facts or inferences conflict. *Id.* However, a plaintiff can recover for negligence only if he establishes that the defendant breached a duty owed to the plaintiff which proximately caused the plaintiff's injuries. *Id.*

Wells contends that Hickman had a duty to control her minor son since she knew or should have known that injury to D.E. was possible and, thus, that this case should be remanded for further proceedings. We disagree.

Whether Indiana recognizes a common law cause of action for parental negligence in the failure to control a minor child is an issue of first impression. While our state has adopted the first three of the four common law exceptions, we have not yet recognized the fourth exception to the general rule that parents are not liable for the tortious acts of their minor children. That exception is at issue in the present case, and we now recognize parental failure to control as a viable cause of action.

The failure to control [cause of action] . . . imposes liability upon the parent for the torts of her minor child. See *Ross,* 619 N.E.2d at 915. Contrary to Wells' contention, however, . . . [it] does not impose vicarious liability based solely upon the familial relationship. Rather, . . . [the] parent's negligence is a separate act of negligence independent of the child's wrongful act. The parent's negligence is nonactionable in the absence of a wrongful act of the child. See *Bankert by Habush v. Threshermen's Mut. Ins. Co.* (1983), 110 Wis.2d 469, 329 N.W.2d 150, 154; see accord *Moore,* 157 Ind.App. 1, 8, 298 N.E.2d 456, 460; see *Prosser and Keeton on Torts* § 123, at 914 (5th ed. 1984) (liability for torts of family may be based upon negligence of defendant himself).

The failure to control exception provides that a parent has a duty to exercise control over her minor child "when the parent knows or should know that injury to another is possible." *K.C.* 577 So.2d at 671. To be liable the parent must know that her child "had a habit of engaging in the particular act or course of conduct which led to the plaintiff's injury." *Id.* The duty to control one's child is described in the Restatement (Second) of Torts as follows:

> A parent is under a duty to exercise reasonable care so to control his minor child as to prevent it from intentionally harming others or from so conducting itself as to create an unreasonable risk of bodily harm to them, if the parent
>
>> (a) knows or has reason to know that he has the ability to control his child, and
>>
>> (b) knows or should know of the necessity and opportunity for exercising such control.

Restatement (Second) of Torts § 316, at 123–24 (1965).

Imposition of a duty is limited to those circumstances where a reasonably foreseeable victim is injured by a reasonably foreseeable harm. *Webb v. Jarvis* (1991), Ind., 575 N.E.2d 992, 997. We conclude that a duty attaches when there has been a failure to control and the parent knows or should have known that injury to another was reasonably foreseeable. Specifically, the parent must know or should have known that the child had a habit of engaging in the particular act or course of conduct which led to the plaintiff's injury. See *K.C.*, 577 So.2d at 671; *Parsons v. Smithey* (1973), 109 Ariz. 49, 53, 504 P.2d 1272, 1276.

The critical issue in this case is foreseeability, and we must determine whether Hickman knew or with due care should have known that L.H. would injure D.E. The facts show that between the Fall of 1990 and October 15, 1991, L.H. had killed a pet dog by beating it in the head and had also killed a pet hamster by throwing it on the ground. On one occasion, L.H. came home from school with injuries indicating he had been in a fight. He also talked about committing suicide. Hickman stated in her deposition that "[L.H.] was full of anger and I didn't know why." Record at 75. She further testified that L.H. seemed to have an "uncontrolled anger" and that "he would get upset with anybody and then he'd get over it." Record at 80. Hickman placed L.H. in counseling where he received minimal treatment.

The record indicates Hickman knew that L.H. was a troubled child and she could anticipate the same type of conduct that he had exhibited in the past. Upon the advice of a school principal and from her personal observations, Hickman was aware that L.H. needed professional help. Nevertheless, we cannot conclude, based upon L.H.'s cruelty to animals and his comment about committing suicide, that it was reasonably foreseeable he would kill a neighborhood friend. The boys apparently had played together previously without incident and Hickman could not have seen L.H.'s behavior as a precursor to homicide or even that L.H. would harm D.E. Neither the type of harm inflicted nor the victim in this case was foreseeable and, thus, cannot support the imposition of a duty upon Hickman. See *Parsons*, 109 Ariz. at 54, 504 P.2d at 1277 (parents could not foresee child would attack another person with hammer and saw off ear); see *K.C.*, 577 So.2d at 671 (unforeseeable that minor child would sexually abuse another child).

Public policy supports the imposition of a duty to control on a parent under the proper circumstances, but it does not in this case. Parents are in a unique position in society because they have a special power to observe and control the conduct of their minor children. See *Prosser and Keeton on Torts* § 123 at 914–15 (5th ed. 1984). The power held by a parent is unlike that held by a child's teachers or peers because a parent has the ability to influence a child's behavior from birth and can observe and modify her child's actions. A parent, unlike a teacher, is in the best position to discover and act upon changes in her child's personality and behavior. Parents have a duty to exercise this power reasonably, especially when they have notice of a child's dangerous tendencies. See *id.* That is not to say that a parent should be responsible for behavior that is not reasonably foreseeable, nor should a parent be held responsible for general incorrigibility or a nasty disposition. See *id.*

We hold that a cause of action for parental negligence in the failure to control may be maintained in Indiana, but we decline to find a duty in this case. A duty may be imposed upon a parent for her failure to control her child when the parent knows or should know that the child has engaged in a particular act or course of conduct and it is reasonably foreseeable that this conduct would lead to the plaintiff's injuries. We conclude, as a matter of law, that Hickman had no duty to exercise control over L.H. because the harm and the victim were not reasonably foreseeable. See *Webb*, 575 N.E.2d at 995. Therefore, summary judgment in favor of Hickman is appropriate.

\* \* \*

Wells next contends that the failure to control exception may be extended to the Grandparents in this case because they assumed a parental role over L.H., their grandson. We cannot agree.

As we have already stated, imposition of a duty under this exception requires that the parent knew or should have known that injury to another was reasonably foreseeable.... [we] concluded that Hickman could not have reasonably foreseen that L.H. would kill or even harm D.E. and, likewise, we conclude that the Grandparents could not have foreseen this occurrence. Therefore, the trial court erred by failing to enter summary judgment in favor of Albert and Geneva Hickman.

Wells also asserts that the Grandparents are liable based on a negligent entrustment theory and claims that because L.H. was entrusted to their care, they are responsible for the death of D.E. Again, we must disagree.

There is a well recognized duty in tort law that persons entrusted with children have a duty to supervise their charges. *Vetor by Weesner v. Vetor* (1994), Ind.App., 634 N.E.2d 513, 515; *Johnson v. Pettigrew* (1992), Ind.App., 595 N.E.2d 747, 753. The duty is to exercise ordinary care on behalf of the child in custody. *Johnson*, 595 N.E.2d at 753. The duty exists whether or not the supervising party has agreed to watch over the child for some form of compensation. *Id.*

Wells argues that *Vetor* and *Johnson* permit the imposition of a duty upon the Grandparents because they supervised L.H. and had a duty to exercise reasonable care over L.H. for the benefit of D.E. Contrary to Wells' assertion, the critical relationship under a negligent entrustment theory is not the relationship between the Grandparents and their grandson, L.H., but rather, the relationship between the Grandparents and D.E. See *id.* Unlike the children in *Johnson* and *Vetor,* who were entrusted to the care of the defendants, D.E. was not entrusted to the Grandparents' care. Indeed, the Grandparents were unaware of D.E.'s presence on their property. There was no relationship between the Grandparents and D.E. that would give rise to a duty under a negligent entrustment theory.

\* \* \*

## NOTES

**1. Parent Liability.** Parents are not under the common law automatically liable for their children's torts, although states are increasingly imposing limited vicarious liability up to a few thousand dollars by statute. Parents under the common law, however, can be held negligent in their supervision of their children. As the principal case indicates, courts can often be very rigorous in restricting negligent liability only for failing to prevent the same kind of harm as the child had previously demonstrated a propensity to engage in. The holding in *Wells v. Hickman* is elaborated by *Nielson v. Spencer,* 287 Wis.2d 273, 704 N.W.2d 390 (Wis.App. 2005), the court notes that "the Restatement's parental duty to control has been interpreted narrowly, both in Wisconsin and elsewhere. \* \* \* Mere knowledge by the parent of a child's mischievous and reckless, heedless or vicious disposition is not of itself sufficient to impose liability with respect to torts of a child. \* \* \* Specifically, the parent must know, or should have known, that the child had a habit of engaging in the particular act or course of conduct which lead to the plaintiff's injury. \* \* \* Simply put, no parental liability exists without notice of a specific type of harmful conduct and an opportunity to interfere with it." See also Jeffrey L. Skaare, Note, *The Development and Current Status of Parental Liability for the Torts of Minors,* 76 N.D.L.Rev. 89 (2000). Consider *Linder v. Bidner,* 50 Misc.2d 320, 270 N.Y.S.2d 427 (N.Y.Sup.Ct.1966), where liability was imposed against the parents for their son's attack against another child. The parents had been informed of their son's propensity to attack smaller children but continued to let him play unsupervised. Do you think this rule and the principal case's strict application of it is appropriate? Note that in any event the parents are only expected to exercise reasonable precautions to protect others from their children.

Consider the following news article in evaluating how aggressively torts should impose civil liability on parents:

MURPHY & HEALY, *WHEN THE SINS OF THE CHILD POINT TO PARENTS, LAW'S GRIP IS TENUOUS*

Los Angeles Times, April 30, 1999, at A1.\*

Should Steven Pfiel's parents have seen the signs of their son's murderous outburst?

At 7, he allegedly set fire to a motor home. As a grammar school student in suburban Chicago, he was accused of singing death chants to a classmate. After the student complained, Pfiel admitted to police that he had vandalized the student's home with a knife and had spray-painted satanic symbols on its side. According to friends, Pfiel dropped rocks on cars from overpasses.

When he was old enough to drive, he would swerve his car in hopes of picking off small animals.

Still, when he turned 17, his birthday gift from his parents was a hunting knife with a serrated, 5–inch blade. And three weeks later, on July 12, 1993, Pfiel used the knife to murder 13–year-old Hillary Norskog, and 17 months later, while awaiting trial, Pfiel beat his brother with a bat, slit his throat and then fled with three of his father's guns.

He is now serving a life prison sentence in Illinois, having pleaded guilty to both murders. And Pfiel's parents, a business executive and a stay-at-home mother who volunteered at his school, are facing a lawsuit from Norskog's mother.

"There are a whole lot of parents out there who act as if being a parent is just their right and it doesn't come with responsibilities," says Donald Pasulka, the Chicago attorney who brought the suit on behalf of Norskog's family.

"We sometimes view the parents as victims," Pasulka said. "When they see the school shootings in Arkansas and Littleton, Colo. and Kentucky, people are starting to wake up and say, 'Wait a minute: If you're not going to control your children, we're going to start controlling them—and you.' "

\* \* \*

### Increasing Cases in Civil Courts

Increasingly, parents are also being held accountable in civil courts for the wrongdoing of their offspring. The National Center for Victims of Crime has tracked as many as 100 cases in the past decade in which parents like the Pfiels have been sued for negligent care. And the volume is rising sharply, said staff attorney Lisa Ferguson.

Parents of school shooters in Jonesboro, Ark., West Paducah, Ky., and Moses Lake, Wash., all face substantial lawsuits from families of the victims—alleging they should have done more to control their children.

\* \* \*

Yet drawing a firm connection between what children do and what their parents could have done to stop it remains difficult and constitutionally problematic, say lawyers and almost any parent who has tried to tell a teenager: "Don't."

In the case of the recent high school shootings in Littleton that left 13 innocent victims dead, authorities have said they are looking at a diary, bomb-making equipment and part of a shotgun found in the home of one of the two teenage assailants, 18–year-old Eric Harris . . . .

"Parents of children in most states are subject to civil liability when they fail to exercise appropriate control over their children and their children cause harm . . . . "

\* \* \*

Tom Higgins, head of the Los Angeles County district attorney's juvenile division, suggests that in balancing a child's right to some measure of privacy and a parent's oversight responsibilities, the principle of probable cause ought to play a role.

"I don't go searching through my kids' bedroom," Higgins said. "They have drawers, they have boxes. I occasionally go in there to tell them to pick their stuff up off the floor, or wake them up when the alarm goes off. But I don't search my kids' room. So, 'should have known' needs to be prefaced with, is there something in their behavior that should have prompted them to search their kid's room?

"And let's just suppose they knew. And let's suppose they said, 'I'm taking that stuff out of your room, and I'm destroying it or I'm calling the cops, make your choice.' If they made the effort, and the kid responded with some expletive, what does a parent do? If there were reasonable efforts made and they failed, then I don't think they would fall under a parental accountability law."

\* \* \*

Lawyers in civil cases need only prove negligence and by a lesser standard than the proof "beyond a reasonable doubt" required in criminal cases.

A Chicago-area family won a $300,000 settlement from the well-to-do parents of 16–year-old David Biro, who broke into a townhome in an affluent suburb and murdered a man and his pregnant wife in 1990. Attorney John Corbett introduced evidence that Biro had previously shot his BB gun out of his bedroom window at passers-by, injuring at least two, and had tried to poison his family by pouring wood alcohol into their milk.

A search of the boy's room, according to evidence introduced at trial, turned up two guns, a set of handcuffs, a bag of burglary tools and a bounty of satanic writings.

"I don't think they ever went into his room," Corbett said of the parents. "They were pretty much oblivious."

A judge in Kentucky last week refused to dismiss a case filed against the parents of Michael Carneal, who pleaded guilty in the shooting deaths of three fellow middle school students in West Paducah in 1997.

"People are appreciating the fact that if they're going to stop the violence in the schools, it's going to have to start someplace, and the home is the best place to do that," said Michael Breen, the attorney representing parents of the victims. "What better way to get Mom and Dad to start taking care of what's going on at home than to start putting them in jail?"

"The analogy is of a vicious dog," added Bobby McDaniel, who is suing the parents of 12–year-old Andrew Golden and 14–year-old Mitchell Johnson on behalf of three of the five students killed at a Jonesboro, Ark., middle school last year. "An owner of a dog is liable for harm inflicted by the dog if the owner knew, or should have known, the dog would do it.

"I believe the law takes the position that a parent cannot say, 'I didn't see this problem, I had no idea, I didn't realize, I looked but I didn't see, I listened but I didn't hear.' The parent must have the responsibility to know, appreciate and understand what their child is doing."

But Michael Borders, the Chicago lawyer defending the Pfeils in a case set to go to trial in October, said it is too easy to "flyspeck" a family's history and come out with a pronouncement that "you should have known."

"Everybody is all too quick to judge parents after something like this," said Borders, who dismisses virtually all of the charges alleged in the Norskog lawsuit as "rumor and innuendo without a shred of evidence."

#### "Children Have Their Own Minds"

Parents who have never experienced this with their own children "can't appreciate that children have their own minds, make their own decisions, not only on the basis of what they learn at home but from society, that teenagers are notorious for not sharing with their parents what they want to hide," Borders added. "It's a tragedy, but it's not going to be cured by dragging a bunch of parents into court."

Indeed, some people caution, holding parents liable for their children's crimes could have the result of further fracturing troubled families.

. . . . Howard Davidson, director of the American Bar Assn.'s Center on Children and the Law [asked] "do we want to promote parents being snoops and informers against their kids?"

### TARASOFF v. THE REGENTS OF THE UNIVERSITY OF CALIFORNIA

Supreme Court of California.
17 Cal.3d 425, 131 Cal.Rptr. 14, 551 P.2d 334 (1976).

TOBRINER, Justice.

On October 27, 1969, Prosenjit Poddar killed Tatiana Tarasoff. Plaintiffs, Tatiana's parents, allege that two months earlier Poddar confided his intention to kill Tatiana to Dr. Lawrence Moore, a psychologist employed by the Cowell Memorial Hospital at the University of California at Berkeley. They allege that on Moore's request, the campus police briefly detained Poddar, but released him when he appeared rational. They further claim that Dr. Harvey Powelson, Moore's superior, then directed that no further action be taken to detain Poddar. No one warned plaintiffs of Tatiana's peril.

\* \* \*

We shall explain that defendant therapists cannot escape liability merely because Tatiana herself was not their patient. When a therapist determines, or pursuant to the standards of his profession should determine, that his patient presents a serious danger of violence to another, he incurs an obligation to use reasonable care to protect the intended victim against such danger. The discharge of this duty may require the therapist to take one or more of various steps, depending upon the nature of the case. Thus it may call for him to warn the intended victim or others likely to apprise the victim of the danger, to notify the police, or to take whatever other steps are reasonably necessary under the circumstances.

\* \* \*

Plaintiffs therefore can amend their complaints to allege that, regardless of the therapists' unsuccessful attempt to confine Poddar, since they knew that Poddar was at large and dangerous, their failure to warn Tatiana or others likely to apprise her of the danger constituted a breach of the therapists' duty to exercise reasonable care to protect Tatiana.

Plaintiffs, however, plead no relationship between Poddar and the police defendants which would impose upon them any duty to Tatiana, and plaintiffs suggest no other basis for such a duty. Plaintiffs have, therefore, failed to show that the trial court erred in sustaining the demurrer of the police defendants without leave to amend.

The second cause of action can be amended to allege that Tatiana's death proximately resulted from defendants' negligent failure to warn Tatiana or others likely to apprise her of her danger. Plaintiffs contend that as amended, such allegations of negligence and proximate causation, with resulting damages, establish a cause of action. Defendants, however, contend that in the circumstances of the present case they owed no duty of care to Tatiana or her parents and that, in the absence of such duty, they were free to act in careless disregard of Tatiana's life and safety.

In analyzing this issue, we bear in mind that legal duties are not discoverable facts of nature, but merely conclusory expressions that, in cases of a particular type, liability should be imposed for damage done. As stated in *Dillon v. Legg* (1968) 68 Cal.2d 728, 734 [69 Cal.Rptr. 72, 441 P.2d 912, 29 A.L.R.3d 1316]: "The assertion that liability must ... be denied because defendant bears no 'duty' to plaintiff 'begs the essential question—whether the plaintiff's interests are entitled to legal protection against the defendant's conduct.... [Duty] is not sacrosanct in itself, but only an expression of the sum total of those considerations of policy which lead the law to say that the particular plaintiff is entitled to protection.' (Prosser, Law of Torts [3d ed. 1964] at pp. 332–333.)"

In the landmark case of *Rowland v. Christian* (1968) 69 Cal.2d 108 [70 Cal.Rptr. 97, 443 P.2d 561, 32 A.L.R.3d 496], Justice Peters recognized that liability should be imposed "for injury occasioned to another by his want of ordinary care or skill" as expressed in section 1714 of the Civil Code. Thus, Justice Peters, quoting from *Heaven* v. *Pender* (1883) 11 Q.B.D. 503, 509 stated: " 'whenever one person is by circumstances placed in such a position with regard to another . . . that if he did not use ordinary care and skill in his own conduct . . . he would cause danger of injury to the person or property of the other, a duty arises to use ordinary care and skill to avoid such danger.' "

We depart from "this fundamental principle" only upon the "balancing of a number of considerations"; major ones "are the foreseeability of harm to the plaintiff, the degree of certainty that the plaintiff suffered injury, the closeness of the connection between the defendant's conduct and the injury suffered, the moral blame attached to the defendant's conduct, the policy of preventing future harm, the extent of the burden to the defendant and consequences to the community of imposing a duty to exercise care with resulting liability for breach, and the availability, cost and prevalence of insurance for the risk involved."

The most important of these considerations in establishing duty is foreseeability. As a general principle, a "defendant owes a duty of care to all persons who are foreseeably endangered by his conduct, with respect to all risks which make the conduct unreasonably dangerous." (*Rodriguez* v. *Bethlehem Steel Corp.* (1974) 12 Cal.3d 382, 399 [115 Cal.Rptr. 765, 525 P.2d 669]; *Dillon* v. *Legg, supra,* 68 Cal.2d 728, 739; *Weirum* v. *RKO General, Inc.* (1975) 15 Cal.3d 40 [123 Cal.Rptr. 468, 539 P.2d 36]; see Civ. Code, § 1714.) As we shall explain, however, when the avoidance of foreseeable harm requires a defendant to control the conduct of another person, or to warn of such conduct, the common law has traditionally imposed liability only if the defendant bears some special relationship to the dangerous person or to the potential victim. Since the relationship between a therapist and his patient satisfies this requirement, we need not here decide whether foreseeability alone is sufficient to create a duty to exercise reasonable care to protect a potential victim of another's conduct.

Although, as we have stated above, under the common law, as a general rule, one person owed no duty to control the conduct of another (*Richards* v. *Stanley* (1954) 43 Cal.2d 60, 65 [271 P.2d 23]; *Wright* v. *Arcade School Dist.* (1964) 230 Cal.App.2d 272, 277 [40 Cal.Rptr. 812]; Rest.2d Torts (1965) § 315), nor to warn those endangered by such conduct (Rest.2d Torts, *supra,* § 314, com. c.; Prosser, Law of Torts (4th ed. 1971) § 56, p. 341), the courts have carved out an exception to this rule in cases in which the defendant stands in some special relationship to either the person whose conduct needs to be controlled or in a relationship to the foreseeable victim of that conduct (see Rest.2d Torts, *supra,* §§ 315–320). Applying this exception to the present case, we note that a relationship of defendant therapists to either Tatiana or Poddar will suffice to establish a duty of care; as explained in section 315 of the Restatement Second of Torts, a duty of care may arise from either "(a) a special relation . . . between the actor and the third person which imposes a duty upon the actor to control the third person's conduct, or

(b) a special relation ... between the actor and the other which gives to the other a right of protection.''

Although plaintiffs' pleadings assert no special relation between Tatiana and defendant therapists, they establish as between Poddar and defendant therapists the special relation that arises between a patient and his doctor or psychotherapist. Such a relationship may support affirmative duties for the benefit of third persons. Thus, for example, a hospital must exercise reasonable care to control the behavior of a patient which may endanger other persons. A doctor must also warn a patient if the patient's condition or medication renders certain conduct, such as driving a car, dangerous to others.

Although the California decisions that recognize this duty have involved cases in which the defendant stood in a special relationship *both* to the victim and to the person whose conduct created the danger, we do not think that the duty should logically be constricted to such situations. Decisions of other jurisdictions hold that the single relationship of a doctor to his patient is sufficient to support the duty to exercise reasonable care to protect others against dangers emanating from the patient's illness. The courts hold that a doctor is liable to persons infected by his patient if he negligently fails to diagnose a contagious disease (*Hofmann v. Blackmon* (Fla.App. 1970) 241 So.2d 752), or, having diagnosed the illness, fails to warn members of the patient's family (*Wojcik* v. *Aluminum Co. of America* (1959) 18 Misc.2d 740 [183 N.Y.S.2d 351, 357–358]; *Davis v. Rodman* (1921) 147 Ark. 385 [227 S.W. 612, 13 A.L.R. 1459]; *Skillings* v. *Allen* (1919) 143 Minn. 323 [173 N.W. 663, 5 A.L.R. 922]; see also *Jones v. Stanko* (1928) 118 Ohio St. 147 [6 Ohio L.Abs. 77, 160 N.E. 456]).

Since it involved a dangerous mental patient, the decision in *Merchants Nat. Bank & Trust Co. of Fargo v. United States* (D.N.D. 1967) 272 F.Supp. 409 comes closer to the issue. The Veterans Administration arranged for the patient to work on a local farm, but did not inform the farmer of the man's background. The farmer consequently permitted the patient to come and go freely during nonworking hours; the patient borrowed a car, drove to his wife's residence and killed her. Notwithstanding the lack of any ''special relationship'' between the Veterans Administration and the wife, the court found the Veterans Administration liable for the wrongful death of the wife.

In their summary of the relevant rulings Fleming and Maximov conclude that the ''case law should dispel any notion that to impose on the therapists a duty to take precautions for the safety of persons threatened by a patient, where due care so requires, is in any way opposed to contemporary ground rules on the duty relationship. On the contrary, there now seems to be sufficient authority to support the conclusion that by entering into a doctor-patient relationship the therapist becomes sufficiently involved to assume some responsibility for the safety, not only of the patient himself, but also of any third person whom the doctor knows to be threatened by the patient.'' (Fleming & Maximov, *The Patient or His Victim: The Therapist's Dilemma* (1974) 62 Cal. L.Rev. 1025, 1030.)

Defendants contend, however, that imposition of a duty to exercise reasonable care to protect third persons is unworkable because therapists cannot accurately predict whether or not a patient will resort to violence. In support of this argument amicus representing the American Psychiatric Association and other professional societies cites numerous articles which indicate that therapists, in the present state of the art, are unable reliably to predict violent acts; their forecasts, amicus claims, tend consistently to overpredict violence, and indeed are more often wrong than right. Since predictions of violence are often erroneous, amicus concludes, the courts should not render rulings that predicate the liability of therapists upon the validity of such predictions.

\* \* \*

We recognize the difficulty that a therapist encounters in attempting to forecast whether a patient presents a serious danger of violence. Obviously, we do not require that the therapist, in making that determination, render a perfect performance; the therapist need only exercise "that reasonable degree of skill, knowledge, and care ordinarily possessed and exercised by members of [that professional specialty] under similar circumstances." (*Bardessono v. Michels* (1970) 3 Cal.3d 780, 788 [91 Cal.Rptr. 760, 478 P.2d 480, 45 A.L.R.3d 717]; *Quintal v. Laurel Grove Hospital* (1964) 62 Cal.2d 154, 159–160 [41 Cal.Rptr. 577, 397 P.2d 161]; see 4 Witkin, Summary of Cal. Law (8th ed. 1974) Torts, § 514 and cases cited.) Within the broad range of reasonable practice and treatment in which professional opinion and judgment may differ, the therapist is free to exercise his or her own best judgment without liability; proof, aided by hindsight, that he or she judged wrongly is insufficient to establish negligence.

In the instant case, however, the pleadings do not raise any question as to failure of defendant therapists to predict that Poddar presented a serious danger of violence. On the contrary, the present complaints allege that defendant therapists did in fact predict that Poddar would kill, but were negligent in failing to warn.

\* \* \*

The risk that unnecessary warnings may be given is a reasonable price to pay for the lives of possible victims that may be saved. We would hesitate to hold that the therapist who is aware that his patient expects to attempt to assassinate the President of the United States would not be obligated to warn the authorities because the therapist cannot predict with accuracy that his patient will commit the crime.

Defendants further argue that free and open communication is essential to psychotherapy (see *In re Lifschutz* (1970) 2 Cal.3d 415, 431–434 [85 Cal.Rptr. 829, 467 P.2d 557, 44 A.L.R.3d 1]); that "Unless a patient ... is assured that ... information [revealed by him] can and will be held in utmost confidence, he will be reluctant to make the full disclosure upon which diagnosis and treatment ... depends." (Sen. Com. on Judiciary, comment on Evid. Code, § 1014.) The giving of a warning, defendants contend, constitutes a breach of trust which entails the revelation of confidential communications.

We recognize the public interest in supporting effective treatment of mental illness and in protecting the rights of patients to privacy (see *In re Lifschutz, supra*, 2 Cal.3d at p. 432), and the consequent public importance of safeguarding the confidential character of psychotherapeutic communication. Against this interest, however, we must weigh the public interest in safety from violent assault. The Legislature has undertaken the difficult task of balancing the countervailing concerns. In Evidence Code section 1014, it established a broad rule of privilege to protect confidential communications between patient and psychotherapist. In Evidence Code section 1024, the Legislature created a specific and limited exception to the psychotherapist-patient privilege: "There is no privilege ... if the psychotherapist has reasonable cause to believe that the patient is in such mental or emotional condition as to be dangerous to himself or to the person or property of another and that disclosure of the communication is necessary to prevent the threatened danger."

We realize that the open and confidential character of psychotherapeutic dialogue encourages patients to express threats of violence, few of which are ever executed. Certainly a therapist should not be encouraged routinely to reveal such threats; such disclosures could seriously disrupt the patient's relationship with his therapist and with the persons threatened. To the contrary, the therapist's obligations to his patient require that he not disclose a confidence unless such disclosure is necessary to avert danger to others, and even then that he do so discreetly, and in a fashion that would preserve the privacy of his patient to the fullest extent compatible with the prevention of the threatened danger. (See Fleming & Maximov, *The Patient or His Victim: The Therapist's Dilemma* (1974) 62 Cal.L.Rev. 1025, 1065–1066.)

The revelation of a communication under the above circumstances is not a breach of trust or a violation of professional ethics; as stated in the Principles of Medical Ethics of the American Medical Association (1957), section 9: "A physician may not reveal the confidence entrusted to him in the course of medical attendance ... *unless he is required to do so by law or unless it becomes necessary in order to protect the welfare of the individual or of the community*." (Italics added.) We conclude that the public policy favoring protection of the confidential character of patient-psychotherapist communications must yield to the extent to which disclosure is essential to avert danger to others. The protective privilege ends where the public peril begins.

Our current crowded and computerized society compels the interdependence of its members. In this risk-infested society we can hardly tolerate the further exposure to danger that would result from a concealed knowledge of the therapist that his patient was lethal. If the exercise of reasonable care to protect the threatened victim requires the therapist to warn the endangered party or those who can reasonably be expected to notify him, we see no sufficient societal interest that would protect and justify concealment. The containment of such risks lies in the public interest. For the foregoing reasons, we find that plaintiffs' complaints can be amended to state a cause of action against defendants Moore, Powelson, Gold, and Yandell and against the Regents as their employer, for breach of a duty to exercise reasonable care to protect Tatiana.

\* \* \*

Turning now to the police defendants, we conclude that they do not have any such special relationship to either Tatiana or to Poddar sufficient to impose upon such defendants a duty to warn respecting Poddar's violent intentions. (See *Hartzler v. City of San Jose* (1975) 46 Cal.App.3d 6, 9–10 [120 Cal.Rptr. 5]; *Antique Arts Corp.* v. *City of Torrance* (1974) 39 Cal.App.3d 588, 593 [114 Cal.Rptr. 332].) Plaintiffs suggest no theory, and plead no facts that give rise to any duty to warn on the part of the police defendants absent such a special relationship. They have thus failed to demonstrate that the trial court erred in denying leave to amend as to the police defendants. (See *Cooper v. Leslie Salt Co.* (1969) 70 Cal.2d 627, 636 [75 Cal.Rptr. 766, 451 P.2d 406]; *Filice v. Boccardo* (1962) 210 Cal.App.2d 843, 847 [26 Cal.Rptr. 789].)

\* \* \*

[Another portion of the decision addressing governmental and public official immunity is printed at page 466, infra.]

### *NOTES*

**1. The Impact of *Tarasoff*.** Ordinarily there is no obligation to control the acts of a third person. As the previous principal case indicates, certain relationships like that between parent and child can create an obligation to protect others from a third party. As the relationship becomes less custodial, assertions that there is an obligation to control another become more controversial. See Diamond, Levine, & Madden, *Understanding Torts* § 8.02 (2nd ed. 2000); Keeton, *Prosser and Keeton On the Law of Torts* § 56 (5th ed. 1984); and Dobbs, *The Law of Torts* §§ 331–332 (2000).

The principal case has generated national debate. Numerous jurisdictions have joined *Tarasoff* in holding that a therapist has an obligation to act to protect their patients' potential victims. Most therapists are instructed to give so-called "*Tarasoff* warnings" in appropriate cases.

Does a therapist have a sufficient relationship to a patient to obligate the therapist to control or otherwise protect others from the patient? Should the obligation be extended to attorneys or other professionals who think clients may act dangerously? See Kohn, *Infecting Attorney–Client Confidentiality: The Ethics of HIV Disclosure*, 9 Georgetown Journal of Legal Ethics 547 (1996).

In *Thompson v. County of Alameda*, 27 Cal.3d 741, 167 Cal.Rptr. 70, 614 P.2d 728 (1980), discussed in the next principal case, California restricted the *Tarasoff*'s duty to warn only "readily identifiable" victims. Furthermore, section 43.92 of the California Civil Code limits the obligation of therapists to warn only when the patient makes "a serious threat of physical violence against a reasonable identifiable victim." In addition, in *Bellah v. Greenson*, 81 Cal.App.3d 614, 146 Cal.Rptr. 535 (1928), the court held that a psychiatrist had no duty to warn a patient's parents about his suicidal tendencies or that he was placing himself in danger by associating with heroin addicts. Other jurisdictions have been less cautious in imposing obligations on therapists. But see *Gregory v. Kilbride*, 150 N.C.App. 601, 565 S.E.2d 685 (2002), where the Court of Appeals of North Carolina acknowledged the landmark status of Tarasoff but declined to follow it.

See *Ewing v. Northridge Hospital Medical Center*, 120 Cal.App.4th 1289, 16 Cal.Rptr.3d 591 (Cal.App. 2 Dist. 2004), in which the Court of Appeals in California expanded the duty of therapists, holding that under Section 43.92, the psychotherapist has a duty to warn a third party even *if the information did not come from the patient himself.* The Court maintained that when a communication of a serious threat of grave bodily injury is conveyed by immediate family and is shared for the purpose of facilitating and furthering the patient's treatment, it is immaterial that the family member is not a patient; the psychotherapist has a duty to warn. In *Ewing*, the patient's father brought the patient to the hospital seeking help and told the psycho-therapist, Capilla, that the patient threatened to kill Ewing and then himself. Capilla interviewed the patient in the presence of hospital security, seemingly out of fear for his own safety. Capilla determined that the patient met the criteria for involuntary commitment but instead persuaded the patient to commit himself because of the repercussions it might have for his career as an LAPD officer. The following day, the patient obtained a discharged, murdered Ewing, and then committed suicide a day later. The Court held that a jury could easily infer from the evidence that Capilla believed the patient's father's statements, thereby making Capilla's failure to take reasonable steps to warn and protect Ewing actionable.

Does *Tarasoff* injure the doctor-patient relationship? Should therapists be obligated to reveal the patients' confidences when it endangers others?

**2. Serving Alcohol.** In some jurisdictions, business establishments that serve alcohol have a duty to prevent intoxicated patrons from driving home drunk and injuring someone. Some of these jurisdictions have imposed the duty by court decision, others by statutes known as "dram shop acts". The duty in these cases typically is limited to commercial suppliers who serve alcohol to visibly intoxicated patrons. Others are limited to situations that involve the serving of alcohol to a minor. Should this duty be extended to social hosts as well? In *Kelly v. Gwinnell*, 96 N.J. 538, 476 A.2d 1219 (1984), the court did extend a duty to control to social hosts, but limited it to social hosts who continue to serve liquor directly to a guest whom the host knows is beyond the point of intoxication and plans to drive home. What policy arguments militate for this kind of an extension of duty? Against? See Diamond, Levine, and Madden, supra, § 8.02[B][1][b].

**3. Duty to Protect: Special Relationship with Victim.** Courts also impose a duty to protect another from harm when the defendant has a special relationship with the victim. These cases are discussed in the notes, supra after the *Ayres v. Hicks* case.

**4. Attorney Failure to Warn.** Suppose a client tells an attorney not to prepare a cross-examination since the witness will be eliminated. Should the attorney have an obligation to warn the witness or police? There is little authority on point. Consider *Hawkins v. King County, Dept. of Rehabilitative Services*, 24 Wash.App. 338, 602 P.2d 361 (1979), where one court recognized that a cause of action existed for attorney failure to warn, but declined to find it under the facts of the case. The court noted that "the obligation to warn, when confidentiality would be compromised to the client's detriment, must be permissive at most, unless it appears beyond a reasonable doubt that the client has formed a firm intention to inflict serious personal injuries on an unknowing third person (internal quotations omitted)." *Id.* at 344. Because in this case the plaintiff, the mother of a mentally disturbed man whom the defendant attorney had assisted in obtaining release on bail, was aware of her son's propensity for violence, this exacting standard was not met.

See also Miller, Timothy J., *The Attorney's Duty to Reveal a Client's Intended Future Criminal Conduct*, 1984 Duke L.J. 582 (1984), where Miller argues that attorney disclosure of a client's intended criminal conduct should only be allowed for serious crimes, and even in such cases, should be discretionary.

## DAVIDSON v. CITY OF WESTMINSTER

Supreme Court of California.
32 Cal.3d 197, 185 Cal.Rptr. 252, 649 P.2d 894 (1982).

KAUS, J.

Plaintiffs Yolanda Davidson and her husband appeal from a judgment of dismissal entered in favor of defendants City of Westminster (city) and Police Officers Varner and Rosenwirth, after defendants' general demurrer was sustained with leave to amend and plaintiffs elected not to do so. We affirm.

According to the complaint, Yolanda Davidson was stabbed four times by Jack Blackmun while in a public laundromat. On three earlier occasions women had been stabbed at the same or nearby laundromats. The evening before Yolanda's stabbing, two police officers had the laundromat under surveillance when another stabbing occurred; the police chased the suspect but failed to catch him. The next evening the officers had the laundromat under surveillance for the purpose of preventing assaults and apprehending the felon. The officers were aware of Yolanda's presence in the laundromat throughout the surveillance. After about an hour of surveillance, they saw a man on the premises who closely resembled the attacker of the previous evening and, while watching him for 15 minutes, identified him as the likely perpetrator of that assault. As the officers watched, the suspect entered and left the laundromat "several times." The officers did not warn Yolanda. Eventually she was stabbed.

Yolanda seeks to recover from the city and the officers on the basis of causes of action for ... failure to protect, and failure to warn. The causes of action in negligence allege that special relationships existed between Yolanda and the officers as well as between the assailant and the officers, each of which imposed a duty of care on the officers.

Defendants demurred, contending (1) that no "special relationship" giving rise to a duty of care existed under the allegations of the complaint.... Without indicating the grounds for its ruling, the trial court sustained the demurrer. On this appeal, plaintiffs maintain that neither of the defendants' arguments support the trial court judgment.

\* \* \*

As a general rule, one owes no duty to control the conduct of another, nor to warn those endangered by such conduct. Such a duty may arise, however, if "(a) a special relation exists between the actor and the third person which imposes a duty upon the actor to control the third person's conduct, or (b) a special relation exists between the actor and the other which gives the other a right to protection." (Rest. 2d. Torts (1965) § 315; *Thompson v. County of Alameda* (1980) 27 Cal.3d 741, 751–752 [167 Cal.Rptr. 70, 614 P.2d 728]; *Tarasoff v. Regents of University of California* (1976) 17 Cal.3d 425 [131 Cal.Rptr. 14, 551 P.2d 334, 83 A.L.R.3d 1166].) Plaintiffs urge that defendants are liable under both theories.

In determining the existence of a duty of care in a given case, pertinent factors to consider include the "foreseeability of harm to the plaintiff, the degree of certainty that the plaintiff suffered injury, the closeness of the connection between the defendant's conduct and the injury suffered, the moral blame attached to the defendant's conduct, the policy of preventing future harm, the extent of the burden to the defendant and consequences to the community of imposing a duty to exercise care with resulting liability for breach, and the availability, cost, and prevalence of insurance for the risk involved." (*Rowland* v. *Christian* (1968) 69 Cal.2d 108, 113 [70 Cal.Rptr. 97, 443 P.2d 561, 32 A.L.R.3d 496].) "When public agencies are involved, additional elements include 'the extent of [the agency's] powers, the role imposed upon it by law and the limitations imposed upon it by budget; ...' (*Raymond* v. *Paradise Unified School Dist.* (1963) 218 Cal.App.2d 1, 8 [31 Cal.Rptr. 847]; see *Smith v. Alameda County Social Services Agency, supra*, 90 Cal.App.3d 929 [153 Cal.Rptr. 712].)" (*Thompson, supra*, 27 Cal.3d at p. 750.)

This court has considered the duty of care owed by police or correctional officials in a trilogy of cases, *Tarasoff v. Regents of University of California, supra*, 17 Cal.3d 425, *Thompson v. County of Alameda, supra*, 27 Cal.3d 741, and the earlier case of *Johnson v. State of California* (1968) 69 Cal.2d 782 [73 Cal.Rptr. 240, 447 P.2d 352].

In *Johnson*, the plaintiff was attacked by a minor who was placed in her foster home by the Youth Authority with no warning of the minor's known homicidal tendencies. We held that the state owed a duty of care to plaintiff: "As the party placing the youth with Mrs. Johnson, the state's relationship to plaintiff was such that its duty extended to warning of latent, dangerous qualities suggested by the parolee's history or character. [Citations.] These cases impose a duty upon *those who create a foreseeable peril*, not readily discoverable by endangered persons, to warn them of such potential peril." (69 Cal.2d at pp. 785–786; italics added.)

In *Tarasoff*, where a particular individual (Tatiana) was the subject of threats by an eventual assailant (Poddar), we held that the defendant therapists who heard the threats had a duty to exercise due care to warn the potential victim. The duty arose from the special relation between a patient and his doctor or psychotherapist, generally recognized as supporting an affirmative duty for the benefit not only of the patient but of other persons as well. (17 Cal.3d at p. 436; *Vistica* v. *Presbyterian Hospital* (1967) 67 Cal.2d 465, 469 [62 Cal.Rptr. 577, 432 P.2d 193].)

Nevertheless, as to certain police defendants, who had briefly detained and then released Poddar, we concluded that "they do not have any such special relationship to either Tatiana or to Poddar sufficient to impose upon such defendants a duty to warn respecting Poddar's violent intentions. (See *Hartzler v. City of San Jose* (1975) 46 Cal.App.3d 6, 9–10 [120 Cal.Rptr. 5]; *Antique Arts Corp.* v. *City of Torrance* (1974) 39 Cal.App.3d 588, 593 [114 Cal.Rptr. 332].) Plaintiffs suggest no theory, and plead no facts that give rise to any duty to warn on the part of the police defendants absent such a special relationship." (17 Cal.3d at p. 444; fn. omitted.) We further considered and rejected the possibility that a cause of action could be stated under the principles of Restatement Second of Torts, section 321, that "If the actor does an act, and subsequently realizes or should realize that it has created an unreasonable risk of causing physical harm to another, he is under a duty to exercise reasonable care to prevent the risk from taking effect."

*Thompson*, like *Tarasoff*, came to this court at the pleading stage. The county was sued for negligence in failing to warn the local police and the parents of neighborhood children that a juvenile offender who was dangerous and posed a threat to young children was being released into the community and in failing to warn the juvenile's mother of his dangerous propensities. The juvenile then killed a neighborhood child. Basing our decision in part on policy considerations and in part upon an analysis of "foreseeability" within the context of the case, we concluded that the county had no duty to warn the local police, the neighborhood parents, or the juvenile's custodian. Of significance to this case is the court's comments regarding the county's duty to warn the police: "In our view, warnings to the police as urged by plaintiffs ordinarily would be of little benefit in preventing assaults upon members of the public by dangerous persons unless we were simultaneously and additionally to impose a concurrent duty on the police to act upon such warnings. As we noted in *Tarasoff, supra* [17 Cal.3d 425] no such duty to act exists." (27 Cal.3d at p. 756.)

Guided by the principles set forth in *Johnson, Tarasoff,* and *Thompson*, we examine the relationship between the officers and the assailant and between Yolanda and the officers to decide whether sufficient factors are present to justify the imposition of a duty to warn or otherwise protect Yolanda.

### Special Relationship Between Officers and Assailant

It is alleged that the officers recognized Blackmun as a potential assailant because of his resemblance to the suspect of the assault of the prior evening. However, a person's mere proximity to an assailant, even with knowledge of his assaultive tendencies or status as a felon, does not establish a relation imposing a duty to control the assailant's conduct. Yet the assertion of a special relationship between the officers and the assailant derives entirely from the officers' status as policemen and their recognition of the assailant as a dangerous person.[3] On the minimal connection here—a visual identification from a distance—we find no relationship sufficient to impose a duty of care based upon a "special relationship" between the officer and the potential assailant.

### Special Relationship Between Yolanda and the Officers

The factors allegedly giving rise to a special relationship between Yolanda and the officers include the decision to conduct the surveillance, the observation of the potential assailant in the laundromat where Yolanda was also present, the recognition of the assailant as the likely perpetrator of a previous assault, the dependence of Yolanda upon the officers to secure her safety, and their failure to intervene by warning or otherwise protecting her.

In *Hartzler v. City of San Jose, supra*, 46 Cal.App.3d 6, referred to with approval in *Tarasoff*, 17 Cal.3d at p. 444, the court rejected a claim by the administrator of the estate of a woman who was killed by her estranged husband where the police had failed to respond to a plea some 45 minutes before the homicide. In dictum, the court determined that no special relationship existed between the police and the victim justifying any reliance on them for protection. The court noted that the common theme running through the cases in which a special relationship had been found was the voluntary assumption by the public entity or official of a duty toward the injured party.

The court concluded: "Appellant has failed to plead facts supporting an assumption that a special relationship existed between decedent and the San Jose Police Department. The allegation that the police had responded 20 times to her calls and had arrested her husband once does not indicate that the department had assumed a duty toward decedent greater than the duty owed to another member of the public. The police may have responded repeatedly to her calls, only to discover that she was not in danger. Absent an indication that the police had induced decedent's reliance on a promise, express or implied, that they would provide her with protection, it must be concluded that no special relationship existed and that appellant has not stated a cause of action." (*Hartzler, supra*, 46 Cal.App.3d at p. 10; see also *McCorkle v. City of Los Angeles* (1969) 70 Cal.2d 252 [74 Cal.Rptr. 389, 449 P.2d 453] [officer investigating accident directed plaintiff to follow him into middle of intersection where plaintiff was hit by another car; held city liable]; *Martinez v. State* (1978) 85 Cal.App.3d 430 [149 Cal.Rptr. 519] [no duty to warn victim of a potential assault by dangerous prisoner being released from custody, where no continuing relationship between state and victim]; *Antique Arts Corp. v. City of Torrance, supra*, 39 Cal.App.3d 588 [police radio dispatcher delayed 10 minutes after alert before broadcasting burglary in progress; held city not liable]; *McCarthy v. Frost, supra*, 33 Cal.App.3d 872 [complaint alleged decedent was driving on state highway at a particular time and place, highway patrolmen failed to find him, and death caused by failure to receive timely medical aid; held state and

---

**3.** Note that no duty to warn was imposed on the police in *Tarasoff* where a stronger connection existed between them and Poddar—he had been in custody and was released with knowledge of potential for violence against a specific victim.

patrolmen not liable]; *Morgan v. County of Yuba* (1964) 230 Cal.App.2d 938 [41 Cal.Rptr. 508] [deputy sheriff voluntarily promised to warn decedent if a prisoner, who had made threats on her life, was released; the prisoner was released, but sheriff did not warn; heirs had cause of action against county].)

Plaintiffs correctly point out that a finding of special relationship does not require a promise or reliance thereon in order to impose a duty of care. They cite *Johnson* v. *State of California, supra,* 69 Cal.2d 782 and *Mann v. State of California* (1977) 70 Cal.App.3d 773 [139 Cal.Rptr. 82], for the proposition that a special relationship may be predicated upon a victim's *dependence* upon the police for protection. In *Mann,* a highway patrolman placed his car with flashing lights behind two cars stalled on the freeway. After a tow truck arrived, the officer departed without warning. He placed no protective flares. Minutes later the stalled car was sideswiped by a passing car and the persons nearby were injured. Holding there was a special relationship imposing a duty to protect, the court reasoned that the injured party was dependent upon the officer who was an expert in traffic safety and the officer, having chosen to investigate and discovering their plight, had a duty to exercise reasonable care.

*Mann* and *Johnson* differ from the instant case in significant respects however. In *Johnson,* for example, the state put the parolee in the victim's home and failed to warn of homicidal tendencies; thus the state *placed* the victim in danger. Here the police were in no way responsible for the presence of either the assailant or the victim in the laundromat.

In *Mann,* the police officer's conduct contributed to, increased, or changed the risk which would have otherwise existed. The officer stopped to provide assistance, lulling the injured parties into a false sense of security and perhaps preventing other assistance from being sought. After calling the tow truck, the officer withdrew without advising those present that he was leaving, withdrawing the protection of his flashing lights which he had furnished to them and of which they were aware. (Cf. *Mikialian v. City of Los Angeles* (1978) 79 Cal.App.3d 150, 165 [144 Cal.Rptr. 794].)

Stripped of its immunity issue, *Johnson* is a straightforward case of liability based on failure to warn of a foreseeable peril created by the defendant and not readily discoverable by the potential victim. (Rest.2d Torts, § 321.) *Mann,* properly read, is a simple application of the "good Samaritan" doctrine. (Rest.2d Torts, §§ 323, 324; see also *Coffee v. McDonnell–Douglas Corp.* (1972) 8 Cal.3d 551, 557–558 [105 Cal.Rptr. 358, 503 P.2d 1366]; *Keene v. Wiggins* (1977) 69 Cal.App.3d 308, 316 [138 Cal.Rptr. 3]; *McGuigan v. Southern Pac. Co.* (1952) 112 Cal.App.2d 704, 718 [247 P.2d 415].)

Neither of these doctrines applies here. Obviously the peril to Yolanda was not created by the officers. She was unaware of their presence and did not rely on them for protection. Their conduct did not change the risk which would have existed in their absence: There is simply no reason to speculate that anyone—Yolanda or Blackmun, victim or assailant—would have acted differently had the officers not placed the laundromat under surveillance.

Nevertheless, we are urged that mere knowledge of Yolanda's danger imposed on the officers a duty to warn the potential victim. We disagree. The very facts of this case confirm us in our belief, voiced in *Tarasoff* (17 Cal.3d at p. 444, fn. 18), that under such circumstances the recognition of a cause of action against police defendants, based on a duty to warn, would raise difficult problems of causation and public policy.

Imposition of a duty to warn Yolanda, premised on the theory that she was a potential victim of a potential assailant, necessarily implies a general duty to warn other potential victims in the vicinity. (See *Thompson v. County of Alameda, supra*, 27 Cal.3d at p. 758.) While under some circumstances the police may conclude that such a course of conduct is prudent and necessary, our past decisions teach that it is inappropriate to impose such a duty—which may paralyze a neighborhood—under pain of tort liability. (See *Hayes v. State of California* (1974) 11 Cal.3d 469, 473 [113 Cal.Rptr. 599, 521 P.2d 855].)

In sum, we conclude that no causes of action for negligence are stated by plaintiffs. Although the facts as alleged may establish that Yolanda, or indeed any other woman using the laundromat, was a reasonably foreseeable victim as in *Tarasoff*, that factor alone does not suffice to establish a special relationship with the officers imposing upon them a duty to warn or protect.

\* \* \*

### NOTES

**1. No Police Duty to Protect.** Most courts have consistently found that police officers are not deemed to have a sufficient relationship with the public to create an exception to the general rule and thus, police officials generally have no duty to the public. See Diamond, Levine & Madden, *Understanding Torts* § 8.02 (1996). See also Keeton, *Prosser and Keeton on The Law of Torts* § 131 (5th ed. 1984).

How far should courts go in protecting police discretion? Consider *Hernandez v. City of Pomona*, 49 Cal.App.4th 1492, 57 Cal.Rptr.2d 406 (1996), in which the police induced the plaintiff's 16–year-old son into revealing incriminating evidence while being questioned concerning a murder trial against fellow gang members. One week after his statement was used at trial, he was murdered in retaliation by fellow gang members. Although the police assured him that he would suffer no harm as a result of the questioning, the court said that the plaintiff's son was fully aware of the potential danger and there was no allegation that this assurance amounted to an undertaking of the police to protect him. Thus, the court held that the police had no such duty to protect the boy:

> Although plaintiff alleges the police officers *assured* Torrez that no harm would come to him by giving a statement, there is no allegation that this *assurance* amounted to a specific or implicit undertaking to provide any protection for Torrez prior to, during, or after trial. The allegation is conclusory and far off the mark of a

specific promise to protect Torrez from his fellow gang members. Although the trial court gave plaintiff the opportunity to amend her complaint, she did not in any way allege that in giving this assurance the police promised, expressly or impliedly, to protect Torrez, or that Torrez relied on this statement as a guarantee of his safety. Though given ample opportunity, the plaintiff did not allege that the statement " 'induced a false sense of security and thereby worsened' " Torrez's position. (See *Carpenter v. City of Los Angeles*, supra, 230 Cal.App.3d at pp. 931–932, quoting *Williams v. State of California* (1983) 34 Cal.3d 18, 28 [192 Cal.Rptr. 233, 664 P.2d 137].) *As such, the alleged statement by the police officers did not give rise to a special relationship between defendants and Torrez out of which a duty to protect arose.*

\* \* \*

Although it was not alleged here that there were any specific threats made against Torrez, we hardly doubt that a gang member harbors a justified fear of harm if he gives any assistance to law enforcement in the prosecution of gang-related crimes. Furthermore, it is a common circumstance for us to be confronted with incidents of this sort in criminal cases appealed to this court. In fact, in the prosecution of gang-related crimes the police must and regularly do interview and take statements from gang members. It is an unfortunate, and perhaps unavoidable, incident of gang affiliation that gang members who do cooperate with law enforcement may themselves become victims of gang violence.

While Torrez's fear unfortunately proved to be well founded in hindsight, the defendants had no duty to take special precautions to protect him from his fellow gang members. The complexity of providing such protection is obvious. When would a protection plan begin, how long would it last and how much of law enforcement's resources should be expended?

\* \* \*

57 Cal.Rptr.2d at 412–413.

A concurring opinion joined in the court's legal conclusion but criticized the behavior of the assistant district attorney, observing that "in order to obtain a conviction, the life of a witness was deliberately put in jeopardy if not outright sacrificed by the prosecution."

Do you agree with the court's ruling?

**2. Finding a Duty.** Some courts are rejecting the majority rule that there is no special relationship between the police and the public. Consider *Burdette v. Marks*, 244 Va. 309, 421 S.E.2d 419 (1992), in which the court held that a violation of a special duty owed to a particular, identifiable individual or class of persons with whom the police had a special relationship would "give rise to civil liability of a public official." In *Burdette*, the plaintiff pulled over to the scene of a car accident to give assistance. When he saw one of the drivers strike the other driver during an altercation, he attempted to give the injured driver aid. The other driver then attacked him, first with his fists and then with a shovel. The plaintiff tried to remove his young son to safety when the driver attacked him again, this time with an iron pipe. The defendant, a deputy sheriff on the scene, observed these beatings but failed to give any assistance. The court reasoned that there was a special relationship between the officer and the defendant since the sheriff was on duty as a uniformed officer at the time and from this it could reasonably be inferred that he was armed and capable of subduing the aggressive driver. The court held that the sheriff breached this duty by not giving aid when he knew or should have known that the plaintiff was in grave danger of serious bodily harm.

Similarly, in *Austin v. City of Scottsdale*, 140 Ariz. 579, 684 P.2d 151 (1984), the court found that since the City of Scottsdale had opted to provide general police protection, it had a duty to use reasonable care in protecting the public. The court held that the police department breached this duty when they did not pursue an anonymous emergency phone call that a particular prisoner, who was to be released from prison on a weekend pass, would be in serious danger if let out. The prisoner was found dead the day after his release, with approximately twenty-five stab wounds. See generally, Diamond, Levine and Madden, supra § 8.02 and Keeton, supra, § 131.

**3. Exceptions to the No–Duty Rule.** Despite the general rule of no special relationship between the police and the public, police officers are subject to the standard exceptions to the no-duty rule discussed previously. See the notes following *L.S. Ayres & Company v. Hicks*, supra. See, for example, *DeLong v. County of Erie*, 89 A.D.2d 376, 455 N.Y.S.2d 887 (N.Y.App.Div.1982), in which the court held that police must act reasonably once they undertake to give assistance or protection. The plaintiff in *DeLong* had called 911 when she saw a burglar behind her house. The complaint writer accidentally wrote down the wrong address and as a result of the police's failure to properly respond, the plaintiff suffered seven knife wounds, one of which was fatal. The court held that by holding out the 911 number as a means of contacting help in an emergency, the police induced reliance. Because they failed to carry out their duty reasonably, the police were found liable. Consider also *Natrona County v. Blake*, 81 P.3d 948 (Wyo. 2003), in which the Supreme Court of Wyoming held that the county correctional facility did in fact owe a duty to a victim murdered by the escape of prison inmates. The correctional facility allowed Graumann, a dangerous criminal with a history of escaping from incarceration, and several others to go to the exercise yard at nighttime, unsupervised. Both the correctional facility and the prisoners knew that there were blind spots in the cameras monitoring them and the prisoners managed to rope their way over a fence in one of those spots despite the fact that a citizen saw them and called the facility to warn that an escape was in progress. That warning and a second warning that the prisoners had actually succeeded to get over the fence and escape were ignored.

Other courts, however, have refused to find a special relationship, even when the police undertook to act. Consider *Williams v. California*, 34 Cal.3d 18, 192 Cal.Rptr. 233, 664 P.2d 137 (1983), in which the plaintiff alleged that the highway patrol's negligence in conducting an investigation of an accident scene caused her to lose her opportunity to recover for her injuries. She alleged that the police failed to determine the identity of the driver of a truck from which a brake part fell off and flew threw her window. Nor did they identify any witnesses. The court held that "stopping to aid a motorist does not, in itself, create a special relationship which would give rise to such a duty." The court reasoned that in the absence of the other exceptions to the general rule, there were no factors supporting the imposition of a special duty on the police even though they undertook an investigation when they arrived at the scene.

**4. Domestic Violence.** In *Dore v. City of Fairbanks*, 31 P.3d 788 (Alaska 2001), the plaintiffs brought suit against the city after their father killed their mother and then committed suicide. The Supreme Court of Alaska held that the city police department had no duty to arrest the plaintiffs' father after a warrant was issued for his arrest for harassing their mother, or to otherwise protect their mother from harm by the father. The court reasoned that there was no duty here under the limited duty imposed on "one who takes control of a third person whom he knows or should know to be likely to cause bodily harm to others if not controlled" because the police were not in control of the plaintiffs' father and they did not know or have reason to know that he was likely to cause serious bodily harm if not controlled. But see *Massee v. Thompson*, 321 Mont. 210, 90 P.3d 394 (2004), in which the Supreme Court of Montana, applying a domestic violence statute, held that the sheriff had a special duty to the victim because the victim was a member of a statutorily protected class of domestic violence victims, a category of the special relationship exception to the general no duty rule. The court also found enough evidence to support the jury's verdict that the Sheriff breached that duty because he failed to provide the victim a notice of rights as a victim of domestic violence and failed to provide her information on community resources at any point in the three-year period when he responded to domestic violence calls at her residence, both requirements imposed by the statute. See also *Beal v. City of Seattle*, 134 Wash.2d 769, 954 P.2d 237 (1998), in which the Supreme Court of Washington found a special relationship creating a duty between the police officer and victim who had called 911 to ask for police protection so that she could remove her clothes from the apartment she shared with her husband against whom she had a restraining order. She received assurances by the city that police were coming, but they had not yet come twenty-two minutes later when her husband showed up and killed her. The court held that "a municipality may be liable in tort for failure to protect another person from criminal acts of third parties where a relationship exists or has developed between plaintiff and municipality's agents giving rise to a duty to perform a mandated act for the benefit of a particular person or class of persons. Such a relationship arises, the court set forth where (1) there is direct contact or privity between public official and injured plaintiff which sets the latter apart from the general public, and (2) there are express assurances given by a public official, which (3) gives rise to justifiable reliance on the part of the plaintiff."

**5. Governmental Immunity.** Even if a court does find that a duty to the public exists, either through an extended special relationship or some other exception to the general no-duty rule, it may conclude that the police are protected from liability by governmental immunity. See Chapter 2, Sec. J., infra, for materials on the issues raised by such immunity.

**6. The Rodney King Case.** Supervisory responsibility over other police officers can lead to civil and criminal liability if the supervising officers unreasonably fail to intervene. Consider the following passage, excerpted in *Allen v. City of Los Angeles*, 92 F.3d 842 (9th Cir.1996) (King's civil suit). Rodney King was viciously assaulted by police officers in Los Angeles. The police attack received national attention since a private citizen was able to videotape the police misconduct and the tape was broadcast nationally. The text is from the criminal indictment against Stacey Koon, one of the police officers in the Rodney King beating case, which the court relied on in establishing part of King's civil claim. It charges that Koon,

> ... then a sergeant with the Los Angeles Police Department, while acting under color of the laws of California, did willfully permit other Los Angeles Police Officers in his presence and under his supervision, namely Laurence M. Powell, Timothy E. Wind, and Theodore J. Briseno, unlawfully to strike with batons, kick, and stomp Rodney Glen [sic] King, an inhabitant of the State of California, while Rodney Glen [sic] King was in the custody of those officers, and did willfully fail to prevent this unlawful assault; resulting in bodily injury to Rodney Glen [sic] King, and thereby did willfully deprive Rodney Glen [sic] King of the right preserved and protected by the Constitution of the United States not to be deprived of liberty without due process of law, including the right to be kept free from harm while in official custody, all in violation of Title 18, United States Code, Section 242.

Is the failure to prevent an egregious wrong less morally culpable than the commission of that wrong? Note that officers who neither personally attacked Mr. King nor had supervisory responsibilities over the attacking officers were not held civilly or criminally liable for failure to intervene.

## 2.  Mental Distress

# THING v. LA CHUSA

Supreme Court of California.
48 Cal.3d 644, 257 Cal.Rptr. 865, 771 P.2d 814 (1989).

EAGLESON, Justice.

The narrow issue presented by the parties in this case is whether the Court of Appeal correctly held that a mother who did not witness an accident in which an automobile struck and injured her child may recover damages from the negligent driver for the emotional distress she suffered when she arrived at the accident scene. The more important question this issue poses for the court, however, is whether the "guidelines" enunciated by this court in *Dillon* v. *Legg* (1968) 68 Cal.2d 728 [69 Cal.Rptr. 72, 441 P.2d 912, 29 A.L.R.3d 1316] are adequate, or if they should be refined to create greater certainty in this area of the law.

Although terms of convenience identify the cause of action here as one for negligent infliction of emotional distress (NIED) and the plaintiff as a "bystander" rather than a "direct victim," the common law tort giving rise to plaintiff's claim is negligence. (*Dillon v. Legg, supra*, 68 Cal.2d 728, 730; *Amaya v. Home Ice, Fuel & Supply Co.* (1963) 59 Cal.2d 295, 314–315 [29 Cal.Rptr. 33, 379 P.2d 513].) It is in that context that we consider the appropriate application of the concept of "duty" in an area that has long divided this court—recognition of the right of persons, whose only injury is emotional distress, to recover damages when that distress is caused by knowledge of the injury to a third person caused by the defendant's negligence. Although we again find ourselves divided, we shall resolve some of the uncertainty over the parameters of the NIED action, uncertainty that has troubled lower courts, litigants, and, of course, insurers.

Upon doing so, we shall conclude that the societal benefits of certainty in the law, as well as traditional concepts of tort law, dictate limitation of bystander recovery of damages for emotional distress. In the absence of physical injury or impact to the plaintiff himself, damages for emotional distress should be recoverable only if the plaintiff: (1) is closely related to the injury victim, (2) is present at the scene of the injury-producing event at the time it occurs and is then aware that it is causing injury to the victim and, (3) as a result suffers emotional distress beyond that which would be anticipated in a disinterested witness.

## I

On December 8, 1980, John Thing, a minor, was injured when struck by an automobile operated by defendant James V. La Chusa. His mother, plaintiff Maria Thing, was nearby, but neither saw nor heard the accident. She became aware of the injury to her son when told by a daughter that John had been struck by a car. She rushed to the scene where she saw her bloody and unconscious child, who she believed was dead, lying in the roadway. Maria sued defendants, alleging that she suffered great emotional disturbance, shock, and injury to her nervous system as a result of these events, and that the injury to John and emotional distress she suffered were proximately caused by defendants' negligence.

\* \* \*

### Limitations in Negligence Actions

... Initially ... in negligence cases the right to recover for emotional distress had been limited to circumstances in which the victim was himself injured and emotional distress was a "parasitic" item of damages, or if a plaintiff who had been in the "zone of danger" did not suffer injury from impact, but did suffer physical injury as a result of the emotional trauma. (See *Webb v. Francis J. Lewald Coal Co.* (1931) 214 Cal. 182, 184 [4 P.2d 532, 77 A.L.R. 675]; *Lindley v. Knowlton* (1918) 179 Cal. 298, 301–302 [176 P. 440].)

\* \* \*

... *Amaya v. Home Ice, Fuel & Supply Co., supra,* 59 Cal.2d 295, ... after confirming that the "impact rule" making a contemporaneous physical impact a prerequisite to recovery for negligently induced fright or shock was not applicable in California, held damages could not be recovered by persons outside the zone of danger created by the defendant's negligence even when that shock was reflected in physiological symptoms. . . .

The court explained the restriction on the right to recover damages for emotional distress in negligence actions on the ground that the defendant had not breached a legal duty to the plaintiff. The court concluded that existence of a duty could not be defined, or left to the jury to find, on the basis of whether the injury was foreseeable. Rather the existence and scope of the defendant's duty in this context was one for the court.

Several factors led to that conclusion.... Ultimately ... the court weighed the interest of the plaintiff in freedom from invasion of mental tranquility against the costs involved in recognizing a duty and concluded that factors militating against recognition of a legal duty to the third party plaintiff predominated.

First among these policy considerations was efficient administration of justice. The court's concern here was the possibility of fraud and the difficulty in resolving disputes among witnesses over the extent and severity of the injury where negligent conduct ... allegedly produced the emotional distress. A second important administrative factor was concern that it would be impossible to limit the circumstances in which liability would exist for emotional distress caused by apprehension of danger or injury not to the plaintiff but to a third person. The court concluded, also, that socioeconomic and moral factors mandate that there be some limit to the liability of the negligent actor. (*Amaya, supra,* 59 Cal.2d at pp. 312–313.)

\* \* \*

The *Amaya* view was short lived, however. Only five years later, the decision was overruled in *Dillon v. Legg, supra,* 68 Cal.2d 728.

In *Dillon* itself, the issue was limited. The mother and sister of a deceased infant each sought damages for "great emotional disturbance and shock and injury to her nervous system" which had caused them great mental pain and suffering. Allegedly these injuries were caused by witnessing the defendant's negligently operated vehicle collide with and roll over the infant as she lawfully crossed a street. The mother was not herself endangered by the defendant's conduct. The sister may have been. The trial court had therefore granted the defendant's motion for judgment on the pleadings as to the mother, but had denied it with respect to the sister of the decedent. Faced with the incongruous result demanded by the "zone of danger" rule which denied recovery for emotional distress and consequent physical injury unless the plaintiff himself had been threatened with injury, the court overruled *Amaya.*

Reexamining the concept of "duty" as applicable to the *Dillon* facts, the court now rejected the argument that the possibility of fraudulent claims justified denial of recovery, at least insofar as a mother who sees her child killed is concerned, as "no one can seriously question that fear or grief for one's child is as likely to cause physical injury as concern over one's own well-being." (*Dillon v. Legg, supra,* 68 Cal.2d 728, 736.) The court held instead that the right to recover should be determined by application of "the neutral principles of foreseeability, proximate cause and consequential injury that generally govern tort law." (*Id.,* at p. 737.)

The difficulty in defining the limits on recovery anticipated by the *Amaya* court was rejected as a basis for denying recovery, but the court did recognize that "to limit the otherwise potentially infinite liability which would follow every negligent act, the law of torts holds defendant amenable only for injuries to others which to defendant at the time were reasonably foreseeable." (*Dillon, supra*, 68 Cal.2d at p. 739.)....

In adopting foreseeability of the injury as the basis of a negligent actor's duty, the *Dillon* court identified the risks that could give rise to that duty as both physical impact and emotional disturbance brought on by the conduct. Having done so, the *Dillon* court conceded: "We cannot now predetermine defendant's obligation in every situation by a fixed category; no immutable rule can establish the extent of that obligation for every circumstance of the future." (68 Cal.2d at p. 740.) In an effort to give some initial definition to this newly approved expansion of the cause of action for NIED the court enunciated "guidelines" that suggested a limitation on the action to circumstances like those in the case before it.

"We note, first, that we deal here with a case in which plaintiff suffered a shock which resulted in physical injury and we confine our ruling to that case. In determining, in such a case, whether defendant should reasonably foresee the injury to plaintiff [mother], or in other terminology, whether defendant owes plaintiff a duty of due care, the courts will take into account such factors as the following: (1) Whether plaintiff was located near the scene of the accident as contrasted with one who was a distance away from it. (2) Whether the shock resulted from a direct emotional impact upon plaintiff from the sensory and contemporaneous observance of the accident, as contrasted with learning of the accident from others after its occurrence. (3) Whether plaintiff and the victim were closely related, as contrasted with an absence of any relationship or the presence of only a distant relationship.

"The evaluation of these factors will indicate the *degree* of the defendant's foreseeability; obviously defendant is more likely to foresee that a mother who observes an accident affecting her child will suffer harm than to foretell that a stranger witness will do so. Similarly, the degree of foreseeability of the third person's injury is far greater in the case of his contemporaneous observance of the accident than that in which he subsequently learns of it. The defendant is more likely to foresee that shock to the nearby, witnessing mother will cause physical harm than to anticipate that someone distant from the accident will suffer more than a temporary emotional reaction. All of these elements, of course, shade into each other; the fixing of the obligation, intimately tied into the facts, depends upon each case.

"In light of these factors the court will determine whether the accident and harm was *reasonably* foreseeable. Such reasonable foreseeability does not turn on whether the particular [defendant] as an individual would have in actuality foreseen the exact accident and loss; it contemplates that *courts, on a case-to-case basis, analyzing all the circumstances, will decide what the ordinary man under such circumstances should reasonably have foreseen*. The courts thus mark out the areas of liability, excluding the remote and unexpected." (*Dillon, supra*, 68 Cal.2d at p. 741. Italics added.)

The *Dillon* court anticipated and accepted uncertainty in the short term in application of its holding, but was confident that the boundaries of this NIED action could be drawn in future cases. In sum, as former Justice Potter Stewart once suggested with reference to that undefinable category of materials that are obscene, the *Dillon* court was satisfied that trial and appellate courts would be able to determine the existence of a duty because the court would know it when it saw it. Underscoring the questionable validity of that assumption, however, was the obvious and unaddressed problem that the injured party, the negligent tortfeasor, their insurers, and their attorneys had no means short of suit by which to determine if a duty such as to impose liability for damages would be found in cases other than those that were "on all fours" with *Dillon*. Thus, the only thing that was foreseeable from the *Dillon* decision was the uncertainty that continues to this time as to the parameters of the third party NIED action.

*  *  *

## V

### *Clarification of the Right to Recover for NIED*

Not surprisingly, this "case-to-case" or ad hoc approach to development of the law that misled the Court of Appeal in this case has not only produced inconsistent rulings in the lower courts, but has provoked considerable critical comment by scholars who attempt to reconcile the cases. (See Rabin, *Tort Recovery for Negligently Inflicted Economic Loss: A Reassessment* (1985) 37 Stan.L.Rev. 1513, 1524–1526, hereafter *Rabin*; Diamond, *Dillon* v. *Legg Revisited: Toward a Unified Theory of Compensating Bystanders and Relatives for Intangible Injuries* (1984) 35 Hastings L.J. 477, hereafter *Diamond*; Bell, *The Bell Tolls: Toward Full Tort Recovery for Psychic Injury* (1984) 36 U.Fla.L.Rev. 333; Pearson, *Liability for Negligently Inflicted Psychic Harm: A Response to Professor Bell* (1984) 36 U.Fla.L.Rev. 413; Nolan & Ursin, *Negligent Infliction of Emotional Distress: Coherence Emerging from Chaos* (1982) 33 Hastings L.J. 583, 620; Miller, *The Scope of Liability for Negligent Infliction of Emotional Distress: Making "The Punishment Fit the Crime"* (1979) 1 Hawaii L.Rev. 1, hereafter *Miller*; Pearson, *Liability to Bystanders for Negligently Inflicted Emotional Harm—A Comment on the Nature of Arbitrary Rules* (1982) 34 U.Fla.L.Rev. 477; Comment, Dillon Revisited: Toward a Better Paradigm for Bystander Cases (1982) 43 Ohio St. L.J. 931, 948; Note, *Limiting Liability for the Negligent Infliction of Emotional Distress: The "Bystander Recovery" Cases* (1981) 54 So.Cal.L.Rev. 847; Note, *Molien* v. *Kaiser Foundation Hospitals: California's New Tort of Negligent Infliction of Serious Emotional Distress* (1982) 18 Cal. Western L.Rev. 101; Note, *Negligent Infliction of Emotional Distress: Reconciling the Bystander and Direct Victim Causes of Action* (1983) 18 U.S.F. L.Rev. 145.)

Proposals to eliminate the arbitrary results of the proliferating, inconsistent and often conflicting *Dillon* progeny include the suggestion that recovery be allowed in any case in which recovery for physical injury is permitted. (See *Ochoa v. Superior Court, supra,* 39 Cal.3d 159, 178 [conc. opn. of Grodin, J.].) Another would limit recovery to the close-relatives class contemplated by *Dillon*, but allow recovery whenever mental distress to the plaintiff was foreseeable. (*Id.* at p. 196, conc. & dis. opn. of Bird, C.J.) At the other extreme, respondent here and amicus curiae Association for California Tort Reform argue, in essence, that the *Dillon* "guidelines" should be recognized as substantive limitations or elements of the tort.

In his thoughtful article documenting the conflicting and sometimes arbitrary results of attempts by lower courts to apply *Dillon* and *Molien*, Professor Diamond analyzes the "flaws" in the *Dillon* analysis which he believes have contributed to the problem. He concludes that the *Dillon*-based cause of action identifies a "duty" on the basis of the purely fortuitous circumstances in which an injury occurs. As a result, when recovery for emotional distress alone is permitted under the *Dillon* guidelines, "foreseeability" is not a realistic indicator of potential liability and does not afford a rational limitation on recovery. Nor, Diamond suggests, do the *Dillon* guidelines, particularly under the expanded right to recovery created by *Molien* (and, we note, *Ochoa*), provide such limitation. In his view, only one of the *Dillon* guidelines is even relevant to foreseeability—the relationship of the plaintiff to the person suffering physical injury—because it is foreseeable that the emotional distress suffered by a close relative on witnessing that injury will be greater than that of a stranger. (*Diamond, supra*, 35 Hastings L.J., at pp. 487–489.)

Diamond argues that the fact that it is foreseeable that a close relative will suffer psychological trauma at witnessing the injury does not adequately limit liability for damages for such intangible losses. When recovery for emotional distress was permitted only as an item of "parasitic" damage suffered by a plaintiff who had been physically injured, the defendant's exposure was limited by more predictable factors. Foreseeability that various activities may cause physical injury limits the potential universe of persons who may be harmed. This, in turn, by limiting the negligent actor's exposure makes it possible to protect potential victims and the defendant through insurance or other risk-spreading mechanisms whose cost is more closely related to the risk, and ensures that this exposure bears a more rational relationship to the defendant's culpability. (*Diamond, supra*, 35 Hastings L.J., at pp. 490–493.)

Another scholar suggests that any foreseeable plaintiff be permitted to recover for NIED and loss of filial consortium, but only for economic loss, thereby reconciling the divergent paths and limitations on recovery for noneconomic damages in these related torts with that permitted in actions for wrongful life. (See *Miller, supra*, 1 Hawaii L.Rev., at pp. 39–41.) Diamond agrees that this solution would permit recovery by all foreseeable plaintiffs in "intangible" tort cases, while restricting recovery to "economically acceptable" limits. (*Diamond, supra*, 35 Hastings L.J., at p. 480.)

In the NIED context, however, permitting recovery of economic damages by all foreseeable plaintiffs would expose defendants to risks no less arbitrary and unacceptable than those presently existing. While the recovery by individual victims might be less, the number of potential plaintiffs traumatized by reason of defendant's negligent conduct toward another, would turn on fortuitous circumstances wholly unrelated to the culpability of the defendant.

Our own prior decisions identify factors that will appropriately circumscribe the right to damages, but do not deny recovery to plaintiffs whose emotional injury is real even if not accompanied by out-of-pocket expense. Notwithstanding the broad language in some of those decisions, it is clear that foreseeability of the injury alone is not a useful "guideline" or a meaningful restriction on the scope of the NIED action. The *Dillon* experience confirms, as one commentator observed, that "[f]oreseeability proves too much. ...Although it may set tolerable limits for most types of physical harm, it provides virtually no limit on liability for nonphysical harm." (*Rabin, supra*, 37 Stan. L. Rev. at p. 1526.) It is apparent that reliance on foreseeability of injury alone in finding a duty, and thus a right to recover, is not adequate when the damages sought are for an intangible injury. In order to avoid limitless liability out of all proportion to the degree of a defendant's negligence, and against which it is impossible to insure without imposing unacceptable costs on those among whom the risk is spread, the right to recover for negligently caused emotional distress must be limited.

\* \* \*

Among the concerns of the *Amaya* court was the social cost of imposing liability on a negligent tortfeasor for all foreseeable emotional distress suffered by relatives who witnessed the injury....

*Ochoa v. Superior Court, supra*, 39 Cal.3d 159, 165, footnote 6,[9] offers additional guidance, justifying what we acknowledge must be arbitrary lines to similarly limit the class of potential plaintiffs if emotional injury absent physical harm is to continue to be a recoverable item of damages in a negligence action. The impact of personally observing the injury-producing event in most, although concededly not all, cases distinguishes the plaintiff's resultant emotional distress from the emotion felt when one learns of the injury or death of a loved one from another, or observes pain and suffering but not the traumatic cause of the injury. Greater certainty and a more reasonable limit on the exposure to liability for negligent conduct is possible by limiting the right to recover for negligently caused emotional distress to plaintiffs who personally and contemporaneously perceive the injury-producing event and its traumatic consequences.

**9.** "[A] distinction between distress caused by personal observation of the injury and by hearing of the tragedy from another is justified because compensation should be limited to abnormal life experiences which cause emotional distress. While receiving news that a loved one has been injured or has died may cause emotional distress, it is the type of experience for which in a general way one is prepared, an experience which is common. By contrast few persons are forced to witness the death or injury of a loved one or to suddenly come upon the scene without warning in situations where tortious conduct is involved. In the present case, for example, while it is common to visit a loved one in a hospital and to be distressed by the loved one's pain and suffering, it is highly uncommon to witness the apparent neglect of the patient's immediate medical needs by medical personnel." (*Ochoa v. Superior Court, supra*, 39 Cal.3d 159, 165, fn. 6.)

Similar reasoning justifies limiting recovery to persons closely related by blood or marriage since, in common experience, it is more likely that they will suffer a greater degree of emotional distress than a disinterested witness to negligently caused pain and suffering or death. Such limitations are indisputably arbitrary since it is foreseeable that in some cases unrelated persons have a relationship to the victim or are so affected by the traumatic event that they suffer equivalent emotional distress. As we have observed, however, drawing arbitrary lines is unavoidable if we are to limit liability and establish meaningful rules for application by litigants and lower courts.

No policy supports extension of the right to recover for NIED to a larger class of plaintiffs. Emotional distress is an intangible condition experienced by most persons, even absent negligence, at some time during their lives. Close relatives suffer serious, even debilitating, emotional reactions to the injury, death, serious illness, and evident suffering of loved ones. These reactions occur regardless of the cause of the loved one's illness, injury, or death. That relatives will have severe emotional distress is an unavoidable aspect of the "human condition." The emotional distress for which monetary damages may be recovered, however, ought not to be that form of acute emotional distress or the transient emotional reaction to the occasional gruesome or horrible incident to which every person may potentially be exposed in an industrial and sometimes violent society. Regardless of the depth of feeling or the resultant physical or mental illness that results from witnessing violent events, persons unrelated to those injured or killed may not now recover for such emotional upheaval even if negligently caused. Close relatives who witness the accidental injury or death of a loved one and suffer emotional trauma may not recover when the loved one's conduct was the cause of that emotional trauma. The overwhelming majority of "emotional distress" which we endure, therefore, is not compensable.

Unlike an award of damages for intentionally caused emotional distress which is punitive, the award for NIED simply reflects society's belief that a negligent actor bears some responsibility for the effect of his conduct on persons other than those who suffer physical injury. In identifying those persons and the circumstances in which the defendant will be held to redress the injury, it is appropriate to restrict recovery to those persons who will suffer an emotional impact beyond the impact that can be anticipated whenever one learns that a relative is injured, or dies, or the emotion felt by a "disinterested" witness. The class of potential plaintiffs should be limited to those who because of their relationship suffer the greatest emotional distress. When the right to recover is limited in this manner, the liability bears a reasonable relationship to the culpability of the negligent defendant.

The elements which justify and simultaneously limit an award of damages for emotional distress caused by awareness of the negligent infliction of injury to a close relative are those noted in *Ochoa*—the traumatic emotional effect on the plaintiff who contemporaneously observes both the event or conduct that causes serious injury to a close relative and the injury itself. Even if it is "foreseeable" that persons other than closely related percipient witnesses may suffer emotional distress, this fact does not justify the imposition of what threatens to become unlimited liability for emotional distress on a defendant whose conduct is simply negligent. Nor does such abstract "foreseeability" warrant continued reliance on the assumption that the limits of liability will become any clearer if lower courts are permitted to continue approaching the issue on a "case-to-case" basis some 20 years after *Dillon*.

We conclude, therefore, that a plaintiff may recover damages for emotional distress caused by observing the negligently inflicted injury of a third person if, but only if, said plaintiff: (1) is closely related to the injury victim; (2) is present at the scene of the injury-producing event at the time it occurs and is then aware that it is causing injury to the victim; and (3) as a result suffers serious emotional distress—a reaction beyond that which would be anticipated in a disinterested witness and which is not an abnormal response to the circumstances. . . .

. . . . Experience has shown that, contrary to the expectation of the *Dillon* majority, and with apology to Bernard Witkin, there are clear judicial days on which a court can foresee forever and thus determine liability but none on which that foresight alone provides a socially and judicially acceptable limit on recovery of damages for that injury.

### Disposition

The undisputed facts establish that plaintiff was not present at the scene of the accident in which her son was injured. She did not observe defendant's conduct and was not aware that her son was being injured. She could not, therefore, establish a right to recover for the emotional distress she suffered when she subsequently learned of the accident and observed its consequences. The order granting summary judgment was proper.

The judgment of the Court of Appeal is reversed.

\* \* \*

BROUSSARD, Justice, dissenting.

I dissent.

"[T]he problem [of negligent infliction of emotional distress] should be solved by the application of the principles of tort, not by the creation of exceptions to them. Legal history shows that artificial islands of exceptions, created from the fear that the legal process will not work, usually do not withstand the waves of reality and, in time, descend into oblivion." (*Dillon v. Legg* (1968) 68 Cal.2d 728, 747 [69 Cal.Rptr. 72, 441 P.2d 912, 29 A.L.R.3d 1316] [Tobriner, J., admonishing this court not to do what the majority do today].)

The majority grope for a "bright line" rule for negligent infliction of emotional distress actions, only to grasp an admittedly arbitrary line which will deny recovery to victims whose injuries from the negligent acts of others are very real. In so doing, the majority reveal a myopic reading of *Dillon v. Legg, supra*, 68 Cal.2d 728. They impose a strict requirement that plaintiff be present at the scene of the injury-producing event at the time it occurs and is aware that it is causing injury to the victim. This strict requirement rigidifies what *Dillon* forcefully told us should be a flexible rule, and will lead to arbitrary results. I would follow the mandate of *Dillon* and maintain that foreseeability and duty determine liability, with a view toward a policy favoring reasonable limitations on liability. There is no reason why these general rules of tort law should not apply to negligent infliction of emotional distress actions.

## I.

We held in *Dillon* that a mother who witnesses the negligent infliction of death or injury on her child may recover for the resulting emotional distress even though the mother does not fear imminent physical harm. We recognized that the primary consideration in finding liability was foreseeability (*Dillon, supra*, 68 Cal.2d at pp. 730–740) and rejected the "hopeless artificiality" of the zone-of-danger rule. (*Id.* at p. 733.)

The majority themselves note that "foreseeability of the injury [is] the basis of a negligent actor's duty," (maj. opn. at p. 654) and quote from *Dillon* that this issue must necessarily be adjudicated only upon "a case-by-case basis." (Maj. opn. at p. 655, quoting *Dillon, supra*, 68 Cal.2d at p. 741.) " 'We cannot now predetermine defendant's obligation in every situation by a fixed category; *no immutable rule* can establish the extent of that obligation for every circumstance of the future.' " (Maj. opn. at p. 654, quoting *Dillon, supra*, 68 Cal.2d at p. 740, italics added.)

Though *Dillon* made foreseeability its lodestar, it provided three factors for courts to consider in determining whether a negligent infliction of emotional distress cause of action was stated in a particular case: "(1) Whether plaintiff was located near the scene of the accident as contrasted with one who was a distance away from it. (2) Whether the shock resulted from a direct emotional impact upon plaintiff from the sensory and contemporaneous observance of the accident, as contrasted with learning of the accident from others after its occurrence. (3) Whether plaintiff and the victim were closely related, as contrasted with an absence of any relationship or the presence of only a distant relationship." (*Dillon, supra*, 68 Cal.2d at pp. 740–741.)

*Dillon* denounced "artificial abstractions which bar recovery contrary to the general rules" of tort law, and emphasized that "mechanical rules of thumb which are at variance with these principles do more harm than good. [Citation.]" (68 Cal.2d at pp. 746–747.) However, some courts have rigidly and mechanically applied the *Dillon* guidelines—many times at the cost of injustice to a victim of a tortfeasor's negligent act. Professor Diamond, although quoted extensively by the majority, warned against a strict application of the *Dillon* guidelines: "[C]ourts have applied the *Dillon* guidelines mechanically, viewing them as strict preconditions to recovery. This mechanical application has led to the erection of arbitrary limitations on recovery bearing little relation to the principles of foreseeability espoused so forcefully in *Dillon*. While in some instances mental distress is compensated, other equally foreseeable mental injuries are not. The result is feast or famine for the plaintiff depending on the fortuities of time, location, or characterization of the plaintiff as 'direct' or 'indirect.' " (Diamond, *Dillon v. Legg Revisited: Toward a Unified Theory of Compensating Bystanders and Relatives for Intangible Injuries* (1984) 35 Hastings L.J. 477, 477–478.)

The majority ignore the fundamental mandate of *Dillon* to consider foreseeability and duty in finding liability. Their only justification for this and a strict rule that will limit liability at the cost of arbitrary results is an amorphous "policy" one. . . .

. . . They freely admit to "drawing arbitrary lines" but complain that it is "unavoidable if we are to limit liability and establish meaningful rules for application by litigants and lower courts." (Maj. opn. at p. 666.) Thus what in *Dillon* were guidelines to assist courts in assessing liability become a tripartite test, which includes the above-mentioned strict and arbitrary requirement, and displaces the consideration of foreseeability.

Under the majority's strict requirement, a mother who arrives moments after an accident caused by another's negligence will not be permitted recovery. No matter that the mother would see her six-year-old son immediately after he was electrocuted, lying in a puddle of water in a dying state, gagging and choking in his own vomit, as in *Hathaway* v. *Superior Court* (1980) 112 Cal.App.3d 728 [169 Cal.Rptr. 435]. No matter that the mother would be following her daughters' car and would come upon the wreckage of the car "before the dust had settled" to find the mangled bodies of her daughters, who were dead or dying, as in *Parsons* v. *Superior Court* (1978) 81 Cal.App.3d 506, 509 [146 Cal.Rptr. 495].

\* \* \* As *Dillon* instructed, there is "no good reason why the general rules of tort law, including the concepts of negligence, proximate cause, and foreseeability, long applied to all other types of injury, should not govern the case now before us." (*Id.* at p. 746.) *Dillon*'s test of reasonable foreseeability "facilitates rational risk spreading and correlates liability with the risks that the defendant should expect." (Diamond, *supra,* 35 Hastings L.J. at p. 500.)

\* \* \*

. . . . The majority's strict requirement that plaintiff be present at the scene of the injury-producing event at the time it occurs and is then aware that it is causing injury to the victim will only bring about arbitrary results that will frustrate justice for victims of the negligent acts of others. We should apply the concepts of foreseeability and duty to negligent infliction of emotional distress actions, with a view toward a policy favoring reasonable restrictions on liability. This is a principled basis for determining liability and would also conform this area with other areas of negligence law.

The majority charge that, as former Supreme Court Justice Potter Stewart once said about obscenity, the *Dillon* guidelines mistakenly assumed that a court would know "duty" when it saw it. But more appropriate to the majority's opinion and the arbitrary and unjust results it will soon engender is what Potter Stewart said, very simply, upon being appointed to the United States Supreme Court: "Fairness is what justice really is." (*The Young Justice* (Oct. 20, 1958) Time, at p. 24.)

## NOTES

1. **The Physical Impact Rule.** Traditionally, courts would allow a plaintiff to recover damages for negligently inflicted emotional distress only where the plaintiff was physically impacted by the negligent act. The mental distress recoverable was, in essence, the pain and suffering associated with a negligently caused physical injury, such as a broken leg. The rule constituted a "limited duty" restricting liability for negligence causing mental distress to cases where physical impact was caused.

Virtually all courts have abandoned the physical impact rule. See Keeton, *Prosser and Keeton on* The Law of Torts, § 57 (5th ed. 1984); see also Diamond, Levine & Madden, *Understanding Torts* § 10.01 (2nd ed. 2000); Dobbs, *The Law of Torts* §§ 308–309 (2000). Certain factual patterns tended to discredit the rule. Consider *Christy Bros. Circus v. Turnage*, 38 Ga.App. 581, 144 S.E. 680 (Ga.Ct.App.1928), where the plaintiff, a spectator at a circus, was allowed to recover for mental distress, since technically the plaintiff suffered an impact, namely, horse droppings. Since the plaintiff suffered no physical injuries, the essence of the claim was pure mental distress. The injustice in the rule was further illustrated in *Mitchell v. Rochester Ry. Co.*, 151 N.Y. 107, 45 N.E. 354 (1896). The plaintiff suffered severe fright when she was nearly trampled by the defendant's on-coming horses. Her mental distress was so strong that it caused her to have a miscarriage. But since there was no physical impact, she was denied recovery. This led to the general adoption of the zone of danger rule discussed in Note 2, infra.

2. **The Zone of Danger Rule.** A slight majority of courts today limit recovery for negligently inflicted mental distress only to plaintiffs who either actually suffered impact or were in the zone of the physical risk of impact. The *Amaya* decision, discussed in the principal case but subsequently rejected by the California Supreme Court, utilized this approach. Consider *Tobin v. Grossman*, 24 N.Y.2d 609, 301 N.Y.S.2d 554, 249 N.E.2d 419 (1969), where a mother witnessed the immediate aftermath of an accident where her son was run over and seriously injured. The New York Court of Appeals reaffirmed its adherence to the majority zone of physical danger requirement and rejected the mother's negligent infliction of mental distress claim. The court noted that allowing recovery for some eyewitnesses to recover would provide "no rational practical boundary to limit liability.... It is enough that the law establishes liability in favor of those directly or intentionally harmed."

3. **The *Dillon* Factors.** A substantial minority of states expand liability for negligently inflicted mental distress to include, in addition to victims in the zone of physical danger, bystanders who satisfy the factors first formulated in *Dillon v. Legg*, 68 Cal.2d 728, 69 Cal.Rptr. 72, 441 P.2d 912 (1968), discussed in the principal case. The *Dillon* rule requires using the following guidelines to determine whether the defendant should be held liable for a bystander's mental distress: (1) whether the plaintiff was present at the scene of the accident; (2) whether the plaintiff's distress was caused by the sensory and contemporaneous observance of the accident; and (3)

whether the plaintiff has a close relationship with the victim. The Restatement 3rd notes that *Dillon* is in fact approaching a majority.

While not a specific requirement, some courts suggested that the event witnessed must be a sudden traumatic event. See *Fernandez v. Walgreen Hastings Co.*, 126 N.M. 263, 968 P.2d 774 (1998), in which a 22–month old died after a prescription medication failed to keep her airway unblocked because it was mis-filled. The grandmother claimed to be the "guardian, caretaker, and provider of parental affection" for the child as she cared for her during the workday. After her condition worsened despite doses of the medication, the mother drove them to the hospital; en route, the child stopped breathing and died in the grandmother's arms. The court held that "the hallmark of NIE is observation of a *sudden, traumatic, injury-producing event* and awareness that the event is causing injury to the victim. Because the occlusion of the granddaughter's airway was a progressive internal medical condition, and the grandmother did not know their cause and witnessed no causal event, the plaintiff did not meet the requirement of contemporaneous sensory perception of the accident."

**4. *Dillon*'s Direct, Contemporaneous Perception Requirement.** The requirement that the plaintiff have direct, contemporaneous sensory perception may be satisfied by non-visual perception of the accident. For example, in *Krouse v. Graham*, 19 Cal.3d 59, 137 Cal.Rptr. 863, 562 P.2d 1022 (1977), the plaintiff was sitting in his car while his wife unloaded groceries from the backseat. At this time, the defendant collided with the car and killed the plaintiff's wife. Although the husband did not see the collision, he nonetheless heard and perceived it and was allowed to recover. Jurisdictions following *Dillon*-like approaches differ over how strictly to apply the guideline that the third party perceive the accident while it is taking place.

The principal case represents California's decision to apply strictly the requirements as to who can recover for mental distress for bystanders under the minority *Dillon* approach. Some of the other states using the *Dillon* approach are more flexible and allow recovery for plaintiffs who have witnessed the immediate aftermath of an accident. Consider, for example, *Ferriter v. Daniel O'Connell's Sons, Inc.*, 381 Mass. 507, 413 N.E.2d 690 (1980), in which the wife and children of an employee injured in a construction accident sued for bystander mental distress. The plaintiffs were not present when the accident happened. Nor did they arrive on the scene immediately afterwards. The plaintiffs first saw the victim when they went to visit him in the hospital. Nevertheless, the court allowed their claim to proceed, commenting that "[s]o long as the shock follows closely on the heels of the accident," the action may be maintained.

By contrast, consider *Cortez v. Macias*, 110 Cal.App.3d 640, 167 Cal. Rptr. 905 (Cal.Ct.App.1980), consistent with the strict approach of the principal case, where the plaintiff was not allowed to recover. In *Cortez*, the plaintiff had unwittingly witnessed her child's death, believing only that the child was falling asleep. It was not until some time later, after she had paid her hospital bill, that she was informed that she had seen the child die. The court based its decision to deny recovery on the fact that the mental distress was triggered not by the observation itself, but by the subsequent information of what she had observed.

Consider also *Hathaway v. Superior Court*, 112 Cal.App.3d 728, 169 Cal.Rptr. 435 (1980), criticized by Justice Broussard in his dissent in the principal case. Plaintiffs' son was electrocuted by an evaporative cooler outside their house. The parents heard a scream and a cry to "let go," but were not alarmed. "A minute or two" later, a playmate of plaintiffs' son summoned the parents outside. Their son was "lying in a puddle of water by the cooler." He still had a "recognizable pulse and was gagging and spitting up." The father picked him up and watched fruitless efforts to revive the boy in a "dying state." Since the boy "was no longer gripping the water cooler and receiving the electrical charge ... the event which caused the accident had ended ... and the plaintiffs did not sensorially perceive the injury-causing event." Consequently, the court denied recovery for negligently inflicted mental distress to the parents.

How would the principal case justify *Hathaway* and *Cortez*? Are you persuaded? Did the *Ferriter* case draw a more appropriate line where recovery should be allowed or does the majority zone of danger view seem the best approach?

**5.** ***Dillon*'s Close Relationship Requirement.** The requirement of a close relationship has been construed by most jurisdictions using the *Dillon* rule as including married spouses, parents, children and siblings. For example, in *Elden v. Sheldon*, 46 Cal.3d 267, 250 Cal.Rptr. 254, 758 P.2d 582 (1988), the Supreme Court of California denied recovery for mental distress to a man who had witnessed the death of a woman with whom he had had a relationship "which was both stable and significant and parallel to a marital relationship." In reaching its decision, the court cited the importance of legal marriage, the burden on the courts that would be created by a need to inquire into non-marriage relationships, and the need to circumscribe defendants' potential liability. Some courts interpret the "close relationship requirement very strictly." Consider *Grotts v. Zahner*, 115 Nev. 339, 989 P.2d 415 (1999), in which the court denied recovery to a woman who witnessed the death of her fiancé on the ground that "any non-family relationship fails, as a matter of law, to qualify or NIED standing." Consider also *Moon v. Guardian Postacute Services*, 95 Cal.App.4th 1005, 116 Cal. Rptr.2d 218 (2002), where a California court denied recovery under *Dillon* to a son-in-law who went to visit his mother-in-law in a nursing home and found her with infected wounds and black and purple blisters on her feet. The court noted that a footnote in *Thing* suggested that a person who was not an immediate family member might be able to recovery in "exceptional circumstances," but that the fact that the plaintiff's mother-in-law had lived with him for five months did not suffice to create exceptional circumstances. What are the arguments against this restriction?

In 2001, California legislature passed a bill allowing registered "domestic partners" to recover for both NIED and wrongful death. Under this law, same sex couples, as well as opposite sex couples over the age of 62 are able to create a domestic partnership by filing with the secretary of state which requires that both partners share a common residence and agree to be jointly responsible for each other's care and living expenses. Cal.Fam.Code § 297, Cal.Civ.Code § 1714.01.

**6. Physical Manifestations of Mental Distress.** Most states, including both those following the majority zone of danger rule and those following the minority *Dillon* rule, require that the mental distress be evidenced by physical manifestations. A heart attack would certainly satisfy this requirement, and some courts have even allowed stomach trouble to constitute a physical manifestation. In *Olson v. Connerly*, 151 Wis.2d 663, 445 N.W.2d 706 (Wis.Ct.App.1989), a Wisconsin appellate court allowed severe abdominal pain to suffice. But in *Robbins v. Kass*, 163 Ill.App.3d 927, 114 Ill.Dec. 868, 516 N.E.2d 1023 (Ill. App. Ct. 1987), an Illinois appellate court held that crying, insomnia and migraine headaches were not a sufficient physical manifestation.

Other states, however, including California subsequent to *Dillon*, have eliminated the requirement that the patient produce evidence of physical manifestations. Consider, for example, *Hedlund v. Superior Court*, 34 Cal.3d 695, 194 Cal.Rptr. 805, 669 P.2d 41 (1983), in which the defendant psychotherapists allegedly failed to warn the plaintiff of the serious threat posed to her by one of their patients. The patient eventually carried out his threat and shot the plaintiff with a shotgun. The plaintiff's son, also a plaintiff, sued for negligently inflicted emotional distress, alleging that he had only suffered "emotional injuries and psychological trauma." The court held that this was adequate to state a cause of action and rejected the defendants' demurrer. Recall that most states do not require physical manifestation for intentional infliction of emotional distress. (See Chapter 1, Sec. F, supra.) Are there reasons to require physical manifestation?

**7. The Foreseeability Approach.** Some jurisdictions have experimented with allowing recovery whenever the plaintiff would be foreseeably distressed. Consider *Rodrigues v. State*, 52 Haw. 156, 472 P.2d 509 (Haw. 1970), in which the Supreme Court of Hawaii used the foreseeability standard to allow a plaintiff to maintain his suit for the mental distress he suffered when his new home flooded as the result of the defendant's alleged negligence. Since *Rodrigues*, however, Hawaii has retreated from this position. In *Kelley v. Kokua Sales & Supply, Ltd.*, 56 Haw. 204, 532 P.2d 673 (Haw. 1975), a grandfather was in California when he was told that his daughter and granddaughter had been killed and another granddaughter had been injured in an automobile accident allegedly due to the defendants' negligence. The court denied recovery, noting that even though the cause of action did not require a showing of physical impact, physical injury, or a blood relationship, it did require a showing that the plaintiff was within a reasonable distance of the scene of the accident. California was not within such a distance. Consider also *Wages v. First National Insurance Company of America*, 318 Mont. 232, 79 P.3d 1095 (2003), where the Supreme Court of Montana adopted a forseeability approach to NIED. In that case, the father of a child who was hit by a truck in the trailer park where he lived and suffered "bilateral pelvic fractures and complete uretheral disruption" sued to recover for NIED despite having been at work at the time of the accident, where he was notified and rushed to the hospital. The court noted that "duty and foreseeability are inextricably linked" and that a court may not "rely exclusively on the fact that a plaintiff was not a bystander to conclude that such a plaintiff is an unforeseeable plaintiff. Does this strike you as arbitrary? Does foreseeability sufficiently limit liability?

**8. Special Cases Permitting Recovery.** There are a few contexts in which courts may allow recovery for negligently inflicted mental distress without satisfying the majority zone of danger rule or minority *Dillon*-type requirements or require physical manifestation. These situations include improper handling of a relative's corpse or mistakenly informing the plaintiff that a relative has died. See Keeton § 54. Some courts have also even allowed a plaintiff to recover for the mental distress caused by a defendant's negligent damage of the plaintiff's chattel. Such cases, however, are typically limited to chattels that have a strong sentimental value.

Should property damage give rise to a claim for negligently inflicted mental distress? An Arizona appellate court answered this question in the negative in *Roman v. CarrolI*, 127 Ariz. 398, 621 P.2d 307 (Ariz.Ct.App. 1980), in which the plaintiff sued after witnessing the defendants' St. Bernard dismember her poodle.

In addition to allowing recovery when the conditions of the principal case are met, the California Supreme Court has allowed recovery when the plaintiff is characterized as a "direct victim." In *Molien v. Kaiser Foundation Hospitals*, the California court allowed a husband to recover for negligently inflicted mental distress when his wife was incorrectly diagnosed as having syphilis. The court reasoned that while the husband did not witness the negligent misdiagnosis, the physician also instructed the plaintiff to be tested, and consequently he was not a mere bystander but a direct victim.

In *Marlene F. v. Affiliated Psychiatric Medical Clinic*, 48 Cal.3d 583, 257 Cal.Rptr. 98, 770 P.2d 278 (1989), the California Supreme Court limited what constituted a direct victim to situations where the negligent defendant had a significant pre-existing relationship with the plaintiff or either assumed or had a legally imposed duty to the plaintiff. In *Marlene F.* the mother was able to recover for mental distress caused by a therapist who molested her son since the mother, as well as the son, had a professional relationship with the therapist. In *Schwarz v. Regents of University of California*, 226 Cal.App.3d 149, 276 Cal.Rptr. 470 (Cal.App. 1990), however, a father could not recover for emotional distress caused by his son's therapist's negligent treatment since the father was not also a patient.

Consider also the next principal case where the court had to evaluate in another context the limits to recovery for negligent infliction of mental distress.

## POTTER v. FIRESTONE TIRE AND RUBBER CO.

Supreme Court of California.

6 Cal.4th 965, 25 Cal.Rptr.2d 550, 863 P.2d 795 (1993).

BAXTER, Justice

\* \* \*

### I.

#### FACTUAL AND PROCEDURAL BACKGROUND

This is a toxic exposure case brought by four landowners living adjacent to a landfill. As a result of defendant Firestone's practice of disposing of its toxic wastes at the landfill, the landowners were subjected to prolonged exposure to certain carcinogens. While none of the landowners currently suffers from any cancerous or precancerous condition, each faces an enhanced but unquantified risk of developing cancer in the future due to the exposure.

\* \* \*

From 1963 until 1980, Firestone operated a tire manufacturing plant near Salinas. In 1967, Firestone contracted with Salinas Disposal

Service and Rural Disposal (hereafter SDS), two refuse collection companies operating the Crazy Horse landfill (hereafter Crazy Horse), for disposal of its industrial waste. Firestone agreed to deposit its waste in dumpsters provided by SDS located at the plant site. SDS agreed to haul the waste to Crazy Horse and deposit it there.

Crazy Horse, a class II sanitary landfill owned by the City of Salinas, covers approximately 125 acres suitable for the disposal of household and commercial solid waste. Unlike dump sites that are classified class I, class II landfills such as Crazy Horse prohibit toxic substances and liquids because of the danger that they will leach into the groundwater and cause contamination.

At the outset of their contractual relationship, SDS informed Firestone that no solvents, cleaning fluids, oils or liquids were permitted at Crazy Horse. Firestone provided assurances that these types of waste would not be sent to the landfill.

Notwithstanding its assurances, Firestone sent large quantities of liquid waste to Crazy Horse, including banbury drippings (a by-product of the tire manufacturing process) containing a combination of semiliquid toxic chemicals. Firestone also sent liquid waste oils, liquid tread end cements, and solvents to the landfill.

In May 1977, Firestone's plant engineer, who was in charge of all environmental matters, sent a memorandum to Firestone's plant managers and department heads. The memorandum, reflecting official plant policy, explained liquid waste disposal procedures and described the particular waste materials involved and the proper method of handling them.

In order to comply with this policy, Firestone initially made efforts to take the waste materials to a class I dump site. However, Firestone accumulated more waste than had been anticipated and disposing of the waste proved costly. When noncompliance with the policy became widespread, the plant engineer sent another memorandum to plant management complaining about the lack of compliance and pointing out that the policy was required by California law.

During this time, the Salinas plant operated under a production manager who had been sent from Firestone's company headquarters in Akron, Ohio, for the purpose of "turning the plant around" and making it more profitable. This manager became angered over the costs of the waste disposal program and decided to discontinue it. As a consequence, Firestone's hazardous waste materials were once again deposited at Crazy Horse.

Frank and Shirley Potter owned property and lived adjacent to Crazy Horse. Joe and Linda Plescia were their neighbors.

In 1984, the Potters and the Plescias (hereafter plaintiffs) discovered that toxic chemicals had contaminated their domestic water wells. The chemicals included: benzene; toluene; chloroform; 1,1–dichloroethene; methylene chloride; tetrachloroethene; 1,1,1–trichloroethane; trichloroethene; and vinyl chloride. Of these, both benzene and vinyl chloride are known to be human carcinogens. Many of the others are strongly suspected to be carcinogens.

\* \* \*

## II.

### DISCUSSION

\* \* \*

"Fear of cancer" is a term generally used to describe a present anxiety over developing cancer in the future. Claims for fear of cancer have been increasingly asserted in toxic tort cases as more and more substances have been linked with cancer. Typically, a person's likelihood of developing cancer as a result of a toxic exposure is difficult to predict because many forms of cancer are characterized by long latency periods (anywhere from 20 to 30 years), and presentation is dependent upon the interrelation of myriad factors.

The availability of damages for fear of cancer as a result of exposure to carcinogens or other toxins in negligence actions is a relatively novel issue for California courts. . . .

We must now consider whether, pursuant to California precedent, emotional distress engendered by the fear of developing cancer in the future as a result of a toxic exposure is a recoverable item of damages in a negligence action.

#### 1. *Parasitic Recovery: Immune System Impairment and/or Cellular Damage as Physical Injury*

Because it initially appeared plaintiffs might have suffered damage to their immune systems, we solicited the views of the parties on whether such damage constitutes physical injury. We did so because it is settled in California that in ordinary negligence actions for physical injury, recovery for emotional distress caused by that injury is available as an item of parasitic damages. (*Crisci v. Security Insurance Co.* (1967) 66 Cal.2d 425, 433 [58 Cal.Rptr. 13, 426 P.2d 173]; *Merenda v. Superior Court* (1992) 3 Cal.App.4th 1, 8–9 [4 Cal.Rptr.2d 87].) Where a plaintiff can demonstrate a physical injury caused by the defendant's negligence, anxiety specifically due to a reasonable fear of a future harm attributable to the injury may also constitute a proper element of damages. (E.g., *Jones v. United Railroads of San Francisco* (1921) 54 Cal.App. 744 [202 P. 919] [affirming damages for emotional distress endured up to time of trial where plaintiff reasonably feared permanent disability in the future as direct and proximate result from physical injury received in accident].)

Although the availability of parasitic damages for emotional distress engendered by a fear of developing cancer in the future appears to be an issue of first impression in California, other jurisdictions have concluded that such damages are recoverable when they are derivative of a claim for serious physical injuries. For example, the court in *Ferrara v. Galluchio* (1958) 5 N.Y.2d 16, 21–22 [176 N.Y.S.2d 996, 1000, 152 N.E.2d 249, 71 A.L.R.2d 331] upheld an award of emotional distress damages based on the plaintiff's fear of cancer where she had been negligently burned in X-ray treatments and later advised by a dermatologist to have her tissue examined every six months as cancer might develop. (Accord, *Dempsey v. Hartley* (E.D.Pa. 1951) 94 F.Supp. 918, 920–921 [fear of breast cancer due to traumatic breast injury]; *Alley v. Charlotte Pipe & Foundry Co.* (1912) 159 N.C. 327 [74 S.E. 885, 886] [fear stemming from sarcoma liable to ensue from burn wound].) In these cases, the existence of a present physical injury, rather than the degree of probability that the disease may actually develop, is determinative.

No California cases address whether impairment of the immune system response and cellular damage constitute "physical injury" sufficient to allow recovery for parasitic emotional distress damages. Courts in other jurisdictions that have considered this issue recently have come to differing conclusions.

\* \* \*

. . . . The statement of decision by the trial court does not include an express finding that plaintiffs' exposure to the contaminated well water resulted in physical injury, cellular damage or immune system impairment. The court made no mention of plaintiffs' immune system response, cellular systems or cells, and made no specific determination of damage or impairment thereto. While the trial court concluded that plaintiffs do have an enhanced "susceptibility" or "risk" for developing cancer and other maladies, it characterized this as a "presently existing physical condition," not as a physical injury. We conclude, therefore, that we lack an appropriate factual record for resolving whether impairment to the immune response system or cellular damage constitutes a physical injury for which parasitic damages for emotional distress ought to be available.

### 2. *Nonparasitic Fear of Cancer Recovery*

\* \* \*

We turn now to Firestone's argument that fear of cancer should be compensable only where the fear is based upon knowledge that cancer is probable, i.e., that it is more likely than not that cancer will develop. In evaluating this argument, we first consider whether it is reasonable for a person to genuinely and seriously fear a disease that is not probable, and if so, whether the emotional distress engendered by such fear warrants recognition as a compensable harm.

We cannot say that it would never be reasonable for a person who has ingested toxic substances to harbor a genuine and serious fear of cancer where reliable medical or scientific opinion indicates that such ingestion has significantly increased his or her risk of cancer, but not to a probable likelihood. Indeed, we would be very hard pressed to find that, as a matter of law, a plaintiff faced with a 20 percent or 30 percent chance of developing cancer cannot genuinely, seriously and reasonably fear the prospect of cancer. Nonetheless, we conclude, for the public policy reasons identified below, that emotional distress caused by the fear of a cancer that is not probable should generally not be compensable in a negligence action.

As a starting point in our analysis, we recognize the indisputable fact that all of us are exposed to carcinogens every day. As one commentator has observed, "[i]t is difficult to go a week without news of toxic exposure. Virtually everyone in society is conscious of the fact that the air they breathe, water, food and drugs they ingest, land on which they live, or products to which they are exposed are potential health hazards. Although few are exposed to all, few also can escape exposure to any." (Dworkin, *Fear Of Disease And Delayed Manifestation Injuries: A Solution Or A Pandora's Box?* (1984) 53 Fordham L. Rev. 527, 576, fns. omitted.)

Thus, all of us are potential fear of cancer plaintiffs, provided we are sufficiently aware of and worried about the possibility of developing cancer from exposure to or ingestion of a carcinogenic substance. The enormity of the class of potential plaintiffs cannot be overstated; indeed, a single class action may easily involve hundreds, if not thousands, of fear of cancer claims. (See Willmore, *In Fear of Cancerphobia* (Sept. 28, 1988) 3 Toxics L. Rptr. (Bur.Nat. Affairs) 559, 563 [hereafter Willmore].)

With this consideration in mind, we believe the tremendous societal cost of otherwise allowing emotional distress compensation to a potentially unrestricted plaintiff class demonstrates the necessity of imposing some limit on the class. (See *Borer v. American Airlines, Inc.* (1977) 19 Cal.3d 441, 447 [138 Cal.Rptr. 302, 563 P.2d 858] [hereafter *Borer*] [refusing to recognize a child's right to recover for the loss of a parent's consortium]; see also *Thing, supra,* 48 Cal.3d at pp. 664–665 [limiting bystander recovery of damages for negligent infliction of emotional distress].) . . .

A second policy concern that weighs in favor of a more likely than not threshold is the unduly detrimental impact that unrestricted fear liability would have in the health care field. As amicus curiae California Medical Association points out, access to prescription drugs is likely to be impeded by allowing recovery of fear of cancer damages in negligence cases without the imposition of a heightened threshold. To wit, thousands of drugs having no known harmful effects are currently being prescribed and utilized. New data about potentially harmful effects may not develop for years. If and when negative data are discovered and made public, however, one can expect numerous lawsuits to be filed by patients who currently have no physical injury or illness but who nonetheless fear the risk of adverse effects from the drugs they used. . . .

\* \* \*

A third policy concern to consider is that allowing recovery to all victims who have a fear of cancer may work to the detriment of those who sustain actual physical injury and those who ultimately develop cancer as a result of toxic exposure. That is, to allow compensation to all plaintiffs with objectively reasonable cancer fears, even where the threatened cancer is not probable, raises the very significant concern that defendants and their insurers will be unable to ensure adequate compensation for those victims who actually develop cancer or other physical injuries. Consider, for instance, that in this case damages totalling $800,000 for fear of cancer were awarded to four plaintiffs. If the same recovery were to be allowed in large class actions, liability for this one type of injury alone would be staggering. As one commentator astutely noted: "It would be a regrettable irony if in the rush to compensate the psychically injured we make it impossible to compensate those suffering of permanent and serious physical injuries." (Willmore, *supra*, 3 Toxics L. Rptr. at p. 563.)

A fourth reason supporting the imposition of a more likely than not limitation is to establish a sufficiently definite and predictable threshold for recovery to permit consistent application from case to case. (See *Thing, supra*, 48 Cal.3d at p. 664; *Elden v. Sheldon* (1988) 46 Cal.3d 267, 276 [250 Cal.Rptr. 254, 758 P.2d 582].) Indeed, without such a threshold, the likelihood of inconsistent results increases since juries may differ over the point at which a plaintiff's fear is a genuine and reasonable fear, i.e., one jury might deem knowledge of a 2 or 5 percent likelihood of future illness or injury to be sufficient (cf. *Heider v. Employers Mutual Liability Ins. Co.* (La.Ct.App. 1970) 231 So.2d 438, 442 [affirming award for plaintiff's fear of becoming epileptic where experts estimated likelihood at 2 to 5 percent]), while another jury might not. A more definite threshold will avoid inconsistent results and may contribute to early resolution or settlement of claims.

Finally, while a more likely than not limitation may foreclose compensation to many persons with genuine and objectively reasonable fears, it is sometimes necessary to "limit the class of potential plaintiffs if emotional injury absent physical harm is to continue to be a recoverable item of damages in a negligence action." (*Thing, supra*, 48 Cal.3d at p. 666.) We have recognized, in analogous contexts, that restricting the liability of a negligent tortfeasor for emotional loss may be warranted in consideration of the following factors: the intangible nature of the loss, the inadequacy of monetary damages to make whole the loss, the difficulty of measuring the damage, and the societal cost of attempting to compensate the plaintiff.... These considerations are equally relevant to fear of cancer claims in toxic exposure cases.

\* \* \*

To summarize, we hold with respect to negligent infliction of emotional distress claims arising out of exposure to carcinogens and/or other toxic substances: Unless an express exception to this general rule is recognized, in the absence of a present physical injury or illness, damages for fear of cancer may be recovered only if the plaintiff pleads and proves that (1) as a result of the defendant's negligent breach of a duty owed to the plaintiff, the plaintiff is exposed to a toxic substance which threatens cancer; *and* (2) the plaintiff's fear stems from a knowledge, corroborated by reliable medical or scientific opinion, that it is more likely than not that the plaintiff will develop the cancer in the future due to the toxic exposure. Under this rule, a plaintiff must do more than simply establish knowledge of a toxic ingestion or exposure and a significant increased risk of cancer. The plaintiff must further show that based upon reliable medical or scientific opinion, the plaintiff harbors a serious fear that the toxic ingestion or exposure was of such magnitude and proportion as to likely result in the feared cancer.

\* \* \*

## NOTES

1. **Fear of Future Harm.** Cases involving a fear of future harm typically arise in the context of toxic environmental torts or HIV exposure. Unlike the previous principal case, the mental distress is not induced by witnessing an injury or near injury, but anxiety over the risk of future harm or disease. The Fifth Circuit reached a more generous result in *Hagerty v. L. & L. Marine Services, Inc.*, 788 F.2d 315 (5th Cir.1986), which involved a seaman who had accidentally been drenched with toxic chemicals. The court held that "[w]ith or without physical injury or impact, a plaintiff is entitled to recover damages for serious mental distress arising from fear of developing cancer where his fear is reasonable and causally related to the defendant's negligence." Id. at 318. Did the court in *Potter* reach a sensible resolution? Is there a reason to be cautious about compensating for distress in these cases?

2. **Fear of Infectious Diseases.** Consider cases involving a fear of having contracted an infectious disease. In *Heiner v. Moretuzzo*, 73 Ohio St.3d 80, 652 N.E.2d 664 (Ohio 1995), the plaintiff alleged that the defendant negligently misdiagnosed her as being HIV positive. The plaintiff had a second test performed and found that she was in fact negative. She brought an action for negligent infliction of emotional distress caused by the fear she felt after the misdiagnosis. The court rejected her claim, holding that it would not allow recovery where the plaintiff was never actually at risk of any physical peril. A similar result was reached in *Montalbano v. Tri–Mac Enterprises of Port Jefferson, Inc.*, 236 A.D.2d 374, 652 N.Y.S.2d 780 (N.Y. Sup. Ct. App. Div. 1997), where a customer sued a fast food franchise after eating french fries which he later discovered had been covered with blood. The plaintiff alleged that he suffered mental distress from his fear of contracting HIV. Since the plaintiff did not demonstrate that he had in fact contracted the virus, or that there was even a plausible way for it to have entered his bloodstream, the court dismissed his claim.

In *Madrid v. Lincoln County Medical Center*, 122 N.M. 269, 923 P.2d 1154 (1996), the plaintiff sued the defendant medical center for her fear of having contracted HIV after open paper cuts on her hand were exposed to bloody fluids. She handled the fluids while transporting medical samples for the defendant. The court allowed the plaintiff to maintain her claim since there was a medically feasible means of transmission of the virus. The court remanded the case for findings of fact pertaining to when, if at all, the plaintiff found out (1) that the containers leaked and (2) whether the samples contained HIV. The court held, however, that the plaintiff did *not* need to prove that she was actually exposed to HIV. The court found persuasive the plaintiff's arguments distinguishing fear of cancer cases like *Potter* on the grounds that exposure to HIV is less common than exposure to carcinogens; that the period of fear of HIV contraction will be limited to six months, the time it takes for the disease to register in tests; and the fact that the required showing of a medically recognized means of transmission will limit the number of potential plaintiffs.

For a discussion of the causation issues raised in toxic tort cases, including medical monitoring, see Chapter 2, Sec. E, supra.

### 3. Wrongful Death and Survival Actions

Compare the different approaches used by the following three principal cases addressing wrongful death:

## GARY v. SCHWARTZ

Supreme Court, Trial Term, Nassau County.
72 Misc.2d 332, 339 N.Y.S.2d 39 (1972).

DANIEL G. ALBERT, Justice.

This is a wrongful death action brought by a mother, Barbara Gary, on behalf of her 16–year-old son, Robert, who suffered fatal injuries on the evening of October 27, 1969 when the bicycle on which he was riding was struck by the motor vehicle being driven by the defendant's 20–year-old son, David Schwartz. After a four-day trial the jury returned a verdict for the plaintiff in the amount of $100,510.40, comprised of special damages of $2,510.40 and general damages of $98,000.

The following morning both counsel appeared in the court's chambers and defendant's attorney presented his post-trial motion to set aside the verdict pursuant to article 44 of the CPLR on the grounds that the verdict was contrary to the weight of the evidence insofar as liability was concerned and that it was excessive insofar as the amount of damages was concerned. The motion is denied in all respects.

\* \* \*

It was established that on the evening in question, October 27, 1969 at 7:30 p.m., night had fallen. It was dark, the street lights were on, the intersection where the accident occurred was well lighted, visibility was good and defendant's headlights were on. (While the sole defendant is actually the owner of the vehicle and mother of the operator thereof, the term defendant shall be used for convenience to refer to the driver, since the owner's liability is based upon the conduct of the operator.) The decedent, Robert Gary, two months short of his 17th birthday, had been working on a term paper at his home which was located two houses in on Third Street just south of Waukena Avenue in Oceanside, Nassau County, the intersection where the fatal accident occurred. A senior in the local public high school, Robert left his house to go approximately three blocks to a candy store in order to purchase a stamp so that he could mail a college application that evening, and he rode his 14–year-old brother's bright orange small-wheeled bike which had a reflector and was covered with iridescent stickers, but which bore no light. As he returned home in a southerly direction along Third Street at about 7:30 p.m. and crossed Waukena Avenue, less than 50 yards from his house, his bike was struck by the motor vehicle driven westbound by the defendant. The decedent's mother, in the bathroom of her home, heard a crash which "shook the house," and when she rushed out along with her neighbors to discover what had happened she found her son lying on the northerly side of Waukena Avenue about three fourths of the way down to Fourth Street.

\* \* \*

While the plaintiff was not entitled to judgment as a matter of law, it was clearly within the province of the jury to conclude from the evidence presented that the defendant was negligent in the operation of his motor vehicle because he was speeding or driving recklessly or carelessly and failed to observe the decedent in sufficient time to avoid the accident, and similarly it could reasonably have concluded that the decedent used that measure of due care to be expected from a 16–year-old lad and that he did not fail to stop for the stop sign on Third Street at the corner of Waukena Avenue.

\* \* \*

Turning now to the second and far more troublesome branch of defendant's motion, i.e., to set the verdict for $100,510.40 aside as excessive, I am confronted with a state of the law which would appear to impose a simple accounting formula for ascertaining the pecuniary loss to a parent whose child has been wrongfully killed: probable wages of the child less cost of upkeep until the infant would have reached 21 years, a formula which "would almost always result in a minus figure." *Hoyt v. United States*, 286 F. 2d 356, 361 (5th Cir.1961). A perfunctory application of such a formula results in the irresistible conclusion that the verdict in this case is excessive in its entirety, and such a conclusion causes me to pause and reflect upon the circumstances of this case and the redress which should be available to a person such as the plaintiff herein, a widowed mother whose older son was tragically killed as a result of the defendant's negligence.

The decedent Robert Gary was not a 16–month-old baby whose character, personality, intellect and potential would be undefined and incalculable. On the contrary, he was a 16–year-old student, a highly intelligent, industrious and talented individual, a senior in high school, headed for premedical college and a dental career thereafter. He was short in height, his health was excellent, he participated in wrestling activities in school and loved all sports. According to the testimony adduced at the trial, he had passed his driver education course in high school and, had he lived, would have received his driver's license but two months after the fatal bicycle accident. He was a quiet, conservative lad who neither drank nor smoked, who dressed neatly, obeyed his parents, went to summer school to obtain better grades (although he had never failed any of his courses) and who did odd jobs in local shops and neighbors' homes since he was 13 years old in order to raise pin money with which he bought gifts for the family (a toaster, for example, as well as pearl earrings for mother, bathrobe for father), depositing the balance of any such moneys in the bank for college and other expenses. Robert was cautious when using tools; he did minor repair work and performed gardening tasks for his own family as well as for neighbors. One such neighbor, in fact, testified that Robert Gary did the gardening work around her home twice a week, that he worked hard and did a beautiful job, that he was a fine boy and that she "would have been proud to have had him as her grandson." Similarly, one of Robert's teachers who had known the boy for over five years testified that he would have been proud to have had Robert "as a son."

Thus we have a fairly accurate portrait of this 16–year-old youth, just two months shy of his 17th birthday, a high school senior preparing for college and a probable career in dentistry. He is now dead, and the jury is given the most difficult burden of determining the pecuniary loss to his mother and his younger brother on account of such death.

It is well known that a cause of action for wrongful death did not exist at common law, and perceiving the terrible inequities in such a state of the law our legislative bodies remedied the situation by enacting so-called wrongful death statutes, starting with Parliament in 1846 (Lord Campbell's Act) and culminating in this State with the adoption of part 4 of article 5 of EPTL in 1967.

Section 5–4.1 reads in pertinent part:

"The personal representative, duly appointed in this state or any other jurisdiction, of a decedent who is survived by distributees may maintain an action to recover damages for a wrongful act, neglect or default which caused the decedent's death against a person who would have been liable to the decedent by reason of such wrongful conduct if death had not ensued."

The amount which may be recovered in such an action is prescribed in section 5–4.3, which reads as follows:

"The damages awarded to the plaintiff may be such sum as the jury or, where issues of fact are tried without a jury, the court or referee deems to be fair and just compensation for the pecuniary injuries resulting from the decedent's death to the persons for whose benefit the action is brought. In every such action, in addition to any other lawful element of recoverable damages, the reasonable expenses of medical aid, nursing and attention incident to the injury causing death and the reasonable funeral expenses of the decedent paid by the distributees, or for the payment of which any distributee is responsible, shall also be proper elements of damage. Interest upon the principal sum recovered by the plaintiff from the date of the decedent's death shall be added to and be a part of the total sum awarded."

\* \* \*

.... What standard did the jury apply in this case to reach its conclusion that plaintiff Barbara Gary should receive $2,510.40 in special damages and $98,000 in general damages for the wrongful death of her 16–year-old son Robert? The court's instructions to the jury on the law of damages in this case, culled from the applicable statutory and decisional law, as well as the relevant Pattern Jury Instruction and the comments thereto (PJI 2:320), read as follows, without exception by either party:

"In the event, after applying the rules of law applicable to this case as I have charged, you find for the plaintiff Barbara Gary on her claim herein, then, in determining the damages sustained by the plaintiff you must apply the following rules of law.

\* \* \*

"With respect to plaintiff's cause of action the measure of damages is fixed by statute at 'such a sum as the jury . . . deems to be a fair and just compensation for the pecuniary injuries, resulting from the decedent's death, to the person or persons, for whose benefit the action is brought.' The present action is brought on behalf of decedent's mother, since his father died in July, 1972. Since the statute limits recovery to pecuniary injury, you may not consider or make any award for sorrow, mental anguish or injury to feeling or loss of companionship. You must appraise in an impartial manner to the best of your ability the pecuniary or money value of decedent to his mother and to his brother.

"In fixing that value you should take into consideration decedent's character, habits and ability; the circumstances and condition of his widowed mother, the services he would have performed for his mother had he lived; the portion of any earnings that he would in the future have applied to the care and support of his mother; decedent's age and life expectancy and the age and life expectancy of his mother. The evidence is that decedent was, at the time of his death 16 years of age and, according to the mortality tables, had a life expectancy of 53.24 years, and that his mother was then 38 years of age and had a life expectancy of 37.48 years. Mortality or life expectancy tables are, of course, nothing more than statistical averages. They neither assure the life spans that I have given nor assure that decedent's life span might not have been or that his mother's will not be greater. The figures I have given you are not binding upon you but may be considered by you together with the evidence you have heard concerning the health, habits, employment and activities of decedent prior to his death and of his mother in determining what their respective life expectancies were at the time he died.

"As I have stated, it is the pecuniary value of decedent to his mother that you must fix. That value is incapable of exact proof since it is prospective and contingent. Considering all of the elements to which I have referred, you must exercise your own common sense and sound judgment in fixing the amount of the pecuniary injuries suffered by decedent's mother. To the sum thus determined, you will add the reasonable expenses for medical aid, nursing and attention incident to the injury causing death, and for the funeral of and a burial lot for decedent, which were testified to as being $2,510.40. The total thus ascertained by you will constitute your verdict, if you find for the plaintiff.

"Where the decedent is a child, the pecuniary loss of the parent is measured by the services of the child during minority less the cost of his maintenance and education during that period, and in addition all the probable, or even possible, pecuniary benefits which might result to the parent from his life, modified as you the members of the jury find by all the chances of failure and misfortune. In considering benefits likely to result to the decedent's parent after the decedent had reached the age of 21 years, you must realize that the parent has no legal claim on the earnings of her adult child unless she becomes unable to support herself. The plaintiff's loss also includes the probability that she would benefit from earnings the child might have accumulated."

\* \* \*

. . . . I feel the jury in this case was eminently justified in granting this widow a pecuniary award of $100,000 for the wrongful death of her 16–year-old son who in all likelihood, based upon the evidence adduced at trial, would have faithfully borne the burden of caring for his mother and in aiding his younger brother, if necessary, upon the completion of his education.[2]

[The appellate court reviewing this decision of the trial court reduced the award without discussion to $52,510.40 including $2,510.40 for medical and funeral expenses. See *Gary v. Schwartz*, 349 N.Y.S.2d 322 (1973).]

## SELDERS v. ARMENTROUT
Supreme Court of Nebraska.
192 Neb. 291, 220 N.W.2d 222 (1974).

BOSLAUGH, Justice.

This is an action for damages for the wrongful death of Marcella Selders, Doureen Selders, and Gary Selders, minor children of Earl Selders and Ila Selders. The children died as a result of injuries sustained in an automobile accident on February 3, 1967.

The issue of the defendants' liability was determined in a previous trial. See *Selders v. Armentrout*, 190 Neb. 275, 207 N.W.2d 686. The sole issue tried in the lower court was the amount of damages which the plaintiffs should recover. The jury returned verdicts for the plaintiffs in the amount of $1,500 on each cause of action. The plaintiffs appeal, contending the verdicts were inadequate. . . .

\* \* \*

At the time of the accident which resulted in the death of the children the plaintiffs were separated. A decree of divorce had been

---

**2.** Evidence as to the widowed status of decedent's mother, whose husband died from a heart attack but four months prior to trial, was introduced without objection, but fairness and compassion, which have not yet been eradicated from our judicial precepts, would have dictated the admissibility of such evidence in any event, since it reduces in great part the degree of speculation in which the jury was required to indulge.

entered on October 10, 1966. The custody of the children had been awarded to Mrs. Selders, and they were living with her.

The verdicts included all pecuniary loss sustained by the plaintiffs including medical, hospital, and funeral expenses. Doureen was killed instantly in the accident. The medical and hospital expenses for Marcella and Gary amounted to $297.10. The funeral expenses for the three children amounted to $3,395. It was a question for the jury whether the funeral expense was reasonable in view of the ages of the children and all the facts and circumstances.

Marcella was 15 years of age, Doureen was 13, and Gary was 9. The evidence showed the deceased children had made no contribution of earnings other than to their own support. The evidence concerning the two other children in the family who were not involved in the accident showed they had left home when they became self-supporting and had contributed very little of a pecuniary nature to their parents.

The amount which should be awarded in any wrongful death case is incapable of computation and is largely a matter for the jury. As stated in *Dorsey v. Yost*, 151 Nev. 66, 36 N.W.2d 574, 14 A.L.R.2d 544: "The amount to which a parent is entitled cannot be accurately determined because of the numerous contingencies involved. The amount being very problematical, it is peculiarly for the jury to determine, after hearing all the evidence bearing upon the situation, including the parent's position in life, the physical and mental condition of the child, his surroundings and prospects, and any other matter that sheds light upon the subject. Members of juries generally have children of their own and have information as to the pecuniary value of children's services and the expense involved in their care and education. A jury is peculiarly fitted to determine the loss sustained by a parent in such a case. At best, the verdict can only be an approximation as no yardstick exists by which the correct answer can be found with exactness."

The evidence in this case was such that the jury could have concluded the pecuniary loss to the parents, including the value of society and companionship, was relatively small. We are unable to say under all the facts and circumstances the verdicts were inadequate.

\* \* \*

## COMPANIA DOMINICANA de AVIACION v. KNAPP

District Court of Appeal of Florida, Third District.
251 So.2d 18 (Fla.Dist.Ct.App.1971).

This action arose out of an airplane crash which took the lives of two of plaintiff's three sons when the aircraft crashed into the automobile paint and body shop on N.W. 36th Street in Miami where the boys were working at the time. On June 23, 1969 an airplane owned and operated by the defendant Compania Dominicana de Aviacion and insured by the defendant, Underwriters at Lloyds, London, took off from Miami International Airport. Immediately upon take-off, mechanical difficulties arose and the plane, in a matter of minutes, crashed in the N.W. 36th Street area as the pilot attempted to return to the airport.

Defendants appeal from a final judgment for plaintiff, Charles Knapp, as father of Clifford Knapp, a deceased minor, and as husband of Ethyle Knapp. The final judgment in this action for the wrongful death of one of the deceased sons was in the amount of $1,800,000 rendered on a jury verdict for the plaintiff. § 768.03, Fla.Stat., F.S.A.

We turn to appellant's contention that the jury verdict of $1,800,000 was excessive. If we had been members of the jury our verdict might not have been the same; but our function is to review the award made by the jury.

Wigginton, J., Dissenting in *Gresham v. Courson*, Fla.App.1965, 177 So.2d 33, 40, discussed both the elements of damages and the scope of appellate review of jury verdicts as follows:

"It is established law of this state that the determination by a trial jury of the amount of damages to be awarded in a given case is entitled to great weight and should not be disturbed by an appellate court merely because the individual members of the court disagree with the amount awarded and prefer to substitute their judgment for that of the jury. This is particularly true when the jury's verdict has been approved by the judge who tried the case, heard the evidence and is in position to better judge whether the verdict is illegal and should be set aside.

"The award by the jury to the plaintiffs in this case was for loss of services of their child which they could reasonably expect to receive prior to his maturity, and for the pain and suffering experienced by them as a result of his death."

This court in *Talcott v. Holl*, Fla.App.1969, 224 So.2d 420, 422, in reviewing a jury verdict for $1,500,000 in a personal injury action recently reiterated that a party who challenges the excessiveness of a jury verdict has the burden of showing a lack of support in the evidence or influence by prejudice. That case did not involve the instantaneous death of a minor child, and so is factually distinguishable.

Many of the Florida cases cited by appellants for reversal deal with awards to children younger than the deceased here, and many of these cases date between 1913 and the early 1940's. Two cases in particular merit discussion. First, *Seaboard Air Line Railroad Co. v. Gay*, Fla.App. 1967, 201 So.2d 238, affirmed an award of $80,000.00 for the death of a minor child, aged 12, to the surviving mother alone. This case was the largest verdict for the death of a minor child approved by a Florida appellate court. In *Seaboard Air Line Railroad Company v. Gay*, a twelve year old girl was killed as the result of a cartrain collision. The decision does not reveal whether the youngster had some extraordinary income-producing attributes but the court did say that it was " * * * confronted primarily with one element, the value of the mother's mental pain and anguish * * *." The second case is *Gresham v. Courson*, Fla.App.1965, 177 So.2d 33, where the First District Court over Judge Wigginton's dissent, reduced a $100,000.00 judgment to $50,000.00 entered in a wrongful death action for the death of an eleven month old only child of parents unable to have other children. The damages there were primarily for the past and future mental pain and suffering of both parents. Cf. *Holland Paving Co. v. Dann*, Fla.App.1964, 169 So.2d 849 and *Coast Cities Coaches, Inc. v. Donat*, Fla.App.1958, 106 So.2d 593.

In their brief opposing the motion for a new trial appellees cited numerous million dollar jury verdicts and several more recent cases were noted in their brief on appeal. Many are mere reports of trial verdicts which are not binding as precedent; they are also factually distinguishable as not being awards for the wrongful death of a minor.

The substance of the testimony of the numerous witnesses who testified as to the damages suffered is that Clifford Knapp was a fifteen year old graduate of junior high school about to enter high school in the fall. At the time of his death he was working at his father's paint and body shop, at no pay, for the summer. He was a good student, and a friendly, polite, warm, active and religious boy. He served as an acolyte at church. The Knapps had a close family relationship. He had his first and only date just two weeks prior to the crash. His church and recreational activities were detailed. A teacher testified that he stood head and shoulders above his contemporaries.

A psychiatrist, the long-time family physician, and family friends testified to the grief and anguish of the parents. Medication continued to be required after the funeral; a vacation to escape the tragedy was cut short because of Mrs. Knapp's continued depression.

Mrs. Knapp had been speaking to Clifford on the telephone when the plane crashed. Mr. Knapp was outside the building, and saw the tragedy unfold.

In conclusion, the verdict was determined by a carefully chosen jury after a lengthy trial before an experienced and knowledgeable judge with the assistance of the expert counsel for the parties. The judge who presided, in the exercise of his discretion, declined to grant a new trial or reduce the award because of claimed excessiveness. See generally *Cloud v. Fallis*, Fla.1959, 110 So.2d 669.

No one doubts that the verdict is large. No one doubts the enduring pain which the parents have suffered. Mr. Justice Terrell in *Winner v. Sharp*, Fla.1950, 43 So.2d 634, 636—637, explained with understanding the helpless anxiety caused by an unexpected, tragic death of a child.

It is our conclusion that the verdict and judgment are supported in law and fact, and no reversible error has been made to appear. Therefore the judgment appealed is affirmed.

Affirmed.

### NOTES

**1. No Action Under Common Law.** Historically, if the victim of a tort dies because of that tort, her relatives could not recover any damages. Influencing this common law view was the perception that it would be immoral to compensate a third party for someone's death. This position led to the awkward result that there would be an economic incentive to kill rather than to merely injure a victim and thereby avoid tort liability. While undoubtedly this incentive was mitigated by potential criminal liability, the potential injustice of a wealthy defendant causing a family to go destitute because of a tortious killing of the family's breadwinner (historically the husband/father) prompted states to modify the no-recovery rule for wrongful death by statute. This common law position has been altered by state statutes which authorize specific family members to sue when their relative dies from a tort. See Diamond, Levine & Madden, *Understanding Torts* § 10.03 (2nd ed. 2000); Keeton, *Prosser and Keeton On* The Law of Torts § 127 (5th ed. 1984) and Dobbs, *The Law of Torts*, §§ 296–297 (2000). See also *Sluder v. Marple*, 134 S.W.3d 15 (Ky.App.2003).

**2. Family Members Can Recover.** Generally, recovery in wrongful death actions is limited to family members, or "close relatives." These usually include a surviving spouse, parents, and children. Which relatives are included depends on the state's wrongful death statute. The requirement that the relative be indicated in the statute will operate to exclude long-term partners who are not legally married and close friends. Consequently, even a survivor who suffers loss due to a tortiously caused death will not be able to recover if she is not a qualifying relative. Note that all losses must be established with some degree of certainty, usually with reference to actuarial tables used to determine the value of the support the decedent would have provided to the particular claimant. A small number of statutes depart from this approach and compensate based on the decreased value of the decedent's estate due to his premature death.

Consider *Aspinall v. McDonnell Douglas Corp.*, 625 F.2d 325 (9th Cir.1980), in which the decedent had been living with a woman for four years and had been the sole support of her and her children. When he was killed in an airplane crash, the woman and her children sued to recover for his wrongful death. Because they were not defined as his heirs under the applicable probate code, the court denied recovery. The court reiterated that a wrongful death cause of action is strictly defined by statute and that the court was thus obligated to deny recovery. As obscured in Note 5 following Thing v. La Chusa supra, California extends wrongful death recovery to same-sex couples and opposite-sex couples over 62 in registered domestic partnerships. Cal. Fam. Code § 297, Cal. Civil Code § 714.01.

**3. Adopted Relatives.** How should adoption impact on the right to recover? Consider *Phraner v. Cote Mart, Inc.*, 55 Cal.App.4th 166, 63 Cal. Rptr.2d 740 (1997), where an adopted child could not recover in a suit for the wrongful death of her biological mother. The court looked to the California Probate Code in defining the parent-child relationship. In doing so, it held that the adoption had severed that relationship and that the plaintiff therefore was not legally a "child" of the victim.

Contrast *Phraner* with *Estate of Jones v. Howell*, 687 So.2d 1171 (Miss.1996), where relatives brought suit to determine whether the decedent's natural son, who had been adopted by another man, was a wrongful death beneficiary. The court held that even though the decedent's son might have a difficult time establishing particular damages in the wrongful death action, he may nevertheless bring a claim seeking the present net cash value of the father's life expectancy, and loss of companionship and society of the father between the time of injury and death, and punitive damages.

**4. Unborn Children.** Courts vary as to whether parents can recover for the wrongful death of an unborn child. For example, in *Wiersma v. Maple*

*Leaf Farms*, 543 N.W.2d 787 (S.D.1996), parents brought a wrongful death action against a frozen foods company for the seven-week-pregnant wife's miscarriage due to salmonella. The court held that South Dakota's wrongful death statute provided a cause of action for the loss of a non-viable unborn child.

**5. Damages.** The three principal cases reflect three different methods for measuring the amount of damages surviving relatives can recover in a wrongful death action. The historical and still majority position allows recovery for the pecuniary loss actually suffered by the plaintiffs. Under this theory, a surviving wife, for example, would have to prove how much monetary loss she suffered from the death of her husband. In such a case, the court would have to consider the husband's life expectancy, income potential, and generosity toward his wife. The economic value of a family member includes not only his cash gifts, but also the value of any services performed for the family, such as work in the home. Note that where courts rely on pecuniary loss, there may be less incentive to protect lower income workers or children. In the case of children, some commentators have advocated allowing parents to recoup their investment as the measurement of value for wrongful death.

An increasing number of states are allowing plaintiffs in wrongful death actions to recover not only pecuniary loss, but also the value of the companionship they have lost. Measuring the value of companionship is obviously a more subjective process than evaluating pecuniary loss. States adopting this position clearly think that pecuniary loss is an inadequate measurement. This is particularly true in cases involving deceased children and dependent elderly where courts may be hard pressed to find any economic loss, since the death may actually produce a net economic benefit once the cost of caring for the deceased is considered. The subjectivity involved with measuring the value of companionship may lead to surprisingly disparate results as the principal cases demonstrate. Consider also *Knowles v. Superior Court of San Diego County*, 118 Cal.App. 4th 1290, 13 Cal.Rptr.3d 700 (4 Dist. 2004), where the physician argued that because the mentally disabled child of the decedent believed his father was still alive, he could not establish wrongful death loss of companionship damages and therefore should be barred from recovery (his siblings were also suing for wrongful death). The court held that just because Nard believed his father was still alive, it did not mean that he did not suffer damages and does not appreciate the loss of his loved one. The children of a decedent in a wrongful death action are "entitled to reasonable compensation of the loss of love, companionship, comfort, affection, society, solace or moral support suffered as a result of the death." Suffering from mental retardation does not necessarily render a person less able to suffer loss of companionship damages.

The third approach, used by only a few states, allows recovery of damages for grief, in addition to compensation for pecuniary loss and lost companionship. Note that wrongful death actions are in addition to potential negligent infliction of mental distress claims (see Chapter 2, Sec. H, supra).

Which approach do you find preferable? Which is the fairest? Do you find any of the approaches objectionable?

# MURPHY v. MARTIN OIL CO.

Supreme Court of Illinois.

56 Ill.2d 423, 308 N.E.2d 583 (1974).

WARD, Justice:

The plaintiff, Charryl Murphy, as administratrix of her late husband, Jack Raymond Murphy, and individually, and as next friend of Debbie Ann Murphy, Jack Kenneth Murphy and Carrie Lynn Murphy, their children, filed a complaint in the circuit court of Cook County against the defendants, Martin Oil Company and James Hocker. Count I of the complaint claimed damages for wrongful death under the Illinois Wrongful Death Act and count II sought damages for conscious pain and suffering, loss of wages and property damage. The circuit court allowed the defendants' motion to strike the second count of the complaint on the ground that it failed to state a cause of action. When the court further ordered that there was no just reason for delaying enforcement or appeal from this order the plaintiffs then appealed the dismissal under Rule 304 (50 Ill.2d R. 304) to the appellate court. That court affirmed the dismissal of count II of the complaint as to its allegations of pain and suffering and reversed the judgment as to its allegations of loss of wages and property damage. The cause was remanded with directions to reinstate as much of count II as related to loss of wages and property damage. (4 Ill.App.3d 1015, 283 N.E.2d 243.) We granted the plaintiff's petition for leave to appeal.

The first count set out the factual background for the complaint. It alleged that on June 11, 1968, the defendants owned and operated a gasoline station in Oak Lawn, Cook County, and that on that date the plaintiff's decedent, Jack Raymond Murphy, while having his truck filled with gasoline, was injured through the defendants' negligence in a fire on the defendants' premises. Nine days later he died from the injuries. Damages for wrongful death were claimed under the Illinois Wrongful Death Act. (Ill.Rev.Stat.1971, ch. 70, pars. 1 and 2.) The language of section 1 of the statute is:

> "Whenever the death of a person shall be caused by wrongful act, neglect or default, and the act, neglect or default is such as would, if death had not ensued, have entitled the party injured to maintain an action and recover damages in respect thereof, then and in every such case the person who or company or corporation which would have been liable if death had not ensued, shall be liable to an action for damages, notwithstanding the death of the person injured, and although the death shall have been caused under such circumstances as amount in law to felony."

The second count of the complaint asked for damages for the decedent's physical and mental suffering, for loss of wages for the nine-day period following his injury and for the loss of his clothing worn at the time of injury. These damages were claimed under the common law and under our survival statute, which provides that certain rights of action survive the death of the person with the right of action. (Ill.Rev. Stat.1971, ch. 3, par. 339.) The statute states:

> "In addition to the actions which survive by the common law, the following also survive: actions of replevin, actions to recover damages for an injury to the person (except slander and libel), actions to recover damages for an injury to real or personal property or for the detention or conversion of personal property, actions against officers for misfeasance, malfeasance, or nonfeasance of themselves or their deputies, actions for fraud or deceit, and actions provided in Section 14 of Article VI of 'An Act relating to alcoholic liquors', approved January 31, 1934, as amended."

On this appeal we shall consider: (1) whether the plaintiff can recover for the loss of wages which her decedent would have earned during the interval between his injury and death; (2) whether the plaintiff can recover for the destruction of the decedent's personal property (clothing) at the time of the injury; (3) whether the plaintiff can recover damages for conscious pain and suffering of the decedent from the time of his injuries to the time of death.

This State in 1853 enacted the Wrongful Death Act and in 1872 enacted the so-called Survival Act (now section 339 of the Probate Act). This court first had occasion to consider the statutes in combination in 1882 in *Holton v. Daly*, 106 Ill. 131. The court declared that the effect of the Wrongful Death Act was that a cause of action for personal injuries, which would have abated under the common law upon the death of the injured party from those injuries, would continue on behalf of the spouse or the next of kin and would be "enlarged to embrace the injury resulting from the death." (106 Ill. 131, 140.) In other words, it was held that the Wrongful Death Act provided the exclusive remedy available when death came as a result of given tortious conduct. In considering the Survival Act the court stated that it was intended to allow for the survival of a cause of action only when the injured party died from a cause other than that which caused the injuries which created the cause of action. Thus, the court said, an action for personal injury would not survive death if death resulted from the tortious conduct which caused the injury.

This construction of the two statutes persisted for over 70 years. (E.g., *Wilcox v. International Harvester Co.* (1917), 278 Ill. 465, 472, 116 N.E. 151; *Susemiehl v. Red River Lumber Co.* (1941), 376 Ill. 138, 33 N.E.2d 211.) Damages, therefore, under the Wrongful Death Act were limited to pecuniary losses, as from loss of support, to the surviving spouse and next of kin as a result of the death. (*Ohnesorge v. Chicago City Ry. Co.* (1913), 259 Ill. 424, 102 N.E. 819.) Under the survival statute damages recoverable in a personal injury action, as for conscious pain and suffering, loss of earnings, medical expenses and physical disability, could be had only if death resulted from a cause other than the one which gave rise to the personal injury action.

This court was asked in 1941 to depart from its decision in *Holton v. Daly* and to permit, in addition to a wrongful death action, an action for personal injuries to be brought, though the injuries had resulted in the death of the injured person. This court acknowledged that there had been other jurisdictions which held contrary to *Holton v. Daly* and permitted the bringing of both actions, but the court said that any change in the rule in *Holton* must come from the legislature. (*Susemiehl v. Red River Lumber Co.* (1941), 376 Ill. 138, 33 N.E.2d 211.) In 1960, however, in *Saunders v. Schultz*, 20 Ill.2d 301, 170 N.E.2d 163, this court noted the absence of legislative action and permitted a widow to recover for funeral and medical expenses in an action which was independent of and in addition to an action brought by her for damages under the Wrongful Death Act. It was said:

> "Viewing the situation realistically, this liability of the surviving spouse for such expenses constitutes very real damages. Since that liability results from defendant's tortious conduct, it is only legally sound, and in accordance with basic negligence principles, that the burden of such damages should fall, not on the innocent victim, but upon the tortfeasor.

> The estate or the spouse, either or both as the circumstances indicate, are entitled to recover for pecuniary losses suffered by either or both which are not recoverable under the Wrongful Death Act, and all cases holding the contrary are overruled." 20 Ill.2d 301, 310—311, 170 N.E.2d 163, 168.

Later, in *Graul v. Adrian* (1965), 32 Ill.2d 345, 205 N.E.2d 444, this court approved an action brought for medical and funeral expenses of a child, which had been concurrently brought with an action brought under the Wrongful Death Act.

While the specific ground of decision in Graul was the family-expense section of the Husband and Wife Act (Ill.Rev.Stat.1961, ch. 68, par. 15), and though some have contended that *Saunders v. Schultz* was based on the liability of the widow there under the Husband and Wife Act, it has become obvious that the Wrongful Death Act is no longer regarded as the exclusive remedy available when the injuries cause death. Too, it is clear that the abatement of actions is not favored.

This disapproval of abatement was expressed in *McDaniel v. Bullard* (1966), 34 Ill.2d 487, 216 N.E.2d 140, where the parents and sister of an infant, Yvonne McDaniel, Daniel, had been killed in an automobile collision. An action was begun on behalf of Yvonne under the Wrongful Death Act and shortly after the filing of the action Yvonne died from causes which were unrelated to the collision. This court rejected the defendant's contention that the pending action under the Wrongful Death Act was abated or extinguished upon Yvonne's death. In holding that an action under the Wrongful Death Act survived under the terms of the Survival Act upon the death of the victim's next of kin, this court said, at pages 493–494, 216 N.E.2d at page 144: "Today damages from most torts are recognized as compensatory rather than punitive, and there is no reason why an estate that has been injured or depleted by the wrong of another should not be compensated whether the injured party is living or not. (Citation.) The rule of abatement has its roots in archaic conceptions of remedy which have long since lost their validity. The reason having ceased the rule is out of place and ought not to be perpetuated." We concluded that under the Survival Act the action for wrongful death did not abate but might be maintained for the benefit of Yvonne's estate.

This disfavoring of abatement and enlarging of survival statutes has been general. In Prosser, Handbook of *The Law of Torts* (4th ed. 1971), at page 901, it is said: "(T)he modern trend is definitely toward the view that tort causes of action and liabilities are as fairly a part of the estate of either plaintiff or defendant as contract debts, and that the question is rather one of why a fortuitous event such as death should extinguish a valid action. Accordingly, survival statutes gradually are being extended; and it may be expected that ultimately all tort actions will survive to the same extent as those founded on contract." And at page 906 Prosser observes that where there have been wrongful death and survival statutes the usual holding has been that actions may be concurrently maintained under those statutes. The usual method of dealing with the two causes of action, he notes, is to allocate conscious pain and suffering, expenses and loss of earnings of the decedent up to the date of death to the survival statute, and to allocate the loss of benefits of the survivors to the action for wrongful death.

As the cited comments of Prosser indicate, the majority of jurisdictions which have considered the question allow an action for personal injuries in addition to an action under the wrongful death statute, though death is attributable to the injuries. Recovery for conscious pain and suffering is permitted in most of these jurisdictions. (See Speiser, Recovery For Wrongful Death, sec. 11:31 (1966).) Permitting decisions include: *Louisville & N.R.R. Co. v. Porter* (1920), 205 Ala. 131, 87 So. 288; *Erhart v. Hummonds* (1960), 232 Ark. 133, 334 S.W.2d 869; *McCoy v. Raucci* (1968), 156 Conn. 115, 239 A.2d 689;*Coulson v. Shirks Motor Express Corp.* (1954), 9 Terry 561, 48 Del. 561, 107 A.2d 922; *Smith v. Laskey* (Fla.App.1969), 222 So.2d 773; *Rosenthal v. O'Neal* (1963), 108 Ga.App. 54, 132 S.E.2d 150; *Furumizo v. United State* (D.Hawaii 1965), 245 F.Supp. 981, aff'd (9 Cir. 1967), 381 F.2d 965; *Fitzgerald v. Hale* (1956), 247 Iowa 1194, 78 N.W.2d 509; *J. Wilton Jones Co. v. Liberty Mutual Insurance Co.* (1970 La.App.), 248 So.2d 878, appeal denied (1971), 259 La. 61, 249 So.2d 202; *Campbell v. Romanos* (1963), 346 Mass. 361, 191 N.E.2d 764; *Gabrish v. Morse* (1960), 361 Mich. 39, 104 N.W.2d 757; *Sandifer Oil Co. v. Dew* (1954), 220 Miss. 609, 71 So.2d 752; *Marinkovich v. Tierney* (1932), 93 Mont. 72, 17 P.2d 93; *Foster v. Maldonado* (D.N.J.1970), 315 F.Supp. 1179, appeal denied (3 Cir.) 433 F.2d 348; *Stang v. Hertz Corp.* (N.M.App.1969), 81 N.M. 69, 463 P.2d 45, aff'd (1970), 81 N.M. 348, 467 P.2d 14; *O'Neil v. State* (Ct.Cl.1971), 66 Misc.2d 936, 323 N.Y.S.2d 56; *Fielder v. Ohio Edison Co.* (1952), 158 Ohio St. 375, 109 N.E.2d 855; *Skoda v. West Penn. Power Co.* (1963), 411 Pa. 323, 191 A.2d 822; *Brooks v. United States* (D.S.C.1967), 273 F.Supp. 619; *Plank v. Heirigs* (1968), 83 S.D. 173, 156 N.W.2d 193; *Louisville & N.R.R. Co. v. Tucker* (6th Cir. 1954), 211 F.2d 325; *Mitchell v. Akers* (Tex.Civ.App.1966), 401 S.W.2d 907; *Legg v. Britton* (1890), 64 Vt. 652, 24 A. 1016; *Ide v. Wamser* (1964), 22 Wis.2d 325, 126 N.W.2d 59.

Too, recovery is allowed under the Federal Employers' Liability Act for a decedent's conscious pain and suffering provided it was not substantially contemporaneous with his death. *Great Northern R.R. Co. v. Capital Trust Co.* (1916), 242 U.S. 144, 37 S.Ct. 41, 61 L.Ed. 208; *Wetherbee v. Elgin, Joliet & Eastern Ry. Co.* (7th Cir. 1951), 191 F.2d 302.

We consider that those decisions which allow an action for fatal injuries as well as for wrongful death are to be preferred to this court's holding in *Holton v. Daly* that the Wrongful Death Act was the only remedy available when injury resulted in death.

The holding in *Holton* was not compelled, we judge, by the language or the nature of the statutes examined. The statutes were conceptually separable and different. The one related to an action arising upon wrongful death; the other related to a right of action for personal injury arising during the life of the injured person.

The remedy available under *Holton* will often be grievously incomplete. There may be a substantial loss of earnings, medical expenses, prolonged pain and suffering, as well as property damage sustained, before an injured person may succumb to his injuries. To say that there can be recovery only for his wrongful death is to provide an obviously inadequate justice. Too, the result in such a case is that the wrongdoer will have to answer for only a portion of the damages he caused. Incongruously, if the injury caused is so severe that death results, the wrongdoer's liability for the damages before death will be extinguished. It is obvious that in order to have a full liability and a full recovery there must be an action allowed for damages up to the time of death, as well as thereafter. Considering "It is more important that the court should be right upon later and more elaborate consideration of the cases than consistent with previous declarations" (*Barden v. Northern Pacific R.R. Co.* (1894), 154 U.S. 288, 322, 14 S.Ct. 1030, 1036, 38 L.Ed. 992, 1000), we declare *Holton* and the cases which have followed it overruled. What this court observed in *Molitor v. Kaneland Community Unit Dist. No. 302* (1959), 18 Ill.2d 11, 26, 163 N.E.2d 89, 96, may appropriately be said again:

> "We have repeatedly held that the doctrine of *stare decisis* is not an inflexible rule requiring this court to blindly follow precedents and adhere to prior decisions, and that when it appears that public policy and social needs require a departure from prior decisions, it is our duty as a court of last resort to overrule those decisions and establish a rule consonant with out present day concepts of right and justice. (*Bradley v. Fox*, 7 Ill.2d 106, 111, 129 N.E.2d 699; *Nudd v. Matsoukas*, 7 Ill.2d 608, 615, 131 N.E.2d 525; *Amann v. Faidy*, 415 Ill. 422, 114 N.E.2d 412.)"

For the reasons given, the judgment of the appellate court is affirmed insofar as it held that an action may be maintained by the plaintiff for loss of property and loss of wages during the interval between injury and death, and that judgment is reversed insofar as it held that the plaintiff cannot maintain an action for her decedent's pain and suffering.

Affirmed in part; reversed in part.

## NOTES

**1. Survival Actions.** Historically a victim's tort claims died with the victim. Survival statutes allow the heirs of the decedent to inherit the victim's potential tort actions and pursue those claims in court. While jurisdictions generally allow property torts to survive, many will not allow survival of a tort providing for recovery of a purely intangible injury, such as mental distress. Personal injury actions often survive, although some states, such as California, will allow only the economic consequences of the personal injury, and not the pain and suffering, to survive. See C.C.P. 377.60. See also Diamond, Levine and Madden, Understanding Torts § 10.03[D] (2nd Ed. 2000). Should a deceased plaintiff's pain and suffering survive her death?

While the principal case utilizes a survival action where the wrongful death action is also being brought, most survival actions involve a decedent who already had an action pending at the time of their death, but who died for unrelated reasons before the proceedings could be completed. For example, if A is suing B for a negligence, but A dies before the suit is adjudicated, A's heirs can continue prosecuting A's negligence suit against B. Since a tort action is devisable by will, it does not need to be brought by a close relative of the decedent, unlike a wrongful death action. Typically, the decedent's will does not mention the decedent's tort action. In such cases, those designated to receive the decedent's residual property receive the right to bring the survival action.

**2. Claims Must be Viable to Survive.** Consider *Nelson v. American National Red Cross*, 26 F.3d 193 (D.C.Cir.1994), in which the son of a patient who received blood contaminated with HIV brought a survival action against the hospital and blood supplier. The court held that because the statute of limitations would have barred the patient at the time of his death from bringing a negligence action, the patient's son could not maintain a survival action after his father's death. Similarly, in *Alexander v. Whitman*, 114 F.3d 1392 (3d Cir.1997), a mother brought a survival action on behalf of her stillborn child. The court, citing *Roe v. Wade*, 410 U.S. 113, 93 S.Ct. 705, 35 L.Ed.2d 147 (1973), held that the lower court's dismissal of the claim did not violate due process since the fetus could not be considered a person and thus had no equal protection under the laws.

**3. Bringing Claims Together.** Considering the value of a victim's pain and suffering which most states allow to survive and the possible additional value of lost wages during the injury prior to death when the death is not immediate, plaintiffs seeking to maximize their recovery will bring both a wrongful death action and a survival action. What claims were brought in the principal case?

**4. The O.J. Simpson Case.** Although O.J. Simpson was acquitted for criminal homicide charges alleging that he killed Nicole Simpson and Ronald Goldman, he was found liable for wrongful death and survival claims under tort law. The wrongful death claim under California law would include pecuniary and companionship losses suffered by the surviving relatives. California does not, however, permit punitive damages for a wrongful death action except where the defendant has been convicted of felonious homicide. See Civ.Code § 3294(d). Since Mr. Simpson was acquitted of the criminal charges, it was strategic for the plaintiffs to bring a claim alleging property torts, however minor, suffered by the victims during the period of the alleged attack, since those torts survive the decedent's death and allowed the heirs of the victims to be awarded 25 million dollars in punitive damage awards. See *Rufo v. Simpson*, 86 Cal.App.4th 573, 103 Cal.Rptr.2d 492 (2001). See also Weinstein, "Size of Punitive Damages is Justified Legal Experts Say," *Los Angeles Times* (2/11/99), A19.

Consider also *Stencel Aero Engineering Corp. v. Superior Court*, 56 Cal.App.3d 978, 128 Cal.Rptr. 691 (1976). The pilot of an airplane was killed during a sequence of events which commenced while piloting the aircraft on the ground. The pilot activated an ejection mechanism intended to project him into the air where his parachute was designed to open and allow his safe descent to the ground. The pilot was killed on impact after his parachute failed to open. The pilot's personal property, consisting of a watch, a wallet, and a small kit containing personal articles was alleged to have been damaged by the rocket blast of the ejection mechanism. Since the pilot's personal effects, valued at over $200, were damaged "seconds—no more, but not less" prior to the pilot's death, the court ruled the pilot's property damage tort survived his death and could be basis for awarding $10,000 in punitive damage. As noted above, California law precluded punitive damages for the wrongful death action, but not for torts against a decedent which preceded his death.

### 4.  Loss of Consortium and Society

## BORER v. AMERICAN AIRLINES, INC.

Supreme Court of California, In Bank.
19 Cal.3d 441, 138 Cal.Rptr. 302, 563 P.2d 858 (1977).

TOBRINER, Acting Chief Justice.

In *Rodriguez v. Bethlehem Steel Corp.* (1974) 12 Cal.3d 382 [115 Cal.Rptr. 765, 525 P.2d 669], we held that a married person whose spouse had been injured by the negligence of a third party may maintain a cause of action for loss of "consortium." We defined loss of "consortium" as the "loss of conjugal fellowship and sexual relations" (12 Cal.3d at p. 385), but ruled that the term included the loss of love, companionship, society, sexual relations, and household services. Our decision carefully avoided resolution of the question whether anyone other than the spouse of a negligently injured person, such as a child or a parent, could maintain a cause of action analogous to that upheld in *Rodriguez*. We face that issue today: the present case presents a claim by nine children for the loss of the services, companionship, affection and guidance of their mother; the companion case of *Baxter v. Superior Court, post*, page 461 [138 Cal.Rptr. 315, 563 P.2d 871] presents the claim of a mother and father for the loss of the companionship and affection of their 16-year-old son.

* * *

... Plaintiffs, the nine children of Patricia Borer, allege that on March 21, 1972, the cover on a lighting fixture at the American Airlines Terminal at Kennedy Airport fell and struck Patricia. Plaintiffs further assert that as a result of the physical injuries sustained by Patricia, each of them has been "deprived of the services, society, companionship, affection, tutelage, direction, guidance, instruction and aid in personality development, all with its accompanying psychological, educational and emotional detriment, by reason of Patricia Borer being unable to carry on her usual duties of a mother." The complaint sets forth causes of action based upon negligence, breach of warranty, and manufacture of a defective product; it names as defendants American Airlines, two companies which manufactured and assembled the lighting fixture, and various fictitious defendants. Each plaintiff seeks damages of $100,000.

\* \* \*

Our analysis of plaintiffs' appeal begins with our decision in *Rodriguez v. Bethlehem Steel Corp., supra*, 12 Cal.3d 382. In holding that a spouse has a cause of action for loss of consortium, we considered the proffered argument that such a holding would logically require us to uphold an analogous cause of action in the parent-child context or in even more distant relationships; we rejected that contention.

\* \* \*

The decision whether to limit liability for loss of consortium by denying a cause of action in the parent-child context, or to permit that action but deny any claim based upon more remote relationships, is thus a question of policy. As explained by Justice Fleming in *Suter* v. *Leonard* (1975) 45 Cal.App.3d 744, 746 [120 Cal.Rptr. 110]: "Plaintiff's claim, viewed in the abstract and divorced from its surroundings, carries both logical and sympathetic appeal.... Certain aspects of spousal relationship are similar to those of the parent-child relationship, and there can be little question of the reality of the loss suffered by a child deprived of the society and care of its parent. Nevertheless our decision must take into account considerations in addition to logical symmetry and sympathetic appeal.... [N]ot every loss can be made compensable in money damages, and legal causation must terminate somewhere. In delineating the extent of a tortfeasor's responsibility for damages under the general rule of tort liability (Civ. Code, § 1714), the courts must locate the line between liability and nonliability at some point, a decision which is essentially political."

In the first instance, strong policy reasons argue against extension of liability to loss of consortium of the parent-child relationship. Loss of consortium is an intangible, nonpecuniary loss; monetary compensation will not enable plaintiffs to regain the companionship and guidance of a mother; it will simply establish a fund so that upon reaching adulthood, when plaintiffs will be less in need of maternal guidance, they will be unusually wealthy men and women. To say that plaintiffs have been "compensated" for their loss is superficial; in reality they have suffered a loss for which they can never be compensated; they have obtained, instead, a future benefit essentially unrelated to that loss.

We cannot ignore the social burden of providing damages for loss of parental consortium merely because the money to pay such awards comes initially from the "negligent" defendant or his insurer. Realistically the burden of payment of awards for loss of consortium must be borne by the public generally in increased insurance premiums or, otherwise, in the enhanced danger that accrues from the greater number of people who may choose to go without any insurance.

\* \* \*

A second reason for rejecting a cause of action for loss of parental consortium is that, because of its intangible character, damages for such a loss are very difficult to measure.

Plaintiffs point out that similar policy arguments could be, and to some extent were, raised in *Rodriguez*, and that our decision to uphold the wife's action for loss of consortium rejected those arguments. We do not, however, read *Rodriguez* as holding that arguments based upon the intangible character of damages and the difficulty of measuring such damages do not merit consideration. Such a holding would imply an indefinite extension of liability for loss of consortium to all foreseeable relationships, a proposition *Rodriguez* plainly repudiates.

*Rodriguez*, then, holds no more than that in the context of a spousal relationship, the policy arguments against liability do not suffice to justify a holding denying a cause of action. Plaintiffs contend, however, that no adequate ground exists to distinguish a cause of action for loss of spousal consortium from one for loss of parental consortium. We reject the contention for three reasons.

First, as *Rodriguez* pointed out, the spousal action for loss of consortium rests in large part on the "impairment or destruction of the sexual life of the couple." (12 Cal.3d 382, 405.) No similar element of damage appears in a child's suit for loss of consortium.

Second, actions by children for loss of parental consortium create problems of multiplication of actions and damages not present in the spousal context.

\* \* \*

The instant case illustrates the point. Patricia Borer has nine children, each of whom would possess his own independent right of action for loss of consortium. Even in the context of a consolidated action, the assertion of nine independent causes of action for the children in addition to the father's claim for loss of consortium and the mother's suit for ordinary tort damages, demonstrates the extent to which recognition of plaintiffs' asserted cause of action will multiply the tort liability of the defendant.

Finally, the proposition that a spouse has a cause of action for loss of consortium, but that a child does not, finds overwhelming approval in the decisions of other jurisdictions. . . .

We reject, finally, plaintiffs' claim that denial of a cause of action for loss of parental consortium is inconsistent with the principles of tort law laid down in prior decisions of this court.

Plaintiffs place particular emphasis on *Dillon v. Legg* (1968) 68 Cal.2d 728 [69 Cal.Rptr. 72, 441 P.2d 912, 29 A.L.R.3d 1316], which upheld a cause of action for injuries flowing from a mother's emotional trauma in witnessing the death of her child. We suggested that the cause of action should be sustained whenever the injury was "reasonably foreseeable" (p. 741), and that one factor to be considered was "whether plaintiff and the victim were closely related." (*Ibid*.) Plaintiffs urge that we follow that paradigm for decision of the instant case.

In *Dillon*, however, we carefully limited our ruling to a case in which the plaintiff suffered physical injury. (68 Cal.2d at p. 740.) Subsequent decisions, interpreting our holding in *Dillon*, have refused to recognize a cause of action in a case in which the plaintiff suffered no physical injury himself as a result of witnessing the infliction of injury upon a family member. (See *Krouse v. Graham, ante*, p. 59 at pp. 77–78 [137 Cal.Rptr. 863, 562 P.2d 1022]; Capelouto v. *Kaiser Foundation Hospitals* (1972) 7 Cal.3d 889, 892 fn. 1 [103 Cal.Rptr. 856, 500 P.2d 880]; *Hair v. County of Monterey, supra*, 45 Cal.App.3d 538, 542.) Thus *Dillon* and subsequent authority support our decision in this case to deny a cause of action founded upon purely intangible injury.

We therefore conclude that we should not recognize a cause of action by a child for loss of parental consortium.[3] Plaintiffs contend, however, that such a conclusion would distinguish between the rights of the child in the present context and the rights afforded him in a wrongful death action, without any rational basis for the distinction in contravention of the equal protection of the laws.

\* \* \*

We perceive two significant distinctions between the child whose parent is killed and one whose parent is disabled, both of which flow from the fact that in the latter case the living victim retains his or her own cause of action. The first distinction relates to the historical purpose of the wrongful death statutes. By 1846, the date of the enactment of the first wrongful death statute, the common law courts had settled that the heirs of a deceased victim could not bring a cause of action against the tortfeasor. (See 1 Speiser, Recovery for Wrongful Death (2d ed. 1975) §§ 1.1, 1.2.) "The result was that it was more profitable for the defendant to kill the plaintiff than to scratch him, and that the most grievous of all injuries left the bereaved family of the victim, who frequently were destitute, without a remedy." (Prosser, Torts (4th ed. 1971) p. 902.) This loophole in the law curtailed the deterrent function of tort recovery, providing to tortfeasors a substantial incentive to finish off their victims. The wrongful death statutes thus met an obvious logical and social need.

Similar policy reasons led the courts to permit the bereaved to recover for the loss of the affection and society of the deceased. As stated in *Krouse v. Graham*, "if damages truly were limited to 'pecuniary' loss, recovery frequently would be barred by the heirs' inability to prove such loss. The services of children, elderly parents, or nonworking spouses

---

**3.** The considerations which lead us to reject a cause of action for negligent injury to consortium in a parent-child context do not bar an action for intentional interference with parental consortium. An action for intentional interference with consortium, recognized by precedent in California (see *Rosefield* v. *Rosefield* (1963) 221 Cal. App.2d 431 [34 Cal.Rptr. 479]) is a relatively unusual tort that presents no danger of multiplication of claims or damages. The ruling, moreover, may serve to deter child stealing and similar antisocial conduct.

often do not result in measurable net income to the family unit, yet unquestionably the death of such a person represents a substantial 'injury' to the family." (*Ante*, at p. 68.) Recovery for loss of affection and society in a wrongful death action thus fulfills a deeply felt social belief that a tortfeasor who negligently kills someone should not escape liability completely, no matter how unproductive his victim.

A suit for loss of consortium of a disabled parent presents a wholly different picture. Here the tortfeasor cannot escape with impunity, for the immediate victim of his tort retains a cause of action for the injuries inflicted. The claim by the child in this setting is not essential to prevent the tortfeasor from totally escaping liability.

Secondly, the wrongful death action serves as the only means by which the family unit can recover compensation for the loss of parental care and services in the case of the wrongful death of the parent. While the parent lives, however, "the tangible aspects of the child's loss can be compensated in the parent's *own* cause of action. As put by Stainback, J., in *Halberg v. Young, supra*, 41 Hawaii 634, 640 . . . , 'where a parent has been injured by the negligent act of another the parent will recover from the other full damage which he has sustained, including such inability, if any, to properly care for his children, and thus the parent's ability to carry out his duty to support and maintain the child has not, in a legal sense, been destroyed or impaired by the injury to him.' " (*Suter v. Leonard, supra*, 45 Cal.App.3d 744, 748.)

We conclude that the distinction between the award of damages for loss of affection and society to a child whose parent has been tortiously killed, and the denial of such damages to a child whose parent has been disabled, rests upon a rational basis. Plaintiffs' constitutional argument therefore fails.

In summary, we do not doubt the reality or the magnitude of the injury suffered by plaintiffs. We are keenly aware of the need of children for the love, affection, society and guidance of their parents; any injury which diminishes the ability of a parent to meet these needs is plainly a family tragedy, harming all members of that community. We conclude, however, that taking into account all considerations which bear on this question, including the inadequacy of monetary compensation to alleviate that tragedy, the difficulty of measuring damages, and the danger of imposing extended and disproportionate liability, we should not recognize a nonstatutory cause of action for the loss of parental consortium.

The judgment is affirmed.

### NOTES

**1. Loss of Consortium.** Loss of consortium actions compensate the plaintiff for the loss of society and companionship suffered when another person is injured or the relationship is otherwise tortiously disrupted. Historically, only a husband could sue for loss of consortium when his wife was tortiously injured. The reason for this was that the wife was viewed as a mere possession of the husband. The case was analogous to seeking property damages. Therefore, the husband was entitled to compensation for the loss of services, companionship and sexual relations occasioned by an injury to the wife. The husband's action was in addition to the wife's primary action for the injury. As the principal case indicates, modern courts allow a wife to bring a loss of consortium action when her husband has been injured. See Diamond, Levine & Madden, *Understanding Torts* § 10.03 (1996). See also Keeton, *Prosser and Keeton On* The Law of Torts § 127 (5th ed. 1984).

    **2. Who Can Recover.** Loss of consortium actions usually are permitted only in the spousal context, and even then are almost always limited to legally married spouses. Should significant others be able to recover?

    Contrary to the principal case, a minority of other courts have allowed parents and children to sue for loss of consortium. The cases are generally based on a serious injury to the victim. Even in those states that do allow parent-child loss of consortium cases to go forward, courts may refuse to expand the right to recover any further. Consider *Hutchinson v. Broadlawns Medical Center*, 459 N.W.2d 273 (Iowa 1990), where the court held that the plaintiff could not sue for the loss of consortium of her grandfather, even though the grandfather had provided care, support and discipline as would a parent. Similarly, in *Miller v. Boden*, 103 Ohio App.3d 73, 658 N.E.2d 809 (Ohio Ct.App.1995), the court held that the plaintiff stepmother, who had assumed a parental role, was precluded from recovering loss of consortium damages resulting from the death of her stepdaughter since the biological mother had not "disclaimed or abandoned her parental rights."

    Loss of consortium can be based on intentional torts as well as negligence claims. For example, an intentional battery can lead to a claim for intentionally inflicted loss of consortium. In these cases, some states, such as California, as noted in the principal case, are more willing to allow parents and children to recover for loss of consortium.

    **3. Types of Harm.** Many loss of consortium cases address a direct interference with the plaintiff's relations with the third party. For example, in *Ex parte N.P. (K.P. v. Reed)*, 676 So.2d 928 (Ala.1996), when a husband brought a malpractice suit related to his penis surgery, his wife brought a derivative claim for loss of consortium. The court held that the evidence was sufficient to prove that the wife had suffered loss of consortium due to the defendant's malpractice. But see *Zwicker v. Altamont Emergency Room Physicians Medical Group*, 98 Cal.App.4th 26, 118 Cal.Rptr.2d 912 (Cal.App. 3 Dist. 2002), where the court did not allow recovery for an injury to the testicle when the injury occurred prior to marriage. Here the Court of Appeals of California held that a wife could not sue for loss of consortium for the physician's failure to diagnose her husband's condition in time to prevent the loss of his testicle and his subsequent infertility, because she was not married to him at the time. She suffered no actionable loss as the result of the physician's alleged negligence, even though she discovered he was permanently infertile some time after the marriage.

    Courts have also sustained loss of consortium claims even where the interference is not derived from a physical injury to the spouse. Consider *Molien v. Kaiser Foundation Hospitals*, 27 Cal.3d 916, 167 Cal.Rptr. 831, 616 P.2d 813 (1980), in which the defendant had misdiagnosed the plaintiff's wife as having syphilis, leading to the wife's assumption that the plaintiff had committed adultery. The plaintiff brought a loss of consortium claim in addition to his mental distress claim for the interference with his marriage. The court sustained his claims.

To allow recovery, the defendant's conduct must have been tortious. Thus, in *Tate v. Derifield*, 510 N.W.2d 885 (Iowa 1994), when a wife filed suit for loss of consortium against a police informant and the government agencies responsible for her husband's arrest and incarceration, the court rejected her claim since the defendants' conduct had not been wrongful; the lawfulness of the arrest and incarceration had been established by the husband's conviction.

**4. Distinguishing Wrongful Death Claims.** Although not the traditional majority rule, an increasing number of states allow surviving relatives in wrongful death actions to sue for "loss of companionship" in addition to "pecuniary" losses narrowly defined. The loss of consortium tort addresses such damages during the period of time when the spouse is injured while wrongful death addresses loss of companionship after death. (See Chapter 2, Sec. 3, supra). It is possible an injury, where the victim dies after an extended period of time, will lead to a loss of consortium and wrongful death claim by a surviving relative.

## 5. Wrongful Life and Wrongful Birth

### TURPIN v. SORTINI

Supreme Court of California.

31 Cal.3d 220, 182 Cal.Rptr. 337, 643 P.2d 954 (1982).

KAUS, Justice.

This case presents the question of whether a child born with an hereditary affliction may maintain a tort action against a medical care provider who—before the child's conception—negligently failed to advise the child's parents of the possibility of the hereditary condition, depriving them of the opportunity to choose not to conceive the child. Although the overwhelming majority of decisions in other jurisdictions recognize the right of *the parents* to maintain an action under these circumstances, the out-of-state cases have uniformly denied *the child's* right to bring what has been commonly termed a "wrongful life" action. In *Curlender v. Bio–Science Laboratories* (1980) 106 Cal.App.3d 811 [165 Cal.Rptr. 477], however, the Court of Appeal concluded that under California common law tort principles, an afflicted child could maintain such an action and could "recover damages for the pain and suffering to be endured during the limited life span available to such a child and any special pecuniary loss resulting from the impaired condition" (*id.*, at p. 831), including the costs of medical care to the extent such costs were not recovered by the child's parents. In the case at bar, a different panel of the Court of Appeal disagreed with the conclusion in *Curlender* and affirmed a trial court judgment dismissing the child's cause of action on demurrer. We granted a hearing to resolve the conflict.

I

The allegations of the complaint disclose the following facts. On September 24, 1976, James and Donna Turpin, acting on the advice of their pediatrician, brought their first—and at that time their only— daughter, Hope, to the Leon S. Peters Rehabilitation Center at the Fresno Community Hospital for evaluation of a possible hearing defect.

Hope was examined and tested by Adam J. Sortini, a licensed professional specializing in the diagnosis and treatment of speech and hearing defects.

The complaint alleges that Sortini and other persons at the hospital negligently examined, tested and evaluated Hope and incorrectly advised her pediatrician that her hearing was within normal limits when, in reality, she was "stone deaf" as a result of an hereditary ailment. Hope's parents did not learn of her condition until October 15, 1977, when it was diagnosed by other specialists. According to the complaint, the nature of the condition is such that there is a "reasonable degree of medical probability" that the hearing defect would be inherited by any offspring of James and Donna.

The complaint further alleges that in December 1976, before learning of Hope's true condition and relying on defendants' diagnosis, James and Donna conceived a second child, Joy. The complaint avers that had the Turpins known of Hope's hereditary deafness they would not have conceived Joy. Joy was born August 23, 1977, and suffers from the same total deafness as Hope.

On the basis of these facts, James, Donna, Hope and Joy filed a complaint setting forth four causes of action against defendants Sortini, the hospital, the rehabilitation center and various Does.... The second cause of action—the only cause before us on this appeal—was brought on behalf of Joy and seeks (1) general damages for being "deprived of the fundamental right of a child to be born as a whole, functional human being without total deafness" and (2) special damages for the "extraordinary expenses for specialized teaching, training and hearing equipment" which she will incur during her lifetime as a result of her hearing impairment.

Defendants demurred to the second and fourth causes of action, and after briefing and argument, the trial court sustained the demurrer without leave to amend. Thereafter, the court entered a judgment dismissing the action as to Joy. As noted, Joy's action is the only matter before us on this appeal.

## II

Although this is the first case in which we have faced the question of potential tort liability in a "wrongful life" or "wrongful birth" context, there is no dearth of authority in this area. In recent years, many courts in other jurisdictions have confronted similar claims brought by both parents and children against medical professionals whose negligence had allegedly proximately caused the birth of hereditarily afflicted children. The overwhelming majority of the recent cases have permitted parents to recover at least some elements of damage in such actions. (See, e.g., *Robak v. United States* (7th Cir. 1981) 658 F.2d 471; *Schroeder* v. *Perkel* (1981) 87 N.J. 53 [432 A.2d 834]; *Berman v. Allan* (1979) 80 N.J. 421 [404 A.2d 8, 13–15]; *Becker* v. *Schwartz* (1978) 46 N.Y.2d 401 [413 N.Y.S.2d 895, 386 N.E.2d 807, 813–814]; *Speck v. Finegold* (1981) 497 Pa. 77 [439 A.2d 110, 111–112]; *Jacobs v. Theimer* (Tex. 1975) 519 S.W.2d 846; *Dumer v. St. Michael's Hospital* (1975) 69 Wis.2d 766 [233

N.W.2d 372, 376–377, 83 A.L.R.3d 1].) At the same time, the out-of-state authorities have uniformly rejected the children's own claims for general damages. (See, e.g., *Berman v. Allan, supra,* 404 A.2d at pp. 11–13; *Becker v. Schwartz, supra,* 386 N.E.2d at pp. 811–812; *Speck v. Finegold, supra,* 439 A.2d at p. 112, affirming by an equally divided ct. (1979) 268 Pa. Super. 342 [408 A.2d 496, 508]; *Dumer v. St. Michael's Hospital, supra,* 233 N.W.2d at pp. 374–376; *Elliot v. Brown* (Ala. 1978) 361 So.2d 546.)

The explanation for the divergent results is that while courts have been willing to permit parents to recover for medical costs or—in some cases—other harms which the parents would not have incurred "but for" the defendants' negligence, they have been reluctant to permit the child to complain when, but for the defendant's negligence, he or she would not have been born at all. In this context the recent decisions have either concluded that the child has sustained no "legally cognizable injury" or that appropriate damages are impossible to ascertain.

While our court has not yet spoken on the question, three California Court of Appeal decisions have addressed somewhat related claims. *Custodio v. Bauer* (1967) 251 Cal.App.2d 303 [59 Cal.Rptr. 463, 27 A.L.R.3d 884], the earliest California case in this area, involved an action brought solely by parents against a physician whose negligence in performing a sterilization operation failed to prevent the plaintiff wife's pregnancy and the birth of a healthy child—the family's 10th. The *Custodio* court, applying generally applicable tort principles, upheld the parents' right to bring the action. Although the court did not define the full scope of recoverable damages in such an action (*Id.,* at pp. 318–326), it did indicate the that numerous items of damage normally recoverable in a tort action could properly be awarded. (*Id.,* at pp. 318–326.)

In the second case, *Stills v. Gratton* (1976) 55 Cal.App.3d 698 [127 Cal.Rptr. 652], both an unmarried mother and her healthy son brought consolidated actions against several doctors who had negligently performed a therapeutic abortion, leading to the unexpected and unwanted birth of the child. With respect to the mother's claim, the *Stills* court followed *Custodio* and permitted the action, concluding that she could recover "all the damages to which she is entitled under ordinary tort principles [subject to] . . . any offsets for benefits conferred and amounts chargeable to a plaintiff under her duty to mitigate damages." (*Id.,* at p. 709.)

With respect to the son's claim, however, the court determined that no cause of action would lie. Although the child had alleged that "he was born out of wedlock and that 'various reasons' affect him to his detriment" (*Id.,* at p. 705), the *Stills* court noted that the testimony at trial disclosed that the boy "was and is a healthy, happy youngster who is a joy to his mother" (*ibid.*) and thus that "[h]is only damages, if any, caused by the respondents' conduct is in being born." (*Ibid.*) Relying on earlier Illinois and New York decisions which had rejected similar wrongful life claims by healthy children of unmarried parents (*Zepeda v. Zepeda* (1963) 41 Ill.App.2d 240 [190 N.E.2d 849]; *Williams v. State* (1966) 25 App.Div.2d 906 [269 N.Y.S.2d 786]), the *Stills* court denied the son's action, suggesting that "[t]he issue involved is more theological or philosophical than legal." (55 Cal.App.3d at p. 705.)

The third and most recent Court of Appeal decision in this area is *Curlender v. Bio–Science Laboratories, supra,* 106 Cal.App.3d 811, an action brought solely on behalf of a child, not her parents. Unlike *Custodio* and *Stills,* in which the defendants' negligence had led to the births of healthy, albeit unplanned, children, in *Curlender* the child-plaintiff was afflicted with Tay–Sachs disease, a fatal illness "characterized by partial or complete loss of vision, mental underdevelopment, softness of the muscles, convulsions, etc." in which the child has a very reduced life span. (*Id.,* at p. 815, fn. 4, quoting Schmidt's Attorneys' Dict. of Medicine (1980).) The principal defendant in *Curlender* was a medical laboratory which allegedly had been negligent in performing blood tests which the child's parents had undergone for the specific purpose of determining if their offspring were likely to suffer from Tay–Sachs disease.

In *Curlender,* the court reviewed the out-of-state and California precedents in this area at some length. The court distinguished *Stills* as a case in which the unwanted but healthy child had suffered no "injury," and concluded that the severely afflicted child in the case before it had suffered an injury which could properly be the basis of an action in tort. ( *Id.,* at p. 825.) Disagreeing with the out-of-state decisions which had found that a child who has been born with serious hereditary defects as opposed to not being born at all has suffered no legally cognizable injury, the *Curlender* court stated: "The reality of the 'wrongful life' concept is that such a plaintiff *exists* and *suffers,* due to the negligence of others. It is neither necessary nor just to retreat into meditation on the mysteries of life. We need not be concerned with the fact that had defendants not been negligent, the plaintiff might not have come into existence at all. The certainty of genetic impairment is no longer a mystery. In addition, a reverent appreciation of life compels recognition that plaintiff, however impaired she may be, has come into existence.as a living person with certain rights." (Original italics.) (*Id.,* at p. 829.)

Taking up the issue of damages, the *Curlender* court rejected the plaintiff's request for damages "based upon an actuarial life expectancy ... of more than 70 years—the life expectancy if plaintiff had been born without Tay–Sachs disease" (*id.,* at p. 830) but, at the same time, also rejected "the notion that a 'wrongful life' cause of action involves any attempted evaluation of a claimed right *not* to be born." (Original italics.) (*Id.,* at pp. 830–831.) Instead, the court held that in such an action a child may "recover damages for the pain and suffering to be endured during the limited life span available to such a child and any special pecuniary loss resulting from the impaired condition." (*Id.,* at p. 831.) The court also made it clear that, to the extent that the costs of care were not recovered by the child's parents in a separate or consolidated action, the child should be permitted to recover such costs in her own suit. (*Ibid.*)

Plaintiff, of course, relies heavily—indeed exclusively—on the *Curlender* decision in support of her action in this case. Before analyzing

*Curlender* and the out-of-state wrongful life decisions, however, we briefly consider the effect of a new statute enacted in the wake of *Curlender*.

## III

As noted, the defendant in *Curlender* was a medical laboratory which allegedly had been negligent in conducting blood tests. In the course of its opinion, however, the *Curlender* court indicated in dictum that in an appropriate case parents of a seriously impaired infant, who, with full knowledge of the child's likely condition, "made a conscious choice to proceed with a pregnancy" (*id.*, at p. 829) could be held liable "for the pain, suffering and misery which they have wrought upon their offspring." (*Ibid.*)

In evident response to this suggestion of possible parental liability for deciding to conceive or failing to abort a potentially defective child, the Legislature enacted section 43.6 of the Civil Code, effective January 1, 1982. Section 43.6 relieves the parents of any liability in this situation and also provides that the parents' decision shall neither be "a defense in any action against a third party" nor "be considered in awarding damages in any such action." (Stats. 1981, ch. 331, § 1.)

We conclude that section 43.6 has no significant effect on the issue before us. In this case, of course, the child is suing allegedly negligent providers of medical services, not her parents, and thus the statute clearly poses no explicit bar to the action. Although subdivision (b) of the provision implicitly recognizes that, under *Curlender*, a wrongful life action may lie against a "third party," we do not think that the statute can properly be viewed as a legislative codification of the *Curlender* holding, transforming the common law tort perceived in *Curlender* into a statutory cause of action. Both the Legislative Counsel's Digest accompanying the bill, and the adjacent sections in the Civil Code (see, e.g., Civ. Code, §§ 43.4, 43.5, 43.5, subd. (a), 43.7, 43.8, 43.9), suggest that the purpose of the legislation was simply to eliminate any liability or other similar economic pressure which might induce potential parents to abort or decline to conceive a potentially defective child. Nothing in the statutory language or legislative history suggests that the new provision was intended to impose liability on any party. Under these circumstances, the section cannot properly be read as creating a *statutory* wrongful life cause of action against third parties. In sum, the new statute does not change the fact that the issue before our court is whether, and to what extent, such a cause of action should be recognized as a matter of California common law.

## IV

In analyzing *Curlender, Stills* and the numerous out-of-state cases, it may be helpful to recognize that although the cause of action at issue has attracted a special name—"wrongful life"—plaintiff's basic contention is that her action is simply one form of the familiar medical or professional malpractice action. The gist of plaintiff's claim is that she has suffered harm or damage as a result of defendants' negligent performance of their professional tasks, and that, as a consequence, she is entitled to recover under generally applicable common law tort principles.

\* \* \*

[D]efendants' basic position—supported by the numerous out-of-state authorities—is that Joy has suffered no legally cognizable injury or rationally ascertainable damages as a result of their alleged negligence. Although the issues of "legally cognizable injury" and "damages" are intimately related and in some sense inseparable, past cases have generally treated the two as distinct matters and, for purposes of analysis, it seems useful to follow that approach.

With respect to the issue of legally cognizable injury, the parties agree that the difficult question here does not stem from the fact that defendants' allegedly negligent act and plaintiff's asserted injury occurred before plaintiff's birth. Although at one time the common law denied recovery for injuries inflicted before birth, California—in tune with other American jurisdictions—has long abandoned that arbitrary limitation. (See Civ. Code, § 29; *Scott v. McPheeters* (1939) 33 Cal.App.2d 629 [92 P.2d 678]. See generally Robertson, *Toward Rational Boundaries of Tort Liability for Injury to the Unborn: Prenatal Injuries, Preconception Injuries and Wrongful Life* (1978) 1978 Duke L.J. 1401, 1402–1413.) Thus, if Joy's deafness was caused by negligent treatment of her mother during pregnancy, or if it resulted from a tort committed upon her mother before conception (see, e.g., *Renslow v. Mennonite Hospital* (1977) 67 Ill.2d 348 [367 N.E.2d 1250]; *Bergstreser* v. *Mitchell* (8th Cir. 1978) 577 F.2d 22; Annot. (1979) 91 A.L.R.3d 316), it is clear that she would be entitled to recover against the negligent party.

\* \* \*

.... In this case ... the obvious tragic fact is that plaintiff never had a chance "to be born as a whole, functional human being without total deafness"; if defendants had performed their jobs properly, she would not have been born with hearing intact, but—according to the complaint—would not have been born at all.

\* \* \*

.... [I]n fixing damages in a tort case the jury generally compares the condition plaintiff would have been in but for the tort, with the position the plaintiff is in now, compensating the plaintiff for what has been lost as a result of the wrong. Although the valuation of pain and suffering or emotional distress in terms of dollars and cents is unquestionably difficult in an ordinary personal injury action, jurors at least have some frame of reference in their own general experience to appreciate what the plaintiff has lost—normal life without pain and suffering. In a wrongful life action, that simply is not the case, for what the plaintiff has "lost" is not life without pain and suffering but rather the unknowable status of never having been born. In this context, a rational, nonspeculative determination of a specific monetary award in accordance with normal tort principles appears to be outside the realm of human competence.

The difficulty in ascertaining or measuring an appropriate award of general damages in this type of case is also reflected in the application of what is sometimes referred to as the "benefit" doctrine in tort damages. Section 920 of the Restatement Second of Torts—which embodies the general California rule on the subject (see, e.g., *Maben* v. *Rankin* (1961) 55 Cal.2d 139, 144 [10 Cal.Rptr. 353, 358 P.2d 681])—provides that "[w]hen the defendant's tortious conduct has caused harm to the plaintiff ... and in so doing has conferred a special benefit to the interest of the plaintiff that was harmed, the value of the benefit conferred is considered in mitigation of damages, to the extent that this is equitable."

In requesting general damages in a wrongful life case, the plaintiff seeks monetary compensation for the pain and suffering he or she will endure because of his or her hereditary affliction. Under section 920's benefit doctrine, however, such damages must be offset by the benefits incidentally conferred by the defendant's conduct "to the interest of the plaintiff that was harmed." With respect to general damages, the harmed interest is the child's general physical, emotional and psychological well-being, and in considering the benefit to this interest which defendant's negligence has conferred, it must be recognized that as an incident of defendant's negligence the plaintiff has in fact obtained a physical existence with the capacity both to receive and give love and pleasure as well as to experience pain and suffering. Because of the incalculable nature of both elements of this harm-benefit equation, we believe that a reasoned, nonarbitrary award of general damage is simply not obtainable.

* * *

## V

Although we have determined that the trial court properly rejected plaintiff's claim for general damages, we conclude that her claim for the "extraordinary expenses for specialized teaching, training and hearing equipment" that she will incur during her lifetime because of her deafness stands on a different footing.

As we have already noted, in the corresponding "wrongful birth" actions parents have regularly been permitted to recover the medical expenses incurred on behalf of such a child. (See, e.g., *Schroeder* v. *Perkel, supra,* 87 N.J. 53 [432 A.2d 834, 841]; *Speck* v. *Finegold, supra,* 439 A.2d 110, 111; *Robak* v. *United States, supra,* 658 F.2d 471, 478; *Becker* v. *Schwartz, supra,* 386 N.E.2d 807, 813; *Dumer* v. *St. Michael's Hospital, supra,* 233 N.W.2d 372, 377; *Jacobs* v. *Theimer, supra,* 519 S.W.2d at p. 849.) In authorizing this recovery by the parents, courts have recognized (1) that these are expenses that would not have been incurred "but for" the defendants' negligence and (2) that they are the kind of pecuniary losses which are readily ascertainable and regularly awarded as damages in professional malpractice actions.

Although the parents and child cannot, of course, both recover for the same medical expenses, we believe it would be illogical and anomalous to permit only parents, and not the child, to recover for the cost of the child's own medical care. If such a distinction were established, the afflicted child's receipt of necessary medical expenses might well depend on the wholly fortuitous circumstance of whether the parents are available to sue and recover such damages or whether the medical expenses are incurred at a time when the parents remain legally responsible for providing such care.

\* \* \*

Moreover, permitting plaintiff to recover the extraordinary, additional medical expenses that are occasioned by the hereditary ailment is also consistent with the established parameters of the general tort "benefit" doctrine discussed above. As we have seen, under that doctrine an offset is appropriate only insofar as the defendant's conduct has conferred a special benefit "to the interest of the plaintiff that was harmed." Here, the harm for which plaintiff seeks recompense is an economic loss, the extraordinary, out-of-pocket expenses that she will have to bear because of her hereditary ailment. Unlike the claim for general damages, defendants' negligence has conferred no incidental, offsetting benefit to this interest of plaintiff. (Cf. *Schroeder v. Perkel, supra,* 432 A.2d at p. 842.) Accordingly, assessment of these special damages should pose no unusual or insoluble problems.

## VI

In sum, we conclude that while a plaintiff-child in a wrongful life action may not recover general damages for being born impaired as opposed to not being born at all, the child—like his or her parents—may recover special damages for the extraordinary expenses necessary to treat the hereditary ailment.

The judgment is reversed and the case is remanded to the trial court for further proceedings consistent with this opinion.

### *NOTES*

**1. Wrongful Life.** The birth of a child can prompt tort litigation in different ways. The principal case addresses the most controversial claim, wrongful life. Under wrongful life, the child claims the defendant's negligence caused the child's own birth. The child is *not* alleging the defendant caused any health disability she may suffer from, only that the child would otherwise have not been born. Potential defendants include physicians who negligently perform an abortion or vasectomy or provide incorrect genetic counseling. As the principal case notes the California legislature enacted a law protecting parents from their child's claims that her own parents were negligent in conceiving or not aborting her. *Turpin* limits the child's recovery to the extra expenses that are prompted by the child's disability, although as noted above there is no allegation the defendant caused the disability. Consequently a healthy child, however dissatisfied with being born, is precluded from bringing a wrongful life claim in California.

Almost all other states reject the concept that a child can sue for being born. New Jersey, however, follows the California approach. Consider *Pro-*

*canik v. Cillo*, 97 N.J. 339, 478 A.2d 755 (1984) where a physician negligently failed to diagnose the mother's German measles during the first trimester of pregnancy. The seriously disabled baby was allowed to sue for extraordinary medical expenses occasioned by his disability. As in the principal case there was no allegation the physician could have prevented the disability, but only that a correct diagnosis might have prompted action to prevent the birth. In *Moscatello v. University of Medicine and Dentistry of New Jersey*, 342 N.J.Super. 351, 776 A.2d 874 (2001), the court noted that "the validity of the wrongful life cause of action in New Jersey has been reaffirmed on several occasions since the *Procanik* decision." See Diamond, Levine & Madden, *Understanding Torts* § 10.02 (2d ed. 2000); Keeton, *Prosser and Keeton on Torts* § 55 (5th ed. 1984); and Dobbs, *The Law of Torts* §§ 291–293 (2000).

Consider also *Anderson v. St. Francis–St. George Hospital, Inc.*, 77 Ohio St.3d 82, 671 N.E.2d 225 (Ohio 1996) where the court rejected a claim that the plaintiff's life had been wrongfully extended when resuscitation efforts were undertaken against the patient's instruction to the hospital.

Consider *Hummel v. Reiss*, 129 N.J. 118, 608 A.2d 1341 (1992), where the New Jersey Supreme Court held that "no wrongful-life cause of action exists for children who were born before *Roe v. Wade*." The court noted that the cause of action for wrongful-life is tied in to the availability of lawful eugenic abortions, and because there was no guarantee of this right prior to *Roe v. Wade* children born before that decision could not bring such a claim.

**2. Negligent Injury to Fetus.** Unlike wrongful life, courts routinely allow a child to recover for injuries suffered while a fetus. Recall the DES litigation in the cause-in-fact section, supra, Chapter 2, Sec. E.

**3. Wrongful Conception.** Wrongful conception is the label most courts now use to describe a parent's tort claim for the birth of an unwanted, but healthy child. Unlike wrongful life, most courts allow negligent actions for wrongful conception. Recovery is often limited to medical and other costs prompted by the mother's pregnancy. Some courts, however, have allowed more expanded recovery. Consider *Zehr v. Haugen*, 318 Or. 647, 871 P.2d 1006 (1994) where a physician negligently performed a tubal ligation sterilization on the mother resulting in an unwanted pregnancy. The court held that damages could include the expense of raising the child and even college tuition. Other courts will only award child rearing expenses if the parents can prove they intended not to have the child out of financial concerns. See *Burke v. Rivo*, 406 Mass. 764, 551 N.E.2d 1 (1990). What damages if any, do you think should be awarded in wrongful conception cases?

Can non-medical tortious conduct support a wrongful conception claim? In *Jevning v. Cichos*, 499 N.W.2d 515 (Minn. Ct. App. 1993), the plaintiff fathered a healthy child at the age of 15, while a victim of statutory rape.

The father alleged wrongful conception against his child's mother in an attempt to reduce his child support obligations which had been imposed on the young man despite his status as a statutory rape victim. The court held that wrongful conception suits were "prohibited except in medical malpractice actions."

**4. Wrongful Birth.** The term wrongful birth is generally used by courts to characterize a parent's action against a defendant for negligently causing the birth of an unwanted child with a health disability. It should again be emphasized that the action does not allege that the defendant is responsible for the baby's disability but only for causing the birth. Many courts recognize wrongful birth and allow some limited recovery, often the cost of the mother's pregnancy and the extra cost of rearing a child with a disability. Some courts, however, allow more expansive recovery. Consider *Smith v. Cote*, 128 N.H. 231, 513 A.2d 341 (1992) where the Supreme Court of New Hampshire recognized that according to the normal rule of tort damages in wrongful birth cases, the plaintiff should receive the entire cost of rearing a child. However, the court rejected this measure of damages, noting that the "extraordinary costs" rule is the prevailing rule, and that despite criticism that such a rule is unprincipled, it can be justified by the contract rule of damages. "Under this view of the problem, ordinary child-rearing costs are analogous to a price the plaintiffs were willing to pay in order to achieve an expected result." In contrast, in *Viccaro v. Milunsky*, 406 Mass. 777, 551 N.E.2d 8 (1990) the plaintiff parents alleged that negligent genetic counseling led them to conceive a child who was born with serious disabilities. The court allowed plaintiff to recover the extraordinary expenses associated with raising the disabled child plus any emotional distress which was not offset by the emotional gain of parenting the child. Consider also *Lodato v. Kappy*, 353 N.J.Super. 439, 803 A.2d 160 (2002), where the court held that the defendant in a wrongful birth case should not be entitled to an offset of emotional distress damages based on the joy parents derive from raising a disabled child. The court noted that such an offset is incompatible with the measure of damages in a wrongful birth case, the extraordinary medical costs and mental distress associated with raising a disabled child, because such an award is "predicated on the needs of living rather than the concept that non-life is preferable to an impaired life (internal quotations omitted)." And "unlike the situations of a doctor who has performed an operation or medical procedure that has both harmed and benefited the patient, a defendant who, in some way, tortiously interferes with procreative choice has no actual role in bringing about the conception or birth of the child."

Not all disabilities may qualify for a wrongful birth action. Consider *Rice v. Veleanu*, 227 A.D.2d 607, 643 N.Y.S.2d 213 (N.Y. App. Div. 1996) where the court held, a child who was born healthy but later developed mild asthma, fallen arches, and weak ankles was not sufficiently disabled to justify a wrongful birth claim.

Are wrongful birth claims an appropriate way to deter negligent genetic counseling and negligent sterilization procedures? Is it offensive to compensate for the birth of a baby?

**5. Further Study.** For further study, see Gold, *An Equality Approach to Wrongful Birth Statutes*, 65 Fordham L. Rev. 1005 (1996), which contends that a ban on wrongful birth torts is a gender-based distinction that warrants scrutiny under the Equal Protection Clause. See also Hanson, *Suits for Wrongful Life, Counterfactuals and the Nonexistence Problem*, 5 S. Cal. Interdisciplinary L.J. 1 (1996), which discusses how biomedical technology has made it possible to determine in advance whether a child will be born with certain defects, how these advances bring with them the possibility of their negligent application, and what the resulting causes of action may involve. For a discussion of wrongful birth as a cause of action and a particular plaintiff's suit, see Cavanagh, *Tort Law—A Cause of Action Exists for Wrongful Birth Claim Where Physician Negligently Fails to Perform Test Which May Have Detected Birth Defects, Even Though the Likelihood of Detection in Less Than Fifty Percent*, 74 U. Det. Mercy L. Rev. 169 (1996).

## 6. Landowners and Occupiers

## YOUNCE v. FERGUSON

Supreme Court of Washington.
106 Wash.2d 658, 724 P.2d 991 (1986).

GOODLOE, Justice.

In this case, we determine whether the common law classifications of entrants as invitees, licensees, or trespassers should continue to be determinative of the standard of care owed by an owner or occupier of land and whether the status of the entrant in this case was correctly determined. We answer both questions affirmatively and affirm the trial court.

Appellant Lisa Younce appeals the dismissal of respondents Charles, Thelma, and Dean Strunk from the suit. Lisa was injured when a car driven by Tamera Ferguson ran into her on a parcel of Strunk property, where a high school graduation "kegger" party was being held.

Dean Strunk, the son of Charles and Thelma Strunk, was a member of the 1977 Evergreen High School graduating class. Class members planned a graduation party to follow commencement exercises on June 7, 1977. Tickets to the party were sold for $4.00 to purchase beer, food, and music. Dean made arrangements to and did buy 15 kegs of beer from a local tavern for the party with ticket proceeds. The party was originally scheduled to be held on another class member's property, but during the commencement exercises it was generally agreed that the party would be moved to the Strunk property on 109th Avenue.

The 109th Avenue property was the largest of eight parcels of land that Charles and Thelma Strunk had under lease for farming purposes. The property was located 6 miles or 8–9 minutes driving time from the Strunk residence. Dean and his younger brother, Brad, took care of family duties at the property.

\* \* \*

When Dean arrived at the 109th Avenue property around 11 p.m. with the kegs, 100–400 minors were present, including graduating seniors, school mates, students from other schools, and other minors not attending school. Brad was collecting tickets, directing cars to parking areas, and advising cars' occupants of the kegs' location.

.... Lisa Younce, a minor, arrived around 11:30 p.m. with Judy Bock, who had previously bought two tickets for their admission....

When the accident occurred, at approximately 12:15 a.m.,.... Lisa was standing in a dimly lit grassy and gravel area near the main barn and approximately 150 feet away from the kegs. Lisa was hit from behind by a Volkswagen driven by Tamera. The car hit her in the right knee and knocked her to the ground. Lisa was not under the influence of or affected by alcohol at the time she was hit. Tamera left or was taken from the scene. Lisa was taken to the hospital.

\* \* \*

Lisa sued Tamera. The trial court found that Tamera had negligently injured Lisa and entered judgment for $69,543.31. Tamera did not appear at trial and has not appealed.

Lisa also sued the Strunks.... Lisa's ... theory which is the basis of the entire appeal relates to the common law classifications between invitee, licensee, and trespasser and the duty of care owed by the owner or occupier of land.

The trial court found that liability on the part of the Strunks depended upon Lisa's status on the property. The court found Lisa was a social guest, and therefore only a licensee. Applying the duty of care applicable to licensees and articulated in Restatement (Second) of Torts § 332 (1965), the trial court found the duty had not been breached. The Strunks were dismissed with prejudice. The court explained in its memorandum opinion, however, that if Lisa had been an invitee and the duty of care therefore had been one of reasonable care under all the circumstances, the court would have concluded that the Strunks had breached their duty to Lisa. The court also noted, however, that this was a case where Lisa could appreciate the dangers or conditions of the premises. Lisa appealed....

Two issues must be addressed. First, we must decide whether in a claim for injury against an owner or occupier of land, the standard of care owed should continue to turn upon the common law distinctions between invitee, licensee, and trespasser, or whether such distinctions should be replaced by a negligence standard of reasonable care under all the circumstances. Because we retain the common law classifications, we must also decide whether Lisa Younce was properly characterized as a licensee or whether she should have been characterized as an invitee.

Lisa argues that the common law distinctions of invitee, licensee, and trespasser should no longer determine the applicable standard of care owed by an owner or occupier of land in Washington. She urges they be abandoned and replaced by a standard of reasonable care under all the circumstances. *See* 16 Gonz.L.Rev. 479 (1981). Washington relies upon and has adopted many of the definitions and corresponding duties outlined in Restatement (Second) of Torts (1965). *Egede-Nissen v. Crystal Mt., Inc.,* 93 Wash.2d 127, 131–32, 606 P.2d 1214 (1980).

In *Egede-Nissen* we acknowledged past questioning of the common law classification scheme, *see Ward v. Thompson,* 57 Wash.2d 655, 660, 359 P.2d 143 (1961) ("timeworn distinctions"); *Mills v. Orcas Power & Light Co.,* 56 Wash.2d 807, 820, 355 P.2d 781 (1960) ("ancient categories"), but decided that we were not ready then to totally abandon the traditional categories and adopt a unified standard. *Egede-Nissen,* 93 Wash.2d at 131, 606 P.2d 1214. We still are not ready and reaffirm use of common law classifications to determine the duty of care owed by an owner or occupier of land.

A recent annotation, Annot., *Modern Status of Rules Conditioning Landowner's Liability Upon Status of Injured Party as Invitee, Licensee, or Trespasser,* 22 A.L.R.4th 294 (1983), outlines the current positions of the different jurisdictions on this issue. Retention of the common law classifications continues to be the majority position.

Nine jurisdictions have abolished use of the common law classifications of invitees, licensees, and trespassers as determinative of the landowner's or land occupier's duty of care. *See Annot.,* at 301–307; *Rowland v. Christian,* 69 Cal.2d 108, 443 P.2d 561, 70 Cal.Rptr. 97, 32 A.L.R.3d 496 (1968); *Pickard v. City & Cy. of Honolulu,* 51 Hawaii 134, 452 P.2d 445 (1969); *Mile High Fence Co. v. Radovich,* 175 Colo. 537, 489 P.2d 308 (1971); *Smith v. Arbaugh's Restaurant, Inc.,* 152 U.S.App. D.C. 86, 469 F.2d 97 (D.C.Cir.1972); *Mariorenzi v. Joseph Di Ponte Inc.,* 114 R.I. 294, 333 A.2d 127 (1975); *Ouellette v. Blanchard,* 116 N.H. 552, 364 A.2d 631 (1976); *Basso v. Miller,* 40 N.Y.2d 233, 352 N.E.2d 868, 386 N.Y.S.2d 564 (1976); *Cates v. Beauregard Elec. Coop., Inc.,* 328 So.2d 367 (La.1976); *Webb v. Sitka,* 561 P.2d 731 (Alaska 1977); *Hudson v. Gaitan,* 675 S.W.2d 699 (Tenn.1984).

\* \* \*

The cases rejecting the classifications list the subtleties and subclassifications created in their respective jurisdictions. The opinions explain that it is difficult to justify a system with so many exceptions and that while the distinctions were justified in feudal times, they are not justified in modern society.

\* \* \*

The reasons proffered for continuing the distinctions include that the distinctions have been applied and developed over the years, offering a degree of stability and predictability and that a unitary standard would not lessen the confusion. Furthermore, a slow, piecemeal development rather than a wholesale change has been advocated. Some courts fear a wholesale change will delegate social policy decisions to the jury with minimal guidance from the court. *See* Hawkins, *Premises Liability After Repudiation of the Status Categories: Allocation of Judge and Jury Functions* Utah L.Rev. 15 (1981). Also, it is feared that the landowner could be subjected to unlimited liability.

We find these reasons to be compelling. As noted by the Kansas court in *Gerchberg*, 223 Kan. at pages 450–51, 576 P.2d 593: "The traditional classifications were worked out and the exceptions were spelled out with much thought, sweat and even tears". We are not ready to abandon them for a standard with no contours.

Lisa argues alternatively that, if the common law classifications are retained, she was incorrectly characterized as a licensee at trial. Lisa argues that she should have been characterized as an invitee under the facts of this case. Lisa's status on the property determines the standard of care owed her by the Strunks.

In *McKinnon v. Washington Fed. Sav. & Loan Ass'n,* 68 Wash.2d 644, 650, 414 P.2d 773 (1966), this court adopted the Restatement (Second) of Torts § 332 (1965) definition of invitee. An invitee is owed a duty of ordinary care.

Section 332 defines an invitee as follows:

(1) An invitee is either a public invitee or a business visitor.

(2) A public invitee is a person who is invited to enter or remain on land as a member of the public for a purpose for which the land is held open to the public.

(3) A business visitor is a person who is invited to enter or remain on land for a purpose directly or indirectly connected with business dealings with the possessor of the land.

A licensee is defined as "a person who is privileged to enter or remain on land only by virtue of the possessor's consent." Restatement, § 330. A licensee includes a social guest, that is, a person who has been invited but does not meet the legal definition of invitee. In *Memel v. Reimer,* 85 Wash.2d 685, 689, 538 P.2d 517 (1975), this court replaced the willful and wanton misconduct standard of care toward licensees with a duty to exercise reasonable care toward licensees where there is a known dangerous condition on the property which the possessor can reasonably anticipate the licensee will not discover or will fail to realize the risks involved. *Memel* specifically adopted the standard of care for licensees outlined in Restatement, § 342:

A possessor of land is subject to liability for physical harm caused to *licensees* by a condition on the land *if, but only if,*

(a) the possessor knows or has reason to know of the condition and should realize that it involves an *unreasonable risk of harm* to such licensees, *and* should expect that they will not discover or realize the danger, *and*

(b) he fails to exercise reasonable care to make the condition safe, or to warn the licensees of the condition and the risk involved, *and*

(c) *the licensees do not know or have reason to know of the condition and the risk involved.*

(Italics ours.) *Memel,* at 689, 691, 538 P.2d 517. The possessor fulfills his duty by making the condition safe or warning of its existence.

Lisa contends that she was a member of the public on the land for a purpose for which the land is held open and therefore is an invitee. We disagree. The facts of this case do not parallel the facts of other cases where the plaintiff was found to be a public invitee. In *McKinnon*, a federal savings and loan association posted a sign saying it had meeting rooms available for public use. The plaintiff in *McKinnon* was part of a Girl Scout group using the room for Scout meetings. In *Fosbre v. State*, 70 Wash.2d 578, 424 P.2d 901 (1967), the plaintiff was injured at a recreational area on a National Guard fort. The area had been improved and maintained for use by National Guard families of which plaintiff was a member. In these "invitee" cases, "the occupier, *by his arrangement of the premises or other conduct,* has led the entrant to believe that the premises were intended to be used by visitors, as members of the public, for the purpose which the entrant was pursuing, and *that reasonable care was taken to make the place safe for those who enter for that purpose.*" (Italics ours.) *McKinnon*, 68 Wash.2d at 649, 414 P.2d 773. *See* W. Prosser, *Torts* § 61, at 388–89 (4th ed. 1971); Restatement, § 332, comment *d*.

This implied assurance helps to distinguish between invitees and social guests, who are considered licensees. As explained in comment *h*(3) to Restatement, § 330:

> The explanation usually given by the courts for the classification of social guests as licensees is that there is a common understanding that the guest is expected to take the premises as the possessor himself uses them, and does not expect and is not entitled to expect that they will be prepared for his reception, or that precautions will be taken for his safety, in any manner in which the possessor does not prepare or take precautions for his own safety, or that of the members of his family.

Under the facts of this case, it is hard to imagine how the Strunks could have prepared or could have been expected to prepare a dairy farm for a kegger.

We are not persuaded by Lisa's argument that payment of a $4.00 admission price made her an invitee. Analysis in cases where an admission was paid and the plaintiff was characterized as an invitee did not focus on the money as indicative of the plaintiff's status as an invitee. *Hooser v. Loyal Order of Moose, Inc.*, 69 Wash.2d 1, 416 P.2d 462, 15 A.L.R.3d 1008 (1966) ( $1.00 for New Year's Eve Party held at Moose Lodge); *Dickinson v. Tesia*, 2 Wash.App. 262, 467 P.2d 356 (1970) ($2.00 for picnic in recreational area).

The trial court correctly identified Lisa as a licensee. She was privileged to enter or remain on the land only by virtue of the owner's consent. We question whether Charles and Thelma did consent to her presence on the property, but recognize that Dean did consent. In any event, we find the duty owed licensees was not breached because no known dangerous condition existed of which Lisa was not aware or of which she did not realize the risks involved. Lisa had knowledge of the risks involved by staying on the property. We affirm the trial court.

## *NOTES*

**1. Limits on the Duty of Landowners and Occupiers of Land Toward Visitors.** Traditionally courts have long limited the duty of care required by either the owner or occupier (e.g., tenant in possession) of land for the benefit of many of the visitors to the land. While historically this undoubtedly reflected the high status and legal protection accorded by landed gentry in English society, these rules, albeit modified, continue to be favored by a majority of American states today.

The amount of protection from negligence liability afforded to the owner or occupier depends on the legal status of the visitor to the land. The three categories, as noted in the principal case, are invitees, licensees, and trespassers. See Diamond, Levine & Madden, *Understanding Torts* § 9.02 (2nd ed. 2000); Keeton, *Prosser and Keeton on* The Law of Torts §§ 58–64 (5th ed. 1984) and Dobbs, *The Law of Torts*, §§ 232–238 (2000).

**2. Trespassers.** Trespassers are visitors to the land who come without permission or privilege. It should be noted, however, that permission need not be explicit but can be implied by the owner's or occupier's actions or simply by community customs. In the absence of the notice to the contrary, for example, a visitor who walks through the front yard path to knock on the front door would have implied consent.

Historically, trespassers enjoyed very little protection. Landowners and occupiers could not intentionally or willfully injure trespassers, except under an applicable privilege, such as self-defense. Consequently, it was also unlawful for landowners and occupiers to set up intentional traps (such as spring gun devices) to injure trespassers.

While some jurisdictions still maintain this traditional view, limiting liability for only willful or wanton injury, many others have substantially expanded protection of trespassers. The Restatement (Second) of Torts, for example would impose a complete reasonable person standard on landowners and occupiers when they are engaging in activities (such as using machinery) when it is known trespassers are present or in locations trespassers should reasonably be anticipated to be present because of constant trespassing in specific portions, such as a trail, on the defendant's land. See Restatement (Second) of Torts § 334, 336.

In addition, the Restatement would require landowners or occupiers to warn or make safe known concealed artificial (human made) conditions that involve the risk of death or serious bodily injury. While this does not impose a duty to inspect for hazards (such as exposed electrical wires) or to repair them, it does require reasonable warning of known concealed hazards. See Restatement (Second) of Torts § 336–337.

Do you agree this expansion in responsibility for known and anticipated trespassers is appropriate or should trespassers take the property as they find it? The common law provides special protection for children, discussed in the next principal case and notes. See Diamond, Levine & Madden, *Understanding Torts* § 9.02 (1996).

**3. Licensees.** Licensees are visitors who enter onto the land with permission or are otherwise privileged to enter but do not qualify as invitees discussed in the next note. The primary example of a licensee is a social guest, although traditionally and somewhat controversially, firefighters and police entering the property are also considered licensees and not invitees.

While licensees originally were given very limited protection, many courts now give much more expanded protection. Just as with trespassers, many jurisdictions now require the landowner or occupier to act like a reasonable person when engaging in activities such as mowing her lawn.

Many courts today also expand the protection provided to licensees for conditions of the land (such as cracks on walkways). The Restatement, for example, requires landowners and occupiers to warn of all known concealed conditions (whether artificial or natural) posing an unreasonable risk of any harm. See Restatement (Second) of Torts § 342. While inspections to discover dangerous conditions and repairs are not required, the Restatement standard expands upon what is required for known and anticipated trespassers. The licensee must be given reasonable warning for all dangerous conditions and not merely artificial conditions threatening death or serious injury. See Restatement (Second) of Torts § 342.

Consider *Singleton v. Jackson,* 85 Wash.App. 835, 935 P.2d 644 (1997), where a member of a religious group was injured as she approached defendant's home with the intent to engage in religious solicitation and fell on a slippery wood deck. The court held that the plaintiff was a licensee because all homeowners give implied consent for strangers to approach front entrances to make contact with the home's occupants. Since the owner was unaware of the dangerous condition of the deck, he owed no duty to the licensee plaintiff to warn him of the risk, and he owed no further duty to the injured plaintiff. Consider also *Carter v. Kinney*, 896 S.W.2d 926 (Mo.1995), where an individual attending a Bible study in the home of a fellow church member slipped and fell on an icy driveway. The court barred recovery because the plaintiff was a licensee to whom the landowner owed only the duty to warn of, or make safe, known dangers. Since the ice had accumulated overnight, the homeowner was unaware of the dangerous condition of the driveway and thus not held responsible for the injury.

Land occupiers are also not responsible for warning licensees of dangers that are obvious or apparent. Consider *King v. Jackson,* 302 Ark. 540, 790 S.W.2d 904 (1990), where an individual visited the home of a neighbor to inquire about a parcel of land for sale. When the plaintiff learned that the neighbors did not in fact own the parcel, she left the home and tripped over a pair of shoes that had been left out on the porch. Although the plaintiff suffered serious injury, she was not permitted to recover from the homeowners since the dangerous condition that caused her to fall (the shoes) was an open and obvious one. Therefore, the land occupiers did not have a duty to warn their licensee guest of the apparent danger and thus had not breached their standard of care.

**4. Invitees.** Invitees are the most protected class of visitors to land. Invitees include those entering the land for the business interest of the landowner or as a members of the public when the land is open to the public (e.g., a visitor to a public museum or library). The classic invitee is the customer or client entering a store or business building. Business visits can, of course, also occur at private homes and can range from garbage pick-up to negotiations over a corporate take-over. See Restatement (Second) of Torts § 343.

There is in essence no limit on the duty of a landowner or occupier to act reasonably to protect the invitee. Obviously, therefore the landowner or occupier must act reasonably when engaging in activities such as using machinery. In addition, the landowner must act reasonably to ensure conditions on the land are reasonably safe for invitees. This includes not merely a warning about known dangers, but reasonable inspection to discover hazards and reasonable repairs when a mere warning of a hazard would be inadequate.

The duty to invitees is only to behave like the reasonable person and not necessarily to eliminate all risks. Consider *Kay v. Kay*, 306 Ark. 322, 812 S.W.2d 685 (1991), where a maid attempted to recover from her homeowner employers for injuries she suffered from the bite of a brown recluse spider. The maid was an invitee to whom was owed the duty of reasonable care, including the duty to take reasonable steps to maintain safe working conditions in the home. While the maid had complained of spiders in the dwelling, the court refused to extend liability to the homeowners to include protection from such an unexpected occurrence as the appearance of a brown recluse. Thus, the defendants did not breach the duty of reasonable care.

**5. Evaluating to the Status of a Visitor.** As the principal case indicates, determining the status of a visitor can be subtle and challenging. Do you agree that a landowner's or occupier's liability should depend on the status of the visitor? Consider *Barmore v. Elmore*, 83 Ill.App.3d 1056, 38 Ill.Dec. 751, 403 N.E.2d 1355 (1980), where the plaintiff, a member of a fraternal organization, visited the home of one of his fellow lodge members to discuss group business. While in the home he was attacked and stabbed by the homeowner's son, a 47-year-old who suffered from mental deficiencies. Although plaintiff argued his status as a business invitee, the court determined he was instead a licensee because the material benefit of the meeting ran to the lodge and not to the defendant. Thus, the homeowner did not have a duty to protect the plaintiff from the dangerous condition on his land, namely his mentally ill child. An individual's status on the land is also subject to change during the duration of or after a visit is complete. Consider *Buzzell v. Jones*, 151 Vt. 4, 556 A.2d 106 (1989), where a county forester was injured while attempting to flee from a landowner's dogs. Although the forester had initially been invited onto the land and thus held the status of business invitee, he later returned unannounced to complete his business. The court held that the forester exceeded the time limitation of the first invitation and thus reentered the land as a trespasser to whom the landowner owed no duty of protection from the dangerous condition presented by his dogs (see Note 2, supra). Consider also *Graves v. Warner Bros.*, 253 Mich. App. 486, 656 N.W.2d 195 (2002), in which the plaintiff's decedent was murdered three days after appearing on the Jenny Jones show. On the show, the decedent, Scott Amedure, revealed to his friend, Jonathan Schmitz, that he had a secret crush on him. On the morning of the murder, Schmitz found a sexually suggestive note from Amedure on his door. He went to the bank and withdrew money which he used to purchase a shotgun, he then drove to Amedure's trailer and confronted him about the note. Amedure smiled at him, and Schmitz told him he had to shut off his car, retrieved the shotgun and returned and shot Amedure in the chest. The court noted the "long established rule that there is no general duty to anticipate and prevent criminal activity * * * Here the only special relationship, if any, that ever existed between defendants and Schmitz, was that of business invitor to invitee. However, any duty ends when the relationship ends." Despite the plaintiff's contention that violence was a reasonably foreseeable consequence of surprising guests with the fact that their friends have homosexual crushes on them, the court rejected this, noting that "this case presents no exceptional circumstances warranting departure from the normal rule."

## UNITED ZINC & CHEMICAL CO. v. BRITT

Supreme Court of the United States.

258 U.S. 268, 42 S.Ct. 299, 66 L.Ed. 615 (1922).

MR. JUSTICE HOLMES delivered the opinion of the Court.

This is a suit brought by the respondents against the petitioner to recover for the death of two children, sons of the respondents. The facts that for the purposes of decision we shall assume to have been proved are these. The petitioner owned a tract of about twenty acres in the outskirts of the town of Iola, Kansas. Formerly it had there a plant for the making of sulphuric acid and zinc spelter. In 1910 it tore the buildings down but left a basement and cellar, in which in July, 1916, water was accumulated, clear in appearance but in fact dangerously poisoned by sulphuric acid and zinc sulphate that had come in one way or another from the petitioner's works, as the petitioner knew. The respondents had been traveling and encamped at some distance from this place. A traveled way passed within 120 or 100 feet of it. On July 27, 1916, the children, who were eight and eleven years old, came upon the petitioner's land, went into the water, were poisoned and died. The petitioner saved the question whether it could be held liable. At the trial the Judge instructed the jury that if the water looked clear but in fact was poisonous and thus the children were allured to it the petitioner was liable. The respondents got a verdict and judgment, which was affirmed by the Circuit Court of Appeals. 264 Fed. 785.

*Union Pacific Ry. Co. v. McDonald*, 152 U. S. 262, 14 Sup. Ct. 619, 38 L. Ed. 434, and kindred cases were relied upon as leading to the result, and perhaps there is language in that and in *Sioux City & Pacific Ry. Co. v. Stout*, 17 Wall. 657, 21 L. Ed. 745, that might seem to justify it; but the doctrine needs very careful statement not to make an unjust and impracticable requirement. If the children had been adults they would have had no case. They would have been trespassers and the owner of the land would have owed no duty to remove even hidden danger; it would have been entitled to assume that they would obey the law and not trespass. The liability for spring guns and mantraps arises from the fact that the defendant has not rested on that assumption, but on the contrary has expected the trespasser and prepared an injury that is no more justified than if he had held the gun and fired it. *Chenery v. Fitchburg R. R. Co.*, 160 Mass, 211, 213, 35 N. E. 554, 22 L. R. A. 575. Infants have no greater right to go upon other people's land than adults, and the mere fact that they are infants imposes no duty upon landowners to expect them and to prepare for their safety. On the other hand the duty of one who invites another upon his land not to lead him into a trap is well settled, and while it is very plain that temptation is not invitation, it may be held that knowingly to establish and expose, unfenced, to children of an age when they follow a bait as mechanically as a fish, something that is certain to attract them, has the legal effect of an invitation to them although not to an adult. But the principle if accepted must be very cautiously applied.

In *Railroad Co. v. Stout*, 17 Wall. 657, 21 L. Ed. 745, the well-known case of a boy injured on a turntable, it appeared that children had played there before to the knowledge of employees of the railroad, and in view of that fact and the situation of the turntable near a road without visible separation, it seems to have been assumed without much discussion that the railroad owed a duty to the boy. Perhaps this was as strong a case as would be likely to occur of maintaining a known temptation, where temptation takes the place of invitation. A license was implied and liability for a danger not manifest to a child was declared in the very similar case of *Cooke v. Midland Great Western Ry. of Ireland* [1909], A. C. 229.

In the case at bar it is at least doubtful whether the water could be seen from any place where the children lawfully were and there is no evidence that it was what led them to enter the land. But that is necessary to start the supposed duty. There can be no general duty on the part of a land-owner to keep his land safe for children, or even free from hidden dangers, if he has not directly or by implication invited or licensed them to come there. The difficulties in the way of implying a license are adverted to in *Chenery v. Fitchburg R. R. Co.*, 160 Mass. 211, 212, 35 N. E. 554, 22 L. R. A. 575, but need not be considered here. It does not appear that children were in the habit of going to the place; so that foundation also fails.

*Union Pacific Ry. Co. v. McDonald*, 152 U. S. 262, 14 Sup. Ct. 619, 38 L. Ed. 434, is less in point. There a boy was burned by falling into burning coal slack close by the side of a path on which he was running homeward from other boys who had frightened him. It hardly appears that he was a trespasser and the path suggests an invitation; at all events boys habitually resorted to the place where he was. Also the defendant was under a statutory duty to fence the place sufficiently to keep out cattle. The decision is very far from establishing that the petitioner is liable for poisoned water not bordering a road, not shown to have been the inducement that led the children to trespass, if in any event the law would deem it sufficient to excuse their going there, and not shown to have been the indirect inducement because known to the children to be frequented by others. It is suggested that the roads across the place were invitations. A road is not an invitation to leave it elsewhere than at its end.

*Judgment reversed.*

Mr. Justice CLARKE, dissenting.

The courts of our country have sharply divided as to the principles of law applicable to "attractive nuisance" cases, of which this one is typical.

The dimensions of the pool of poisoned water were about 20 x 45 feet. It was 2 ½ to 3 feet deep in part and in part 10 or more feet deep. A photograph in the record gives it the appearance of an attractive swimming pool, with brick sides and the water coming nearly to the top of the wall. The water is described by the witnesses as appearing to be clear and pure, and, on the hot summer day on which the children perished, attractively cool.

This pool is indefinitely located within a tract of land about 1,000 feet wide by 1,200 feet long, about which there had not been any fence whatever for many years, and there was no sign or warning of any kind indicating the dangerous character of the water in the pool. There were several paths across the lot, a highway ran within 100 to 120 feet of the pool, and a railway track was not far away. The land was immediately adjacent to a city of about 10,000 inhabitants, with dwelling houses not far distant from it. The testimony shows that not only the two boys who perished had been attracted to the pool at the time, but that there were two or three other children with them, whose cries attracted men who were passing near by, who, by getting into the water, succeeded in recovering the dead body of one child and in rescuing the other in such condition that, after lingering for a day or a two, he died. The evidence shows that the water in the pool was highly impregnated with sulphuric acid and zinc sulphate, which certainly caused the death of the children, and that the men who rescued the boys suffered seriously, one of them for as much as two weeks, from the effects of the poisoned water.

The case was given to the jury in a clear and comprehensive charge, and the judgment of the District Court upon the verdict was affirmed by the Circuit Court of Appeals. The court charged the jury that if the water in the pool was not poisonous and if the boys were simply drowned there could be no recovery, but that if it was found, that the defendant knew or in the exercise of ordinary care should have known that the water was impregnated with poison, that children were likely to go to its vicinity, that it was in appearance clear and pure and attractive to young children as a place for bathing, and that the death of the children was caused by its alluring appearance and by its poisonous character, and because no protection or warning was given against it, the case came within the principle of the "attractive nuisance" or "turntable" cases and recovery would be allowed.

\* \* \*

Believing as I do that the doctrine of the *Stout* and *McDonald* Cases, giving weight to, and making allowance, as they do, for, the instincts and habitual conduct of children of tender years, is a sound doctrine, calculated to make men more reasonably considerate of the safely of the children of their neighbors, than will the harsh rule which makes trespassers of little children which the court is now substituting for it, I cannot share in setting aside the verdict of the jury in this case, approved by the judgments of two courts, upon what is plainly a disputed question of fact and in thereby overruling two decisions which have been accepted as leading authorities for half a century, and I therefore dissent from the judgment and opinion of the court.

The CHIEF JUSTICE and Mr. Justice DAY concur in this opinion.

# RESTATEMENT (SECOND) OF TORTS § 339*

## ARTIFICIAL CONDITIONS HIGHLY DANGEROUS TO TRESPASSING CHILDREN

A possessor of land is subject to liability for physical harm to children trespassing thereon caused by an artificial condition upon the land if

(a) the place where the condition exists is one upon which the possessor knows or has reason to know that children are likely to trespass, and

(b) the condition is one of which the possessor knows or has reason to know and which he realizes or should realize will involve an unreasonable risk of death or serious bodily harm to such children, and

(c) the children because of their youth do not discover the condition or realize the risk involved in intermeddling with it or in coming within the area made dangerous by it, and

(d) the utility to the possessor of maintaining the condition and the burden of eliminating the danger are slight as compared with the risk to children involved, and

(e) the possessor fails to exercise reasonable care to eliminate the danger or otherwise to protect the children.

Caveat:

The Institute expresses no opinion as to whether the rule stated in this Section may not apply to natural conditions of the land.

## *NOTES*

**1. Child Trespassers.** As the principal case by Justice Holmes suggests, children trespassers have been granted by courts special protection not provided to adult trespassers under the "attractive nuisance" doctrine. Historically, the doctrine required the artificial hazard to attract the child visitor onto the land. Contrast this with the Restatement position, quoted above, which instead considers whether children are likely to trespass.

Consider *McGettigan v. National Bank of Washington*, 320 F.2d 703 (D.C.Cir.1963), where a boy while trespassing at an abandoned house discovered a flare. The boy brought the flare to his home where it ignited and injured his brother. The court held that, although the child had not been attracted to the property by the hazard, "the value of the lives of children" required that the landowners remove dangerous conditions where children would foreseeably trespass. But also consider *Carroll v. Jagoe Homes*, 677 N.E.2d 612 (Ind.Ct.App.1997) where a child was injured while trespassing at a construction site. The court expressly rejected the Restatement view and held that a child to benefit from the attractive nuisance exception had to prove the site would "likely . . . incite the curiosity of a child" from afar, and rejected the contention that all construction sites were sufficiently alluring to automatically constitute attractive nuisance.

Note also that the Restatement factors consider the age of the child trespasser and his ability to appreciate the hazard.

Consider, for example, *Hollis v. Norfolk Southern Railway Co.,* 667 So.2d 727 (Ala.1995) where the court held a trespassing teenager who fell from a cliff was old enough to appreciate from previous visits to the property the hazards and could not benefit from an attractive nuisance doctrine. Note that in any event, the Restatement's caveat, cited above, reserves decision on whether the exception for trespassing children applies for natural conditions. See also *Texas Utilities Electric Co. v. Timmons,* 947 S.W.2d 191 (Tex.1997) holding that a 14–year-old teenager should appreciate the risk of electrical lines and consequently could not benefit from the attractive nuisance doctrine after trespassing onto the electric transmission tower.

Consider also that the Restatement requires the landowners to take precautions only when the hazards substantially exceed the burden of the precaution. Is this sufficient protection for children? See Diamond, Levine & Madden, *Understanding Torts* § 9.02 (2nd ed. 2000) and Dobbs, *The Law of Torts,* § 236 (2000).

**2. Current Adult Protection.** As indicated after the previous principal case, protections for adult trespassers have expanded in many jurisdictions in more recent years. Should landowners be required to post warnings for the benefit of adult trespassers?

## ROWLAND v. CHRISTIAN

Supreme Court of California.
69 Cal.2d 108, 70 Cal.Rptr. 97, 443 P.2d 561 (1968).

PETERS, Justice.

Plaintiff appeals from a summary judgment for defendant Nancy Christian in this personal injury action.

In his complaint plaintiff alleged that about November 1, 1963, Miss Christian told the lessors of her apartment that the knob of the cold water faucet on the bathroom basin was cracked and should be replaced; that on November 30, 1963, plaintiff entered the apartment at the invitation of Miss Christian; that he was injured while using the bathroom fixtures, suffering severed tendons and nerves of his right hand; and that he has incurred medical and hospital expenses. He further alleged that the bathroom fixtures were dangerous, that Miss Christian was aware of the dangerous condition, and that his injuries were proximately caused by the negligence of Miss Christian. Plaintiff sought recovery of his medical and hospital expenses, loss of wages, damage to his clothing, and $100,000 general damages. It does not appear from the complaint whether the crack in the faucet handle was obvious to an ordinary inspection or was concealed.

\* \* \*

In the instant case, Miss Christian's affidavit and admissions made by plaintiff show that plaintiff was a social guest and that he suffered injury when the faucet handle broke; they do not show that the faucet handle crack was obvious or even nonconcealed. Without in any way contradicting her affidavit or his own admissions, plaintiff at trial could establish that she was aware of the condition and realized or should have realized that it involved an unreasonable risk of harm to him, that defendant should have expected that he would not discover the danger, that she did not exercise reasonable care to eliminate the danger or warn him of it, and that he did not know or have reason to know of the danger. Plaintiff also could establish, without contradicting Miss Christian's affidavit or his admissions, that the crack was not obvious and was concealed. Under the circumstances, a summary judgment is proper in this case only if, after proof of such facts, a judgment would be required as a matter of law for Miss Christian. The record supports no such conclusion.

Section 1714 of the Civil Code provides: "Every one is responsible, not only for the result of his willful acts, but also for an injury occasioned to another by his want of ordinary care or skill in the management of his property or person, except so far as the latter has, willfully or by want of ordinary care, brought the injury upon himself. ..." This code section, which has been unchanged in our law since 1872, states a civil law and not a common law principle. (*Fernandez v. Consolidated Fisheries, Inc.*, 98 Cal.App.2d 91, 96 [219 P.2d 73].)

Nevertheless, some common law judges and commentators have urged that the principle embodied in this code section serves as the foundation of our negligence law. Thus in a concurring opinion, Brett, M. R. in *Heaven v. Pender* (1883) 11 Q.B.D. 503, 509, states: "whenever one person is by circumstances placed in such a position with regard to another that every one of ordinary sense who did think would at once recognize that if he did not use ordinary care and skill in his own conduct with regard to those circumstances he would cause danger of injury to the person or property of the other, a duty arises to use ordinary care and skill to avoid such danger."

\* \* \*

A departure from this fundamental principle involves the balancing of a number of considerations; the major ones are the foreseeability of harm to the plaintiff, the degree of certainty that the plaintiff suffered injury, the closeness of the connection between the defendant's conduct and the injury suffered, the moral blame attached to the defendant's conduct, the policy of preventing future harm, the extent of the burden to the defendant and consequences to the community of imposing a duty to exercise care with resulting liability for breach, and the availability, cost, and prevalence of insurance for the risk involved. (Citations omitted).

One of the areas where this court and other courts have departed from the fundamental concept that a man is liable for injuries caused by his carelessness is with regard to the liability of a possessor of land for injuries to persons who have entered upon that land. It has been suggested that the special rules regarding liability of the possessor of land are due to historical considerations stemming from the high place which land has traditionally held in English and American thought, the dominance and prestige of the landowning class in England during the formative period of the rules governing the possessor's liability, and the heritage of feudalism. (2 Harper and James, *The Law of Torts, supra,* p. 1432.)

The departure from the fundamental rule of liability for negligence has been accomplished by classifying the plaintiff either as a trespasser, licensee, or invitee and then adopting special rules as to the duty owed by the possessor to each of the classifications. Generally speaking a trespasser is a person who enters or remains upon land of another without a privilege to do so; a licensee is a person like a social guest who is not an invitee and who is privileged to enter or remain upon land by virtue of the possessor's consent, and an invitee is a business visitor who is invited or permitted to enter or remain on the land for a purpose directly or indirectly connected with business dealings between them. (*Oettinger v. Stewart,* 24 Cal.2d 133, 136 [148 P.2d 19, 156 A.L.R. 1221].)

In refusing to adopt the rules relating to the liability of a possessor of land for the law of admiralty, the United States Supreme Court stated: "The distinctions which the common law draws between licensee and invitee were inherited from a culture deeply rooted to the land, a culture which traced many of its standards to a heritage of feudalism. In an effort to do justice in an industrialized urban society, with its complex economic and individual relationships, modern common-law courts have found it necessary to formulate increasingly subtle verbal refinements, to create subclassifications among traditional common-law categories, and to delineate fine gradations in the standards of care which the landowner owes to each. Yet even within a single jurisdiction, the classifications and subclassifications bred by the common law have produced confusion and conflict. As new distinctions have been spawned, older ones have become obscured. Through this semantic morass the common law has moved, unevenly and with hesitation, towards 'imposing on owners and occupiers a single duty of reasonable care in all the circumstances.'" (Footnotes omitted.) (*Kermarec v. Compagnie Generale,* 358 U.S. 625, 630–631 [3 L.Ed.2d 550, 554–555, 79 S.Ct. 406].

There is another fundamental objection to the approach to the question of the possessor's liability on the basis of the common law distinctions based upon the status of the injured party as a trespasser, licensee, or invitee. Complexity can be borne and confusion remedied where the underlying principles governing liability are based upon proper considerations. Whatever may have been the historical justifications for the common law distinctions, it is clear that those distinctions are not justified in the light of our modern society and that the complexity and confusion which has arisen is not due to difficulty in applying the original common law rules—they are all too easy to apply in the original formulation—but is due to the attempts to apply just rules in our modern society within the ancient terminology.

Without attempting to labor all of the rules relating to the possessor's liability, it is apparent that the classifications of trespasser, licensee, and invitee, the immunities from liability predicated upon those classifications, and the exceptions to those immunities, often do not reflect the major factors which should determine whether immunity should be conferred upon the possessor of land. Some of those factors, including the closeness of the connection between the injury and the defendant's conduct, the moral blame attached to the defendant's conduct, the policy of preventing future harm, and the prevalence and availability of insurance, bear little, if any, relationship to the classifications of trespasser, licensee and invitee and the existing rules conferring immunity.

Although in general there may be a relationship between the remaining factors and the classifications of trespasser, licensee, and invitee, there are many cases in which no such relationship may exist. Thus, although the foreseeability of harm to an invitee would ordinarily seem greater than the foreseeability of harm to a trespasser, in a particular case the opposite may be true. The same may be said of the issue of certainty of injury. The burden to the defendant and consequences to the community of imposing a duty to exercise care with resulting liability for breach may often be greater with respect to trespassers than with respect to invitees, but it by no means follows that this is true in every case. In many situations, the burden will be the same, i.e., the conduct necessary upon the defendant's part to meet the burden of exercising due care as to invitees will also meet his burden with respect to licensees and trespassers. The last of the major factors, the cost of insurance, will, of course, vary depending upon the rules of liability adopted, but there is no persuasive evidence that applying ordinary principles of negligence law to the land occupier's liability will materially reduce the prevalence of insurance due to increased cost or even substantially increase the cost.

Considerations such as these have led some courts in particular situations to reject the rigid common law classifications and to approach the issue of the duty of the occupier on the basis of ordinary principles of negligence.... And the common law distinctions after thorough study have been repudiated by the jurisdiction of their birth. (Occupiers' Liability Act, 1957, 5 and 6 Eliz. 2, ch. 31.)

A man's life or limb does not become less worthy of protection by the law nor a loss less worthy of compensation under the law because he has come upon the land of another without permission or with permission but without a business purpose. Reasonable people do not ordinarily vary their conduct depending upon such matters, and to focus upon the status of the injured party as a trespasser, licensee, or invitee in order to determine the question whether the landowner has a duty of care, is contrary to our modern social mores and humanitarian values. The common law rules obscure rather than illuminate the proper considerations which should govern determination of the question of duty.

It bears repetition that the basic policy of this state set forth by the Legislature in section 1714 of the Civil Code is that everyone is responsible for an injury caused to another by his want of ordinary care or skill in the management of his property. The factors which may in particular cases warrant departure from this fundamental principle do not warrant the wholesale immunities resulting from the common law classifications, and we are satisfied that continued adherence to the common law distinctions can only lead to injustice or, if we are to avoid injustice, further fictions with the resulting complexity and confusion. We decline to follow and perpetuate such rigid classifications. The proper test to be applied to the liability of the possessor of land in accordance with section 1714 of the Civil Code is whether in the management of his property he has acted as a reasonable man in view of the probability of injury to others, and, although the plaintiff's status as a trespasser, licensee, or invitee may in the light of the facts giving rise to such status have some bearing on the question of liability, the status is not determinative.

Once the ancient concepts as to the liability of the occupier of land are stripped away, the status of the plaintiff relegated to its proper place in determining such liability, and ordinary principles of negligence applied, the result in the instant case presents no substantial difficulties. As we have seen, when we view the matters presented on the motion for summary judgment as we must, we must assume defendant Miss Christian was aware that the faucet handle was defective and dangerous, that the defect was not obvious, and that plaintiff was about to come in contact with the defective condition, and under the undisputed facts she neither remedied the condition nor warned plaintiff of it. Where the occupier of land is aware of a concealed condition involving in the absence of precautions an unreasonable risk of harm to those coming in contact with it and is aware that a person on the premises is about to come in contact with it, the trier of fact can reasonably conclude that a failure to warn or to repair the condition constitutes negligence. Whether or not a guest has a right to expect that his host will remedy dangerous conditions on his account, he should reasonably be entitled to rely upon a warning of the dangerous condition so that he, like the host, will be in a position to take special precautions when he comes in contact with it.

It may be noted that by carving further exceptions out of the traditional rules relating to the liability to licensees or social guests, other jurisdictions reach the same result (see Rest.2d Torts, *supra*, § 342; Annot., Duty of a possessor of land to warn adult licensees of danger (1957) 55 A.L.R.2d 525; 49–55 A.L.R.2d, Later Case Service (1967) 485; but cf. *Hansen v. Richey, supra,* 237 Cal.App.2d 475, 478– 479; *Saba v. Jacobs,* 130 Cal.App.2d 717, 719 [279 P.2d 826]; *Ward v. Oakley Co.,* 125 Cal.App.2d 840, 844–845 [271 P.2d 536]; *Fisher v. General Petroleum Corp.,* 123 Cal.App.2d 770, 779–780 [267 P.2d 841]), that by continuing to adhere to the strained construction of active negligence or possibly, by applying the trap doctrine the result would be reached on the basis of some California precedents (e.g., *Hansen v. Richey, supra,* 237 Cal.App.2d 475, 481), and that the result might even be reached by a continued expansion of the definition of the term 'invitee' to include all persons invited upon the land who may thereby be led to believe that the host will exercise for their protection the ordinary care of a reasonable man (cf. *O'Keefe v. South End Rowing Club,* 64 Cal.2d 729, 737–739 [51 Cal.Rptr. 534, 414 P.2d 830, 16 A.L.R.3d 1]). However, to approach the problem in these manners would only add to the confusion, complexity, and fictions which have resulted from the common law distinctions.

The judgment is reversed.

BURKE, Justice (dissenting).

I dissent. In determining the liability of the occupier or owner of land for injuries, the distinctions between trespassers, licensees and invitees have been developed and applied by the courts over a period of many years. They supply a reasonable and workable approach to the problems involved, and one which provides the degree of stability and predictability so highly prized in the law. The unfortunate alternative, it appears to me, is the route taken by the majority in their opinion in this case; that such issues are to be decided on a case by case basis under the application of the basic law of negligence, bereft of the guiding principles and precedent which the law has heretofore attached by virtue of the relationship of the parties to one another.

Liability for negligence turns upon whether a duty of care is owed, and if so, the extent thereof. Who can doubt that the corner grocery, the large department store, or the financial institution owes a greater duty of care to one whom it has invited to enter its premises as a prospective customer of its wares or services than it owes to a trespasser seeking to enter after the close of business hours and for a nonbusiness or even an antagonistic purpose? I do not think it unreasonable or unfair that a social guest (classified by the law as a licensee, as was plaintiff here) should be obliged to take the premises in the same condition as his host finds them or permits them to be. Surely a homeowner should not be obliged to hover over his guests with warnings of possible dangers to be found in the condition of the home (e.g., waxed floors, slipping rugs, toys in unexpected places, etc., etc.). Yet today's decision appears to open the door to potentially unlimited liability despite the purpose and circumstances motivating the plaintiff in entering the premises of another, and despite the caveat of the majority that the status of the parties may "have some bearing on the question of liability ...," whatever the future may show that language to mean.

In my view, it is not a proper function of this court to overturn the learning, wisdom and experience of the past in this field. Sweeping modifications of tort liability law fall more suitably within the domain of the Legislature, before which all affected interests can be heard and which can enact statutes providing uniform standards and guidelines for the future.

I would affirm the judgment for defendant.

### NOTES

**1. Rejecting Duty Based on Visitor's Status.** A small minority of states now follows the principal case and rejects limited duties based on whether the plaintiff is a trespasser, licensee, or invitee. Do you find the principal case's decision persuasive? Would the result in the principal case arguably be the same under the traditional status approach now that most modern courts require licensee's to be warned of known hidden dangers?

**2. Excluding Trespassers.** One particularly controversial aspect of the principal case's approach is the imposition of a reasonable person standard for trespassers. Consequently, some courts have merged the invitee and licensee category, but maintained a limited duty for trespassers. Consider the editorial quoted below:

## The San Francisco Chronicle Wednesday, February 27, 1985*
### EDITORIAL CORRECTING THE COURT'S ERROR

IN A 1968 case, the California Supreme Court threw common law and common sense to the winds. There is now an opportunity to restore a little of both at the current session of the Legislature.

Before the 1968 decision, common law, accepted and enforced by California courts, held that trespassers could not sue land or homeowners for injuries they suffered while their presence was unwanted. But that year the court ruled, in effect, that trespassers had the same rights as any other accident victim to seek damages for injuries.

The result has been bizarre. Two extreme cases which offend public sensibilities have been cited by Assemblyman Alister McAlister, author of the new legislation, and by Lee A. Phelps, chairman of ACTIV, an organization seeking to undo part of the Supreme Court's bad work.

In Shasta County, a man attempting burglary climbed atop a school building. He fell through a skylight and suffered spinal injuries. He brought suit against the school district and the City of Redding, alleging that he had not been warned that the skylight was unsafe. In an out-of-court settlement based on the 1968 decision, the public agencies agreed to pay $260,000 in damages and $1200 monthly for the lifetime of the would-be burglar.

IN A SAN BENITO County case, a thief went joyriding on a stolen motorcycle. Far from the scene of the theft, he drove across a farmer's field, where he rode into a pothole and was thrown from the stolen bike, suffering serious injuries. The trespassing thief sued the farmer and won almost $500,000 in damages.

Assemblyman McAlister has entered Assembly Bill 200 which would rectify some of the folly produced by the Supreme Court decision. The bill would provide that an owner of property, including a governmental agency, would be free of liability for any injury suffered by a person during that person's commission of a felony, attempted felony or after the commission of a felony.

A similar bill did not even get out of the Assembly Judiciary Committee in the last session. ACTIV sees a connection between the committee vote and the fact that major campaign contributions have been made to committee members by the California Trial Lawyers Association. We will watch the committee to see how it votes this time around.

WE DO NOT think that a burglar should be able to sue a householder if he breaks his leg going down the front steps with the family piano. That is the case today and it simply does not make moral, legal or reasonable sense.

## NOTES

**1. Legislative Reaction.** The California legislature adopted the statutory proposal urged in the above editorial. See Cal. Civ. Code § 847. Trespassers, committing or attempting to commit enumerated felonies, can only recover from landowner or occupier for willful or wanton injuries. What are the arguments for and against the statute? Does California now give less protection to trespassing criminals than states following a traditional approach?

**2. Climbing School Buildings.** The editorial above describes a "burglar" on top of a school roof. Suppose the trespasser was an 18-year-old high school senior attempting a prank. Should the school provide warnings that portions of the roof would not support a person's weight when the weakness of a portion of the roof is not readily apparent? Should the school or a university be liable if it fails to provide warnings knowing students and others sometimes unlawfully go on the roof?

## 7. Landowners' Liability to Plaintiffs Off Land

### SPEARS v. BLACKWELL

Court of Appeals of Indiana.
666 N.E.2d 974 (1996).

BARTEAU, Judge.

\* \* \*

### FACTS

In the afternoon of June 14, 1991, Tim Spears was driving his car in a southerly direction on Ladoga Road in Montgomery County, Indiana. The Blackwells owned six acres of real estate ("Property") abutting the west side of Ladoga Road, including a house located approximately 500 feet from Ladoga Road. The Property was in a rural area, with farmers' fields in the immediate area.

.... Due to the height of the vegetation, described as weeds, growing on [defendant's] land, .... [the other driver, who collided with Spears] nor Tim Spears saw each other's car ... [on] Ladoga Road, at which point Tim Spears's car struck the side of Brier's car. Tim Spears sustained various injuries from the accident.

\* \* \*

### DISCUSSION

The key issue is whether the Blackwells, as owners of the realty in a rural area, owed Tim Spears, as a user of the public thoroughfare of Ladoga Road, a duty of care to maintain the vegetation in a way that protected him from harm that could result from the condition of the vegetation.

The Spearses' claim is a negligence action. To prevail in a negligence action, the plaintiff must prove the elements of a cause of action for negligence, being: (1) defendants' duty to conform their conduct to a standard of care arising from their relationship with the plaintiff; (2)

breach of that duty; and (3) injury to the plaintiff resulting from that breach. *Webb v. Jarvis,* 575 N.E.2d 992, 995 (Ind.1991), *reh'g denied.* Here, we are asked to address the issue of whether a duty exists. If the Blackwells owed no duty to Tim Spears under these facts, then no breach and no recovery can occur under a negligence cause of action. *Hawn v. Padgett,* 598 N.E.2d 630, 632 (Ind.Ct.App.1992).

Generally, the court decides as a matter of law whether a duty exists. *Webb,* 575 N.E.2d at 995; *Clyde E. Williams and Assocs., Inc., v. Boatman,* 176 Ind.App. 430, 434, 375 N.E.2d 1138, 1140 (1978). However, at times the fact finder must determine a preliminary factual issue, the existence of which will lead the trial court to determine the legal issue of whether a duty of care arises. *Boatman,* 176 Ind.App. at 435, 375 N.E.2d at 1140–42. In such cases, the determination of the existence of a duty becomes a mixed question of law and fact, which the fact finder ultimately resolves. *State v. Cornelius,* 637 N.E.2d 195, 198 (Ind.Ct.App. 1994), *trans. denied.*

Generally, an owner of realty does not owe a duty to passersby using an adjacent public thoroughfare to protect them from harm that could result from natural conditions of the land. *Valinet v. Eskew,* 574 N.E.2d 283 (Ind.1991). Conversely, such a duty is owed regarding an artificial condition of the land about which the landowner knew or should have known. *Holiday Rambler Corp. v. Gessinger,* 541 N.E.2d 559 (Ind.Ct. App.1989), *trans. denied; Pitcairn v. Whiteside,* 109 Ind.App. 693, 34 N.E.2d 943 (1941).

The trial court granted summary judgment because it determined that the vegetation was a natural condition. The Spearses contend that the trial court erred when it determined that the vegetation was a natural condition, contending that the issue of whether the vegetation was a natural or an artificial condition is a genuine issue of material fact. We agree.

The Restatement defines natural conditions as land that was not changed by any acts of humans, including the possessor or any predecessors in interest. Restatement (Second) of Torts § 363 cmt. b (1965). Natural conditions also include the natural growth of vegetation, such as weeds, on land that is not artificially made receptive to them. *Id.* Also, vegetation that humans plant is non-natural despite whether they are inherently harmful or become so only because of subsequent changes due to natural forces. *Id.* Additionally, the Restatement defines "natural condition" of land to be "a condition that is not in any way the result of human activity." Restatement (Second) of Torts § 840 cmt. a (1979). "Natural condition" includes "soil that has not been cultivated, graded or otherwise disturbed." *Id.* Vegetation is not considered a "natural condition" if it "grows on land only because it has been plowed," even if no one planted or cultivated the vegetation. *Id.*

The vegetation on the raised area is described as having been tall weeds at the time of the accident. Before the Blackwells' ownership of the property, the owners of the property had planted juniper shrubs and a rock garden in the area where the vegetation was growing. Evidence of this rock and juniper garden was still present in August of 1993 when a large amount of rock and dirt was removed from the area where the vegetation was growing. Also, a corn field existed in the vicinity of the raised area when the Blackwells first acquired the property. And, on at least one occasion before the accident, the Blackwells mowed the area of the vegetation.

The Spearses presented evidence from which a reasonable trier of fact could determine that the vegetation was not a natural condition. This created a genuine issue of material fact precluding summary judgment. See Ind.Trial Rule 56(C); *ACONA,* 621 N.E.2d at 1119. We reverse the entry of summary judgment and remand this case to the trial court.

Reversed.

## NOTES

**1. Duty to Plaintiffs Off the Land.** Under the common law, landowners or occupiers are not liable for most natural conditions on their land that can cause injury to those off the land. This rule limits the duty of landowners or occupiers to act reasonably to protect those off the land from hazards, such as naturally formed rocks or mud, that could injure plaintiffs on neighboring roads and property.

This is in contrast to artificial (human made) conditions, such as roof tiles, for which the land owner or occupier is fully liable for injuries to those off the land caused by land occupier's negligence.

As the principal case indicates the distinction between natural and artificial (human made) conditions, given the cultivation of land, can be subtle and contentious.

Note also that the plaintiff in the principal case was off the defendant's land and consequently was not a visitor to the defendant's land. Therefore the status of the plaintiff, e.g., licensee, is not relevant.

**2. Exception for Trees.** Most courts make an exception to the general rule discussed in Note 1 and require urban land owners and occupiers to inspect and reasonably care for trees that could endanger those off the land. Some courts have extended this duty to trees in rural locations as well. See, for example, *Valinet v. Eskew,* 557 N.E.2d 702 (Ind.Ct.App. 1990) holding a rural landowner liable for a tree that hit a motorist on an adjacent highway. While this arguably provides better protection to the public and neighbors, some environmentalists have argued this encourages excessive clearing of trees near roadsides to avoid the cost of reasonable inspection or potential liability. Which view is more persuasive?

**3. Liability for all Natural Conditions.** Some courts have imposed a full duty of reasonable care on landowners and occupiers for all natural conditions. Consider *Sprecher v. Adamson Companies,* 30 Cal.3d 358, 178 Cal.Rptr. 783, 636 P.2d 1121 (1981), where the court imposed a duty on the landowner to act reasonably to protect neighbors from the danger of a mud slide. While imposing the duty, the court emphasized that it was not necessarily suggesting that the defendant land occupier had in fact any reasonable options that would have prevented the slide.

## 8. Negligent Misrepresentation

# BILY v. ARTHUR YOUNG & CO.

Supreme Court of California.

3 Cal.4th 370, 11 Cal.Rptr.2d 51, 834 P.2d 745 (1992).

LUCAS, Chief Justice.

We granted review to consider whether and to what extent an accountant's duty of care in the preparation of an independent audit of a client's financial statements extends to persons other than the client.

Since Chief Judge Cardozo's seminal opinion in *Ultramares Corp. v. Touche* (1931) 255 N.Y. 170 [174 N.E. 441, 74 A.L.R. 1139] (*Ultramares*), the issue before us has been frequently considered and debated by courts and commentators. Different schools of thought have emerged. At the center of the controversy are difficult questions concerning the role of the accounting profession in performing audits, the conceivably limitless scope of an accountant's liability to nonclients who may come to read and rely on audit reports, and the effect of tort liability rules on the availability, cost, and reliability of those reports.

### I.

#### SUMMARY OF FACTS AND PROCEEDINGS BELOW

This litigation emanates from the meteoric rise and equally rapid demise of Osborne Computer Corporation (hereafter the company). Founded in 1980 by entrepreneur Adam Osborne, the company manufactured the first portable personal computer for the mass market. Shipments began in 1981. By fall 1982, sales of the company's sole product, the Osborne I computer, had reached $10 million per month, making the company one of the fastest growing enterprises in the history of American business.

Plaintiffs in this case were investors in the company. They include individuals as well as pension and venture capital investment funds....

The company retained defendant Arthur Young & Company (hereafter Arthur Young), one of the then-"Big Eight" public accounting firms, to perform audits and issue audit reports on its 1981 and 1982 financial statements. (Arthur Young has since merged with Ernst & Whinney to become Ernst & Young, now one of the "Big Six" accounting firms.) ...

Arthur Young issued unqualified or "clean" audit opinions on the company's 1981 and 1982 financial statements....

\* \* \*

Plaintiffs' principal expert witness, William J. Baedecker, reviewed the 1982 audit and offered a critique identifying more than 40 deficiencies in Arthur Young's performance amounting, in Baedecker's view, to gross professional negligence.... He found the liabilities on the company's financial statements to have been understated by approximately $3 million. As a result, the company's supposed $69,000 operating profit was, in his view, a loss of more than $3 million. He also determined that

Arthur Young had discovered material weaknesses in the company's accounting controls, but failed to report its discovery to management.

\* \* \*

## III.

### APPROACHES TO THE PROBLEM OF AUDITOR LIABILITY TO THIRD PERSONS

The complex nature of the audit function and its economic implications has resulted in different approaches to the question whether CPA auditors should be subjected to liability to third parties who read and rely on audit reports. Although three schools of thought are commonly recognized, there are some variations within each school and recent case law suggests a possible trend toward merger of two of the three approaches.

A substantial number of jurisdictions follow the lead of Chief Judge Cardozo's 1931 opinion for the New York Court of Appeals in *Ultramares, supra,* 174 N.E. 441, by denying recovery to third parties for auditor negligence in the absence of a third party relationship to the auditor that is "akin to privity." (See pt. III(A), *post.*) In contrast, a handful of jurisdictions, spurred by law review commentary, have recently allowed recovery based on auditor negligence to third parties whose reliance on the audit report was "foreseeable." (See pt. III(B), *post.*)

Most jurisdictions, supported by the weight of commentary and the modern English common law decisions cited by the parties, have steered a middle course based in varying degrees on Restatement Second of Torts section 552, which generally imposes liability on suppliers of commercial information to third persons who are intended beneficiaries of the information. . . .

\* \* \*

### A. *Privity of Relationship*

In *Ultramares, supra,* 174 N.E. 441, plaintiff made three unsecured loans totalling $165,000 to a company that went bankrupt. Plaintiff sued the company's auditors, claiming reliance on their audit opinion that the company's balance sheet "present[ed] a true and correct view of the financial condition of [the company]." (*Id.* at p. 442.) Although the balance sheet showed a net worth of $1 million, the company was actually insolvent. The company's management attempted to mask its financial condition; the auditors failed to follow paper trails to "off-the-books" transactions that, if properly analyzed, would have revealed the company's impecunious situation.

The jury, precluded by the trial judge from considering a fraud cause of action, returned a verdict in plaintiff's favor based on the auditor's negligence in conducting the audit. The New York Court of Appeals, speaking through Chief Judge Cardozo, reinstated the fraud cause of action but set aside the negligence verdict.

The auditor in *Ultramares* knew the company was in need of capital and that its audit opinion would be displayed to third parties "as the basis of financial dealings." (*Ultramares, supra,* 174 N.E. at p. 442.) In this regard, it supplied to the company 32 copies of the opinion "with serial numbers as counterpart originals." (*Ibid.*) Plaintiff's name, however, was not mentioned to the auditor nor was the auditor told about any actual or proposed credit or investment transactions in which its audit opinion would be presented to a third party.

With respect to the negligence claim, the court found the auditor owed no duty to the third party creditor for an "erroneous opinion." In an often quoted passage, it observed: "If liability for negligence exists, a thoughtless slip or blunder, the failure to detect a theft or forgery beneath the cover of deceptive entries, may expose accountants to a liability in an indeterminate amount for an indeterminate time to an indeterminate class. The hazards of a business conducted on these terms are so extreme as to enkindle doubt whether a flaw may not exist in the implication of a duty that exposes to these consequences." (*Ultramares, supra,* 174 N.E. at p. 444.)

Although acknowledging the demise of privity of contract as a limitation on tort liability in the context of personal injury and property damage, the court distinguished between liability arising from a "physical force" and "the circulation of a thought or the release of the explosive power resident in words." (*Ultramares, supra,* 174 N.E. at p. 445.) It also distinguished its own prior decision in *Glanzer v. Shepherd* (1922) 233 N.Y. 236 [135 N.E. 275, 23 A.L.R. 1425], in which a seller of beans requested the operator of a public scale to give a certificate of weight to the buyer. When the certificate proved inaccurate and the buyer sued, the court held the operator liable for negligence. As the court explained, the difference between the cases was that "the transmission of the certificate [in *Glanzer*] was not merely one possibility among many, but the '*end and aim of the transaction*,' as certain and immediate and deliberately willed as if a husband were to order a gown to be delivered to his wife, or a telegraph company, contracting with the sender of a message, were to telegraph it wrongly to the damage of the person expected to receive it." (174 N.E. at p. 445, italics added.)

In summarizing its holding, the court emphasized that it was not releasing auditors from liability to third parties for fraud but merely for "honest blunder." (*Glanzer v. Shepherd, supra,* 174 N.E. at p. 448.) It questioned "whether the average business man receiving a certificate without paying for it, and receiving it as one of a multitude of possible investors, would look for anything more." (*Ibid.*)

In cases following *Ultramares,* the New York Court of Appeals has not required privity of contract as a universal prerequisite to third party suits against auditors; rather, on occasion, it has found an equivalent privity of relationship between the auditor and the plaintiff. . . .

\* \* \*

The New York Court of Appeals restated the law in light of *Ultramares,* . . . and other cases in *Credit Alliance v. Arthur Andersen & Co.* (1985) 65 N.Y.2d 536 [493 N.Y.S.2d 435, 483 N.E.2d 110]. . . .

The New York court promulgated the following rule for determining auditor liability to third parties for negligence: "Before accountants may be held liable in negligence to noncontractual parties who rely to their detriment on inaccurate financial reports, certain prerequisites must be satisfied: (1) the accountant must have been aware that the financial reports were to be used for a particular purpose or purposes; (2) in the furtherance of which a known party or parties was intended to rely; and (3) there must have been some conduct on the part of the accountants linking them to that party or parties, which evinces the accountants' understanding of that party or parties' reliance." (*Credit Alliance v. Arthur Andersen & Co., supra,* 483 N.E.2d at p. 118.)

\* \* \*

From the cases cited by the parties, it appears at least nine states purport to follow privity or near privity rules restricting the liability of auditors to parties with whom they have a contractual or similar relationship. . . .

### B. Foreseeability

Arguing that accountants should be subject to liability to third persons on the same basis as other tortfeasors, Justice Howard Wiener advocated rejection of the rule of *Ultramares* in a 1983 law review article. (Wiener, *Common Law Liability of the Certified Public Accountant for Negligent Misrepresentation* (1983) 20 San Diego L.Rev. 233 [hereafter Wiener].) In its place, he proposed a rule based on foreseeability of injury to third persons. Criticizing what he called the "anachronistic protection" given to accountants by the traditional rules limiting third person liability, he concluded: "Accountant liability based on foreseeable injury would serve the dual functions of compensation for injury and deterrence of negligent conduct. Moreover, it is a just and rational judicial policy that the same criteria govern the imposition of negligence liability, regardless of the context in which it arises. The accountant, the investor, and the general public will in the long run benefit when the liability of the certified public accountant for negligent misrepresentation is measured by the foreseeability standard." (*Id.* at p. 260.) Under the rule proposed by Justice Wiener, "[f]oreseeability of the risk would be a question of fact for the jury to be disturbed on appeal only where there is insufficient evidence to support the finding." (*Id.* at pp. 256–257.)

Following in part Justice Wiener's approach, the New Jersey Supreme Court upheld a claim for negligent misrepresentation asserted by stock purchasers against an auditor who had rendered an unqualified audit report approving fraudulently prepared financial statements. (*Rosenblum v. Adler* (1983) 93 N.J. 324 [461 A.2d 138, 35 A.L.R.4th 199].) The court found no reason to distinguish accountants from other suppliers of products or services to the public and no reason to deny to third party users of financial statements recovery for economic loss resulting from negligent misrepresentation. (*Id.* at pp. 142–146.) From its review of the purpose and history of the audit function, it concluded: "The auditor's function has expanded from that of a watchdog for management to an independent evaluator of the adequacy and fairness of financial statements issued by management to stockholders, creditors, and others." (*Id.* at p. 149.) Noting the apparent ability of accounting firms to obtain insurance against third party claims under the federal securities laws, the court posited the same or similar protection would be available for common law negligent misrepresentation claims. (*Ibid.*)

From a public policy standpoint, the court emphasized the potential deterrent effect of a liability-imposing rule on the conduct and cost of audits: "The imposition of a duty to foreseeable users may cause accounting firms to engage in more thorough reviews. This might entail setting up stricter standards and applying closer supervision, which should tend to reduce the number of instances in which liability would ensue. Much of the additional cost incurred either because of more thorough auditing review or increased insurance premiums would be borne by the business entity and its stockholders or its customers." (*Rosenblum v. Adler, supra,* 461 A.2d at p. 152.)

\* \* \*

Two other state high courts—those of Wisconsin and Mississippi—have endorsed foreseeability rules. . . .

\* \* \*

In the nearly 10 years since it was formally proposed, the foreseeability approach has not attracted a substantial following. . . .

The foreseeability approach has also encountered substantial criticism from commentators, who have questioned, among other matters, its failure to consider seriously the problem of indeterminate liability and its prediction of a significant deterrent effect that will improve the quality of audit reporting. Other commentators have disagreed. The body of scholarly and practical literature is substantial.

### C.   The Restatement: Intent to Benefit Third Persons

Section 552 of the Restatement Second of Torts covers "Information Negligently Supplied for the Guidance of Others." It states a general principle that one who negligently supplies false information "for the guidance of others in their business transactions" is liable for economic loss suffered by the recipients in justifiable reliance on the information. (*Id.,* subd. (1).) But the liability created by the general principle is expressly limited to loss suffered: "(a) [B]y the person or one of a limited group of persons for whose benefit and guidance he intends to supply the information or knows that the recipient intends to supply it; and (b) through reliance upon it in a transaction that he intends the information to influence or knows that the recipient so intends or in a substantially similar transaction." (*Id.,* subd. (2).) To paraphrase, a supplier of information is liable for negligence to a third party only if he or she intends to supply the information for the benefit of one or more third parties in a specific transaction or type of transaction identified to the supplier.

Comment (h) to subdivision (2) of section 552, Restatement Second of Torts, observes that the liability of a negligent supplier of information is appropriately more narrowly restricted than that of an intentionally fraudulent supplier. It also notes that a commercial supplier of information has a legitimate concern as to the nature and scope of the client's transactions that may expand the supplier's exposure liability. As the comment states: "In many situations the identity of the person for whose guidance the information is supplied is of no moment to the person who supplies it, although the number and character of the persons to be reached and influenced, and the nature and extent of the transaction for which guidance is furnished may be vitally important. *This is true because the risk of liability to which the supplier subjects himself by undertaking to give the information, while it may not be affected by the identity of the person for whose guidance the information is given, is vitally affected by the number and character of the persons, and particularly the nature and the extent of the proposed transaction.*" (*Ibid.,* italics added.)

To offer a simple illustration of comment (h) to subdivision (2) of section 552, Restatement Second of Torts, an auditor engaged to perform an audit and render a report to a third person whom the auditor knows is considering a $10 million investment in the client's business is on notice of a specific potential liability. It may then act to encounter, limit or avoid the risk. In contrast, an auditor who is simply asked for a generic audit and report to the client has no comparable notice.

\* \* \*

Although the parties debate precisely how many states follow the Restatement rule, a review of the cases reveals the rule has somewhat more support than the privity of relationship rule and much more support than the foreseeability rule. At least 17 state and federal decisions have endorsed the rule in this and related contexts. Whatever the exact number of states that have endorsed it, the Restatement rule has been for many, if not most, courts a satisfactory compromise between their discomfort with the traditional privity approach and the "specter of unlimited liability." (*Briggs v. Sterner* (S.D.Iowa 1981) 529 F.Supp. 1155, 1177.)

\* \* \*

Of the approaches we have reviewed, Restatement Second of Torts section 552, subdivision (b) is most consistent with the elements and policy foundations of the tort of negligent misrepresentation. The rule expressed there attempts to define a narrow and circumscribed class of persons to whom or for whom representations are made. In this way, it recognizes commercial realities by avoiding both unlimited and uncertain liability for economic losses in cases of professional mistake and exoneration of the auditor in situations where it clearly intended to undertake the responsibility of influencing particular business transactions involving third persons. The Restatement rule thus appears to be a sensible and moderate approach to the potential consequences of imposing unlimited negligence liability which we have identified.

We recognize the rule expressed in the Restatement Second of Torts has been criticized in some quarters as vague and potentially arbitrary. In his article advocating a foreseeability rule, Justice Wiener generally criticized the Restatement rule as resting "solely on chance considerations" and "fortuitousness" (e.g., the "state of the mind of the accountant" and the scope of his engagement) having, in his view, nothing to do with increasing the flow of accurate information. (Wiener, *supra*, 20 San Diego L.Rev. at p. 252.)

We respectfully disagree. In seeking to identify a specific class of persons and a transaction that the supplier of information "intends the information to influence," the authors of the Restatement Second of Torts have applied basic factors of tort liability recognized in this state and elsewhere (see *Biakanja, supra,* 49 Cal.2d 647). By confining what might otherwise be unlimited liability to those persons whom the engagement is designed to benefit, the Restatement rule requires that the supplier of information receive notice of potential third party claims, thereby allowing it to ascertain the potential scope of its liability and make rational decisions regarding the undertaking. The receipt of such notice justifies imposition of auditor liability for conduct that is merely negligent.

Moreover, the identification of a limited class of plaintiffs to whom the supplier itself has directed its activity establishes a closer connection between the supplier's negligent act and the recipient's injury, thereby ameliorating the otherwise difficult concerns of causation and of credible evidence of reliance. Finally, no unfairness results to those recipients who are excluded from the class of beneficiaries because they have means of private ordering—among other things, they can establish direct communication with an auditor and obtain a report for their own direct use and benefit. For these reasons, the rule expressed in the Restatement Second of Torts represents a reasoned, not an arbitrary, approach to the problem before us.

\* \* \*

# V.

### DISPOSITION

This case was tried on the assumption that the general negligence rule and foreseeability approach of *International Mortgage Co. v. John P. Butler Accountancy Corp., supra,* 177 Cal.App.3d 806, represented California law. The jury was instructed in accordance with that approach. For the reasons stated above, we have rejected the rule of *International Mortgage Co.* in favor of a negligent misrepresentation rule substantially in accord with section 552 of the Restatement Second of Torts. As a result, plaintiffs' judgment based on the general negligence rule must be set aside. Because plaintiffs were not clients of Arthur Young, they were not entitled to recover on a general negligence theory.

\* \* \*

### *NOTES*

**1. Pure Economic Loss.** Generally courts are quite hesitant to award pure economic loss for negligence. Instead economic loss is usually only awarded when it flows from a negligently inflicted personal injury or property damage. Such economic loss is deemed parasitic to the property or personal injury suffered by the plaintiff. Consequently, if A's negligence while driving caused personal injury to B, B's recovery includes lost wages and other economic expenses proximately caused by the personal injury. If on the other hand, A's negligent automobile accident causes C to be delayed in traffic and therefore lose compensation for being late to work, C is precluded from recovery. In essence, there is no legal duty under negligence to refrain from causing pure economic loss.

**2.  Negligent Misrepresentation.** Negligent misrepresentation, is a generally accepted exception to the rule that the negligent defendant is not liable for pure economic loss. The Restatement (Second) of Torts defines negligent misrepresentation as follows:

(1) One who, in the course of his business, profession, or employment, or in any other transaction in which he has a pecuniary interest, supplies false information for the guidance of others in their business transactions, is subject to liability for pecuniary loss caused to them by their justifiable reliance upon the information, if he fails to exercise reasonable care or competence in obtaining or communicating the information.

(2) Except as stated in subsection (3), the liability stated in subsection (1) is limited to loss suffered

(a) by the person or one of a limited group of persons for whose benefit and guidance he intends to supply the information or knows that the recipient intends to supply it; and

(b) through reliance upon it in a transaction that he intends the information to influence or knows that the recipient so intends or in a substantially similar transaction

(3) The liability of one who is under a public duty to give the information extends to loss suffered by any of the class of persons for whose benefit the duty is created, in any of the transactions in which it is intended to protect them.

Restatement (Second) of Torts § 552.

**3.  Requirement of Business Relationship and Justifiable Reliance.** Negligent misrepresentation as the Restatement in Note 2, supra, indicates is limited to information supplied in a business, professional or employment relationship. Some courts do not go as far as the Restatement and require a special business relationship. Accountants and investment advisors typify professionals potentially liable for the economic consequence of their malpractice. Since most of the injuries caused by their professional negligence result in only pure economic loss and no physical injuries, without imposing liability for pure economic loss, these professions would not be accountable to their clients for negligence. Courts generally recognize a special business relationship between these professionals and their clients.

But consider cases where courts determined that there was no "special relationship" giving rise to a duty to impart correct information. In *Andres v. LeRoy Adventures, Inc.,* 201 A.D.2d 262, 607 N.Y.S.2d 261 (1994), persons who hired a restaurant for a wedding reception, later brought suit against the restaurant for negligent misrepresentation arising from the restaurant's failure to disclose relevant information. The Supreme Court, Appellate Division, held that the plaintiffs failed to show that the restaurant made negligent misrepresentations, as no special relationship between the parties could be discerned from the casual dealings between the parties. Similarly, in *Barden v. Harpercollins Publishers Inc.,* 863 F.Supp. 41 (1994), a book buyer brought an action against a publisher to recover for the alleged misrepresentation about an attorney's qualifications listed in the book. The District Court of Massachusetts held that the publisher did not owe a duty to the book buyer even though the publisher sought a profit, as requiring publishers to check every fact in books they publish would be impractical.

Consider also *Conway v. Pacific University*, 129 Or.App. 307, 879 P.2d 201 (1994) where a university professor claimed he was denied tenure because of poor student evaluations. The professor alleged the university had negligently misrepresented in hiring negotiations that student evaluations would not affect his tenure decision. The court held there was no special relationship justifying liability since the alleged misrepresentation occurred in the context of negotiations where each party had "divergent rather than common interests."

But in contrast, consider *McCullough v. USAir, Inc.*, 1990 WL 127751 (E.D.Pa.1990) where the airline's alleged negligent misrepresentation effectively concealed the name of the passenger who had injured the plaintiff by dropping baggage from the overhead compartment. The court recognized the case was not "an archetypical application" of (Restatement) Section 552 but concluded that the misrepresentation satisfied the standard since they were made in the course of a business and pecuniary relationship.

**4. Third Party Recovery.** The principal case outlines the debate over when third parties should recovery for negligent misrepresentation. Historically, a contractual relationship (privity) or at least near privity was required. A majority of states now follow the Restatement view expanding liability as indicated above to a limited group, for which the information supplier intends to supply the information or knows the recipient so intends for a substantially similar transaction, *see* Restatement (Second) of Torts § 552(2) supra. A third more aggressive approach holding the information supplier responsible for all foreseeable recipients is rarely followed as noted by the principal case.

Why do most courts hesitate to impose the ordinary foreseeable person standard in the context of negligently supplied information? Does the problem of potentially crushing liability against an accountant or investment advisor justify a stricter limit? Do scandals, such as Enron, where the financial viability of a company was misrepresented, argue for greater accountant liability? Should stockholders be able to recover losses resulting from the negligent failure of accountants to discover and report corporations in finacial distress? Is the potential for liability comparable to negligent inflection of emotional distress?

**5. Further Study.** For further study, see Peter Hanauer, LL.B., *Fraud and Deceit*, 60 NYJUR FRAUD § 126 (1997), which discusses the limited circumstances under which New York adheres to the view that negligent representations are actionable. See also Jeanne E. Irving, *What a Difference a Decade Makes—Chipping away at the Bily Club* 1438 PLI/Corp 195 (2004), where Irving argues that in the decade since *Bily v. Arthor Young and Co.* was decided that the pendulum has swung back in the direction of expanding liability, as courts have become less concerned about limiting liability and more concerned about "the danger posed by societal injuries resulting from unchecked accounting misstatements," such as a loss of consumer confidence in the stock market. See also, Richard P. Salgado, *Negligent Misrepresentation and The Economic Loss Rule*, 22 Colo.Law 1689 (1993), which discusses the issues to be considered when evaluating an action based on negligent misrepresentation.

## 9. Economic Loss

# J'AIRE CORP. v. GREGORY

Supreme Court of California.

24 Cal.3d 799, 157 Cal.Rptr. 407, 598 P.2d 60 (1979).

BIRD, Chief Justice.

Appellant, a lessee, sued respondent, a general contractor, for damages resulting from the delay in completion of a construction project at the premises where appellant operated a restaurant. Respondent demurred successfully and the complaint was dismissed. This court must decide whether a contractor who undertakes construction work pursuant to a contract with the owner of premises may be held liable in tort for business losses suffered by a lessee when the contractor negligently fails to complete the project with due diligence.

### I

The facts as pleaded are as follows. Appellant, J'Aire Corporation, operates a restaurant at the Sonoma County Airport in premises leased from the County of Sonoma. Under the terms of the lease the county was to provide heat and air conditioning. In 1975 the county entered into a contract with respondent for improvements to the restaurant premises, including renovation of the heating and air conditioning systems and installation of insulation.

As the contract did not specify any date for completion of the work, appellant alleged the work was to have been completed within a reasonable time as defined by custom and usage. (Civ. Code, § 1657.) Despite requests that respondent complete the construction promptly, the work was not completed within a reasonable time. Because the restaurant could not operate during part of the construction and was without heat and air conditioning for a longer period, appellant suffered loss of business and resulting loss of profits.

Appellant alleged two causes of action in its third amended complaint. The first cause of action was based upon the theory that it was a third party beneficiary of the contract between the county and respondent. The second cause of action sounded in tort and was based upon negligence in completing the work within a reasonable time. Damages of $50,000 were claimed.

Respondent demurred on the ground that the complaint did not state facts sufficient to constitute a cause of action. (Code Civ. Proc., § 430.10, subd. (e).) The trial court sustained the demurrer without leave to amend and the complaint was dismissed. On appeal only the sustaining of the demurrer to the second cause of action is challenged.

### II

In testing the sufficiency of a complaint, a reviewing court must assume the truth of all material allegations in the complaint (*Serrano v. Priest* (1971) 5 Cal.3d 584, 591 [96 Cal.Rptr. 601, 487 P.2d 1241]), including the allegations of negligence and cause in fact. The only question before this court is whether a cause of action for negligent loss of expected economic advantage may be maintained under these facts.

Liability for negligent conduct may only be imposed where there is a duty of care owed by the defendant to the plaintiff or to a class of which the plaintiff is a member. (*Richards v. Stanley* (1954) 43 Cal.2d 60, 63 [271 P.2d 23].) A duty of care may arise through statute or by contract. Alternatively, a duty may be premised upon the general character of the activity in which the defendant engaged, the relationship between the parties or even the interdependent nature of human society. (See *Valdez v. J.D. Diffenbaugh Co.* (1975) 51 Cal.App.3d 494, 505 [124 Cal.Rptr. 467].) Whether a duty is owed is simply a shorthand way of phrasing what is " 'the essential question—whether the plaintiff's interests are entitled to legal protection against the defendant's conduct.' " (*Dillon v. Legg* (1968) 68 Cal.2d 728, 734 [69 Cal.Rptr. 72, 441 P.2d 912, 29 A.L.R.3d 1316], quoting from Prosser, Law of Torts (3d ed. 1964) pp. 332–333. See also Prosser, Law of Torts (4th ed. 1971) pp. 324–327; Fleming, An Introduction to *The Law of Torts* (1967) pp. 43–50.)

This court has held that a plaintiff's interest in prospective economic advantage may be protected against injury occasioned by negligent as well as intentional conduct. For example, economic losses such as lost earnings or profits are recoverable as part of general damages in a suit for personal injury based on negligence. (*Connolly v. Pre–Mixed Concrete Co.* (1957) 49 Cal.2d 483, 489 [319 P.2d 343]; *Neumann v. Bishop* (1976) 59 Cal.App.3d 451, 462 [130 Cal.Rptr. 786].) Where negligent conduct causes injury to real or personal property, the plaintiff may recover damages for profits lost during the time necessary to repair or replace the property. (*Reynolds v. Bank of America* (1959) 53 Cal.2d 49, 50–51 [345 P.2d 926].)

Even when only injury to prospective economic advantage is claimed, recovery is not foreclosed. Where a special relationship exists between the parties, a plaintiff may recover for loss of expected economic advantage through the negligent performance of a contract although the parties were not in contractual privity. *Biakanja v. Irving* (1958) 49 Cal.2d 647 [320 P.2d 16, 65 A.L.R.2d 1358], *Lucas v. Hamm* (1961) 56 Cal.2d 583 [15 Cal.Rptr. 821, 364 P.2d 685] and *Heyer v. Flaig* (1969) 70 Cal.2d 223 [74 Cal.Rptr. 225, 449 P.2d 161] held that intended beneficiaries of wills could sue to recover legacies lost through the negligent preparation of the will. (See also Prosser, Law of Torts (4th ed. 1971) p. 952.)

In each of the above cases, the court determined that defendants owed plaintiffs a duty of care by applying criteria set forth in *Biakanja v. Irving, supra*, 49 Cal.2d at page 650. Those criteria are (1) the extent to which the transaction was intended to affect the plaintiff, (2) the foreseeability of harm to the plaintiff, (3) the degree of certainty that the plaintiff suffered injury, (4) the closeness of the connection between the defendant's conduct and the injury suffered, (5) the moral blame attached to the defendant's conduct and (6) the policy of preventing future harm. (See also *Connor v. Great Western Sav. & Loan Assn.* (1968) 69 Cal.2d 850, 865 [73 Cal.Rptr. 369, 447 P.2d 609, 39 A.L.R.3d 224].)

Applying these criteria to the facts as pleaded, it is evident that a duty was owed by respondent to appellant in the present case. (1) The contract entered into between respondent and the county was for the renovation of the premises in which appellant maintained its business. The contract could not have been performed without impinging on that business. Thus respondent's performance was intended to, and did, directly affect appellant. (2) Accordingly, it was clearly foreseeable that any significant delay in completing the construction would adversely affect appellant's business beyond the normal disruption associated with such construction. Appellant alleges this fact was repeatedly drawn to respondent's attention. (3) Further, appellant's complaint leaves no doubt that appellant suffered harm since it was unable to operate its business for one month and suffered additional loss of business while the premises were without heat and air conditioning. (4) Appellant has also alleged that delays occasioned by the respondent's conduct were closely connected to, indeed directly caused its injury. (5) In addition, respondent's lack of diligence in the present case was particularly blameworthy since it continued after the probability of damage was drawn directly to respondent's attention. (6) Finally, public policy supports finding a duty of care in the present case. The wilful failure or refusal of a contractor to prosecute a construction project with diligence, where another is injured as a result, has been made grounds for disciplining a licensed contractor. (Bus. & Prof. Code, § 7119.) Although this section does not provide a basis for imposing liability where the delay in completing construction is due merely to negligence, it does indicate the seriousness with which the Legislature views unnecessary delays in the completion of construction.

In light of these factors, this court finds that respondent had a duty to complete construction in a manner that would have avoided unnecessary injury to appellant's business, even though the construction contract was with the owner of a building rather than with appellant, the tenant. (7) It is settled that a contractor owes a duty to avoid injury to the person or property of third parties. (See *Stewart v. Cox* (1961) 55 Cal.2d 857, 862–863 [13 Cal.Rptr. 521, 362 P.2d 345].) As appellant points out, injury to a tenant's business can often result in greater hardship than damage to a tenant's person or property. Where the risk of harm is foreseeable, as it was in the present case, an injury to the plaintiff's economic interests should not go uncompensated merely because it was unaccompanied by any injury to his person or property.

To hold under these facts that a cause of action has been stated for negligent interference with prospective economic advantage is consistent with the recent trend in tort cases. This court has repeatedly eschewed overly rigid common law formulations of duty in favor of allowing compensation for foreseeable injuries caused by a defendant's want of ordinary care. (See, e.g., *Dillon v. Legg, supra,* 68 Cal.2d at p. 746 [liability for mother's emotional distress when child killed by defendant's negligence]; *Rowland v. Christian* (1968) 69 Cal.2d 108, 119 [70 Cal. Rptr. 97, 443 P.2d 561, 32 A.L.R.3d 496] [liability of host for injury to social guest on premises]; cf. *Brown v. Merlo* (1973) 8 Cal.3d 855 [106

Cal.Rptr. 388, 506 P.2d 212, 66 A.L.R.3d 505] [liability of automobile driver for injury to nonpaying passenger]; *Rodriguez* v. *Bethlehem Steel Corp.* (1974) 12 Cal.3d 382 [115 Cal.Rptr. 765, 525 P.2d 669] [liability for loss of consortium].) Rather than traditional notions of duty, this court has focused on foreseeability as the key component necessary to establish liability: "While the question whether one owes a duty to another must be decided on a case-by-case basis, every case is governed by the rule of general application that all persons are required to use ordinary care to prevent others from being injured as the result of their conduct. ...[F]oreseeability of the risk is a primary consideration in establishing the element of duty." (*Weirum v. RKO General, Inc.* (1975) 15 Cal.3d 40, 46 [123 Cal.Rptr. 468, 539 P.2d 36], fn. omitted.) Similarly, respondent is liable if his lack of ordinary care caused foreseeable injury to the economic interests of appellant.

In addition, this holding is consistent with the Legislature's declaration of the basic principle of tort liability, embodied in Civil Code section 1714, that every person is responsible for injuries caused by his or her lack of ordinary care. (See *Rowland v. Christian, supra,* 69 Cal.2d at p. 119.) That section does not distinguish among injuries to one's person, one's property or one's financial interests. Damages for loss of profits or earnings are recoverable where they result from an injury to one's person or property caused by another's negligence. Recovery for injury to one's economic interests, where it is the foreseeable result of another's want of ordinary care, should not be foreclosed simply because it is the only injury that occurs.

Respondent cites *Fifield Manor v. Finston* (1960) 54 Cal.2d 632 [7 Cal.Rptr. 377, 354 P.2d 1073, 78 A.L.R.2d 813] for the proposition that recovery may not be had for negligent loss of prospective economic advantage. *Fifield* concerned the parallel tort of interference with contractual relations. (See Prosser, *supra,* Law of Torts (4th ed.) at p. 952.) There a nonprofit retirement home that had contracted with Ross to provide him with lifetime medical care sued a driver who negligently struck and killed Ross. The plaintiff argued it had become liable under the contract for Ross' medical bills and sought recovery from the driver, on both a theory of direct liability and one of subrogation. Recovery was denied.

The critical factor of foreseeability distinguishes *Fifield* from the present case. Although it was reasonably foreseeable that defendant's negligence might cause injury to Ross, it was less foreseeable that it would injure the retirement home's economic interest. Defendant had not entered into any relationship or undertaken any activity where negligence on his part was reasonably likely to affect plaintiff adversely. Thus, the nexus between the defendant's conduct and the risk of the injury that occurred to the plaintiff was too tenuous to support the imposition of a duty owing to the retirement home. (*Id.,* at p. 637.) In contrast, the nexus in the present case between the injury that occurred and respondent's conduct is extremely close. *Fifield* does not entirely foreclose recovery for negligent interference with prospective economic advantage.

Respondent also relies on *Adams v. Southern Pac. Transportation Co.* (1975) 50 Cal.App.3d 37 [123 Cal.Rptr. 216]. In *Adams* plaintiff employees were held unable to sue the railroad whose cargo of bombs exploded, destroying the factory where they worked. It should be noted that the Court of Appeal in *Adams* clearly believed that plaintiffs should be permitted to maintain an action for negligent interference with prospective economic interests. It reluctantly held they could not only under the belief that *Fifield* precluded such recovery. Adhering to the *Fifield* rule, the Court of Appeal in *Adams* did not determine whether the railroad owed plaintiffs a duty of care. The *Fifield* case has been the subject of some criticism. In addition to *Adams v. Southern Pac. Transportation Co., supra*, 50 Cal.App.3d 37, see, e.g., Note (1964) 16 Stan. L.Rev. 664, 671; Comment (1961) 34 So.Cal. L.Rev. 467; Comment (1961) 46 Iowa L.Rev. 876; Prosser, *supra*, Law of Torts (4th ed.) at page 940. (50 Cal.App.3d at p. 47.) In the present case, plaintiff's injury stemmed directly from conduct intended to affect plaintiff and was more readily foreseeable than the damage to the employer's property in *Adams*. To the extent that *Adams* holds that there can be no recovery for negligent interference with prospective economic advantage, it is disapproved.

The chief dangers which have been cited in allowing recovery for negligent interference with prospective economic advantage are the possibility of excessive liability, the creation of an undue burden on freedom of action, the possibility of fraudulent or collusive claims and the often speculative nature of damages. (See, e.g., Prosser, *supra*, Law of Torts (4th ed.) at p. 940 and Note, *Negligent Interference With Economic Expectancy: The Case for Recovery* (1964) 16 Stan.L.Rev. 664, 679–693, neither of which considers these fears to justify denial of recovery in all cases.) Central to these fears is the possibility that liability will be imposed for remote consequences, out of proportion to the magnitude of the defendant's wrongful conduct.

However, the factors enumerated in *Biakanja* and applied in subsequent cases place a limit on recovery by focusing judicial attention on the foreseeability of the injury and the nexus between the defendant's conduct and the plaintiff's injury. These factors and ordinary principles of tort law such as proximate cause are fully adequate to limit recovery without the drastic consequence of an absolute rule which bars recovery in all such cases. (See *Dillon v. Legg, supra*, 68 Cal.2d at p. 746.) Following these principles, recovery for negligent interference with prospective economic advantage will be limited to instances where the risk of harm is foreseeable and is closely connected with the defendant's conduct, where damages are not wholly speculative and the injury is not part of the plaintiff's ordinary business risk.

## III

Accordingly, this court holds that a contractor owes a duty of care to the tenant of a building undergoing construction work to prosecute that work in a manner which does not cause undue injury to the tenant's business, where such injury is reasonably foreseeable. The demurrer to appellant's second cause of action should not have been sustained. The judgment of dismissal is reversed.

## NOTES

**1. Allowing Pure Economic Loss Beyond Misrepresentation.** With the exception of misrepresentation of information in a business or professional context, as discussed in the previous principal case and notes, most courts do not allow recovery of pure economic loss under negligence. The principal case is an unusual exception. Do you think it is justified? Consider also *People Express Airlines, Inc. v. Consolidated Rail Corp.,* 100 N.J. 246, 495 A.2d 107 (1985), where the New Jersey Supreme Court allowed People Express Airline to recover for lost profits caused by a negligently started fire which forced the terminal to close. The airline suffered no physical damage but was deemed "particularly foreseeable" victim and allowed recovery. Does *People Express* have as a compelling a claim to economic recovery as the plaintiff in the principal case? Should the employees of a bombed factory as noted in the principal case be entitled to recovery? Despite foreseeability, most courts find the spectrum of unrestricted liability for pure economic loss too excessive to impose liability.

**2. Attorney Liability to Third Parties.** In limited circumstances attorneys have been held liable to non-client third parties. Consider *Lucas v. Hamm*, 56 Cal.2d 583, 15 Cal.Rptr. 821, 364 P.2d 685 (1961) where beneficiaries of a will complained they were inadvertently precluded from benefitting because of the attorney's alleged negligent failure to avoid an invalid will under the rule against perpetuity. Although finding the general practitioner was not negligent given the law's complexity, the court did find a duty was owed to the beneficiaries. Similarly a public notary was held liable to beneficiaries of a will for his negligence. See *Biakanja v. Irving*, 49 Cal.2d 647, 320 P.2d 16 (Cal. 1958) cited in the principal case.

# SECTION I.   DEFENSES TO NEGLIGENCE

## 1.   Contributory and Comparative Negligence

### MARK v. PACIFIC GAS AND ELECTRIC CO.

Supreme Court of California.
7 Cal.3d 170, 101 Cal.Rptr. 908, 496 P.2d 1276 (1972).

BURKE, Justice.

Plaintiffs appeal from a judgment of nonsuit entered by the San Francisco Superior Court at the close of plaintiffs' case in a wrongful death action. Plaintiffs' decedent, Calvin Mark, was electrocuted while attempting to remove or unscrew a light bulb from a street lamp located outside his apartment bedroom window. Plaintiffs sued, under various theories of liability, Calvin's landlord (Mr. and Mrs. Chase), the City and County of San Francisco ("City"), and Pacific Gas and Electric Company ("PG & E"). We have concluded that although a nonsuit was properly entered in favor of the landlord and City, there was ample evidence to support a jury verdict against PG & E, and that the judgment of nonsuit in favor of PG & E should be reversed.

\* \* \*

Viewed in the light most favorable to plaintiffs, the evidence disclosed the following facts: Calvin and his three roommates moved into the Chases' apartment building in June 1964. At once the boys discovered that the light from a street lamp pole standing adjacent to their bedroom window was so bright that it disturbed their sleep; even with the drapes drawn and room lights extinguished the boys were able to read by the light cast by the street lamp. Calvin and his roommates complained to the Chases regarding the light, and Mr. Chase contacted PG & E which advised him to call City's street and lighting department. Chase did so and the City directed PG & E to examine the lamp. Thereupon a PG & E inspector attempted to reduce the light's glare by partly blackening a portion of the plastic globe or canopy surrounding the bulb; subsequently Chase also blackened part of the globe with aluminum paint. These efforts, however, had no measurable effect in reducing the intensity of the light. The boys themselves called City and PG & E to complain of the matter, but the light remained undiminished in its intensity.

In September 1964 an automobile crashed into the lamp pole, breaking the bulb, knocking the canopy off the top, and bending the pole toward the Chases' apartment building. Although PG & E replaced bulb and canopy, the pole remained unstraightened. In its bent condition, the pole was only 10 inches away from the edge of a fire escape located just outside the bedroom window, and 55 inches from the window itself, thereby making the lamp easily accessible to the occupants of the room. Having received no effective assistance from Chase, City or PG & E, the boys decided to employ self-help, and from time to time thereafter they extinguished the light simply by removing the plastic canopy and unscrewing the bulb. The boys were able to unscrew the bulb without incident upon several occasions prior to Calvin's death. Twining (Calvin's roommate) testified that there was nothing about the light to indicate that the current flowing through the lamp was high voltage, and that there was no reason to believe that it was any different "than the one you would have in your room."

Each time the bulb was unscrewed and the light extinguished, employees of PG & E were called to the scene to correct the deficiency. The evidence showed that Luth, a PG & E employee, had screwed the bulb back in place on January 26, 1965, and again on February 6, 1965. On March 3, 1965, another employee, Rosner, was dispatched to correct an outage and was informed by Luth that someone had been tampering with the light fixture; PG & E records confirm that Rosner had been directed to "check for tampering." Rosner found the bulb unscrewed, was aware that someone had tampered with it, appreciated the danger involved, and attempted, without success, to locate someone in the apartment to warn. Rosner confirmed that there was nothing on the light to indicate that it contained high voltage; he testified that the bulb is "just a little bit larger" than an ordinary light bulb and can be unscrewed in the same manner as an ordinary bulb.

On March 9, 1965, Calvin's roommate, Twining, stepped onto the fire escape, removed the protective canopy surrounding the bulb by releasing a wire catch, and attempted to remove the bulb with a towel, but was unable to do so because of inadequate friction. Consequently, Calvin put on his ski gloves to insulate his hands from the heat and was electrocuted while attempting to remove the bulb. Apparently, his hand contacted an uninsulated wire lead which provided electricity for the light. Although photographic evidence indicates that there were two thick copper leads terminating below the porcelain bulb socket, Twining testified that he had never observed wires of any kind in or around the light bulb or at its base.

* * *

### DECEDENT'S CONTRIBUTORY NEGLIGENCE

The trial court also held, in nonsuiting plaintiffs, that decedent was contributorily negligent[8] as a matter of law. Ordinarily, the issue of contributory negligence is one for the jury. (*Pike v. Frank G. Hough Co.*, 2 Cal.3d 465, 469 [85 Cal.Rptr. 629, 467 P.2d 229]; *Elmore v. American Motors Corp.*, 70 Cal.2d 578, 583 [75 Cal.Rptr. 652, 451 P.2d 84].) Thus, "The rule is that 'Where the evidence on the issue of contributory negligence is conflicting, and would support a finding either way, the question is one of fact and not of law, and must be decided by the trier of the facts.' [Citation.] (8) '[C]ontributory negligence is not established as a matter of law unless the only reasonable hypothesis is that such negligence exists; that reasonable or sensible men could have drawn that conclusion and none other ...' [Citation.]" (*Hogue v. Southern Pacific Co.*, 1 Cal.3d 253, 259 [81 Cal.Rptr. 765, 460 P.2d 965].)

Contributory negligence generally falls within one of two categories: (1) voluntary exposure to the danger arising from defendant's negligence, or (2) other conduct falling below the standard of due care, i.e., for an adult, the conduct of a reasonable man under like circumstances. (See 2 Witkin, Summary of Cal. Law, *supra*, Torts, § 325, pp. 1521–1522; Rest.2d Torts, *supra*, § 466.) In order for voluntary exposure to danger to constitute contributory negligence, plaintiff "must have knowledge of such facts that, as a reasonable man, he should realize the danger involved," and "his intentional exposure of himself to the known danger must be unreasonable. In order that it may be unreasonable it is necessary that a reasonable man in his position would not expose himself to it." (Rest.2d Torts, *supra*, § 466, com. at p. 512.)

Thus, our courts have often held that one who knowingly touches a high voltage power line or wire may be held contributorily negligent as a

---

**8.** "Contributory negligence is conduct on the part of the plaintiff which falls below the standard to which he should conform for his own protection, and which is a legally contributing cause co-operating with the negligence of the defendant in bringing about the plaintiff's harm." (Rest.2d Torts, § 463.) "Unless the actor is a child or an insane person, the standard of conduct to which he must conform for his own protection is that of a reasonable man under like circumstances." (*Id.*, § 464, subd. (1).)

matter of law, since the danger of electrical shock from such high voltage lines is "presumed to be familiar to men of average intelligence." (*Andrews* v. *Valley Ice Co.*, 167 Cal. 11, 20 [138 P. 699] [power lines: decedent was a construction worker who "must have known the danger of getting near highly charged wires"]; see *Shade v. Bay Counties Power Co.*, 152 Cal. 10, 12 [92 P. 62] [hanging power lines: decedent was warned not to touch lines and "knew the danger of live wires"]; cf. *Mosley v. Arden Farms Co.*, 26 Cal.2d 213, 217 [157 P.2d 372, 158 A.L.R. 872] [all men are charged with knowledge of "the qualities, characteristics, and capacities of things and forces in so far as they are matters of common knowledge at the time and in the community ..."]; Rest.2d Torts, *supra*, § 290, and illus. 1 [one who grabs high voltage power line is negligent notwithstanding ignorance of danger if danger is matter of common knowledge in community].)

The evidence in the instant case failed to establish that Calvin himself knew or suspected that the lamp carried high voltage current, or that he appreciated the risk he took in attempting to unscrew the bulb. He had seen his roommates remove the bulb successfully upon several occasions, and there was nothing about the lamp pole or bulb to indicate any possible danger. Although the jury might have concluded that a 24–year-old college student[9] such as Calvin must have known the risk involved, the trial court removed that issue from its consideration.

Therefore, we are left with the question whether, under an objective standard, Calvin, as a reasonable man, should have appreciated the risk of substantial injury or death. Although the authorities indicate that all reasonable men may be deemed to know the risks inherent in touching overhead power lines, we cannot say on the present record that it is a matter of common knowledge either that ordinary street lamps contain high voltage current, or that one risks substantial injury by attempting to unscrew a street lamp bulb of the nature involved herein. As noted above, plaintiffs' expert, Oliphant, testified that there was nothing about the lamp pole which would indicate that it contained high voltage, and that only an expert could make that determination. Moreover, the fact that the bulb was removed on several occasions without causing an electrical shock is, at least, some indication that Calvin's death resulted from an unusual combination of factors with which no lay person may be said to have common knowledge.

It should be kept in mind that upon retrial of this case, defendant PG & E will have the opportunity of establishing, to the jury's satisfaction, that decedent knew or should have known the danger involved in attempting to unscrew the bulb in question. For example, defendant may be able to show, by expert testimony or otherwise, that it is a matter of common knowledge in the community that such a danger exists. Nothing in the present record, however, establishes that proposition, and we are unable to say that the matter is so beyond reasonable dispute as to be subject to judicial notice. (Evid. Code, § 452, subds. (g) and (h).)

**9.** The record indicates that none of Calvin's courses at college involved the physical sciences, and the expert witness, Oliphant, testified that "It doesn't make any difference what his age is unless he is aware of the voltage that is there."

We return to the rule, set forth above, that contributory negligence is not established as a matter of law unless reasonable men could have drawn that conclusion *and no other.* (*Hogue v. Southern Pacific Co., supra,* 1 Cal. 3d 253, 259.) A natural disinclination to tamper with any electric force would, perhaps, lead many reasonable men to conclude that Calvin acted negligently. Other reasonable men, acknowledging the dilemma which confronted the boys, the various steps they took to resolve their problem before resorting to self-help, and the presence of highly technical factors involved in appraising the dangers of electrical shock, might conclude that Calvin acted as they might have acted under similar circumstances. It is precisely this potential diversity of opinion among reasonable men which leads us to conclude that plaintiffs were entitled to a jury determination of Calvin's contributory negligence.

Defendant PG & E points out, however, that Calvin's conduct violated a public ordinance and urges that such violation constituted contributory negligence per se. Section 585 of the San Francisco Police Code makes it unlawful for "any person ... without authority, to extinguish any public light," and plaintiffs concede that Calvin violated this ordinance. The California cases have held that under certain circumstances, the violation of a statute or other regulation may constitute negligence per se, or at least raise a rebuttable presumption of negligence. (See *Satterlee* v. *Orange Glenn School Dist.,* 29 Cal.2d 581, 587–590 [177 P.2d 279]; 2 Witkin, Summary of Cal. Law, *supra,* Torts, §§ 230–235, pp. 1423–1432, and cases cited.) (11) Similarly such a violation by the plaintiff may constitute *contributory* negligence per se. (*Farole* v. *Eichman,* 39 Cal.2d 822, 824 [249 P.2d 261]; 2 Witkin, *supra,* §§ 334–337, pp. 1534–1539, and cases cited.) The rule of the foregoing cases is now codified in section 669 of the Evidence Code (added 1967), which provides: "(a) The failure of a person to exercise due care is presumed if:

"(1) He violated a statute, ordinance, or regulation of a public entity;

"(2) The violation proximately caused death or injury to person or property;

"(3) The death or injury resulted from an occurrence of the nature which the statute, ordinance, or regulation was designed to prevent; and

"(4) The person suffering the death or the injury to his person or property was one of the class of persons for whose protection the statute, ordinance, or regulation was adopted.

"(b) This presumption may be rebutted by proof that:

"(1) The person violating the statute, ordinance, or regulation did what might reasonably be expected of a person of ordinary prudence, acting under similar circumstances, who desired to comply with the law ... "

It seems apparent to us that the presumption of negligence set forth in section 669 did not form a proper basis for a nonsuit against decedent. First, defendant PG & E has not shown that section 585 was intended to prevent injury or death from electrocution. The complete text of section 585 (adopted in 1903) is as follows: "It shall be unlawful for any person to hitch or fasten any animal to, or to place any placard or notice upon, or in anywise to injure any lamppost or hydrant, or any growing tree, upon any public street, or, without authority, to extinguish any public light." The evident purposes of section 585 are to protect public property and assure adequate lighting of public streets. Thus, the requirement of section 669, subdivision (a), subsection (3), that the death or injury resulted from an occurrence of the nature which the ordinance was designed to prevent, is not satisfied. Further, as section 585 evidently sought to protect the street-using public, by assuring adequate street lighting, it cannot be said that Calvin Mark was, under section 669, subdivision (a), subsection (4), one of the class of persons for whose protection the ordinance was adopted. Accordingly, two essential elements of section 669 remain unfulfilled, and we need not reach the further question whether the jury should have been given the opportunity to determine, under section 669, subdivision (b), subsection (1), whether Calvin acted as a reasonable person would have acted under similar circumstances who desired to comply with the law. (See *Alarid v. Vanier*, 50 Cal.2d 617, 624 [327 P.2d 897], and *Beard* v. *Atchison, Topeka & Santa Fe Ry. Co., supra*, 4 Cal.App.3d 129, 140, regarding the rebuttable nature of the presumption of negligence.)

\* \* \*

We conclude that decedent was not contributorily negligent as a matter of law and that nonsuit should not have been granted in favor of defendant PG & E. The judgments in favor of defendants Chase and City are affirmed; the judgment in PG & E's favor is reversed.

\* \* \*

### NOTES

**1. Complete Bar to Recovery.** Even if the plaintiff proves all the elements required to establish negligence, the defendant historically could prove the plaintiff was contributorily negligent and completely escape liability. In all but a handful of jurisdictions today, as will be discussed, infra, contributory negligence has been converted into comparable negligence and is now only a partial defense. (Comparative negligence will be discussed infra in the discussion of *Li v. Yellow Cab Co. of California*.) The Restatement (Second) of Torts defines contributory negligence as follows:

> Contributory negligence is conduct on the part of the plaintiff which falls below the standard to which he should conform for his own protection, and which is a legally contributing cause co-operating with the negligence of the defendant in bringing about the plaintiff's harm.

Restatement (Second) of Torts § 463.

In essence, the defendant is proving that the plaintiff was negligent toward herself; consequently, the same reasonable person and causation standards applicable to the defendant are in theory applicable to the plaintiff. Since children are generally subject to a more individualized standard of conduct, as noted in Chapter 2, Sec. B, supra, it can be difficult for a defendant to establish a young child's contributory negligence. The majority of courts, consistent with the Restatement, make no dispensation, however, for adult mental disability or insanity. Nevertheless, a growing minority of courts are increasingly tempted to make adjustments for the mentally disabled in the context of contributory or comparative negligence. See Diamond, Levine & Madden, *Understanding Torts* § 15.02 (2nd ed. 2000). See also Keeton, *Prosser and Keeton on* The Law of Torts § 65 (5th ed. 1984); Dobbs, *The Law of Torts*, §§ 199–200 (2000).

As the principal case indicates, negligence per se can apply to contributory negligence. See negligence per se discussion, Chapter 2, Sec. D, supra. See Diamond, Levine & Madden, supra.

Consider *Dunn v. Employers' Liability Assurance Corp.*, 241 So.2d 291 (La.Ct.App.1970), in which the plaintiff tripped over boxes stacked in an aisle of the defendant's market and sustained injuries. The defendant argued that the plaintiff was contributorily negligent. The plaintiff admitted to having seen the boxes before entering the aisle, but claimed that she was momentarily distracted when she saw Vienna sausages on sale and took several cans of them from the shelf. Also, the plaintiff claimed that she had also been engaged in a conversation with a store employee. The court held that neither of these distractions was sufficient to justify forgetting about the presence of the boxes at her feet.

Consider also *Dukat v. Leiserv, Inc.*, 6 Neb.App. 905, 578 N.W.2d 486 (1998), in which the plaintiff was injured when she fell while walking on an icy sidewalk outside the defendant's bowling alley. She left the bowling alley after she had played several games and drunk three beers. Significantly, it was alleged that the plaintiff had noticed the ice on the sidewalk prior to entering the bowling alley. The court upheld an instruction to the jury on contributory negligence since the plaintiff, despite knowing the sidewalk was icy, had not asked the management to spread an ice melting substance on the sidewalk, but instead returned to her car without assistance.

In *Poyner v. Loftus*, 694 A.2d 69 (D.C.1997), the court affirmed that a legally blind pedestrian had been contributorily negligent and could not recover. The pedestrian had fallen from an elevated walkway, after a bush, which the plaintiff had previously relied on for orientation, had been removed. The court noted that the blind plaintiff had neither used a cane or a seeing eye dog to assist her.

Compare however, *Baltimore Gas and Electric Co. v. Flippo*, 348 Md. 680, 705 A.2d 1144 (1998), where the court declined to find plaintiff contributorily negligent as a matter of law. Plaintiff suffered electric shock when he inadvertently touched an electrical wire in a tree. The court held that there was a factual dispute over whether he had been warned of the electrical wire or whether the wire was in plain view.

**2. Defense to Negligence Only.** Contributory negligence acts as a defense only to claims of negligence. It does not function as a defense to intentional torts, or to willful, wanton or reckless conduct. If A throws an intentional punch at B's face, A can't claim B was hit because he was contributory negligent in not ducking quickly enough. Note, however, that in jurisdictions using comparative negligence, recklessness can be offset to some extent by the plaintiff's comparative negligence.

Consider *Adkisson v. City of Seattle*, 42 Wash.2d 676, 258 P.2d 461 (1953), in which the plaintiffs sued for wrongful death. The plaintiff's large automobile collided into a mound of dirt that was dumped on a major road right below an incline that precluded a clear vision of the dirt pile. In addition it was alleged there were inadequate signs or lights to otherwise warn the plaintiff of the hazard in the road. The court held there was sufficient evidence for the jury to find the defendant acted with wanton conduct sufficient to preclude use of contributory negligence as a defense.

**3. Failure to Mitigate Potential Injury.** The failure to take precautions such as wearing a motorcycle helmet or seat belt is not considered contributory negligence since the conduct, even if unreasonable, is not a cause-in-fact of an accident. Instead, such conduct is a failure to mitigate injuries from an accident when they occur. Plaintiffs are obligated to reasonably mitigate injuries. This failure of "anticipatory mitigation" traditionally precluded recovery for the aggravated injury caused by the absence of the seat belt or other precaution. In comparative negligence jurisdictions, the failure to mitigate is usually absorbed into the general defense of comparative negligence.

**4. Causation Must be Proven.** As the principal case indicates, to establish contributory negligence the defendant must, in addition to proving a breach in the standard of conduct, prove that the breach was an actual and proximate cause of the plaintiff's injury.

## DAVIES v. MANN

Court of Exchequer Chamber.
152 Eng. Rep. 588 (1842).

Case for negligence. The declaration stated, that the plaintiff theretofore, and at the time of the committing of the grievance thereinafter mentioned, to wit, on & c, was lawfully possessed of a certain donkey, which said donkey of the plaintiff was then lawfully in a certain highway, and the defendant was then possessed of a certain waggon and certain horses drawing the same, which said waggon and horses of the defendant were then under the care, government, and direction of a certain then servant of the defendant, in and along the said highway; nevertheless the defendant, by his said servant, so carelessly, negligently, unskillfully, and improperly governed and directed his said waggon and horses, that by and through the carelessness, negligence, unskillfulness, and improper conduct of the defendant, by his said servant, the said waggon and horses of the defendant then ran and struck with great violence against the said donkey of the plaintiff, and thereby then wounded, crushed, and killed the same, & c.

The defendant pleaded not guilty.

At the trial, before Erskine, J., at the last Summer Assizes for the county of Worcester, it appeared that the plaintiff, having fettered the fore feet of an ass belonging to him, turned it into a public highway, and at the time in question the ass was grazing on the off side of a road about eight yards wide, when the defendant's waggon, with a team of three horses, coming down a slight descent, at what the witness termed a smartish pace, ran against the ass, knocked it down, and the wheels passing over it, it died soon after. The ass was fettered at the time, and it was proved that the driver of the waggon was some little distance behind the horses. The learned Judge told the jury, that though the act of the plaintiff, in leaving the donkey on the highway so fettered as to prevent his getting out of the way of carriages travelling along it, might be illegal, still, if the proximate cause of the injury was attributable to the want of proper conduct on the part of the driver of the waggon, the action was maintainable against the defendant; and his Lordship directed them if they thought that the accident might have been avoided by the exercise of ordinary care on the part of the driver, to find for the plaintiff. The jury found their verdict for the plaintiff, damages 40s.

Godson now moved for a new trial, on the ground of misdirection. The act of the plaintiff in turning the donkey into the public highway was an illegal one, and, as the injury arose principally from that act, the plaintiff was not entitled to compensation for that injury which, but for his own unlawful act, would never have occurred. [Park, B. The declaration states that the ass was lawfully on the highway, and the defendant has not traversed that allegation; therefore it must be taken to be admitted.] The principle of law, as deducible from the cases, is, that where an accident is the result of faults on both sides, neither party can maintain an action. Thus, in *Butterfield v. Forrester* (11 East, 60), it was held that one who is injured by an obstruction on a highway, against which he fell, cannot maintain an action, if it appear that he was riding with great violence and want of ordinary care, without which he might have seen and avoided the obstruction. So, in *Vennall v. Garner* (1 C. & M. 21), in case for running down a ship, it was held, that neither party can recover when both are in the wrong; and Bayley, B., there says, "I quite agree that if the mischief be the result of the combined negligence of the two, they must both remain in statu quo, and neither party can recover against the other." Here the plaintiff, by fettering the donkey, had prevented him from removing himself out of the way of accident; had his fore feet been free, no accident would probably have happened. *Pluckwell v. Wilson* (5 Carr. & P. 375), *Luxford v. Large* (*ibid.* 421), and *Lynch v. Nurdin* (1 Ad. & E. (N.S.), 29; 4 P. & D. 672), are to the same effect.

PARKE, B. This subject was fully considered by this Court in the case of *Bridge v. The Grand Junction Railway Company* (3 M. & W. 246), where, as appears to me, the correct rule is laid down concerning negligence, namely, that the negligence which is to preclude a plaintiff from recovering in an action of this nature, must be such as that he could, by ordinary care, have avoided the consequences of the defendant's negligence. I am reported to have said in that case, and I believe quite correctly, that "the rule of law is laid down with perfect correctness in the case of *Butterfield v. Forrester*, that, although there may have been negligence on the part of the plaintiff, yet unless he might, by the exercise of ordinary care, have avoided the consequences of the defendant's negligence, he is entitled to recover; if by ordinary care he might have avoided them, he is the author of his own wrong." In that case of *Bridge v. Grand Junction Railway Company*, there was a plea imputing negligence on both sides; here it is otherwise; and the Judge simply told the jury, that the mere fact of negligence on the part of the plaintiff in leaving his donkey on the public highway, was no answer to the action, unless the donkey's being there was the immediate cause of the injury; and that, if they were of opinion that it was caused by the fault of the defendant's servant in driving too fast, or, which is the same thing, at a smartish pace, the mere fact of putting the ass upon the road would not bar the plaintiff of his action. All that is perfectly correct; for, although the ass may have been wrongfully there, still the defendant was bound to go along the road at such a pace as would be likely to prevent mischief. Were this not so, a man might justify the driving over goods left on a public highway, or even over a man lying asleep there, or the purposely running against a carriage going on the wrong side of the road.

GURNEY, B., and ROLFE, B., concurred.

Rule refused.

### NOTES

**1. Last Clear Chance.** The "last clear chance" doctrine nullifies the plaintiff's contributory negligence if the defendant's negligence occurred chronologically *after* the plaintiff's contributory negligence. When the defendant's negligence occurs after the plaintiff's contributory negligence, the plaintiff can therefore recover fully against the defendant. In most states, where comparative negligence has replaced contributory negligence, the last clear chance doctrine has been eliminated. See Diamond, Levine & Madden, *Understanding Torts* § 15.02 (2nd ed. 2000); Keeton, *Prosser and Keeton on Torts* § 66 (5th ed. 1984) and Dobbs, *The Law of Torts*, § 207 (2000).

**2. Rationale.** Is the principal case, which established the last clear chance doctrine, correct when it asserts that without the doctrine, a defendant could intentionally run over a man negligently lying on the road without tort liability? Note that contributory negligence is *not* a defense to intentional torts or even extreme reckless variants of negligence. See Note 2, supra after previous principal case. Is it fair to exclude contributory negligence based on chronology rather than the relative culpability of the plaintiff and defendant?

**3. Determining Who Was Last.** Determining who had the last clear chance is not always easy. States, for example, have disagreed over whether a defendant who was "inattentive" nevertheless had the last clear chance.

Consider *Williams v. Harrison*, 255 Va. 272, 497 S.E.2d 467 (1998). The plaintiff was driving immediately in front of the defendant on a highway lane. Both plaintiff and defendant were speeding. After reaching the top of a hill, the plaintiff braked quickly. The defendant behind turned left in an attempt to avoid hitting the plaintiff, but the plaintiff had also turned left where he was hit by the defendant. The court declined to utilize the last clear chance doctrine to nullify the plaintiff's contributory negligence since there was no evidence the plaintiff was unaware of the hazard of turning left in front of the defendant.

# LI v. YELLOW CAB CO.

Supreme Court of California.

13 Cal.3d 804, 119 Cal.Rptr. 858, 532 P.2d 1226 (1975).

SULLIVAN, Justice.

In this case we address the grave and recurrent question whether we should judicially declare no longer applicable in California courts the doctrine of contributory negligence, which bars all recovery when the plaintiff's negligent conduct has contributed as a legal cause in any degree to the harm suffered by him, and hold that it must give way to a system of comparative negligence, which assesses liability in direct proportion to fault. As we explain in detail *infra*, we conclude that we should. In the course of reaching our ultimate decision we conclude that: (1) The doctrine of comparative negligence is preferable to the "all-or-nothing" doctrine of contributory negligence from the point of view of logic, practical experience, and fundamental justice; (2) judicial action in this area is not precluded by the presence of section 1714 of the Civil Code, which has been said to "codify" the "all-or-nothing" rule and to render it immune from attack in the courts except on constitutional grounds; (3) given the possibility of judicial action, certain practical difficulties attendant upon the adoption of comparative negligence should not dissuade us from charting a new course—leaving the resolution of some of these problems to future judicial or legislative action; (4) the doctrine of comparative negligence should be applied in this state in its so-called "pure" form under which the assessment of liability in proportion to fault proceeds in spite of the fact that the plaintiff is equally at fault as or more at fault than the defendant; and finally (5) this new rule should be given a limited retrospective application.

The accident here in question occurred near the intersection of Alvarado Street and Third Street in Los Angeles. At this intersection Third Street runs in a generally east-west direction along the crest of a hill, and Alvarado Street, running generally north and south, rises gently to the crest from either direction. At approximately 9 p.m. on November 21, 1968, plaintiff Nga Li was proceeding northbound on Alvarado in her 1967 Oldsmobile. She was in the inside lane, and about 70 feet before she reached the Third Street intersection she stopped and then began a left turn across the three southbound lanes of Alvarado, intending to enter the driveway of a service station. At this time defendant Robert Phillips, an employee of defendant Yellow Cab Company, was driving a company-owned taxicab southbound in the middle lane on Alvarado. He came over the crest of the hill, passed through the intersection, and collided with the right rear portion of plaintiff's automobile, resulting in personal injuries to plaintiff as well as considerable damage to the automobile.

The court, sitting without a jury, found as facts that defendant Phillips was traveling at approximately 30 miles per hour when he entered the intersection, that such speed was unsafe at that time and place, and that the traffic light controlling southbound traffic at the intersection was yellow when defendant Phillips drove into the intersection. It also found, however, that plaintiff's left turn across the south-bound lanes of Alvarado "was made at a time when a vehicle was approaching from the opposite direction so close as to constitute an immediate hazard." The dispositive conclusion of law was as follows: "That the driving of Nga Li was negligent, that such negligence was a proximate cause of the collision, and that she is barred from recovery by reason of such contributory negligence." Judgment for defendants was entered accordingly.

I

"Contributory negligence is conduct on the part of the plaintiff which falls below the standard to which he should conform for his own protection, and which is a legally contributing cause cooperating with the negligence of the defendant in bringing about the plaintiff's harm." (Rest. 2d Torts, § 463.) Thus the American Law Institute, in its second restatement of the law, describes the kind of conduct on the part of one seeking recovery for damage caused by negligence which renders him subject to the doctrine of contributory negligence. What the effect of such conduct will be is left to a further section, which states the doctrine in its clearest essence: "Except where the defendant has the last clear chance, the plaintiff's contributory negligence *bars recovery* against a defendant whose negligent conduct would otherwise make him liable to the plaintiff for the harm sustained by him." (Rest. 2d Torts, § 467.) (Italics added.)

This rule, rooted in the long-standing principle that one should not recover from another for damages brought upon oneself (see *Baltimore & P.R. Co. v. Jones* (1877) 95 U.S. 439, 442 [24 L.Ed. 506, 507]; *Buckley v. Chadwick* (1955) 45 Cal.2d 183, 192 [288 P.2d 12, 289 P.2d 242]), has been the law of this state from its beginning. (See *Innis v. The Steamer Senator* (1851) 1 Cal. 459, 460–461; *Griswold v. Sharpe* (1852) 2 Cal. 17, 23–24; *Richmond v. Sacramento Valley Railroad Company* (1861) 18 Cal. 351, 356–358; *Gay v. Winter* (1867) 34 Cal. 153, 162–163; *Needham v. S. F. & S. J. R. Co.* (1869) 37 Cal. 409, 417–423.) Although criticized almost from the outset for the harshness of its operation, it has weathered numerous attacks, in both the legislative and the judicial arenas, seeking its amelioration or repudiation. We have undertaken a thorough reexamination of the matter, giving particular attention to the common law and statutory sources of the subject doctrine in this state. As we have indicated, this reexamination leads us to the conclusion that the "all-or-nothing" rule of contributory negligence can be and ought to be superseded by a rule which assesses liability in proportion to fault.

It is unnecessary for us to catalogue the enormous amount of critical comment that has been directed over the years against the "all-or-nothing" approach of the doctrine of contributory negligence. The essence of that criticism has been constant and clear: the doctrine is inequitable in its operation because it fails to distribute responsibility in proportion to fault. Against this have been raised several arguments in justification, but none have proved even remotely adequate to the task. The basic objection to the doctrine—grounded in the primal concept that in a system in which liability is based on fault, the extent of fault should govern the extent of liability—remains irresistible to reason and all intelligent notions of fairness.

Furthermore, practical experience with the application by juries of the doctrine of contributory negligence has added its weight to analyses of its inherent shortcomings: "Every trial lawyer is well aware that juries often do in fact allow recovery in cases of contributory negligence, and that the compromise in the jury room does result in some diminution of the damages because of the plaintiff's fault. But the process is at best a haphazard and most unsatisfactory one." (Prosser, *Comparative Negligence, supra*, p. 4; fn. omitted.) (See also Prosser, Torts, *supra*, § 67, pp. 436–437; Comments of Malone and Wade in *Comments on Maki v. Frelk—Comparative v. Contributory Negligence: Should the Court or Legislature Decide?* (1968) 21 Vand.L.Rev. 889, at pp. 934, 943; Ulman, A Judge Takes the Stand (1933) pp. 30–34; cf. Comment of Kalven, 21 Vand.L.Rev. 889, 901–904.) It is manifest that this state of affairs, viewed from the standpoint of the health and vitality of the legal process, can only detract from public confidence in the ability of law and legal institutions to assign liability on a just and consistent basis. (See Keeton, *Creative Continuity in the Law of Torts* (1962) 75 Harv.L.Rev. 463, 505; Comment of Keeton in *Comments on Maki v. Frelk, supra*, 21 Vand.L.Rev. 889, at p. 916; Note (1974) 21 U.C.L.A. L.Rev. 1566, 1596–1597.)

It is in view of these theoretical and practical considerations that to this date 25 states, have abrogated the "all-or-nothing" rule of contributory negligence and have enacted in its place general apportionment *statutes* calculated in one manner or another to assess liability in proportion to fault. In 1973 these states were joined by Florida, which effected the same result by judicial decision. (*Hoffman v. Jones* (Fla. 1973) 280 So.2d 431.) We are likewise persuaded that logic, practical experience, and fundamental justice counsel against the retention of the doctrine rendering contributory negligence a complete bar to recovery— and that it should be replaced in this state by a system under which liability for damage will be borne by those whose negligence caused it in direct proportion to their respective fault.

The foregoing conclusion, however, clearly takes us only part of the way. It is strenuously and ably urged by defendants and two of the amici curiae that whatever our views on the relative merits of contributory and comparative negligence, we are precluded from making those views the law of the state by judicial decision. Moreover, it is contended, even if we are not so precluded, there exist considerations of a practical nature which should dissuade us from embarking upon the course which we have indicated. We proceed to take up these two objections in order.

## II

It is urged that any change in the law of contributory negligence must be made by the Legislature, not by this court. Although the doctrine of contributory negligence is of judicial origin—its genesis being traditionally attributed to the opinion of Lord Ellenborough in *Butterfield v. Forrester* (K.B. 1809) 103 Eng. Rep. 926—the enactment of section 1714 of the Civil Code in 1872 codified the doctrine as it stood at that date and, the argument continues, rendered it invulnerable to attack in the courts except on constitutional grounds. Subsequent cases of this court, it is pointed out, have unanimously affirmed that—barring the appearance of some constitutional infirmity—the "all-or-nothing" rule is the law of this state and shall remain so until the Legislature directs otherwise. The fundamental constitutional doctrine of separation of powers, the argument concludes, requires judicial abstention.

We are further urged to observe that a basic distinction exists between the situation obtaining in Florida prior to the decision of that state's Supreme Court abrogating the doctrine (*Hoffman v. Jones, supra,* 280 So.2d 431), and the situation now confronting this court. There, to be sure, the Florida court was also faced with a statute, and the dissenting justice considered that fact sufficient to bar judicial change of the rule. The statute there in question, however, merely declared that the general English common and statute law in effect on July 4, 1776, was to be in force in Florida except to the extent it was inconsistent with federal constitutional and statutory law and acts of the state legislature. (Fla. Stat., § 2.01, F.S.A.) The majority simply concluded that there was no clear-cut common law rule of contributory negligence prior to the 1809 *Butterfield* decision (*Butterfield v. Forrester, supra,* 103 Eng. Rep. 926), and that therefore that rule was not made a part of Florida law by the statute. (280 So.2d at pp. 434–435.) In the instant case, defendants and the amici curiae who support them point out, the situation is quite different: here the Legislature has specifically enacted the rule of contributory negligence as the law of this state. In these circumstances, it is urged, the doctrine of separation of powers requires that any change must come from the Legislature.

We have concluded that the foregoing argument, in spite of its superficial appeal, is fundamentally misguided. As we proceed to point out and elaborate below, it was not the intention of the Legislature in enacting section 1714 of the Civil Code, as well as other sections of that code declarative of the common law, to insulate the matters therein expressed from further judicial development; rather it was the intention of the Legislature to announce and formulate existing common law principles and definitions for purposes of orderly and concise presentation and with a distinct view toward continuing judicial evolution.

\* \* \*

## III

We are thus brought to the second group of arguments which have been advanced by defendants and the amici curiae supporting their position. Generally speaking, such arguments expose considerations of a practical nature which, it is urged, counsel against the adoption of a rule of comparative negligence in this state even if such adoption is possible by judicial means.

The most serious of these considerations are those attendant upon the administration of a rule of comparative negligence in cases involving multiple parties. One such problem may arise when all responsible parties are not brought before the court: it may be difficult for the jury to evaluate relative negligence in such circumstances, and to compound this difficulty such an evaluation would not be res judicata in a subsequent suit against the absent wrongdoer. Problems of contribution and indemnity among joint tortfeasors lurk in the background. (See generally Prosser, *Comparative Negligence, supra,* 41 Cal.L.Rev. 1, 33–37; Schwartz, Comparative Negligence, *supra,* §§ 16.1–16.9, pp. 247–274.)

A second and related major area of concern involves the administration of the actual process of fact-finding in a comparative negligence system. The assigning of a specific percentage factor to the amount of negligence attributable to a particular party, while in theory a matter of little difficulty, can become a matter of perplexity in the face of hard facts. The temptation for the jury to resort to a quotient verdict in such circumstances can be great. (See Schwartz, *supra,* § 17.1, pp. 275–279.) These inherent difficulties are not, however, insurmountable. Guidelines might be provided the jury which will assist it in keeping focussed upon the true inquiry (see, e.g., Schwartz, *supra,* § 17.1, pp. 278–279), and the utilization of special verdicts or jury interrogatories can be of invaluable assistance in assuring that the jury has approached its sensitive and often complex task with proper standards and appropriate reverence. (See Schwartz, *supra,* § 17.4, pp. 282–291; Prosser, *Comparative Negligence, supra,* 41 Cal.L.Rev., pp. 28–33.)

The third area of concern, the status of the doctrines of last clear chance and assumption of risk, involves less the practical problems of administering a particular form of comparative negligence than it does a definition of the theoretical outline of the specific form to be adopted. Although several states which apply comparative negligence concepts retain the last clear chance doctrine (see Schwartz, *supra,* § 7.2, p. 134), the better reasoned position seems to be that when true comparative negligence is adopted, the need for last clear chance as a palliative of the hardships of the "all-or-nothing" rule disappears and its retention results only in a windfall to the plaintiff in direct contravention of the principle of liability in proportion to fault. (See Schwartz, *supra,* § 7.2, pp. 137–139; Prosser, *Comparative Negligence, supra,* 41 Cal.L.Rev., p. 27.) As for assumption of risk, we have recognized in this state that this defense overlaps that of contributory negligence to some extent and in fact is made up of at least two distinct defenses. "To simplify greatly, it has been observed . . . that in one kind of situation, to wit, where a plaintiff *unreasonably* undertakes to encounter a specific known risk imposed by a defendant's negligence, plaintiff's conduct, although he may encounter that risk in a prudent manner, is in reality a form of contributory negligence. . . . Other kinds of situations within the doctrine of assumption of risk are those, for example, where plaintiff is held to agree to relieve defendant of an obligation of reasonable conduct toward him. Such a situation would not involve contributory negligence, but rather a reduction of defendant's duty of care." (*Grey* v. *Fibreboard Paper Products Co.* (1966) 65 Cal.2d 240, 245–246 [53 Cal.Rptr. 545, 418 P.2d 153]; see also *Fonseca* v. *County of Orange* (1972) 28 Cal.App.3d 361, 368–369 [104 Cal.Rptr. 566]; see generally, 4 Witkin, Summary of Cal. Law, Torts, § 723, pp. 3013–3014; 2 Harper & James, The Law of

Torts, *supra*, § 21.1, pp. 1162–1168; cf. Prosser, Torts, *supra*, § 68, pp. 439–441.) We think it clear that the adoption of a system of comparative negligence should entail the merger of the defense of assumption of risk into the general scheme of assessment of liability in proportion to fault in those particular cases in which the form of assumption of risk involved is no more than a variant of contributory negligence. (See generally, Schwartz, *supra*, ch. 9, pp. 153–175.)

\* \* \*

It remains to identify the precise form of comparative negligence which we now adopt for application in this state. Although there are many variants, only the two basic forms need be considered here. The first of these, the so-called "pure" form of comparative negligence, apportions liability in direct proportion to fault in all cases. This was the form adopted by the Supreme Court of Florida in *Hoffman v. Jones, supra*, and it applies by statute in Mississippi, Rhode Island, and Washington. Moreover it is the form favored by most scholars and commentators. (See, e.g., Prosser, *Comparative Negligence, supra*, 41 Cal.L.Rev. 1, 21–25; Prosser, Torts, *supra*, § 67, pp. 437–438; Schwartz, *supra*, § 21.3, pp. 341–348; *Comments on Maki v. Frelk—Comparative v. Contributory Negligence: Should the Court or Legislature Decide?, supra*, 21 Vand.L.Rev. 889 (Comment by Keeton at p. 906, Comment by Leflar at p. 918).) The second basic form of comparative negligence, of which there are several variants, applies apportionment based on fault *up to the point* at which the plaintiff's negligence is equal to or greater than that of the defendant—when that point is reached, plaintiff is barred from recovery. Nineteen states have adopted this form or one of its variants by statute. The principal argument advanced in its favor is moral in nature: that it is not morally right to permit one more at fault in an accident to recover from one less at fault. Other arguments assert the probability of increased insurance, administrative, and judicial costs if a "pure" rather than a "50 percent" system is adopted, but this has been seriously questioned. (See authorities cited in Schwartz, *supra*, § 21.3, pp. 344–346; see also *Vincent v. Pabst Brewing Co.* (1970) 47 Wis.2d 120, 138 [177 N.W.2D 513] (dissenting opn.).)

We have concluded that the "pure" form of comparative negligence is that which should be adopted in this state. In our view the "50 percent" system simply shifts the lottery aspect of the contributory negligence rule to a different ground. As Dean Prosser has noted, under such a system "[i]t is obvious that a slight difference in the proportionate fault may permit a recovery; and there has been much justified criticism of a rule under which a plaintiff who is charged with 49 percent of the total negligence recovers 51 percent of his damages, while one who is charged with 50 percent recovers nothing at all." (Prosser, *Comparative Negligence, supra*, 41 Cal.L.Rev. 1, 25; fns. omitted.) In effect "such a rule distorts the very principle it recognizes, i.e., that persons are responsible for their acts to the extent their fault contributes to an injurious result. The partial rule simply lowers, but does not eliminate, the bar of contributory negligence." (Juenger, *Brief for Negligence Law Section of the State Bar of Michigan in Support of Comparative Negli-*

*gence as Amicus Curiae, Parsonson v. Construction Equipment Company, supra*, 18 Wayne L.Rev. 3, 50; see also Schwartz, *supra*, § 21.3, p. 347.)

\* \* \*

For all of the foregoing reasons we conclude that the "all-or-nothing" rule of contributory negligence as it presently exists in this state should be and is herewith superseded by a system of "pure" comparative negligence, the fundamental purpose of which shall be to assign responsibility and liability for damage in direct proportion to the amount of negligence of each of the parties. Therefore, in all actions for negligence resulting in injury to person or property, the contributory negligence of the person injured in person or property shall not bar recovery, but the damages awarded shall be diminished in proportion to the amount of negligence attributable to the person recovering. The doctrine of last clear chance is abolished, and the defense of assumption of risk is also abolished to the extent that it is merely a variant of the former doctrine of contributory negligence; both of these are to be subsumed under the general process of assessing liability in proportion to negligence. Pending future judicial or legislative developments, the trial courts of this state are to use broad discretion in seeking to assure that the principle stated is applied in the interest of justice and in furtherance of the purposes and objectives set forth in this opinion.

\* \* \*

The judgment is reversed.

## *NOTES*

**1. Comparative Negligence.** Comparative negligence, also known as comparative fault, converts contributory negligence into a potentially partial defense. All but four states have replaced contributory negligence with comparative negligence. The Restatement (Third) of Torts, Apportionment of Liability § 7 adopted by the American Law Institute in 1999 also now endorses comparative negligence. The principal case adopted "pure" comparative negligence where the plaintiff can be 99% at fault and still recover 1% of the damages. Most states have adopted "modified" comparative negligence where the plaintiff is completely barred from any recovery if she is over 50% at fault, or in a few jurisdictions, 50% or more at fault. Under this approach, a plaintiff 49% at fault recovers 51% of the damages, but a plaintiff 51% at fault recovers nothing. The appraisal of "fault" or "responsibility" is subjectively made by the finder of fact, most often the jury. See generally Schwartz, *Comparative Negligence* (3rd ed. 1994). See also Diamond, Levine, & Madden, *Understanding Torts* § 15.03 (2nd ed. 2000); Keeton, *Prosser and Keeton on The Law of Torts* § 67 (5th ed. 1984) and Dobbs, *The Law of Torts* § 201 (2000).

**2. Comparing the Defenses.** Are there arguments for retaining contributory negligence? Should a non-innocent plaintiff be able to recover for an accident that would not have occurred if the plaintiff had taken proper care or precautions? Why is it arguably fairer to draw the line at 50%? Should a plaintiff who is 99% responsible be able to recover 1% from a defendant?

**3. Absorbing Last Clear Chance and Allowing Defense Against Recklessness.** Most jurisdictions adopting comparative negligence have abolished the last clear chance doctrine discussed in the prior principal case. In addition, courts most often allow the comparative negligence defense against even very reckless variants of negligence, where traditionally contributory negligence was precluded as a defense.

## 2. Assumption of Risk

### MURPHY v. STEEPLECHASE AMUSEMENT CO.

Court of Appeals of New York.
250 N.Y. 479, 166 N.E. 173 (1929).

CARDOZO, Ch. J.

The defendant, Steeplechase Amusement Company, maintains an amusement park at Coney Island, New York.

One of the supposed attractions is known as "The Flopper." It is a moving belt, running upward on an inclined plane, on which passengers sit or stand. Many of them are unable to keep their feet because of the movement of the belt, and are thrown backward or aside. The belt runs in a groove, with padded walls on either side to a height of four feet, and with padded flooring beyond the walls at the same angle as the belt. An electric motor, driven by current furnished by the Brooklyn Edison Company, supplies the needed power.

Plaintiff, a vigorous young man, visited the park with friends. One of them, a young woman, now his wife, stepped upon the moving belt. Plaintiff followed and stepped behind her. As he did so, he felt what he describes as a sudden jerk, and was thrown to the floor. His wife in front and also friends behind him were thrown at the same time. Something more was here, as every one understood, than the slowly-moving escalator that is common in shops and public places. A fall was foreseen as one of the risks of the adventure. There would have been no point to the whole thing, no adventure about it, if the risk had not been there. The very name above the gate, the Flopper, was warning to the timid. If the name was not enough, there was warning more distinct in the experience of others. We are told by the plaintiff's wife that the members of her party stood looking at the sport before joining in it themselves. Some aboard the belt were able, as she viewed them, to sit down with decorum or even to stand and keep their footing; others jumped or fell. The tumbling bodies and the screams and laughter supplied the merriment and fun. "I took a chance," she said when asked whether she thought that a fall might be expected.

Plaintiff took the chance with her, but, less lucky than his companions, suffered a fracture of a knee cap. He states in his complaint that the belt was dangerous to life and limb in that it stopped and started violently and suddenly and was not properly equipped to prevent injuries to persons who were using it without knowledge of its dangers, and in a bill of particulars he adds that it was operated at a fast and dangerous rate of speed and was not supplied with a proper railing, guard or other device to prevent a fall therefrom. No other negligence is charged.

We see no adequate basis for a finding that the belt was out of order. It was already in motion when the plaintiff put his foot on it. He cannot help himself to a verdict in such circumstances by the addition of the facile comment that it threw him with a jerk. One who steps upon a moving belt and finds his heels above his head is in no position to discriminate with nicety between the successive stages of the shock, between the jerk which is a cause and the jerk, accompanying the fall, as an instantaneous effect. There is evidence for the defendant that power was transmitted smoothly, and could not be transmitted otherwise. If the movement was spasmodic, it was an unexplained and, it seems, an inexplicable departure from the normal workings of the mechanism. An aberration so extraordinary, if it is to lay the basis for a verdict, should rest on something firmer than a mere descriptive epithet, a summary of the sensations of a tense and crowded moment (Matter of Case, 214 N. Y. 199; *Dochtermann v. Brooklyn Heights R. R. Co.*, 32 App. Div. 13, 15; 164 N. Y. 586; *Foley v. Boston & Maine R. R. Co.*, 193 Mass. 332, 335; *Work v. Boston El. Ry. Co.*, 207 Mass. 447, 448; *N. & W. Ry. Co. v. Birchett*, 252 Fed. Rep. 512, 515). But the jerk, if it were established, would add little to the case. Whether the movement of the belt was uniform or irregular, the risk at greatest was a fall. This was the very hazard that was invited and foreseen (*Lumsden v. Thompson Scenic Ry. Co.*, 130 App. Div. 209, 212, 213).

*Volenti non fit injuria.* One who takes part in such a sport accepts the dangers that inhere in it so far as they are obvious and necessary, just as a fencer accepts the risk of a thrust by his antagonist or a spectator at a ball game the chance of contact with the ball (Pollock; Torts [11th ed.], p. 171; *Lumsden v. Thompson Scenic Ry. Co., supra*; *Godfrey v. Conn. Co.*, 98 Conn. 63; *Johnson v. City of N. Y.*, 186 N. Y. 139, 148; *McFarlane v. City of Niagara Falls*, 247 N. Y. 340, 349; cf. 1 Beven, Negligence, 787; Bohlen, Studies in the Law of Torts, p. 443). The antics of the clown are not the paces of the cloistered cleric. The rough and boisterous joke, the horseplay of the crowd, evokes its own guffaws, but they are not the pleasures of tranquillity. The plaintiff was not seeking a retreat for meditation. Visitors were tumbling about the belt to the merriment of onlookers when he made his choice to join them. He took the chance of a like fate, with whatever damage to his body might ensue from such a fall. The timorous may stay at home.

A different case would be here if the dangers inherent in the sport were obscure or unobserved (*Godfrey v. Conn. Co., supra*; *Tantillo v. Goldstein Bros. Amusement Co.*, 248 N. Y. 286), or so serious as to justify the belief that precautions of some kind must have been taken to avert them (cf. *O'Callaghan v. Dellwood Park Co.*, 242 Ill. 336). Nothing happened to the plaintiff except what common experience tells us may happen at any time as the consequence of a sudden fall. Many a skater or a horseman can rehearse a tale of equal woe. A different case there would also be if the accidents had been so many as to show that the game in its inherent nature was too dangerous to be continued without change. The president of the amusement company says that there had never been such an accident before. A nurse employed at an emergency hospital maintained in connection with the park contradicts him to some extent. She says that on other occasions she had attended patrons of the park who had been injured at the Flopper, how many she could not say. None, however, had been badly injured or had suffered broken bones. Such testimony is not enough to show that the game was a trap for the unwary, too perilous to be endured. According to the defendant's estimate, two hundred and fifty thousand visitors were at the Flopper in a year. Some quota of accidents was to be looked for in so great a mass. One might as well say that a skating rink should be abandoned because skaters sometimes fall.

There is testimony by the plaintiff that he fell upon wood, and not upon a canvas padding. He is strongly contradicted by the photographs and by the witnesses for the defendant, and is without corroboration in the testimony of his companions who were witnesses in his behalf. If his observation was correct, there was a defect in the equipment, and one not obvious or known. The padding should have been kept in repair to break the force of any fall. The case did not go to the jury, however, upon any such theory of the defendant's liability, nor is the defect fairly suggested by the plaintiff's bill of particulars, which limits his complaint. The case went to the jury upon the theory that negligence was dependent upon a sharp and sudden jerk.

The judgment of the Appellate Division and that of the Trial Term should be reversed, and a new trial granted, with costs to abide the event.

* * *

Judgments reversed, etc.

***NOTES***

**1. Assumption of Risk.** The Restatement (Second) of Torts defines the defense of assumption of risk as follows:

> [A] plaintiff who fully understands a risk of harm to himself or his things caused by the defendant's conduct or by the condition of the defendant's land or chattels, and who nevertheless voluntarily chooses to enter or remain, or to permit his things to enter or remain within the area of that risk, under circumstances that manifest his willingness to accept it, is not entitled to recover.

Restatement (Second) of Torts § 496.

As the Restatement definition indicates, the plaintiff must subjectively know and appreciate the risk and voluntarily expose oneself to it. This is in contrast to contributory or comparative negligence where the subjective knowledge of the plaintiff is irrelevant and instead the comparison is to the objective standard of a reasonable person.

Consider *Sayed v. Azizullah*, 238 Ga.App. 642, 519 S.E.2d 732 (1999), where the court rejected the claims of the parents of a 17–year-old teenager against the boy's nephew who allegedly led the boy into dangerous water. The court concluded the boy was old enough and the peril obvious enough that the boy assumed the risk. Therefore, the court barred a negligence claim against the nephew.

Sometimes assumption of risk overlaps with contributory negligence and consequently both defenses are available against the plaintiff. Consider *Gonzalez v. Garcia*, 75 Cal.App.3d 874, 142 Cal.Rptr. 503 (1977) where plaintiff joined the defendant and another friend for an after-work drink at a bar. This was followed by a visit to a liquor store where the three consumed a bottle of tequila and then visited a second bar for more drinks. The plaintiff who had drunk the least liquor initially drove the group to the defendant's car. The plaintiff also attempted to call his wife for a ride home. Ultimately the plaintiff acquiesced to the defendant's insistence that he drive the plaintiff home. The plaintiff was subsequently seriously injured when the intoxicated defendant's driving led to an automobile accident. The court held the plaintiff was both contributorily negligent (since a reasonable person would not have accepted the ride) and assumed the risk (since his actions confirmed he subjectively was aware of the risk).

**2. A Complete Defense.** Traditionally assumption of risk, like contributory negligence, was a complete defense to negligence. As discussed in *Knight v. Jewett, infra* this chapter, implied assumption of risk in many states has become only a partial defense.

**3. Was Defense Necessary in Principal Case?** Was the defense of assumption of risk necessary in the principal case? Did the operators of the Flopper breach their duty of reasonable conduct and care to the plaintiff? Would the defendants have been liable if through inattention or intoxication, the plaintiff had not been subjectively aware of the Flopper's risk? What risk did the riders assume? Would the result be different if the plaintiff had been impaled by a hidden nail as he fell off the Flopper?

# RUSH v. COMMERCIAL REALTY CO.

Supreme Court of New Jersey.
7 N.J.Misc. 337, 145 A. 476 (1929).

PER CURIAM.

The case for the plaintiffs was that they were tenants of the defendant, which controlled the house wherein they lived and also the adjoining house, and provided a detached privy for the use of both houses; that Mrs. Rush having occasion to use this privy, went into it and fell through the floor, or through some sort of trap door therein, descended about nine feet into the accumulation at the bottom, and had to be extricated by use of a ladder. . . .

Taking the facts as the jury were entitled to find them, most favorably for the plaintiffs, the situation was that of a building under the control of the landlord for the use of tenants generally, and maintained by the landlord; a consequent duty of care in maintenance; a defective condition in the floor which the jury might say was due to negligent maintenance by the defendant; and an accident resulting therefrom. In such a situation it would seem that the argument for a nonsuit or for a direction must be restricted to the questions of contributory negligence and assumption of risk. In dealing with these, it should be observed that Mrs. Rush had no choice, when impelled by the calls of nature, but to use the facilities placed at her disposal by the landlord, to wit, a privy with a trap door in the floor, poorly maintained. We hardly think this was the assumption of a risk; she was not required to leave the premises and go elsewhere. . . .

We conclude that there was no error in denying motions to take the case from the jury, and the judgment will accordingly be affirmed.

## EMMETTE L. BARRAN, III v. KAPPA ALPHA ORDER, INC.

Supreme Court of Alabama.
730 So.2d 203 (Ala. 1998).

SEE, Justice

### I.

Viewed in the light most favorable to Jason Jones, the nonmovant, the evidence indicates that he enrolled at Auburn University in 1993; that in September 1993, Jones chose to become, and became, a pledge of the KA fraternity; that within two days, Jones began to experience hazing by the fraternity members; and that the hazing activities continued over the next academic year, and included: (1) having to dig a ditch and jump into it after it had been filled with water, urine, feces, dinner leftovers, and vomit; (2) receiving paddlings to his buttocks; (3) being pushed and kicked, often into walls, pits, and trash cans; (4) eating such foods as peppers, hot sauce, butter, and "yerks" (a mixture of hot sauce, mayonnaise, butter, beans, and other items); (5) doing chores for the fraternity and its members, such as cleaning the fraternity house and yard, serving as designated driver, and running errands; (6) appearing regularly at 2 a.m. "meetings" during which the pledges would be hazed for a couple of hours; and (7) "running the gauntlet," during which the pledges were pushed, kicked, and hit as they ran down a hallway and down a flight of stairs. The evidence further indicates that, despite all of these hazing incidents, and although he was aware that 20% to 40% of the members of his pledge class had elected to withdraw from the pledge program, Jones continued to participate in the hazing, in the hope of becoming a full member of KA; and that Jones continued as a KA pledge and continued to participate in the hazing until Auburn University suspended him from school for poor academic performance.

In October 1995, Jones sued the national and local KA organizations, and several individual members of KA, alleging negligence and/or wantonness, in violation of Ala.Code 1975, § 16–1–23, assault and battery, negligent supervision, conspiracy, and the tort of outrage. Jones alleged that he had suffered "mental and physical injuries" as a result of the hazing engaged in by KA and its members. The trial court granted a motion for summary judgment in favor of each defendant on each claim except for the assault-and-battery claims against Brad Sauls and Jason Hard, KA members. The trial court held that Jones assumed the risk of hazing because he voluntarily entered the pledge class, voluntarily participated in the hazing activities, and could have withdrawn at any time.

\* \* \*

The Court of Civil Appeals then held that the traditional defense of assumption of the risk did not support a summary judgment because the peer pressure associated with fraternity life placed Jones in a coercive environment and, thus, prevented him from voluntarily withdrawing from the pledge class.

## II.

\* \* \*

Alabama has long recognized the affirmative defense of assumption of the risk. See, e.g., *Edwards v. Southern Ry.*, 233 Ala. 65, 66, 169 So. 715, 715 (1936); *Dunklin v. Hanna*, 229 Ala. 242, 243, 156 So. 768, 769 (1934); *Louisville & N.R.R. v. Parker*, 223 Ala. 626, 635, 138 So. 231, 238 (1931). The general principle of assumption of the risk is that "[a] plaintiff who voluntarily assumes a risk of harm arising from the negligent or reckless conduct of the defendant cannot recovery for such harm." Restatement (Second) of Torts § 496A (1965). As Prosser and Keeton explain:

> "[Assumption of the risk occurs] where the plaintiff voluntarily enters into some relation with the defendant, with knowledge that the defendant will not protect him against one or more future risks that may arise from the relation. He may then be regarded as tacitly or impliedly consenting to the negligence, and agreeing to take his own chances. Thus, he accept employment, knowing that he is expected to work with a dangerous horse; or ride in a car with knowledge that the brakes are defective, or the driver incompetent.... [T]he legal result is that the defendant is simply relieved of the duty which would otherwise exist."

Prosser & Keeton, The Law of Torts 481 (5th ed. 1984) (footnotes and emphasis omitted).

Assumption of the risk has two subjective elements: (1) the plaintiff's knowledge and appreciation of the risk; and (2) the plaintiff's voluntary exposure to that risk. *Driver v. National Security Fire & Casualty Co.*, 658 So.2d 390, 393 (Ala.1995).

\* \* \*

First, KA and its members argue that Jones knew and appreciated the risks inherent in hazing. This Court has previously held that the knowledge-and-awareness element of assumption of risk was satisfied, as a matter of law, where a worker who was injured when he slipped on ice had known that the ice was present on the floor, but continued working. *Harris v. Food Equip. Specialist, Inc.* 559 So.2d 1066, 1069 (Ala.1990). Similarly, in *Kemp v. Jackson*, 274 Ala. 29, 33, 145 So.2d 187, 191 (1962), this Court held that the knowledge-and-awareness element of the assumption-of-the-risk defense would be satisfied if a person entered, or continued to ride in, a vehicle with knowledge that the door latch was defective and with an appreciation or consciousness of the hazards involved in doing so.

Jones's deposition indicates that before he became a KA pledge, he was unfamiliar with the specific hazing practices engaged in at KA, but that the hazing began within two days of becoming a pledge; that despite the severe and continuing nature of the hazing, Jones remained a pledge and continued to participate in the hazing activities for a full academic year; that Jones knew and appreciated that hazing was both illegal and against school rules; and that he repeatedly helped KA cover up the hazing by lying about its occurrence to school officials, his doctor, and even his own family. Given Jones's early introduction to the practice of hazing and its hazards, and in light of his own admission that he realized that hazing would continue to occur, the trial court correctly determined that reasonable people would conclude that Jones knew of and appreciated the risks of hazing.

Second, in addition to establishing that Jones both knew of and appreciated the risk, KA and the individual defendants argue that Jones voluntarily exposed himself to the hazing. Jones responds by arguing that a coercive environment hampered his free will to the extent that he could not voluntarily choose to leave the fraternity. The Court of Civil Appeals, in reversing the summary judgment as to KA and the individual defendants, stated that it was not clear that Jones voluntarily assumed the risk of hazing, because the court stated:

> "[I]n today's society, numerous college students are confronted with the great pressures associated with fraternity life and ... compliance with the initiation requirements places the students in a position of functioning in what may be construed as a coercive environment."

*Jones*, 730 So.2d at 200. With respect to the facts in this case, we disagree.

In *Driver*, 658 So.2d at 393, this Court stated that the "voluntary" element of assumption of the risk was satisfied where a plaintiff, who was injured in an automobile accident, had put herself in danger by riding in a vehicle operated by someone she knew had been drinking. Similarly, in *Skipper v. Shannon, Strobel & Weaver, Inc.*, 623 So.2d 1072, 1074 (Ala.1993), this Court stated that the "voluntary" element of assumption of the risk was satisfied where a plaintiff who was injured by tripping over a gap in a floor had put herself in danger by working in an area that she knew was undergoing tile repair.

The record indicates that Jones voluntarily chose to continue his participation in the hazing activities. After numerous hazing events, Jones continued to come back for more two o'clock meetings, more paddlings, and more gauntlet runs, and did so for a full academic year. Auburn University officials, in an effort to help him, asked him if he was being subjected to hazing activities, but he chose not to ask the officials to intervene. Jones's parents, likewise acting in an effort to help him, asked him if he was being subjected to hazing activities, but he chose not to ask his parents for help.

Moreover, we are not convinced by Jones's argument that peer pressure created a coercive environment that prevented him from exercising free choice. Jones had reached the age of majority when he enrolled at Auburn University and pledged the KA fraternity. We have previously noted: "College students and fraternity members are not children. Save for very few legal exceptions, they are adult citizens, ready, able, and willing to be responsible for their own actions." *Rothman v. Gamma Alpha Chapter of Pi Kappa Alpha Fraternity*, 599 So.2d 9, 11 (Ala.1992) (quoting *Campbell v. Board of Trustees*, 495 N.E.2d 227, 232 (Ind.App.1986)). Thus, even for college students, the privileges of liberty are wrapped in the obligations of responsibility. See *Foremost Insurance Co. v. Parham*, 693 So.2d 409, 437–39 (Ala.1997) (see, J., concurring) (discussing the relationship of rights and responsibilities); see, e.g., *Flowers v. State*, 586 So.2d 978, 990 (Ala.Crim.App) (affirming a life sentence for a 15–year-old for the commission of a murder), cert. denied, 596 So.2d 954 (Ala.1991) (table), cert. denied, 504 U.S. 930, 112 S.Ct. 1995, 118 L.Ed.2d 591 (1992).

Jones realized that between 20% and 40% of his fellow pledges voluntarily chose to leave the fraternity and the hazing, but he chose to stay. See, Prosser & Keeton, The Law of Torts 491 ("[W]here there is a reasonably safe alternative open, the plaintiff's choice of the dangerous way is a free one, and may amount to assumption of the risk. . . . "). As a responsible adult in the eyes of the law, Jones cannot be heard to argue that peer pressure prevented him from leaving the very hazing activities that, he admits, several of his peers left.[1]

Jones's own deposition testimony indicates that he believed he was free to leave the hazing activities:

"Q: You didn't have to let this [hazing] happen to you, did you?

"A: No.

"Q: And you could have quit at any time?

"A: Yes.

"Q: But yet you chose to go through with what you have described here in your complaint with the aspirations that you were going to become a brother in the Kappa Alpha Order? You were willing to subject yourself to this for the chance to become a member of the brotherhood . . . were you not?

" . . . .

"A: Yes."

We conclude that Jones's participation in the hazing activities was of his own volition. The trial court correctly determined that reasonable people could reach no conclusion other than that Jones voluntarily

1. We note that the peer pressure that may accompany an individual's desire to joint a voluntary social organization is a far cry from the economic necessity and inequality in bargaining position that have been used to justify determinations that a child cannot assume the risk of a work-related injury where a child-labor law prohibits his employment. See, e.g., *Brilliant Coal Co. v. Sparks*, 16 Ala.App. 665, 667, 81 So. 185, 187 (1919) (stating that the defense of assumption of the risk cannot be invoked by a mine operator for injuries to an employee under 16 years of age); *Boyles v. Hamilton*, 235 Cal.App.2d 492, 498, 45 Cal. Rptr. 399 (1965) (stating that one who employs a child in violation of a statute should not escape responsibility, by reason of the defenses of assumption of the risk or contributory negligence, for injuries sustained by the child).

exposed himself to the hazing. Because we conclude that Jones assumed the risks of hazing, as a matter of law, we pretermit discussion of whether Alabama should recognize a new tort of "hazing" based on the doctrine of negligence per se or based on common-law principles of negligence. See Ex parte *Gentry*, 689 So.2d 916, 920 n. 2 (Ala.1996).

## III

The trial court correctly entered the summary judgment for the defendants with respect to Jones's negligence claims. Therefore, we reverse that portion of the judgment of the Court of Civil Appeals overturning the summary judgment for the defendants with respect to Jones's negligence claims. We remand the case for an order or proceedings not inconsistent with this opinion.

REVERSED AND REMANDED.

### *NOTES*

**1. Voluntary Exposure to Risk.** The principal cases indicate the wide range in how aggressive courts may be in assessing whether the plaintiff's assumption of risk was voluntary. The characterization of conduct as involuntary may be a mechanism for the court to find the defense inapplicable and allow the plaintiff full recovery. Do you agree with the *Rush* court's finding that the plaintiff's action was involuntary or the *Barran III* courts finding that the plaintiff voluntarily assumed the risks of hazing. Consider *McDermott v. Platte County Agricultural Society*, 245 Neb. 698, 515 N.W.2d 121 (1994), where the plaintiff slipped on defendant's icy parking lot while attempting to enter an exhibition hall. The nearest door to the hall was locked. The plaintiff argued that she had no alternative but to attempt to walk on the ice and had therefore not assumed the risk. The court concluded that when "the person against whom the doctrine is applied is deprived of a choice in the matter, the risk is not assumed, although it may be encountered."

Consider also *Jimenez v. Morgan Drive Away, Inc.*, 238 Ga.App. 638, 519 S.E.2d 722 (1999). The plaintiff encountered mechanical problems with his car and consequently parked on the highway's emergency shoulder. A truck collided into the plaintiff seriously injuring him. The court rejected a defense of assumption of risk. The court observed that "[a]ssumption of risk assumes that the actor, without coercion of circumstances, chooses a course of action with full knowledge of its danger and while exercising a free choice as to whether to engage in the act or not."

## WOODALL v. WAYNE STEFFNER PRODUCTIONS, INC.

District Court of Appeal, Second District, California.
201 Cal.App.2d 800, 20 Cal.Rptr. 572 (1962).

ASHBURN, Justice.

Defendants Wayne Steffner Productions, Inc., and Jerome Welo appeal from judgment for plaintiff based on a verdict for $135,000 which was reduced to $70,000 on motion for new trial. The action is one for damages for personal injuries.

Plaintiff had a stunt in which he was lifted over water while suspended by and sitting on the framework of a kite which he had constructed. This he had done often. In March 1959, he made a deal with defendant corporation to come from his Cleveland home to the Los Angeles area and for a consideration of $500 to do the same act, known as "The Human Kite," over land, being drawn by an automobile instead of a boat. It was to be a sequence for a television production entitled "You Asked For It." Briefly, the setup was this: He stood on roller skates with the kite in position, it was tied to the rear axle of an automobile by a 150 foot rope; the auto was to start slowly and increase its speed to 27–30 miles an hour, at which time the kite would take to the air with plaintiff sitting in it. His experience had been such that he was able to control all features of the flight except forward speed; on that he had to rely on the operator of the boat or automobile; it was imperative that the speed be reduced as soon as the kite became airborne; the object of this is to stop the upward climb, when that happens the kite goes forward and can be maneuvered successfully; if the take-off speed is maintained the wind in the back will override the forward speed and cause the kite to dive. Plaintiff further explained: "Once the kite gets up in her flying position, whether it is 50 feet, 75 feet or 100 feet, wherever the kite levels off in this position here (indicating) which is her regular flight position, ... say a gust of wind come along, or the car has a tendency to be two miles over the speed, I can rock up on my bars here and bring the kite into the wind and that automatically creates a brake on the kite, it automatically will slow down the automobile to bring it down to the given speed. In speed boats with 30 horsepower motors I can rock on the kite and bring the boat almost to a standstill just by braking the kite into the wind." But, when 75 feet up in the air "if you don't make a perfect flight it is curtains." Though plaintiff had made but one exhibition flight over land, he had found in 10 or 11 trial flights that the land job was steadier than the one over water. He had one expert driver whom he used for the land flight, one Mannyings. When making the deal with Mr. Chamberlin (television producer for defendant corporation) plaintiff said his main requirement in a driver was that he had been on stunts of that nature before. Asked if it was absolutely necessary for his own driver to come to California he said, "I knew my kite and I could take care of the kite if the man on the ground will listen to instructions, if he was a qualified driver. So at that he said 'We have one of the best stunt drivers in Hollywood,' ... in fact better than my drivers back in Cleveland and I said 'Well, in that case, it would be all right to use your drivers.' ... Q. Was there any discussion in the second conversation again about the qualifications of the driver? A. Yes, we went over that again and he had contacted the drivers that would be used on the program and again he assured me, I reminded him that the man would have to be a top qualified driver and able to listen to orders when given to him, and what not to do. Q. He again assured you, you say? A. Yes." Likewise, Don Henderson (defendant's director-cameraman) "assured me that the drivers they had were qualified drivers." So plaintiff left his own driver at home.

Soon after his arrival in Los Angeles on March 22, 1959, one Hochman drove plaintiff from his hotel to the drag strip where the stunt was to be put on. Hochman said he was to be plaintiff's driver but when plaintiff discovered he had been driving with his emergency brake partially on he refused to have Hochman. So Welo was assigned by defendant to drive in the exhibition flight. Plaintiff gave Welo explicit and repeated instructions as to speed, signals, etc., and Welo was told to slow the car after reaching a speed of 27–30 miles; he agreed to do so. Plaintiff's last word to Welo before the flight was, "Remember, now, don't go over 30 miles an hour," to which Welo agreed. Welo himself testified by deposition: "I have never represented myself to Mr. Woodall or anybody else as being a driver because I am not." In fact Welo never held himself out to Henderson as a stunt driver, had never been used as such by defendant, but had been assigned to this stunt notwithstanding the assurances previously given to plaintiff.

On the occasion in question, according to plaintiff, Welo started too slowly, was given a signal to go faster and was supposed to accelerate at once; the kite jumped along and did not take off; then Welo gave a quick surge forward and the kite rocketed up. Plaintiff started giving the wave-off signal (for an emergency stop); the kite reversed itself, but plaintiff still felt a forward motion, the kite began to fall and he could no longer control it. They were jerked along the ground and plaintiff could feel the rope taut and could feel the forward motion. His estimate was that the car got up to 45 miles.

Welo testified: "Q. Do you recall anything that Mr. Woodall told you with respect to the importance of slowing down after a certain point when he took to the air? A. Yes, I know all that. Q. You know all that? A. Yes. Q. You accelerated, though, is that correct? A. No, I did not. Q. Well, did you slow down when he got into the air? A Did I slow down? Q. Did you slow the speed of the car down when he got in the air? A. I stopped immediately. Q. How far into the air did he get then? A. I would say 70, 75, maybe 80 feet. I am not sure. Q. While he was getting 70, 75 or 80 feet in the air, during that period from the time he left the ground until he got 75 feet in the air, did you slow down any before you made an immediate stop? A. Look, fellow. There wasn't time, it happened so fast." "I said we had a prearranged signal but it happened so fast that I never got the signal. Q. Then you didn't see any signal; is that right? A. That is right." "Q. You were the driver on that day, weren't you? A. I was the driver, if you want to call it that, but I am looking backwards and he [Carlson] is watching the speedometer and everything else. Q. Who is holding the wheel? A. Pardon? Q. Who is holding the wheel? A. I don't remember."

The kite turned over on plaintiff and he was seriously injured. He began to yell, "Too fast, too fast, I told him too fast." A boy who was about five feet from plaintiff when on the ground heard him, less than a minute after the accident, repeating, "I told him not to go too fast." Welo said the car got up to 33–34 miles. Kenneth Carlson, who was in the tow car with Welo assigned to the job of watching the speedometer, testified that when plaintiff was lying on the ground he heard him say, "Too fast" and "My leg, my leg."

An expert witness, William D. Bridgeman, who viewed the film of this unfortunate flight and made computations based thereon, testified that "speed was the cause of the accident"; also, "Speed caused it to come down, that is right." Another expert, Sergeant Donald M. Mac-Lean, of the Los Angeles Police Department, upon the basis of like calculations expressed the opinion that the speed of the tow car got up to 46.5 miles an hour.

In the foregoing statement and upon other factual issues we have accepted as proved all evidence and inferences favorable to respondent which find substantial support in the evidence, for this we are required to do. (*Crawford v. Southern Pacific Co.*, 3 Cal.2d 427, 429 [45 P.2d 183]; *Nichols v. Mitchell*, 32 Cal.2d 598, 600 [197 P.2d 550]; *New v. New*, 148 Cal.App.2d 372, 383 [306 P.2d 987].)

Appellants do not challenge the amount of the verdict as reduced. Their first point is that there was no substantial evidence that appellants were negligent or that negligence of appellants, if any, was a proximate cause of plaintiff's injuries. The foregoing statement of facts seems to answer this contention sufficiently. Actually the burden of the argument is that this was an inherently hazardous stunt and one who engaged in it was negligent as a matter of law or assumed any risks involved in it.

Reliance is placed on *Montijo v. Samuel Goldwyn, Inc.*, 113 Cal.App. 57 [297 P. 949], which does lend considerable apparent support to appellants' position. The cardinal facts are stated at page 58: "In the fall of 1925 respondent was filming a picture known as 'Partners Again,' one of a 'Potash and Perlmutter' series. The plot of the story included an act which involved an airplane and an automobile rushing toward each other at rapid speeds with the airplane avoiding a collision by zooming over the automobile and just missing it. This was characterized as a 'stunt' which was intended to give a 'thrill' to an audience by the apparent and actual danger to those participating in it"; and page 61: "For some reason the stunt did not work as planned, the automobile and airplane coming into collision a short distance west of the center of the field. The left wheel of the airplane struck the radiator of the automobile between a foot and a half and two feet above the ground. This wheel was torn off as well as the lower left wing of the airplane. The balance of the airplane cleared the automobile and rose over some wires at the end of the field when it settled and crashed into a brick wall seriously damaging it." At page 64: "That the stunt was inherently dangerous appears from the testimony of all of the participants in it as well as that of other aviators called as witnesses. ... When the success or failure of an undertaking of this kind depends, first, upon the elements of nature, second, upon the operation of highly intricate machines such as an airplane and an automobile, and, third, upon inconstant human factors controlling the exactness and precision of the operation of these machines, and when a change in any one of these three things might result in serious consequences it would be apparent to anyone that a collision with consequent damage and injury would almost surely result from the frequent repetition of the act. Just when this injury would come would depend upon the failure of one of these three factors to function properly and with the exact precision that the success of the maneuver required. Neither appellant nor anyone else could reasonably expect exact precision in the operation of each of the three elements on repeated occasions. The fact that the accident did not occur during one of the four trials on November 20th could be attributed more to good luck than to any other cause. In making his contract with respondent appellant should and probably did take these risks into consideration and fix his compensation at a sum commensurate with them. He should be held to have assumed the risks of damage to his airplane which were incident to his contract."

This case has no tendency to support the claim that appellants herein were not negligent. At best it argues for assumption of risk, and the argument of appellants really merges into the claim of assumption of risk, later considered and rejected herein.

\* \* \*

Appellants urge that they were released from liability by an instrument reading as follows: "Release Agreement. Pursuant to our telephone conversation, this written agreement hereby releases the Wayne Steffner Productions and any or all of its agents or representatives from any and all responsibility, liability or claims resulting from the performance of my act. /s/ Alphonse Woodall, Human Kite." Without any previous discussion, this document was presented to plaintiff upon his arrival at defendant's office, he was requested to sign, he read it and signed it; there was no further talk about it. The deal was oral, completed by telephone, nothing had been said on this subject, and plaintiff relying upon the deal as made had paid or incurred transportation costs of $224. Without any additional consideration he signed this instrument after arriving in California.

There is in it no mention of negligence and the writing must be strictly construed, with the result that it does not cover defendant's own negligence. (See *Basin Oil Co. v. Baash–Ross Tool Co.*, 125 Cal.App.2d 578, 595 [271 P.2d 122]; 35 Cal.Jur.2d § 6, p. 490.)

\* \* \*

Appellants rely upon *Harvey Machine Co. v. Hatzel & Buehler, Inc.*, 54 Cal.2d 445 [353 P.2d 924], while respondent pins his faith to *Vinnell Co. v. Pacific Elec. Ry. Co.*, 52 Cal.2d 411 [340 P.2d 604]. In *Vinnell* it is said, at page 414: "It would appear that 'to be sufficient as an exculpatory provision against one's own negligence, the party seeking to rely thereon must select words or terms clearly and explicitly expressing that this was the intent of the parties.'" (*Sproul v. Cuddy*, 131 Cal.App.2d 85, 95 [280 P.2d 158].) The language of the present clause, prepared on behalf of the defendant railroad, falls short of so expressing the defendant's intention to exculpate itself. As stated in *Basin Oil Co. v. Baash-Ross Tool Co.*, 125 Cal.App.2d 578, 595 [271 P.2d 122], quoting from *Pacific Indemnity Co. v. California Elec. Works, Ltd.*, 29 Cal.App.2d 260, 274 [84 P.2d 313], "The defendant itself wrote the provision into the contract for its own benefit. It could have plainly stated, if such was the understanding of the parties, that the plaintiff agreed to relieve it in the matter from all liability for its own negligence. As it did not do so, we resolve all doubt, as we should, in favor of the plaintiff, and hold that it was not the intent of the parties to give to the contract as written the effect claimed by the company." At page 416: "Both by precedent and good reason, if an indemnitor such as the plaintiff is to be made responsible for the negligent acts of an indemnitee over whose conduct it has no control, the language imposing such liability should do so expressly and unequivocally so that the contracting party is advised in definite terms of the liability to which it is exposed. The indemnification clause in the present case, by not expressly stating that the defendant was protected against acts of its own negligence, failed to meet this requirement."

\* \* \*

Appellants assert that plaintiff was negligent as a matter of law in attempting such an inherently hazardous stunt and complain of refusal of certain requested instructions along that line. We think that, at best, it was a question of fact. The court submitted it to the jury as such. 35 California Jurisprudence 2d section 225, page 757: "Taking a risk does not amount to contributory negligence unless it is not necessary in order to meet the ordinary requirements of business or pleasure. It constitutes contributory negligence only if it would not have been taken by an ordinarily prudent person in the given situation. A previous assurance of safety, given to the person charged with contributory negligence may have a bearing on the determination whether he acted reasonably in not paying attention to the possibility of the danger involved."

Plaintiff, engaged in the business of television servicing and hi-fi installation, had served as airplane mechanic in the Army Air Force and had studied the basic principles of flight at Sheppard Field, Texas, one of the finest schools in the country. Kite-flying with water skis is a common sport throughout the eastern part of the country, especially in Florida. Plaintiff became interested in the sport when he saw an exhibition of same in Cleveland. This led to the construction of his own kite and the flying of same over water some 225 to 250 times, including a flight across Lake Erie, some 32 miles. At none of these times did he suffer any injury, though he had one or two spills when flying over water. One he related as follows: "Once I had a cruiser went across our wake. We were in a small boat and the bow ran in the wake and it had no choice but stop the forward motion and the kite would stop her forward flight in the center balance point and come straight down like a parachute, and you adjusted your skis and slid into the water." He turned from water to flights over land, which he found smoother and steadier than water. After 10 or 11 trial flights he gave one exhibition over land at Cleveland in October or November, 1958. He understood this to be the first time in history such a flight had been made over dry land, and it was a success. The only danger point lay in possible lack of cooperation on the part of the driver of the tow car. Plaintiff went over the matter about 30 times with Welo who understood the instructions and agreed to conform to them and to the signals given to him. To plaintiff he appeared to be a careful driver, alert and understanding. The assurances given to plaintiff by his employer's officers placed Welo in the class of an expert stunt driver. Every phase of this flight had been canvassed by plaintiff in advance and with utmost care. The evidence discloses that he had so perfected the flight that he could successfully control all elements of danger except that flowing from failure of the driver of the automobile to cooperate according to an agreed plan of action. Plaintiff was not required to anticipate negligence on the part of defendant or its driver— had a right to assume, until alerted to the contrary, that they would exercise ordinary care (35 Cal.Jur.2d § 232, p. 765). The accident was caused by excessive speed of the car driven by Welo, negligently so, and there seems to be no basis for holding that plaintiff was negligent in any respect. Colonel Glenn's flight around the world in outer space certainly was a highly hazardous one but was so carefully planned and executed that, though it might fall within the classification of assumption of risk, it certainly could not be classified as negligence. In lesser degree the same holds true of plaintiff's flight.

The issue of assumption of risk, upon which appellants heavily rely, was left to the jury as one of fact by the instructions, which were as favorable to defendants as they reasonably could expect.

It is doubtless true that plaintiff assumed any risk growing out of inexpert manipulation of the kite, a sudden windstorm, breaking loose of the tow rope which he had fastened, the kite splitting in the air, or any one of many eventualities that were not properly attributable to the two defendants' own activities. Respondent's brief says, at page 63: "Respondent may have assumed the risk of his kite's breaking, his landing's being imperfect, a pothole in the road, a gust of wind. But that respondent assumed the risk of the ridiculous and callous lead-foot on the accelerator, which *in fact* caused the accident, is denied by a mass of testimony. Every case cited by appellants simply underlines this concept. In each and every one of them, the cause of the injury was inherent in the very nature of the thing."

Concerning defendant's part in the flight, it is to be remembered that plaintiff had been assured repeatedly as to the competency and care of the driver to be furnished by defendant. That was the one feature of the venture that he could not control. He obviously surrendered his judgment as to selection of a driver to defendant and did so upon the faith of such assurances given him. Prosser on Law of Torts, 2d edition, page 311, says: "Assumption of risk must be free and voluntary. If it clearly appears from the plaintiff's words or conduct that he does not consent to relieve the defendant of the obligation to protect him, the risk will not be assumed. ... If, however, he surrenders his better judgment upon an assurance of safety or a promise of protection, he does not assume the risk, unless the danger is so obvious and so extreme that there can be no reasonable reliance upon the assurance." 65 Corpus Juris Secundum section 174, page 851: "Thus, if plaintiff surrendered his better judgment on an assurance of safety or a promise of protection he did not assume the risk unless the danger was so obvious and so extreme that there could be no reasonable reliance on the assurance." See also *Fred Harvey Corp. v. Mateas* (9 Cir.), 170 F.2d 612, 615–616; *Whyte v. Idora Park Co.,* 29 Cal.App. 342, 343, 346 [155 P. 1018]; *Weis v. Davis,* 28 Cal.App.2d 240, 244 [82 P.2d 487].

65 Corpus Juris Secundum section 174, page 852, further says: "[O]ne is not required to anticipate that he will be exposed to a hazard not naturally incidental to his situation, but arising from negligence which he has no reason to foresee." *Rogers v. Los Angeles Transit Lines,* 45 Cal.2d 414, 419 [289 P.2d 226]: "While a person, if fully informed, may assume the risk even though the dangerous condition is caused by the negligence of others. (*Prescott v. Ralphs Grocery Co., supra,* 42 Cal.2d 158, 162 [265 P.2d 904]). 'The plaintiff does not assume the risk of any negligence which he has no reason to anticipate, but once he is fully informed of it, it is well settled that the risks arising from such negligence may be assumed.' (Prosser on Torts, p. 385.)" See also 35 California Jurisprudence 2d section 278, page 824.

The parties had a fair trial and the judgment is affirmed; the attempted appeal from the verdict of the jury is dismissed; the order denying motion of defendants Wayne Steffner Productions, Inc., and Jerome Welo for judgment notwithstanding the verdict is affirmed.

## *NOTES*

**1. Assuming a Particular Risk.** The defense of assumption of risk applies to the particular risk the plaintiff is assuming. In addition, the plaintiff must appreciate the risk's magnitude. What risks did the plaintiff assume in the principal case? Consider *Karr v. Brant Lake Camp*, 261 A.D.2d 342, 691 N.Y.S.2d 427 (N.Y.App.Div.1999) where an 11–year-old, playing baseball at camp was hit by a ball thrown by an older counselor who was actively playing with the younger children. The court rejected assumption of risk as a matter of law since the plaintiff, while assuming the risk of being hit by a baseball, did not necessarily assume the enhanced risks of playing with an older counselor.

**2. Express Versus Implied Assumption of Risk.** "Express" assumption of risk is explicitly articulated by the plaintiff often, but not necessarily, in written contractual form. "Implied" assumption of risk is not expressly articulated by the plaintiff but deduced from the plaintiff's behavior. As the principal case demonstrates, both express and implied assumption of risk can be potentially argued in the same case.

**3. Invalidating Express Assumption of Risk.** *Express* assumption of risk can be invalidated by the court if it is deemed to be against public policy. Courts may find express assumption of risk provisions against public policy where the plaintiff's waiver appears coerced by the circumstances or where the waiver of the right to sue for negligence appears otherwise egregiously offensive. For example, in *Tunkl v. Regents of University of California*, 60 Cal.2d 92, 32 Cal.Rptr. 33, 383 P.2d 441 (1963), the California Supreme Court invalidated an express assumption of risk of medical malpractice required of patients to obtain treatment in a hospital emergency room. Express assumption of risk is either completely invalidated or a complete defense. This is in contrast with implied assumption of risk, where in many jurisdictions, it can now be a partial defense. See next principal case, infra.

**4. Assumption of risk is not a defense to intentional torts.** Consider *Janelsins v. Button* 102 Md.App. 30, 648 A.2d 1039 (1994), where the plaintiff was injured when the defendant kicked him in the face. The plaintiff was one of a number of people attempting to force the defendant, who was extremely drunk at the time, into his car despite the fact that he was cursing and screaming that he did not want to be put in the car. The court noted the similarities between the defenses of consent and assumption to risk, but held that only consent was an applicable defense in case of intentional torts.

## KNIGHT v. JEWETT

Supreme Court of California.

3 Cal.4th 296, 11 Cal.Rptr.2d 2, 834 P.2d 696 (1992).

GEORGE, Justice.

In this case, and in the companion case of *Ford v. Gouin, post,* page 339, [11 Cal.Rptr.2d 30, 834 P.2d 724], we face the question of the proper application of the "assumption of risk" doctrine in light of this court's adoption of comparative fault principles in *Li v. Yellow Cab Co.* (1975) 13 Cal.3d 804 [119 Cal.Rptr. 858, 532 P.2d 1226, 78 A.L.R.3d 393]. Although the *Li* decision itself addressed this issue, subsequent Court of Appeal decisions have differed in their interpretation of *Li*'s discussion of this point. We granted review to resolve the conflict among the Courts of Appeal.

I

We begin with a summary of the facts of this case, as set forth in the declarations and deposition transcripts submitted in support of and in opposition to defendant's motion for summary judgment.

On January 25, 1987, the day of the 1987 Super Bowl football game, plaintiff Kendra Knight and defendant Michael Jewett, together with a number of other social acquaintances, attended a Super Bowl party at the home of a mutual friend. During half time of the Super Bowl, several guests decided to play an informal game of touch football on an adjoining dirt lot, using a "peewee" football. Each team had four or five players and included both women and men; plaintiff and defendant were on opposing teams. No rules were explicitly discussed before the game.

Five to ten minutes into the game, defendant ran into plaintiff during a play. According to plaintiff, at that point she told defendant "not to play so rough or I was going to have to stop playing." Her declaration stated that "[defendant] seemed to acknowledge my statement and left me with the impression that he would play less rough prospectively." In his deposition, defendant recalled that plaintiff had asked him to "be careful," but did not remember plaintiff saying that she would stop playing.

On the very next play, plaintiff sustained the injuries that gave rise to the present lawsuit. As defendant recalled the incident, his team was on defense on that play, and he jumped up in an attempt to intercept a pass. He touched the ball but did not catch it, and in coming down he collided with plaintiff, knocking her over. When he landed, he stepped backward onto plaintiff's right hand, injuring her hand and little finger.

Both plaintiff and Andrea Starr, another participant in the game who was on the same team as plaintiff, recalled the incident differently from defendant. According to their declarations, at the time plaintiff was injured, Starr already had caught the pass. Defendant was running toward Starr, when he ran into plaintiff from behind, knocked her down, and stepped on her hand. Starr also stated that, after knocking plaintiff down, defendant continued running until he tagged Starr, "which tag was hard enough to cause me to lose my balance, resulting in a twisting or spraining of my ankle."

The game ended with plaintiff's injury, and plaintiff sought treatment shortly thereafter. After three operations failed to restore the movement in her little finger or to relieve the ongoing pain of the injury, plaintiff's finger was amputated.

\* \* \*

With respect to the effect of the adoption of comparative negligence on the assumption of risk doctrine—the issue before us today—the *Li* decision, *supra,* 13 Cal.3d 804, stated as follows: "As for assumption of risk, we have recognized in this state that this defense overlaps that of contributory negligence to some extent and in fact is made up of at least two distinct defenses. 'To simplify greatly, it has been observed . . . that in one kind of situation, to wit, where a plaintiff unreasonably undertakes to encounter a specific known risk imposed by a defendant's negligence, plaintiff's conduct, although he may encounter that risk in a prudent manner, is in reality a form of contributory negligence. . . . Other kinds of situations within the doctrine of assumption of risk are those, for example, where plaintiff is held to agree to relieve defendant of an obligation of reasonable conduct toward him. Such a situation would not involve contributory negligence, but rather a reduction of defendant's duty of care.' (*Grey v. Fibreboard Paper Products Co.* (1966) 65 Cal.2d 240, 245–246 [53 Cal.Rptr. 545, 418 P.2d 153]; see also *Fonseca v. County of Orange* (1972) 28 Cal.App.3d 361, 368–369 [104 Cal.Rptr. 566]; see generally, 4 Witkin, Summary of Cal. Law [(8th ed. 1974)], Torts, § 723, pp. 3013–3014; 2 Harper & James, The Law of Torts [(1st ed. 1956)] § 21.1, pp. 1162–1168; cf. Prosser, Torts [(4th ed. 1971)] § 68, pp. 439–441.) We think it clear that the adoption of a system of comparative negligence should entail the merger of the defense of assumption of risk into the general scheme of assessment of liability in proportion to fault in those particular cases in which the form of assumption of risk involved is no more than a variant of contributory negligence. (See generally, Schwartz [Comparative Negligence (1st ed. 1974)] ch. 9, pp. 153–175.)" (*Li. supra,* 13 Cal.3d at pp. 824–825, original italics.)

As this passage indicates, the *Li* decision, *supra,* 13 Cal.3d 804, clearly contemplated that the assumption of risk doctrine was to be partially merged or subsumed into the comparative negligence scheme. Subsequent Court of Appeal decisions have disagreed, however, in interpreting *Li,* as to what category of assumption of risk cases would be merged into the comparative negligence scheme.

A number of appellate decisions, focusing on the language in *Li* indicating that assumption of risk is in reality a form of contributory negligence "where a plaintiff unreasonably undertakes to encounter a specific known risk imposed by a defendant's negligence" (13 Cal.3d at p. 824), have concluded that *Li* properly should be interpreted as drawing a distinction between those assumption of risk cases in which a plaintiff "unreasonably" encounters a known risk imposed by a defendant's negligence and those assumption of risk cases in which a plaintiff "reasonably" encounters a known risk imposed by a defendant's negligence. (See, e.g., *Ordway v. Superior Court, supra,* 198 Cal.App.3d 98, 103–105.) These decisions interpret *Li* as subsuming into the comparative fault scheme those cases in which the plaintiff acts unreasonably in encountering a specific known risk, but retaining the assumption of risk doctrine as a complete bar to recovery in those cases in which the plaintiff acts reasonably in encountering such a risk. Although aware of the apparent anomaly of a rule under which a plaintiff who acts reasonably is completely barred from recovery while a plaintiff who acts unreasonably only has his or her recovery reduced, these decisions nonetheless have concluded that this distinction and consequence were intended by the *Li* court.[2]

In our view, these decisions—regardless whether they reached the correct result on the facts at issue—have misinterpreted *Li* by suggesting that our decision contemplated less favorable legal treatment for a plaintiff who reasonably encounters a known risk than for a plaintiff who unreasonably encounters such a risk. Although the relevant passage in *Li* indicates that the assumption of risk doctrine would be merged into the comparative fault scheme in instances in which a plaintiff " 'unreasonably undertakes to encounter a specific known risk imposed by a defendant's negligence' " (13 Cal.3d at p. 824), nothing in this passage suggests that the assumption of risk doctrine should survive as a total bar to the plaintiff's recovery whenever a plaintiff acts reasonably in encountering such a risk. Instead, this portion of our opinion expressly contrasts the category of assumption of risk cases which " 'involve contributory negligence' " (and which therefore should be merged into the comparative fault scheme) with those assumption of risk cases which involve " 'a reduction of defendant's duty of care.' " (*Id.* at p. 825.)

Indeed, particularly when the relevant passage in *Li, supra,* 13 Cal.3d at pages 824–825, is read as a whole and in conjunction with the authorities it cites, we believe it becomes clear that the distinction in assumption of risk cases to which the *Li* court referred in this passage was not a distinction between instances in which a plaintiff unreasonably encounters a known risk imposed by a defendant's negligence and instances in which a plaintiff reasonably encounters such a risk. Rather, the distinction to which the *Li* court referred was between (1) those

**2.** In *Ordway v. Superior Court, supra,* 198 Cal.App.3d 98, the court suggested that the differentiation in the treatment accorded reasonable and unreasonable plaintiffs under an approach viewing "reasonable implied assumption of risk" as a complete bar to recovery was only "superficially anomalous" (*id.* at p. 104), and could be explained by reference to "the expectation of the defendant. He or she is permitted to ignore reasonably assumed risks and is not required to take extraordinary precautions with respect to them. The defendant must, however, anticipate that some risks will be unreasonably undertaken, and a failure to guard against these may result in liability." (*Id.* at p. 105.)

* * *

instances in which the assumption of risk doctrine embodies a legal conclusion that there is "no duty" on the part of the defendant to protect the plaintiff from a particular risk—the category of assumption of risk that the legal commentators generally refer to as "primary assumption of risk"—and (2) those instances in which the defendant does owe a duty of care to the plaintiff but the plaintiff knowingly encounters a risk of injury caused by the defendant's breach of that duty—what most commentators have termed "secondary assumption of risk." Properly interpreted, the relevant passage in *Li* provides that the category of assumption of risk cases that is not merged into the comparative negligence system and in which the plaintiff's recovery continues to be completely barred involves those cases in which the defendant's conduct did not breach a legal duty of care to the plaintiff, i.e., "primary assumption of risk" cases, whereas cases involving "secondary assumption of risk" properly are merged into the comprehensive comparative fault system adopted in *Li*.

Although the difference between the "primary assumption of risk"/"secondary assumption of risk" nomenclature and the "reasonable implied assumption of risk"/"unreasonable implied assumption of risk" terminology embraced in many of the recent Court of Appeal decisions may appear at first blush to be only semantic, the significance extends beyond mere rhetoric. First, in "primary assumption of risk" cases— where the defendant owes no duty to protect the plaintiff from a particular risk of harm—a plaintiff who has suffered such harm is not entitled to recover from the defendant, whether the plaintiff's conduct in undertaking the activity was reasonable or unreasonable. Second, in "secondary assumption of risk" cases—involving instances in which the defendant has breached the duty of care owed to the plaintiff—the defendant is not entitled to be entirely relieved of liability for an injury proximately caused by such breach, simply because the plaintiff's conduct in encountering the risk of such an injury was reasonable rather than unreasonable. Third and finally, the question whether the defendant owed a legal duty to protect the plaintiff from a particular risk of harm does not turn on the reasonableness or unreasonableness of the plaintiff's conduct, but rather on the nature of the activity or sport in which the defendant is engaged and the relationship of the defendant and the plaintiff to that activity or sport. For these reasons, use of the "reasonable implied assumption of risk"/"unreasonable implied assumption of risk" terminology, as a means of differentiating between the cases in which a plaintiff is barred from bringing an action and those in which he or she is not barred, is more misleading than helpful.

Our reading of *Li, supra,* 13 Cal.3d 804, insofar as it draws a distinction between assumption of risk cases in which the defendant has not breached any legal duty to the plaintiff and those in which the defendant has breached a legal duty, is supported not only by the language of *Li* itself and the authorities it cites, but also, and perhaps most significantly, by the fundamental principle that led the *Li* court to replace the all-or-nothing contributory negligence defense with a comparative fault scheme. In "primary assumption of risk" cases, it is consistent with comparative fault principles totally to bar a plaintiff from pursuing a cause of action, because when the defendant has not breached a legal duty of care to the plaintiff, the defendant has not committed any conduct which would warrant the imposition of any liability whatsoever, and thus there is no occasion at all for invoking comparative fault principles. (See Prosser & Keeton on Torts, *supra,* § 68, at pp. 496–497.) By contrast, in the "secondary assumption of risk" context, the defendant has breached a duty of care owed to the plaintiff. When a risk of harm is created or imposed by a defendant's breach of duty, and a plaintiff who chose to encounter the risk is injured, comparative fault principles preclude automatically placing all of the loss on the plaintiff, because the injury in such a case may have been caused by the combined effect of the defendant's and the plaintiff's culpable conduct. To retain assumption of risk as a complete defense in such a case would fly in the face of *Li*'s basic holding that when both parties are partially at fault for an injury, a rule which places all of the loss on one of the parties is inherently inequitable. (See *id.* at pp. 497–498.)

\* \* \*

The dissenting opinion suggests, however, that, even when a defendant has breached its duty of care to the plaintiff, a plaintiff who reasonably has chosen to encounter a known risk of harm imposed by such a breach may be totally precluded from recovering any damages, without doing violence to comparative fault principles, on the theory that the plaintiff, by proceeding in the face of a known risk, has "impliedly consented" to any harm. (See dis. opn. by Kennard, J., *post,* pp. 331–333.) For a number of reasons, we conclude this contention does not withstand analysis.

First, the argument that a plaintiff who proceeds to encounter a known risk has "impliedly consented" to absolve a negligent defendant of liability for any ensuing harm logically would apply as much to a plaintiff who unreasonably has chosen to encounter a known risk, as to a plaintiff who reasonably has chosen to encounter such a risk. As we have seen, however, *Li* explicitly held that a plaintiff who " 'unreasonably undertakes to encounter a specific known risk imposed by a defendant's negligence' " (*Li, supra,* 13 Cal.3d at p. 824) is not completely barred from recovery; instead, the recovery of such a plaintiff simply is reduced under comparative fault principles. Thus, the dissenting opinion's implied consent argument is irreconcilable with *Li* itself.

\* \* \*

An amicus curiae in the companion case has questioned, on a separate ground, the duty approach to the post-*Li* assumption of risk doctrine, suggesting that if a plaintiff's action may go forward whenever a defendant's breach of duty has played some role, however minor, in a plaintiff's injury, a plaintiff who voluntarily engages in a highly dangerous sport—for example, skydiving or mountain climbing—will escape any responsibility for the injury so long as a jury finds that the plaintiff was not "unreasonable" in engaging in the sport. This argument rests on the premise that, under comparative fault principles, a jury may assign some portion of the responsibility for an injury to a plaintiff only if the jury finds that the plaintiff acted unreasonably, but not if the jury finds that the plaintiff knowingly and voluntarily, but reasonably, chose to engage in a dangerous activity. Amicus curiae contends that such a rule frequently would permit voluntary risk takers to avoid all responsibility for their own actions, and would impose an improper and undue burden on other participants.

Although we agree with the general thesis of amicus curiae's argument that persons generally should bear personal responsibility for their own actions, the suggestion that a duty approach to the doctrine of assumption of risk is inconsistent with this thesis rests on a mistaken premise. Past California cases have made it clear that the "comparative fault" doctrine is a flexible, common sense concept, under which a jury properly may consider and evaluate the relative responsibility of various parties for an injury (whether their responsibility for the injury rests on negligence, strict liability, or other theories of responsibility), in order to arrive at an "equitable apportionment or allocation of loss." (See *Daly v. General Motors Corp.* (1978) 20 Cal.3d 725, 734–742 [144 Cal.Rptr. 380, 575 P.2d 1162]; *Safeway Stores, Inc. v. Nest–Kart* (1978) 21 Cal.3d 322, 328–332 [146 Cal.Rptr. 550, 579 P.2d 441]; *Far West Financial Corp. v. D & S Co.* (1988) 46 Cal.3d 796, 804, fn. 7 [251 Cal.Rptr. 202, 760 P.2d 399].)

Accordingly, contrary to amicus curiae's assumption, we believe that under California's comparative fault doctrine, a jury in a "secondary assumption of risk" case would be entitled to take into consideration a plaintiff's voluntary action in choosing to engage in an unusually risky sport, whether or not the plaintiff's decision to encounter the risk should be characterized as unreasonable, in determining whether the plaintiff properly should bear some share of responsibility for the injuries he or she suffered. (See, e.g., *Kirk v. Washington State University* (1987) 109 Wn.2d 448 [746 P.2d 285, 290–291]. See generally Schwartz, Comparative Negligence, *supra*, § 9.5, p. 180; Diamond, *Assumption of Risk After Comparative Negligence: Integrating Contract Theory into Tort Doctrine* (1991) 52 Ohio St. L.J. 717, 748–749.) Thus, in a case in which an injury has been caused by both a defendant's breach of a legal duty to the plaintiff and the plaintiff's voluntary decision to engage in an unusually risky sport, application of comparative fault principles will not operate to relieve either individual of responsibility for his or her actions, but rather will ensure that neither party will escape such responsibility.

It may be helpful at this point to summarize our general conclusions as to the current state of the doctrine of assumption of risk in light of the adoption of comparative fault principles in *Li, supra*, 13 Cal.3d 804, general conclusions that reflect the view of a majority of the justices of the court (i.e., the three justices who have signed this opinion and Justice Mosk (see conc. and dis. opn. by Mosk, J., *post*, p. 321)). In cases involving "primary assumption of risk"—where, by virtue of the nature of the activity and the parties' relationship to the activity, the defendant owes no legal duty to protect the plaintiff from the particular risk of harm that caused the injury—the doctrine continues to operate as a complete bar to the plaintiff's recovery. In cases involving "secondary assumption of risk"—where the defendant does owe a duty of care to the plaintiff, but the plaintiff proceeds to encounter a known risk imposed by the defendant's breach of duty—the doctrine is merged into the comparative fault scheme, and the trier of fact, in apportioning the loss resulting from the injury, may consider the relative responsibility of the parties.

Accordingly, in determining the propriety of the trial court's grant of summary judgment in favor of the defendant in this case, our inquiry does not turn on the reasonableness or unreasonableness of plaintiff's conduct in choosing to subject herself to the risks of touch football or in continuing to participate in the game after she became aware of defendant's allegedly rough play. Nor do we focus upon whether there is a factual dispute with regard to whether plaintiff subjectively knew of, and voluntarily chose to encounter, the risk of defendant's conduct, or impliedly consented to relieve or excuse defendant from any duty of care to her. Instead, our resolution of this issue turns on whether, in light of the nature of the sporting activity in which defendant and plaintiff were engaged, defendant's conduct breached a legal duty of care to plaintiff. We now turn to that question.

## III

As a general rule, persons have a duty to use due care to avoid injury to others, and may be held liable if their careless conduct injures another person. (See Civ. Code, § 1714.) Thus, for example, a property owner ordinarily is required to use due care to eliminate dangerous conditions on his or her property. (See, e.g., *Rowland v. Christian* (1968) 69 Cal.2d 108 [70 Cal.Rptr. 97, 443 P.2d 561, 32 A.L.R.3d 496].) In the sports setting, however, conditions or conduct that otherwise might be viewed as dangerous often are an integral part of the sport itself. Thus, although moguls on a ski run pose a risk of harm to skiers that might not exist were these configurations removed, the challenge and risks posed by the moguls are part of the sport of skiing, and a ski resort has no duty to eliminate them. (See generally Annot. (1987) 55 A.L.R.4th 632.) In this respect, the nature of a sport is highly relevant in defining the duty of care owed by the particular defendant.

Although defendants generally have no legal duty to eliminate (or protect a plaintiff against) risks inherent in the sport itself, it is well established that defendants generally do have a duty to use due care not to increase the risks to a participant over and above those inherent in the sport. Thus, although a ski resort has no duty to remove moguls from a ski run, it clearly does have a duty to use due care to maintain its towropes in a safe, working condition so as not to expose skiers to an increased risk of harm. The cases establish that the latter type of risk, posed by a ski resort's negligence, clearly is not a risk (inherent in the sport) that is assumed by a participant. (See generally Annot. (1979) 95 A.L.R.3d 203.)

In some situations, however, the careless conduct of others is treated as an "inherent risk" of a sport, thus barring recovery by the plaintiff. For example, numerous cases recognize that in a game of baseball, a player generally cannot recover if he or she is hit and injured by a carelessly thrown ball (see, e.g., *Mann v. Nutrilite, Inc.* (1955) 136 Cal.App.2d 729, 734–735 [289 P.2d 282]), and that in a game of basketball, recovery is not permitted for an injury caused by a carelessly extended elbow (see, e.g., *Thomas v. Barlow* (1927) 5 N.J. Misc. 764 [138 A. 208]). The divergent results of the foregoing cases lead naturally to the question how courts are to determine when careless conduct of another properly should be considered an "inherent risk" of the sport that (as a matter of law) is assumed by the injured participant.

Contrary to the implied consent approach to the doctrine of assumption of risk, discussed above, the duty approach provides an answer which does not depend on the particular plaintiff's subjective knowledge or appreciation of the potential risk. Even where the plaintiff, who falls while skiing over a mogul, is a total novice and lacks any knowledge of skiing whatsoever, the ski resort would not be liable for his or her injuries. (See *Brown v. San Francisco Baseball Club* (1950) 99 Cal. App.2d 484, 488–492 [222 P.2d 19] [baseball spectator's alleged ignorance of the game did not warrant imposing liability on stadium owner for injury caused by a carelessly thrown ball].) And, on the other hand, even where the plaintiff actually is aware that a particular ski resort on occasion has been negligent in maintaining its towropes, that knowledge would not preclude the skier from recovering if he or she were injured as a result of the resort's repetition of such deficient conduct. In the latter context, although the plaintiff may have acted with knowledge of the potential negligence, he or she did not consent to such negligent conduct or agree to excuse the resort from liability in the event of such negligence.

Rather than being dependent on the knowledge or consent of the particular plaintiff, resolution of the question of the defendant's liability in such cases turns on whether the defendant had a legal duty to avoid such conduct or to protect the plaintiff against a particular risk of harm. As already noted, the nature of a defendant's duty in the sports context depends heavily on the nature of the sport itself. Additionally, the scope of the legal duty owed by a defendant frequently will also depend on the defendant's role in, or relationship to, the sport.

\* \* \*

In the present case, defendant was a participant in the touch football game in which plaintiff was engaged at the time of her injury, and thus the question before us involves the circumstances under which a participant in such a sport may be held liable for an injury sustained by another participant.

The overwhelming majority of the cases, both within and outside California, that have addressed the issue of coparticipant liability in such a sport, have concluded that it is improper to hold a sports participant liable to a coparticipant for ordinary careless conduct committed during the sport—for example, for an injury resulting from a carelessly thrown ball or bat during a baseball game—and that liability properly may be imposed on a participant only when he or she intentionally injures another player or engages in reckless conduct that is totally outside the range of the ordinary activity involved in the sport. (See, e.g., *Gauvin v. Clark* (1989) 404 Mass. 450 [537 N.E.2d 94, 96–97] and cases cited.)

In reaching the conclusion that a coparticipant's duty of care should be limited in this fashion, the cases have explained that, in the heat of an active sporting event like baseball or football, a participant's normal energetic conduct often includes accidentally careless behavior. The courts have concluded that vigorous participation in such sporting events likely would be chilled if legal liability were to be imposed on a participant on the basis of his or her ordinary careless conduct. The cases have recognized that, in such a sport, even when a participant's conduct violates a rule of the game and may subject the violator to internal sanctions prescribed by the sport itself, imposition of legal liability for such conduct might well alter fundamentally the nature of the sport by deterring participants from vigorously engaging in activity that falls close to, but on the permissible side of, a prescribed rule.

A sampling of the cases that have dealt with the question of the potential tort liability of such sports participants is instructive. In *Tavernier v. Maes, supra,* 242 Cal.App.2d 532, for example, the Court of Appeal upheld a verdict denying recovery for an injury sustained by the plaintiff second baseman as an unintended consequence of the defendant baserunner's hard slide into second base during a family picnic softball game. Similarly, in *Gaspard v. Grain Dealers Mutual Insurance Company* (La.Ct.App. 1961) 131 So.2d 831, the plaintiff baseball player was denied recovery when he was struck on the head by a bat which accidentally flew out of the hands of the defendant batter during a school game.

\* \* \*

By contrast, in *Griggas v. Clauson* (1955) 6 Ill.App.2d 412 [128 N.E.2d 363], the court upheld liability imposed on the defendant basketball player who, during a game, wantonly assaulted a player on the opposing team, apparently out of frustration with the progress of the game.

\* \* \*

In our view, the reasoning of the foregoing cases is sound. Accordingly, we conclude that a participant in an active sport breaches a legal duty of care to other participants—i.e., engages in conduct that properly may subject him or her to financial liability—only if the participant intentionally injures another player or engages in conduct that is so reckless as to be totally outside the range of the ordinary activity involved in the sport.[7]

**7.** As suggested by the cases described in the text, the limited duty of care applicable to coparticipants has been applied in situations involving a wide variety of active sports, ranging from baseball to ice hockey and skating. Because the touch football game at issue in this case clearly falls within the rationale of this rule, we have no occasion to decide whether a comparable limited duty of care appropriately should be applied to other less active sports, such as archery or golf. We note that because of the special danger to others posed by the sport of hunting, past cases generally have found the ordinary duty of care to be applicable to hunting accidents. (See, e.g., *Summers v. Tice* (1948) 33 Cal.2d 80, 83 [199 P.2d 1, 5 A.L.R.2d 91].)

As applied to the present case, the foregoing legal principle clearly supports the trial court's entry of summary judgment in favor of defendant. The declarations filed in support of and in opposition to the summary judgment motion establish that defendant was, at most, careless or negligent in knocking over plaintiff, stepping on her hand, and injuring her finger. Although plaintiff maintains that defendant's rough play as described in her declaration and the declaration of Andrea Starr properly can be characterized as "reckless," the conduct alleged in those declarations is not even closely comparable to the kind of conduct—conduct so reckless as to be totally outside the range of the ordinary activity involved in the sport—that is a prerequisite to the imposition of legal liability upon a participant in such a sport.

Therefore, we conclude that defendant's conduct in the course of the touch football game did not breach any legal duty of care owed to plaintiff. Accordingly, this case falls within the primary assumption of risk doctrine, and thus the trial court properly granted summary judgment in favor of defendant. Because plaintiff's action is barred under the primary assumption of risk doctrine, comparative fault principles do not come into play.

The judgment of the Court of Appeal, upholding the summary judgment entered by the trial court, is affirmed.

## NOTES

1. **Implied Assumption of Risk as a Partial Defense.** The modern trend is to allow all implied assumption of risk to be a partial defense. The finder of fact, just as with the conversion of contributory negligence into comparative negligence, must allocate a percentage deduction from the plaintiff's recovery based on a finding of implied assumption of risk. Since in many jurisdictions, implied assumption of risk and contributory negligence are both comparative, the two defenses are merged together into "comparative fault" or what is still called comparative negligence but includes comparative implied assumption of risk.

As the principal case indicates, the finder of fact must translate the implied assumption of risk into a percentage. As with the conversion of contributory negligence into comparative negligence, this conversion is a subjective, mostly intuitive, evaluation. Since implied assumption of risk can be reasonable, as arguably in the case of a well-trained athlete's willing exposure to a poorly maintained athletic field, percentage deductions for implied assumption of risk can exist even if the implied assumption of risk doesn't constitute fault. In such instances, the finder of fact is simply allocating partial "responsibility" for the accident to the plaintiff's assumption of risk.

2. **Merging Only Unreasonable Implied Assumption of Risk into Comparative Fault.** The principal case and most courts reject the approach of only merging "unreasonable" implied assumption of risk into comparative fault and allowing "reasonable" implied assumption of risk to remain a complete defense. Under this "Alice in Wonderland" approach, the plaintiff's attorney would argue the plaintiff's assumption of risk was at least slightly unreasonable to allow recovery, while the defendant's attorney

would claim the plaintiff's implied assumption of risk was entirely reasonable and consequently barred any recovery. Are there any justifications for this approach? Is it persuasive to argue that a "reasonably" assumed risk is a "fair" deal, but an "unreasonable" assumption of risk means the plaintiff has been "victimized?"

**3. Maintaining Implied Assumption of Risk as a Complete Defense.** A third approach to implied assumption of risk accepted by only a few courts, maintains implied assumption of risk as a complete defense even when contributory negligence is converted to the partial defense of comparative negligence. Does implied assumption of risk effectively constitute a consent to the defendant's negligence and thereby justify denying the plaintiff any recovery? Consider *Kennedy v. Providence Hockey Club*, 119 R.I. 70, 376 A.2d 329 (1977) where a spectator at a hockey match was hit by a hockey puck. The court held that the spectator had assumed the risk and that implied assumption of risk should continue to constitute a complete defense.

**4. Creation of Limited Duty.** The principal case, in addition to making all implied assumption of risk, a partial instead of complete defense and merging it into comparative fault, also creates a new "limited duty" precluding participants from recovery for mere negligence against other participants in football and other similar sports. This limited duty requires a finding of reckless conduct that is totally outside the range of the ordinary activity involved in the sport before a participant is liable to another participant. Why should the law treat sports differently from other activities and exempt participants from liability for ordinary negligence?

The principal case characterized this new limited duty as a type of "primary" assumption of risk since no duty has been breached. Does the court gain anything by using this terminology or is it simply a potentially confusing and superfluous use of language to describe a specific limited duty? Professor James invented the term "primary" assumption of risk to refer to cases where the defendant was not liable because she had not breached a duty, but where the decision had mistakenly been viewed as an assumption of risk case. Recall the first principal case under assumption of risk. Had the operators of the Flopper breached a duty of care? Was assumption of risk actually required as a defense? See Diamond, *Assumption of Risk After Comparative Negligence: Integrating Contract Theory Into Tort Doctrine*, 52 Ohio St.L.J. 717 (1991), Sugarman, *Assumption of Risk*, 31 Val.U.C.Rev. 833 (1997).

In *Kahn v. East Side Union High School District*, 31 Cal.4th 990, 4 Cal.Rptr.3d 103, 75 P.3d 30 (2003), the California Supreme Court held that the limited duty for participation in sports also applied with respect to alleged negligence on the part of coaches in pushing players beyond their skill level. In this case, the coach of a high school junior varsity swim program told a student that she had to dive from the diving block into shallow water despite the fact that she had repeatedly expressed concern about doing so, and had not been properly trained in the technique, which resulted in the student breaking her neck. The court held that there was a triable issue of fact as to whether the coach was reckless in requiring the student to dive, or merely negligent (which would not have resulted in liability). Consider also *Pfister v. Shusta*, 167 Ill.2d 417, 212 Ill.Dec. 668, 657 N.E.2d 1013 (1995), where the Supreme Court of Illinois held that the contact sports exception was applicable to a spontaneous and informal game of kick the can played in a dormitory hallway. The court noted that participants in contact sports are immunized from liability except for intentional or reckless and wanton conduct. Despite the fact that the game being played by plaintiff was not organized sport, he had still assumed the risks attendant to a contact sport. Consider also *Avila v. Citrus Community College District*, 38 Cal.4th 148, 41 Cal.Rptr.3d 299, 131 P.3d 383 (2006), where the California Supreme Court rejected the claims of a baseball player allegedly intentionally hit by a pitch. The court noted that "being *intentionally* hit by a pitch is likewise an inherent risk of the sport [or baseball] so accepted by custom that a pitch intentionally thrown at a batter has its own terminology." Because such behavior did not fall "totally outside the range of the ordinary activity involved in the sport (internal quotations omitted) there was no liability on the part of the college for failure to prevent such behavior. *Id.* at 165.

**5. Firefighters' Rule.** Most jurisdictions preclude firefighters and often police from recovering for negligence ordinarily encountered in their jobs. In essence, these professionals have assumed these risks by their employment. Consequently, a firefighter injured fighting a fire cannot sue the negligent homeowner who caused the fire. Is it appropriate to limit a firefighter's recovery for negligence? Does it encourage potential defendants to request help? Are such employees already adequately compensated for these risks? Historically, assumption of risk was utilized to preclude all employees from suing for injuries sustained from obviously unsafe working conditions. Is the firefighters' rule an inappropriate vestige of this restriction?

# SECTION J. IMMUNITIES

## GIBSON v. GIBSON

Supreme Court of California.

3 Cal.3d 914, 92 Cal.Rptr. 288, 479 P.2d 648 (1971).

SULLIVAN, Justice.

We are asked to reexamine our holding in *Trudell v. Leatherby* (1931) 212 Cal. 678 [300 P. 7] that an unemancipated minor child may not maintain an action against his parent for negligence. That decision, announced 40 years ago, was grounded on the policy that an action by a child against his parent would "bring discord into the family and disrupt the peace and harmony of the household." (*Id.* at p. 680.) If this rationale ever had any validity, it has none today. We have concluded that parental immunity has become a legal anachronism, riddled with exceptions and seriously undermined by recent decisions of this court. Lacking the support of authority and reason, the rule must fall.

James A. Gibson, plaintiff herein, is the minor son of defendant, Robert Gibson. James' complaint alleges in substance as follows. In January 1966 he was riding at night in a car which was being driven by his father and which was towing a jeep. His father negligently stopped the car on the highway and negligently instructed James to go out on the roadway to correct the position of the jeep's wheels. While following these directions, James was injured when another vehicle struck him.

Defendant filed a general demurrer on the theory that a minor child has no right of action against his parent for simple negligence. Judgment of dismissal was entered on an order sustaining the demurrer without leave to amend. This appeal followed.

The doctrine of parental immunity for personal torts is only 80 years old, an invention of the American courts. Although the oft-compared rule of interspousal immunity reached back to the early common law, English law books record no case involving a personal tort suit between parent and child. (*Dunlap v. Dunlap* (1930) 84 N.H. 352, 356 [150 A. 905, 71 A.L.R. 1055]; Prosser, Torts (3d ed. 1964) § 116, p. 886; Annot. (1951) 19 A.L.R.2d 423, 425; see McCurdy, *Torts Between Persons in Domestic Relation* (1930) 43 Harv.L.Rev. 1030, 1059–1060.) Since children have long been allowed to sue their parents in matters involving property, however, some scholars have concluded that "there is no good reason to think that the English law would not permit actions for personal torts as well. ..." (Prosser, *op. cit. supra.*, § 116, p. 886 (citing Reeve, Domestic Relations (1816) p. 287; Eversley, Domestic Relations (3d ed. 1906) p. 578); *Dunlap v. Dunlap, supra.*, 84 N.H. 352, 356.) Modern decisions in Scotland and Canada have recognized such personal injury suits. (*Young v. Rankin* (Scotland 1934) Sess. Cas. 499; *Deziel v. Deziel* (Canada 1953) 1 D.L.R. 651, 653–654; see Prosser, *op. cit. supra.*, § 116, p. 886.)

In 1891, however, the Mississippi Supreme Court laid the egg from which parental immunity was hatched. Citing no authorities in *Hewlett v. George* (1891) 68 Miss. 703 [9 So. 885], the Mississippi court barred a minor daughter's false imprisonment action against her mother who had wrongfully committed her to an insane asylum. The court declared that the "peace of society, and of the families composing society, and a sound public policy, designed to subserve the repose of families and the best interests of society" would be disturbed by such an action and concluded that a child's only protection against parental abuse was to be found in the criminal law. (*Id.* at p. 711.) This "compelling" logic soon led the Washington Supreme Court to conclude that family peace and harmony would be irreparably destroyed if a 15–year-old girl were allowed to sue her father for rape. (*Roller v. Roller* (1905) 37 Wash. 242 [79 P. 788]; see also *McKelvey v. McKelvey* (1903) 111 Tenn. 388 [77 S.W. 664], upholding a demurrer to a minor's complaint seeking damages for "cruel and inhuman treatment" by her father and stepmother.)

Other states quickly adopted the rule of *Hewlett* and *Roller*, applying it to actions for negligence as well as for intentional torts, occasionally with more emotion than reason. (See, e.g., *Mesite v. Kirchenstein* (1929) 109 Conn. 77 [145 A. 753]; *Sorrentino v. Sorrentino* (1928) 248 N.Y. 626 [162 N.E. 551]; *Wick v. Wick* (1927) 192 Wis. 260 [212 N.W. 787, 52 A.L.R. 1113]; *Elias v. Collins* (1926) 237 Mich. 175 [211 N.W. 88, 52 A.L.R. 1118]; *Matarese v. Matarese* (1925) 47 R.I. 131 [131 A. 198, 42 A.L.R. 1360]; *Small v. Morrison, supra.*, 185 N.C. 577; *Taubert v. Taubert* (1908) 103 Minn. 247 [114 N.W. 763].)

*Trudell v. Leatherby, supra.*, 212 Cal. 678, decided in 1931, involved an action by a minor plaintiff for damages for personal injuries sustained while a passenger in a car driven by his stepmother. After a discussion of barely one page on the issue of parental immunity, it was there concluded, "That a minor child, unemancipated by its parents, cannot sustain an action against its parents seems to be well settled by the authorities." (*Id.* at p. 680.) In support were cited "well considered" cases from eight states, and even a passage from *Hewlett* (as quoted in 20 R.C.L. 631). *Trudell's* only rationale was the threat of family discord.

No sooner had American courts, including our own, embraced the parental immunity doctrine than they began to fashion a number of qualifications and exceptions to it. In *Martinez v. Southern Pacific Co., supra.*, 45 Cal.2d 244, we allowed an emancipated minor to sue her parent for simple negligence; in *Emery v. Emery* (1955) 45 Cal.2d 421 [289 P.2d 218], we held that wilful or malicious torts were not within the scope of the immunity. Courts in other states compounded the doctrine's idiosyncrasies in decisions permitting tort actions by minors against the estate of a deceased parent (*Davis v. Smith* (3d Cir. 1958) 253 F.2d 286; *Dean v. Smith* (1965) 106 N.H. 314 [211 A.2d 410]; *Brennecke v. Kilpatrick* (Mo. 1960) 336 S.W.2d 68); against the parent in his business capacity (*Signs v. Signs* (1952) 156 Ohio St. 566 [103 N.E.2d 743]; *Borst v. Borst* (1952) 41 Wn.2d 642 [251 P.2d 149]; *Lusk v. Lusk* (1932) 113 W.Va. 17 [166 S.E. 538]; *Dunlap v. Dunlap, supra.*, 84 N.H. 352); and against the parent's employer under *respondeat superior* for the tort of the parent within the scope of his employment. (*Stapleton v. Stapleton* (1952) 85 Ga.App. 728 [70 S.E. 156]; *O'Connor v. Benson Coal Co.* (1938) 301 Mass. 145 [16 N.E.2d 636]; *Mi-Lady Cleaners v. McDaniel* (1938) 235 Ala. 469 [179 So. 908, 116 A.L.R. 639]; *Chase v. New Haven Waste Material Corporation* (1930) 111 Conn. 377 [150 A. 107, 68 A.L.R. 1497].) Although purporting to distinguish the situation of a negligence action directly against a living parent, such cases probably rested as much on growing judicial distaste for a rule of law which in one sweep disqualified an entire class of injured minors.

Apart from this general trend to restrict parental immunity, however, we believe that a trilogy of recent California cases in the area of intra-family tort immunity has weakened, if not eroded, the doctrinal underpinnings of the rule. In *Emery v. Emery, supra.*, 45 Cal.2d 421, we recognized the right of an injured minor to sue her father for wilful or malicious tort and to sue her brother for negligence. In *Self v. Self* (1962) 58 Cal.2d 683 [26 Cal.Rptr. 97, 376 P.2d 65] and *Klein v. Klein* (1962) 58 Cal.2d 692 [26 Cal.Rptr. 102, 376 P.2d 70], we abrogated *interspousal* immunity for intentional and negligent torts. We think that the reasoning of those decisions has totally destroyed two of the three grounds traditionally advanced in support of parental immunity: (1) disruption of family harmony and (2) fraud or collusion between family "adversaries." The third ground, the threat to parental authority and discipline, although of legitimate concern, cannot sustain a total bar to parent-child negligence suits. We shall examine these arguments one by one.

The danger to family harmony was the only rationale for immunity mentioned in *Trudell*. In *Self*, however, we termed this argument "illogical and unsound." Observing that spouses commonly sue each other over property matters, we concluded that "It would not appear that such assumed conjugal harmony is any more endangered by tort actions than by property actions.... " (58 Cal.2d 683, 690.) Indeed, as we shall discuss, *infra.*, the risk of family discord is much less in negligence actions, where an adverse judgment will normally be satisfied by the defendant family member's insurance carrier, than in property actions, where it will generally be paid out of the defendant's pocket. Since the law has long allowed a child to sue his parent over property matters (*King v. Sells* (1938) 193 Wash. 294 [75 P.2d 130]; *Lamb v. Lamb* (1895) 146 N.Y. 317 [41 N.E. 26]), the rationale of *Self* is equally applicable to parent-child tort suits.

We found the family harmony argument similarly unpersuasive in *Emery* when advanced to bar a suit between a minor sister and her minor brother. We said: "Exceptions to the general principle of liability (Civ. Code, § 3523 ['For every wrong there is a remedy.']) ... are not to be lightly created, and we decline to create such an exception on the basis of the speculative assumption that to do so would preserve family harmony. An uncompensated tort is no more apt to promote or preserve peace in the family than is an action between minor brother and sister to recover damages for that tort." (45 Cal.2d 421, 430–431.)

Arguments based on the fear of fraudulent actions are also adequately answered by reference to *Emery*, *Self*, and *Klein*. While some danger of collusion cannot be denied, the peril is no greater when a minor child sues his parent than in actions between husbands and wives, brothers and sisters, or adult children and parents, all of which are permitted in California. In short, as we stated in *Klein*: "The possibility of fraud or perjury exists to some degree in all cases. But we do not deny a cause of action to a party because of such a danger.... It would be a sad commentary on the law if we were to admit that the judicial processes are so ineffective that we must deny relief to a person otherwise entitled because in some future case a litigant may be guilty of fraud or collusion. Once that concept were accepted, then all causes of action should be abolished. Our legal system is not that ineffectual." (58 Cal.2d 692, 695–696.)

Moreover, we pointed out in *Emery* that concern with collusion is entirely inconsistent with the dire predictions of familial discord. The collusion argument assumes that the suit is in reality aimed not at the defendant family member but at his insurance carrier. In such case, the tort action poses no threat whatever to family tranquility; in fact, "domestic harmony will not be disrupted so much by allowing the action as by denying it." (Prosser, *op. cit. supra.*, § 116, p. 889.) As we concluded in *Emery*, "The interest of the child in freedom from personal injury caused by the tortious conduct of others is sufficient to outweigh any danger of fraud or collusion." (45 Cal.2d 421, 431.)

The threat to parental authority and discipline is the only one of the traditional arguments for immunity which was not fully answered by *Self*, *Klein*, and *Emery*. "Preservation of the parent's right to discipline his minor children has been the basic policy behind the rule of parental immunity from tort liability." (*Emery v. Emery*, *supra.*, 45 Cal.2d 421, 429.) Since *Self* and *Klein* dealt with suits between spouses, who are equals, we were not called upon to consider this issue. Nor does *Emery* adequately deal with this contention, for it involved parental misconduct which, because of its wilful or malicious character, forfeited all claim to immunity under the cloak of parental authority.

However, the absence of precedent on this point is not decisive. In our view, the possibility that some cases may involve the exercise of parental authority does not justify continuation of a blanket rule of immunity. In many actions, no question of parental control will arise. Thus, the parent who negligently backs his automobile into his child or who carelessly maintains a lawnmower, which injures the child, cannot claim that his parental role will be threatened if the infant is permitted to sue for negligence. To preserve the rule of immunity in such cases, where the reason for it fails, appears indefensible.

We do recognize, however, that issues of parental discretion and supervision will occasionally be raised when children sue their parents in tort. In such situations, some jurisdictions, although abrogating a broad doctrine of immunity (see *infra.*), have nevertheless retained a limited one where basic parental functions are involved. For example, in *Goller v. White, supra.*, 20 Wis.2d 402, the Wisconsin Supreme Court, while ending parental immunity in general, delineated two areas where immunity should remain: "(1) [w]here the alleged negligent act involves an exercise of parental authority over the child; and (2) where the alleged negligent act involves an exercise of ordinary parental discretion with respect to the provision of food, clothing, housing, medical and dental services, and other care." (*Id.* at p. 413.)

We agree with this approach in its recognition of the undeniable fact that the parent-child relationship is unique in some aspects, and that traditional concepts of negligence cannot be blindly applied to it. Obviously, a parent may exercise certain authority over a minor child which would be tortious if directed toward someone else. For example, a parent may spank a child who has misbehaved without being liable for battery, or he may temporarily order the child to stay in his room as punishment, yet not be held responsible for false imprisonment.

However, we reject the implication of *Goller* that within certain aspects of the parent-child relationship, the parent has carte blanche to act negligently toward his child. As we noted in *Emery*, "Since the law imposes on the parent a duty to rear and discipline his child and confers the right to prescribe a course of reasonable conduct for its development, the parent has a wide discretion in the performance of his parental functions, but that discretion does not include the right wilfully to inflict personal injuries *beyond the limits of reasonable parental discipline*." (45 Cal.2d 421, 430.) (Italics added.) Although *Emery* involved *wilful* parental misconduct, we think this reasoning is applicable to a parent's *negligent* exercise of his familial duties and powers. In short, although a parent has the prerogative and the duty to exercise authority over his minor child, this prerogative must be exercised within reasonable limits. The standard to be applied is the traditional one of reasonableness, but viewed in light of the parental role. Thus, we think the proper test of a parent's conduct is this: what would an ordinarily reasonable and prudent *parent* have done in similar circumstances?

We choose this approach over the *Goller*-type formula for several reasons. First, we think that the *Goller* view will inevitably result in the drawing of arbitrary distinctions about when particular parental conduct falls within or without the immunity guidelines. Second, we find intolerable the notion that if a parent can succeed in bringing himself within the "safety" of parental immunity, he may act negligently with impunity.

In deciding to abrogate parental immunity, we are also persuaded by several policy factors. One is the obvious but important legal principle that "when there is negligence, the rule is liability, immunity is the exception." (*Muskopf v. Corning Hospital Dist.* (1961) 55 Cal.2d 211, 219 [11 Cal.Rptr. 89, 359 P.2d 457].) As we stated in *Klein*, this fundamental doctrine of compensation for injury proximately caused by the act of another governs "in the absence of statute or compelling reasons of public policy." (58 Cal.2d 692, 695.) Of course, no statute requires parental immunity, and as we have already explained, public policy compels liability, not immunity.

Secondly, we feel that we cannot overlook the widespread prevalence of liability insurance and its practical effect on intra-family suits. Although it is obvious that insurance does not create liability where none otherwise exists (*Emery v. Emery, supra.*, 45 Cal.2d 421, 431), it is unrealistic to ignore this factor in making an informed policy decision on whether to abolish parental negligence immunity. (See *Goller v. White, supra.*, 20 Wis.2d 402, 412.) We can no longer consider child-parent actions on the outmoded assumption that parents may be required to pay damages to their children. As Professor James has observed: "Recovery by the unemancipated minor child against his parent is almost uniformly denied for a variety of reasons which involve the integrity of the family unit and the family exchequer and the importance of parental discipline. But in truth, virtually no such suits are brought except where there is insurance. And where there is, none of the threats to the family exists at all." (James, *Accident Liability Reconsidered: The Impact of Liability Insurance* (1948) 57 Yale L.J. 549, 553.)

By our decision today we join 10 other states which have already abolished parental tort immunity. We think it is significant that since 1963, when the Wisconsin Supreme Court drove the first wedge (*Goller v. White, supra.*, 20 Wis.2d 402), other jurisdictions have steadily hacked away at this legal deadwood. Of particular interest from our viewpoint is *Hebel v. Hebel* (Alaska 1967) 435 P.2d 8, where the Alaska Supreme Court relied in part on our decisions in *Self* and *Klein*. Other states which now allow children to sue their parents in tort include Kentucky (*Rigdon v. Rigdon* (Ky. Dec. 18, 1970) 39 U.S.L. Week 2350); New Jersey (*France v. A.P.A. Transport Corp.* (1970) 56 N.J. 500 [267 A.2d 490]); Arizona (*Streenz v. Streenz* (1970) 106 Ariz. 86 [461 P.2d 186]); New York (*Gelbman v. Gelbman* (1969) 23 N.Y.2d 434 [297 N.Y.S.2d 529, 245 N.E.2d 192]); Illinois (*Schenk v. Schenk* (1968) 100 Ill.App.2d 199 [241 N.E.2d 12]); Minnesota (*Silesky v. Kelman* (1968) 281 Minn. 431 [161

N.W.2d 631]); North Dakota (*Nuelle v. Wells* (N.D. 1967) 154 N.W.2d 364); and New Hampshire (*Briere v. Briere* (1966) 107 N.H. 432 [224 A.2d 588]).

Applying what we have said above to the case at bench, we hold that the trial court erred in sustaining the defendant's demurrer in reliance on *Trudell v. Leatherby*. We overrule *Trudell*, and hold that an unemancipated minor child may maintain an action for negligence against his parent. Consequently, plaintiff's complaint stated a cause of action and was not vulnerable to demurrer.

The judgment is reversed and the cause is remanded to the trial court with directions to overrule the demurrer and to allow the defendant a reasonable time within which to answer.

### NOTES

**1. Immunity from Tort Liability.** When compelling policy reasons are present, courts may hold that a certain class of defendants is immune from tort liability. The traditional classes include parents and children, spouses, charities, the government, and government officials. While the modern trend has been to scale back such immunities, some courts have held onto them as a way to restrain tort litigation in general. See Diamond, Madden & Levine, *Understanding Torts* § 15.05 (2nd ed. 2000); Keeton, *Prosser and Keeton on the Law of Torts* § 131 (5th ed. 1984) and Dobbs, *The Law of Torts*, § 225 (2000).

**2. Parent–Child Immunity.** Parent-child immunity applies to suits between parents and their unemancipated minor children. The immunity precludes tort liability for personal injuries caused by negligence, but not for economic harm. It also traditionally precludes suits for certain intentional torts, including assault and battery. Unlike its rejection in the principal case, parent-child immunity is still recognized to a certain extent in most American jurisdictions, largely because of judicial reluctance to interfere with family relations. As noted in the principal case, parent-child immunity was not derived from English common law, but is an American invention. Yet, as observed by the North Carolina Supreme Court in a footnote in an omitted portion of the principal case, "If this restraining doctrine were not announced by any of the writers of the common law, because no such case was ever brought before the courts of England, it was unmistakably and indelibly carved upon the tablets of Mount Sinai." *Small v. Morrison*, 118 S.E. 12, 16 (N.C.1923).

As the principal case indicates, some states have abrogated parent-child immunity. Still others have partially abolished parent-child immunity. For example, in *Goller v. White*, 20 Wis.2d 402, 122 N.W.2d 193 (Wis. 1963), the Wisconsin Supreme Court, as noted in the principal case, abrogated general parent-child immunity, but effectively retained a limited duty restricting negligent liability for negligent parenting.

Consider *Mohorn v. Ross*, 205 Ga.App. 443, 422 S.E.2d 290 (1992), in which a mother brought suit against the father of her child alleging that the child had been injured due to the father's negligent operation of a vehicle. The court held that the father enjoyed parental immunity for the injuries. It reasoned that even though the family was separated, the parents were not divorced, there was no evidence of domestic unrest, and therefore the underlying policy of "preserving domestic tranquility, family resources, and parental discipline remained." Consider also *Squeglia v. Squeglia*, 34 Conn. App. 866, 644 A.2d 378 (1994), where a minor child sued his father to recover for personal injuries sustained when he was attacked by the father's dog. The court held that the doctrine of parental immunity barred the suit, even though the action did not actually sound in negligence but was based on a statute imposing strict liability on dog owners to third parties for injuries caused by the animal. The court reasoned that despite the statute, the policy of parental immunity to "preserve the integrity of and unity of the family" was still applicable.

In *Reale v. Herco, Inc.*, 183 A.D.2d 163, 589 N.Y.S.2d 502 (N.Y.App.Div. 1992), a child who was injured when he fell from a slide at summer camp sued the corporation that owned the camp. The defendant, in turn, asserted a claim against the child's parents based on the parents' failure to provide proper parental supervision. The court held that under New York law, there is no recognized tort actionable by the child for parents' failure to supervise. Thus, a third party cannot seek contribution from a child's parents on that basis.

Among those jurisdictions that retain parent-child immunity, there is some disagreement as to who qualifies as a parent. In *Mitchell v. Davis*, 598 So.2d 801 (Ala.1992), an action was brought against foster parents to recover for the injury to and wrongful death of their foster children. The Supreme Court of Alabama held that the parental immunity doctrine protected foster parents from claims of simple negligence, as foster parents provide food, shelter, discipline, and emotional support for their foster children. But in *Warren v. Warren*, 336 Md. 618, 650 A.2d 252 (1994), a mother and father brought suit on behalf of their child against the child's stepmother to recover for injuries sustained in an automobile accident. The Court of Appeals of Maryland held that the doctrine of parental immunity did not apply to stepparents regardless of whether they stand in loco parentis to the injured child. The court reasoned that "parent-child immunity is required only for natural parents because the obligations between natural parent and child are reciprocal."

Like the principal case, some courts have completely eliminated parent-child immunity. Consider *Broadbent v. Broadbent*, 184 Ariz. 74, 907 P.2d 43 (1995), where a minor sued his mother to recover for injuries he sustained when he nearly drowned. The court held that the doctrine of parental immunity had been abolished. Thus, the relevant question was whether the mother had acted reasonably and prudently with respect to the act or omission that caused her child's injury. Similarly, in *Hartman v. Hartman*, 821 S.W.2d 852 (Mo.1991), minor children sued their father, mother, and grandfather for injuries sustained while the family had been on vacation. The court held that since the parental immunity doctrine no longer existed in Missouri, the case would have to be remanded for a finding as to whether the defendants had acted as reasonable prudent parents.

**3. Policy Debate on Parent–Child Immunity.** Should the parent-child immunity be retained at least as a limited duty in reference to parental supervision? Some argue that the immunity is a vestige of the courts' hesitancy to involve itself in family domestic affairs. Just as spousal and child abuse may be under-prosecuted, the family immunity reflected an inappropriate deference to the more powerful family member's wrongdoing to other family members.

On the other hand, some argue that judicial supervision of the parents' behavior toward their children through tort liability will potentially restrict culturally diverse styles of parenting. It has also been noted that liability for negligent parenting allows parents of an injured child, to be impleaded as defendants for negligent supervision, when their children sue a negligent third party defendant, thereby reducing the family unit's recovery. See discussion on contribution and indemnification, Chapter 2, Sec. K, infra. Which arguments most persuade you?

**4. Spousal Immunity.** Under traditional common law, a wife was considered the property of her husband and thus had no legal autonomy; her rights were his rights. Courts would not recognize a suit between spouses since the married couple was seen as a single legal entity incapable of suing itself. Over time, this basis for spousal immunity gave way to less abstract arguments. These have included arguments that spousal suits disrupt family harmony and that there is a high risk of conspiracy to take advantage of insurance policies. But even these relatively recent arguments have been exposed as lacking merit. For instance, litigation tends to come out of families that already have problems, rather than to be the source of those problems. As for arguments of collusive suits, such suits can occur in any context and there is no reason to believe they are any more common in the context of a spousal tort suit than elsewhere. Under pressure from critics who point out the lack of a reasonable foundation for supporting spousal immunity, the majority of jurisdictions have abrogated spousal immunity. See Diamond, Levine & Madden, supra. See also Keeton, supra, § 122.

Consider *Beattie v. Beattie*, 630 A.2d 1096 (Del.1993), where a woman sued her husband for injuries sustained while a passenger in an automobile driven by her husband. The Supreme Court of Delaware abrogated the doctrine of spousal immunity and permitted the suit. The court reasoned that it had no basis for believing that allowing negligence suits between spouses would lead to the destruction of family harmony or the proliferation of fraudulent suits. Similarly, in *Marriage of J.T.*, 77 Wash.App. 361, 891 P.2d 729 (1995), a woman sued her former husband for negligent infliction of emotional distress occasioned by the defendant's extramarital affair. The court held that since the rule of spousal immunity was abolished, the suit was not barred. In *Doe v. Doe*, 122 Md.App. 295, 712 A.2d 132 (Md. Ct. Spec. App. 1998), a man sued his wife for intentional infliction of emotional distress and fraud, alleging that his wife had had an adulterous affair and deliberately concealed from her husband the true paternity of the resulting children. The court permitted the suit.

Even in those states that still recognize spousal immunity, courts are increasingly unlikely to apply the immunity to economic or intentional torts. In *Waite v. Waite*, 593 So.2d 222 (Fla.Dist.Ct.App.1991), a woman sued her former husband to recover for injuries she sustained when the defendant attacked her with a machete. The court held that the doctrine of interspousal immunity did not bar the woman's post-dissolution suit against her former husband. The court reasoned that even though the parties were married as of the time of the attack, given its extreme nature, there was little risk of disrupting family harmony or that the plaintiff would conspire with the defendant to defraud an insurer.

**5. Charitable Immunity.** Traditionally charitable organizations enjoyed immunity from tort suits. Today most states have abolished the immunity. Other states severely limit when the immunity can be invoked. Proponents of the immunity, advance a number of rationales. First, it allows charities to continue providing their services to society without the expense of defending against tort suits. Additionally, it protects people who donate to charities against having their money used for a purpose other than charitable services. Third, in the context of suits by beneficiaries of the charity, it has been argued that those beneficiaries waived the right to sue the charity when they accepted its services. Opponents of the immunity argue that many charities are sophisticated organizations capable of purchasing insurance to protect themselves from tort liability and providing compensation to victims of their torts. See Diamond, Levine & Madden, supra. See also Keeton, supra § 133.

In the majority of states where charitable immunity is abolished, charities are subject to the ordinary liability for intentional and negligent torts. For example in *Gibson v. Brewer*, 952 S.W.2d 239 (Mo.1997), the plaintiff alleged a priest had sexually fondled him during a sleepover conducted at a parish rectory. The court held the diocese was not immune.

Some states have limited charitable immunity. For example, New Jersey by statute, precludes beneficiaries of charities and other non-profits from suing the organizations. Consider *Graber v. Richard Stockton College of New Jersey*, 313 N.J.Super. 476, 713 A.2d 503 (N.Y.App.Div. 1998) where a student was injured when she fainted in a college physiology class while witnessing the vivisection of a laboratory rat. The plaintiff's injuries included broken teeth, a split gum and required ten stitches. The court held the plaintiff was precluded from suing the college despite paying tuition to the college. The court reasoned that students were per se beneficiaries of a college or university. See also *Morales v. New Jersey Academy of Aquatic Sciences*, 302 N.J.Super. 50, 694 A.2d 600 (N.J.Super.Ct.App.Div.1997) where the plaintiff slipped while visiting an aquarium on a school trip. The court ruled the visitor was precluded by the immunity from recovering for alleged negligence.

Should charities be immune from negligence? Should beneficiaries be precluded from suing?

**6. Further Study.** For a discussion of how the majority of states have either abrogated or strictly limited the parental immunity doctrine, see Tolch, *Will Junior's First Words Be "I'll See You in Court!"?*, 58 Mo. L. Rev. 251 (1993). For an analysis of modern cases concerning parental immunity, see Eclavea, *Liability of Parent for Injury to Unemancipated Child Caused by Parent's Negligence—Modern Cases*, 6 A.L.R.4th 1066 (1997). A discussion of cases addressing the issue of spousal immunity in personal injury tort suits may be found in Foster, *Modern Status of Interspousal Tort Immunity in Personal Injury and Wrongful Death Actions*, 92 A.L.R.3d 901 (1997). For a discussion of the history of charitable immunity, see Fairchild, *Tort Immunity of Nongovernmental Charities—Modern Status*, 25 A.L.R.4th 517 (1981).

# TARASOFF v. THE REGENTS OF THE UNIVERSITY OF CALIFORNIA

Supreme Court of California.

17 Cal.3d 425, 131 Cal.Rptr. 14, 551 P.2d 334, (1976).

[The government employed therapists and police were sued by the parents of a murder victim for failure to warn the victim or family or to detain the patient who told therapists he intended to kill the victim. See first part of decision, *supra* page 305.]

\* \* \*

We address the issue of whether defendant therapists are protected by governmental immunity for having failed to warn Tatiana or those who reasonably could have been expected to notify her of her peril. We postulate our analysis on section 820.2 of the Government Code. That provision declares, with exceptions not applicable here, that "a public employee is not liable for an injury resulting from his act or omission where the act or omission was the result of the exercise of the discretion vested in him, whether or not such discretion [was] abused."

\* \* \*

Noting that virtually every public act admits of some element of discretion, we drew the line in *Johnson v. State of California* (1968) 69 Cal.2d 782 [73 Cal.Rptr. 240, 447 P.2d 352], between discretionary policy decisions which enjoy statutory immunity and ministerial administrative acts which do not. We concluded that section 820.2 affords immunity only for "*basic* policy decisions." (Italics added.) (See also *Elton v. County of Orange* (1970) 3 Cal.App.3d 1053, 1057–1058 [84 Cal.Rptr. 27]; 4 Cal. Law Revision Com. Rep. (1963) p. 810; Van Alstyne, Supplement to Cal. Government Tort Liability (Cont. Ed. Bar 1969) § 5.54, pp. 16–17; Comment, *California Tort Claims Act: Discretionary Immunity* (1966) 39 So.Cal.L.Rev. 470, 471; cf. James, *Tort Liability of Governmental Units and Their Officers* (1955) 22 U.Chi.L.Rev. 610, 637–638, 640, 642, 651.)

We also observed that if courts did not respect this statutory immunity, they would find themselves "in the unseemly position of determining the propriety of decisions expressly entrusted to a coordinate branch of government." (*Johnson v. State of California, supra*, at p. 793.) It therefore is necessary, we concluded, to "isolate those areas of quasilegislative policy-making which are sufficiently sensitive to justify a blanket rule that courts will not entertain a tort action alleging that careless conduct contributed to the governmental decision." (*Johnson v. State of California, supra*, at p. 794.) After careful analysis we rejected, in *Johnson*, other rationales commonly advanced to support governmental immunity and concluded that the immunity's scope should be no greater than is required to give legislative and executive policymakers sufficient breathing space in which to perform their vital policymaking functions.

Relying on *Johnson*, we conclude that defendant therapists in the present case are not immune from liability for their failure to warn of

Tatiana's peril. *Johnson* held that a parole officer's determination whether to warn an adult couple that their prospective foster child had a background of violence "present[ed] no ... reasons for immunity" (*Johnson v. State of California, supra,* at p. 795), was "at the lowest, ministerial rung of official action" (*id.,* at p. 796), and indeed constituted "a classic case for the imposition of tort liability." (*Id.,* p. 797; cf. *Morgan* v. *County of Yuba, supra,* 230 Cal.App.2d 938, 942–943.) Although defendants in *Johnson* argued that the decision whether to inform the foster parents of the child's background required the exercise of considerable judgmental skills, we concluded that the state was not immune from liability for the parole officer's failure to warn because such a decision did not rise to the level of a "basic policy decision."

We also noted in *Johnson* that federal courts have consistently categorized failures to warn of latent dangers as falling outside the scope of discretionary omissions immunized by the Federal Tort Claims Act. (See *United Air Lines, Inc. v. Wiener* (9th Cir. 1964) 335 F.2d 379, 397–398, cert. den. *sub nom. United Air Lines, Inc. v. United States,* 379 U.S. 951 [13 L.Ed.2d 549, 85 S.Ct. 452] (decision to conduct military training flights was discretionary but failure to warn commercial airline was not); *United States v. State of Washington* (9th Cir. 1965) 351 F.2d 913, 916, (decision where to place transmission lines spanning canyon was assumed to be discretionary but failure to warn pilot was not); *United States* v. *White* (9th Cir. 1954) 211 F.2d 79, 82 (decision not to "dedud" army firing range assumed to be discretionary but failure to warn person about to go onto range of unsafe condition was not); *Bulloch v. United States* (D.Utah 1955) 133 F.Supp. 885, 888 (decision how and when to conduct nuclear test deemed discretionary but failure to afford proper notice was not); *Hernandez v. United States* (D.Hawaii 1953) 112 F.Supp. 369, 371 (decision to erect road block characterized as discretionary but failure to warn of resultant hazard was not).

We conclude, therefore, that the therapist defendants' failure to warn Tatiana or those who reasonably could have been expected to notify her of her peril does not fall within the absolute protection afforded by section 820.2 of the Government Code. We emphasize that our conclusion does not raise the specter of therapists employed by the government indiscriminately being held liable for damage despite their exercise of sound professional judgment. We require of publicly employed therapists only that quantum of care which the common law requires of private therapists. The imposition of liability in those rare cases in which a public employee falls short of this standard does not contravene the language or purpose of Government Code section 820.2.

### 4. Defendant Therapists Are Immune From Liability for Failing to Confine Poddar.

We sustain defendant therapists' contention that Government Code section 856 insulates them from liability under plaintiffs' first and fourth causes of action for failing to confine Poddar. Section 856 affords public entities and their employees absolute protection from liability for "any injury resulting from determining in accordance with any applicable enactment ... whether to confine a person for mental illness." ...

\* \* \*

5. DEFENDANT POLICE OFFICERS ARE IMMUNE FROM LIABILITY FOR FAILING TO CONFINE PODDAR IN THEIR CUSTODY.

Confronting, finally, the question whether the defendant police officers are immune from liability for releasing Poddar after his brief confinement, we conclude that they are. The source of their immunity is section 5154 of the Welfare and Institutions Code, which declares that: "[t]he professional person in charge of the facility providing 72–hour treatment and evaluation, his designee, *and the peace officer responsible for the detainment of the person* shall not be held civilly or criminally liable for any action by a person released at or before the end of 72 hours...." (Italics added.)

\* \* \*

7. *Conclusion*

For the reasons stated, we conclude that plaintiffs can amend their complaints to state a cause of action against defendant therapists by asserting that the therapists in fact determined that Poddar presented a serious danger of violence to Tatiana, or pursuant to the standards of their profession should have so determined, but nevertheless failed to exercise reasonable care to protect her from that danger. To the extent, however, that plaintiffs base their claim that defendant therapists breached that duty because they failed to procure Poddar's confinement, the therapists find immunity in Government Code section 856. Further, as to the police defendants we conclude that plaintiffs have failed to show that the trial court erred in sustaining their demurrer without leave to amend.

\* \* \*

## NOTES

**1. Governmental Immunity.** Historically, governmental immunity followed from the notion that the monarch could not be sued. The immunity was absolute. Modern statutes, however, allow tort suits against the government under certain circumstances. A major exception to the rule of governmental immunity involves suits over injuries caused by ministerial, as opposed to discretionary, governmental function. Discretionary functions encompass policy decisions, such as a legislative enactment. Ministerial functions involve the implementation of governmental policies. Driving a government vehicle would constitute a ministerial activity. The rationale behind this approach is that discretionary functions are the domain of the legislative and executive branches of government and thus should not be subject to judicial second-guessing. Nevertheless, as the principal case suggests, it may be difficult to distinguish between discretionary and ministerial functions.

In addition to distinguishing between ministerial and discretionary functions, the federal government maintains immunity from suits for many intentional torts, strict liability, and injuries arising out of military activities and mail handling. See Diamond, Madden & Levine, *Understanding Torts* § 15.05 (2nd ed. 2000); Keeton, *Prosser and Keeton on the Law of Torts* § 131 (5th ed. 1984) and Dobbs, *The Law of Torts*, §§ 260–272 (2000).

Consider *Feres v. United States*, 340 U.S. 135, 71 S.Ct. 153, 95 L.Ed. 152 (1950), in which military servicemen, while on active non-combat duty in the military, sustained injuries as a result of the government's alleged negligence. The Court interpreted the Federal Tort Claims Act to preclude the government from being held liable for the harm. The Court noted the availability of compensation through the soldiers' pension plan and a system similar to workers' compensation. Are there legitimate justifications for maintaining governmental immunity today?

**2. Public Official Immunity.** Public officials, such as judges and elected representatives, are generally immune from liability for injuries they cause while acting in their official capacities. Other government officials are afforded varying degrees of immunity. See Diamond, Madden & Levine, supra. See also Keeton, supra § 132; Dobbs, supra, §§ 273–274.

**3. Civil Rights Action.** State government officials enjoy less immunity for violations under the Civil Rights Act of 1871 (42 U.S.C.A. § 1983) than for tort liability. In addition, federal officials can be liable for implied cause of actions derived from the Constitution. See Diamond, Levine & Madden, supra, § 15.05; Dobbs, supra, §§ 275–278; Antieau & Meechum, *Tort Liability of Government Officers and Employees* (1990).

# SECTION K.  JOINT AND SEVERAL LIABILITY

## AMERICAN MOTORCYCLE ASSOCIATION v. SUPERIOR COURT

Supreme Court of California.

20 Cal.3d 578, 146 Cal.Rptr. 182, 578 P.2d 899 (1978).

TOBRINER, Justice.

Three years ago, in *Li* v. *Yellow Cab Co.* (1975) 13 Cal.3d 804 [119 Cal.Rptr. 858, 532 P.2d 1226, 78 A.L.R.3d 393], we concluded that the harsh and much criticized contributory negligence doctrine, which totally barred an injured person from recovering damages whenever his own negligence had contributed in any degree to the injury, should be replaced in this state by a rule of comparative negligence, under which an injured individual's recovery is simply proportionately diminished, rather than completely eliminated, when he is partially responsible for the injury. In reaching the conclusion to adopt comparative negligence in *Li*, we explicitly recognized that our innovation inevitably raised numerous collateral issues, "[t]he most serious [of which] are those attendant upon the administration of a rule of comparative negligence in cases involving multiple parties." (13 Cal.3d at p. 823.) Because the *Li* litigation itself involved only a single plaintiff and a single defendant, however, we concluded that it was "neither necessary nor wise" (13 Cal.3d at

p. 826) to address such multiple party questions at that juncture, and we accordingly postponed consideration of such questions until a case directly presenting such issues came before our court. The present mandamus proceeding presents such a case, and requires us to resolve a number of the thorny multiple party problems to which *Li* adverted.

For the reasons explained below, we have reached the following conclusions with respect to the multiple party issues presented by this case. First, we conclude that our adoption of comparative negligence to ameliorate the inequitable consequences of the contributory negligence rule does not warrant the abolition or contraction of the established "joint and several liability" doctrine; each tortfeasor whose negligence is a proximate cause of an indivisible injury remains individually liable for all compensable damages attributable to that injury. Contrary to petitioner's contention, we conclude that joint and several liability does not logically conflict with a comparative negligence regime. Indeed, as we point out, the great majority of jurisdictions which have adopted comparative negligence have retained the joint and several liability rule; we are aware of no judicial decision which intimates that the adoption of comparative negligence compels the abandonment of this long-standing common law rule. The joint and several liability doctrine continues, after *Li*, to play an important and legitimate role in protecting the ability of a negligently injured person to obtain adequate compensation for his injuries from those tortfeasors who have negligently inflicted the harm.

Second, although we have determined that *Li* does not mandate a diminution of the rights of injured persons through the elimination of the joint and several liability rule, we conclude that the general principles embodied in *Li* do warrant a reevaluation of the common law equitable indemnity doctrine, which relates to the allocation of loss *among* multiple tortfeasors. As we explain, California decisions have long invoked the equitable indemnity doctrine in numerous situations to permit a "passively" or "secondarily" negligent tortfeasor to shift his liability completely to a more directly culpable party. While the doctrine has frequently prevented a more culpable tortfeasor from completely escaping liability, the rule has fallen short of its equitable heritage because, like the discarded contributory negligence doctrine, it has worked in an "all-or-nothing" fashion, imposing liability on the more culpable tortfeasor only at the price of removing liability altogether from another responsible, albeit less culpable, party.

Prior to *Li*, of course, the notion of apportioning liability on the basis of comparative fault was completely alien to California common law. In light of *Li*, however, we think that the long-recognized common law equitable indemnity doctrine should be modified to permit, in appropriate cases, a right of partial indemnity, under which liability among multiple tortfeasors may be apportioned on a comparative negligence basis. As we explain, many jurisdictions which have adopted comparative negligence have embraced similar comparative contribution or comparative indemnity systems by judicial decision. Such a doctrine conforms to *Li's* objective of establishing "a system under which liability for damage will be borne by those whose negligence caused it in direct proportion to their respective fault." (13 Cal.3d at p. 813.)

Third, we conclude that California's current contribution statutes do not preclude our court from evolving this common law right of comparative indemnity. In *Dole v. Dow Chemical Company* (1972) 30 N.Y.2d 143 [331 N.Y.S.2d 382, 282 N.E.2d 288, 53 A.L.R.3d 175] the New York Court of Appeals recognized a similar, common law partial indemnity doctrine at a time when New York had a contribution statute which paralleled California's present legislation. Moreover, the California contribution statute, by its own terms, expressly subordinates its provisions to common law indemnity rules; since the comparative indemnity rule we recognize today is simply an evolutionary development of the common law equitable indemnity doctrine, the primacy of such right of indemnity is expressly recognized by the statutory provisions. In addition, the equitable nature of the comparative indemnity doctrine does not thwart, but enhances, the basic objective of the contribution statute, furthering an equitable distribution of loss among multiple tortfeasors.

Fourth, and finally, we explain that under the governing provisions of the Code of Civil Procedure, a named defendant is authorized to file a cross-complaint against any person, whether already a party to the action or not, from whom the named defendant seeks to obtain total or partial indemnity. Although the trial court retains the authority to postpone the trial of the indemnity question if it believes such action is appropriate to avoid unduly complicating the plaintiff's suit, the court may not preclude the filing of such a cross-complaint altogether.

In light of these determinations, we conclude that a writ of mandate should issue, directing the trial court to permit petitioner-defendant to file a cross-complaint for partial indemnity against previously unjoined alleged concurrent tortfeasors.

1.  *The facts.*

In the underlying action in this case, plaintiff Glen Gregos, a teenage boy, seeks to recover damages for serious injuries which he incurred while participating in a cross-country motorcycle race for novices. Glen's second amended complaint alleges, in relevant part, that defendants American Motorcycle Association (AMA) and the Viking Motorcycle Club (Viking)—the organizations that sponsored and collected the entry fee for the race—negligently designed, managed, supervised and administered the race, and negligently solicited the entrants for the race. The second amended complaint further alleges that as a direct and proximate cause of such negligence, Glen suffered a crushing of his spine, resulting in the permanent loss of the use of his legs and his permanent inability to perform sexual functions. Although the negligence count of the complaint does not identify the specific acts or omissions of which plaintiff complains, additional allegations in the complaint assert, inter alia, that defendants failed to give the novice participants reasonable instructions that were necessary for their safety, failed to segregate the entrants into reasonable classes of equivalently skilled participants, and failed to limit the entry of participants to prevent the racecourse from becoming overcrowded and hazardous.

AMA filed an answer to the complaint, denying the charging allegations and asserting a number of affirmative defenses, including a claim that Glen's own negligence was a proximate cause of his injuries. Thereafter, AMA sought leave of court to file a cross-complaint, which purported to state two causes of action against Glen's parents. The first cause of action alleges that at all relevant times Glen's parents (1) knew that motorcycle racing is a dangerous sport, (2) were "knowledgeable and fully cognizant" of the training and instruction which Glen had received on the handling and operation of his motorcycle, and (3) directly participated in Glen's decision to enter the race by signing a parental consent form. This initial cause of action asserts that in permitting Glen's entry into the race, his parents negligently failed to exercise their power of supervision over their minor child; moreover, the cross-complaint asserts that while AMA's negligence, if any, was "passive," that of Glen's parents was "active." On the basis of these allegations, the first cause of action seeks indemnity from Glen's parents if AMA is found liable to Glen.

In the second cause of action of its proposed cross-complaint, AMA seeks declaratory relief. It reasserts Glen's parents' negligence, declares that Glen has failed to join his parents in the action, and asks for a declaration of the "allocable negligence" of Glen's parents so that "the damages awarded [against AMA], if any [may] be reduced by the percentage of damages allocable to cross-defendants' negligence." As more fully explained in the accompanying points and authorities, this second cause of action is based on an implicit assumption that the *Li* decision abrogates the rule of joint and several liability of concurrent tortfeasors and establishes in its stead a new rule of "proportionate liability," under which each concurrent tortfeasor who has proximately caused an indivisible harm may be held liable only for a *portion* of plaintiff's recovery, determined on a comparative fault basis.

\* \* \*

2. *The adoption of comparative negligence in Li does not warrant the abolition of joint and several liability of concurrent tortfeasors.*

In evaluating the propriety of the trial court's ruling, we begin with a brief review of the established rights of injured persons vis-a-vis negligent tortfeasors under current law. Under well-established common law principles, a negligent tortfeasor is generally liable for all damage of which his negligence is *a* proximate cause; stated another way, in order to recover damages sustained as a result of an indivisible injury, a plaintiff is not required to prove that a tortfeasor's conduct was *the sole* proximate cause of the injury, but only that such negligence was *a* proximate cause. (See generally 4 Witkin, Summary of Cal. Law (8th ed. 1974) Torts, § 624, pp. 2906–2907 and cases cited; Rest.2d Torts, §§ 432, subd. (2), 439.) This result follows from Civil Code section 1714's declaration that "[e]very one is responsible . . . for an injury occasioned to another by his want of ordinary care or skill. . . ." A tortfeasor may not escape this responsibility simply because another act—either an "innocent" occurrence such as an "act of God" or other negligent conduct—may also have been a cause of the injury.

In cases involving multiple tortfeasors, the principle that each tortfeasor is personally liable for any indivisible injury of which his negligence is a proximate cause has commonly been expressed in terms of "joint and several liability." As many commentators have noted, the "joint and several liability" concept has sometimes caused confusion because the terminology has been used with reference to a number of distinct situations. (See, e.g., Prosser, Law of Torts (4th ed. 1971) §§ 46, 47, pp. 291–299; 1 Harper & James, Law of Torts (1956) § 10.1, pp. 692–709.) The terminology originated with respect to tortfeasors who acted in concert to commit a tort, and in that context it reflected the principle, applied in both the criminal and civil realm, that all members of a "conspiracy" or partnership are equally responsible for the acts of each member in furtherance of such conspiracy.

Subsequently, the courts applied the "joint and several liability" terminology to other contexts in which a preexisting relationship between two individuals made it appropriate to hold one individual liable for the act of the other; common examples are instances of vicarious liability between employer and employee or principal and agent, or situations in which joint owners of property owe a common duty to some third party. In these situations, the joint and several liability concept reflects the legal conclusion that one individual may be held liable for the consequences of the negligent act of another.

In the concurrent tortfeasor context, however, the "joint and several liability" label does not express the imposition of any form of vicarious liability, but instead simply embodies the general common law principle, noted above, that a tortfeasor is liable for any injury of which his negligence is a proximate cause. Liability attaches to a concurrent tortfeasor in this situation not because he is responsible for the acts of other independent tortfeasors who may also have caused the injury, but because he is responsible for all damage of which his own negligence was a proximate cause. When independent negligent actions of a number of tortfeasors are each a proximate cause of a single injury, each tortfeasor is thus personally liable for the damage sustained, and the injured person may sue one or all of the tortfeasors to obtain a recovery for his injuries; the fact that one of the tortfeasors is impecunious or otherwise immune from suit does not relieve another tortfeasor of his liability for damage which he himself has proximately caused.

Prior to *Li*, of course, a negligent tortfeasor's liability was limited by the draconian contributory negligence doctrine; under that doctrine, a negligent tortfeasor escaped liability for injuries which he had proximately caused to another whenever the injured person's lack of due care for his own safety was also a proximate cause of the injury. In *Li*, however, we repudiated the contributory negligence rule, recognizing with Dean Prosser that "[p]robably the true explanation [of the doctrine's development in this country was] that the courts [of the 19th century] found in this defense, along with the concepts of duty and proximate cause, a convenient instrument of control over the jury, by which the liabilities of rapidly growing industry were curbed and kept within bounds." (13 Cal.3d at p. 811, fn. 4 (quoting Prosser, *Comparative Negligence* (1953) 41 Cal.L.Rev. 1, 4); cf. *Dillon v. Legg* (1968) 68 Cal.2d

728, 734–735 [69 Cal.Rptr. 72, 441 P.2d 912, 29 A.L.R.3d 1316].) Concluding that any such rationale could no longer justify the complete elimination of an injured person's right to recover for negligently inflicted injury, we held in *Li* that "in all actions for negligence resulting in injury to person or property, the contributory negligence of the person injured in person or property shall not bar recovery, but the damages awarded shall be diminished in proportion to the amount of negligence attributable to the person recovering." (13 Cal.3d at p. 829.)

In the instant case AMA argues that the *Li* decision, by repudiating the all-or-nothing contributory negligence rule and replacing it by a rule which simply diminishes an injured party's recovery on the basis of his comparative fault, in effect undermined the fundamental rationale of the entire joint and several liability doctrine as applied to concurrent tortfeasors. In this regard AMA cites the following passage from *Finnegan v. Royal Realty Co.* (1950) 35 Cal.2d 409, 433–434 [218 P.2d 17]: "Even though persons are not acting in concert, if the result[s] produced by their acts are indivisible, each person is held liable for the whole. . . . *The reason for imposing liability on each for the entire consequences is that there exists no basis for dividing damages and the law is loath to permit an innocent plaintiff to suffer as against a wrongdoing defendant.* This liability is imposed where each cause is sufficient in itself as well as where each cause is required to produce the result." (Italics added.) Focusing on the emphasized sentence, AMA argues that after *Li* (1) there is a basis for dividing damages, namely on a comparative negligence basis, and (2) a plaintiff is no longer necessarily "innocent," for *Li* permits a negligent plaintiff to recover damages. AMA maintains that in light of these two factors it is logically inconsistent to retain joint and several liability of concurrent tortfeasors after *Li*. As we explain, for a number of reasons we cannot accept AMA's argument.

First, the simple feasibility of apportioning fault on a comparative negligence basis does not render an indivisible injury "divisible" for purposes of the joint and several liability rule. As we have already explained, a concurrent tortfeasor is liable for the whole of an indivisible injury whenever his negligence is a proximate cause of that injury. In many instances, the negligence of each of several concurrent tortfeasors may be sufficient, in itself, to cause the entire injury; in other instances, it is simply impossible to determine whether or not a particular concurrent tortfeasor's negligence, acting alone, would have caused the same injury. Under such circumstances, a defendant has no equitable claim vis-à-vis an injured plaintiff to be relieved of liability for damage which he has proximately caused simply because some other tortfeasor's negligence may also have caused the same harm. In other words, the mere fact that it may be possible to assign some percentage figure to the relative culpability of one negligent defendant as compared to another does not in any way suggest that each defendant's negligence is not a proximate cause of the entire indivisible injury.

Second, abandonment of the joint and several liability rule is not warranted by AMA's claim that, after *Li*, a plaintiff is no longer "innocent." Initially, of course, it is by no means invariably true that after *Li* injured plaintiffs will be guilty of negligence. In many instances a plaintiff will be completely free of all responsibility for the accident, and yet, under the proposed abolition of joint and several liability, such a completely faultless plaintiff, rather than a wrongdoing defendant, would be forced to bear a portion of the loss if any one of the concurrent tortfeasors should prove financially unable to satisfy his proportioned share of the damages.

Moreover, even when a plaintiff is partially at fault for his own injury, a plaintiff's culpability is not equivalent to that of a defendant. In this setting, a plaintiff's negligence relates only to a failure to use due care for his own protection, while a defendant's negligence relates to a lack of due care for the safety of others. Although we recognized in *Li* that a plaintiff's self-directed negligence would justify reducing his recovery in proportion to his degree of fault for the accident,[2] the fact remains that insofar as the plaintiff's conduct creates only a risk of self-injury, such conduct, unlike that of a negligent defendant, is not tortious. (See Prosser, Law of Torts, *supra*, § 65, p. 418.)

Finally, from a realistic standpoint, we think that AMA's suggested abandonment of the joint and several liability rule would work a serious and unwarranted deleterious effect on the practical ability of negligently injured persons to receive adequate compensation for their injuries. One of the principal by-products of the joint and several liability rule is that it frequently permits an injured person to obtain full recovery for his injuries even when one or more of the responsible parties do not have the financial resources to cover their liability. In such a case the rule recognizes that fairness dictates that the "wronged party should not be deprived of his right to redress," but that "[t]he wrongdoers should be left to work out between themselves any apportionment." (*Summers v. Tice* (1948) 33 Cal.2d 80, 88 [199 P.2d 1, 5 A.L.R.2d 91].) The *Li* decision does not detract in the slightest from this pragmatic policy determination.

\* \* \*

3. *Upon reexamination of the common law equitable indemnity doctrine in light of the principles underlying Li, we conclude that*

**2.** A question has arisen as to whether our *Li* opinion, in mandating that a plaintiff's recovery be diminished in proportion to the plaintiff's negligence, intended that the plaintiff's conduct be compared with each individual tortfeasor's negligence, with the cumulative negligence of all named defendants or with all other negligent conduct that contributed to the injury. The California BAJI Committee, which specifically addressed this issue after *Li*, concluded that "the contributory negligence of the plaintiff must be proportioned to the combined negligence of plaintiff and of all the tort-feasors, whether or not joined as parties ... whose negligence proximately caused or contributed to plaintiff's injury." (Use note, BAJI No. 14.90 (5th ed. 1975 pocket pt.) p. 152.)

We agree with this conclusion, which finds support in decisions from other comparative negligence jurisdictions. (See, e.g., *Pierringer* v. *Hoger* (1963) 21 Wis.2d 182 [124 N.W.2d 106]; *Walker* v. *Kroger Grocery & Baking Co.* (1934) 214 Wis. 519 [252 N.W. 721, 727–728].) In determining to what degree the injury was due to the fault of the plaintiff, it is logically essential that the plaintiff's negligence be weighed against the combined total of all other causative negligence; moreover, inasmuch as a plaintiff's actual damages do not vary by virtue of the particular defendants who happen to be before the court, we do not think that the damages which a plaintiff may recover against defendants who are joint and severally liable should fluctuate in such a manner.

*the doctrine should be modified to permit partial indemnity among concurrent tortfeasors on a comparative fault basis.*

Although, as discussed above, we are not persuaded that our decision in *Li* calls for a fundamental alteration of the rights of injured plaintiffs vis-a-vis concurrent tortfeasors through the abolition of joint and several liability, the question remains whether the broad principles underlying *Li* warrant any modification of this state's common law rules governing the allocation of loss *among* multiple tortfeasors. As we shall explain, the existing California common law equitable indemnity doctrine—while ameliorating inequity and injustice in some extreme cases—suffers from the same basic "all-or-nothing" deficiency as the discarded contributory negligence doctrine and falls considerably short of fulfilling *Li's* goal of "a system under which liability for damage will be borne by those whose negligence caused it in direct proportion to their respective fault." (13 Cal.3d at p. 813.) Taking our cue from a recent decision of the highest court of one of our sister states, we conclude—in line with *Li's* objectives—that the California common law equitable indemnity doctrine should be modified to permit a concurrent tortfeasor to obtain partial indemnity from other concurrent tortfeasors on a comparative fault basis.

In California, as in most other American jurisdictions, the allocation of damages among multiple tortfeasors has historically been analyzed in terms of two, ostensibly mutually exclusive, doctrines: contribution and indemnification. In traditional terms, the apportionment of loss between multiple tortfeasors has been thought to present a question of contribution; indemnity, by contrast, has traditionally been viewed as concerned solely with whether a loss should be entirely shifted from one tortfeasor to another, rather than whether the loss should be shared between the two. (See, e.g., *Alisal Sanitary Dist. v. Kennedy* (1960) 180 Cal.App.2d 69, 74–75 [4 Cal.Rptr. 379]; *Atchison, T. & S. F. Ry. Co. v. Lan Franco* (1968) 267 Cal.App.2d 881, 886 [73 Cal.Rptr. 660].) As we shall explain, however, the dichotomy between the two concepts is more formalistic than substantive,[3] and the common goal of both doctrines, the equitable distribution of loss among multiple tortfeasors, suggests a need for a reexamination of the relationship of these twin concepts. (See generally Werner, *Contribution and Indemnity in California* (1969) 57 Cal.L.Rev. 490.)

Early California decisions, relying on the ancient law that "the law will not aid a wrongdoer," embraced the then ascendant common law rule denying a tortfeasor any right to contribution whatsoever. (See, e.g., *Dow* v. *Sunset Tel. & Tel. Co.* (1912) 162 Cal. 136 [121 P. 379].) In 1957, the California Legislature enacted a bill to ameliorate the harsh effects of that "no contribution" rule; this legislation did not, however, sweep aside the old rule altogether, but instead made rather modest inroads into the contemporary doctrine, restricting a tortfeasor's statutory right of contribution to a narrow set of circumstances. We discuss the effect of

---

**3.** As Judge Learned Hand observed more than a quarter of a century ago: "[I]ndemnity is only an extreme form of contribution." (*Slattery v. Marra Bros.* (2d Cir. 1951) 186 F.2d 134, 138.)

the 1957 contribution legislation in more detail below; at this point it is sufficient to note that the passage of the 1957 legislation had the effect of foreclosing any evolution of the California common law contribution doctrine beyond its pre–1957 "no contribution" state. Over the past two decades, common law developments with respect to the allocation of loss between joint tortfeasors in this state have all been channeled instead through the equitable indemnity doctrine. (Cf. *Bielski v. Schulze* (1962) 16 Wis.2d 1 [114 N.W.2d 105, 107–111]; *Packard v. Whitten* (Me. 1971) 274 A.2d 169, 179–180.)

\* \* \*

In order to attain … a system, in which liability for an indivisible injury caused by concurrent tortfeasors will be borne by each individual tortfeasor "in direct proportion to [his] respective fault," we conclude that the current equitable indemnity rule should be modified to permit a concurrent tortfeasor to obtain partial indemnity from other concurrent tortfeasors on a comparative fault basis. In reaching this conclusion, we point out that in recent years a great number of courts, particularly in jurisdictions which follow the comparative negligence rule, have for similar reasons adopted, as a matter of common law, comparable rules providing for comparative contribution or comparative indemnity. (See, e.g., *United States v. Reliable Transfer Co.* (1975) 421 U.S. 397, 405–411 [44 L.Ed.2d 251, 258–262, 95 S.Ct. 1708]; *Kohr v. Allegheny Airlines, Inc.* (7th Cir. 1974) 504 F.2d 400, 405; *Gomes v. Brodhurst* (3d Cir. 1967) 394 F.2d 465, 467–470; *Packard v. Whitten, supra,* 274 A.2d 169, 179–180; *Bielski v. Schulze, supra,* 114 N.W.2d 105, 107–114; cf. *Lincenberg v. Issen* (Fla. 1975) 318 So.2d 386, 389–391. See also U. Comp. Fault Act, § 4, subd. (a).)

\* \* \*

.... Moreover, to preserve the incentive to settle which section 877 provides to injured plaintiffs, we conclude that a plaintiff's recovery from nonsettling tortfeasors should be diminished only by the amount that the plaintiff has actually recovered in a good faith settlement, rather than by an amount measured by the settling tortfeasor's proportionate responsibility for the injury. (See Fleming, *Foreword: Comparative Negligence At Last—By Judicial Choice* (1976) 64 Cal.L.Rev. 239, 258–259.)

> 5. *Under the allegations of the cross-complaint, AMA may be entitled to obtain partial indemnification from Glen's parents, and thus the trial court, pursuant to Code of Civil Procedure section 428.10 et seq., should have granted AMA leave to file the cross-complaint.*

Having concluded that a concurrent tortfeasor enjoys a common law right to obtain partial indemnification from other concurrent tortfeasors on a comparative fault basis, we must finally determine whether, in the instant case, AMA may properly assert that right by cross-complaint against Glen's parents, who were not named as codefendants in Glen's amended complaint. As we explain, the governing provisions of the Code of Civil Procedure clearly authorize AMA to seek indemnification from a previously unnamed party through such a cross-complaint. Accordingly, we conclude that the trial court erred in denying AMA leave to file its pleading.

\* \* \*

Accordingly, we conclude that under the governing statutory provisions a defendant is generally authorized to file a cross-complaint against a concurrent tortfeasor for partial indemnity on a comparative fault basis, even when such concurrent tortfeasor has not been named a defendant in the original complaint. In the instant case, the allegations of AMA's cross-complaint are sufficient to suggest that Glen's parents' negligence may possibly have been a concurrent cause of Glen's injuries. While we, of course, intimate absolutely no opinion as to the merits of the claim, if it is established that the parents were indeed negligent in supervising their son and that such negligence was a proximate cause of injury, under the governing California common law rule Glen's parents could be held liable for the resulting damages. (See, e.g., *Gibson v. Gibson* (1971) 3 Cal.3d 914 [92 Cal.Rptr. 288, 479 P.2d 648].) Thus, we believe that AMA's cross-complaint states a cause of action for comparative indemnity and that the trial court should have permitted its filing.

6. *Conclusion*

In the instant case we have concluded that the force of *Li's* rationale applies equally to the allocation of responsibility between two or more negligent defendants and requires a modification of this state's traditional all-or-nothing common law equitable indemnity doctrine. Again, we concur with Dean Prosser's observation in a related context that "[there] is obvious lack of sense and justice in a rule which permits the entire burden of a loss, for which two defendants were ... unintentionally responsible, to be shouldered onto one alone, ... while the latter goes scot free." (Prosser, Law of Torts, *supra*, § 50, p. 307.) From the crude all-or-nothing rule of traditional indemnity doctrine, and the similarly inflexible per capita division of the narrowly circumscribed contribution statute, we have progressed to the more refined stage of permitting the jury to apportion liability in accordance with the tortfeasors' comparative fault.

Accordingly, we hold that under the common law equitable indemnity doctrine a concurrent tortfeasor may obtain partial indemnity from cotortfeasors on a comparative fault basis.

Let a peremptory writ of mandate issue directing the trial court (1) to vacate its order denying AMA leave to file its proposed cross-complaint, and (2) to proceed in accordance with the views expressed in this opinion. Each party shall bear its own costs.

CLARK, Justice, dissenting.

I

Repudiating the existing contributory negligence system and adopting a system of comparative negligence, this court in *Li v. Yellow Cab Co.* (1975) 13 Cal.3d 804 [119 Cal.Rptr. 858, 532 P.2d 1226, 78 A.L.R.3d 393] repeatedly—like the tolling bell—enunciated the principle that the extent of liability must be governed by the extent of fault. Thus, the court stated, "the extent of fault should govern the extent of liability" (*id.*, at p. 811), "liability for damage will be borne by those whose negligence caused it in direct proportion to their respective fault" (*id.*, at p. 813), and "the fundamental purpose of [the rule of pure comparative negligence] shall be to assign responsibility and liability for damage in direct proportion to the amount of negligence of each of the parties" (*id.*, at p. 829). And in a cacophony of emphasis this court explained that the "basic objection to the doctrine [of contributory negligence]—grounded in the primal concept that in a system in which liability is based on fault, the extent of fault should govern the extent of liability—remains irresistible to reason and all intelligent notions of fairness." (*Id.*, at p. 811.)

Now, only three years later, the majority of my colleagues conclude that the *Li* principle is not irresistible after all. Today, in the first decision of this court since *Li* explaining the operation of the *Li* principle, they reject it for almost all cases involving multiple parties.

The majority reject the *Li* principle in two ways. First, they reject it by adopting joint and several liability holding that each defendant—including the marginally negligent one—will be responsible for the loss attributable to his codefendant's negligence. To illustrate, if we assume that the plaintiff is found 30 percent at fault, the first defendant 60 percent, and a second defendant 10 percent, the plaintiff under the majority's decision is entitled to a judgment for 70 percent of the loss against each defendant, and the defendant found only 10 percent at fault may have to pay 70 percent of the loss if his codefendant is unable to respond in damages.

The second way in which the majority reject *Li's* irresistible principle is by its settlement rules. Under the majority opinion, a good faith settlement releases the settling tortfeasor from further liability, and the "plaintiff's recovery from nonsettling tortfeasors should be diminished only by the amount that the plaintiff has actually recovered in a good faith settlement, rather than by an amount measured by the settling tortfeasor's proportionate responsibility for the injury." (*Ante*, p. 604.)[1] The settlement rules announced today may turn *Li's* principle upside down—the extent of dollar liability may end up in inverse relation to fault.

Whereas the joint and several liability rules violate the *Li* principle when one or more defendants are absent or unable to respond in damages, the settlement rules will ordinarily preclude effecting the

---

**1.** Although one of the most important matters determined by today's decision, the issue of pro rata reduction or dollar amount reduction was barely mentioned and the relative merits of the two systems were not briefed or argued by the parties or by any of the numerous amici. The overwhelming weight of authority—contrary to the majority—is for pro rata reduction rather than settlement amount reduction. (Ark. Stats. Ann., § 34–1005; Hawaii Rev.Laws § 663–15; *Nebben v. Kosmalski* (1976) 307 Minn. 211 [239 N.W.2d 234, 236]; *Theobald* v. *Angeles* (1965) 44 N.J. 228 [208 A.2d 129,

131]; *Rogers* v. *Spady* (1977) 147 N.J.Super. 274 [371 A.2d 285, 287]; N.Y.Gen.Obl.Law, § 15–108; R.I.Gen.Laws (1956) § 10–6–8; S.D.Codified Laws 15–8–18; Tex.Rev.Civ. Stat., art. 2212a, § 2(e); Utah Code 78–27–43; *Gomes* v. *Brodhurst* (3d Cir. 1967) 394 F.2d 465; *Pierringer* v. *Hoger* (1963) 21 Wis.2d 182 [124 N.W.2d 106]; Wyo.Stat. Ann. § 1–7.6; but cf.Fla.Stat.Ann. § 768.31; Mass.Laws Ann., ch. 231B, § 4.) Although I believe it is improper for the court to reach such an important issue without the aid of counsel, I am compelled to discuss the problem because the majority has determined it.

majority's principle in cases when all defendants are involved in the litigation and are solvent. To return to my 30–60–10 illustration and further assuming both defendants are solvent, the plaintiff is ordinarily eager to settle quickly to avoid the long delay incident to trial. Further, he will be willing to settle with either defendant because under the majority's suggested rules, he may then pursue the remaining defendant for the balance of the recoverable loss (70 percent) irrespective whether the remaining defendant was 10 percent at fault or 60 percent at fault. The defendants' settlement postures will differ substantially. Realizing the plaintiff is eager for quick recovery and is capable of pursuing the codefendant, the defendant 60 percent liable for the loss will be prompted to offer a sum substantially below his share of fault, probably paying 20 to 40 percent of the loss. The defendant only 10 percent at fault will be opposed to such settlement, wishing to limit his liability. To compete with his codefendant in settlement offers he will be required to offer substantially in excess of his 10 percent share of the loss, again frustrating the *Li* principle that the extent of liability should be governed by the extent of fault. Should he fail to settle, the 10 percent at fault defendant runs the risk that his codefendant will settle early for perhaps half of his own liability, while the lesser negligent person must eventually pay the remainder, not only frustrating the *Li* principle but turning it upside down. In any event, it is extremely unlikely he can settle for his 10 percent share.

The foregoing demonstrates that under the majority's joint and several liability and settlement rules, only rarely will the *Li* principle be carried out in multi-party litigation. The principle will be frustrated if one or more defendants are unavailable, insolvent, or have settled. Prior to *Li*, the overwhelming majority of accident cases were settled in whole or in part, and assuming this practice continues, the *Li* principle will not be realized in those cases. In a substantial number of the remaining cases it can be expected that one of the tortfeasors will not be able to respond in damages, again frustrating the *Li* principle. In sum, although the majority devote approximately half of their opinion to asserted maintenance of the *Li* principle (pts. 3, 4, and 5), in only a very small number of multiple party cases will the loss be shared in accordance with that principle.

Attempting to justify their repudiation of the *Li* principle in favor of joint and several liability, the majority suggest three rationales. First, we are told that the feasibility of apportioning fault on a comparative basis does not "render an indivisible injury 'divisible,'" each defendant's negligence remaining a proximate cause of the entire indivisible injury. (*Ante*, p. 588.) The argument proves too much. Plaintiff negligence is also a proximate cause of the entire indivisible injury, and the argument, if meritorious, would warrant repudiation of *Li* not only in the multiple party case but in all cases.

The second rationale of the majority lies in two parts. First, we are told that after *Li* there is no reason to assume that plaintiffs will "invariably" be guilty of negligence. (*Ante*, p. 589.) Obviously this is true. The basis of joint and several liability prior to *Li* was that between an innocent plaintiff and two or more negligent defendants, it was proper to hold the defendants jointly and severally liable. The innocent plaintiff should not suffer as against a wrongdoing defendant. (*Ante*, p. 588.) (*Finnegan v. Royal Realty Co.* (1950) 35 Cal.2d 409, 433–434 [218 P.2d 17].) Accordingly, it is not unreasonable to reject the *Li* principle when we are comparing the plaintiff's innocence and defendants' negligence. But the issue presented by this case is whether joint and several liability shall be extended to *Li* cases, cases where the plaintiff *by definition* is negligent. While we cannot know whether a plaintiff will be found negligent until trial, we also cannot know whether any given defendant will be found at fault until trial. Since liability is not to be determined until after trial, there is no reason not to deal with the real issue before us whether joint and several liability should be applied in cases where the plaintiff is found negligent—i.e., cases where by definition the plaintiff is "invariably" found negligent.

\* \* \*

## NOTES

**1. Joint and Several Liability.** Defendants often share responsibility for their torts with other defendants also found liable for a plaintiff's injury. Such liable defendants or "tortfeasors" are traditionally under the common law "jointly and severally" liable for the damages they wrongfully inflicted on the plaintiff. The term indicates that all the liable defendants are each fully responsible for the entire injury.

A court may use one of three theories to find that multiple tortfeasors are joint tortfeasors. First, the defendants may have engaged in concerted action that caused the tort. Second, the defendants, through completely independent acts, may have produced a single, indivisible injury. Third, the defendants may be jointly and severally liable because of vicarious liability. See Diamond, Levine & Madden, *Understanding Torts* § 13.01 (2nd ed. 2000); Keeton, *Prosser and Keeton on the Law of Torts* § 46 (5th ed. 1984) and Dobbs, *The Law of Torts* §§ 385–396 (2000). The first two of these theories are discussed below. For a discussion of vicarious liability, see Chapter 6, infra.

**2. Acting in Concert.** If one person gives aid or encouragement to another person to commit a tort, then those two people are said to be acting in concert to commit that tort. The aid or encouragement need only be a factor that has some effect on the aided party; it does not need to be a "but for" cause of the tort. This is the tort equivalent to the criminal law rule that accessories and co-conspirators are responsible for the other's crimes. For example, in *Bierczynski v. Rogers*, 239 A.2d 218 (Del. Super. Ct. 1968), two defendants were racing their automobiles when one racer injured the plaintiff. The court held that the defendants were acting in concert and were thus jointly and severally liable for the plaintiff's injuries.

It is important to note that the aid must be tortious; innocent conduct that inadvertently aids a tortfeasor will not suffice to constitute concerted action. Consider *Day v. Walton*, 199 Tenn. 10, 281 S.W.2d 685 (1955), where armed bouncers at a dance hall ejected a rowdy patron and subsequently had a confrontation with him outside. When the bouncers seized the patron, the patron struck one of the bouncers and fled. During the pursuit, one of the bouncers shot near the patron, but the bullet ricocheted and hit the plaintiff, an innocent bystander. The court noted that firing a gun at a person suspected of only a misdemeanor is unlawful. The plaintiff was thus entitled to go to a jury in her suit against the bouncer who shot the gun. In determining whether the other bouncers who participated in the chase could be held liable for the shooting, the court noted "where there is no joint negligence, no encouragement to do the particular act, no *unlawful* common enterprise or objective, then there is no joint liability for an unlawful act committed by one of the several parties." (Emphasis in original.) Since the other bouncers only participated in the attempt to apprehend the patron, but did not aid or encourage the shooting, they could not be held liable for the plaintiff's injury.

**3. Independent Torts Causing Indivisible Injury.** A court will also find that multiple defendants are joint tortfeasors if they committed separate torts which combined to produce a single, indivisible injury to the plaintiff. Suppose, for example, that A and B each drop a brick at the same time on C's right foot, causing an injury. Since there is only one injury and it cannot be said who caused how much damage, both A and B would be held jointly and severally liable for the harm. Consider *Bartlett v. New Mexico Welding Supply, Inc.*, 98 N.M. 152, 646 P.2d 579 (N.M.Ct.App.1982), in which the plaintiff was in an automobile accident with two other automobiles. Since the automobiles struck the plaintiff simultaneously, there was no way to attribute certain injuries to one defendant or to another. Similarly, in *Coney v. J.L.G. Industries, Inc.*, 97 Ill.2d 104, 73 Ill.Dec. 337, 454 N.E.2d 197 (1983), the plaintiff's decedent died when he fell from a hydraulic work platform. The plaintiff sued the platform manufacturer on a strict products liability theory, alleging that the platform was defective. The plaintiff also sued the decedent's employer, alleging that the employer was negligent in not training the decedent in how to operate the platform and in not maintaining additional personnel on the ground. The plaintiff argued that the defendants should be held jointly and severally liable; the court agreed and so held.

Where a plaintiff's injuries are divisible and can be attributed to individual defendants, then the indivisible injury theory of joint and several liability may not be used. To illustrate, suppose that in the careless masons' hypothetical above A dropped her brick on C's right foot and B dropped hers on C's left foot. In such a case, there are two separate injuries, each of which may be attributed to the separate plaintiffs, and thus the indivisible injury theory would not apply.

**4. Allocating Responsibility.** Although under joint and several liability, each tortfeasor is fully responsible for the plaintiff's entire injury, when more than one tortfeasor is available to pay, traditionally liability was divided evenly on a pro rated basis. For example, two tortfeasors would pay half, three would each pay a third.

Today many courts, as in the principal case, allocate responsibility on a percentage basis. One defendant may be found 70% responsible, the other 30%. Furthermore, courts generally now allow defendants of negligent tort actions to implead as additional defendants other potential defendants under the jurisdiction of the court, such as the parents in the principal case, even if the plaintiff chose not to sue these other defendants. Most courts call this division among liable defendants "comparative contribution," although the principal case used the term "comparative indemnification" to evade prior legislative restrictions on when a tortfeasor could seek a contribution from other tortfeasors.

**5.  Rejecting Joint and Several Liability.** Despite the willingness of courts to allow comparative allocation of liability under comparative contribution or indemnification, as the principal case indicates this does not necessarily result in the abolition of joint and several liability. If, for example, a tortfeasor judged 70% responsible is unable to pay, the other defendants must make up the missing share and are assessed according to their percentage of responsibility. In some jurisdictions the plaintiff, if judged to be comparatively negligent, is allocated his percentage of the defaulting tortfeasor's share.

In many states tort reform statutes have either abolished or modified joint and several liability. For example, in California, a ballot proposition, passed by voters, modified the principal case so that joint and several liability exists only for economic damages, including medical expenses, lost income and damaged property. For pain and suffering, loss of consortium and other intangible damages, the defendants are only liable for their percentage share. Under this reform approach, the plaintiff is not compensated for a defendant's share of the intangible loss, if he is unable or unavailable to pay it. The policy debate over joint and several liability is considered in the editorial and notes following it, *infra*.

**6.  Settlements.** Most litigation is resolved through settlements between the plaintiffs and the defendants. As the dissent in the principal case indicates, some courts require those tortfeasors who do not settle in a multi-defendant case to pay not only their percentage of liability, but the difference between the jury's total damage assessment and the amount paid out in settlement to the plaintiff by other defendants.

Consider for example that defendant B settles for $12,000 with plaintiff A. Joint tortfeasor C does not settle and goes to the trial where the jury finds C 10% responsible for $100,000 worth of damages to plaintiff A, and B responsible for 90%. B has already settled and is not responsible for paying the plaintiff any additional amount. Nevertheless, under the settlements rules used by the principal case, the remaining defendant must not pay merely his allotted 10% or $10,000 of the $100,000 judgment, but the $100,000 minus what the other defendant paid in his settlement or $88,000. This approach encourages settlements by the plaintiff since he can still recover fully from remaining defendants. Likewise defendants are encourages to settle rather than be left responsible for large amounts of the awarded damages. Do you agree or disagree with Justice Clark's criticism of this approach? The procedure does require the settlements to be approved by a court in a "good faith" hearing that is intended to prevent settlements designed to unfairly skirt responsibility to another defendant. Nevertheless, given the uncertainty of a jury's verdict, including issues of liability and measurement of damages, much discretion is usually allowed the settling parties.

A majority of states disagree with the principal case and deduct the settling defendant's allocated percentage as the jury later determines it at a trial for the defendants who did not settle. In the example above, defendant C would only be responsible for his 10% or $10,000. The plaintiff would not be compensated for the difference between B's $12,000 settlement and 90% of the damages or $90,000 allocated to B. A would receive only a small percentage of his potential recovery. This approach is endorsed by the Uniform Comparative Fault Act and the Restatement (Third) of Torts, Apportionment of Liability § 16 (adopted 1999). Which of these two approached do you find preferable? These settlement approaches are applicable only in the context of joint and several liability. Otherwise, each defendant is always only liable for his allocated share of the damages.

**7. Contribution and Indemnification Distinguished.** Where one of several joint tortfeasors has been required to pay for all of the plaintiff's damages, that tortfeasor may seek contribution from the other tortfeasors for their share of the liability. This was not allowed historically, but now the majority rule is to allow such actions outside the context of intentional torts. Most courts still bar contribution actions prosecuted by intentional tortfeasors on the grounds that judicial resources should not be spent to help intentional tortfeasors. Nevertheless, the Restatement (Third) of Torts, Apportionment of Liability § 1, comment C (1999) now endorses contribution for intentional torts. See also *Southern Pacific Transportation Co. v. State of California*, 115 Cal.App.3d 116, 171 Cal.Rptr. 187 (1981) allowing contribution claims where there is willful misconduct.

In order to be liable for contribution, the defendant must typically be someone who would have been liable to the original plaintiff. Thus, if the tortfeasor was immune from the suit by the original plaintiff, she will not generally be liable for contribution. See Chapter 2, Sec. J, supra, for a discussion of immunities.

Indemnification, unlike contribution, involves a shift of total liability. Historically, this occurred where one joint tortfeasor was only slightly or technically responsible for the injury, while another joint tortfeasor was primarily at fault. Such a situation might arise where one tortfeasor is liable only on a theory of vicarious liability. In such cases, the "passive" tortfeasor forced to compensate the plaintiff, could seek reimbursement from the "active" tortfeasor. Indemnification also arises in cases where parties have entered into indemnification contracts. In jurisdictions that utilize a comparative fault system of liability, the trend is to have indemnification, outside of contractual or vicarious liability indemnification cases, subsumed by comparative contribution.

**8. Policy Issues Surrounding Joint and Several Liability.** A number of arguments may be advanced for and against joint and several liability. Some argue that it should be retained, since it affords the plaintiff a greater likelihood of full recovery and leaves it to the culpable defendants to worry about their individual shares of liability. On the other hand, joint and several liability often results in a deep pocket defendant paying large amounts that are far out of proportion to their level of culpability. Consider the arguments for and against joint and several liability as you read the following editorial.

Editorial, *Torts Gone Wild* San Francisco
Chronicle, Sunday Punch[1]
Dec. 1, 1985.

THE LAST TWO decades have been times of social upheaval: Minorities, including women, have achieved new rights and power. Gays

---

**1.** © The San Francisco Chronicle reprinted with permission.

have come roaring out of the closet. The folks who didn't want to trust anyone over 30 are well past that age and contending for the power they distrusted.

But another major change is now occurring. We think most Americans don't realize what is happening. Yet the change is profound, sweeping, affects all of us and is bringing great change to our lives. Judicial activism is increasing, and the nation is suffering from the effects of what the New Republic recently called "as an explosion of torts" liability law. The legal doctrine of joint and several liability is literally changing American life.

That doctrine means that a solvent defendant can be held responsible for all of the costs of a damage award if he was as little as one percent responsible for an accident or mishap—if the other defendants are insolvent, usually by not being insured. This is the theory known as the "deep pocket" doctrine.

Judicial acceptance of the deep pocket doctrine has sent insurance rates out of sight. In some cases it has made insurance simply unavailable. The insurance industry, which was in a competitive rate war just a few years ago, has suffered billions of dollars in losses over the last two years, so some insurance companies are getting out of the business of insuring people or institutions that are apt to be targets of costly damage suits. All agencies of local government fall into this unfortunate category, along with companies and individuals making or selling all sorts of goods and services.

While we have previously expressed alarm about the extent of this problem in California, it is now of national concern. The latest issue of State Legislatures, the publication of the National Conference of State Legislatures, reports that "A chorus of cries for relief is rising in the state houses. The voices are those of mayors, county commissioners and other local officials just back from court or from meetings with their insurance companies."

"Local governments are discovering that no company wants to insure them against the kinds of suits being filed. Bridgefield, Conn., for example, was told by its insurer that its $25 million umbrella liability insurance policy couldn't be renewed without modification. Coverage would be lowered to $3 million and the premium would rise from a rate of $16,500 to $215,000."

\* \* \*

BRIDGEFIELD OFFICIALS may have it easy, it seems. The cities of Oakland and Berkeley have been unable to find insurers and are among a group of 34 California cities that either have no insurance now or will have none once current policies expire.

California cities, counties, school districts and special-purpose districts are in serious trouble. Because huge damage awards have become typical, government agencies are increasingly negotiating large settlements of damage suits even when their liability is known to be minor.

Contra Costa County, for instance, recently negotiated a $1.1 million settlement of a suit brought by a driver who, while allegedly drunk, drove his pickup truck through a barrier in Crockett. The truck went down an embankment, and in the ensuing crash the young driver was crippled for life. The driver's misbehavior was not an issue in the settlement; the effectiveness and safety of the barrier were. The county's attorney believes that a jury would have made a much greater damage award.

The terrible truth is that settlements of this type are not at all unusual. Court decisions have created a precedent by which individuals are no longer held responsible for the consequences of their misbehavior. The taxpayers are repeatedly stuck under the joint and several liability doctrine.

We think that it is time for a major change.

### NOTES

Do you find the editorial persuasive? Is the example at the end of the editorial appropriate? What counterarguments can you advance? Note that many states have enacted statutes to limit joint and several liability. California is one such state. Sections 1431 and 1431.2 of the California Civil Code limits joint and several liability to economic harm. Are these statutes a good idea? Who is most likely to benefit from such statutes? Who loses?

# Chapter III

# STRICT LIABILITY AND PRODUCTS LIABILITY

## SECTION A. TRADITIONAL STRICT LIABILITY

### SIEGLER v. KUHLMAN

Supreme Court of Washington, En Banc.
81 Wash.2d 448, 502 P.2d 1181 (1972).

HALE, Associate Justice.

Seventeen-year-old Carol J. House died in the flames of a gasoline explosion when her car encountered a pool of thousands of gallons of spilled gasoline. She was driving home from her after-school job in the early evening of November 22, 1967, along Capitol Lake Drive in Olympia; it was dark but dry; her car's headlamps were burning. There was a slight impact with some object, a muffled explosion, and then searing flames from gasoline pouring out of an overturned trailer tank engulfed her car. The result of the explosion is clear, but the real causes of what happened will remain something of an eternal mystery.

Aaron L. Kuhlman had been a truck driver for nearly 11 years after he completed the tenth grade in high school and after he had worked at other jobs for a few years. He had been driving for Pacific Intermountain Express for about 4 months, usually the night shift out of the Texaco bulk plant in Tumwater. That evening of November 22nd, he was scheduled to drive a gasoline truck and trailer unit, fully loaded with gasoline, from Tumwater to Port Angeles. Before leaving the Texaco plant, he inspected the trailer, checking the lights, hitch, air hoses and tires. Finding nothing wrong, he then set out, driving the fully loaded truck tank and trailer tank, stopping briefly at the Trail's End Café for a cup of coffee. It was just a few minutes after 6 p.m., and dark, but the roads were dry when he started the drive to deliver his cargo—3,800 gallons of gasoline in the truck tank and 4,800 gallons of gasoline in the trailer tank. With all vehicle and trailer running lights on, he drove the truck and trailer onto Interstate Highway 5, proceeded north on that freeway at about 50 miles per hour, he said, and took the offramp about

1 mile later to enter Highway 101 at the Capitol Lake interchange. Running downgrade on the offramp, he felt a jerk, looked into his left-hand mirror and then his right-hand mirror to see that the trailer lights were not in place. The trailer was still moving but leaning over hard, he observed, onto its right side. The trailer then came loose. Realizing that the tank trailer had disengaged from his tank truck, he stopped the truck without skidding its tires. He got out and ran back to see that the tank trailer had crashed through a chain-link highway fence and had come to rest upside down on Capitol Lake Drive below. He heard a sound, he said, "like somebody kicking an empty fifty-gallon drum and that is when the fire started." The fire spread, he thought, about 100 feet down the road.

The trailer was owned by defendant Pacific Intermountain Express. It had traveled about 329,000 miles prior to November 22, 1967, and had been driven by Mr. Kuhlman without incident down the particular underpass above Capitol Lake Drive about 50 times. When the trailer landed upside down on Capitol Lake Drive, its lights were out, and it was unilluminated when Carol House's car in one way or another ignited the spilled gasoline.

\* \* \*

Why the tank trailer disengaged and catapulted off the freeway down through a chain-link fence to land upside down on Capitol Lake Drive below remains a mystery. What caused it to separate from the truck towing it, despite many theories offered in explanation, is still an enigma. Various theories as to the facts and cause were advanced in the trial. Plaintiff sought to prove both negligence on the part of the driver and owner of the vehicle and to bring the proven circumstances within the res ipsa loquitur doctrine. Defendants sought to obviate all inferences of negligence and the circumstances leading to the application of res ipsa loquitur by showing due care in inspection, maintenance and operation.

\* \* \*

The jury apparently found that defendants had met and overcome the charges of negligence.

\* \* \*

In the Court of Appeals, the principal claim of error was directed to the trial court's refusal to give an instruction on res ipsa loquitur, and we think that claim of error well taken. Our reasons for ruling that an instruction on res ipsa loquitur should have been given and that an inference of negligence could have been drawn from the event are found, we believe, in our statement on the subject: *ZeBarth v. Swedish Hosp. Medical Center*, 81 Wash.2d 12, 499 P.2d 1 (1972); *Miles v. St. Regis Paper Co.*, 77 Wash.2d 828, 467 P.2d 307 (1970); *Douglas v. Bussabar-ger*, 73 Wash.2d 476, 438 P.2d 829 (1968); *Pederson v. Dumouchel*, 72 Wash.2d 73, 431 P.2d 973 (1967). We think, therefore, that plaintiff was entitled to an instruction permitting the jury to infer negligence from the occurrence.

But there exists here an even more impelling basis for liability in this case than its derivation by allowable inference of fact under the res ipsa loquitur doctrine, and that is the proposition of strict liability arising as a matter of law from all of the circumstances of the event.

Strict liability is not a novel concept; it is at least as old as *Fletcher v. Rylands*, L.R. 1 Ex. 265, 278 (1866), *affirmed*, House of Lords, 3 H.L. 330 (1868). In that famous case, where water impounded in a reservoir on defendant's property escaped and damaged neighboring coal mines, the landowner who had impounded the water was held liable without proof of fault or negligence. Acknowledging a distinction between the natural and nonnatural use of land, and holding the maintenance of a reservoir to be a nonnatural use, the Court of Exchequer Chamber imposed a rule of strict liability on the landowner. The ratio decidendi included adoption of what is now called *strict liability*, and at page 278 announced, we think, principles which should be applied in the instant case:

> [T]he person who for his own purposes brings on his lands and collects and keeps there anything likely to do mischief if it escapes, must keep it in at his peril, and, if he does not do so, is prima facie answerable for all the damage which is the natural consequence of its escape.

All of the Justices in *Fletcher v. Rylands, supra,* did not draw a distinction between the natural and nonnatural use of land, but such a distinction would, we think, be irrelevant to the transportation of gasoline. The basic principles supporting the *Fletcher* doctrine, we think, control the transportation of gasoline as freight along the public highways the same as it does the impounding of waters and for largely the same reasons. See Prosser, Torts, § 78 (4th ed. 1971).

In many respects, hauling gasoline as freight is no more unusual, but more dangerous, than collecting water. When gasoline is carried as cargo—as distinguished from fuel for the carrier vehicle—it takes on uniquely hazardous characteristics, as does water impounded in large quantities. Dangerous in itself, gasoline develops even greater potential for harm when carried as freight—extraordinary dangers deriving from sheer quantity, bulk and weight, which enormously multiply its hazardous properties. And the very hazards inhering from the size of the load, its bulk or quantity and its movement along the highways presents another reason for application of the *Fletcher v. Rylands, supra,* rule not present in the impounding of large quantities of water—the likely destruction of cogent evidence from which negligence or want of it may be proved or disproved. It is quite probable that the most important ingredients of proof will be lost in a gasoline explosion and fire. Gasoline is always dangerous whether kept in large or small quantities because of its volatility, inflammability and explosiveness. But when several thousand gallons of it are allowed to spill across a public highway—that is, if, while in transit as freight, it is not kept impounded—the hazards to third persons are so great as to be almost beyond calculation. As a consequence of its escape from impoundment and subsequent explosion and ignition, the evidence in a very high percentage of instances will be destroyed, and the reasons for and causes contributing to its escape will quite likely be lost in the searing flames and explosions.

That this is a sound case for the imposition of a rule of strict liability finds strong support in Professor Cornelius J. Peck's analysis in *Negligence and Liability Without Fault in Tort Law*, 46 Wash.L.Rev. 225 (1971). Pointing out that strict liability was imposed at common law prior to *Fletcher v. Rylands, supra*, that study shows the application of a rule of strict liability in a number of instances, *i.e.*, for harm done by trespassing animals; on a bona fide purchaser of stolen goods to their true owner; on a bailee for the misdelivery of bailed property regardless of his good faith or negligence; and on innkeepers and hotels at common law.

\* \* \*

The rule of strict liability rests not only upon the ultimate idea of rectifying a wrong and putting the burden where it should belong as a matter of abstract justice, that is, upon the one of the two innocent parties whose acts instigated or made the harm possible, but it also rests on problems of proof:

> One of these common features is that the person harmed would encounter a difficult problem of proof if some other standard of liability were applied. For example, the disasters caused by those who engage in abnormally dangerous or extra-hazardous activities frequently destroy all evidence of what in fact occurred, other than that the activity was being carried on. Certainly this is true with explosions of dynamite, large quantities of gasoline, or other explosives. It frequently is the case with falling aircraft. Tracing the course followed by gases or other poisons used by exterminators may be difficult if not impossible. The explosion of an atomic reactor may leave little evidence of the circumstances which caused it. Moreover, application of such a standard of liability to activities which are not matters of common experience is well-adapted to a jury's limited ability to judge whether proper precautions were observed with such activities.

> Problems of proof which might otherwise have been faced by shippers, bailors, or guests at hotels and inns certainly played a significant role in shaping the strict liabilities of carriers, bailees, and innkeepers. Problems of proof in suits against manufacturers for harm done by defective products became more severe as the composition and design of products and the techniques of manufacture became less and less matters of common experience; this was certainly a factor bringing about adoption of a strict liability standard. (Footnote omitted.) C. Peck, *Negligence and Liability Without Fault in Tort Law*, 46 Wash.L.Rev. 225, 240 (1971). See, also, *G. P. Fletcher, Fairness and Utility in Tort Theory*, 85 Harv.L.Rev. 537 (1972), for an analysis of the judicial philosophy relating to tort liability as affecting or affected by concepts of fault and negligence; and *Comment, Liability*

*Without Fault: Logic and Potential of a Developing Concept,*
1970 Wis.L.Rev. 1201.

Thus, the reasons for applying a rule of strict liability obtain in this
case. We have a situation where a highly flammable, volatile and
explosive substance is being carried at a comparatively high rate of
speed, in great and dangerous quantities as cargo upon the public
highways, subject to all of the hazards of high-speed traffic, multiplied by
the great dangers inherent in the volatile and explosive nature of the
substance, and multiplied again by the quantity and size of the load.
Then we have the added dangers of ignition and explosion generated
when a load of this size, that is, about 5,000 gallons of gasoline, breaks
its container and, cascading from it, spreads over the highway so as to
release an invisible but highly volatile and explosive vapor above it.

Danger from great quantities of gasoline spilled upon the public
highway is extreme and extraordinary, for any spark, flame or appreciable heat is likely to ignite it. The incandescent filaments from a broken
automobile headlight, a spark from the heat of a tailpipe, a lighted
cigarette in the hands of a driver or passenger, the hot coals from a
smoker's pipe or cigar, and the many hot and sparking spots and units of
an automobile motor from exhaust to generator could readily ignite the
vapor cloud gathered above a highway from 5,000 gallons of spilled
gasoline. Any automobile passing through the vapors could readily have
produced the flames and explosions which killed the young woman in
this case and without the provable intervening negligence of those who
loaded and serviced the carrier and the driver who operated it. Even the
most prudent and careful motorist, coming unexpectedly and without
warning upon this gasoline pool and vapor, could have driven into it and
ignited a holocaust without knowledge of the danger and without leaving
a trace of what happened to set off the explosion and light the searing
flames.

Stored in commercial quantities, gasoline has been recognized to be
a substance of such dangerous characteristics that it invites a rule of
strict liability—even where the hazard is contamination to underground
water supply and not its more dangerous properties such as its explosiveness and flammability. See *Yommer v. McKenzie*, 255 Md. 220, 257 A.2d
138 (1969). It is even more appropriate, therefore, to apply this principle
to the more highly hazardous act of transporting it as freight upon the
freeways and public thoroughfares.

Recently this court, while declining to apply strict liability in a
particular case, did acknowledge the suitability of the rule in a proper
case. In *Pacific Northwest Bell Tel. Co. v. Port of Seattle*, 80 Wash.2d 59,
491 P.2d 1037 (1971), we observed that strict liability had its beginning
in *Fletcher v. Rylands, supra,* but said that it ought not be applied in a
situation where a bursting water main, installed and maintained by the
defendant Port of Seattle, damaged plaintiff telephone company's underground wires. There the court divided—not on the basic justice of a rule
of strict liability in some cases—but in its application in a particular case
to what on its face was a situation of comparatively minor hazards. Both
majority and dissenting justices held, however, that the strict liability

principles of *Fletcher v. Rylands, supra,* should be given effect in some cases; but the court divided on the question of whether underground water mains there constituted such a case.

The rule of strict liability, when applied to an abnormally dangerous activity, as stated in the Restatement (Second) of Torts § 519 (Tent. Draft No. 10, 1964), was adopted as the rule of decision in this state in *Pacific Northwest Bell Tel. Co. v. Port of Seattle, supra,* at 64, 491 P.2d, at 1039, 1040, as follows:

> (1) One who carries on an abnormally dangerous activity is subject to liability for harm to the person, land or chattels of another resulting from the activity, although he has exercised the utmost care to prevent such harm.
>
> (2) Such strict liability is limited to the kind of harm, the risk of which makes the activity abnormally dangerous.

As to what constitutes an abnormal activity, § 520 states:

> In determining whether an activity is abnormally dangerous, the following factors are to be considered:
>
> (a) Whether the activity involves a high degree of risk of some harm to the person, land or chattels of others;
>
> (b) Whether the gravity of the harm which may result from it is likely to be great;
>
> (c) Whether the risk cannot be eliminated by the exercise of reasonable care;
>
> (d) Whether the activity is not a matter of common usage;
>
> (e) Whether the activity is inappropriate to the place where it is carried on; and
>
> (f) The value of the activity to the community.

Applying these factors to this system, we do not find the activity to be abnormally dangerous. There has never been a break in the system before, absent an earthquake, and the pipe could have been expected to last many more years. It is a system commonly used for fire protection, and its placement under ground is, of course, appropriate. We do not find § 519 of the Restatement, (Tent.Draft No. 10, 1964), or *Rylands v. Fletcher, supra,* applicable.

It should be noted from the above language that we rejected the application of strict liability in *Pacific Northwest Bell Tel. Co. v. Port of Seattle, supra,* solely because the installation of underground water mains by a municipality was not, under the circumstances shown, an abnormally dangerous activity. Had the activity been found abnormally dangerous, this court would have applied in that case the rule of strict liability.

Contrast, however, the quiet, relatively safe, routine procedure of installing and maintaining and using underground water mains as described in *Pacific Northwest Bell v. Port of Seattle, supra,* with the activity of carrying gasoline as freight in quantities of thousands of gallons at freeway speeds along the public highway and even at lawful lesser speeds through cities and towns and on secondary roads in rural districts. In comparing the quiescence and passive job of maintaining underground water mains with the extremely heightened activity of carrying nearly 5,000 gallons of gasoline by truck, one cannot escape the conclusion that hauling gasoline as cargo is undeniably an abnormally dangerous activity and on its face possesses all of the factors necessary for imposition of strict liability as set forth in the Restatement (Second) of Torts § 519 (Tent.Draft No. 10, 1964), above.

Transporting gasoline as freight by truck along the public highways and streets is obviously an activity involving a high degree of risk; it is a risk of great harm and injury; it creates dangers that cannot be eliminated by the exercise of reasonable care. That gasoline cannot be practicably transported except upon the public highways does not decrease the abnormally high risk arising from its transportation. Nor will the exercise of due and reasonable care assure protection to the public from the disastrous consequences of concealed or latent mechanical or metallurgical defects in the carrier's equipment, from the negligence of third parties, from latent defects in the highways and streets, and from all of the other hazards not generally disclosed or guarded against by reasonable care, prudence and foresight. Hauling gasoline in great quantities as freight, we think, is an activity that calls for the application of principles of strict liability.

The case is therefore reversed and remanded to the trial court for trial to the jury on the sole issue of damages.

### NOTES

**1. Traditional Strict Liability.** Strict liability is not based on the defendant's standard of conduct, but on the type of activity in which she is engaged. The activity must, depending upon the jurisdiction, be characterized as "abnormally dangerous" or "ultrahazardous". Strict liability is not absolute liability. The plaintiff must still establish that the defendant owed a duty and that the activity was the actual and proximate cause of the damage. The damage must be the type of harm that causes the activity to be ultrahazardous or abnormally dangerous (again, depending on the jurisdiction). See Diamond, Levine & Madden, *Understanding Torts* § 16.01 (2nd Ed. 2000); Keeton, *Prosser and Keeton on the Law of Torts* § 75 (5th ed. 1984) and Dobbs, *The Law of Torts* §§ 342–351 (2000).

Strict liability for activities should be distinguished from the concept of strict products liability, discussed in Chapter 3 Sec. B infra.

**2. Origin of Strict Liability.** The early English case of *Rylands v. Fletcher*, 3 L.R.-E. & I. App. 330 (1868), discussed in the principal case, has been credited with establishing the doctrine of strict liability. In *Rylands*, the defendant constructed a water reservoir on his land. When the reservoir was full, it broke and flooded underground coal mine shafts that connected to the plaintiff's property. The trial court found for the defendant because he was not negligent and because he did not intend for the water to go to his neighbor's land. On appeal, the Exchequer Chamber reversed, holding that the landowner's duty was an "absolute duty to keep it [the water] in at his peril." The court reasoned as follows:

[I]t seems but reasonable and just that the neighbor, who has brought something on his own property which was not naturally there, harmless to others so long as it is confined to his own property, but which he knows to be mischievous if it gets on his neighbour's, should be obliged to make good the damage which ensues if he does not succeed in confining it to his own property. But for his act in bringing it there no mischief could have accrued, and it seems but just that he should at his peril keep it there so that no mischief may accrue, or answer for the natural and anticipated consequences.

*Fletcher v. Rylands*, L.R. 1 Ex. 265 (1866). The court also held that the level of care the defendant took was irrelevant.

The House of Lords in *Rylands v. Fletcher* affirmed the Exchequer Chamber:

[T]he question in general is not whether the Defendant has acted with due care and caution, but whether his acts have occasioned the damage.... And the doctrine is founded on good sense. For when one person, in managing his own affairs, causes, however innocently, damage to another, it is obviously only just that he should be the party to suffer.

The court stated that relief to the plaintiff would not have been available had this been a "natural use" of the land; the defendant's reservoir had not been such a use. By "natural," the English court meant conventional or common. The construction of the reservoir was highly unconventional in the area.

Dean Prosser argued that soon after the English decision, it was misinterpreted by the American courts that rejected it. Cases in New York, New Hampshire and New Jersey interpreted *Rylands* as "holding that the defendant is absolutely liable in all cases whenever anything whatever under his control escapes and causes damage." They applied *Rylands* even though what was involved in each of those cases was a customary natural use. However, the rule of *Rylands*, Prosser argued, is "that the defendant will be liable when he damages another by a thing or activity unduly dangerous and inappropriate to the place where it is maintained, in the light of the character of that place and its surroundings." Prosser, *The Principle of* Rylands v. Fletcher, in Prosser, *Selected Topics on the Law of Torts* 135 (1954). See also Keeton, supra, § 78.

**3. The Restatements.** The Restatement (First) of Torts (1938) adopted the principle of *Rylands v. Fletcher* in imposing strict liability for ultrahazardous activities:

One who carries on an ultrahazardous activity is liable to another whose person, land, or chattels the actor should recognize as likely to be harmed by the unpreventable miscarriage of the activity for harm resulting thereto from that which makes the activity ultrahazardous, although the utmost care is exercised to prevent the harm.

Restatement (First) of Torts, § 519. The Restatement (First) then went on to define "ultrahazardous":

An activity is ultrahazardous if it

(a) necessarily involves a risk of serious harm to the person, land or chattels of others which cannot be eliminated by the exercise of the utmost care, and

(b) is not a matter of common usage.

Id. § 520.

The Restatement (Second) of Torts (1977), however, changed the standard:

(1) One who carries on an abnormally dangerous activity is subject to liability for harm to the person, land, or chattels of another resulting from the activity, although he has exercised the utmost care to prevent the harm.

(2) This strict liability is limited to the kind of harm, the possibility of which makes the activity abnormally dangerous.

Restatement (Second) of Torts § 519. The Restatement (Second) uses a multi-factor analysis to discern the level of danger:

In determining whether an activity is abnormally dangerous, the following factors are to be considered:

a) existence of a high degree of risk of some harm to the person, land or chattels of others;

b) likelihood that the harm that results from it will be great;

c) inability to eliminate the risk by the exercise of reasonable care;

d) extent to which the activity is not a matter of common usage;

e) inappropriateness of the activity to the place where it is carried on; and

f) extent to which its value to the community is outweighed by its dangerous attributes.

Id. § 520.

Notice that the Restatement (Second) requires that the activity be "abnormally dangerous" rather than "ultrahazardous." The difference is meant to reflect the fact that the characterization of the activity is based on a balancing test, which includes consideration of the appropriateness of the location of the activity and the value of the activity to the community. Consequently, an activity such as the use of dynamite, which had always been characterized as an ultrahazardous activity subject to strict liability under the Restatement (First), could in certain circumstances not be characterized as abnormally dangerous and subject to strict liability under the Restatement (Second) if the court concluded the location of the activity was sufficiently appropriate and the value of the activity sufficiently high to outweigh the other factors.

**4. Resistance to the Second Restatement's Approach.** Some courts disagree with the Restatement (Second) of Torts' approach to strict liability and choose not to apply it. In *Yukon Equipment, Inc. v. Fireman's Fund Insurance Co.*, 585 P.2d 1206 (Alaska 1978), thieves set off a powerful explosion that registered 1.8 on the Richter scale at an earthquake observation station some thirty miles away. The court asserted that the six factor balancing test of section 520 seemed too similar to a negligence standard and therefore would not be appropriate to a case involving the use and storage of explosives:

> The Restatement (Second) approach requires an analysis of degrees of risk and harm, difficulty of eliminating risk, and appropriateness of place, before absolute liability may be imposed. Such factors suggest a negligence standard. The six factor analysis may well be necessary where damage is caused by unique hazards and the question is whether the general rule of absolute liability applies, but in cases involving the storage and use of explosives we take that question to have been resolved by more than a century of judicial decisions.

> The reasons for imposing absolute liability on those who have created a grave risk of harm to others by storing or using explosives are largely independent of considerations of locational appropriateness. We see no reason for making a distinction between the right of a homesteader to recover when his property has been damaged by a blast set off in a remote corner of the state, and the right to compensation of an urban resident whose home is destroyed by an explosion originating in a settled area. In each case, the loss is properly to be regarded as a cost of the business of storing or using explosives. Every incentive remains to conduct such activities in locations which are as safe as possible, because there the damages resulting from an accident will be kept to a minimum.

Do you think the section 520 rubric is a useful way to determine whether strict liability should attach to certain activities?

**5. Abnormally Dangerous Activities.** Consider *Klein v. Pyrodyne Corp.*, 117 Wash.2d 1, 810 P.2d 917 (1991), where spectators who were injured by a fireworks shell sued the company that was conducting the fireworks display. The plaintiffs alleged the following:

> [T]hat [defendant] Pyrodyne failed to properly bury the mortar tubes prior to detonation, failed to provide a diagram of the display and surrounding environment to the local government, failed to provide crowd control monitors, and failed to keep the invitees at the mandated safe distance.... During the fireworks display, one of the 5 inch mortars was knocked into a horizontal position. From this position a shell inside was ignited and discharged. The shell flew 500 feet in a trajectory parallel to the earth and exploded near the crowd of onlookers. Plaintiffs Danny and Marion Klein were injured by the explosion. Mr. Klein's clothing was set on fire, and he suffered facial burns and serious injury to his eyes.

The question presented before the court was whether a fireworks show constituted an abnormally dangerous activity as a matter of law under the Restatement (Second) of Torts § 520. The court applied section 520 and found that

> the factors stated in clauses (a),(b), and (c) are all present in the case of fireworks displays. Any time a person ignites aerial shells or rockets with the intention of sending them aloft to explode in the presence of large crowds of people, a high risk of serious personal injury or property damage is created. That risk arises because of the possibility that a shell or rocket will malfunction or be misdirected.

Furthermore, no matter how much care pyrotechnicians exercise, they cannot entirely eliminate the high risk inherent in setting off powerful explosives such as fireworks near crowds.... The factors stated in clauses (a), (b), and (c) together, and sometimes one of them alone, express what is commonly meant by saying that an activity is ultrahazardous.

The court then turned to the other factors in the section 520 analysis. As for (d), whether the activity is a matter of "common usage," the court noted that "relatively few persons conduct public fireworks displays. Therefore, presenting public fireworks displays is not a matter of common usage." The court found that (e) (appropriateness of location) "is not present in this case." As for the last factor, the activity's value to the community the court found as follows:

> We do not find that this factor is present here. This country has a long-standing tradition of fireworks on the 4th of July. That tradition suggests that we as a society have decided that the value of fireworks on the day celebrating our national independence and unity outweighs the risk of injuries and damage. In sum, we find that setting off public fireworks displays satisfies four of the six conditions under the Restatement test; that is, it is an activity that is not "of common usage" and that presents an ineliminably high risk of serious bodily injury or property damage. We therefore hold that conducting public fireworks displays is an abnormally dangerous activity justifying the imposition of strict liability.

But consider *Cadena v. Chicago Fireworks Manufacturing Company,* 297 Ill.App.3d 945, 232 Ill.Dec. 60, 697 N.E.2d 802 (1998), where the Illinois Appellate Court, also using the Restatement Second's analysis, held that fireworks did not constitute an ultrahazardous activity giving rise to strict liability. The court agreed that the factors stated in (a) and (b) were both present because fireworks presented a high degree of risk, and likelihood that any resultant harm will be great. However, the court declined "to follow *Klein,* and disagree with the court's determination that the risk involved in fireworks displays cannot be sufficiently reduced and that the value of fireworks displays to the community does not outweigh their dangerous attributes."

Consider *Green v. Ensign–Bickford Co.,* 25 Conn.App. 479, 595 A.2d 1383 (1991), in which an explosives manufacturer was sued under a strict liability theory after the plaintiff was injured by an explosion.

> The defendant corporation has been a manufacturer of explosives in Simsbury for more than 150 years. Ancillary to its manufacturing, the defendant conducts research and development of new explosives. Some of the research takes place in a frangible structure designed to allow its detached wooden roof to blow off and its cinder block walls to fall outward in the event of an explosion. The structure was situated on a concrete slab surrounded on three sides by twenty foot high earthen berm with the fourth side open towards a heavily wooded area known as Powder Forest.
>
> On the day of the explosion, three of the defendant's employees, all experienced professional chemists, were engaged in a research project in this building. The project entailed mixing chemicals in a reactor located twelve to fourteen feet above the floor. For reasons

that will probably never be known, a colossal explosion took place, killing the researchers and completely destroying the building. At the time of the explosion, the plaintiff was in bed on the second story of his wood frame house located approximately seven eighths of a mile from the accident.... The plaintiff testified that the explosion lifted him upward from his bed and threw him across the room causing him serious injuries.

The court explained its interpretation of why section 519 exists. "It is founded upon a policy of law that imposes upon anyone who for his own purposes creates an abnormal risk of harm to his neighbors, the responsibility of relieving against the harm when it does in fact occur." The court went on to analyze the defendant's activity under section 520:

> The first three factors all involve the degree of risk, harm and difficulty of eliminating the risk inherent in the activity. Here, the defendant's activity, the use of a highly volatile chemical in a specially designed building located away from the defendant's main facility, satisfied these three factors. The fourth factor, that the activity not be a matter of common usage, is also easily met. In fact, the defendant's activity is expressly addressed in comment (i) which states that "the manufacture, storage, transportation and use of high explosives ... are carried on by only a comparatively small number of persons and therefore are not matters of common usage."

> The fifth factor, inappropriateness of the activity to the place where it is carried on, is satisfied by the defendant's experimentation with explosives in a residential area. The sixth factor encompasses the extent to which the activity's value to the community is outweighed by its dangerous attributes. The record is devoid of facts to satisfy this but, as stated earlier, all six factors do not need to be satisfied in order to find that the defendant's activity is ultrahazardous. Comment (h) provides that "[a] combination of the factors stated in clauses (a), (b), and (c), or sometimes any of them alone, is commonly expressed by the saying the activity is 'ultrahazardous' or 'extra hazardous....' "

> In light of our review of the six factors required by § 520 and our conclusion that five of these factors were satisfied by the defendant's research activity, we conclude that the defendant is strictly liable for any damage caused by the explosion.

In *T & E Industries, Inc. v. Safety Light Corp.*, 123 N.J. 371, 587 A.2d 1249 (N.J. 1991), the Supreme Court of New Jersey considered whether the processing, handling and disposal of radium was an abnormally dangerous activity.

> [A]lthough the risks involved in the processing and disposal of radium might be curtailed, one cannot safely dispose of radium by dumping it onto the vacant portions of an urban lot. Because of the extraordinarily hazardous nature of radium, the processing and disposal of that substance is particularly inappropriate in an urban setting. We conclude that despite the usefulness of radium, defendant's processing, handling, and disposal of that substance under the facts of this case constituted an abnormally dangerous activity. Plaintiff's property is befouled with radium because of defendant's

abnormally dangerous activity. Radiation levels at the site exceed those permitted under governmental health regulations. Moreover, the property has been earmarked as a Superfund site.... Because plaintiff vacated the premises in response to the health concerns posed by the radium-contaminated site and because the danger to health is "the kind of harm, the possibility of which [made defendant's] activity abnormally dangerous," defendant is strictly liable for the resulting harm.

Consider *Goodwin v. Reilley*, 176 Cal.App.3d 86, 221 Cal.Rptr. 374 (1985), where the court focused on the nature and purpose of strict liability in determining that driving a motorcycle drunk was not an activity for which strict liability should be imposed. The plaintiffs in this case attempted to get around the limitations of negligent infliction of emotional distress, by premising liability for their emotional injury on a strict liability theory. The court noted that "the tort concept of abnormally dangerous or ultrahazardous activity presupposes that the activity has some social value and that reasonable care is insufficient to eliminate its harm." The court held that "driving under the influence of alcohol, although unquestionably dangerous and hazardous-in-fact, does not come within the rubric of an ultrahazardous or abnormally dangerous activity for purposes of tort liability, and that to hold the defendant strictly liable for the consequences of his driving would not, in any event, extend his liability beyond that imposed for negligence."

## INDIANA HARBOR BELT RAILROAD CO. v. AMERICAN CYANAMID CO.
### United States Court of Appeals, Seventh Circuit.
### 916 F.2d 1174 (1990).

POSNER, Circuit Judge.

American Cyanamid Company, the defendant in this diversity tort suit governed by Illinois law, is a major manufacturer of chemicals, including acrylonitrile, a chemical used in large quantities in making acrylic fibers, plastics, dyes, pharmaceutical chemicals, and other intermediate and final goods. On January 2, 1979, at its manufacturing plant in Louisiana, Cyanamid loaded 20,000 gallons of liquid acrylonitrile into a railroad tank car that it had leased from the North American Car Corporation. The next day, a train of the Missouri Pacific Railroad picked up the car at Cyanamid's siding. The car's ultimate destination was a Cyanamid plant in New Jersey served by Conrail rather than by Missouri Pacific. The Missouri Pacific train carried the car north to the Blue Island railroad yard of Indiana Harbor Belt Railroad, the plaintiff in this case, a small switching line that has a contract with Conrail to switch cars from other lines to Conrail, in this case for travel east. The Blue Island yard is in the Village of Riverdale, which is just south of Chicago and part of the Chicago metropolitan area.

The car arrived in the Blue Island yard on the morning of January 9, 1979. Several hours after it arrived, employees of the switching line noticed fluid gushing from the bottom outlet of the car. The lid on the outlet was broken. After two hours, the line's supervisor of equipment was able to stop the leak by closing a shut-off valve controlled from the top of the car. No one was sure at the time just how much of the contents of the car had leaked, but it was feared that all 20,000 gallons had, and since acrylonitrile is flammable at a temperature of 30Ë Fahrenheit or above, highly toxic, and possibly carcinogenic (*Acrylonitrile,* 9 International Toxicity Update, no. 3, May-June 1989, at 2, 4), the local authorities ordered the homes near the yard evacuated. The evacuation lasted only a few hours, until the car was moved to a remote part of the yard and it was discovered that only about a quarter of the acrylonitrile had leaked. Concerned nevertheless that there had been some contamination of soil and water, the Illinois Department of Environmental Protection ordered the switching line to take decontamination measures that cost the line $981,022.75, which it sought to recover by this suit.

One count of the two-count complaint charges Cyanamid with having maintained the leased tank car negligently. The other count asserts that the transportation of acrylonitrile in bulk through the Chicago metropolitan area is an abnormally dangerous activity, for the consequences of which the shipper (Cyanamid) is strictly liable to the switching line, which bore the financial brunt of those consequences because of the decontamination measures that it was forced to take.

The question whether the shipper of a hazardous chemical by rail should be strictly liable for the consequences of a spill or other accident to the shipment en route is a novel one in Illinois. . . .

\* \* \*

The parties agree that the question whether placing acrylonitrile in a rail shipment that will pass through a metropolitan area subjects the shipper to strict liability is, as recommended in Restatement (Second) of Torts § 520, comment *l* (1977), a question of law, so that we owe no particular deference to the conclusion of the district court. They also agree (and for this proposition, at least, there is substantial support in the *Fallon* and *Continental* opinions) that the Supreme Court of Illinois would treat as authoritative the provisions of the Restatement governing abnormally dangerous activities. The key provision is section 520, which sets forth six factors to be considered in deciding whether an activity is abnormally dangerous and the actor therefore strictly liable.

The roots of section 520 are in nineteenth-century cases. The most famous one is *Rylands v. Fletcher,* 1 Ex. 265, aff'd, L.R. 3 H.L. 300 (1868), but a more illuminating one in the present context is *Guille v. Swan,* 19 Johns. (N.Y.) 381 (1822). A man took off in a hot-air balloon and landed, without intending to, in a vegetable garden in New York City. A crowd that had been anxiously watching his involuntary descent trampled the vegetables in their endeavor to rescue him when he landed. The owner of the garden sued the balloonist for the resulting damage, and won. Yet the balloonist had not been careless. In the then state of ballooning it was impossible to make a pinpoint landing.

*Guille* is a paradigmatic case for strict liability. (a) The risk (probability) of harm was great, and (b) the harm that would ensue if the risk materialized could be, although luckily was not, great (the balloonist could have crashed into the crowd rather than into the vegetables). The confluence of these two factors established the urgency of seeking to prevent such accidents. (c) Yet such accidents could not be prevented by the exercise of due care; the technology of care in ballooning was insufficiently developed. (d) The activity was not a matter of common usage, so there was no presumption that it was a highly valuable activity despite its unavoidable riskiness. (e) The activity was inappropriate to the place in which it took place—densely populated New York City. The risk of serious harm to others (other than the balloonist himself, that is) could have been reduced by shifting the activity to the sparsely inhabited areas that surrounded the city in those days. (f) Reinforcing (d), the value to the community of the activity of recreational ballooning did not appear to be great enough to offset its unavoidable risks.

These are, of course, the six factors in section 520. They are related to each other in that each is a different facet of a common quest for a proper legal regime to govern accidents that negligence liability cannot adequately control. The interrelations might be more perspicuous if the six factors were reordered. One might for example start with (c), inability to eliminate the risk of accident by the exercise of due care. *Erbrich Products Co. v. Wills,* 509 N.E.2d 850, 857 n. 3 (Ind.App.1987). The baseline common law regime of tort liability is negligence. When it is a workable regime, because the hazards of an activity can be avoided by being careful (which is to say, nonnegligent), there is no need to switch to strict liability. Sometimes, however, a particular type of accident cannot be prevented by taking care but can be avoided, or its consequences minimized, by shifting the activity in which the accident occurs to another locale, where the risk or harm of an accident will be less ((e)), or by reducing the scale of the activity in order to minimize the number of accidents caused by it ((f)). *Bethlehem Steel Corp. v. EPA,* 782 F.2d 645, 652 (7th Cir.1986); Shavell, *Strict Liability versus Negligence,* 9 J. Legal Stud. 1 (1980). By making the actor strictly liable—by denying him in other words an excuse based on his inability to avoid accidents by being more careful—we give him an incentive, missing in a negligence regime, to experiment with methods of preventing accidents that involve not greater exertions of care, assumed to be futile, but instead relocating, changing, or reducing (perhaps to the vanishing point) the activity giving rise to the accident. *Anderson v. Marathon Petroleum Co.,* 801 F.2d 936, 939 (7th Cir.1986). The greater the risk of an accident ((a)) and the costs of an accident if one occurs ((b)), the more we want the actor to consider the possibility of making accident-reducing activity changes; the stronger, therefore, is the case for strict liability. Finally, if an activity is extremely common ((d)), like driving an automobile, it is unlikely either that its hazards are perceived as great or that there is no technology of care available to minimize them; so the case for strict liability is weakened.

The largest class of cases in which strict liability has been imposed under the standard codified in the Second Restatement of Torts involves the use of dynamite and other explosives for demolition in residential or urban areas. Restatement, *supra,* § 519, comment d; *City of Joliet v. Harwood,* 86 Ill. 110 (1877). Explosives are dangerous even when handled carefully, and we therefore want blasters to choose the location of the activity with care and also to explore the feasibility of using safer substitutes (such as a wrecking ball), as well as to be careful in the blasting itself. Blasting is not a commonplace activity like driving a car, or so superior to substitute methods of demolition that the imposition of liability is unlikely to have any effect except to raise the activity's costs.

Against this background we turn to the particulars of acrylonitrile. Acrylonitrile is one of a large number of chemicals that are hazardous in the sense of being flammable, toxic, or both; acrylonitrile is both, as are many others. A table in the record, drawn from Glickman & Harvey, Statistical Trends in Railroad Hazardous Material Safety, 1978 to 1984, at pp. 63–65 (Draft Final Report to the Environmental & Hazardous Material Studies Division of the Association of American Railroads, April 1986) (tab. 4.1), contains a list of the 125 hazardous materials that are shipped in highest volume on the nation's railroads. Acrylonitrile is the fifty-third most hazardous on the list. Number 1 is phosphorus (white or yellow), and among the other materials that rank higher than acrylonitrile on the hazard scale are anhydrous ammonia, liquified petroleum gas, vinyl chloride, gasoline, crude petroleum, motor fuel antiknock compound, methyl and ethyl chloride, sulphuric acid, sodium metal, and chloroform. The plaintiff's lawyer acknowledged at argument that the logic of the district court's opinion dictated strict liability for all 52 materials that rank higher than acrylonitrile on the list, and quite possibly for the 72 that rank lower as well, since all are hazardous if spilled in quantity while being shipped by rail. Every shipper of any of these materials would therefore be strictly liable for the consequences of a spill or other accident that occurred while the material was being shipped through a metropolitan area. The plaintiff's lawyer further acknowledged the irrelevance, on her view of the case, of the fact that Cyanamid had leased and filled the car that spilled the acrylonitrile; all she thought important is that Cyanamid introduced the product into the stream of commerce that happened to pass through the Chicago metropolitan area. Her concession may have been incautious. One might want to distinguish between the shipper who merely places his goods on his loading dock to be picked up by the carrier and the shipper who, as in this case, participates actively in the transportation. But the concession is illustrative of the potential scope of the district court's decision.

No cases recognize so sweeping a liability. Several reject it, though none has facts much like those of the present case. *Hawkins v. Evans Cooperage Co.,* 766 F.2d 904, 907 (5th Cir.1985); *New Meadows Holding Co. v. Washington Power Co.,* 102 Wash.2d 495, 687 P.2d 212 (1984); *Ozark Industries, Inc. v. Stubbs Transports, Inc.,* 351 F.Supp. 351, 357 (W.D.Ark.1972).

\* \* \*

*Siegler v. Kuhlman,* 81 Wash.2d 448, 502 P.2d 1181 (1972), also imposed strict liability on a transporter of hazardous materials, but the circumstances were again rather special. A gasoline truck blew up, obliterating the plaintiff's decedent and her car. The court emphasized that the explosion had destroyed the evidence necessary to establish whether the accident had been due to negligence; so, unless liability was strict, there would be no liability—and this as the very consequence of the defendant's hazardous activity. 81 Wash.2d at 454–55, 502 P.2d at 1185. But when the Supreme Court of Washington came to decide the *New Meadows* case, *supra,* it did not distinguish *Siegler* on this ground, perhaps realizing that the plaintiff in *Siegler* could have overcome the destruction of the evidence by basing a negligence claim on the doctrine of res ipsa loquitur. Instead it stressed that the transmission of natural gas through underground pipes, the activity in *New Meadows,* is less dangerous than the transportation of gasoline by highway, where the risk of an accident is omnipresent. 102 Wash.2d at 502–03, 687 P.2d at 216–17. We shall see that a further distinction of great importance between the present case and *Siegler* is that the defendant there was the transporter, and here it is the shipper.

Cases such as *McLane v. Northwest Natural Gas Co.,* 255 Or. 324, 467 P.2d 635 (1970); *Langlois v. Allied Chemical Corp.,* 258 La. 1067, 249 So.2d 133 (1971); *State Dept. of Environmental Protection v. Ventron,* 94 N.J. 473, 488, 468 A.2d 150, 157–60 (N.J.1983); *Cities Service Co. v. State,* 312 So.2d 799 (Fla.App.1975), and *Sterling v. Velsicol Chemical Corp.,* 647 F.Supp. 303, 315–16 (W.D.Tenn.1986), aff'd in part and rev'd in part, on other grounds, 855 F.2d 1188 (6th Cir.1988); but see *Standard Equipment, Inc. v. Boeing Co.,* 1987 U.S.Dist.Lexis 15137, at [*19–20] (W.D.Wash.1987), that impose strict liability for the storage of a dangerous chemical provide a potentially helpful analogy to our case. But they can be distinguished on the ground that the storer (like the transporter, as in *Siegler*) has more control than the shipper.

So we can get little help from precedent, and might as well apply section 520 to the acrylonitrile problem from the ground up. To begin with, we have been given no reason, whether the reason in *Siegler* or any other, for believing that a negligence regime is not perfectly adequate to remedy and deter, at reasonable cost, the accidental spillage of acrylonitrile from rail cars. Cf. *Bagley v. Controlled Environment Corp.,* 127 N.H. 556, 560, 503 A.2d 823, 826 (1986). Acrylonitrile could explode and destroy evidence, but of course did not here, making imposition of strict liability on the theory of the *Siegler* decision premature. More important, although acrylonitrile is flammable even at relatively low temperatures, and toxic, it is not so corrosive or otherwise destructive that it will eat through or otherwise damage or weaken a tank car's valves although they are maintained with due (which essentially means, with average) care. No one suggests, therefore, that the leak in this case was caused by the *inherent* properties of acrylonitrile. It was caused by carelessness—whether that of the North American Car Corporation in failing to maintain or inspect the car properly, or that of Cyanamid in failing to maintain or inspect it, or that of the Missouri Pacific when it had custody of the car, or that of the switching line itself in failing to notice the ruptured lid, or some combination of these possible failures of care. Accidents that are due to a lack of care can be prevented by taking care; and when a lack of care can (unlike *Siegler*) be shown in court, such accidents are adequately deterred by the threat of liability for negligence.

It is true that the district court purported to find as a fact that there is an inevitable risk of derailment or other calamity in transporting "large quantities of anything." 662 F.Supp. at 642. This is not a finding of fact, but a truism: anything can happen. The question is, how likely is this type of accident if the actor uses due care? For all that appears from the record of the case or any other sources of information that we have found, if a tank car is carefully maintained the danger of a spill of acrylonitrile is negligible. If this is right, there is no compelling reason to move to a regime of strict liability, especially one that might embrace all other hazardous materials shipped by rail as well. This also means, however, that the amici curiae who have filed briefs in support of Cyanamid cry wolf in predicting "devastating" effects on the chemical industry if the district court's decision is affirmed. If the vast majority of chemical spills by railroads are preventable by due care, the imposition of strict liability should cause only a slight, not as they argue a substantial, rise in liability insurance rates, because the incremental liability should be slight. The amici have momentarily lost sight of the fact that the feasibility of avoiding accidents simply by being careful is an argument *against* strict liability.

This discussion helps to show why *Siegler* is indeed distinguishable even as interpreted in *New Meadows*. There are so many highway hazards that the transportation of gasoline by truck is, or at least might plausibly be thought, inherently dangerous in the sense that a serious danger of accident would remain even if the truckdriver used all due care (though *Hawkins* and other cases are *contra*). Which in turn means, contrary to our earlier suggestion, that the plaintiff really might have difficulty invoking res ipsa loquitur, because a gasoline truck might well blow up without negligence on the part of the driver. The plaintiff in this case has not shown that the danger of a comparable disaster to a tank car filled with acrylonitrile is as great and might have similar consequences for proof of negligence. And to repeat a previous point, if the reason for strict liability is fear that an accident might destroy the critical evidence of negligence we should wait to impose such liability until such a case appears.

The district judge and the plaintiff's lawyer make much of the fact that the spill occurred in a densely inhabited metropolitan area. Only 4,000 gallons spilled; what if all 20,000 had done so? Isn't the risk that this might happen even if everybody were careful sufficient to warrant giving the shipper an incentive to explore alternative routes? Strict liability would supply that incentive. But this argument overlooks the fact that, like other transportation networks, the railroad network is a hub-and-spoke system. And the hubs are in metropolitan areas. Chicago is one of the nation's largest railroad hubs. In 1983, the latest year for which we have figures, Chicago's railroad yards handled the third highest volume of hazardous-material shipments in the nation. East St. Louis, which is also in Illinois, handled the second highest volume. Office of Technology Assessment, Transportation of Hazardous Materials 53 (1986). With most hazardous chemicals (by volume of shipments) being at least as hazardous as acrylonitrile, it is unlikely—and certainly not demonstrated by the plaintiff—that they can be rerouted around all the metropolitan areas in the country, except at prohibitive cost. Even if it were feasible to reroute them one would hardly expect shippers, as distinct from carriers, to be the firms best situated to do the rerouting. Granted, the usual view is that common carriers are not subject to strict liability for the carriage of materials that make the transportation of them abnormally dangerous, because a common carrier cannot refuse service to a shipper of a lawful commodity. Restatement, *supra*, § 521. Two courts, however, have rejected the common carrier exception. *National Steel Service Center, Inc. v. Gibbons,* 319 N.W.2d 269 (Ia.1982); *Chavez v. Southern Pacific Transportation Co.,* 413 F.Supp. 1203, 1213–14 (E.D.Cal.1976). If it were rejected in Illinois, this would weaken still further the case for imposing strict liability on shippers whose goods pass through the densely inhabited portions of the state.

The difference between shipper and carrier points to a deep flaw in the plaintiff's case. Unlike *Guille,* and unlike *Siegler,* and unlike the storage cases, beginning with *Rylands* itself, here it is not the actors—that is, the transporters of acrylonitrile and other chemicals—but the manufacturers, who are sought to be held strictly liable. Cf. *City of Bloomington v. Westinghouse Elec. Corp., supra,* 891 F.2d at 615–16. A shipper can in the bill of lading designate the route of his shipment if he likes, 49 U.S.C. § 11710(a)(1), but is it realistic to suppose that shippers will become students of railroading in order to lay out the safest route by which to ship their goods? Anyway, rerouting is no panacea. Often it will increase the length of the journey, or compel the use of poorer track, or both. When this happens, the probability of an accident is increased, even if the consequences of an accident if one occurs are reduced; so the expected accident cost, being the product of the probability of an accident and the harm if the accident occurs, may rise. Glickman, Analysis of a National Policy for Routing Hazardous Materials on Railroads (Department of Transportation, Research and Special Programs Administration, Transportation Systems Center, May 1980). It is easy to see how the accident in this case might have been prevented at reasonable cost by greater care on the part of those who handled the tank car of acrylonitrile. It is difficult to see how it might have been prevented at reasonable cost by a change in the activity of transporting the chemical. This is therefore not an apt case for strict liability.

We said earlier that Cyanamid, because of the role it played in the transportation of the acrylonitrile—leasing, and especially loading, and also it appears undertaking by contract with North American Car Corporation to maintain, the tank car in which the railroad carried Cyanamid's acrylonitrile to Riverdale—might be viewed as a special type of shipper (call it a "shipper-transporter"), rather than as a passive shipper. But neither the district judge nor the plaintiff's counsel has attempted to distinguish Cyanamid from an ordinary manufacturer of chemicals on this ground, and we consider it waived. Which is not to say that had it not been waived it would have changed the outcome of the case. The very fact that Cyanamid participated actively in the transportation of the acrylonitrile imposed upon it a duty of due care and by doing so brought into play a threat of negligence liability that, for all we know, may provide an adequate regime of accident control in the transportation of this particular chemical.

In emphasizing the flammability and toxicity of acrylonitrile rather than the hazards of transporting it, as in failing to distinguish between the active and the passive shipper, the plaintiff overlooks the fact that ultrahazardousness or abnormal dangerousness is, in the contemplation of the law at least, a property not of substances, but of activities: not of acrylonitrile, but of the transportation of acrylonitrile by rail through populated areas. *Cropper v. Rego Distribution Center, Inc.,* 542 F.Supp. 1142, 1149 (D.Del.1982). Natural gas is both flammable and poisonous, but the operation of a natural gas well is not an ultrahazardous activity. Cf. *Williams v. Amoco Production Co.,* 241 Kan. 102, 115, 734 P.2d 1113, 1123 (1987). Whatever the situation under products liability law (section 402A of the Restatement), the manufacturer of a product is not considered to be engaged in an abnormally dangerous activity merely because the product becomes dangerous when it is handled or used in some way after it leaves his premises, even if the danger is foreseeable. *City of Bloomington v. Westinghouse Elec. Corp., supra,* 891 F.2d at 616–17; *Erbrich Products Co. v. Wills, supra.* The plaintiff does not suggest that Cyanamid should switch to making some less hazardous chemical that would substitute for acrylonitrile in the textiles and other goods in which acrylonitrile is used. Were this a feasible method of accident avoidance, there would be an argument for making manufacturers strictly liable for accidents that occur during the shipment of their products (how strong an argument we need not decide). Apparently it is not a feasible method.

The relevant activity is transportation, not manufacturing and shipping. This essential distinction the plaintiff ignores. But even if the defendant is treated as a transporter and not merely a shipper, the plaintiff has not shown that the transportation of acrylonitrile in bulk by rail through populated areas is so hazardous an activity, even when due care is exercised, that the law should seek to create—perhaps quixotically—incentives to relocate the activity to nonpopulated areas, or to reduce the scale of the activity, or to switch to transporting acrylonitrile by road rather than by rail, perhaps to set the stage for a replay of *Siegler v. Kuhlman.* It is no more realistic to propose to reroute the shipment of all hazardous materials around Chicago than it is to propose the relocation of homes adjacent to the Blue Island switching yard to more distant suburbs. It may be less realistic. Brutal though it may seem to say it, the inappropriate use to which land is being put in the Blue Island yard and neighborhood may be, not the transportation of hazardous chemicals, but residential living. The analogy is to building your home between the runways at O'Hare.

The briefs hew closely to the Restatement, whose approach to the issue of strict liability is mainly *allocative* rather than *distributive.* By this we mean that the emphasis is on picking a liability regime (negligence or strict liability) that will control the particular class of accidents in question most effectively, rather than on finding the deepest pocket and placing liability there. At argument, however, the plaintiff's lawyer invoked distributive considerations by pointing out that Cyanamid is a huge firm and the Indiana Harbor Belt Railroad a fifty-mile-long switching line that almost went broke in the winter of 1979, when the accident occurred. Well, so what? A corporation is not a living person but a set of contracts the terms of which determine who will bear the brunt of liability. Tracing the incidence of a cost is a complex undertaking which the plaintiff sensibly has made no effort to assume, since its legal relevance would be dubious. We add only that however small the plaintiff may be, it has mighty parents: it is a jointly owned subsidiary of Conrail and the Soo line.

The case for strict liability has not been made. Not in this suit in any event. We need not speculate on the possibility of imposing strict liability on shippers of more hazardous materials, such as the bombs carried in *Chavez v. Southern Pacific Transportation Co., supra,* any more than we need differentiate (given how the plaintiff has shaped its case) between active and passive shippers. We noted earlier that acrylonitrile is far from being the most hazardous among hazardous materials shipped by rail in highest volume. Or among materials shipped, period. The Department of Transportation has classified transported materials into sixteen separate classes by the degree to which transporting them is hazardous. Class number 1 is radioactive material. Class number 2 is poisons. Class 3 is flammable gas and 4 is nonflammable gas. Acrylonitrile is in Class 5. 49 C.F.R. §§ 172.101, Table; 173.2(a).

\* \* \*

The defendant concedes that if the strict liability count is thrown out, the negligence count must be reinstated, as requested by the cross-appeal.

The judgment is reversed (with no award of costs in this court) and the case remanded for further proceedings, consistent with this opinion, on the plaintiff's claim for negligence.

### NOTES

**1.   Rejecting of Strict Liability.** While most American states apply some form of strict liability, a few states do not accept strict liability for any activities. Consider *Jones v. Texaco, Inc.*, 945 F.Supp. 1037 (S.D.Tex.1996), in which buyers of land sued the seller, claiming that the seller should be strictly liable for the contamination of the land. The court noted that

> Texas courts have repeatedly repudiated the general rule announced in *Rylands. Turner v. Big Lake Oil Co.*, 128 Tex. 155, 96 S.W.2d 221, 222, 226 (Tex.1936). As the Texas Supreme Court observed in *Turner*, "By making the liability absolute, the rule in *Fletcher v. Rylands*, taken literally, imposes an unqualified restriction upon the right of an owner of land to put it to a use lawful in itself." 96 S.W.2d at 223. Texas, likewise, has not adopted §§ 519 and 520 of the Restatement. In fact, Texas courts, when confronted with the opportunity to apply strict liability for ultrahazardous activities, have declined to do so and have consistently required some other showing, such as negligence or trespass, for recovery.

**2.   Strict Liability and Economic Theory.** Judge Richard Posner, a prominent proponent of economic analysis of tort law, is generally critical of utilizing strict liability. See Posner, *Strict Liability: A Comment*, 2 J. Legal Stud. 205. While strict liability on its face seems to be the more ethical choice (since the injurer is required to compensate the injured), Posner notes that this does not mean it is the most efficient choice. Strict liability as a global standard for tort law does not maximize society's resources because it does take into account that one's conduct affects others:

> Although both strict liability and negligence appear to provide efficient solutions to problems of conflicting resource uses, they do not have identical economic effects. The difference comes in cases where the efficient solution is for neither party to the interference to do anything. This is the category of interferences known in negligence law as "unavoidable accidents." They are rarely unavoidable in the literal sense. But frequently the cost either to injurer or to victim of taking measures to prevent an accident exceeds the expected accident cost and in such a case efficiency requires that the accident be permitted to occur. Under a negligence standard, the injurer is not liable; under strict liability, he is.

Posner argues that not all social harms need be deterred. Rather, where the social benefits of allowing a harm exceed the social costs of avoiding it, the harm should be allowed:

> Compare two different tracts of land that are identical in every respect except that one is immediately adjacent to a railroad line and one is well back from any railroad line. If the railroad is strictly liable for crop damage inflicted by engine sparks there will be no incentive to use the tract near the railroad line for fire-insensitive uses and to shift the growing of flammable crops to the tract that is remote from a railroad line, even though such a rearrangement may eliminate all crop damage at zero cost.

Strict liability proponents assert that since under strict liability the injurer has to pay if she causes the harm, there is an incentive for her to do research and development to reduce accidents. Posner dispels this myth that strict liability encourages higher safety levels than negligence:

> Rather than creating an incentive to engage in research on safety, a rule of strict liability merely shifts that incentive. Under the negligence standard the cost of unavoidable accidents is borne by the victims of accidents. They can reduce this cost in the long run by financing research into and development of cost-justified measures by which to protect themselves. The victims will not themselves organize for research, but they will provide the market for firms specializing in the development of new safety appliances.

Strict liability advocates also argue that since strict liability is a simpler rule and results in more certain liability, it translates into a more efficient system of justice. Posner, however, adopts a larger perspective on whether strict liability is really cheaper than negligence:

> It might appear that strict liability would reduce the costs of tort litigation, both by simplifying the issues in a trial and thereby reducing its costs and by removing an element of uncertainty and thereby facilitating settlements, which are cheaper than trials. But the matter is more complex than this. By increasing the scope of liability, strict liability enlarges the universe of claims, so even if the

fraction of cases that go to trial is smaller the absolute number may be larger. And, by increasing the certainty that the plaintiff will prevail, strict liability encourages him to spend more money on the litigation; conceivably, therefore, the costs of trials might actually increase.

A leading proponent of strict liability, Professor Richard A. Epstein, posits that tort law should not be limited to consideration of economic efficiency. He notes that "even among those who analyze tort in economic terms there is acknowledgment of certain questions of 'justice' or 'fairness' rooted in common sense beliefs that cannot be explicated in terms of economic theory." Epstein, *A Theory of Strict Liability*, 2 J. Legal Stud. 151 (1973).

Epstein's justification for tort law rests upon a theory known as corrective justice. This theory, in the words of Professor Borgo, states that "when one man harms another the victim has a moral right to demand, and the injurer a moral duty to pay to him, compensation for the harm." Borgo, *Causal Paradigms in Tort Law*, 8 J. Legal Stud. 419 (1979).

One commentator summarizes the differences between Epstein and Posner.

> Whereas Posner understands autonomy and liberty to be means to the end of wealth maximization [most efficiently using societal resources], Epstein understands them to be ends in themselves, and to consist in a kind of inviolability that is not found in the world inhabited by Posner's transacting parties, where boundaries are permeable, everything is negotiable, and what law there is exists to facilitate, or mimic, that negotiation. In Epstein's world, in contrast, law exists to preserve the individual, inviolate, in his possession of liberties and wealth; these make up a " 'natural' set of entitlements ... deserving of absolute protection and vindication." Weston, *The Metaphysics of Modern Tort Theory*, 28 Val. U. L. Rev. 919 (1994), quoting Epstein, *Causation and Corrective Justice: A Reply to Two Critics*, 8 J. Legal Stud. 477 (1979).

**3. Strict Liability and Moral Theory.** Consider an alternative to the debate represented by Posner and Epstein. Professor Fletcher, a moral theorist, points out that in comparing strict liability and negligence, it is important to understand whose interests are being taken into consideration:

> The conflict is whether judges should look solely at the claims and interests of the parties before the court, or resolve seemingly private disputes in a way that serves the interests of the community as a whole.

Fletcher, *Fairness and Utility in Tort Theory*, 85 Harv. L. Rev. 537 (1972). Fletcher proposes that liability should be imposed where there are nonreciprocal risks. Fletcher discusses negligence and strict liability in these terms:

> [B]oth strict liability and negligence express the rationale of liability for unexcused, nonreciprocal risk-taking. The only difference is that reciprocity in strict liability cases is analyzed relative to the background of innocuous risks in the community, while reciprocity in ... negligence cases ... is measured against the background of risk generated in specific activities like motoring and skiing.

Professor Fletcher argues that strict liability for abnormally dangerous activities is appropriate since the actor is imposing unusual risks that are not normally imposed (reciprocated) by others. For common activities, negligence liability is appropriate since the actor is liable only when the risk imposed is beyond what society condones.

**4. Exception for Common Carriers.** As indicated in the principal case, some courts do not apply strict liability to abnormally dangerous activities if that activity is in pursuit of a public duty. This view is endorsed by the Restatement (Second) of Torts:

> The rules as to strict liability for abnormally dangerous activities do not apply if the activity is carried on in pursuance of a public duty imposed upon the actor as a public officer or employee or as a common carrier.

Restatement (Second) of Torts § 521.

This exception, however, is not allowed in some jurisdictions. Consider, for example, *National Steel Service Center, Inc. v. Gibbons*, 319 N.W.2d 269 (Iowa 1982), in which the Supreme Court of Iowa chose to impose strict liability on a common carrier when railroad cars full of propane derailed and exploded. The court refused to recognize the common carrier exception, noting that common carriers are in a position to spread their losses over a large population by passing along their costs and thus achieve efficient resource allocation:

> Here we have two parties without fault. One of them, the carrier, engaged in an abnormally dangerous activity under the compulsion of public duty. The other who was injured was wholly innocent. The carrier was part of the dangerous enterprise, and the victim was not. The carrier was in a better position to investigate and identify the case of the accident. When an accident destroys the evidence of causation, it is fairer for the carrier to bear the cost of that fortuity. Apart from the risk distribution concept, the carrier is also in a better position than the ordinary victim to evaluate and guard against the risk financially.
>
> Furthermore, the carrier is in a superior position to develop safety technology to prevent such accidents....

**5. Animals.** In addition to strict liability for abnormally dangerous activity, courts impose strict liability on the possession of certain classes of animals. The Restatement (Second) of Torts separates animals into two classes: wild and domesticated. The possessor of a wild animal is strictly liable for any harm that results from the animal's "dangerous propensity". The possessor of a domesticated animal, on the other hand, is strictly liable only if she knew or should have known of a dangerous propensity in the particular animal. Otherwise, she is subject to a negligence standard of liability. In addition, it is not uncommon for jurisdictions to have specific statutory provisions addressing liability for dog bites. See Diamond, Levine & Madden, *Understanding Torts* § 16.02 (2nd ed. 2000); Keeton, *Prosser and Keeton on the Law of Torts* § 76 (5th ed. 1984) and Dobbs, *The Law of Torts* §§ 343–345 (2000).

## KELLEY v. R.G. INDUSTRIES, INC.

Court of Appeals of Maryland.
304 Md. 124, 497 A.2d 1143 (1985).

ELDRIDGE, Judge.

\* \* \*

Olen J. Kelley was injured when an unnamed assailant shot him in the chest during an armed robbery of the grocery store where he was employed. The weapon used in the crime was a Rohm Revolver Handgun Model RG–38S, Serial Number 0152662, designed and marketed by Rohm Gesellschaft, a West German corporation. The handgun was assembled and initially sold by R.G. Industries, Inc., a Miami-based corporation which is a subsidiary of the West German corporation.

Kelley and his wife filed a tort action against Rohm Gesellschaft and R.G. Industries in the Circuit Court for Montgomery County, setting forth several theories for recovery. The first count was based on strict liability, with the plaintiffs claiming that the handgun was "abnormally dangerous." . . .

\* \* \*

. . . . First, Kelley asserts that the manufacturer or marketer is strictly liable because the manufacturing or marketing of handguns is an "abnormally dangerous activity." Restatement (Second) of Torts, §§ 519–520. . . .

\* \* \*

Kelley's first premise for the imposition of liability is under the Restatement (Second) of Torts, §§ 519 and 520. These sections recognize the liability of one engaged in an abnormally dangerous or ultrahazardous activity even though that person may have exercised the utmost care to prevent harm. Whether an activity is "abnormally dangerous" under these sections depends on its satisfying the following six factors, specified in § 520:

> "(a) existence of a high degree of risk of some harm to the person, land or chattels of others;
>
> (b) likelihood that the harm that results from it will be great;
>
> (c) inability to eliminate the risk by the exercise of reasonable care;
>
> (d) extent to which the activity is not a matter of common usage;
>
> (e) inappropriateness of the activity to the place where it is carried on; and
>
> (f) extent to which its value to the community is outweighed by its dangerous attributes."

Regardless, however, of whether a handgun might satisfy these factors, Maryland law would not permit liability to be imposed on a handgun manufacturer or marketer under this theory. This Court has refused to extend the abnormally dangerous activity doctrine to instances in which the alleged tortfeasor is not an owner or occupier of land. *Toy v. Atlantic Gulf & Pacific Co.,* 176 Md. 197, 4 A.2d 757 (1939). *See also Yommer v. McKenzie,* 255 Md. 220, 257 A.2d 138 (1969); *Kirby v. Hylton,* 51 Md.App. 365, 443 A.2d 640 (1982).

The thrust of the doctrine is that the activity be abnormally dangerous in relation to the area where it occurs. If a gasoline station owner has faulty tanks which leak gasoline into the underground water supply, that might be abnormally dangerous if the land in which the tanks are buried is located in a well populated area. In such a situation, the hazard bears a relation to the occupation and location of the land on which the activity occurs. See *Yommer v. McKenzie, supra.* The dangers inherent in the use of a handgun in the commission of a crime, on the other hand, bear no relation to any occupation or ownership of land. Therefore, the abnormally dangerous activity doctrine does not apply to the manufacture or marketing of handguns.

Other jurisdictions which have addressed the issue are in accord. *See, e.g., Perkins v. F.I.E. Corp.,* 762 F.2d 1250, 1268 (5th Cir.1985), *rev'g Richman v. Charter Arms Co.,* 571 F.Supp. 192 (E.D.La.1983) ("[marketing handguns] is not a land-related activity, and the injuries of which the plaintiffs complain were not caused by the marketing itself, but rather resulted only when there was substandard conduct on the part of third parties"); *Martin v. Harrington and Richardson, Inc.,* 743 F.2d 1200, 1203–1204 (7th Cir.1984) (ultrahazardous activity doctrine applies only to the use of a product, not to its manufacture or sale); *Riordan v. International Armament Corp.,* 132 Ill.App.3d 642, 87 Ill.Dec. 765, 769, 477 N.E.2d 1293, 1297 (1985) ("We have found no decision other than *Richman* that has held that the lawful sale of a non-defective product can be an ultrahazardous activity."); *Burkett v. Freedom Arms,* 299 Or. 551, 704 P.2d 118 (1985). *See also* Note, *Legal Limits of a Handgun Manufacturer's Liability for the Criminal Acts of Third Persons,* 49 Mo.L.Rev. 830 (1984) (criticizing the imposition of liability under the ultrahazardous activity doctrine).

\* \* \*

Questions of law answered as herein set forth. Each party to pay its own costs.

### NOTES

**1. Dangerous Products.** Some plaintiffs have attempted to apply traditional strict liability to manufacturers of dangerous products. Generally, courts have rejected the application of strict liability in this context since the manufacturing of the product, as opposed to its use, is not an abnormally dangerous activity.

Consider *Gaines-Tabb v. ICI Explosives USA, Inc.,* 995 F.Supp. 1304 (W.D.Okla.1996), in which the victims of the Oklahoma City bombing brought a class action suit against the manufacturer of the ammonium nitrate (AN) that Timothy McVeigh and Terry Nichols used to make the bomb. The plaintiffs characterized the marketing of the fertilizer as ultra-hazardous and alleged that "ICI owed a high degree of care to others not to permit the ultrahazardous substance to injure or cause damage to the Plaintiffs; and that Defendant ICI is strictly liable to the Plaintiffs." The court was not convinced and held that "the mere sale of [AN] does not and cannot constitute an abnormally dangerous activity under the facts alleged by Plaintiffs."

In *Perkins v. F.I.E. Corp.*, 762 F.2d 1250 (5th Cir.1985), victims of criminal shootings alleged that the manufacture and sale of small caliber handguns should be regarded as an abnormally dangerous activity and thus be subject to strict liability. Two cases were consolidated on appeal. In the first case, Perkins was shot by Nichols who used a gun manufactured by F.I.E. Corporation. Nichols had been involved in a fight in the parking lot of a bar and decided to enter the bar and shoot the person with whom he had been fighting. One of Nichols' bullets hit Perkins, an innocent bystander, and paralyzed him from the waist down. In the second case, Kathy Newman, a third-year medical student at Tulane University, was kidnapped at gun-point from the University parking lot. She was forced to drive the kidnapper to a deserted area, where she was robbed, raped, and then shot in the back of the head. The court of appeals refused to impose strict liability for the manufacture and sale of small handguns:

> The marketing of handguns to the general public falls far beyond the boundaries of the Louisiana doctrine of ultrahazardous activities. It is not a land-related activity, and the injuries of which the plaintiffs complain were not caused by the marketing itself, but rather resulted only when there was substandard conduct on the part of third parties. We agree with the Seventh Circuit that a ruling that the marketing of handguns constitutes an ultrahazardous activity "would in practice drive manufacturers out of business" and "would produce a handgun ban by judicial fiat." *Martin v. Harrington & Richardson*, 7 Cir.1984, 743 F.2d 1200, 1204.

The court also noted that applying strict liability to manufacturers of guns in this case would make them insurers and would have other far-reaching implications:

> [T]he logic of the plaintiffs' arguments is essentially without bound-aries. Because liability for ultrahazardous activities is absolute under Louisiana law, liability under the doctrine "virtually makes the enterpriser an insurer." *Kent v. Gulf States Utilities Co.*, La.1982, 418 So.2d 493, 498. If we were to classify the marketing of handguns as an ultrahazardous activity, handgun manufacturers might be liable, not only as insurers against every criminal misuse of a handgun, but also, for example, to the families of suicide victims, and to victims or their families who were shot by home-owners in legitimate self-defense or mistakenly shot by hunters or the police. There is also nothing inherent in the logic of the plaintiffs' arguments that would prevent their application to the manufacturers of any instrumentality that can be used dangerously, such as knives, lead pipes, explosives, automobiles, alcohol, and rolling pins. Indeed, most consumer products marketed to the general public have both legitimate and harmful uses. We cannot accept the argument that the manufacturer should become an

insurer of all uses of those products, both legitimate and illegitimate, simply by virtue of having marketed them.

Consider also *Delahanty v. Hinckley*, 564 A.2d 758 (D.C.1989), where a District of Columbia policeman who was shot during the assassination attempt on President Reagan sued the gun manufacturer on a theory of strict products liability. The court rejected the appellant's argument that marketing that type of handgun was "inherently and abnormally dangerous with no social value." The court held that the applicable Restatement section referred to the activity itself and that gun marketing was not an "inherently dangerous" activity. Do you think there is an argument for applying strict liability against the sellers of dangerous products such as handguns and dynamite?

**2. Distinguishing Traditional Strict Liability From Strict Products Liability.** Efforts to impose liability against product manufacturers under traditional strict liability for engaging in abnormally dangerous activities should be distinguished from efforts to impose *strict product liability* on manufacturers. Strict products liability is a distinct theory from traditional strict liability and requires proof of a product "defect." For example, a gun without a trigger lock may arguably be defective. For a discussion of strict products liability, see this Chapter, Sec. B, infra. See also Diamond, *Eliminating the "Defect" in Design Strict Products Liability Theory*, 34 Hastings L.J. 529 (1983).

### FOSTER v. PRESTON MILL CO.
Supreme Court of Washington.
44 Wash.2d 440, 268 P.2d 645 (1954).

HAMLEY, Justice.

Blasting operations conducted by Preston Mill Company frightened a mother mink owned by B. W. Foster, and caused the mink to kill their kittens. Foster brought this action against the company to recover damages. His second amended complaint, upon which the case was tried, sets forth a cause of action on the theory of absolute liability, and, in the alternative, a cause of action on the theory of nuisance.

After a trial to the court without a jury, judgment was rendered for plaintiff in the sum of $1,953.68. . . .

\* \* \*

The modern doctrine of strict liability for dangerous substances and activities stems from Justice Blackburn's decision in *Rylands v. Fletcher*, 1 Exch. 265, decided in 1866 and affirmed two years later in *Fletcher v. Rylands*, L.R. 3 H.L. 330. Prosser on Torts, 449, § 59. As applied to blasting operations, the doctrine has quite uniformly been held to establish liability, irrespective of negligence, for property damage sustained as a result of casting rocks or other debris on adjoining or neighboring premises. *Patrick v. Smith*, 75 Wash. 407, 134 P. 1076, 48 L.R.A.,N.S., 740; *Schade Brewing Co. v. Chicago*, M. & P. S. R. Co., 79 Wash. 651, 140 P. 897; *Bedell v. Goulter, Or.*, 261 P.2d 842; *Exner v. Sherman Power Const. Co.*, 2 Cir., 54 F.2d 510, 80 A.L.R. 686. But see *Klepsch v. Donald*, 4 Wash. 436, 30 P. 991.

\* \* \*

[T]he authorities ... appear to be agreed that strict liability should be confined to consequences which lie within the extraordinary risk whose existence calls for such responsibility. Prosser on Torts, 458, § 60; Harper, Liability Without Fault and Proximate Cause, 30 Mich.L.Rev. 1001, 1006; 3 Restatement of Torts, 41, § 519. This limitation on the doctrine is indicated in the italicized portion of the rule as set forth in Restatement of Torts, *supra*:

"Except as stated in §§ 521–4, one who carries on an ultrahazardous activity is liable to another whose person, land or chattels the actor should recognize as likely to be harmed by the unpreventable miscarriage of the activity for harm resulting thereto *from that which makes the activity ultrahazardous*, although the utmost care is exercised to prevent the harm." (Italics supplied.)

This restriction which has been placed upon the application of the doctrine of absolute liability is based upon considerations of policy. As Professor Prosser has said:

" * * * It is one thing to say that a dangerous enterprise must pay its way within reasonable limits, and quite another to say that it must bear responsibility for every extreme of harm that it may cause. The same practical necessity for the restriction of liability within some reasonable bounds, which arises in connection with problems of 'proximate cause' in negligence cases, demands here that some limit be set. * * * This limitation has been expressed by saying that the defendant's duty to insure safety extends only to certain consequences. More commonly, it is said that the defendant's conduct is not the 'proximate cause' of the damage. But ordinarily in such cases no question of causation is involved, and the limitation is one of the policy underlying liability." Prosser on Torts, 457, § 60.

Applying this principle to the case before us, the question comes down to this: Is the risk that any unusual vibration or noise may cause wild animals, which are being raised for commercial purposes, to kill their young, one of the things which make the activity of blasting ultrahazardous?

We have found nothing in the decisional law which would support an affirmative answer to this question. The decided cases. as well as common experience, indicate that the thing which makes blasting ultrahazardous is the risk that property or persons may be damaged or injured by coming into direct contact with flying debris, or by being directly affected by vibrations of the earth or concussions of the air.

* * *

It is our conclusion that the risk of causing harm of the kind here experienced, as a result of the relatively minor vibration, concussion, and noise from distant blasting, is not the kind of risk which makes the activity of blasting ultrahazardous. The doctrine of absolute liability is therefore inapplicable under the facts of this case, and respondent is not entitled to recover damages.

The judgment is reversed.

### NOTES

**1. Duty and Proximate Cause.** Traditional strict liability requires proof of duty and, as the principal case indicates, proximate cause. Indeed, given that the defendant in strict liability is less blameworthy than a negligent tortfeasor, courts may be less inclined to find proximate cause in borderline cases. See Dobbs, *The Law of Torts* § 349 (2000).

**2. Defenses to Strict Liability.** Contributory negligence, while a complete defense to claims of negligence, is *not* a defense to strict liability. In comparative fault jurisdictions, the trend is to allow comparative fault as a partial defense to strict liability. Assumption of risk, on the other hand *is* a defense to strict liability. See Diamond, Levine & Madden, Understanding Torts § 16.03 [D] (2nd ed. 2000); and Dobbs, supra, § 350, Keeton, *Prosser and Keeton on the Law of Torts* § 79 (5th ed. 1984). For an extended discussion of comparative negligence as a defense to strict products liability see *Daly v. General Motors Corp.*, 20 Cal.3d 725, 144 Cal.Rptr. 380, 573 P.2d 1162 (1978), reprinted in Sec. B of this chapter on page 573, infra.

# SECTION B. PRODUCTS LIABILITY

## 1. The Development of Alternative Theories of Liability

### PILLARS v. R. J. REYNOLDS TOBACCO CO.

Supreme Court of Mississippi, Division B.
117 Miss. 490, 78 So. 365 (1918).

COOK, P. J.

The appellant sued the Corr–Williams Tobacco Company, distributors, and R. J. Reynolds Tobacco Company, manufacturer, of "Brown Mule Chewing Tobacco," for damages resulting to the appellant from Chewing a piece of Brown Mule tobacco in which was concealed a decomposed human toe. The evidence disclosed that R. J. Reynolds Tobacco Company was the sole manufacturer of the tobacco, and that this company manufactured the identical plug which contained the rotten toe; the tobacco in question was sold by the manufacturer to the other defendant, the Corr–Williams Company, and resold by the latter company to a retailer in Jackson, and was bought by appellant from the retailer. It seems that appellant consumed one plug of his purchase, which measured up to representations, that it was tobacco unmixed with human flesh, but when appellant tackled the second plug it made him sick, but, not suspecting the tobacco, he tried another chew, and still another, until he bit into some foreign substance, which crumbled like dry bread, and caused him to foam at the mouth, while he was getting "sicker and sicker." Finally, his teeth struck something hard; he could not bite through it. After an examination he discovered a human toe, with flesh and nail intact. We refrain from detailing the further harrowing and nauseating details. The appellant consulted a physician, who testified that appellant exhibited all of the characteristic symptoms of ptomaine poison. The physician examined the toe and identified it as a human toe in a state of putrefaction, and said, in effect, that his condition was caused by the poison generated by the rotten toe. At the close of the evidence for plaintiff the trial judge, at the request of the defendants, directed a verdict for the defendants, and from a judgment responsive to this instruction, an appeal is prosecuted to this court.

Generally speaking, the rule is that the manufacturer is not liable to the ultimate consumer for damages resulting from the defects and impurities of the manufactured article. This rule is generally based upon the theory that there is no contractual relations existing between the ultimate consumer and the manufacturer. From time to time, the courts have made exceptions to the rule. The manufacturers of food, beverages, drugs, condiments, and confections have been held liable to ultimate consumers for damages resulting from the negligent preparation of their products. The contention of the defendants here is that the limit has been reached by the courts, and that the facts of this case do not warrant an exception in favor of the plaintiff, and this view was adopted by the learned trial court. The exceptions already made were for the protection of the health of the people, and to insure a scrupulous care in the preparation of those articles of commerce so as to reduce to a minimum all danger to those using them.

If poisons are concealed in food, or in beverages, or in confections or in drugs, death or the impairment of health will be the probable consequence. We know that chewing tobacco is taken into the mouth, that a certain proportion will be absorbed by the mucous membrane of the mouth, and that some, at least, of the juice or pulp will and does find its way into the alimentary canal, there to be digested and ultimately to become a part of the blood. Tobacco may be relatively harmless, but decaying flesh, we are advised, develops poisonous ptomaines, which are certainly dangerous and often fatal. Anything taken into the mouth there to be masticated should be free of those elements which may endanger the life or health of the user. No one would be so bold as to contend that the manufacturer would be free from liability if it should appear that he purposely mixed human flesh with chewing tobacco, or chewing gum. If the manufacturer would be liable for intentionally feeding putrid human flesh to any and all consumers of chewing tobacco, does it not logically follow that he would be liable for negligently bringing about the same result? It seems to us that this question must be answered in the affirmative.

\* \* \*

We have read with care the very able and instructive brief for the appellee, in which he argues and we think proves that tobacco is not food for human beings at least, no matter how much tobacco worms or the town goat may relish it, but we are of opinion that we are not restricted to this narrow question, nor have we reached the limit when we admit that tobacco is not a beverage, or a condiment, or a drug.

The fact that the courts have at this time made only the exceptions mentioned to the general rule does not prevent a step forward for the health and life of the public. The principles announced in the cases which recognize the exceptions, in our opinion, apply, with equal force, to this case.

We believe that the way the tobacco is to be used furnishes the reason for great care in its preparation. If we eat food or drink beverages containing substances which under certain conditions may endanger our lives, for obvious reasons, he who prepares the food or drink should be required to exercise great care to prevent the dangerous conditions. It appears sufficiently certain that chewing tobacco with poisonous ptomaines hidden in it is dangerous to the consumer, as was proven in this case.

We can imagine no reason why, with ordinary care, human toes could not be left out of chewing tobacco, and if toes are found in chewing tobacco, it seems to us that somebody has been very careless.

We will reverse the judgment of the lower court as to the manufacturer and affirm the judgment for the distributor. The distributor could not have suspected that human toes were concealed in the plug, and was not negligent in not discovering the noxious contents of the plug.

Reversed in part and affirmed in part.

## NOTES

**1. Products Liability.** Products liability is not today a single theory of liability, but a cluster of tort and contract actions that a plaintiff can utilize to recover for injuries and losses resulting from defective products. Liability as will be discussed in subsequent cases can be based on negligence, express warranty, implied warranty, misrepresentation and strict products liability. Although the Restatement (Third) of Torts: Products Liability (1998) urges a single unified theory of products liability, it is far from clear that courts will adopt this approach (see Sec. B(4), infra, this chapter).

Potential defendants include the manufacturer, wholesaler, and retailer of the product. Historically, in defective product cases, courts required privity between the parties in order for one to be liable for negligence. By "privity," the court means that the plaintiff and defendant had a direct relationship with each other. Thus, where an ultimate consumer sued a manufacturer in production of the product, the consumer would lose if there were intermediate parties such as wholesalers and retailers that interrupted the parties' privity. Furthermore, in many product cases, the retailers could not be held liable for negligence since they had no reason to know the product was defective. As the principal case makes clear, courts came to recognize exceptions to the privity rule in cases involving food, beverages, drugs, and cosmetics. See Diamond, Levine & Madden, *Understanding Torts* § 17.01 (2nd ed. 2000); Keeton, *Prosser and Keeton on the Law of Torts* §§ 95–97 (5th ed. 1984); and Dobbs, *The Law of Torts* §§ 351–353 (2000).

The privity rule came under further attack in the landmark case of *MacPherson v. Buick Motor Co.*, 217 N.Y. 382, 111 N.E. 1050 (N.Y. 1916), in which the Court of Appeals of New York held that a manufacturer's duty for negligence liability extended not only to those in privity with the manufacturer, but to anyone who could foreseeably be injured by a potentially dangerous product it had sold.

Negligence liability for product manufacturer, wholesaler, and seller is today based on the same rules that apply to negligence liability generally. The plaintiff must establish that each of the potential defendants, such as the manufacturer and retailer, didn't behave like a reasonable person and was the proximate cause of his or her injury. For example, the manufacturer may have carelessly designed or constructed the products. While less frequent, it is also possible the retailer was negligent as, for example, by storing milk for sale in an inadequately refrigerated location.

**2. Tobacco Litigation.** Note the dictum in *Pillars* that "[t]obacco may be relatively harmless." In recent decades, numerous plaintiffs have tried to prove otherwise. Should cigarettes be considered defective? Might there be other viable theories of recovery for harm caused by tobacco products? See *Roysdon v. R.J. Reynolds Tobacco Co.*, infra page 532, in this chapter, and *New Jersey Carpenters Health Fund v. Philip Morris, Inc.* in Chapter 1, Sec. J at page 125, supra.

# GREENMAN v. YUBA POWER PRODUCTS, INC.

Supreme Court of California.
59 Cal.2d 57, 27 Cal.Rptr. 697, 377 P.2d 897 (1963).

TRAYNOR, J.

Plaintiff brought this action for damages against the retailer and the manufacturer of a Shopsmith, a combination power tool that could be used as a saw, drill, and wood lathe. He saw a Shopsmith demonstrated by the retailer and studied a brochure prepared by the manufacturer. He decided he wanted a Shopsmith for his home workshop, and his wife bought and gave him one for Christmas in 1955. In 1957 he bought the necessary attachments to use the Shopsmith as a lathe for turning a large piece of wood he wished to make into a chalice. After he had worked on the piece of wood several times without difficulty, it suddenly flew out of the machine and struck him on the forehead, inflicting serious injuries. About 10 1/2 months later, he gave the retailer and the manufacturer written notice of claimed breaches of warranties and filed a complaint against them alleging such breaches and negligence.

After a trial before a jury, the court ruled that there was no evidence that the retailer was negligent or had breached any express warranty and that the manufacturer was not liable for the breach of any implied warranty. Accordingly, it submitted to the jury only the cause of action alleging breach of implied warranties against the retailer and the causes of action alleging negligence and breach of express warranties against the manufacturer. The jury returned a verdict for the retailer against plaintiff and for plaintiff against the manufacturer in the amount of $65,000. The trial court denied the manufacturer's motion for a new trial and entered judgment on the verdict. The manufacturer and plaintiff appeal. Plaintiff seeks a reversal of the part of the judgment in favor of the retailer, however, only in the event that the part of the judgment against the manufacturer is reversed.

Plaintiff introduced substantial evidence that his injuries were caused by defective design and construction of the Shopsmith. His expert witnesses testified that inadequate set screws were used to hold parts of the machine together so that normal vibration caused the tailstock of the lathe to move away from the piece of wood being turned permitting it to fly out of the lathe. They also testified that there were other more positive ways of fastening the parts of the machine together, the use of which would have prevented the accident. The jury could therefore reasonably have concluded that the manufacturer negligently construct- ed the Shopsmith. The jury could also reasonably have concluded that statements in the manufacturer's brochure were untrue, that they constituted express warranties,[1] and that plaintiff's injuries were caused by their breach.

The manufacturer contends, however, that plaintiff did not give it notice of breach of warranty within a reasonable time and that therefore his cause of action for breach of warranty is barred by section 1769 of the Civil Code. Since it cannot be determined whether the verdict against it was based on the negligence or warranty cause of action or both, the manufacturer concludes that the error in presenting the warranty cause of action to the jury was prejudicial.

Section 1769 of the Civil Code provides: "In the absence of express or implied agreement of the parties, acceptance of the goods by the buyer shall not discharge the seller from liability in damages or other legal remedy for breach of any promise or warranty in the contract to sell or the sale. But, if, after acceptance of the goods, the buyer fails to give notice to the seller of the breach of any promise or warranty within a reasonable time after the buyer knows, or ought to know of such breach, the seller shall not be liable therefor."

Like other provisions of the Uniform Sales Act (Civ. Code, §§ 1721– 1800), section 1769 deals with the rights of the parties to a contract of sale or a sale. It does not provide that notice must be given of the breach of a warranty that arises independently of a contract of sale between the parties. Such warranties are not imposed by the sales act, but are the product of common-law decisions that have recognized them in a variety of situations. (See *Gagne v. Bertran*, 43 Cal.2d 481, 486–487 [275 P.2d 15], and authorities cited; *Peterson v. Lamb Rubber Co.*, 54 Cal.2d 339, 348 [5 Cal.Rptr. 863, 353 P.2d 575]; *Klein v. Duchess Sandwich Co., Ltd.*, 14 Cal.2d 272, 276–283 [93 P.2d 799]; *Burr v. Sherwin Williams Co.*, 42 Cal.2d 682, 695–696 [268 P.2d 1041]; *Souza & McCue Constr. Co., Inc. v. Superior Court*, 57 Cal.2d 508, 510–511 [20 Cal.Rptr. 634, 370 P.2d 338].) It is true that in many of these situations the court has invoked the sales act definitions of warranties (Civ. Code, §§ 1732, 1735) in defining the defendant's liability, but it has done so, not because the statutes so required, but because they provided appropriate standards for the court to adopt under the circumstances presented. (See *Clinks- cales v. Carver*, 22 Cal.2d 72, 75 [136 P.2d 777]; *Dana v. Sutton Motor Sales*, 56 Cal.2d 284, 287 [14 Cal.Rptr. 649, 363 P.2d 881].)

The notice requirement of section 1769, however, is not an appropri- ate one for the court to adopt in actions by injured consumers against manufacturers with whom they have not dealt. (*La Hue v. Coca-Cola*

---

**1.** In this respect the trial court limited the jury to a consideration of two state- ments in the manufacturer's brochure. (1) "WHEN SHOPSMITH IS IN HORIZON- TAL POSITION–RUGGED construction of frame provides rigid support from end to end. Heavy centerless-ground steel tubing insures perfect alignment of components." (2) "SHOPSMITH maintains its accuracy because every component has positive locks that hold adjustments through rough or precision work."

*Bottling, Inc.,* 50 Wn.2d 645 [314 P.2d 421, 422]; *Chapman v. Brown,* 198 F. Supp. 78, 85, affd. *Brown v. Chapman,* 304 F. 2d 149.) "As between the immediate parties to the sale [the notice requirement] is a sound commercial rule, designed to protect the seller against unduly delayed claims for damages. As applied to personal injuries, and notice to a remote seller, it becomes a booby-trap for the unwary. The injured consumer is seldom 'steeped in the business practice which justifies the rule,' [James, *Product Liability,* 34 Texas L. Rev. 44, 192, 197] and at least until he has had legal advice it will not occur to him to give notice to one with whom he has had no dealings." (Prosser, *Strict Liability to the Consumer,* 69 Yale L. J. 1099, 1130, footnotes omitted.) It is true that in *Jones v. Burgermeister Brewing Corp.,* 198 Cal.App.2d 198, 202–203 [18 Cal.Rptr. 311]; *Perry v. Thrifty Drug Co.,* 186 Cal.App.2d 410, 411 [9 Cal.Rptr. 50], *Arata v. Tonegato,* 152 Cal.App.2d 837, 841 [314 P.2d 130], and *Maecherlein v. Sealy Mattress Co.,* 145 Cal.App.2d 275, 278 [302 P.2d 331], the court assumed that notice of breach of warranty must be given in an action by a consumer against a manufacturer. Since in those cases, however, the court did not consider the question whether a distinction exists between a warranty based on a contract between the parties and one imposed on a manufacturer not in privity with the consumer, the decisions are not authority for rejecting the rule of the *La Hue* and *Chapman* cases, *supra.* (*Peterson v. Lamb Rubber Co.,* 54 Cal.2d 339, 343 [5 Cal.Rptr. 863, 353 P.2d 575]; *People v. Banks,* 53 Cal.2d 370, 389 [1 Cal.Rptr. 669, 348 P.2d 102].) We conclude, therefore, that even if plaintiff did not give timely notice of breach of warranty to the manufacturer, his cause of action based on the representations contained in the brochure was not barred.

Moreover, to impose strict liability on the manufacturer under the circumstances of this case, it was not necessary for plaintiff to establish an express warranty as defined in section 1732 of the Civil Code.[2] A manufacturer is strictly liable in tort when an article he places on the market, knowing that it is to be used without inspection for defects, proves to have a defect that causes injury to a human being. Recognized first in the case of unwholesome food products, such liability has now been extended to a variety of other products that create as great or greater hazards if defective. (*Peterson v. Lamb Rubber Co.,* 54 Cal.2d 339, 347 [5 Cal.Rptr. 863, 353 P.2d 575] [grinding wheel]; *Vallis v. Canada Dry Ginger Ale, Inc.,* 190 Cal.App.2d 35, 42–44 [11 Cal.Rptr. 823] [bottle]; *Jones v. Burgermeister Brewing Corp.,* 198 Cal.App.2d 198, 204 [18 Cal.Rptr. 311] [bottle]; *Gottsdanker v. Cutter Laboratories,* 182 Cal.App.2d 602, 607 [6 Cal.Rptr. 320] [vaccine]; *McQuaide v. Bridgeport Brass Co.,* 190 F. Supp. 252, 254 [insect spray]; *Bowles v. Zimmer Manufacturing Co.,* 277 F. 2d 868, 875 [surgical pin]; *Thompson v. Reedman,* 199 F. Supp. 120, 121 [automobile]; *Chapman v. Brown,* 198 F. Supp. 78, 118, 119, affd. *Brown v. Chapman,* 304 F. 2d 149 [skirt]; *B. F. Goodrich Co. v. Hammond,* 269 F. 2d 501, 504 [automobile tire];

---

**2.** "Any affirmation of fact or any promise by the seller relating to the goods is an express warranty if the natural tendency of such affirmation or promise is to induce the buyer to purchase the goods, and if the buyer purchases the goods relying thereon. No affirmation of the value of the goods, nor any statement purporting to be a statement of the seller's opinion only shall be construed as a warranty."

*Markovich v. McKesson & Robbins, Inc.,* 106 Ohio App. 265 [149 N.E. 2d 181, 186–188] [home permanent]; *Graham v. Bottenfield's, Inc.,* 176 Kan. 68 [269 P.2d 413, 418] [hair dye]; *General Motors Corp. v. Dodson,* 47 Tenn.App. 438 [338 S.W. 2d 655, 661] [automobile]; *Henningsen v. Bloomfield Motors, Inc.,* 32 N.J. 358 [161 A. 2d 69, 76–84, 75 A.L.R. 2d 1] [automobile]; *Hinton v. Republic Aviation Corp.,* 180 F. Supp. 31, 33 [airplane].)

Although in these cases strict liability has usually been based on the theory of an express or implied warranty running from the manufacturer to the plaintiff, the abandonment of the requirement of a contract between them, the recognition that the liability is not assumed by agreement but imposed by law (see e.g., *Graham v. Bottenfield's, Inc.,* 176 Kan. 68 [269 P.2d 413, 418]; *Rogers v. Toni Home Permanent Co.,* 167 Ohio St. 244 [147 N.E. 2d 612, 614, 75 A.L.R. 2d 103]; *Decker & Sons v. Capps,* 139 Tex. 609, 617 [164 S.W. 2d 828, 142 A.L.R. 1479]), and the refusal to permit the manufacturer to define the scope of its own responsibility for defective products (*Henningsen v. Bloomfield Motors, Inc.,* 32 N.J. 358 [161 A. 2d 69, 84–96, 75 A.L.R. 2d 1]; *General Motors Corp. v. Dodson,* 47 Tenn.App. 438 [338 S.W. 2d 655, 658–661]; *State Farm Mut. Auto Ins. Co. v. Anderson–Weber, Inc.,* 252 Iowa 1289 [110 N.W. 2d 449, 455–456]; *Pabon v. Hackensack Auto Sales, Inc.,* 63 N.J. Super. 476 [164 A. 2d 773, 778]; *Linn v. Radio Center Delicatessen,* 169 Misc. 879 [6 N.Y.S. 2d 110, 112]) make clear that the liability is not one governed by the law of contract warranties but by the law of strict liability in tort. Accordingly, rules defining and governing warranties that were developed to meet the needs of commercial transactions cannot properly be invoked to govern the manufacturer's liability to those injured by its defective products unless those rules also serve the purposes for which such liability is imposed.

We need not recanvass the reasons for imposing strict liability on the manufacturer. They have been fully articulated in the cases cited above. (See also 2 Harper and James, Torts, §§ 28.15–28.16, pp. 1569–1574; Prosser, *Strict Liability to the Consumer,* 69 Yale L.J. 1099; *Escola v. Coca Cola Bottling Co.,* 24 Cal.2d 453, 461 [150 P.2d 436], concurring opinion.) The purpose of such liability is to insure that the costs of injuries resulting from defective products are borne by the manufacturers that put such products on the market rather than by the injured persons who are powerless to protect themselves. Sales warranties serve this purpose fitfully at best. (See Prosser, *Strict Liability to the Consumer,* 69 Yale L.J. 1099, 1124–1134.) In the present case, for example, plaintiff was able to plead and prove an express warranty only because he read and relied on the representations of the Shopsmith's ruggedness contained in the manufacturer's brochure. Implicit in the machine's presence on the market, however, was a representation that it would safely do the jobs for which it was built. Under these circumstances, it should not be controlling whether plaintiff selected the machine because of the statements in the brochure, or because of the machine's own appearance of excellence that belied the defect lurking beneath the surface, or because he merely assumed that it would safely do the jobs it was built to do. It should not be controlling whether the details of the sales from manufacturer to retailer and from retailer to plaintiff's wife were such that one or more of the implied warranties of the sales act arose. (Civ. Code, § 1735.) "The remedies of injured consumers ought not to be made to depend upon the intricacies of the law of sales." (*Ketterer v. Armour & Co.*, 200 F. 322, 323; *Klein v. Duchess Sandwich Co., Ltd.*, 14 Cal.2d 272, 282 [93 P.2d 799].) To establish the manufacturer's liability it was sufficient that plaintiff proved that he was injured while using the Shopsmith in a way it was intended to be used as a result of a defect in design and manufacture of which plaintiff was not aware that made the Shopsmith unsafe for its intended use.

The manufacturer contends that the trial court erred in refusing to give three instructions requested by it. It appears from the record, however, that the substance of two of the requested instructions was adequately covered by the instructions given and that the third instruction was not supported by the evidence.

The judgment is affirmed.

### NOTES

**1. Express and Implied Warranty Liability.** In addition to negligence, products liability cases may also be based on the defendant's breach of a warranty. Warranty cases are actually controlled by contract law, not tort law, and are thus controlled by the appropriate Uniform Commercial Code (UCC) provisions. A warranty, which is part of the terms of the contract covering the sale, may be express or implied.

Express warranties are created when the seller makes factual assertions about characteristics of the product. These should be distinguished, however, from a seller's opinions about the product, or "puffing." Express warranties may be created in a wide variety of ways, including a salesperson's verbal assertions, advertisements, and brochures. Express warranty by promising a product characteristic, such as a watch being waterproof, can raise the consumer's legitimate levels of expectation about what a product can do.

The UCC provides for two types of implied warranty. Implied warranties are not expressly articulated by the sellers, but are imposed by law on the seller. The first, created by UCC § 2–314, is the implied warranty of merchantability. The implied warranty of merchantability is a guarantee by the seller that the goods sold reasonably conform to their description and are safe for their intended use. It is automatically implied in contracts where the seller is a "merchant," meaning that the seller is engaged in selling that product professionally. The other type of UCC implied warranty, imposed by § 2–315, is the warranty of fitness for a particular purpose. This warranty enters the parties' agreement when the seller has reason to know that the buyer is purchasing goods for some special purpose and is relying on the seller's knowledge or skill in furnishing the goods. For example, if A tells B that she wishes to purchase a boat capable of pulling a water skier and that she is deferring to B's expertise in selecting such a boat, then the boat that B sells A will have a warranty of being fit for towing a water skier. Unlike the implied warranty of merchantability, the warranty of fitness for a particular purpose does not require that the seller be a merchant.

One of the advantages of basing a products liability case on a warranty theory is that liability is strict; the plaintiff need not prove negligence. In addition, warranty theory, unlike negligence in product liability, can compensate for pure economic loss unaccompanied by personal injury or property damage, such as when a computer fails to operate causing a business loss. Under negligence theory in product liability, economic loss must derive from a personal injury or property damage to be compensated. The drawback for warranty theory, however, is that sellers may limit their liability by limiting remedies or disclaiming warranties altogether, although consumer protection provisions may limit such disclaimers. Also, a plaintiff who is not in contractual privity with the defendant may face privity barriers depending on which version of the UCC's privity rules it adopts. In § 2–318, the UCC offers three alternatives for privity limitations for third parties, ranging from family members and household guests of the buyer (Alternative A) to any person who might with reasonable foreseeability be affected by the product (Alternative C). Historically, as the next principal case indicates, warranty also includes strict requirements that the victim give prompt, timely notice of dissatisfaction to the defendant. See Diamond, Levine & Madden, Understanding Torts, § 17.03 (2nd Ed. 2000).

**2. Misrepresentation.** In addition to negligence and warranty theory, product liability can be based on misrepresentation. Misrepresentation is very similar to liability based on an express warranty, but is a tort theory. For example, a seller can misrepresent that a watch is waterproof. The Restatement (Second) of Torts articulates the majority rule as follows:

> One engaged in the business of selling chattels who, by advertising, labels, or otherwise, makes to the public a misrepresentation of a material fact concerning the character or quality of a chattel sold by him is subject to liability for physical harm to a consumer of the chattel caused by justifiable reliance upon the misrepresentation, even though

> (a) it is not made fraudulently or negligently, and

> (b) the consumer has not bought the chattel from or entered into any contractual relation with the seller.

Restatement (Second) Torts § 402B. Claims based on misrepresentation for products do not require proof of intent or negligence on the part of the defendants who are in the business of selling chattels. See Diamond, Levine & Madden, supra, § 17.06. For a discussion of intentional and negligent misrepresentation, see Chapter 1, Sec. J and Chapter 2, Sec. H, supra, respectively.

**3. Strict Products Liability.** In addition to liability for negligence, express and implied warranty, and misrepresentation, contemporary courts impose liability for strict product liability. Plaintiffs will most often allege multiple theories of liability to increase the chances of a successful lawsuit. In the principal case, Justice Traynor, writing for the California Supreme Court, invents the strict product liability tort with much debt owed to implied warranty theory. In essence strict product liability has evolved to impose responsibility for personal and property injuries proximately caused by a defective product. The tort imposes liability against the manufacturer, wholesaler, and retailer selling new products without reference to whether they are negligent or the potential limitations of warranty theory noted above. Left unresolved by the principal case was the sometimes difficult problem of defining when a product is in fact defective. The issue is considered in subsequent principal cases in this chapter.

## 2. Strict Products Liability

# LEE v. CROOKSTON COCA–COLA BOTTLING CO.

Supreme Court of Minnesota.
290 Minn. 321, 188 N.W.2d 426 (1971).

ROGOSHESKE, Justice.

Appeal from an order denying a new trial after a jury verdict for defendant, Crookston Coca–Cola Bottling Company. The action is one for personal injury and consequential damages caused by an "exploding" bottle of carbonated beverage, and the appeal raises questions concerning the trial court's submission of the issue of contributory negligence and its refusal to submit the issue of liability on the theory of strict liability, as plaintiffs requested. We find reversible error and grant a new trial.

Plaintiff Helen Lee, a waitress, while working at the Norman Steak House at Ada, Minnesota, was injured when a quart (26–ounce) Coca–Cola bottle exploded in her hand and a glass fragment of the bottle punctured the median nerve at the level of her right wrist. Mrs. Lee and her husband, Claire, brought this action to recover damages upon pleaded theories of breach of implied warranty, negligence, and strict tort liability. The case was tried and submitted to a jury on the theories of breach of implied warranty and of negligence under the doctrine of res ipsa loquitur. The jury returned a general verdict for defendant, presumably upon a finding either of no breach of warranty or no negligence or of contributory negligence. On this appeal, plaintiffs principally contend that the trial court erred ... in refusing to submit their claim against defendant upon the theory of strict liability in tort.

The evidence relating to the injury-producing incident is not in substantial dispute. Defendant's driver delivered a 12–bottle case of Coca–Cola and other beverages to the steak house shortly before noon on the day of the accident. Using a handcart, he stacked the Coca–Cola case in the dining room area of the steak house behind a bar or counter about 2 feet from a waist-high, sliding-top-three-door-type, refrigerated cooler. The case and the bottles remained undisturbed until between 12:30 and 1 p.m., when Mrs. Lee (hereafter plaintiff) undertook to transfer the bottles from the Coca–Cola case into the cooler. Without moving the case, she grasped one bottle at a time with her right hand, moved it laterally to her right, and lowered it into the cooler. While she was lowering the third bottle into the cooler, it "exploded" in her hand, the neck of the bottle with a cap intact remaining in her hand. . . .

\* \* \*

A new trial is ... necessary because we hold that the circumstantial evidence justifying submission of the issue of liability to the jury on the theory of negligence also justified submission of the issue on the theory of strict liability in tort, as pleaded and requested by plaintiffs.

Our intention to apply the rule of strict liability to manufacturers and sellers of defective products was announced in *McCormack v. Hankscraft Co. Inc.*, 278 Minn. 322, 154 N.W.2d 488. This decision was based on policy considerations expressed in our prior case law and a host of other authorities alluded to in the *Hankscraft* case. Summarized, these policy considerations are: (1) The public interest in safety will be promoted by discouraging the marketing of defective products which constitute a menace to consumers not equipped to protect themselves from products they are induced to purchase through modern advertising methods by persuasive representations that the product is suitable and safe for its intended use; (2) the burden of loss caused by placing a defective product on the market should be borne by the manufacturer, who is best able to distribute it by insuring against inevitable hazards as a part of the cost of the product; (3) maximum legal protection should be afforded the consumer to promote product safety and to encourage the growing practice of reputable manufacturers and sellers of settling valid claims without litigation; and (4) one injured by a defective product should be entitled to bring action directly against the party responsible for putting the product on the market without becoming involved in the delay and expense of joining other sellers in the chain of distribution, as frequently occurs when liability is sought to be determined under warranty provisions of the Uniform Commercial Code.

The rule of strict liability, as revised and adopted by the American Law Institute in 1964, is embodied in Restatement, Torts (2d) s 402A.[7] It imposes liability, without proof of negligence or privity of contract, upon a manufacturer or seller for injury caused by a dangerously defective product. To recover under the rule, the injured party must present evidence, direct or circumstantial, from which the jury can justifiably find that (1) the product was in fact in a defective condition, unreasonably dangerous for its intended use; (2) such defect existed when the product left defendant's control; and (3) the defect was the proximate cause of the injury sustained.

The greatest difficulty in establishing liability under this rule is in proving that the product was defective and that the defect existed when the product left defendant's control.... Thus, strict liability does not mean that the defendant is held liable as an insurer of his product regardless of circumstances....

The narrow question presented here, however, is whether circumstantial evidence, the core of the res ipsa loquitur doctrine, is sufficient

---

**7.** Restatement, Torts (2d) § 402A, provides:

"(1) One who sells any product in a defective condition unreasonably dangerous to the user or consumer or to his property is subject to liability for physical harm thereby caused to the ultimate user or consumer, or to his property, if

"(a) the seller is engaged in the business of selling such a product, and

"(b) it is expected to and does reach the user or consumer without substantial change in the condition in which it is sold.

"(2) The rule stated in Subsection (1) applies although

"(a) the seller has exercised all possible care in the preparation and sale of his product, and

"(b) the user or consumer has not bought the product from or entered into any contractual relation with the seller."

to take the case to the jury on the theory of strict liability as well as on the theory of negligence....

\* \* \*

Under the theory of strict liability, the elements of proof as noted above are few and uncomplicated. The significant difference is that under strict liability the jury need not infer from the circumstantial evidence that defendant was negligent in order to impose liability. It is sufficient that the evidence establishes that the manufacturer placed a dangerously defective product on the market, knowing that it is to be used without inspection for defects....

Where res ipsa is relied upon as the theory of recovery, plaintiff is not required to allege or prove specific claims of negligence or, as in this case, a specific defect. *Anderson v. Eastern Minn. Power Co.*, 197 Minn. 144, 266 N.W. 702; *Segal v. Bloom Brothers Co.*, 249 Minn. 367, 82 N.W.2d 359. Indeed, plaintiff's inability to determine the specific defect or cause, coupled with the fact that the defendant is in a better position to present evidence as to the cause of the accident, is itself a fundamental reason for the res ipsa rule. The same reasoning applies with equal force to excuse plaintiff from proving a specific defect when pursuing recovery on the theory of strict liability. This is especially true in exploding-bottle cases and similar situations where the product is destroyed by reason of the defect, which is also obliterated, or where the defective part alone is destroyed by the incident. *Grant v. Malkerson Sales, Inc.*, 259 Minn. 419, 108 N.W.2d 347; *Franks v. National Dairy Products Corp.* (W.D.Tex.) 282 F.Supp. 528. In short, under the theory of strict liability plaintiff should not be required to prove specifically what defect caused the incident, but may rely upon circumstantial evidence from which it can reasonably be inferred that it is more probable than not that the product was defective when it left defendant's control.

\* \* \*

Thus, the trial court's refusal to submit plaintiffs' claim upon the theory of strict liability in tort must also be regarded as reversible error. The court's ruling deprived plaintiffs of a legitimate choice of theories on which to submit the case. Plaintiffs are entitled to attempt to prove their case on either or both theories—that defendant was negligent or that it put a dangerously defective product on the market.

It could be argued that the case in effect was submitted to the jury on strict liability, since the jury was instructed on implied warranty. Although strict liability in tort and in warranty are very similar, we cannot view the court's instructions as sufficient to constitute submission of the question for strict liability in tort to the jury. The jury was told that defendant warranted that the bottle of Coca-Cola "was reasonably fit for the ordinary and usual handling as it might reasonably anticipate in the exercise of reasonable care." This language falls short of conveying to the jury that if a defect existed in defendant's product when it left its control, defendant should be found liable for the injuries caused by such defect.

Reversed and new trial granted.

* * *

***NOTES***

**1. The Restatement (Second) of Torts Approach.** The Restatement (Second) of Torts, cited in the principal case, articulates the following approach to strict products liability:

> (1) One who sells any product in a defective condition unreasonably dangerous to the user or consumer or to his property is subject to liability for physical harm thereby caused to the ultimate user or consumer, or to his property, if
>
>> (a) the seller is engaged in the business of selling such a product, and
>>
>> (b) it is expected to and does reach the user or consumer without substantial change in the condition in which it is sold.
>
> (2) The rule stated in Subsection (1) applies although
>
>> (a) the seller has exercised all possible care in the preparation and sale of his product, and
>>
>> (b) the user or consumer has not bought the product from or entered into any contractual relation with the seller.

Restatement (Second) Torts § 402A. Just what constitutes a "defective condition" that is "unreasonably dangerous" is open to debate. According to the comments following § 402A, strict products liability attaches "only where the product is, at the time it leaves the seller's hands, in a condition not contemplated by the ultimate consumer, which will be unreasonably dangerous to him." Restatement (Second) of Torts § 402A cmt. g. This approach has been described as the "consumer expectations" test and has been widely adopted, although as subsequent principal cases indicate, an increasing number of courts and the new Restatement (Third) on products liability (see *Potter v. Chicago Pneumatic Tool*, infra at page 565) are rejecting it. The next principal case explores the consumer expectation test further. See Diamond, Levine & Madden, *Understanding Torts* § 17.04 (2nd ed. 2000), and Dobbs, *The Law of Torts* §§ 355–356 (2000).

**2. Res Ipsa Loquitur.** In the context of a negligence suit, res ipsa loquitur is used to establish causation where the accident normally does not occur without negligence on the part of the defendant. See Chapter 2, Sec. G, supra. In the context of strict products liability, res ipsa loquitur may be used to prove that a product is somehow defective, even though the plaintiff cannot prove what specifically was defective.

**3. Strict Product Liability Applies to Merchants of New Products.** Courts traditionally limit strict product liability to merchants who "sell" new products and not those who merely provide a service. An interesting number of courts also apply strict liability to the leasing of new goods (see Note 4, infra, at page 558).

Consider *Speyer, Inc. v. Humble Oil & Refining Co.*, 403 F.2d 766 (3d Cir.1968), where a garage and sixty-five taxicabs were destroyed in a fire caused by a leaky gas pump. According to the evidence, a replacement hose had ruptured the pump's casting when a cab driver tried to drive away with the hose still attached to his gas tank. The owners of the garage and the cabs sued the gasoline supplier and the successor of the pump manufacturer under a products liability theory. The court struck down their claim, noting the gas supplier was merely supplying gas, not selling the pump. The gas and the pump were not considered to be one unit. The court also absolved the manufacturer of the pump, holding that replacement of the hose was a "substantial change" within the meaning of the Restatement.

Consider also, *Acosta-Mestre v. Hilton Intern. of Puerto Rico*, 156 F.3d 49 (1st Cir.1998), where a hotel guest caught his finger in a collapsing lounge chair. Sustaining considerable injuries, he brought suit against the hotel alleging negligence and strict products liability. The defendant prevailed on a jury verdict for the negligence claim, and as a matter of law on the products liability claim. The appellate court held the products liability claim barred because the hotel was not in the business of the manufacture or sale of lounge chairs.

# GRAY v. MANITOWOC COMPANY
United States Court of Appeals, Fifth Circuit.
771 F.2d 866 (1985).

W.  EUGENE DAVIS, Circuit Judge.

\* \* \*

Gray was struck in two separate incidents by the butt end of the boom of a Manitowoc 4100W crane while working as an ironworker foreman on a construction project near Port Gibson, Mississippi. These incidents occurred while Gray's crew was changing sections of the crane's boom and had placed the boom in a plane roughly parallel to the ground (the "boom down" position). Gray was standing on the left side of the crane, supervising this operation, as the crane operator swung the lowered boom in Gray's direction, striking Gray in the back.

Testimony at trial established that the operator's vision to the left side of the Manitowoc crane is obscured by the boom when the crane is operated in the "boom down" position. To compensate for the operator's incomplete field of vision, users of cranes such as the 4100W place a signalman at various locations on the ground to guide the operator. This procedure was followed by Gray's employer during both incidents in which Gray alleged that he was struck. Gray contends, however, that Manitowoc should have provided mirrors, closed circuit television cameras or other devices to enable the operator to see to the left side of the crane when the crane is operated in the "boom down" position. Gray asserts that had these safety devices been placed on the crane, the crane operator would have seen Gray standing on the left side of the boom and would have avoided hitting him with the boom.

Manitowoc responds that even if mirrors or other devices would have permitted the operator to observe the area on the left side of the crane, the omission of these devices did not render the crane defective. Manitowoc argues that the hazards of operating the crane in the boom down position were open and obvious to ordinary users of the crane and that Mississippi law does not permit recovery under any theory of products liability for a manufacturer's failure to correct such patent dangers.

* * *

Under Mississippi's version of strict liability for hazardous products, manufacturers are not insurers of the products they produce; the existence of a product defect must be established before recovery may be obtained for a resulting injury. *Walton v. Chrysler Motor Corp.,* 229 So.2d 568, 572 (Miss.1969); *General Motors Corp. v. Howard,* 244 So.2d 726, 728 (Miss.1971). *See also Jones v. Babst,* 323 So.2d 757, 759 (Miss.1975). Mississippi has adopted the following formulation of the doctrine of strict liability for product defects (as it applies to manufacturers) from *The Restatement (Second) of the Law of Torts,* § 402A(1) (1965): "One who sells any product in a defective condition unreasonably dangerous to the consumer or to his property is subject to liability for physical harm thereby caused to the ultimate user or consumer, or to his property . . . ." *Jackson v. Johns-Manville Sales Corp.,* 727 F.2d 506, 511 (5th Cir.1984), *reinstated en banc in relevant respects,* 750 F.2d 1314, 1317 (1985); *State Stove Manufacturing Co. v. Hodges,* 189 So.2d 113, 118 (Miss.1966), *cert. denied, sub nom. Yates v. Hodges,* 386 U.S. 912, 87 S.Ct. 860, 17 L.Ed.2d 784 (1967); *Ford Motor Co. v. Matthews,* 291 So.2d 169, 171 (Miss.1974).

Comment (g) to the Restatement § 402A defines the term "defective condition": "The rule stated in this Section applies only where the product is, at the time it leaves the seller's hands, in a condition not contemplated by the ultimate consumer, which will be unreasonably dangerous to him." Comment (i), in turn, gives substance to the phrase "unreasonably dangerous":

> The rule stated in this Section applies only where the defective condition of the product makes it unreasonably dangerous to the user or consumer. . . . The article sold must be dangerous to an extent beyond that which would be contemplated by the ordinary consumer who purchases it, with the ordinary knowledge common to the community as to its characteristics.

As these comments illustrate, the consumer expectation test of section 402A is rooted in the warranty remedies of contract law, and requires that harm and liability flow from a product characteristic that frustrates consumer expectations. *See* Keeton, *Product Liability and the Meaning of Defect,* 5 St. Mary's L.J. 30, 37 (1973).

. . . . Hence, we conclude that the Grays' right to recover under the theory of strict liability depends upon whether the evidence was sufficient to permit the jury to find that the 4100W crane was "dangerous to an extent not contemplated by the ordinary consumer who purchased it, with the ordinary knowledge common to the community as to its characteristics." *See Ford Motor Co.,* 291 So.2d at 169.

We are persuaded that the record does not support a finding that the blind spot in the 4100W was a latent hazard. The evidence was overwhelming that the existence of this blind spot was common knowledge in the construction industry. Gray's supervisor, testifying as Gray's witness, stated that the existence of a blind spot in the crane operator's field of vision had been widely discussed at the Grand Gulf job site. . . .

. . . . [8] In light of the overwhelming evidence indicating that the existence of a blind spot in the 4100W was common knowledge in the construction trade, we must conclude that the testimony of Gray and his inexperienced co-worker did not create a jury question as to the knowledge or expectations of the *ordinary* observer or consumer. We conclude that no reasonable jury could have found that the blind spot of the Manitowoc 4100W was not open and obvious, nor could any reasonable jury have concluded that the 4100W was dangerous to a degree not anticipated by the ordinary consumer of that product.

Since the Grays failed to establish that the Manitowoc 4100W crane was defectively designed under any proper theory of Mississippi law, the district court erred in refusing to grant defendant's motion for judgment notwithstanding the verdict. We therefore REVERSE and RENDER the judgment.

### NOTES

**1. Types of Defects.** A product can be defective in three ways. A manufacturing defect is an error in the construction of the particular product. The plaintiff is, in essence, complaining that he or she got the "broken" one. The error may be the result of poor quality control by the manufacturer, but under strict product liability it is not necessary to prove the defendant was negligent in the manufacturing process. The manufacturer, wholesaler, and retailer are all liable for any "defect" that existed when they sold the product.

A design defect indicates that the product has an error in its design or blueprint. The problem is not that individual products were constructed incorrectly, but that the entire product line is defective because of its design. The economic consequences to the defendants of a product design defect can be enormous. As in the case of a manufacturing defect, under strict liability, it is not necessary to prove sellers of the product were negligent.

A warning defect occurs when the product lacks adequate warnings or instructions. Unless the warning or instructions have inadvertently been excluded from a particular product because of a manufacturing defect type error, a warning defect is usually a type of design defect affecting the entire product line. Nevertheless, courts are increasingly categorizing warning defects as a distinct typology. As with the other two types of defects, strict liability imposes liability on all the sellers (e.g., manufacturer, wholesaler, and retailer) even if none or only one of them (e.g., manufacturer) was in fact negligent.

**2. "Consumer Expectations" Test.** In those jurisdictions that adopt the "consumer expectations" test of the Restatement (Second) of Torts, the plaintiff must prove that an ordinary consumer would not discover the unsafe characteristic of the product. As the principal case indicates, the inquiry is an objective one, analyzed from the point of view of a typical consumer in the community. The Restatement (Second) utilizes the same consumer expectation test to ascertain any kind of defect without differentiating between design, manufacturing, or warning defect. See Diamond,

---

**8.** Gray's actual ignorance or awareness of the crane's blind spot hazard would be dispositive only if an assumption of risk issue were before us. See *Alexander v. Conveyors & Dumpers, Inc.*, 731 F.2d 1221, 1223–24 (5th Cir.1984).

Levine & Madden, *Understanding Torts* § 17.04 (2nd ed. 2000); Dobbs *The Law of Torts* § 356 (2000). The new Restatement (Third), as discussed in sec. B(4), this chapter, infra, rejects the consumer expectations.

Proponents of the consumer expectation test note that it does not require plaintiffs to necessarily hire experts and technologically demonstrate a defect, but bases liability on an ordinary consumer's expectation. Critics question whether liability should be limited by consumer expectations which may be excessively low or inadequately informed. Do you agree with the result in the principal case?

Consider *Jennings v. BIC Corp.*, 181 F.3d 1250 (11th Cir.1999), where a three-year-old playing with a lighter caught his brother's pajamas on fire. Their mother sued BIC, the manufacturer, and others. Her cause of action claimed the lighter was defective (unreasonably dangerous because it was not child-proof) and thus BIC should be liable in negligence and strict products liability. The district court granted partial summary judgment, ruling that a manufacturer has no duty under Florida law to child-proof its lighters. The Eleventh Circuit affirmed, holding that the defectiveness of product design is determined in an objective sense, not the viewpoint of any specific user, such as a child. The normal public expectation, therefore, is that lighters can start fires and should be handled with care. A non-childproof lighter is not "defective" under the objective standard.

## ROYSDON v. R.J. REYNOLDS TOBACCO CO.

United States Court of Appeals, Sixth Circuit.
849 F.2d 230 (1988).

RYAN, Circuit Judge.

Floyd Roysdon began smoking "Camel" cigarettes, a product of the R.J. Reynolds Company, in 1946. In the 1960's, he switched brands to "Winston," another Reynolds product. Due to his addiction, Mr. Roysdon has been unable to stop smoking. On November 30, 1983, Mr. Roysdon had surgery on his left foot. Two surgical incisions on the foot failed to heal due to severe peripheral atherosclerotic vascular disease, and Mr. Roysdon's left leg had to be amputated below the knee. At the trial, there was testimony linking smoking to vascular disease and Mr. Roysdon's doctors testified that his vascular disease was caused by his smoking.

Thereafter, Mr. Roysdon and his wife filed this products liability action against Reynolds on July 5, 1984, in a Tennessee Circuit Court. The case was removed to the United States District Court for the Eastern District of Tennessee pursuant to 28 U.S.C. § 1441(a), based on the existence of diversity jurisdiction....

* * *

[T]he Roysdons ... alleged that Reynolds cigarettes were "defective and unreasonably dangerous due to their harmful contents...." According to the district court's opinion, the parties conceded that Tennessee law required the Roysdons to show that cigarettes were *both* defective and unreasonably dangerous, and the court applied the parties' interpretation of the law to the facts. *Roysdon*, 623 F.Supp. at 1191. Accordingly, the court directed a verdict in Reynolds' favor because the court determined that the Roysdons had failed to establish a *prima facie* case that the cigarettes were "unreasonably dangerous." Regardless of whether the parties agree upon an interpretation of the law, the district court has an independent duty to determine if that interpretation is correct.

Therefore, as a preliminary matter, we must determine whether, under Tennessee law, a products liability action will lie where the product is *either* defective or unreasonably dangerous, or only when the product is *both* defective and unreasonably dangerous. The Tennessee General Assembly enacted Public Acts of 1978, Chapter 703, § 5, which has been codified as Tenn.Code Ann. § 29–28–105(a). That section provides:

> (a) A manufacturer or seller of a product shall not be liable for any injury to person or property caused by the product unless the product is determined to be in a defective condition *or* unreasonably dangerous at the time it left the control of the manufacturer or seller.

*Id.* (emphasis added).

Prior to the enactment of § 29–28–105, Tennessee had judicially adopted § 402A of the Restatement (Second) of Torts (1966), which requires the plaintiff to prove that the product was both defective and unreasonably dangerous. *Ellithorpe v. Ford Motor Co.*, 503 S.W.2d 516 (Tenn.1973). However, it is clear from the plain language of the statute and its legislative history that the criteria for liability were intended to be read in the disjunctive ("or") rather than the conjunctive ("and")....

\* \* \*

Clearly, the Tennessee legislature intended to deviate from § 402A and allow a products liability action when the product is either defective or unreasonably dangerous.

\* \* \*

Tennessee law defines a "defective condition" as "a condition of a product that renders it unsafe for normal or anticipatable handling and consumption." Tenn.Code Ann. § 29–28–102(2). Thus, consumer knowledge about the risks inherent in the use of a product is one factor to be considered when determining if a product is defective. The normal use of cigarettes is known by ordinary consumers to present grave health risks, but that is not to say that defendant's cigarettes, when they left the hands of the manufacturer or seller, were flawed in the sense that they were "improperly manufactured" or contained "dangerous impurities." *Pemberton v. American Distilled Spirits Co.*, 664 S.W.2d 690, 692 (Tenn. 1984). Moreover, the Roysdons make no allegation and offered no proof that these cigarettes were "improperly manufactured" or contained "dangerous impurities." They claim simply that since Mr. Roysdon suffered illness that was caused by smoking the defendant's product, the product was therefore defective. But that is not the sense in which the

*Pemberton* court, speaking in the context of the consumption of an excessive amount of an alcoholic beverage, defined "defective condition."

Because the record contains no evidence whatever that the use of the defendant's cigarettes presents risks greater than those known to be associated with smoking, we find that a reasonable jury could not find that the cigarettes were defective. Therefore, unless there is a jury question with respect to whether the defendant's cigarettes are "unreasonably dangerous," the verdict in favor of Reynolds was proper.

A product is "unreasonably dangerous" if it is "dangerous to an extent beyond that which could be contemplated by the ordinary consumer who purchases it with the ordinary knowledge common to the community as to its characteristics." Tenn.Code Ann. § 29–28–102(8). According to the Supreme Court of Tennessee, this can be determined from the "knowledge of the ordinary consumers of the products." *Pemberton,* 664 S.W.2d at 692. With this in mind, the district court took judicial notice that "tobacco has been used for over 400 years and that its characteristics have also been fully explored. Knowledge that cigarette smoking is harmful to health is widespread and can be considered part of the common knowledge of the community." *Roysdon,* 623 F.Supp. at 1192. Remembering that this action was limited to the ten years preceding the filing of this complaint, we think this approach was appropriate. The extensive information regarding the risks of smoking available to the public during that time precluded the existence of a jury question as to whether cigarettes are unreasonably dangerous. We find that whether there was knowledge regarding Mr. Roysdon's specific medical problem is irrelevant in light of the serious nature of the other diseases known at that time to be caused by cigarette smoking.

For the above reasons we AFFIRM the district court's dismissal of the Roysdons' failure to warn claim and order directing a verdict in Reynolds' favor on the defective or unreasonably dangerous product issue.

### NOTES

**1. Tobacco Litigation Strategies.** As discussed in the previous principal case, Section 402A of the Restatement (Second) of Torts is not triggered if the danger inherent in the product is commonly known in the community. See Restatement (Second) of Torts § 402A cmt. i. Thus, plaintiffs alleging that a product such as cigarettes, chewing tobacco, or alcohol is defective faces the problem of proving that the dangers of these products are not commonly known. As the principal case shows, this barrier is not easily surmounted. But consider *Dewey v. R.J. Reynolds Tobacco Co.,* 121 N.J. 69, 577 A.2d 1239 (1990), in which the Supreme Court of New Jersey rejected the defendants' argument that it should not be liable for harm caused by its product since the hazards of tobacco are widely known. The court challenged the premise that the dangers of cigarette smoking are common knowledge:

> Defendants' argument completely ignores the extensive efforts of the tobacco manufacturers to saturate the public with information regarding the benefits of cigarette smoking, the aim of which is to rebut the assertions of public-health advocates and the Surgeon

General.... Public opinion surveys as well as Federal Trade Commission reports suggest that the tobacco companies' efforts at rebuttal have been successful, thus raising a material issue of fact regarding consumer awareness of the dangers of smoking.

Plaintiffs' claims against tobacco products have been strengthened by documents and testimony indicating the industry actively withheld information about the dangers of their tobacco products. Claims based on fraudulent misrepresentation, such as *New Jersey Carpenters Health Fund v. Philip Morris, Inc.* (see Chapter 1, Sec. J, supra, at page 125) have, on occasion, survived dismissal. See *Steamfitters Local Union 420 v. Philip Morris, Inc.*, 171 F.3d 912 (3d Cir. 1999), dismissing union insurance fund action against tobacco company but noting 9 out of 20 similar cases have allowed some actions against tobacco company to survive dismissal. Claims by governments and the health industry claiming economic injury based on such misrepresentations can avoid the need to prove the tobacco products "defective" and also avoid defenses, such as assumption of risk, which claims by tobacco smokers must face. Smokers may, however, claim certain information, such as the addictive nature of tobacco, may have been withheld. In addition, as noted infra Sec. B(6), defenses to strict liability are increasingly only comparative. Under what, if any, circumstances do you think tobacco products should be held defective?

## BARKER v. LULL ENGINEERING COMPANY, INC.

Supreme Court of California.

20 Cal.3d 413, 143 Cal.Rptr. 225, 573 P.2d 443 (1978).

TOBRINER, Acting Chief Justice.

In August 1970, plaintiff Ray Barker was injured at a construction site at the University of California at Santa Cruz while operating a high-lift loader manufactured by defendant Lull Engineering Co. and leased to plaintiff's employer by defendant George M. Philpott Co., Inc. Claiming that his injuries were proximately caused, inter alia, by the alleged defective design of the loader, Barker instituted the present tort action seeking to recover damages for his injuries. The jury returned a verdict in favor of defendants, and plaintiff appeals from the judgment entered upon that verdict, contending primarily that in view of this court's decision in *Cronin v. J. B. E. Olson Corp.* (1972) 8 Cal.3d 121 [104 Cal.Rptr. 433, 501 P.2d 1153], the trial court erred in instructing the jury "that strict liability for a defect in design of a product is based on a finding that the product was unreasonably dangerous for its intended use...."

As we explain, we agree with plaintiff's objection to the challenged instruction and conclude that the judgment must be reversed.

\* \* \*

As *Cronin* acknowledged, in the past decade and a half California courts have frequently recognized that the defectiveness concept defies a simple, uniform definition applicable to all sectors of the diverse product liability domain. Although in many instances—as when one machine in a million contains a cracked or broken part—the meaning of the term "defect" will require little or no elaboration, in other instances, as when a product is claimed to be defective because of an unsafe design or an inadequate warning, the contours of the defect concept may not be self-evident. In such a case a trial judge may find it necessary to explain more fully to the jury the legal meaning of "defect" or "defective." We shall explain that *Cronin* in no way precluded such elucidation of the defect concept, but rather contemplated that, in typical common law fashion, the accumulating body of product liability authorities would give guidance for the formulation of a definition.

As numerous recent judicial decisions and academic commentaries have recognized, the formulation of a satisfactory definition of "design defect" has proven a formidable task; trial judges have repeatedly confronted difficulties in attempting to devise accurate and helpful instructions in design defect cases. Aware of these problems, we have undertaken a review of the past California decisions which have grappled with the design defect issue, and have measured their conclusions against the fundamental policies which underlie the entire strict product liability doctrine.

As we explain in more detail below, we have concluded from this review that a product is defective in design either (1) if the product has failed to perform as safely as an ordinary consumer would expect when used in an intended or reasonably foreseeable manner, or (2) if, in light of the relevant factors discussed below, the benefits of the challenged design do not outweigh the risk of danger inherent in such design. In addition, we explain how the burden of proof with respect to the latter "risk-benefit" standard should be allocated.

This dual standard for design defect assures an injured plaintiff protection from products that either fall below ordinary consumer expectations as to safety, or that, on balance, are not as safely designed as they should be. At the same time, the standard permits a manufacturer who has marketed a product which satisfies ordinary consumer expectations to demonstrate the relative complexity of design decisions and the trade-offs that are frequently required in the adoption of alternative designs. Finally, this test reflects our continued adherence to the principle that, in a product liability action, the trier of fact must focus on the *product*, not on the *manufacturer's conduct*, and that the plaintiff need not prove that the manufacturer acted unreasonably or negligently in order to prevail in such an action.

1. *The facts of the present case*

Plaintiff Barker sustained serious injuries as a result of an accident which occurred while he was operating a Lull High–Lift Loader at a construction site. The loader, manufactured in 1967, is a piece of heavy construction equipment designed to lift loads of up to 5,000 pounds to a maximum height of 32 feet. The loader is 23 feet long, 8 feet wide and weighs 17,050 pounds; it sits on 4 large rubber tires which are about the height of a person's chest, and is equipped with 4–wheel drive, an automatic transmission with no park position and a hand brake. Loads are lifted by forks similar to the forks of a forklift.

The loader is designed so that the load can be kept level even when the loader is being operated on sloping terrain. The leveling of the load is controlled by a lever located near the steering column, and positioned between the operator's legs. The lever is equipped with a manual lock that can be engaged to prevent accidental slipping of the load level during lifting.

The loader was not equipped with seat belts or a roll bar. A wire and pipe cage over the driver's seat afforded the driver some protection from falling objects. The cab of the loader was located at least nine feet behind the lifting forks.

On the day of the accident the regular operator of the loader, Bill Dalton, did not report for work, and plaintiff, who had received only limited instruction on the operation of the loader from Dalton and who had operated the loader on only a few occasions, was assigned to run the loader in Dalton's place. The accident occurred while plaintiff was attempting to lift a load of lumber to a height of approximately 18 to 20 feet and to place the load on the second story of a building under construction. The lift was a particularly difficult one because the terrain on which the loader rested sloped sharply in several directions.

Witnesses testified that plaintiff approached the structure with the loader, leveled the forks to compensate for the sloping ground and lifted the load to a height variously estimated between 10 and 18 feet. During the course of the lift plaintiff felt some vibration, and, when it appeared to several coworkers that the load was beginning to tip, the workers shouted to plaintiff to jump from the loader. Plaintiff heeded these warnings and leaped from the loader, but while scrambling away he was struck by a piece of falling lumber and suffered serious injury.

Although the above facts were generally not in dispute, the parties differed markedly in identifying the responsible causes for the accident. Plaintiff contended, inter alia, that the accident was attributable to one or more design defects of the loader. Defendant, in turn, denied that the loader was defective in any respect, and claimed that the accident resulted either from plaintiff's lack of skill or from his misuse of its product. . . .

\* \* \*

2. *The trial court erred in instructing the jurors that "strict liability for a defect in design . . . is based on a finding that the product was unreasonably dangerous for its intended use."*

Plaintiff principally contends that the trial court committed prejudicial error in instructing the jury "that strict liability for a defect in design of a product is based on a finding that the product was unreasonably dangerous for its intended use. . . ."[4] Plaintiff maintains that this

---

**4.** The challenged instruction reads in full: "I instruct you that strict liability for the defect in design of a product is based on a finding that the product was unreasonably dangerous for its intended use, and in turn the unreasonableness of the danger must necessarily be derived from the state of the art at the time of the design. The manufacturer or lessor are not insurers of their products. However, an industry cannot set its own standards."

Plaintiff's challenge is limited to the portion of the instruction which provides that "strict liability for the defect in design of a product is based on a finding that the product was unreasonably dangerous for its intended use," and accordingly we express no

instruction conflicts directly with this court's decision in *Cronin*, decided subsequently to the instant trial, and mandates a reversal of the judgment. Defendants argue, in response, that our *Cronin* decision should not be applied to product liability actions which involve "design defects" as distinguished from "manufacturing defects."

The plaintiff in *Cronin*, a driver of a bread delivery truck, was seriously injured when, during an accident, a metal hasp which held the truck's bread trays in place broke, permitting the trays to slide forward and propel plaintiff through the truck's windshield. Plaintiff brought a strict liability action against the seller, contending that his injuries were proximately caused by the defective condition of the truck. Evidence at trial established that the metal hasp broke during the accident "because it was extremely porous and had a significantly lower tolerance to force than a nonflawed aluminum hasp would have had" (8 Cal.3d at p. 124), and, on the basis of this evidence, the jury returned a verdict in favor of plaintiff.

On appeal, defendant in *Cronin* argued that the trial court had erred "by submitting a definition of strict liability which failed to include, as defendant requested, the element that the defect found in the product be 'unreasonably dangerous.'" (8 Cal.3d at pp. 127–128 (fns. omitted).) Relying upon section 402A of the Restatement Second of Torts[5] and a number of California decisions which had utilized the "unreasonably dangerous" terminology in the product liability context, the defendant in *Cronin* maintained that a product's "unreasonable dangerousness" was an essential element that a plaintiff must establish in any product liability action.

\* \* \*

As we noted in *Cronin*, the Restatement draftsmen adopted the "unreasonably dangerous" language primarily as a means of confining the application of strict tort liability to an article which is "dangerous to an extent beyond that which would be contemplated by the ordinary consumer who purchases it, with the ordinary knowledge common to the community as to its characteristics." (Rest.2d Torts, § 402A, com. i.) In *Cronin*, however, we flatly rejected the suggestion that recovery in a products liability action should be permitted *only* if a product is more dangerous than contemplated by the average consumer, refusing to permit the low esteem in which the public might hold a dangerous product to diminish the manufacturer's responsibility for injuries caused by that product. As we pointedly noted in *Cronin*, even if the "ordinary consumer" may have contemplated that Shopsmith lathes posed a risk of loosening their grip and letting a piece of wood strike the operator, "another Greenman" should not be denied recovery. (8 Cal.3d at p. 133.) Indeed, our decision in *Luque v. McLean* (1972) 8 Cal.3d 136 [104 Cal.Rptr. 443, 501 P.2d 1163]—decided the same day as *Cronin*—aptly reflects our disagreement with the restrictive implications of the Restate-

opinion as to the propriety of the remaining portions of the instruction.

**5.** Section 402A provides, inter alia, that one is strictly liable in tort if he "sells any product in a defective condition unreasonably dangerous to the user or consumer or to his property...."

ment formulation, for in *Luque* we held that a power rotary lawn mower with an unguarded hole could properly be found defective, in spite of the fact that the defect in the product was patent and hence in all probability within the reasonable contemplation of the ordinary consumer.

Thus, our rejection of the use of the "unreasonably dangerous" terminology in *Cronin* rested in part on a concern that a jury might interpret such an instruction, as the Restatement draftsman had indeed intended, as shielding a defendant from liability so long as the product did not fall below the ordinary consumer's expectations as to the product's safety.[7] As *Luque* demonstrates, the dangers posed by such a misconception by the jury extend to cases involving design defects as well as to actions involving manufacturing defects: indeed, the danger of confusion is perhaps more pronounced in design cases in which the manufacturer could frequently argue that its product satisfied ordinary consumer expectations since it was identical to other items of the same product line with which the consumer may well have been familiar.

Accordingly, contrary to defendants' contention, the reasoning of *Cronin* does not dictate that that decision be confined to the manufacturing defect context. Indeed, in *Cronin* itself we expressly stated that our holding applied to design defects as well as to manufacturing defects (8 Cal.3d at pp. 134–135), and in *Henderson v. Harnischfeger Corp.* (1974) 12 Cal.3d 663, 670 [117 Cal.Rptr. 1, 527 P.2d 353], we subsequently confirmed the impropriety of instructing a jury in the language of the "unreasonably dangerous" standard in a design defect case. (See also *Foglio v. Western Auto Supply* (1976) 56 Cal.App.3d 470, 475 [128 Cal.Rptr. 545].)[8] Consequently, we conclude that the design defect instruction given in the instant case was erroneous.[9]

---

**7.** This is not to say that the expectations of the ordinary consumer are irrelevant to the determination of whether a product is defective, for as we point out below we believe that ordinary consumer expectations are frequently of direct significance to the defectiveness issue. The flaw in the Restatement's analysis, in our view, is that it treats such consumer expectations as a "ceiling" on a manufacturer's responsibility under strict liability principles, rather than as a "floor." As we shall explain, past California decisions establish that *at a minimum* a product must meet ordinary consumer expectations as to safety to avoid being found defective.

**8.** One commentator has observed that, in addition to the deficiencies in the "unreasonably dangerous" terminology noted in *Cronin*, the Restatement's language is potentially misleading because "[i]t may suggest an idea like ultrahazardous, or abnormally dangerous, and thus give rise to the impression that the plaintiff must prove that the product was unusually or extremely dangerous." (Wade, *On the Nature of Strict Tort Liability for Products* (1973) 44 Miss.L.J. 825, 832.) We agree with this crit-

icism and believe it constitutes a further reason for refraining from utilizing the "unreasonably dangerous" terminology in defining a defective product. (8 Cal.3d at p. 126.)

**9.** Indeed, the challenged instruction (see fn. 4, *ante*) was additionally erroneous because it suggested that in evaluating defectiveness, only the "intended use" of the product is relevant, rather than the product's "reasonably foreseeable use." In *Cronin*, we specifically held that the adequacy of a product must be determined in light of its reasonably foreseeable use, declaring that "[t]he design and manufacture of products should not be carried out in an industrial vacuum but with recognition of the realities of their everyday use."

Because, in the instant case, the jury may have concluded that the use of the loader by a relatively inexperienced worker was not an "intended use" of the loader, but was a "reasonably foreseeable use," this aspect of the instruction may well have prejudiced the plaintiff.

3.  *A trial court may properly formulate instructions to elucidate the "defect" concept in varying circumstances. In particular, in design defect cases, a court may properly instruct a jury that a product is defective in design if (1) the plaintiff proves that the product failed to perform as safely as an ordinary consumer would expect when used in an intended or reasonably foreseeable manner, or (2) the plaintiff proves that the product's design proximately caused injury and the defendant fails to prove, in light of the relevant factors, that on balance the benefits of the challenged design outweigh the risk of danger inherent in such design.*

\* \* \*

In *Cronin*, we reaffirmed the basic formulation of strict tort liability doctrine set forth in *Greenman*: "A manufacturer is strictly liable in tort when an article he places on the market, knowing that it is to be used without inspection for defects, proves to have a defect that causes injury to a human being. . . ." (8 Cal.3d at p. 130 (quoting 59 Cal.2d at p. 62).) We held in *Cronin* that a plaintiff satisfies his burden of proof under *Greenman*, in both a "manufacturing defect" and "design defect" context, when he proves the existence of a "defect" and that such defect was a proximate cause of his injuries. (8 Cal.3d at pp. 133–134.) In reaching this conclusion, however, *Cronin* did not purport to hold that the term "defect" must remain undefined in all contexts (see *Baker v. Chrysler Corp.* (1976) 55 Cal.App.3d 710, 715 [127 Cal.Rptr. 745]), and did not preclude a trial court from framing a definition of defect, appropriate to the circumstances of a particular case, to guide the jury as to the standard to be applied in determining whether a product is defective or not.

As this court has recognized on numerous occasions, the term defect as utilized in the strict liability context is neither self-defining nor susceptible to a single definition applicable in all contexts. In *Jiminez v. Sears, Roebuck & Co., supra*, 4 Cal.3d 379, 383, for example, we stated: "A defect may be variously defined, and as yet no definition has been formulated that would resolve all cases or that is universally agreed upon." Indeed, in *Cronin* itself, we expressly recognized "the difficulties inherent in giving content to the defectiveness standard" and suggested that the problem could best be resolved by resort to the "cluster of useful precedents" which have been developed in the product liability field in the past decade and a half. (8 Cal.3d at p. 134, fn. 16 (citing Traynor, *The Ways and Meanings of Defective Products and Strict Liability* (1965) 32 Tenn.L.Rev. 363, 373).)

Resort to the numerous product liability precedents in California demonstrates that the defect or defectiveness concept has embraced a great variety of injury-producing deficiencies, ranging from products that cause injury because they deviate from the manufacturer's intended result (e.g., the one soda bottle in ten thousand that explodes without explanation (*Escola v. Coca Cola Bottling Co.* (1944) 24 Cal.2d 453 [150 P.2d 436])), to products which, though "perfectly" manufactured, are unsafe because of the absence of a safety device (e.g., a paydozer without rear view mirrors (*Pike v. Frank G. Hough Co., supra*, 2 Cal.3d 465)), and including products that are dangerous because they lack adequate warnings or instructions (e.g., a telescope that contains inadequate instructions for assembling a "sun filter" attachment (*Midgley* v. *S. S. Kresge Co.* (1976) 55 Cal.App.3d 67 [127 Cal.Rptr. 217])).

Commentators have pointed out that in view of the diversity of product deficiencies to which the defect rubric has been applied, an instruction which requires a plaintiff to prove the existence of a product defect, but which fails to elaborate on the meaning of defect in a particular context, may in some situations prove more misleading than helpful. As Professor Wade has written: "[The] natural application [of the term 'defective'] would be limited to the situation in which something went wrong in the manufacturing process, so that the article was defective in the sense that the manufacturer had not intended it to be in that condition. To apply [the term 'defective'] also to the case in which a warning is not attached to the chattel or the design turns out to be a bad one or the product is likely to be injurious in its normal condition ... [and] [t]o use it without defining it to the jury is almost to ensure that they will be misled." (Wade, *On the Nature of Strict Tort Liability for Products, supra*, 44 Miss.L.J. 825, 831–832 (fns. omitted); see also Keeton, *Product Liability and the Meaning of Defect* (1973) 5 St. Mary's L.J. 30, 32; Hoenig, *Product Designs and Strict Tort Liability: Is There a Better Approach?* (1976) 8 Sw.U.L.Rev. 108, 118; Note (1973) 49 Wash. L.Rev. 231, 250.)

Our decision in *Cronin* did not mandate such confusion. Instead, by observing that the problem in defining defect might be alleviated by reference to the "cluster of useful precedents," we intended to suggest that in drafting and evaluating instructions on this issue in a particular case, trial and appellate courts would be well advised to consider prior authorities involving similar defective product claims.

Since the rendition of our decision in *Cronin*, a number of thoughtful Court of Appeal decisions have wrestled with the problem of devising a comprehensive definition of design defect in light of existing authorities. (See, e.g., *Hyman v. Gordon* (1973) 35 Cal.App.3d 769 [111 Cal.Rptr. 262]; *Self v. General Motors Corp.* (1974) 42 Cal.App.3d 1 [116 Cal.Rptr. 575]; *Baker* v. *Chrysler Corp., supra*, 55 Cal.App.3d 710; *Buccery v. General Motors Corp.* (1976) 60 Cal.App.3d 533 [132 Cal.Rptr. 605].) As these decisions demonstrate, the concept of defect raises considerably more difficulties in the design defect context than it does in the manufacturing or production defect context.

In general, a manufacturing or production defect is readily identifiable because a defective product is one that differs from the manufacturer's intended result or from other ostensibly identical units of the same product line. For example, when a product comes off the assembly line in a substandard condition it has incurred a manufacturing defect. (E.g., *Lewis v. American Hoist & Derrick Co.* (1971) 20 Cal.App.3d 570, 580 [97 Cal.Rptr. 798].) A design defect, by contrast, cannot be identified simply by comparing the injury-producing product with the manufacturer's plans or with other units of the same product line, since by definition the plans and all such units will reflect the same design. Rather than applying any sort of deviation-from-the-norm test in determining whether a product is defective in design for strict liability purposes, our cases have employed two alternative criteria in ascertaining, in Justice Traynor's words, whether there is something "wrong, if not in the manufacturer's manner of production, at least in his product." (Traynor, *The Ways and Meanings of Defective Products and Strict Liability, supra*, 32 Tenn.L.Rev. 363, 366.)

First, our cases establish that a product may be found defective in design if the plaintiff demonstrates that the product failed to perform as safely as an ordinary consumer would expect when used in an intended or reasonably foreseeable manner. This initial standard, somewhat analogous to the Uniform Commercial Code's warranty of fitness and merchantability (Cal.U.Com. Code, § 2314), reflects the warranty heritage upon which California product liability doctrine in part rests. As we noted in *Greenman*, "implicit in [a product's] presence on the market ... [is] a representation that it [will] safely do the jobs for which it was built." (59 Cal.2d at p. 64.) When a product fails to satisfy such ordinary consumer expectations as to safety in its intended or reasonably foreseeable operation, a manufacturer is strictly liable for resulting injuries. (*Greenman, supra*; *Pike v. Frank G. Hough Co., supra*, 2 Cal.3d 465, 477; *Hauter v. Zogarts* (1975) 14 Cal.3d 104, 121 [120 Cal.Rptr. 681, 534 P.2d 377, 74 A.L.R.3d 1282]; *Self* v. *General Motors Corp., supra*, 42 Cal. App.3d 1, 6; *Culpepper* v. *Volkswagen of America, Inc.* (1973) 33 Cal. App.3d 510, 517–518 [109 Cal.Rptr. 110]; *Van Zee v. Bayview Hardware Store* (1968) 268 Cal.App.2d 351, 361 [74 Cal.Rptr. 21].) Under this standard, an injured plaintiff will frequently be able to demonstrate the defectiveness of a product by resort to circumstantial evidence, even when the accident itself precludes identification of the specific defect at fault. (*Vandermark v. Ford Motor Co.* (1964) 61 Cal.2d 256, 260 [37 Cal.Rptr. 896, 391 P.2d 168]; *Culpepper v. Volkswagen of America, Inc., supra*, 33 Cal.App.3d at p. 518; *Elmore v. American Motors Corp.* (1969) 70 Cal.2d 578, 580–584 [75 Cal.Rptr. 652, 451 P.2d 84].)

As Professor Wade has pointed out, however, the expectations of the ordinary consumer cannot be viewed as the exclusive yardstick for evaluating design defectiveness because "[i]n many situations ... the consumer would not know what to expect, because he would have no idea how safe the product could be made." (Wade, *On the Nature of Strict Tort Liability for Products, supra*, 44 Miss.L.J. 825, 829.) Numerous California decisions have implicitly recognized this fact and have made clear, through varying linguistic formulations, that a product may be found defective in design, even if it satisfies ordinary consumer expectations, if through hindsight the jury determines that the product's design embodies "excessive preventable danger," or, in other words, if the jury finds that the risk of danger inherent in the challenged design outweighs the benefits of such design. (E.g., *Self v. General Motors Corp., supra*, 42 Cal.App.3d at p. 6; *Hyman v. Gordon, supra*, 35 Cal.App.3d at p. 773; *Buccery v. General Motors Corp., supra*, 60 Cal.App.3d at p. 547.)[10]

---

**10.** In the instant case we have no occasion to determine whether a product which entails a substantial risk of harm may be found defective even if no safer alternative

A review of past cases indicates that in evaluating the adequacy of a product's design pursuant to this latter standard, a jury may consider, among other relevant factors, the gravity of the danger posed by the challenged design, the likelihood that such danger would occur, the mechanical feasibility of a safer alternative design, the financial cost of an improved design, and the adverse consequences to the product and to the consumer that would result from an alternative design....

Although our cases have thus recognized a variety of considerations that may be relevant to the determination of the adequacy of a products design, past authorities have generally not devoted much attention to the appropriate allocation of the burden of proof with respect to these matters. (Cf. *Self v. General Motors Corp., supra,* 42 Cal.App.3d at p. 8 with *Baker v. Chrysler Corp., supra,* 55 Cal.App.3d at p. 716.) The allocation of such burden is particularly significant in this context inasmuch as this court's product liability decisions, from *Greenman* to *Cronin,* have repeatedly emphasized that one of the principal purposes behind the strict product liability doctrine is to relieve an injured plaintiff of many of the onerous evidentiary burdens inherent in a negligence cause of action. Because most of the evidentiary matters which may be relevant to the determination of the adequacy of a product's design under the "risk-benefit" standard—e.g., the feasibility and cost of alternative designs—are similar to issues typically presented in a negligent design case and involve technical matters peculiarly within the knowledge of the manufacturer, we conclude that once the plaintiff makes a prima facie showing that the injury was proximately caused by the product's design, the burden should appropriately shift to the defendant to prove, in light of the relevant factors, that the product is not defective. Moreover, inasmuch as this conclusion flows from our determination that the fundamental public policies embraced in *Greenman* dictate that a manufacturer who seeks to escape liability for an injury proximately caused by its product's design on a risk-benefit theory should bear the burden of persuading the trier of fact that its product should not be judged defective, the defendant's burden is one affecting the burden of proof, rather than simply the burden of producing evidence. (See Evid. Code, § 605; cf. *Harris v. Irish Truck Lines* (1974) 11 Cal.3d 373, 378 [113 Cal.Rptr. 489, 521 P.2d 481]; *Estate of Gelonese* (1974) 36 Cal.App.3d 854, 862 [111 Cal.Rptr. 833]; *Perales v. Dept. of Human Resources Dev.* (1973) 32 Cal.App.3d 332 [108 Cal.Rptr. 167]; *Rebmann* v. *Major* (1970) 5 Cal.App.3d 684, 688 [85 Cal.Rptr. 399].)

Thus, to reiterate, a product may be found defective in design, so as to subject a manufacturer to strict liability for resulting injuries, under either of two alternative tests. First, a product may be found defective in design if the plaintiff establishes that the product failed to perform as safely as an ordinary consumer would expect when used in an intended or reasonably foreseeable manner. Second, a product may alternatively be found defective in design if the plaintiff demonstrates that the

design is feasible. As we noted in *Jiminez v. Sears, Roebuck & Co., supra,* 4 Cal.3d 379, 383, Justice Traynor has "suggested that liability might be imposed as to products whose norm is danger." (Citing Traynor, *The Ways and Meaning of Defective Products and Strict Liability, supra,* 32 Tenn. L.Rev. 363, 367 et seq.)

product's design proximately caused his injury and the defendant fails to establish, in light of the relevant factors, that, on balance, the benefits of the challenged design outweigh the risk of danger inherent in such design.

Although past California decisions have not explicitly articulated the two-pronged definition of design defect which we have elaborated above, other jurisdictions have adopted a somewhat similar, though not identical, dual approach in attempting to devise instructions to guide the jury in design defect cases. (See, e.g., *Henderson v. Ford Motor Co.* (Tex. 1974) 519 S.W.2d 87, 92; *Welch* v. *Outboard Marine Corporation* (5th Cir. 1973) 481 F.2d 252, 254.) As we have indicated, we believe that the test for defective design set out above is appropriate in light of the rationale and limits of the strict liability doctrine, for it subjects a manufacturer to liability whenever there is something "wrong" with a product's design—either because the product fails to meet ordinary consumer expectations as to safety or because, on balance, the design is not as safe as it should be—while stopping short of making the manufacturer an insurer for all injuries which may result from the use of its product. This test, moreover, explicitly focuses the trier of fact's attention on the adequacy of the product itself, rather than on the manufacturer's conduct, and places the burden on the manufacturer, rather than the plaintiff, to establish that because of the complexity of, and trade-offs implicit in, the design process, an injury-producing product should nevertheless not be found defective.

\* \* \*

Finally, contrary to the suggestion of amicus CTLA, an instruction which advises the jury that it may evaluate the adequacy of a product's design by weighing the benefits of the challenged design against the risk of danger inherent in such design is not simply the equivalent of an instruction which requires the jury to determine whether the manufacturer was negligent in designing the product. (See, e.g., Wade, *On the Nature of Strict Tort Liability for Products, supra*, 44 Miss.L.J. 825, 835.) It is true, of course, that in many cases proof that a product is defective in design may also demonstrate that the manufacturer was negligent in choosing such a design. As we have indicated, however, in a strict liability case, as contrasted with a negligent design action, the jury's focus is properly directed to the condition of the product itself, and not to the reasonableness of the manufacturer's conduct. (See, e.g., *Ault* v. *International Harvester Co.* (1974) 13 Cal.3d 113, 121 [117 Cal.Rptr. 812, 528 P.2d 1148, 74 A.L.R.3d 986]; *Escola v. Coca Cola Bottling Co., supra*, 24 Cal.2d 453, 462 (Traynor, J. conc.).)

Thus, the fact that the manufacturer took reasonable precautions in an attempt to design a safe product or otherwise acted as a reasonably prudent manufacturer would have under the circumstances, while perhaps absolving the manufacturer of liability under a negligence theory, will not preclude the imposition of liability under strict liability principles if, upon hindsight, the trier of fact concludes that the product's design is unsafe to consumers, users, or bystanders. (See *Foglio* v. *Western Auto Supply, supra*, 56 Cal.App.3d 470, 477.)

### 4. *Conclusion*

The technological revolution has created a society that contains dangers to the individual never before contemplated. The individual must face the threat to life and limb not only from the car on the street or highway but from a massive array of hazardous mechanisms and products. The radical change from a comparatively safe, largely agricultural, society to this industrial unsafe one has been reflected in the decisions that formerly tied liability to the fault of a tortfeasor but now are more concerned with the safety of the individual who suffers the loss. As Dean Keeton has written, "The change in the substantive law as regards the liability of makers of products and other sellers in the marketing chain has been from fault to defect. The plaintiff is no longer required to impugn the maker, but he is required to impugn the product." (Keeton, *Product Liability and the Meaning of Defect* (1973) 5 St. Mary's L.J. 30, 33.)

If a jury in determining liability for a defect in design is instructed only that it should decide whether or not there is "a defective design," it may reach to the extreme conclusion that the plaintiff, having suffered injury, should without further showing, recover; on the other hand, it may go to the opposite extreme and conclude that because the product matches the intended design the plaintiff, under no conceivable circumstance, could recover. The submitted definition eschews both extremes and attempts a balanced approach.

We hold that a trial judge may properly instruct the jury that a product is defective in design (1) if the plaintiff demonstrates that the product failed to perform as safely as an ordinary consumer would expect when used in an intended or reasonably foreseeable manner, or (2) if the plaintiff proves that the product's design proximately caused his injury and the defendant fails to prove, in light of the relevant factors discussed above, that on balance the benefits of the challenged design outweigh the risk of danger inherent in such design.

Because the jury may have interpreted the erroneous instruction given in the instant case as requiring plaintiff to prove that the high-lift loader was ultrahazardous or more dangerous than the average consumer contemplated, and because the instruction additionally misinformed the jury that the defectiveness of the product must be evaluated in light of the product's "intended use" rather than its "reasonably foreseeable use" (see fn. 9, *ante*), we cannot find that the error was harmless on the facts of this case. In light of this conclusion, we need not address plaintiff's additional claims of error, for such issues may not arise on retrial.

The judgment in favor of defendants is reversed.

### *NOTES*

**1. Risk–Utility Replacing Consumer Expectations Tests.** The modern trend among American courts is towards allowing recovery using the risk-utility test instead of the consumer expectations test. This is true even of courts that do not follow the *Barker* approach of allowing plaintiffs to use either theory. A primary rationale of moving away from the consumer expectations test is that consumers often do not know what to expect in terms of the hazards associated with a product. Indeed, in *Soule v. General Motors Corp.*, 8 Cal.4th 548, 34 Cal.Rptr.2d 607, 882 P.2d 298 (1994), the Supreme Court of California held that, where an evaluation of defectiveness involves complex technical information, the plaintiff may not rely on the consumer expectations prong of *Barker* and must only use the risk/utility prong to establish defectiveness. *Soule* concerned an evaluation of whether an automobile was defective where a collision caused the front wheel to detach and move rearward, smashing the floorboards against the driver's feet. But, consider also *McCabe v. American Honda Motor Co.*, 100 Cal. App.4th 1111, 123 Cal.Rptr.2d 303 (2002), where the Court of Appeals reversed a granting of summary judgment based on a finding that the consumer expectation test was barred in a case where the driver's side airbag failed to deploy in a collision. The court held that "whether a product is within the ordinary experience of every day consumers and thus suscepti-ble to consumer expectation, analysis cannot be looked at in isolation but rather must be considered in the context of the facts surrounding its failure. The critical question is whether the circumstances of the products failure permit an inference that the products design performed below the legitimate commonly accepted minimum safety assumptions of its ordinary consum-ers." Noting that "at a minimum, triable issues of the fact as to the circumstances of the accident preclude a determination that the consumer expectation test of design defect is inapplicable as a matter of law" the court held that a jury could conclude that the airbag failed to meet common expectation as to its safety. In light of the increasing complexity of technolo-gy, which approach to evaluating defectiveness makes the most sense?

The risk versus benefit test evaluates the product's design in light of a variety of factors including cost, and the gravity of danger. In *Cepeda v. Cumberland Engineering Co., Inc.*, 76 N.J. 152, 386 A.2d 816 (1978), the New Jersey Supreme Court endorsed Professor Wade's listing of factors to be evaluated in balancing the risk versus benefit of a product design:

(1) The usefulness and desirability of the product—its utility to the user and to the public as a whole.

(2) The safety aspects of the product—the likelihood that it will cause injury, and the probable seriousness of the injury.

(3) The availability of a substitute product which would meet the same need and not be as unsafe.

(4) The manufacturer's ability to eliminate the unsafe charac-ter of the product without impairing its usefulness or making it too expensive to maintain its utility.

(5) The user's ability to avoid danger by the exercise of care in the use of the product.

(6) The user's anticipated awareness of the dangers inherent in the product and their avoidability, because of general public knowl-edge of the obvious condition of the product, or of the existence of suitable warnings or instructions.

(7) The feasibility, on the part of the manufacturer, of spread-ing the loss by setting the price of the product or carrying liability insurance.

See also Wade, *On the Nature of Strict Liability for Products*, 44 Miss. L.J. 825 (1973); Dobbs, *The Law of Torts* § 361 (2000).

2. **Test for Manufacturing Defect and Warning Defect.** While the Restatement (Second) of Torts § 402A, consumer expectation test for product defects under strict product liability, does not delineate between different types of defects, the principal case does. While the risk versus benefit or consumer expectation test is applied to design defects, a manufacturing defect is characterized as when a product is different than its ostensibly similar units. Is it useful to have different tests to ascertain different types of defects? In practice, manufacturing defects are not difficult to identify under whatever test is utilized. Even a five-year-old at his birthday party will quickly identify a manufacturing defect among the toys given him based on his knowledge of what the toy is supposed to look like. Identifying design defects is more complex since the entire product line is alleged to be wrongly conceived.

Warning defects are most often subject to the same analysis as design defects since, in most instances, they reflect on an intentional manufacturer decision on what information should be provided with all the products. Warning defects are considered further in the next principal case, infra.

3. **Comparing Strict Product Liability and Negligence.** The court in the principal case devotes considerable effort attempting to distinguish strict product liability from liability for products under ordinary negligence. Is the court's reasoning persuasive? Negligence focuses on the behavior of the defendants. Strict product liability focuses on whether the product is defective. How does the principal case's risk versus benefit mechanism for evaluating whether a product is defectively designed differ significantly from whether the designer of the product unreasonably designed the product? Will the results be identical for the manufacturer who is responsible for the design under negligence but different for wholesalers and retailers who cannot be held accountable under negligence for the manufacturer's poor design decisions (at least in the absence of reasonable notice that they are selling a defective product)?

Traditionally the defenses to strict product liability differed from defenses to negligence, but as discussed infra in this section in *Daly v. General Motors Corp.* at page 573, the distinctions in defenses are increasingly being eliminated. While the principal case shifts the burden and requires the defendant under the *Barber* test to prove the benefits of the design outweigh the risks in a strict product liability, most courts utilizing a risk-benefit analysis to determine design defect do not.

Strict product liability and negligence liability for product defects are more easily distinguishable for manufacturing as opposed to design defects. Under negligence, the manufacturer is only responsible for construction errors which are the result of negligent construction procedures and quality controls. The wholesaler and retailer, in the absence of notice of potential defects, would rarely be held negligent. Under strict product liability any manufacturing defect would lead to liability to all the sellers (manufacturer through retailer) in the chain of distribution.

4. **State of the Art.** One question left unresolved in the principal case is whether a product should be evaluated based on the technology available at the time of manufacture or the technology and knowledge available at the time of trial. The issue is considered further in the next principal case.

**5. Firearms and Products Liability.** Plaintiffs have tried suing handgun manufacturers on product liability theories, but have found difficulty in proving a "defect." See, e.g., *Perkins v. F.I.E. Corp.*, 762 F.2d 1250 (5th Cir.1985). Another approach has been to allege that the manufacture and distribution of handguns constitutes a public nuisance. See Butterfield, *Chicago is Suing Over Guns for Suburbs*, N.Y. Times, Nov. 13, 1998 at A16. For materials on nuisance, see Chapter 4, infra.

Do you agree that manufacturers of dangerous but legal products should be held liable for negligent marketing? Consider *Moning v. Alfono*, 400 Mich. 425, 254 N.W.2d 759 (1977) where the court reversed a directed verdict against a plaintiff alleging that slingshot manufacturers were negligent for marketing slingshots directly to children. In *Moning*, the plaintiff, a child, was blinded in one eye from a pellet shot from his playmate's slingshot. Reconsider *Kelley v. R.G. Industries, Inc.*, 304 Md. 124, 497 A.2d 1143 (1985), discussed at page 511, supra, where the court rejected characterizing the selling of guns as an abnormally dangerous activity. Do you agree that handguns are not "defective" and, therefore, there is no liability under strict product liability?

As acknowledged in *Whitfield v. Heckler and Koch, Inc.*, 98 Cal.Rptr.2d 820 (2000), Section 1714.4 of California Civil Code prevents the balancing test for products liability developed in *Barker* from being applied to firearms, providing specifically that "in a products liability action, no firearm or ammunition shall be deemed defective in design on the basis that the benefits of the product do not outweigh the risk of injury posed by its potential to cause serious injury, damage, or death when discharged." As a result, the court in this case was barred from evaluating the plaintiff's argument that the guns used in a bank heist were defective in design sine there was no lawful purpose or reason for being as powerful, or discharging as rapidly as they did.

# BESHADA v. JOHNS–MANVILLE PRODUCTS CORP.

Supreme Court of New Jersey.
90 N.J. 191, 447 A.2d 539 (1982).

PASHMAN, J.

The sole question here is whether defendants in a product liability case based on strict liability for failure to warn may raise a "state of the art" defense. Defendants assert that the danger of which they failed to warn was undiscovered at the time the product was marketed and that it was undiscoverable given the state of scientific knowledge at that time. The case comes to us on appeal from the trial court's denial of plaintiffs' motion to strike the state-of-the-art defense. For the reasons stated below, we reverse the trial court judgment and strike the defense.

I

These six consolidated cases are personal injury and wrongful death actions brought against manufacturers and distributors of asbestos products. Plaintiffs are workers, or survivors of deceased workers, who claim to have been exposed to asbestos for varying periods of time. They allege that as a result of that exposure they contracted asbestosis (a non-malignant scarring of the lungs), mesothelioma (a rare cancer of the lining of the chest, the pleura, or the lining of the abdomen, the peritoneum) and other asbestos-related illnesses.

These cases involve asbestos exposure dating back perhaps as far as the 1930's. The suits are first arising now because of the long latent period between exposure and the discernible symptoms of asbestosis and mesothelioma. See *Borel v. Fibreboard Paper Products Corporation*, 493 *F.*2d 1076, 1083 (5th Cir. 1973). Plaintiffs have raised a variety of legal theories to support their claims for damages. The important claim, for purposes of this appeal, is strict liability for failure to warn. Prior to the 1960's, defendants' products allegedly contained no warning of their hazardous nature. Defendants respond by asserting the state-of-the-art defense. They allege that no one knew or could have known that asbestos was dangerous when it was marketed.

There is substantial factual dispute about what defendants knew and when they knew it. A trial judge in the Eastern District of Texas, the forum for numerous asbestos-related cases, has concluded that "[k]nowledge of the danger can be attributed to the industry as early as the mid–1930's...." *Hardy v. Johns–Manville Sales Corp.*, 509 *F.Supp.* 1352, 1355 (E.D.Texas 1981) (footnote omitted). Defendants respond, however, that it was not until the 1960's that the medical profession in the United States recognized that a potential health hazard arose from the use of insulation products containing asbestos. Before that time, according to defendants, the danger from asbestos was believed limited to workers in asbestos textile mills, who were exposed to much higher concentrations of asbestos dust than were the workers at other sites, such as shipyards. Defendants claim that it was not discovered until recently that the much smaller concentrations those workers faced were also hazardous.

We need not resolve the factual issues raised. For purposes of plaintiffs' motion to strike the defense, we assume the defendants' version of the facts. The issue is whether the medical community's presumed unawareness of the dangers of asbestos is a defense to plaintiffs' claims.

\* \* \*

### III

Our inquiry starts with the principles laid down in *Freund v. Cellofilm Properties, Inc., supra, Suter v. San Angelo Foundry & Machine Company, supra*, and *Cepeda v. Cumberland Engineering Company, Inc.*, 76 *N.J.* 152, 386 *A.*2d 816 (1978). In *Suter*, we summarized the principle of strict liability as follows:

> If at the time the seller distributes a product, it is not reasonably fit, suitable and safe for its intended or reasonably foreseeable purposes so that users or others who may be expected to come in contact with the product are injured as a result thereof, then the seller shall be responsible for the ensuing damages. [*Id.* at 169, 406 *A.*2d 140 (footnote omitted)]

The determination of whether a product is "reasonably fit, suitable and safe" depends on a comparison of its risks and its utility (risk-utility equation).

Central to this theory is the risk-utility equation for determining liability. The theory is that only safe products should be marketed—a safe product being one whose utility outweighs its inherent risk, provided that risk has been reduced to the greatest extent possible consistent with the product's continued utility. [*Freund*, 87 *N.J.* at 238, n.1, 432 *A.*2d 925]

In *Cepeda*, we explained that in the context of design defect liability, strict liability is identical to liability for negligence, with one important caveat: "The only qualification is as to the requisite of foreseeability by the manufacturer of the dangerous propensity of the chattel manifested at the trial—this being imputed to the manufacturer." *Cepeda*, 76 *N.J.* at 172, 386 *A.*2d 816. *See Freund v. Cellofilm Properties, Inc.*, 87 *N.J.* at 239, 439 *A.*2d 925. In so holding, we adopted the explication of strict liability offered by Dean Wade:

> The time has now come to be forthright in using a tort way of thinking and tort terminology [in cases of strict liability in tort]. There are several ways of doing it, and it is not difficult. The simplest and easiest way, it would seem, is to assume that the defendant knew of the dangerous condition of the product and ask whether he was then negligent in putting it on the market or supplying it to someone else. In other words, the scienter is supplied as a matter of law, and there is no need for the plaintiff to prove its existence as a matter of fact. Once given this notice of the dangerous condition of the chattel, the question then becomes whether the defendant was negligent to people who might be harmed by that condition if they came into contact with it or were in the vicinity of it. Another way of saying this is to ask whether the magnitude of the risk created by the dangerous condition of the product was outweighed by the social utility attained by putting it out in this fashion. [Wade, "On the Nature of Strict Tort Liability for Products," 44 *Miss.L.J.* 825, 834–35 (1973), quoted in *Cepeda*, 76 *N.J.* at 172, 386 *A.*2d 816]

Stated differently, negligence is conduct-oriented, asking whether defendant's actions were reasonable; strict liability is product-oriented, asking whether the product was reasonably safe for its foreseeable purposes. *Freund*, 87 *N.J.* at 238, 432 *A.*2d 925.[3]

"Warning" cases constitute one category of strict liability cases. Their relation to the strict liability principles set forth above can best be analyzed by focusing on the definition of safe products found in footnote 1 of *Freund*. *See supra* at 544. For purposes of analysis, we can

---

**3.** The imputation of knowledge is, of course, a legal fiction. It is another way of saying that for purposes of strict liability the defendant's knowledge of the danger is irrelevant. *See Freund v. Cellofilm Products, Inc.*, 87 *N.J.* at 239, 432 *A.*2d 925, quoting Keeton, "Products Liability—Inadequacy of Information," 48 *Tex.L.Rev.* 398, 407–08 (1970). The imputation of knowledge does not represent any presumption that defendants knew or even that they could have known of the product's dangers.

distinguish two tests for determining whether a product is safe: (1) does its utility outweigh its risk? and (2) if so, has that risk been reduced to the greatest extent possible consistent with the product's utility? *Id.* at 238, n. 1, 432 A.2d 925. The first question looks to the product as it was in fact marketed. If that product caused more harm than good, it was not reasonably fit for its intended purposes. We can therefore impose strict liability for the injuries it caused without having to determine whether it could have been rendered safer. The second aspect of strict liability, however, requires that the risk from the product be reduced to the greatest extent possible without hindering its utility. Whether or not the product passes the initial risk-utility test, it is not reasonably safe if the same product could have been made or marketed more safely.[4]

Warning cases are of this second type.[5] When plaintiffs urge that a product is hazardous because it lacks a warning, they typically look to the second test, saying in effect that regardless of the overall cost-benefit calculation the product is unsafe because a warning could make it safer at virtually no added cost and without limiting its utility. *Freund* recognized this, noting that in cases alleging "an inadequate warning as to safe use, the utility of the product, as counter-balanced against the risks of its use, is rarely at issue." *Id.* at 242, 432 A.2d 925.

*Freund* is our leading case on strict liability for failure to warn. In *Freund*, Justice Handler applied the principles set forth above, initially laid down in *Suter* and *Cepeda*, to warning cases. The issue there was whether there is any difference between negligence and strict liability in warning cases. We stated unequivocally that there is. That difference is the same difference that we noted in *Suter* and *Cepeda* concerning other design defect cases:

> when a plaintiff sues under strict liability, there is no need to prove that the manufacturer knew or should have known of any dangerous propensities of its product—such knowledge is imputed to the manufacturer. [*Freund v. Cellofilm Properties, Inc.*, 87 N.J. at 239, 432 A.2d 925]

Thus, we held in *Freund* that it was reversible error for the trial judge to instruct the jury only with a negligence charge.

With these basic principles of design defect strict liability in New Jersey as our framework for analysis, we turn now to a discussion of the state-of-the-art defense.

---

**4.** This dichotomy is created only for purposes of analysis, because it will help explain the role of state-of-the-art in strict liability cases. In actuality, the only test for product safety is whether the benefit outweighs the risk. However, in calculating the benefit from any product, one must consider alternate products that can yield the same benefit at lower risk. Wade, 44 *Miss. L.J.* at 837–38.

**5.** This two-part distinction can best be clarified by looking at how it would apply to automobiles without seatbelts. Because of the great utility of cars, few would dispute that even without seatbelts, a car's utility to society outweighs its risks. Thus, cars would be considered safe under the first aspect of the test. However, since seatbelts make cars safer without hindering utility, cars without seatbelts are deemed unsafe by virtue of the second part of the *Freund* test. Warnings are like seatbelts: regardless of the utility and risk of a product without warnings, a warning can generally be added without diminishing utility. *Freund v. Cellofilm Properties, Inc.*, 87 N.J. at 238–39, n. 1, 432 A.2d 925.

IV

As it relates to warning cases, the state-of-the-art defense asserts that distributors of products can be held liable only for injuries resulting from dangers that were scientifically discoverable at the time the product was distributed. Defendants argue that the question of whether the product can be made safer must be limited to consideration of the available technology at the time the product was distributed. Liability would be absolute, defendants argue, if it could be imposed on the basis of a subsequently discovered means to make the product safer since technology will always be developing new ways to make products safer. Such a rule, they assert, would make manufacturers liable whenever their products cause harm, whether or not they are reasonably fit for their foreseeable purposes.

Defendants conceptualize the scientific unknowability of the dangerous propensities of a product as a technological barrier to making the product safer by providing warnings. Thus, a warning was not "possible" within the meaning of the *Freund* requirement that risk be reduced "to the greatest extent possible."

In urging this position, defendants must somehow distinguish the *Freund* holding that knowledge of the dangers of the product is imputed to defendants as a matter of law. A state-of-the-art defense would contravene that by requiring plaintiffs to prove at least that knowledge of the dangers was scientifically available at the time of manufacture.

Defendants argue that *Freund* did not specify precisely what knowledge is imputed to defendants. They construe *Freund* to impute only that degree of knowledge of the product's dangerousness that existed at the time of manufacture or distribution.

While we agree that *Freund* did not explicitly address this question, the principles laid down in *Freund* and our prior cases contradict defendants' position. Essentially, state-of-the-art is a negligence defense. It seeks to explain why defendants are not culpable for failing to provide a warning. They assert, in effect, that because they could not have known the product was dangerous, they acted reasonably in marketing it without a warning. But in strict liability cases, culpability is irrelevant. The product was unsafe. That it was unsafe because of the state of technology does not change the fact that it was unsafe. Strict liability focuses on the product, not the fault of the manufacturer. "If the conduct is unreasonably dangerous, then there should be strict liability without reference to what excuse defendant might give for being unaware of the danger." Keeton, 48 *Tex.L.Rev.* at 408.

When the defendants argue that it is unreasonable to impose a duty on them to warn of the unknowable, they misconstrue both the purpose and effect of strict liability. By imposing strict liability, we are not requiring defendants to have done something that is impossible. In this sense, the phrase "duty to warn" is misleading. It implies negligence concepts with their attendant focus on the reasonableness of defendant's behavior. However, a major concern of strict liability—ignored by defendants—is the conclusion that if a product was in fact defective, the distributor of the product should compensate its victims for the misfortune that it inflicted on them.

If we accepted defendants' argument, we would create a distinction among fact situations that defies common sense. Under the defendants' reading of *Freund*, defendant would be liable for failure to warn if the danger was knowable even if defendants were not negligent in failing to discover it. Defendants would suffer no liability, however, if the danger was undiscoverable. But, as Dean Keeton explains,

> if a defendant is to be held liable for a risk that is discoverable by some genius but beyond the defendant's capacity to do so, why should he not also be liable for a risk that was just as great but was not discoverable by anyone? [Keeton, 48 *Tex.L.Rev.* at 409]

We are buttressed in our conclusion that the state-of-the-art defense is inconsistent with *Freund* by the recent decision of Judge Ackerman in *Marcucci v. Johns–Manville Sales Corp.*, Nos. 76–414, 76–604 and 76–1510 (D.N.J. Feb. 19, 1982), in which he applied New Jersey law to strike defendants' state-of-the-art-defense.

The most important inquiry, however, is whether imposition of liability for failure to warn of dangers which were undiscoverable at the time of manufacture will advance the goals and policies sought to be achieved by our strict liability rules. We believe that it will.

*Risk Spreading.* One of the most important arguments generally advanced for imposing strict liability is that the manufacturers and distributors of defective products can best allocate the costs of the injuries resulting from it. The premise is that the price of a product should reflect all of its costs, including the cost of injuries caused by the product. This can best be accomplished by imposing liability on the manufacturer and distributors. Those persons can insure against liability and incorporate the cost of the insurance in the price of the product. In this way, the costs of the product will be borne by those who profit from it: the manufacturers and distributors who profit from its sale and the buyers who profit from its use. "It should be a cost of doing business that in the course of doing that business an unreasonable risk was created." Keeton, 48 *Tex.L.Rev.* at 408. *See* Prosser, *The Law of Torts*, § 75, p. 495 (4th Ed. 1971).

Defendants argue that this policy is not forwarded by imposition of liability for unknowable hazards. Since such hazards by definition are not predicted, the price of the hazardous product will not be adjusted to reflect the costs of the injuries it will produce. Rather, defendants state, the cost "will be borne by the public at large and reflected in a general, across the board increase in premiums to compensate for unanticipated risks." There is some truth in this assertion, but it is not a bad result.

First, the same argument can be made as to hazards which are deemed scientifically knowable but of which the manufacturers are unaware. Yet it is well established under our tort law that strict liability is imposed even for defects which were unknown to the manufacturer. It is precisely the imputation of knowledge to the defendant that distinguishes strict liability from negligence. *Freund*, 87 *N.J.* at 240, 432 *A.2d* 925. Defendants advance no argument as to why risk spreading works better for unknown risks than for unknowable risks.

Second, spreading the costs of injuries among all those who produce, distribute and purchase manufactured products is far preferable to imposing it on the innocent victims who suffer illnesses and disability from defective products. This basic normative premise is at the center of our strict liability rules. It is unchanged by the state of scientific knowledge at the time of manufacture.

Finally, contrary to defendants' assertion, this rule will not cause the price and production level of manufactured products to diverge from the so-called economically efficient level. Rather, the rule will force the price of any particular product to reflect the cost of insuring against the possibility that the product will turn out to be defective.

*Accident Avoidance.* In *Suter*, we stated:

> Strict liability in a sense is but an attempt to minimize the costs of accidents and to consider who should bear those costs. *See* the discussion in Calabresi & Hirschoff, "Toward a Test for Strict Liability in Torts," 81 *Yale L.J.* 1055 (1972), in which the authors suggest that the strict liability issue is to decide which party is the 'cheapest cost avoider' or who is in the best position to make the cost-benefit analysis between accident costs and accident avoidance costs and to act on that decision once it is made. *Id.* at 1060. Using this approach, it is obvious that the manufacturer rather than the factory employee is 'in the better position both to judge whether avoidance costs would exceed foreseeable accident costs and to act on that judgment.' *Id.*
> [*Suter v. San Angelo Foundry*, 81 *N.J.* at 173–74, 406 *A.2d* 140]

Defendants urge that this argument has no force as to hazards which by definition were undiscoverable. Defendants have treated the level of technological knowledge at a given time as an independent variable not affected by defendants' conduct. But this view ignores the important role of industry in product safety research. The "state-of-the-art" at a given time is partly determined by how much industry invests in safety research. By imposing on manufacturers the costs of failure to discover hazards, we create an incentive for them to invest more actively in safety research.

*Fact finding process.* The analysis thus far has assumed that it is possible to define what constitutes "undiscoverable" knowledge and that it will be reasonably possible to determine what knowledge was technologically discoverable at a given time. In fact, both assumptions are highly questionable. The vast confusion that is virtually certain to arise from any attempt to deal in a trial setting with the concept of scientific knowability constitutes a strong reason for avoiding the concept altogether by striking the state-of-the-art defense.

Scientific knowability, as we understand it, refers not to what in fact was known at the time, but to what *could have been* known at the time. In other words, even if no scientist had actually formed the belief that asbestos was dangerous, the hazards would be deemed "knowable" if a scientist could have formed that belief by applying research or performing tests that were available at the time. Proof of what could have been known will inevitably be complicated, costly, confusing and time-consuming. Each side will have to produce experts in the history of science and technology to speculate as to what knowledge was feasible in a given year. We doubt that juries will be capable of even understanding the concept of scientific knowability, much less be able to resolve such a complex issue. Moreover, we should resist legal rules that will so greatly add to the costs both sides incur in trying a case.

The concept of knowability is complicated further by the fact, noted above, that the level of investment in safety research by manufacturers is one determinant of the state-of-the-art at any given time. Fairness suggests that manufacturers not be excused from liability because their prior inadequate investment in safety rendered the hazards of their product unknowable. Thus, a judgment will have to be made as to whether defendants' investment in safety research in the years preceding distribution of the product was adequate. If not, the experts in the history of technology will have to testify as to what would have been knowable at the time of distribution if manufacturers had spent the proper amount on safety in prior years. To state the issue is to fully understand the great difficulties it would engender in a courtroom.

In addition, discussion of state-of-the-art could easily confuse juries into believing that blameworthiness is at issue. Juries might mistakenly translate the confused concept of state-of-the-art into the simple question of whether it was defendants' fault that they did not know of the hazards of asbestos. But that would be negligence, not strict liability.

For precisely this reason, Professor Keeton has urged that negligence concepts be carefully avoided in strict liability cases.

> My principal thesis is and has been that theories of negligence should be avoided altogether in the products liability area in order to simplify the law, and that if the sale of a product is made under circumstances that would subject someone to an unreasonable risk in fact, liability for harm resulting from those risks should follow. [Keeton, 48 *Tex.L.Rev.* at 409 (footnote omitted)]

This Court has expressed the same concern in *Freund*, reversing the trial court's jury charge because the "terminology employed by the trial judge was riddled with references to negligence, knowledge and reasonable care on the part of a manufacturer." 87 *N.J.* at 243, 432 *A.2d* 925. "[W]e must be concerned with the effect of the trial judge's articulation upon the jury's deliberative processes." *Id.* at 244, 432 *A.2d* 925.

## V

For the reasons expressed above, we conclude that plaintiffs' position is consistent with our holding in *Freund* and prior cases and will achieve the various policies underlying strict liability. The burden of illness from dangerous products such as asbestos should be placed upon those who profit from its production and, more generally, upon society at large, which reaps the benefits of the various products our economy manufactures. That burden should not be imposed exclusively on the innocent victim. Although victims must in any case suffer the pain involved, they should be spared the burdensome financial consequences of unfit products. At the same time, we believe this position will serve the salutary goals of increasing product safety research and simplifying tort trials.

Defendants have argued that it is unreasonable to impose a duty on them to warn of the unknowable. Failure to warn of a risk which one could not have known existed is not unreasonable conduct. But this argument is based on negligence principles. We are not saying what defendants should have done. That is negligence. We are saying that defendants' products were not reasonably safe because they did not have a warning. Without a warning, users of the product were unaware of its hazards and could not protect themselves from injury. We impose strict liability because it is unfair for the distributors of a defective product not to compensate its victims. As between those innocent victims and the distributors, it is the distributors—and the public which consumes their products—which should bear the unforeseen costs of the product.

The judgment of the trial court is reversed; the plaintiff's motion to strike the state-of-the-art defense is granted.

### NOTES

**1. Warnings.** A strong argument in favor of warnings is that they afford consumers safety at little cost to manufacturers. Parties may differ as to what constitutes a sufficient warning. The inquiry may include analysis of the nature of the harm to be warned against and how the warning is communicated. See Diamond, Levine & Madden, *Understanding Torts* § 17.05 (2nd ed. 2000) and Dobbs, *The Law of Torts*, §§ 363–368 (2000).

See *Young v. Elmira Transit Mix, Inc.*, 52 A.D.2d 202, 383 N.Y.S.2d 729 (N.Y.App.Div.1976), where a man working on his cellar floor came in physical contact with wet cement supplied by the defendant. A chemical in the cement caused the man serious burns, and he sued the manufacturer on a theory of products liability. The plaintiff's contention was that defendant could reasonably foresee that the cement was dangerous if used as intended, but that defendant had failed to provide adequate warnings. The jury awarded the plaintiff damages, and the appellate court affirmed, noting that the defendant had knowledge of the need to use protective clothing, but had not warned the plaintiff.

Consider *Johnson v. Johnson Chemical Co., Inc.*, 183 A.D.2d 64, 588 N.Y.S.2d 607 (N.Y.App.Div.1992), where a woman spraying her kitchen with roach spray negligently failed to read the manufacturer's warning not to use the product near a pilot light. When her kitchen exploded, she brought a products liability suit against the defendant. The court ruled that a manufacturer may be held liable for failure to warn of hazards which may follow from use of the product in some abnormal way when it is proved that abnormal use of the product was reasonably foreseeable. The court focused on the intensity of the warning and the prominence of the label as factors to consider in determining adequacy of the warning.

As courts continue to hold manufacturers liable for failure to warn, manufacturers can be expected to increase their use of warnings. Indeed, consider the following warning attached to a Batman costume marketed for children: "Warning: This Batman cape will not allow wearer to fly." Morse, *Life May Be Hazardous to Your Health*, S.F. Examiner, Feb. 26, 1999 at A2. See also Henderson & Twerski, *Doctrinal Collapse in Products Liability: The Empty Shell of Failure to Warn*, 65 N.Y.U. L. Rev. 265 (1990).

Under a risk versus benefit analysis, the cost of a warning is so nominal, it is tempting, within reason, for juries to fault a product for not providing one against a hazard some potential consumer may not anticipate. But also consider *Mazda Motor of America, Inc. v. Rogowksi,* 105 Md.App. 318, 659 A.2d 391 (1995), where a man fell asleep at the wheel of his pickup truck and hit a tree at approximately 30 miles per hour. He sued the manufacturer, alleging that the seat belt restraint system was defective and unreasonably dangerous, and that the manufacturer should have warned him that the seat belt would not protect him from injury in an accident. At trial, the jury found no defect in design or manufacture, but held the defendant liable for failure to warn, awarding damages to the plaintiff. The appellate court reversed, holding that the manufacturer did not owe a duty to warn because the risk about which the plaintiff complained was open and obvious. The court noted that strict liability would not attach because persons of ordinary intelligence could be expected to know that a seat belt could not absolutely protect the occupants of a vehicle from injury, no matter how well it was designed and made.

Should warnings be written in languages other than English when the product's marketed consumers include many non-English-speaking users in the United States? In *Ramirez v. Plough, Inc.,* 6 Cal.4th 539, 25 Cal.Rptr.2d 97, 863 P.2d 167 (1993), the court held only English was required for an aspirin that had been marketed in part with Spanish language advertisements. See Dobbs, supra, at § 364, noting that other decisions have supported the use of universal warning symbols to accommodate nonreaders.

**2. State-of-the Art Defense.** Although the Supreme Court of New Jersey rejected the state-of-the-art defense in *Beshada*, it later held, in *Feldman v. Lederle Laboratories*, 97 N.J. 429, 479 A.2d 374 (N.J. 1984), that the defense would be allowed in other contexts. In *Feldman* the plaintiff suffered unanticipated tooth discoloration after taking a drug manufactured by the defendant. Consider also *Fischer v. Johns–Manville Corp.,* 103 N.J. 643, 512 A.2d 466 (1986) where New Jersey held that "a defendant's knowledge, or state of knowledge, although inadmissible for a claim of compensatory damages on a theory of strict liability, could be admissible on a claim for punitive damages." See for example *Carlin v. Superior Court* 13 Cal.4th 1104, 56 Cal.Rptr.2d 162, 920 P.2d 1347 (1996), where the California Supreme Court held in relation to prescription drugs that "the manufacturer should bear the cost, in terms of preventable injury or death, of its own failure to provide adequate warnings of known or reasonable scientifically knowable risks." Conversely, no liability should be imposed where the danger alleged was unknowable based on the then present state of scientific knowledge. This is consistent with the majority trend, which is to allow the state-of-the-art defense.

**3. Unavoidably Unsafe Products.** Certain products are necessarily dangerous and cannot be made any safer for their intended use. The

Restatement (Second) of Torts § 402A, cmt. k, supports this position and negates any consumer expectation to the contrary. Drugs, such as vaccines with occasional side effects, most often are included in this category. In jurisdictions using the risk/utility approach to determining if a product is defective, the utility of such products must be high enough to outweigh the irreducible danger. Additionally, although the product itself cannot be made safer, there will typically be a need to include an appropriate warning with the product. The Restatement (Third) of Torts: Products Liability (1998), discussed in this chapter at (B)(4), infra, also concludes a specific provision addressing prescription drugs and medical devices. Section 6(d) provides that drugs and medical devices are not defective as long as they are sufficiently therapeutic to justify a reasonable health provider, knowing its foreseeable risks, to prescribe the drug or device for any class of patient. See Diamond, Levine & Madden, supra, § 17.05 and Dobbs, supra, § 365.

4. **Strict Liability in Special Contexts.** Although the focus of the preceding cases and notes has been on products acquired through sales (see Note 3 at page 528, supra), most courts allow strict liability recovery in cases against commercial lessors, bailors and licensors. Professionally provided services, on the other hand, are generally not permitted to be the subject strict liability suits. Blood products are also usually barred by special statutes from giving rise to strict liability claims. The rationale for such "blood shield" statutes tends to focus on the public interest in protecting blood banks from excessive liability. Consider *Weishorn v. Miles–Cutter*, 721 A.2d 811 (Pa. Super. Ct. 1998), where a woman with a blood disorder was a regular recipient of platelet transfusions. Hospitalized in 1992, she intravenously received a plasma preparation manufactured by the defendant. Not long after, she was diagnosed with the Hepatitis–B and Hepatitis–C viruses. She brought suit for strict liability, negligence, and breach of implied warranty. The defendant filed a motion for summary judgment. The negligence claim was dismissed by the trial court, and the applicable blood shield statute was held to bar the strict liability and warranty claims. The court noted two types of blood shield statutes: one characterizing blood-related transactions as rendering a service (not a sale) and thus protected from strict liability, and the other a broader statute granting immunity to those involved with blood transfusion or handling blood products. The court held that under the second type of statute, even a commercial supplier of blood products is protected from such claims because of the overwhelming public policy considerations and the fact that no test can guarantee that the product is absolutely safe. See Diamond, Levine & Madden, § 17.04, supra and Dobbs, supra, §§ 375–476.

### 3.   Federal Pre–Emption

## RIEGEL v. MEDTRONIC, INC.

Supreme Court of the United States.

—— U.S. ——, 128 S.Ct. 999 (2008).

Judge Scalia delivered the opinion of the Court.

### I

### A

The Federal Food, Drug, and Cosmetic Act (FDCA), 52 Stat. 1040, as amended, 21 U.S.C. § 301 *et seq.*, has long required FDA approval for the introduction of new drugs into the market. Until the statutory enactment at issue here, however, the introduction of new medical devices was left largely for the States to supervise as they saw fit. See *Medtronic, Inc. v. Lohr,* 518 U.S. 470, 475–476, 116 S.Ct. 2240, 135 L.Ed.2d 700 (1996).

The regulatory landscape changed in the 1960's and 1970's, as complex devices proliferated and some failed. Most notably, the Dalkon Shield intrauterine device, introduced in 1970, was linked to serious infections and several deaths, not to mention a large number of pregnancies. Thousands of tort claims followed. R. Bacigal, The Limits of Litigation: The Dalkon Shield Controversy 3 (1990). In the view of many, the Dalkon Shield failure and its aftermath demonstrated the inability of the common-law tort system to manage the risks associated with dangerous devices. See, *e.g.,* S. Foote, Managing the Medical Arms Race 151–152 (1992). Several States adopted regulatory measures, including California, which in 1970 enacted a law requiring premarket approval of medical devices. 1970 Cal. Stats. ch. 1573, §§ 26670–26693; see also Leflar & Adler, The Preemption Pentad: Federal Preemption of Products Liability Claims After Medtronic, 64 Tenn. L.Rev. 691, 703, n. 66 (1997) (identifying 13 state statutes governing medical devices as of 1976).

Congress stepped in with passage of the Medical Device Amendments of 1976(MDA), 21 U.S.C. § 360c et seq., which swept back some state obligations and imposed a regime of detailed federal oversight. The MDA includes an express pre-emption provision that states:

"Except as provided in subsection (b) of this section, no State or political subdivision of a State may establish or continue in effect with respect to a device intended for human use any requirement—

"(1) which is different from, or in addition to, any requirement applicable under this chapter to the device, and

"(2) which relates to the safety or effectiveness of the device or to any other matter included in a requirement applicable to the device under this chapter." § 360k(a).

The exception contained in subsection (b) permits the FDA to exempt some state and local requirements from pre-emption.

The new regulatory regime established various levels of oversight for medical devices, depending on the risks they present. Class I, which includes such devices as elastic bandages and examination gloves, is subject to the lowest level of oversight: "general controls," such as labeling requirements. § 360c(a)(1)(A); FDA, Device Advice: Device Classes, http://www.fda.gov/cdrh/devadvice/3132. html (all Internet materials as visited Feb. 14, 2008, and available in Clerk of Court's case file). Class II, which includes such devices as powered wheelchairs and surgical drapes, *ibid.,* is subject in addition to "special controls" such as performance standards and postmarket surveillance measures, § 360c(a)(1)(B).

The devices receiving the most federal oversight are those in Class III, which include replacement heart valves, implanted cerebella stimulators, and pacemaker pulse generators, FDA, Device Advice: Device

Classes, *supra*. In general, a device is assigned to Class III if it cannot be established that a less stringent classification would provide reasonable assurance of safety and effectiveness, and the device is "purported or represented to be for a use in supporting or sustaining human life or for a use which is of substantial importance in preventing impairment of human health," or "presents a potential unreasonable risk of illness or injury." § 360c(a)(1)(C)(ii).

Although the MDA established a rigorous regime of premarket approval for new Class III devices, it grandfathered many that were already on the market. Devices sold before the MDA's effective date may remain on the market until the FDA promulgates, after notice and comment, a regulation requiring premarket approval. §§ 360c(f)(1), 360e(b)(1). A related provision seeks to limit the competitive advantage grandfathered devices receive. A new device need not undergo premarket approval if the FDA finds it is "substantially equivalent" to another device exempt from premarket approval. § 360c(f)(1)(A). The agency's review of devices for substantial equivalence is known as the § 510(k) process, named after the section of the MDA describing the review. Most new Class III devices enter the market through § 510(k). In 2005, for example, the FDA authorized the marketing of 3,148 devices under § 510(k) and granted premarket approval to just 32 devices. P. Hutt, R. Merrill, & L. Grossman, Food and Drug Law 992 (3d ed.2007).

Premarket approval is a "rigorous" process. *Lohr,* 518 U.S., at 477, 116 S.Ct. 2240. A manufacturer must submit what is typically a multivolume application. FDA, Device Advice–Premarket Approval (PMA) 18, http://www.fda.gov/cdrh/devadvice/pma/printer.html. It includes, among other things, full reports of all studies and investigations of the device's safety and effectiveness that have been published or should reasonably be known to the applicant; a "full statement" of the device's "components, ingredients, and properties and of the principle or principles of operation"; "a full description of the methods used in, and the facilities and controls used for, the manufacture, processing, and, when relevant, packing and installation of, such device"; samples or device components required by the FDA; and a specimen of the proposed labeling. § 360e(c)(1). Before deciding whether to approve the application, the agency may refer it to a panel of outside experts, 21 CFR § 814.44(a)(2007), and may request additional data from the manufacturer, § 360e(c)(1)(G).

The FDA spends an average of 1,200 hours reviewing each application, *Lohr, supra,* at 477, 116 S.Ct. 2240, and grants premarket approval only if it finds there is a "reasonable assurance" of the device's "safety and effectiveness," § 360e(d). The agency must "weig[h] any probable benefit to health from the use of the device against any probable risk of injury or illness from such use." § 360c(a)(2)(C). It may thus approve devices that present great risks if they nonetheless offer great benefits in light of available alternatives. It approved, for example, under its Humanitarian Device Exemption procedures, a ventricular assist device for children with failing hearts, even though the survival rate of children using the device was less than 50 percent. FDA, Center for Devices and

Radiological Health, Summary of Safety and Probable Benefit 20 (2004), online at http://www.fda.gov/cdrh/pdf3/H030003b.pdf.

The premarket approval process includes review of the device's proposed labeling. The FDA evaluates safety and effectiveness under the conditions of use set forth on the label, § 360c(a)(2)(B), and must determine that the proposed labeling is neither false nor misleading, § 360e(d)(1)(A).

After completing its review, the FDA may grant or deny premarket approval. § 360e(d). It may also condition approval on adherence to performance standards, 21 CFR § 861.1(b)(3), restrictions upon sale or distribution, or compliance with other requirements, § 814.82. The agency is also free to impose device-specific restrictions by regulation. § 360j(e)(1).

\* \* \*

Once a device has received premarket approval, the MDA forbids the manufacturer to make, without FDA permission, changes in design specifications, manufacturing processes, labeling, or any other attribute, that would affect safety or effectiveness. § 360e(d)(6)(A)(i). If the applicant wishes to make such a change, it must submit, and the FDA must approve, an application for supplemental premarket approval, to be evaluated under largely the same criteria as an initial application. § 360e(d)(6); 21 CFR § 814.39(c).

After premarket approval, the devices are subject to reporting requirements. § 360i. These include the obligation to inform the FDA of new clinical investigations or scientific studies concerning the device which the applicant knows of or reasonably should know of, 21 CFR § 814.84(b)(2), and to report incidents in which the device may have caused or contributed to death or serious injury, or malfunctioned in a manner that would likely cause or contribute to death or serious injury if it recurred, § 803.50(a). The FDA has the power to withdraw premarket approval based on newly reported data or existing information and must withdraw approval if it determines that a device is unsafe or ineffective under the conditions in its labeling. § 360e(e)(1); see also § 360h(e) (recall authority).

### B

\* \* \*

Charles Riegel underwent coronary angioplasty in 1996, shortly after suffering a myocardial infarction. App. to Pet. for Cert. 56a. His right coronary artery was diffusely diseased and heavily calcified. Riegel's doctor inserted the Evergreen Balloon Catheter into his patient's coronary artery in an attempt to dilate the artery, although the device's labeling stated that use was contraindicated for patients with diffuse or calcified stenoses. The label also warned that the catheter should not be inflated beyond its rated burst pressure of eight atmospheres. Riegel's doctor inflated the catheter five times, to a pressure of 10 atmospheres; on its fifth inflation, the catheter ruptured. Complaint 3. Riegel developed a heart block, was placed on life support, and underwent emergency coronary bypass surgery.

Riegel and his wife Donna brought this lawsuit in April 1999, in the United States District Court for the Northern District of New York. Their complaint alleged that Medtronic's catheter was designed, labeled, and manufactured in a manner that violated New York common law, and that these defects caused Riegel to suffer severe and permanent injuries. The complaint raised a number of common-law claims. The District Court held that the MDA pre-empted Riegel's claims of strict liability; breach of implied warranty; and negligence in the design, testing, inspection, distribution, labeling, marketing, and sale of the catheter. App. to Pet. for Cert. 68a; Complaint 3–4. It also held that the MDA pre-empted a negligent manufacturing claim insofar as it was not premised on the theory that Medtronic violated federal law. App. to Pet. for Cert. 71a. Finally, the court concluded that the MDA pre-empted Donna Riegel's claim for loss of consortium to the extent it was derivative of the pre-empted claims. *Id.,* at 68a; see also *id.,* at 75a.[1]

* * *

## II

Since the MDA expressly pre-empts only state requirements "different from, or in addition to, any requirement applicable . . . to the device" under federal law, § 360k(a)(1), we must determine whether the Federal Government has established requirements applicable to Medtronic's catheter. If so, we must then determine whether the Riegels' common-law claims are based upon New York requirements with respect to the device that are "different from, or in addition to" the federal ones, and that relate to safety and effectiveness. § 360k(a).

We turn to the first question. In *Lohr,* a majority of this Court interpreted the MDA's pre-emption provision in a manner "substantially informed" by the FDA regulation set forth at 21 CFR § 808.1(d). 518 U.S., at 495, 116 S.Ct. 2240; see also *id.,* at 500–501, 116 S.Ct. 2240. That regulation says that state requirements are pre-empted "only when the Food and Drug Administration has established specific counterpart regulations or there are other specific requirements applicable to a particular device. . . ." 21 CFR § 808.1(d). Informed by the regulation, we concluded that federal manufacturing and labeling requirements applicable across the board to almost all medical devices did not pre-empt the common-law claims of negligence and strict liability at issue in *Lohr.* The federal requirements, we said, were not requirements specific to the device in question—they reflected "entirely generic concerns about device regulation generally." 518 U.S., at 501, 116 S.Ct. 2240. While we disclaimed a conclusion that general federal requirements could never pre-empt, or general state duties never be pre-empted, we

---

**1.** The District Court later granted summary judgment to Medtronic on those claims of Riegel it had found not pre-empted, viz., that Medtronic breached an express warranty and was negligent in manufacturing because it did not comply with federal standards. App. to Pet. for Cert. 90a. It consequently granted summary judgment as well on Donna Riegel's derivative consortium claim. *Ibid.* The Court of Appeals affirmed these determinations, and they are not before us.

held that no pre-emption occurred in the case at hand based on a careful comparison between the state and federal duties at issue. *Id.,* at 500–501, 116 S.Ct. 2240.

Even though substantial-equivalence review under § 510(k) is device specific, *Lohr* also rejected the manufacturer's contention that § 510(k) approval imposed device-specific "requirements." We regarded the fact that products entering the market through § 510(k) may be marketed only so long as they remain substantial equivalents of the relevant pre–1976 devices as a qualification for an exemption rather than a requirement. *Id.,* at 493–494, 116 S.Ct. 2240; see also *id.,* at 513, 116 S.Ct. 2240 (O'Connor, J., concurring in part and dissenting in part).

Premarket approval, in contrast, imposes "requirements" under the MDA as we interpreted it in *Lohr.* Unlike general labeling duties, premarket approval is specific to individual devices. And it is in no sense an exemption from federal safety review-it *is* federal safety review. Thus, the attributes that *Lohr* found lacking in § 510(k) review are present here. While § 510(k) is " 'focused on *equivalence,* not safety,' " *id.,* at 493, 116 S.Ct. 2240 (opinion of the Court), premarket approval is focused on safety, not equivalence. While devices that enter the market through § 510(k) have "never been formally reviewed under the MDA for safety or efficacy," *ibid.,* the FDA may grant premarket approval only after it determines that a device offers a reasonable assurance of safety and effectiveness, § 360e(d). And while the FDA does not " 'require' " that a device allowed to enter the market as a substantial equivalent "take any particular form for any particular reason," *ibid.,* at 493, 116 S.Ct. 2240, the FDA requires a device that has received premarket approval to be made with almost no deviations from the specifications in its approval application, for the reason that the FDA has determined that the approved form provides a reasonable assurance of safety and effectiveness.

### III

We turn, then, to the second question: whether the Riegels' common-law claims rely upon "any requirement" of New York: law applicable to the catheter that is "different from, or in addition to" federal requirements and that "relates to the safety or effectiveness of the device or to any other matter included in a requirement applicable to the device." § 360k(a). Safety and effectiveness are the very subjects of the Riegels' common-law claims, so the critical issue is whether New York's tort duties constitute "requirements" under the MDA.

### A

In *Lohr,* five Justices concluded that common-law causes of action for negligence and strict liability do impose "requirement[s]" and would be pre-empted by federal requirements specific to a medical device. See 518 U.S., at 512, 116 S.Ct. 2240 (opinion of O'Connor, J., joined by Rehnquist, C. J., and Scalia and Thomas, JJ.); *id.,* at 503–505, 116 S.Ct. 2240 (opinion of Breyer, J.). We adhere to that view. * * *

Congress is entitled to know what meaning this Court will assign to terms regularly used in its enactments. Absent other indication, reference to a State's "requirements" includes its common-law duties. As the plurality opinion said in *Cipollone,* common-law liability is "premised on the existence of a legal duty," and a tort judgment therefore establishes that the defendant has violated a state-law obligation. *Id.,* at 522, 112 S.Ct. 2608. And while the common-law remedy is limited to damages, a liability award " 'can be, indeed is designed to be, a potent method of governing conduct and controlling policy.' " *Id.,* at 521, 112 S.Ct. 2608.

In the present case, there is nothing to contradict this normal meaning. To the contrary, in the context of this legislation excluding common-law duties from the scope of pre-emption would make little sense. State tort law that requires a manufacturer's catheters to be safer, but hence less effective, than the model the FDA has approved disrupts the federal scheme no less than state regulatory law to the same effect. Indeed, one would think that tort law, applied by juries under a negligence or strict-liability standard, is less deserving of preservation. A state statute, or a regulation adopted by a state agency, could at least be expected to apply cost-benefit analysis similar to that applied by the experts at the FDA: How many more lives will be saved by a device which, along with its greater effectiveness, brings a greater risk of harm? A jury, on the other hand, sees only the cost of a more dangerous design, and is not concerned with its benefits; the patients who reaped those benefits are not represented in court. As Justice Breyer explained in *Lohr,* it is implausible that the MDA was meant to "grant greater power (to set state standards 'different from, or in addition to' federal standards) to a single state jury than to state officials acting through state administrative or legislative lawmaking processes." 518 U.S., at 504, 116 S.Ct. 2240. That perverse distinction is not required or even suggested by the broad language Congress chose in the MDA, and we will not turn somersaults to create it.

\* \* \*

## IV

State requirements are pre-empted under the MDA only to the extent that they are "different from, or in addition to" the requirements imposed by federal law. § 360k(a)(1). Thus, § 360k does not prevent a State from providing a damages remedy for claims premised on a violation of FDA regulations; the state duties in such a case "parallel," rather than add to, federal requirements. *Lohr,* 518 U.S., at 495, 116 S.Ct. 2240; see also *id.,* at 513, 116 S.Ct. 2240 (O'Connor, J., concurring in part and dissenting in part). The District Court in this case recognized that parallel claims would not be pre-empted, see App. to Pet. for Cert. 70a–71a, but it interpreted the claims here to assert that Medtronic's device violated state tort law notwithstanding compliance with the relevant federal requirements, see *id.,* at 68a. Although the Riegels now argue that their lawsuit raises parallel claims, they made no such contention in their briefs before the Second Circuit, nor did they raise this argument in their petition for certiorari. We decline to address that argument in the first instance here.

\* \* \*

For the foregoing reasons, the judgment of the Court of Appeals is *Affirmed.*

## NOTE

Do you agree that when a federal agency specifically approves a product design, state tort law actions asserting design defects based on negligence and strict product liability should be preempted? Do you agree with the Supreme Court that products substantially similar to Federal Drug Administration(FDA) approved medical products should not be immune from state tort law determination of a design defect? Do torts or government regulations provide the best approach to insuring safe products? Should Congress enact federal products liability law to replace state products liability law for all nationally distributed products?

### 4. Restatement (Third) of Torts: Products Liability: A Proposed Consolidated Theory of Liability

## POTTER v. CHICAGO PNEUMATIC TOOL CO.

Supreme Court of Connecticut.
241 Conn. 199, 694 A.2d 1319 (1997).

KATZ, Associate Justice.

This appeal arises from a products liability action brought by the plaintiffs against the defendants, Chicago Pneumatic Tool Company (Chicago Pneumatic), Stanley Works and Dresser Industries, Inc. (Dresser). The plaintiffs claim that they were injured in the course of their employment as shipyard workers at the General Dynamics Corporation Electric Boat facility (Electric Boat) in Groton as a result of using pneumatic hand tools manufactured by the defendants. Specifically, the plaintiffs allege that the tools were defectively designed because they exposed the plaintiffs to excessive vibration, and because the defendants failed to provide adequate warnings with respect to the potential danger presented by excessive vibration.

The defendants appeal from the judgment rendered on jury verdicts in favor of the plaintiffs. . . .

\* \* \*

Although courts have widely accepted the concept of strict tort liability, some of the specifics of strict tort liability remain in question. In particular, courts have sharply disagreed over the appropriate definition of defectiveness in design cases. As the Alaska Supreme Court has stated: "Design defects present the most perplexing problems in the field of strict products liability because there is no readily ascertainable external measure of defectiveness. While manufacturing flaws can be evaluated against the intended design of the product, no such objective standard exists in the design defect context." *Caterpillar Tractor Co. v. Beck,* 593 P.2d 871, 880 (Alaska 1979).

\* \* \*

The defendants propose that it is time for this court to abandon the consumer expectation standard and adopt the requirement that the plaintiff must prove the existence of a reasonable alternative design in order to prevail on a design defect claim. We decline to accept the defendants' invitation.

In support of their position, the defendants point to the second tentative draft of the Restatement (Third) of Torts: Products Liability (1995) (Draft Restatement [Third]), which provides that, as part of a plaintiff's prima facie case, the plaintiff must establish the availability of a reasonable alternative design. Specifically, § 2(b) of the Draft Restatement (Third) provides: "[A] product is defective in design when the foreseeable risks of harm posed by the product could have been reduced or avoided by the adoption of a reasonable alternative design by the seller or other distributor, or a predecessor in the commercial chain of distribution, and the omission of the alternative design renders the product not reasonably safe." The reporters to the Draft Restatement (Third) state that "[v]ery substantial authority supports the proposition that [the] plaintiff must establish a reasonable alternative design in order for a product to be adjudged defective in design." Draft Restatement (Third), *supra*, § 2, reporters' note to comment (c), p. 50.

We point out that this provision of the Draft Restatement (Third) has been a source of substantial controversy among commentators. See, e.g., J. Vargo, "The Emperor's New Clothes: The American Law Institute Adorns a 'New Cloth' for Section 402A Products Liability Design Defects—A Survey of the States Reveals a Different Weave," 26 U.Mem. L.Rev. 493, 501 (1996) (challenging reporters' claim that Draft Restatement (Third)'s reasonable alternative design requirement constitutes "consensus" among jurisdictions); P. Corboy, "The Not-So–Quiet Revolution: Rebuilding Barriers to Jury Trial in the Proposed Restatement (Third) of Torts: Products Liability," 61 Tenn.L.Rev. 1043, 1093 (1994) ("[t]he decisional support for [the reasonable alternative design requirement], however, appears to be overstated by the Reporters, who claim that [eighteen] states support the rule"); F. Vandall, "The Restatement (Third) of Torts: Products Liability Section 2(b): The Reasonable Alternative Design Requirement," 61 Tenn.L.Rev. 1407, 1428 (1994) ("The centerpiece of the Restatement (Third) of Torts: Products Liability is the requirement that the plaintiff present evidence of a reasonable alternative design as part of her prima facie case. This requirement is not supported by the majority of the jurisdictions that have considered the question."). Contrary to the rule promulgated in the Draft Restatement (Third), our independent review of the prevailing common law reveals that the majority of jurisdictions *do not* impose upon plaintiffs an absolute requirement to prove a feasible alternative design.

In our view, the feasible alternative design requirement imposes an undue burden on plaintiffs that might preclude otherwise valid claims from jury consideration. Such a rule would require plaintiffs to retain an expert witness even in cases in which lay jurors can infer a design defect from circumstantial evidence. . . .

Moreover, in some instances, a product may be in a defective condition unreasonably dangerous to the user even though no feasible alternative design is available. In such instances, the manufacturer may be strictly liable for a design defect notwithstanding the fact that there are no safer alternative designs in existence. See, e.g., *O'Brien v. Muskin Corp.*, 94 N.J. 169, 184, 463 A.2d 298 (1983) ("other products, including some for which no alternative exists, are so dangerous and of such little use that ... a manufacturer would bear the cost of liability of harm to others"); *Wilson v. Piper Aircraft Corp.*, 282 Or. 61, 71 n. 5, 577 P.2d 1322 (1978) ("Our holding should not be interpreted as a requirement that [the practicability of a safer alternative design] must in all cases weigh in [the] plaintiff's favor before the case can be submitted to the jury. There might be cases in which the jury would be permitted to hold the defendant liable on account of a dangerous design feature even though no safer design was feasible (or there was no evidence of a safer practicable alternative)."); *Sumnicht v. Toyota Motor Sales, U.S.A., Inc.*, 121 Wis.2d 338, 371, 360 N.W.2d 2 (1984) ("[a] product may be defective and unreasonably dangerous even though there are no alternative, safer designs available"). Accordingly, we decline to adopt the requirement that a plaintiff must prove a feasible alternative design as a sine qua non to establishing a prima facie case of design defect.

\* \* \*

### NOTES

**1. Restatement (Third) of Torts Approach.** The approach of the Restatement (Third) of Torts is to consolidate theories of recovery (negligence, warranty, strict products liability) into one unified approach:

> One engaged in the business of selling or otherwise distributing products who sells or distributes a defective product is subject to liability for harm to persons or property caused by the defect.

Restatement (Third) of Torts: Products Liability § 1 (1998). The focus is on defects, which continue to be divided into one of the three traditional categories:

> A product is defective when, at the time of sale or distribution, it contains a manufacturing defect, is defective in design, or is defective because of inadequate instructions or warnings. A product:
>
> (a) contains a manufacturing defect when the product departs from its intended design even though all possible care was exercised in the preparation and marketing of the product;
>
> (b) is defective in design when the foreseeable risks of harm posed by the product could have been reduced or avoided by the adoption of a reasonable alternative design by the seller or other distributor, or a predecessor in the commercial chain of distribution, and the omission of the alternative design renders the product not reasonably safe;
>
> (c) is defective because of inadequate instructions or warnings when the foreseeable risks of harm posed by the product could have been reduced or avoided by the provision of reasonable instructions or warnings by the seller or other distributor, or a

predecessor in the commercial chain of distribution, and the omission of the instructions or warnings renders the product not reasonably safe.

Restatement (Third) of Torts: Products Liability § 2 (1998).

**2. Consolidation of Theories.** Currently plaintiffs in a product liability action would ordinarily bring claims based on negligence, warranty theories, and strict product liability. The Restatement (Third) of Torts advocates consolidating the different theories into the product liability action. Do you think there is any value in maintaining distinct theories?

**3. Restatement (Third) Controversial Positions.** As § 1(b) of the Restatement (Third) quoted above in Note 1 indicates, a product is defective only if there are foreseeable risks that could not be avoided by a reasonable alternative design. This effectively allows the state-of-art technology at the time of manufacture to be a defense. More dramatically, the Restatement (Third) requires that there be a reasonable alternative design for the product to be deemed defective. The Restatement (Third) cites firearms and above ground swimming pools as products that cannot be found defective unless a safer alternative design is feasible. Critics note that, under ordinary negligence, liability for a product design does not require proof of an alternative design to find the product is unreasonably dangerous. Consequently, Restatement (Third) eliminates design strict product liability with a new approach even more onerous to plaintiffs than ordinary negligence. See, e.g., Vandall, *The Restatement (Third) of Torts: Product Liability Section 2(b): The Reasonable Alternative Design*, 61 Tenn. L.Rev. 1407 (1994). The Restatement (Third) does include an exception for "manifestly dangerous" unreasonable designs (e.g., a toy pellet gun) for which no alternative design may be possible. (See Restatement (Third) of Products Liability § 2, cmt. e, and § 360). See Dobbs, *The Law of Torts* § 361 (2000). Is the requirement of an alternative reasonable design an appropriate requirement? How does such a requirement impact on efforts to find firearms or tobacco defective?

## 5. Types of Recoverable Damages

### TWO RIVERS COMPANY v. CURTISS BREEDING SERVICE

United States Court of Appeals, Fifth Circuit.
624 F.2d 1242 (1980).

THORNBERRY, Circuit Judge.

This action was brought by Two Rivers Company (Two Rivers), alleging that it purchased from Hi–Pro Feeds, Inc. (Hi–Pro) semen used for artificial insemination of its cattle, and that the semen caused syndactylism in the offspring of its cattle. The semen was marketed by Curtiss Breeding Service, Division of Searle Agriculture, Inc. (Curtiss). Two Rivers' claim for damages against Curtiss and Hi–Pro is based on the doctrines of strict liability and implied warranty.

This appeal arises from a jury verdict in favor of Two Rivers. The jury apparently found that Curtiss was strictly liable for the sale of defective semen and that Curtiss breached its implied warranty of merchantability. The jury also found that Two Rivers was entitled to damages in the sum of $52,900.00. This amount represents the damage to the reputation of Two Rivers' herd of cattle as computed by the loss of the prospective market value of the cattle. The court entered judgment for plaintiff in the amount found by the jury and denied Curtiss's motion for judgment notwithstanding the verdict. We hold that, under Texas law, the district court erred in that Two Rivers is not entitled to a recovery of damages based on either strict liability or implied warranty.

Curtiss markets semen around the world that is used to artificially inseminate cattle. Because federal regulations prohibit direct importation of certain bulls into the United States, Curtiss maintains its bulls in other countries and imports semen into the United States. The process of artificial insemination allows one sire to artificially inseminate thousands of cattle in its lifetime while a bull in natural service can sire no more than 125–150 offspring in the same span of time. These techniques allow a breeder access to many different bulls without incurring the cost of maintaining a large number of bulls.

Curtiss markets the semen of many different breeds of cattle, including the Chianina breed. In 1972, Curtiss entered into an agreement with a Canadian firm to market in the United States the semen from a Chianina bull known as Farro AC–35. . . .

\* \* \*

### TYPES OF LOSS

The critical question presented in this case is whether Two Rivers is entitled to an award of damages pursuant to section 402A of the Restatement (Second) of Torts, the implied warranties of the Uniform Commercial Code, or under both theories. To analyze this issue, it is necessary to distinguish the four types of property loss which are recognized in Texas. A different legal analysis attaches to each type of loss.

The first type of loss involves personal injury to the user (or consumer) or physical injury to the property of the user (or consumer). It is specifically covered by the language of section 402A of the Restatement (Second) of Torts which states that. . . .

\* \* \*

The second type of loss, on the complete opposite end of the spectrum, can be classified as economic loss resulting from a product with defective workmanship or materials. This category of loss was examined in *Nobility Homes of Texas v. Shivers*, 557 S.W.2d 77 (Tex. 1977), where an individual who purchased a mobile home sought to recover damages for economic loss suffered as the result of defects in the product. The mobile home was negligently constructed and was not fit for the purposes for which it was sold. The consumer was awarded $8,750 as the difference between the purchase price and the market value of the mobile home for his economic loss.

The court held in *Nobility Homes* that an individual may not recover for economic loss under section 402A. The court stated that an individual must instead seek damages under the implied warranties of the Uniform Commercial Code and the theory of common law negligence. Strict liability was not extended to instances of economic loss because the distinction that exists between physical damage and commercial loss had to be recognized. The Uniform Commercial Code governs the case of a mere loss of value resulting from the failure of the product to perform according to the contractual bargain and the expectations of the consumer.

A third type of loss consists of "economic loss to the purchased product itself." *Mid Continent Aircraft Corp. v. Curry County Spraying Service*, 572 S.W.2d 308 (Tex.1978). In *Mid Continent Aircraft*, plaintiff sought damages for physical injury to an airplane (damage to fuselage and wings) and for loss of its use value when it made a forced landing because an individual negligently failed to install a crankshaft gear bolt lock plate. Noting that the explicit language of section 402A applied only to physical harm to a person or his other property, the court stated that in a commercial sale, strict liability should not be extended to cover a loss resulting from damage to the product itself. The court stated that "when no physical injury has occurred to persons or other property, injury to the defective product itself is an economic loss governed by the Uniform Commercial Code." 572 S.W.2d at 313. This is because the damage to the product is merely a loss to the purchaser of the benefit of the bargain with the seller.

The fourth type of loss is a hybrid involving physical harm to a plaintiff's other property as well as to the product itself. This fact pattern was presented in *Signal Oil* where a defective isomax reactor charge heater exploded. The explosion and ensuing fire at Signal Oil's Houston refinery destroyed not only the heater, but also a significant portion of the refinery (other property). It is clear that the damage to the refinery presents a strict liability cause of action under section 402A since a buyer is entitled to recover for damage to his other property. But the court went even further and held that:

> [W]here such collateral property damage exists in addition to damage to the product itself, recovery for such damages are recoverable under Section 402A of the Restatement (Second) of Torts as damage to property or under the Texas Business and Commerce Code, Section 2.715, as consequential damages for a breach of an implied warranty. To the extent that the product itself has become part of the accident risk or the tort by causing collateral property damage, it is properly considered as part of the property damages, rather than as economic loss. 572 S.W.2d at 325 (emphasis added).

Therefore, if both the product and other property are damaged, a plaintiff has a cause of action under strict liability and the U.C.C.

### STRICT LIABILITY

Two Rivers asserts a cause of action based on the doctrine of strict liability against Curtiss, alleging that Curtiss sold a genetically defective product that was unreasonably dangerous. Two Rivers sought damages for the loss of the market value of the entire herd and for the value of the four calves born with syndactylism. In assessing Two Rivers' claim, the herd of calves must be divided into two groups: a group composed of those calves that received a gene for syndactyl from Farro semen (including the four syndactyl calves) and a second group composed of those calves that were not artificially inseminated with Farro semen.

Only 22 of the 98 calves born alive were the product of Farro's semen. Two Rivers claims that it is entitled to damages equal to the reduction in the market value of the 76 non-Farro calves (the second group) because of the stigma caused by having as many as 22 carriers in the herd.

After an examination of the controlling Texas case law, it is clear that Two Rivers has not stated a cause of action under strict liability with respect to the second group of calves. If anything, any damage incurred upon discovering and making publicly known a latent physical defect in the herd of one-half blood Chianina heifers purchased by Two Rivers constitutes economic loss governed by the rules of commercial law. A plaintiff in Texas is precluded from recovering for economic loss under strict liability.

First, it is obvious that this injury does not come within either the first or fourth category of loss, discussed *supra*, each of which provides for recovery under the doctrine of strict liability. There was obviously no physical injury to any of the 76 calves merely because the other 22 calves were artificially inseminated with Farro semen. Second, a decrease in market value can best be described as an intangible commercial loss. Keeton, Private Law Torts, 25 S.W.L.J. 1 (1971)....

With respect to the first group of calves (artificially inseminated with Farro semen), the question is much more difficult. These calves were either born with a syndactyly gene or were possible carriers of syndactylism. The damage suffered by Two Rivers does not fit neatly into any one of the four categories discussed above.

On the one hand, it could be argued that this case presents a situation merely involving injury to the product itself. Therefore, it would only involve economic loss governed by *Mid Continent* and the U.C.C....

On the other hand, it could just as easily be argued that the product (bull semen) is a constituent part of a new product (the calf) which is other property. Because there is damage to other property, *Signal Oil* would provide for recovery under the doctrine of strict liability.

\* \* \*

Because there are no Texas Supreme Court cases on point dealing with the situation where one product is biologically combined with another to form, by a natural process, a continuation of those products, we must decide whether the Texas Supreme Court would view this case as one that should be governed by the doctrine of strict liability or the rules of commercial law....

The law of sales has been carefully articulated to govern the economic relations between suppliers and consumers of goods. The history of the doctrine of strict liability in tort indicates that it was designed, not to undermine the warranty provisions of the sales act or of the Uniform Commercial Code but, rather, to govern the distinct problem of physical injuries.

The distinction that the law has drawn between tort recovery for physical injuries and warranty recovery for economic loss is not arbitrary and does not rest on the "luck" of one plaintiff in having an accident causing physical injury. The distinction rests, rather, on an understanding of the nature of the responsibility a manufacturer must undertake in distributing his products. He can appropriately be held liable for physical injuries caused by defects by requiring his goods to match a standard of safety defined in terms of conditions that create unreasonable risks of harm. He cannot be held for the level of performance of his products in the consumer's business unless he agrees that the product was designed to meet the consumer's demands.

* * *

The loss claimed by Two Rivers, represented by the decrease in market value of the herd, can best be described as an intangible commercial loss. . . .

The Farro bull semen satisfied Two Rivers' business demands since it had a satisfactory conception rate. It did not cause physical harm to individuals or to Two Rivers' dams or bulls. Strict liability evolved to provide a remedy for physical injuries. It was not designed to replace the U.C.C. in governing commercial transactions. The damages claimed by Two Rivers are not the type protected by the social policy of strict liability to protect consumers and distribute the costs to the consuming public. The public need not be burdened with additional costs because of a consumer's unfulfilled commercial expectations. The socio-economic policy and enterprise theory behind strict liability was not designed to provide a remedy for a disappointed buyer. Sales & Perdue, *supra*, at 148–49. This is a case of economic loss that must be governed by commercial law.

### Implied Warranty

Because this case presents a situation involving the principles of commercial law, the provisions of the Uniform Commercial Code govern the outcome. *Nobility Homes, supra; Mid Continent, supra.* The U.C.C. was designed to deal with obligations imposed by law for commercial losses and it provides both express and implied warranties. Two Rivers does not claim that Curtiss made an express warranty, but it does contend that the judgment of the trial court may be affirmed on the theory of breach of an implied warranty.

* * *

[I]n Texas the type of loss presented in this case is governed by the U.C.C. and the law of warranty. But Curtiss successfully disclaimed any and all implied warranties in this case. Therefore, the district court incorrectly allowed Two Rivers to receive damages based on the theories of strict liability and breach of an implied warranty of merchantability.

REVERSED.

\* \* \*

### NOTES

**1. No Recovery for Economic Loss Without Personal or Property Injury.** As the principal case indicates, claims based on strict products liability allow recovery for economic loss only where there is an accompanying personal injury or property damage. For example, suppose A purchases a computer and uses it to place stock trades. If the computer malfunctions and A is unable to place the trades, she will not be able to recover against the manufacturer on a strict liability theory unless the computer injures her or another person, as by an electric shock, or damages some other property, as another piece of equipment. Generally negligence also does not support recovery for pure economic loss (see Chapter 2, Sec. H(9), supra). As the principal case indicates pure economic loss is recoverable under UCC warranty theories. See Keeton, *Prosser and Keeton on the Law of Torts*, § 101 (5th ed. 1984).

### 6.   Defenses

## DALY v. GENERAL MOTORS CORP.

Supreme Court of California.

20 Cal.3d 725, 144 Cal.Rptr. 380, 575 P.2d 1162 (1978).

RICHARDSON, J.

The most important of several problems which we consider is whether the principles of comparative negligence expressed by us in *Li* v. *Yellow Cab Co.* (1975) 13 Cal.3d 804 [119 Cal.Rptr. 858, 532 P.2d 1226, 78 A.L.R.3d 393], apply to actions founded on strict products liability. We will conclude that they do. We also inquire whether evidence of "compensating" safety devices installed in a motor vehicle by its manufacturer is admissible to offset alleged design deficiencies, and whether, under the particular facts herein, evidence of a driver's claimed intoxication or of his asserted failure to use his vehicle's safety equipment may be considered. While agreeing that evidence of compensating design characteristics is admissible, we will further determine that under the circumstances herein prejudicial error requiring reversal occurred upon the admission of evidence of the decedent's alleged intoxication and failure to use safety devices in his vehicle.

\* \* \*

#### THE FACTS AND THE TRIAL

Although there were no eyewitnesses, the parties agree, generally, on the reconstruction of the accident in question. In the early hours of October 31, 1970, decedent Kirk Daly, a 36–year-old attorney, was driving his Opel southbound on the Harbor Freeway in Los Angeles. The vehicle, while travelling at a speed of 50–70 miles per hour, collided with and damaged 50 feet of metal divider fence. After the initial impact between the left side of the vehicle and the fence the Opel spun counterclockwise, the driver's door was thrown open, and Daly was forcibly ejected from the car and sustained fatal head injuries. It was equally undisputed that had the deceased remained in the Opel his injuries, in all probability, would have been relatively minor.

Plaintiffs, who are decedent's widow and three surviving minor children, sued General Motors Corporation, Boulevard Buick, Underwriter's Auto Leasing, and Alco Leasing Company, the successive links in the Opel's manufacturing and distribution chain. The sole theory of plaintiffs' complaint was strict liability for damages allegedly caused by a defective product, namely, an improperly designed door latch claimed to have been activated by the impact. It was further asserted that, but for the faulty latch, decedent would have been restrained in the vehicle and, although perhaps injured, would not have been killed. Thus, the case involves a so-called "second collision" in which the "defect" did not contribute to the original impact, but only to the "enhancement" of injury.

At trial the jury heard conflicting expert versions as to the functioning of the latch mechanism during the accident. Plaintiffs' principal witness testified that the Opel's door was caused to open when the latch button on the exterior handle of the driver's door was forcibly depressed by some protruding portion of the divider fence. It was his opinion that the exposed push button on the door constituted a design "defect" which caused injuries greatly in excess of those which Daly would otherwise have sustained. Plaintiffs also introduced evidence that other vehicular door latch designs used in production models of the same and prior years afforded substantially greater protection. Defendants' experts countered with their opinions that the force of the impact was sufficiently strong that it would have caused the door to open resulting in Daly's death even if the Opel had been equipped with door latches of the alternative designs suggested by plaintiffs.

Over plaintiffs' objections, defendants were permitted to introduce evidence indicating that: (1) the Opel was equipped with a seat belt-shoulder harness system, and a door lock, either of which if used, it was contended, would have prevented Daly's ejection from the vehicle; (2) Daly used neither the harness system nor the lock; (3) the 1970 Opel owner's manual contained warnings that seat belts should be worn and doors locked when the car was in motion for "accident security"; and (4) Daly was intoxicated at the time of collision, which evidence the jury was advised was admitted for the limited purpose of determining whether decedent had used the vehicle's safety equipment. After relatively brief deliberations the jury returned a verdict favoring all defendants, and plaintiffs appeal from the ensuing adverse judgment.

### Strict Products Liability And Comparative Fault

In response to plaintiffs' assertion that the "intoxication-nonuse" evidence was improperly admitted, defendants contend that the deceased's own conduct contributed to his death. Because plaintiffs' case rests upon strict products liability based on improper design of the door latch and because defendants assert a failure in decedent's conduct, namely, his alleged intoxication and nonuse of safety equipment, without which the accident and ensuing death would not have occurred, there is thereby posed the overriding issue in the case, should comparative principles apply in strict products liability actions?

It may be useful to refer briefly to certain highlights in the historical development of the two principles—strict and comparative liability. Tort law has evolved from a legal obligation initially imposed without "fault," to recovery which, generally, was based on blameworthiness in a moral sense. For reasons of social policy and because of the unusual nature of defendants' acts, liability without fault continued to be prescribed in a certain restricted area, for example, upon keepers of wild animals, or those who handled explosives or other dangerous substances, or who engaged in ultrahazardous activities. Simultaneously, and more particularly, those who were injured in the use of personal property were permitted recovery on a contract theory if they were the purchasers of the chattel or were in privity. Subsequently, liability was imposed in negligence upon the manufacturer of personalty in favor of the general consumer. (For a comprehensive historical review, see Prosser, Law of Torts (4th ed. 1971) § 96, pp. 641–644; 2 Harper & James, The Law of Torts (1956) § 12.2 and foll., p. 747 and foll.) Evolving social policies designed to protect the ultimate consumer soon prompted the extension of legal responsibility beyond negligence to express or implied warranty. Thus, in the area of food and drink a form of strict liability predicated upon warranty found wide acceptance. Warranty actions, however, contained their own inherent limitations requiring a precedent notice to the vendor of a breach of the warranty, and absolving him from loss if he had issued an adequate disclaimer.

General dissatisfaction continued with the conceptual limitations which traditional tort and contract doctrines placed upon the consumers and users of manufactured products, this at a time when mass production of an almost infinite variety of goods and products was responding to a myriad of ever-changing societal demands stimulated by wide-spread commercial advertising. From an historic combination of economic and sociological forces was born the doctrine of strict liability in tort.

\* \* \*

Those counseling against the recognition of comparative fault principles in strict products liability cases vigorously stress, perhaps equally, not only the conceptual, but also the semantic difficulties incident to such a course. The task of merging the two concepts is said to be impossible, that "apples and oranges" cannot be compared, that "oil and water" do not mix, and that strict liability, which is not founded on negligence or fault, is inhospitable to comparative principles. The syllogism runs, contributory negligence was only a defense to negligence, comparative negligence only affects contributory negligence, therefore comparative negligence cannot be a defense to strict liability. (See *Butaud v. Suburban Marine & Sport. Goods, Inc.* (Alaska 1976) 555 P.2d 42, 47 (dis. opn. by Burke, J.), noted by Masin (1977) 4 Western St.U. L.Rev. 283, 284.) While fully recognizing the theoretical and semantic distinctions between the twin principles of strict products liability and traditional negligence, we think they can be blended or accommodated.

The inherent difficulty in the "apples and oranges" argument is its insistence on fixed and precise definitional treatment of legal concepts. In the evolving areas of both products liability and tort defenses, however, there has developed much conceptual overlapping and interweaving in order to attain substantial justice. The concept of strict liability itself, as we have noted, arose from dissatisfaction with the wooden formalisms of traditional tort and contract principles in order to protect the consumer of manufactured goods. Similarly, increasing social awareness of its harsh "all or nothing" consequences led us in *Li* to moderate the impact of traditional contributory negligence in order to accomplish a fairer and more balanced result. We acknowledged an intermixing of defenses of contributory negligence and assumption of risk and formally effected a type of merger, "As for assumption of risk, we have recognized in this state that this defense overlaps that of contributory negligence to some extent...." (*Li, supra,* 13 Cal.3d at p. 824.) In *Li,* we further reaffirmed our observation in *Grey* v. *Fibreboard Paper Products Co.* (1966) 65 Cal.2d 240, 245 [53 Cal.Rptr. 545, 418 P.2d 153]: " '[T]hat in one kind of situation, to wit, where a plaintiff *unreasonably* undertakes to encounter a specific known risk imposed by a defendant's negligence, plaintiff's conduct, although he may encounter that risk in a prudent manner, is in reality a form of contributory negligence....' We think it clear that the adoption of a system of comparative negligence should entail the merger of the defense of assumption of risk into the general scheme of assessment of liability in proportion to fault in those particular cases in which the form of assumption of risk involved is no more than a variant of contributory negligence." (13 Cal.3d at pp. 824–825, quoting *Grey, supra,* 65 Cal.2d at pp. 245–246, italics in original.)

Furthermore, the "apples and oranges" argument may be conceptually suspect. It has been suggested that the term "contributory negligence," one of the vital building blocks upon which much of the argument is based, may indeed itself be a misnomer since it lacks the first element of the classical negligence formula, namely, a duty of care owing to another. A highly respected torts authority, Dean William Prosser, has noted this fact by observing, "It is perhaps unfortunate that contributory negligence is called negligence at all. 'Contributory fault' would be a more descriptive term. Negligence as it is commonly understood is conduct which creates an undue risk of harm to others. Contributory negligence is conduct which involves an undue risk of harm to the actor himself. Negligence requires a duty, an obligation of conduct to another person. Contributory negligence involves no duty, unless we are to be so ingenious as to say that the plaintiff is under an obligation to protect the defendant against liability for the consequences of his own negligence." (Prosser, Law of Torts, *supra,* § 65, p. 418.)

We think, accordingly, the conclusion may fairly be drawn that the terms "comparative negligence," "contributory negligence" and "assumption of risk" do not, standing alone, lend themselves to the exact measurements of a micrometer-caliper, or to such precise definition as to divert us from otherwise strong and consistent countervailing policy considerations. Fixed semantic consistency at this point is less important than the attainment of a just and equitable result. The interweaving of concept and terminology in this area suggests a judicial posture that is flexible rather than doctrinaire.

We pause at this point to observe that where, as here, a consumer or user sues the manufacturer or designer alone, technically, neither fault nor conduct is really compared functionally. The conduct of one party in combination with the product of another, or perhaps the placing of a defective article in the stream of projected and anticipated use, may produce the ultimate injury. In such a case, as in the situation before us, we think the term "equitable apportionment or allocation of loss" may be more descriptive than "comparative fault."

Given all of the foregoing, we are, in the wake of *Li*, disinclined to resolve the important issue before us by the simple expedient of matching linguistic labels which have evolved either for convenience or by custom. Rather, we consider it more useful to examine the foundational reasons underlying the creation of strict products liability in California to ascertain whether the purposes of the doctrine would be defeated or diluted by adoption of comparative principles. We imposed strict liability against the manufacturer and in favor of the user or consumer in order to relieve injured consumers "from *problems of proof* inherent in pursuing negligence ... and warranty ... remedies, ..." (*Cronin v. J. B. E. Olson Corp., supra*, 8 Cal.3d at p. 133, italics added; *Greenman v. Yuba Power Products, Inc., supra*, 59 Cal.2d at p. 63; *Escola v. Coca Cola Bottling Co.* (1944) 24 Cal.2d 453, 461–462 [150 P.2d 436] (conc. opn. by Traynor, J.).) As we have noted, we sought to place the burden of loss on manufacturers rather than " ... injured persons *who are powerless to protect themselves....*" (*Greenman, supra*, 59 Cal.2d at p. 63, italics added; see *Escola, supra*, 24 Cal.2d at p. 462; *Price v. Shell Oil Co.* (1970) 2 Cal.3d 245, 251 [85 Cal.Rptr. 178, 466 P.2d 722] ["*protection of otherwise defenseless victims* of manufacturing defects and the spreading throughout society of the cost of compensating them"] italics added.)

The foregoing goals, we think, will not be frustrated by the adoption of comparative principles. Plaintiffs will continue to be relieved of proving that the manufacturer or distributor was negligent in the production, design, or dissemination of the article in question. Defendant's liability for injuries caused by a defective product remains strict. The principle of protecting the defenseless is likewise preserved, for plaintiff's recovery will be reduced *only* to the extent that his own lack of reasonable care contributed to his injury. The cost of compensating the victim of a defective product, albeit proportionately reduced, remains on defendant manufacturer, and will, through him, be "spread among society." However, we do not permit plaintiff's own conduct relative to the product to escape unexamined, and as to that share of plaintiff's damages which flows from his own fault we discern no reason of policy why it should, following *Li*, be borne by others. Such a result would directly contravene the principle announced in *Li*, that loss should be assessed equitably in proportion to fault.

We conclude, accordingly, that the expressed purposes which persuaded us in the first instance to adopt strict liability in California would not be thwarted were we to apply comparative principles. What would be forfeit is a degree of semantic symmetry. However, in this evolving area of tort law in which new remedies are judicially created, and old defenses judicially merged, impelled by strong considerations of equity and fairness we seek a larger synthesis. If a more just result follows from the expansion of comparative principles, we have no hesitancy in seeking it, mindful always that the fundamental and underlying purpose of *Li* was to promote the equitable allocation of loss among all parties legally responsible in proportion to their fault.

A second objection to the application of comparative principles in strict products liability cases is that a manufacturer's incentive to produce safe products will thereby be reduced or removed. While we fully recognize this concern we think, for several reasons, that the problem is more shadow than substance. First, of course, the manufacturer cannot avoid its continuing liability for a defective product even when the plaintiff's own conduct has contributed to his injury. The manufacturer's liability, and therefore its incentive to avoid and correct product defects, remains; its exposure will be lessened only to the extent that the trier finds that the victim's conduct contributed to his injury. Second, as a practical matter a manufacturer, in a particular case, cannot assume that the user of a defective product upon whom an injury is visited will be blameworthy. Doubtless, many users are free of fault, and a defect is at least as likely as not to be exposed by an entirely innocent plaintiff who will obtain full recovery. In such cases the manufacturer's incentive toward safety both in design and production is wholly unaffected. Finally, we must observe that under the present law, which recognizes assumption of risk as a complete defense to products liability, the curious and cynical message is that it profits the manufacturer to make his product so defective that in the event of injury he can argue that the user had to be aware of its patent defects. To that extent the incentives are inverted. We conclude, accordingly, that no substantial or significant impairment of the safety incentives of defendants will occur by the adoption of comparative principles.

In passing, we note one important and felicitous result if we apply comparative principles to strict products liability. This arises from the fact that under present law when plaintiff sues in negligence his own contributory negligence, however denominated, may diminish but cannot wholly defeat his recovery. When he sues in strict products liability, however, his "assumption of risk" *completely bars* his recovery. Under *Li*, as we have noted, "assumption of risk" is merged into comparative principles. (13 Cal.3d at p. 825.) The consequence is that after *Li* in a negligence action, plaintiff's conduct which amounts to "negligent" assumption of risk no longer defeats plaintiff's recovery. Identical conduct, however, in a strict liability case acts as a complete bar under rules heretofore applicable. Thus, strict products liability, which was developed to free injured consumers from the constraints imposed by traditional negligence and warranty theories, places a consumer plaintiff in a worse position than would be the case were his claim founded on simple negligence. This, in turn, rewards adroit pleading and selection of theories. The application of comparative principles to strict liability obviates this bizarre anomaly by treating alike the defenses to both negligence and strict products liability actions. In each instance the defense, if established, will reduce but not bar plaintiff's claim.

A third objection to the merger of strict liability and comparative fault focuses on the claim that, as a practical matter, triers of fact, particularly jurors, cannot assess, measure, or compare plaintiff's negligence with defendant's strict liability. We are unpersuaded by the argument and are convinced that jurors are able to undertake a fair apportionment of liability.

\* \* \*

We find equally unpersuasive a final objection that the merger of the two principles somehow will abolish or adversely affect the liability of such intermediate entities in the chain of distribution as retailers (*Vandermark v. Ford Motor Co.* (1964) 61 Cal.2d 256, 263 [37 Cal.Rptr. 896, 391 P.2d 168]), and bailors (*Price* v. *Shell Oil Co., supra,* 2 Cal.3d 245, 253.) We foresee no such consequence. Regardless of the identity of a particular defendant or of his position in the commercial chain the basis for his liability remains that he has marketed or distributed a defective product. If, as we believe, jurors are capable of assessing fully and fairly the legal responsibility of a manufacturer on a strict liability basis, no reason appears why they cannot do likewise with respect to subsequent distributors and vendors of the product.

We note that the majority of our sister states which have addressed the problem, either by statute or judicial decree, have extended comparative principles to strict products liability.

\* \* \*

MOSK, Justice, dissenting.

I dissent.

This will be remembered as the dark day when this court, which heroically took the lead in originating the doctrine of products liability (*Greenman v. Yuba Power Products, Inc.* (1963) 59 Cal.2d 57 [27 Cal. Rptr. 697, 377 P.2d 897, 13 A.L.R.3d 1049]) and steadfastly resisted efforts to inject concepts of negligence into the newly designed tort (*Cronin v. J. B. E. Olson Corp.* (1972) 8 Cal.3d 121 [104 Cal.Rptr. 433, 501 P.2d 1153]), inexplicably turned 180 degrees and beat a hasty retreat almost back to square one. The pure concept of products liability so pridefully fashioned and nurtured by this court for the past decade and a half is reduced to a shambles.

The majority inject a foreign object—the tort of negligence—into the tort of products liability by the simple expedient of calling negligence something else: on some pages their opinion speaks of "comparative fault," on others reference is to "comparative principles," and elsewhere the term "equitable apportionment" is employed, although this is clearly not a proceeding in equity. But a rose is a rose and negligence is negligence; thus the majority find that despite semantic camouflage they must rely on *Li v. Yellow Cab Co.* (1975) 13 Cal.3d 804 [119 Cal.Rptr. 858, 532 P.2d 1226, 78 A.L.R.3d 393], even though *Li* is purely and simply a negligence case which merely rejects contributory negligence and substitutes therefor comparative negligence.

\* \* \*

The defective product is comparable to a time bomb ready to explode; it maims its victims indiscriminately, the righteous and the evil, the careful and the careless. Thus when a faulty design or otherwise defective product is involved, the litigation should not be diverted to consideration of the negligence of the plaintiff. The liability issues are simple: was the product or its design faulty, did the defendant inject the defective product into the stream of commerce, and did the defect cause the injury? The conduct of the ultimate consumer-victim who used the product in the contemplated or foreseeable manner is wholly irrelevant to those issues.

The majority devote considerable effort to rationalizing what has been described as a mixture of apples and oranges. Their point might be persuasive if there were some authority recognizing a defense of contributory products liability, for which they are now substituting comparative products liability. However, all our research to discover such apples and oranges has been fruitless. The conclusion is inescapable that the majority, in avoiding approval of comparative negligence in name as a defense to products liability, are thereby originating a new defense that can only be described as comparative products liability. We may now anticipate similar defenses in the vast number of other tort actions. Can comparative libel, comparative slander of title, comparative wrongful litigation, comparative nuisance, comparative fraud, be far behind? By whatever name, negligence, heretofore just one subtopic in the elaborate spectrum of torts—which require six volumes and appendices of the Restatement Second of Torts to cover—now seems destined to envelop the entire tort field.

\* \* \*

## NOTES

**1. Defenses.** Where a plaintiff relies on a theory of negligence to recover for harm caused by a product, the defendant may assert the defenses of contributory negligence and/or assumption of risk. Defenses in the context of strict products liability tend to parallel those in traditional strict liability cases. Thus, in a strict products liability case, the defendant may use assumption of risk as a defense, but may *not* use contributory negligence as a defense. In those jurisdictions that use a comparative fault scheme, the modern trend is to allow comparative fault to be a partial defense in strict products liability cases. For a discussion of contributory and comparative fault and assumption of risk, see Chapter 2, Sec. I, supra. How persuasive is Justice Mosk's strongly worded dissent? See Keeton, *Prosser and Keeton on the Law of Torts*, § 102 (5th ed. 1984). Consider *Whitehead v. Toyota Motor Sales, U.S.A., Inc.*, 897 S.W.2d 684 (Tenn.1995), where a man driving his truck crossed the center line into a head-on collision with an oncoming vehicle. He sued the manufacturer and seller of the truck for strict products liability, alleging that the seatbelt system of the truck was defective, thus increasing his injuries. The defendant brought the defense of comparative fault, and insisted there were no defects in the truck. The court ruled that comparative fault may be used as a defense in a strict products liability action.

Some courts, however, are more limited than the principal case in allowing comparative negligence to always be a defense to strict product liability. See also *Hernandez v. Barbo Machinery Co.*, 141 Or.App. 34, 917 P.2d 30 (1996) where the plaintiff mechanic came upon a new saw at his workplace and, being unfamiliar with its operation, decided to service it. Since the saw was partially enclosed in a cabinet, plaintiff looked for the on-off switch. He did not know the saw was running until he opened it, slipped on some sawdust, and put his hand inside, sustaining injuries. Subsequently, he sued the manufacturer under a strict products liability theory. The manufacturer raised the defense of comparative negligence. The plaintiff argued that comparative negligence should not be a defense when such negligence consists merely in a failure to discover the defect in the product, or to guard against the possibility of its existence. The court held that the defendant must offer some evidence from which the jury could infer that the plaintiff's conduct or omission was something other than the failure to discover or guard against the defect that made the product dangerously defective. If a reasonable juror could only find from the evidence that the injury resulted from the failure to discover the defect, the giving of a comparative fault instruction would be improper.

# Chapter IV

# TRESPASS AND NUISANCE

## HANNABALSON v. SESSIONS

Supreme Court of Iowa.
116 Iowa 457, 90 N.W. 93 (1902).

WEAVER, J.

Plaintiff and defendant live upon adjoining lots. There is frequent war between the families. The casus belli in the present instance is to be found in the following circumstances: Upon the boundary line between the lots is a tight board fence, a part of which was built by plaintiff's husband; but, unfortunately, this barrier, while all sufficient to prevent the passage of the dove of peace, is neither high enough nor tight enough to prevent the interchange of brick bats or the bandying of opprobrious epithets. On May 30, 1898, the defendant, while at work in his garden, claimed to have narrowly escaped a brick hurled in his direction by one of plaintiff's children, and in his indignation at the unprovoked bombardment threatened the lad with arrest. Plaintiff and her husband, being at work near by, heard the threat, and took up the quarrel. About this time plaintiff's husband discovered that a ladder belonging to defendant was hanging upon a peg or block attached to the partition fence, and, conceiving this to be a cloud upon his title, he forthwith attempted to remove it, while defendant, seeing the peril in which his property was placed, rushed to its defense. Whether plaintiff herself laid violent hands on the ladder is a matter of grave dispute. She denies it, and says that the height and depth of her offending consisted in her leaning up against the fence with one arm quietly hanging over the top thereof, and in stimulating her husband's zeal by audible remarks about the "crazy fool" who was bearing down upon them from the other side. She further avers that while occupying this position of strict neutrality the defendant assaulted her vi et armis, and with his clenched fist struck the arm which protruded over the fence top into his domain. Defendant denies the striking, and says that plaintiff, instead of being a peaceable and impartial observer of the skirmish, was herself a principal actor, and that in aid of her husband she climbed upon some convenient pedestal, and, hanging herself across the fence, reached down, and with malice aforethought seized the ladder and wrenched it from its resting place. Thereupon, actuated by a natural and lawful desire to protect his

**582**

property from such ravishments, and being goaded on by statements from the other side of the fence reflecting upon his mother and casting doubt upon his proper rank in the animal kingdom, he gently, and without unreasonable force, laid his open hand upon plaintiff's arm, and mildly but firmly suggested the propriety of her "keeping on her own side of the fence." As is usual in cases of this kind the testimony of the principal parties is entirely irreconcilable, and, as is also usual, each is supported by partisan witnesses in a very emphatic manner. More than a year after the alleged assault this action for damages was begun, and plaintiff swears that, as a result of the blow upon her arm, she has during all that time been sick, weak, nervous, suffering great pain and anguish, and is to a great extent a physical and nervous wreck. On the other hand, some of defendant's witnesses testify, in effect, that, whatever may be plaintiff's bodily ills, they have existed for many years, while others tell us that since the alleged assault they have seen her performing outdoor labor with all the apparent strength of an athlete. Her physician, who was a witness in her behalf, says that, while "she is not quite so fleshy as she was a year ago, she is still fleshy enough," and the jury, who saw her at the trial, seem to have adopted his conservative estimate.

\* \* \*

.... The mere fact that plaintiff did not step across the boundary line does not make her any less a trespasser if she reached her arm across the line, as she admits she did. It is one of the oldest rules of property known to the law that the title of the owner of the soil extends, not only downward to the center of the earth, but upward *usque ad coelum*, although it is, perhaps, doubtful whether owners as quarrelsome as the parties in this case will ever enjoy the usufruct of their property in the latter direction. The maxim, "Ubi pars est ibi est totum,"—that where the greater part is there is the whole,—does not apply to the person of a trespasser, and the court and jury could therefore not be expected to enter into any inquiry as to the side of the boundary line upon which plaintiff preponderated, as she reached over the fence top. It was enough that she thrust her hand or arm across the boundary to technically authorize the defendant to demand that she cease the intrusion, and to justify him in using reasonable and necessary force required for the expulsion of so much of her person as he found upon his side of the line, being careful to keep within the limits of the rule, "Molliter manus imposuit," so far as was consistent with his own safety. Under the instructions of the court, the jury must have found that defendant kept within the scope of his legal rights in this respect, and that the alleged assault was not established by the evidence.

\* \* \*

## NOTES

**1. Trespass.** The law of trespass protects the plaintiff's right to the exclusive possession of her land. Even trivial intrusions are sufficient to give rise to a trespass claim. See Diamond, Levine & Madden, *Understanding Torts* § 18.02 (2nd ed. 2000); Keeton, *Prosser and Keeton on the Law of*

*Torts* § 13 (5th ed. 1984) and Dobbs, *The Law of Torts* §§ 50–58 (2000). The Restatement (Second) of Torts articulates the law of trespass as follows:

> One is subject to liability to another for trespass, irrespective of whether he thereby causes harm to any legally protected interest of the other, if he intentionally
>
> (a) enters land in the possession of the other, or causes a thing or a third person to do so, or
>
> (b) remains on the land, or
>
> (c) fails to remove from the land a thing which he is under a duty to remove.

Restatement (Second) of Torts § 158.

Consider *Giddings v. Rogalewski*, 192 Mich. 319, 158 N.W. 951 (1916), in which the defendant entered the plaintiff's land in order to go fishing. The lake on which the defendant sought to fish was entirely surrounded by the plaintiff's farm and thus did not benefit from a state law protecting access to "meandering" waters for fishing. The court held that the entry was a trespass and affirmed the lower court's judgment for the plaintiff in the payment of six cents.

Also, consider *Food Lion, Inc. v. Capital Cities/ABC, Inc.*, 951 F.Supp. 1217 (1996), where the court held that material misrepresentations could nullify consent which would otherwise preclude trespass claims. In this case, two *Primetime Live* employees falsified employment applications and obtained employment in order to obtain behind the scenes footage for a TV expose. Because consent to entry was obtained based on misrepresentation, the jury could find that such consent would not have been given absent the falsifications, making the defendants' presence a trespass.

**2. Intent.** Trespass like battery must be intentional—the defendant's entry must have been either desired by the defendant or she must know it is a substantially certain result of her actions. Thus, negligent entry is controlled by the law of negligence and not trespass. For example, if A negligently loses control of her car and intrudes onto B's property, this would not be an intentional trespass. Mistake, by contrast, is not a defense to a claim of trespass; the defendant need only intend the entry. If A, reasonably relying on a surveyor's map of property lines, walks onto B's property thinking it's her own, it is a trespass. Similarly, suppose X invites Y to her house and tells Y to go to the only purple house in the neighborhood. If it turns out that there is another purple house nearby and Y enters it with the mistaken belief that it is X's house, Y has committed a trespass. For a discussion of mistake and issues of transferred intent pertinent to trespass, see Chapter 1, Sec. D, supra.

**3. Trespass to Area Above and Below the Surface.** Just how far into the air should a property owner's right to exclusive enjoyment extend? According to the Restatement (Second) of Torts, any intrusion of the airspace above the plaintiff's land is a trespass, with the exception of aircraft that stay out of the immediate reaches of the land and do not interfere with the owner's use of the land. Restatement (Second) of Torts § 159. This would include such items as a frisbee or, as in the principal case, an arm. Other approaches to the air space problem have included finding a trespass only over those areas actually occupied, dividing air space into upper and lower strata and protecting the plaintiff's property interest in the latter only, and treating the case as one of nuisance. See generally Keeton, supra § 13.

Trespass may also occur where the defendant invades the earth underneath the plaintiff's land, as where the defendant seeks to conduct mining activities under the plaintiff's land or to tunnel through it. But consider *Boehringer v. Montalto*, 142 Misc. 560, 254 N.Y.S. 276 (N.Y.Sup.Ct.1931), where the defendant had constructed sewer lines 150 feet underneath the plaintiff's land. The court held that the property interest extends below only so far as the plaintiff might actually use the land. Since the plaintiff could not make use of the earth at a depth of 150 feet, there was no invasion. Id.

**4. Requirement of a Tangible Invasion.** Most courts require that a trespass consist of an intrusion of something tangible. This would exclude sound, light, and odors since they are intangible. Consider, for example, *Amphitheaters, Inc. v. Portland Meadows*, 184 Or. 336, 198 P.2d 847 (1948), in which light from the defendant's horse racing track shone on the plaintiff's drive-in movie theater, making it impossible to see the movies. The court rejected the plaintiff's claim for trespass on the grounds that light is not a physical invasion.

The tangible/intangible distinction was questioned in *Martin v. Reynolds Metals Co.*, 221 Or. 86, 342 P.2d 790 (1959), in which the defendant's aluminum reduction plant discharged fluorides in the form of gases and particulates onto the plaintiff's land. The court noted that with modern understandings of microscopic particles, the common law distinction between tangible and intangible invasions was less viable. Although frequently discussed, *Martin* has not been widely followed, and plaintiff's must generally prove a tangible invasion. Nevertheless, in such cases a plaintiff may have a remedy under nuisance law. Consider the next principal case.

## BROWN v. COUNTY COMMISSIONERS OF SCIOTO COUNTY

Court of Appeals of Ohio, Fourth District, Scioto County.
87 Ohio App.3d 704, 622 N.E.2d 1153 (1993).

HARSHA, Presiding Judge.

Jack D. Brown and Barbara Brown filed a complaint which alleged that the Scioto County Commissioners had failed to properly maintain and operate a sewage treatment plant and thereby created a nuisance and trespass to the Browns' neighboring property. After the trial court granted the commissioners' motion for summary judgment, Barbara Brown took this appeal.

\* \* \*

In 1983, the Browns filed a complaint seeking damages and injunctive relief against appellees and Sewer District No. Four. The Browns subsequently filed a third amended complaint naming appellees, the state of Ohio, Department of Rehabilitation and Correction, and the superintendent of the Southern Ohio Correctional Facility ("SOCF") as defendants. Their third amended complaint alleged that the defendants had created a nuisance and trespassed on their property by negligently and/or willfully and wantonly constructing, operating, and maintaining a sewage treatment plant in the immediate vicinity of the Browns' real property. As a result of the defendants' tortious conduct, noxious gases and odors were emitted from the plant which settled on and diminished the value of the Browns' and their neighbors' property, created health hazards, denied them the use and enjoyment of their property, and caused extreme emotional and "intestinal" distress. The Browns sought injunctive relief against "each defendant" and compensatory and punitive damages against appellees in the total amount of $500,000.

\* \* \*

For the sum of $50,000, the Browns purchased a house located approximately one-quarter of a mile from the sewage treatment plant. They moved into the house on March 12, 1978. Prior to moving into the house, they did not perceive any odor from the plant. However, within the first week after they moved in, they noticed some odor coming from the plant. The odor was not very noticeable the first few years, but became worse and more frequent during the early 1980s. The odor was particularly bad when the weather was hot and humid or when the wind was blowing in a particular direction. The worst period for the noxious odors emanating from the sewage treatment plant was the summer of 1983, when there was an odor comparable to having their septic tank cleaned. The extreme odor during that period lasted twenty-four hours every day and prompted the Browns to file their initial complaint. Additionally, the odors from the plant increased the number of insects of all kinds on the Browns' property, requiring them to call an exterminating company two or three times a month during one period of time. The Browns became nauseated due to the odors, and in 1984, a physician indicated that it was a "probability" that appellant's stomach problems, including loss of appetite, were related to the treatment plant odors. The odors made it uncomfortable and, at times, impossible to be outside their house.

According to Jack D. Brown, the sewage treatment plant emitted germs and bacteria that rotted the ears off two rabbits that the Browns owned. Although unsure of the exact date, the Browns had their home listed for sale at $65,000 and a woman interested in purchasing it was driven away by the plant odors. Although the Browns and several neighbors complained to appellees, as well as state and federal officials, no action was taken by appellees to remedy the problems associated with their operation and maintenance of the sewage treatment plant.

Appellees operated the sewage treatment plant from its inception under a lease with the state. The lease was extended for a few brief periods until it was determined that the state could more efficiently operate the plant. Accordingly, appellees relinquished operation and maintenance of the plant to the state on June 1, 1985. During appellees' period of operation of the plant, the condition of the plant was deplorable. The Ohio Environmental Protection Agency cited the plant for violations concerning the level of bacteria and suspended solids contained in the effluent discharged into an adjacent stream. Most of the equipment was old and worn out. A comminutor, which was utilized to break down the raw sewage, had not been operable for several months, and the screen used to filter the sewage through the treatment process had a large hole in it. One of the two oxidation ditches was idle and the other ditch was only operating at twenty-five to fifty percent of its capacity. The idle oxidation ditch had become septic, breeding anaerobic bacteria that emitted the gaseous substance causing the noxious odors.

* * *

As stated by Professor Keeton in Prosser & Keeton, The Law of Torts (5 Ed.1984) 616, Section 86: "There is perhaps no more impenetrable jungle in the entire law than that which surrounds the word 'nuisance.' " Nuisance describes two separate fields of tort liability that through the accident of historical development are called by the same name. See Restatement of the Law 2d, Torts (1979) 84, Introductory Note. One of these two fields of liability bears the name of public nuisance and covers the invasion of public rights, *i.e.,* rights common to all members of the public. Historically, public nuisance was criminal in nature and recovery in damages is limited to those who can show particular harm of a kind different from that suffered by the general public. *Id.*

The other field of liability is called private nuisance. This tort covers the invasion of the private interest in the use and enjoyment of land. As such, plaintiff's action must always be founded upon her interest in the land. *Id.* . . .

Restatement of the Law 2d, Torts (1979) 87, Section 821B, defines public nuisance as an unreasonable interference with a right common to the general public. Conduct does not become a public nuisance merely because it interferes with a large number of people. At common law, there must be some interference with a public right which is common to all members of the general public. In addition to common-law public nuisance, Ohio has adopted statutes and administrative regulations which define certain conduct as being a public nuisance. These statutes amount to a legislative declaration that the proscribed conduct is an unreasonable interference with a public right.

Restatement of the Law 2d, Torts (1979) 100, Section 821D, defines private nuisance as a nontrespassory invasion of another's interest in the private use and enjoyment of land. Section 822 of Restatement of the Law 2d, Torts provides that in order to be actionable, the invasion must be either (a) intentional and unreasonable, or (b) unintentional and caused by negligent, reckless or abnormally dangerous conduct (negligent and reckless conduct carry with them a degree of unreasonableness; abnormally dangerous activity is not treated in the same sense, but the balancing effort necessary to determine liability has the same effect). *Id.* at 113–115.

While the law in Ohio is far from clear in this area, absolute nuisance and nuisance *per se* seem to be the same. The essence of these two characterizations of nuisance is that no matter how careful one is, such activities are inherently injurious and cannot be conducted without damaging someone else's property or rights. See *Metzger v. Pennsylva-*

*nia, Ohio & Detroit RR. Co.* (1946), 146 Ohio St. 406, 32 O.O. 450, 66 N.E.2d 203, paragraph one of the syllabus; *Curtis v. Ohio State Univ.* (1986), 29 Ohio App.3d 297, 301, 29 OBR 363, 366–367, 504 N.E.2d 1222, 1226; *Blair v. Ohio Dept. of Rehab. & Corr.* (1989), 61 Ohio Misc.2d 649, 658, 582 N.E.2d 673, 678. They are based upon either intentional conduct or abnormally dangerous conditions, and as such the rule of absolute liability applies. *Jennings Buick, Inc. v. Cincinnati* (1978), 56 Ohio St.2d 459, 465, 10 O.O.3d 545, 549, 384 N.E.2d 303, 307. A modern example would be a neighborhood "crack house."

Conversely, qualified nuisance is premised upon negligence. It consists of a lawful act that is so negligently or carelessly done as to have created an unreasonable risk of harm which in due course results in injury to another. *Metzger, supra,* at paragraph two of the syllabus; *State ex rel. Schoener v. Hamilton Cty. Bd. of Commrs.* (1992), 84 Ohio App.3d 794, 619 N.E.2d 2. Obviously, both public and private nuisances may be either absolute or qualified.

Having reviewed the appropriate law, we look first to see if appellant has presented sufficient evidence to allow her complaint to proceed in the area of either common law or statutory public nuisance....

\* \* \*

A public nuisance as such does not afford a basis for recovery of damages in tort unless there is particular harm to the plaintiff that is of a different kind than that suffered by the public in general. See Restatement of the Law 2d, Torts (1979) 94, Section 821C(1). When the particular harm involved consists of interference with the use and enjoyment of land, the landowner may recover either on the basis of the particular harm to her resulting from the public nuisance or on the basis of private nuisance. See Restatement of the Law 2d, Torts (1979) 93, Section 821B, Comment *h.* Here appellant contends that she lost an opportunity to sell her property and was unable to use and enjoy it. This is a sufficiently distinct or particular harm from the public right so as to allow recovery under a statutory public nuisance theory.

.... In *Schoener, supra,* the First District Court of Appeals held that a regulated solid waste disposal facility could not be subject to liability as an absolute nuisance. In order for a duly licensed and regulated sanitary landfill to be found liable for maintaining a nuisance, negligence must be established, *i.e.,* a qualified nuisance. The *Schoener* court based its holding upon the following rationale:

> "A standard of strict liability is not appropriate under these circumstances, where the public policy of Ohio has clearly chosen to allow operators such as Rumpke to do business in this state subject to the limitations imposed under what can only be termed a comprehensive and vigilant regulatory scheme. Once an operator becomes licensed by the state, we think it fair to say in law that part of the quid pro quo for the submission to such exacting regulatory oversight is the operator's insulation from liability under a theory of strict liability. Therefore, we conclude

that the trial court did not err when it declined to instruct the jury concerning absolute nuisance.''

As stated above, appellant introduced no evidence that appellees were not licensed to operate the sewage disposal plant. See *Wing, supra.* Consequently, pursuant to *Schoener,* she failed to raise a genuine issue of material fact as to the presence of absolute public nuisance, but may proceed on the theory of qualified statutory nuisance.

We turn now to the cause of action for private nuisance. First, we note that *Schoener* is equally applicable to public and private nuisance claims. Accordingly, appellant did not present sufficient evidence to withstand a motion for summary judgment on the issue of absolute private nuisance.

A civil action based upon the maintenance of a qualified private nuisance is essentially an action in tort for the negligent maintenance of a condition, which, of itself, creates an unreasonable risk of harm, ultimately resulting in injury. *Allen Freight Lines, Inc. v. Consol. Rail Corp.* (1992), 64 Ohio St.3d 274, 275, 595 N.E.2d 855, 856. In such a case, negligence must be alleged and proven to warrant a recovery. *Id.* at 276, 595 N.E.2d at 856, citing *Taylor v. Cincinnati* (1944), 143 Ohio St. 426, 441, 28 O.O. 369, 375, 55 N.E.2d 724, 731.

Appellees contend that there was no evidence of a qualified nuisance since there was no indication that appellant suffered any injury during the period when appellees operated the plant. We note that appellant's appraisal of her property value was made over five years after appellees relinquished operation of the plant and, thus, was too remote to establish injury at that time. However, there was evidence that a prospective purchaser was lost due to the offensive odors from the plant. There was also evidence that appellant suffered nausea and was unable to fully use her property. To entitle adjoining property owners to recover damages for the maintenance of a nuisance, it is not necessary that they should be driven from their dwellings, or that the defendants' acts create a positive unhealthy condition; it is enough that their enjoyment of life and property is rendered uncomfortable, for in some circumstances discomfort and annoyance may constitute a nuisance. See, generally, 61 American Jurisprudence 2d (1981) 950, Pollution Control, Section 531. Accordingly, there remains a genuine issue of material fact as to whether appellees' conduct constituted a qualified private nuisance.

\* \* \*

Appellees further claim that there was no showing of trespass. The essential elements necessary to state a cause of action in trespass are: (1) an unauthorized intentional act, and (2) entry upon land in the possession of another. See, *e.g., Blashinsky v. Topazio* (Apr. 17, 1987), Lake App. No. 11–113, unreported, 1987 WL 9942. Traditionally, an invasion of the exclusive possession of land by intangible substances, such as an airborne pollutant, was usually held by the courts not to constitute a trespass since a trespass involved a physical invasion by tangible matters. See Annotation, Recovery in Trespass for Injury to Land Caused by Airborne Pollutants (1980), 2 A.L.R. 4 th 1054. However, there has been a growing trend among jurisdictions to hold that the test for whether an invasion of a property interest is a trespass does not depend upon whether the intruding agent is an intangible or tangible substance, but whether the intrusion interferes with the right to the exclusive possession of property. *Id.* at 1055. However, odors emanating from a facility, see *Born v. Exxon Corp.* (Ala.1980), 388 So.2d 933, or mere diminution of value, see *Maddy v. Vulcan Materials Co.* (D.Kan.1990), 737 F.Supp. 1528, are insufficient to state a trespass claim even under the modern view.

The Supreme Court of Alabama in *Born* cited its previous decision in *Borland v. Sanders Lead Co., Inc.* (Ala.1979), 369 So.2d 523, 530, to note the following distinction between trespass under the modern trend and nuisance at 388 So.2d at 934:

> "For an indirect invasion to amount to an actionable trespass, there must be an interference with plaintiff's exclusive possessory interest; that is, through the defendant's intentional conduct, and with reasonable foreseeability, some substance has entered upon the land itself, affecting its nature and character, and causing substantial actual damage to the res. For example, if the smoke or polluting substance emitting from a defendant's operation causes discomfort and annoyance to the plaintiff in his use and enjoyment of the property, then the plaintiff's remedy is for nuisance; but if, as a result of the defendant's operation, the polluting substance is deposited upon the plaintiff's property, thus interfering with his exclusive possessory interest by causing substantial damage to the res, then the plaintiff may seek his remedy in trespass, though his alternative remedy in nuisance may co-exist."

There is no summary judgment evidence of the polluting substance, *i.e.,* noxious odors, depositing particulate matter on appellant's real property or causing physical damage to it. We are persuaded that under either the traditional or modern views, since appellant has failed to adduce summary judgment evidence of physical damage to her real property, appellees were entitled to summary judgment on appellant's trespass claim.

\* \* \*

### COMMONWEALTH v. DANNY'S NEW ADAM AND EVE BOOKSTORE

Commonwealth Court of Pennsylvania.
625 A.2d 119, 155 Pa.Cmwlth. 281 (1993).

NARRICK, Senior Judge

Appellants' establishments are adult bookstores located in Philadelphia. Both establishments sell video tapes, books and magazines, sexual in nature. Both stores also contain video viewing booths equipped with coin-operated video monitors upon which patrons can view sexually-oriented videos. Each video viewing booth adjoins the booth next to it with a common wall between the booths. Agents, conducting an investigation for the Appellee, discovered that a number of the booths had a three-by-five inch hole located between the booths that allowed patrons to have sexual activity with persons in the adjacent booth.

Additionally, the Book Bin East contained a floor designated as the "California Couch Dancing" area where two rooms are divided by a glass wall. Appellee's agent observed a woman through the glass, as she performed lewd strip-tease dancing. The agent was also offered sex for money.

On July 29, 1992, Appellee filed complaints in equity which sought to abate the use of Appellants' premises as a nuisance pursuant to Section 1 of the Uses of Property Act, Act of June 23, 1931, P.L. 1178, 68 P.S. § 467. Appellee further filed petitions for temporary injunctions (temporary restraining orders) and preliminary injunctions, enjoining the operations of video viewing booths and the "California Couch Dancing area." The Philadelphia County Court of Common Pleas granted the temporary injunctions and scheduled a hearing pursuant to Pa.R.C.P. No. 1531. The trial court held a two-day hearing, limited to the issue of whether the temporary injunctions should become preliminary injunctions, pending a hearing on the merits. On September 3, 1992, the trial court granted the preliminary injunctions, reasoning in part:

The citizens of Commonwealth of Pennsylvania will suffer irreparable harm if defendants continue to maintain video viewing booths and areas utilized "California Couch Dancing" where sexual activity has taken place which could lead to the spread of Human Immunodeficiency Virus (HIV) which may result in the fatal illness known as "Acquired Immune Deficiency Syndrome" (AIDS).

* * *

In *Muehlieb v. City of Philadelphia*, 133 Pa.Commonwealth Ct. 133, 574 A.2d 1208 (1990), this court adopted the Restatement (Second) of Torts definition of a public nuisance as "an unreasonable interference with a right common to the general public." *Id.* at 140, 574 A.2d at 1211, quoting Restatement (Second) of Torts § 821B. One set of circumstances which support a conclusion that an interference with a public right is unreasonable is whether the conduct in question poses a significant threat to the public health. *Id.* Among other health and scientific groups, the Advisory Health Board of the Pennsylvania Department of Health has declared AIDS to be a communicable disease. 28 Pa.Code § 27.2.

Competent evidence exists in the record to support the trial court's conclusion that sexual conduct, occurring on the Appellants' premises, could lead to the spread of HIV which may result in AIDS. Expert witnesses for both the Appellants and the Appellee testified to this fact. In addition, Ralph Taylor, a patron of Appellants' establishments, testified that he was infected with HIV and that he had, on several occasions, engaged in intercourse in the Appellants' establishments. It is well-settled that even a lawful business may be enjoined from operation if it is shown that, under the particular circumstance, its operation constitutes a public nuisance. *Ranck v. Bonal Enterprises, Inc.*, 467 Pa. 569, 359 A.2d 748 (1976).

The testimony of Taylor and Appellee's agents and expert witnesses also supports a conclusion that greater harm would have resulted from denying the injunction. The threat to the public health was ongoing.

\* \* \*

Concerning Appellants' argument that the trial court's reliance upon the Act violated their First Amendment rights, we find this argument meritless. The Superior Court held the Act applicable to adult bookstores in *Commonwealth ex rel. Lewis v. Allouwill Realty Corp.*, 330 Pa.Superior Ct. 32, 478 A.2d 1334 (1984). Allouwill concerned two adult bookstores in the Harrisburg area that had video viewing booths with holes between the common walls. Harrisburg Police Officers observed sexual activity occurring in the booths. The Superior Court upheld an injunction which padlocked the two adult bookstores as public nuisances pursuant to the Act.

In *Arcara v. Cloud Books, Inc.*, 478 U.S. 697, 106 S.Ct. 3172, 92 L.Ed.2d 568 (1968), the United States Supreme Court held that statutes such as the Act do not offend the First Amendment. In *Arcara*, a bookstore was closed pursuant to a section of the New York Public Health Law which defined places of prostitution, lewdness and assignation, as public health nuisances. The Court held that the closure statute did not single out bookstores or others engaged in First Amendment protected activities. The closure statute was directed at unlawful conduct (i.e., illicit sexual activity) which had nothing to do with books or other expressive activity, protected under the First Amendment. Further, the Court held that the sexual activity carried on in a bookstore manifests no element of protected expression. "First Amendment values may not be invoked merely by linking the words 'sex' and 'books'." 478 U.S. at 705, 106 S.Ct. at 3176.

Like the New York Public Health Law, in *Arcara*, Pennsylvania's Act does not single out bookstores for the imposition of its burden. The Act is aimed at any building used for illicit or illegal sexual conduct. That the Appellants' buildings were coincidentally adult bookstores does not excuse the unlawful sexual activity occurring on their premises.

The preliminary injunction here is narrow in scope and aimed at stopping the sexual activity occurring in the video viewing booths and the "California Couch Dancing" area of Appellants' establishments. The status quo is restored, as Appellants' establishments return to being utilized for what is assumed to be their original purpose, as adult bookstores, where Appellants are free to continue selling books, magazines and videos, thereby exercising their First Amendment rights.

Accordingly, we affirm the trial court's grant of preliminary injunction pending a full hearing on the merits.

### NOTES

**1. Private and Private Nuisance.** There are two kinds of nuisance: private and public. A private nuisance is one that interferes with an individual's right to the private use and enjoyment of land. The Restatement (Second) of Torts articulates the law of private nuisance as follows:

> One is subject to liability for a private nuisance if, but only if, his conduct is a legal cause of an invasion of another's interest in the private use and enjoyment of land, and the invasion is either
>
> > (a) intentional and unreasonable, or
> >
> > (b) unintentional and otherwise actionable under the rules controlling liability for negligent or reckless conduct, or for abnormally dangerous conditions or activities.

Restatement (Second) of Torts § 822. See Diamond, Levine & Madden, *Understanding Torts* § 18.01 (2nd ed. 2000); Keeton, *Prosser and Keeton on the Law of Torts* § 87 (5th ed. 1984) and Dobbs, *The Law of Torts* §§ 462–468 (2000).

A public nuisance, on the other hand, is one that interferes with the general public's health or safety or a public right. The Restatement (Second) of Torts defines the law of public nuisance as follows:

> (1) A public nuisance is an unreasonable interference with a right common to the general public.
>
> (2) Circumstances that may sustain a holding that an interference with a public right is unreasonable include the following:
>
> > (a) whether the conduct involves a significant interference with the public health, the public safety, the public peace, the public comfort or the public convenience, or
> >
> > (b) whether the conduct is proscribed by a statute, ordinance or administrative regulation, or
> >
> > (c) whether the conduct is of a continuing nature or has produced a permanent or long-lasting effect, and, as the actor knows or has reason to know, has a significant effect upon the public right.

Restatement (Second) of Torts § 821B. See Diamond, Levine & Madden, supra, and Keeton, supra, § 90; Dobbs, supra, §§ 462–468.

A nuisance can be both a public and private nuisance where it unreasonably interferes with both private property rights and the safety or other rights of the public. For example in *German v. Federal Home Loan Mortgage Corp.*, 885 F.Supp. 537 (S.D.N.Y.1995) the court held that the failure to remove lead paint from apartment buildings could constitute both a public and private nuisance by interfering both with public safety and the use and enjoyment of private land.

Should the sale of guns in quantities that raise questions concerning the intended use and potential illegal resale of the weapons be characterized as a public nuisance? Several local governments are making such claims. Does such marketing unreasonably interfere with the public safety? See Butterfield, "Chicago is Suing Over Guns for Suburbs," *N.Y. Times* (11/13/98) at A16. See also *Hamilton v. Accu–Tek*, 62 F.Supp.2d 802 (E.D.N.Y. 1999) discussing negligent marketing.

Consider *In Re Starlink Corn Products Liability Litigation*, 212 F.Supp.2d 828 (2002), where the court held that farmers alleging a nuisance in that genetically modified corn was allowed to commingle and thus contaminate their crops, had stated a claim for both private and public nuisance. The court agreed that "drifting pollen can constitute an invasion, and that contaminating neighbors' crops interferes with their enjoyment of land." Even though the defendants themselves were no longer in control of the seeds at the time of the alleged contamination, the fact that defendants had an EPA mandate duty to control the use of their product "arguably put Aventis in a position to control the nuisance." The plaintiffs also stated a claim for public nuisance, because they alleged a general injury to the public in the contamination of the food supply, and a special injury to themselves as corn growers who suffered the financial burden of the contamination.

**2. Role of Equity.** Certain equitable factors may affect a court's willingness to find a nuisance. Zoning is one such factor and impacts on whether the interference is unreasonable. Another concerns instances where the plaintiff comes to the nuisance, as was the case in the article that follows:

BRAGG, *COUNTRY CLUB MEETS ENEMY: COUNTRY, AND PIGS\**

N.Y. Times, April 11, 1999 at A16.

Two worlds collide, on the 15th tee.

On one side of the skinny blacktop road, the manicured fairways of the Florida Club golf course meander through the palmetto scrub, where a solitary golfer with a retirement tan hacks hard at the ball and then chases it down in his golf cart, like a duck after a June bug.

On the other side, 165 mud-spattered pigs wallow, grunt, scratch and squeal under the skimpy shade of the same southeast Florida scrub, and the stench, from the animals, the manure and the mounds of rotting lettuce, tomatoes and moldy bread that they consume, hits the people who turn in the sandy driveway like a punch in the nose.

Country music—at the moment the Dixie Chicks, singing on WIRK radio about crying mamas and wide open spaces—mingles with the smell and the heat and the squeals, and the whole experience drifts across the scrub, across the road and onto the carefully tended greens of the Florida Club course.

The pigs' owner, a big, ruddy-faced, white-haired, sunburned man named Paul Thompson, sits in the shade beside the fly-blown pens and shakes his head.

"Now who," Mr. Thompson said, "would choose to build a golf course next to a pig farm? Didn't they read the sign? It says 'pig farm,' not 'rose garden.' "

He shakes his head again.

"And they say I'm crazy."

Such a confrontation of old and new Florida, here in this corner of Martin County about 30 minutes north of Palm Beach, was bound to lead to lawyers. But it is the music, not the smell, that has Mr. Thompson in court, defending his right to play Merle Haggard,

Garth Brooks and Dolly Parton for his pigs. He swears it improves their disposition.

The Florida Club, a golf course and subdivision with homes that sell for around $300,000, is suing Mr. Thompson, 60, and another farmer, claiming that the country music they play bothers the golfers.

Mr. Thompson says he is being told how to live his life by the new, richer residents who are encroaching on what used to be a wild, simple place, "just one more case of the rich developers running over the little guy."

Asked how he knew the developers were rich, he smiled.

"Because I've never seen a poor developer," he said.

A trial date has not been set.

Greg Cotten, the general manager of the Florida Club, insists that its members only want to play in peace, and that the legal challenge is a simple lawsuit intended to halt a nuisance. The club seeks no damages, just reduced volume.

"This guy is persisting with his story of the big developers squeezing him out," which is false, Mr. Cotten said. "He's welcome to stay there."

Lawyers for the club have said that Mr. Thompson and the neighbor who also raises music-accented pork, Tom Rossano, want the club to buy their properties at an inflated price, to gain peace and quiet.

Mr. Cotten said Mr. Thompson also liked being courted by the media. "He's just a lonely guy who's enjoying the attention," Mr. Cotten said.

Asked whether he was playing the country music in an effort to get the club to buy his three acres, Mr. Thompson said no.

He was here first, in 1957, 38 years before the country club, he said.

But when asked whether he would consider selling his property, Mr. Thompson replied that "everything is for sale, if someone is willing to sell and someone is willing to buy."

"But I can't force anybody to buy me out," and certainly, he said, not by playing country music.

"When I pulled up in my car here for the first time, in '57, there was country music on the radio," Mr. Thompson said. Over the years, he read studies about how music made cows give more milk, made chickens lay more eggs and even made small children in day care centers happier.

What was good for humans must be good for pigs, he reasoned. He found that the music soothed the pigs, and made them less prone to attack each other in their tight surroundings.

The pigs, Mr. Thompson said, do not know the difference between styles of music, between Handel and Hank Williams.

"I play country," he said, "because I like country."

The golfers, bent over their Big Bertha drivers, trying to cleanly strike a small white sphere, have found that hard to do with George Jones warbling: "It's that teeny-weeny, itsy-bitsy thing we call the love bug."

Mr. Thompson has no sympathy for them. He does not play golf.

He considers the golfers hypocrites, people who do not want to know where their pork comes from.

"Standing around moaning about me, with a pork chop in their mouth," he said.

The battle with the country club has been raging for the past year, and so far the law seems to be on the pig farmers' side.

Checks on the noise level of the music by deputies of the Martin County Sheriff's Department and the neighboring St. Lucie County Sheriff's Department found that the music at both Mr. Thompson's and Mr. Rossano's farms was below the 60 decibels allowed in residential areas.

"There is no violation," said Jenell Atlas, the public information officer for the Martin County Sheriff's Department. Mr. Thompson has "been out there many, many years. As far as we're concerned, he's not breaking the law."

On the face of it, it seems a lopsided battle. One of the country club's lawyers is State Representative Tom Warner, a Republican from Stuart.

And within the past year, the country club pushed for and won a new ordinance that set a decibel level for residential areas—the very one that Mr. Thompson has been obeying.

But Mr. Thompson is no backwoods farmer, despite the pig flop on his boots. He has his own Web site—www.pigfarmer.com—and now he has his own legal defense fund, the Paul Thompson–Pig Farmer Legal Defense Fund, to be precise.

It will give him a chance, he said, against the country club.

Why not just turn the music down, he is asked. Well, he said, the pigs could not hear it, and worse than that, it would be giving up.

And when he gives up, he said, it will be only when "they're carrying me out of here, walking slow and singing low."

Appropriately, John Anderson comes on the radio a few minutes later, singing about a dying way of life in Florida.

*Blow, blow Seminole wind*

*Blow like it's never gonna blow again*

It is hard to tell if the pigs are impressed.

Where a plaintiff comes to a nuisance, courts may be more hesitant to find that the defendant's pre-existing activities constitute a nuisance. This is not an absolute rule, however, as courts recognize the need to allow for changes in land use. What was once not a nuisance may become one.

To what extent should notions of equity permit a land user to impede on a neighbor's right to quiet use and enjoyment? Consider *Armory Park Neighborhood Association v. Episcopal Community Services in Arizona*, 148 Ariz. 1, 712 P.2d 914 (1985), in which the defendants offered free meals to indigent persons, thus drawing large numbers of visitors to the plaintiff's neighborhood. The visitors frequently trespassed on the residents' property, littered, and caused other problems. The plaintiff association sued for an injunction. The court held that even though the defendant's activities were praiseworthy and complied with zoning laws, it would uphold the lower court's granting of a preliminary injunction.

## IMPELLIZERRI v. JAMESVILLE FEDERATED CHURCH

Supreme Court, Onondaga County, New York.
104 Misc.2d 620, 428 N.Y.S.2d 550 (1979).

TENNEY, Justice.

Anthony and Luana Impellizerri are seeking an injunction to restrain the Jamesville Federated Church from playing its carillon. They contend that the playing of the carillon is . . . a nuisance. The carillon is a series of bells which are played in various musical arrangements. It is played three times a day and four times on Sundays at regular hours for a period of approximately four minutes each time. Many attempts have been made to compromise. The speakers have been moved, playing time curtailed and the sound intensity reduced to no avail. Plaintiffs want it stopped. There is no dispute as to the facts and neither party has requested a hearing.

Life is full of sounds. The same sound can be pleasant in one moment and unpleasant in another. Children at play can be a refreshing sound to some and an annoyance to others. Unwanted sound is called noise, and it can produce unwanted effects. It may even reach the point where it becomes a restrainable pollutant. (See discussion 45A NY Jur, Pollution Control and Conservation Laws, § 143.) However, there are many noises which are part of life and which all of us have to learn to accept. Plaintiffs admit that on occasion the normal village and traffic sounds drown out the bells.

In an industrial society, there are many noises which the courts have considered and have found not subject to restraint; trains and whistles, low flying planes, manufacturing noises, loud music *(Peters v. Moses*, 171 Misc 441), road traffic *(Sperry v. State of New York*, 50 AD2d 618), contra stock car racing *(State of New York v. Waterloo Stock Car Raceway*, 96 Misc 2d 350), fans *(Hunt v. Eschen*, 136 NYS2d 136).

In each case, the court has tried to consider the effect in determining the existence of a nuisance. A nuisance may be merely a right thing in a wrong place. *(Euclid v. Amber Co.*, 272 U.S. 365, 388.)

The plaintiffs contend that the volume of the bells effects their son who has a neurological disease and is kept awake. Luana Impellizerri claims she has migraine headaches and muscle spasms as the result of an accident which are aggravated by the bells. Generally, the claim is that conversation is disrupted, and the sounds cause severe anxiety and emotional stress to plaintiffs.

Bells in one form or another are a tradition throughout the world. In the Koran, they are considered the music of God. In the Christian world, every church is proud of its bells. The bells are rung for joy, for sadness, for warnings and for worship.

There are people who find total beauty in the sounds of bells in the Tower of Parliament in London or the daily ritual ringing at the Cathedral of Notre Dame in Paris. There is little question that the sound is often deafening when these bells start to ring, but for the general enjoyment of the public, it is considered acceptable.

It is often said that what is beauty to one may be ugly to another. A person with a special problem or an extra sensitive ear will be upset by any but the purest sound. That is not enough to justify the interference of the law.

The right to make a reasonable use of one's property has been long protected. Such a right is limited only if it unreasonably interferes with the rights of others. *McCarty v. Natural Carbonic Gas Co.* (189 NY 40, 50), 81 N.E. 549 at page 551:

> "The use made of property may be unpleasant, unsightly or, to some extent, annoying and disagreeable to the occupants of neighboring property without creating a nuisance."

There must be a material interference with the physical comfort and financial injury before there can be a nuisance. Stated another way, an early Massachusetts case held that the test should be the "common care of persons of ordinary prudence" and not as to those with "peculiar condition[s]". *(Rogers v. Elliott,* 146 Mass 349, 353.) The alleged nuisance must be such as would cause an unwanted effect on the health and comfort of an ordinary person in the same or a similar situation. (58 Am Jur 2d, Nuisances, §§ 65–67.)

It seems that the plaintiffs have a special problem because of their own special condition. There are no other complainants, although there are several neighbors who live closer to the church than plaintiffs. It cannot be said that the ringing of the bell is such that would produce an unwanted effect on the ordinary person in the same circumstances.

\* \* \*

Therefore, the plaintiffs' motion for an injunction is denied, and the defendant's cross motion to dismiss the complaint is granted.

### NOTES

**1. Evaluating Nuisance Objectively.** Hypersensitive plaintiffs are generally not allowed to recover for private nuisance. The Restatement (Second) of Torts states:

> There is liability for a nuisance only to those to whom it causes significant harm, of a kind that would be suffered by a normal

person in the community or by property in normal condition and used for a normal purpose.

Restatement (Second) of Torts § 821F.

Consider *Layton v. Yankee Caithness Joint Venture*, 774 F.Supp. 576 (D.Nev.1991), in which the court found that one of the plaintiffs was "exceptionally sensitive" to the noise of a neighboring geothermal power plant and therefore would not be able to recover for his injuries. The court reasoned:

> Any injury suffered by [the plaintiff] is due to his unusual sensitivity to noise. The law holds YCJV to the standards of normal persons in the locality. It is undisputed that YCJV's conduct satisfies that standard.

Even if there is economic harm to the plaintiff, the defendant will not be liable under private nuisance unless his actions constitute a cognizable injury. In *Adkins v. Thomas Solvent Co.*, 440 Mich. 293, 487 N.W.2d 715 (1992), the court considered a property owner's contention that:

> [A] claim for relief may be maintained by plaintiffs who claim the right to damages in nuisance for property depreciation caused by environmental contamination of ground water despite testimony by both plaintiffs' and defendants' experts that their properties were not and would never be subject to ground water contamination emanating from the defendants' property.

The court then went on to summarize its interpretation of the relevant Restatement sections.

> According to the Restatement, an actor is subject to liability for private nuisance for a nontrespassory invasion of another's interest in the private use and enjoyment of land if (a) the other has property rights and privileges in respect to the use or enjoyment interfered with, (b) the invasion results in significant harm, (c) the actor's conduct is the legal cause of the invasion, and (d) the invasion is either (i) intentional and unreasonable, or (ii) unintentional and otherwise actionable under the rules governing liability for negligent, reckless, or ultrahazardous conduct.

The court then held that an ungrounded fear cannot form the basis of a private nuisance claim.

> In short, we do not agree with the dissent's suggestion that wholly unfounded fears of third parties regarding the conduct of a lawful business satisfy the requirement for a legally cognizable injury as long as property values decline. Indeed, we would think it is not only "odd" ... but anachronistic that a claim of nuisance in fact could be based on unfounded fears regarding persons with AIDS moving into a neighborhood, the establishment of otherwise lawful group homes for the disabled, or unrelated person living together, merely because the fears experienced by third parties would cause a decline in property values.

# BOOMER v. ATLANTIC CEMENT CO.

Court of Appeals of New York.

26 N.Y.2d 219, 309 N.Y.S.2d 312, 257 N.E.2d 870 (1970).

BERGAN, Judge.

Defendant operates a large cement plant near Albany. These are actions for injunction and damages by neighboring land owners alleging injury to property from dirt, smoke and vibration emanating from the plant. A nuisance has been found after trial, temporary damages have been allowed; but an injunction has been denied.

\* \* \*

The cement making operations of defendant have been found by the court at Special Term to have damaged the nearby properties of plaintiffs in these two actions. That court, as it has been noted, accordingly found defendant maintained a nuisance and this has been affirmed at the Appellate Division. The total damage to plaintiffs' properties is, however, relatively small in comparison with the value of defendant's operation and with the consequences of the injunction which plaintiffs seek.

The ground for the denial of injunction, notwithstanding the finding both that there is a nuisance and that plaintiffs have been damaged substantially, is the large disparity in economic consequences of the nuisance and of the injunction. This theory cannot, however, be sustained without overruling a doctrine which has been consistently reaffirmed in several leading cases in this court and which has never been disavowed here, namely that where a nuisance has been found and where there has been any substantial damage shown by the party complaining an injunction will be granted.

\* \* \*

. . . . The total of permanent damages to all plaintiffs thus found was $185,000 . . . . \*

\* \* \*

One alternative is to grant the injunction but postpone its effect to a specified future date to give opportunity for technical advances to permit defendant to eliminate the nuisance; another is to grant the injunction conditioned on the payment of permanent damages to plaintiffs which would compensate them for the total economic loss to their property present and future caused by defendant's operations. For reasons which will be developed the court chooses the latter alternative.

If the injunction were to be granted unless within a short period—e.g., 18 months—the nuisance be abated by improved methods, there would be no assurance that any significant technical improvement would occur.

\* \* \*

---

\* Respondent's investment in the plant is in excess of $45,000,000. There are over 300 people employed there.

On the other hand, to grant the injunction unless defendant pays plaintiffs such permanent damages as may be fixed by the court seems to do justice between the contending parties. All of the attributions of economic loss to the properties on which plaintiffs' complaints are based will have been redressed.

\* \* \*

Thus it seems fair to both sides to grant permanent damages to plaintiffs which will terminate this private litigation. The theory of damage is the "servitude on land" of plaintiffs imposed by defendant's nuisance. (See *United States v. Causby*, 328 U. S. 256, 261, 262, 267, where the term "servitude" addressed to the land was used by Justice Douglas relating to the effect of airplane noise on property near an airport.)

The judgment, by allowance of permanent damages imposing a servitude on land, which is the basis of the actions, would preclude future recovery by plaintiffs or their grantees (see *Northern Indiana Public Serv. Co. v. Vesey*, supra, p. 351).

This should be placed beyond debate by a provision of the judgment that the payment by defendant and the acceptance by plaintiffs of permanent damages found by the court shall be in compensation for a servitude on the land.

Although the Trial Term has found permanent damages as a possible basis of settlement of the litigation, on remission the court should be entirely free to re-examine this subject. It may again find the permanent damage already found; or make new findings.

The orders should be reversed, without costs, and the cases remitted to Supreme Court, Albany County to grant an injunction which shall be vacated upon payment by defendant of such amounts of permanent damage to the respective plaintiffs as shall for this purpose be determined by the court.

## NOTES

**1. Remedies for Nuisance**. Consider the following summary of the four basic judicial responses to a nuisance:

\* \* \*

Before *Boomer*, New York courts understood nuisance law to include two possible outcomes. One was a classic injunction when there was any substantial interference with the use and enjoyment of the land of another. The other was no remedy at all. The first compelled the polluter to adjourn operations, or "pay off" the victim to allow continuation of the nuisance. This placed the victim in a position of immense power. The second left the "victim" with no hope for recourse, unless he could convince the polluter to accept payment to abate the alleged nuisance.

\* \* \*

Most scholars today would assert that there are four theoretical outcomes for nuisance litigation, short of securing a public official's action.

## A. No Remedy

The plaintiff loses and receives no assistance from the courts. The only possible remedy is to attempt to "bribe" the polluter to stop polluting.

\* \* \*

## B. Compensated Injunctions

The victim obtains an injunction abating the nuisance but must compensate the polluter for the losses incurred from the injunction. This remedy has strong scholarly support, but appears to have been adopted only once.

\* \* \*

## C. Damages

The third possible remedy is damages under a "liability rule." The victims receive compensation for the harm they suffer, but an injunction is not granted. This is the essentially the remedy employed in *Boomer*.

\* \* \*

## D. Conventional Injunctions

The fourth outcome is the conventional injunction under a "property rule." The victims have the right to abate the nuisance. This puts the polluter in the position of "bribing" the victim for the right to pollute, thus settling the lawsuit.

Holezer, *Boomer Revisited: Using Experimental and Partial Injunctions in Private Nuisance Actions*, 64 Def. Couns. J. 99 (1997) [footnotes omitted]. See Calabresi & Melamed, *One View of the Cathedral*, 85 Harv. L. Rev. 1089 (1972); Diamond, Levine & Madden, *Understanding Torts* § 18.01 (2nd ed. 2000); Keeton, *Prosser and Keeton on the Law of Torts*, § 89 (5th ed. 1984) and Dobbs, *The Law of Torts* § 468 (2000).

Consider *Spur Industries, Inc. v. Del E. Webb Development Co.*, 108 Ariz. 178, 494 P.2d 700 (1972), alluded to in the above excerpt as an example of a compensation injunction. Spur Industries ran a cattle feedlot that adversely affected its residential neighbors, who had bought their homes from Del E. Webb. The court found that the feedlot was a nuisance. However, since Del E. Webb developed around the feedlot, the injunction against the feedlot would only be granted if Del E. Webb would pay the reasonable relocation fees of the feedlot.

**2. Response to *Boomer*.** Do cases like *Boomer* and *Spur* offer a sensible solution to environmental and property issues? Consider the following commentary:

> When *Boomer* and its satellite, *Spur Industries v. Del E. Webb Development Co.*, appeared above the legal horizon in the early seventies, they caused a great stir as harbingers, for good or ill, of a new era in environmental and property law. These decisions seemed to stand for a new idea: that property rights could be treated like the right to be free from personal harm. The infringement of these rights would call forth not the thunderbolts of equity, but rather simple damage awards. The entitlements of smallholders would be acknowledged, in all fairness, and the remedy for their loss would be monetary, not equitable, as efficiency demanded.

Halper, *Nuisance, Courts and Markets in the New York Court of Appeals, 1850–1915*, 54 Alb. L. Rev. 301 (1990).

**3. Nuisance Law and the Coase Theorem.** Arguably the court injunction in a nuisance case will not affect the ultimate use of the land. The Coase theorem states that the initial assignment of property rights does not affect how the property will be ultimately used in the absence of transaction costs. Professor Ronald Coase developed his theorem with nuisance specifically in mind. Absent substantial transaction costs, even if there was an injunction, the land would still be used in the most efficient way because the parties would simply negotiate among themselves to use the land in the most efficient manner. If the injunction was against the polluter, then the polluter would buy out the injunction against him as long as the benefit of the pollution causing activity exceeds the cost of the harm caused by the pollution. If no injunction is imposed, then the plaintiff will pay the polluter not to pollute up the point the benefits of no pollution exceed the costs of paying for it. See Coase, *The Problem of Social Cost*, 3 Journal of Law & Economics (1960). See generally Rabin, Nuisance Law: Rethinking Fundamental Assumptions, 63 Va. L. Rev. 1299 (1977).

# Chapter V

## DAMAGES

---

### SECTION A.  COMPENSATORY DAMAGES

#### McDOUGALD v. GARBER

Court of Appeals of New York.

73 N.Y.2d 246, 538 N.Y.S.2d 937, 536 N.E.2d 372 (1989).

WACHTLER, Chief Judge.

This appeal raises fundamental questions about the nature and role of nonpecuniary damages in personal injury litigation. By nonpecuniary damages, we mean those damages awarded to compensate an injured person for the physical and emotional consequences of the injury, such as pain and suffering and the loss of the ability to engage in certain activities. Pecuniary damages, on the other hand, compensate the victim for the economic consequences of the injury, such as medical expenses, lost earnings and the cost of custodial care.

The specific questions raised here deal with the assessment of nonpecuniary damages and are (1) whether some degree of cognitive awareness is a prerequisite to recovery for loss of enjoyment of life and (2) whether a jury should be instructed to consider and award damages for loss of enjoyment of life separately from damages for pain and suffering. We answer the first question in the affirmative and the second question in the negative.

I.

On September 7, 1978, plaintiff Emma McDougald, then 31 years old, underwent a Caesarean section and tubal ligation at New York Infirmary. Defendant Garber performed the surgery; defendants Armengol and Kulkarni provided anesthesia. During the surgery, Mrs. McDougald suffered oxygen deprivation which resulted in severe brain damage and left her in a permanent comatose condition. This action was brought by Mrs. McDougald and her husband, suing derivatively, alleging that the injuries were caused by the defendants' acts of malpractice.

**604**

A jury found all defendants liable and awarded Emma McDougald a total of $9,650,102 in damages, including $1,000,000 for conscious pain and suffering and a separate award of $3,500,000 for loss of the pleasures and pursuits of life. The balance of the damages awarded to her were for pecuniary damages—lost earnings and the cost of custodial and nursing care. Her husband was awarded $1,500,000 on his derivative claim for the loss of his wife's services. On defendants' posttrial motions, the Trial Judge reduced the total award to Emma McDougald to $4,796,728 by striking the entire award for future nursing care ($2,353,-374) and by reducing the separate awards for conscious pain and suffering and loss of the pleasures and pursuits of life to a single award of $2,000,000 (*McDougald v. Garber*, 132 Misc 2d 457). Her husband's award was left intact. On cross appeals, the Appellate Division affirmed (135 AD2d 80) and later granted defendants leave to appeal to this court.

## II.

We note at the outset that the defendants' liability for Emma McDougald's injuries is unchallenged here, except for a claim by Dr. Garber that liability against her was predicated on a theory not asserted in the complaint or bill of particulars. We agree with the Appellate Division, for the reasons stated by that court (*see,* 135 AD2d 80, 95–96, *supra*), that Dr. Garber's claim does not warrant a new trial on liability.

Also unchallenged are the awards in the amount of $770,978 for loss of earnings and $2,025,750 for future custodial care—that is, the pecuniary damage awards that survived defendants' posttrial motions.

What remains in dispute, primarily, is the award to Emma McDougald for nonpecuniary damages. At trial, defendants sought to show that Mrs. McDougald's injuries were so severe that she was incapable of either experiencing pain or appreciating her condition. Plaintiffs, on the other hand, introduced proof that Mrs. McDougald responded to certain stimuli to a sufficient extent to indicate that she was aware of her circumstances. Thus, the extent of Mrs. McDougald's cognitive abilities, if any, was sharply disputed.

The parties and the trial court agreed that Mrs. McDougald could not recover for pain and suffering unless she were conscious of the pain. Defendants maintained that such consciousness was also required to support an award for loss of enjoyment of life. The court, however, accepted plaintiffs' view that loss of enjoyment of life was compensable without regard to whether the plaintiff was aware of the loss. Accordingly, because the level of Mrs. McDougald's cognitive abilities was in dispute, the court instructed the jury to consider loss of enjoyment of life as an element of nonpecuniary damages separate from pain and suffering. The court's charge to the jury on these points was as follows:

"If you conclude that Emma McDougald is so neurologically impaired that she is totally incapable of experiencing any unpleasant or painful sensation, then, obviously, she cannot be awarded damages for conscious pain * * *.

"It is for you to determine the level of Emma McDougalds perception and awareness. Suffering relates primarily to the emotional reaction of the injured person to the injury. Thus, for an injured person to experience suffering, there, again, must be some level of awareness. If Emma McDougald is totally unaware of her condition or totally incapable of any emotional reaction, then you cannot award her damages for suffering. If, however, you conclude that there is some level of perception or that she is capable of an emotional response at some level, then damages for pain and suffering should be awarded * * *.

"Damages for the loss of the pleasures and pursuits of life, however, require no awareness of the loss on the part of the injured person. Quite obviously, Emma McDougald is unable to engage in any of the activities which constitute a normal life, the activities she engaged in prior to her injury * * * Loss of the enjoyment of life may, of course, accompany the physical sensation and emotional responses that we refer to as pain and suffering, and in most cases it does. It is possible, however, for an injured person to lose the enjoyment of life without experiencing any conscious pain and suffering. Damages for this item of injury relate not to what Emma McDougald is aware of, but rather to what she has lost. What her life was prior to her injury and what it has been since September 7, 1978 and what it will be for as long as she lives."

We conclude that the court erred, both in instructing the jury that Mrs. McDougald's awareness was irrelevant to their consideration of damages for loss of enjoyment of life and in directing the jury to consider that aspect of damages separately from pain and suffering.

### III.

We begin with the familiar proposition that an award of damages to a person injured by the negligence of another is to compensate the victim, not to punish the wrongdoer (see, Sharapata v. Town of Islip, 56 NY2d 332, 335; Prosser and Keeton, Torts, at 7 [5th ed]). The goal is to restore the injured party, to the extent possible, to the position that would have been occupied had the wrong not occurred (1 Minzer, Nates, Kimball, Axelrod & Goldstein, Damages in Tort Actions §§ 1.00, 1.02). To be sure, placing the burden of compensation on the negligent party also serves as a deterrent, but purely punitive damages—that is, those which have no compensatory purpose—are prohibited unless the harmful conduct is intentional, malicious, outrageous, or otherwise aggravated beyond mere negligence (see, Sharapata v. Town of Islip, supra, at 335; Prosser and Keeton, Torts, at 9–10 [5th ed]; 1 Minzer, op. cit., § 1.03).

Damages for nonpecuniary losses are, of course, among those that can be awarded as compensation to the victim. This aspect of damages, however, stands on less certain ground than does an award for pecuniary damages. An economic loss can be compensated in kind by an economic gain; but recovery for noneconomic losses such as pain and suffering and loss of enjoyment of life rests on "the legal fiction that money damages can compensate for a victim's injury" (Howard v. Lecher, 42 NY2d 109, 111). We accept this fiction, knowing that although money will neither ease the pain nor restore the victim's abilities, this device is as close as the law can come in its effort to right the wrong. We have no hope of evaluating what has been lost, but a monetary award may provide a measure of solace for the condition created (see, Skelton v. Collins, 115 CLR 94, 130, 39 ALJR 480, 495 [Austl H C]).

Our willingness to indulge this fiction comes to an end, however, when it ceases to serve the compensatory goals of tort recovery. When that limit is met, further indulgence can only result in assessing damages that are punitive. The question posed by this case, then, is whether an award of damages for loss of enjoyment of life to a person whose injuries preclude any awareness of the loss serves a compensatory purpose. We conclude that it does not.

Simply put, an award of money damages in such circumstances has no meaning or utility to the injured person. An award for the loss of enjoyment of life "cannot provide [such a victim] with any consolation or ease any burden resting on him * * * He cannot spend it upon necessities or pleasures. He cannot experience the pleasure of giving it away" (Flannery v. United States, 718 F2d 108, 111, cert denied 467 US 1226).

We recognize that, as the trial court noted, requiring some cognitive awareness as a prerequisite to recovery for loss of enjoyment of life will result in some cases "in the paradoxical situation that the greater the degree of brain injury inflicted by a negligent defendant, the smaller the award the plaintiff can recover in general damages" (McDougald v. Garber, 132 Misc 2d 457, 460, supra). The force of this argument, however—the temptation to achieve a balance between injury and damages—has nothing to do with meaningful compensation for the victim. Instead, the temptation is rooted in a desire to punish the defendant in proportion to the harm inflicted. However relevant such retributive symmetry may be in the criminal law, it has no place in the law of civil damages, at least in the absence of culpability beyond mere negligence.

Accordingly, we conclude that cognitive awareness is a prerequisite to recovery for loss of enjoyment of life. We do not go so far, however, as to require the fact finder to sort out varying degrees of cognition and determine at what level a particular deprivation can be fully appreciated. With respect to pain and suffering, the trial court charged simply that there must be "some level of awareness" in order for plaintiff to recover. We think that this is an appropriate standard for all aspects of nonpecuniary loss. No doubt the standard ignores analytically relevant levels of cognition, but we resist the desire for analytical purity in favor of simplicity. A more complex instruction might give the appearance of greater precision but, given the limits of our understanding of the human mind, it would in reality lead only to greater speculation.

We turn next to the question whether loss of enjoyment of life should be considered a category of damages separate from pain and suffering.

## IV.

There is no dispute here that the fact finder may, in assessing nonpecuniary damages, consider the effect of the injuries on the plaintiff's capacity to lead a normal life. Traditionally, in this State and elsewhere, this aspect of suffering has not been treated as a separate category of damages; instead, the plaintiff's inability to enjoy life to its fullest has been considered one type of suffering to be factored into a general award for nonpecuniary damages, commonly known as pain and suffering.

\* \* \*

We do not dispute that distinctions can be found or created between the concepts of pain and suffering and loss of enjoyment of life. If the term "suffering" is limited to the emotional response to the sensation of pain, then the emotional response caused by the limitation of life's activities may be considered qualitatively different (*see*, Comment, *Loss of Enjoyment of Life as a Separate Element of Damages*, 12 Pac LJ 965, 969–973). But suffering need not be so limited—it can easily encompass the frustration and anguish caused by the inability to participate in activities that once brought pleasure. Traditionally, by treating loss of enjoyment of life as a permissible factor in assessing pain and suffering, courts have given the term this broad meaning.

The advocates of separate awards contend that because pain and suffering and loss of enjoyment of life can be distinguished, they must be treated separately if the plaintiff is to be compensated fully for each distinct injury suffered. We disagree. Such an analytical approach may have its place when the subject is pecuniary damages, which can be calculated with some precision. But the estimation of nonpecuniary damages is not amenable to such analytical precision and may, in fact, suffer from its application. Translating human suffering into dollars and cents involves no mathematical formula; it rests, as we have said, on a legal fiction. The figure that emerges is unavoidably distorted by the translation. Application of this murky process to the component parts of nonpecuniary injuries (however analytically distinguishable they may be) cannot make it more accurate. If anything, the distortion will be amplified by repetition.

Thus, we are not persuaded that any salutary purpose would be served by having the jury make separate awards for pain and suffering and loss of enjoyment of life. We are confident, furthermore, that the trial advocate's art is a sufficient guarantee that none of the plaintiff's losses will be ignored by the jury.

\* \* \*

TITONE, Judge (dissenting).

The majority's holding represents a compromise position that neither comports with the fundamental principles of tort compensation nor furnishes a satisfactory, logically consistent framework for compensating nonpecuniary loss. Because I conclude that loss of enjoyment of life is an objective damage item, conceptually distinct from conscious pain and suffering, I can find no fault with the trial court's instruction authorizing separate awards and permitting an award for "loss of enjoyment of life" even in the absence of any awareness of that loss on the part of the injured plaintiff. Accordingly, I dissent.

It is elementary that the purpose of awarding tort damages is to compensate the wronged party for the actual loss he or she has sustained

(1 Minzer, Nates, Kimball, Axelrod & Goldstein, Damages in Tort Actions § 1.00, at 1–3). Personal injury damages are awarded "to restore the injured person to the state of health he had prior to his injuries because that is the only way the law knows how to recompense one for personal injuries suffered" *(Romeo v. New York City Tr. Auth.,* 73 Misc 2d 124, 126; *see, Thompson v. National R. R. Passenger Corp.,* 621 F2d 814, 824, *cert denied* 449 US 1035). Thus, this court has held that "[t]he person responsible for the injury must respond for all damages resulting directly from and as a natural consequence of the wrongful act" *(Steitz v. Gifford,* 280 NY 15, 20).

The capacity to enjoy life—by watching one's children grow, participating in recreational activities, and drinking in the many other pleasures that life has to offer—is unquestionably an attribute of an ordinary healthy individual. The loss of that capacity as a result of another's negligent act is at least as serious an impairment as the permanent destruction of a physical function, which has always been treated as a compensable item under traditional tort principles *(e.g., Simpson v. Foundation Co.,* 201 NY 479 [loss of sexual potency]; *see, Robison v. Lockridge,* 230 App Div 389, 390). Indeed, I can imagine no physical loss that is more central to the quality of a tort victim's continuing life than the destruction of the capacity to enjoy that life to the fullest.

Unquestionably, recovery of a damage item such as "pain and suffering" requires a showing of some degree of cognitive capacity. Such a requirement exists for the simple reason that pain and suffering are wholly subjective concepts and cannot exist separate and apart from the human consciousness that experiences them. In contrast, the destruction of an individual's capacity to enjoy life as a result of a crippling injury is an objective fact that does not differ in principle from the permanent loss of an eye or limb. As in the case of a lost limb, an essential characteristic of a healthy human life has been wrongfully taken, and, consequently, the injured party is entitled to a monetary award as a substitute, if, as the majority asserts, the goal of tort compensation is "to restore the injured party, to the extent possible, to the position that would have been occupied had the wrong not occurred" (majority opn., at 254, at 939 of 538 N.Y.S.2d, at 374 of 536 N.E.2d).

\* \* \*

## NOTES

**1. Types of Damages.** Tort damages may be classified into one of three types: nominal, compensatory, and punitive. Nominal damages are awarded where the tort causes no actual harm, such as a technical trespass. Such damages are usually awarded where the plaintiff seeks only to affirm or vindicate some right.

Compensatory damages are awarded to compensate the plaintiff for harm caused by the tort. Compensable harm may consist of pecuniary loss or non-pecuniary loss or both. Where a plaintiff sues for damage to property, pecuniary losses may include the diminution of value of the property, the cost of repair or replacement, or the cost of obtaining some other appropriate substitute. In the context of personal injury, pecuniary loss may include the cost of medical treatment, lost wages, and diminished earning capacity. Personal injury may also give rise to a claim for non-pecuniary damages, such as for pain and suffering, loss of consortium, and other types of non-economic harm.

As the principal case indicates, the victim must be conscious to be compensated for pain and suffering, which generally encompasses loss of enjoyment as a result of the injury. Should an unconscious victim be able to be compensated for loss of enjoyment of life? Should pain and suffering be compensated at all?

Punitive damages are awarded to punish a tortfeasor who has committed a tort with malice. The award is usually paid to the plaintiff, although in some states the government receives at least a portion of the award. See Sec. C, infra.

See generally Dobbs, *Law of Remedies: Damages, Equity, Restitution* (2nd ed. 1993); Diamond, Levine & Madden, *Understanding Torts* § 14.01 (2nd ed. 2000); Dobbs, *The Law of Torts*, §§ 377–380 (2000).

**2. Mitigation of Damages.** When a plaintiff sustains an injury from a tort defendant, she has a duty to mitigate the damages as much as she reasonably can. Thus, if a defendant causes personal injury to the plaintiff, the plaintiff must make a reasonable effort to give proper medical attention to the injury.

Related to the duty to mitigate is the obligation to engage in anticipatory mitigation. This addresses situations where the plaintiff fails to take safety precautions and thereby subjects herself to the risk of greater injury. For example, a passenger in an automobile who fails to wear a seatbelt may suffer greater injuries than she would have if she had been utilizing the seatbelt. The failure to mitigate is not considered contributory negligence, which would, under traditional doctrine, completely bar the plaintiff's claim, since the lack of precaution does not contribute to the occurrence of the accident—it merely makes the potential harm from an accident more serious. Thus, in contributory negligence jurisdictions, the plaintiff can still maintain the action, with damages reflecting the harm that the plaintiff would have suffered had she taken the proper precautions. In comparative fault jurisdictions, the notion of anticipatory mitigation is now usually simply subsumed into the comparative negligence analysis. See Chapter 2, Sec. 1, supra, for discussion of contributory and comparative negligence. See Dobbs, id.; Diamond, Levine & Madden, supra, § 17.04.

# SECTION B. COLLATERAL SOURCE RULE

## HELFEND v. SOUTHERN CALIFORNIA RAPID TRANSIT DISTRICT

Supreme Court of California.
2 Cal.3d 1, 84 Cal.Rptr. 173, 465 P.2d 61 (1970).

TOBRINER, Acting Chief Justice.

Defendants appeal from a judgment of the Los Angeles Superior Court entered on a verdict in favor of plaintiff, Julius J. Helfend, for

$16,400 in general and special damages for injuries sustained in a bus-auto collision that occurred on July 19, 1965, in the City of Los Angeles.

We have concluded that the judgment for plaintiff in this tort action against the defendant governmental entity should be affirmed. The trial court properly followed the collateral source rule in excluding evidence that a portion of plaintiff's medical bills had been paid through a medical insurance plan that requires the refund of benefits from tort recoveries.

1. *The facts.*

Shortly before noon on July 19, 1965, plaintiff drove his car in central Los Angeles east on Third Street approaching Grandview. At this point Third Street has six lanes, four for traffic and one parking lane on each side of the thoroughfare. While traveling in the second lane from the curb, plaintiff observed an automobile driven by Glen A. Raney, Jr., stopping in his lane and preparing to back into a parking space. Plaintiff put out his left arm to signal the traffic behind him that he intended to stop; he then brought his vehicle to a halt so that the other driver could park.

At about this time Kenneth A. Mitchell, a bus driver for the Southern California Rapid Transit District, pulled out of a bus stop at the curb of Third Street and headed in the same direction as plaintiff. Approaching plaintiff's and Raney's cars which were stopped in the second lane from the curb, Mitchell pulled out into the lane closest to the center of the street in order to pass. The right rear of the bus sideswiped plaintiff's vehicle, knocking off the rear-view mirror and crushing plaintiff's arm, which had been hanging down at the side of his car in the stopping signal position.

\* \* \*

Plaintiff filed a tort action against the Southern California Rapid Transit District, a public entity, and Mitchell, an employee of the transit district. At trial plaintiff claimed slightly more than $2,700 in special damages, including $921 in doctor's bills, a $336.99 hospital bill, and about $45 for medicines.[1] Defendant requested permission to show that about 80 percent of the plaintiff's hospital bill had been paid by plaintiff's Blue Cross insurance carrier and that some of his other medical expenses may have been paid by other insurance. The superior court thoroughly considered the then very recent case of *City of Salinas v. Souza & McCue Constr. Co.* (1967) 66 Cal.2d 217 [57 Cal.Rptr. 337, 424 P.2d 921], distinguished the *Souza* case on the ground that *Souza* involved a contract setting, and concluded that the judgment should not be reduced to the extent of the amount of insurance payments which plaintiff received. The court ruled that defendants should not be permitted to show that plaintiff had received medical coverage from any collateral source.

---

**1.** The plaintiff claimed special damages of $2,737.99 of which $1,302.99 represented medical expenses, $35 repair of plaintiff's watch, about $1,350 expenses and costs incurred as a result of hiring another man to do the work plaintiff normally performed, and $50 plaintiffs share of the automobile repair costs.

After the jury verdict in favor of plaintiff in the sum of $16,400, defendants appealed, raising only two contentions: (1) The trial court committed prejudicial error in refusing to allow the introduction of evidence to the effect that a portion of the plaintiff's medical bills had been paid from a collateral source. (2) The trial court erred in denying defendant the opportunity to determine if plaintiff had been compensated from more than one collateral source for damages sustained in the accident.

We must decide whether the collateral source rule applies to tort actions involving public entities and public employees in which the plaintiff has received benefits from his medical insurance coverage.

2. *The collateral source rule.*

The Supreme Court of California has long adhered to the doctrine that if an injured party receives some compensation for his injuries from a source wholly independent of the tortfeasor, such payment should not be deducted from the damages which the plaintiff would otherwise collect from the tortfeasor. (See, e.g., *Peri v. Los Angeles Junction Ry. Co.* (1943) 22 Cal.2d 111, 131 [137 P.2d 441].) As recently as August 1968 we unanimously reaffirmed our adherence to this doctrine, which is known as the "collateral source rule." (*De Cruz v. Reid* (1968) 69 Cal.2d 217, 223–227 [70 Cal.Rptr. 550, 444 P.2d 342]; see *City of Salinas v. Souza & McCue Constr. Co., supra.*, 66 Cal.2d 217, 226.)

Although the collateral source rule remains generally accepted in the United States, nevertheless many other jurisdictions have restricted or repealed it. In this country most commentators have criticized the rule and called for its early demise. . . .

\* \* \*

The collateral source rule as applied here embodies the venerable concept that a person who has invested years of insurance premiums to assure his medical care should receive the benefits of his thrift. The tortfeasor should not garner the benefits of his victim's providence.

The collateral source rule expresses a policy judgment in favor of encouraging citizens to purchase and maintain insurance for personal injuries and for other eventualities. Courts consider insurance a form of investment, the benefits of which become payable without respect to any other possible source of funds. If we were to permit a tortfeasor to mitigate damages with payments from plaintiff's insurance, plaintiff would be in a position inferior to that of having bought no insurance, because his payment of premiums would have earned no benefit. Defendant should not be able to avoid payment of full compensation for the injury inflicted merely because the victim has had the foresight to provide himself with insurance.

Some commentators object that the above approach to the collateral source rule provides plaintiff with a "double recovery," rewards him for the injury, and defeats the principle that damages should compensate the victim but not punish the tortfeasor. We agree with Professor Fleming's observation, however, that "double recovery is justified only in the face of some exceptional, supervening reason, as in the case of accident or life insurance, where it is felt unjust that the tortfeasor should take advantage of the thrift and prescience of the victim in having paid the premium." (Fleming, Introduction to the Law of Torts (1967) p. 131.) As we point out *infra.*, recovery in a wrongful death action is not defeated by the payment of the benefit on a life insurance policy.

Furthermore, insurance policies increasingly provide for either subrogation or refund of benefits upon a tort recovery, and such refund is indeed called for in the present case. (See Fleming, *The Collateral Source Rule and Loss Allocation in Tort Law, supra.*, 54 Cal.L.Rev. 1478, 1479.) Hence, the plaintiff receives no double recovery; the collateral source rule simply serves as a means of by-passing the antiquated doctrine of non-assignment of tortious actions and permits a proper transfer of risk from the plaintiff's insurer to the tortfeasor by way of the victim's tort recovery. The double shift from the tortfeasor to the victim and then from the victim to his insurance carrier can normally occur with little cost in that the insurance carrier is often intimately involved in the initial litigation and quite automatically receives its part of the tort settlement or verdict.

Even in cases in which the contract or the law precludes subrogation or refund of benefits, or in situations in which the collateral source waives such subrogation or refund, the rule performs entirely necessary functions in the computation of damages. For example, the cost of medical care often provides both attorneys and juries in tort cases with an important measure for assessing the plaintiff's general damages. (Cf., e.g., *Rose v. Melody Lane* (1952) 39 Cal.2d 481, 489 [247 P.2d 335].) To permit the defendant to tell the jury that the plaintiff has been recompensed by a collateral source for his medical costs might irretrievably upset the complex, delicate, and somewhat indefinable calculations which result in the normal jury verdict. (See *Hoffman v. Brandt* (1966) 65 Cal.2d 549, 554–555 [55 Cal.Rptr. 417, 421 P.2d 425]; *Garfield v. Russell* (1967) 251 Cal.App.2d 275, 279 [59 Cal.Rptr. 379].)

We also note that generally the jury is not informed that plaintiff's attorney will receive a large portion of the plaintiff's recovery in contingent fees or that personal injury damages are not taxable to the plaintiff and are normally deductible by the defendant. Hence, the plaintiff rarely actually receives full compensation for his injuries as computed by the jury. The collateral source rule partially serves to compensate for the attorney's share and does not actually render "double recovery" for the plaintiff. Indeed, many jurisdictions that have abolished or limited the collateral source rule have also established a means for assessing the plaintiff's costs for counsel directly against the defendant rather than imposing the contingent fee system. In sum, the plaintiffs recovery for his medical expenses from both the tortfeasor and his medical insurance program will not usually give him "double recovery," but partially provides a somewhat closer approximation to full compensation for his injuries.

If we consider the collateral source rule as applied here in the context of the entire American approach to the law of torts and damages, we find that the rule presently performs a number of legitimate and even indispensable functions. Without a thorough revolution in the American approach to torts and the consequent damages, the rule at least with respect to medical insurance benefits has become so integrated within our present system that its precipitous judicial nullification would work hardship. In this case the collateral source rule lies between two systems for the compensation of accident victims: the traditional tort recovery based on fault and the increasingly prevalent coverage based on non-fault insurance. Neither system possesses such universality of coverage or completeness of compensation that we can easily dispense with the collateral source rule's approach to meshing the two systems. (Cf., e.g., *Bilyeu v. State Employees' Retirement System* (1962) 58 Cal.2d 618, 629 [24 Cal.Rptr. 562, 375 P.2d 442] (concurring opn. of Peters, J.).) The reforms which many academicians propose cannot easily be achieved through piecemeal common law development; the proposed changes, if desirable, would be more effectively accomplished through legislative reform. In any case, we cannot believe that the judicial repeal of the collateral source rule, as applied in the present case, would be the place to begin the needed changes.

\* \* \*

The judgment is affirmed.

### NOTES

**1. Collateral Source Rule.** The traditional approach to awarding damages is to not allow the jury to know of compensation that the plaintiff has received from other sources, such as insurance companies. Thus, suppose that A is tortiously injured by B and sustains personal injuries. A may have medical insurance and be fully compensated from that source. Nevertheless, B is still liable to A for the total cost of the harm, and B will not be allowed to introduce evidence of A's insurance policy. The collateral source rule has been modified in many states by tort reform statutes. See this Chapter, Sec. D, infra. See Diamond, Levine & Madden, *Understanding Torts* § 14.06 (2nd ed. 2000); Dobbs, *The Law of Torts* § 380 (2000).

**2. Subrogation Clauses.** Many insurance policies contain what are known as subrogation clauses. A subrogation clause entitles the insurer to any tort damages for the same injury awarded to the insured plaintiff, up to the amount paid by the insurer. This allows insurance companies to recover the cost of the claim from the tortfeasor, while still affording the plaintiff full compensation. See Diamond, Levine & Madden, supra.

# SECTION C.  PUNITIVE DAMAGES

## STATE FARM MUTUAL AUTOMOBILE INS. CO. v. CAMPBELL
Supreme Court of the United States.
538 U.S. 408, 123 S.Ct. 1513, 155 L.Ed.2d 585 (2003).

Justice KENNEDY delivered the opinion of the Court.

We address once again the measure of punishment, by means of punitive damages, a State may impose upon a defendant in a civil case.

The question is whether, in the circumstances we shall recount, an award of $145 million in punitive damages, where full compensatory damages are $1 million, is excessive and in violation of the Due Process Clause of the Fourteenth Amendment to the Constitution of the United States.

I

In 1981, Curtis Campbell (Campbell) was driving with his wife, Inez Preece Campbell, in Cache County, Utah. He decided to pass six vans traveling ahead of them on a two-lane highway. Todd Ospital was driving a small car approaching from the opposite direction. To avoid a head-on collision with Campbell, who by then was driving on the wrong side of the highway and toward oncoming traffic, Ospital swerved onto the shoulder, lost control of his automobile, and collided with a vehicle driven by Robert G. Slusher. Ospital was killed, and Slusher was rendered permanently disabled. The Campbells escaped unscathed.

In the ensuing wrongful death and tort action, Campbell insisted he was not at fault. Early investigations did support differing conclusions as to who caused the accident, but "a consensus was reached early on by the investigators and witnesses that Mr. Campbell's unsafe pass had indeed caused the crash." 65 P.3d 1134, 1141 (Utah, 2001). Campbell's insurance company, petitioner State Farm Mutual Automobile Insurance Company (State Farm), nonetheless decided to contest liability and declined offers by Slusher and Ospital's estate (Ospital) to settle the claims for the policy limit of $50,000 ($25,000 per claimant). State Farm also ignored the advice of one of its own investigators and took the case to trial, assuring the Campbells that "their assets were safe, that they had no liability for the accident, that [State Farm] would represent their interests, and that they did not need to procure separate counsel." *Id.*, at 1142. To the contrary, a jury determined that Campbell was 100 percent at fault, and a judgment was returned for $185,849, far more than the amount offered in settlement.

At first State Farm refused to cover the $135,849 in excess liability. Its counsel made this clear to the Campbells: " 'You may want to put for sale signs on your property to get things moving.' " *Ibid.* Nor was State Farm willing to post a supersedeas bond to allow Campbell to appeal the judgment against him. Campbell obtained his own counsel to appeal the verdict. During the pendency of the appeal, in late 1984, Slusher, Ospital, and the Campbells reached an agreement whereby Slusher and Ospital agreed not to seek satisfaction of their claims against the Campbells. In exchange, the Campbells agreed to pursue a bad-faith action against State Farm and to be represented by Slusher's and Ospital's attorneys. The Campbells also agreed that Slusher and Ospital would have a right to play a part in all major decisions concerning the bad-faith action. No settlement could be concluded without Slusher's and Ospital's approval, and Slusher and Ospital would receive 90 percent of any verdict against State Farm.

\* \* \*

## II

We recognized in *Cooper Industries, Inc. v. Leatherman Tool Group, Inc.*, 532 U.S. 424, 121 S.Ct. 1678, 149 L.Ed.2d 674 (2001), that in our judicial system, compensatory and punitive damages, although usually awarded at the same time by the same decisionmaker, serve different purposes. *Id.* at 432, 121 S.Ct. 1678. Compensatory damages "are intended to redress the concrete loss that the plaintiff has suffered by reason of the defendant's wrongful conduct." *Ibid.* (citing Restatement (Second) of Torts § 903, pp. 453–454 (1979)). By contrast, punitive damages serve a broader function; they are aimed at deterrence and retribution. *Cooper Industries, supra*, at 432, 121 S.Ct. 1678; see also *Gore, supra*, at 568, 116 S.Ct. 1589 ("Punitive damages may properly be imposed to further a State's legitimate interests in punishing unlawful conduct and deterring its repetition"); *Pacific Mut. Life Ins. Co. v. Haslip*, 499 U.S. 1, 19, 111 S.Ct. 1032, 113 L.Ed.2d 1 (1991) ("[P]unitive damages are imposed for purposes of retribution and deterrence").

While States possess discretion over the imposition of punitive damages, it is well established that there are procedural and substantive constitutional limitations on these awards. *Cooper Industries, supra*; *Gore, supra*, at 559, 116 S.Ct. 1589; *Honda Motor Co. v. Oberg*, 512 U.S. 415, 114 S.Ct. 2331, 129 L.Ed.2d 336 (1994); TXO Production Corp. v. Alliance Resources Corp., 509 U.S. 443, 113 S.Ct. 2711, 125 L.Ed.2d 366 (1993); *Haslip, supra*.

\* \* \*

Although these awards serve the same purposes as criminal penalties, defendants subjected to punitive damages in civil cases have not been accorded the protections applicable in a criminal proceeding. This increases our concerns over the imprecise manner in which punitive damages systems are administered. We have admonished that "[p]unitive damages pose an acute danger of arbitrary deprivation of property. Jury instructions typically leave the jury with wide discretion in choosing amounts, and the presentation of evidence of a defendant's net worth creates the potential that juries will use their verdicts to express biases against big businesses, particularly those without strong local presences." *Honda Motor, supra*, at 432, 114 S.Ct. 2331; see also *Haslip, supra*, at 59, 111 S.Ct. 1032 (O'CONNOR, J., dissenting).

\* \* \*

In light of these concerns, in *Gore, supra*, we instructed courts reviewing punitive damages to consider three guideposts: (1) the degree of reprehensibility of the defendant's misconduct; (2) the disparity between the actual or potential harm suffered by the plaintiff and the punitive damages award; and (3) the difference between the punitive damages awarded by the jury and the civil penalties authorized or imposed in comparable cases. *Id.*, at 575, 116 S.Ct. 1589. We reiterated the importance of these three guideposts in *Cooper Industries* and mandated appellate courts to conduct de novo review of a trial court's application of them to the jury's award. 532 U.S. 424, 121 S.Ct. 1678. Exacting appellate review ensures that an award of punitive damages is based upon an " 'application of law, rather than a decisionmaker's caprice.' " *Id.* at 436, 121 S.Ct. 1678 (quoting *Gore, supra,* at 587 116 S.Ct. 1589 (BREYER, J., concurring)).

III

Under the principles outlined in *BMW of North America, Inc. v. Gore,* this case is neither close nor difficult. It was error to reinstate the jury's $145 million punitive damages award. We address each guidepost of *Gore* in some detail.

A.

[T]he most important indicium of the reasonableness of a punitive damages award is the degree of reprehensibility of the defendant's conduct .. " *Gore,* 517 U.S., at 575, 116 S.Ct. 1589. We have instructed courts to determine the reprehensibility of a defendant by considering whether: the harm caused was physical as opposed to economic; the target of the conduct had financial vulnerability; the conduct involved repeated actions or was an isolated incident; and the harm was the result of intentional malice, trickery, or deceit, or mere accident. *Id.,* at 576–577, 116 S.Ct. 1589. The existence of any one of these factors weighing in favor of a plaintiff may not be sufficient to sustain a punitive damages award; and the absence of all of them renders any award suspect. It should be presumed a plaintiff has been made whole for his injuries by compensatory damages, so punitive damages should only be awarded if the defendant's culpability, after having paid compensatory damages, is so reprehensible as to warrant the imposition of further sanctions to achieve punishment or deterrence. *Id.,* at 575, 116 S.Ct. 1589.

Applying these factors in the instant case, we must acknowledge that State Farm's handling of the claims against the Campbells merits no praise. The trial court found that State Farm's employees altered the company's records to make Campbell appear less culpable. State Farm disregarded the overwhelming likelihood of liability and the near-certain probability that, by taking the case to trial, a judgment in excess of the policy limits would be awarded. State Farm amplified the harm by first assuring the Campbells their assets would be safe from any verdict and by later telling them, postjudgment, to put a for-sale sign on their house. While we do not suggest there was error in awarding punitive damages based upon State Farm's conduct toward the Campbells, a more modest punishment for this reprehensible conduct could have satisfied the State's legitimate objectives, and the Utah courts should have gone no further.

This case, instead, was used as a platform to expose, and punish, the perceived deficiencies of State Farm's operations throughout the country.

* * *

B

Turning to the second *Gore* guidepost, we have been reluctant to identify concrete constitutional limits on the ratio between harm, or potential harm, to the plaintiff and the punitive damages award. 517 U.S., at 582, 116 S.Ct. 1589 ("[W]e have consistently rejected the notion that the constitutional line is marked by a simple mathematical formula, even one that compares actual and potential damages to the punitive award"), *TXO, supra,* at 458, 113 S.Ct. 2711. We decline again to impose a bright-line ratio which a punitive damages award cannot exceed. Our jurisprudence and the principles it has now established demonstrate, however, that, in practice, few awards exceeding a single-digit ratio between punitive and compensatory damages, to a significant degree, will satisfy due process. In *Haslip,* in upholding a punitive damages award, we concluded that an award of more than four times the amount of compensatory damages might be close to the line of constitutional impropriety. 499 U.S., at 23–24, 111 S.Ct. 1032. We cited that 4–to–1 ratio again in *Gore,* 517 U.S., at 581, 116 S.Ct. 1589. The Court further referenced a long legislative history, dating back over 700 years and going forward to today, providing for sanctions of double, treble, or quadruple damages to deter and punish. *Id.* at 581, and n. 33, 116 S.Ct. 1589. While these ratios are not binding, they are instructive. They demonstrate what should be obvious: Single-digit multipliers are more likely to comport with due process, while still achieving the State's goals of deterrence and retribution, than awards with ratios in range of 500 to 1, *id.,* at 582, 116 S.Ct. 1589, or, in this case, of 145 to 1.

Nonetheless, because there are no rigid benchmarks that a punitive damages award may not surpass, ratios greater than those we have previously upheld may comport with due process where "a particularly egregious act has resulted in only a small amount of economic damages." *Ibid;* see also *ibid.* (positing that a higher ratio might be necessary where "the injury is hard to detect or the monetary value of noneconomic harm might have been difficult to determine"). The converse is also true, however. When compensatory damages are substantial, then a lesser ratio, perhaps only equal to compensatory damages, can reach the outermost limit of the due process guarantee. The precise award in any case, of course, must be based upon the facts and circumstances of the defendant's conduct and the harm to the plaintiff.

In sum, courts must ensure that the measure of punishment is both reasonable and proportionate to the amount of harm to the plaintiff and to the general damages recovered. In the context of this case, we have no doubt that there is a presumption against an award that has a 145–to–1 ratio. The compensatory award in this case was substantial; the Campbells were awarded $1 million for a year and a half of emotional distress. This was complete compensation. The harm arose from a transaction in the economic realm, not from some physical assault or trauma; there were no physical injuries; and State Farm paid the excess verdict before the complaint was filed, so the Campbells suffered only minor economic injuries for the 18–month period in which State Farm refused to resolve the claim against them. The compensatory damages for the injury suffered here, moreover, likely were based on a component which was duplicated in the punitive award. Much of the distress was caused by the outrage and humiliation the Campbells suffered at the actions of their insurer; and it is the major role of punitive damages to condemn such conduct. Compensatory damages, however, already contain this punitive element. See Restatement (Second of Torts) § 908, Comment c., p.466 (1977) ("In many cases in which compensatory damages include an amount for emotional distress, such as humiliation or indignation aroused by the defendant's act, there is no clear line of demarcation between punishment and compensation and a verdict for a specified amount frequently includes elements of both").

\* \* \*

### C

The third guidepost in *Gore* is the disparity between the punitive damages award and the "civil penalties authorized or imposed in comparable cases." *Id*. at 575, 116 S.Ct. 1589. We note that, in the past, we have also looked to criminal penalties that could be imposed. *Id*. at 583, 116 S.Ct. 1589; *Haslip*, 499 U.S., at 23, 111 S.Ct. 1032. The existence of a criminal penalty does have bearing on the seriousness with which a State views the wrongful action. When used to determine the dollar amount of the award, however, the criminal penalty has less utility. Great care must be taken to avoid use of the civil process to assess criminal penalties that can be imposed only after the heightened protections of a criminal trial have been observed, including, of course, its higher standards of proof. Punitive damages are not a substitute for the criminal process, and the remote possibility of a criminal sanction does not automatically sustain a punitive damages award.

Here, we need not dwell long on this guidepost. The most relevant civil sanction under Utah state law for the wrong done to the Campbells appears to be a $10,000 fine for an act of fraud, 65 P.3d, at 1154, an amount dwarfed by the $145 million punitive damages award. The Supreme Court of Utah speculated about the loss of State Farm's business license, the disgorgement of profits, and possible imprisonment, but here again its references were to the broad fraudulent scheme drawn from evidence of out-of-state and dissimilar conduct. This analysis was insufficient to justify the award.

### IV

An application of the *Gore* guideposts to the facts of this case, especially in light of the substantial compensatory damages awarded (a portion of which contained a punitive element), likely would justify a punitive damages award at or near the amount of compensatory damages. The punitive award of $145 million, therefore, was neither reasonable nor proportionate to the wrong committed, and it was an irrational and arbitrary deprivation of the property of the defendant. The proper calculation of punitive damages under the principles we have discussed should be resolved, in the first instance, by the Utah courts.

The judgment of the Utah Supreme Court is reversed, and the case is remanded for further proceedings not inconsistent with this opinion.

It is so ordered.

## NOTES

**1. Punitive Damages.** Punitive damages are awarded to punish the defendant and deter others inclined to repeat the defendant's wrong. Punitive damages are in addition to any damages awarded to the plaintiff to compensate for her losses. Juries have discretion to award punitive damages when the defendant acted with malice, usually, defined as ill will, hatred, or reckless disregard to the rights of the defendant. The jury is allowed to consider the wealth of the defendant in determining the amount of the punitive damages to award. See Diamond, Levine & Madden, *Understanding Torts* § 14.05 (2nd ed. 2000); Dobbs, *The Law of Torts* §§ 381–384.

In *Pacific Mutual Life Insurance Co. v. Haslip*, 499 U.S. 1, 111 S.Ct. 1032, 113 L.Ed.2d 1 (1991), the Court upheld an Alabama procedure for scrutinizing the appropriateness of a punitive damage award. The procedure required an evaluation of seven factors, including (1) the relationship between the punitive damage award, the potential harm that could have occurred, and the harm that did occur, (2) the reprehensibility, frequency, and duration of the defendant's conduct, (3) the profitability of the defendant's conduct, (4) the defendant's financial position, (5) the cost of the litigation, (6) any criminal sanctions already imposed on the defendant, and (7) any civil judgments already rendered against the defendant.

In *Philip Morris v. Williams*, ___ U.S. ___, 127 S.Ct. 1057, 166 L.Ed.2d 940 (2007), the Supreme Court held that a jury may not award punitive damages for harm done to nonparties to the litigation. In this case, which arose out of the death of long time smoker, Jesse Williams, the jury found that Williams smoked in large part because he believed it was safe to do so, and that Phillip Morris falsely and knowingly lead him to so believe. The plaintiff's attorney in this case told the jury "to think about how many other Jesse Williamses in the state of Oregon there have been." The Supreme Court, reviewing the record from the trial court upon a challenge by Phllip Morris of the jury's nearly 80 million dollar punitive damages award, held that "the Constitution's Due Process Clause forbids a state to use a punitive damages award to punish a defendant for injury that it inflicts upon nonparties or those whom they directly represent, *i.e.,* injury that it inflicts upon those who are, essentially, strangers to the litigation." The court noted that to allow such damages would lead to standardless awards of punitive damages, and would constitute a taking of property without Due Process. Evidence of harm to those not parties to the litigation can still be introduced for the purpose of determining the reprehensibility of the defendant's conduct, but Due Process requires that states "cannot authorize procedures that create an unreasonable risk of" juries awarding punitive damages as a punishment for harm done to nonparties. In this case, because the lower court had not applied the correct standard for punitive damages, the Court remanded without specifically addressing whether the award of nearly 80 million dollars in punitive damages was constitutionally excessive in light of the $800,000 award for compensatory damages for wrongful death.

**2. Policy Debate Surrounding Punitive Damages.** Punitive damages constitute a powerful weapon in tort liability. Some argue it provides an important deterrence against tortious conduct committed with malice. The controversy has been debated in the United States Congress in the context whether Health Maintenance Organizations (HMOs) should be subject to punitive damages for wrongfully failing to authorize appropriate medical treatment. See Robert Pear, *House Passes Bill to Expand Rights on Medical Care*, New York Times, October 8, 1999, p.1. Arguably it could be cheaper to deprive an elderly patient of appropriate health treatment and pay the wrongful death claim based on the patient's life expectancy. (See Wrongful Death, Chapter 2, Sec. H, supra.) Imposing punitive damages when medical treatment is deprived with malice (as defined in Note 1, supra) can deter this conduct. Awarding punitive damages also rewards and thereby encourages the plaintiffs and their attorneys who go after malicious conduct. Opponents of punitive damages argue that it inappropriately turns torts from a compensation system to a quasi-criminal system without the safeguards of criminal procedure or even specific fines. The size of the awards also concern critics who argue the cost borne by business from punitive damages will be passed along to consumers. Furthermore, large punitive damage awards can deplete funds available to compensate other victims who sue after the original plaintiff was awarded punitive damages. See Dobbs, *Law of Remedies: Damages, Equity and Restitution* (2nd ed. 1993); Diamond, Levine & Madden, supra, § 14.05; Dobbs, *The Law of Torts* § 381 (2000). Which arguments most persuade you?

# SECTION D.   TORT REFORM STATUTES

## FEIN v. PERMANENTE MEDICAL GROUP

Supreme Court of California.
38 Cal.3d 137, 211 Cal.Rptr. 368, 695 P.2d 665 (1985).

KAUS, Justice.

In this medical malpractice action, both parties appeal from a judgment awarding plaintiff about $1 million in damages. Defendant claims that the trial court committed reversible error during the selection of the jury, in instructions on liability as well as damages, and in failing to order that the bulk of plaintiff's award be paid periodically rather than in a lump sum. Plaintiff defends the judgment against defendant's attacks, but maintains that the trial court, in fixing damages, should not have applied two provisions of the Medical Injury Compensation Reform Act of 1975 (MICRA): Civil Code section 3333.2, which limits noneconomic damages in medical malpractice cases to $250,000, and Civil Code section 3333.1, which modifies the traditional "collateral source" rule in such litigation. Plaintiff's claims are based on a constitutional challenge similar to the challenges to other provisions of MICRA that we recently addressed and rejected in *American Bank & Trust Co. v. Community Hospital* (1984) 36 Cal.3d 359 [204 Cal.Rptr. 671, 683 P.2d 670], *Barme v. Wood* (1984) 37 Cal.3d 174 [207 Cal.Rptr. 816, 689 P.2d 446], and *Roa v. Lodi Medical Group, Inc.* (1985) 37 Cal.3d 920 [211 Cal.Rptr. 77, 695 P.2d 164]. We conclude that the judgment should be affirmed in all respects.

I

On Saturday, February 21, 1976, plaintiff Lawrence Fein, a 34–year-old attorney employed by the Legislative Counsel Bureau of the California State Legislature in Sacramento, felt a brief pain in his chest as he was riding his bicycle to work. The pain lasted a minute or two. He noticed a similar brief pain the following day while he was jogging, and then, three days later, experienced another episode while walking after lunch. When the chest pain returned again while he was working at his office that evening, he became concerned for his health and, the following morning, called the office of his regular physician, Dr. Arlene Brandwein, who was employed by defendant Permanente Medical Group, an affiliate of the Kaiser Health Foundation (Kaiser).

Dr. Brandwein had no open appointment available that day, and her receptionist advised plaintiff to call Kaiser's central appointment desk for a "short appointment." He did so and was given an appointment for 4 p.m. that afternoon, Thursday, February 26. Plaintiff testified that he did not feel that the problem was so severe as to require immediate treatment at Kaiser Hospital's emergency room, and that he worked until the time for his scheduled appointment.

When he appeared for his appointment, plaintiff was examined by a nurse practitioner, Cheryl Welch, who was working under the supervision of a physician-consultant, Dr. Wintrop Frantz; plaintiff was aware that Nurse Welch was a nurse practitioner and he did not ask to see a doctor. After examining plaintiff and taking a history, Nurse Welch left the room to consult with Dr. Frantz. When she returned, she advised plaintiff that she and Dr. Frantz believed his pain was due to muscle spasm and that the doctor had given him a prescription for Valium. Plaintiff went home, took the Valium, and went to sleep.

That night, about 1 a.m., plaintiff awoke with severe chest pains. His wife drove him to the Kaiser emergency room where he was examined by Dr. Lowell Redding about 1:30 a.m. Following an examination that the doctor felt showed no signs of a heart problem, Dr. Redding ordered a chest X-ray. On the basis of his examination and the X-ray results, Dr. Redding also concluded that plaintiff was experiencing muscle spasms and gave him an injection of Demerol and a prescription for a codeine medication.

Plaintiff went home but continued to experience intermittent chest pain. About noon that same day, the pain became more severe and constant and plaintiff returned to the Kaiser emergency room where he was seen by another physician, Dr. Donald Oliver. From his initial examination of plaintiff Dr. Oliver also believed that plaintiff's problem was of muscular origin, but, after administering some pain medication, he directed that an electrocardiogram (EKG) be performed. The EKG showed that plaintiff was suffering from a heart attack (acute myocardial infarction). Plaintiff was then transferred to the cardiac care unit.

Following a period of hospitalization and medical treatment without surgery, plaintiff returned to his job on a part-time basis in October 1976, and resumed full-time work in September 1977. By the time of trial, he had been permitted to return to virtually all of his prior recreational activities—e.g., jogging, swimming, bicycling and skiing.

In February 1977, plaintiff filed the present action, alleging that his heart condition should have been diagnosed earlier and that treatment should have been given either to prevent the heart attack or, at least, to lessen its residual effects. The case went to judgment only against Permanente.

At trial, Dr. Harold Swan, the head of cardiology at the Cedars–Sinai Medical Center in Los Angeles, was the principal witness for plaintiff. Dr. Swan testified that an important signal that a heart attack may be imminent is chest pain which can radiate to other parts of the body. Such pain is not relieved by rest or pain medication. He stated that if the condition is properly diagnosed, a patient can be given Inderal to stabilize his condition, and that continued medication or surgery may relieve the condition.

Dr. Swan further testified that in his opinion any patient who appears with chest pains should be given an EKG to rule out the worst possibility, a heart problem. He stated that the symptoms that plaintiff had described to Nurse Welch at the 4 p.m. examination on Thursday, February 26, should have indicated to her that an EKG was in order. He also stated that when plaintiff returned to Kaiser late that same night with his chest pain unrelieved by the medication he had been given, Dr. Redding should also have ordered an EKG. According to Dr. Swan, if an EKG had been ordered at those times it could have revealed plaintiff's imminent heart attack, and treatment could have been administered which might have prevented or minimized the attack.

Dr. Swan also testified to the damage caused by the attack. He stated that as a result of the attack a large portion of plaintiff's heart muscle had died, reducing plaintiff's future life expectancy by about one-half, to about 16 or 17 years. Although Dr. Swan acknowledged that some of plaintiff's other coronary arteries also suffer from disease, he felt that if plaintiff had been properly treated his future life expectancy would be decreased by only 10 to 15 percent, rather than half.

Nurse Welch and Dr. Redding testified on behalf of the defense, indicating that the symptoms that plaintiff had reported to them at the time of the examinations were not the same symptoms he had described at trial. Defendant also introduced a number of expert witnesses—not employed by Kaiser—who stated that on the basis of the symptoms reported and observed before the heart attack, the medical personnel could not reasonably have determined that a heart attack was imminent. Additional defense evidence indicated (1) that an EKG would not have shown that a heart attack was imminent, (2) that because of the severe disease in the coronary arteries which caused plaintiff's heart attack, the attack could not have been prevented even had it been known that it was about to occur, and finally (3) that, given the deterioration in plaintiff's other coronary arteries, the heart attack had not affected plaintiff's life expectancy to the degree suggested by Dr. Swan.

In the face of this sharply conflicting evidence, the jury found in favor of plaintiff on the issue of liability and, pursuant to the trial court's instructions, returned special verdicts itemizing various elements of damages. The jury awarded $24,733 for wages lost by plaintiff to the time of trial, $63,000 for future medical expenses, and $700,000 for wages lost in the future as a result of the reduction in plaintiff's life expectancy. Finally, the jury awarded $500,000 for "noneconomic damages," to compensate for pain, suffering, inconvenience, physical impairment and other intangible damages sustained by plaintiff from the time of the injury until his death.

After the verdict was returned, defendant requested the court to modify the award and enter a judgment pursuant to three separate provisions of MICRA: (1) Civil Code section 3333.2—which places a $250,000 limit on noneconomic damages, (2) Civil Code section 3333.1—which alters the collateral source rule, and (3) Code of Civil Procedure section 667.7—which provides for the periodic payment of damages. The trial court, which had rejected plaintiff's constitutional challenge to Civil Code sections 3333.2 and 3333.1 in a pretrial ruling, reduced the noneconomic damages to $250,000, reduced the award for past lost wages to $5,430—deducting $19,303 that plaintiff had already received in disability payments as compensation for such lost wages—and ordered defendant to pay the first $63,000 of any future medical expenses not covered by medical insurance provided by plaintiff's employer, as such expenses were incurred. At the same time, the court declined to order that the award for future lost wages or noneconomic damages be paid periodically pursuant to Code of Civil Procedure section 667.7, determining that the statute was not "mandatory" and that "under the unique facts and circumstances of this case" a periodic payment award of such damages would "defeat rather than promote" the purpose of section 667.7.

\* \* \*

## VI

After the jury returned its verdict, defendant requested the trial court to enter a judgment—pursuant to section 667.7 of the Code of Civil Procedure—providing for the periodic payment of future damages, rather than a lump-sum award. Although the trial court rejected plaintiff's constitutional challenge to the periodic payment provision—a conclusion consistent with our recent decision in *American Bank*—it nonetheless denied defendant's request, interpreting section 667.7 as affording a trial court discretion in determining whether to enter a periodic payment judgment and concluding that on the facts of this case the legislative purpose of section 667.7 "would be defeated rather than promoted by ordering periodic payments rather than a lump sum award." Defendant contends that the trial court misinterpreted the statute and erred in failing to order periodic payment of all future damages.

We agree with defendant that the trial court was in error insofar as it interpreted section 667.7 as "discretionary" rather than "mandatory." The statute provides that "[i]n any [medical malpractice action], a superior court *shall*, at the request of either party, *enter a judgment ordering that money damages* or its equivalent *for future damages* of the judgment creditor *be paid in whole or in part by periodic payments rather than by a lump-sum payment* if the award equals or exceeds fifty thousand dollars ($50,000) in future damages." (Italics added.) Although in some contexts the use of the term "shall" may be consistent with a "discretionary" rather than a "mandatory" meaning (see, e.g., *Estate of*

*Mitchell* (1942) 20 Cal.2d 48, 50–52 [123 P.2d 503]), the legislative history of section 667.7 leaves little doubt that here the Legislature intended to impose a mandatory duty on the trial court to enter a periodic payment judgment in cases falling within the four corners of the section.

\* \* \*

### VII

We now turn to plaintiff's contentions.

As noted, although the jury by special verdict set plaintiff's noneconomic damages at $500,000, the trial court reduced that amount to $250,000 pursuant to Civil Code section 3333.2.[13] Plaintiff challenges this ruling, contending that section 3333.2 is unconstitutional on a number of grounds. In many respects, plaintiff's argument tracks the constitutional objections to other provisions of MICRA that we have recently rejected in *American Bank, Barme* and *Roa.*

We begin with the claim that section 3333.2 denies due process because it limits the potential recovery of medical malpractice claimants without providing them an adequate quid pro quo. In rejecting a similar challenge to the periodic payment provision at issue in *American Bank*, we explained that "[i]t is well established that a plaintiff has no vested property right in a particular measure of damages, and that the Legislature possesses broad authority to modify the scope and nature of such damages. (See, e.g., Werner v. Southern Cal. etc. Newspapers (1950) 35 Cal.2d 121, 129 [216 P.2d 825, 13 A.L.R.2d 2522]; Feckenscher v. Gamble (1938) 12 Cal.2d 482, 499–500 [85 P.2d 8855]; Tulley v. Tranor (1878) 53 Cal. 274, 280.) Since the demise of the substantive due process analysis of Lochner v. New York (1905) 198 U.S. 45 [49 L.Ed. 937, 25 S.Ct. 539], it has been clear that the constitutionality of measures affecting such economic rights under the due process clause does not depend on a judicial assessment of the justifications for the legislation or of the wisdom or fairness of the enactment [i.e., the "adequacy" of the quid pro quo]. So long as the measure is rationally related to a legitimate state interest, policy determinations as to the need for, and the desirability of, the enactment are for the Legislature."* (Italics added.) (*American Bank, supra*, 36 Cal.3d 359, 368–369.)

It is true, of course, that section 3333.2 differs from the periodic payment provision in *American Bank* inasmuch as the periodic payment provision—in large measure—simply postpones a plaintiff's receipt of damages whereas section 3333.2 places a dollar limit on the amount of noneconomic damages that a plaintiff may obtain. That difference, however, does not alter the applicable due process standard of review. As our language in *American Bank* itself suggests, our past cases make clear that the Legislature retains broad control over *the measure*, as well as

---

**13.** Section 3333.2 provides in relevant part: "(a) In any [medical malpractice] action ... the injured plaintiff shall be entitled to recover noneconomic losses to compensate for pain, suffering, inconvenience, physical impairment, disfigurement and other nonpecuniary damage. [b] In no action shall the amount of damages for noneconomic losses exceed two hundred fifty thousand dollars ($250,000)."

*the timing*, of damages that a defendant is obligated to pay and a plaintiff is entitled to receive, and that the Legislature may expand or limit recoverable damages so long as its action is rationally related to a legitimate state interest. In *Werner v. Southern Cal. etc. Newspapers, supra*, 35 Cal.2d 121, for example, our court applied the "rational relationship" standard in dismissing a due process attack on a statute— Civil Code section 48a—which permitted a plaintiff who brought a libel or slander action against a newspaper generally to obtain only "special damages," largely eliminating the traditional right to obtain "general damages" that such a plaintiff had enjoyed before the statute.

In light of our discussion of the legislative history and purposes of MICRA in *American Bank, Barme* and *Roa*, it is clear that section 3333.2 is rationally related to legitimate state interests. As we explained in those decisions, in enacting MICRA the Legislature was acting in a situation in which it had found that the rising cost of medical malpractice insurance was posing serious problems for the health care system in California, threatening to curtail the availability of medical care in some parts of the state and creating the very real possibility that many doctors would practice without insurance, leaving patients who might be injured by such doctors with the prospect of uncollectible judgments. In attempting to reduce the cost of medical malpractice insurance in MICRA, the Legislature enacted a variety of provisions affecting doctors, insurance companies and malpractice plaintiffs.

Section 3333.2, like the sections involved in *American Bank, Barme* and *Roa*, is, of course, one of the provisions which made changes in existing tort rules in an attempt to reduce the cost of medical malpractice litigation, and thereby restrain the increase in medical malpractice insurance premiums. It appears obvious that this section—by placing a ceiling of $250,000 on the recovery of noneconomic damages—is rationally related to the objective of reducing the costs of malpractice defendants and their insurers.

There is no denying, of course, that in some cases—like this one— section 3333.2 will result in the recovery of a lower judgment than would have been obtained before the enactment of the statute. It is worth noting, however, that in seeking a means of lowering malpractice costs, the Legislature *placed no limits whatsoever on a plaintiff's right to recover for all of the economic, pecuniary damages—such as medical expenses or lost earnings—resulting from the injury*, but instead confined the statutory limitations to the recovery of *noneconomic damages*, and— even then—permitted up to a $250,000 award for such damages. Thoughtful jurists and legal scholars have for some time raised serious questions as to the wisdom of awarding damages for pain and suffering in any negligence case, noting, inter alia, the inherent difficulties in placing a monetary value on such losses, the fact that money damages are at best only imperfect compensation for such intangible injuries and that such damages are generally passed on to, and borne by, innocent consumers. While the general propriety of such damages is, of course, firmly imbedded in our common law jurisprudence (see, e.g., *Capelouto v. Kaiser Foundation Hospitals* (1972) 7 Cal.3d 889, 892–893 [103 Cal.Rptr. 856, 500 P.2d 880]), no California case of which we are aware has ever suggested that the right to recover for such noneconomic injuries is constitutionally immune from legislative limitation or revision. (See, e.g., *Werner v. Southern Cal. etc. Newspapers, supra*, 35 Cal.2d 121, 126–128; fn. 15, *ante*. See generally Morris, *Liability for Pain and Suffering* (1959) 59 Colum.L.Rev. 476 [urging legislative revision of rules relating to damages for pain and suffering].)

Faced with the prospect that, in the absence of some cost reduction, medical malpractice plaintiffs might as a realistic matter have difficulty collecting judgments for *any* of their damages—pecuniary as well as nonpecuniary—the Legislature concluded that it was in the public interest to attempt to obtain some cost savings by limiting noneconomic damages. Although reasonable persons can certainly disagree as to the wisdom of this provision, we cannot say that it is not rationally related to a legitimate state interest.

\* \* \*

Plaintiff alternatively contends that the section violates the equal protection clause, both because it impermissibly discriminates between medical malpractice victims and other tort victims, imposing its limits only in medical malpractice cases, and because it improperly discriminates within the class of medical malpractice victims, denying a "complete" recovery of damages only to those malpractice plaintiffs with noneconomic damages exceeding $250,000.

With respect to the first contention, it should be evident from what we have already said that the Legislature limited the application of section 3333.2 to medical malpractice cases because it was responding to an insurance "crisis" in that particular area and that the statute is rationally related to the legislative purpose. *American Bank, Barme* and *Roa* make clear that under these circumstances, plaintiff's initial equal protection claim has no merit. (See *American Bank, supra*, 36 Cal.3d 359, 370–374; *Barme, supra*, 37 Cal.3d 174, 181–182; *Roa, supra*, 37 Cal.3d 920, 930–931.)

As for the claim that the statute violates equal protection because of its differential effect within the class of malpractice plaintiffs, the constitutional argument is equally unavailing. First, as we have already explained, the Legislature clearly had a reasonable basis for drawing a distinction between economic and noneconomic damages, providing that the desired cost savings should be obtained only by limiting the recovery of noneconomic damage. (See pp. 159–160, *ante*.) The equal protection clause certainly does not require the Legislature to limit a victim's recovery for out-of-pocket medical expenses or lost earnings simply because it has found it appropriate to place some limit on damages for pain and suffering and similar noneconomic losses. (See, e.g., *Werner v. Southern Cal. etc. Newspapers, supra*, 35 Cal.2d 121, 126–128.)

Accordingly, we conclude that section 3333.2 is constitutional. The trial court did not err in reducing the noneconomic damage award pursuant to its terms.

## VIII

For similar reasons, plaintiff's constitutional challenge to Civil Code section 3333.1—which modifies this state's common law "collateral source" rule—is also without merit.

Under the traditional collateral source rule, a jury, in calculating a plaintiff's damages in a tort action, does not take into consideration benefits—such as medical insurance or disability payments—which the plaintiff has received from sources other than the defendant—i.e., "collateral sources"—to cover losses resulting from the injury. (See, e.g., *Helfend v. Southern Cal. Rapid Transit Dist.* (1970) 2 Cal.3d 1 [84 Cal.Rptr. 173, 465 P.2d 61, 77 A.L.R.3d 398].) Section 3333.1 alters this rule in medical malpractice cases.[20] Under section 3333.1, subdivision (a), a medical malpractice defendant is permitted to introduce evidence of such collateral source benefits received by or payable to the plaintiff; when a defendant chooses to introduce such evidence, the plaintiff may introduce evidence of the amounts he has paid—in insurance premiums, for example—to secure the benefits. Although section 3333.1, subdivision (a)—as ultimately adopted—does not specify how the jury should use such evidence, the Legislature apparently assumed that in most cases the jury would set plaintiff's damages at a lower level because of its awareness of plaintiff's "net" collateral source benefits.

In addition, section 3333.1, subdivision (b) provides that whenever such collateral source evidence is introduced, the source of those benefits is precluded from obtaining subrogation either from the plaintiff or from the medical malpractice defendant. As far as the malpractice plaintiff is concerned, subdivision (b) assures that he will suffer no "double deduction" from his tort recovery as a result of his receipt of collateral source benefits; because the jury that has learned of his benefits may reduce his tort award by virtue of such benefits, the Legislature eliminated any right the collateral source may have had to obtain repayment of those benefits from the plaintiff. As for the malpractice defendant, subdivision (b) assures that any reduction in malpractice awards that may result from the jury's consideration of the plaintiff's collateral source benefits will inure to its benefit rather than to the benefit of the collateral source.

In our recent case of *Barme* v. *Wood, supra,* 37 Cal.3d 174, we addressed a constitutional challenge to section 3333.1, subdivision (b) brought by a "collateral source" whose subrogation rights against a malpractice defendant had been eliminated by the statute. In upholding

---

**20.** Section 3333.1 provides in relevant part: "(a) In the event the defendant so elects, in an action for personal injury against a health care provider based upon professional negligence, he may introduce evidence of any amount payable as a benefit to the plaintiff as a result of the personal injury pursuant to the United States Social Security Act, any state or federal income disability or worker's compensation act, any health, sickness or income-disability insurance, accident insurance that provides health benefits or income-disability coverage, and any contract or agreement of any group, organization, partnership, or corporation to provide, pay for, or reimburse the cost of medical, hospital, dental, or other health care services. Where the defendant elects to introduce such evidence, the plaintiff may introduce evidence of any amount which the plaintiff has paid or contributed to secure his right to any insurance benefits concerning which the defendant has introduced evidence. (b) No source of collateral benefits introduced pursuant to subdivision (a) shall recover any amount against the plaintiff nor shall it be subrogated to the rights of the plaintiff against a defendant."

the section's constitutionality, we explained that a collateral source has no vested due process right to subrogation and that section 3333.1, subdivision (b) is rationally related to the purposes of MICRA since it reduces the costs imposed on medical malpractice defendants by shifting some of the costs in the area to other insurers.

This case is not controlled by *Barme*, because here plaintiff challenges the validity of subdivision (a), rather than subdivision (b), and contends that the statute violates the rights of a malpractice plaintiff, rather than the rights of a collateral source. Nonetheless, plaintiff's constitutional challenge is still without merit.

Again, we begin with the due process objections to the statute. Although, by its terms, subdivision (a) simply adds a new category of evidence that is admissible in a medical malpractice action, we recognize that in reality the provision affects the measure of a plaintiff's damage award, permitting the jury to reduce an award on the basis of collateral source benefits of which—but for the statute—the jury would be unaware. Nonetheless, as we have already explained in our discussion of section 3333.2, a plaintiff has no vested property right in a particular measure of damages. Thus, the fact that the section may reduce a plaintiff's award does not render the provision unconstitutional so long as the measure is rationally related to a legitimate state interest.

Because section 3333.1, subdivision (a) is likely to lead to lower malpractice awards, there can be no question but that this provision—like section 3333.2—directly relates to MICRA's objective of reducing the costs incurred by malpractice defendants and their insurers. And, as we have seen, the Legislature could reasonably have determined that the reduction of such costs would serve the public interest by preserving the availability of medical care throughout the state and by helping to assure that patients who were injured by medical malpractice in the future would have a source of medical liability insurance to cover their losses.

Moreover, the Legislature clearly did not act irrationally in choosing to modify the collateral source rule as one means of lowering the costs of malpractice litigation. In analyzing the collateral source rule more than a decade ago in *Helfend v. Southern Cal. Rapid Transit District, supra*, 2 Cal.3d 1, we acknowledged that most legal commentators had severely criticized the rule for affording a plaintiff a "double recovery" for "losses" he had not in reality sustained, and we noted that many jurisdictions had either restricted or repealed it. (*Id.*, at pp. 6–7, & fns. 4, 5 & 6.) Although we concluded in *Helfend* that a number of policy considerations counseled against judicial abolition of the rule, we in no way suggested that it was immune from legislative revision, but, on the contrary, stated that the changes proposed by legal commentators "if desirable, would be more effectively accomplished through legislative reform." (*Id.*, at p. 13.) In the mid–1970's, California was only one of many states to include a modification of the collateral source rule as a part of its medical malpractice reform legislation (see Comment, *An Analysis of State Legislative Responses to the Medical Malpractice Crisis* (1975) Duke L.J. 1417, 1447–1450), and the American Bar Association's Commission on Medical Professional Liability also recommended abolition of the rule as one appropriate response to the medical malpractice "crisis." (See Rep. of Com. on Medical Professional Liability, *supra*, 102 ABA Ann. Rep. 786, 849–850.) Under the circumstances, we think it is clear that the provision is rationally related to a legitimate state interest and does not violate due process.

Plaintiff's equal protection challenge to section 3333.1 is equally without merit. As with all of the MICRA provisions that we have examined in recent cases, the Legislature could properly restrict the statute's application to medical malpractice cases because the provision was intended to help meet problems that had specifically arisen in the medical malpractice field.

Accordingly, the trial court did not err in upholding section 3333.1.

## NOTES

**1.  Tort Reform in the Context of Medical Malpractice.** Many states have enacted tort reform statutes that limit recovery in specific contexts like medical malpractice suits or more generally. Given that many people have health insurance, a common approach is to abrogate the collateral source rule (see Note 1 following *Helfend v. Southern California Rapid Transit District*, supra). Some states require that the plaintiff's award in tort cases be reduced by the amount of compensation that the plaintiff receives from the collateral source (e.g., insurance). Other states do not require such a reduction, but do permit the jury to consider compensation from other sources in calculating the plaintiff's award. The effect of such statutes tends to be a shifting of cost from doctors, hospitals, and their insurers onto the insurers of patients. This protects health providers, but can be expected to increase the cost of health insurance. See Diamond, Levine & Madden, *Understanding Torts* § 14.06 (2nd ed. 2000); Dobbs, *The Law of Torts* § 384 (2000).

**2.  Limiting Recovery for Pain and Suffering.** Another common tort reform is to limit recovery for pain and suffering. In part, this reflects ambiguity as to whether pain and suffering should be compensated at all and whether monetary compensation can be equated with pain and suffering. See, e.g., Justice Traynor's dissent in *Seffert v. Los Angeles Transit Lines*, 56 Cal.2d 498, 15 Cal.Rptr. 161, 364 P.2d 337 (1961), cited in an omitted portion of the principal case. On the other hand, pain and suffering represents an authentic loss which should not be discounted in deterring the potential tortfeasor or compensating the victim. Also note that ordinarily the plaintiff lawyer's contingent fee comes from the recovery. Pain and suffering recovery allows that recovery to come from noneconomic losses suffered by the victim. Do you agree that caps should be utilized to limit noneconomic losses such as pain and suffering?

**3.  Limiting the Attorney's Recovery.** Some jurisdictions limit the percentage a plaintiff's attorney can recover of the plaintiff's judgment in a tort case. To enable plaintiffs with good tort claims to hire good attorneys, contingent fee arrangements are very common in tort cases. The victim may have little or no money to pay an attorney. By accepting a contingent fee arrangement, the plaintiff's attorney agrees to be compensated by a percentage of what the client ultimately recovers. This percentage can be 35 percent or higher. Advocates of limits on contingent fees argue plaintiff lawyers are being excessively compensated, putting pressure for plaintiffs to demand higher settlements. Opponents argue that limiting fees interferes with free market negotiation between clients and attorneys and discourages the best attorneys from representing plaintiffs in tort actions.

**4.  Cost of Insurance.** One of the major arguments for limiting recovery in torts is the impact of high insurance premiums. These premiums are reflected in the cost of doing business, and consequently when passed on by businesses, increases the cost to the consumer. In some instances, the cost of insurance may be so high that the business cannot pass along the costs and is forced out of business.

Others argue that pressure on insurance costs is often more the product of a falling stock market and other low yielding investments. Insurance companies receive premiums from the insured which they invest until some funds must be paid out in response to claims. So long as investments are sufficiently profitable, insurance companies will be able to keep rates low despite some high payouts.

Do higher insurance costs justify limiting injured plaintiffs' recoveries?

# Chapter VI

# VICARIOUS LIABILITY

## SECTION A.  EMPLOYERS' VICARIOUS LIABILITY FOR EMPLOYEES

### RODGERS v. KEMPER CONSTRUCTION CO.

Court of Appeal, Fourth District, Division 2, California.
50 Cal.App.3d 608, 124 Cal.Rptr. 143 (1975).

TAMURA, Acting P. J.

A subcontractor on a construction project appeals from a judgment entered on a jury verdict holding it liable for injuries sustained by two employees of the general contractor as a result of an assault committed upon them by employees of the subcontractor.

The assault occurred at the site of the state's Cedar Springs Dam project. Plaintiffs (Rodgers and Kelley) were employed as heavy equipment operators by the general contractor for the project. Defendant Kemper Construction Co. (Kemper) was a subcontractor on the same job. Defendants Herd and O'Brien were employees of Kemper.

Kemper maintained its office in a movable trailer on the job site. Near the office trailer was a "dry house" trailer equipped with a shower room and lockers for Kemper's employees. Kemper's subcontract involved construction of tunnels and other work under the spillway. Its employees wore special clothing which they kept in the dry house lockers. After work Kemper's employees usually showered before putting on their own clothing.

Work on the Cedar Springs project continued around the clock during the week but no work was performed on Saturday or Sunday. Kemper's employees worked in three shifts, the day shift from 8 a.m. to 4 p.m., the swing shift from 4 p.m. to 12 midnight, and the night shift from 12 midnight to 8 a.m. When in need of extra help, Kemper's supervisors would sometimes look in the dry house to see whether any of the men who had just completed a shift would be willing to work overtime.

Although the dry house had a sign prohibiting alcohol, it was not unusual for the men to drink beer there after a shift. Particularly on

Friday nights there was usually beer in the dry house. Kemper's supervisors made no effort to stop the drinking and in fact they frequently joined in.

On Friday, July 18, 1969, Herd and O'Brien worked the day shift for Kemper, ending at 4 p.m. After work they went to the dry house, changed clothes, and then worked on O'Brien's pickup in the Kemper parking area adjacent to the dry house. There was beer in a styrofoam chest in the dry house and Herd and O'Brien had three or four beers each. Dieffenbauch, Kemper's office manager, was present and also drank beer.

About 8 p.m. Herd and O'Brien set out on foot across the job site to look for a friend from whom they planned to borrow money to continue drinking in a nearby town. Herd and O'Brien approached Rodgers who was operating a bulldozer on the spillway and signaled him to stop. O'Brien climbed on the tractor and asked Rodgers for a ride which Rodgers refused because it was against regulations. Both Herd and O'Brien then fell on Rodgers, beating him with their fists and with rocks.

When the two men left, Rodgers drove to where Kelley was working and asked for help in obtaining the identities of the assailants. Rodgers and Kelley proceeded to the Kemper parking area where they saw Herd and O'Brien getting into O'Brien's pickup. As Rodgers began to write down the license number of the pickup, O'Brien got out and hit Kelley knocking him down. Rodgers threw a rock at O'Brien which missed and cracked the windshield of the pickup. Herd got out and began fighting with Rodgers. At this point Dieffenbauch entered the scene and hit Rodgers from behind rendering him unconscious. Herd beat Kelley about the head with a hard hat and Dieffenbauch jumped on Kelley's legs and kicked them. The fight ended when another employee of the general contractor arrived and managed to remove Rodgers and Kelley.

Rodgers sustained serious multiple injuries to his right hip, left shoulder and low back necessitating numerous surgeries. He has been permanently disabled from working as a heavy equipment operator. Kelley sustained a permanent diplopia (double vision) requiring corrective lenses. The jury returned a verdict in favor of Rodgers and against Kemper, Herd and O'Brien in the sum of $220,442.07, and in favor of Kelley and against the same defendants in the sum of $1,500. Kemper appeals from the judgment on the jury verdict.

\* \* \*

From the analysis which follows, we have concluded there is substantial evidence in support of Kemper's liability under the doctrine of *respondeat superior*.

\* \* \*

Under *respondeat superior*, an employer is vicariously liable for the torts of his employees committed within the scope of the employment. The doctrine, which departs from the normal tort principle that liability follows fault, is an ancient one but its scope and stated rationale have varied widely from period to period. (See 2 Harper & James, The Law of Torts, pp. 1361–1374; Prosser, Torts (4th ed. 1971) pp. 458–459.) It has been aptly stated that "Respondeat superior has long been a rule in search of a guiding rationale." (Note, 82 Harv.L.Rev. 1568, 1569.)

California has adopted the rationale that the employer's liability should extend beyond his actual or possible control over the employees to include risks inherent in or created by the enterprise because he, rather than the innocent injured party, is best able to spread the risk through prices, rates or liability insurance. (*Hinman v. Westinghouse Elec. Co.*, 2 Cal.3d 956, 959–960 [88 Cal.Rptr. 188, 471 P.2d 988]; *Johnston v. Long*, 30 Cal.2d 54, 63–64 [181 P.2d 645]; *Fields v. Sanders*, 29 Cal.2d 834, 841 [180 P.2d 684, 172 A.L.R. 525]; *Carr v. Wm. C. Crowell Co.*, 28 Cal.2d 652, 655–656 [171 P.2d 5]; *Strait v. Hale Constr. Co.*, 26 Cal.App.3d 941, 948–949 [103 Cal.Rptr. 487].) In some respects this rationale is akin to that underlying the modern doctrine of strict tort liability for defective products. (See *Escola v. Coca Cola Bottling Co.*, 24 Cal.2d 453, 461–462 [150 P.2d 436], concurring opn. of Traynor, J.; *Greenman v. Yuba Power Products, Inc.*, 59 Cal.2d 57, 63 [27 Cal.Rptr. 697, 377 P.2d 897, 13 A.L.R.3d 1049].) But this does not mean that *respondeat superior* is merely a justification for reaching a "deep pocket" or that it is based only upon an elaborate economic theory regarding optimal resource allocation. It is grounded upon "a deeply rooted sentiment that a business enterprise cannot justly disclaim responsibility for accidents which may fairly be said to be characteristic of its activities." (*Ira S. Bushey & Sons, Inc. v. United States*, 398 F.2d 167, 171, noted in 82 Harv.L.Rev. 1568–1575. See generally, Keeton, *Conditional Fault in the Law of Torts*, 72 Harv.L.Rev. 401.)

One way to determine whether a risk is inherent in, or created by, an enterprise is to ask whether the actual occurrence was a generally foreseeable consequence of the activity. However, "foreseeability" in this context must be distinguished from "foreseeability" as a test for negligence. In the latter sense "foreseeable" means a level of probability which would lead a prudent person to take effective precautions whereas "foreseeability" as a test for *respondeat superior* merely means that in the context of the particular enterprise an employee's conduct is not so unusual or startling that it would seem unfair to include the loss resulting from it among other costs of the employer's business. (2 Harper & James, The Law of Torts, pp. 1377–1378. See *Ira S. Bushey & Sons, Inc. v. United States, supra*, at pp. 171–172.) In other words, where the question is one of vicarious liability, the inquiry should be whether the risk was one "that may fairly be regarded as typical of or broadly incidental" to the enterprise undertaken by the employer. (2 Harper & James, The Law of Torts, p. 1376.)

Under the modern rationale for *respondeat superior*, the test for determining whether an employer is vicariously liable for the tortious conduct of his employee is closely related to the test applied in workers' compensation cases for determining whether an injury arose out of or in the course of employment. (*Hinman v. Westinghouse Elec. Co., supra*, 2 Cal.3d 956, 962, fn. 3.) This must necessarily be so because the theoretical basis for placing the loss on the employer in both the tort and workers' compensation fields is the allocation of the economic cost of an injury resulting from a risk incident to the enterprise. (*Huntsinger v. Glass Containers Corp.*, 22 Cal.App.3d 803, 808 [99 Cal.Rptr. 666]; 2 Harper & James, The Law of Torts, pp. 1376–1378.) Consequently, our high court has on many occasions relied upon workers' compensation cases in tort cases. (E.g., *Hinman v. Westinghouse Elec. Co., supra*, at pp. 961–962; *George* v. *Bekins Van & Storage Co.*, 33 Cal.2d 834, 843 [205 P.2d 1037]; *Fields v. Sanders, supra*, 29 Cal.2d 834, 841; *Carr v. Wm. C. Crowell Co., supra*, 28 Cal.2d 652, 656.) Since the instant case involves an unusual factual situation which, to our knowledge, has never been previously considered by a reviewing court, it is particularly appropriate and instructive to draw on the experience in the workers' compensation field. We shall do so in the ensuing discussion.

Turning to the present case, Kemper contends the evidence fails to establish its liability under *respondeat superior* because: (a) The assault occurred after Herd and O'Brien had completed their work shift and (b) the assault was the result of personal malice unrelated to the work. Those contentions must be rejected.

Although on the day in question Herd and O'Brien had finished their shift at 4 p.m., they were still on the job site when the fight occurred sometime between 8 and 9 p.m. There was evidence that as a matter of mutual convenience, Kemper customarily permitted its employees to remain on the premises in or about the dry house long after their work shift had ended. When Kemper needed additional workers for later shifts, it frequently contacted employees who remained in or about the dry house. It was customary, particularly on Friday evenings, for employees to sit around the dry house after their work shift and talk and drink beer, often, as on the evening in question, joined by their supervisors.

In the field of workers' compensation under varied circumstances an employee may be acting in the scope of employment even though the injury occurred during an off-duty period. Thus, an employee has been held to be acting within the scope of employment while properly traversing the employer's premises in going to or returning from work so long as there is no unreasonable delay. (*Peterson v. Moran*, 111 Cal.App.2d 766, 768 [245 P.2d 540]. See *Greydanus* v. *Industrial Acc. Com.*, 63 Cal.2d 490 [47 Cal.Rptr. 384, 407 P.2d 296]; *Van Cleve* v. *Workmen's Comp. App. Bd.*, 261 Cal.App.2d 228 [67 Cal.Rptr. 757]; *Bethlehem Steel Co. v. Ind. Acc. Com.*, 70 Cal.App.2d 382 [161 P.2d 59].) And, under the "bunkhouse rule," an employee who lives on his employer's premises may be acting within the scope of his employment even while engaged in leisure pursuits on an off-duty day provided the employee is making a reasonable use of the employer's premises. (*Argonaut Ins. Co. v. Workmen's Comp. App. Bd.*, 247 Cal.App.2d 669, 677–678 [55 Cal.Rptr. 810].) Our Supreme Court recently held that where social or recreational pursuits on the employer's premises after hours are endorsed by the express or implied permission of the employer and are "conceivably" of some benefit to the employer *or*, even in the absence of proof of benefit, if such activities have become "a customary incident of the employment relationship," an employee engaged in such pursuits after hours is still acting within the scope of his employment. (*McCarty v. Workmen's Comp. Appeals Bd.*, 12 Cal.3d 677, 681–683 [117 Cal.Rptr. 65, 527 P.2d 617].)

In the case at bench, it was neither unusual nor unreasonable for Herd and O'Brien to be on the job site at the time the incident occurred. Their continued presence after completion of their work shift was "conceivably" of some benefit to Kemper. It was a convenience to Kemper to be able to recruit additional help by simply contacting employees remaining in or about the job site. Also, apart from benefit to the employer, there was substantial evidence that the after-hours social activity in and about the dry house—talking and drinking beer—was with the express or implied permission of the employer and was a customary incident of the employment relationship. Thus, the mere fact that the assault occurred after working hours does not compel the conclusion that it occurred outside the scope of employment.

Nor does the evidence establish, as a matter of law, that the assault was the result of personal malice unconnected with the employment relationship.

*Respondeat superior* includes liability for an employee's intentional tort as well as negligence. Traditionally, before an employer could be held vicariously liable for an employee's assault, proof was required that the employee intended to benefit or further the interest of the employer. (See 2 Harper & James, The Law of Torts, p. 1392.) However, the "motive test," though still the "majority rule," has been abandoned in California. (*Fields v. Sanders, supra*, 29 Cal.2d 834, 838–839; *Carr v. Wm. C. Crowell Co., supra*, 28 Cal.2d 652, 654; Note, 35 Cal.L.Rev. 126–128) and by federal courts applying federal tort law (*Ira S. Bushey & Sons, Inc. v. United States, supra*, 398 F.2d 167, 170–171.) In this state, the test applied is virtually identical to that used for an employee's negligent torts. If the assault was motivated by personal malice not engendered by the employment, the employer is not vicariously liable; but otherwise, liability may be found if the injury results from "a dispute arising out of the employment." (*Carr v. Wm. C. Crowell Co., supra*, at p. 654.)

In the case at bench, there was no evidence of personal malice unrelated to the employment. In *Carr v. Wm. C. Crowell Co., supra*, an employee of a general building contractor became angry with an employee of a subcontractor and threw a hammer at him, causing serious injuries. Affirming judgment against the general contractor, the Supreme Court explained there could be no personal malice where the assailant and his victim were strangers: "Not only did the altercation leading to the injury arise solely over the performance of Enloe's duties, but his entire association with plaintiff arose out of his employment on the building under construction. He had never seen plaintiff before the day preceding the accident, and had never conversed with him before the dispute ..." (28 Cal.2d 652, at p. 657.) So also in the case at bench, Rodgers and Kelley, as they testified, were complete strangers to Herd and O'Brien.

Not only was there a lack of evidence of personal malice, there was substantial evidence that the dispute which was the proximate cause of the assault arose out of the employment. The initial conflict resulted from O'Brien's request for a ride on Rodgers' bulldozer. The jury could permissibly infer from O'Brien's testimony that he believed his status as an employee of the subcontractor carried with it the fringe benefit of free rides on the general contractor's heavy equipment. When Rodgers refused to recognize this perquisite, taking the position that all free rides were forbidden, O'Brien apparently lost his temper. Had O'Brien not been employed on that project, had he been a mere visitor, it may be inferred that he would not have felt privileged to ask for a ride or, if he did, would not have been so deeply offended at Rodgers' refusal. As previously mentioned, California does not require that an employee intend by his assault to benefit the employer.

In holding that the assault in *Carr v. Wm. C. Crowell Co., supra*, 28 Cal.2d 652, was an outgrowth of the employment, the court observed: "[D]efendant's enterprise required an association of employees with third parties, attended by the risk that someone might be injured. 'The risk of such associations and conditions were risks of the employment.' (Cardozo, J., in *Leonbruno v. Champlain Silk Mills*, 229 N. Y. 470, 472 [128 N.E. 711, 13 A.L.R. 522].) Such associations 'include the faults and derelictions of human beings as well as their virtues and obediences. Men do not discard their personal qualities when they go to work. Into the job they carry their intelligence, skill, habits of care and rectitude. Just as inevitably they take along also their tendencies to carelessness and camaraderie, as well as emotional makeup.... These expressions of human nature are incidents inseparable from working together. They involve risks of injury and these risks are inherent in the working environment.' [Citations.]" (*Carr v. Wm. C. Crowell Co., supra*, 28 Cal.2d 652, 656. See also *Fields* v. *Sanders, supra*, 29 Cal.2d 834, 841 [employer liable for an assault by its truck driver on a motorist resulting from a collision on a highway].)

In the instant case, it was reasonably to be expected that Kemper's employees would come in contact with employees of other contractors on the same project. The risk of such association, as explained in *Carr* and *Fields*, extends to expressions of normal human traits which, unhappily, include occasional emotional flareups and propensity for violence. In the case at bench the quarrel on the job site, though between employees of different contractors, arose over the rights and privileges of Kemper's off-duty employees. It was manifestly an outgrowth of the employment relationship and a risk which may fairly be considered as typical of, or incidental to, the employment. The incident which led to plaintiff's injuries was such as might normally be expected to occur during the course of a major construction job.

Kemper relies on *Yates v. Taft Lodge No. 1527*, 6 Cal.App.2d 389 [44 P.2d 409], and *Lane v. Safeway Stores, Inc.*, 33 Cal.App.2d 169 [91 P.2d 160]. In *Yates*, the defendant rented picnic grounds from the plaintiff for a single day and hired one Dear as gatekeeper for that day. While so engaged, Dear became embroiled in an argument with plaintiff-landlord about the terms of the lease during the course of which Dear assaulted the plaintiff. Defendant's demurrer to plaintiff's complaint was sustained and the ensuing judgment of dismissal was affirmed on appeal on the ground that Dear was not acting within the scope of his employment. Although *Yates* had never been overruled, it is inconsistent with the spirit of *Carr v. Wm. C. Crowell Co., supra,* 28 Cal.2d 652, *Fields v. Sanders, supra,* 29 Cal.2d 834, and other more recent decisions and has been distinguished in a number of later cases (see *Sullivan v. Matt,* 130 Cal.App.2d 134, 139–141 [278 P.2d 499]; *Haworth* v. *Elliott,* 67 Cal. App.2d 77, 81–82 [153 P.2d 804]; and *Hiroshima* v. *Pacific Gas & Elec. Co.,* 18 Cal.App.2d 24, 28 [63 P.2d 340]). The precedential value of *Yates* has thus been eroded.

In *Lane v. Safeway Stores, Inc., supra,* 33 Cal.App.2d 169, plaintiff, a nine-year old boy, was sent to defendant store to purchase an item. While consummating the purchase, he was kicked by the clerk. In a nonjury trial, the court found in favor of plaintiff and against the clerk but found in favor of Safeway on the ground the clerk was not acting in the scope of his employment. The trial judge commented that it appeared the boy was "fooling around this store" and was "mischievous" and that the clerk merely kicked him playfully. The appellate court affirmed the judgment on the ground the clerk was acting outside the scope of his employment when he engaged in horseplay with the customer. The court cited as its principal authority *Stephenson v. Southern Pac. Co.,* 93 Cal. 558 [29 P. 234]. However, *Stephenson* was expressly overruled in *Carr v. Wm. C. Crowell Co., supra,* 28 Cal.2d 652, at page 656, as being contrary to the course of subsequent decisions. *Lane* is therefore no longer a valid precedent.

Although the facts in the instant case are somewhat unusual and there appears to be no case authority precisely in point, we conclude that the jury's implied finding of Kemper's liability under *respondeat superior* is consistent with the current rationale for the doctrine and is supported by substantial evidence.

* * *

Judgment is affirmed.

### NOTES

**1. Vicarious Liability and Respondeat Superior.** In certain situations, a defendant may be held vicariously liable for the torts of another, without any finding of negligence or intent on the part of the defendant. This occurs most commonly where an employer is held vicariously liable for the tort of an employee acting within the scope of employment. In such suits, which rely on the doctrine of "respondeat superior", litigation tends to center around defining the scope of employment. See Diamond, Levine & Madden, *Understanding Torts* § 13.02 (2nd ed. 2000); Keeton, *Prosser and Keeton on The Law of Torts* §§ 69–70 (5th ed. 1984) and Dobbs, *The Law of Torts* §§ 333–335 (2000). As the principal case indicates, employer liability for employees' acts "within the scope of employment" can be broadly construed to include both negligence and intentional torts that are attributable to the employment. The older rationale that the employer has "control" of the employee and should be responsible for his or her torts is increasingly being supplanted by notions that the employer's business should be responsible for risks the enterprise imposes on the community.

Vicarious liability is, in effect, strict liability imposed on the employer for the employees' torts. The employer is liable even if he or she did not behave negligently in hiring or supervising the employee. Vicarious liability adds liability to the employer, but does not eliminate the liability the employee has for his or her own tort. Since the employer ordinarily has more economic resources (the "deep pocket"), plaintiffs look most often to the employer for recovery. See also Keeton, *Prosser and Keeton on the Law of Torts* § 69 (5th ed. 1984).

Consistent with the doctrine of respondeat superior, partners may generally be held liable for torts committed by others in furtherance of the partnership. See Diamond, Levine & Madden, supra, and Keeton, supra, § 72. Consider *Royal Bank and Trust Co. v. Weintraub, Gold & Alper*, 68 N.Y.2d 124, 506 N.Y.S.2d 151, 497 N.E.2d 289 (1986), in which one of the named partners of a law firm signed a note indicating that a check issued by the plaintiff as a loan would be placed in escrow in the firm's account and returned on a specified date. The other partners of the firm sought to disavow liability for the unreturned check by asserting that they had privately dissolved the firm prior to issuance of the check. But since the firm had not made the dissolution public, the court rejected the argument:

> Nearly two years after alleged dissolution, the public indicia of the partnership remained undisturbed. Where the firm space, telephone number, telephone book listing and stationery continued in use by the individuals, with no discernible sign of dissolution, we conclude that the partnership continued to be liable as such to a party reasonably relying to its detriment on the impression of an ongoing entity.

The court thus held the other partners liable.

## CALDWELL v. A.R.B., INC.

Court of Appeal, Fifth District, California.
176 Cal.App.3d 1028, 222 Cal.Rptr. 494 (1986).

### The Case

Plaintiff filed a complaint for damages against Bruce Wayne Brandon, charging him with negligently operating his vehicle and causing it to collide with plaintiff's vehicle. The complaint further alleged that Brandon was acting in the scope of his employment. At the time of the accident, Brandon was employed by defendant A.R.B., and A.R.B. was named later as a defendant in the suit. A.R.B. filed a motion for summary judgment on the ground that Brandon was not acting within the scope of his employment at the time of the accident. The motion was granted, and plaintiff appeals.

### The Facts

On January 20, 1982, plaintiff was driving his van on Highway 58 in Kern County when he was involved in a car accident. Plaintiff's van and a vehicle driven by Brandon collided head-on. Brandon was killed, and plaintiff suffered severe injuries as a result of the accident.

Brandon was an apprentice pipefitter and had been hired by A.R.B. to work at the Shell Oil dehydration plant project, which was located north of McKittrick approximately 35 to 40 miles from Bakersfield. As a pipefitter, Brandon was a member of the United Association Local Union No. 460 and was subject to the terms and conditions of the working agreement between Union Local No. 460 and the Plumbing and Mechanical Contractors Association of Kern, Inyo and Mono Counties. Defendant A.R.B. was a member of the Plumbing and Mechanical Contractors Association and, as such, also was subject to the union contract.

January 20, 1982, was a regular workday for the apprentice pipefitters working at the McKittrick jobsite, and Brandon had reported for work that day. The workday, however, ended early at approximately 11 a.m. due to the onset of heavy rain. The rain caused working conditions around the pipe to be unsafe, plus the welders were unable to work in the rain. Under these conditions, the workers were sent home and were not subject to recall on that day. The employees were to assume the next day was a regular workday unless they were notified the following morning not to show up. The employees then received pay for working from 7 a.m. to 11 a.m.

Sometime that morning, Brandon offered to give a coworker, Jeff Richardson, a ride home. Richardson normally commuted to work with another employee, David Solar, but Solar had fallen into a mud puddle, and the company sent Solar home so that he would not get sick. Afterwards, the job was shut down early, and Richardson and Brandon left the jobsite around noon. On their way back to Bakersfield from work, their vehicle was involved in the car accident that killed Brandon and injured plaintiff.

Richardson and Ernest Choukalos, construction foreman for A.R.B., both gave information in their depositions about the conditions of employment with A.R.B. The employees were to report directly to the jobsite each day, which was about 35 to 40 miles from Bakersfield. There was no public transportation from Bakersfield to McKittrick. Richardson usually carpooled with a coworker. All the carpooling was informally organized by the individual employees. Choukalos also stated no public transportation existed from the union hall to the jobsite. The employees had to use their own vehicles to get out to the jobsite, or they simply would not work.

\* \* \*

Under the doctrine of respondeat superior, an employer is liable for the torts of his employees committed within the scope of their employment. (*Ducey v. Argo Sales Co.* (1979) 25 Cal.3d 707, 721 [159 Cal.Rptr. 835, 602 P.2d 755].)

Generally, whether an act of an employee is committed within the scope of employment is a question of fact. (*Ducey v. Argo Sales Co.*, *supra.*, 25 Cal.3d at p. 722.) However, when the facts of a case are undisputed and conflicting inferences may not be drawn from those facts, whether an employee is acting within the scope of his employment is a question of law. (*Golden West Broadcasters, Inc. v. Superior Court* (1981) 114 Cal.App.3d 947, 956 [171 Cal.Rptr. 95].)

Case law has established the general rule that an employee is outside the scope of his employment while engaged in his ordinary commute to and from his place of work. (*Ducey v. Argo Sales Co.* , *supra.*, 25 Cal.3d at p. 722.) This principle is known as the "going-and-coming rule" and is based on several theories. One is that the employment relationship is suspended from the time the employee leaves his job until he returns. Another is that during the commute, the employee is not rendering services to his employer. (*Hinman v. Westinghouse Elec. Co.* (1970) 2 Cal.3d 956, 961 [88 Cal.Rptr. 188, 471 P.2d 988].) The courts, however, have recognized several exceptions to the "going-and-coming" rule. (*Id.*, at pp. 961–962.) One exception is the special mission or errand exception and another is a travel expense or allowance exception.

Plaintiff relies on workmen's compensation cases as well as tort cases in support of his contention that the special mission or errand exception and the travel expense exception are applicable in this case. Although the California courts often cite tort and workmen's compensation cases interchangeably, the latter are not controlling with respect to exceptions to the "going-and-coming" rule when liability is predicated upon respondeat superior principles. (1 Witkin, Summary of Cal. Law (1984 supp.) Agency and Employment, § 167, pp. 266–267; see *Ducey v. Argo Sales Co.* , *supra.*, 25 Cal.3d 707, 722; *Munyon v. Ole's, Inc.* (1982) 136 Cal.App.3d 697, 703 [186 Cal.Rptr. 424]; *Church v. Arko* (1977) 75 Cal.App.3d 291, 300 [142 Cal.Rptr. 92].)

We first reject a contention raised by plaintiff at oral argument. Citing to *Santa Rosa Junior College v. Workers' Comp. Appeals Bd.* (1985) 40 Cal.3d 345 [220 Cal.Rptr. 94, 708 P.2d 673], plaintiff argued the employee's commute fell into the special risk exception to the going-and-coming rule. The argument was that in sending the employees home early in hazardous weather, the employer subjected the employees to a risk causally related to employment.

In the *Santa Rosa* case, the Supreme Court set forth the following test to determine the applicability of the special risk exception in workmen's compensation cases:

> "[T]he exception will apply (1) if 'but for' the employment the employee would not have been at the location where the injury occurred and (2) if 'the risk is distinctive in nature or quantitatively greater than risks common to the public.' " (*Santa Rosa Junior College v. Workers' Comp. Appeals Bd.*, *supra.*, 40 Cal.3d at p. 354.)

Assuming, without deciding, that the special risk exception is applicable to employer tort liability cases, the facts of the present case fail to satisfy the second prong of the test. Plaintiff is correct that these employees were subjected to the risk of driving home in hazardous weather, but all drivers in the vicinity were exposed to the same risks in driving their automobiles under the prevailing weather conditions. We conclude that the risk suffered by A.R.B. employees was not " ' ...

distinctive in nature or quantitatively greater than risks common to the public.' "

A. *Special Errand Exception*

Another exception to the going-and-coming rule both in tort and workmen's compensation cases occurs when the employee commits a negligent act while engaged in a "special errand" or "special mission" for the employer. (*Munyon v. Ole's, Inc.*, *supra.*, 136 Cal.App.3d 697, 703.) In describing the special errand exception, the Court of Appeal in *Boynton v. McKales* stated:

> "If the employee is not simply on his way from his home to his normal place of work or returning from said place to his home for his own purpose, but is coming from his home or returning to it on a special errand either as part of his regular duties or at a specific order or request of his employer, the employee is considered to be in the scope of his employment from the time that he starts on the errand until he has returned or until he deviates therefrom for personal reasons. [Citations.] To such special missions the general test as to scope of employment applies. It is not necessary that the servant is directly engaged in the duties which he was employed to perform, but included are also missions which incidentally or indirectly contribute to the service, incidentally or indirectly benefit the employer." (*Boynton v. McKales* (1956) 139 Cal.App.2d 777, 789 [294 P.2d 733].)

The following activities have been considered special errands: picking up or returning tools used on the job, attendance at an employment social function when an employee's attendance is expected and it benefits the employer, and a trip in which the employee responds to a service call when the employee is on call for the employer's business. (*Munyon v. Ole's, Inc., supra.*, 136 Cal.App.3d at p. 703.)

Plaintiff argues the special mission exception is applicable to this case because (1) in giving a coworker a ride home, Brandon performed a work-related service for defendant A.R.B., and (2) when the jobsite was shut down and the employees were sent home early, defendant received a benefit by not having to pay the employees a full day's salary and by avoiding possible liability for workplace injuries caused by hazardous working conditions. We conclude as a matter of law that the special errand exception is not applicable in this case.

The facts surrounding Brandon's providing Jeff Richardson with a ride home are as follows: Richardson had commuted to work with a coworker. That morning the coworker slipped and fell into a mud puddle and was sent home by defendant so the coworker would not get sick by working further in the rain. Thereafter, Brandon offered to give Richardson a ride home. The facts do not indicate that defendant requested or invited Brandon to provide Richardson with transportation.

According to *Boynton* and other cases discussing the special mission exception, an employee may be on a "special errand either as part of his regular duties or at a specific order or request of his employer, ..."

(*Boynton v. McKales, supra.*, 139 Cal.App.2d at p. 789; *Munyon v. Ole's, Inc., supra.*, 136 Cal.App.3d at p. 703.) Since providing coemployees with transportation was not a part of Brandon's routine duties, to have the special mission exception apply, A.R.B. must have made a specific order or request that Richardson be taken home by Brandon. On the facts of this case, no such request or order may be found.

Plaintiff contends, relying on *C. L. Pharris Sand & Gravel, Inc. v. Workers' Comp. Appeals Bd.*, that an express request by the employer is not necessary to the application of the special errand exception. In that case, the court held that a prerequisite to the exception is a request or invitation by the employer, which may be either express or implied. (*C. L. Pharris Sand & Gravel, Inc. v. Workers' Comp. Appeals Bd.* (1982) 138 Cal.App.3d 584, 591 [187 Cal.Rptr. 899].) Even assuming that the law in a workers' compensation case is applicable to a vicarious tort liability case, the facts still do not show any type of request or invitation, either express or implied. Brandon's offering to take Richardson home was purely gratuitous. Defendant A.R.B. never paid or offered to pay Brandon for his services. Nothing in the facts suggests that A.R.B. ever requested or suggested that certain employees provide transportation for other employees.

It is possible for a special mission to be present when an employee gives a ride home to another employee. (See *Harvey v. D & L Construction Co.* (1967) 251 Cal.App.2d 48, 52–53 [59 Cal.Rptr. 255].) In that case, unlike the present case, however, the facts presented a reasonable inference not only that the employer had requested his employee to give a coworker a ride home, but that providing such transportation was a part of the employee's routine duties.

\* \* \*

## B.  *Transportation Exception*

Plaintiff argues that because there was some evidence that defendant provided a crew truck to transport employees from its yard in Bakersfield to the McKittrick jobsite and in addition paid the employees a travel allowance, the going-and-coming rule was inapplicable to Brandon's commute at the time of the accident. This argument is specious. Brandon was driving his own vehicle returning to Bakersfield and was not utilizing any means of transportation provided by defendant.

## C.  *Travel Allowance Exception*

Plaintiff's final contention is that the going-and-coming rule does not apply because defendant paid a travel allowance to its employees. According to Choukalos and Richardson, A.R.B. employees were not paid for their travel time, but they were paid for travel expenses. Richardson testified all the employees received what was called a subsistence pay, which was to compensate the employee for expenses in the use of his car. All employees received this pay as a part of their check each week whether or not the employee actually drove his own vehicle. Richardson believed the travel allowance for this job was about $10 a day. According to the union contract, the employees were to receive a specified travel allowance when the jobsite was more than 15 miles from the union dispatch office in Bakersfield. The amount of the allowance varied with the distance between jobsite and union office. For example, if a job was 30 to 35 miles from the dispatch office the employee would receive $10 travel allowance. If the job was 35 to 40 miles away the employee would receive $13 a day travel allowance. This travel allowance was given even when the employees worked a short day due to weather conditions.

\* \* \*

In *Hinman v. Westinghouse Elec. Co., supra.*, 2 Cal.3d 956, the employees were paid for their travel time to and from the jobsite and also paid travel expenses. The Supreme Court first indicated that exceptions to the going-and-coming rule will be made "where the trip involves an incidental benefit to the employer, not common to commute trips by ordinary members of the work force." (*Id.*, at p. 962.) The court then stated that the payment of travel expenses and payment for travel time benefited the employer because such payments allowed the employer to enlarge the labor market. The employer's reaching out to a distant or larger labor market increases the risk of injury in transportation and the costs of this risk inherent in the employer's enterprise should be paid for by the employer. The *Hinman* court then concluded:

> "We are satisfied that, where, as here, the employer and employee have made the travel time part of the working day by their contract, the employer should be treated as such during the travel time."

\* \* \*

Recognizing that the answer to the question here addressed is not truly a legal one but one of public policy, and also noting that the Supreme Court has not overruled or disapproved the holding in *Harris v. Oro–Dam Constructors, supra.*, 269 Cal.App.2d 911, we follow the reasoning of Justice Freidman and hold that the mere payment of a travel allowance as shown in the present case does not reflect a sufficient benefit to defendant so that it should bear responsibility for plaintiff's injuries.

We have considered and rejected plaintiff's other contentions.

The judgment is affirmed. Defendant to have its costs on appeal.

### NOTES

**1. "Coming and Going" Rule.** Torts committed by an employee during the course of ordinary commuting are generally not considered as having occurred within the scope of employment. This rule does not apply, however, if the trip also involves an errand for the employer or is part of a special, compensated trip. See Diamond, Levine & Madden, *Understanding Torts* § 13.02 (2nd ed. 2000). See also Keeton, *Prosser and Keeton on the Law of Torts* § 70 (5th ed. 1984); Dobbs, *The Law of Torts* § 335 (2000).

Consider *Simpson v. United States*, 484 F.Supp. 387 (W.D. Penn. 1980), in which the plaintiff sued the government after his decedent was involved in an accident with a military vehicle. The court noted that the presence of a defendant's name on a commercial vehicle raises a rebuttable presumption that the driver is acting within the scope of employment. The vehicle in *Simpson* bore the insignia of the Marine Corps and government license plates and thus gave rise to the presumption. Additionally, the driver was in full military dress. The government sought to rebut the presumption by arguing that the driver was on a personal outing, noting that there had been beer cans and members of the opposite sex present in the vehicle. The court rejected the argument, however, pointing out that, the driver was a recruiter and that, of the passengers, one was a potential recruit and the other was a valuable contact for finding other recruits.

Consider also *Fruit v. Schreiner*, 502 P.2d 133 (Alaska 1972), in which the defendant insurance company sent its salesman to a conference using his own transportation, for which he would be compensated. As part of the conference, the salesman was encouraged to socialize with out-of-town guests. He thus left the resort hosting the convention and drove to another restaurant expecting to find other conventioneers there. Finding none, he headed back towards the resort at approximately 2:00 a.m. On his way back he collided with the plaintiff's disabled automobile, crushing the plaintiff between the two vehicles. The court held that the defendant insurance company could be held vicariously liable as the salesman's drive was within the scope of employment.

## MAVRIKIDIS v. PETULLO

Supreme Court of New Jersey.
153 N.J. 117, 707 A.2d 977 (1998).

GARIBALDI, J.

In this case, we revisit the parameters of the vicarious liability doctrine as it pertains to whether a contractee may be vicariously liable for the negligence of its independent contractor....

### I

This case arose from an automobile accident that resulted in severe injury to plaintiff Alice Mavrikidis (Mavrikidis or plaintiff), including second- and third-degree burns over twenty-one percent of her body. On September 11, 1990, the intersection collision occurred after defendant Gerald Petullo, operating a dump truck registered to Petullo Brothers, Inc. (Petullo Brothers), drove through a red light, struck plaintiff's car, hit a telephone pole, and then overturned, spilling the truck's contents onto Mavrikidis's car. At the time of the accident, Gerald was transporting 10.99 tons of hot asphalt, which had been loaded onto the truck by Newark Asphalt Corporation (Newark Asphalt), to his job site at Clar Pine Servicenter (Clar Pine), a retail gasoline and automotive repair shop in Montclair.

Prior to the accident, Clar Pine's owner, Karl Pascarello (Pascarello), decided to renovate the station because he was switching gasoline brands from Getty to Gulf Oil. Those renovations included the installation of new pumps and canopies....

Because Pascarello had no experience in the construction or paving business, he hired Gerald's father, Angelo Petullo, to perform the asphalt and concrete work as part of the renovation of his service station. Pascarello had known Angelo since 1972 and, prior to hiring him, Pascarello examined other paving jobs that Angelo had completed. Pascarello hired Angelo by verbal agreement to participate in the station's renovations based on Angelo's reputation as an excellent mason and, to a lesser extent, the debt owed Clar Pine under the Petullo Brothers' account. Over the years, Angelo and Gerald had charged gas and small repairs to their company account. In exchange for the asphalt work, both parties orally agreed that the Petullos would receive a $6,800 credit toward a $12,000 to $20,000 debt that Petullo Brothers had accumulated.

\* \* \*

The Petullos supplied the labor, equipment, concrete, and most of the asphalt needed for the job, until Angelo "ran out of money" in the midst of the renovations. As a result, Pascarello provided him with a blank check made out to Newark Asphalt to purchase the asphalt on the day of the accident. Pascarello testified that he supplied Angelo with a check because he "[was] the type of person you don't give cash to." Nevertheless, it is undisputed that Pascarello was not involved in supervising the Petullos' work on a daily basis. Other than general supervision and periodic consultation, Pascarello's limited participation in the asphalt work consisted of payment for three loads of asphalt, including the one involved in this accident, as well as his direction to lay the asphalt in front of the service station's bay doors first to enable him to continue his automotive repairs while the gas station was out of service. As part of its regular course of business, Clar Pine repaired cars and small trucks. During completion of the paving job, Clar Pine remained open for business, servicing cars but not selling gasoline.

\* \* \*

## II

The first question is whether Clar Pine is vicariously liable for plaintiff's injuries. As we explained in *Majestic, supra,* the resolution of this issue must be approached with an awareness of the long settled doctrine that ordinarily where a person engages a contractor, who conducts an independent business by means of his own employees, to do work not in itself a nuisance (as our cases put it), he is not liable for the negligent acts of the contractor in the performance of the contract. [30 N.J. at 430–31, 153 A.2d 321.]

*See also Bahrle v. Exxon Corp.,* 145 *N.J.* 144, 156, 678 A.2d 225 (1996) ("Ordinarily, an employer that hires an independent contractor is not liable for the negligent acts of the contractor in the performance of the contract."); *Baldasarre v. Butler,* 132 *N.J.* 278, 291, 625 A.2d 458 (1993) ("Generally ... the principal is not vicariously liable for the torts of the independent contractor if the principal did not direct or participate in them.").

The initial inquiry in our analysis is to examine the status of the Petullos in relation to Clar Pine. Despite plaintiff's alternate theories to the contrary, the Petullos were independent contractors rather than servants of Clar Pine.

> The important difference between an employee and an independent contractor is that one who hires an independent contractor "has no right of control over the manner in which the work is to be done, it is to be regarded as the contractor's own enterprise, and he, rather than the employer is the proper party to be charged with the responsibility for preventing the risk, and administering and distributing it." [*Baldasarre, supra,* 132 *N.J.* at 291, 625 *A.*2d 458 (quoting *W. Page Keeton, Prosser & Keeton on the Law of Torts* § 71 (5th ed.1984)).]

In contrast, a servant is traditionally one who is "employed to perform services in the affairs of another, whose physical conduct in the performance of the service is controlled, or is subject to a right of control, by the other." W. Page Keeton, *Prosser & Keeton, supra,* § 70 at 501.

In determining whether a contractee maintains the right of control, several factors are to be considered. The *Restatement (Second) of Agency* sets forth these factors, including:

> (a) the extent of control which, by the agreement, the master may exercise over the details of the work;

> (b) whether or not the one employed is engaged in a distinct occupation or business;

> \* \* \*

> (d) the skill required in the particular occupation;

> (e) whether the employer or the workman supplies the instrumentalities, tools, and the place of work for the person doing the work;

> (f) the length of time for which the person is employed;

> (g) the method of payment, whether by the time or by the job;

> (h) whether or not the work is a part of the regular business of the employer; [and]

> (i) whether or not the parties believe they are creating the relation of master and servant....

[*Restatement (Second) of Agency* § 220(2) (1958).]

Applying those Restatement factors, it is evident that neither Angelo nor Gerald was a servant of Clar Pine. The masonry work required a skilled individual. Although Pascarello paid for three loads of asphalt, the Petullos provided their own tools and the remainder of the needed materials, other than bolts and plywood supplied by Pascarello to install the canopies. Their work did not involve the regular business of Clar Pine. In addition, the period of employment spanned only the time it took to lay the asphalt and concrete. Following the accident, the Petullos continued the job for which they were hired, which was approved by the Building Inspector of Montclair. In exchange for their services, the

Petullos were not paid by the hour or month; instead, they received a discharge of the portion of their debt.

Based on that threshold determination, we now must determine whether this case falls within any exceptions to the general rule of nonliability of principals/contractees for the negligence of their independent contractors. There are three such exceptions, as delineated by the *Majestic* Court: "(a) where the landowner [or principal] retains control of the manner and means of the doing of the work which is the subject of the contract; (b) where he engages an incompetent contractor; or (c) where ... the activity contracted for.... [is inherently dangeous]."

\* \* \*

### III

We now discuss each of the *Majestic* exceptions in turn. Under the first *Majestic* exception, the reservation of control "of the manner and means" of the contracted work by the principal permits the imposition of vicarious liability. 30 *N.J.* at 431, 153 *A.2d* 321. "In such a case the employer is responsible for the negligence of the independent contractor even though the particular control exercised and its manner of exercise had no causal relationship with the hazard that led to the injury, just as in the case of a simple employer-employee situation." *Bergquist v. Penterman,* 46 *N.J.Super.* 74, 85, 134 *A.2d* 20 (App.Div.), *certif. denied,* 25 *N.J.* 55, 134 *A.2d* 832 (1957). Under that test, the reservation of control over the equipment to be used, the manner or method of doing the work, or direction of the employees of the independent contractor may permit vicarious liability. *Trecartin v. Mahony–Troast Constr. Co.,* 18 *N.J.Super.* 380, 387, 87 *A.2d* 349 (App.Div.1952), *aff'd,* 21 *N.J.* 1, 120 *A.2d* 733 (1956).

However, supervisory acts performed by the contractee will not give rise to vicarious liability under that exception. As indicated by the language of the exception, application of principles of *respondeat superior* are not warranted where the contractee's "supervisory interest relates [only] to the result to be accomplished, not to the means of accomplishing it." *Majestic, supra,* 30 *N.J.* at 431, 153 *A.2d* 321; *see also Marion v. Public Serv. Elec. & Gas Co.,* 72 *N.J.Super.* 146, 154–55, 178 *A.2d* 57 (App.Div.1962) (explaining that retention of broad supervisory power rather than "right to direct and control" did not subject contractee to vicarious liability for independent contractor's actions); *Trecartin, supra,* 18 *N.J.Super.* at 386, 87 *A.2d* 349 (recognizing that "[a] general contractor ... exercising only such general superintendence as is necessary to see that the subcontractor performs the contract, ordinarily has no duty to protect an employee of the subcontractor").

Pascarello's actions did not exceed the scope of general supervisory powers so as to subject Clar Pine to vicarious liability for Gerald's negligence. Providing blueprints, paying for some of the asphalt, and directing that a portion of the concrete be completed first are clearly within the scope of a contractee's broad supervisory powers....

IV

Under the second *Majestic* exception, a principal may be held liable for injury caused by its independent contractor where the principal hires an incompetent contractor. As the Appellate Division explained in this case, "[t]he gravamen of th[is] exception is selection of a contractor who is incompetent. The selection of a competent contractor who negligently causes injury, does not render a [principal] liable." No presumption as to the negligence of an employer in hiring an independent contractor arises from the fact that, after being hired, the contractor is negligent in the performance of his duties and injures the person or property of another. *See* Reuben I. Friedman, Annotation, *When is Employer Chargeable with Negligence in Hiring Careless, Reckless, or Incompetent Independent Contractor,* 78 *A.L.R.*3d 910, 919 (1977).

\* \* \*

Because the second *Majestic* prong may include causes of action for both direct and vicarious liability, there is no reason to set out a separate tort for negligently hiring an independent contractor. To hold an employer liable under the second *Majestic* exception to the general rule of nonliability of principals for the negligence of their independent contractors, it is necessary to show both (1) that the contractor was incompetent or unskilled to perform the job for which he was hired, and (2) that the principal knew or had reason to know of the contractor's incompetence. The Petullos were skilled and experienced paving contractors. There is no evidence that the Petullos were unqualified to perform the masonry work for which they were hired. In fact, Pascarello visited other job sites that Angelo had paved in order to check the quality of his work. Viewing the evidence most favorably to plaintiffs, we find that the evidence does not support a finding that the Petullos were incompetent to perform the paving work for which they were engaged; hence, there is no basis for holding Clar Pine liable, either vicariously or directly, for plaintiff's injuries.

\* \* \*

V

Next, we consider the application of the third *Majestic* exception—whether the work engaged in by Petullo Brothers was inherently dangerous. In formulating this exception, the *Majestic* Court explained,

> "where work is to be done that may endanger others, there is no real hardship in holding the party for whom it is done responsible for neglect in doing it. Though he may not be able to do it himself, or intelligently supervise it, he will nevertheless be the more careful in selecting an agent to act for him." [*Majestic, supra,* 30 *N.J.* at 440, 153 *A.*2d 321 (quoting *Covington & Cincinnati Bridge Co. v. Steinbrock,* 61 *Ohio St.* 215, 55 *N.E.* 618, 621 (1899)).]

We observed that "nuisance per se" could be equated with "inherently dangerous." *Id.* at 434–35, 153 *A.*2d 321. Namely, work can be considered to be inherently dangerous if it is an activity which can be carried on safely only by the exercise of special skill and care, and which involves grave risk of danger to persons or property if negligently done. The term signifies that danger inheres *in the activity itself at all times, so as to require special precautions to be taken with regard to it to avoid injury. It means more than simply danger arising from the casual or collateral negligence of persons engaged in it under particular circumstances.* [*Ibid.* (citations omitted) (emphasis added).]

*See also Prosser & Keeton, supra,* § 71 at 512–16.

The definition of inherently dangerous set forth in *Majestic* comports with the discussion in sections 413, 416, and 427 of the *Restatement (Second) of Torts* (1965) regarding a contractee's nondelegable duty to take special precautions against dangers that arise from inherently dangerous work. The comments and illustrations following those sections explain that in cases in which the work relates to the transport of materials, the contractee is not responsible for the ordinary risks or dangers associated with faulty brakes or poor driving. In discussing the meaning of "[p]eculiar risk and special precautions," comment b to section 413 states:

It is obvious that an employer of an independent contractor may always anticipate that if the contractor is in any way negligent toward third persons, some harm to such persons may result. Thus one who hires a trucker to transport his goods must, as a reasonable man, always realize that if the truck is driven at an excessive speed, or with defective brakes, some collision or other harm to persons on the highway is likely to occur.... [Routine] precautions are the responsibility of the contractor.... [*Restatement (Second) of Torts, supra,* § 413 comment b.]

A peculiar risk is different "from the common risks to which persons in general are commonly subjected by the ordinary forms of negligence." *Id.* § 416 comment d. As a result, "the [contractee] is not liable for the contractor's failure to inspect the brakes on his truck, or for his driving in excess of the speed limit, because the risk is in no way a peculiar one, and only an ordinary precaution is called for." *Ibid.*

In *Ek v. Herrington,* 939 F.2d 839 (9th Cir.1991), the Ninth Circuit applied the three sections of the *Restatement (Second) of Torts* discussed above. In that case, decedent's heirs sued an independent contractor, who was hired to haul logs, and the owner of the logging operation, after the logs broke loose from the truck, landing on decedent's vehicle and causing her death. There, the brakes on the truck were defective and the truck was overloaded by at least 10,000 pounds. Addressing the issue of whether vicarious liability should be imposed on the logging operation for the hauler's negligence, the court held:

We accept the Restatement's suggestion that the risk posed by malfunctioning brakes is an ordinary one that an employer of an independent contractor has no duty to provide against. Similarly, we hold that the risk posed by overloading a logging truck is not a peculiar risk that arises in the normal course of logging and for which special precautions must be taken. It is a risk that would not arise, *but for the independent contractor's negligence, and which can be avoided by the ordinary precaution of not overloading the truck. An employer of an independent contractor is justified in presuming that a careful contractor will not create that risk . . . .* The duty rests solely on the shoulders of the independent contractor. [*Id.* at 844 (emphasis added).]

Moreover, in a case with facts almost identical to those presented here, a California appellate court refused to impose vicarious liability on a contractee whose independent contractor struck and killed the plaintiff's decedent with his dump truck, which was loaded with asphalt. *A. Teichert & Son, Inc. v. Superior Court,* 179 *Cal.App.*3d 657, 225 *Cal. Rptr.* 10 (1986). In its decision, the court noted that "[the truck driver's] negligence, if any, entailed nothing more than ordinary failure to exercise due care in the operation of a motor vehicle. This is not sufficient to invoke the 'special risk' exception to the rule of non-liability for the negligence of an independent contractor." *Id.* 225 *Cal.Rptr.* at 12.

\* \* \*

## NOTES

**1. Independent Contractor Rule.** In the context of respondeat superior suits, courts generally do not hold a defendant liable for torts committed by an independent contractor. An independent contractor is not considered a servant of the employer, and therefore while hired usually for specific tasks, such as plumber or electrician services, does not ordinarily subject those who employ them to vicarious liability. The line between a servant employee and independent contractor can be vague. Factors in favor of finding independent contractor status include the workers' use of his own equipment, freedom from direct supervision from those who employ him, and the number of other clients the worker serves. See Diamond, Levine & Madden, *Understanding Torts* § 13.02 (2nd ed. 2000); Keeton, *Prosser and Keeton on the Law of Torts* § 71 (5th ed. 1984); Dobbs, *The Law of Torts* § 336 (2000).

**2. Freedom From Control.** Even if the employee can be characterized as an "independent contractor," the independent contractor rule may not be applied if the employer is closely involved with the details of the contractor's work. In *Fisher v. Townsends, Inc.,* 695 A.2d 53 (Del.1997), plaintiff was injured while a passenger in the bed of a pickup truck driven by Reid, a weighmaster for Townsends' chicken processing business, when the truck swerved and hit a telephone pole. Plaintiff sued Townsends, alleging that Reid was its agent. The Superior Court held that Reid was an independent contractor, and, as a matter of law, could not have his negligence imputed to the defendants. On appeal, the court stated that one exception to the independent contractor rule turns on the amount of control retained or exercised by the owner. If the owner or contractee's control or direction dominates the manner or means of the work performed, the non-agent status of the independent contractor can be destroyed for the purposes of vicarious liability. Thus the issue becomes one of fact.

See also *Moore v. Vision Quest,* 1999 WL 51802 (N.D.Ill.1999), where a salesman for Vision Quest on his way to dinner with a client drove through an intersection and struck the plaintiff with his car. The salesman (Vantil) had signed a non-exclusive Independent Contract Agreement to sell products for Vision Quest. The agreement included provisions that he would document the movement of inventory in his sales territory, follow Vision Quest's specifications, discounts, prices and other conditions of sale. Vision Quest assigned goals for gross sales revenue. Additionally, Vision Quest had access to the salesman's computer files, required him to keep up-to-date records, attend sales meetings, respond to Vision Quest messages within four hours, and carry a pager at all times. Defendant claimed it did not control the details or the method of Vantil's work because he determined his own schedule, hours, vacation and sick time. The court denied summary judgement, holding that Vision Quest had not overcome its burden of showing it did not have control over Vantil.

**3. Non–Delegable Duty Exception.** An additional exception to the independent contractor rule involves situations where the contractor's activities constitute a "non-delegable duty", in which case the employer retains responsibility for the worker's tortious acts. In *Rizzuto v. L.A. Wenger Contracting Co., Inc.*, 91 N.Y.2d 343, 670 N.Y.S.2d 816, 693 N.E.2d 1068 (1998), plaintiff plumbing foreman was replacing a submersible pipe in the fuel station area of a bus depot, while two Transit Authority employees prepared to pressure-test an underground tank for leakage. Plaintiff's immediate work area was suddenly sprayed with diesel fuel, covering him and the floor. As he attempted to leave the area, he slipped and sustained serious injuries. The court held that a non-delegable duty of reasonable care is imposed upon owners and contractors to provide reasonable and adequate protection and safety to persons employed in or lawfully frequenting all areas in which construction, excavation, or demolition work is being performed.

See also *Alabama Power Co. v. Pierre*, 236 Ala. 521, 183 So. 665 (1938), where Alabama Power Company sold electrical fixtures to the Pierres for their newly-built home. Alabama Power agreed to install the fixtures at no cost; for which task it contracted with a third party. During the installation the subcontractors inadvertently set the house on fire. The Pierres sued Alabama Power, alleging that the installation of the fixtures was a non-delegable duty. The court held that one who by his contract or by law is due certain obligations to another cannot divest himself of liability for a negligent performance by reason of the employment of such contractor. Thus, by contract this installation was a non-delegable duty on defendant's part so far as these plaintiffs were concerned, and the contractor may be treated in law as the agent or servant of defendant, though as between the parties and in a strict legal sense such a relationship did not in fact exist.

**4. Dangerous Activity Exception.** Courts may also refuse to apply the independent contractor rule where the work constitutes an inherently dangerous activity. Consider *Waite v. American Airlines, Inc.*, 73 F.Supp.2d 349 (S.D.N.Y.1999), where a baggage handler working for an independent contractor was injured in a conveyer belt accident and sued the owner-airline, claiming vicarious liability (after recovering workers' compensation from his direct employer). The court held that the fact that a thing or activity causes frequent or severe injury is not enough to make it abnormally or inherently dangerous under law: There must be a union of the harmfulness of the thing or activity with it being "unnatural" or "inappropriate" to its context. The court held the presence of a baggage conveyer in an airport baggage handling area clearly failed the inappropriateness or unnaturalness requirement.

Compare *Rohlfs v. Weil*, 271 N.Y. 444, 3 N.E.2d 588 (1936), where an independent contractor painting a building negligently built its scaffolding such that its worker fell from the scaffolding onto the plaintiff walking below. The owner of the building site who had employed the independent contractor was held liable to the pedestrian. The court noted the natural tendency of the presence of a scaffold above a street without barricades or warning signals to create danger and to inflict injury on the traveling public.

# SECTION B.   VICARIOUS LIABILITY FOR CHILDREN

## WELLS v. HICKMAN

Court of Appeals of Indiana.
657 N.E.2d 172 (1995).

NAJAM, Judge.

[Another portion of this opinion is printed on page 298, supra.]

Cheryl Wells ("Wells") filed a complaint for the wrongful death of her son, D.E., at the hands of L.H., the son of Gloria Hickman ("Hickman") and the grandson of Albert and Geneva Hickman (the "Grandparents"). L.H. beat D.E. to death while the two boys were in the woods behind the Grandparents' home. Wells alleged that Hickman and the Grandparents failed to control L.H. when they were aware or should have been aware that injury to D.E. was possible and that their negligence resulted in D.E.'s death.

\* \* \*

D.E. and his mother, Cheryl Wells, were neighbors to L.H. and his mother, Gloria Hickman. L.H. and Hickman lived in a trailer located on land owned by L.H.'s grandparents, Albert and Geneva Hickman. The trailer was parked within 100 feet of the Grandparents' house and L.H. was often at their home. Hickman worked the night shift and usually left for work at 10:00 p.m. The Grandparents cared for L.H. while Hickman was at work, and L.H. often ate his meals and snacks at the Grandparents' home. Either Hickman or the Grandparents always knew L.H.'s whereabouts.

Between the Fall of 1990 and October 15, 1991, L.H. killed a pet dog by beating it to death, and he killed a pet hamster. L.H. had also expressed his desire to commit suicide. L.H. often exhibited anger and, on one occasion, he came home from school with a black eye, cuts and bruises. Upon the recommendation of his school principal, L.H. attended counseling sessions at Southern Hills Counseling Center.

On October 15, 1991, D.E. was celebrating his twelfth birthday. After school, fifteen year old L.H. invited D.E. over to play video games. Wells, D.E.'s mother, agreed. The boys did not play video games and neither Hickman nor the Grandparents were aware that D.E. and L.H. were together. Around 6:30 p.m., L.H. returned home and appeared to be very nervous. Later, L.H. told his mother that he thought he had killed D.E. After a search, D.E.'s body was found lying beside a fallen tree on the Grandparents' property.

\* \* \*

Wells contends that Indiana Code § 34–4–31–1 does not limit Hickman's liability to $3,000.00 and does not preclude the recovery of damages in a common law action based on parental negligence. Wells argues that the trial court erred when it granted Hickman's motion for summary judgment and, in effect, determined that the statute was the exclusive remedy for the acts of L.H.

As a general rule, the common law does not hold a parent liable for the tortious acts of her minor children. *Moore v. Waitt* (1973), 157 Ind.App. 1, 9, 298 N.E.2d 456, 461. Indiana Code § 34–4–31–1, however, imposes liability upon a parent for the harm or damage caused by the knowing, intentional or reckless act of her minor child. Subsection (1) of this statute states in pertinent part:

> (a) As used in this section, "child" means an unemancipated person who is less than eighteen (18) years of age.

> (b) A parent is liable for not more than three thousand dollars ($3,000) in actual damages arising from harm to a person or damage to property knowingly, intentionally, or recklessly caused by the parent's child if:

> > (1) the parent has custody of the child; and

> > (2) the child is living with the parent.

IND.CODE § 34–4–31–1. The imposition of liability under this statute is in derogation of the common law. *Johnson v. Toth* (1987), Ind.App., 516 N.E.2d 85, 86.

Statutes in derogation of the common law must be strictly construed against limitations on a claimant's right to bring suit. *Bartrom v. Adjustment Bureau, Inc.* (1993), Ind., 618 N.E.2d 1, 10. This court presumes that the legislature is aware of the common law and does not intend to make a change in the common law beyond its declaration either by express terms or by unmistakable implication. *Hinshaw v. Board of Commissioners of Jay County* (1993), Ind., 611 N.E.2d 637, 639. In cases of doubt, a statute is construed as not changing the common law. *Bartrom,* 618 N.E.2d at 10. We examine and interpret the statute as a whole with the foremost objective to determine and give effect to the legislative intent. *Duvall v. ICI Americas, Inc.* (1993), Ind.App., 621 N.E.2d 1122, 1125.

The plain language of Indiana Code § 34–4–31–1 imposes liability on a parent for not more than $3,000.00 in actual damages for harm to a person or damage to property knowingly, intentionally, or recklessly caused by the parent's child. The parent is liable if the tortious child is a minor and lives with the parent, and that parent has legal custody of the child. There is no requirement under the statute that the parent be found negligent for liability to attach. In sum, the statute makes a parent strictly liable for the knowing, intentional or reckless tortious acts of the parent's minor child.

In addition to Indiana Code § 34–4–31–1, there are four common law exceptions to the general rule that a parent is not liable for the tortious acts of her child.

> (1) where the parent entrusts the child with an instrumentality which, because of the child's lack of age, judgment, or experience, may become a source of danger to others; (2) where the child committing the tort is acting as the servant or agent of its parents; (3) where the parent consents, directs, or sanctions the wrongdoing; and (4) where the parent fails to exercise control over the minor child although the parent knows or with due care should know that injury to another is possible.

*K.C. v. A.P.* (1991), Fla.App., 577 So.2d 669, 671. Wells' claim is based on the fourth common law exception. She alleges that Hickman was negligent because Hickman failed to control her minor son when she knew or should have known that L.H. would injure D.E.

As we have noted, Indiana Code § 34–4–31–1 holds a parent strictly liable for certain acts of her minor child. Unlike the statute, the first and fourth exceptions focus on the negligent act or omission of the parent. The second and third exceptions are virtually indistinguishable and are based on principles of agency with liability attaching when there is a direct nexus between the parent's control and the child's activity. Unlike the statute, all four common law exceptions require more than the existence of a parent-child relationship for liability to attach. Liability under these exceptions is based upon the negligent act or omission of a parent or the parent's direct control over her child, which creates the opportunity for the child to cause the injury. *See Moore,* 157 Ind.App. at 8, 298 N.E.2d at 460. While Indiana Code § 34–4–31–1 confers liability on a parent for the reckless, knowing, or intentional acts of her minor child, the statute was not intended to limit a parent's liability from her own negligence or from her direct control of her minor child. Rather, the purpose of the statute is to protect innocent victims from damage caused by irresponsible judgment proof minors. *See Hyman v. Davies* (1983), Ind.App., 453 N.E.2d 336, 338.

Under Hickmans interpretation, the statute would vitiate the common law exceptions. If we were to interpret the statute as Hickman suggests, a $3,000.00 payment would be the extent of a parent's liability regardless of the type of injury, amount of damages, parental negligence, or direct control over a child's behavior. We do not believe that the legislature intended to place such a limit on a parent's liability. The common law causes of action are separate and distinct from a strict liability claim made under the statute, and any damages which may be recovered under the common law exceptions are not limited by the statute. Contrary to the trial court's conclusion, Indiana Code § 34–4–31–1 is not Well's exclusive remedy and does not preclude a common law cause of action based on the negligence of the parent. We hold that Indiana Code § 34–4–31–1 does not limit a parent's damages to $3,000.00 when the parent is found to be liable under one of the four exceptions stated above. However, any payment a plaintiff recovers pursuant to the statute will reduce the damage award received under a common law exception by the same amount.

\* \* \*

The judgment of the trial court is affirmed in part, reversed in part, and remanded with instructions to enter judgment for Albert and Geneva Hickman and against Cheryl Wells, and for Cheryl Wells and against Gloria Hickman in the amount of $3,000.00.

## NOTES

**1. Parents Not Liable for Children's Torts.** Under the common law, parents are generally not held vicariously liable for torts committed by their children. However, statutes in many states impose a vicarious liability on parents for harm caused by their children's torts. Parent liability under these statutes is usually limited to a few thousand dollars. Liability is, however, not based on alleging parental fault, but automatically imposed on the parents. As discussed in the portion of the principal case excerpted in the Failure to Act section, supra at page 298, parents may also be held liable for their personal negligence in failing to control their children. (Indeed, gross parental negligence may also lead to criminal liability.) Unlike vicarious liability statutes, parental negligence liability is not limited. Establishing liability under failure to control is difficult.

Vicarious liability can be very useful to victims of a child's vandalism. Should parents be liable for a child's actions vicariously, even when the parents have not done anything wrong? Should an uncontrollable teenager be able to cost parents thousands of dollars? Reconsider the Los Angeles Times article reprinted in Chapter 2, Sec. H at page 302, supra. See Diamond, Levine & Madden, *Understanding Torts* § 13.02 (2nd ed. 2000); Keeton, *Prosser and Keeton on the Law of Torts* § 123 (5th ed. 1984); and Dobbs, *The Law of Torts* § 340.

**2. Automobile Owners.** Automobile owners are generally not vicariously liable for torts caused by persons authorized to borrow their vehicle. As with parental liability, however, statutes may impose limited liability in such situations. Also, in some situations vehicle owners may be liable under a theory of negligent entrustment when a reasonable person would not have loaned the automobile to the driver because the driver was obviously intoxicated or otherwise not competent to drive.

# Chapter VII

## STATUTORY REPLACEMENTS AND LIMITS ON TORTS

### SECTION A.  WORKERS' COMPENSATION

#### BLETTER v. HARCOURT, BRACE & WORLD, INC.
Supreme Court, Appellate Division, Third Department, New York.
30 A.D.2d 601, 290 N.Y.S.2d 59 (1968).

GIBSON, Presiding Justice.

Appeal from a decision which awarded compensation benefits; appellants employer and carrier contending that claimant's accidental fall, which they concede occurred in the course of the employment, did not arise out of the employment.

Claimant, age 33, was employed as an associate editor of high school textbooks by Harcourt, Brace & World, Inc., a publisher, which occupied about half of the space in the Harcourt, Brace & World building where claimant was employed. Employees were permitted to take an hour for lunch and either to leave the building or to make use of the company cafeteria. On the day of the accident claimant ate in the cafeteria with two co-workers in his department and, because they were busy at the time, "probably" cut short their lunch time. While returning on a self-service elevator from the fourth floor cafeteria to his eighth floor office, claimant, because, as he testified, "I was in good spirits because of the fact I was enjoying the job, that I had good friends there and I was generally feeling good", attempted to do a dance step but fell and fractured his thigh. Questioned further as to his "good spirits", he said, "I felt things were going well in my position with the company and I was enjoying the people I was working with and my supervisor, and was generally in good spirits."

The board's decision was, in pertinent part, as follows: "The Board finds that claimant's casual indulgence in a little dance step on the employer's premises and while in a swiftly moving elevator, was not an unreasonable activity in view of his feeling of well-being created by his liking for both the job and his co-workers, so as to be deemed a deviation from the employment. Under the circumstances here, the Board finds that the act in question was a work related incident and that the injuries then sustained arose out of and in the course of the employment."

We agree with the board's conclusion that this spontaneous, perhaps irrepressible outburst of exuberance and good feeling was engendered by, and arose out of the employment and, of course, and as appellants concede, occurred in the course of the employment. Even had the act constituted a deviation, it was momentary and would have to be found so brief and minor as not to have interrupted the employment. . . .

\* \* \*

. . . . As in the horse play cases, to which this is akin, claimant during the enforced waiting period "was not required to remain immobile [but] was at liberty to indulge in any reasonable activity" (*Matter of Ingraham v. Lane Constr. Corp.*, 285 App. Div. 572, 573, affd. 309 N. Y. 899; *Matter of Sarriera v. Axel Electronics*, 25 A D 2d 592; and see *Matter of Manville v. New York State Dept. of Labor*, 294 N. Y. 1, 4; *Matter of Miles v. Gibbs & Hill*, 225 App. Div. 839, affd. 250 N. Y. 590; 1 Larson, Workmen's Compensation Law, §§ 21.21 [c], 23.62 [b], 23.63). We cannot find either unreasonable or a substantial deviation this claimant's expression or gesture of approval of his work and work relationships, spontaneously manifested to those with whom he worked.

Decision affirmed, with costs to the Workmen's Compensation Board.

## RALPHS GROCERY CO. v. WORKERS' COMP. APPEALS BD.

Court of Appeal, Second District, Division 1, California.
58 Cal.App.4th 647, 68 Cal.Rptr.2d 161, (1997).

ORTEGA, Acting P. J.

Petitioner Ralphs Grocery Company seeks to annul the respondent Workers' Compensation Appeals Board's award of death benefits to an employee's surviving minors. We conclude the injury was noncompensable and annul the award.

### Facts

Mark Moeller was a 32-year-old meatcutter employed by Ralphs for 10 years when he died of a heart attack while at home on a Sunday evening, June 1, 1992. Moeller had not worked at Ralphs since October 29, 1991, when he went on disability leave due to an industrial injury to his finger. Because of declining sales, Ralphs laid off Moeller in November 1991, while he was still on disability leave. On June 1, 1992, the day before Moeller was scheduled to return to work from the layoff, he suddenly collapsed and died of a heart attack.

On the date of death, which is also the date of the alleged industrial injury, Ralphs telephoned Moeller at home and told him to report back to work the next day, June 2, 1992. Ralphs offered Moeller a part-time meatcutter's position without benefits. This offer was less than what Moeller, who was in financial difficulty, had hoped to receive.

Moeller had been diagnosed with colon cancer in May 1991, and the layoff had eliminated his medical insurance benefits. After the layoff, Moeller had to deplete the family savings to pay for chemotherapy and radiation treatments. Moeller's wife worked part time as a nurse and the couple had three young children to support. When Moeller received the back-to-work phone call, the news that he would be working only part time without benefits was so stressful to him that it triggered a sudden heart arrhythmia which, due to Moeller's congenital heart muscle disease, caused a fatal heart attack.

\* \* \*

The WCJ [worker's compensation judge] found, accepting Mrs. Moeller's expert medical witness's opinion and rejecting Ralphs' conflicting medical evidence, that the back-to-work phone call was so stressful it triggered a sudden arrhythmia and fatal heart attack. The WCJ further found the phone call arose out of and occurred during the course of employment, despite the undisputed evidence that Moeller had not worked at Ralphs since October 29, 1991, had been laid off since November 1991, and had died the day before he was to return to work.

After the board rejected Ralphs' petition for reconsideration, Ralphs filed a writ petition seeking to vacate the award. We issued a writ of review.

### DISCUSSION

We conclude the injury did not occur in the course of employment because it happened while Moeller was off duty, off premises, and performing no special business or service for his employer.

The workers' compensation system provides for compensation to injured employees "for any injury ... arising out of and in the course of the employment and for the death of any employee if the injury proximately causes death...." (Lab. Code, § 3600.) This requirement is to be liberally construed in favor of awarding benefits. (Lab. Code, § 3202.)

An injury is said to arise out of employment when it " 'occur[s] by reason of a condition or incident of [the] employment....' [Citation.] That is, the employment and the injury must be linked in some causal fashion. [Citation.] However, '[i]f we look for a causal connection between the employment and the injury, such connection need not be the sole cause; it is sufficient if it is a contributory cause. [Citation]' [Citation.]" (*Maher v. Workers' Comp. Appeals Bd.* (1983) 33 Cal.3d 729, 733–734 [190 Cal.Rptr. 904, 661 P.2d 1058], fn. omitted.) Here, Ralphs does not challenge the finding that the injury arose out of employment. Ralphs states in its petition: "While the telephone call that occurred may be deemed to arise out of decedent's employment with Petitioner as it dealt with his returning to work, the subsequent death of Mark Moeller sometime *after* said telephone call was not in the *course and scope* of his employment with Petitioner."

The course of employment requirement " 'ordinarily refers to the time, place, and circumstances under which the injury occurs.' [Citation.] Thus ' "[a]n employee is in the 'course of his employment' when he does those reasonable things which his contract with his employment expressly or impliedly permits him to do." ' [Citation.] And, ipso facto, an employee acts within the course of his employment when ' "performing a duty imposed upon him by his employer and one necessary to perform before the terms of the contract [are] mutually satisfied." [Citation.]' [Citation.]" (*Maher v. Workers' Comp. Appeals Bd.*, *supra*, 33 Cal.3d at p. 733.)

When he was injured, Moeller was off duty, at home, and spending time with his family on a Sunday evening. He was engaged in no special errand or activity for Ralphs. It would be a stretch of the imagination to say that answering his home phone was an act in the course of Moeller's employment as a meat cutter with Ralphs.

When an employee is off duty, the employer-employee relation is temporarily suspended until the employee reenters the employer's service. In general, "... the employment relationship is deemed suspended from the time the employee leaves work until the time the employee resumes work. (*Kobe v. Industrial Acc. Com.* (1950) 35 Cal.2d 33, 35....)" (*State Lottery Com. v. Workers' Comp. Appeals Bd.* (1996) 50 Cal.App.4th 311, 315 [57 Cal.Rptr.2d 745].)

Accepting that Moeller sustained an injury when he learned of the job reassignment which triggered the fatal heart attack, we conclude Moeller was not performing a service incidental to his employment when he was injured. He was at home, on his own time, conducting his own affairs. By picking up the telephone and learning of the job assignment, Moeller discussed matters of mutual concern with his employer, but performed no service growing out of and incidental to his employment. Where there is liability under the compensation law, " ... the right to an award is founded not 'upon the fact that the injury grows out of and is incidental to [the employee's] employment,' but rather, 'upon the fact that the *service* [the employee] is rendering at the time of the injury grows out of and is incidental to the employment.' ..." (*Santa Rosa Junior College v. Workers' Comp. Appeals Bd.* (1985) 40 Cal.3d 345, 351 [220 Cal.Rptr. 94, 708 P.2d 673].) Although "liability under the compensation law has been extended to cover personal acts necessary to the comfort, convenience and welfare of the employee," that exception has been limited to instances where "the employee at the time of injury was at work and either on the employer's premises [citations] or on a business errand off the premises [citation]." (*Fireman's Fund etc. Co. v. Ind. Acc. Com.* (1952) 39 Cal.2d 529, 532 [247 P.2d 707].)

The rationale underlying our determination also applies to the going and coming rule of nonliability. "Ordinarily an employee cannot obtain workers' compensation for an injury suffered while going to or coming from the workplace (the 'going and coming' rule), because the employment relationship is deemed suspended from the time the employee leaves work until the time the employee resumes work. [Citation.] Alternatively, the injury is not compensable because when going to or coming from work the employee is rendering no service to the employer. [Citation.]" (*State Lottery Com. v. Workers' Comp. Appeals Bd.*, *supra*, 50 Cal.App.4th at p. 315.)

Had Moeller suffered a heart attack while commuting to work the morning after the back-to-work phone call, the employer-employee relationship would not yet have reattached, and Moeller would not have been rendering any service to Ralphs while commuting to work. (See *Santa Rosa Junior College v. Workers' Comp. Appeals Bd.*, *supra*, 40 Cal.3d at p. 348.) The going and coming rule of nonliability applies even when an employee who voluntarily and regularly takes work home is injured while commuting. (*Ibid.*) In this case, the heart attack occurred the night before Moeller was to return to work, well before the employer-employee relationship could reattach.

We conclude, as a matter of law, that the injury did not occur in the course of employment.

## DISPOSITION

The decision of the board is annulled. The case is remanded to the board with directions to enter a new order denying the claim.

## *NOTES*

**1. The Purpose of Workers' Compensation.** Workers' compensation systems, as the principal case indicates, provide specific compensation for injuries workers suffer "arising out of and in the course of employment." The workers' compensation system replaces the tort system for injuries occurring as a result of employment. The statutory system exists in all states and provides compensation for injuries to employees without the need for the worker to prove the employer is liable for negligence or another tort. Without workers' compensation, the employee could recover only when the employer was liable for a tort. Assumption of risk and contributory negligence, along with the need to prove all the prima facie elements of negligence, often precluded recovery. In addition, historically, an employee's recovery against an employer was made more onerous by the "fellow servant rule." The "fellow servant rule" attributed to a plaintiff, as contributory negligence, the negligence of any co-employee that helped cause the plaintiff's injury.

The adoption of workers' compensation represented a political compromise between the interests of employers and employees. Under workers' compensation, the employee is precluded from suing the employer for negligence, traditional strict liability in the case of abnormally dangerous activities, and in some states certain intentional torts even when the employee could easily win the tort case against the employer. Although the employee can alternatively recover in workers' compensation, there is a significant downside. In order to make it economically feasible (and sufficiently politically attractive to employers' interests to have been legislatively enacted) to compensate all injuries whether or not the employer is negligent, the amount of the compensation under workers' compensation systems are substantially less than for tort recovery. See generally Carlin & Fairman, *Squeeze Play: Workers' Compensation and the Professional Athlete*, 12 U.

Miami Ent. & Sports L. Rev. (1994). See also Dobbs, *The Law of Torts* §§ 392–396 (2000).

**2. Compensation Schedules.** Compensation schemes under workers' compensation often reflect a percentage of lost economic capacity resulting from an injury and often include maximum limits. Accidents resulting in death also often reflect lost wages to the decedent's dependents. Workers' compensation also provides for medical costs attributed to the work-related injury. Unlike torts, however, full economic loss resulting from the injury is rarely recovered. Most significantly, intangible losses such as pain and suffering (including loss of enjoyment of life) and punitive damages are not generally part of a workers' compensation system. *Id.*

**3. Does the Adoption of Workers' Compensation Reflect Good Policy?** By replacing the tort system, employees can recover without going to court and proving tortious liability. Administrative hearing officers subject to judicial review provide quicker and arguably more efficient resolution of claims. All employees get compensated for injuries arising out of and in the course of employment. On the other hand, employees are not fully compensated even if the employer's clearly tortious conduct caused the injury. The employer is therefore not subject to the same level of deterrence for maintaining unsafe working conditions which the full array of tort recovery, including punitive damages, would provide. Does torts or workers' compensation provide the best approach? Should a similar statutory system be extended to other areas?

The Supreme Court of Ohio, in *Guy v. Arthur H. Thomas Co.*, 55 Ohio St.2d 183, 378 N.E.2d 488 (Ohio 1978), justified the necessity of workers' compensation as follows: "The genesis of workers' compensation in the United States and Ohio was the inability of the common-law remedies to cope with modern industrialism and its inherent injuries to workers." Do you agree?

Consider the Fourth Circuit's comparison of workers' compensation to pension systems in *Bowen v. Hockley*, 71 F.2d 781 (4th Cir.1934):

> A business is more than the property which it employs. It represents all of the intangible human values which are put into it including the labor and loyalty of its employees. The purpose of the compensation act is that this business, this going concern, shall bear the burden of industrial accidents, instead of the unfortunate injured employee. He has contributed to the building of the business. He has made one of the sacrifices which with statistical regularity it demands. He is to be compensated by a charge which the law imposes upon the business as a fixed expense. Uninjured laborers contribute by their labor to the operation of the business and are paid on the basis of that contribution. The employee who is injured or killed has made his contribution just as the superannuated employee has made his; and in equity and good conscience the compensation award should be held a charge on the income of the business, just as is the wage of the laborer or the pension of the superannuated employee.

The court also stated that the purpose of workers' compensation acts "was to grant injured employees certain and speedy compensation; and they should not be defeated of that compensation, or be delayed in obtaining it."

Does workers' compensation or torts better serve this goal?

**4. Types of Compensable Injuries.** Generally, there is a two-part test to determine whether injuries are compensable. The employee's injuries must "arise out of and in the course of employment." As the principal cases indicated, both prongs must be satisfied for an employee to recover. Consider *Sills v. Wert*, 139 N.Y.S.2d 132 (N.Y.Sup.Ct.1955), in which the court elaborates on the two-part test:

> The words "arising out of and in the course of employment" are conjunctive, and relief can be had under the act only when the accident arose both "out of" and "in the course of" employment. The injury must be received: (1) While the workman is doing the duty he is employed to perform; and also (2) as a natural incident of the work. It must be one of the risks connected with the employment, flowing therefrom as a natural consequence and directly connected with the work.

Workers' compensation is to redress work-related injuries, not merely those injuries suffered at work. Consider *LaTourette v. Workers' Compensation Appeals Board*, 17 Cal.4th 644, 72 Cal.Rptr.2d 217, 951 P.2d 1184 (1998), where the widow of an employee who had suffered a fatal heart attack during a business trip was seeking death benefits from workers' compensation. The court denied the widow benefits because the heart attack did not arise out of the employment since there was insufficient evidence work-related stress rather than a pre-existing medical condition caused the heart attack.

Momentary deviations from work-related activity during the course of employment may not, however, preclude recovery. Consider *Bashwinger v. Cath–Fran Construction Co.*, 200 A.D.2d 791, 606 N.Y.S.2d 435 (N.Y.App. Div.1994), in which the court stated:

> It is well settled that "[t]o be compensable, an injury must arise out of and in the course of employment".... Although activities that are purely personal pursuits are not within the scope of employment, and, hence, no recovery may be had for injuries sustained while engaging in them, "[m]omentary deviation[s] from the work routine for a customary and accepted purpose will not bar a claim for benefits. The determination of what is reasonable activity and what is unreasonable, and thus a deviation, is factual and the Board is afforded wide latitude in deciding whether the employee's conduct is disqualifying...."

What constitutes a compensable injury varies greatly by jurisdiction. Some states virtually require a very obvious immediate physical accident during and obviously caused by the work, while other jurisdictions are more prepared to consider repetitive aggravations that only gradually result in a manifested injury. A major controversy is whether mental or physical disabilities resulting from job-related stress should be compensated. Impacting on the debate on what workers' compensation should compensate is concern by some states that too much generosity to employees will increase the cost of doing business and thereby discourage industry from locating in the state.

Do you agree with the results in the two principal cases? Which of the two required prongs noted above are in contention in the two principal cases?

# JOHNSON v. STRATLAW, INC.

Court of Appeal, Third District, California.
224 Cal.App.3d 1156, 274 Cal.Rptr. 363 (1990).

CARR, J.

In this appeal from a summary judgment entered in favor of defendant, plaintiffs assert the court erred in ruling their suit is barred by the exclusive remedy provisions of the Workers' Compensation Act. (Lab. Code, § 3200 et seq.) We shall affirm the judgment.

## FACTUAL AND PROCEDURAL BACKGROUND

This case involves an automobile accident in which plaintiffs' 16–year-old son, Daryl, was killed. Daryl worked part time at a Straw Hat pizza parlor owned and operated by defendant. Daryl's father, Robert, also worked at the restaurant.

On Friday, September 4, 1987, Daryl worked as a dishwasher at the pizzeria from 5 p.m. to its closing at 1 a.m. He completed his chores after 2 a.m. and left the premises with his father, who had also been working. They got into their cars and started to drive home, each taking a different route to their house some 15 miles away. Daryl's father arrived home first. Ten minutes later, when his son had still not arrived, Robert left to find him. Two miles from the house he came upon a sheriff's car at an accident scene. Daryl had been involved in a single-car accident and emergency personnel were working to extricate him from the wreckage. Daryl later died from the injuries he sustained.

In their second amended complaint, plaintiffs alleged two causes of action against defendant. The first alleged a cause of action for wrongful death, asserting defendant "carelessly and negligently directed, supervised, managed and controlled the activities at said Straw Hat Pizza and particularly the activities of decedent ... so as to require him to work from 5 p.m. until after 2 a.m. on a non-schoolday in violation of California Labor Code § 1391."

The complaint continued: "As a direct and proximate result of defendants ... negligently and carelessly requiring the decedent to work until after 2 a.m. and for a period in excess of eight hours, in violation of Labor Code § 1391 as stated above, the decedent, while driving home after work was tired and/or exhausted, fell asleep or was otherwise drowsy, causing him to be involved in an automobile accident."

The second cause of action, for negligent infliction of emotional distress, alleged plaintiffs watched the rescue efforts and "suffered shock resulting from the sensory and contemporaneous observance of their son's accident."

Defendant demurred to the complaint, asserting inter alia that plaintiffs' sole remedy lay in a workers' compensation claim and further, that plaintiffs were precluded from asserting a claim for negligent infliction of emotional distress because they had not observed Daryl's accident. The trial court sustained the demurrer as to the mother's cause of action for emotional distress but overruled the demurrer on all other grounds.

Defendant answered the complaint and moved for summary judgment and/or summary adjudication, again arguing workers' compensation was the appropriate forum for plaintiffs' claims and that no claim for negligent infliction of emotional distress could be made because there had been no contemporaneous observance of the accident. The trial court granted summary adjudication in favor of defendant on the cause of action for emotional distress but denied the motion as to the first cause of action.

One month later, defendant once more moved for summary judgment, reiterating its earlier arguments that this matter fell within workers' compensation provisions. The trial court agreed and granted summary judgment in favor of defendant. This appeal followed.

### DISCUSSION

"A defendant is entitled to summary judgment if the record establishes as a matter of law that none of plaintiff's asserted causes of action can prevail. [Citation.] To succeed, the defendant must conclusively negate a necessary element of the plaintiff's case, and demonstrate that under no hypothesis is there a material issue of fact that requires the process of a trial. [Citation.]" (*Molko v. Holy Spirit Assn.* (1988) 46 Cal.3d 1092, 1107 [252 Cal.Rptr. 122, 762 P.2d 46].)

The central question in this case is whether plaintiffs' complaint is barred by the exclusive remedy provisions of the Workers' Compensation Act. We conclude it is.

Labor Code section 3600 provides "[l]iability for the compensation provided by this division, in lieu of any other liability whatsoever to any person except as otherwise specifically provided ... shall, without regard to negligence, exist against an employer for any injury sustained by his or her employees arising out of and in the course of the employment and for the death of any employee if the injury proximately causes death" if certain conditions are met.[2] One of these conditions, subdivision (a)(2), requires that "at the time of the injury, the employee is performing service growing out of and incidental to his or her employment and is acting within the course of his or her employment."

Plaintiffs contend their claim does not fall within the workers' compensation provisions because their son had left work and was therefore no longer in the course of his employment at the time of his accident.

The principles involved in the instant case were discussed at length in *Parks v. Workers' Comp. Appeals Bd.* (1983) 33 Cal.3d 585 [190 Cal.Rptr. 158, 660 P.2d 382]: "One of the rules the courts have fashioned

---

**2.** "In the course of employment" refers to the time and place of the injury while the phrase "arise out of employment" refers to a causal connection between the injury and the employment. (*West American Ins. Co. v. California Mutual Ins. Co.* (1987) 195 Cal. App.3d 314, 320 [240 Cal.Rptr. 540].)

to aid in determining whether an injury occurred in the 'course of employment' is the 'going and coming' rule. Broadly stated, the rule prohibits compensation for injuries received by an employee while traveling to and from work. Courts have reasoned that the employment relationship is suspended during this period and, therefore, injuries occurring when an employee is engaged in off-duty travel, off of the employer's premises, are not within the 'course of employment' for purposes of the Workers' Compensation Act.

"Normally, when an injury occurs during the commute to or from work, the going and coming rule will apply to prevent compensation unless the injury can be found to fit within one of the many exceptions to the rule. One of the exceptions which has been devised to implement the rule in marginal situations is the 'special risk' exception.

"An employee will be 'entitled to compensation, if the employment creates a special risk, for injuries sustained within the field of that risk. Such a risk may attend the employee as soon as he enters the employer's premises or the necessary means of access thereto, even when the latter is not under the employer's control or management. . . .'

"This principle applies when the employee is entering or leaving the employer's premises. Furthermore, '[t]he fact[] that an accident happens upon a public road and that the danger is one to which the general public is likewise exposed ... do[es] not preclude the existence of a causal relationship between the accident and the employment if the danger is one to which the employee, by reason of and in connection with his or her employment, is subjected peculiarly or to an abnormal degree. . . .'

"Synthesizing concepts from these and other older cases, this court in *Chairez* [*General Ins. Co. v. Workers' Comp. Appeals Bd.* (1976) 16 Cal.3d 595 (128 Cal.Rptr. 417, 546 P.2d 1361)] devised a two prong test to determine applicability of the special risk-exception. *Chairez* held that the exception will apply (1) if 'but for' the employment the employee would not have been at the location where the injury occurred and (2) if 'the risk is distinctive in nature or quantitatively greater than risks common to the public.' " (Citations, fns. and italics omitted; *Parks v. Workers' Comp. Appeals Bd., supra,* 33 Cal.3d at pp. 588–590.)

In *Chairez, supra,* 16 Cal.3d 595, an employee parked his car in front of his place of employment, got out of the car, and was struck by a passing motorist. (*Id.* at p. 598.) The court concluded "Chairez' injury was causally related to his employment. But for his job, Chairez would not have been on La Cienega that morning. However, Chairez' death does not come within the second requirement of the special risk exception-that the risk is distinctive in nature or quantitatively greater than risks common to the public. Chairez was parked on a public street at a time and in a location where parking is available to the general public. The fact that he was struck by a passing motorist, while tragic, is a type of risk the public is subject to daily. Moreover, nothing in the facts indicates Chairez was exposed to a greater risk from passing motorists than was anyone else on La Cienega that morning." (*Id.* at p. 601.)

*Parks, supra,* 33 Cal.3d 585, presented a different set of circumstances. In that case, a teacher left a school parking lot to drive home. She found herself stopped by departing schoolchildren who were crossing the street between cars. While she was stopped, three youths opened the driver's door on Parks' car, wrestled her purse away from her, and ran away. Parks sought workers' compensation benefits for the disability she suffered as a result of the attack. (*Id.* at pp. 587–588.) The court distinguished this situation from that in *Chairez,* finding that Parks was "regularly subjected at the end of each day's work to the risk of becoming blocked by school children in traffic and becoming a 'sitting duck' for an assault.... Her risk was clearly 'quantitatively greater' than that to which passing motorists might be subjected on a sporadic or occasional basis. [Citations.] Parks' employment required her to pass through the zone of danger each day. As such, her employment created a special risk in leaving the school parking lot." (*Id.* at pp. 592–593, italics omitted.) The court concluded the going and coming rule did not apply to bar compensation. (*Id.* at p. 593.)

Here, plaintiffs assert their case is more like *Chairez* than *Parks.* Plaintiffs acknowledge the first prong of the *Chairez* test is met: but for Daryl's employment, he would not have been on the road where the accident occurred. Plaintiffs center their arguments on the second part of this test, the nature of the risk involved. They assert the risk of accident was no greater for Daryl than for the public at large, given that the accident occurred on a public highway miles away from defendant's restaurant. Plaintiffs' characterization of the risk involved ignores the pleadings set forth in their complaint.

Plaintiffs charged defendant violated Labor Code section 1391 in requiring their son to work until after 2 a.m. on a nonschool day, thereby causing Daryl to become tired and involved in an automobile accident. These pleadings allege a special risk: Daryl, a minor, was in an accident because he became tired after being kept at work by defendant long past the legal hours. Indeed, without such an allegation, plaintiffs could not establish any nexus linking defendants to Daryl's accident. The language of plaintiffs' complaint demonstrates a special risk was involved, one rooted in requiring a minor to work until after 2 a.m. Unlike *Chairez,* the risk outlined in plaintiffs' complaint is not one to which the public is generally exposed.

This case is distinguishable from *Baroid v. Workers' Comp. Appeals Bd.* (1981) 121 Cal.App.3d 558 [175 Cal.Rptr. 633], a case relied upon by plaintiffs. In *Baroid,* an employee was injured in a car accident while on his way to work. The Workers' Compensation Appeals Board had found the injury compensable under another exception to the going and coming rule, the "special mission" exception. The Court of Appeal grappled with this doctrine and another exception to the going and coming rule, the "wage payment or travel time" exception, and remanded the matter to the Workers' Compensation Appeals Board for further findings. In dicta, the court noted: "[W]e also do not find that the 'special risk' exception to the going and coming rule ... applies herein. Applicant has not shown that traveling to work at [5 a.m.] subjected him to a greater risk of injury or that the employer's premises in any way contributed to the creation of such risk." (Fn. omitted; *id.* at p. 574.) Here, however, plaintiffs' own pleadings allege it was defendant's employment practices with respect to Daryl that created the risk of injury.

Under these circumstances, the "special risk" exception to the going and coming rule applies and plaintiffs' complaint is barred by the exclusive remedy provisions of the workers' compensation system. The trial court properly granted summary judgment for defendant.

DISPOSITION

The judgment is affirmed.

*NOTES*

**1. Going and Coming Rule.** Usually, the commute of an employee is not compensable under workers' compensation under an exception known as the "going and coming rule." See Dobbs, *The Law of Torts* § 393 (2000). Consider *State Lottery Commission v. Workers' Compensation Appeals Board*, 50 Cal.App.4th 311, 57 Cal.Rptr.2d 745 (Cal.Ct.App.1996), where a police officer was denied workers' compensation benefits when he was hurt because of a fall on an icy sidewalk on way to his car:

> Ordinarily an employee cannot obtain workers' compensation for an injury suffered while going to or coming from the workplace (the "going and coming" rule), because the employment relationship is deemed suspended from the time the employee leaves work until the time the employee resumes work. Alternatively, the injury is not compensable because when going to or coming from work the employee is rendering no service to the employer.

Consider also *Santa Rosa Junior College v. Workers' Compensation Appeals Board*, 40 Cal.3d 345, 220 Cal.Rptr. 94, 708 P.2d 673 (1985), where the Supreme Court of California denied death benefits of the widow of a college professor who was killed on his way back from his college in order to do work at home. The court applied the going and coming rule in order to exclude benefits for the employee's widow. The court declined to find that the professor's home was a second job site nor that he was required to do work at home.

There are exceptions, as noted in the principal case, to the coming and going rule where workers' compensation will apply. These generally include special risks in the commutation imposed by the job as in the principal case, travel to special activities for the benefit of the employer, and during travel where the employer is compensating the employee for the travel time.

**2. Preference for Non–Coverage in Workers' Compensation.** In many instances the employee is eager to be covered under workers' compensation. As the principal case demonstrates, however, the employee may prefer to sue in torts against the employer when he or she has a strong tort case against the employer and the tort case is likely to compensate the victim more than workers' compensation. While the employee is free to sue a third party who has committed a tort against her, she is precluded from suing the employer if workers' compensation is applicable.

The next principal case further explores the preemptive impact on workers' compensation on the plaintiff's right to sue the employer in torts.

## FERMINO v. FEDCO, INC.

Supreme Court of California.

7 Cal.4th 701, 30 Cal.Rptr.2d 18, 872 P.2d 559 (1994).

MOSK, Justice.

In this case we consider whether an employee subject to false imprisonment at the hands of her employer may sue that employer in a civil action, or whether such a suit is barred by the exclusivity provisions of the Workers' Compensation Act (Lab. Code, §§ 3600, 3602). We conclude that her suit would not be barred, because an employer that falsely imprisons its employee has stepped outside its proper role, and an injury resulting therefrom is beyond the scope of what we have termed the "compensation bargain."

\* \* \*

The facts, as stated in plaintiffs second amended complaint, are as follows. Plaintiff Fermino was employed as a salesclerk in defendant's department store, working in the jewelry department. The store's personnel manager summoned her to a windowless room, and proceeded to interrogate her concerning her alleged theft of the proceeds of a $4.95 sale to a customer. The personnel manager was joined by the store's loss prevention manager and by two security agents. One of the security agents stated that a customer and an employee, who were waiting in the next room, had witnessed the theft. He then demanded that Fermino confess. He told her that the interrogation could be handled in two ways: the "Fedco way" or the "system way." The "Fedco way" was to award points each time she denied her guilt. When 14 points were reached, she would be handled the "system" way, i.e., handed over to the police. After each of plaintiff's repeated and vehement denials, the security agent said "one point." The loss prevention manager "hurled profanities" and demanded that Fermino confess.

Fermino's repeated requests to leave the room and to call her mother were denied. She was physically compelled to remain in the room for more than one hour. At one point Fermino rose out of her chair and walked toward the door of the interrogation room in an attempt to leave; however, as soon as she made a move toward the door, one of the security guards slid in front of the door, threw up a hand and gestured her to stop.

Finally, Fermino became hysterical, and broke down in tears. At this point her interrogators departed from the room. Upon returning, they admitted no employee or customer was waiting to testify against her. They further stated they believed her, and that she could leave.

As the result of this incident, Fermino sustained unspecified physical injury and "shock and injury to her nervous system and person," as well as "mental anguish and emotional distress." Fermino sued for false imprisonment, as well as intentional and negligent infliction of emotional distress. She claimed that the false imprisonment resulted from a method of interrogation that was approved company policy.

Defendant Fedco demurred on the grounds that Fermino's claim was barred by the Workers' Compensation Act (hereafter the Act), and in particular the exclusivity provisions of Labor Code sections 3600 and 3602, (hereafter the exclusivity rule). The trial court sustained the demurrer. A divided Court of Appeal upheld the trial court, relying on the statute, and on our decisions in *Shoemaker v. Myers* (1990) 52 Cal.3d 1 [276 Cal.Rptr. 303, 801 P.2d 1054, 20 A.L.R.5th 1016] (hereafter *Shoemaker*) and *Cole v. Fair Oaks Fire Protection Dist.* (1987) 43 Cal.3d 148 [233 Cal.Rptr. 308, 729 P.2d 743] (hereafter *Cole*). Only the false imprisonment claim has been raised in Fermino's petition for review with this court.

Labor Code section 3600, subdivision (a), provides that, subject to certain particular exceptions and conditions, workers' compensation liability, "in lieu of any other liability whatsoever" will exist "against an employer for any injury sustained by his or her employees arising out of and in the course of the employment." As we have recognized, the basis for the exclusivity rule in workers' compensation law is the "presumed 'compensation bargain,' pursuant to which the employer assumes liability for industrial personal injury or death without regard to fault in exchange for limitations on the amount of that liability. The employee is afforded relatively swift and certain payment of benefits to cure or relieve the effects of industrial injury without having to prove fault but, in exchange, gives up the wider range of damages potentially available in tort." (*Shoemaker, supra,* 52 Cal.3d at p. 16.)

We recognized in *Shoemaker* and elsewhere, however, that certain types of injurious employer misconduct remain outside this bargain. There are some instances in which, although the injury arose in the course of employment, the employer engaging in that conduct " 'stepped out of [its] proper role[ ]' " or engaged in conduct of " 'questionable relationship to the employment.' " (*Shoemaker, supra,* 52 Cal.3d at p. 16, quoting *Cole, supra,* 43 Cal.3d at p. 161.)

\* \* \*

This court returned to the subject of intentional torts and workers' compensation in *Cole, supra,* 43 Cal.3d 148. In *Cole,* we considered a fire captain's claims against a fire department and its chief for intentional infliction of emotional distress. He alleged that he had been unfairly demoted, that the demotion proceedings were tantamount to a " 'kangaroo' " court, and that as the result of the demotion he was compelled to perform " 'humiliating and menial duties.' " (*Id.* at pp. 152–153.)

We held, nonetheless, that his claim was barred by workers' compensation. We reasoned that a supervisor's conduct was "inherently 'intentional.' In order to properly manage its business, every employer must on occasion review, criticize, demote, transfer and discipline employees. Employers are necessarily aware that their employees ... may consider any such adverse action to be improper and outrageous." (*Cole, supra,* 43 Cal.3d at p. 160.)

We concluded that "when the misconduct attributed to the employer is actions which are a normal part of the employment relationship, such as demotions, promotions, criticism of work practices, and frictions in negotiations as to grievances, an employee suffering emotional distress causing disability may not avoid the exclusive remedy provisions of the Labor Code by characterizing the employer's decisions as manifestly unfair, outrageous, harassment, or intended to cause emotional disturbance resulting in disability." (*Cole, supra,* 43 Cal.3d at p. 160.) This conclusion was necessitated by the reality that "If characterization of conduct normally occurring in the workplace as unfair or outrageous were sufficient to avoid the exclusive remedy provisions of the Labor Code, the exception would permit the employee to allege a cause of action in every case where he suffered mental disability merely by alleging an ulterior purpose of causing injury." (*Ibid.*)

\* \* \*

.... In *Hart v. National Mortgage & Land Co.* (1987) 189 Cal. App.3d 1420 [235 Cal.Rptr. 68] (hereafter *Hart*), the court considered whether a civil action for intentional infliction of emotional distress and battery, based on a supervisor's persistent personal harassment of an employee that included acts of physical molestation and deliberate humiliation, was barred by the exclusivity rule. In holding that the action for intentional infliction of emotional distress was permitted, the court distinguished the case from *Cole.* Unlike the demotion in *Cole,* the campaign of harassment directed against the plaintiff-employee "had a questionable relationship to employment, and [was] neither a risk, an incident, nor a normal part of Hart's employment...." (*Hart, supra,* 189 Cal.App.3d at p. 1430.)

The *Hart* court therefore distinguished its case from *Cole* by looking to the employer's conduct, rather than its state of mind. The employer, in engaging in this campaign of harassment, used behavior that could not be considered a normal risk of employment. (*Hart, supra,* 189 Cal.App.3d at p. 1430; see also *Livitsanos v. Superior Court, supra,* 2 Cal.4th 744, 756 [concluding that campaign of harassment that involved possible defamation and economic coercion presented a question for remand as to whether such action was a normal part of the employment relationship].)

In *Gantt v. Sentry Insurance* (1992) 1 Cal.4th 1083 [4 Cal.Rptr.2d 874, 824 P.2d 680] (hereafter *Gantt*), we further clarified the "proper role" exception to the exclusivity rule. In that case, the plaintiff was demoted and constructively discharged for no reason other than his support for a fellow employee, who was the victim of sexual harassment, and his refusal to testify untruthfully or withhold testimony in the course of the Department of Fair Employment and Housing investigation. (*Id.* at p. 1096.) We concluded that "[w]hen an employer's decision to discharge an employee results from an animus that violates the fundamental policy of this state ... , such misconduct cannot under any reasonable viewpoint be considered a 'normal part of the employment relationship.' " (*Id.* at p. 1100.)

\* \* \*

The crime of false imprisonment is defined by Penal Code section 236 as the "unlawful violation of the personal liberty of another." The tort is identically defined. (*Molko v. Holy Spirit Assn.* (1988) 46 Cal.3d 1092, 1123 [252 Cal.Rptr. 122, 762 P.2d 46].) As we recently formulated it, the tort consists of the " 'nonconsensual, intentional confinement of a person, without lawful privilege, for an appreciable length of time, however short.' " (*Ibid.*) That length of time can be as brief as 15 minutes. (*Alterauge v. Los Angeles Turf Club* (1950) 97 Cal.App.2d 735, 736 [218 P.2d 802].) Restraint may be effectuated by means of physical force (*Moffat v. Buffums' Inc.* (1937) 21 Cal.App.2d 371, 374 [69 P.2d 424]), threat of force or of arrest (*Vandiveer v. Charters* (1930) 110 Cal.App. 347, 351 [294 P. 440]), confinement by physical barriers (*Schanafelt v. Seaboard Finance Co.* (1951) 108 Cal.App.2d 420, 423 [239 P.2d 42]), or by means of any other form of unreasonable duress. (See Rest.2d Torts, § 40A.)

The only mental state required to be shown to prove false imprisonment is the intent to confine, or to create a similar intrusion. (Prosser & Keeton, Torts (5th ed. 1984) § 11, pp. 52–53; cf. *Weaver v. Bank of America* (1963) 59 Cal.2d 428, 433–435 [30 Cal.Rptr. 4, 380 P.2d 644] [bank's act of failing to honor check, inadvertently leading to the plaintiff's arrest and imprisonment, cognizable as a tort of negligence].) Thus, the intent element of false imprisonment does not entail an intent or motive to cause harm; indeed false imprisonments often appear to arise from initially legitimate motives. (See, e.g., *Schanafelt v. Seaboard Finance Co.*, *supra*, 108 Cal.App.2d 420, 422–423 [judgment against defendant upheld where defendant used false imprisonment in repossession of plaintiff's furniture after payment delinquency].)

\* \* \*

Fedco argues that its own actions were a normal part of employment. It correctly claims for itself the right to "monitor the security at its workplace," and, indeed, to "*insist* on its right to investigate employee theft even if the suspected employee wishes not to be questioned." Therefore, it concludes that "[t]he right to question a salesperson employee regarding a possible theft" means that its interrogation of Fermino is to be considered within the scope of the compensation bargain.

We agree that all reasonable attempts to investigate employee theft, including employee interrogation, are a normal part of the employment relationship. It is also true that all such reasonable interrogation or voluntary confinement cannot be regarded as false imprisonment and is not actionable. (Pen. Code, § 490.5, subd. (f)(1); *Collyer v. S.H. Kress & Co.*, *supra*, 5 Cal.2d at pp. 180–181.) The question we must decide is whether an employer's actions that go beyond the bounds of reasonable interrogation and detention, and constitute false imprisonment, are entitled to the same protections of the exclusivity rule as would a reasonable detention.

\* \* \*

What matters, then, is not the label that might be affixed to the employer conduct, but whether the conduct itself, concretely, is of the kind that is within the compensation bargain. In this case, Fermino does not contend, as the plaintiff did in *Cole*, that seemingly ordinary employer disciplinary actions become tortious when seen in light of the employer's malicious state of mind. Rather, Fermino here claims that the acts themselves were prima facie outside the employer's "proper role," irrespective of Fedco's intent to harm, because they criminally deprived her of her liberty and therefore were beyond the scope of the compensation bargain. *Cole* therefore does not dispose of the present case. What we must decide is whether false imprisonment is the sort of employer conduct that can ever be viewed as a normal aspect of the employment relationship.

\* \* \*

Unlike the tort of intentional infliction of emotional distress considered in *Cole*, the tort of false imprisonment involves *criminal conduct* against the employee's person, not permissible conduct that only becomes intentionally tortious in light of the employer's supposed malicious state of mind. Thus, permitting an employee's civil action for false imprisonment presents none of the dangers recognized in *Cole* and *Johns-Manville* that allowance of such exceptions would undermine the exclusivity provisions of the workers' compensation system. Rather, in order to plead false imprisonment in a civil action, a plaintiff/employee would have to allege rather specific, and fairly uncommon, acts of involuntary and criminal confinement.

It is true that whether a false imprisonment did indeed take place in this case is a closer question than that posed in the *Meyer*, *Iverson*, or *Moffat* cases cited above. The justification here for the confinement was arguably more substantial than in the former two cases, and the duration of the confinement was considerably shorter than in the third. We do not deny the right of an employer to reasonably detain an employee suspected of theft, and indeed to discharge an employee—consistent with the employee's contractual or other employment rights—if he or she refuses to cooperate with a reasonable investigation. But the question whether Fedco's actions were reasonable, justifiable, or privileged goes to the factual question *whether* its actions constituted false imprisonment— a question we cannot and do not resolve on the pleadings. Once it is determined, however, that a false imprisonment has indeed taken place, then such action cannot be said to be a normal aspect of the employment relationship, however legitimate its initial justification, any more than an assault on an employee can be brought within the scope of the exclusivity rule by claiming it was motivated by the need for employee discipline. (See *Miller v. Reed* (1986) 27 Ohio.App.3d 70 [499 N.E.2d 919, 922] [civil action permitted when supervisor "with force and violence, act[s] to discipline the plaintiff for disobedience of his directions"].) We conclude therefore that false imprisonment committed by an employer against an employee is always outside the scope of the compensation bargain.

Turning to the present case, we conclude that plaintiff has stated a cause of action for false imprisonment. Like the plaintiff in *Parrott v. Bank of America, supra,* 97 Cal.App.2d at page 22, plaintiff here has pleaded that she was held against her will by her employer for an appreciable time under threat of force and threat of arrest for an apparently ill-founded reason. As such, her cause of action for false imprisonment cannot be defeated on demurrer by raising the claim that it is barred by sections 3600 and 3602.

The judgment of the Court of Appeal is reversed.

### NOTES

**1. Intentional Injury Exception.** Workers' compensation ordinarily provides employees their exclusive remedy against the employers for workplace injuries. Consequently, an employee usually cannot recover for torts the employer has inflicted against him. Many workers' compensation statutes make an exception to the exclusive remedy rule and allow employees to sue employers for intentional torts. Jurisdictions are divided over whether the employer's intent can be satisfied by "substantial certainty" or whether "desire" to injure is required to escape the exclusive remedy rule. See Chapter 1, Sec. A, supra. See Dobbs, *The Law of Torts* § 395 (2000).

Consider *Peay v. U.S. Silica Co.,* 313 S.C. 91, 437 S.E.2d 64 (1993), in which the employer, U.S. Silica, "knew that unprotected and excessive exposure to respirable silica dust was hazardous and could, under certain circumstances, cause personal injury to some people." The employee contracted silicosis in part from his exposure to respirable silica. Nevertheless, the Supreme Court of South Carolina denied the action in tort because the employer did not have the specific intent to injure the employee. But see *Woodson v. Rowland,* 329 N.C. 330, 407 S.E.2d 222 (1991), allowing employees to sue for intentional torts based on "substantial certainty." Consider the following passage from an article discussing whether North Dakota's workers' compensation statute bars employees from recovering damages for assaults. Do you agree with the author?

> [I]n a compulsory, no-fault system which relegates injured employees solely to accident recovery, it would seem doubtful that any legislature intended to *completely* abrogate an employee's right to recover damages in a civil action. It is equally true that precluding injured workers from maintaining tort claims directly against their employers or co-employees by virtue of a blind and rigid adherence to the rule of exclusivity cannot be justified in *all* instances.

> Workers' compensation was specifically designed to provide an alternative system of compensation for those risks inherent in the workplace. Workers' compensation statutes prescribe standards for segregating compensable work-related injuries from those that are not compensable in order to carve out strictly *employment risks* from the general body of hazards that beset all humankind.... The "accident" requirement is the benchmark by which the boundary and applicability of the exclusive-remedy rule should generally be measured. An examination of the origin and evolution of the law of

workers' compensation unequivocally supports this proposition for most work-related injuries.

The sole function of exclusivity in workers' compensation is to impart efficacy to the compensation bargain. Although the workers' compensation bargain clearly contemplates a reciprocal yielding of common-law rights for new and enlarged rights and remedies, the *quid pro quo* concerns work-related "accidents"; intentionally injurious conduct by an employer or co-employee was not a part of the bargain. The original bargain *never* contemplated the relinquishment of an employee's common-law rights for intentionally caused injuries which were by way of legal definition unaffected by the traditional common-law defenses available to an employer or co-employee in a *negligence* action. Simply because a legislature intended through the enactment of workers' compensation legislation to limit and diffuse liability for accidental injuries does not likewise compel the conclusion that a legislature intended to limit and diffuse liability for intentional injuries. Intended wrongs introduce an ingredient of "moral hazard" which was never intended to be governed *exclusively* by a set of rules specifically designed to redress accidental injuries. Similarly, intentional harms are not the type of wrongs intended to be a bar to maintaining a common-law suit against an employer or employee notwithstanding the breadth of the exclusive-remedy provisions of most compensation acts. . . .

To view intentional harms as an inevitable accompaniment of industrial production, whose costs, like any other cost of production, should be borne exclusively by the industry and ultimately by the consumer would seem repugnant to the very purpose for which workers' compensation legislation was promulgated. Intentionally injurious conduct would seem to be the type of behavior that every legislature in the United States would most want to discourage. Subjecting intentional harms to the rule of exclusivity would be counterproductive to that end and would in essence allow intentional tortfeasors to shift their liability to a fund generally financed with employer-paid premiums. Such a result permits an employer to effectively "cost-out" safety issues in disregard of potential injuries as investment decisions. The immunity afforded by workers' compensation should not give employers the unfettered right to carry on their enterprises without regard to the life and limb of those who serve in their employ. Furthermore, a tortfeasor who affirmatively commits an intentionally tortious act such as an assault can not reasonably aver that the resultant injury is a risk or condition incident to the employment.

* * *

Singer, *Workers' Compensation: The* Assault *on the Shield of Immunity— Coming to Blows with the Exclusive–Remedy Provisions of the North Dakota Workers' Compensation Act,* 70 N.D. L. Rev. 905 (1994).***

**2. Dual Capacity Doctrine.** The dual capacity doctrine recognizes that an employer may also have a separate distinct relationship with the employee, such as the product manufacturer of a product used in the workplace. Many, but not all jurisdictions allow the employee to sue the employer outside of workers' compensation for this separate role. Consider *Short v. State Farm Fire and Casualty Co.*, 719 So.2d 519 (La.Ct.App.1998), where a legal secretary was injured because of a negligently maintained parking lot (she stepped on a roofing nail), owned by her employer:

> The dual capacity doctrine recognizes that in some instances an employer or co-employee may function in two roles simultaneously. Under the dual capacity doctrine, one of those roles could involve obligations that are outside the scope of workers' compensation and, thereby, expose the employer or co-employee to tort liability.

> [I]n 1994, the supreme court [of Louisiana] further explained the dual capacity doctrine as follows:

>> In a true dual capacity case, an employer or co-employee must wear two hats simultaneously, as is the case with a company doctor. At the time of the work-related injury, the company doctor has two relationships with the plaintiff: doctor and co-employee. Another example of dual capacity is when an employee is injured on the job using a product manufactured by his employer. In such situations, an employer's second capacity is inextricably intertwined with his capacity as employer. [Citation omitted.]

> . . .

> In the instant case, Mr. Lane's status as partner of the law firm contemplates the normal course and scope of the partner's duties with the partnership. Mr. Lane practiced law and functioned as a managing partner of the firm. However, he also functioned separately as a landowner and lessor. In furtherance of these business interests, he leased the ERS/BR lot [the negligently maintained parking lot] and then subleased it to the law firm. Such activities were in his own interest, not those of the firm. Therefore, in leasing the EBR lot to the law firm he was not acting in the course and scope of his status as partner with the firm. There is no reason to interpret statutory immunity as protecting the employer when that employer is functioning as a totally separate business capacity.... This conclusion is consistent with the supreme court's conclusion that the legislature did not intend for "the exclusive remedy provision of the Workers' Compensation Law to relieve employers from tort liability for negligence unrelated to the employment relationship."

Consider also *Duprey v. Shane*, 39 Cal.2d 781, 249 P.2d 8 (1952), where plaintiff nurse, sued her employer for malpractice which led to the worsening of an injury initially received at work. The court noted that there was no question that the initial injury occurred in the course of the plaintiff's employment and, thus, her exclusive remedy was worker's compensation, but held that she could still maintain her claims against her employer for any worsening of her condition arising out of their malpractice. "It is our conclusion that, when employing doctor elected to treat the industrial injury, the doctor assumed the same responsibilities that any doctor would have assumed had he been called in on the case."

**3. Fraudulent Concealment Exception.** Another exception to the exclusive remedy rule is the aggravation of injury or fraudulent concealment rule, which allows suit where the employer deceives the employee regarding the employee's condition and this results in a worsening of that condition.

Consider *Johns-Manville Products Corp. v. Superior Court*, 27 Cal.3d 465, 165 Cal.Rptr. 858, 612 P.2d 948 (1980), where an employer allegedly deceived an employee regarding an asbestos-related illness. The court held that, even though the employee could not recover in tort for the original illness, he could recover damages for any additional harm caused by the concealment.

# SECTION B.   NO FAULT MOTOR VEHICLE INSURANCE

Consider Professor Mark M. Hager's analysis of the arguments for and against substituting torts in auto accidents with a system that requires drivers to purchase insurance that will compensate them regardless of whose, if anyone's, negligence caused the accident. As Professor Hager indicates, most jurisdictions that utilize a "no-fault" system only use it for minor injuries and allow larger claims to be pursued by victims in tort cases. This mixed use complicates evaluation of how the two alternative systems serve the goals of compensation, deterrence, and corrective justice.

Mark M. Hager, *No-Fault Drives Again: A Contemporary Primer*
52 U. Miami L. Rev. 793 (1998).*

[most footnotes omitted]

I.   Introduction

There are signs that the United States may be entering a second wave of "no-fault" reforms to traditional auto accident tort law. A first wave, with both academic and legislative initiatives, peaked in the 1960s and early 1970s and then subsided. Today, twenty-six states plus the District of Columbia and Puerto Rico have some sort of auto no-fault system. In recent years, three states—Georgia, Nevada, and Connecticut—have repealed no-fault, no state has enacted no-fault in the past twenty years, and California voters have rejected a no-fault ballot initiative.

First-wave no-fault systems now have a record for study and evaluation. Meanwhile, the contemporary second wave is impelled by several converging factors: advocacy by no-fault proponents, a generalized interest in anti-liability "tort reform," and persisting concern over high auto insurance costs. No-fault bills and ballot initiatives have proliferated, prompting an occasion for debate and assessment. . . .

\* \* \*

In some respects, the new debate simply recapitulates issues and arguments from the first no-fault wave, but at the same time there are new complexities in the debate for two reasons. First, there has now been actual experience with no-fault schemes, and studies and evaluations have been made. Second, there are novel no-fault proposals, not just in response to criticisms of traditional tort, but also in response to criticisms of existing first-wave no-fault schemes. Compared with the first-wave, the second-wave debate may be both more sophisticated and more confusing.

Tort law delivers compensation to accident victims from the pocket of the driver at fault, or from that driver's insurer. No-fault compensation schemes depart from this in two crucial respects. First, tort suits for auto accident injuries are curtailed. Second, compensation comes without proof of any party's fault from the victim's own first-party accident insurance coverage, which he is required to carry. Essentially, no-fault narrows auto accident victims' rights to seek compensation from culprits, requiring victims to accept compensation instead from coverage they have been forced to buy. The principal argument for such an arrangement is that it benefits victims by delivering compensation more rationally, efficiently, and cost-effectively than the tort system does. The main arguments against no-fault are that it does not function more effectively than the tort system, and that no-fault carries disadvantages that outweigh its advantages. No-fault's disadvantages are chiefly two-fold: (1) loss of tort law's purported role in deterring unsafe driving; and (2) loss of tort law's purported corrective justice function in securing recompense for injury victims from culprits who inflict injury.

\* \* \*

II.   Basic Insurance Critiques of Tort

Advocacy for no-fault originates in criticism of the tort system as a costly, inefficient, and irrational means of delivering compensation to auto accident victims. It focuses on tort as a system of compensation, to the exclusion of other objectives associated with tort: deterrence and corrective justice. To the extent one views tort exclusively as a compensation system, no-fault is likely to appear superior. On the other hand, to whatever extent one credits or values tort's deterrent and corrective justice aspects, no-fault will appear less advantageous, or even detrimental.

Several compensation-oriented critiques of the tort system are dominant. First, tort litigation costs and attorneys' fees drain extravagant portions of insurance premium funds away from victim compensation. Hence, by eliminating tort suits, expanded compensation and/or reduced premiums could be achieved.

Second, tort confines compensation to victims of negligent driving, thereby excluding many who are comparably injured and needy, but who receive nothing because they cannot prove that some other party was at fault. One study suggests that only thirty-seven percent of auto accident victims receive a tort recovery, while twenty-three percent receive no compensation at all. The low level of recovery stems, in part, from the requirement of proving negligence to recover in tort. By eliminating fault as a prerequisite to recovery, no-fault delivers compensation more widely and less arbitrarily.

Third, tort systematically produces over-compensation of less-severely injured victims and under-compensation of poor or more seriously injured ones. Because litigation is risky and costly, defendants often settle small claims at inflated levels attractive to plaintiffs. By contrast, plaintiffs with large claims and poor plaintiffs tend to avoid the prolonged litigation needed to secure full compensation, opting instead to settle early for less.

Fourth, the tort litigation process delays delivery of compensation, compared with how long a straightforward first-party insurance system takes.

Fifth, auto accident cases strain court systems by their sheer numbers. Many cases may be too commonplace or trivial to warrant such resource drain.

Finally, the tort system creates incentives to create fraudulent claims and to overstate injuries. Fraud ranges from the staging of accidents to more genteel forms. Overstatement is inherently in the interest of particular claimants.

There is little that tort defenders can say directly in response to these critiques. The premium drain point is undeniable. Tort entails litigation that is superfluous to a first-party compensation scheme, diverting premium dollars away from compensation. There is no response in defense of the tort system except to say that it is not solely a compensation system.

Tort defenders would also note that first-party compensation schemes will generate their own litigation costs and lawyer fees, while avoiding those of tort. Litigation issues under no-fault would include scope of policy coverage and other contractual ambiguities, cause of accident, and degree of damage. Premiums will be drained away from compensation in order to resolve such issues. One can only guess how these drains compare with current tort-system drains. I have found no study addressing the question. A reasonable guess is that the no-fault drain, though substantial, should be smaller than the tort drain. In a first-party insurance market, underwriters can compete to offer low premiums to customers by finding ways to minimize dispute-driven premium drain through contractual clarity and low-cost dispute resolution. Equivalent market forces to reduce dispute costs cannot so easily operate in a tort system between adversarial parties not covered by prior contracts.

Requiring proof of fault also excludes many victims from compensation. Again, the charge cannot be denied, but only answered by pointing out that a fault-based tort system is not the same animal as a loss-based compensation system. Another possible response is to propose a non-fault-based (strict liability) recovery rule for auto tort cases. The merits and demerits of that suggestion, however, are beyond the scope of this analysis. Nevertheless, such a reform is not in the current political winds. Contemporary no-fault debate focuses on first-party insurance coverage, not third-party tort recovery.

Charges of over-and under-compensation in tort actions are difficult to deny. It has been estimated that for out-of-pocket losses under $500, victims on average receive four and a half times their loss from the tort system, while victims with over $25,000 in out-of-pocket losses receive, on average, only around a third of their losses. This feature emerges from tort's adversarial and fault-based aspects. If loss-based indemnity is the only object, these compensation "errors" can be curtailed.

The charge of delay is equally undeniable. Delivery of compensation is undoubtedly quicker if it does not turn on proving fault in litigation. The strain on courts point is true, as well. If fewer cases get litigated, court burdens lighten. Of course, this is no more true of auto cases than of medical malpractice, product liability, toxic tort, or business tort cases. These other types of cases, though less numerous than auto cases, tax courts in a different way by virtue of their complexity. In varying degrees, they could also be swept from the dockets by enacting no-fault compensation schemes.

Similarly, the fraud and overstatement charge is also true, though whether it is truer of auto than of other tort cases is unproved. Curtailing tort suits might diminish some such abuse, but it will by no means, eliminate abuse, since temptations to commit fraud and to overstate injuries also characterize straightforward insurance schemes. Successful reduction of incentives toward abuse may depend on whether a given no-fault scheme succeeds in reducing access to the pain and suffering damages offered under tort law. Availability of such damages may fan the flames of temptation toward fraud and overstatement.

III.  No–Fault, Tort, and Deterrence

Critics of no-fault contend that curtailing tort suits will cause traffic injuries to rise because dangerous driving will not be checked by the fear of lawsuits. Defenders of no-fault essentially make two responses to this criticism—one weak, the other stronger.

The first response is that no-fault schemes can provide meaningful deterrence against unsafe driving through an experience-rated premium device. Because unsafe motorists would be charged higher premiums, drivers would feel a direct financial interest in driving safely. This argument is dubious. At best, it holds true only if drivers can be classified with meaningful precision so that premium charges can be accurately gauged to reflect driver safety. The only conceivably affordable mechanism for this is to set premiums based on the number and severity of moving violations and accidents. But, the incidence of tickets and accidents is far too multi-causal and random to correlate substantially with driver dangerousness.

Premium-setting based on the number and severity of accidents might be rational from the standpoint of underwriter profitability because it predicts average likelihood of payout. For that reason, such premium-setting makes as much sense under no-fault as it does under tort. But, such premium-setting has little power, in itself, to induce safe driving because, within a broad range of driving habits, a driver's number or severity of accidents is poorly correlated with how dangerously he drives. It correlates more strongly with general accident rates in the areas where he drives.

Underwriters cannot easily implement true safety rating in a profitable manner. They maximize profit by correlating the premiums charged to any insured with the likelihood of making payouts to that insured. The elaborate information gathering needed to implement meaningful safety rating would probably cost far more than any benefit provided in improving the correlation between premiums charged and driver safety.

Sophisticated data would have to be developed on relationships between driving records and the likelihood of causing accidents. Information on moving violations would have to be analyzed along with accident and claim records. Huge uncertainties would stem from undetected traffic violations, unreported accidents, and vagaries in criminal adjudications. No strong evidence indicates that underwriters systematically link premiums to driver dangerousness. Even weaker is evidence that motorists change their driving habits in response to premium rates.

Though safety-rating is not a strong response to the lost-deterrence critique of no-fault, a stronger response exists—that the tort system does not substantially deter unsafe driving in the first place. If the deterrent effect of tort liability is weak, little is lost in moving to no-fault. Some studies suggest that tort plays a substantial role in deterring auto negligence. Other studies indicate that tort's deterrent effect is weak. Analysis of the debate on this point is set out below.

If tort has little effect in reducing accident rates, it is not difficult to grasp why: driving may not be the kind of activity upon which liability can exert strong incentive effects. Tort liability's financial incentives operate most powerfully on activities pursued with financial gain in mind. Motoring is generally not such an activity. Key incentives for safe driving include concern for safety of self, loved ones, and strangers; desire to prove competence and mastery; desire to avoid the hassle of accidents; and fear of losing driving privileges. Fear of tort liability probably ranks well behind all these other safe-driving incentives, especially because motorists generally carry liability insurance to shield themselves from having to pay tort judgments. If so, moving to a no-fault system will leave adequately powerful safety incentives in place.

Not only is the effect of tort liability on driving habits weak, but the relationship between driving habits and accidents is also attenuated. Most auto carelessness has a low correlation with injury. Common unsafe practices—excess speed, momentary lapses of attention, cheating on traffic signals, failures to anticipate—rarely produce accidents. If they did, they would not be so common. Nearly all drivers commit such sins regularly, though not grievously, and rarely cause accidents. No given motorist can greatly reduce his or her odds of an accident by reducing such careless habits, though many accidents in general are caused by them. This is because accidents are often caused by the interplay of conditions with actions and decisions taken by several drivers. Given this general low correlation between safety zeal and accident avoidance, no safety incentives of any kind are likely to have a meaningful impact on the majority of drivers—except perhaps drastic sanctions for unsafe practices.

A different analysis may, at first glance, seem warranted for egregiously reckless drivers. Their habits seem especially prone to deterrence, because they lie so far from the norm and could be altered easily without great hardship or superhuman vigilance. But, this apparent susceptibility to deterrence is probably illusory. Young males and the inebriated, the two chief classes of deviantly bad drivers, are not likely to respond to tort liability with safer driving, because their dangerous behavior stems from impaired judgment from the start. Thus, it seems unlikely that tort law substantially constrains the level of drunk driving or young male recklessness. For these drivers, under either no-fault or tort, meaningful deterrence can arise only if they risk forfeiture of driving privileges or other harsh sanctions, even if they have not yet caused an accident.

One odd feature of this debate is the self-contradictory posture each side may sometimes stake out. Defenders of tort who criticize no-fault on lost-deterrence grounds contend that motorists respond to possible tort liability with safer driving, but do not respond similarly to possible premium hikes under no-fault. That makes no more sense than denying that tort promotes safe driving while at the same time insisting that premium hikes under no-fault do. It makes equal sense to expect that either fear of suits or fear of premiums will promote safe driving. In fact, for motorists with liability insurance, fear of suits is pretty much the same thing as fear of premium hikes, because tort judgments themselves will be paid by underwriters. It would take solid empirical evidence to prove that such minor financial stakes have a major impact on highway safety, under either tort or no-fault.

There is one likely respect in which experience rating may affect safety—by inducing some high-risk motorists to drive less in order to keep their premiums down. Though it may fail to affect individual driving habits, experience rating may improve the ratio of low-risk to high-risk drivers on the road. This effect could operate under either tort or no-fault and is, therefore, not a safety advantage for preferring either system over the other.

Most discussion of injury prevention under no-fault focuses on whether no-fault undermines deterrence by weakening incentives to drive safely. An argument can be made, however, that no-fault actually promotes injury prevention because, in a first-party coverage system, underwriters will offer low premiums to motorists driving collision-safe cars. They do this, of course, because safe cars reduce payout risks. Underwriters can, therefore, compete by cutting costs to attract customers who drive safe cars. This safety incentive is missing under tort where the damage pay-out goes to a third-party victim, not to the underwriter's own customer.

It is likely that safety premiums would indeed emerge on discrete safety items, like air bags and anti-lock brakes, but unlikely that they would reach more subtle design elements. Crashworthiness can be sharply affected by even such minor design changes as occur year-to-year within continuing models. Gathering meaningful safety data on such items is painstaking at best and nearly impossible for new models.

Though safe-car discounts could theoretically produce injury reductions, I have seen no study showing they do so in fact. There are reasons to suspect they might not. Discounts would bring injury reductions only if they strongly affect the number of motorists choosing air bags, anti-lock breaks, crash-proof construction, and the like. The actual effect may be small, however, because personal safety, not insurance cost, is arguably the major motive for choosing protective features. In addition, safety-indifferent motorists will not be tempted by premium discounts which fail to offset the added costs of these optional safety features. In short, safe-car discounts—nice as they are for those who get them—may not have much impact on safe-car choices. Safety-minded motorists will choose safety features even without discounts and safety-indifferent ones will reject them, discounts or no.

IV.   Corrective Justice: Now You See It, Now You Don't

In addition to deterrence, another key value attributed to tort law is corrective justice: the fairness of exacting victim recompense from the culpable party. With no-fault, corrective justice falls by the wayside, and as a result, could be judged a serious loss, though not everyone agrees. Concern over corrective justice strikes some as trivial and precious compared with tangible goals like compensation and deterrence. However, why worry about corrective justice if no-fault can deliver compensation more rationally than tort without sacrificing deterrence?

Moreover, no-fault proponents doubt whether auto tort law truly represents corrective justice. The notion of corrective justice starts with an image of injustice inflicted by the defendant upon the plaintiff. Because the defendant is "guilty" and the plaintiff "innocent," and because the defendant operated at the plaintiff's expense, he or she owes the plaintiff. Liability "corrects" the injustice.

It is not clear that this model makes sense for typical auto accidents. As suggested above, low-level auto negligence is ubiquitous. The vast majority of accidents involve the large group of drivers with low accident frequency. Most motorists make driving mistakes frequently, once every two miles according to one study. Though negligence is ubiquitous, the incidence of actual harm is highly random, resembling "acts of God" in the selection of victims. Moreover, the risks imposed are highly reciprocal. Typically, the victim is about as "bad" a driver as the culprit. These aspects becloud the picture of auto tort liability as a form of corrective justice. If there is little corrective justice in auto tort law to start with, little is lost in moving to no-fault.

The corrective justice picture is also beclouded by insurance. Underwriters, not negligent drivers, usually pay tort damages. All drivers finance those payments through their premiums. Hence, payment ultimately comes from the pockets of the driving public, including victims. The notion that payment goes to innocent victims from negligent culprits is misguided. The negligent motorist becomes merely the moral scapegoat in an insurance delivery system.

Nevertheless, anxiety over lost corrective justice cannot simply be dismissed. Those who dismiss corrective justice concerns may hold a simplistic conception of them. The link between liability and corrective justice may be important, even if it is hazy and imperfect. Auto tort liability is not the only area where negligence law's link to corrective justice is hazy. In medical malpractice, for example, liability seldom turns on the notion that the doctor has done an "injustice" to the injured patient or is, so to speak, a "bad" doctor. Good doctors make mistakes just as the best athletes do.

But when such a mistake harms another, there may be injustice in failure to take responsibility for the mistake, even if "injustice" seems too strong a word for the defendant's actions toward the plaintiff. Hence, malpractice law may perform a corrective justice function, albeit a weaker one than pronouncing upon good and evil. The analogy between auto tort and medical malpractice can be pushed even further. Consumers ultimately absorb the cost of medical malpractice damages, because doctors will raise fees in order to pay insurance premiums. As in auto tort, where the driving public collectively makes payments to negligently injured members, the collective consumers of health care wind up paying malpractice victims. Hence, the corrective justice function of tort seems essentially symbolic for both auto tort law and medical malpractice. Both systems identify mistakes and attribute responsibility to culpable parties, though the victim's compensation comes not from the culprit but from elsewhere.

If corrective justice becomes purely symbolic, its value lies only in ritual assessments of responsibility. Such assessments delineate and fortify a sense of moral order by identifying how and by whom damage has been done. This may be meaningful to victims and other concerned parties, though it serves no instrumental function. An American Bar Association report [Special Committee on the Tort Liability System, Towards a Jurisprudence of Injury: The Continuing Creation of a System of Substantive Justice in American Tort Law (1984)] notes that "the tort system provides an important psychological outlet for seriously injured victims who would be dissatisfied with 'no-fault' benefits and desirous of an impartial hearing of their substantive case." To devalue tort law on the grounds that its corrective justice role is inconsequential or vestigial may ignore subtle but important concerns and experiences.

Still, it might be argued that corrective justice is especially overrated when it comes to auto tort law. A driver's negligence—as opposed to bad luck—seems less "responsible" for a given accident injury than a doctor's negligence is for medical mishaps. If so, the blame game may be misplaced or downright harmful. On the other hand, tort suits do allow fact-finders to weigh doubts about assigning responsibility. Such deliberations can be performed on a flexible case-by-case basis. But where no-fault prevails, all regularized inquest into responsibility for accidents is banished.

Is the symbolic corrective justice of auto negligence law worth all its lawyer fees and litigation costs? Such funds could be channeled into broader and/or deeper compensation, or be saved through premium reduction. Do all victims of harmful negligence have a "right" to corrective justice? In states that have adopted no-fault, some polls show majority support for a return to tort. Such polls may reveal frustration with continuing high premiums under no-fault. But they may also reveal a moral sense that corrective justice for negligence is valuable, even if the negligence in question is as pervasive as auto carelessness is, implicating everyone, and even if corrective justice is costly.

V.   Types of Existing No–Fault Schemes

Although no state has ever enacted a pure no-fault system, three states—Michigan, New York, and Florida—have adopted schemes which eliminate substantial proportions of auto tort suits. Though they are technically "partial" no-fault, these schemes approximate "pure" no-fault. Michigan's scheme comes closest to pure no-fault. It bars suits for economic damages, except those intentionally inflicted under a narrow definition of intention. It bars pain and suffering suits except for harm that is exceedingly serious or intentionally-inflicted.

Partial and pure no-fault schemes can be compared with each other and with traditional tort systems still operating in many states. All three systems—partial no-fault, pure no-fault, and tort—can further be compared with new "choice" proposals that allow motorists to choose between a pre-existing tort or partial no-fault scheme on the one hand, and an alternative scheme closer to pure no-fault, on the other hand.

Partial no-fault schemes provide first-party compensation for economic loss, up to the limits of coverage purchased, without proof of fault. A few also compensate for noneconomic damages (e.g., pain and suffering), but most do not. Some, but not all, eliminate the right to sue for economic damages to the extent such damages are covered by no-fault benefits. Schemes that do not eliminate such suits usually let first-party insurers who make pay-outs to victims claim subrogation rights over tort judgments awarded to those same victims. This prevents double recovery by victims and discourages them from bringing tort suits, because damages from suits have to be paid to insurers as reimbursement for benefits paid.

Partial schemes ban pain and suffering claims for minor injuries, but allow them for major ones. All allow suits for death and egregious injury. They differ in how minor an injury can be and still be major enough for lawsuit eligibility.

Two different systems or types of thresholds exist for separating major from minor injuries. One is a "verbal" threshold, which descriptively defines injuries eligible for law suits—for example, broken bones, "permanent serious disfigurement," or "significant and permanent loss of an important bodily function." The other type of threshold is "monetary," a minimum dollar amount of medical damages. Hence, depending on the type of threshold and on whether economic damages are entirely excluded from tort, there can be several major types of partial no-fault schemes. Partial no-fault schemes that most fully eliminate the tort option for economic damages and place a high threshold for suits for non-economic damages approximate pure no-fault. Currently, Michigan, New York, and Florida have no-fault systems of this type.

## VI.   Evaluation Overview

The most significant no-fault experiences to date have been with "partial" schemes which continue to allow tort suits for certain damages. There is now enough experience with such schemes to allow meaningful, though tentative, assessment. To compare no-fault meaningfully with traditional tort, one would ideally assess each major type with respect to at least four major factors: (1) rationality and efficiency in delivering compensation; (2) success in deterrence; (3) fidelity to values of corrective justice; and (4) effect on low-income motorists. No study has attempted such a thorough evaluation, but less comprehensive evaluations have been offered, based unavoidably on incomplete information and debatable value judgments.

Attempts to evaluate no-fault have focused on compensation and deterrence. With respect to compensation, the controversy centers less upon the observed effects of no-fault than upon how they should be evaluated from the standpoint of wise public policy. With respect to deterrence, by contrast, the empirical controversy is thick, focusing on whether no-fault leads to increased highway danger. With respect to corrective justice, controversy over no-fault remains purely normative, focusing on the value and tangibility of corrective justice as delivered by auto tort litigation and how corrective justice should be weighed against compensation goals which may be better served by abandoning it.

## VII.   No–Fault as a Compensation System

In general, studies have found existing no-fault schemes superior to tort for rational and efficient delivery of compensation. This is unsurprising, since the chief inspiration for no-fault is the deficiency of tort as a compensation system. It would be strange if no-fault, designed specifically to meet compensation goals alone, failed to excel in meeting those goals compared with tort, where compensation goals are compromised by additional and partially competing goals like deterrence and corrective justice. On the other hand, there are several ambiguities in evaluating whether no-fault indeed exceeds tort in compensation rationality and efficiency.

Before exploring those ambiguities, it is worthwhile to itemize the different ways in which no-fault seems to successfully serve rationality and efficiency in compensation.

No–Fault Pays a Higher Proportion of Premium Income to Claimants Than Do Tort Systems. For each premium dollar, no-fault states deliver 50.2 cents in victim benefits, while tort states deliver only 43.2 cents. Again, this is no surprise, because a goal of no-fault is to reduce the drain of premium dollars into lawyer fees and other litigation costs. Because most existing no-fault schemes are partial, the figures above understate the potential premium savings of no-fault. Under pure no-fault, the savings on fees and costs would almost certainly be higher and a larger gap would open between no-fault and tort states in the delivery of premium dollars to victims.

No–Fault Delivers Auto Insurance Compensation to More Accident Victims Than Does Tort. Compared with tort, many more victims receive auto insurance compensation under no-fault. Estimates for the increase range between roughly 25% and roughly 100%. This is expected, since a basic purpose of no-fault is to widen the delivery of compensation by removing proof of some adverse party's fault as a prerequisite to compensation.

No–Fault Reduces Over-and Under–Compensation. Under no-fault, compensation delivered matches economic damages— mainly medical expenses and lost income—more closely than under tort. This unsurprising result stems from two chief factors. First, no-fault plans focus on compensating economic losses and on curtailing compensation for pain and suffering. Second, no-fault delivers compensation with far less delay and strategic maneuvering between adverse litigants.

No–Fault Delivers Compensation More Quickly Than Does Tort. One year after filing notice of their claim, no-fault claimants have received, on average, over 95% of all they will ever receive, while most tort claimants have received less than 52%. This comes as no surprise, because no-fault avoids the delays of tort litigation by handling compensation as a simple insurance claim matter.

No–Fault Cuts the Number of Lawsuits. Since barring suits is at the heart of no-fault, this could scarcely fail to be true. Reduction in suits depends, of course, on the degree of "purity" in no-fault plans. Abolition of no-fault restores higher lawsuit volume.

Conclusions. No-fault successfully achieves some goals it is designed to achieve. From this, one could conclude that no-fault exceeds tort in compensation rationality and efficiency. But before drawing that conclusion, several ambiguities need to be cleared up.

Existing no-fault has not brought reduced premiums, despite claims by advocates that it should. If anything, premiums appear to be higher in no-fault states than in traditional tort states, despite savings on lawyer fees and litigation costs. There are two main reasons. First, no-fault compensates more people. Second, thresholds against tort suits have not been high enough to prevent the continued frequent filing of suits. Premiums in partial no-fault states reflect not only victim compensation, but also the costs and lawyer fees associated with persistent tort litigation. Premiums could be reduced by moving toward pure no-fault. This means reduced litigation costs and lawyers' fees. Of course, it also means curtailed corrective justice. Though experience with partial no-fault suggests a slight average hike in premiums compared with tort states, this could be viewed as a good bargain, because premiums under no-fault are paying for compensation to far more victims. But what seems like a bargain may trouble consumers concerned only with keeping their own premiums down. They may not care that hiked premiums under no-fault provide them guaranteed compensation for auto accident injury. Given a choice, many might waive guaranteed compensation in return for lower premiums. If so, no-fault undermines rationality and efficiency by delivering more compensation than people truly value. The tort fault system is, therefore, arguably better.

\* \* \*

### VIII.   No–Fault and Deterrence

With respect to deterrence, the crucial question is whether no-fault is inferior to tort. Conclusions on lost deterrence—increased accidents due to decreased care in driving—are mixed. The issue has been hotly contested in a series of studies reaching various results. At this point, no firm conclusion can be drawn on whether no-fault produces higher accident rates, and if so, why or how much. What follows is a brief review of several of the significant studies and issues.

In one early study, Elizabeth M. Landes looked at auto fatality rates for the 1967–76 period, running a regression analysis designed to isolate the impact of no-fault.[71] She concluded that at a $1,500 lawsuit threshold, fatal accidents would rise 10% over what would happen under tort.[72]

Landes' study was hotly criticized by O'Connell and Levmore.[73] They chide failure to control for such variables as weather, police enforcement, road quality, driver training, urban-rural differences, and medical care. It was also criticized for focusing on fatalities, not injuries generally, and its implicit assumption that motorists will ignore their own safety, increasing their recklessness due to no-fault's protection against tort suits.[74] All of these criticisms seem well-taken except for the focus-on-fatalities point. The critics puzzlingly suggest that a fatalities hike proves nothing about any difference between tort and no-fault, because tort recovery for fatalities remains available anyway under all state no-fault plans. But if no-fault's reduced exposure to tort liability makes drivers more reckless, an increase in fatalities is very much what one could expect, even if fatalities remain subject to tort suits under no-fault. Of course, this is not to say that Landes has indeed proved that curtailing tort will in fact cause increased recklessness.

**71.**  See Elisabeth M. Landes, Insurance, Liability, and Accidents: A Theoretical and Empirical Investigation of the Effects of No–Fault Accidents, *25 J.L. & Econ.* 49, 62 (1982).

**72.**  See *id.*

**73.**  See generally Jeffrey O'Connell & Saul Levmore, A Reply to Landes: A Faulty Study of No–Fault's Effect on Fault?, 48 Mo. L. Rev. 649 (1983).

**74.**  See *id.* at 650–51.

. . . . A U.S. Department of Transportation study comparing no-fault with tort states, found no statistically significant difference in highway fatalities or injuries.

\* \* \*

IX.   No–Fault and Corrective Justice

Corrective justice inherently defies empirical measurement or study. Hence, any corrective justice comparison between tort and no-fault schemes is ineffable. If pure no-fault abandons all corrective justice (because tort suits are thrown out entirely), comparing it with tort quickly reduces to two questions: (1) how valuable is corrective justice; and (2) how much does auto tort litigation embody it?

Comparisons grow even more ineffable when tort is compared with partial no-fault, which retains vestiges of corrective justice, and when partial no-fault is compared with pure no-fault. The comparisons become ones between varying types and degrees of corrective justice. How close to or far from the tort law "norm" for corrective justice do the various partial no-fault schemes lie? How much does it matter? How should any sacrifices in corrective justice be weighed against gains in compensation rationality and efficiency? Can meaningful corrective justice be reconciled with substantial gains in compensation rationality and efficiency?

X.   "Choice" No–Fault: The Simple Version

Current assessments of no-fault are further complicated by proposals for so-called "choice" no-fault plans. Under the simplest choice scheme, each motorist would opt either for a type of no-fault coverage or for retention of whatever tort lawsuit rights, full or partial, exist prior to enactment of the choice scheme. . . .

The appeal of choice is to offer motorists the option of no-fault's projected low premiums and ensure compensation without forcing it on anyone who prefers tort's corrective justice and higher possible recoveries. . . .

Choice proponents predict substantial premium reductions for motorists who select no-fault. Since this is the proposal's main purpose, this prediction is unsurprising. By removing pain and suffering, lawyer fees, and litigation costs from the compensation system for no-fault insureds, the scheme is able to offer them reduced premiums. Participants get reduced premiums, guaranteed compensation without proof of fault, and immunity from suits for pain and suffering in exchange for waiving access to pain and suffering damages. Though this assertedly achieves superior rationality and efficiency in compensation, pain and suffering damages must be sacrificed in order to obtain no-fault's advantages. This upends no-fault's claim to economic superiority. In technical economic terms: there is no free lunch.

For those who choose the no-fault option under a simple choice plan, results compare to what one could expect from a pure no-fault plan that bars compensation for pain and suffering. Meanwhile, those opting for tort under a simple choice plan can expect premiums to remain basically as they were under the pre-existing tort or partial no-fault systems, because accident risks and litigation expenses would not change much. Minor changes might occur, because for accidents between defendants under PIP [the no-fault optional, called Personal Injury Protection] and plaintiffs under tort, pain and suffering indemnity would come from first-party coverage, known as tort maintenance coverage, not from adversary lawsuits as under tort or partial no-fault. This difference could affect average premiums paid by tort-system motorists.

New Jersey and Pennsylvania have recently enacted simple choice systems. They basically allow motorists to choose between partial no-fault coverage and the traditional tort system. . . .

XI.  The Congressional Choice Initiative: "Neo–Partial" No–Fault

In the Auto Choice Reform Act of 1997, Congress considered a plan different in one crucial respect from the simple choice plan described above. Under the Congressional choice plan, all motorists, whether covered under PIP [Personal Injury Protection, the no-fault system] or under tort maintenance, could sue for pain and suffering where the injuring driver was under the influence of drugs or alcohol or engaged in intentional misconduct. This exception to no-fault preemption of pain and suffering suits separates the Congressional plan from the simple choice scheme. Essentially, the Congressional plan substitutes a severity-of-misconduct threshold to pain and suffering suits for the severity-of-injury thresholds found in partial no-fault schemes. Hence, the Congressional plan could be called "neo-partial" no-fault.

\* \* \*

The Congressional plan dreams of major premium cuts while retaining the crucial moral core of corrective justice. But that circle will not square, precisely because drunk driving suits are key both to corrective justice and to high costs and premiums. In terms of corrective justice, a misconduct-based threshold is superior to an injury-based one. But preserving this heart of corrective justice requires losing a substantial slice of potential cost cuts.

\* \* \*

XIII.  Low–Income Motorists

Because high premiums are a major factor in prompting advocacy for no-fault, it is especially relevant to consider the place of low-income drivers under tort and no-fault. Benefits or detriments to low-income drivers may warrant special emphasis in policy evaluation. Tort has been criticized as particularly harmful and inequitable to low-income motorists.

First, high premiums are especially unaffordable for low-income motorists, who sometimes spend staggering proportions of their total incomes on auto insurance. This expense may be inescapable for those who drive to work.

Second, due to urban residence, low-income motorists may pay average premiums higher in absolute terms, not just in proportion to income.

Third, low-income drivers on average receive less in tort compensation than high-income drivers, because their lost income component is lower, and possibly also because their medical care is furnished by lower-cost providers. Their premiums are not reduced in proportion to this compensation deficit, because an insured's income is a weak predictor of the third-party payout risk he imposes on an underwriter. Low-income motorists are as likely as wealthy ones to cause damage an insurer might need to indemnify. Because they receive less compensation than the rich from the tort/insurance system but pay nearly as much, low-income motorists subsidize compensation for wealthier motorists. In effect, they pay for insurance to cover their well-to-do neighbors.

Fourth, low-income motorists get lower average settlements for equivalent loss, probably due to inferior education, sophistication, and lawyering, combined with higher need for quick cash.

It would be good, somehow, to offer low-income motorists relief from these burdens and inequities. Some observers contend that no-fault can accomplish this by reducing premiums overall and by calibrating low premiums to the low incomes that would yield reduced payouts in first-party coverage. Because partial no-fault does not deliver premium reductions and retains tort to a substantial degree, relief for low-income motorists is not found there. Pure no-fault and choice plans may be different. There is reason to hope they might deliver reduced premiums overall by eliminating noneconomic damages, lawyer fees, and litigation costs. Arguably, they could also provide specially reduced premiums to the poor.... Because low-income victims would file smaller claims than the rich, underwriters might offer them reduced premiums.

\* \* \*

Choice proposals introduce one further critical issue. I suggest above that a choice system might quickly evolve into a uniform no-fault system, with pain and suffering damages wiped from the scene by failure in the first-party insurance market for them, leaving only PIP coverage for all. If that is not the case, however, what may emerge instead is a class system of access to pain and suffering damages.

Under choice, low-income motorists will be more likely to opt for low-premium no-fault coverage than high-income motorists who can better afford the high premiums associated with tort. Wealthy motorists would be more inclined than the poor to retain tort rights to pain and suffering damages. No-fault's guarantee of compensation without proof of fault means less to the wealthy whose medical expenses are probably covered by job-linked health insurance and whose lost income from physical injury averages less, because they do not live off manual labor. Though many high-income motorists will choose no-fault anyway and some low-income motorists will stay with tort, the predictable result is a class system in which average wealthy victims receive pain and suffering damages (for fault-based accidents), while average low-income victims do not.

The implications grow more troubling when one considers that pain and suffering (along with other non-economic damages) act as a compensation equalizer between poor and wealthy under tort. The poor may receive less for lost income and medical expenses, but they suffer the same pain as the rich for mangled limbs and gashed faces, and receive roughly equivalent pain and suffering damages.

In this light, the tort system seems to affirm equal human worth between rich and poor, better than a pure no-fault system that eliminates pain and suffering compensation or a choice system that eliminates it disproportionately for the poor. Hence, no-fault may subject the poor to an unintended but very real indignity. True, this indignity may seem weightless compared with the tangible benefit of providing the poor with more affordable insurance. But damaged dignity is a paramount feature of serious personal injury. Redressing and minimizing dignitarian damage are key purposes of delivering compensation and administering corrective justice. Thus, there is reason to pause before adopting compensation schemes that might themselves engender new forms of dignitarian insult.

\* \* \*

## XIV. Conclusion

Agitation and debate over auto no-fault are likely to accelerate in coming years. Fueled mainly by high and rising premiums, the discussion will call attention to no-fault's apparent advantages as a compensation system. Cost and compensation advantages are greatest when no-fault is closest to pure. Among existing schemes, this is best approximated by partial no-fault schemes with stringent verbal thresholds against pain and suffering suits.

Though studies are mixed, it seems unlikely that no-fault seriously undermines road safety. It is also unlikely to augment it.

No-fault's cost and compensation advantages must be weighed against disadvantages in preempting corrective justice values that tort may vindicate. Neo-partial no-fault, its pain and suffering lawsuit threshold based on severe misconduct, may strike a reasonable compromise between attaining no-fault's compensation advantages in modest degree and preserving corrective justice where it matters most. Whether it can deliver substantial premium cuts is more doubtful.

Choice plans, inspired by consumer sovereignty, may fail to serve it. They may instead yield no-fault for all, as underwriters and motorists respond to market incentives, pressures, and failures.

All existing and seriously discussed systems visit hardships and even inequities upon the poor. On other hand, insofar as they are uninsured, the poor deal hardships and even inequities upon others. Policy options should be weighed for their impacts on the poor with respect to both of these dimensions.

### *NOTES*

**1. The Policy Debate.** Which arguments seem most persuasive in favor of the tort system for automobile accidents? Which arguments most strongly support no-fault systems?

**2. Compromise Plans.** Does the compromise of a partial no-fault and traditional tort system seem appealing or do the two approaches working together remove each other's advantages? How appealing is the consumer choice approach, allowing drivers to choose between torts and no-fault?

# Chapter VIII

# DEFAMATION

## SECTION A.  DEFAMATORY ASSERTION OF FACT

### KAPLAN v. NEWSWEEK MAGAZINE, INC.
United States Court of Appeals for the Ninth Circuit.
October 24, 1985.*

BROWNING, C.J., ANDERSON and NELSON, J.J.

In October 1983, appellee published an article entitled "A Giggle of Guts," describing "an all-American team of 11 gut courses," including a course taught by appellant. Appellant requested retraction of comments about his course. . . . Appellee did not retract, but instead published most of appellant's demand letter, a correction acknowledging that appellant's midterm examination was not a take-home, and a disclaimer that appellee "did not intent to suggest that just because a course is popular and fairly painless it is without worth or intellectual merit."

Appellant sued, alleging libel in count I. . . .

The district court dismissed the action. This appeal followed. We affirm on the ground that the statements complained of are either nondefamatory as a matter of law or are protected because they are statements of opinion rather than of fact.

### I.

Many statements in the paragraph of the article that refer specifically to appellant's course are statements of fact, but appellant virtually concedes, and we agree,[1] that this paragraph, standing alone, is not

---

* This disposition is not appropriate for publication and may not be cited to or by the courts of this circuit except as provided by 9th Cir. R. 21. [The federal courts in many instances decline to officially publish an otherwise binding judicial decision or authorize it to be cited as controlling precedence in unrelated litigation.]

1. Under California Law, whether a statement is reasonably susceptible of defamatory meaning is a question of law for the court to decide. *MacLeod v. Tribune Publishing Co.*, 52 Cal.2d 536, 546 (1959); *Yorty v. Chandler*, 13 Cal. App. 3d 467, 475 (1970). This is the common-law rule followed by most states. *See* Restatement of Torts (Second), § 614(1) (1977).

defamatory.[2] It says nothing directly about appellant, his ability, or his integrity. One must stretch things greatly even to infer anything regarding appellant, other than the fact that he is *not* an easy grader. Criticism of the substance of a professor's course should not be interpreted as defamatory of the author personally, just as similar criticism of books, movies and plays is not. *See Exner v. American Medical Association*, 12 Wash. App. 215, 218–19 (1974). Moreover, it is a sizable step to infer anything derogatory about appellant's course: the implication that it must be worthless because some students believe it to be easy is strained.

Even if the article reflected upon appellant, the implication would be nondefamatory; comments more pejorative and more directly attacking an individual have been held nondefamatory at the pleading stage. *See, e.g., Yorty v. Chandler*, 13 Cal. App. 3d 467, 475 (1970); *Miller v. Bakersfield News–Bulletin, Inc.*, 44 Cal. App. 3d 899, 903 (1975).

## II.

Appellant relies primarily upon a second paragraph—the article's lead paragraph—referring to the group of courses as (1) "Micks," "guts," or "blowoffs"; (2) "all good for the grade-point average"; (3) "pleasant ways to compile credits"; (4) "painless courses"; (5) courses for which one can "study for about an hour for a test and get a 98" (6) "an all-American team of 11 gut courses."

With the exception of (5), the statements are subjective evaluations of the courses; they are expressions of opinion, not fact. Statement (5) presents a closer case but, in context, is also one of opinion. It is obvious hyperbole and a figurative description of an easy course, not fairly readable as a literal statement of fact. It is settled law that statements of opinion are not actionable, *Gertz v. Robert Welch, Inc.*, 418 U.S. 323, 339–40 (1974); *Carr v. Warden*, 159 Cal. App. 3d 1166, 1170 (1984), and it is routinely held that uncomplimentary evaluations, such as appellee's appraisal of the eleven selected courses, fall in the protected category. *See, e.g., Mr. Chow of New York v. Ste. Jour Azur S.A.*, 759 F.2d 219, 227–31 (2d Cir.1985); *Lauderback v. American Broadcasting Companies*, 741 F.2d 193, 196–98 (8th Cir.1984). Appellant relies on *Ollman v. Evans*, 750 F.2d 970 (D.C.Cir.1984) (en banc), but *Ollman* held that, in context, a statement that Professor Ollman had "no status within the [teaching] profession but is a pure and simple activist," is an expression of opinion, not fact, and thus is protected. *Id.* at 989–92.

Appellant contends the article implies it was based on a poll of students and, if this is untrue or if the poll was unsound, the statements,

**2.** The specific statements about appellant's course are as follows:

(1) it "is recognized as the easiest five credits" at Stanford;

(2) lectures are broadcast on campus radio, and students listen while sunning themselves by the pool;

(3) The requirements are few—a take-home midterm and a multiple choice final;

(4) the grades exactly mirror the curve for all grades given at Stanford;

(5) one student who took the final outdoors and finished in fifty minutes got an "A";

(6) two students took the final in black tie while sipping champagne.

even though opinion, are actionable. An opinion implicitly based on unstated defamatory fact may be actionable, Restatement (Second) of Torts § 566 (1977), but this rule does not reach appellant's case. The rule supports a cause of action when the implied fact itself is untrue and defamatory, but not when, although untrue, it is not defamatory. *See Carr v. Warden*, 159 Cal. App. 3d at 1170. Appellant's argument is that the asserted nomination of his course to the "Mick" hall-of-fame may have been fraudulent, but since the implied fact, if any, is not defamatory, he has no cause of action. Count I was properly dismissed.

\* \* \*

AFFIRMED.

### *NOTES*

**1.  Common Law Defamation.** The common law tort of defamation consists of the (1) defamatory assertion of fact against the plaintiff (2) intentionally or negligently published. The term "published," as will be discussed infra at Sec. C, is a term of art which simply means communication of the defamation to at least one person other than the victim of the defamation. The common law also provides defenses, discussed infra at Sec. E. The most notable defense is proof that the defamatory statement is truthful. Under the traditional common law, the defamatory assertion is presumed false and the defendant has the burden of proving the assertion true. In addition, under the common law (with the exception of limited common law privileges when adopted by the jurisdiction), the defendant who "published" defamation would be liable for asserting the falsehoods even when a reasonable person would have mistakenly concluded the defamatory assertion was true. In this sense traditional common law defamation imposes strict liability on the speaker for an error in fact. The harshness of this rule and its chilling effect on speech has prompted the United States Supreme Court to interpret the First Amendment of the United States Constitution (guaranteeing free speech and a free press) to require in some, but not all, instances that the defendant in effect be either negligent or in other cases reckless toward the truth. These constitutional requirements, superimposed on traditional defamation, are discussed infra at Sec. D. In addition, constitutional cases have also in some, but not all, instances shifted the burden on the plaintiff to prove the defamation is false. See Diamond, Levine & Madden, *Understanding Torts* § 21.02 (2nd ed. 2000). Keeton, *Prosser and Keeton on the Law of Torts* § 111 (5th ed. 1984), and Dobbs, *The Law of Torts* §§ 400–401 (2000); See generally, Franklin, Anderson & Cate, Mass Media Law (6th ed. 2000).

**2.  Defining "Defamatory".** A defamatory statement is typically described as one that exposes the plaintiff to hatred, contempt, ridicule, or scorn, or causes the plaintiff to be avoided. Id. The Restatement (Second) of Torts offers a somewhat more expansive definition:

> "A communication is defamatory if it tends so to harm the reputation of another as to lower him in the estimation of the community or to deter third persons from associating or dealing with him."

Restatement (Second) of Torts § 559. See *Gorman v. Swaggart*, 524 So.2d 915 (La.App.1988), where a noted religious minister sued for defamation when he was publicly accused of adultery, immoral conduct, embezzlement, and involvement with organized crime. The suit included a claim against defendants for attacking the business practices of plaintiff's nonprofit corporation before creditors and television stations. The court ruled that the allegations against the corporation and minister were defamatory.

In *Decker v. Princeton Packet, Inc.*, 116 N.J. 418, 561 A.2d 1122 (1989), a newspaper printed an obituary without first confirming its accuracy. Plaintiff, who was still alive, sued the newspaper for defamation, even though a retraction had been published. The court held that no per se cause of action existed, because announcement of the plaintiff's death was not by itself harmful to her reputation.

See also *Talens v. Bernhard*, 669 F.Supp. 251 (E.D.Wis.1987), where a doctor from the Philippines who did his residency at an American medical center sued its chairman for defamation. The defendant had originally written positive letters of recommendation for the plaintiff, but upon discovering that plaintiff did not intend to return to the Philippines, he wrote another set of letters casting plaintiff in a negative light. The court ruled that the plaintiff had established sufficient questions of fact as to whether the letters were defamatory, and thus summary judgment was denied.

Consider also *Tatur v. Solsrud*, 174 Wis.2d 735, 498 N.W.2d 232 (1993), where a false description of an incumbent politician's voting record on taxes was held not to be defamatory under the Restatement standard quoted above, even though it caused some people not to vote for him. See generally Keeton, supra, § 111; Diamond, Levine, and Madden, supra § 21.02[A]; and Dobbs, supra, § 403.

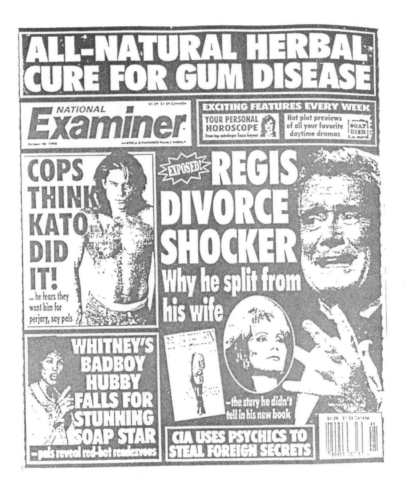

**3. Misleading Headlines.** Consider *Kaelin v. Globe Communications Corp.*, 162 F.3d 1036 (9th Cir.1998) where the plaintiff complained that headlines in the National Examiner, reprinted above, misled readers into thinking that the police thought he had murdered O.J. Simpson's former wife and her friend. The tabloid argued the text of the story clarified the headline. Consider the court's analysis:

* * *

[T]he front page headline consists of two sentences. The first—"COPS THINK KATO DID IT!"—states what the cops supposedly think. The second—"... he fears they want him for perjury, say pals"—is what Kato's pals supposedly said. These two sentences express two different thoughts and are not mutually exclusive.

California courts in libel cases have emphasized that "the publication is to be measured, not so much by its effect when subjected to the critical analysis of a mind trained in the law, but by the natural and probable effect upon the mind of the average reader." *Bates v. Campbell*, 213 Cal. 438, 2 P.2d 383, 385 (Cal. 1931); *see also*

*Corman v. Blanchard*, 211 Cal.App.2d 126, 27 Cal.Rptr. 327, 332 (1962). Since the publication occurred just one week after O.J. Simpson's highly publicized acquittal for murder, we believe that a reasonable person, at that time, might well have concluded that the "it" in the first sentence of the cover and internal headlines referred to the murders. Such a reading of the first sentence is not negated by or inconsistent with the second sentence as a matter of logic, grammar, or otherwise. In our view, an ordinary reader reasonably could have read the headline to mean that the cops think that Kato committed the murders *and* that Kato fears that he is wanted for perjury.

Globe argues that the "it" refers to perjury. Even assuming that such a reading is reasonably possible, it is not the only reading that is reasonably possible as a matter of law. So long as the publication is reasonably susceptible of a defamatory meaning, a factual question for the jury exists. *See Kahn v. Bower*, 232 Cal.App.3d 1599, 284 Cal.Rptr. 244, 249–50 (1991); *Weller v. American Broadcasting Companies, Inc.*, 232 Cal.App.3d 991, 283 Cal.Rptr. 644, 651 (1991).

Globe argues that even if the front page headline could be found to be false and defamatory, the totality of the publication is not. Globe's position is that because the text of the accompanying story is not defamatory, the headline by itself cannot be the basis of a libel action under California law.

\* \* \*

Although California courts have not had occasion to opine on whether a headline alone can be the basis of a libel action, it is certainly clear under California law that headlines are not irrelevant, extraneous, or liability-free zones. They are essential elements of a publication. *See Selleck*, 212 Cal.Rptr. at 844; *Davis v. Hearst*, 160 Cal. 143, 116 P. 530, 549 (Cal.1911).

\* \* \*

Globe argues that the entirety of the publication, including the story itself, clears up any false and defamatory meaning that could be found on the cover. Whether it does or not is a question of fact for the jury. The Kaelin story was located 17 pages away from the cover. In this respect, the National Examiner's front page headline is unlike a conventional headline that immediately precedes a newspaper story, and nowhere does the cover headline reference the internal page where readers could locate the article. A reasonable juror could conclude that the Kaelin article was too far removed from the cover headline to have the salutary effect the Globe claims.

\* \* \*

Viewing the facts in the light most favorable to Kaelin as we are required to do, we hold that Kaelin has come forward with clear and convincing evidence to get to a jury on the issue of whether the headlines are susceptible of a false and defamatory meaning.

\* \* \*

162 F.3d at 1039–1041.

**4. Opinion Versus Fact.** The United States Supreme Court in *Milkovich v. Lorain Journal Co.*, 497 U.S. 1, 110 S.Ct. 2695, 111 L.Ed.2d 1 (1990), declined to endorse a constitutional "privilege" for "opinions" but instead requires courts to determine whether the defendant's statement included or implied factual assertions that can be proven false. Only assertions of fact that can be proven false are subject to liability for defamation. In *Milkovich*, the Supreme Court held that an opinion columnist's assertion that a high school coach had committed perjury when he denied his involvement in his team's rumble with an opposing wrestling team constituted an assertion of fact, since it could be proven right or wrong, despite its placement in an opinion column.

## BINDRIM v. MITCHELL

Court of Appeal, Second District, Division 4, California.
92 Cal.App.3d 61, 155 Cal.Rptr. 29 (1979).

KINGSLEY, J.

This is an appeal taken by Doubleday and Gwen Davis Mitchell from a judgment for damages in favor of plaintiff-respondent Paul Bindrim, Ph.D. The jury returned verdicts on the libel counts against Doubleday and Mitchell and on the contract count against Mitchell.

The court denied defendants' motion for judgment NOV and granted a new trial subject to the condition that new trial would be denied if plaintiff would consent to (1) a reduction of the libel verdict against Mitchell from $38,000 to $25,000; (2) a striking of the $25,000 punitive damage award against Doubleday on the libel count; and (3) a striking of the $12,000 damage award on the contract count against Mitchell.

Plaintiff consented without prejudice on these issues in any appeal to be taken from the judgment. Defendants appealed and plaintiff cross-appealed from the judgment reducing the original jury verdict.

Plaintiff is a licensed clinical psychologist and defendant is an author. Plaintiff used the so-called "Nude Marathon" in group therapy as a means of helping people to shed their psychological inhibitions with the removal of their clothes.

Defendant Mitchell had written a successful best seller in 1969 and had set out to write a novel about women of the leisure class. Mitchell attempted to register in plaintiff's nude therapy but he told her he would not permit her to do so if she was going to write about it in a novel. Plaintiff said she was attending the marathon solely for therapeutic reasons and had no intention of writing about the nude marathon. Plaintiff brought to Mitchell's attention paragraph B of the written contract which reads as follows:

> "The participant agrees that he will not take photographs, write articles, or in any manner disclose who has attended the workshop or what has transpired. If he fails to do so he releases all parties from this contract, but remains legally liable for damages sustained by the leaders and participants."

Mitchell reassured plaintiff again she would not write about the session, she paid her money and the next day she executed the agreement and attended the nude marathon.

Mitchell entered into a contract with Doubleday two months later and was to receive $150,000 advance royalties for her novel.

Mitchell met Eleanor Hoover for lunch and said she was worried because she had signed a contract and painted a devastating portrait of Bindrim.

Mitchell told Doubleday executive McCormick that she had attended a marathon session and it was quite a psychological jolt. The novel was published under the name "Touching" and it depicted a nude encounter session in Southern California led by "Dr. Simon Herford."

Plaintiff first saw the book after its publication and his attorneys sent letters to Doubleday and Mitchell. Nine months later the New American Library published the book in paperback.

The parallel between the actual nude marathon sessions and the sessions in the book "Touching" was shown to the jury by means of the tape recordings Bindrim had taken of the actual sessions. Plaintiff complains in particular about a portrayed session in which he tried to encourage a minister to get his wife to attend the nude marathon. . . .

\* \* \*

Plaintiff asserts that he was libeled by the suggestion that he used obscene language which he did not in fact use. Plaintiff also alleges various other libels due to Mitchell's inaccurate portrayal of what actually happened at the marathon. Plaintiff alleges that he was injured in his profession and expert testimony was introduced showing that Mitchell's portrayal of plaintiff was injurious and that plaintiff was identified by certain colleagues as the character in the book, Simon Herford.

\* \* \*

Appellants claim that, even if there are untrue statements, there is no showing that plaintiff was identified as the character, Simon Herford, in the novel "Touching."

Appellants allege that plaintiff failed to show he was identifiable as Simon Herford, relying on the fact that the character in "Touching" was described in the book as a "fat Santa Claus type with long white hair, white sideburns, a cherubic rosy face and rosy forearms" and that Bindrim was clean shaven and had short hair. Defendants rely in part on *Wheeler v. Dell Publishing Co.* (7th Cir. 1962) 300 F.2d 372, which involved an alleged libel caused by a fictional account of an actual murder trial. The *Wheeler* court said (at p. 376):

> "In our opinion, any reasonable person who read the book and was in a position to identify Hazel Wheeler with Janice Quill would more likely conclude that the author created the latter in an ugly way so that none would identify her with Hazel Wheeler. It is important to note that while the trial and locale might

suggest Hazel Wheeler to those who knew the Chenoweth family, suggestion is not identification. In *Levy* [*Levey v. Warner Bros. Pictures* (S.D.N.Y. 1944) 57 F.Supp. 40] the court said those who had seen her act may have been reminded of her by songs and scenes, but would not reasonably identify her."

However, in *Wheeler* the court found that no one who knew the real widow could possibly identify her with the character in the novel. In the case at bar, the only differences between plaintiff and the Herford character in "Touching" were physical appearance and that Herford was a psychiatrist rather than psychologist. Otherwise, the character Simon Herford was very similar to the actual plaintiff.

\* \* \*

In the case at bar, apart from some of those episodes allegedly constituting the libelous matter itself, and apart from the physical difference and the fact that plaintiff had a Ph.D., and not an M.D., the similarities between Herford and Bindrim are clear, and the transcripts of the actual encounter weekend show a close parallel between the narrative of plaintiff's novel and the actual real life events. Here, there were many similarities between the character, Herford, and the plaintiff Bindrim. . . .

\* \* \*

Defendants contend that the fact that the book was labeled as being a "novel" bars any claim that the writer or publisher could be found to have implied that the characters in the book were factual representations not of the fictional characters but of an actual nonfictional person. That contention, thus broadly stated, is unsupported by the cases. The test is whether a reasonable person, reading the book, would understand that the fictional character therein pictured was, in actual fact, the plaintiff acting as described. (*Middlebrooks v. Curtis Publishing Co.* (4th Cir. 1969) *supra.*, 413 F.2d 141, 143.) Each case must stand on its own facts. In some cases, such as *Greenbelt Pub. Assn. v. Bresler* (1970) *supra.*, 398 U.S. 6, an appellate court can, on examination of the entire work, find that no reasonable person would have regarded the episodes in the book as being other than the fictional imaginings of the author about how the character he had created would have acted. Similarly, in *Hicks v. Casablanca Records* (S.D.N.Y. 1978) 464 F.Supp. 426, a trier of fact was able to find that, considering the work as a whole, no reasonable reader would regard an episode, in a book purporting to be a biography of an actual person, to have been anything more than the author's imaginative explanation of an episode in that person's life about which no actual facts were known. We cannot make any similar determination here. Whether a reader, identifying plaintiff with the "Dr. Herford" of the book, would regard the passages herein complained of as mere fictional embroidering or as reporting actual language and conduct, was for the jury. Its verdict adverse to the defendants cannot be overturned by this court.

\* \* \*

### *NOTES*

**1. Liability for Fiction.** As the principal case indicates, simply labeling a story as fiction is only one factor in determining whether the publisher's statements can be reasonably construed as an assertion of fact subjecting the defendant to potential liability for defamatory assertions.

In an omitted portion of the principal case, the court refers to *Middlebrooks v. Curtis Publishing Co.*, 413 F.2d 141 (4th Cir.1969). In that case, a writer used his boyhood friend's nickname in a fictitious story about a character who resorted to theft to keep up his automobile. Plaintiff initially congratulated the author, but objected to the use of his name when the story was sold to The Saturday Evening Post. The writer renamed the character somewhat, but plaintiff sued for impairment of reputation and subjection to ridicule. The District Court held that although the story was libelous as to the fictitious character, readers could not conclude reasonably that the character was in fact or intended to be, the plaintiff. Nor would it be sufficient to establish a cause of action that someone said he understood that the character depicted the plaintiff. The court cited several countervailing considerations: the story was an obvious work of fiction, there were age and employment differences between plaintiff and the character, and plaintiff was absent at the time of principal events depicted. The court justified the use of actual place names, stating that authors of necessity must rely on their own backgrounds and experiences in writing fiction. Should labeling a book or play fictitious immunize the publisher from liability?

**2. Inducement and Innuendo.** A statement may be defamatory even though its defamatory quality is not immediately apparent. If so, the plaintiff must allege any additional facts necessary to establish the statement's defamatory quality; such allegations are known as the "inducement." The plaintiff must also establish how these facts produce a defamatory meaning, thus proving the "innuendo." For example, if the defendant says A married B yesterday, this would not be defamatory on its face. If, however, A is already currently married to C, the first statement supplemented with this additional information, known to some listener (the inducement), would create the actionable innuendo that A is a bigamist. Where the defendant's statement is sufficiently defamatory on its face, this is called libel per se. Where extrinsic evidence is needed to supplement an otherwise innocuous statement, this is labeled libel per quod. In a minority of states this classification can be significant. See Sec. B, Note 1, infra. See Diamond, Levine & Madden, *Understanding Tort* § 21.02[B] (2nd ed. 2000); Keeton, Prosser and Keeton on *The Law of Torts* § 111 (5th ed. 1984) and Dobbs, *The Law on Torts* § 405.

**3. Interpreting a Defamatory Statement.** In determining whether a statement is defamatory, the court views the statement in context and interprets it as would a reasonable person. The statement must be defamatory according to the Restatement to at least a "substantial and respected minority." Restatement (Second) of Torts § 559, cmt. c. Consider *Agnant v. Shakur*, 30 F.Supp.2d 420 (S.D.N.Y.1998), where plaintiff sued a musician for defamation, claiming defendant's song wrongly accused him of being an undercover federal informant. The court ruled that even if the accusation was unfounded and caused the plaintiff to suffer damages, to be actionable, such libel must hold him up to ridicule or scorn in the minds of "right-thinking persons." The court held the allegation was not defamatory since people who would ridicule someone for legitimately cooperating with law enforcement are not "right-thinking" people.

Consider also *Connelly v. McKay*, 176 Misc. 685, 28 N.Y.S.2d 327 (1941), holding that a false assertion that a restaurant catering to truckers that was reporting vehicle violations to the Interstate Commerce Commission did not constitute defamation despite its obvious potential to injure the restaurant economically. See also Franklin, Anderson and Cate, *Mass Media Law* (6th ed. 2000). In what is obviously a highly controversial application of this standard, courts have allowed defamation actions to proceed based on statements characterizing a plaintiff's sexual orientation. See, e.g., *Matherson v. Marchello*, 100 A.D.2d 233, 473 N.Y.S.2d 998 (N.Y.App.Div.1984).

**4. Colloquium.** In order to be actionable, a defamatory statement must also refer to the plaintiff. If it is not obvious that the statement refers to the plaintiff, the plaintiff must prove "colloquium"—those facts necessary to establish that the statement refers to the plaintiff. For example, if the defendant refers to "Bill," the plaintiff must prove the reference was reasonably understood as referring to him. As in the principal case, proof of colloquium in the context of a novel can be a very contentious and critical issue in the litigation.

**5. Group Defamation.** The common law does not recognize defamation of large groups. Consequently, to defame all lawyers is not actionable. The traditional rule effectively bars defamation liability for ethnic or racial disparagement. Individuals in small groups can generally sue for defamation if all or, in many jurisdictions, a significant unnamed number of the small group is defamed on the theory that each individual in the small group has been hurt by the defamation. In *Neiman-Marcus v. Lait*, 13 F.R.D. 311 (S.D.N.Y.1952), 15 of 25 salesmen sued authors of a book stating "most are fairies" and 30 saleswomen out of 382 sued for a statement suggesting they were prostitutes. The salesmen's action was deemed actionable, but the saleswomen's action was deemed to involve too large a group to be actionable. See Keeton, *Prosser and Keeton on the Law of Torts* § 111 (5th ed. 1984); Diamond, Levine & Madden, *Understanding Torts* § 21.02 (2nd ed. 2000); and Dobbs, *The Law of Torts* § 406 (2000).

# SECTION B.   LIBEL VERSUS SLANDER

There are two kinds of defamation: libel and slander. As the excerpt from the Restatement below explains in more detail, libel includes written defamation while slander includes spoken defamation. The rules applicable to defamation apply equally to libel and slander. The significance of the distinction is that slander, except four categories of slander called slander per se, requires proof of "special" or pecuniary damages as a prerequisite to recovery for nonpecuniary damages including emotional distress. For libel, in most states, there is never any requirement that "special" damages be proven as a prerequisite to recover emotional distress caused by the defamation. After reading the Restatement excerpt below, consider whether the distinction between libel and slander is justified.

# RESTATEMENT (SECOND) OF TORTS*

## § 568. LIBEL AND SLANDER DISTINGUISHED

(1) Libel consists of the publication of defamatory matter by written or printed words, by its embodiment in physical form or by any other form of communication that has the potentially harmful qualities characteristic of written or printed words.

(2) Slander consists of the publication of defamatory matter by spoken words, transitory gestures or by any form of communication other than those stated in Subsection (1).

(3) The area of dissemination, the deliberate and premeditated character of its publication and the persistence of the defamation are factors to be considered in determining whether a publication is a libel rather than a slander.

\* \* \*

b. *Historical note.* It is impossible to define and difficult to describe with precision the two forms of defamation, slander and libel. Oral defamation is tortious if the words spoken fall within a limited class of cases in which the words are actionable per se, or if they cause special damages. Written defamation is actionable per se. For two centuries and a half the common law has treated the tort of defamation in two different ways on a basis of mere form. Yet no respectable authority has ever attempted to justify the distinction on principle; and in modern times, with the discovery of new methods of communication, many courts have condemned the distinction as harsh and unjust. This anomalous and unique distinction is in fact a survival of historical exigencies in the development of the common law jurisdiction over defamation.

Throughout the Middle Ages the ecclesiastical courts exercised general jurisdiction over defamation. It was not until the reign of Henry VIII that the common law courts entered this field. The contest was short and decisive. At the end of the sixteenth century the common law courts had absorbed most of the ecclesiastical jurisdiction in these cases. The common law offered the only remedy then available, an action on the case for words. Certain consequences followed inevitably from the nature of the remedy. Damage, not insult, was the gist of the action; publication to a third person was essential; truth was a defense. Since the defamation then dealt with was still almost without exception oral, the usual designation of the wrong was slander; but there was no distinction in form. The kinds of oral defamation actionable per se, as we now know them, were then developed, not on theoretical grounds of principle, but merely as practical expedients in extending the jurisdiction of the common law courts; they were the classes of slander that the common law courts found it possible by fictions or other expedients to wrest from ecclesiastical jurisdiction. The result was simply that certain types of slander, having certain characteristics and consequences, came within common law jurisdiction; and the remaining types stayed within ecclesiastical jurisdiction.

Meanwhile the Star Chamber had assumed jurisdiction over printing in the interest of the public peace. It undertook to deal with defamation generally. Its practice, so far as known, was not always consistent, but it did develop a definite attitude toward libels, which exercised vast influence in later times. Adapting the Roman criminal law (first reported by Coke in 1609 in the case De Libellis Famois, 5 Co.Rep. 125, 77 Eng.Rep. 250) applicable to pasquinades, which, being in their nature anonymous and scurrilous, were regarded as peculiarly dangerous, the Star Chamber introduced into English law for the first time a new type of defamation based upon mere form. But in the Roman law the crime was based, not upon the form of the publication, but upon the character of the matter published, its anonymous nature and the extent of its diffusion. It is apparent that the Star Chamber adopted the Roman law without regard to Roman limitations and with certain additions of its own, chief among which was the fundamental principle that a libel is punishable as a crime because it tends to a breach of the peace. The latter ground alone involved consequences that distinguished it from the common law doctrine. Truth was no defense, for injuries should be redressed in the courts, not avenged by defamation. Publication to a third person was not essential, for communication to the person defamed was more likely to provoke a breach of the peace.

When the Star Chamber was abolished in 1641, the common law courts succeeded to its jurisdiction in defamation. The offense became a common law misdemeanor, the wrong a tort. The characteristics of the tort required definition. The limited scope of the common law doctrine of slander was wholly inadequate in such turbulent times as a general doctrine. Influenced, probably, by the breach-of-the-peace theory of the Star Chamber, the common law courts after the Restoration held that libel, as distinguished from slander, was a wrongful act from which damage would be presumed, thus fixing upon the law a distinction in form. This rule was first announced in 1670 by Hale, who said: "Although such general words spoken once without writing or publishing them would not be actionable, yet here, they being writ and published, which contains more malice than if they had been once spoken, they are actionable." This view was subsequently followed by Holt and Hardwicke, and was finally settled in 1812 on the ground that the doctrine, although indefensible in principle, was too well established to be repudiated. A generation later a committee of the leading English judges of the day advised Parliament on certain methods of reforming the law of defamation. Among other things they recommended the abolition of the distinction in form, "which rests upon no solid foundation." And there it still rests.

\* \* \*

d. *When publication libel, when slander.* The publication of defamatory matter by written or printed words constitutes a libel. Common methods of publishing a libel are by newspapers, books, magazines, letters, circulars and petitions. The writing or printing may be made upon paper, parchment, metal, wood, stone or any other substance and may be accomplished by the use of pencil, pen, chalk or a mechanical device such as the printing press, typewriter, or mimeographing machine. Defamatory pictures, caricatures, statues and effigies are libels because the defamatory publication is embodied in physical form. There are, however, other methods of publishing a libel. The wide area of dissemination, the fact that a record of the publication is made with some substantial degree of permanence and the deliberation and premeditation of the defamer are important factors for the court to consider in determining whether a particular communication is to be treated as a libel rather than a slander. The publication of defamatory matter may be made by conduct which by reason of its persistence it may be more appropriate to treat as a libel than a slander. On the other hand, the use of a mere transitory gesture commonly understood as a substitute for spoken words such as a nod of the head, a wave of the hand or a sign of the fingers is a slander rather than a libel.

**Illustrations:**

1. A procures two men to "shadow" B. They follow him from one public place to another until the "shadowing" becomes notorious in the community. A has libeled B.

2. A makes a gesture with his fingers in the presence of B which indicates that C has the "evil eye," a characterization that is highly disparaging in the community. A has slandered but not libeled C.

3. A prepares a wax figure recognizable as a representation of B and places it among a number of effigies of famous murderers in "The Chamber of Horrors," where it is seen by a number of persons. A has libeled B.

e. *Reading aloud defamatory writing.* A publication of a libel may be made by reading aloud a defamatory writing. In this case, although the third person obtains knowledge of the defamatory imputation by hearing it, nevertheless the fact that the reader has given publicity to matter already recorded in permanent form is sufficient to make his conduct libelous as well as slanderous. It is not material that the person who hears the reading does or does not know that a writing is being read.

f. *Oral communication to be written down.* A publication of a libel may be made by an oral communication that is intended to be, and is, reduced to writing. Thus one who dictates to a stenographer a letter that defames a third person may become liable for libel on the basis of the oral communication when the stenographer takes it down, even though no other person sees it. The same is true when a message is telephoned to a telegraph office where it is reduced to writing, or when a statement is given orally to a newspaper reporter and is published in the paper. In this case the oral communication takes on the character of libel because of the intended and actual embodiment in permanent form.

\* \* \*

h. *Concurrence of various factors important in distinction between libel and slander.* In doubtful cases, it is not always necessary that all the factors stated in Subsection (3) concur in order for a publication of a defamatory communication to be regarded as libel rather than slander. Any one of these factors or the concurrence of less than all of them may in a particular case be of sufficient importance to make it proper for the publication to be regarded as libelous. On the other hand, the existence of all of the factors may not be sufficient invariably to induce the court to regard the publication as a libel. The importance of the factors stated will depend upon the circumstances of each particular case.

## § 568A. RADIO AND TELEVISION

Broadcasting of defamatory matter by means of radio or television is libel, whether or not it is read from a manuscript.

Comment:

a. This Section is a special application of the rule stated in § 568, under which defamation by any form of communication that has the potentially harmful qualities characteristic of written or printed words is to be treated as libel. The wide dissemination that results from broadcasting over radio and television, together with the prestige and potential effect upon the public mind of a standardized means of publication that many people tend automatically to accept as conveying truth, are such as to put the broadcaster upon the same footing as the publisher of a newspaper.

b. The rule stated in this Section is regulated by statute in a number of states. Some of these statutes have provided that radio or television broadcasting of defamatory matter constitutes libel; others provide that it constitutes slander.

## § 569. LIABILITY WITHOUT PROOF OF SPECIAL HARM—LIBEL

One who falsely publishes matter defamatory of another in such a manner as to make the publication a libel is subject to liability to the other although no special harm results from the publication.

## § 570. LIABILITY WITHOUT PROOF OF SPECIAL HARM—SLANDER

One who publishes matter defamatory to another in such a manner as to make the publication a slander is subject to liability to the other although no special harm results if the publication imputes to the other

(a) a criminal offense . . . or

(b) a loathsome disease . . . or

(c) matter incompatible with his business, trade, profession, or office . . . or

(d) serious sexual misconduct. . . .

## § 575. SLANDER CREATING LIABILITY BECAUSE OF SPECIAL HARM

One who publishes a slander that, although not actionable per se, is the legal cause of special harm to the person defamed, is subject to liability to him.

Comment:

* * *

*b. Special harm.* Special harm, as the words are used in this Chapter, is the loss of something having economic or pecuniary value. In its origin, this goes back to the ancient conflict of jurisdiction between the royal and the ecclesiastical courts, in which the former acquired jurisdiction over some kinds of defamation only because they could be found to have resulted in "temporal" rather than "spiritual" damage. The limitation has persisted in the requirement that special harm, to serve as the foundation of an action for slander that is not actionable per se, must be "temporal," "material," pecuniary or economic in character.

The more modern decisions have shown some tendency to liberalize the old rule, and to find pecuniary loss when the plaintiff has been deprived of benefit which has a more or less indirect financial value to him. Thus the loss of the society, companionship and association of friends may be sufficient when their hospitality or assistance has been such that it can be found to have a money value. The tendency has been in the direction of finding an indirect benefit to be sufficient.

Special harm must result from the conduct of a person other than the defamer or the one defamed and must be legally caused by the defamation. It is, however, immaterial whether the harmful action is taken because the person who takes it believes the defamation, or because he is unwilling to deal or to associate with one whose reputation has been impaired by it. Loss of reputation alone is not enough to make the defamer liable under the rule stated in this Section unless it is reflected in some kind of economic or pecuniary loss. So too, lowered social standing and its purely social consequences are not sufficient. Thus the fact that a slander has caused the person defamed to lose caste in the eyes of his friends and so has deprived him of many pleasant social contacts is not special harm. If, however, the loss of reputation results in material loss capable of being measured in money, the fact that the lowered social standing resulting from the slander itself causes the acts that produce the loss does not prevent the tangible loss from being special harm. Thus, while a slander that has been so widely disseminated as to cause persons previously friendly to the plaintiff to refuse social intercourse with him is not of itself special harm, the loss of the material advantages of their hospitality is sufficient. Special harm may be a loss of presently existing advantage, as a discharge from employment. It may also be a failure to realize a reasonable expectation of gain, as the denial of employment which, but for the currency of the slander, the plaintiff would have received. It is not necessary that he be legally entitled to receive the benefits that are denied to him because of the slander. It is enough that the slander has disappointed his reasonable expectation of receiving a gratuity.

## § 623.  EMOTIONAL DISTRESS AND RESULTING BODILY HARM

One who is liable to another for a libel or slander is liable also for emotional distress and bodily harm that is proved to have been caused by the defamatory publication.

Comment:

a.  As stated in § 575, Comment c, neither emotional distress nor bodily harm resulting from it is special harm sufficient to support an action for a slander that is not actionable per se. If, however, the defamation is slander actionable per se or libel or there is proof of special harm as described in § 575, Comment b, the emotional distress caused by it and any physical harm resulting from the distress are elements of the damages recoverable.

### NOTES

**1.  Minority Position.** A minority of states, in addition to requiring special damages for slander (excluding the four categories of slander per se), also require proof of special damages for libel per quod. As noted earlier (see Note 2, Sec. A, on page 705, supra), libel per quod constitutes libel (written defamation) which is not defamatory on its face but requires extrinsic evidence to supplement the defendant's statement to create a defamatory meaning. This is in contrast to libel per se, which is defamatory on its face and which in all jurisdictions does not require proof of special damages.

Consider, for example, *Aycock v. Padgett*, 134 N.C.App. 164, 516 S.E.2d 907 (1999), where a losing candidate for a political seat brought a defamation suit in response to a public allegation that he was not a resident of the town in which he was running for office. The court concluded special damages (which were not established) were required since the accusation was only libel per quod and not libel per se. The accusation of being a nonresident was not defamatory on its face but required extrinsic knowledge that the victim was a candidate and knowledge that election law required a candidate to be a town resident.

**2.  Policy Issues.** Should special damages be required for slander as a prerequisite to recovery? Is libel necessarily more damaging or serious than slander? Do the slander per se exceptions make sense to you?

# SECTION C.  PUBLICATION

## WEIDMAN v. KETCHAM
Court of Appeals of New York.
278 N.Y. 129, 15 N.E.2d 426 (1938).

RIPPEY, J.

This action was brought to recover damages for libel. After a verdict was rendered for plaintiff, a motion by defendant to set it aside was granted and defendant's motion to dismiss the complaint at the close of plaintiff's case and renewed at the close of all the evidence, upon which decision had been reserved, was granted. The Appellate Division reversed the judgment entered for defendant and reinstated the verdict. Defendant does not question here that there was sufficient evidence to warrant the jury to find that the written words constituted a libel. He asserts that there was no evidence of publication, without which no action will lie.

There can be no actionable libel unless the defamatory writing, through some act or the carelessness of the defendant, is read by or otherwise communicated to someone other than the person defamed who understood its meaning and knew to whom it referred (*Youmans v. Smith*, 153 N. Y. 214, 218; *Snyder v. Andrews*, 6 Barb. 43, 46; *Ostrowe v. Lee*, 256 N. Y. 36, 38; Townshend on Slander and Libel [4th ed.], § 95; Seelman on the Law of Libel and Slander, § 121). The author may directly publish it. He may read it and give information as to whom it relates to a third party. He may treat the writing in such a way that the natural or reasonably expected result will be that it will come into the hands of a third party before it reaches the person defamed. He might then be required to pay for his improper conduct if the writing is defamatory, malicious, untrue, and not privileged. But if he keeps the writing to himself or communicates it only to the one to whom it relates, there is no publication upon which any suit for damages may be based. Plaintiff set forth in his complaint and attempted to establish at the trial that the libel was published within the meaning of the above (1) at the post office at Schoharie, New York, and (2) at the home of the plaintiff. The question as to whether there was publication at either place was submitted to the jury. It is necessary to consider the testimony in its aspect most favorable to the plaintiff to determine whether or not there was evidence of publication of the libel at either place.

For evidence that the libel was published at the post office, plaintiff must rely on the testimony of the postmaster and that of defendant. If the jury discarded that, there was no evidence concerning the happenings in the post office. The following appeared from their testimony. The defendant was the assistant postmaster at Schoharie, New York. Early in the morning of October 8, 1934, he wrote upon a postcard which was addressed to the plaintiff at Esperance, New York, the following words: "You want to come and pay for those apples that you have stole out of my orchard or I will have you arrested. Yours, Elmer Ketcham." The postmaster was present in the office at the time the writing was done but was from fifteen to eighteen feet from defendant and did not see the writing on the card. No other person was present. Defendant said to the postmaster that he was sending a card to a man who had been in his orchard stealing apples. The postmaster did not see the address on the card and was not told to whom it was to be sent, nor was the name of any person mentioned. Defendant was either told by the postmaster or decided for himself that the card should not be sent through the mail without being inclosed in an envelope. He thereupon procured a stamped envelope, placed the postcard in the envelope, sealed the envelope and addressed it to the plaintiff. There is no evidence that the postmaster saw the address on the envelope or knew to whom it was to be sent. Defendant's duties were to make up the mail that left the post office each morning in bundles and put them in the mailbag for delivery. He took the sealed envelope, placed it in a bundle with other mail matter, placed the bundle in a bag for delivery and gave the bag to the carrier. Without evidence that the postmaster knew to whom the defamatory card or its containing envelope was addressed or to whom it referred, there was no publication within the meaning of that requirement in the law of defamation (*Miller v. Maxwell*, 16 Wend. 9; *Northrop v. Tibbles*, 215 Fed. Rep. 99). It is asserted that the jury might infer the postmaster knew and must have known to whom the card was sent. The evidence may have furnished food for speculation. But imagination and speculation are no substitute for proof. From the evidence here adduced, the jury could not infer the essential fact that the postmaster knew to whom the libel referred. . . .

### NOTES

**1. Requirement of Publication.** In order to establish defamation, the plaintiff must prove that the defamatory statement concerning the plaintiff was "published." Publication, in the context of a defamation suit, means that the statement was intentionally or negligently communicated to someone besides the defamed party. See Restatement (Second) of Torts § 577. See Diamond, Levine & Madden, *Understanding Torts* § 21.02 (2nd ed. 2000); Keeton, *Prosser and Keeton on the Law of Torts* § 111 (5th ed. 1984); Dobbs, *The Law of Torts* § 402 (2000).

**2. Republication.** A defendant may be held liable for defamation even where she properly attributes the statement to another source. Thus, if D, a newspaper reporter, hears from X that X witnessed P commit murder, when in fact this is not true, D may be liable for defamation if she publishes an article to the effect that, "according to a witness, P committed murder." There are, however, privileges to republish, such as fair reporting of a public meeting or proceeding, that are discussed infra Sec. E.

# SECTION D.  CONSTITUTIONAL CULPABILITY REQUIREMENT

## NEW YORK TIMES CO. v. SULLIVAN

Supreme Court of the United States.
376 U.S. 254, 84 S.Ct. 710, 11 L.Ed.2d 686 (1964).

Mr. Justice BRENNAN delivered the opinion of the Court.

We are required in this case to determine for the first time the extent to which the constitutional protections for speech and press limit a State's power to award damages in a libel action brought by a public official against critics of his official conduct.

Respondent L. B. Sullivan is one of the three elected Commissioners of the City of Montgomery, Alabama. He testified that he was "Commissioner of Public Affairs and the duties are supervision of the Police

Department, Fire Department, Department of Cemetery and Department of Scales." He brought this civil libel action against the four individual petitioners, who are Negroes and Alabama clergymen, and against petitioner the New York Times Company, a New York corporation which publishes the New York Times, a daily newspaper. A jury in the Circuit Court of Montgomery County awarded him damages of $500,000, the full amount claimed, against all the petitioners, and the Supreme Court of Alabama affirmed. 273 Ala. 656, 144 So.2d 25.

Respondent's complaint alleged that he had been libeled by statements in a full-page advertisement that was carried in the New York Times on March 29, 1960.[1] . . .

The text appeared over the names of 64 persons, many widely known for their activities in public affairs, religion, trade unions, and the performing arts. Below these names, and under a line reading "We in the south who are struggling daily for dignity and freedom warmly endorse this appeal," appeared the names of the four individual petitioners and of 16 other persons, all but two of whom were identified as clergymen in various Southern cities. The advertisement was signed at the bottom of the page by the "Committee to Defend Martin Luther King and the Struggle for Freedom in the South," and the officers of the Committee were listed.

\* \* \*

It is uncontroverted that some of the statements contained in the two paragraphs were not accurate descriptions of events which occurred in Montgomery. Although Negro students staged a demonstration on the State Capital steps, they sang the National Anthem and not "My Country, 'Tis of Thee." Although nine students were expelled by the State Board of Education, this was not for leading the demonstration at the Capitol, but for demanding service at a lunch counter in the Montgomery County Courthouse on another day. Not the entire student body, but most of it, had protested the expulsion, not by refusing to register, but by boycotting classes on a single day; virtually all the students did register for the ensuing semester. The campus dining hall was not padlocked on any occasion, and the only students who may have been barred from eating there were the few who had neither signed a preregistration application nor requested temporary meal tickets. Although the police were deployed near the campus in large numbers on three occasions, they did not at any time "ring" the campus, and they were not called to the campus in connection with the demonstration on the State Capitol steps, as the third paragraph implied. Dr. King had not been arrested seven times, but only four; and although he claimed to have been assaulted some years earlier in connection with his arrest for loitering outside a courtroom, one of the officers who made the arrest denied that there was such an assault.

\* \* \*

1. A copy of the advertisement is printed in the Appendix, pages 740 and 741.

The general proposition that freedom of expression upon public questions is secured by the First Amendment has long been settled by our decisions. The constitutional safeguard, we have said, "was fashioned to assure unfettered interchange of ideas for the bringing about of political and social changes desired by the people." *Roth v. United States*, 354 U.S. 476, 484, 77 S.Ct. 1304, 1308, 1 L.Ed.2d 1498. "The maintenance of the opportunity for free political discussion to the end that government may be responsive to the will of the people and that changes may be obtained by lawful means, an opportunity essential to the security of the Republic, is a fundamental principle of our constitutional system." *Stromberg v. California*, 283 U.S. 359, 369, 51 S.Ct. 532, 536, 75 L.Ed. 1117. "(I)t is a prized American privilege to speak one's mind, although not always with perfect good taste, on all public institutions," *Bridges v. California*, 314 U.S. 252, 270, 62 S.Ct. 190, 197, 86 L.Ed. 192, and this opportunity is to be afforded for "vigorous advocacy" no less than "abstract discussion." *N.A.A.C.P. v. Button*, 371 U.S. 415, 429, 83 S.Ct. 328, 9 L.Ed.2d 405. The First Amendment, said Judge Learned Hand, "presupposes that right conclusions are more likely to be gathered out of a multitude of tongues, than through any kind of authoritative selection. To many this is, and always will be, folly; but we have staked upon it our all." *United States v. Associated Press*, 52 F.Supp. 362, 372 (D.C.S.D.N.Y.1943).

Thus we consider this case against the background of a profound national commitment to the principle that debate on public issues should be uninhibited, robust, and wide-open, and that it may well include vehement, caustic, and sometimes unpleasantly sharp attacks on government and public officials. See *Terminiello v. Chicago*, 337 U.S. 1, 4, 69 S.Ct. 894, 93 L.Ed. 1131; *De Jonge v. Oregon*, 299 U.S. 353, 365, 57 S.Ct. 255, 81 L.Ed. 278. The present advertisement, as an expression of grievance and protest on one of the major public issues of our time, would seem clearly to qualify for the constitutional protection. The question is whether it forfeits that protection by the falsity of some of its factual statements and by its alleged defamation of respondent.

\* \* \*

A rule compelling the critic of official conduct to guarantee the truth of all his factual assertions—and to do so on pain of libel judgments virtually unlimited in amount—leads to a comparable "self-censorship." Allowance of the defense of truth, with the burden of proving it on the defendant, does not mean that only false speech will be deterred. Even courts accepting this defense as an adequate safeguard have recognized the difficulties of adducing legal proofs that the alleged libel was true in all its factual particulars. See, e.g., *Post Publishing Co. v. Hallam*, 59 F. 530, 540 (C.A.6th Cir. 1893); see also Noel, Defamation of Public Officers and Candidates, 49 Col.L.Rev. 875, 892 (1949). Under such a rule, would-be critics of official conduct may be deterred from voicing their criticism, even though it is believed to be true and even though it is in fact true, because of doubt whether it can be proved in court or fear of the expense of having to do so. They tend to make only statements which "steer far wider of the unlawful zone." *Speiser v. Randall, supra*, 357 U.S., at 526,

78 S.Ct. at 1342, 2 L.Ed.2d 1460. The rule thus dampens the vigor and limits the variety of public debate. It is inconsistent with the First and Fourteenth Amendments.

The constitutional guarantees require, we think, a federal rule that prohibits a public official from recovering damages for a defamatory falsehood relating to his official conduct unless he proves that the statement was made with "actual malice"—that is, with knowledge that it was false or with reckless disregard of whether it was false or not. . . .

\* \* \*

Applying these standards, we consider that the proof presented to show actual malice lacks the convincing clarity which the constitutional standard demands, and hence that it would not constitutionally sustain the judgment for respondent under the proper rule of law. The case of the individual petitioners requires little discussion. Even assuming that they could constitutionally be found to have authorized the use of their names on the advertisement, there was no evidence whatever that they were aware of any erroneous statements or were in any way reckless in that regard. The judgment against them is thus without constitutional support.

As to the Times, we similarly conclude that the facts do not support a finding of actual malice. The statement by the Times' Secretary that, apart from the padlocking allegation, he thought the advertisement was "substantially correct," affords no constitutional warrant for the Alabama Supreme Court's conclusion that it was a "cavalier ignoring of the falsity of the advertisement (from which), the jury could not have but been impressed with the bad faith of The Times, and its maliciousness inferable therefrom." The statement does not indicate malice at the time of the publication; even if the advertisement was not "substantially correct"—although respondent's own proofs tend to show that it was—that opinion was at least a reasonable one, and there was no evidence to impeach the witness' good faith in holding it. The Times' failure to retract upon respondent's demand, although it later retracted upon the demand of Governor Patterson, is likewise not adequate evidence of malice for constitutional purposes. . . .

Finally, there is evidence that the Times published the advertisement without checking its accuracy against the news stories in the Times' own files. The mere presence of the stories in the files does not, of course, establish that the Times "knew" the advertisement was false, since the state of mind required for actual malice would have to be brought home to the persons in the Times' organization having responsibility for the publication of the advertisement. With respect to the failure of those persons to make the check, the record shows that they relied upon their knowledge of the good reputation of many of those whose names were listed as sponsors of the advertisement, and upon the letter from A. Philip Randolph, known to them as a responsible individual, certifying that the use of the names was authorized.

\* \* \*

The judgment of the Supreme Court of Alabama is reversed and the case is remanded to that court for further proceedings not inconsistent with this opinion.

Reversed and remanded.

---

THE NEW YORK TIMES, TUESDAY, MARCH 29, 1960.　　　　　　　L.　　25

[APPENDIX.]

*"The growing movement of peaceful mass demonstrations by Negroes is something new in the South, something understandable.... Let Congress heed their rising voices, for they will be heard."*

—*New York Times editorial
Saturday, March 19, 1960*

# Heed Their Rising Voices

As the whole world knows by now, thousands of Southern Negro students are engaged in widespread non-violent demonstrations in positive affirmation of the right to live in human dignity as guaranteed by the U. S. Constitution and the Bill of Rights. In their efforts to uphold these guarantees, they are being met by an unprecedented wave of terror by those who would deny and negate that document which the whole world looks upon as setting the pattern for modern freedom. ...

In Orangeburg, South Carolina, when 400 students peacefully sought to buy doughnuts and coffee at lunch counters in the business district, they were forcibly ejected, tear-gassed, soaked to the skin in freezing weather with fire hoses, arrested en masse and herded into an open barbed-wire stockade to stand for hours in the bitter cold.

In Montgomery, Alabama, after students sang "My Country, 'Tis of Thee" on the State Capitol steps, their leaders were expelled from school, and truckloads of police armed with shotguns and tear-gas ringed the Alabama State College Campus. When the entire student body protested to state authorities by refusing to re-register, their dining hall was padlocked in an attempt to starve them into submission.

In Tallahassee, Atlanta, Nashville, Savannah, Greensboro, Memphis, Richmond, Charlotte, and a host of other cities in the South, young American teenagers, in face of the entire weight of official state apparatus and police power, have boldly stepped forth as protagonists of democracy. Their courage and amazing restraint have inspired millions and given a new dignity to the cause of freedom.

Small wonder that the Southern violators of the Constitution fear this new, non-violent brand of freedom fighter ... even as they fear the upswelling right-to-vote movement. Small wonder that they are determined to destroy the one man who, more than any other, symbolizes the new spirit now sweeping the South—the Rev. Dr. Martin Luther King, Jr., world-famous leader of the Montgomery Bus Protest. For it is his doctrine of non-violence which has inspired and guided the students in their widening wave of sit-ins; and it is this same Dr. King who founded and is president of the Southern Christian Leadership Conference—the organization which is spearheading the surging right-to-vote movement. Under Dr. King's direction the Leadership Conference conducts Student Workshops and Seminars in the philosophy and technique of non-violent resistance.

Again and again the Southern violators have answered Dr. King's peaceful protests with intimidation and violence. They have bombed his home almost killing his wife and child. They have assaulted his person. They have arrested him seven times—for "speeding," "loitering" and similar "offenses." And now they have charged him with "perjury"—a felony under which they could imprison him for ten years. Obviously, their real purpose is to remove him physically as the leader to whom the students and millions of others—look for guidance and support, and thereby to intimidate all leaders who may rise in the South. Their strategy is to behead this affirmative movement, and thus to demoralize Negro Americans and weaken their will to struggle. The defense of Martin Luther King, spiritual leader of the student sit-in movement, clearly, therefore, is an integral part of the total struggle for freedom in the South.

Decent-minded Americans cannot help but applaud the creative daring of the students and the quiet heroism of Dr. King. But this is one of those moments in the stormy history of Freedom when men and women of good will must do more than applaud the rising-to-glory of others. The America whose good name hangs in the balance before a watchful world, the America whose heritage of Liberty these Southern Upholders of the Constitution are defending, is our America as well as theirs ...

We must heed their rising voices—yes—but we must add our own.

We must extend ourselves above and beyond moral support and render the material help so urgently needed by those who are taking the risks, facing jail, and even death in a glorious re-affirmation of our Constitution and its Bill of Rights.

We urge you to join hands with our fellow Americans in the South by supporting, with your dollars, this Combined Appeal for all three needs—the defense of Martin Luther King—the support of the embattled students—and the struggle for the right-to-vote.

## Your Help Is Urgently Needed . . . NOW!!

| | | | |
|---|---|---|---|
| Stella Adler | Dr. Alan Knight Chalmers | Anthony Franciosa | John Killens | L. Joseph Overton | Maureen Stapleton |
| Raymond Pace Alexander | Richard Coe | Lorraine Hansbury | Eartha Kitt | Clarence Pickett | Frank Silvera |
| Harry Van Arsdale | Nat King Cole | Rev. Donald Harrington | Rabbi Edward Klein | Shad Polier | Hope Stevens |
| Harry Belafonte | Cheryl Crawford | Nat Hentoff | Hope Lange | Sidney Poitier | George Tabori |
| Julie Belafonte | Dorothy Dandridge | James Hicks | John Lewis | A. Philip Randolph | Rev. Gardner C. |
| Dr. Algernon Black | Ossie Davis | Mary Hinkson | Viveca Lindfors | John Raitt | Taylor |
| Nora Blatzein | Sammy Davis, Jr. | Van Heflin | Carl Murphy | Elmer Rice | Norman Thomas |
| William Branch | Ruby Dee | Langston Hughes | Don Murray | Jackie Robinson | Kenneth Tynan |
| Marlon Brando | Dr. Philip Elliott | Morris Iushewitz | John Murray | Mrs. Eleanor Roosevelt | Charles White |
| Mrs. Ralph Bunche | Dr. Harry Emerson | Mahalia Jackson | A. J. Muste | Bayard Rustin | Shelley Winters |
| Diahann Carroll | Fosdick | Mordecai Johnson | Frederick O'Neal | Robert Ryan | Max Youngstein |

*We in the south who are struggling daily for dignity and freedom warmly endorse this appeal*

| | | | |
|---|---|---|---|
| Rev. Ralph D. Abernathy *(Montgomery, Ala.)* | Rev. Matthew D. McCollom *(Orangeburg, S. C.)* | Rev. Walter L. Hamilton *(Norfolk, Va.)* | Rev. A. L. Davis *(New Orleans, La.)* |
| Rev. Fred L. Shuttlesworth *(Birmingham, Ala.)* | Rev. William Holmes Borders *(Atlanta, Ga.)* | I. S. Levy *(Columbia, S. C.)* | Mrs. Katie E. Whickham *(New Orleans, La.)* |
| Rev. Kelley Miller Smith *(Nashville, Tenn.)* | | Rev. Martin Luther King, Sr. *(Atlanta, Ga.)* | Rev. W. H. Hall *(Hattiesburg, Miss.)* |
| Rev. W. A. Dennis *(Chattanooga, Tenn.)* | Rev. Douglas Moore *(Durham, N. C.)* | Rev. Henry C. Bunton *(Memphis, Tenn.)* | Rev. J. E. Lowery *(Mobile, Ala.)* |
| Rev. C. K. Steele *(Tallahassee, Fla.)* | Rev. Wyatt Tee Walker *(Petersburg, Va.)* | Rev. S. S. Seay, Sr. *(Montgomery, Ala.)* | Rev. T. J. Jemison *(Baton Rouge, La.)* |
| | | Rev. Samuel W. Williams *(Atlanta, Ga.)* | |

**COMMITTEE TO DEFEND MARTIN LUTHER KING AND THE STRUGGLE FOR FREEDOM IN THE SOUTH**
312 West 125th Street, New York 27, N. Y. UNiversity 6-1700

*Chairmen:* A. Philip Randolph, Dr. Gardner C. Taylor; *Chairmen of Cultural Division:* Harry Belafonte, Sidney Poitier; *Treasurer:* Nat King Cole; *Executive Director:* Bayard Rustin; *Chairman of Church Division:* Father George B. Ford, Rev. Harry Emerson Fosdick, Rev. Thomas Kilgore, Jr., Rabbi Edward E. Klein; *Chairman of Labor Division:* Morris Iushewitz.

*Please mail this coupon TODAY!*

╔══════════════════════════════╗
**Committee To Defend Martin Luther King**
**and**
**The Struggle For Freedom In The South**
312 West 125th Street, New York 27, N. Y.
UNiversity 6-1700

I am enclosing my contribution of $.......
for the work of the Committee.

Name ...........................
(PLEASE PRINT)

Address .........................

City .......... Zone .... State ....

☐ I want to help　☐ Please send further information

*Please make checks payable to:*
**Committee To Defend Martin Luther King**
╚══════════════════════════════╝

## NOTES

**1. Defamation of a Public Official.** In order for a defamation plaintiff who is a public official to recover damages, she must prove that the defendant acted with actual or *"New York Times"* malice. The plaintiff must prove *New York Times* malice in addition to the ordinary common law elements of defamation. The malice element is satisfied where the plaintiff proves by clear and convincing evidence, a more demanding standard than the preponderance standard generally applicable to civil cases, that the defendant either had actual knowledge that the statement was false or acted recklessly in not ascertaining whether it was false. While the protection may apply to all defendants, the Supreme Court has never expressly extended the *New York Times* rule beyond media defendants. See *Philadelphia Newspapers, Inc. v. Hepps*, 475 U.S. 767, 106 S.Ct. 1558, 89 L.Ed.2d 783 (1986), noting court had never ruled on this question. See also *Hutchinson v. Proxmire*, 443 U.S. 111, 99 S.Ct. 2675, 61 L.Ed.2d 411 (1979), fn. 16.

The Supreme Court's use of the term "actual malice" is potentially confusing since the term has traditionally been defined to mean ill-will, hatred, or reckless disregard toward the rights of the victim. This traditional definition of common law malice is used to establish the malice required for punitive damages. See Chapter 5, Sec. C, supra. It is important to recognize that it is *New York Times* malice and not the common law definition of malice that is required to satisfy the constitutionally required culpability for a public official to recover for defamation. Common law malice is still used to establish punitive damages once the basic elements of the tort and the *New York Times* malice standard are met.

In *St. Amant v. Thompson*, 390 U.S. 727, 88 S.Ct. 1323, 20 L.Ed.2d 262 (1968), the Supreme Court defined "recklessness" in ascertaining whether the statement was false to mean that "the defendant in fact entertained serious doubts as to the truth of the publication." Consequently, under the *New York Times* standard, the defendant must know the statement is false or subjectively entertain serious doubts as to its truth. This subjective element justifies discovery into the thought processes of the journalist. See *Herbert v. Lando*, 441 U.S. 153, 99 S.Ct. 1635, 60 L.Ed.2d 115 (1979), allowing plaintiff lawyer to ask defendants, journalists whose report on CBS's "60 Minutes" allegedly defamed the plaintiff, a military officer, questions concerning the state of mind of the journalists while preparing the report. See Diamond, Levine & Madden, *Understanding Torts* § 21.02 (2nd ed. 2000). See also Keeton, *Prosser and Keeton on the Law of Torts* § 111 (5th ed. 1984); Dobbs, *The Law of Torts* § 417–419 (2000).

**2. Determining Who is a Public Official.** The First Amendment protections afforded by the principal case are not triggered unless the plaintiff is a public official, the rationale being that parties should be able to speak freely in criticizing the government. Public officials are generally those who are in a position to shape government policy. This would include politicians such as members of congress, city mayors, and county commissioners. But the lower the official's position in the governmental hierarchy, the less likely he would be considered a public official for the purpose of bringing the case within the ambit of *Sullivan*. See Diamond, Levine & Madden, supra, § 21.03. In *Staheli v. Smith*, 548 So.2d 1299 (Miss.1989), a college professor at a state university who had been denied tenure sued the dean for defamation based on statements made by the dean recommending against his nomination. The court ruled that the professor, though a public employee, was not in that class of higher-level decision-making public employees that required proof of *New York Times* malice. Interestingly, police officers, given public interest in their performance, are often characterized as public officials. In *Kassel v. Gannett Co.*, 875 F.2d 935 (1st Cir.1989), the court, in determining that a staff psychologist employed by the Veteran's Administration was not a public official, listed as factors in its evaluation whether the government position is important enough to warrant public interest in the official's qualification, the official has access to the media and the official assumed the risk of public criticism.

Should candidates for public office also be considered public officials in defamation cases? Consider *Monitor Patriot Co. v. Roy*, 401 U.S. 265, 91 S.Ct. 621, 28 L.Ed.2d 35 (1971), where a newspaper referred to a senatorial candidate as a "former small-time bootlegger." The Supreme Court held that statements bearing on a candidate's fitness for public office were entitled to constitutional protection.

**3. Evaluating the Standard.** Most professionals are evaluated by a negligence standard. As a result of the *New York Times* standard, only conscious intentional or reckless conduct leads to liability for journalists who defame public officials. Given the sensationalism and irresponsibility of some media coverage, do you think the *New York Times* standard provides the media too much protection? Would liability for negligence excessively chill free speech?

**4. Criticism Against Government.** The *Sullivan* decision also held it was unconstitutional for government agencies to sue for defamation. Since the plaintiff commissioner in the *Sullivan* case was not personally attacked in the *New York Times* advertisement, the court characterized his defamation action as an attempt to "sidestep this obstacle by transmuting criticism of the government, however impersonal it may seem on its face, into personal criticism, and hence potential libel, of the officials of whom the government is composed." This constituted another basis for reversal.

## GERTZ v. ROBERT WELCH, INC.
Supreme Court of the United States.
418 U.S. 323, 94 S.Ct. 2997, 41 L.Ed.2d 789, (1974).

Mr. Justice POWELL delivered the opinion of the Court.

This Court has struggled for nearly a decade to define the proper accommodation between the law of defamation and the freedoms of speech and press protected by the First Amendment. With this decision we return to that effort. We granted certiorari to reconsider the extent of a publisher's constitutional privilege against liability for defamation of a private citizen. 410 U.S. 925, 93 S.Ct. 1355, 35 L.Ed.2d 585 (1973).

I

In 1968 a Chicago policeman named Nuccio shot and killed a youth named Nelson. The state authorities prosecuted Nuccio for the homicide and ultimately obtained a conviction for murder in the second degree. The Nelson family retained petitioner Elmer Gertz, a reputable attorney, to represent them in civil litigation against Nuccio.

Respondent publishes American Opinion, a monthly outlet for the views of the John Birch Society. Early in the 1960's the magazine began to warn of a nationwide conspiracy to discredit local law enforcement agencies and create in their stead a national police force capable of supporting a Communist dictatorship. As part of the continuing effort to alert the public to this assumed danger, the managing editor of American Opinion commissioned an article on the murder trial of Officer Nuccio. For this purpose he engaged a regular contributor to the magazine. In March 1969 respondent published the resulting article under the title "FRAME–UP: Richard Nuccio And The War On Police." The article purports to demonstrate that the testimony against Nuccio at his criminal trial was false and that his prosecution was part of the Communist campaign against the police.

In his capacity as counsel for the Nelson family in the civil litigation, petitioner attended the coroner's inquest into the boy's death and initiated actions for damages, but he neither discussed Officer Nuccio with the press nor played any part in the criminal proceeding. Notwithstanding petitioner's remote connection with the prosecution of Nuccio, respondent's magazine portrayed him as an architect of the "frame-up." According to the article, the police file on petitioner took "a big, Irish cop to lift." The article stated that petitioner had been an official of the "Marxist League for Industrial Democracy, originally known as the Intercollegiate Socialist Society, which has advocated the violent seizure of our government." It labeled Gertz a "Leninist" and a "Communist-fronter." It also stated that Gertz had been an officer of the National Lawyers Guild, described as a Communist organization that "probably did more than any other outfit to plan the Communist attack on the Chicago police during the 1968 Democratic Convention."

These statements contained serious inaccuracies. The implication that petitioner had a criminal record was false. Petitioner had been a member and officer of the National Lawyers Guild some 15 years earlier, but there was no evidence that he or that organization had taken any part in planning the 1968 demonstrations in Chicago. There was also no basis for the charge that petitioner was a "Leninist" or a "Communist-fronter." And he had never been a member of the "Marxist League for Industrial Democracy" or the "Intercollegiate Socialist Society."

The managing editor of American Opinion made no effort to verify or substantiate the charges against petitioner. Instead, he appended an editorial introduction stating that the author had "conducted extensive research into the Richard Nuccio Case." And he included in the article a photograph of petitioner and wrote the caption that appeared under it: "Elmer Gertz of Red Guild harasses Nuccio." Respondent placed the issue of American Opinion containing the article on sale at newsstands throughout the country and distributed reprints of the article on the streets of Chicago.

\* \* \*

## II

The principal issue in this case is whether a newspaper or broadcaster that publishes defamatory falsehoods about an individual who is neither a public official nor a public figure may claim a constitutional privilege against liability for the injury inflicted by those statements.

\* \* \*

We begin with the common ground. Under the First Amendment there is no such thing as a false idea. However pernicious an opinion may seem, we depend for its correction not on the conscience of judges and juries but on the competition of other ideas. But there is no constitutional value in false statements of fact. Neither the intentional lie nor the careless error materially advances society's interest in "uninhibited, robust, and wide-open" debate on public issues. *New York Times Co. v. Sullivan*, 376 U.S., at 270, 84 S.Ct., at 721. They belong to that category of utterances which "are no essential part of any exposition of ideas, and are of such slight social value as a step to truth that any benefit that may be derived from them is clearly outweighed by the social interest in order and morality." *Chaplinsky v. New Hampshire*, 315 U.S. 568, 572, 62 S.Ct. 766, 769, 86 L.Ed. 1031 (1942).

Although the erroneous statement of fact is not worthy of constitutional protection, it is nevertheless inevitable in free debate. As James Madison pointed out in the Report on the Virginia Resolutions of 1798: "Some degree of abuse is inseparable from the proper use of every thing; and in no instance is this more true than in that of the press." 4 J. Elliot, Debates on the Federal Constitution of 1787, p. 571 (1876).

\* \* \*

Some tension necessarily exists between the need for a vigorous and uninhibited press and the legitimate interest in redressing wrongful injury. As Mr. Justice Harlan stated, "some antithesis between freedom of speech and press and libel actions persists, for libel remains premised on the content of speech and limits the freedom of the publisher to express certain sentiments, at least without guaranteeing legal proof of their substantial accuracy." *Curtis Publishing Co. v. Butts, supra*, 388 U.S., at 152, 87 S.Ct., at 1990. In our continuing effort to define the proper accommodation between these competing concerns, we have been especially anxious to assure to the freedoms of speech and press that 'breathing space' essential to their fruitful exercise. *NAACP v. Button*, 371 U.S. 415, 433, 83 S.Ct. 328, 338, 9 L.Ed.2d 405 (1963). To that end this Court has extended a measure of strategic protection to defamatory falsehood.

The *New York Times* standard defines the level of constitutional protection appropriate to the context of defamation of a public person. Those who, by reason of the notoriety of their achievements or the vigor and success with which they seek the public's attention, are properly classed as public figures and those who hold governmental office may recover for injury to reputation only on clear and convincing proof that the defamatory falsehood was made with knowledge of its falsity or with reckless disregard for the truth. This standard administers an extremely powerful antidote to the inducement to media self-censorship of the common-law rule of strict liability for libel and slander. And it exacts a correspondingly high price from the victims of defamatory falsehood.

Plainly many deserving plaintiffs, including some intentionally subjected to injury, will be unable to surmount the barrier of the *New York Times* test. . . .

\* \* \*

[W]e have no difficulty in distinguishing among defamation plaintiffs. The first remedy of any victim of defamation is self-help—using available opportunities to contradict the lie or correct the error and thereby to minimize its adverse impact on reputation. Public officials and public figures usually enjoy significantly greater access to the channels of effective communication and hence have a more realistic opportunity to counteract false statements then private individuals normally enjoy. Private individuals are therefore more vulnerable to injury, and the state interest in protecting them is correspondingly greater.

More important than the likelihood that private individuals will lack effective opportunities for rebuttal, there is a compelling normative consideration underlying the distinction between public and private defamation plaintiffs. An individual who decides to seek governmental office must accept certain necessary consequences of that involvement in public affairs. . . .

Those classed as public figures stand in a similar position. Hypothetically, it may be possible for someone to become a public figure through no purposeful action of his own, but the instances of truly involuntary public figures must be exceedingly rare. For the most part those who attain this status have assumed roles of especial prominence in the affairs of society. Some occupy positions of such persuasive power and influence that they are deemed public figures for all purposes. More commonly, those classed as public figures have thrust themselves to the forefront of particular public controversies in order to influence the resolution of the issues involved. In either event, they invite attention and comment.

\* \* \*

We hold that, so long as they do not impose liability without fault, the States may define for themselves the appropriate standard of liability for a publisher or broadcaster of defamatory falsehood injurious to a private individual.

Our accommodation of the competing values at stake in defamation suits by private individuals allows the States to impose liability on the publisher or broadcaster of defamatory falsehood on a less demanding showing than that required by *New York Times*. This conclusion is not based on a belief that the considerations which prompted the adoption of the *New York Times* privilege for defamation of public officials and its extension to public figures are wholly inapplicable to the context of private individuals. Rather, we endorse this approach in recognition of the strong and legitimate state interest in compensating private individuals for injury to reputation. But this countervailing state interest extends no further than compensation for actual injury. For the reasons stated below, we hold that the States may not permit recovery of presumed or punitive damages, at least when liability is not based on a showing of knowledge of falsity or reckless disregard for the truth.

The common law of defamation is an oddity of tort law, for it allows recovery of purportedly compensatory damages without evidence of actual loss. Under the traditional rules pertaining to actions for libel, the existence of injury is presumed from the fact of publication. Juries may award substantial sums as compensation for supposed damage to reputation without any proof that such harm actually occurred. The largely uncontrolled discretion of juries to award damages where there is no loss unnecessarily compounds the potential of any system of liability for defamatory falsehood to inhibit the vigorous exercise of First Amendment freedoms. . . .

. . . . We need not define "actual injury," as trial courts have wide experience in framing appropriate jury instructions in tort actions. Suffice it to say that actual injury is not limited to out-of-pocket loss. Indeed, the more customary types of actual harm inflicted by defamatory falsehood include impairment of reputation and standing in the community, personal humiliation, and mental anguish and suffering. Of course, juries must be limited by appropriate instructions, and all awards must be supported by competent evidence concerning the injury, although there need be no evidence which assigns an actual dollar value to the injury.

We also find no justification for allowing awards of punitive damages against publishers and broadcasters held liable under state-defined standards of liability for defamation. In most jurisdictions jury discretion over the amounts awarded is limited only by the gentle rule that they not be excessive. . . . They are not compensation for injury. Instead, they are private fines levied by civil juries to punish reprehensible conduct and to deter its future occurrence. In short, the private defamation plaintiff who establishes liability under a less demanding standard than that stated by *New York Times* may recover only such damages as are sufficient to compensate him for actual injury.

\* \* \*

Notwithstanding our refusal to extend the *New York Times* privilege to defamation of private individuals, respondent contends that we should affirm the judgment below on the ground that petitioner is either a public official or a public figure. There is little basis for the former assertion. Several years prior to the present incident, petitioner had served briefly on housing committees appointed by the mayor of Chicago, but at the time of publication he had never held any remunerative governmental position. Respondent admits this but argues that petitioner's appearance at the coroner's inquest rendered him a "de facto public official." Our cases recognized no such concept. Respondent's suggestion would sweep all lawyers under the *New York Times* rule as officers of the court and distort the plain meaning of the "public official" category beyond all recognition. We decline to follow it.

Respondent's characterization of petitioner as a public figure raises a different question. That designation may rest on either of two alternative bases. In some instances an individual may achieve such pervasive fame or notoriety that he becomes a public figure for all purposes and in all contexts. More commonly, an individual voluntarily injects himself or is drawn into a particular public controversy and thereby becomes a public figure for a limited range of issues. In either case such persons assume special prominence in the resolution of public questions.

Petitioner has long been active in community and professional affairs. He has served as an officer of local civic groups and of various professional organizations, and he has published several books and articles on legal subjects. Although petitioner was consequently well known in some circles, he had achieved no general fame or notoriety in the community. . . . Absent clear evidence of general fame or notoriety in the community, and pervasive involvement in the affairs of society, an individual should not be deemed a public personality for all aspects of his life. It is preferable to reduce the public-figure question to a more meaningful context by looking to the nature and extent of an individual's participation in the particular controversy giving rise to the defamation.

In this context it is plain that petitioner was not a public figure. He played a minimal role at the coroner's inquest, and his participation related solely to his representation of a private client. He took no part in the criminal prosecution of Officer Nuccio. Moreover, he never discussed either the criminal or civil litigation with the press and was never quoted as having done so. He plainly did not thrust himself into the vortex of this public issue, nor did he engage the public's attention in an attempt to influence its outcome. We are persuaded that the trial court did not err in refusing to characterize petitioner as a public figure for the purpose of this litigation.

We therefore conclude that the *New York Times* standard is inapplicable to this case and that the trial court erred in entering judgment for respondent. Because the jury was allowed to impose liability without fault and was permitted to presume damages without proof of injury, a new trial is necessary. We reverse and remand for further proceedings in accord with this opinion.

* * *

Reversed and remanded.

## NOTES

**1. Defamation of a Public Figure.** Public figures, like public officials, must prove actual or *New York Times* malice in order to recover in a defamation action. This is in addition to establishing the common law elements of the tort. There are two types of public figure. The first type is the all-purpose public figure. An example would be a nationally known celebrity. The other type is someone who is a public figure for a limited purpose. This would include someone who is well known in the context of a specific public issue or controversy. Once a court finds that a defamation plaintiff is a public figure, that plaintiff must surmount the potentially difficult obstacle of proving actual malice, either for all matters if an all-purpose public figure or for limited matters if only a public figure in certain contexts. See Diamond, Levine & Madden, *Understanding Torts* § 21.03 (2nd ed. 2000); Keeton, *Prosser and Keeton on the Law of Torts* § 113 (5th ed. 1984) and Dobbs, *The Law of Torts* § 419–420 (2000). Consider *Brewer v. Rogers*, 211 Ga.App. 343, 439 S.E.2d 77 (1993), where a high school football coach brought a defamation action against a superintendent of schools, television station and news reporter, after a television news report alleged the plaintiff had made grade changes for a football-playing student and had been involved in illegal gambling. The coach was considered a public figure within the context of the alleged grade changing and was thus required to show actual malice.

In *Hutchinson v. Proxmire*, 443 U.S. 111, 99 S.Ct. 2675, 61 L.Ed.2d 411 (1979), another portion of which is reprinted infra at Sec. E, the Supreme Court discusses further factors which help determine whether a plaintiff should be characterized as a public figure. The plaintiff in *Hutchinson* served as director of research at a mental hospital and had received federal grants to study aggression by observing the behavior patterns of animals.

It is not contended that Hutchinson attained such prominence that he is a public figure for all purposes. Instead, respondents have argued that the District Court and the Court of Appeals were correct in holding that Hutchinson is a public figure for the limited purpose of comment on his receipt of federal funds for research projects. That conclusion was based upon two factors: first, Hutchinson's successful application for federal funds and the reports in local newspapers of the federal grants; second, Hutchinson's access to the media, as demonstrated by the fact that some newspapers and wire services reported his response to the announcement of the Golden Fleece Award. Neither of those factors demonstrates that Hutchinson was a public figure prior to the controversy engendered by the Golden Fleece Award; his access, such as it was, came after the alleged libel.

On this record, Hutchinson's activities and public profile are much like those of countless members of his profession. His published writings reach a relatively small category of professionals concerned with research in human behavior. To the extent the subject of his published writings became a matter of controversy, it was a consequence of the ... [defendant's defamation]. Clearly, those charged with defamation cannot, by their own conduct, create their own defense by making the claimant a public figure. See *Wolston v. Reader's Digest Assn., Inc.*, 443 U.S. 157, 167–168, 99 S.Ct. 2701, 2708, 61 L.Ed.2d 450.

Hutchinson did not thrust himself or his views into public controversy to influence others. Respondents have not identified such a particular controversy; at most, they point to concern about general public expenditures. But that concern is shared by most and relates to most public expenditures; it is not sufficient to make Hutchinson a public figure. If it were, everyone who received or benefited from the myriad public grants for research could be classified as a public figure—a conclusion that our previous opinions have rejected. The "use of such subject-matter classifications to determine the extent of constitutional protection afforded defamatory falsehoods may too often result in an improper balance between the competing interests in this area." *Time, Inc. v. Firestone, supra,* 424 U.S., at 456, 96 S.Ct., at 966.

Moreover, Hutchinson at no time assumed any role of public prominence in the broad question of concern about expenditures. Neither his applications for federal grants nor his publications in professional journals can be said to have invited that degree of public attention and comment on his receipt of federal grants essential to meet the public figure level. The petitioner in *Gertz v. Robert Welch, Inc.,* had published books and articles on legal issues; he had been active in local community affairs. Nevertheless, the Court concluded that his activities did not make him a public figure.

Finally, we cannot agree that Hutchinson had such access to the media that he should be classified as a public figure. Hutchinson's access was limited to responding to the announcement of the Golden Fleece Award. He did not have the regular and continuing access to the media that is one of the accouterments of having become a public figure.

Earlier in *Time, Inc. v. Firestone,* 424 U.S. 448, 96 S.Ct. 958, 47 L.Ed.2d 154 (1976), the Supreme Court declined to characterize as a limited public figure in the context of a highly publicized divorce, Mrs. Firestone, a figure in Palm Beach, Florida high society and member of a very wealthy American family. The Supreme Court noted that public interest in her did not suffice to make her a public figure and she had not "thrust herself to the forefront of any particular public controversy." See also *Wolston v. Reader's Digest Ass'n,* 443 U.S. 157, 99 S.Ct. 2701, 61 L.Ed.2d 450 (1979), which held an individual convicted years earlier for contempt charges in an espionage investigation was not a public figure.

**2. Private Plaintiffs in Matters of Public Controversy.** A private figure is not constitutionally required to prove *New York Times* malice to recover in a defamation action. The Supreme Court does require that the private plaintiff must in a matter of public controversy prove fault, generally understood to mean negligence toward the truth, a much less demanding standard than *New York Times* malice. If the plaintiff only proves negligence, she is, however, limited to recovery for "actual" injuries. It is important to note that actual injuries is far more expansive than "special" or pecuniary damages required to recover for most slander. It includes all "proven" losses, including proven mental distress. Under *Gertz*, the plaintiff after proving negligence toward the truth must introduce evidence of reputational and mental damage in order to recover for these injuries. How onerous is this requirement? Under traditional common law defamation, a jury was free to presume the defamation caused the victim reputational and emotional injuries. In order to recover more than "actual" losses, most notably punitive damages, the private plaintiff must, as a constitutional prerequisite, prove *New York Times* malice, as well as satisfying the jurisdiction's ordinary prerequisite for punitive damages in any tort action, common law malice (e.g., ill-will, hatred). (See Chapter 5, Sec. C, supra).

# DUN & BRADSTREET, INC. v. GREENMOSS BUILDERS, INC.

Supreme Court of the United States.

472 U.S. 749, 105 S.Ct. 2939, 86 L.Ed.2d 593(1985).

Justice POWELL announced the judgment of the Court and delivered an opinion, in which Justice REHNQUIST and Justice O'CONNOR joined.

In *Gertz v. Robert Welch, Inc.*, 418 U.S. 323, 94 S.Ct. 2997, 41 L.Ed.2d 789 (1974), we held that the First Amendment restricted the damages that a private individual could obtain from a publisher for a libel that involved a matter of public concern. More specifically, we held that in these circumstances the First Amendment prohibited awards of presumed and punitive damages for false and defamatory statements unless the plaintiff shows "actual malice," that is, knowledge of falsity or reckless disregard for the truth. The question presented in this case is whether this rule of *Gertz* applies when the false and defamatory statements do not involve matters of public concern.

## I

Petitioner Dun & Bradstreet, a credit reporting agency, provides subscribers with financial and related information about businesses. All the information is confidential; under the terms of the subscription agreement the subscribers may not reveal it to anyone else. On July 26, 1976, petitioner sent a report to five subscribers indicating that respondent, a construction contractor, had filed a voluntary petition for bankruptcy. This report was false and grossly misrepresented respondent's assets and liabilities. . . .

\* \* \*

Respondent then brought this defamation action in Vermont state court. It alleged that the false report had injured its reputation and sought both compensatory and punitive damages. The trial established that the error in petitioner's report had been caused when one of its employees, a 17–year-old high school student paid to review Vermont bankruptcy pleadings, had inadvertently attributed to respondent a bankruptcy petition filed by one of respondent's former employees. Although petitioners representative testified that it was routine practice to check the accuracy of such reports with the businesses themselves, it did not try to verify the information about respondent before reporting it.

After trial, the jury returned a verdict in favor of respondent and awarded $50,000 in compensatory or presumed damages and $300,000 in punitive damages. Petitioner moved for a new trial. It argued that in *Gertz v. Robert Welch, Inc., supra*, at 349, 94 S.Ct., at 3011, this Court had ruled broadly that "the States may not permit recovery of presumed or punitive damages, at least when liability is not based on a showing of knowledge of falsity or reckless disregard for the truth," and it argued that the judge's instructions in this case permitted the jury to award such damages on a lesser showing....

\* \* \*

We have never considered whether the *Gertz* balance obtains when the defamatory statements involve no issue of public concern. To make this determination, we must employ the approach approved in *Gertz* and balance the State's interest in compensating private individuals for injury to their reputation against the First Amendment interest in protecting this type of expression. This state interest is identical to the one weighed in *Gertz*....

\* \* \*

The First Amendment interest, on the other hand, is less important than the one weighed in *Gertz*. We have long recognized that not all speech is of equal First Amendment importance. It is speech on " 'matters of public concern' " that is "at the heart of the First Amendment's protection." *First National Bank of Boston v. Bellotti*, 435 U.S. 765, 776, 98 S.Ct. 1407, 1415, 55 L.Ed.2d 707 (1978), citing *Thornhill v. Alabama*, 310 U.S. 88, 101, 60 S.Ct. 736, 743, 84 L.Ed. 1093 (1940)....

\* \* \*

In contrast, speech on matters of purely private concern is of less First Amendment concern. *Id.,* at 146–147, 103 S.Ct., at 1689–1690. As a number of state courts, including the court below, have recognized, the role of the Constitution in regulating state libel law is far more limited when the concerns that activated *New York Times* and *Gertz* are absent. In such a case,

> "[t]here is no threat to the free and robust debate of public issues; there is no potential interference with a meaningful dialogue of ideas concerning self-government; and there is no threat of liability causing a reaction of self-censorship by the press. The facts of the present case are wholly without the First Amendment concerns with which the Supreme Court of the United States has been struggling." *Harley-Davidson Motorsports, Inc. v. Markley,* 279 Or. 361, 366, 568 P.2d 1359, 1363 (1977).

\* \* \*

While such speech is not totally unprotected by the First Amendment, see *Connick v. Myers, supra,* 461 U.S., at 147, 103 S.Ct., at 1690, its protections are less stringent. In *Gertz,* we found that the state interest in awarding presumed and punitive damages was not "substantial" in view of their effect on speech at the core of First Amendment concern. 418 U.S., at 349, 94 S.Ct., at 3011. This interest, however, *is* "substantial" relative to the incidental effect these remedies may have on speech of significantly less constitutional interest. The rationale of the common-law rules has been the experience and judgment of history that "proof of actual damage will be impossible in a great many cases where, from the character of the defamatory words and the circumstances of publication, it is all but certain that serious harm has resulted in fact." W. Prosser, Law of Torts § 112, p. 765 (4th ed. 1971); accord, *Rowe v. Metz, supra,* 195 Colo., at 425–426, 579 P.2d, at 84; Note, Developments in the Law—Defamation, 69 Harv.L.Rev. 875, 891–892 (1956). As a result, courts for centuries have allowed juries to presume that some damage occurred from many defamatory utterances and publications. Restatement of Torts § 568, Comment *b*, p. 162 (1938) (noting that Hale announced that damages were to be presumed for libel as early as 1670). This rule furthers the state interest in providing remedies for defamation by ensuring that those remedies are effective. In light of the reduced constitutional value of speech involving no matters of public concern, we hold that the state interest adequately supports awards of presumed and punitive damages—even absent a showing of "actual malice."

The only remaining issue is whether petitioner's credit report involved a matter of public concern. In a related context, we have held that "[w]hether ... speech addresses a matter of public concern must be determined by [the expression's] content, form, and context ... as revealed by the whole record." *Connick v. Myers, supra,* 461 U.S., at 147–148, 103 S.Ct., at 1690. These factors indicate that petitioner's credit report concerns no public issue. It was speech solely in the individual interest of the speaker and its specific business audience. Cf. *Central Hudson Gas & Elec. Corp. v. Public Service Comm'n of New York,* 447 U.S. 557, 561, 100 S.Ct. 2343, 2348, 65 L.Ed.2d 341 (1980). This particular interest warrants no special protection when—as in this case—the speech is wholly false and clearly damaging to the victim's business reputation. Cf. *id.,* at 566, 100 S.Ct., at 2351; *Virginia Pharmacy Bd. v. Virginia Citizens Consumer Council, Inc.,* 425 U.S. 748, 771–772, 96 S.Ct. 1817, 1830–1831, 48 L.Ed.2d 346 (1976). Moreover, since the credit report was made available to only five subscribers, who, under the terms of the subscription agreement, could not disseminate it further, it cannot be said that the report involves any "strong interest in the free flow of commercial information." *Id.,* at 764, 96 S.Ct., at 1827. There is simply no credible argument that this type of credit reporting requires special protection to ensure that "debate on public issues [will] be uninhibited, robust, and wide-open." *New York Times Co. v. Sullivan,* 376 U.S., at 270, 84 S.Ct., at 720.

* * *

We conclude that permitting recovery of presumed and punitive damages in defamation cases absent a showing of "actual malice" does not violate the First Amendment when the defamatory statements do not involve matters of public concern. Accordingly, we affirm the judgment of the Vermont Supreme Court.

*It is so ordered.*

### *NOTES*

**1. Defamation of a Private Party in a Private Matter.** In addition to distinguishing between public and private plaintiffs to determine whether the plaintiff must prove *New York Times* malice to recover any damages in defamation, it is necessary in the case of a private plaintiff to determine whether the defamation concerns a matter of "public concern." The *Gertz* constitutional rule requiring the private plaintiff to prove fault (generally construed as negligence toward the truth) to recover "actual injuries" and *New York Times* malice to recover presumed and punitive damages, applies to defamation involving a matter of "public concern." In the principal case, the Supreme Court determined the credit report in question was not a matter of public concern. See Diamond, Levine & Madden, *Understanding Torts* § 21.03 (2nd ed. 2000); Dobbs, *The Law of Torts* §§ 417, 420 (2000).

The principal case does not expressly address what, if any, constitutional limits are imposed on a private plaintiff suing for defamation in a private matter. The requirement to prove *New York Times* malice to recover presumed and punitive damages is eliminated. An open question is whether in private defamation negligence toward the truth will be required or whether strict liability for private defamation is constitutionally acceptable. At present, while the states are free to impose culpability standards, common law defamation involving a private plaintiff in a private matter would appear to be unrestricted by any constitutionally imposed culpability requirements derived from the First Amendment. Do you think constitutional requirements should be imposed in private defamation?

2. ***Philadelphia Newspapers, Inc. v. Hepps*, 475 U.S. 767, 106 S.Ct. 1558, 89 L.Ed.2d 783 (1986).** In the *Hepps* case, the Supreme Court held that a private plaintiff accused of bribing a public official constituted a matter of public concern and was therefore subject to the *Gertz* rules. Nevertheless, the line between private matters and issues of public concern remains not entirely clear at the boundaries.

The *Hepps* case also added a requirement applicable to plaintiffs subject to the *New York Times* and *Gertz* standard. In these cases involving public officials, public figures and private plaintiffs suing over defamatory matters of public concern, the plaintiff now has the burden of proving the defamation is false in order to recover damages. This changes the common law approach where the defamation is presumed true and the defendant has the burden of proving truth as a defense.

The Supreme Court in *Hepps* also reiterated that it had never expressly decided whether non-media defendants enjoy the constitutional protection afforded by the *New York Times* and *Gertz* cases. Nevertheless most scholars and lower courts take the position that non-media defendants are protected by the *New York Times* and *Gertz* rules.

# SECTION E.   PRIVILEGES

## HUTCHINSON v. PROXMIRE
Supreme Court of the United States.
443 U.S. 111, 99 S.Ct. 2675, 61 L.Ed.2d 411 (1979).

Mr. Chief Justice BURGER delivered the opinion of the Court.

\* \* \*

Ronald Hutchinson, a research behavioral scientist, sued respondents, William Proxmire, a United States Senator, and his legislative assistant, Morton Schwartz, for defamation arising out of Proxmire's giving what he called his "Golden Fleece" award. The "award" went to federal agencies that had sponsored Hutchinson's research. Hutchinson alleged that in making the award and publicizing it nationwide, respondents had libeled him, damaging him in his professional and academic standing, and had interfered with his contractual relations. . . .

\* \* \*

Respondent Proxmire is a United States Senator from Wisconsin. In March 1975, he initiated the "Golden Fleece of the Month Award" to publicize what he perceived to be the most egregious examples of wasteful governmental spending. The second such award, in April 1975, went to the National Science Foundation, the National Aeronautics and Space Administration, and the Office of Naval Research, for spending almost half a million dollars during the preceding seven years to fund Hutchinson's research.

At the time of the award, Hutchinson was director of research at the Kalamazoo State Mental Hospital. Before that he had held a similar position at the Ft. Custer State Home. Both the hospital and the home are operated by the Michigan State Department of Mental Health; he was therefore a state employee in both positions. During most of the period in question he was also an adjunct professor at Western Michigan University. When the research department at Kalamazoo State Mental Hospital was closed in June 1975, Hutchinson became research director of the Foundation for Behavioral Research, a nonprofit organization. The research funding was transferred from the hospital to the foundation.

The bulk of Hutchinson's research was devoted to the study of emotional behavior. In particular, he sought an objective measure of aggression, concentrating upon the behavior patterns of certain animals, such as the clenching of jaws when they were exposed to various aggravating stressful stimuli. The National Aeronautics and Space Agency and the Navy were interested in the potential of this research for resolving problems associated with confining humans in close quarters for extended periods of time in space and undersea exploration.

The Golden Fleece Award to the agencies that had sponsored Hutchinson's research was based upon research done for Proxmire by Schwartz. While seeking evidence of wasteful governmental spending, Schwartz read copies of reports that Hutchinson had prepared under grants from NASA. Those reports revealed that Hutchinson had received grants from the Office of Naval Research, the National Science Foundation, and the Michigan State Department of Mental Health. Schwartz also learned that other federal agencies had funded Hutchinson's research. After contacting a number of federal and state agencies, Schwartz helped to prepare a speech for Proxmire to present in the Senate on April 18, 1975; the text was then incorporated into an advance press release, with only the addition of introductory and concluding sentences. Copies were sent to a mailing list of 275 members of the news media throughout the United States and abroad.

Schwartz telephoned Hutchinson before releasing the speech to tell him of the award; Hutchinson protested that the release contained an inaccurate and incomplete summary of his research. Schwartz replied that he thought the summary was fair.

In the speech, Proxmire described the federal grants for Hutchinson's research, concluding with the following comment:[3]

"The funding of this nonsense makes me almost angry enough to scream and kick or even clench my jaw. It seems to me it is outrageous.

"Dr. Hutchinson's studies should make the taxpayers as well as his monkeys grind their teeth. In fact, the good doctor has made a fortune from his monkeys and in the process made a monkey out of the American taxpayer.

"It is time for the Federal Government to get out of this 'monkey business.' In view of the transparent worthlessness of Hutchinson's study of jaw-grinding and biting by angry or hard-drinking monkeys, it is time we put a stop to the bite Hutchinson and the bureaucrats who fund him have been taking of the taxpayer." 121 Cong.Rec. 10803 (1975).

In May 1975, Proxmire referred to his Golden Fleece Awards in a newsletter sent to about 100,000 people whose names were on a mailing list that included constituents in Wisconsin as well as persons in other states. The newsletter repeated the essence of the speech and the press release. Later in 1975, Proxmire appeared on a television interview program where he referred to Hutchinson's research, though he did not mention Hutchinson by name.

The final reference to the research came in a newsletter in February 1976. In that letter, Proxmire summarized his Golden Fleece Awards of 1975. The letter did not mention Hutchinson's name, but it did report:

"—The NSF, the Space Agency, and the Office of Naval Research won the 'Golden Fleece' for spending jointly $500,000 to determine why monkeys clench their jaws.

\* \* \*

"All the studies on why monkeys clench their jaws were dropped. No more monkey business." App. 168–171.

After the award was announced, Schwartz, acting on behalf of Proxmire, contacted a number of the federal agencies that had sponsored the research. In his deposition he stated that he did not attempt to dissuade them from continuing to fund the research but merely discussed the subject. Hutchinson, by contrast, contends that these calls

---

**3.** Proxmire is not certain that he actually delivered the speech on the Senate floor. He said that he might have merely inserted it into the Congressional Record. App. 220–221. In light of that uncertainty, the question arises whether a nondelivered speech printed in the Congressional Record is covered by the Speech or Debate Clause. This Court has never passed on that question and neither the District Court nor the Court of Appeals seemed to think it was important. Nevertheless, we assume, without deciding, that a speech printed in the Congressional Record carries immunity under the Speech or Debate Clause as though delivered on the floor.

were intended to persuade the agencies to terminate his grants and contracts.

\* \* \*

## IV

In support of the Court of Appeals holding that newsletters and press releases are protected by the Speech or Debate Clause, respondents rely upon both historical precedent and present-day congressional practices. They contend that impetus for the Speech or Debate Clause privilege in our Constitution came from the history of parliamentary efforts to protect the right of members to criticize the spending of the Crown and from the prosecution of a Speaker of the House of Commons for publication of a report outside of Parliament. Respondents also contend that in the modern day very little speech or debate occurs on the floor of either House; from this they argue that press releases and newsletters are necessary for Members of Congress to communicate with other Members. For example, in his deposition Proxmire testified:

> "I have found in 19 years in the Senate that very often a statement on the floor of the Senate or something that appears in the Congressional Record misses the attention of most members of the Senate, and virtually all members of the House, because they don't read the Congressional Record. If they are handed a news release, or something, that is going to call it to their attention. . . ." App., at 220.

Respondents also argue that an essential part of the duties of a Member of Congress is to inform constituents, as well as other Members, of the issues being considered.

Whatever imprecision there may be in the term "legislative activities," it is clear that nothing in history or in the explicit language of the Clause suggests any intention to create an absolute privilege from liability or suit for defamatory statements made outside the Chamber. In *Brewster, supra,* 408 U.S., at 507, 92 S.Ct., at 2535, we observed:

> "The immunities of the Speech or Debate Clause were not written into the Constitution simply for the personal or private benefit of Members of Congress, but to protect the integrity of the legislative process by insuring the independence of individual legislators."

Claims under the Clause going beyond what is needed to protect legislative independence are to be closely scrutinized.

\* \* \*

A speech by Proxmire in the Senate would be wholly immune and would be available to other Members of Congress and the public in the Congressional Record. But neither the newsletters nor the press release was "essential to the deliberations of the Senate" and neither was part of the deliberative process.

Respondents, however, argue that newsletters and press releases are essential to the functioning of the Senate; without them, they assert, a

Senator cannot have a significant impact on the other Senators. We may assume that a Member's published statements exert some influence on other votes in the Congress and therefore have a relationship to the legislative and deliberative process. But in *Brewster*, 408 U.S., at 512, we rejected respondents' expansive reading of the Clause:

"It is well known, of course, that Members of the Congress engage in many activities other than the purely legislative activities protected by the Speech or Debate Clause. These include ... preparing so-called 'news letters' to constituents, news releases, and speeches delivered outside the Congress."

There we went on to note that *United States v. Johnson*, 383 U.S. 169, 86 S.Ct. 749, 15 L.Ed.2d 681 (1966), had carefully distinguished between what is only "related to the due functioning of the legislative process," and what constitutes the legislative process entitled to immunity under the Clause:

"In stating that those things [Johnson's attempts to influence the Department of Justice] 'in no wise related to the due functioning of the legislative process' were *not* covered by the privilege, the Court did not in any sense imply as a corollary that everything that 'related' to the office of a Member was shielded by the Clause. Quite the contrary in *Johnson* we held, citing *Kilbourn v. Thompson, supra*, that only acts generally done in the course of the process of enacting legislation were protected.

\* \* \*

"In no case has this Court ever treated the Clause as protecting all conduct *relating* to the legislative process.

\* \* \*

"... In its narrowest scope, the Clause is a very large, albeit essential, grant of privilege. It has enabled reckless men to slander [by speech or debate] and even destroy others with impunity, but that was the conscious choice of the Framers. 408 U.S., at 513–516, 92 S.Ct., at 2538–2539. (Emphasis in original.)

We are unable to discern any "conscious choice" to grant immunity for defamatory statements scattered far and wide by mail, press, and the electronic media.

Respondents also argue that newsletters and press releases are privileged as part of the "informing function" of Congress. Advocates of a broad reading of the "informing function" sometimes tend to confuse two uses of the term "informing." In one sense, Congress informs itself collectively by way of hearings of its committees. It was in that sense that Woodrow Wilson used "informing" in a statement quoted by respondents. In reality, Wilson's statement related to congressional efforts to learn of the activities of the Executive Branch and administrative agencies; he did not include wide-ranging inquiries by individual Members on subjects of their choice. Moreover, Wilson's statement itself clearly implies a distinction between the *informing* function and the *legislative* function:

> "Unless Congress have and use every means of acquainting itself with the acts and the disposition of the administrative agents of the government, the country must be helpless to learn how it is being served; and unless Congress both scrutinize these things and sift them by every form of discussion, the country must remain in embarrassing, crippling ignorance of the very affairs which it is most important that it should understand and direct. The informing function of Congress should be preferred even to its legislative function.... [T]he only really self-governing people is that people which discusses and interrogates its administration." W. Wilson, Congressional Government 303 (1885).

It is in this narrower Wilsonian sense that this Court has employed "informing" in previous cases holding that congressional efforts to inform itself through committee hearings are part of the legislative function.

The other sense of the term, and the one relied upon by respondents, perceives it to be the duty of Members to tell the public about their activities. Valuable and desirable as it may be in broad terms, the transmittal of such information by individual Members in order to inform the public and other Members is not a part of the legislative function or the deliberations that make up the legislative process. As a result, transmittal of such information by press releases and newsletters is not protected by the Speech or Debate Clause.

*Doe v. McMillan*, 412 U.S. 306, 93 S.Ct. 2018, 36 L.Ed.2d 912 (1973), is not to the contrary. It dealt only with reports from congressional committees, and held that Members of Congress could not be held liable for voting to publish a report. Voting and preparing committee reports are the individual and collective expressions of opinion within the legislative process. As such, they are protected by the Speech or Debate Clause. Newsletters and press releases, by contrast, are primarily means of informing those outside the legislative forum; they represent the views and will of a single Member. It does not disparage either their value or their importance to hold that they are not entitled to the protection of the Speech or Debate Clause.

\* \* \*

We therefore reverse the judgment of the Court of Appeals and remand the case to the Court of Appeals for further proceedings consistent with this opinion.

*Reversed and remanded.*

\* \* \*

Mr. Justice BRENNAN, dissenting.

I disagree with the Court's conclusion that Senator Proxmire's newsletters and press releases fall outside the protection of the speech-or-debate immunity. In my view, public criticism by legislators of unnecessary governmental expenditures, whatever its form, is a legislative act shielded by the Speech or Debate Clause. I would affirm the judgment below. . . .

## *NOTES*

1. **Absolute Privilege.** An absolute privilege protects the speaker from defamation liability no matter how intentional or malicious the defamation. Independent policy reasons against potential liability override the interest in allowing the victim to be vindicated and compensated in a lawsuit. In addition to the constitutional privilege provided members of Congress, the common law privilege, generally recognized in jurisdictions, gives absolute protection to statements made in legislatures, relevant statements made by participants (including witnesses) in judicial proceedings, and at least high government executive officials speaking in an official capacity. See Diamond, Levine & Madden, *Understanding Torts* § 21.02 (2nd ed. 2000). See also Keeton, *Prosser and Keeton on the Law of Torts* § 114 (5th ed. 1984); Dobbs, *The Law of Torts* § 412 (2000). See *Barr v. Matteo*, 360 U.S. 564, 79 S.Ct. 1335, 3 L.Ed.2d 1434 (1959), where two former employees of the Office of Rent Stabilization sued their director for issuing a libelous press release stating his intent to suspend them for conduct that had reflected poorly on the agency. The Supreme Court reversed a lower court holding, and granted absolute immunity to the official. In *Hugel v. Milberg, Weiss, Bershad, Hynes & Lerach, LLP*, 175 F.3d 14 (1st. Cir.1999), plaintiff claimed he was defamed by allegations in a complaint filed in a federal securities fraud case, to which he was not a party. The court dismissed the claim concluding the charges were privileged statements pursuant to judicial proceedings.

In addition to the legislative, judicial and executive absolute privilege, conversations between spouses (not communicated to others) are also absolutely protected from defamation liability.

2. **Policy Debate.** An absolute protection from defamation liability protects legislatures, other governmental officials, and even judicial witnesses from threats of civil suits alleging defamation. Does the need for this protection justify removing the victim's right to sue? In the 1950s, Senator McCarthy's famous attack on alleged communists was uninhibited by defamation suits. On balance, do you agree with the privilege?

## BROWN v. KELLY BROADCASTING CO.

Supreme Court of California.
48 Cal.3d 711, 257 Cal.Rptr. 708, 771 P.2d 406 (1989).

EAGLESON, Justice.

The sole issue in this case is whether Civil Code section 47, subdivision 3, affords a broad privilege, sometimes referred to as a "public-interest privilege," to the news communications industry (news media) to make false statements regarding a private individual.

Section 47(3) provides a privilege to communications made without malice on occasions in which the speaker and the recipient of the communication share a common interest. Defendants (a television station and its reporter) and several amici curiae argue that when the news media publish and broadcast matters of public interest they have a common interest with their audiences and that the publications and broadcasts should be privileged under section 47(3). Under that privilege, the plaintiff in a defamation action would be required to prove malice by the news media defendant to recover compensatory damages.

As we will explain, there is no such privilege for the news media under section 47(3). We hold that a publication or broadcast by a member of the news media to the general public regarding a private person is not privileged under section 47(3) regardless of whether the communication pertains to a matter of public interest. Thus, a private-person plaintiff is not required by section 47(3) to prove malice to recover compensatory damages.

### FACTS

Defendant Kelly Broadcasting Company (Kelly) owns and operates KCRA–TV, a television station broadcasting on Channel 3 in Sacramento. Defendant Brad Willis (Willis) was employed by Kelly as a reporter and appeared on Channel 3 programs. Willis narrated two stories in May 1984 concerning plaintiff on "Call 3 for Action" (Call 3), a consumer affairs segment of KCRA's daily news show. The stories were about two homeowners who had received home improvement loans made by the federal government and administered by the Sacramento Housing and Redevelopment Agency (SHRA). One of the homeowners, Lawson, had entered into a home improvement contract with plaintiff Brown, a licensed contractor.

In the first broadcast, Willis claimed that Lawson was the victim of a failure of the SHRA to correct mistakes made by plaintiff in remodeling Lawson's home. Willis alleged that Lawson had suffered through "a series of warped doors, and is still left with peeling paint, cracking plaster, blistered wallpaper, shoddy work, inside and out." The story included pictures of various problems including bubbling and peeling wallcovering, peeling paint, cracked plaster, and faulty doors. Willis asserted that Call 3 had attempted to call plaintiff to discuss the remodeling problems but that she had not returned the calls. He also said that plaintiff had returned $225 to Lawson and had been released by SHRA from further responsibility for the remodeling.

\* \* \*

Defamation has two forms—libel and slander. (§ 44.) Each is statutorily defined as "a false and *unprivileged* publication." (§ 45 [libel] and § 46 [slander], italics added.) Section 47(3) provides a privilege to specified communications made "without malice." For purposes of section 47(3), malice has been defined as "a state of mind arising from hatred or ill will, evidencing a willingness to vex, annoy or injure another person." (*Agarwal v. Johnson* (1979) 25 Cal.3d 932, 944 [160 Cal.Rptr. 141, 603 P.2d 58].) If section 47(3) applies to the occasion on which a communication is made *and* if it was made without malice, it is privileged and cannot constitute a defamation under California law.

With this understanding of how section 47(3) operates, we turn to the issue of whether it provides a special public-interest privilege to the news media. We begin with the fundamental rule that our primary task in construing a statute is to determine the Legislature's intent. (*Moyer v. Workmen's Comp. Appeals Bd.* (1973) 10 Cal.3d 222, 230 [110 Cal.Rptr. 144, 514 P.2d 1224].) "The court turns first to the words themselves for the answer." (*People* v. *Knowles* (1950) 35 Cal.2d 175, 182 [217 P.2d 1]; *Committee of Seven Thousand v. Superior Court* (1988) 45 Cal.3d 491, 501 [247 Cal.Rptr. 362, 754 P.2d 708].) Section 47 states: "A privileged publication or broadcast is one made ... In a communication, without malice, to a person interested therein, (1) by one who is also interested, or (2) by one who stands in such relation to the person interested as to afford a reasonable ground for supposing the motive for the communication innocent, or (3) who is requested by the person interested to give the information."

The statutory language contains no reference to a "*public* interest" or any *special* privilege for the news media. If the Legislature had intended to create a broad public-interest privilege for the news media, the Legislature could easily have done so in reasonably clear language.

* * *

Most important, the privilege sought by defendants would be so broad that it would apply to almost every defamatory communication. Presumably, the news media generally publish and broadcast only matters that the media believe are of public interest, and the media defendant in every defamation action would therefore argue that the communication was a matter of public interest. We think it would be a rare case in which a media defendant would contend that its viewers or readers were not interested in the communication or that the defendant itself was not also interested. Thus, the practical result sought by the news media would be that nearly everything they publish and broadcast would be privileged. A privilege is an exception to a general rule of liability, but under defendants' view of section 47(3), the privilege would be the general rule for the news media and liability would be the exception. We believe the Legislature would have made clear its intention for such a drastic restriction on the common law of defamation, especially because the statute was enacted when strict liability was the standard of fault for defamation actions. (See discussion at pp. 726–727, *post.*)

The statutory language does not suggest the broad public-interest privilege claimed by defendants. To the contrary, subdivision 3, and section 47 as a whole, show that no such privilege was contemplated by the Legislature.

*Legislative history confirms that section 47(3) is narrow in scope.*

Although we need not look beyond the clear language of the statute, we find strong support for our conclusion in the legislative history of section 47(3). It was enacted as part of the Civil Code in 1872. At that time, in the common law of England and the United States, defamation was subject to strict liability, that is, liability without fault as to truth or falsity. (Eldredge, *supra*, § 5, pp. 14–25; Prosser & Keeton, The Law of

Torts (5th ed. 1984) § 113, p. 804.) The standard of liability was succinctly phrased in Lord Mansfield's often quoted statement that, "Whenever a man publishes he publishes at his peril." (*The King v. Woodfall* (1774) Loftt 776, 781 [98 Eng. Rep. 914, 916].) Justice Holmes subsequently stated the rule in equally clear fashion: "If the publication was libellous the defendant took the risk." (*Peck v. Tribune Co.* (1909) 214 U.S. 185, 189 [53 L.Ed. 960, 962, 29 S.Ct. 554]; "libellous" is now archaic spelling.)

To ameliorate the harshness of the strict-liability standard, certain privileges and defenses developed in the common law. The one that is most relevant to the question before us is the common-interest privilege, which protected communications made in good faith on a subject in which the speaker and hearer shared an interest or duty. This privilege applied to a narrow range of private interests. The interest protected was private or pecuniary; the relationship between the parties was close, e.g., a family, business, or organizational interest; and the request for information must have been in the course of the relationship. (*Rancho La Costa, Inc.* v. *Superior Court* (1980) 106 Cal.App.3d 646, 664–665 [165 Cal.Rptr. 347] [describing limited nature of privilege]; see, e.g., *Brewer v. Second Baptist Church* (1948) 32 Cal.2d 791, 796 [197 P.2d 713] [recognizing that a privilege ordinarily exists for communications among church members]; Cate, *Defining California Civil Code Section 47(3): The Resurgence of Self–Governance* (1987) 39 Stan.L.Rev. 1201, 1204–1205 (hereafter Cate).)

The legislative history of section 47(3) indicates the Legislature intended to codify the narrow common law privilege of common interest, not to create any broad news-media privilege. We find special significance in *Wilson v. Fitch* (1871) 41 Cal. 363, which we decided only one year before section 47(3) was enacted. The plaintiff was an owner of a mining corporation; defendants were the editors of a general circulation newspaper that had published an article suggesting financial wrongdoing by the corporation towards its investors. In response to a libel suit, the defendants contended their article was privileged because "... it was published by public journalists as a matter of general and peculiar public interest, and related to the conduct of the plaintiff...." (*Id.*, at p. 382.) We squarely rejected this argument: "Nor can a defamatory publication in a public journal be said to be privileged *simply because it relates to a subject of public interest*, and was published in good faith, without malice, and from laudable motives. No adjudicated case, that I am aware of, has ever gone so far." (*Id.*, at pp. 382–383, italics added.) We noted a "due regard to the freedom of the press" but explained that the privilege sought by the newspaper would result in "little security for private character." (*Id.*, at p. 383.)

\* \* \*

We also find significance in the drafters' comments to section 47(3). The wording of section 47(3) was identical to that of section 31 of the original New York Civil Code published in 1865 as a codification of the common law (N.Y. Civ. Code, § 31 (Field 1865)). In the comments following section 47(3), its drafters cited two New York cases dealing with the common-interest privilege. (Cal. Civ. Code Ann., § 47 annotation (Haymond & Burch 1872).) Neither involved a privilege even remotely similar to that claimed by defendants in the present case.

The first case cited was *Lewis and Herrick v. Chapman* (1857) 16 N.Y. 369. A banker had received for collection from a mercantile house a note payable at the bank and drawn by plaintiffs. When the banker remitted payment for the note he informed the payee in a confidential letter that payment had been as an accommodation to the plaintiffs, suggesting that they had insufficient funds to pay the note. The court found the communication privileged on the ground that a banker entrusted by a creditor with the collection of the note has a privilege to inform the holder of the note of the inability of the maker to pay at maturity. (*Id.*, at p. 375.) The common interest involved was private and pecuniary. No news report was involved and there was not even a question as to the public interest.

The other case cited by section 47(3)'s drafters was *Thorn* v. *Moser* (N.Y. Sup. Ct. 1845) 1 Denio 488, in which the plaintiff sought to recover for statements by the payee of a check drawn by plaintiff charging him with forgery of the check. The court found no privilege on the facts of the case. Moreover, neither a news report nor the public interest were at issue.

The drafters also cited a treatise on the common law, Hilliard, The Law of Torts or Private Wrongs (1859) chapter XIV, page 317. We have found nothing in that work to support the privilege claimed by defendants. Although not referring to a common-interest privilege by name, the author discussed communications made in connection "with some matter of lawful business" and communications by "employers, in reference to the character of their servants." (Hilliard, *supra*, (3d ed. 1866) at pp. 347 and 351.) There is no discussion of a general public-interest privilege to make false accusations against a private person.

The authorities cited by section 47(3)'s drafters suggest no intent to extend the common-interest privilege to the news media. Quite the contrary, they demonstrate that the privilege was meant to be quite limited. It had previously applied to essentially *private* interests, not matters of public interest, and there had to be a genuine *common* interest. (*Rancho La Costa, Inc. v. Superior Court, supra*, 106 Cal.App.3d 646, 664–665, quoting 4 Witkin, Summary of Cal. Law (8th ed. 1974) Torts, §§ 306–309, pp. 2577–2580; Cate, *supra*, 39 Stan.L.Rev. 1201, 1204–1205.) The interest a news publisher has in a story may or may not be shared by its audience. Even if there is a shared interest, it is not "common" within the meaning of the common-interest privilege codified in section 47(3). Moreover, under the common law it was clear that, "A newspaper proprietor has no greater privileges than any other person. He is to stand or fall by the same rules and principles of law." (Folkard, Starkie on Libel and Slander (4th ed. 1877) § 266, p. 326; Townshend, Libel and Slander (3d ed. 1877) § 252, p. 482; Newell, Slander and Libel (4th ed. 1924) § 441, pp. 477–478.)

We find nothing in the legislative history or background of section 47(3) to indicate any legislative intent to create a public-interest privilege for the news media.

*  *  *

## NOTES

1. **Qualified Privilege.** Defamation defendants may, in appropriate cases, assert a defense of a qualified privilege. Such a privilege usually applies where the defendant makes a defamatory statement in an effort to protect a legitimate interest of his own or the person he is speaking with. A typical context would be an employment reference. In order to encourage honest and, when necessary, negative reports, common law qualified privileges protect speakers from possible strict liability for potentially defamatory errors. The privilege is particularly useful in the context of purely private defamation where *New York Times* and even *Gertz* culpability requirements are not clearly applicable. See Note 1, page 721 supra. Unlike an absolute privilege, however, a qualified privilege can be lost by abuse such as bad faith, recklessness, or excessive communication to those not legitimately in need of the information. Qualified privileges vary from jurisdiction to jurisdiction. See Diamond, Levine & Madden, *Understanding Torts* § 21.02 (2nd ed. 2000). See also Keeton, *Prosser and Keeton on the Law of Torts* § 115 (5th ed. 1984); Dobbs, *The Law of the Torts* §§ 413–416 (2000). See *Present v. Avon Products, Inc.*, 253 A.D.2d 183, 687 N.Y.S.2d 330 (1999), where a former employee sued his employer for defamation after he was fired and criminally prosecuted for falsification of billing records and misappropriation of company property. The employer's communications to the police were held to be subject to the qualified common interest privilege, because the employer had investigated the matter and confirmed it with disinterested parties prior to making the report. The court held that to overcome the qualified privilege, plaintiff must show malice by a lack of good faith on the part of the defendants. The court held the plaintiff failed to meet the burden and the complaint was dismissed.

2. **Fair and Accurate Report.** The fair and accurate report privilege allows journalists and others to republish a defamatory statement in the course of reporting on an official action, proceeding, or public meeting. The privilege is important since the repetition or republication of defamation is not generally protected. In *Smith v. Reed*, 944 S.W.2d 623 (Tenn.Ct.App. 1996), a day care center employee put a hot pepper in the mouth of one of the children, who had been biting others. After being acquitted of child abuse charges, the day care center sued a newspaper for defamation, citing inaccuracies in the wording of an article on the case. The newspaper had written "forced" rather than "placed" to describe how the pepper got into the child's mouth. The court held that this was a reasonable interpretation of the testimony and that the fair reporting privilege protects newspapers that report judicial proceedings to inform the public, subject to elements of balance and neutrality.

Controversy exists over when the media should be privileged to quote defamatory assertions in contexts outside of governmental proceedings and public meetings. In *Edwards v. National Audubon Society, Inc.*, 556 F.2d 113 (2d Cir. 1977), the court ruled the *New York Times* was privileged to quote a prominent responsible organization's serious charge against a public official in a fair, neutral, and accurate manner. This "neutral reportage privilege" extends the privilege to republish beyond the traditional fair reporting privilege of official proceedings and public meetings and is not accepted by all courts. See *Dickey v. CBS, Inc.,* 583 F.2d 1221 (3d Cir. 1978), rejecting *Edwards.* Other courts have extended the fair reporting privilege to the reporting of defamatory statements concerning private individuals appearing in non-public FBI files containing unverified accusations. See *Medico v. Time, Inc.,* 643 F.2d 134 (3d Cir. 1981). See Franklin, Anderson & Cate, *Mass Media Law* (6th ed. 2000).

Should the media and others be privileged to repeat defamatory charges or rumors?

**3. Retraction.** When a potential defendant retracts a defamatory statement, the action may mitigate the harm caused by the tort and thus reduce the amount of damages for which the defendant may be held liable.

The nature of the mitigation depends on the applicable statute and thus varies state by state. Section 48(a) of the California Civil Code, for example, states that a plaintiff may recover only special damages when a newspaper or radio broadcast is promptly retracted. Cal. Civ. Code § 48(a) (West 1999). The statute was applied in *Burnett v. National Enquirer, Inc.,* 144 Cal. App.3d 991, 193 Cal.Rptr. 206 (Cal.Ct.App.1983), in which the defendant printed the following item:

> "In a Washington restaurant, a boisterous Carol Burnett had a loud argument with another diner, Henry Kissinger. Then she traipsed around the place offering everyone a bite of her dessert. But Carol really raised eyebrows when she accidentally knocked a glass of wine over one diner and started giggling instead of apologizing. The guy wasn't amused and 'accidentally' spilled a glass of water over Carol's dress."

Since the item contained several false statements, Burnett's attorney demanded a retraction or correction. The defendant subsequently printed the following retraction:

> "An item in this column on March 2 erroneously reported that Carol Burnett had an argument with Henry Kissinger at a Washington restaurant and became boisterous, disturbing other guests. We understand these events did not occur and we are sorry for any embarrassment our report may have caused Miss Burnett."

After holding that the National Enquirer was not a newspaper within the meaning of the statute, the court stated in dicta that, even if the National Enquirer had qualified for protection under the statute, the retraction was not legally sufficient. The court noted that the retraction was incomplete, evasive, and less conspicuous than the original piece.

**4. Defamation and the Internet.** In 1996 a federal statute, 47 U.S.C. § 230, granted immunity to internet providers who republish a third party's defamation. The federal provision was in response to concerns internet providers, unlike traditional media publishers, could not effectively review the volume of third party communications distributed to subscribers by the providers. In *Blumenthal v. Drudge,* 992 F.Supp. 44 (D.D.C. 1998), the court, relying on the statutory immunity, held America On Line (AOL) was not liable for false defamatory accusation made online by Matt Drudge ("The Drudge Report") asserting a White House press assistant beat his wife. The immunity applied even though AOL paid Mr. Drudge to prepare his report and make it available to AOL subscribers. The court noted that Mr. Drudge, himself, was not immune. Consider also *Zeran v. America Online, Inc.*, 129 F.3d 327 (4th Cir. 1997). The court held America Online immune from liability for defamation based on allegations the internet provider failed to promptly remove, despite repeated requests by the plaintiff, an anonymously submitted message posted on its bulletin board. The message falsely indicated the plaintiff was selling T-shirts and other items exploiting the bombing of the Oklahoma federal building and prompted death threats against him. How much protection should internet publishers be given from liability for defamation?

# Chapter IX

## PRIVACY

---

## SECTION A.  INTRUSION UPON SECLUSION

### PEARSON v. DODD

United States Court of Appeals District of Columbia Circuit.
410 F.2d 701 (1969).

J. SKELLY WRIGHT, Circuit Judge.

This case arises out of the exposure of the alleged misdeeds of Senator Thomas Dodd of Connecticut by newspaper columnists Drew Pearson and Jack Anderson. The District Court has granted partial summary judgment to Senator Dodd, appellee here, finding liability on a theory of conversion. At the same time, the court denied partial summary judgment on the theory of invasion of privacy. Both branches of the court's judgment are before us on interlocutory appeal. We affirm the District Court's denial of summary judgment for invasion of privacy and reverse its grant of summary judgment for conversion.

The undisputed facts in the case were stated by the District Court as follows:

"* * * On several occasions in June and July, 1965, two former employees of the plaintiff, at times with the assistance of two members of the plaintiff's staff, entered the plaintiff's office without authority and unbeknownst to him, removed numerous documents from his files, made copies of them, replaced the originals, and turned over the copies to the defendant Anderson, who was aware of the manner in which the copies had been obtained. The defendants Pearson and Anderson thereafter published articles containing information gleaned from these documents."

### I

The District Court ruled that appellants' six newspaper columns concerning appellee, which were attached to appellee's complaint, did not establish liability for the tort of invasion of privacy. That tort, whose historical origin lies in the famous Warren and Brandeis article of 1890,[3] is recognized in the District of Columbia. It has always been considered a defense to a claim of invasion of privacy by publication, however, that the published matter complained of is of general public interest. The columns complained of here gave appellants' version of appellee's relationship with certain lobbyists for foreign interests, and gave an interpretive biographical sketch of appellee's public career. They thus clearly bore on appellee's qualifications as a United States Senator, and as such amounted to a paradigm example of published speech not subject to suit for invasion of privacy.

Indeed, appellee has not urged with any vigor on appeal the theory that appellants' publications in themselves tortiously invaded his privacy. Rather he has argued that the District Court misapprehended his privacy claim, which went rather to the manner in which the information in the columns was obtained than to the matter contained in them.

Appellee proceeds under a branch of privacy theory which Dean Prosser has labeled "intrusion," and which has been increasingly recognized by courts and commentators in recent years. Thus it has been held that unauthorized bugging of a dwelling, tapping a telephone, snooping through windows, and overzealous shadowing amount to invasions of privacy, whether or not accompanied by trespasses to property.

Unlike other types of invasion of privacy, intrusion does not involve as one of its essential elements the publication of the information obtained. The tort is completed with the obtaining of the information by improperly intrusive means.

"Intrusion" has not been either recognized or rejected as a tort in the District of Columbia. It has been recognized by a number of state courts, most recently by the New Hampshire Supreme Court in *Hamberger v. Eastman*. Hamberger found liable a defendant who eavesdropped upon the marital bedroom of plaintiffs by electronic means, holding that "the invasion of the plaintiffs' solitude or seclusion * * * was a violation of their right of privacy."

We approve the extension of the tort of invasion of privacy to instances of intrusion, whether by physical trespass or not, into spheres from which an ordinary man is a plaintiff's position could reasonably expect that the particular defendant should be excluded. Just as the Fourth Amendment has expanded to protect citizens from government intrusions where intrusion in not reasonably expected, so should tort law protect citizens from other citizens. The protection should not turn exclusively on the question of whether the intrusion involves a technical trespass under the law of property. The common law, like the Fourth Amendment, should "protect people, not places."

The question then becomes whether appellants Pearson and Anderson improperly intruded into the protected sphere of privacy of appellee Dodd in obtaining the information on which their columns were based. In determining this question, we may assume, without deciding, that appellee's employees and former employees did commit such an

**3.** Warren and Brandeis, The Right to Privacy, 4 Harv.L.Rev. 193 (1890).

improper intrusion when they removed confidential files with the intent to show them to unauthorized outsiders.

Although appellee's complaint charges that appellants aided and abetted in the removal of the documents, the undisputed facts, narrowed by the District Judge with the concurrence of counsel, established only that appellants received copies of the documents knowing that they had been removed without authorization. If we were to hold appellants liable for invasion of privacy on these facts, we would establish the proposition that one who receives information from an intruder, knowing it has been obtained by improper intrusion, is guilty of a tort. In an untried and developing area of tort law, we are not prepared to go so far. A person approached by an eavesdropper with an offer to share in the information gathered through the eavesdropping would perhaps play the nobler part should he spurn the offer and shut his ears. However, it seems to us that at this point it would place too great a strain on human weakness to hold one liable in damages who merely succumbs to temptation and listens.

\* \* \*

Of course, appellants did more than receive and peruse the copies of the documents taken from appellee's files; they published excerpts from them in the national press. But in analyzing a claimed breach of privacy, injuries from intrusion and injuries from publication should be kept clearly separate. Where there is intrusion, the intruder should generally be liable whatever the content of what he learns. An eavesdropper to the marital bedroom may hear marital intimacies, or he may hear statements of fact or opinion of legitimate interest to the public; for purposes of liability that should make no difference. On the other hand, where the claim is that private information concerning plaintiff has been published, the question of whether that information is genuinely private or is of public interest should not turn on the manner in which it has been obtained. Of course, both forms of invasion may be combined in the same case.

Here we have separately considered the nature of appellant's publications concerning appellee, and have found that the matter published was of obvious public interest. The publication was not itself an invasion of privacy. Since we have also concluded that appellants' role in obtaining the information did not make them liable to appellee for intrusion, their subsequent publication, itself no invasion of privacy, cannot reach back to render that role tortious.

\* \* \*

So ordered.

TAMM, Circuit Judge (concurring):

Some legal scholars will see in the majority opinion—as distinguished from its actual holding—an ironic aspect. Conduct for which a law enforcement officer would be soundly castigated is, by the phraseology of the majority opinion, found tolerable; conduct which, if engaged in by government agents would lead to the suppression of evidence obtained by these means, is approved when used for the profit of the press.

There is an anomaly lurking in this situation: the news media regard themselves as quasi-public institutions yet they demand immunity from the restraints which they vigorously demand be placed on government. That which is regarded as a mortal taint on information secured by any illegal conduct of government would appear from the majority opinion to be permissible as a technique or modus operandi for the journalist. Some will find this confusing, but I am not free to act on my own views under the doctrine of stare decisis which I consider binding upon me.

* * *

## DIETEMANN v. TIME, INC.

United States Court of Appeals, Ninth Circuit.
449 F.2d 245 (1971).

HUFSTEDLER, Circuit Judge:

This is an appeal from a judgment for plaintiff in an action for invasion of privacy. Jurisdiction was grounded in diversity. The parties agreed that California law governed. After a court trial plaintiff was awarded $1000 general damages. On appeal we are asked to consider significant questions involving the relationship between personal privacy and the freedom of the press.

The district court's decision is reported in *Dietemann v. Time, Inc.*, 284 F.Supp. 925 (1968). The facts, as narrated by the district court, are these:

"Plaintiff, a disabled veteran with little education, was engaged in the practice of healing with clay, minerals, and herbs—as practiced, simple quackery.

"Defendant, Time, Incorporated, a New York corporation, publishes Life Magazine. Its November 1, 1963 edition carried an article entitled 'Crackdown on Quackery.' The article depicted plaintiff as a quack and included two pictures of him. One picture was taken at plaintiff's home on September 20, 1963, previous to his arrest on a charge of practicing medicine without a license, and the other taken at the time of his arrest.

"Life Magazine entered into an arrangement with the District Attorney's Office of Los Angeles County whereby Life's employees would visit plaintiff and obtain facts and pictures concerning his activities. Two employees of Life, Mrs. Jackie Metcalf and Mr. William Ray, went to plaintiff's home on September 20, 1963. When they arrived at a locked gate, they rang a bell and plaintiff came out of his house and was told by Mrs. Metcalf and Ray that they had been sent there by a friend, a Mr. Johnson. The use of Johnson's name was a ruse to gain entrance. Plaintiff admitted them and all three went into the house and into plaintiff's den.

"The plaintiff had some equipment which could at best be described as gadgets, not equipment which had anything to do with the practice of medicine. Plaintiff, while examining Mrs. Metcalf, was photographed by Ray with a hidden camera without the consent of plaintiff. One of the pictures taken by him appeared in Life Magazine showing plaintiff with his hand on the upper portion of Mrs. Metcalf's breast while he was looking at some gadgets and holding what appeared to be a wand in his right hand. Mrs. Metcalf had told plaintiff that she had a lump in her breast. Plaintiff concluded that she had eaten some rancid butter 11 years, 9 months, and 7 days prior to that time. Other persons were seated in the room during this time.

"The conversation between Mrs. Metcalf and plaintiff was transmitted by radio transmitter hidden in Mrs. Metcalf's purse to a tape recorder in a parked automobile occupied by Joseph Bride, Life employee, John Miner of the District Attorney's Office, and Grant Leake, an investigator of the State Department of Public Health. While the recorded conversation was not quoted in the article in Life, it was mentioned that Life correspondent Bride was making notes of what was being received via the radio transmitter, and such information was at least referred to in the article.

"The foregoing events were photographed and recorded by an arrangement among Miner of the District Attorney's Office, Leake of the State Department of Pubic Health, and Bride, a representative of Life. It had been agreed that Life would obtain pictures and information for use as evidence, and later could be used by Life for publication.

"Prior to the occurrences of September 20, 1963, on two occasions the officials had obtained recordings of conversations in plaintiff's home; however, no pictures had been secured. Life employees had not participated in obtaining the recordings on these occasions.

"On October 15, 1963, plaintiff was arrested at his home on a charge of practicing medicine without a license in violation of Section 26280, California Health and Safety Code. At the time of his arrest, many pictures were made by Life of plaintiff at his home. Plaintiff testified that he did not agree to pose for the pictures but allowed pictures because he thought the officers could require it. Also present were newspaper men who had also been invited by the officials to be present at the time of arrest.

"Defendant contends that plaintiff posed for pictures at the time of his arrest and thus permission was given to take those pictures. As hereinafter pointed out, it is unnecessary to decide whether or not permission was given to take pictures at the time of his arrest.

"Plaintiff, although a journeyman plumber, claims to be a scientist. Plaintiff had no listings and his home had no sign of any kind. He did not advertise, nor did he have a telephone. He made no charges when he attempted to diagnose or to prescribe herbs and minerals. He did accept contributions.

"Life's article concerning plaintiff was not published until after plaintiff was arrested but before his plea on June 1, 1964 of nolo contendere for violations of Section 2141 of the California Business and Professions Code and Section 26280 of the California Health and Safety Code (misdemeanors).

"* * *

"Defendant's claim that the plaintiff's house was open to the public is not sustained by the evidence. The plaintiff was administering his so-called treatments to people who visited him. He was not a medical man of any type. He did not advertise. He did not have a phone. He did have a lock on his gate. To obtain entrance it was necessary to ring a bell. He conducted his activities in a building which was his home. The employees of defendant gained entrance by a subterfuge."

The district court concluded: "The publication in Life Magazine on November 1, 1963 of plaintiff's picture taken without his consent in his home on September 20, 1963 was an invasion of his privacy under California law for which he is entitled to damages...."

\* \* \*

The appeal presents three ultimate issues: (1) Under California law, is a cause of action for invasion of privacy established upon proof that defendant's employees, by subterfuge, gained entrance to the office portion of plaintiff's home wherein they photographed him and electronically recorded and transmitted to third persons his conversation without his consent as a result of which he suffered emotional distress? (2) Does the First Amendment insulate defendant from liability for invasion of privacy because defendant's employees did those acts for the purpose of gathering material for a magazine story and a story was thereafter published utilizing some of the material thus gathered?

\* \* \*

In jurisdictions other than California in which a common law tort for invasion of privacy is recognized, it has been consistently held that surreptitious electronic recording of a plaintiff's conversation causing him emotional distress is actionable. Despite some variations in the description and the labels applied to the tort, there is agreement that publication is not a necessary element of the tort, that the existence of a technical trespass is immaterial, and that proof of special damages is not required. (*E.g., Nader v. General Motors Corp.* (1970) 25 N.Y.2d 560, 307 N.Y.S.2d 647, 255 N.E.2d 765 (applying District of Columbia law); *Hamberger v. Eastman* (1964) 106 N.H. 107, 206 A.2d 239; *Roach v. Harper* (1958) 143 W.Va. 869, 105 S.E.2d 564; *McDaniel v. Atlanta Coca–Cola Bottling Co.* (1939) 60 Ga.App. 92, 2 S.E.2d 810; *cf. Pearson v. Dodd*, 133 U.S.App.D.C. 279; 410 F.2d 701, cert denied (1969) 395 U.S. 947, 89 S.Ct. 2021, 23 L.Ed.2d 465).

Although the issue has not been squarely decided in California, we have little difficulty in concluding that clandestine photography of the plaintiff in his den and the recordation and transmission of his conversation without his consent resulting in his emotional distress warrants recovery for invasion of privacy in California. California began developing a common law privacy tort in 1931 with the decision of *Melvin v. Reid*, 112 Cal.App. 285, 297 P. 91. Since then, the California Supreme Court has decided a number of privacy cases in some of which there are indications that California would recognize the plaintiff's claim.

The most recent expression is found in Briscoe v. Reader's Digest Ass'n, *supra,* 4 Cal.3d at [529], 93 Cal.Rptr. at 869, 483 P.2d at 37, a privacy action based upon the publication of an article disclosing plaintiff's conviction of a felony 11 years earlier. The court equated the growing acceptance of the right of privacy with "the increasing capability of * * * electronic devices with their capacity to destroy an individual's anonymity, intrude upon his most intimate activities, and expose his most personal characteristics to public gaze. * * *"

* * *

In *Gill v. Hearst Publishing Co.* (1953) 40 Cal.2d 224, 230, 253 P.2d 441, 444, which denied recovery for invasion of privacy to plaintiffs whose picture was taken in a public market and later published without their consent, the court stressed that the picture had not been "surreptitiously snapped on private grounds, but rather was taken of plaintiffs in a pose voluntarily assumed in a public market place."

Concurrently with the development of privacy law, California had decided a series of cases according plaintiffs relief from unreasonable penetrations of their mental tranquility based upon the tort of intentional inflection of emotional distress. (*E.g., Alcorn v. Anbro Engineering, Inc.* (1970) 2 Cal.3d 493, 86 Cal.Rptr. 88, 468 P.2d 216; *State Rubbish Collectors Ass'n v. Siliznoff* (1952) 38 Cal.2d 330, 240 P.2d 282; *Fletcher v. Western Nat'l Life Ins. Co.* (1970) 10 Cal.App.3d 376, 89 Cal.Rptr. 78.) Although these cases are not direct authority in the privacy area, they are indicative of the trend of California law to protect interests analogous to those asserted by plaintiff in this case.

We are convinced that California will "approve the extension of the tort of invasion of privacy to instances of intrusion, whether by physical trespass or not, into spheres from which an ordinary man in plaintiff's position could reasonably expect that the particular defendant should be excluded." (*Pearson v. Dodd, supra,* 410 F.2d at 704.)

Plaintiff's den was a sphere from which he could reasonably expect to exclude eavesdropping newsmen. He invited two of defendant's employees to the den. One who invites another to his home or office takes a risk that the visitor may not be what he seems, and that the visitor may repeat all he hears and observes when he leaves. But he does not and should not be required to take the risk that what is heard and seen will be transmitted by photograph or recording, or in our modern world, in full living color and hi-fi to the public at large or to any segment of it that the visitor may select. A different rule could have a most pernicious effect upon the dignity of man and it would surely lead to guarded conversations and conduct where candor is most valued, *e.g.,* in the case of doctors and lawyers.

The defendant claims that the First Amendment immunizes it from liability for invading plaintiff's den with a hidden camera and its concealed electronic instruments because its employees were gathering news and its instrumentalities "are indispensable tools of investigative reporting." We agree that newsgathering is an integral part of news dissemination. We strongly disagree, however, that the hidden mechanical contrivances are "indispensable tools" of newsgathering. Investigative reporting is an ancient art; its successful practice long antecedes the invention of miniature cameras and electronic devices. The First Amendment has never been construed to accord newsmen immunity from torts or crimes committed during the course of newsgathering. The First Amendment is not a license to trespass, to steal, or to intrude by electronic means into the precincts of another's home or office. It does not become such a license simply because the person subjected to the intrusion is reasonably suspected of committing a crime.

Defendant relies upon the line of cases commencing with *New York Times Co. v. Sullivan* (1964) 376 U.S. 254, 84 S.Ct. 710, 11 L.Ed.2d 686 and extending through *Rosenbloom v. Metromedia, Inc.* (1971) 403 U.S. 29, 91 S.Ct. 1811, 29 L.Ed.2d 296 (1971) to sustain its contentions that (1) publication of news, however tortiously gathered, insulates defendant from liability for the antecedent tort, and (2) even of it is not thus shielded from liability, those cases prevent consideration of publication as an element in computing damages.

As we previously observed, publication is not an essential element of plaintiff's cause of action. Moreover, it is not the foundation for the invocation of a privilege. Privilege concepts developed in defamation cases and to some extent in privacy actions in which publication is an essential component are not relevant in determining liability for intrusive conduct antedating publication. (*Cf.* Nimmer, "The Right to Speak From Time to Time: First Amendment Theory Applied to Libel and Misapplied to Privacy" (1968) 56 Calif.L.Rev. 935, 957.) Nothing in *New York Times* or its progeny suggests anything to the contrary. Indeed, the Court strongly indicates that there is no First Amendment interest in protecting news media from calculated misdeeds. (*E.g., Time, Inc. v. Hill, supra,* 385 U.S. at 389–390 and 384 n. 9.)

No interest protected by the First Amendment is adversely affected by permitting damages for intrusion to be enhanced by the fact of later publication of the information that the publisher improperly acquired. Assessing damages for the additional emotional distress suffered by a plaintiff when the wrongfully acquired data are purveyed to the multitude chills intrusive acts. It does not chill freedom of expression guaranteed by the First Amendment. A rule forbidding the use of publication as an ingredient of damages would deny to the injured plaintiff recovery for real harm done to him without any countervailing benefit to the legitimate interest of the public in being informed. The same rule would encourage conduct by news media that grossly offends ordinary men.

The judgment is affirmed.

\* \* \*

## NOTES

**1. Privacy.** The tort of invasion of privacy is of relatively recent origin, having come into acceptance in the last century. According to section 652A of the Restatement (Second) of Torts, invasion of privacy may be established by one of four theories: (1) intrusion upon seclusion; (2) unauthorized use of a party's name or likeness; (3) giving unreasonable publicity to private matters; and (4) publicly characterizing the party in a false light. See Diamond, Levine & Madden, *Understanding Torts* § 22.01 (2nd ed.

2000); Keeton, *Prosser and Keeton on the Law of Torts* § 117 (5th ed. 1984); and Dobbs, *The Law of Torts*, § 426 (2000).

**2. Intrusion Upon Seclusion.** The Restatement defines Intrusion upon Seclusion as follows:

> "One who intentionally intrudes, physically or otherwise, upon the solitude or seclusion of another or his private affairs or concerns, is subject to liability to the other for invasion of his privacy, if the intrusion would be highly offensive to a reasonable person."

Restatement (Second) of Torts § 652B.

As the principal cases indicate, damages may be recovered where the defendant intrudes upon the plaintiff's seclusion. In order to be actionable, the intrusion must be highly offensive when evaluated objectively. The tort is committed by the intrusion—there is no requirement the information obtained be communicated. As for the intrusion, it need not be trespassory— eavesdropping from a distance could suffice. Finally, it is no defense to assert that the matter is of public concern. Perhaps the classic example of intrusion upon seclusion is *Hamberger v. Eastman*, 106 N.H. 107, 206 A.2d 239 (1964), where the defendant placed a microphone under the matrimonial mattress.

**3. Media Liability.** The privacy tort of intrusion upon seclusion raises questions of how far the media can go in pursuit of a story. In *Deteresa v. American Broadcasting Companies*, 121 F.3d 460 (9th Cir.1997), a producer for the ABC television network went to the plaintiff's condominium entrance. The plaintiff served as an attendant on the flight O.J. Simpson had been on soon after the murders of his ex-wife, Nicole Simpson, and Ronald Goldman. The producer identified himself as working for ABC and requested an on-camera interview. The plaintiff declined. In fact, ABC surreptitiously made a video and audio tape of the preliminary conversation that took place outside the condominium's front door. The court held that the plaintiff was in public view and spoke freely to an identified reporter and consequently there was an insufficient expectation of privacy to support the tort.

Compare *Deteresa* with another case involving an ABC reporter, *Sanders v. American Broadcasting Companies*, 20 Cal.4th 907, 85 Cal.Rptr.2d 909, 978 P.2d 67 (1999). In *Sanders*, the ABC reporter obtained a job as a "telepsychic" and proceeded to surreptitiously videotape conversations with co-employees by concealing the camera in her hat at the shared office space where the psychic worked. The court concluded intrusion upon seclusion was actionable:

> "To summarize, we conclude that in the workplace, as else-where, the reasonableness of a person's expectation of visual and aural privacy depends not only on who might have been able to observe the subject interaction, but on the identity of the claimed intruder and the means of intrusion. (*Shulman, supra*, 18 Cal.4th at pp. 233–235, 74 Cal.Rptr.2d 843, 955 P.2d 469; *Dietemann v. Time, Inc., supra*, 449 F.2d at p. 249; *Huskey v. National Broadcasting Co., Inc., supra*, 632 F.Supp. at pp. 1287–1288; *Nader v. General Motors Corporation, supra*, 307 N.Y.S.2d at p. 655, 255 N.E.2d 765; *Pearson v. Dodd, supra*, 410 F.2d at p. 704; *Walker v. Darby, supra*, 911 F.2d at p. 1579.) For this reason, we answer the briefed question affirmatively: a person who lacks a reasonable expectation

of complete privacy in a conversation, because it could be seen and overheard by coworkers (but not the general public), may nevertheless have a claim for invasion of privacy by intrusion based on a television reporter's covert videotaping of that conversation.

Defendants warn that 'the adoption of a doctrine of *per se* workplace privacy would place a dangerous chill on the press' investigation of abusive activities in open work areas, implicating substantial First Amendment concerns. (Italics in original.) We adopt no such per se doctrine of privacy. We hold only that the possibility of being overheard by coworkers does not, as a matter of law, render unreasonable an employee's expectation that his or her interactions within a nonpublic workplace will not be videotaped in secret by a journalist. In other circumstances, where, for example, the workplace is regularly open to entry or observation by the public or press, or the interaction that was the subject of the alleged intrusion was between proprietor (or employee) and customer, any expectation of privacy against press recording is less likely to be deemed reasonable. Nothing we say here prevents a media defendant from attempting to show, in order to negate the offensiveness element of the intrusion tort, that the claimed intrusion, even if it infringed on a reasonable expectation of privacy, was 'justified by the legitimate motive of gathering the news.' (*Shulman, supra*, 18 Cal.4th at pp. 236–237, 74 Cal.Rptr.2d 843, 955 P.2d 469.)" *Id.* at 77.

What do you think should be the limits of journalistic deception and surreptitious recording? In a related matter, the United States Supreme Court recently in *Wilson v. Layne*, 526 U.S. 603, 119 S.Ct. 1692, 143 L.Ed.2d 818 (1999) held that it was a violation of the Fourth Amendment's protection against unreasonable search and seizure "for the police to bring members of the media or other third parties into a home during the execution of a warrant when the presence of the third parties in the home was not in aid of the execution of the warrant."

# SECTION B. APPROPRIATION OF NAME OR LIKENESS AND PUBLICITY OF PRIVATE LIFE

## NEFF v. TIME, INC.
United States District Court, W.D. Pennsylvania.
406 F.Supp. 858 (1976).

MARSH, District Judge.

This diversity action was removed from the Court of Common Pleas of Allegheny County, Pennsylvania, where a complaint had been filed by John W. Neff, the plaintiff, against Time, Inc., the defendant. The complaint was verified by Neff and alleged that the defendant is the owner of a magazine known as Sports Illustrated sold weekly throughout Pennsylvania; that Neff is a private citizen employed in education; that in its issue of August 5, 1974, the defendant's magazine used Neff's picture without his prior knowledge and consent to illustrate an article entitled "A Strange Kind of Love;" that the photograph shows Neff with the front zipper of his trousers completely opened implying that he is a "crazy, drunken slob," and combined with the title of the article, "a sexual deviate." Neff alleges that the unauthorized publication and circulation of his picture to illustrate the article invaded his right of privacy and subjected him to public ridicule and contempt, injured his personal esteem and the esteem of his profession, reflected on his character, diminished his high standing reputation among his family, friends, neighbors and business associates, destroyed his peace of mind and caused him severe mental and emotional distress to his damage in excess of $5,000, amended to aver in excess of $10,000.

\* \* \*

The affidavits establish that the photograph was taken about 1:00 o'clock P.M. November 25, 1973, while Neff was present on a dugout with a group of fans prior to a professional football game at Cleveland between the Cleveland Browns and the Pittsburgh Steelers. The photographer was on the field intending to take pictures of the Steeler players as they entered the field from the dugout. Neff and others were jumping up and down in full view of the fans in the stadium; they were waving Steeler banners and drinking beer; they all seemed to be slightly inebriated. One of the group asked the photographer for whom he was working and was told Sports Illustrated, whereupon the group began to act as if a television camera had been put on them; as the pictures were taken they began to react even more, screaming and howling and imploring the photographer to take more pictures. The more pictures taken of the group, the more they hammed it up. All were aware that the photographer was covering the game for Sports Illustrated. There were no objections; they wanted to be photographed. Thirty pictures were taken of the group on the dugout from different angles.

During the period from July through December, 1973, this photographer took 7,200 pictures pursuant to his assignment to cover the Steelers. As part of his duty he edited the pictures and submitted one hundred to the magazine for selection by a committee of five employees. After several screenings of the thirty pictures of the group on the dugout, the committee selected Neff's picture with his fly open. Although Neff's fly was not open to the point of being revealing, the selection was deliberate and surely in utmost bad taste; subjectively, as to Neff, the published picture could have been embarrassing, humiliating and offensive to his sensibilities. Without doubt the magazine deliberately exhibited Neff in an embarrassing manner.

It appears that the pictures were taken to illustrate a book being written by one Blount about the Steeler fans, and three excerpts from the book were published in the magazine. Only three pictures, including Neff's, accompanied the article of August 5, 1974. The title to this article "A Strange Kind of Love" could convey to some readers a derogatory connotation. Neff is not mentioned by name in the article; the Steeler–Cleveland game of November, 1973, is not mentioned in the article; Neff's photograph was not selected on the basis of its relationship to that game. The caption appearing adjacent to the photograph reads:

"In the fading autumn Sundays at Three Rivers, the fans joined the players in mean pro dreams."

Three Rivers is the name of the stadium in Pittsburgh. Neff's photograph was selected because "it represented the typical Steeler fan: a rowdy, strong rooter, much behind his team, having a good time at the game," and "it fitted in perfectly with the text of the story." (See affidavit of Richard M. Gangel, Art Director for Sports Illustrated).

It seems to us that art directors and editors should hesitate to deliberately publish a picture which most likely would be offensive and cause embarrassment to the subject when many other pictures of the same variety are available. Notwithstanding, "[t]he courts are not concerned with establishing canons of good taste for the press or the public." *Aquino v. Bulletin Company*, 190 Pa.Super. 528, 154 A.2d 422, 425 (1959).

The right of privacy is firmly established in Pennsylvania despite the fact that its perimeter is not yet clearly defined and its contours remain amorphous. *Vogel v. W. T. Grant Company*, 458 Pa. 124, 327 A.2d 133 (1974).

From *Vogel* it seems that Pennsylvania follows the rules promulgated by the Restatement (Second) of Torts Secs. 652 B through E (Tent. Draft No. 13, 1967); that invasion of privacy is actionable under any one of four distinct, but coordinate, torts. These are concisely paraphrased in *Goldman v. Time, Inc.*, 336 F.Supp. 133, 136 (N.D.Cal.1971) as follows:

"1. Intrusion upon the plaintiff's seclusion or solitude, or into his private affairs.

2. Public disclosure of embarrassing private facts about the plaintiff.

3. Publicity which places the plaintiff in a false light in the public eye.

4. Appropriation, for the defendant's advantage, of the plaintiff's name or likeness. Prosser on Torts at 837 et seq. (3d ed. 1964); Prosser, "Privacy," 48 Cal.L.Rev. 383, 389 (1960)."

See also Sec. 652 A, Restatement (Second) of Torts (Tent. Draft No. 21, 1975).

Plaintiff's claim is based on "appropriation of name or likeness" and "publicity given to private life," i.e., 4 and 2, supra. Plaintiff's brief, page 5.

As to 4, *supra*, Sec. 652 C of the Restatement (Second) of Torts (Tent. Draft No. 21, 1975) states:

"One who appropriates to his own use or benefit the name or likeness of another is subject to liability to the other for unreasonable invasion of his privacy."

It is settled that this section is not applicable when a person's picture is used in a non-commercial article dealing with an accident, or the picture of a bystander at a political convention, or parade, *Murray v. N.Y. Magazine Co.*, 27 N.y.2d 406, 318 N.Y.S.2d 474, 267 N.E.2d 256

(1971), or generally in the reporting of news. We think actions of excited fans at a football game are news as is a story about the fans of a professional football team. As stated in *Gautier v. Pro–Football, Inc.,* 278 App.Div. 431, 435, 106 N.Y.S.2d 553, 557 (1st Dept. 1951), aff'd 304 N.Y. 354, 107 N.E.2d 485 (1953): "Once an item has achieved the status of newsworthiness, it retains that status even when no longer current." See also *Jenkins v. Dell Publishing Company,* 251 F.2d 447 (3rd Cir. 1958); Murray v. N.Y. Magazine Co., supra. The fact that Sports Illustrated is a magazine published for profit does not constitute a "commercial appropriation of Neff's likeness." The fact that Neff was photographed in a public place for a newsworthy article, entitles the defendant to the protection of the First Amendment. *Time, Inc. v. Hill,* 385 U.S. 374, 397, 87 S.Ct. 534, 17 L.Ed.2d 456 (1967); *New York Times Co. v. Sullivan,* 376 U.S. 254, 84 S.Ct. 710, 11 L.Ed.2d 686 (1964). The tort described in 4, supra, and Sec. 652 C Restatement (Second) of Torts is not applicable to the facts in this case.

Of course, we are concerned that Neff's picture was deliberately selected by an editorial committee from a number of similar pictures and segregated and published alone. If his picture had appeared as part of the general crowd scene of fans at a game, even though embarrassing, there would be no problem. Although we have some misgivings, it is our opinion that the publication of Neff's photograph taken with his active encouragement and participation, and with knowledge that the photographer was connected with a publication, even though taken without his express consent, is protected by the Constitution.

An appropriate order will be entered.

## NOTES

**1. Appropriation of Name or Likeness.** Unauthorized appropriation of the name or picture of another for one's own use constitutes the second of four privacy torts recognized by the Restatement. The Restatement defines the tort as:

> "One who appropriates to his own use or benefit the name or likeness of another is subject to liability to the other for invasion of his privacy."

Restatement (Second) of Torts § 652C.

For example, using a person's image to promote a product, as on a box of cereal, would be actionable. The tort does not, however, prohibit the use of a name or picture in magazines, news articles, or even an unauthorized biography. This activity is protected by the First Amendment. Consequently, magazines may regularly print photographs of celebrities and others on the cover of magazines and do feature articles and photo spreads. The line between tortious appropriation of name or likeness and legitimate use can be fuzzy. Suppose magazine covers are reprinted as posters? Consider *Montana v. San Jose Mercury News, Inc.,* 34 Cal.App.4th 790, 40 Cal.Rptr.2d 639 (Cal. Ct. App. 1995), where a newspaper reprinted pictures from several of its Superbowl issues in poster format and sold them to the general public. Celebrity football player Joe Montana depicted in those issues sued the paper for commercial misappropriation of his name, photograph and likeness. The defendant moved for summary judgment, claiming the action was barred by the First Amendment and by the statute of limitations. The court granted the motion, stating first that the pictures were items of public interest, and second that a newspaper has a constitutional right to promote itself by reproducing its originally protected articles or photographs.

But consider *Titan Sports, Inc. v. Comics World Corp.*, 870 F.2d 85 (2d Cir.1989), where publisher of a magazine included up to ten full color, oversized photographs of professional wrestlers. The posters had to be detached from the magazine for full view. The court held this constituted appropriation for purposes of trade under the applicable New York statute. Where should courts draw the line? See also *Namath v. Sports Illustrated*, 39 N.Y.2d 897, 386 N.Y.S.2d 397, 352 N.E.2d 584 (1976), where another celebrity football quarterback argued Sports Illustrated had misappropriated his picture by reprinting a picture of him in the magazine in its advertising. The court noted the magazine's use of the picture did not imply the football player's endorsement and that the magazine was allowed to display its content including plaintiff's picture when seeking subscribers. See Diamond, Levine & Madden, *Understanding Torts* § 22.03 (2nd ed. 2000); Keeton, *Prosser and Keeton on the Law of Torts* § 117 (5th ed. 1984); Dobbs, *The Law of Torts* § 425 (2000).

**2. Beyond Name and Picture.** Courts have also attempted to resolve what aspects of the identity of celebrities besides their names and pictures might constitute appropriation of their identity under the tort. In *Midler v. Ford Motor Co.*, 849 F.2d 460 (9th Cir.1988), the court found the defendant liable for imitating Midler's distinctive voice in an advertisement; another court found defendant liable for naming portable toilets, "Here's Johnny," the announcement phrase used to introduce Jay Leno's late night television host predecessor, Johnny Carson. See *Carson v. Here's Johnny Portable Toilets, Inc.*, 698 F.2d 831 (6th Cir.1983). See also Franklin, Anderson, & Cate, *Mass Media Law* (6th ed. 2000).

In *Zacchini v. Scripps–Howard Broadcasting Co.*, 433 U.S. 562, 97 S.Ct. 2849, 53 L.Ed.2d 965 (1977), the Supreme Court sustained an appropriation claim against a television station for its broadcast of the entire 15–second human cannonball act at a county fair in a newscast. The Court rejected First Amendment arguments that the television broadcast was reporting legitimate news instead of appropriating the plaintiff's exhibition rights.

**3. Right of Publicity.** Celebrities, who clearly have an economic investment in their names and images, generally can also sue under what is known as a right of publicity tort, violation of which is established in the same manner as the tortious appropriation of name or likeness. The distinction is important insofar as the right of publicity, unlike the appropriation tort, is inheritable in many states. In essence, however, the right of publicity protects the same interest as the appropriation tort. Consider *Sagan v. Apple Computer, Inc.*, 874 F.Supp. 1072 (C.D.Cal.1994), where a famous scientist threatened to sue a computer manufacturer when it was revealed in the media that the defendant was using the plaintiff's name as a code word for a new computer. The defendant changed the code word to "Butt–Head Astronomer," and the new code word was published by the defendant and appeared in various media. The court consolidated the plaintiff's claims for misappropriation of the right to publicity and the right to privacy, emphasizing the two torts protect the same rights.

# SIPPLE v. CHRONICLE PUBLISHING CO.

Court of Appeal, First District, Division 4, California.
154 Cal.App.3d 1040, 201 Cal.Rptr. 665 (1984).

CALDECOTT, Presiding Justice.

On September 22, 1975, Sara Jane Moore attempted to assassinate President Gerald R. Ford while the latter was visiting San Francisco, California. Plaintiff Oliver W. Sipple (hereafter appellant or Sipple) who was in the crowd at Union Square, San Francisco, grabbed or struck Moore's arm as the latter was about to fire the gun and shoot at the President. Although no one can be certain whether or not Sipple actually saved the President's life, the assassination attempt did not succeed and Sipple was considered a hero for his selfless action and was subject to significant publicity throughout the nation following the assassination attempt.

Among the many articles concerning the event was a column written by Herb Caen and published by the San Francisco Chronicle on September 24, 1975. The article read in part as follows: "One of the heroes of the day, Oliver 'Bill' Sipple, the ex-Marine who grabbed Sara Jane Moore's arm just as her gun was fired and thereby may have saved the President's life, was the center of midnight attention at the Red Lantern, a Golden Gate Ave. bar he favors. The Rev. Ray Broshears, head of Helping Hands, and Gay Politico, Harvey Milk, who claim to be among Sipple's close friends, describe themselves as 'proud—maybe this will help break the stereotype'. Sipple is among the workers in Milk's campaign for Supervisor."

Thereafter, the Los Angeles Times and numerous out-of-state newspapers published articles which, referring to the primary source (i.e., the story published in the San Francisco Chronicle), mentioned both the heroic act shown by Sipple and the fact that he was a prominent member of the San Francisco gay community. Some of those articles speculated that President Ford's failure to promptly thank Sipple for his heroic act was a result of Sipple's sexual orientation.

Finding the articles offensive to his private life, on September 30, 1975, Sipple filed an action against the California defendants, the Chronicle Publishing Company, Charles de Young Thieriot, the publisher of the Chronicle, Herb Caen, a columnist for the Chronicle, the Times Mirror Company, the owner and publisher of the Los Angeles Times, and Otis Chandler (hereafter together respondents) and numerous out-of-state newspapers. The complaint was predicated upon the theory of invasion of privacy and alleged in essence that defendants without authorization and consent published private facts about plaintiff's life by disclosing that plaintiff was homosexual in his personal and private sexual orientation; that said publications were highly offensive to plaintiff inasmuch as his parents, brothers and sisters learned for the first time of his homosexual orientation; and that as a consequence of disclosure of private facts about his life plaintiff was abandoned by his family, exposed to contempt and ridicule causing him great mental anguish, embarrassment and humiliation. Plaintiff finally alleged that defendants' conduct amounted to malice and oppression calling for both compensatory and punitive damages.

* * *

Appellant's principal contention on appeal is that the trial court prejudicially erred in granting summary judgment in favor of respondents. More precisely, appellant argues that the individual elements of the invasion of privacy (i.e., public disclosure of private facts; the offensiveness of the public disclosure; and the newsworthiness of the publication as an exception to tort liability) constituted a factual determination which could not be resolved or adjudicated by way of summary procedure.

Before discussing appellant's contentions on the merit, as an initial matter we set out the legal principles governing the case. It is well settled that there are three elements of a cause of action predicated on tortious invasion of privacy. First, the disclosure of the private facts must be a *public disclosure* (*Porten v. University of San Francisco* (1976) 64 Cal.App.3d 825, 828 [134 Cal.Rptr. 839]). Second, the facts disclosed must be *private facts*, and not public ones (*Kapellas v. Kofman* (1969) 1 Cal.3d 20, 35 [81 Cal.Rptr. 360, 459 P.2d 912]; *Coverstone v. Davies* (1952) 38 Cal.2d 315, 323 [239 P.2d 876]). Third, the matter made public must be one which would be *offensive* and objectionable to a reasonable person of ordinary sensibilities (*Forsher v. Bugliosi* (1980) 26 Cal.3d 792, 808–809 [163 Cal.Rptr. 628, 608 P.2d 716]; *Gill v. Hearst Publishing Co.* (1953) 40 Cal.2d 224 [253 P.2d 441]). It is likewise recognized, however, that due to the supreme mandate of the constitutional protection of freedom of the press even a tortious invasion of one's privacy is exempt from liability if the publication of private facts is truthful and newsworthy. The latter proposition finds support primarily in Restatement Second of Torts section 652D which provides that "One who gives publicity to a matter concerning the private life of another is subject to liability to the other for invasion of his privacy, if the matter publicized is of a kind that (a) would be highly offensive to a reasonable person, and (b) is not of legitimate concern to the public."

In interpreting the cited section, the cases and authorities emphasize that the privilege to publicize newsworthy matters incorporated in section 652D is not only immunity accorded by the common law, but also one of constitutional dimension based upon the First Amendment of the United States Constitution. As tersely stated in comment d to section 652D: "When the subject-matter of the publicity is of legitimate public concern, there is no invasion of privacy. This has now become a rule not just of common law of torts, but of the Federal Constitution as well." (Accord *Cox Broadcasting Corp. v. Cohn* (1975) 420 U.S. 469 [43 L.Ed.2d 328, 95 S.Ct. 1029]; *Time, Inc. v. Hill* (1967) 385 U.S. 374, 383 [17 L.Ed.2d 456, 464, 87 S.Ct. 534]; *Virgil v. Time, Inc.* (9th Cir. 1975) 527 F.2d 1122, 1129; see also *Forsher v. Bugliosi, supra.*, 26 Cal.3d at pp. 809–810; *Briscoe v. Reader's Digest Association, Inc.* (1971) 4 Cal.3d 529, 541 [93 Cal.Rptr. 866, 483 P.2d 34, 57 A.L.R.3d 1]; *Kapellas v. Kofman, supra.*, 1 Cal.3d at pp. 35–36.)

As an additional preliminary matter, it also bears emphasis that a motion for summary judgment in First Amendment cases is an approved procedure because unnecessarily protracted litigation would have a chilling effect upon the exercise of First Amendment rights and because speedy resolution of cases involving free speech is desirable (*Good Government Group of Seal Beach, Inc. v. Superior Court* (1978) 22 Cal.3d 672, 685 [150 Cal.Rptr. 258, 586 P.2d 572]; *Desert Sun Publishing Co. v. Superior Court* (1979) 97 Cal.App.3d 49, 53 [158 Cal.Rptr. 519]). While the crucial test as to whether to grant a motion for summary judgment remains the same in free speech cases (i.e., whether there is a triable issue of fact presented in the case), the courts impose more stringent burdens on one who opposes the motion and require a showing of high probability that the plaintiff will ultimately prevail in the case. In the absence of such showing the courts are inclined to grant the motion and do not permit the case to proceed beyond the summary judgment stage (i.e., *United Medical Laboratories v. Columbia Broadcasting Sys.* (9th Cir. 1968) 404 F.2d 706, 712–713; *Time, Inc. v. McLaney* (5th Cir. 1969) 406 F.2d 565, 572–573; *Time, Inc. v. Johnston* (4th Cir. 1971) 448 F.2d 378, 383–384; *Belli v. Curtis Pub. Co.* (1972) 25 Cal.App.3d 384, 388 [118 Cal.Rptr. 370]).

When viewed in light of the aforegoing principles, the summary judgment in this case must be upheld on two grounds. First, as appears from the record properly considered for the purposes of summary judgment, the facts disclosed by the articles were not private facts within the meaning of the law. Second, the record likewise reveals on its face that the publications in dispute were newsworthy and thus constituted a protective shield from liability based upon invasion of privacy.

(A) *The facts published were not private.*

As pointed out earlier, a crucial ingredient of the tort premised upon invasion of one's privacy is a public disclosure of *private facts* (*Forsher v. Bugliosi, supra.*, 26 Cal.3d at p. 808; *Kapellas v. Kofman, supra.*, 1 Cal.3d at p. 35), that is, the unwarranted publication of intimate details of one's private life which are outside the realm of legitimate public interest (*Johnson v. Harcourt, Brace, Jovanovich, Inc.* (1974) 43 Cal. App.3d 880, 891 [118 Cal.Rptr. 370]). In elaborating on the notion, the cases explain that there can be no privacy with respect to a matter which is already public (*Werner v. Times–Mirror Co.* (1961) 193 Cal.App.2d 111, 117 [14 Cal.Rptr. 208]) or which has previously become part of the "public domain" (*Kapellas v. Kofman, supra.*, 1 Cal.3d at pp. 36–37, fn. 24). Moreover, it is equally underlined that there is no liability when the defendant merely gives further publicity to information about the plaintiff which is already public or when the further publicity relates to matters which the plaintiff leaves open to the public eye (*Virgil v. Time, Inc., supra.*, 527 F.2d at p. 1126; see also com. c to § 652D of Rest. 2d Torts).

The case at bench falls within the aforestated rules. The undisputed facts reveal that prior to the publication of the newspaper articles in question appellant's homosexual orientation and participation in gay community activities had been known by hundreds of people in a variety of cities, including New York, Dallas, Houston, San Diego, Los Angeles and San Francisco. Thus, appellant's deposition shows that prior to the assassination attempt appellant spent a lot of time in "Tenderloin" and "Castro," the well-known gay sections of San Francisco; that he frequented gay bars and other homosexual gatherings in both San Francisco and other cities; that he marched in gay parades on several occasions; that he supported the campaign of Mike Caringi for the election of "Emperor"; that he participated in the coronation of the "Emperor" and sat at Caringi's table on that occasion; that his friendship with Harvey Milk, another prominent gay, was well-known and publicized in gay newspapers; and that his homosexual association and name had been reported in gay magazines (such as Data Boy, Pacific Coast Times, Male Express, etc.) several times before the publications in question. In fact, appellant quite candidly conceded that he did not make a secret of his being a homosexual and that if anyone would ask, he would frankly admit that he was gay. In short, since appellant's sexual orientation was already in public domain and since the articles in question did no more than to give further publicity to matters which appellant left open to the eye of the public, a vital element of the tort was missing rendering it vulnerable to summary disposal.

Although the conclusion reached above applies with equal force to all respondents, we cannot help observing that respondents Times Mirror and its editor are exempt from liability on the additional ground that the Los Angeles Times only republished the Chronicle article which implied that appellant was gay. It is, of course, axiomatic that no right of privacy attaches to a matter of general interest that has already been publicly released in a periodical or in a newspaper of local or regional circulation (*Sperry Rand Corporation v. Hill* (1st Cir. 1966) 356 F.2d 181, 185 [23 A.L.R.3d 853]).

(B) *The publication was newsworthy.*

But even aside from the aforegoing considerations, the summary judgment dismissing the action against respondents was justified on the additional, independent basis that the publication contained in the articles in dispute was newsworthy.

As referred to above, our courts have recognized a broad privilege cloaking the truthful publication of all newsworthy matters. Thus, in *Briscoe v. Reader's Digest Association, Inc., supra.*, 4 Cal.3d at page 541, our Supreme Court stated that a truthful publication is protected if (1) it is newsworthy and (2) it does not reveal facts so offensive as to shock the community notions of decency. While it has been said that the general criteria for determining newsworthiness are (a) the social value of the facts published; (b) the depth of the article's intrusion into ostensibly private affairs; and (c) the extent to which the individual voluntarily acceded to a position of public notoriety (*Briscoe v. Reader's Digest Association, Inc., supra.*, at p. 541; see also *Forsher v. Bugliosi, supra.*, 26 Cal.3d at pp. 811–812; *Kapellas v. Kofman, supra.*, 1 Cal.3d at p. 36), the cases and authorities further explain that the paramount test of newsworthiness is whether the matter is of legitimate public interest which in turn must be determined according to the community mores.

As pointed out in *Virgil v. Time, Inc., supra.*, 527 F.2d at page 1129: " ' In determining what is a matter of legitimate public interest, account must be taken of the customs and conventions of the community; and in the last analysis what is proper becomes a matter of the community mores. *The line is to be drawn when the publicity ceases to be the giving of information to which the public is entitled, and becomes a morbid and sensational prying into private lives for its own sake,* with which a reasonable member of the public, with decent standards, would say that he had no concern.' " (Italics added.) (Accord Rest. 2d Torts, § 652D, com. h.)

In the case at bench the publication of appellant's homosexual orientation which had already been widely known by many people in a number of communities was not so offensive even at the time of the publication as to shock the community notions of decency. Moreover, and perhaps even more to the point, the record shows that the publications were not motivated by a morbid and sensational prying into appellant's private life but rather were prompted by legitimate political considerations, i.e., to dispel the false public opinion that gays were timid, weak and unheroic figures and to raise the equally important political question whether the President of the United States entertained a discriminatory attitude or bias against a minority group such as homosexuals. Thus appellant's case squarely falls within the language of *Kapellas* in which the California Supreme Court emphasized that "when, [as here] the legitimate public interest in the published information is substantial, a much greater intrusion into an individual's private life will be sanctioned, especially if the individual willingly entered into the public sphere." (*Kapellas v. Kofman, supra.*, 1 Cal.3d at p. 36.)

Appellant's contention that by saving the President's life he did not intend to enter into the limelight and become a public figure can be easily answered. In elaborating on involuntary public figures, Restatement Second of Torts section 652D, comment f, sets out in part as follows: "There are other individuals who have not sought publicity or consented to it, but through their own conduct or otherwise have become a legitimate subject of public interest. They have, in other words, becomes 'news.' . . . These persons are regarded as properly subject to the public interest, and publishers are permitted to satisfy the curiosity of the public as to its heroes, leaders, villains and victims, and those who are closely associated with them. As in the case of the voluntary public figure, the authorized publicity is not limited to the event that itself arouses the public interest, and to some reasonable extent includes publicity given to facts about the individual that would otherwise be purely private." (See also com. g.) (Accord *Virgil v. Time, Inc., supra.*, 527 F.2d at p. 1129.)

In summary, appellant's assertion notwithstanding, the trial court could determine as a matter of law that the facts contained in the articles were not private facts within the purview of the law and also that the publications relative to the appellant were newsworthy. Since the record thus fails to present any triable issue of fact, the trial court was justified (if not mandated) in granting summary judgment and dismiss the case against respondents by way of summary procedure.

The purported appeal from the order denying a motion for new trial is dismissed as the order is not an appealable order.

The judgment is affirmed.

## NOTES

**1. Publicity Given to Private Life.** A third privacy tort and perhaps the one most intuitively associated with privacy is Publicity Given to Private Life. See Diamond, Levine & Madden, *Understanding Torts* § 22.05 (1996); Keeton, *Prosser and Keeton on the Law of Torts*, § 117 (5th ed. 1984). The Restatement defines the tort as follows:

"One who gives publicity to a matter concerning the private life of another is subject to liability to the other for invasion of his privacy, if the matter publicized is of a kind that

(a) would be highly offensive to a reasonable person and

(b) is not of legitimate concern to the public."

Restatement (Second) of Torts § 652D.

**2. Private Facts.** As the principal case illustrates, courts are rigorous in requiring the facts disclosed be highly private to find liability under the tort. The tort poses First Amendment issues because it punishes truthful information. Indeed, the United States Supreme Court has been, as a matter of constitutional First Amendment law, extremely aggressive in invalidating privacy claims where the facts were in public records made available to the press. In *Cox Broadcasting Corp. v. Cohn*, 420 U.S. 469, 95 S.Ct. 1029, 43 L.Ed.2d 328 (1975), the Supreme Court invalidated on First Amendment grounds a privacy action against a broadcasting company when a television reporter broadcast the name of a teenage girl who had been raped and murdered. Although it was a crime in the state to publish the name of a rape victim, the television reporter was allowed to inspect court records with the name of the victim. Since the records with the victim's name were open to public inspection, the privacy claim was held unconstitutional.

In *Florida Star v. B.J.F.*, 491 U.S. 524, 109 S.Ct. 2603, 105 L.Ed.2d 443 (1989), the Supreme Court invalidated a newspaper's liability under a state statute imposing civil liability for the mass media to disclose the victim of a sexual offense. The newspaper had obtained the victim's name from a police report that had inadvertently been made available for public inspection. The Supreme Court held that "where a newspaper publishes truthful information which it has lawfully obtained, punishment may lawfully be imposed, if at all, only when narrowly tailored to a state interest of the highest order ..." which the Court found did not exist in the case. See Diamond, Levine & Madden, *Understanding Torts* § 22.05 (2nd ed. 2000); Dobbs, *The Law of Torts* § 427 (2000). The Supreme Court decisions raise questions of when, if ever, publicizing information about individuals from obscure but public records could ever be the basis for liability for publicity to a private fact.

**3. Highly Offensive to a Reasonable Person.** As the Restatement states, the disclosure of the private fact must be highly offensive to a reasonable person. Consider *Johnson v. Harcourt, Brace, Jovanovich, Inc.*, 43 Cal.App.3d 880, 118 Cal.Rpt. 370 (Cal.Ct.App.1974), where a janitor sued a publisher of a high school textbook for reporting that the janitor had returned thousands of dollars lost by an armored truck. The plaintiff's friends and associates had mocked him for his honesty, but the court held the disclosure of honesty was not offensive.

**4. Legitimate Concern to the Public.** In addition to proving the disclosure concerned a private fact, highly offensive to a reasonable person, the plaintiff to recover for publicity of private fact must also prove the disclosure was not of legitimate public concern. Consider *Sidis v. F–R Publishing Corp.*, 113 F.2d 806 (2d Cir.1940). The New Yorker magazine reported that a former child prodigy, who 40 years ago had won national radio quiz shows, was now living in a squalid apartment, collecting subway tokens, and employed in a menial job. The court held the disclosure satisfied a legitimate public concern to know the ultimate success of a once prominent child prodigy. Consider also *Jones v. WTXF–Fox 29*, 26 Phila.Co.Rptr. 291, 1993 WL 1156080 (Com. Pleas 1993), where the plaintiff-fugitive's surrender to a news columnist was featured on the television program "America's Most Wanted." She sued the network for invading her privacy by giving unreasonable publicity to her private life. The court held that the plaintiff had failed to show that her exposure would be highly offensive to a reasonable person, or that it was not of legitimate public concern. The court also noted that her conviction was on public court records and thus not private.

**5. Publicity.** Unlike defamation which requires only "publication" or communication to one person other than the victim, the publicity of private fact privacy tort requires, as the Restatement puts it, "that the matter is made public, by communicating it to the public at large, or to so many persons that the matter must be regarded as substantially certain to become one of public knowledge." Restatement (Second) of Torts at 652D, ct. A.

# SECTION C.  FALSE LIGHT

## CANTRELL v. FOREST CITY PUBLISHING CO.

Supreme Court of the United States.
419 U.S. 245, 95 S.Ct. 465, 42 L.Ed.2d 419 (1974).

Mr. Justice STEWART delivered the opinion of the Court.

Margaret Cantrell and four of her minor children brought this diversity action in a Federal District Court for invasion of privacy against the Forest City Publishing Co., publisher of a Cleveland newspaper, the Plain Dealer, and against Joseph Eszterhas, a reporter formerly employed by the Plain Dealer, and Richard Conway, a Plain Dealer photographer. The Cantrells alleged that an article published in the Plain Dealer Sunday Magazine unreasonably placed their family in a false light before the public through its many inaccuracies and untruths. The District Judge struck the claims relating to punitive damages as to all the plaintiffs and dismissed the actions of three of the Cantrell children in their entirety, but allowed the case to go to the jury as to Mrs. Cantrell and her oldest son, William. The jury returned a verdict against all three of the respondents for compensatory money damages in favor of these two plaintiffs.

The Court of Appeals for the Sixth Circuit reversed, holding that, in the light of the First and Fourteenth Amendments, the District Judge should have granted the respondents' motion for a directed verdict as to all the Cantrells' claims. 484 F.2d 150. We granted certiorari, 418 U.S. 909, 94 S.Ct. 3202, 41 L.Ed.2d 1156.

## I

In December 1967, Margaret Cantrell's husband Melvin was killed along with 43 other people when the Silver Bridge across the Ohio River at Point Pleasant, W.Va., collapsed. The respondent Eszterhas was assigned by the Plain Dealer to cover the story of the disaster. He wrote a "news feature" story focusing on the funeral of Melvin Cantrell and the impact of his death on the Cantrell family.

Five months later, after conferring with the Sunday Magazine editor of the Plain Dealer, Eszterhas and photographer Conway returned to the Point Pleasant area to write a follow-up feature. The two men went to the Cantrell residence, where Eszterhas talked with the children and Conway took 50 pictures. Mrs. Cantrell was not at home at any time during the 60 to 90 minutes that the men were at the Cantrell residence.

Eszterhas' story appeared as the lead feature in the August 4, 1968, edition of the Plain Dealer Sunday Magazine. The article stressed the family's abject poverty; the children's old, ill-fitting clothes and the deteriorating condition of their home were detailed in both the text and accompanying photographs. As he had done in his original, prize-winning article on the Silver Bridge disaster, Eszterhas used the Cantrell family to illustrate the impact of the bridge collapse on the lives of the people in the Point Pleasant area.

It is conceded that the story contained a number of inaccuracies and false statements. Most conspicuously, although Mrs. Cantrell was not present at any time during the reporter's visit to her home, Eszterhas wrote, "Margaret Cantrell will talk neither about what happened nor about how they are doing. She wears the same mask of non-expression she wore at the funeral. She is a proud woman. Her world has changed. She says that after it happened, the people in town offered to help them out with money and they refused to take it." Other significant misrepresentations were contained in details of Eszterhas' descriptions of the poverty in which the Cantrells were living and the dirty and dilapidated conditions of the Cantrell home.

The case went to the jury on a so-called "false light" theory of invasion of privacy. In essence, the theory of the case was that by publishing the false feature story about the Cantrells and thereby making them the objects of pity and ridicule, the respondents damaged Mrs. Cantrell and her son William by causing them to suffer outrage, mental distress, shame, and humiliation.

## II

In *Time, Inc. v. Hill*, 385 U.S. 374, 87 S.Ct. 534, 17 L.Ed.2d 456, the Court considered a similar false-light, invasion-of-privacy action. The New York Court of Appeals had interpreted New York Civil Rights Law, McKinney's Consol.Laws, c. 6, ss 50—51 to give a "newsworthy person" a right of action when his or her name, picture or portrait was the subject of a "fictitious" report or article. Material and substantial falsification was the test for recovery. 385 U.S., at 384—386, 87 S.Ct. at 540—541. Under this doctrine the New York courts awarded the plaintiff James Hill compensatory damages based on his complaint that Life Magazine had falsely reported that a new Broadway play portrayed the Hill family's experience in being held hostage by three escaped convicts. This Court, guided by its decision in *New York Times Co. v. Sullivan,* 376 U.S. 254, 84 S.Ct. 710, 11 L.Ed.2d 686, which recognized constitutional limits on a State's power to award damages for libel in actions brought by public officials, held that the constitutional protections for speech and press precluded the application of the New York statute to allow recovery for "false reports of matters of public interest in the absence of proof that the defendant published the report with knowledge of its falsity or in reckless disregard of the truth." 385 U.S., at 388, 87 S.Ct., at 542. Although the jury could have reasonably concluded from the evidence in the *Hill* case that Life had engaged in knowing falsehood or had recklessly disregarded the truth in stating in the article that "the story re-enacted" the Hill family's experience, the Court concluded that the trial judge's instructions had not confined the jury to such a finding as a predicate for liability as required by the Constitution. Id., at 394, 87 S.Ct., at 545.

The District Judge in the case before us, in contrast to the trial judge in *Time, Inc. v. Hill,* did instruct the jury that liability could be imposed only if it concluded that the false statements in the Sunday Magazine feature article on the Cantrells had been made with knowledge of their falsity or in reckless disregard of the truth. No objection was made by any of the parties to this knowing-or-reckless-falsehood instruction. Consequently, this case presents no occasion to consider whether a State may constitutionally apply a more relaxed standard of liability for a publisher or broadcaster of false statements injurious to a private individual under a false-light theory of invasion of privacy, or whether the constitutional standard announced in *Time, Inc. v. Hill* applies to all false-light cases. Cf. *Gertz v. Robert Welch, Inc.,* 418 U.S. 323, 94 S.Ct. 2997, 41 L.Ed.2d 789. Rather, the sole question that we need decide is whether the Court of Appeals erred in setting aside the jury's verdict.

### III

At the close of the petitioners' case-in-chief, the District Judge struck the demand for punitive damages. He found that Mrs. Cantrell had failed to present any evidence to support the charges that the invasion of privacy "was done maliciously within the legal definition of that term." The Court of Appeals interpreted this finding to be a determination by the District Judge that there was no evidence of knowing falsity or reckless disregard of the truth introduced at the trial. Having made such a determination, the Court of Appeals held that the District Judge should have granted the motion for a directed verdict for respondents as to all the Cantrells' claims. 484 F.2d, at 155.

The Court of Appeals appears to have assumed that the District Judge's finding of no malice "within the legal definition of that term" was a finding based on the definition of "actual malice" established by this Court in *New York Times Co. v. Sullivan,* 376 U.S., at 280, 84 S.Ct., at 726: "with knowledge that (a defamatory statement) was false or with reckless disregard of whether it was false or not." As so defined, of course, "actual malice" is a term of art, created to provide a convenient shorthand expression for the standard of liability that must be established before a State may constitutionally permit public officials to recover for libel in actions brought against publishers. As such, it is quite different from the common-law standard of "malice" generally required under state tort law to support an award of punitive damages. In a false-light case, common-law malice—frequently expressed in terms of either personal ill will toward the plaintiff or reckless or wanton disregard of the plaintiff's rights—would focus on the defendant's attitude toward the plaintiff's privacy, not toward the truth or falsity of the material published. See *Time, Inc. v. Hill*, 385 U.S., at 396 n. 12, 87 S.Ct., at 546 n. 12. See generally W. Prosser, Law of Torts 9–10 (4th ed.).

Although the verbal record of the District Court proceedings is not entirely unambiguous, the conclusion is inescapable that the District Judge was referring to the common-law standard of malice rather than to the *New York Times* "actual malice" standard when he dismissed the punitive damages claims. For at the same time that he dismissed the demands for punitive damages, the District Judge refused to grant the respondents' motion for directed verdicts as to Mrs. Cantrell's and William's claims for compensatory damages. And, as his instructions to the jury made clear, the District Judge was fully aware that the *Time, Inc. v. Hill* meaning of the *New York Times* "actual malice" standard had to be satisfied for the Cantrells to recover actual damages. Thus, the only way to harmonize these two virtually simultaneous rulings by the District Judge is to conclude, contrary to the decision of the Court of Appeals, that in dismissing the punitive damages claims he was not determining that Mrs. Cantrell had failed to introduce any evidence of knowing falsity or reckless disregard of the truth. This conclusion is further fortified by the District Judge's subsequent denial of the respondents' motion for judgment n.o.v. and alternative motion for a new trial.

Moreover, the District Judge was clearly correct in believing that the evidence introduced at trial was sufficient to support a jury finding that the respondents Joseph Eszterhas and Forest City Publishing Co. had published knowing or reckless falsehoods about the Cantrells. There was no dispute during the trial that Eszterhas, who did not testify, must have known that a number of the statements in the feature story were untrue. In particular, his article plainly implied that Mrs. Cantrell had been present during his visit to her home and that Eszterhas had observed her "wear[ing] the same mask of nonexpression she wore [at her husband's] funeral." These were "calculated falsehoods," and the jury was plainly justified in finding that Eszterhas had portrayed the Cantrells in a false light through knowing or reckless untruth.

The Court of Appeals concluded that there was no evidence that Forest City Publishing Co. had knowledge of any of the inaccuracies contained in Eszterhas' article. However, these was sufficient evidence for the jury to find that Eszterhas' writing of the feature was within the scope of his employment at the Plain Dealer and that Forest City Publishing Co. was therefore liable under traditional doctrines of respondeat superior. Although Eszterhas was not regularly assigned by the Plain Dealer to write for the Sunday Magazine, the editor of the magazine testified that as a staff writer for the Plain Dealer, Eszterhas frequently suggested stories he would like to write for the magazine. When Eszterhas suggested the follow-up article on the Silver Bridge disaster, the editor approved the idea and told Eszterhas the magazine would publish the feature if it was good. From this evidence, the jury could reasonably conclude that Forest City Publishing Co., publisher of the Plain Dealer, should be held vicariously liable for the damage caused by the knowing falsehoods contained in Eszterhas' story.

For the foregoing reasons, the judgment of the Court of Appeals is reversed and the case is remanded to that court with directions to enter a judgment affirming the judgment of the District Court as to the respondents Forest City Publishing Co. and Joseph Eszterhas.

It is so ordered.

### NOTES

**1. False Light.** In addition to intrusion upon seclusion, appropriation of name or likeness, and publicity of private fact, the Restatement (Second) of Torts and most courts recognize invasion of privacy on a theory of portraying the plaintiff in a false light. False light is established where the defendant publicizes false, objectionable information about the plaintiff. The Restatement defines it as follows:

"One who gives publicity to a matter concerning another that places the other before the public in a false light is subject to liability to the other for invasion of his privacy, if

(a) the false light in which the other was placed would be highly offensive to a reasonable person, and

(b) the actor had knowledge of or acted in reckless disregard as to the falsity of the publicized matter and the false light in which the other would be placed."

Restatement (Second) of Torts § 652E.

**2. False Light Compared with Defamation.** False light is remarkably similar to defamation (see Chapter 8, supra). The tort is different in a few ways. First, publicity is required for false light, while defamation only requires "publication." Publicity, as discussed in the context of publicity of private facts, requires that the information be communicated to the general public while "publication" only requires communication to one person other than the victim of the defamation.

Secondly, both private and public figures must prove *New York Times* malice (knowledge of falsity or reckless disregard as to the truth or falsity of the statement). In defamation, only public officials and public figures are required to prove *New York Times* malice to recover at least some damages (see Chapter 8, Sec. D, supra). As the principal case indicates, *New York Times* malice should be clearly distinguished from common law malice (e.g., ill will, hatred) required for punitive damages.

Thirdly, defamation requires that the victim's reputation be seriously damaged by the defendant's false assertions. False light has a lower threshold and only requires that the false statement would be highly offensive to a reasonable person. For example, falsely portraying in a docudrama that the unmarried male hero was romantically involved with an unmarried female associate could be highly offensive and therefore false light, but not defamatory.

Nevertheless, in most cases defamation and false light overlap. This raises the issue whether the false light is worth accepting or maintaining as a separate action. Although false light does not distinguish between libel and slander like defamation, courts are resistant to efforts to utilize the false light tort to evade slander's special damage requirements for nonwritten defamation. Also defamation defenses are usually applied, where applicable, to false light. See Diamond, Levine & Madden, *Understanding Torts* § 22.04 (2nd ed. 2000); Keeton, *Prosser and Keeton on the Law of Torts* § 117 (5th ed. 1984); Dobbs, *The Law of Torts* § 428 (2000), Franklin, Anderson, & Cate, *Mass Media Law* (6th ed. 2000).

Consider *Bridgman v. New Trier High School District*, 128 F.3d 1146 (7th Cir.1997), where a high school student under suspicion of drug use was searched and examined by school authorities, who also called his mother. He and his mother brought suit against the school district, alleging the tort of false light invasion of privacy. The claim failed because the court found that he had not alleged facts sufficient to prove either publicity or actual malice, both essential elements of the claim. See also *Cook v. Mardi Gras Casino Corp.*, 697 So.2d 378 (Miss.1997), where a casino jackpot winner was portrayed in a newspaper as having won $235,000. Because of a dispute with casino owners over the payment plan, she claimed (without basis) that she had won only $70,000. She sued the paper and the casino for misrepresentation and false light, claiming harassment and embarrassment in the community. The court dismissed her claim, noting that it was doubtful that a reasonable person would be offended that others knew that she had won a large sum of money. The fact that she had posed for the picture supported this conclusion. The court also noted that it could not be shown that the defendant had acted in reckless disregard of any falsity since it was undisputed that Cook had won over $235,000. But see *Dempsey v. National Enquirer*, 702 F.Supp. 934 (D.Me.1989), allowing a celebrity to maintain a false light claim against the tabloid for inaccurately implying he had interviewed with the newspaper.

**3. Rejecting False Light.** While most states follow the Restatement and accept false light as a privacy tort, some states have rejected the tort. Some courts express concern that liability for falsehoods that do not seriously damage the victim's reputation unduly chills free speech. Courts have also questioned whether the overlap between defamation and false light in most cases justifies the tort. See *Cain v. Hearst Corp.*, 878 S.W.2d 577 (Tex.1994). Should the tort of false light exist?

# Index

References are to pages

### References are to pages